DANIEL DEFOE: MASTER OF FICTIONS

Defoe in the Pillory from a pirated edition of *Jure Divino*

DANIEL DEFOE

MASTER OF FICTIONS

HIS LIFE AND IDEAS

Maximillian E. Novak

OXFORD

UNIVERSITY PRESS

Great Clarendon Street, Oxford, OX2 6DP

Oxford University Press is a department of the University of Oxford.
It furthers the University's objective of excellence in research, scholarship,
and education by publishing worldwide in

Oxford New York

Athens Auckland Bangkok Bogotá Buenos Aires Calcutta
Cape Town Chennai Dar es Salaam Delhi Florence Hong Kong Istanbul
Karachi Kuala Lumpur Madrid Melbourne Mexico City Mumbai
Nairobi Paris São Paulo Shanghai Singapore Taipei Tokyo Toronto Warsaw

and associated companies in Berlin Ibadan

Published in the United States
by Oxford University Press Inc., New York

First published 2001

British Library Cataloguing in Publication Data

Data available

Library of Congress Cataloging in Publication Data

Data available

ISBN-0-19-812686-7

1 3 5 7 9 10 8 6 4 2

Typeset in Fournier by Regent Typesetting, London
Printed in Great Britain
on acid-free paper by
T.J. International Ltd,
Padstow, Cornwall

To Estelle, Ralph, Daniel, and Rachel, my family instructors

ACKNOWLEDGEMENTS

I never expected this project to take as long as it did, but as tedious and arduous as the work sometimes was, it gave me an understanding of the period from 1660 to 1731 that I could never have gained without it. From that standpoint, it has been an enriching experience. After I had been working on this biography for several years, Paula R. Backscheider and I began collaborating. The partnership ended when she decided to write a biography on her own. We never came to the point of working out a joint approach to Defoe's character, but we did share the results of some of our research. I am particularly grateful for the help she provided in using the Public Records Office in Edinburgh. My indebtedness to past scholars, from William Lee to William Trent, from James Sutherland to John Robert Moore, may be found on every page of my text. I found new ways of seeing Defoe's life by extensive reading in contemporary pamphlets and periodicals and by reinterpreting documentary evidence. However, with but few exceptions, all of these scholars had viewed the same documents I examined and served as my guide to these materials.

I also want to thank the staffs of the many libraries and institutions I used, particularly the William Andrews Clark Memorial Library, the Henry H. Huntington Library, the Bodleian Library, the Beinecke Library, the British Library, the Boston Public Library, the John Rylands Library, and the Public Records Office at Chancery Lane, Kew, and Colchester. I received generous grants to work on this project from the National Endowment for the Humanities, the Beinecke Library, the University of California in the form of a President's Fellowship, and the Henry H. Huntington Library. I also had continuing support from the Research Council of the University of California, Los Angeles. Finally, I want to thank my wife, Estelle, who read and edited the entire work.

CONTENTS

LIST OF ILLUSTRATIONS

Frontispiece Defoe in the Pillory from a pirated edition of *Jure Divino*

(Between pages 372 and 373)

1. Defoe by Van der Gucht after the painting by Jeremiah Taverner
2. Popish Plot playing card: the Fire of London
3. Popish Plot playing card: Titus Oates before Charles II
4a and b. Title-page and illustration of debtors in prison from Moses Pitt, *The Cry of the Oppressed*, 1691
5. Portrait of King William engraved by Smith after the painting by Sir Godfrey Kneller
6. Portrait of Robert Harley, Earl of Oxford
7. Sacheverell Trial playing card showing Queen Anne and Sacheverell
8. Title-page of Defoe's *Review*
9. Frontispiece of the 1719 edition of *Robinson Crusoe*
10. Moll Flanders from a chapbook illustration
11. Frontispiece of the 1724 edition of *Roxana*
12. The Custom House, from Robert Morden and Philip Lea, *A Prospect of London*, c.1700
13. Engraving of Defoe's house at Stoke Newington
14. Peter the Wild Boy, a woodcut after the portrait by William Kent, 1726
15. The frontispiece to *A System of Magick*, 1727
16. Defoe's signature and seal on a deed to the Colchester property
17. Portrait of Henry Baker engraved by Nutter after the painting by Thomson

Frontispiece and illustrations 4a and b, 9, 11, 12, and 15 are courtesy of the William Andrews Clark Memorial Library; 1 and 5 are courtesy of the Mary Evans Picture Library; 2, 3, 6 and 7 are courtesy of the Huntington Library and Art Gallery; 8 is reproduced from the facsimile edition published by Columbia University Press, 1938, edited by Arthur W. Secord; 10 and 14 are courtesy of the British Library, London; 13 is private collection; 16 is courtesy of the Essex Record Office; and 17 is courtesy of the National Portrait Gallery, London.

ABBREVIATIONS

BL	British Library
C	Chancery Records, PRO
Checklist	John Robert Moore, *A Checklist of the Writings of Daniel Defoe*, 2nd edn. Hamden, Conn.: Archon Books, 1971
CLRO	City of London Records Office
CSPD	Calendar of State Papers Domestic
DNB	*Dictionary of National Biography*
H	*The Letters of Daniel Defoe*, ed. George Harris Healey. Oxford: Clarendon Press, 1955
HMC	Historical Manuscripts Commission
JHC	*Journals of the House of Commons*. London: HMSO, 1803–
JHL	*Journals of the House of Lords*. London: HMSO, 17xx–
Lee	William Lee, *Daniel Defoe: His Life and Recently Discovered Writings: Extending from 1716 to 1729*. 3 vols. London: John Camden Hotten, 1869
Luttrell	Narcissus Luttrell, *A Brief Relation of State Affairs from September 1678 to April 1714*. London, 1857
N&Q	*Notes and Queries*
POAS	*Poems on Affairs of State*, ed. George de F. Lord et al. 7 vols. New Haven, Conn.: Yale University Press, 1963–75
Political State	Abel Boyer, *The Political State of Great Britain* (London, 1711–29)
Portland Papers	*Report on the Manuscripts of His Grace the Duke of Portland, Preserved at Welbeck Abbey*. 6 vols. Norwich: HMSO, 1899

PRO	Public Records Office
PROB	Probate Records, PRO
Review	Daniel Defoe, *A Review of the Affairs of France: and of All Europe, as Influenc'd by That Nation*, ed. Arthur Wellesley Secord. Orig. 9 vols. in 22. New York: Columbia University Press, 1938
Shakespeare Head Edition	*The Shakespeare Head Edition of the Novels and Selected Writings of Daniel Defoe*. 14 vols. Oxford: Blackwell, 1927–8
Tour	Daniel Defoe, *A Tour thru' the Whole Island of Great Britain*, intro. G. D. H. Cole. 2 vols. London: Peter Davies, 1927
Trent Collection	The collection of manuscripts and typescripts at Yale's Beinecke Library, New Haven, by William Peterfield Trent, including 'A Biographical and Bibliographical Study' of Daniel Defoe
True Collection	Daniel Defoe, *A True Collection of the Writings of the Author of the True-Born Englishman*. 2 vols. London: 1703–5

Introduction

Another observation, suggested by the case of De Foe, is that eminent
literary and intellectual merit at length finds its due place in the
Temple of Fame. . . .
  Though his abilities in certain respects were generally acknowledged, full justice was far from being done to his reputation, either
during his life, or for a considerable time after his decease. . . . But the
world has at last become sensible of his great and various talents.

> Andrew Kippis, in *Biographia Britannica*, ed. Andrew Kippis,
> Joseph Towers et al. (London: Longman, 1793), v. 74.

Few writers have had so difficult a path to what Kippis calls 'the Temple of
Fame', and fewer yet have had such a difficult time remaining there.
Compared to the ups and downs of Defoe's reputation, William Blake's or
Emily Dickinson's rise to positions of literary greatness has to appear
steady and continuous. When it first appeared in 1719, Defoe's masterpiece, *Robinson Crusoe*, was attacked viciously by Charles Gildon, as a
vulgarization of art and life, and toward the end of the eighteenth century
he was accused of having plagiarized his work from the Scottish seaman
Alexander Selkirk. A playful modern version of the plagiarism theory
occurs in J. M. Coetzee's *Foe*, in which Defoe has stolen his work from his
own creation, Roxana, who appears as Susan in the text. Even as I write,
Defoe's position as one of the progenitors of the English novel, a masterful
prose stylist, a powerful writer of political poetry, and a brilliant thinker on
social and economic problems is under attack by those who believe he had
no right to usurp the voice of female narrators, those who feel that he
should have made Robinson Crusoe a vegetarian, and those who consider
him a primitive writer of fiction with no idea of how to construct a narrative. As early as the mid-nineteenth century, Charles Dickens, deploring

the political correctness of his time, wondered whether, in the need to produce a text that did not offend anti-war movements, lovers of cannibalism, and those who objected to his drinking rum, Robinson Crusoe would not eventually be 'edited out of his island and the island . . . swallowed up in the editorial ocean'.[1] Yet there have always been readers such as Kippis to admire some aspect of Defoe's many talents.

Kippis was writing at a time when, sixty-two years after his death, Defoe's writings and the events of his life were just being rediscovered. It was the period when the cult of the genius had finally provoked publishers into adding Defoe's name to the many works that had been ascribed to him. Robert Shiels had written an encomiastic life in 1753, and we know that Samuel Johnson, an admirer of *Robinson Crusoe*, offered to make a list of Defoe's writings for Elizabeth Montagu. But it was George Chalmers's life of 1785, along with the expanded edition of 1790, with its extensive bibliography, that prepared the way for Kippis's comments. One problem with this elevation to greatness, by those attempting to view Defoe as a genius, was that, in order for him to qualify fully, his life was supposed to possess a kind of saintly quality. This was rapidly supplied. He was viewed as a martyr to Whiggish political principles, to his religious beliefs, to his supposed belief in free trade. Not until William Minto's debunking biography in 1879 did the bubble burst. What William Lee had found to be more evidence of Defoe's adherence to his principles, Minto read as a sign that Defoe might have been 'the greatest liar that ever lived'.[2]

Since that time judgements have varied widely on Defoe's character and ideas. He has been viewed by some as an amusing scoundrel and by others as a crusading spokesman for a free press and the emerging power of the writer. He has been listed in a dictionary of radical writers and accused of resembling the worst propagandists working for Nazi Germany. And oddly enough, one may find all of these varying opinions about him in the writings of his contemporaries. Matters did not clear up after his death. His most radical attack upon nationalistic pride, *The True-Born Englishman* (1701), which was republished during the American Revolution in Philadelphia as a republican tract, was also printed as a Jacobite tract in the second half of the eighteenth century with a portrait of Bonnie Prince Charlie as a frontispiece.[3] Both his life and his writings lend themselves to what seems to be limitless interpretation and misinterpretation. This process extended itself to his grave in Bunhill Fields. When his bones were

[1] 'Frauds on the Fairies', *Household Words* 8 (1 Oct. 1853), 97–100. I am grateful to my son, Daniel Novak, for providing me with this reference.
[2] *Daniel Defoe* (London: Macmillan, 1879), 169.
[3] I found this copy in the library of Trinity College, Dublin.

disinterred on 16 September 1871 for the purpose of erecting the monument to his achievements, newspaper accounts seemed to be incapable of agreeing about very much. Was there a plaque on his coffin with the name 'Daniel Defoe', as stated by the *Daily News*, or did it, as the *Daily Telegraph* insisted, merely say 'Foe'? The account in *The Times* mentioned nothing about an identifying plate. As it turned out, the event degenerated into a near riot. Police had to be called to guard Defoe's remains from those seeking to carry off a bone or two as a relic, for *Robinson Crusoe* had given its author the status of a saint, whether he deserved it or not.[4]

I

More important than these attacks upon his body have been the wars being fought over the canon of Defoe's writings. During the nineteenth and twentieth century, as more and more became known about his activities as a writer, the number of works ascribed to him grew expeditiously, from the list offered by Chalmers to close to 600 works in the lists of William Trent, John Robert Moore, and Frank Bastian. Defoe almost always disguised himself behind a mask of anonymity. After 1715, aside from one work on which he allowed his initials to be placed on the title-page, he concealed his authorship behind a variety of pseudonyms. He never even acknowledged the three volumes of *Robinson Crusoe* upon which his fame has been based. In the first extensive list of Defoe's writings, published in 1785, George Chalmers limited himself for the most part to the few works that Defoe claimed in his *True Collection of the Writings of the Author of the True-Born Englishman* (1703–5). When reviewers complained about the many works Chalmers had omitted, he responded with an expanded list in 1790.[5] He may have had access to information still circulating in the printing and publishing trade, but he also recognized that to compile a representative list of Defoe's writings it was necessary to search through the vast body of anonymous works produced during Defoe's lifetime for pieces that reflected his particular style and ideas.

The danger in such an endeavour has been that Defoe might be credited with works he may not have written. Robert Shiels, who compiled the first brief list of Defoe's writings in 1753, credited Defoe with a novel

[4] Samuel Horner, *A Brief Account of the Interesting Ceremony of unveiling the Monument erected by the Boys and Girls of England to the Memory of Daniel Defoe* (Southampton: Hampshire Independent Office, 1871), 5–6, 22, 24.

[5] See Spiro Peterson, *Daniel Defoe: A Reference Guide, 1731–1924* (Boston, Mass.: G. K. Hall, 1987), 31, 37–8.

actually written by the Abbé Prévost. Chalmers included among works
certainly by Defoe such doubtful titles as *A Voyage to the World of Cartesius*
and the *History of Addresses*—works which no modern scholar accepts as
belonging in the Defoe canon. Walter Wilson, writing in 1830, thought
that Defoe had started his career as a writer in 1682 with *Speculum Crape-
Gownorum*, and William Lee, in 1869, believed Defoe was the author of *The
Highland Rogue*, a work about Rob Roy. William Peterfield Trent was
convinced that Defoe contributed to a medical controversy concerning the
health of drinking water, and John Robert Moore was guilty of adding
works to the Defoe canon that were revealed to have been written by John
Oldmixon and Arthur Maynwaring. Such errors must be maddening to
librarians and cataloguers, but these scholars added hundreds of genuine
works to the Defoe canon and enabled us to see him as one of the great
writers of his period. Many of their judgements rested on probability rather
than hard evidence, but they based their decisions about the canon on a vast
amount of reading in contemporary pamphlets and newspapers. Sometimes they had little to go on beyond a knowledge of Defoe's interests and
what they thought to be an ability to recognize his style. Those of us who
have continued to write on Defoe owe them an enormous debt and should
forgive them their errors. All of us know that there is no very good external
evidence for Defoe's authorship of works such as *Captain Singleton* or even
Roxana, perhaps the work that most interests modern readers and critics,
but no one who has read extensively in Defoe's writings could doubt his
authorship of such books for a moment. If much of the Defoe canon rests
upon probability rather than certainty, we should acknowledge that, and
demonstrate by the connections we can make between such works and
those works that are more definitely his how strong the probability of his
authorship might actually be.

   While this biography was being written, P. N. Furbank and W. R.
Owens challenged Defoe's authorship of a number of pieces and gradually
expanded this critique to include close to 250 works.[6] I have stated my
objections to this attempt at de-attribution in a number of reviews, and
more recently in a long review article in the *Huntington Library Quarterly*.[7]
If some of the attributions of William Trent, John Robert Moore, and
Frank Bastian appear to rest on doubtful notions of Defoe's style and his
ideas, Furbank and Owens are motivated by their own biases—by the
notion that fewer works by Defoe are better than more, that works of no

   [6] *Defoe De-attributions: A Critique of J. R. Moore's Checklist* (London: Hambledon Press, 1994).
   [7] 'The Defoe Canon: Attribution and De-attribution', *Huntington Library Quarterly* 59 (1997): 189–
207.

real literary merit (in their minds) are best dumped, and by a biographical notion that Defoe did not contradict himself in his printed writings. This latter opinion runs contrary to the evidence in his letters, particularly his letter to the Secretary of State in 1718, as well as his own statements when confronted with such contradictions. After an excellent start with the making of concordances, Furbank and Owen abandoned any notion that Defoe's syntax, style, vocabulary, and use of proverbs and popular phrases was unique. They ignored Defoe's allegiances to certain publishers and were willing to believe that works written in his style, on a subject that interested him, and issued by a publisher he patronized are by some unknown writer. They have proceeded on their path despite the development of the *Eighteenth-Century Short Title Catalogue*, which for the first time gives us access to information about publishers' lists, and new ways of distinguishing Defoe's vocabulary and style from those of his contemporaries through computer analysis.[8]

Andrew Kippis, whom I quoted at the beginning of this introduction, was able to draw upon a nearly contemporary account of Defoe to comment on how quickly he wrote his pamphlets and books.[9] There is actually nothing extraordinary about the numbers of works ascribed to him. He had the ability to write quickly, and possessed a remarkable capacity to illustrate his points with examples drawn from his historical readings and his wide experience. Although Furbank and Owen pretend to be revising a number of relatively obscure bibliographers, in fact they are also dismissing such distinguished biographers and critics of Defoe as James Sutherland, Pierre Dottin, and J. T. Boulton, all of whom believed they were capable of recognizing Defoe's style and ideas. In judging what Defoe actually wrote, I have drawn upon my years of reading his texts and those of his contemporaries. I have not followed the *Checklist* of John Robert Moore in cases where I felt that there was not sufficient evidence for the ascription. I have added a number of works to the canon, from a holograph manuscript I found in the William Andrews Clark Memorial Library to pamphlets which to my mind reflect his style and thought. In each case I have published my reasons for believing these works were by Defoe, and I have not changed my mind about them.

[8] Professor Irving Rothman of the University of Houston has begun work on determining Defoe's authorship through statistical analysis of language, vocabulary, and style.
[9] *Biographia Britannica*, iv. 74.

II

In naming the first half of the eighteenth century 'Defoe's England', the
historian G. M. Trevelyan was presenting something of a paradox.[10] It is
well that we understand that paradox before any attempt to discuss Defoe
in his age. If we are looking for a writer who explored almost every aspect
of the life of his time through his writings and did it with knowledge and
insight, then Defoe is an excellent candidate.[11] The title of Peter Earle's
study, *The World of Defoe*, suggests the same view as that advanced by
Trevelyan. To look at the early eighteenth century through Defoe's eyes is
to see its economic, social, and political realities reveal themselves in a
manner that no other writer affords. He commented on everything from
warfare to street lighting, from the condition of women's education to the
rise of the middle class. And since he loved to give names to his period—
'The Projecting Age', 'The Age of Luxury', 'The Age of Extravagance'—
why not 'The Age of Defoe'?

But his contemporaries would have howled in outrage at the suggestion.
In 1728, the publication of Fontenelle's encomium to Newton, who had
died two years earlier, brought out retrospective assessments of Newton's
life that left little doubt that if the age was to be named, it should belong to
him—'The Age of Newton'. Everyone acknowledged his pre-eminence in
science. He headed the Royal Society and the Mint. Honours were heaped
upon him, and he died a wealthy man. The newspapers were filled with
poems praising his extraordinary powers of mind. As the title of Marjorie
Nicolson's book on the subject suggested, Newton's genius 'demanded'
that the writers of the age celebrate him.[12] And unlike Newton, who was a
wealthy man at his death, Defoe was to die away from his home, hiding
from a creditor who had the power to seize all his goods and throw him into
prison for debt.

Contrary to the example of Newton, in 1726, many in the literate population were probably uncertain whether Defoe was alive or dead in 1731.
Prose fiction was considered an upstart genre. How absurd that the
supposed author of *Robinson Crusoe* might be considered a major contributor to the literature of the period! Addison and Shaftesbury had made
politeness the literary ideal, and Defoe's speciality was the impolite, the
outrageous, and the shocking. And as the author of pamphlets and newspapers, he suffered from a distorted view of who he was and what he had

---

[10] *English Social History* (London: Longmans, Green, 1942), 293.
[11] This was the rationale that Trevelyan gave in his *England under Queen Anne* (3 vols., London:
Longmans, Green, 1930–4), i. 2–4.
[12] The title of Nicolson's book was *Newton Demands the Muse*.

done. A writer in the *Whitehall Evening Post* of 25–7 January 1728, a journal that Defoe had founded and which he had once controlled, decided to use the example of Defoe to suggest to the editor of *The Craftsman*, a newspaper, which was Tory, anti-Walpole (the chief minister), and flirted with Jacobitism, that he might well experience the same fate as Defoe:

A *Gentleman* well known for his works in *Verse* and *Prose*, and *who dealt much in the allegorical and figurative Way of Writing*, happening once to be *too well understood* in a *Court of Justice*, was, for about the Space of an Hour, set up as an *additional Statue*, in the *Area* at *Charing-Cross*, upon a *Pedestal* of the *Law's providing*; where having been sufficiently *Bronzed*, he was ever afterwards found *hardy* enough to write *for* or *against* any *Persons* or *Things* whatsoever: This *Gentleman*, about the latter End of the *late Queen*'s Reign, wrote and publish'd a String of *Pamphlets* under these three alarming Titles,

What if the Queen should dye?
What if the House of *Hanover* should be set aside?
What if the Pretender should come?

The author of this piece managed to get most things wrong. To the outrage of his enemies, Defoe was unharmed by the crowd that usually hurled filth (including faeces) at those placed in the pillory. He turned the occasion into a triumph. The three pamphlets were all anti-Jacobite, and his pardon had come because he was useful to the government, even if they must have been outraged that he would write such pieces. This image of Defoe as an unprincipled journalist who wrote three pro-Jacobite pamphlets and had to be protected by the Queen's pardon was almost all that had survived of his reputation during the later years of his life and the decades following his death—this and the knowledge that he had probably written *Robinson Crusoe*, one of the truly popular and widely respected works of the early eighteenth century. When a false rumour reported Defoe dead in 1718, contemporary newspapers were filled with satires on his descent to the underworld. Compared to these ironic obituaries, anonymity must have seemed a blessing. Shortly after his real death, one editor, who admired Defoe's arguments on a certain issue, felt he had to apologize for printing the work of so '*infamous*' a writer, and justified his action on the grounds that the work had been written 'before his fall into jacobitism', and that it was 'written with great strength of argument, as well as sprightliness of style'.[13]

Thus, although he had created works which were to shape the ideas of his time and continue to influence our own, Defoe was hardly thought of as

---

[13] Quoted from the *The Corn-Cutter's Journal* (1735), No. 74, in *An Alphabetical Catalogue of an Extensive Collection of the Writings of Daniel Defoe* (London: Whitmore & Fenn, 1830), 41.

the *author* of these works. When his *Plan of the English Commerce* was announced as '*This day Published*' in the *Evening Post* of 21–3 March 1723, no author was listed. This was in contrast to the next advertisement, the second edition of *The Henriade*, proudly identified as the work of the already famous Voltaire. Defoe may have understood the price he would pay to posterity for concealing his authorship, but the notoriety he had achieved, during the reigns of William and Mary, William III, and Queen Anne, and its disastrous results may have left him cool to the pleasures of authorial fame.

Although he certainly did not shun the notoriety, Defoe courted anonymity from the beginning of his writing career because he knew that exposing his name might be dangerous. By assuming a mask, as it was called, or writing anonymously, he could attack ideas and persons with a certain freedom. Toward the end of his life, he assumed the mask of Andrew Moreton to give his final advice to his fellow Britains. Most of the knowledgeable audience knew that Moreton was Defoe, and they suspected his presence in every anonymous work. It was as if everyone preferred him to maintain this shadowy existence. As Kippis suggested, his rediscovery at the end of the eighteenth century and his canonization during the following century and in ours may have represented the proof that literary cream rises to the surface, but it would have seemed strange to Defoe's contemporaries. Not that the greatest poet of the age, Alexander Pope, did not recognize his talent.[14] It was just that, in his case, talent was not supposed to be enough.

III

Who then was this Defoe whom some historians feel worthy of being thought of as the hero of his age? I hope that my biography will provide some answers to this question, but I must confess that I came to writing this work reluctantly. Nevertheless, after having written a number of books on Defoe's fiction and ideas, I became convinced that some of the ambiguities in his writing would never become clear unless the writings were viewed in the context of his life. Trevelyan thought of him as a perceptive observer of his age who saw things with 'modern' eyes and who, therefore, speaks to our sensibility. There is some truth in this, but in many ways, he was

---

[14] Pope remarked to Joseph Spence, 'The first part of *Robinson Crusoe*, good. DeFoe wrote a vast many things, and none bad, though none excellent. There's something good in all he has writ.' See Joseph Spence, *Observations, Anecdotes and Characters of Books and Men*, ed. James Osborn (2 vols., Oxford: Clarendon Press, 1966), i. 213 (item 498).

deeply rooted in the past—in the culture that led to and supported the Civil War of the seventeenth century. What made him unique was his ability to see history as a continuum, to see, for example, the inevitable development of Britain toward capitalism and the Industrial Revolution while contrasting the present and future to the ideals of the past. He also had the imagination to turn this sense of time and history into fictions, dramatizing change and development through the lives of a series of brilliantly realized characters.

I have to admit to a personal admiration for many of Defoe's ideas, particularly those of his youth, when he held radical egalitarian principles involving what he considered to be the social and political ideals behind the Glorious Revolution of 1688. Defoe was always at his best when he was revealing the hypocrisy of society—of the wealthy and powerful punishing the weak and poor for the same crimes that they themselves committed. But my major aim was to write a biography that would see him mainly in terms of his development as a writer of fiction and travel literature. This is how we know and appreciate his writings today, and it is those aspects of his life relevant to his writing *Robinson Crusoe*, *Moll Flanders*, *Colonel Jack*, and *Roxana* that have been my major interest. Many of the documents involving Defoe are legal in nature, but I have avoided seeing Defoe's life through court proceedings except where his encounters with the law inform us about his character. Defoe's life was filled with exciting events, and I had no intention of making it less interesting than it actually was.

I

After the Revolution

the enthusiasm, the battle-readiness, the confident emnity, the polemical eagerness, the sense of unity among the brethren, the first pride of self-control—all of these were gone. Something of the tension, vigilance, and excitement they suggest might have been maintained in the holy common-wealth but not in the world of the Restoration and the Whigs.

Michael Walzer, *The Revolution of the Saints*[1]

Daniel Defoe was born in 1660, the year of the Restoration of Charles II to the throne of England. After eighteen years, the nation was to be once more united under a legitimate monarch. The poetry written for the occasion depicted Charles as a new sun dispelling the clouds of civil war and promising to bring the nation a period of brightness and glory. The Interregnum was viewed as a period of darkness and despair. Charles was the son of the martyred Charles I, whose beheading had been viewed by many as a terrible blow to any notion of a universe ruled by a beneficent and all-knowing God whose earthly monarchs ruled as His representatives. Now all might be well again. A world that to a majority of Englishmen seemed turned upside down was to be righted again. For Presbyterians such as Daniel's parents, James and Alice Foe, the Restoration was to prove the reverse—a time of moral corruption and religious persecution.

What Michael Walzer depicts as the deflation of spirit that assailed those who had supported Parliament in its war against the Stuart monarchy was very much part of the milieu into which Defoe was born. He came into the world after the revolution—after the time of great deeds, of victories on the field of battle and victories of the spirit. His attitude toward the age of

---

[1] (New York: Athenaeum, 1969), 320.

heroes that came before was both romantic and nostalgic. He longed to be a hero, a saint, or the helper of some great man, and as the secret agent for William III and for various ministers, he achieved that last ambition. That his true greatness for posterity would depend on his talents as a writer of fiction—as the author of *Robinson Crusoe*, *Moll Flanders*, *A Journal of the Plague Year*, and *Roxana*—might have come as a mild surprise. Yet he would have accepted the recognition of his genius as, perhaps, inevitable. Though vilified by his enemies as an agent of Satan, a leader of the mob, and a turncoat, Defoe had the irritating quality of pretending to complete sincerity and to unruffled moderation.

A few of the unregenerate 'Saints' who had brought about the revolution of 1642 remained in England to brood over the ruin of their hopes to create a new earth in expectation of a new heaven. To the last moment, England's greatest living poet, John Milton, urged the nation to retain its freedom from monarchy. But there were few to listen, and Milton barely escaped punishment. The regicides who had not succeeded in fleeing the country were captured and executed; the bodies of those who had died, including that of the Protector, Oliver Cromwell, were exhumed and subjected to humiliation. Some, such as General Ludlow, fled across the Channel and would occasionally publish a defence of republicanism and of the Pro-tectorate to show that the Old Cause was still alive. But most retired from public life to meditate upon those great years when revolution against the monarchy seemed to be the road that biblical prophecy had ordained, when Charles I had seemed like an agent of Satan who needed to be swept away in the general cleansing of the earth that would precede the second coming of the Messiah.

Such figures, crabby, odd, nostalgic, were frequently brought onto the Restoration stage as objects of amusement. In the comedies of the time, characters who insisted too much upon the wonderful orderliness of life during the Protectorate were mocked and swept aside along with those who looked back even further to the wonders of the 'Last Age', the period preceding 1642. Members of the younger generation such as Hippolita in William Wycherley's *The Gentleman Dancing Master* proclaimed the wonders of the new age. In response to the glorification of the past at the expense of the present by one of her elders, she announced that the world was good enough for her, and that those who didn't like it could step out of the way and leave it to the young who knew how to enjoy it.[2] In expressing her opinion and in dismissing the past and the opinions of the vast popula-tion outside of London where religious attitudes still held sway, Hippolita

[2] *Complete Plays*, ed. Gerald Weales (New York: Doubleday, 1962; Athenaeum, 1969), 139 (I. i).

was giving voice to the views that dominated in the seat of power and influence—the court and the sophisticated 'Town'. The authors of the many 'letters from the country' might rage over the luxury of the court and the corruption of the city. Satires against the behaviour of the King's mistresses were passed around in manuscript. A particular target of such attacks was the Duchess of Portsmouth, Charles's favourite mistress, upon whom he lavished great sums of money. Many considered her little less than a spy for France and Louis XIV. But Charles refused to abandon his pleasures, even though there were times when he expected treatment from his subjects hardly less severe than that visited on his father.

Equally disapproving were the Dissenters. After the Conference of Westminster in 1661 had failed to resolve the differences between Anglican ministers and the Presbyterians, Independents, Baptists, and other sects, those who felt they could not conform to the rules of the Church of England became known as Dissenters. Their ministers were deprived of their positions in the Church and, through a series of Parliamentary Acts, forced out of their ministries. They lived under the threat of continual punishment. They and their followers were often thrown into prison for holding what had become unlawful religious services. Although the acts were enforced unevenly, depending upon the particular political situation of the time, no Dissenter felt himself free from persecution. Not until William and Mary were crowned as joint monarchs of England in 1690, Defoe's 30th year, was a degree of toleration firmly established.

I

The Foe family came from an area north of Peterborough, around the towns of Peakirk and Etton. When Defoe wrote his brilliant poetic attack against the idea of racial purity, *The True-Born Englishman*, one of his enemies accused him of writing as a foreigner, or as one of the descendants of Protestant refugees who had fled Catholic persecution by coming to England, but there is no evidence for this assumption beyond his own frequent praise of the wisdom of Queen Elizabeth for allowing refugees from religious oppression to come to England. There were members of the family in the area of Peakirk and Etton as early as 1529, when the Abbot of Peterborough granted lands with a lease of eighty-one years to Thomas Foe and his wife, Cicilie. The lease was probably renewed in 1610, for Foes are present in the area into the early seventeenth century.[3]

[3] See Frank Bastian, *Defoe's Early Life* (London: Macmillan, 1981), 11.

Peakirk is still a charming village, but James Foe, Daniel Defoe's father, was born in 1630 at Etton, about five miles to the east across what is now the A15 highway. That small community retains its agricultural character even today. The land is flat and filled with gravel, not very productive without the help of fertilizer. That so many younger sons were sent to London from this area to be apprenticed is partly to be ascribed to the general social movement toward the city in this period, but it may also say something about the harsh existence on small farms in this area at this time.[4]

Defoe's father, James Foe, along with his older brother, Henry, followed the road to London and to moderate success as tradesmen and merchants. The youngest of Daniel and Rose Foe's four children, James was born in 1630 at Etton. Daniel died in 1631, leaving £230 to be divided among his children. The oldest son, another Daniel, took over the farm but, like his father, his life came to an early end in 1647. Nothing is known about any descendants he may have had. There are, indeed, no records of a Foe family in the Etton region during Defoe's lifetime. Perhaps the harsh existence of the yeoman and its toll on father and son may have convinced all to move away. Nothing is known of Mary Foe, who was baptized at Etton in 1625, but the Jane Foe who was arrested for being present at an illegal Dissenting religious meeting in 1686 was probably Defoe's aunt.

Although little information exists about James Foe's sisters and brothers, something more is known about Defoe's grandmother, Rose. She had two more husbands after Daniel Foe. In 1633, she married another Etton yeoman, Solomon Fall, and had two children with him. After his death, the date of which is not known, she married Thomas King of Orton Longueville in Huntingdonshire, a widower with two children. His daughter, Ellen King, had married Rose's eldest son, Daniel in 1643. When Thomas King died in 1658, Rose experienced for the third time the fate of being a widow with a family to care for. Her life could not have been easy. Thomas King left her an annuity of only £5. Like her other husbands, he had been a yeoman with a farm of little more than fifty acres. Defoe liked to throw out hints about ancestry who came from the gentry, but his feeling for the common people of England and his sense that the power of governing sprang from them was more likely to have had its roots in the spirit of the English yeomanry from which he was truly descended.

What kind of people were these who came before the revolution? One

⁴ See Richard Grassby, 'Social Mobility and Business Enterprise in Seventeenth-Century England', in *Puritans and Revolutionaries*, ed. Donald Pennington and Keith Thomas (Oxford: Clarendon Press, 1978), 355–60.

biographer of Defoe has suggested that the character of the mother in Defoe's *Due Preparations for the Plague* (1722) may have been modelled on Rose Foe, since she is presented as a widow with three grown children, a daughter and two sons, the latter two living as merchants in London while she resided outside the city.[5] Such interpretation, if made too literally, can result in an absurd selectivity of facts. The mother in *Due Preparations* speaks of her experiences in London with the plagues of 1636, when Rose Foe was unlikely to have been outside the Etton area, but as a portrait of a strong and religious woman of the time, Rose Foe may very well have provided Defoe with some aspects of this character. The mother clearly belongs to that group of 'sober and orderly people' known as Puritans.

Since Defoe was continually attempting to teach the lessons that might be drawn from history to his reading audience, it is hardly surprising that he drew a sharp distinction between the Puritans and his contemporaries, no matter how upright in the conduct of their lives or orthodox in their Christian beliefs. In a manuscript located at the William Andrews Clark Memorial Library, with the motto 'Humanum est Errare' and the title 'Mistakes on All Sides, An Enquiry into the Vulgar Errors of the State', Defoe treated those he called 'Puritans' as those Englishmen of the sixteenth and early seventeenth centuries who wanted to purify themselves and their religion.[6] Some felt so bitterly about the religion that James I had forced on the nation that they fled to New England, and 'they so unanimously flocked thither that had not the Civill Wars afterwards happened, Twas thought all the Soberest people in the Nation had gon away'.[7] Those who remained saw the nation's morals corrupted by the 'Debauching' of James I and by his *Book of Sports*. The Puritans lived in a different world, a world as yet relatively innocent of the 'Luxury' that the Stuarts were to introduce.

But according to Defoe, they would never have broken with the established Church. The break that occurred was 'purely Politicall'. It was the refusal of Charles I to comply with his Parliament in 'matters of liberty, Grievances of State, breaches of Priviledges' that brought about the rebellion.[8] As evidence of the Puritans' willingness to endure what was to them ungodly religious practices without separating from the Church of England, Defoe instanced the 'Shout in the house of Commons, and a

[5] Bastian, *Early Life*, 13. See also P. D. Mundy, 'The Ancestry of Daniel Defoe', *N&Q* 74 (1938), 112–14; 175 (1975), 44.

[6] William Andrews Clark Memorial Library MS D324M1. H918. See my 'Humanum est Errare', *Clark Library Newsletter* 4 (1983), 1–4.

[7] 'Humanum est Errare', fo. 3ʳ.

[8] Ibid.

Universall joy Thro' the whole Nation' upon the King's agreement to the Petition of Right in 1628. Had Charles I not attempted to act against the 'people's libertyes' afterwards, the Civil War would never have divided the nation.[9]

Although Defoe was mainly intent upon describing the errors that led to the refusal of a part of the nation to conform with the Church of England and to distribute the mistakes evenly in accord with his theory of moderation, 'Humanum est Errare' leaves the Puritans wholly innocent. While attributing to Oliver Cromwell the mistake of failing to restore the monarchy, the bulk of the errors are put squarely on the shoulders of the Stuart monarchs. If Defoe proposed to write a pamphlet that might heal divisions, he certainly had not succeeded. But what is important for us is how much it reveals about Defoe's attitudes toward those 'Exact observers of Religious Dutyes, Upright, Harmless, Just, and Charitable' people who were his ancestors.[10]

In Defoe's mind the Puritans had lived at a time when the modern world of corrupt luxury had not made its irreversible impact upon everyday life. Although he accepted this rift in history and made the changes that had occurred a central part of his thinking on social and economic issues, and although in some senses he was very much the 'citizen of the modern world' depicted in John Robert Moore's biography, there was another part of Defoe's soul that longed for the era that he described in his *Memoirs of a Cavalier*, the period of the Thirty Years War and the English Civil War. The volume titled *The Swedish Discipline*, with its combination of military order and religious faith, formed part of his reading as it had for so many of those who fought under Gustavus Adolphus and under Cromwell.[11] The former had rallied the Protestant forces in Germany at a time when Catholic Europe seemed ready to overwhelm the Protestant North, and the latter had shown how Christian faith might be translated into the stuff of military heroism. When, toward the end of the third volume of *Robinson Crusoe*, Defoe's hero punningly called for a new crusade ('Crusadoe') to conquer, civilize, and Christianize the furthest reaches of the earth, Defoe must have been delighted to have found a way to use a fictional character and a fictional form of his own invention as a means of dramatizing and imaginatively fulfilling his daydreams. And when he wrote of the shout that echoed through the House of Commons when Charles I finally agreed to the Petition of Right, who can doubt that Defoe felt himself among those

[9] 'Humanum est Errare', fo. 4^r.
[10] Ibid. fo. 3^r.
[11] As Arthur W. Secord demonstrated, Defoe used this work extensively in writing *Memoirs of a Cavalier*. See *Robert Drury's Journal and Other Studies* (Urbana: University of Illinois Press, 1961), 92.

who had won those basic rights to have some say in how people should be taxed, some right to an impartial legal system, and some ability to resist the military power of the king? If, as one historian has suggested, Englishmen might still be divided according to which side they would have taken in the battle of Marston Moor (1644), when Oliver Cromwell and his Ironsides inflicted a decisive defeat on the king's forces, there is little doubt that Defoe's sympathies would have been with Cromwell. If Defoe had some relative who fought for Parliament against Charles I and his cavaliers, we do not know of them, but who can doubt where the sympathies of the Foe family lay?

Defoe boasted of wearing a ring that had been given at the funeral of Christoper Love, the Presbyterian minister who had been beheaded in 1653 for taking part in a plot to overthrow Cromwell and bring in Charles Stuart, later Charles II, and perhaps there had been some connection between the Foe family and Love. But Love himself had preached excitedly of rebellion in 1645.[12] That the Presbyterians in general were unhappy with the Protectorate is well known, but their attitudes toward the monarchy had not only been shaped by *The Swedish Discipline*. In Defoe's library is another work that was tremendously popular with those on the side of Parliament, John Goodwin's *Anti-Cavalierism* (1642), a work which argued in the strongest possible manner the inevitability as well as the right of resistance against any extra-legal use of force on any individual.[13] When Defoe was to argue that a citizen might justly defend himself against impressment into the army or navy to the extent of killing those attempting to capture him, he was employing arguments which had been forcefully stated by Goodwin and which probably constituted the beliefs of the Foe family.[14]

Although little is known about James Foe and even less about Alice, or Ailce, as her name is recorded in the records of births and marriages, there are enough hints to imagine what they were like. In 1644 James had been apprenticed to John Levitt, a member of the Butchers' Company, who was serving his second term as master of the Company in that year. Levitt was described as a 'tallowchandler', and a similar designation is used for his former apprentice in the Cripplegate registers, but membership in the livery companies of the city seldom indicated very much about the real

---

[12] See Lawrence Kaplan, *Politics and Religion during the English Revolution* (New York: New York University Press, 1976), 104.

[13] Defoe's library was sold with that of the Anglican cleric Phillips Farewell by Olive Payne in 1731. With the exception of books in Latin on ecclesiastical subjects, the catalogue consists mainly of Defoe's books. See *The Libraries of Daniel Defoe and Phillips Farewell*, ed. Helmut Heidenreich (Berlin: printed by W. Hildebrand for the author, 1970), 94 (item 1423c).

[14] See esp. Goodwin's appeals to liberty and equality in *Anti-Cavalierism* (London [1642]), 3–4, 38–9.

occupation of those listed.[15] James probably underwent an apprenticeship in areas associated with his trade, but he functioned for the most part as a tradesman in various goods and, at least in part, as a merchant, in that he imported and exported goods. What is clear from the continued years of service in the Butchers' Company, where he was made Assistant Warden and Warden, is his steadiness and reputation as an honest and dependable businessman. His selection as the trustee in a number of wills suggests that those appointing him thought of him as a person who would be unlikely to misuse the money entrusted to his care. James Foe was probably close to being the ideal tradesman whom Defoe canonized in his *Compleat English Tradesman* (1726–7), the man who regulates his time, knows the language of his trade, and is not distracted by the schemes of projectors or the lure of politics and society. Most of all, he must actually take pleasure in his work:

Now in order to have a man apply heartily, and pursue earnestly the business he is engag'd in, there is yet another thing necessary, namely, that he should delight in it: to follow a trade, and not to love and delight in it, is a slavery, a bondage, not a business: the shop is a *Bridewell*, and the warehouse a house of Correction to the Tradesman, if he does not delight in his trade; while he is bound, as we say, to keep his shop, he is like the galley-slave chain'd down to the oar; he tuggs and labours indeed, and exerts the utmost of his strength for fear of the strapado, and because he is obliged to do it; but when he is on shore, and is out from the bank, he abhors the labour, and hates to come to it again.

To delight in business is making business pleasant and agreeable; and such a Tradesman cannot but be diligent in it: this according to *Solomon* makes him certainly rich, makes him in time, raises him above the world, and able to instruct and encourage those who come after him.[16]

Defoe could wax rhapsodic over his ideal tradesman, but that this picture was not to fit James's son will become clear enough.

James probably married Alice at the end of 1656 or the beginning of 1657 if the birth of their first child, Mary, on 13 November 1657 may be taken as evidence. What kind of family was Alice descended from? Did James meet her in the parish of St Botolph Aldgate while he worked for James Levitt? To marry someone connected with one's master was fairly common. The only 'facts' about her seem less certain the more carefully they are considered. The grandfather Defoe mentioned in the preface to the seventh volume of his journal, the *Review*, who kept a huntsman with a pack of hounds named for the various generals of the Civil War, has conjured up the picture of a large country estate, and since Defoe made some effort to claim descent from a family with the name De Beau Faux, there has been conjecture that there may have been some reality to this picture. But it hardly seems likely that Alice would have been connected with such a family. Defoe had introduced the subject by speaking of the custom of Tory fox-hunters to name their good dogs after Tories and the bad ones after Whigs. He may simply have been using a rhetorical strategy to suggest that names of this kind may be subject to the fluctuations of history.[17] As for another reference to his ancestry, the connection with the family of Sir Walter Raleigh, one can only think with Defoe's biographer, James Sutherland, that if Defoe liked to believe that he had the blood of that earlier explorer and writer in his veins, the strain must have been thin indeed by the time of Defoe's birth.[18] Defoe mentioned his mother only once, and that was by way of illustrating the futility of trying to control the Dutch from trading with the French during the war they, along with their English allies, were fighting against France. Since there was no way of controlling the Dutch, there was no use complaining. He compared the attitude of the English to a time when, as a child, he tried to have his own way against the will of his mother: '*If you Vex me, I'll Eat no Dinner*, said I, when I was a Little Boy, till my Mother taught me to be Wiser, by letting me stay till I was a Hungry.'[19] Although one biographer sees in this incident a somewhat severe mother, the incident seems to suggest that the young Defoe was under the impression that he had considerable power over his parents—the power that children exert through their knowledge of the overwhelming affection that their parents feel for them.[20] If he had to be taught a lesson, it was because his expectation was that he would be able to manoeuvre his mother into doing what he wished by the mere spectre of his suffering the pangs of hunger.

The incident is important because it suggests that James and Alice Foe had what has been called a 'companionate marriage'—a marriage based on the love of the parents for each other and for their children. While it is doubtful that children were ever regarded as merely a 'piece of protein', whose life or death was almost a matter of indifference to the parents, it is also true that the high mortality rate among children had to create a certain hardness toward them. And without the conveniences that accompany the raising of infants in our society today, the rearing of children was far more difficult. If, then, Defoe became an advocate for love as the only valid

---

[17] *Review.*
[18] Sutherland, *Defoe*, 2nd edn. (London: Methuen, 1950), 2.
[19] *Review*, i. 367.
[20] Bastian, *Early Life*, 18, sees this as a sign of the 'calm discipline of a Puritan merchant's home'.

basis for marriage and for the family as the centre of a sane existence, he probably found his model in his own mother and father.[21]

As a return for the difficulties of bringing a child into the world, raising and educating it, the child was to feel gratitude and deep respect. It was not uncommon for children, even after they were adults, to kneel when they came into the presence of their parents. Late in his life, Defoe attacked the wickedness of some children toward their parents as the height of ingratitude:

Let such self-sufficient Persons consider, that it was once in their Parents Power to have abandoned them, then they were more helpless than any other Being to which God has given Life. When they must inevitably have perished, without great Care and Tenderness: and indeed the Divine Wisdom is most manifestly seen in making Man, the Chief of all his earthly Creatures, to require so delicate a Management, and so tender a Nourishment: parental Love being encreas'd by Its Care, as filial Love ought to be, by a Gratitude for that Care it can never too Much acknowledge or repay.[22]

As shall be seen, when Henry Baker came to court Defoe's daughter, Sophia, he asked her if her affections had been given to anyone. She replied that they were given only to her father and to God. Defoe seems to have passed on his attitudes to at least one of his children. This intense love and respect within the family was not universal at the end of the seventeenth century, but Defoe was one of those writers who helped to make it the model for the next century.

II

Like so much in Defoe's life, the exact place and date of his birth are uncertain. The place was probably the London parish of St Giles Cripplegate and the date some time in 1660. The parish registers of St Giles Cripplegate list the birth of his two sisters in a distinct manner. In the list for 1657 there appears:

Mary daught' of James Foe Tallowchandler & of Ailce Not christened but borne November 13.[23]

[21] I take the term 'companionate marriage' from Lawrence Stone, *The Family, Sex, Love, and Marriage in England, 1500–1800* (New York: Harper & Row, 1977).

[22] Defoe, *The Protestant Monastery* (London, 1727 [1726]), 4–5.

[23] St Giles Cripplegate Parish Register, Nov. 1657, Microfilm 6419/5, 6, 7; MS 6419.6.

And for 1659:

Elizab' daugt' of James Foe tallowchand' & of Ailce not Christe: borne June 19.[24]

By the time Defoe was born, the recorders had returned to the custom of including only baptisms rather than births, and like his sisters, Defoe was not baptized. Some biographers have assumed that Defoe must have been born on 30 September, taking this hint from the date of Robinson Crusoe's shipwreck on his island on that date in 1659. Writing in *The Protestant Monastery*, Defoe, under the pseudonym of Andrew Moreton, described himself as 67, but although that work had the title-page date of 1727, it was actually published on 19 November 1726. Admittedly, Defoe may have been aware that his work would appear with a 1727 imprint, but there is another problem. If Andrew Moreton bears a close resemblance to his creator, he is a fictional creation whose claims that he has started writing late in life and that he was having difficulty having his schemes published in the periodical press bear no resemblance to the prolific Daniel Defoe. On the other hand, it is possible that Defoe thought he was a year older than he actually was. At any rate, the birth of Elizabeth in June of 1659 makes some date in 1660, anywhere from late spring to the end of the year, a likely time for the birth of Daniel.

Why were he and his sisters unbaptized? Since the family's religious sympathies were with the Presbyterians, what would cause them to take such a decision? Samuel Annesley, whom Defoe was to eulogize in a poem after his death, was the minister at St Giles Cripplegate church, and it has sometimes been thought that the Foe family attended his sermons after he was ejected from his place following the Restoration settlement. But Annesley allowed his children to be baptized. Defoe's biographer, Frank Bastian, has made the ingenious suggestion that Alice Foe may have been a Quaker. He rightly suggests how rare the entry 'not christened' was in the parish registers, and connects Defoe's interest in the Quakers with their attitudes toward baptism to arrive at what might seem like a plausible explanation.[25]

Bastian may be correct, but he provides no real evidence for his conjecture. And the problem may not be so complicated that it would demand such a radical solution. In describing the Puritans, Defoe noted that despite various disagreements with the Church of England, the Presbyterians would not have separated themselves had there been any effort at

---

[24] St Giles Cripplegate Parish Register, June 1659. On a page with 39 entries this is the only one with an indication that the child was not christened.

[25] Bastian, *Early Life*, 16.

accommodating the differences between the two bodies.[26] One of the major points of differences concerned the use of the Cross in baptism. Richard Baxter, one of the leading dissenting divines, listed this as an important matter of dispute between many of those who decided to dissent and those who found that they could accept the authority of the Church of England. Although the points of disagreement may seem small enough to us, they represented matters of conscience which families such as that of James and Alice Foe considered significant enough to make membership in the Church of England impossible. The differences between a Tillotson, who conformed and became Archbishop of Canterbury, and a Baxter, who dissented and suffered harassment by the government after 1661, were not great. For many, the question turned simply on a sincere examination of the conscience. And after dissenting, the choice of affiliation with Presbyterians or Congregationalists was often a matter of preference. The Foes likely felt that the manner of baptism as practised in their parish church was unacceptable to them. They need not have been Quakers to have come to such a conclusion.[27]

James Foe was probably a little over 30 when Daniel was born. His career was prospering, and his changes of address suggests a certain upward mobility. But there was nothing meteoric about his rise. In 1667 he was living in Jones's Rents, in the parish of St Stephen Coleman Street, and there is some evidence that he had moved there as early as 1665. It may have been a better neighbourhood then than in 1720, when John Strype referred to it as 'a ruinous Place, the Houses ready to fall down', but to a young boy the winding alleys that led to the ancient wall of London must have been continually intriguing.[28] Even now the streets exert a certain fascination. Not far away lived the blind poet John Milton, and from the meeting-house in Swan Alley there poured forth the Fifth Monarchy Men in 1661 to rise against King Charles II in the name of 'King *Jesus*'. It would be along similar streets that Defoe's thieves, Moll Flanders and Colonel Jack, would run in trying to escape their pursuers.[29]

Although James had been described as a tallow chandler in the birth registries of Mary and Elizabeth, he was listed as a 'Merchant and Citizen of London' in a document from 1673, and in his own will, he described him-

[26] 'Humanum est Errare', fo. 3ʳ.

[27] Richard Baxter wrote: 'But that a Man may adjoyn such a human Sacrament as the Cross in Baptism, to God's Sacrament, I am not satisfied in: And cannot Assent or Consent to it, that such a solemn dedicating Sign should be stated in God's Publick Worship by Man.' *The Life of the Reverend Richard Baxter* (London, 1696), 428.

[28] John Stow, *A Survey of the Cities of London and Westminster*, modernized by John Strype (London, 1720), I. iii. 64.

[29] *Review*, i. 27.

self as a 'merchant' as well. This was a more honorific term than 'trades-man', but it is likely that while he dealt in goods which he imported and sold, he also kept a shop or a warehouse where he vended his merchan-dise.[30] Frank Bastian has relied upon Defoe's *A Journal of the Plague Year* for certain facts about the Foe family during these years, including the notion that James Foe may have been the brother of H. F. or Henry Foe, who had travelled as far as Turkey and had recently come from Lisbon. Although the results of such speculation are certainly intriguing, there is no more reason to speculate on James Foe as the brother who went off to Lincolnshire than to think of the two brothers in Defoe's *Due Preparation for the Plague*, both of whom remain in London. Defoe used the initials H. F. for the saddler who narrated the account of the plague, but he likely used his uncle as a figure to anchor his work in the reality of 1665 while allowing his imagination full play.

What we do know is that Henry Foe, James's brother, was a saddler who had a house of six hearths in an area just outside the chains designating the limits of the city; and this corresponds very well with Defoe's H.F., who lived just in that place, 'a populous Conjunction of Alleys, Courts and Passages . . . full of poor People, most of them belonging to the Butchers, or to other Employments depending on the Butchery'.[31] H.F. had a 'Shop and Ware-houses fill'd with Goods', but explains that he had a steady trade 'to the English Colonies in America'.[32] If he sold only leather goods, he would seem to have been unusual. England at this time has been compared to what would be today the economy of a developing country, and under such circumstances a tradesman-merchant is likely to handle all kinds of goods as opportunities present themselves. While the warehouse with the supply of hats that attracts so many ladies in the midst of the plague may not have belonged to James Foe, it would not have been unusual for him to have handled such merchandise, however out of place it might seem for a dealer in candles.

[30] See Bastian, *Early Life*, 10.
[31] Ibid. 21. In the Guildhall Record Room, Box 37, MS 5, for the Cornhill Ward, Henry Foe is listed as living on Barrs Street, which corresponds with H.F.'s description of his living-place in *A Journal of the Plague Year*.
[32] Defoe, *A Journal of the Plague Year*, ed. Louis Landa (London: Oxford University Press, 1969), 8.

III

What Defoe's childhood was like has to be left to the imagination. He was probably pampered by his mother and his older sister, Mary, and he was undoubtedly strongly imbued with the aura of sanctity and work that would have been typical of the household of a dissenting tradesman.[33] But when Defoe was 5 years old, England experienced a series of extraordinary events beginning with the Great Plague in 1665 and concluding in the following year with the London Fire, and a war with the Dutch that featured a number of spectacular sea battles. Portraying events of this kind were to become his speciality as a writer. John Dryden, who was to be one of Defoe's favorite poets, found artistic inspiration in London as a phoenix rising from her ashes and in the glory of exploding ships, but it was for Defoe to find in the plague a rich source of fictional realism, horror, and fascination. How much of the plague could he have remembered from the age of 5? He told of recalling how coins received in exchange for merchandise were dipped in vinegar before anyone would handle them, and this is precisely the kind of detail that a child might recall. Noting that, as a 5-year-old child, Defoe would hardly have been allowed to wander the streets of London to see the bodies being dropped into the plague pits, James Sutherland wondered if there had been a diary left by Henry Foe that Defoe drew upon, and Frank Bastian approached *A Journal of the Plague Year* as a form of history rather than fiction.[34]

These strike me as wrong directions in responding to a work as gripping as this. Defoe, like Wordsworth, was very much a writer of memory—of recalled emotions as well as experiences—and he may have had the ability to remember how people felt during the plague and how terrified he was of the strange disease that seemed to come upon its victims often without warning. Although the narrative seems to come from H.F., the mature saddler and respected citizen of London, the central effect of the work bears some similarity to the works of Gothic horror written at the end of the eighteenth century, with their openness to psychological interpretation. At the age of 5, children often develop an ambivalent fascination for death—a combination of curiosity and terror. The narrative of H.F. may be said to duplicate just that experience. He is drawn compulsively to wander about the half-deserted city in search of the effects of the very disease which terrifies him.

[33] Alice, the first child of James Foe and Alice, probably died in infancy, since there is no record of her after her birth. In the Guildhall Record Room, Box 21.3, a list of the inhabitants of the Coleman Ward for 1667/8 includes James, Alice, and one servant.

[34] Sutherland, *Defoe*, 8–9.

He tells the reader how his 'Curiosity led, or rather drove me to go and see this Pit again, when there had been near 400 People buried in it', and he insists on seeing it at night in spite of the 'strict Order' against it.[35] Another observer near the pit faints as the bodies fall from the cart, and H.F. seems close to fainting as well:

This was a mournful Scene indeed, and affected me almost as much as the rest; but the other was awful, and full of Terror, the Car had in it sixteen or seventeen Bodies, some were wrapt up in Linen Sheets, some in Rugs, some little other than naked, or so loose, that what Covering they had, fell from them in the shooting out of the Cart, and they fell quite naked among the rest; but the Matter was not much to them, or the Indecency much to any one else, seeing they were all dead, and were to be huddled together into the common Grave of mankind, as we may call it, for here was no Difference made, but Poor and Rich went together; there was no other way of Burials, neither was it possible there should, for Coffins were not to be had for the prodigious Numbers that fell in such a Calamity as this.[36]

H.F. is present in the moralizing and in the commentary on the lack of coffins, but the horror of the pit is very much the child's horror of death and the unknown.

And the failure of language to describe the experience is very much the child's failure to find words to communicate his experience. H.F. confesses about his account: 'This may serve a little to describe the dreadful Condition of that Day, tho' it is impossible to say any Thing that is able to give a true Idea of it to those who did not see it, other than this; that it was indeed *very, very, very* dreadful, and such as no Tongue can express.'[37] As we shall see, there was much in the events of 1722 that explains the writing of *A Journal of the Plague Year* at that time, but Defoe was warning about the possibility of a plague and its horror throughout his life. The places where the pits had been were well marked and remained part of the geography of London that he knew so well. It is possible that he was carried by his father into the country—to Lincolnshire, Northhamptonshire, or Bedfordshire—at the first sign of a change in the bills of mortality, or at least long before 50,000 were to die in just two months,[38] but Defoe's anxiety was real enough. For all its details, statistics, and vivid sense of reality, it is those underlying emotions—fear, curiosity, anxiety—that make *A Journal of the Plague Year* a great book. And those feelings were certainly learned in childhood.

[35] Defoe, *Journal of the Plague Year*, 60.
[36] Ibid. 61–2.
[37] Ibid. 60.
[38] These are Defoe's reckonings. See ibid. 99.

The other great event of this decade, the Fire of London, made less of an impression on him. The fascination that fire exerts for children is quite different from that produced by the horrors of death associated with the plague. Though it produced its share of misery, the Fire of London was also accompanied by great excitement and an interest approaching pleasure. The fire started early in the morning of 2 September 1666 at a baker's shop in Pudding Lane, not far from London Bridge. The diarist Samuel Pepys revealed that mixture of sympathy and excitement as he wandered about London attempting to obtain a good view of the conflagration:

Poor Michell's house, as far as the Old Swan, already burned that way and the fire running further, that in a very little time it got as far as the Stillyard while I was there. Everybody endeavouring to remove their goods, and flinging into the River or bringing them into lighters that lay off. Poor people staying in their houses as long as till the very fire touched them, and then running into boats or clambering from one pair of stair by the water-side to another. And among other things the poor pigeons I perceived were loath to leave their houses, but hovered about the windows and balconies till . . . some of them burned . . . their wings, and fell down.[39]

As the fire approached his own house, Pepys began worrying about his goods and became more thoroughly involved in the general misery, but when he wandered toward Moor Fields after the fire was out but the ashes still hot, observing the ruin of the Exchange and the crowds of 'people, and poor wretches carrying their goods there, and everybody keeping his goods together by themselfs', his account of this stroll reveals the degree of pleasure to be found in any adventure.[40]

The fire burned close to the rented home of James Foe in Swan Alley, but there was time to gather together household valuables before it spread too far in that direction. Interestingly enough, both Defoe and Pepys used the phrase 'a sad heart' to describe their emotions. That sadness arose from the futility of trying to put out the flames when, because of an unusual dry period, everything was so combustible. Defoe described how the 'despairing citizens looke on and saw the devastation of their dwellings with a kind of stupidity caused by amazement' (*Review*, i [ix]. 115), and how the water thrown on the flames seemed to add to the fury of the blaze rather than contribute toward extinguishing it.[41] Pepys tells of encountering Sir Thomas

[39] *Diary*, ed. Robert Latham and William Matthews (Berkeley: University of California Press, 1970–83), vii. 268.
[40] Ibid. 276.
[41] *Review*, i [ix]. 115.

Bludworth, the Lord Mayor, and of his lament that his effort at 'pulling down houses' to make a fire break had proved futile, as the fire would over-take them in the midst of their efforts. 'So he left me, and I him, and walked home,' Pepys wrote, 'seeing people all almost distracted and no manner of means used to quench the fire.'[42]

The spectacle of destroying houses to stop the Fire of London from spreading gave Defoe certain images and ideas which he never forgot, and which he used over and over again in his writings. In times of necessity such as a fire, even the sacred laws of property are suspended. Individual property may be sacrificed for the good of the entire society when danger threatens. Perhaps James Foe was one of those who broke down the walls surrounding Moor Fields in order to safeguard the goods in his home and his warehouse. At any rate, his son used the failure of the magistrates to complain about this action as an example of the way ordinary laws are superseded when the lives and properties of a society are threatened.[43] For someone to take advantage of a person during a fire became, for Defoe, one of the more despicable acts, and when Moll Flanders exploits the misery of such people once too often, she is quickly punished by a watchful Providence.

Defoe seldom referred to the naval battles with the Dutch or to the sight of burning and exploding ships that occurred in the same year as the Fire of London, but the spectacle of the city burning from the Tower in the east to Fetter Lane in the west was not easy to forget. Defoe remained fascinated by fire and explosions throughout his life, whether man-made or the result of some natural catclysm such as a volcanic eruption. Doubtless there were some religious associations in Defoe's mind between the violent upheavals of volcanoes and the fiery end predicted for a sinful mankind, but usually he did not make such connections explicit. Rather one might say that his mind tended to dwell upon the numinous implications of the powerful forces of nature. As such visions were to take shape in his writing, they tended to draw upon the uncomfortable sense of human frailty and minute-ness before a mysterious nature and the all-powerful God who ruled it. Whether he had direct experience of the events of 1665–6 or imaginatively re-created them from the excited conversations of his parents and their friends, they left a vivid impression on Defoe's mind and sensibilities.

Such disasters might be referred to a God angry with a humanity that disdained His warnings. The Mother in *Due Preparations for the Plague* tells her son that a plague might reduce the nation to a state of barbarity similar to Hobbes's state of nature: 'all will be filled with horror and desolation,

---

[42] Pepys, *Diary*, vii. 269–70.   [43] Lee, ii. 368.

every one mourning for himself; no composure, no compassion, no affection; no one to comfort, none to assist; nothing but death in all its most dismal shapes, and its most frightful appearances.' And she predicts the coming of the plague in a way that makes her son think of Jonah's warnings to Nineveh. To this she replies that the plague is 'a messenger sent from God to scourge us from our crying sins'.[44] But the fire raised suspicion of a more earthly cause. John Lilly, the astrologer, was called before Parliament to explain the print of a burning city in one of his books of prediction, and Defoe must have heard rumours about the possible involvement of the Jesuits in such an act. A feeling of conspiracy dominated thinking during the Restoration and early eighteenth century, and no group felt it more than those who, like James Foe and his family, belonged to the group known as Nonconformists or Protestant Dissenters.

Parliament passed a series of punitive laws against them that must have given them both a feeling of persecution and a sense that they were like the Israelites in the wilderness—a relatively select and chosen body of people who would eventually lead England to reformation. The Municipal Corporations Act of 1661 established a series of 'tests' including oaths of non-resistance to the King and communion in the Church of England. Since few Dissenters could agree to this, they were deprived of any control of the municipal corporations that sent many members to the House of Commons. The Act of Uniformity insisted that all ministers subscribe to the *Book of Common Prayer*, and resulted in the resignation of more than 1200 clerics. The Conventicle Act imposed punishment for any meeting for religious worship other than in an Anglican church when more than five members of a family were present. The Five Mile Act forbade any minister who had refused to take the oath imposed by the Act of Uniformity from approaching within five miles of a town or parish where he had formerly preached. Although these laws were enforced unevenly, they were effective weapons in the hands of a host of informers who might, at any time, interrupt a meeting and drag those attending off to prison.

The danger was real enough for them to induce a degree of paranoia throughout the entire Nonconformist community. Defoe noted in his *Review* that at one time during the reign of Charles II his family was so alarmed at the possibility that there would be a forced return to the Catholic Church that, fearing a confiscation of their bibles, they decided to copy them out in shorthand. Defoe remarked that although he was only a 'boy', he 'worked like a horse, till I wrote out the whole Pentateuch, and

[44] In *Romances and Narratives by Daniel Defoe*, ed. George A. Aitken (London: Dent, 1901), xvi. 101–2.

then was so tired I was willing to run the risk of the rest'.[45] For the Dissenters there were few moments in English history until the days of the Popish Plot in 1678 that would have conjured up this image of a return to the days of Queen Mary and of Protestants being burned at the stake for their convictions. And feelings of anxiety went far beyond the Nonconformist community. Theories of conspiracy might be set off by anything from the supposed Catholic origins of the Fire of London to the justified suspicion that there might have been a secret clause in the Treaty of Dover, which Charles made with Louis XIV in 1670, that agreed to an attempted restoration of Catholicism in England. Another period of apprehension came in 1672, when Charles issued his Declaration of Indulgence that suspended the penal laws against both Catholics and Dissenters. Since the Dissenters were even more fearful of 'Popery' than of the persecutions visited upon them by Parliament, for the most part they rejected Charles's suspicious gesture in the direction of toleration. In such an atmosphere, many Dissenters preferred the risk of prison to any concessions toward the *real* enemy.

Such events must have left their scars on Defoe's way of thinking, but along with the fear and suspicion came the sense of being right in a bad world. He was reared in a manner that gave him a certainty about his religious beliefs that could never be shaken. James Sutherland commented shrewdly on Defoe's willingness to forgo copying out the rest of the Bible once he had completed the Pentateuch:

The tone in which Defoe refers to this youthful indiscretion is significant. He is looking back on something which he can now regard with tolerant amusement; he is not actually ashamed of his superfluous zeal, but he can afford to smile. The attitude is characteristic of him. He never lost his early seriousness, but he learnt to be cheerful about it. Defoe, in fact, had been given what is perhaps the most valuable of all intellectual trainings: he grew up in a rather too strict household, and was compelled in later life to discard a number of his early prejudices. Whatever effect such a training may have on a child of weak or mediocre wits, there is a great deal to be said for it when the child is mentally robust; it gives him a shape, a point of view. That point of view he may afterwards have to modify, or even reject completely, but he will never be without one afterwards for the rest of his life.

As the judgement of a scholar who grew up at a time when a strict upbringing was still quite common and in a place still imbued with Presbyterianism and yet who was young enough to have lived through what has been called 'the psychoanalytic revolution', this assessment has to be given

[45] *Review*, ii. 498.

considerable attention in weighing Defoe's character. However, it is in
need of both modification and amplification.

Sutherland sees in the picture of the young boy giving up after transcribing the five books of Moses into shorthand a kind of acceptance of his
weakness, but self-mockery would seem a better description of his state of
mind than cheerfulness. The passage implies an ability to laugh at his weaknesses, and some sense that history had revealed the panic that had forced
such an activity upon him to have been an exaggerated response. The
image of the little boy labouring 'like a horse' underscores the comedy.
This historical distancing also implies some capacity to evaluate his own
life and actions in relationship to changing times. He retained his parents'
Christian beliefs unswervingly, but his experience of the world showed
him that the human race was motivated by self-interest and passion rather
than religious principles and reason. He might appeal to the latter two
principles on occasion, but often he contented himself with convincing
others that their self-interest lay on the side for which he was arguing. His
own weaknesses during his first bankruptcy may have come as a surprise to
him, and the experience made him a better and a more humane person. But
at a time when that section of the Athanasian Creed that consigned most of
the human race to damnation was regarded by many writers, from Dryden
to Fielding, as a part of Christian belief that could be disgarded, Defoe
insisted that salvation depended upon a belief that arose from faith, and that
those who did not believe could not be saved.

So Sutherland was correct in stressing Defoe's sense of the certainty of
his opinions, at least in the area of religious principle. And it is also true
that he was capable of making decisions with firmness and considerable
certainty. Much of this was indeed owing to his childhood in the house
of Alice and James Foe. But when he operated in the areas of politics,
economics, and social reform, he saw unresolvable conflict everywhere.
Trade depended upon luxury, upon stimulating consumer interest, and
upon circulating goods through as many hands as possible. He might raise
the moral principles with which such activities clashed, but he applauded
progress and recognized that in the world of his time there would be no
reconciling economics with morality. And in political matters, much as he
deplored faction and parties as an evil within the state during the reigns of
William III and Queen Anne, he came to accept a *'Balance of Parties'* as the
practical working principle of contemporary politics.[46] He came to see the
gulf separating the ideal from reality as a paradoxical part of human

---

[46] *An Appeal to Honour and Justice Though It Be of His Worst Enemies*, in *The Shakespeare Head
Edition of the Novels and Selected Writings of Daniel Defoe* (Oxford: Blackwell, 1927), 193.

existence, and from this awareness came the possibility of writing a type of fiction in which such conflicts were dramatized and often deliberately unresolved.

2

The Education of a Dissenter

Little is known about Defoe's formal education until he enrolled at Charles Morton's Dissenting Academy in Newington Green. Robinson Crusoe speaks of his education as sufficiently good for what it was, 'House-Education and a Country Free School'.[1] Defoe's enemy Charles Gildon mocked the phrase 'House-Education', and Defoe may have been describing his own early lessons in reading a wide selection of religious and moral books. How much time it took for Daniel to transcribe the Pentateuch into shorthand is difficult to say, but for so religious a family as the Foes, reading and even memorizing large portions of the Bible would have constituted a major part of their son's early education. The home in Swan Alley would have been his schoolhouse, and the company of his mother and his sisters would have constituted his schoolfellows. Elizabeth probably died as an infant, but his close relationship with his future brother-in-law, Robert Davis, suggests a continuing affection for his remaining sister, Mary, throughout his life. Perhaps it was the obvious abilities of this elder sister that led Defoe to complain of the kind of education that women usually received:

The soul is placed in the body like a rough diamond, and must be polished, or the lustre of it will never appear: and it is manifest that as the rational soul distinguishes us from brutes, so education carries on the distinction and makes some less brutish than others. . . . But why then should women be denied the benefit of instruction? If knowledge and understanding had been useless additions to the sex, God Almighty would never have given them capacities, for He made nothing needless. Besides, I would ask such what they can see in ignorance that they should think it a necessary ornament to a woman? or how much worse is a wise

---

[1] *The Life and Strange Surprizing Adventures of Robinson Crusoe*, ed. J. Donald Crowley (London: Oxford University Press, 1981), 3. See also Charles Gildon, *The Life and Strange Surprising Adventures of Mr. D-----De F--*, in *Robinson Crusoe Examin'd and Criticis'd*, ed. Paul Dottin (London: Dent, 1923), 86. Gildon found the phrase odd, remarking, 'I never met with [it] before in all my Reading and Conversation.'

woman than a fool? or what has the woman done to forfeit the privilege of being taught? Does she plague us with her pride and impertinence? Why did we not let her learn, that she might have had more wit? Shall we upbraid women with folly, when it is only the error of this inhuman custom that hindered them being made wiser?[2]

This kind of attitude toward women, with its open admiration and lack of condescension, was so rare in the period that it might be doubted that he spent very much time in the schools for boys that tended to produce the type of male chauvinism of which the women of our century have so justly complained.

By 1671, when Daniel was 11, James Foe moved from Jones's Rents to French Court in the parish of St Benet Fink just off Threadneedle Street. This was an area that had been rebuilt after the fire, and the move may have been an indication of his growing prosperity. He was listed among the Livery Men of the Butchers' Company in that year, and his progress to becoming a Warden reveals a steady climb.[3] Although the survey of London published in 1720 suggested that French Court was but 'indifferent well inhabited', it did have a free stone pavement and was closer than James Foe's previous residences to the business centre of the city.[4]

While most of Daniel's life was spent in the city which he was to eulogize in his *Tour Thro' the Whole Island of Great Britain* (1724–7) as 'the great Center of England' and as 'the most glorious Sight without exception, that the whole World at present can show, or perhaps ever cou'd show since the Sacking of *Rome* in the *European*, and the burning the Temple of *Jerusalem* in the *Asian* part of the World',[5] he travelled beyond London on a variety of occasions. When still very young he apparently travelled to Bath in the west and to Ipswich in the east, if his accounts of his travels may be taken as more than a fiction. In the *Tour*, he took a boat from Harwich up the River Orwell to Ipswich and commented on the decay in the number of ships engaged in carrying coals from Newcastle to London that used to have their centre there:

In the Town of *Ipswich* the Masters of these Ships generally dwelt, and there were, as they then told me, above a hundred Sail of them, belonging to the Town at one time, the least of which carried Fifteen-score, *as they compute it*, that is, 300 Chaldron of Coals; this was abut the Year 1668 (when I first knew the Place). This

---

[2] *An Essay upon Projects*, ed. Joyce Kennedy, Michael Seidel, and M. E. Novak (New York: AMS Press, 1999), 108.
[3] James Foe's steady rise may be traced in the Rough Master's and Warden's Accounts now at the Guildhall Library, MS 6441/1–5; MS 6443a. He became one of the Warden's assistants in 1682.
[4] John Stow, *A Survey of the Cities of London and Westminster* (London, 1720), I. ii. 132.
[5] *Tour*, i. 168, 317.

made the Town be at that time so populous for those Masters, as they had good Ships at Sea, so they had large Families, who liv'd plentifully, and in very good Houses in the Town, and several Streets were chiefly Inhabited by such.

In his further account of the town, Defoe remarked on another visit, stating he had been there 'five and Thirty Years before the present Journey', and contrasting the vivid sight of many ships anchored there in his boyhood with the relatively deserted and desolate contemporary harbour. Most of all, it was his mythologizing the past that made his knowledge of Ipswich seem so personal. He spoke of the ships 'so prodigious strong' that they sometimes remained in service for more than fifty years and of the captains who 'as they had good ships at sea, so they had large families, who liv'd plentifully, and in good houses in the town'.[6]

Although Defoe may have visited such places on occasional trips with his parents, he appears to have spent a considerable time at Dorking in Surrey, where the Marsh family lived. One biographer has suggested that Alice Foe was related to the Marsh family. In the will of Lawrence Marsh, who died in July 1665, James Foe is referred to as 'cousin Foe', but the word seems to be applied in the sense of a close friend rather than to a specific relation.[7] Elizabeth, Lawrence Marsh's wife, was originally from London, and she may have been acquainted with Alice Foe and continued the acquaintance as she was giving birth to her four sons between 1656 and 1660. When Elizabeth died in 1671, she left James Foe £50 and, in making him the executor of her will, provided £10 a year for the 'cares and pains' taken in behalf of her children. The children were put under the care of the wife of John Alexander, who had been her neighbour in Budge Row, London.[8]

Daniel Defoe was well acquainted with the Marsh children, and although Lawrence Marsh did not return to Dorking to take up his estate there until 1677, Defoe probably visited there with his friends often enough to know the neighbourhood around Dorking well. When he and William Marsh, the youngest of the sons, were involved in a lawsuit together, Defoe described him as 'an antient acquaintance and familiar friend'.[9] The boys may have been sent to a boarding-school in the town at one point, for Defoe tells of some 'roguish London boys' at such a school who rigged up an old house in the neighbourhood in such a manner as to give it the appearance of a haunted house.

In the Night, one of those unlucky Boys had gotten a dark Lanthorn, which was a

[6] *Tour*, i. 40–2.   [7] PROB 11, 321, fo. 230ᵛ.
[8] Ibid. 11, 337, fo. 353.   [9] C8/548/96. The arguments were filed in July 1692.

thing the Country People did not understand, and with this he walked all about the Orchard, and two or three Closes near the House, sometimes showing the Light on this side, and then his Comrades calling all the old Women about 'em to see it, on a sudden the Light would go out, the Boy closing up the Lanthorn; and then he would run swiftly across the whole Field, and show his Light again on the other side. Now he would be up in a Tree, then in the Road, and then upon the middle of the Heath; so that the Country People made no more question, but that the old Lady walk'd with a Candle in her Hand, than that they saw the Light of it; and in a word it passed for an Apparition as certainly as we, on the other hand, knew what Knavery agitated it all.[10]

The slip in the account from a third person account to 'we' may suggest that Defoe was a member of this group, and it is certainly possible.[11] On the basis of the failure to mention Alice Foe in Elizabeth Marsh's will, Frank Bastian has argued that Alice Foe may have died, that James had remarried, and that the fierce stepmother had packed Defoe off to a boarding-school in Dorking. Such an account is possible, but the evidence is slight indeed. The ghost was supposed to have been that of an 'ancient lady', though Elizabeth Marsh had been but 41 at her death, and the Marsh children could hardly be described as 'some roguish London boys': they had grown up in Dorking. Bastian has Defoe at a school in Dorking run by James Fisher, but there may also have been a school for Presbyterian children run by John Wood. To see the young Defoe as the ringleader of this group of boys, tricking the gullible country people into believing that they had a poltergeist in their midst, is tempting, not so much because it casts him as a Tom Sawyer as because it suggests that his sense of humour was with him when he was very young, and that the trickster who could manoeuvre disguises to confound his enemies had very deep roots. The safest conclusion that may be drawn from this account is that Defoe could find humour in the pranks of these boys, and that if he did not participate in such activities, he at least enjoyed them from some distance.

I

If Defoe lived at Dorking, or, as he called it, Darking, for any length of time, it was during 1676, for he mentions a number of events from that year

[10] *The Secrets of the Invisible World Disclos'd*, 2nd edn. (London, 1735), 373.

[11] See Frank Bastian, *Defoe's Early Life* (London: Macmillan, 1981), 2. The alternative explanation for the shift in pronoun is that Defoe may simply have lapsed from his detached third-person commentary in telling the story, but the rationale for such an error points at least to his personal knowledge of the events if not his participation.

in his *Tour*, from the 'little troop of the young fellows and boys of the town' who were recruited by Sir Adam Brown's son to capture fish that had escaped from local fishponds in the heavy rains to the planting of a unique garden by Mr Howard at Deaden, his residence, with spectacular hills, a cave, and a vineyard. To underestimate Defoe's ability to re-create a scene from information gleaned from books or accounts he had heard is always a mistake, but the picture of the capture of the fish as the water seeped into the ground was likely to have been experienced at first hand:

they built Hutts or Booths, and made Fires, and sent for Victuals and Drink to treat their Young Company, and there they encamp'd, as if they waited some great Event; and so indeed they did, for in about two Nights and a Day, exclusive of the time they took in making their Dams, the Water sunk all away in the Field; and the consequence of that was, that the Fish being surrounded, were catch'd, as it were, in a Trap, for they cou'd not be swallow'd up with the Water; and the Purchase fully recompenc'd their Labour, for the like quantity of Fish, great and small, I believe was never taken at once in this kingdom, out of so small a river.

This story would have nothing wonderful, to make it worth recording, were it not so evident a Demonstration of the manner of this river losing it self under ground, or being *Swallowed up*, as they call it.[12]

Defoe may have had these and other details from his friends the Marsh boys, but the vividness of the account is remarkable even for Defoe.

If Defoe attended school in Dorking, it was probably in order to gain some proficiency at Latin before going on to the Dissenting Academy of Charles Morton. Was he planning on a career as a clergyman? Defoe gave conflicting accounts about the careers for which he had been trained, perhaps because his parents and he went through a number of changes of mind on the subject. In his journal, the *Review*, Defoe addressed his audience on the matter of trade with the personal statement of his qualifications and regrets, '*if I may speak as a Merchant*, to which I had the Misfortune to be bred'.[13] But in the sixth volume of that journal, after stating that he was going to 'preach a little' to his readers, though he was not a clergyman, Defoe remarked, 'It was my Disaster first to be set a-part for, and then to be set a-part from the Honour of that Sacred Employ.'[14] The change in plans may have come with the sudden death of Daniel's uncle, Henry Foe, in late February 1675. Delivering his will 'by word of mouth', he left everything he owned to his brother. His burial on 28 February may have cast a pall over the family of James Foe, and in a mood of renewed piety, they may have decided to spend the money on Daniel's education as

---

[12] *Tour*, i. 151–2.   [13] *Review*, viii. 754.   [14] Ibid. vi. 341.

a Presbyterian minister.[15] Daniel would have been just the right age for such a decision, for if he had studied as a merchant under his father up to this time, a formal apprenticeship to a merchant or tradesman might have been the usual path for a bright boy of 14.

That the choice of the ministry as a career may have been a late decision could be one explanation for his weakness in Latin. He may have had to learn it quickly and late. His enemies often mocked his ignorance of Latin, and while he could probably read it well enough, he made frequent grammatical errors in attempting to quote Roman authors. Provoked by the criticisms of his friendly rival John Tutchin and his enemy Joseph Browne, he retorted:

I easily acknowledge myself blockhead enough to have lost the fluency of expression in the *Latin*, and so far Trade has been a prejudice to me; and yet I think I owe this justice to my ancient father, still living, and in whose behalf I freely testify, that if I am a Blockhead, it was no Bodies Fault but my own, he having spar'd nothing in my Education that might qualify me to match the accurate Dr. B[rowne], or the learned *Observator*.[16]

In responding to the contemptuous remarks of his enemies, Defoe claimed a knowledge of five foreign languages, but he may have learned these languages easily enough in his travels. As for his gratitude toward his father, Defoe must have realized that the decision to employ much of the money left by Henry Foe for his son's education had not been easy for his father.

And the decision could not have been easy for Defoe either. When Defoe would speak of certain interests that he had as a youth, not all of them appear entirely compatible with those one would expect of a clergyman. If we can believe his statement in one of his last works in which he proposed that a national academy of music be established in Britain, he had played on the lute and the viol as a boy and demonstrated some talent. He mentions several times his love of horse-racing and of his attending the races in the time of Charles II when the Duke of Monmouth rode and won, though a heavy man and as much as possible unlike the jockeys of the 1720s (and our own day) who were selected for their light weight.[17] In the *Review*, he informed his enemies that he carried a sword and knew how to use it. Again, in the *Tour*, he told with apparent satisfaction of how a group of youths became indignant over sabbath-breaking at a kind of pleasure

---

[15] PROB, 250, 1675. The will was dated 19 Apr. 1674 and speaks of 'the sicknesse whereof he dyed'. He lived for another 10 months.

[16] *Review*, ii. 153; see also ii. 149–50.

[17] *Tour*, ii. 553.

garden at Box Hill (the place where Mr Knightley deflated Emma's complacency about herself in Jane Austen's novel) and blew it up with explosives.

Without taking anything away from Defoe's undoubted piety, any biographer would have to conclude that the impulse that led his parents to set him aside for the ministry was misguided. Had he been born a half century earlier, he might have found his ideal vocation as an officer under Cromwell or Fairfax, the heroic ideal of his fictional creation, the Cavalier. That his talents needed to find an outlet in the world of action rather than in a clergyman's study is clear enough from a manuscript that he sent to his future wife, Mary Tuffley, in 1683, 'Historical Collections or Memoires of Passages & Stories Collected from Severall Authors', a selection of his 'juvenal reading'.[18] His purpose was probably twofold. He was surely attempting to provide Mary with a gift in the form of some stories that might entertain her, and he must have been trying to give her some key to the kind of person he was by showing her what had interested him when he was a boy. At any rate, too large a number involved tales of great gestures by leaders of nations or of heroism in battle to suggest that the young Defoe was ready for the contemplative life.

I will discuss some of the implications of this work in the next chapter, in considering how Mary Tuffley might have looked upon this collection, but here I want to consider it in relation to Defoe's youthful reading and what the stories that impressed him say about his character. Although almost all these stories are drawn from books which were intended to inculcate excellent morality in young men, Defoe probably copied down the stories that fascinated him into a commonplace book arranged according to various topics. When he copied a selection for Mary, he omitted the moral instruction that usually accompanied the original texts and allowed the fictions to carry their own message. Remarkably enough, the historical figure mentioned most often is Alexander, and most of the anecdotes about him concern illustrations of his behaviour as an ideal hero. Of the 140 separate apophthegms or anecdotes, ten concern Alexander, with other great worthies such as Julius Caesar and Augustus Caesar having three each. The Great Scanderberg, the Albanian hero who fought so bravely against the Turks, appears in several stories, and fifteen concern soldiers or some aspect of the military life. Forty of the stories involve death and execution, and the same number, allowing some overlapping, are con-

---

[18] This MS is in the collection of the William Andrews Clark Memorial Library, MS H6735M3. For a discussion of this work, see my *Realism, Myth, and History in Defoe's Fiction* (Lincoln: University of Nebraska Press, 1983), 18–21.

cerned with matters of religion. And many of the stories involving religious themes also have their share of violence in them.

If, as seems almost certain, these were Defoe's favourite narratives, his typical daydream involved a moment at which a hero triumphed over his adversaries by some remarkable feat of strength or wit. Such fantasies hardly seem unusual for a boy between the ages of 8 and 15, but they hardly seem the kind of fanciful fiction that would entrance a boy whose mind was focused entirely on spiritual matters. The degree of violence in them might seem more suitable for someone planning a military career than for a future clergyman. One of his important sources was Richard Brathwait's *The English Gentleman* (1630), with its argument for gentility based on virtue and self-control and its suggestion that a man might earn gentility through noble deeds. When Defoe was in trouble with the law later in his life, he spoke of himself as a 'gentleman' and offered to lead a regiment of soldiers to fight for Queen Anne against France. That he did not offer, rather, to leave off all activities in the world and spend his time reading devout books was a sign of where his real interests lay.

'Historical Collections' is important for other aspects of Defoe's life, but one of the episodes that is suggestive of his underlying nature is worth considering at this point. That story was drawn from *Speculum Mundi* and involved a renegade Englishman who, being somewhat drunk, decided to go out to kill a lion that had been seen in the area. He took a long knife with him, but the lion was too quick for him, threw him down, and since he had recently satisfied his hunger, decided to sit on the man until he was ready to eat him. The Englishman took advantage of the animal's decision by eventually freeing his hand with the knife, thrusting it into the lion and killing it.[19]

The story is like a nightmare, even to the point of the beast's weight on his intended victim. That this terrifying story touched a deep chord in Defoe is unquestionable. Robinson Crusoe lives in terror of being devoured by wild beasts. He encounters them first on the coast of Africa after his escape from Sallee with Xury and later, on his island, feels certain that he will be made a victim of the beasts on his island. When these prove to be illusory, he discovers the presence of cannibals, and following a visit to the remains of one of their feasts, he retches from a mixture of disgust and horror. After he has been rescued, he encounters a horde of wolves and other ferocious animals in the Pyrenees. Pscychoanalytic critics have always read such fears as evidence of a fear of castration. That such fear is

[19] See 'Historical Collections', item 120. John Swan's *Speculum Mundi* was published in 1635. There were at least three editions of this work during the Restoration.

controlled in 'Historical Collections' by more benign narratives involving animals—the retelling of the familiar story of 'Androcles and the Lion', with the grateful animal refusing to devour the man who had once relieved its pain by removing a thorn from its paw, and in *Robinson Crusoe* having Friday enact a comic killing of a bear—does not lessen its impact.

What may be said of such evidence is tentative, but the strong patriarchal household of the Defoes must have produced the usual dread of the father and desire to replace him that we now call the Oedipus Complex. In most of Defoe's fictions no father is present or, as with Roxana's father, the father dies early. But in *Robinson Crusoe* the action begins with a conflict between the son, who wishes to wander, and the father, who recommends the calm life of the 'middle State, or what might be called the upper Station of *Low Life*', as 'the best State in the World . . . that this Way Men went silently and smoothly thro' the World, and comfortably out of it'. Crusoe deliberately revolts against his father, and refers to his disobedience as his 'Original Sin'. Defoe seems to us to have been entirely obedient to his father's wishes, but a desire to flout the deeply conservative attitudes of his father in his business dealings as well as his political activism may have lain beneath the emotional surface of young Daniel. If nothing in his career approaches the direct disobedience of a Robinson Crusoe, the results of Defoe's actions were perhaps not very different.

II

Had Defoe's parents not been Dissenters, Defoe would have been sent to Oxford or Cambridge for the studies that would have enabled him to take orders as a clergyman. From almost every true educational standpoint, however, attending the Dissenting Academy of Charles Morton at Newington Green was advantageous to him. Unlike the universities, the academies were open to new ideas, even where such ideas were not entirely congenial. For example, Locke's *Treatise concerning Human Understanding*, which was attacked vehemently by Bishop Edward Stillingfleet as a wicked and probably heretical book when it was published in 1690, became a standard text for discussion in the Academies. New books could be introduced because the curriculum of the Dissenting Academies embodied some of the reforms in education that had been proposed in the middle of the century by J. A. Comenius and Samuel Hartlib. Whereas the universities continued to direct their programmes toward rhetoric and grammar, the Dissenting Academies began going in the direction of placing an emphasis upon 'things' rather than 'words', an emphasis that was to find its most forceful exposition almost a century later in Jean-Jacques Rousseau's *Émile*.

The reputation of the universities was so low and that of the Dissenting Academies so high that many parents who were not Nonconformists sent their children to these institutions. Charles Morton's academy at Newington Green may have been the best of those in existence for the twenty years between 1666 and 1685 that he managed the school. Whereas some of these institutions were hardly more than an extension of the home of the teacher, Morton's academy had a garden with a pond and a kind of laboratory with some scientific equipment, among which was an air pump, that icon of science for the age. Incessant harassment by the Anglican Church finally drove Morton to leave England for America, where he became Vice-President of Harvard College, but if the ecclesiastical authorities made him a target of persecution, everyone else seems to have admired him without reserve. Even Samuel Wesley, in an attack upon the Dissenting Academies as a hotbed of political radicalism and immorality, had to confess his admiration for his former tutor.[20] Morton appears to have been one of those great teachers who impresses his students by his love of learning and his moral character. Edward Calamy said of him, 'He had indeed a Peculiar Talent, of winning Youth to a love of Vertue and Learning, both by his Pleasant Conversation, and by a Familiar Way he had of making difficult Subjects easily Intelligible.'[21] Although he was not one of those pupils trained by Morton who entered the ministry, Defoe was to be his most famous student, and while there may be something of the irony of history in this, Defoe became his disciple in a number of ways.

The best exposition of Morton's system of education appeared in Defoe's *The Compleat English Gentleman* in the context of Defoe's insistence that there was no need for a mastery of the learned languages in education. A person might take a more direct route to knowledge by studying subjects such as geography, history, and politics in English. To apply the notion of learning solely to a command of Latin and Greek, Defoe thought, was narrow and stupid. As an instance of his theory, Defoe pointed to a teacher who conducted his lectures entirely in English and also asked for essays from his students in their native language. Although the idea seems perfectly sensible to us, it was a revolutionary scheme for the Restoration. That it was a boon to Defoe with his weak command of Latin

[20] Wesley, *A Letter from a Country Divine to His Friend in London. Concerning the Education of the Dissenters, in Their Private Academies* (London, 1703), 4–5, 7.

[21] Edward Calamy, *An Account of the Ministers, Lecturers, Masters and Fellows of Colleges and School Masters Who Were Ejected or Silenced after the Revolution in 1660*, 2nd edn. (London, 1713), ii. 145.

is beyond question. He characterized Morton as a man of tremendous powers:

I once was accquainted with a tutor of unquestion'd reputacion for learning and who was himself a critick in the learned languages and even in all the oriental tongues, as the Syriac, Chaldee, Arabic, Hebrew; and none could object that he did it for want of skill, but being sencible of the great defficiency I have been speaking of, and how our gentlemen were dropt, as it were, out of the conversation of the learned world, he set up what he call'd an English Academy. He first published his just complaint against the school learning and their locking up, as I have call'd it, all science in the Greek and Latin, compelling all their pupils to learn the sciences in those languages or not at all; but which means many young gentlemen, even the greatest and best proficients in learning, as they understand the word, came finish'd, as they call'd it, out of their hands, and yet had no tast of the English tongue, could neither express themselves fluently upon any subject or write elegantly in their mother tongue. To rectifye this great mistake of the schools, he set up his little Accademy, wherein he taught Physicks, that is to say, Natural Phylosophy, with a system of Astronomy as a seperate science, tho' not exclusiv of the generall system of Nature; he taught also Geography and the use of the maps and globes in a seperate or distinct class: in a word, he taught his pupils all the parts of accademick learning, except Medicine and Surgery. He also had a class for History, ecclesiastic and civil. And all this he taught in English, and gave his pupils draughts of the works of Khiel and Newton and others translated; also he requir'd all the exercises and performances of the gentlemen, his pupils, to be made in English.[22]

Before we consider other aspects of this training, the emphasis on the English language ought to be stressed because it was so unusual. It represented Defoe's first conscious training as a writer, and its importance cannot be ignored. The act of writing, even the very materials of writing—pen, ink, and paper—was his constant subject.

He was to begin his journal, the *Review*, with an attack upon other journals—upon articles that were impossible to decipher, or seeming errors of fact created by the writer's inability to say what he meant. More than twenty years later, after a chapter devoted to introducing his subject, he entered into the main subject-matter of *The Compleat English Tradesman* with a discussion of the improper and proper methods of writing letters. After attacking the tradesman who uses 'a rumbling bombast stile', Defoe argues that the 'easy free concise way of writing' is the best style not only for the tradesman but for everyone:

---

[22] Defoe, *The Compleat English Gentleman*, ed. Karl Bülbring (London: David Nutt, 1890), 218–19. For a discussion of the curriculum at Newington Green Academy, see Lew Girdler, 'Defoe's Education at Newington Green Academy', *Studies in Philology* 50 (1953): 573–91.

easy, plain, and familiar language is the beauty of Speech in general, and is the excellency of all writing, on whatever subject, or to whatever persons they are that we write or speak. The end of Speech is that men might understand one another's meaning; certainly that speech, or that way of speaking which is most easily understood is the best. If any man was to ask me, what I would suppose to be a perfect stile or language, I would answer, that in which a man speaking to five hundred people, of all common and various capacities, Ideots and Lunaticks excepted, should be understood by they all, in the same manner with one another, and in the same sense which the speaker intended to be understood, this would certainly be a most perfect stile.[23]

Although Defoe was addressing tradesmen, he explained that they need not feel deprived of the pleasures of an ornate style. Plainness with energy were the true graces of any good style.

Defoe's training under Morton gave him this special ability to write with clarity and power, and he was to expatiate upon its virtues:

He had a class for eloquence, and his pupils declaim'd weekly in the English tongue, made orations, and wrot epistles twice every week upon such subjects as he prescrib'd to them or upon such as they themselves chose to write upon. Sometimes they were ambassadors and agents abroad at forreign Courts, and wrote accounts of their negotiacions and recepcion in forreign Courts directed to the Secretary of State and some times to the Soveraign himself.

Some times they were Ministers of State, Secretaries and Commissioners at home, and wrote orders and instruccions to the ministers abroad, as by order of the King in Council and the life. Thus he taught his pupils to write a masculine and manly stile, to write the most polite English, and at the same time to kno' how to suit their manner as well to the subject they were to write upon as to the persons or degrees of persons they wer to write to; and all equally free and plain, without foolish flourishes and ridiculous flights of jingling bombast in stile, or dull meanesses of expression below the dignity of the subject or the character of the writer. In a word, his pupils came out of his hands finish'd orators, fitted to speak in the highest presence, to the greatest assem[b]lies, and even in Parliament, Courts of Justice, or any where; and severall of them come afterwards to speak in all those places and capacityes with great applause.[24]

If anyone mastered the art of writing taught at Newington Green, it was Defoe, and there could have been no better training in the creation of character and fictional context than the kind of exercises given by Morton.

In his *History of Parties* (1712), Defoe was later to complain of the lack of facilities in the Dissenting Academies and how much it limited education.

[23] Defoe, *The Complete English Tradesman*, 2nd edn. (London, 1727; repr. New York: Augustus Kelley, 1969), i. 26.
[24] *The Compleat English Gentleman*, 219–20.

But on the whole, he boasted of the training in 'Science' that was unavailable at the universities. He was to tell a story which illustrates some of the problems and some of the advantages of studying at Morton's academy:

I knew a philosopher that was excellently skill'd in the noble science or study of astronomy, who told me he had some years studied for some simily, or proper allusion, to explain to his scholars the phaenomenon of the sun's motion round its own axis, and could never happen upon one to his mind, 'till by accident he saw his maid *Betty* trundling her mop; surpris'd with the exactness of the motion to describe the thing he wanted, he goes into his study, calls his pupils about him, and tells them that *Betty*, who her self knew nothing of the matter, could shew them the sun revolving about itself in a more lively manner than ever he could. Accordingly *Betty* was call'd, and bad bring out her mop, when placing his scholars in a due position, opposite not to the face of the maid, but to her left side, so that they could see the end of the mop, when it whirl'd round upon her arm, they took it immediately; there was the broad headed nail in the center, which was as the body of the sun, and the thrums whisking round, flinging the water about everry way by innumberable little streams, describing exactly the rays of the sun darting light from the center to the whole system.[25]

In context the passage is about learning by making use of what is available. Better equipment might have enabled Morton to have illustrated his point more efficiently. But it would hardly have replaced the excitement of receiving the latest ideas of Newton.

Not everyone saw it that way. Attacked for his ignorance by Swift, Defoe presented an outline of what he knew:

I have also, *Illiterate as I am,* made a little Progress in *Science*; I read *Euclids Elements*, and yet never found the *Mathematical Description* of A SCURRILOUS GENTLEMAN: I have read Logick, but could never see a Syllogism form'd upon the Notion of it—I went some length in Physicks, or Natural Philosophy, and could never find between the two great Ends of Nature, *Generation* and *Corruption*, one Species, out of which such a Creature could be found—I thought my self Master of Geography; and could have set up for a Country *Almanack Maker*, as to my Skill in *Astronomy*; yet could in neither of the Globes, find either in what part of the World such a Heterogeneous Creature lives.[26]

Defoe often lamented the lack of good mathematicians and engineers who could lend their skills to the betterment of society. His enemies might laugh at him then, but in the sciences, and in matters of history, geography, and economics, he was the more knowledgeable.

But to a certain extent Defoe missed the point. He viewed education in

[25] *The Complete English Tradesman*, i. 42–3.   [26] *Review*, viii. 455b.

terms of a body of knowledge that might be mastered and then put to use. In *The Compleat English Gentleman* he set up a litany of rhetorical questions intended to demonstrate his conviction that true learning might be carried on entirely in English. He instanced his ideally educated man as someone whose accomplishments were startlingly like those of Defoe himself. This man could speak modern languages, had a knowledge of modern science, geography, astronomy, history, and the economic condition of his own country; 'yet', repeats Defoe in a chorus of heavy sarcasm, 'he is NO SCHOLLAR'. In contrast there is the product of the universities, the 'meer pedant':

I think our meer scholarrs are a kind of mechanicks in the schools, for they deal in words and syllables as haberdashers deal in small ware. They trade in measure, quantityes, dactyls, and spondaes, as instrument-makers do in quadrants, rules, squares, and compasses; etymologyes, and derivations, prepositions and termina-tions, points, commas, colons and semicolons, etc., are the product of their brain, just as gods and devils are made in Italy by every carver and painter; and they fix them in their proper stations in perspectiv, just as they do in nitches and glass windowes.[27]

The argument is excellent. Defoe argued that the education at the uni-versities made a man into a kind of laborer in words. We should be con-vinced by modern theories of education, however different they may be, that he was right. But what he could not understand or, at least, not accept was the entire set of social premises behind the educational system.

Defoe's future patron, Harley, was to receive an education in a Dissenting Academy, but he came out an Anglican and a defender of the social fabric. The trouble with Defoe was that he represented the very problem against which that social fabric was battling. He was a Presbyterian, and, as Charles II remarked, that was not the proper religion for a gentleman. He believed in the idea of an open society in which the most talented men ought to rise to the top. And he harboured deep within him the sense that all men who worked were useful members of the commonwealth, that the unearned privileges of rank belonged to a feudal structure that was in process of erosion. If his education at Newington Green was the best he could have experienced for the improvement of his mind, it may have hardened some of his attitudes against the education given to those studying for orders in the Church of England at Cambridge and Oxford and drawn him closer to some of the more radical social and political ideals of the Dissenters. When Swift mocked Defoe's ignorance,

[27] *The Compleat English Gentleman*, 201.

he invited the derision of those belonging to a relatively select club toward those outside the group. Although Defoe knew he was an outsider, he never could quite understand why his obvious abilities did not gain for him membership in the club.

III

In addition to the modern subjects that Defoe learned at Newington Green, he claimed to have learned about politics 'as a science', and of course he spent a great deal of time on theological subjects. The politics that Defoe learned must remain a matter of dispute. Samuel Wesley stated that Morton warned against criticizing the government, but that there was an anti-monarchial bias in most of the Dissenting Academies.[28] Even Morton's 'Eutaxia', his political treatise that circulated among the fifty boys at Newington Green, seemed to favour a commonwealth, and various republican tracts were common, according to Wesley. Defoe refuted these charges:

I have now by me the Manuscripts of Science, the Exercises and Actions of his School, and, among the rest those of Politicks in particular, and I must do that Learned Gentleman's Memory that Justice to affirm, that neither in his System of Politicks, Government and Discipline, or in any other the Exercises of that School, was there any thing Taught or Encourag'd that was Antimonarchical, or Destructive to the Government, or Constitution of *England*; and particularly among the Performances of that School, I find a Declamation relating to the benefit of a single Person in a Common Wealth, where in it is declar'd and prov'd from History and Reason, that Monarchy is the best Government, and the best suited to the Nature of Government, and the Defence of Property; which Discourse, together with the said Manuscripts, System of Politicks and Government, as Read in that School, and which are now above 25 Years old, are left at the Publishers of the Book for any one to peruse.[29]

If this passage is read carefully, some doubts must inevitably arise. Was the 'Declamation' by Morton? Or was it one of those exercises, composed by Defoe or one of the other students, intended to argue a position as forcefully as possible? In constant danger of arrest by informers, Morton would have been extremely cautious about speaking against the government, but within the context of teaching the science of politics surely other systems

---

[28] Wesley, *A Reply to Mr. Palmer's Vindication of the Learning, Loyalty, Morals and Most Christian Behaviour of the Dissenters towards the Church of England* (London, 1707), 65–85.
[29] *True Collection*, ii. 276–7.

had to be discussed. With his scientific interests and his connection with Wadham College, Morton might well have had some contact with Locke. Might he not have brought in that philosopher's version of the Constitution of Carolina in the same way as he brought in the latest ideas of Newton? Defoe too believed that monarchy might be the most efficient form of government, but it may not have been an accident that, in his longest discussion of the education among the Dissenters, he wrote of Parliament as 'our Protectors in that Happy Liberty of *speaking plain Truth*, the want of which Liberty makes other Nations Slaves, and comfortably distinguishes *Englishmen* from all the Nations of the World'.[30] Morton's 'Eutaxia' has never been found, but if it was not 'anti-monarchial', it surely did not contain the kind of adulation of the monarch expected by those members of the Church of England who regarded 30 January, the day on which Charles I was beheaded, as rivalling the day on which the Crucifixion took place.

Those writings of Morton that saw print or are retained in manuscript form in the archives of research libraries suggest at least a few specific ideas that Defoe may have picked up from his mentor. Morton's major published work, *The Spirit of Man*, appeared in Boston in 1693 but probably circulated in manuscript in the manner of the works Defoe mentioned. In some ways, given its publication date, it is somewhat old-fashioned. The appeal, at the beginning, to the 'Understanding . . . as a candle . . . to search and find out by its Exercise, all those Inward Acts and Inclinations which would otherwise lie hidden and undiscovered' is reminiscent of the approach of the Cambridge Platonists with their faith in reason, and there is much of the tolerance and sense of exploration associated with that group in Morton's approach to religious subjects.[31] Also a little old-fashioned is the use of the theory of the four humours in discussing human character.[32] The more mechanical theories of the passions of Descartes and Gassendi tended to replace older discussion of the passions early in the Restoration. When Defoe was to write of the workings of the passions, he almost never resorted to discussions of the quality or quantity of the humours in the body.

But Morton held one of the basic beliefs of those who founded the Dissenting Academies—that there was nothing in the mind but what sense

[30] *The Present State of the Parties in Great Britain* (London, 1712), 240.

[31] Charles Morton, *The Spirit of Man* (Boston, 1693), 12. The quotation from Prov. 20: 27 was strongly associated with the Cambridge Platonists, who flourished in the middle of the seventeenth century. On the other hand, philosophers such as Thomas Burnet and John Norris continued to offer some of their ideas in the 1690s.

[32] Ibid. 27–86.

perception brought into it.[33] This resulted in a concern for the environment of learning. 'Men', wrote Morton, 'are much what the Custom and usual practice of the place is, where they live. He that is bred, or much conversant in the country; gets there a simple plain heartedness; or perhaps a Rough Rusticity: He that is much in the City, has more of Civility, Sagacity, and Cunning.'[34] Outward circumstances change human beings, and if a condition prevails for some length of time, it may shape the character of the person. Morton believed in a basic character formed by the particular composition of the humours within the body, but also held that environment and education could give a particular shape to character. And he outlined the effect of particular instruction. Poetry might be an aid to 'quickness of fancy, and *Imagination*', while the study of history might bring a degree of prudence.[35] Defoe, who listed himself among the poets produced by Morton's academy, might have had his interest stirred by his tutor.[36]

A few other ideas presented by Morton may have left an impression as well. Morton argued that gratitude was a trait that was especially human and admirable. Defoe might have gotten such a concept from any number of sources but he considered ingratitude the worst of crimes. Morton had a faith in the progress of knowledge. '*New Observations*', he wrote, 'may be made in one Age, that are not in another but the hints that one Age gives to another, whereby Human Reason (being still the same in all Ages) works on upon former Observations, so as what is begun in one Age, may be perfected in another.'[37] Defoe's belief in the progress of invention, which so startlingly contrasted with the pessimism of his contemporaries Swift and Pope, may have been instilled by Morton. While he was a minister at Blisland in Cornwall, Morton contributed a piece to the *Philosophical Transactions* of the Royal Society on the subject of the use of sea sand containing organic compounds for fertilizer. The essay is made up of close observation, statistics, and an analysis of the sand according to the different shellfish contained in it. In addition to the particular observation of natural phenomena, the essay contains what may be called a 'project' for the increased use of such sands, and is therefore very much in Defoe's projecting mode.[38]

[33] Irene Parker, *Dissenting Academies in England* (Cambridge: Cambridge University Press, 1914), 28.
[34] Morton, *Spirit of Man*, 24.
[35] Ibid. 22.
[36] *The Present State of the Parties*, 319.
[37] Morton, *An Essay Towards the Probable Solution of this Question. Whence Come the Stork and the Turtle, the Crane and the Swallow* (London, 1703), 15.
[38] 'The Improvement of Cornwall by Sea Sand, Communicated by an Intelligent Gentleman well Acquainted in those Parts to Dr. Dan. Cox', *Philosophical Transactions of the Royal Society for the Year 1675* (New York: Johnson Reprint Corp., 1963), x. 293.

But Defoe's major indebtedness to Morton is probably to be found in Morton's theological approach to nature and in his style. Although Morton may have drawn upon Newton for explaining technical problems of gravity, Defoe credits Morton with a 'generall system of Nature'. Newton's view of the universe as a vast body kept in order by a ruling deity was to become the major system of theology in the eighteenth century. Although it was often used to support a natural theology or deism, with its distant, ordering God, it could also be used to buttress a fairly traditional Christian view of man's place in the universe. Morton's view of man as 'that little Pigmy on a Mole-hill' would not have been out of place in one of the many Boyle Lectures that had been established to support a rational and Christian explanation of the universe and man's relationship to it.[39] But he saw no contradiction between the new scientific ideas and what he considered to be orthodox Christianity. Neither did Defoe. The world of his characters is open and spacious, but God's presence is everywhere.

Finally, Morton may have had some influence upon Defoe's style. In two religious treatises, he used dialogue form to create the sense of a balanced discussion. It worked in a manner not very different from Defoe's later use of dialogue without Defoe's vividness of character. On the other hand, when Morton wrote about the debauchery of his times and of rakes 'whose lust will needs assume the name of Love', he assumed a dry, mocking tone that seemed to question the language that would confuse sexual desire with genuine feeling for another person.[40] It was mainly this questioning tone about language that Defoe seems to have borrowed from his teacher. Morton was intent upon making the distinction between words and things that was the hallmark of the new education. In a second dialogue, *The Way of Good Men for Wise Men to Walk in*, published in 1681, when Defoe had just left the Newington Green academy, Logicus leads Ethicus to reach beyond high-sounding words, such as 'Church and Reverend Divines', to the real state of the Church and its ministers. He shows Ethicus that if the Church is composed of self-interested men and the divines merely a group of unworthy ministers, there is no reason to remain a part of such an institution. Logicus' stress upon the 'explication of the words' was to become one of Defoe's prinicipal points of emphasis throughout his writings.[41]

But such demonstrable influences were probably less important than the impact of the man himself and the environment of the school. At the most formative years of his life Defoe came into contact with someone who must

---

[39] Morton, *An Essay Towards the Probable Solution*, 17. Morton argues that God is forced to teach man of the 'vast Magnitudes and Motions' of the universe.

[40] Morton, *The Little Peace-Maker* (London, 1674), 69.

[41] Defoe, *The Way of Good Men for Wise Men to Walk in* (London, 1681), ix. 19.

have been a surrogate for his father—a man learned in science and letters and steady in his religious faith. The experience also involved contact with many students who were far wealthier than James Foe at the very height of his prosperity. Morton himself came from a good family in Nottingham-shire and owned some property in addition to the large house that he used as a boarding-school. The descendant of yeomen farmers and the son of a man who had worked as a lowly apprentice must have found the experience exhilarating and interesting. If Daniel Defoe was not to achieve gentility through leading an army against the Turks, he might yet become a gentle-man and achieve fame as a remarkable preacher. But at some time during his years at Newington Green he knew that it was not to be.

3

Meditating on Matters Spiritual
and Secular

Defoe was silent on the reasons for his abandoning any plans to become a
minister, except to suggest that the decision was not entirely his own. He
may have been implying that he did not feel the call to such a vocation and
that, in a sense, God had made the decision for him. Or his father may have
decided that the times were not propitious. On 17 October 1678 the body of
Sir Edmund Berry Godfrey was found behind some bushes on the south
side of Primrose Hill. As a London magistrate, Godfrey had been hearing
accusations made by Titus Oates and Ezerel Tonge concerning a plot to
murder Charles II, accompanied by a massacre of Protestants, and an
invasion of Ireland by the French. The Duke of York, the future James II,
was to become King and reign under the direction of the Jesuits. The
matter had been brought to the attention of the King's Council during
September, and Oates had testified to the existence of a wide network of
conspirators in a manner so filled with circumstantial details that many of
the councillors were convinced that there had to be some truth in it.

The discovery of the magistrate's body convinced most disbelievers that
some kind of a plot existed, and when the correspondence of Edward
Coleman, a former secretary to the Duke of York, was found to contain
general references to restoring the Catholic faith to England and 'subduing
a pestilent heresy', almost everyone in the nation was convinced that the
Jesuits had hatched a conspiracy to slaughter great numbers of Protestants
and return England to the control of the Catholic Church.[1] As executions
of those supposed to be guilty went on into the following year without anyone confessing his guilt, doubts began to grow about the veracity of Titus
Oates, but anxieties raised by the supposed Plot concerning a Catholic

---

[1] See John Kenyon, *The Popish Plot* (London: Heinemann, 1972), 88.

succession brought about an attempt to exclude the Duke of York from the throne.[2]

The Exclusion Crisis which engaged the energies of Parliament and the King until 28 March 1681, when Charles II dissolved the Parliament in the midst of its deliberations over removing James from the line of succession, may be seen as a continuation of the events stirred up by Titus Oates—as a general fear of a resurgence of Catholic power throughout Europe. But others viewed it as a separate phenomenon, as the effort of a single, ambitious man, Anthony Ashley Cooper, the First Earl of Shaftesbury, to satisfy his thirst for power or as an attempt to return to the unfinished political business of the Interregnum. Suspicious of Charles II's relationship with Louis XIV, many Englishmen thought the time had come to reassess the entire Restoration settlement. Andrew Marvell's magnificent treatise, *An Account of the Growth of Popery and Arbitrary Government* (1678), was regarded as a kind of prophetic programme for the events that were to occur at the end of that year. Dissatisfaction was not hard to find. The merchants in the City had never forgiven Charles for closing the Exchange in 1672, while the nation as a whole seemed to feel that Charles's relationship with the Duchess of Portsmouth was unendurable. Those who were not morally outraged by Charles's behaviour could point to its political impropriety; and everyone suspected that she received vast amounts of the nation's revenue through secret funds. The House of Commons actually drew up charges against her, and she wisely took a temporary vacation in her native France. Charles II, who well remembered his father's fate, felt uncertain if he would succeed in weathering the storm.

I

By 1680 Newington Green was already a suburb of London, but Defoe must have found the life of a student at Charles Morton's academy too remote from what must have seemed a world filled with excitement. 'In the Times of the *Popish* Plot, and when every Day gave us new Accounts and Discoveries of the hidden Mysteries of that yet not compleatly-discover'd Contrivance of Hell and its Agents; Every Body's Business you may be sure, was to enquire what News, what News?'[3] He used this as a prelude to a story about the tricking of one poor man who was convinced that six Frenchmen had attempted to steal the monument to the London Fire, after

[2] For the move from the Popish Plot to Exclusion, see ibid. 87–8.
[3] *Review*, iv. 530–1.

some wags swore to the truth of the story. Defoe assured his readers that he was a witness to this scene in which a hunger for news produced incredible gullibility. He also experienced the sense of fear spread by the rumour that a general massacre might be ordered by the Jesuits at any time:

I remember in the Time of the *Popish Plot*, when Murthering Men in the Dark was pretty much in fashion, and every honest Man walk'd the streets in danger of his Life, a very pretty Invention was found out, which soon put an end to the *Doctrine of Assassination*, and the Practice too, and clear'd our Streets of the Murthering Villains of that Day, and this was *a Protestant Flail*.

   Now this *Protestant Flail* is an Excellent Weapon, a Pistol is a Fool to it, it laughs at the Sword, or the Cane, for you know *there's no Fence against a Flail*; for my part, I have frequently walked with one about me, in the Old *Popish* Days, and tho' I never set up for a Hero, yet when Arm'd with this *Scourge for a Papist*, I remember I fear'd nothing . . . the very Apprehension of it soon put an end to the Murthers and Assassinations, that then began to be practised in the Streets, and otherwise, as upon *Godfrey*, *Arnold*, *Julien*, *Johnston*, and others.[4]

In stating that he 'never set up for a Hero', Defoe was certainly trying to fend off the ridicule with which his opponents might regard this image of himself wandering about the streets looking for secret Jesuit assassins to knock on the head. But anyone who might have had access to the now lost commonplace book that formed the basis for the 'Historical Collections', which he would present to Mary Tuffley in a few years, would have had no doubt that, while carrying about this Protestant Flail, Defoe imagined himself a heroic defender of the Protestant cause.

   Defoe never for a moment questioned the existence of some kind of a plot, and although he came to mistrust some of the hysterical claims made at the time, for him, the villains were the 'Tories', a term whose transformation from a description of Irish outlaws to that of a faction supporting absolute monarchy Defoe ascribed to Titus Oates:

These Men for their Eminent Preying upon their Country, and their Cruel, Blood Disposition began to shew themselves so like the *Irish* Thieves and Murtherers . . . that they quickly got the Name of *Tories*— Their real Godfather and who gave them the Name, was *Titus Oats*, and the Occasion as follows; the Author of this happened to be present—There was a Meeting of some Honest People in the City, upon the Occasion of the Discovery of some Attempt, to stifle the Evidence of the Witnesses, and Tampering with *Bedlow* and *Stephen Dugdale*—And among the Discourse Mr. *Bedlow* said he had Letters from *Ireland*, that there were some *Tories* to be brought over hither, who were privately to Murther Dr. *Oats*, and the said *Bedlow*. The Doctor whose Zeal was very hot, could never hear any Man

[4] *Review*, viii. 614.

after this talk against the Plot, or against the Witnesses, but he Thought he
was one of these *Tories*, and call'd almost every Man a *Tory* that oppos'd him in
Discourse, till at last, the Word Tory became Popular.[5]

Although he hints at a degree of paranoia in the character and pronouncements of Titus Oates, Defoe tended to include as Tories all who doubted
the reality of the Popish Plot, all who opposed the attempt to exclude James
from the throne, and all who stood by while Charles II proceeded to undermine all opposition in cities and towns by removing their charters. The
term 'Whig', on the other hand, was applied to the 'unmercifully
Persecuted' religious folk of the Western Highlands of Scotland, deriving
from a liquor that they were accustomed to drink. Defoe used the origins of
the words to imply that Whigs were ardent defenders of Protestantism
while the Tories were those willing to surrender their country to '*Popery*
and *Arbitrary Power*, under the pretence of Passive Obedience and Non
Resistance'.[6]

There is no reason to doubt Defoe's claim that he witnessed these events
in London during his vacations from Morton's Academy, and the chances
are that he may have found his fascination with the political events of the
time had diminished his zeal for becoming a clergyman. That Defoe should
recall the massacres that occurred in Ireland in 1641 while discussing
the Popish Plot of 1680 and 1681 is hardly surprising. Contemporary
Dissenters found the study of what might be called comparative massacres
of Protestants endlessly fascinating. Pamphlets such as *A Seasonable Warning to Protestants from the Cruelty and Treachery of the Parisian Massacre,
August the 24th 1572* (1680) or *A Memento for English Protestants* (1681)
linked the massacres of Queen Mary's reign in England and the St
Bartholomew's Day's Massacre in Paris with similar slaughters of martyrs
in the Protestant cause. John Owen, in his *A Brief and Impartial Account of
the Nature of the Protestant Religion* (1682), praised the greatness of the
'Cause' and argued that the time was right for a counter-attack: 'There is
evidently at present a Spirit of Courage . . . to do and suffer whatever they
shall Lawfully be called unto, for the defence of this *Protestant* Religion.'[7]
Defoe may have thought the times more ripe for 'some Cromwell guiltless
of his country's blood' than for another clergyman.

After all, Protestantism itself seemed to be embattled, not merely in
England but on the Continent. In France, Louis XIV was already threatening to revoke the Edict of Nantes that had given French Protestants

---

[5] *Review*, vii. 297. Defoe's statement about being in the midst of this action should be noted.
[6] Ibid.
[7] I am using the edition published in London, 1690, iii. 36.

freedom of worship. Defoe wrote about a meeting at the church at Charenton around the year 1681 at which Mr Cloud, following his formal sermon, began to prophesy about the sufferings the French Protestants, or Huguenots, would undergo before they would once more emerge as a powerful church. Defoe remarks on the 'Minutes I took long ago of these things' (*Review*, iv. 359) as if he had been present.[8] Defoe was uniquely talented in his capacity to create such scenes as if he had been on the spot, but he may very well have been at Charenton. One of Defoe's biographers suggests that he was there as part of a grand tour that he took at this time that gave him a familiarity with Germany, France, and Italy. Admittedly, grand tours were coming into fashion as part of the education of young gentlemen, but that James Foe would have considered such a tour as a means of polishing Daniel's manners or even as a useful preparation for becoming a merchant seems as unlikely as his taking such a journey without his father's approval. If he was present at this gathering of French Protestants, he more than likely went specifically for the occasion. Perhaps he was even sent by members of the Dissenting community. Morton may have noticed that Defoe's real talent was for action and accurate recording of events rather than for the more abstruse apects of theology, and suggested that one so adept at shorthand might prove useful in bringing an accurate report of the events at Charenton for the English Dissenters. What is most certain as well as most significant is his involvement with the Protestant cause on an international level. It was to be no accident that Defoe's earliest work was concerned with another threat to that cause and to all of European Christianity—the siege of Vienna by the Turks in 1683.

If political events may have been taking up Defoe's interests at this time, occurrences at home may also have exerted some pressures that drew him away from any thought he may have given to becoming the minister of a Dissenting congregation. On 20 May 1679 his sister Mary married Francis Barham, a shipwright and son of the owner of a shipyard near Execution Dock. Defoe may have been less involved with Francis Barham than he was to be with her second husband, Robert Davis, but like Francis, Davis too was a shipwright. Davis married Mary after she had given birth to two children in her marriage to Francis. Defoe had a lifelong interest in the navy, in ships, and in seamen, and his relationship with Barham and later with Davis may have opened up possibilities for him that seemed more attractive than a more studious life. Typically enough, Defoe's one known engagement in shipbuilding was a project—the perfecting of a

[8] *Review*, iv. 359.

diving-engine which might be used to search for treasure. When he had been established for years as a shipbuilder at Leith, Robert Davis wrote to Harley to remind him that he had perfected a diving-engine and that people could testify that he had descended successfully, singing the hundreth psalm while under water. Perhaps Defoe had spent more time at the Newington Green Academy experimenting with Charles Morton's air pump than he had in exploring the complexities of religious doctrine.[9]

Meanwhile James Foe was reaching the height of his prosperity at this time. In 1680 he assumed the position of Renter Warden in order to relieve the Master of his financial duties, and in 1681–2 was listed, in the books of the Butchers' Company preserved at the Guildhall Library, as one of the Warden's Assistants. In 1683–4 he was elected as the fourth warden of the Company. He was an efficient keeper of the books of the Company, and when his son was to write of the importance of keeping neat and accurate books in his *Complete English Tradesman* with something approaching religious fervour, he may have had his father's example in mind. Something may have happened in 1683 that brought an end to James Foe's activities in the Company, for after this date his name appears simply as a Liveryman. This was the year in which he moved from French Court back to the Coleman Street Ward, where he had lived when his children were young. He appeared in a list as a lodger with Widow Scopelong in the same house in Jones's Rents, Swan Alley, where he had lived before. The reason for this change might not have involved a decline in fortune, but there was an obvious retrenchment. His surviving daughter, Mary, was married. His son, Daniel was launched in the world, and it is likely that his first wife, Alice was dead. He was probably not ready to retire, but at fifty three, he may have considered that the hopes of the family rested with his very able son, Daniel.

II

On Sunday 20 February 1681, Defoe was in London listening to the first of a series of sermons delivered by John Collins. He had left the Academy of the Reverend Charles Morton and was taking down the sermon word for word. Collins was considered by many to be the best preacher in the area of London. He was also reluctant about having anything printed, and Defoe may have regarded himself as preserving the work of a great man for

[9] See Historical Manuscripts Commission, xxix: *Reports on the MS. of His Grace the Duke of Portland*, xxix (Norwich, 1899).

posterity.[10] The decision about his vocation had probably been already made, but Defoe might still have had some lingering doubts as he took down what amounted to an exposition of orthodox Christian doctrine Sunday after Sunday. It was the period between the proroguing of the Parliament which, on 7 January 1681, had voted not to grant Charles II any money until the Exclusion Bill had been passed and the fatal meeting of Charles's last Parliament at the end of March. Charles was just about to make a secret treaty with Louis XIV that would make him financially independent of Parliament. But as these events were coming to a climax, Defoe, at least for these Sundays, could turn his mind entirely to his religious faith.

Collins's sermons, along with a series of poetic meditations that record his inner spiritual struggles at the time, in Defoe's hand are preserved in the Huntington Library in San Marino. The 'Meditations' and the sermons are related. Collins preached on Mark 16: 15 and 16: 'And he said unto them, go yet into all the world, and preach the gospel to every creature. He that believeth and is baptized shall be saved; but he that believeth not shall be damned.'[11] There was nothing particularly controversial about Collins's text, but Defoe listed him along with the great preachers who had enriched religious life among the Dissenters.[12] This must have meant that he preached with something of the zeal that Jonathan Swift considered almost equivalent to madness. In a clear reference to Swift's contemptuous *Mechanical Operation of the Spirit*, Defoe complained in 1712 of the coldness of modern preaching and lamented that truly inspirational pulpit oratory was derided as 'the Mechanism of the Spirit'.[13]

On that Sunday and on 26 March, 15 May, 12 June, 25 September, and one following date that Defoe omitted, John Collins preached of salvation through belief and faith, of justification and grace, and of the damnation of those who did not believe. Defoe was 'Absent in the Country' on 10 July and missed one of the sermons on verse 16, but he took down every word of those he heard.[14] With pagans and Jews Christ has no 'treaty', Collins argued.[15] They are in the same state of sin as Adam after the Fall. No longer was man in the image of God in which he had been made but rather in the image of the Devil who had brought sin to Adam and Eve in the Garden of Eden. Human beings are prone to sin, and no amount of good works can

[10] See A. G. Matthews, *Calamy Revised* (Oxford: Clarendon Press, 1934), 127–8.

[11] Defoe recorded the quotation from Mark in an elaborate imitation of a title-page and with the statement, 'Preached by Mr John Collins Feb. 20th 1680'.

[12] Daniel Defoe, *The Present State of the Parties in Great Britain* (London, 1712), 352.

[13] Ibid. 323.

[14] Huntington Library MS, fo. 118.

[15] Ibid. fo. 38.

save their souls. But those who believe in Jesus as their saviour may achieve 'a stability of grace' that will sustain them throughout their lives.[16] This belief should be accompanied by repentance for past sins, and that repentance removes the heart of stone. Once that is achieved, Collins preached, 'it is impossible that the Spirit of Corruption should bring such a one to Abuse the spirit of that grace'.[17] The fact that Defoe made an error in transcription at this point may suggest that he had some difficulty with this idea. But whether his mark in the margin was intended to alert a future printer or for his own attention is difficult to say.

He made only a few marks of this kind. Collins's text involved advice to those who would go out to preach the gospel, and next to the idea of appealing to the sinner's sense that he might never have another opportunity to make a successful conversion, Defoe put 'read more'.[18] He also noted Collins's distinction between a faith of our own making ('one of the Dreadfullest things in the world') and a faith made by God. The latter brings with it a sense of peace and contentment. Collins had a strong sense of a covenant or 'treaty' between the believer and Christ; it was the 'business' of Jesus to save the sinner. Defoe seems to have been struck by this idea as well as Collins's insistence that the person in a state of grace will have experienced a 'glorious Supernaturall powre of the spirit'.[19] The true believer should experience something like a mystical 'Union' with Christ, and unless he had this sense of union, he could not be confident of his salvation.

At the end of Collins's sermons, following the quotation from Proverbs 9: 35–6, 'For whoso findeth me findeth life, and shall obtain favour of the Lord. But he that sinneth against me wrongeth his own soul: all they that hate me love death', Defoe wrote, 'So much for this Doctrine' and 'Finis'.[20] Was there something about Collins's sermons that he did not like? Did he find the emphasis upon salvation to all believers uncongenial? Did he feel that the group elected for salvation was smaller than that suggested by these sermons? Some of Defoe's remarks might lead to such a suspicion. Collins, after all, was an Independent or Congregationalist, and while there were major areas of agreement between the two groups, the union attempted in 1691 was to last only until 1694. It came to an abrupt end with the Congregationalists suspecting their Presbyterian brothers of antinomianism.

Curiously enough, in the *Meditations* that follow Collins's sermons in this manuscript volume, there are some suggestions of Defoe's fear of

[16] Huntington Library MS, fo. 52.   [17] Ibid. fo. 65.   [18] Ibid. fo. 117.
[19] Ibid. fo. 123.   [20] Ibid. fo. 171.

excessive confidence in his own election. Such confidence often led to antinomianism or the feeling that since salvation was assured, no action could change God's decision. What followed from such certainty was often a sense that all might be permitted. His concern about such a condition appears in references to 'all That Gawdy Righteousness of Myne' and his 'Self . . . On which my Soul Would Splitt and Drown'.[21] However, reading the 'Meditations' in this way leads to several difficulties. Although the religious meditation in verse was a common seventeenth-century form, the purpose of such meditations was to bring the writer into closer association with God. In the mystical meditation, the intention was a genuine fusing of the self with the deity, resulting in an annihilation of the self and a religious rapture, but for most Christians an intense focus on various aspects of the religious experience was sufficient. The Mannerist extremes of a poem such as John Donne's famous sonnet beginning 'Batter my heart three-personed God' would not be expected of a poet writing in 1681, but certain aspects of the poetic meditation remained stable. For example, some judgement has to be made about the degree to which the works are public—available for everyone to read in print—or strictly private, purely for the purpose of solitary meditation. Defoe never published his *Meditations*, but he kept them all of his life. We will probably never know whether he did this out of a sentimental attachment to one of his earliest poetic productions or because he went back to them in those moments when he wanted to look deeply into his soul.

Perhaps the best way to consider them would be in terms of two very different kinds of poets who wrote religious poetry: John Bunyan, who wrote meditations at the beginning of the Restoration and William Cowper, who wrote during the second half of the eighteenth century. John Bunyan published his *Profitable Meditations* (1661) as 'public' religious poetry. His aim was to lay down some of the tenets of Christianity in pleasing form. He stated his purpose clearly at the beginning:

> Tis not the Method but the Truth alone
> Should please a Saint and Mollifie his heart
> Truth in or out of Meeter is but one;
> And this thou knowst, if thou a Christian art.[22]

His 'A Discourse between Death and a Saint' is not properly a meditation at all but simply a poetic dialogue in which the religious man confronts

---

[21] Daniel Defoe, *The Meditations*, ed. George Healey (Cummington, Mass.: Cummington Press, 1946), v. 5.

[22] *The Poems*, ed. Graham Midgley, in *Miscellaneous Works of John Bunyan*, ed. Roger Sharrock (Oxford: Clarendon Press, 1980), vi. 5.

death without fear, rejecting the 'sting' of death that might injure his body yet never hurt his soul. Bunyan's language is simple, strong, and direct.[23] Since Charles Morton recommended that his pupils should hear Bunyan preach when he made an appearance in Newington Green, Defoe might have gone to listen along with his instructor; but too much has been made of such a doubtful encounter.[24] Defoe may have learned something about writing dialogue from Bunyan and may even have imitated aspects of his direct and powerful prose style, but he had no copy of *Pilgrim's Progress* in his library or any other work by Bunyan. Any connection between Bunyan's poetry and Defoe's may be limited to the stress that both writers gave to the content of poetry rather than to a polished style.

The most obvious comment to make about the first page of Defoe's *Meditations* is that he had obviously been reading Dryden. He ends his series of couplets with a triplet of which the final line is an alexandrine. The unrhymed half-line before the triplet is equally typical of the writer who was generally considered the best poet in England as well as Poet Laureate. Even the extended metaphor of the cities of refuge bears some resemblance to the kinds of extended similes that Dryden was to use in his rhymed heroic dramas. That Dryden was essentially a secular poet apparently did not make very much difference to Defoe. Dryden was to remain one of Defoe's favourite poets throughout his life. A second secular poet who appears as an influence is more problematic—the Earl of Rochester. The first stanza of 'Thou Hast Made Us & Not We' depicts his pride in acting as

> If I my Self my Own First Being gave
> And From That Primitive Nill
> Into The Present Something Then Arose
> Of my Meer Power & Will
> And Been my Self That Contradicction
> Of Being, of its Self From Nothing Grown
> Then I had been Indeed of Right My Owne.[25]

There are clear echoes from Rochester's 'Upon Nothing' and even some suggestion of the ideas present in his 'Satire upon Mankind'. Neither of these poems was obscene, but Samuel Wesley argued that the most porno-graphic productions of England's most obscene poet were read at Morton's Academy. Along with Dryden, the recently deceased Rochester was England's leading poet at the time, and someone such as Defoe, who had

[23] *The Poems*, vi. 25.
[24] Samuel Wesley, *A Defence of a Letter concerning the Education of the Dissenters in Their Private Academies* (London, 1704), 48.
[25] *Meditations*, 15.

aspirations toward gaining fame as a poet, was clearly looking toward these writers rather than toward Bunyan. He may even have regarded Bunyan's method of identifying his religious references by a marginal gloss as old-fashioned.

That Defoe adapted his poetry to the new poetic forms of his time does not mean that the poems were not intensely personal. He supplemented his flirtation with the controlled couplet by making use of the irregular 'Pindarick' stanza form that was considered the proper contemporary poetic medium for the expression of deep emotion. The themes he chose were drawn from the Old and New Testaments and therefore part of the public poetic material available to all Christian believers, but they clearly had profound significance for him. For example, the first poem, 'Fleeing for Refuge to the Hope Sett before Us', draws upon the concept of the six cities of refuge that were set up 'for the manslayer, that he may flee thither' (Num. 35: 6), but goes far beyond such a prescribed idea. The image of the destruction that waits behind the murderer recalls Lot's flight from Sodom and Gomorrah, his eyes facing forward because what waits behind is too terrible to watch. It recalls Defoe's frequent descriptions of the murderer trying to flee from his guilt, and finally, on a deeper level, it conjures up the nightmare in which the dreamer finds himself rushing toward some place of safety as a tidal wave or something like death itself pursues and threatens to overtake him. Defoe uses this profound image to speak of his fleeing to God from the sins and character flaws that would prevent his arriving at his destination. Here, as elsewhere, he attacks his

> False Confidence,
> And all The Aery joy That Flow's From Thence.
> From all my Brain begotten Faith,
> From all my Doubt,
> And all my Foolish Thoughts about
> What Heaven Sayeth.
> From all my Growth in Morralls schoole,
> With which I Mock't my Maker, & My Soule.[26]

The apparent self-confidence and egotism may have been real enough. It seems only half-concealed in his attack upon his 'Growth in Morralls schoole', or in his mastery of the corpus of ethics and theology taught at Morton's Academy. Even as he is blaming himself for placing too much emphasis on such outward manifestations of his knowledge, he seems to be complimenting himself for his abilities. And he may have been aware

---

[26] *Meditations*, 5.

enough of these traits in asking God to cure certain sins that he found himself unable to conquer:

> Ile Bring My Tainted heart
> For Thee to Cure;
> My False and Hyppocritick Part,
> For Thee to Make Sinceer.[27]

Perhaps the best of the group as poetry is that drawn from Isaiah 45: 9:
'Shall the Clay say to him that fashioneth it, What makest thou?' Defoe
uses the concept in much the same way Browning was to do in 'Rabbi Ben
Ezra', where the aged but still optimistic speaker urges the usefulness of
work and effort. In the same spirit Defoe's potter, angry at the protestation
of the pot who objected to being made for a useful task rather than for
ornament (Now I/Must bee A Drudge & This a Dish of qualitye'), returns
the clay pot to its formless state, saying:

> Be Now What Untill Now you Were
> For Ever Shapeless Useless Unemploy'd.[28]

In the final poem, 'The Seige Raised', Defoe creates a conventional
psychomachia, or conflict within the soul, figured forth as a battle between
Reason and the rebellious faculties of will and passion. The ultimate
victory of Reason is achieved through Conscience which moves Reason to
turn to Soveraign Grace for aid.

All of these poems tell us much about Defoe as a young man. He was
confident, unquestionably too confident, about his abilities. He felt a kind
of exhilaration produced by a sense of grace, justification, and election. He
believed that with his powers of reason and his faith he could master the
world about him. If he was not going to be the most powerfully moving
preacher in England, he was still able to conquer a different kind of world.
He would become a wealthy merchant capable of putting into operation
projects that would change the world. And he might write poetry on the
side, poetry that would equal the best of John Dryden and John Wilmot,
Earl of Rochester.

At the end of the eighteenth century, the poet William Cowper suffered
a number of emotional crises. He feared that he would be damned for
eternity, that God, who would choose those to be saved and those who
would be sent to Hell, had not selected him for an eternity of bliss. Such an
emotional state was typical of the age of sensibility, and in our own age of
doubt, anxiety, or dread, Cowper's terror of the unknown exerts an appeal

---

[27] *Meditations*, 7.   [28] Ibid. 18.

even if most of his poetry, with its fear of confronting what might stir up the horror of damnation, has been valued less than that of the Romantic poets, with their interest in the confrontation between the self and the work of art. The closer Cowper approaches the abyss that threatens to swallow him, the more interesting we think him; hence the relative popularity of a poem like 'The Castaway' compared to his less despairing works. When he wrote his *Olney Hymns*, he employed what might be called 'public' Christian imagery. And he wrote them in the four-line ballad or hymn stanza that Emily Dickinson was to employ for some of the greatest poetry written in the nineteenth century. Defoe has one of his *Meditations* in this form, and it approximates the traditional Christian poetry written by Bunyan and Cowper:

> Down to ye Shades of Black Despair
> My helpless Soul Made hast
> Sorrows as Thickning Clouds ye Air
> My Comforts Over cast

After brooding over false friends, he sighingly turns to God and receives an instant reward:

> Twas But A Sigh with Staggering Faith
> And Doubting Soul I Sent
> Yet Swift as Lightning Strikes a Path
> I'th' Liquid Element.[29]

Aside from not being very good poetry or sensible English, the immediate response of Heaven which will bring back his good spirits lacks all subtlety. Not only was Cowper a better poet than Defoe, but he knew that neither the world nor God provided instant remedies for the terrors of existence. Fortunately experience was to make Defoe a wiser and better man.

III

The confidence that Defoe revealed in his *Meditations* must have translated itself into a tremendous output of energy as he launched himself into a career as a businessman and set out to find a wife. Perhaps this turn to private affairs was helped by a turn in politics against the Whigs and the Dissenters. After 28 March 1681, when Charles dismissed the Parliament at Oxford and turned back what was threatening to be a radical seizure of

---

[29] *Meditations*, 22.

power, there followed a period which one historian has called 'The Stuart Revenge'. On 31 August of that year, Stephen College, a militant member of the Oxford Parliament and the inventor of the 'Protestant flail' that Defoe had carried about with him to bash the papists, was executed after a trial which set the pattern for a series of 'judicial murders' of those who favoured Exclusion and the Whig cause. Two months earlier, on 2 July, Shaftesbury had been sent to the Tower on charges of treason. The London jury refused to find him guilty, but their verdict, announced to the accompaniment of cheers from the spectators, was close to being the last successful act of defiance against a monarchy bent on suppressing its enemies. From this point on, the Whigs had to be content with successful escapes from prosecution or prison.

In praising the English legal system and its protection of individual liberties, Defoe instanced the verdict on Shaftesbury as the one great moment during 'the cruel Days' of Charles II.[30] They were certainly cruel for the Dissenters. The diary kept by Narcissus Luttrell from September 1678 until April 1714 recorded a sudden upswing in persecutions of Nonconformists from 16 December 1681, when he made an entry on the monarch's promise to suppress the Dissenters. On 1 February 1682 he noted the severe measures taken by the Justices of the Peace for Middlesex and the vow by the authorities in other counties to follow their lead. In October Richard Baxter, a Dissenter respected for his learning and piety by many members of the Church of England, was arrested and punished for violating the Five-Mile Act. Luttrell reported at the beginning of 1683 that the King was angry with three important churchmen, Tillotson, Stillingfleet, and Burnet, for their lack of enthusiasm about these persecutions. On 16 February he wrote, 'The conventicles in and about this citty are prosecuted more violently then ever, so that those that doe meet, doe it either early in the morning or late at night; nothwithstanding which severall of them have been disturbed, and the principall hearers taken, and made to pay the penalties the law has inflicted.'[31] Defoe's former tutor, Charles Morton had to go into hiding at this time, and among the Dissenters an atmosphere of fear was a day-to-day experience.[32]

Among the 8000 Dissenters captured at supposedly illegal religious meetings who died in the filth and disease of the prisons that opened their doors wide to receive them was Thomas Delaune, whom Defoe mentioned frequently as an example of the repression of the time. Delaune was

[30] *Review*, vi. 94a.
[31] Luttrell, i. 250.
[32] See F. L. Harris, 'Charles Morton: Minister, Academy Master and Emigrant (1627–1697)', *Journal of the Royal Institution of Cornwall*, n.s. 4 (1963): 326–52.

arrested in November 1683, tried on 17 January of the following year, and forced to pay a fine beyond his means. Delaune returned to Newgate, where he died after witnessing the deaths of his wife and two children in that chamber of horrors, the very name of which was to send Moll Flanders into paroxysms of fear. Meanwhile, Charles II moved against his political as well as religious enemies. After the revelation of a supposed conspiracy to assassinate both Charles and James—named the Rye House Plot for the place where the act was to be committed, a house with a moat which Charles II was to pass on his way to or from the races at Newmarket—the number of 'judicial murders' swelled to include the writer on political theory Algernon Sidney.[33] After the judge, Jeffreys, argued that a person holding such ideas would always be capable of treason, Sidney was found guilty and executed on 17 December 1683, less than a month before Defoe was to marry Mary Tuffley at the church of St Botolph Aldgate, not far from where his uncle, Henry Foe, had once lived.

Somehow, amid all this turmoil of plots and religious persecution, Defoe had found time to court a young woman whose dowry of £3700 must have made her an extraordinarily desirable match. Defoe had been courting her from some time in 1682 when, as has been mentioned, he presented her with a volume of what were called apophthegms—short narratives directed to a particular moral point. The stories appear to be taken from what must have been an anthology of his 'Juvenal Readings'. He speaks of them as 'Abruptly Transcribed', but the volume is prepared with such care that the task must have taken some time even for so fast a writer as Defoe. Given his new dedication to his commercial career and his sudden interest in Mary Tuffley, Defoe must have found himself too busy to be involved very deeply in politics.

But there was one involvement that he mentioned, and that was his writing what has been called his 'Tract against the Turks'. Defoe was to mention it as the first occasion he came to disagree with those 'on the *Whigs* Side'—the party with which he was usually associated and which had accused him of betrayal:

The first Time I had the Misfortune to differ with my Freinds, was about the Year 1683, when the *Turks* were besieging *Vienna*, and the *Whigs* in *England*, generally speaking, were for the *Turks* taking it; which I having read the History of the Cruelty and perfidious Dealings of the *Turks* in their Wars, and how they had rooted out the Name of the Christian Religion in above threescore and Ten Kingdoms, could by no means agree with: and tho' then but a young Man, and

---

[33] For the term 'judicial murders', see Steven Zwicker, *Politics and Language in Dryden's Poetry* (Princeton, NJ: Princeton University Press, 1984), 27, 53.

a younger Author, I opposed it, and wrote against it; which was taken very unkindly indeed.[34]

Moore's surmises on this piece may be in error on a number of grounds. Defoe does not say that the work was a prose tract, and his target was not the Turks, from whom he expected nothing but brutality, but the '*Whigs*'. And in reality, those who were the most enthusiastic supporters of a Turkish victory were the Dissenters, who believed that the Hungarians, led by Count Teckely,[35] who were fighting alongside the Turks, were attempting to assert a Protestant position in their revolt against the Austrian monarchy. Defoe was to devote a large part of the first volume of the *Review* to this subject, but in 1683 and 1684 the seeming contradictions appealed mainly to the writers of poetic satire. As one anonymous wit wrote,

> Next Paint our English Mufties of the Tub,
> Those great Promoters of the *Teckelites* Club.
> Draw me them praying for the Turkish Cause,
> And for the overthrow of Christian Laws.[36]

If Defoe felt bitter both about the failure of the Dissenters to help Delaune and his family and about their mistaken ideas about the Turks, he may well have found in his affection for Mary and the possibility of starting his own family a welcome retreat from the turmoil of the political repression that was going on about him.

IV

As suggested before, given the content of 'Historical Collections', Defoe must have been attempting to afford Mary some idea of the kind of person he was as well as providing her with narratives that might entertain her. Perhaps the impulse came from her. She wanted to know what kind of person he was, and he had the idea of showing her, as a key to his character, the kind of stories that had fascinated him when he was a very young man. The name of the volume convinced Defoe's biographers that it must have

[34] *An Appeal to Honour and Justice Tho' It Be of His Worst Enemies*, in *The Shortest Way with the Dissenters and Other Pamphlets*, *Shakespeare Head Edition*, 233. The Turks reached Vienna on 7 July 1683. Two months later, their siege of the city was broken by a decisive battle on 12 Sept. See David Ogg, *Europe in the Seventeenth Century* (London: Adam & Charles Black, 1946), 492–6.

[35] More properly transcribed as Thököly, but I have used the spelling that most contemporary English writers employed.

[36] *Third Part of Advice to the Painter, Concerning the Great Turk* (London, 1684), 1.

been composed mainly of a number of parallel historical dates which revealed God's design in human history. That it contains a series of narratives must come as a delightful surprise to anyone interested in England's first great writer of prose fiction, but nothing, perhaps, is as surprising as the opening dedication of the work:

The Dedication To Clarinda

The Sence of your Knowledge and The Knowledge of your Sence Excellent & Incomparable Clarinda Brings The Dedication of a Few Remarks stories and Sayeings, Roughly composed, and as Abruptly Transcribed out of my Juvenal Readings To your Feet. Most Easy is it For a Fool To Speak the Words of wise men, But the Words of Wisdome come not Originally From Such heads. The Same Sence Therefore of my own Ignorance & Insufficiency, Made me Resolve Not To put in a word of my own Either in stile or story. For I hold it more Ingenuous To acknowledge Folly Than to Boast of Wisdome much more when There is none to Boast of. Know Then Divine Lady That Nothing Herein but The Collecting Transcribing and Dedicating This Piece is the worke of The Authour. For the Imperfections of the First and the Impertinence of the last of which He asks your Pardon & Begs That his penalty may Be the Happyness of continueing For Ever

What he now is

The Meanest

&

Truest

of

Your Adorers & Servants

Bellmour F

Is this really Defoe? Thomas Hardy had one of his characters, searching for a way of saying, 'Let us talk direct and plain prose so that we may understand each other', state, 'Let's talk Defoe.' Should we ever have imagined that Defoe would write like this?

The answer to this more than rhetorical question is a hesitant and very much after the fact . . . yes. Defoe was not merely a young man in love; he was a believer in what he considered to be genuine love. When the social historian Lawrence Stone wrote of the growth of what he called 'the companionate marriage', in this period and in the eighteenth century, it was Defoe to whom he gave considerable space as a fierce spokesman for marriage and the family and against marriage for any reason but love based on mutual esteem.[37] Defoe called marriage for wealth and position merely a

[37] Lawrence Stone, *The Family, Sex, and Marriage in England, 1500–1800* (New York: Harper & Row, 1977), 325–404.

form of legalized prostitution. It suggests that the belief he expressed in women's equal capability with men from *An Essay upon Projects* in 1697 to *The Use and Abuse of the Marriage Bed* in 1727 was a basic tenet in his life.

More surprising is the style. Defoe was a good mimic of styles, and this was fairly typical of the ornate prose of the contemporary love letter. Attempting to be as elegant as possible, Defoe drew upon an ornate, Ciceronian rhetoric that was common enough in the late sixteenth and early seventeenth centuries. It appears nowhere else in 'Historical Collections', and he pointedly avoided it for the rest of his life. Perhaps he considered such writing an essential part of the romance tradition to which the names of Clarinda and Bellmour belonged. That such elegant love-making had travelled down to the middle and even to the lower classes has long been known. When Henry Baker paid court to Sophia Defoe in 1725, he addressed her as his Amanda. Sophia and Mary probably expected no less.

A comparison of Defoe's dedication with contemporary love letters suggests that rather than emphasize his passion, Defoe preferred to appeal to Mary's 'sence' and 'knowledge' by presenting her with 'Words of wise men'. There is none of John Dunton's swooning, platonic ecstasy over his Valeria and little of the kind of sensuality that might be found in the circle about Ephelia (Joan Philips). For all his exaggerated humility, Mary Tuffley's Bellmour is presenting her with a volume of what he considered to be wisdom, and he must have known her well enough to think that she would appreciate such a gesture. Perhaps it was what convinced her to accept one who called himself the 'meanest . . . of . . . [her] Adorers'.

What we know of her shows that Defoe chose wisely. She was apparently courageous enough to go before the Earl of Nottingham to plead for her husband when he was in hiding from the authorities in 1703. Defoe wrote to his patron, Harley, of her general character and of her behaviour during that ordeal with true appreciation:

But I was Ruin'd *The shortest way* and Now Sir had Not your Favour and her Majties Bounty Assisted it must ha' been One of the worst Sorts of Ruine. I do Not mean as to Bread; I firmly and I Thank God Comfortably Depend on the Divine Goodness That I shall Never want That, But a Large and Promiseing family, a vertuous and excellent Mother to Seaven Beautifull and hopefull Children, a woman whose fortunes I have Ruin'd, with whom I have had 3700 £, and yet who in the worst of my afflictions when my Ld N. first Insulted her Then Tempted her, scorn'd So much as to Move me to Complye with him, and Rather Encourag'd me to Oppose him.[38]

[38] H 17.

What we have here is something akin to the kind of feeling that was common enough in fiction published in the middle of the eighteenth century, when writers such as Richardson and Fielding were idealizing women as the guardian of virtue and cautious common sense within the family. Defoe was to do much to shape this notion in his works on the family, and Mary may have sat for the portraits of such women in these works.

If Defoe was trying to give Mary some idea of the kind of person she might be marrying through the selection of 'Histories' in 'Historical Collections', she might well have wondered about elements of character in this 'meanest of her Adorers'. I have already mentioned the presence of a great deal of violence in these narratives, but one might also wonder about her reaction to the fifteen stories in which a character managed to gain great wealth through some stroke of fortune or an apt sentence. Mary might well have suspected that her future husband would be a wanderer and an adventurer rather than a steady business man.

In reading 'Historical Collections', she would have learned that Daniel was intensely serious about his religious beliefs: forty stories treat some aspect of religion. This is less surprising than his elimination of very much moralizing over such narratives. Defoe drew many of his examples from works such as Thomas Brook's *Apples of Gold*, but Brooks never told a story without making a careful application and exhorting the young men he imagined his readers to be to follow a straight and narrow path:

Ah! Young men, Young Men, 'tis onely heaven that is above all winds, storms, and tempests, nor hath God cast man out of Paradise for him to think to finde out another Paradise in this world; the main reason, why many young men dote upon the world, is, because they are not acquainted with a greater glory. . . . Ah! Young men; were you but cloathed with the Sun of Righteousness, and had you a Crown set upon your heads, by the hand of Faith, you would have all things of this World, which are as low bespotted, and mutable, as the Moon under your feet.[39]

Whatever his reason for leaving out such moralizing, Defoe allowed his stories to stand by themselves, and when he did add marginal comments, they were mainly secular. For example, next to the material he was later to use in *Memoirs of a Cavalier*, about the Swedish soldier who came upon a hoard of money in a town the troops had captured after his commander had told the troops they might keep whatever spoils they found, Defoe noted that such 'abstinence' from greed was rare. And in a comment longer than the original story, he launched into an attack on Bajazet as a tyrant who

---

[39] Thomas Brooks, *Apples of Gold* (London, 1662).

deserved whatever punishment he received. Even in his marginal glosses, Defoe's imagination seems to dwell upon fighting against tyrants and winning some great reward. Of religious material, then, there is more than enough for modern taste, but compared with the 'Meditations', these narratives seem to reflect a turn to the world of action.

Several of the stories concern Jews in one or another degrading situation. Since Defoe was often to preach to his enemies about toleration for the Dissenters, and was occasionally to extend his arguments to all religious groups, it might have been hoped that even as a young man he would have shown a generous spirit toward other religious groups. But the priggishness that some critics found in Defoe's religious attitudes reveals itself throughout 'Historical Collections' in a strong antipathy for Catholics, Muslims, and Jews as well as certain national prejudices, particularly against Italians. Defoe tells a few stories about noble gestures by Muslims and individual Catholics, but his Jews are always ignoble. In this attitude Defoe did not transcend his time. Jews were regarded by various Protestant sects as agents of Satan, having incurred God's curse in rejecting Christ as the Messiah. On the other hand, Defoe's attitude toward the Jews accords well with his concept of the rigid separation between those destined for future salvation and those who must be damned.

As one of the narratives illustrates effectively, Defoe believed that God would be a severe judge:

A Certaine man being risen from the dead, And being Asked how he found things to be Ordered in the other world? he Answered no man doth beleive, no man doth beleive, no man doth Beleive, and being further Asked what he meant by that repetition, replyed, no man doth Beleive how Exactly God Examineth, how strictly God Judgeth, how Severely God Punisheth.

I have already remarked that at this time in his life, in his own assurance of salvation, Defoe's attitude was close to being antinomian. His sense of his own rightness on issues of conscience, and his unwillingness to accept the possibility that he might have acted improperly, may have proceeded from a profound conviction that since he was among those elected for eternal salvation, he could never be very wrong in any matter of importance. Even if the world at large would come to regard him as a turncoat and a mercenary who would write for any side that paid him sufficiently, he retained a conviction of his integrity.

V

One highly significant anecdote in 'Historical Collections', drawn indirectly from Richard Knolles' *Historie of the Turks*, is the same episode from which Johnson was to take the plot of his *Irene*. Defoe tells how Mahomet the Great was so deeply in love with a beautiful Greek captive named Irene that he spent much of his time with her. His troops became restless, thinking that he was sunk in luxury to the extent that he was no longer capable of governing the state. Ordering his soldiers to assemble, Mahomet brought out his beloved Irene dressed in a manner that struck everyone with her beauty. All who are present agree that she is a woman worthy of an emperor. Having accomplished this, Mahomet pronounced her doom: 'But my affections must be Bridled by you my Slaves, and drawing out his scimitar at one Blow he cut of her head. Before them all; saying, "now know that your Emperour is able to conquer his Affections as well as his Enemies".' This might seeem an odd story to be telling to any woman before marriage. But Mary was not supposed to read it as a warning that her future husband might be capable of murdering her; rather, she was supposed to see it as a fantasy of self-control, as a manifestation of Daniel's ability to abandon what he most desired in the name of duty.

Charles Dickens told his friend, Foster, that from what he could gather, Defoe must have been a passionless (and therefore nasty) fellow. But quite the opposite is suggested here. Mahomet's love for Irene is of the kind that might be felt by an heroic figure, by a man capable of a great passion. But his ability to control that passion required a kind of greatness as well. Why would he want to tell Mary Tuffley this? In part, Defoe seemed to be suggesting that he possessed the kind of heroic self-discipline that his puritan forebears admired so much. But may he not also be suggesting that even were she to marry him, she would not have to have sexual intercourse with him every time he felt a twinge of desire? With women dying tragically in childbirth after sixteen or seventeen births and with miscarriages a common part of contemporary existence, surely every woman of sense, such as Mary Tuffley appears to have been, had to be concerned with this aspect of marriage. Mary had eight children, and Defoe praised her as a marvellous mother, but would she have wanted the seventeen pregnancies undergone by the wife of Defoe's son, Benjamin Norton? Defoe thought that women had the worst part of most marriages, and he despised the double standard accepted at the time by which a husband might sleep with a prostitute and pass on a venereal disease to his innocent wife. In an age without any cure for such diseases, sexual intercourse could be a form of murder and self-control over sexual desire a genuine virtue.

Along with his admiration for self-control, Defoe also seems to have been drawn toward the bold gesture, particularly from those who might be expected to show humility. He tells the story of the pirate who audaciously informed Alexander that but for the difference in the size of their forces, they were in the same profession. In a similar vein is the gesture made by the soldiers defending Agria in Hungary who, though besieged by a Turkish force thirty times their number, hung a coffin draped in black over the town walls to indicate that they would sooner die than surrender. Alexander rewarded the pirate for his boldness, and the town of Agria was never taken by the Turks. Defoe must have fantasized about such moments at which fear was held at bay, as well as about moments of the highest magnanimity such as Alexander's refusing to take a drink of water until his solders had relieved their thirst. Such a sense of heroism is all the more poignant because by 1691, in the midst of his first bankruptcy, Defoe must have felt less like Alexander and more like Conrad's Lord Jim, who, having thought all his life that he would one day act out the part of a hero, found himself playing the part of a fool and a coward—the very reverse of what he thought to be his real self. But that confrontation between his image of himself that is so apparent in 'Historical Collections' and the realities of life was still nine years in the future.

4

Marriage and Rebellion

On the first day of January 1684 Daniel Foe married Mary Tuffley, the only daughter of John Tuffley and his wife, Joan, formerly Joan Rawlins. Tuffley was a cooper, and Defoe may have become acquainted with him and his family in connection with one of his major business activities— buying, selling, and importing wines. The event took place at St Botolph Aldgate, a parish church located just outside the 'bars' marking the limits of the old city of London and not very far from where Defoe's uncle, Henry Foe, had lived in his spacious house with six chimneys. They were married more than a year after Defoe had presented Mary with his gift of 'Historical Collections'. The manuscript at the Clark Library is bound in a white vellum embossed with green and gold. Whether this was in any way connected with the original binding is impossible to determine. Pages seem to have been added in the nineteenth century, but it would certainly have been the kind of decorative volume that an 'Adorer', such as Defoe professed himself to be, might have presented to the woman he wished to marry.

In that work, Defoe quoted one wise man on the folly of marrying young, but Mary was just 20 and Daniel about 24, young for someone just beginning his career as a merchant. The equivalent of the modern marriage licence had been obtained on 28 December 1683 and appears in the *Allegations for Marriage Licences Issued by the Vicar-General of the Archbishop of Canterbury* as follows:

Daniel Foe, of St. Michaell, Cornehill, Lond., Merchant, Bachelor, about 24, & Mrs. Mary Tuffley, of St. Bottolph's, Aldgate, Lond., Spinster, about 20, with consent of her father; alleged by Charles Lodwick, of St. Michaell's aforesaid; at St. Bottolph's aforesaid, St. Lawrence, Jewry, or St. Giles, Cripplegate, London.[1]

The formula is the same as that used for hundreds of other couples and

---

[1] Ed. George J. Armytrage, Harleian Society 30 (1890), 155.

contains no surprises. Marriages at the time were often made for advantage. In a passage that John Robert Moore thought aimed at Defoe, Swift has Lemuel Gulliver comment on the progress of his life, 'I took Part of a small House in the *Old Jury*; and being advised to alter my Condition, I marrried Mrs. *Mary Burton*, second Daughter to Mr. *Edmond Burton*, Hosier in *Newgate-street*, with whom I received four Hundred Pounds for a Portion.'[2] In this account, the nature of the dowry is given as the important matter. Passion has no part in his selection of a wife, and but for her name, we are told nothing about her, as if such information would be insignificant; but when Defoe was to tell Harley about his wife, he spoke with feeling about her as a person. If Swift was trying to depict what he considered to be the impassivity and lack of imagination among the middle classes he could hardly have done better. But Defoe was certainly no Lemuel Gulliver. He was unquestionably deeply in love with his Clarinda—Mary Tuffley.

I

The day of the marriage must have been extraordinarily cold, cold enough to have made all the participants eager to get before a roaring fire. This was no ordinary English winter. Luttrell described the weather as 'freezing very bitter'.[3] The Thames, only a few streets away, had frozen over, allowing Londoners the opportunity to hold a 'Frost Fair' on the ice by way of celebration. Although the 'whole Streets of Shedds' that was to turn the Thames into a small city did not go up until the middle of January, there was already some activity at the beginning of the month.[4] Luttrell remarked on the 'great row of booths crosse the Thames, where is sold diverse liquors and meat roasted', and the scene inspired a number of poets to describe the crowds of people and the cries of the vendors:

> . . . *Good Beer* and *Ale*,
> *Coffee or Mum or Wine, the heart to chear,*
> *Roast Beef, or Mutton boil'd, or Brandy clear.*[5]

Defoe regarded marriage as a solemn and crucial occasion. ''Tis one of the

[2] Jonathan Swift, *Gulliver's Travels*, in *Prose Writings*, ed. Herbert Davis (14 vols., Oxford: Blackwell, 1959), xi. 20. See John Robert Moore, 'A Defoe Allusion in *Gulliver's Travels*', *Notes & Queries* 3 (1940), 79–80.

[3] Luttrell, i. 295.

[4] Thomas Tryon, *Modest Observations* (London, 1684), 1.

[5] See the contemporary broadside, *Thamasis's Advice to the Painter from her Frigid Zone: or Wonder upon the Water*; and Luttrell, i. 295

most Weighty Affairs of Life,' he wrote, 'and ought no more to be trifled with; all that we call Happiness in this Life, depending upon it.'[6] But he was also fascinated by extraordinary natural phenomena. Certainly he could hardly have resisted taking his young bride for a stroll through the booths, however vain he may have considered many of the attractions of the fair. He had chosen to live in the world of trade and business, which to John Bunyan was 'Vanity Fair' itself, and he could not have refused Mary a sight so wonderful.

Before his wedding Defoe may have used his father's shop and warehouse as his place of business, but after his marriage he moved into his own residence in Freeman's Yard, a court on the north side of Cornhill close to that centre of commerce, the Royal Exchange. He appears on the records of Cornhill Ward as a junior member of the Petty Jury for 1684. He is listed simply as 'Foe' with no Christian name attached, a newcomer to the group.[7] Mary's dowry probably financed this move to so splendid an area. By 1711 Defoe was famous enough to have a wholesaler of gowns, Henry Bright, advertise that his establishment, which could be entered directly from the street, had formerly been 'the Ware-House of Mr. Daniel Defoe'.[8] Defoe probably had his rooms for conducting business above the warehouse area and his residence on the top floor. It was a part of London which, at the time, had been 'fill'd with Wholesale-Men, and Rich Shopkeepers . . . and such People who managed the necessary Appendices of Trade',[9] an ideal place for a young man eager to make his fortune as an importer of wines and as a middleman in selling stockings.

II

So little is known of Defoe's business ventures, so busy does his life as a writer and as a secret agent seem without this knowledge, that it is easy enough to ignore this part of his life entirely. The most spectacular facts of his business dealings are his two bankruptcies in 1692 and in 1703. In our time, when a bankruptcy may simply be carrying on regular business by somewhat extraordinary means, conceiving of how terrible an experience such an event must have been is difficult. In some seventeenth-century utopias, bankruptcy was made *the* significant crime and indeed a capital

---

[6] *Review*, i. 379.
[7] Cornhill Ward Jury Duty Wardmote, Guildhall MS 4069/2, fo. 358. He is the only person without a first name.
[8] Frank Bastian, *Defoe's Early Life* (London: Macmillan, 1981), 101.
[9] *Review*, viii. 507.

offence. Defoe was continually inveighing against the absurdity of putting bankrupts in prison and therefore making it almost impossible for them to pay their debts. The reasonableness as well as the humanity of his pleas were listened to appreciatively, but bankruptcy continued to be regarded as the unforgivable sin for a businessman. In 1704 one writer, who was no friend of Defoe or his political principles, left a manuscript with the title of 'A Character of Daniell de Foe writer of the Pamphlet Called the Review' that has a few comments on his business reputation:

Daniel Defoe the Author of the Review is no French man, but born here in England, bred an Hozier, and followd that trade till he broke for a considerable Sum. His Creditors run him into an Execution of Bankrupcy, but to no purpose, he haveing fraudulently, as they seem assur'd, Conceald his Effects. So that His Reputation amongst ye fair Dealers of the City is very Foule. He is a profest Dissenter, tho' reckond of no Morals.[10]

Although there are a number of errors in this account (for example, Defoe was certainly not trained to be a hosier), this was probably the way his enemies viewed him. That some of his creditors felt he had cheated them seems likely enough. Most of his biographers prefer to adopt the view that the reasons for his failures may be discovered in a certain incompatibility between the daydreaming future novelist and the man of business.

But entering into trade in London during the late seventeenth century was risky even with the best financial backing and finest training. One modern historian has noted that without influential connections and good luck success was impossible. At least ten years were necessary for becoming established; the merchant who died young also died poor:

The risks of trade cannot be underestimated, particularly for a young man starting on his own . . . All trades were subject to arbitrary factors—both human and acts of God—seasonal fluctuations, disruptions through weather or war, fire, earthquake, piracy, price movements, fiscal exactions, the failures of other merchants, the condition of the currency, sudden shifts in demand. The speed with which a ship reached a market could turn on the wind or the temperature or the timing of arrival could mean profit or ruin on a cargo. The unpredictable nature of events could be modified to a certain extent by insurance, by distributing cargoes between several ships, by adjusting profit margins and prices to risk. But as Michael Blackett wrote, 'I never yet Adventured anything but which I durst trust God withall to let his will be done.' Time and good luck were essential.[11]

    [10] (1704), BL MS 28,094, fo. 165.
    [11] Richard Grassby, 'Social Mobility and Business Enterprise in Seventeenth-Century England', in *Puritans and Revolutionaries*, ed Donald Pennington and Keith Thomas (Oxford: Clarendon Press, 1978), 368.

Like Michael Blackett, Defoe preferred to believe in a ruling Providence rather than chance or fortune, but even he might have allowed that his 'luck' was not the best.

The economy of England at this time resembled that of what is now called a developing nation. Under such conditions, the businessman was likely to deal in a variety of goods. Although Defoe was most familiar with the clothing industry and with wines and brandies, he also handled whatever products seemed to offer an opportunity for profit. John Robert Moore once tried to show that, when Defoe was attempting to convince the Scots that he was in Scotland to establish himself in business, the many lines of trade in which he pretended to be interested were actually areas that he knew well. Recently discovered letters from John Russell, Defoe's factor in Edinburgh, reveal that Defoe was trading in horses as well as wines and liquors.[12] *The Compleat English Tradesman* reveals his knowledge of all kinds of merchandise, from linen cloth to products connected with gardening and planting. He traded for tobacco and lumber from America in his early years, sending hose and woollen cloth to the colonies, and purchased large amounts of oysters and cheese when he was in his 60s. He seems to have known something about manufacturing bricks as well as of commercial fishing for herring and cod. He thought that a good tradesman should be capable of handling any kind of business, and after listing a number of successful transformations from one branch of trade to another, he concluded that a tradesman ought to know a wide variety of areas and be prepared to do business in any one of them that seemed capable of yielding him a profit.[13] Defoe's ideal tradesman was akin to a universal genius, or, perhaps, something like Defoe himself.

III

In his *Compleat English Tradesman*, Defoe gave ample enough illustrations of the ways in which a tradesman might encounter disaster. His first example involved the failure to learn thoroughly enough in the fifth and sixth years of an apprenticeship. Defoe may have grown up in close contact with his father's business, but at the very time when he might have been learning to appraise the value of goods bought and sold, he was at Morton's

---

[12] See Paula Backscheider, 'John Russell to Daniel Defoe: Fifteen Unpublished Letters from Scotland', *Philological Quarterly* 61 (1982): 161–77.

[13] *The Complete English Tradesman* (2 vols., London, 1727), i. 35, ii. 73. Although the publisher changed the title to the more modern-looking 'Complete', within the text Defoe always spelled the word as I have indicated. Although I will refer to the title as furnished by the publisher of the 2nd edition in my footnotes, I will use Defoe's preferred spelling in my references within my text.

Dissenting Academy in Newington Green. 'If a young man neglects this part,' Defoe wrote, 'and passes over the season for such improvement, he very rarely ever recovers it; for this part has its season, and that more remarkable than in many other cases, and that season lost never comes again; a judgment in goods taken in early is never lost, as a judgment taken in late, is seldom good.'[14] Defoe was learning much at Morton's Academy, but the value of goods was not part of that education. Nevertheless Defoe followed this warning with a personal anecdote of how he avoided being cheated by a seller of brandies:

I liked the goods very well, but the merchant, as they call'd him, that is to say, the knave appointed to cheat the poor strangers, was cunningly out of the way; so that no bargain was to be made that night. But as I had said that I lik'd the brandies, the same person who brought me an account of them, and who was indeed the owner of the goods, comes to my lodging to treat with me about a price. We did not make many words: I bad him the current price which I had bought for, some days before, and after a few struggles for five crowns a ton more, he came to my price . . . and as I had seen the goods already, he thought there was nothing to do but to make a Bargain, and order the goods to be deliver'd.

But as young as I was, I was too old for that too, and told him, I could not tell positively how many I should take, but that I would come in the afternoon, and taste them over again, and mark out what I wanted.[15]

When the owner of the goods speaks of other customers, Defoe answers 'coldly' that he should sell to whomever he wished. On tasting the brandy again, Defoe discovers that the seller has extended his supply by adding other ingredients and refuses to buy more than three casks. Defoe may have had a number of problems in importing wines and brandies, but he showed a native shrewdness in dealing with this 'knave'.

Three other reasons that he gave for business failures involved excessive involvements with literature, with giving the appearance of a gentleman, and with contemporary politics. In illustrating all of these certain roads to ruin, Defoe was surely attempting to exorcise certain demons that he felt within himself. Although he seemed shrewd enough in turning the tables on the seller of brandies, 'Historical Collections' reveals a strongly idealistic attitude toward trade that may have tended to undercut Defoe's native shrewdness. Similarly, his mockery of the wit, the tradesman with a hankering after gentility, and the shopkeeper eagerly following every shift in the wind of politics should not blind us to his own ability to see himself in the mirror of his satire.

[14] *The Complete English Tradesman*, i. 7.
[15] Ibid. i. 9.

The second distraction, then, may have been his fancying himself a man of letters superior to the concerns of trade. Defoe certainly ridicules the tradesman who carries a love of literature into the counting house. 'He that affects a rumbling and bombast stile, and fills his letters with long harangues, compliments, and flourishes, should turn Poet instead of Tradesman, and set up for a wit, not a shopkeeper,' Defoe warned.[16] Did Defoe have his mind on poetry rather than hosiery? Although Defoe mentioned only his attack against the English supporters of Teckely and the Hungarians as an example of his early writing, he more than likely contributed something to the mass of political poetry composed during this period, even if such works sometimes circulated only in manuscript. His first published poem was hardly the work of a novice. He would have been unlikely to have assigned himself the entire poetical province of the lampoon in his *Pacificator* (1700) had he not written a fair amount in that genre. And he was probably a member of an academy, perhaps that established by the poet Lord Roscommon around 1683.[17] However, the evidence for his membership in such a group is slight indeed. Frank Bastian remarked that in his discussion of a 'small Society' of which he had been a member that had dedicated itself 'to Refine and Correct' the English language, Defoe had quoted from Roscommon's *Essay on Translated Verse* published in 1684. This is the only link between Defoe and what is known as 'Roscommon's Academy', and to dismiss it as wild speculation would be easy enough. The trouble is that this is precisely the way Defoe liked to communicate little pieces of information. Readers may have been able to recognize the allusion to Roscommon's effort to continue the work begun and abandoned by a committee of the Royal Society in the 1660s. But why would this academy have wanted Defoe in their midst? The answer to that is simple. Seventeenth-century academies tried to avoid a bias toward scholarly and pedantic language. As a young, literate merchant with a turn for poetry and as the product of a Dissenting Academy famous for its dedication to excellent English style, Defoe would have brought to such a group a knowledge of commercial terminology and an ability to make distinctions between jargon of the counting-house and true English. And since a dictionary and a grammar were among the usual products of such academies, Defoe could have been useful in one of the major projects of such a society.

If Defoe was indeed part of this group, he may have been introduced into

---

[16] *The Complete English Tradesman*, i. 17.

[17] See *An Essay upon Projects*, ed. Joyce Kennedy, Michael Seidel, and Maximillian E. Novak, in *The Stoke Newington Daniel Defoe Edition* (New York: AMS Press, 1999), 89. For some other candidates for this academy of which he was a member, see the note on p. 192.

their company by Francis Lodowick, the uncle of his friend Charles Lodowick, who signed as a witness at Defoe's wedding. Francis Lodowick (1619–94) did not become a Fellow of the Royal Society until he was 60, but he had contact with scientists such as Hooke and Wilkins for several decades. He was fascinated by the idea of a universal language, and his scheme for a phonetic alphabet appeared in the *Philosophical Transactions* of the Royal Society in 1686. His desire for a language that would 'truly express things', along with his fascination for hieroglyphics and shorthand, may have had a direct influence on Defoe. It is also possible that Lodowick himself and a group of admirers constituted the 'Academy' to which Defoe was referring, but if not, he would certainly have been the most likely contact between Defoe and the Roscommon group. Yet it seems questionable that such a group would have taken up very much of Defoe's time, or that whatever poetry Defoe might have written during these years would have detracted from his involvement in the world of commerce.

A third possibility among the negative examples provided by Defoe as the source of ruin in business is what Moll Flanders calls 'this amphibious Creature, this *Land-water-thing*, calll'd, *a Gentleman-Tradesman*'. Moll realizes that her second husband managed to be a 'Rake, Gentleman, Shop keeper, and Beggar all together'.[18] Doubtless she would have preferred someone who was not a beggar, but she desired a husband who would carry a sword and show no sign of the shop apron when he was not working; and she found him in her extraordinary Draper:

Vanity is the perfection of a Fop; my Husband had this Excellence, that he valued nothing of Expence, and as his History you may be sure has very little weight in it; 'tis enough to tell you, that in about two Years and a Quarter he Broke, and was not so happy to get over into the *Mint*, but got into a *Spunging-House*, being Arrested in an Action too heavy for him to give Bail to, so he sent for me to come to him.[19]

Moll's husband eventually closes his shop and flees to France with whatever money he can raise. And he does this at the expense of his creditors before a formal 'Commission of Bankrupt' could seize them.[20]

Moll feels somewhat confused about her longings after gentility, or rather the appearance of it, and perhaps Defoe shared some of her bewilderment. His decision to change his name to Defoe or De Foe, his references to himself as a gentleman, his discussion of the family of the De Beaux Faux in his *Tour Thro' the Whole Island of Great Britain*, his hint

[18] *Moll Flanders*, ed. G. S. Starr (London: Oxford University Press, 1971), 60–1.
[19] Ibid. 62.
[20] Ibid. 63.

that he carried a sword—all these outward trappings of gentility that he treasured, despite his insistence that true gentility came from a combination of virtue and knowledge, suggest some leanings in the direction of Moll's 'Gentleman Tradesman'. Yet it would be impossible to conceive of Defoe taking an expensive trip to Oxford in the manner of Moll and her husband during which they flaunted their suppposed wealth and status. According to contemporary wisdom, a tradesman could not be a gentleman. In fact, Defoe was contemptuous of the idle aristocracy, and by way of contrast, almost every page that Defoe wrote about commerce was filled with interest and excitement. If there may have been something of the gentleman tradesman in Defoe during the years he was starting his family in Hackney, of extravagance and pretence to gentility, the evidence suggests his main failing lay elsewhere.

A fourth way in which someone like Defoe might have strayed from the rigid demands of the tradesman's calling would have been an excessive involvement in the politics of the time. Politics was to dominate so much of his life that we might ask the question: was it involvement in the anxiety of having James as King followed by the excitement of William's reign that detracted from the concern he should have shown over his accounts? Defoe warned against this temptation:

In order then to direct the Tradesman how to furnish himself thus with a needful stock of trading knowledge, first, I shall propose to him to converse with tradesmen chiefly: he that will be a Tradesman should confine himself within his own sphere: never was the gazette so full of the advertisements of commissions of bankrupt as since our shop-keepers are so much engaged in Parties, form'd into clubs to hear news, read journals, and study politicks; in short, when tradesmen turn statesmen, they should either shut up their shops, or hire some body else to look after them.

The known story of the upholsterer is very instructive, who, in his abundant concern for the publick, run himself out of this business into a jayl; and even when he was in prison, could not sleep for the concern he had for the liberties of his dear country: the man was a good Patriot, but a bad shopkeeper; indeed he should rather have shut up his shop, and got a commission in the army, and then he had served his country in the way of his calling.[21]

The upholsterer of whom Defoe speaks so mockingly would probably have been hopelessly inept in the realities of politics as in the terrors of the field. The lesson of all of these admonitions is—stick to your trade. 'Trade was the Whore I doated on,' wrote Defoe in the last number of the *Review*. Although he was speaking of writing about economic subjects, the image

---

[21] *The Complete English Tradesman*, i. 38.

might be extended further. Whores are not wives to whom one remains faithful; they belong to the illicit activities of life, mistaken and unfortunate adventures which could prove fatal. He seems to have treated business as a kind of adventure. The drudgery of keeping books and handling the routine of business does not seem to have interested him at all. He was able to write about the importance of careful bookkeeping, but he does not appear to have relished it himself. As a businessman, he was essentially a gambler, excited by new deals, new prospects.[22] What we see in many of the speculations that led to his bankruptcy is an almost compulsive interest in taking risks. The youthful Defoe, who abandoned his business interests and his young wife to fight for the Duke of Monmouth, was hardly the steady, dependable tradesman Defoe sometimes idealized.

Finally, it should be noted that the kinds of business that attracted him were connected with a new consumer society. His involvement with civet cats, whose glands exuded a strong and lasting scent, brought him into the manufacture of perfume. His hosiery trade was associated with the booming fashion industry, and his importation of wines and brandy from Spain was also among the trades that many considered part of the new luxury that was supposed to be destroying the moral fibre of England. Everything suggests that Defoe belonged with those thinkers such as Nicholas Barbon who defended the expanded building in London and luxury in general as part of a new consumer society. His business transactions belonged to that new world of changing tastes in luxuries and fashion—a world in which business failures and bankruptcy were to become more and more commonplace.

IV

Certainly Defoe did not help his prospects as a business man by riding forth in the manner of Don Quixote to join the forces of the Duke of Monmouth after he landed at Lyme Regis on the afternoon of 11 June 1685. He had been married for just a year and a half and had everything to lose. Did Mary say nothing more than 'Be careful'? Was her family so caught up in the persecution of the Dissenters at the time that she would have thought that her husband was merely doing his duty? What would the steady and cautious James Foe have thought? Why would Defoe do such a thing

---

[22] Defoe's many legal problems appear to have stemmed from this aspect of his character. On 15 Oct. 1684, long before the suits between 1688 and 1692 that were a sign of his growing difficulties, Defoe lost a suit with a William Whetton which involved his paying 'all claymes & demands'. Guildhall London Records Office, Lord Mayor's Waiting Book, xiv. 32.

unless, somewhere in his imagination, he envisioned himself as one of those great heroes whose mighty deeds he recorded in his 'Historical Collections'? Of course he was not alone. The army was composed of just such enthusiasts who had left their shops and their young wives to fight against James II who, after the death of Charles II, had assumed the throne. Defoe was not the only student of Charles Morton in the group either. Years later, he was to list some of his former schoolmates who, had they not lost their lives in Monmouth's Rebellion, might have been great poets.[23]

Of course, these young Dissenters thought that they were fighting to preserve their religion and their freedom, and those who, like Defoe, kept a careful watch over events in France thought they could see in James II another Louis XIV, and in their own future the same experiences that the Huguenots were undergoing in the years before the final revocation of the Edict of Nantes in 1685. Defoe was to write about those events in France later in his life with something of the same emotion as he must have felt when he was 25. After describing the original Edict, which had permitted the French Protestants to retain their religious freedom, he heaped scorn on the King who ignored such a solemn promise:

But in Contempt of God and Man, and to the eternal Infamy of Popery, and of the very Name and Memory of the late *Lewis* XIV it was disown'd, revok'd, and rescinded by the particular Order of that Prince in the Year 1685, and the Protestants thereupon treated with such Cruelty and Inhumanity, as can scarce be express'd by Words; and which in some Cases was more insupportable than Death even by Torments; and therefore it may be justly said to exceed the Cruleties of the Ten primitive Persecutions, such in particular as the ravishing Children and Women in the Presence of their Parents and Husbands, besides inumerable Cruelties studied by the most refin'd Understandings to wound even the Souls of the Sufferers, and which surpass the Wounds of the Body, as much as the Soul is more capable of Resentment.[24]

'I must be Blind', wrote Defoe in his journal, the *Review*, '. . . if I do not see a most exact Connection of Measures and Circumstances, between the Prosecution and Destruction of that Innocent People in *France*, and the present Steps a Party among us take at this time to Ruin and Extirpate the *Dissenters* among us.'[25] If Defoe could write this in 1712, how much more serious this parallel must have seemed to him in 1685, when refugees arriving in England from France had spread news of torture and massacres.

[23] *The Present State of the Parties in Great Britain* (London, 1712), 319.
[24] *Atlas Maritimus & Commercialis* (London, 1728), 57.
[25] *Review*, viii. 593.

Whereas Defoe's fellow journalist and friendly rival for the hearts of the Whig audience during the reign of Queen Anne, John Tutchin, emphasized his participation in Monmouth's Rebellion and wrote in celebration of the 'Western Martyrs', Defoe mentioned the event sparingly. One biographer imagines his riding to look over the rebel forces on 6 July 1685, during the battle of Sedgemoor, and, after observing the disorder among Monmouth's forces, deciding wisely to retreat. Indeed, James II's regular forces inflicted a devastating defeat upon the raw recruits who composed Monmouth's army. Admittedly, this attempt to cast Defoe in the role of Stendhal's Fabrizio in *The Charterhouse of Parma*, as the hero who somehow misses the great romantic moment in which he so longs to participate, has its attractions. Two of Defoe's fictional heroes, Colonel Jack and the Cavalier, miss the main part of such a crucial day, and so perhaps did Defoe. But Defoe remarked in the *Review* of 31 March 1713 that if, of those who talked so boldly about fighting for the Duke of Monmouth, 'half of them had as boldly joyn'd him Sword in Hand, he had never been routed at Kings-sedg-moor; and as they kept their Hands off from acting, so when he was defeated, we heard but little of their Tongues neither afterwards.'[26] Defoe was in an extremely vulnerable position at this time, and had he not himself fought with Monmouth's forces, there would have been hundreds of his enemies who could have attacked him either for cowardice on the field of battle or for claiming for himself a soldierly role that was false. That no such enemy stepped forward suggests that, in the general rout that occurred at Sedgemoor, Defoe's conduct was no worse than that of most of Monmouth's troops. If he was among the mounted troops led by Lord Grey, like many of those among this inexperienced cavalry, he may have found that his horse, unaccustomed to the sounds of cannon and rifles, was uncontrollable and carried him away from the battle before he could gain command.[27] Apparently Defoe did not enjoy recalling what happened at Sedgemoor. Defeat is never pleasant, and the aftermath was terrifying enough to make his avoidance of the subject understandable.

One other piece of evidence of Defoe's participation is a remarkable picture of the kind of suffering that an army must endure in the intervals between battles. Criticizing those who object to the pleasure-seeking soldier off-duty, Defoe painted a grim picture of the soldier's life:

But if they did but see them in a Rainy Season, when the whole Country about them is trod into a Chaos, and in such intolerable Marches, Men and Horses dying and dead together, and the best of them glad of a bundle of Straw to lay down their

[26] *Review*, ix. 154.
[27] See Peter Earle, *Monmouth's Rebels* (New York: St. Martin's Press, 1977), 127–8.

wet and weary Limbs: If they did but see a Siege, besides the daily danger and expectation of Death, which is common to all, from the General to the Sentinel; the Watches, the Labours, the Cares which attend the greatest; the ugly Sights, the Stinks of Mortality, the Grass all wither'd and black with the Smoke of Powder, the horrid Noises all Night and all Day, and Spoil and Destruction on every side; I am sure they would be perswaded, that a State of War, to those who are engag'd in it, must needs be a state of Labour and Misery.[28]

Although caution might suggest that Defoe could have described such a scene through imagination and wide reading, a preponderance of detail would suggest that he had been through a campaign. What he describes are exactly the kinds of observation that never appear in print. It was rain on the night of 23 June that caused Monmouth to delay his abortive attack on Bristol, and Defoe probably witnessed the six hours of cannonading between the two armies through a rainy night at Phillips Norton a few days later. He could have learned of the horror of sieges by reading of the taking of Magdenburgh in the Thirty Years War, but something of the rain and mud of Somerset in 1685 and a desperate rebellion seeps through this passage. He was there.

Somehow, perhaps by managing to flee the country or by going into hiding, Defoe escaped the vicious reprisals that followed the failure of the rebellion. James II wanted the rebels hanged for all to see, and with the aid of his Chief Justice, Jeffreys, men were hunted down throughout the region. Some of the prisoners were sold as transported felons, others fled to Holland and even to New England. Many of those hanged were given the full punishment, their entrails burned, their bodies quartered, and the remains displayed all over the South West of England. The wives and children of those executed were often reduced to begging. Only the Amnesty of March 1686 put an end to the butchery, but a profitable trade in transporting the prisoners to the West Indies coninued for some time.[29] Defoe was to receive a special pardon in 1687, probably the kind that, at this late date, could be purchased for £60.[30] Under any circumstance, his business must have suffered during 1685 and 1686, and some of his troubles may really have dated from that time.

All of these matters considered, we must revise our understanding of Defoe's character somewhat along the lines of his hero, Robinson Crusoe. For Crusoe was an extraordinarily successful businessman when he applied himself to his various trades. As he remarked to his partner, who had

---

[28] *A Short Narrative of the Life of His Grace John D. of Marlborough* (London, 1711), 41.
[29] See David Ogg, *England in the Reign of James II and William III* (Oxford: Clarendon Press, 1966), 152–7.
[30] CSPD, 31 May 1687.

upbraided him for a certain slackness in the pursuit of gain, despite his hatred of 'sitting still', once he embarked on a business venture, he pursued it with remarkable industry.[31] Crusoe's problem is his 'Wandering Fancy', his desire to travel, and such a romantic motivation must be laid to Defoe's account in the affair of the Monmouth Rebellion. He was industrious enough, and he loved the idea of trade with a passion, but with not so much of a passion as he loved his various causes. For them, particularly for his political causes, he would put on the armour of the knight errant and charge at the nearest windmill.

V

With the prospect of James's revenge—of the bodies of rebels hanging along the roads from Somerset to London—where did Defoe go in the confusion of the defeat at Sedgemoor on 6 July 1685? He had a relative at Martock, fifteen miles away, who ran a free school which Defoe had visited on various occasions, but a thorough search was being made throughout the West Country. Houses were invaded without any legal ceremony, and the trials were almost modelled on those of the Queen in *Alice in Wonderland*, with the verdict first and the trial after. Defoe would have been wise to have left the country, at least until a pardon was obtained. Certainly he would never have had a better time to take a voyage to some of those lands he was to visit imaginatively in his fiction.

How far he went and how long he stayed are perplexing questions. His knowledge of the places of the earth and their products was so extensive that he was chosen to write the commentary on this subject for *Atlas Maritimus & Commercialis* (1728), a large undertaking by a consortium of publishers. He did this in conjunction with the famous contemporary scientist Edmund Halley, who supplied the maps. But Defoe often boasted of the power of the imagination to recreate places never seen. In *Captain Singleton*, he was to send his hero across parts of Africa that were unknown in Defoe's day, and he did much the same for the South Pacific in *A New Voyage Round the World*. The descriptions are vivid enough, yet he was surely never in either place. In describing a person who was a 'SCHOLLAR' in Defoe's eyes despite his ignorance of the classical

---

[31] After listening to a criticism of his 'indolent Temper', Crusoe remarks, 'I begin to be a Convert to the Principles of Merchandizing; but I must tell you . . . you do not know what I am doing; foir if once I conquer my backwardness, and embark heartily; as old as I am, I shall harrass you up and down the World, till I tire you; for I shall pursue it so eagerly, I shall never let you lye still.' *The Farther Adventures of Robinson Crusoe*, in *Shakespeare Head Edition* (1927–8), iii. 112.

languages, Defoe listed his knowledge of geography: 'You can not name any country in the known part of Europe but he can give you extempore an account of its situation, latitude, rivers, chief towns, its commerce, and, nay, and some thing of its history and of its political interests.'[32] If such a person had the imaginative and creative abilities of Defoe, he could make places come alive in such a way that we might conclude he had surely been there. And for the most part, Defoe's accounts of foreign parts are probably nothing more than an imagined reality.

On occasions, he will speak of certain events that occurred to him when he was in another country. Such statements have to be examined with scepticism, particularly when they occur in a work such as his *Tour thro' the Whole Island of Great Britain*, which he published between 1724 and 1727. This work is written in a series of 'Familiar Letters', and the narrator is supposed to be a world traveller capable of comparing gardens, buildings, and the natural landscape with similar features in other parts of the world. For example, in his description of Wilton House in Wiltshire, he remarks that a statue of Venus was unmatched by any sculpture in England and only equalled by artefacts to be seen in Italy: 'In Italy, and especially at Romne and Naples, we see a great variety of fine columns, and some of them of excellent workmanship, and antiquity, and at some of the Courts of the Princes of Italy the like is seen; as especially at the Court of Florence; but in England I do not remember to have seen any thing like this.'[33] While Defoe may have wandered about Italy sampling the best in art and culture, what is most important about this passage is that we feel we are in the presence of a connoisseur. The same is true when he shifts to what seems like a confession of a direct experience. Commenting on a bas-relief of Marcus Aurelius in the same collection, he states, 'I never saw any thing like what appears here, except in the chamber of rarieties at Munick in Bavaria.'[34]

As Samuel Johnson, quoting Castiglione, was to remark about writing in a 'Mask' or under the disguise of anonymity, it confers certain privileges, and among them was a release from an excessive regard for the truth.[35] Defoe may have actually viewed the great art treasures of western Europe; he was curious about everything in the world around him, but whatever travelling he did, it probably had little resemblance to the 'Grand Tour' taken by gentlemen as part of their education during the eighteenth century. As with his Robinson Crusoe, such travel would usually have had as its ostensible goal some interest in trade. Merchants often travelled a great deal. His friend Charles Lodwick and Lodwick's half-brother

[32] *The Compleat English Gentleman*, 200.
[33] *Tour*, i. 193–4.
[34] Ibid. 195.
[35] Samuel Johnson, *The Rambler*, No. 208.

Matthew Clarkson both travelled to New York, where they acted as factors on behalf of Defoe, and Defoe had firm links with Spain, probably through his dealing in wines. France and Holland lay but a short distance across the Channel. He seems to have visited Germany and Italy, and perhaps, like his own Colonel Jack, his French was good enough to pass for a native of that country. That one of his aliases was 'Claude Guilot' may suggest that he thought he would not be detected in such a disguise.

At any rate, in fleeing for his life after the defeat at Sedgemoor, Defoe may have used his contacts as a merchant to board the first available ship to the Continent. A likely place for him to have gone would have been Holland. It was to Holland that Shaftesbury had fled after being freed by the London jury, and as the most tolerant of Europe's states, it held attractions for a large number of those who fled the wrath of James II. Many were to return to England from Holland with William of Orange in 1688. But none of the exiles mention an ardent young Englishman named Daniel Foe in any of their correspondence.[36] At this point in his career, he would have been more interested in keeping his business going than in political intrigue among professional plotters such as Robert Ferguson and Major Wildman. He appears to have returned even before 10 March 1686, when James issued his general pardon. On 24 January 1686 he posted bail for a relative, Jane Foe, and for a Mary Deering, who had been arrested for attending an illegal conventicle at Tenter Alley in Little Moor Fields.[37] He may have already paid a ransom that assured his safety, but as has been mentioned, he appears on a list for 31 May 1687 of those pardoned.[38] Individual entrepreneurs purchased such lists at a flat rate to make what money could be earned at so late a date. Defoe's is among the names of those purchased by a George Penne—names of those who were to be transported to the West Indies. When Defoe depicted the servitude of Colonel Jack in Virginia, he may have experienced a vicarious sense of relief at his hero's ability to overcome his situation. In real life, the rebels transported to the West Indies were fortunate if they survived the voyage itself.

The Petty Jury list for the Cornhill Ward lists Defoe's name for 1685 and 1686. His name does not appear for 1687, but he was back on the Petty Jury in 1688.[39] Much of the fervour had gone out of the search for the rebels by 1686, and Penne may have been content with £60 or £65. Ransoms of

---

[36] Frank Bastian presents some evidence for a Dutch connection, but nothing entirely persuasive. See *Defoe's Early Life*, 118–20.

[37] Guildhall, London Records Office, Lord Mayor's Waiting Book, vol. 14, 503. He also paid for a Maria Deering.

[38] CSPD, 31 May 1687.

[39] Cornhill Ward, Jury Duty Wardmote, Guildhall Library MS 4069/2, fo. 379.

£15,000, such as Edward Prideaux paid to the King and to Chief Justice Jeffreys, were no longer to be obtained.[40] On 4 April 1687 James II had issued his Declaration of Indulgence, hoping that by suspending the Test Acts against Dissenters and Catholics, he would be able to manipulate these two groups against the reigning Anglican establishment in both church and state. Toleration was the important notion he was attempting to sell to the nation. One of the most respected Dissenters, Richard Baxter, was released from prison, and James actively courted the Quaker William Penn. In posing as the newfound friend of the Dissenters, James could hardly wish to revive memory of the Bloody Assizes. Defoe could not have felt seriously endangered by his involvement in the Monmouth affair at this point in time.

He apparently felt confident enough to write a work in which he urged his fellow Dissenters to reject the King's overtures. In *An Appeal to Honour and Justice,* he described his disagreement with many among the Dissenters who believed that James II ought to be trusted as his second disagreement with his fellow Nonconformists after he had upbraided them for support-ing the Turks during the siege of Vienna:

The next Time I differed with my Friends was when King *James* was wheedling the *Dissenters* to take off the Penal Laws and Test, which I could by no means come into. And as *in the first* I used to say, I had rather the Popish House of *Austria* should ruin the Protestants in *Hungaria*, than the Infidel House of *Ottoman* should ruin both Protestant and Papist, by over-running *Germany*; So in the other, I told the *Dissenters* I had rather the Church of *England* should pull our Cloaths off by Fines and Forfeitures, than the Papists should fall both upon the *Church*, and the *Dissenters*, and pull our Skins off by Fire and Fagot.[41]

Some of his fellow Dissenters believed that there was some advantage to be gained in lifting the state of siege under which they had lived during the last years of Charles II and under James II. In the period between Monmouth's rebellion and James's declaration of a new toleration of Dissenters and Catholics, the King had encouraged brutal treatment toward anyone attending illegal conventicles or violating the other laws that had been passed to discourage religious dissent, and a horde of spies and informers were only too eager to collect rewards for testimony against some of the most distinguished of the Nonconformists. Defoe's teacher, Charles Morton, was among those who found the climate in England impossible and left for New England. But rather than making him eager for accommodation, such violations of what Defoe considered to be religious

---

[40] See Ogg, *James II and William III*, 153.
[41] *An Appeal to Honour and Justice*, in *Shakespeare Head Edition*, 233.

freedom simply made him angry. He was already showing the extra-ordinary resilience that was to mark his entire life. A fugitive just a few months before and perhaps still on a secret list of known traitors, he was ready to attack a policy which he saw as the prelude to an attempt to turn England back into a Catholic nation.

John Robert Moore identified *A Letter to a Dissenter from his Friend at the Hague, Concerning the Penal Laws and the Test* as the work to which Defoe was referring, suggesting that there was another production in 1687 attack-ing those 'Addresses' who congratulated James on his generosity in suspending the Test Acts. Such Addresses continued to be published in the London Gazette until the end of James's reign, and he repeated his Declaration of Indulgence on 27 April 1688, a year after the first.[42] This makes the dating of Defoe's work difficult. The brief four-page pamphlet named by Moore, with its argument for the Test Acts as a way of keeping the Catholics from power, hardly seems the kind of work that would have angered any large section of the Dissenters at such a late date. The irony directed against James II is very much in the style of Defoe, but he may indeed have written a longer and more explicit attack earlier.

VI

William III landed at Torbay on 5 November 1688, blown there by what seemed, to those who looked for the signs of Providence in history, a miraculous 'Protestant Wind'. With this event began what was called the Glorious Revolution, as James found his power slipping from him and, after one abortive attempt at departing, finally left England for France on 23 December. Perhaps no event in English history has been the occasion of such revisionist thinking as the Glorious Revolution. Advocates of the 'Whig theory of history' saw in this event a crucial moment in English history and, indeed, in the history of the world, a moment when England progressed toward liberal democracy and toward everything that the nine-teenth century regarded as the modern world. Many modern historians have argued that William succeeded by various subterfuges, that for the most part the idea of 'Revolution Principles' remained meaningless for the greater part of the population, and that the introduction of a society based firmly on the rights of property created a heartless exploitation of the poor. It also gave England a monarch whose right to the throne was dependent not upon a divinely ordained succession but rather upon the necessity of a

---

[42] Ogg, *England in the Reigns of James II and William III*, 186.

state apparatus to maintain law and order. It ushered into England what has been called the 'Financial Revolution' by one modern historian and an atmosphere described by a contemporary poet as 'The Corruption of the World by Money'.[43] Even if we now can perceive that there are at least two ways of seeing the Glorious Revolution, we should not surrender to the kind of nostalgia that afflicted those who longed for a return of James II and his family to the throne of England—those who became known as Jacobites. If absolutism seemed to many contemporaries the correct political direction of the future, we know that it was not: that whatever evils came in with the creation of a state geared for capitalist expansion and for the eventual development of liberal democracy, it was a far better system than one governed by the caprice of a single monarch. Defoe was to be the enthusiastic propagandist, political theorist, and economic prophet for the Glorious Revolution and for its hero, William III. He thought that the Dissenters should have gained more from it—more, that is, than toleration of their dissent—but he never criticized the political settlement created by the Glorious Revolution.

To demonstrate his pleasure in the extraordinary turn of events, Defoe participated in the Lord Mayor's Show on 29 October 1689, to which William III had been invited. John Oldmixon noted that it was more elaborate than anything the magistrates of the city of London had ever staged before:

and what deserv'd to be particularly mention'd, says a Reverend Historian, was a Royal Regiment of Volunteer Horse, made up of the chief Citizens, who being gallantly mounted and richley accoutred, were led by the Earl of Monmouth, now Earl of Petersborough, and attended their Majesties from Whitehall. Among these Troopers, who were for the most part Dissenters, was Daniel Foe, at that time a Hosier in Freeman's Yard, Cornhill; the same who afterwards was Pillory'd for writing an ironical invective against the Church, and did after that list in the service of Mr. Robert Harley ...[44]

How proud Defoe must have been to have ridden with a troop led by the son of the man for whom he fought at Sedgemoor! No one watching at the time would have seen the vision that Oldmixon attempted to give his readers by projecting the future upon the past, by projecting an image of Defoe, the future traitor, upon that of the young merchant proudly playing out his role as a soldier enlisted in the cause of King William.

[43] The modern historian was P. G. M. Dickson, whose book *The Financial Revolution* was published in 1967. The contemporary poet was Robert Gould.
[44] John Oldmixon, *The History of England during the Reigns of King William and Queen Mary* (London, 1735), 37.

Although the next few years were to bring some genuine pleasures, they were certainly mixed with the anxieties of family life and the uncertainties of business. But on that day in October, Defoe must have seen before him the prospect of a brilliant future. He was 29. His wife, Mary, had either just given birth to their second daughter, Maria, or was pregnant with her.[45] On the other hand, Defoe's excitement over the successful invasion by William of Orange, now William III, ruling jointly with his wife, Queen Mary, would certainly have been tempered by his grief over the death of his first child. On 7 September 1688, he had buried Mary in the parish church of St Michael Cornhill.[46] Although some historians have argued that the high mortality rate among children must have inured parents to feelings of excessive grief over the deaths of their children, such 'evidence' contradicts everything that we know about individual grief. For someone as oriented toward family life as Defoe, the death of a child must have come as a stunning blow. Concern over the wellbeing of new children being born may have relieved some of the sadness in the home, but we should not let modern statistics of mortality blind us to our sense of what must have been tremendous sorrow. It was to be Defoe's genius in *A Journal of the Plague Year* to contrast the individual, tragic death with the Bills of Mortality, and his insight into the disparity between the cold numbers and the reality of whole families being wiped out makes that work so poignant and believable.

So little is known of Defoe's children that his biographers tend to avoid the subject. James Sutherland, wonderful scholar that he was, limited himself to a discussion of the supposed illegitimacy of Benjamin Norton Defoe, who was probably Defoe's third child, concluding that Defoe's sins were probably 'not those of the flesh' and that the charge, coming from the unreliable Richard Savage, was doubtful. The little that we know is that Defoe had eight children in all: Mary, Maria, Hannah, Benjamin, Henrietta, Daniel, Margaret, and, finally, Sophia, in December 1701. All of these children, all of Mary's pregnancies, must have made the Defoe household a busy place, full of excitement and affection. If Mary were to live through the experience of having eight children in so short a time, she would obviously need help, and by 6 March 1692 the poll tax list revealed not only a second child but five servants. Richard Addis was apparently there to assist Defoe in his business, but Ralph Besey, Mary, Anne, and 'Nourse' were there to help with the burdens of the household and the

---

[45] The taxation rolls of the Cornhill Ward for 1690, Box 6, MS 10, at the Guildhall list Defoe as living with his wife, one child, and two servants, a man and a woman.

[46] See *The Register of St. Michael's Cornhill 1546–1754* (London: Harleian Society, 1882), 270.

nursery. In this list, Defoe is listed as a 'Whole Sale Hosier' rather than as the 'Merchant' he described himself as in his marriage licence.[47]

In a sense, Defoe had really settled down for the first time since his marriage. That there were no children in the first few years is hardly surprising. Until the general pardon was issued for the participants in Monmouth's Rebellion, he probably made only brief appearances at his home, and perhaps not until the particular pardon at the end of May 1687 did he really feel secure. But as suggested, arrangements for that pardon may have been made long in advance, for on 12 January 1687 he applied for the status of Livery Man in the Butchers' Company on the basis of his father's membership. He agreed to pay a fine of £10 15s. for the privilege of being discharged of any obligations to serve as an officer or of any duties.[48] He thereby assumed his rights as a citizen of London.

VII

Four years after the Glorious Revolution, on 29 October 1692, Defoe was in the Fleet prison, his career as a merchant and tradesman sliding toward ruin. He was sentenced by Sir John Powell on a suit brought by Walter Ridley, Cornelius Shadwell, Jerome Whichcote, and Nicholas Barrett. Walter Ridley is identified as a 'haberdasher', and all four were probably associated with Defoe's dealings in hosiery. Pat Rogers, who first uncovered the records of this incarceration, suggested that it threw doubt on Defoe's claims of being a merchant. He was deeply involved with these London tradesmen, Rogers argued, and it was in this area rather than that of marine insurance that Defoe met disaster.[49] But as Frank Bastian has demonstrated, Defoe's business dealings were immensely varied, and, as the records of the Port and Custom Books at the Public Records Office reveal, he was engaged in importing and exporting goods.[50] Considering that only a small portion of his dealings were recorded in such records and court cases, everything suggests that he dabbled in anything that might enable him to turn a profit.

He apparently owned a vessel with the provocative name *Desire*, for we know he attempted to sell it to a Robert Harrison for £260 on 13 August 1688. Harrison could only manage to raise £195, leaving Defoe with a

[47] Guildhall Library, Poll Book, Mar. 1692, Cornhill Ward, 1st Precinct.

[48] Guildhall Library, Court Minutes, MS 6443–1.

[49] Pat Rogers, 'Defoe in Fleet Street Prison', *Notes & Queries* 216 (1971): 451–5.

[50] His name appears in the records of the Collector of Customs, E.90. 144/1 on 28 Mar. 1688 (item 10); and Port Books, 145/1 for 3 July (item 51) and 6 July (item 39). His dealings were relatively small compared to merchants such as William Joliffe.

quarter share.[51] Just a few months before, on 18 June, he had signed an agreement with Humphrey Ayles to transport merchandise and passengers to Boston, New York, and Maryland, and to return with a specified cargo, a transaction that was to end in litigation.[52] And in July he was being dunned by a merchant from Kings Lynn named Joseph Braban for £396 7s. 1d. not yet collected from his customers. Defoe agreed to pay Braban the money in monthly instalments, a sure sign that he had extended his credit far beyond any cash that he had to hand.[53] In fact, this was the period that saw a huge expansion in the use of credit in financial transactions. Defoe was to extol the magic powers of Lady Credit in his later writings, but for a relatively young merchant, the ability to obtain unlimited credit was dangerous. Given Defoe's exhuberant temperament, the temptation to invest in seemingly exciting projects must have been irresistible.

The two projects that brought him the most grief were his investment in a diving-engine to search for treasure and in a civet cat farm for the extraction of ingredients used in making perfume from the urine of these animals. The image of diving into the depths of the ocean for gold and sifting the urine of civet cats for perfume seems to combine utopian dreams with the kind of scientific project that Swift was to satirize in the wonderful academy of Lagado in the third book of *Gulliver's Travels*, but as Defoe was to remind the readers of his *Essay upon Projects*, deciding on whether a scheme is completely mad or a stroke of genius is not always so easy:

There is, 'tis true, a great difference between *New Inventions* and *Projects*, between Improvement of Manufactures or Lands, which tend to the immediate Benefit of the Public and Imploying of the Poor, and projects framed by subtle Heads, with a sort a *Deceptio Visus* and *Legerdemain*, to bring people to run needless and unusual hazards. I grant it, and give a due preferenct to the first, and yet Success has so sanctifi'd some of those other sorts of projects, that 'twou'd be a kind of Blashemy against Fortune to disallow 'em: witness *Sir William Phip's* Voyage to the Wreck; 'twas a mere Project, a Lottery of a Hundred thousand to One odds; a hazard which, if it had fail'd, every body would have been asham'd to have own'd themselves concern'd in, a Voyage that wou'd have been as much ridicul'd as *Don Quixot's Adventure upon the Windmill*.[54]

Even as he speaks of the £200,000 that Sir William Phipps managed to salvage from the Spanish wreck off Florida, the reader can feel Defoe's eyes glowing and his excitement returning.

[51] See PRO. C7. 179/188.
[52] Ibid. C7/122/36; C7/122/9.
[53] Ibid. C8. 548/96. For an excellent summary of these cases, see James Sutherland, 'Some Early Troubles of Daniel Defoe', *Review of English Studies* 9 (1933), 275–90.
[54] *An Essay upon Projects*, 11.

After mentioning diving-engines among some doubtful projects, Defoe noted, 'I could give a very diverting history of a patent-monger whose cully was nobody but myself.' The person Defoe had in mind was Joseph Williams, who experimented with such a machine in May 1691 off the coast of Scotland. He patented the machine on 17 October of that year and formed a company. Defoe purchased ten shares with £200 and was voted secretary-treasurer. An additional 10s. per share was added to provide working capital. Williams, who received 400 shares of stock for his invention paid Defoe partly in money and partly in notes, but by 3 February 1693 he was suing Defoe for having cashed some of his notes. The diving-engine proved to be unsuccessful. Whether Williams managed to recover any of the money and notes he gave Defoe is unknown, but at the very least, Defoe lost the £200. That Defoe's enthusiasm for such a discovery was undiminished is shown by a letter from his brother-in-law Robert Davis to Defoe's patron, Robert Harley, on 30 October 1713. After mentioning Defoe's name and obvious approval of his scheme, Davis provided testimony to his going down in an engine and singing the hundreth psalm under water in September 1704. More important than this moment in the history of music was the recovery of several silver bars from a wreck. Defoe may have pictured himself as the naive victim of Williams, but he apparently never gave up hope that he would find a diving machine that would make him rich.[55]

Defoe's adventure into the perfume trade was both more expensive and more questionable from the standpoint of his business practices. On 21 April 1692, he agreed to take over a civet cat farm owned by John Barksdale for the sum of £852 15s. He borrowed £400 from an old acquaintance, Samuel Stancliffe, to whom he already owed £1100, but almost £800 came from his mother-in-law, Joan Tuffley. When the sixty-nine cats were seized by the Sheriffs of London, Sir Thomas Lane and Sir Thomas Cooke, they were appraised at half the value, and the operation was taken over by Sir Thomas Estcourt. Joan Tuffley sued Defoe for misrepresenting the price of the civet cats, charging 'manifest fraud' and referring to Defoe as a 'gay deceiver'.[56] By July of that year Defoe, faced with a Chancery suit over a bill for £40, admitted that he owed the money and that he did not have the money to meet the note. At this point he was obviously bankrupt.

The question of Defoe's guilt in all of this has been a point of contention between his biographers. When Theodore Newton first discussed Defoe's

[55] *Portland Papers*, 350–1.
[56] PRO C7.373/33. Joan Tuffley filed to recover her investment on 17 May 1693. Sir Thomas Estcourt replied on 2 June and John Barksdale on 12 June of that year.

involvement in the transactions over the civet cat farm, he accused Defoe of doing anything to save himself, and that included deceiving his own relatives. John Robert Moore rushed to the defence of Defoe's character. The lawsuit of Joan Tuffley, he argued, was actually an attempt to get Sir Thomas Estcourt to disgorge some of his money. James Sutherland, balancing the evidence, thought that Defoe could not be excused from practising a degree of deception upon Joan Tuffley.

Such views have the benefit of hindsight but do not suggest the misery that Defoe must have experienced at the time. Sutherland aptly quoted a number of the *Review* for 19 February 1706, in which Defoe confessed, 'I freely name myself, with those, that are ready to own, that they have in the Extremities and Embarrassments in Trade, done those things, which their own Principles Condemn'd, which they are not Asham'd to Blush for, which they look back on with Regret, and strive to make Reparation for, with their utmost Diligence.'[57] As evidence for Defoe's innocence, Professor Moore argued that Defoe remained on excellent terms with the Tuffley family, but Defoe clearly took money from them and others which he used to balance out other accounts rather than those in which they thought they were investing. That he was later to move his family into the Tuffley home may show that they found him a likeable human being and that they thought his financial problems were more the result of inexperience and youth than of malicious intent. But there appears to be no question about his misuse of funds.[58]

Defoe expressed his thoughts on bankruptcy most tellingly in *The Compleat English Tradesman*, where the subject occupies 100 pages near the beginning of the second edition of 1727. The positioning of this discussion shows how close to Defoe's feelings was this experience, and the warning against 'over-trading' suggests that he considered this to have been his chief error:

Over-trading is among tradesmen as over-lifting is among strong men; such people vain of their strength, and their pride prompting them to put it to the utmost trial, at last lift at something too heavy for them, over-strain their sinews, break some of Nature's bands, and are cripples ever after. I take Over-trading to be to a shop-keeper, as ambition is to a prince. The late King of France, the great King Lewis is a flagrant example. . . . Thus the strong man in the fable, who by

---

[57] *Review*, iii. 86b.
[58] For a balanced approach, see James Sutherland, *Defoe*, 2nd edn. (London: Methuen, 1950), 41–2. Sutherland concludes that the apparent anger shown by Joan Tuffley in her law suit was real enough. On the other hand, he may underestimate the nature of family unity at the time. She may have been acting in a practical manner, attempting to salvage something from the general wreckage of Defoe's finances, but she must have been angry at Defoe's apparent duplicity.

main strength us'd to rive a tree, undertaking one at last which was too strong for him, it clos'd upon his fingers and held him till the wild beasts came and devour'd him.[59]

Defoe reached back into his 'Historical Collections', to the story of Milo Crotoniates, for this fable of the man who overestimates his powers. His most detailed comparison for the able tradesman who overestimates his strength is drawn from history—the attempts of Louis XIV to conquer all of Europe and his ultimate defeat at the hands of the forces he succeeded in uniting in opposition to him; Spain, England, and Holland. Both examples suggest his tendency to mythologize the fall of his 'compleat tradesman' and his own bankruptcy. Of course Defoe did not refer specifically to himself in this discussion, but those readers who could guess at the author might sense a certain lack of modesty in Defoe's picture of the ruin of a powerful entrepreneur.

In urging the tradesman to 'break' early, before his situation becomes desperate, Defoe was clearly thinking of the horrors of his own situation. He imagines the entire scene as an epic struggle. The tradesman is like a fighter knocked down, unable to resist, or like a 'soldier surrounded with enemies, he must be kill'd; so the debtor must sink, it cannot be prevented'.[60] Defoe believed strongly that he would always be able to overcome difficulties by his skill or cleverness. Bankruptcy taught him that, in certain situations, capitulation was the only recourse. Before the final disaster, he probably tried to retrench as much as possible. He gives a dialogue between a tradesman and his wife in which the husband is reluctant to worry his wife. It is she who insists on knowing the true state of his affairs and who offers to cut back from five maids and a footman to just two maids. He, on the other hand, is reluctant to give up his horses and groom: 'It is very hard, I han't your spirit my Dear.'[61] That this was a version of a conversation between Mary Foe and her husband is the more likely because the details of the family depicted, including numbers of servants and children, are very close to those of the family of Daniel Foe.

As has been mentioned, by the end of October 1692 all efforts at saving his business had failed. His debts totalled £17,000. Of 140 creditors, all but four agreed to accept 15s. to the pound, the amount that Defoe considered fair in his *Complete English Tradesman*, but four of the creditors holding debts amounting to £2000 refused to accept the agreement. This ended efforts at a reasonable solution. After his imprisonment on 29 October, he was again committed to the Fleet on 4 November for a debt of £700 owed

---

[59] *The Complete English Tradesman*, i. 57–8.   [60] Ibid. 77–8.   [61] Ibid. 143.

to Thomas Martin and an unstipulated sum owed to Henry Fairfax. As with his arrest in October, he was quickly removed to the King's Bench Prison. From there, he may have gone to the Mint, a sanctuary for debtors, but like his heroine, Moll Flanders, who passed some time there only to find that she was 'not wicked enough' for such company, he probably left as soon as he could.[62] Moll's observations, made despite her feeling that preaching was not her particular 'Talent', express what must have been Defoe's horror at seeing the ideals of the commercial world flaunted by the inhabitants of this sanctuary:

It was indeed a Subject of strange Reflection to me, to see Men who were over-whelm'd in perplex'd Circumstances; who were reduc'd some Degrees below being Ruin'd; whose Families were Objects of their own Terror and other Peoples Charity; yet while a Penny lasted, nay, even beyond it, endeavouring to drown their Sorrow in their Wickedness; heaping up more Guilt upon themselves, labouring to forget former things, which now it was the proper time to remember, making more Work for Repentance, and Sinning on, as a Remedy for Sin past. . . . I have heard them, turning about, fetch a deep Sigh, and cry *what a Dog am I!* Well *Betty*, my Dear, I'll drink thy Health tho' *meaning the Honest Wife*, that perhaps had not a Half a Crown for herself and three or four Children: The next Morning they are at their Penitentials again, and perhaps the poor weeping Wife comes over to him, either brings him some Account of what his Creditors are doing, and how she and the Children are turn'd out of Doors, or some other dreadful News; and this adds to his self Reproaches; but when he has Thought and Por'd on it till he is almost Mad, having no Principles to Support him nothing within him, or above him, to Comfort himn; but finding it all Darkness on every Side, he flyes to the same Relief again, (viz.) to Drink it away.[63]

That Defoe understood how it felt to experience this sense of helplessness and despair there can be no doubt. If he sensed within him a conviction that somehow he would recover from his bankruptcy—a conviction supplied both by an invincible faith in his own abilities and by his religious beliefs— he nevertheless understood what these men were suffering. Bankruptcy was a disaster for Defoe in all kinds of ways, but it supplied him with an understanding of human anguish that was to be the making of a great writer of fiction.

Like the families of these men, Defoe's family was living upon charity. Mary Foe and her children had taken refuge in the house of Joan Tuffley and her son, Samuel, at Kingsland, and Daniel joined her there some time in 1693. The home in Freeman's Yard was gone, though Defoe continued

⁶² *Moll Flanders*, 66.   ⁶³ Ibid. 65.

his hosiery business with the help of two assistants, Richard Addis and James Moyer. He had not abandoned his business career, but the fear of arrest through the demands of his creditors must have made his life uncomfortable. Indeed, it may have been the secret kind of life he had to live in evading arrests for debt that introduced him to various other forms of secrecy. Apparently he even thought it unsafe to attend public worship on Sunday, since he was to mention how he had been deprived of that pleasure.

And as if matters were not bad enough, he may have experienced further financial disaster when, on 26 June 1693, the Smyrna fleet of 400 ships was attacked by a French force of fifty men-of-war. In his *Continuation of the Letters of a Turkish Spy* (1718) Defoe was to describe this battle as a great victory for the French, with sixty-six ships captured or destroyed, 'most of them richly laden'.[64] Defoe's name was among those on the 'Merchant Insurers Bill' which passed through the Commons and went to the House of Lords, where it was rejected on 9 March 1694. If it had passed, Defoe would have been able to make suitable arrangements with his creditors for paying off his debts, for he already had agreements from two-thirds of those to whom money was owed. The bill stated that if two-thirds agreed to a certain composition, the others would have to accept the amount agreed upon. John Robert Moore argues conclusively that as a late applicant among the nineteen, Defoe would have had his credentials examined very carefully.[65] This means that some of his losses must have involved his insuring ships. Was he still investing in insurance in 1693? His late application may suggest that he was taking advantage of the mishandling of the naval protection of the Smyrna fleet to make claims for some insurance disasters earlier in the war. These may have been the shocks that forced him into the desperate measures at the end of 1692.

In some ways Defoe could count his blessings. At least he was free to recover his fortunes. What might have been is suggested by a volume published in 1691 by Moses Pitt with the title *The Cry of the Oppress'd*. Pitt, a former book publisher, was unable to find the means to get out of prison. He printed a series of horror stories of debtors around the country who were forced to suffer unspeakable indignities. Some were forced to capture and devour rats to stay alive. Their wives were attacked sexually by the prison guards; they were often kept under the filthiest conditions; and they sometimes had to live alongside the corpses of fellow prisoners who had died from their sufferings.[66] A number of published proposals for projects

---

[64] Daniel Defoe, *Continuation of the Letters of a Turkish Spy* (London, 1718), 299.
[65] Moore, *Daniel Defoe* (Chicago: University of Chicago Press, 1958), 92–4.
[66] Pitt added illustrations to his work to make his descriptions even more vivid.

that would help the nation came from men who claimed that they need only be released from prison to put their schemes into effect. Defoe was to be imprisoned several more times during his life, but it never ceased to be the nightmare that haunted his soul.

5

Financial Woes and Recovery

While Defoe was experiencing all these tribulations in his business affairs, he was also emerging as an author, or rather it may be argued that his sufferings and experience of change transformed his character and intellectual vision in such a manner as to give him the viewpoint of an author— of someone sufficiently outside the mainstream of society to be capable of seeing it in an original way. Lucien Goldmann argued that the typical author of the eighteenth century was a member of the bourgeoisie who had somehow been cast down from his former social status—someone who understood the life of those in the middle orders but who was no longer entirely a part of that life. While the young Defoe must have been something of a prig, his experience of bankruptcy and the various legal actions brought against him introduced him to two powerful and transforming emotional experiences—shame and humiliation.

Even after the government's attempt to humanize the process of bankruptcy in the law of 1706, there continued to be a taint of immorality adhering to the bankrupt.[1] Defoe had cheated his mother-in-law and involved his best friends in lawsuits. One case, involving his old friend William Marsh, saw him cashing a bill of £100 which was to be drawn on the account of John Hoyle, who had recently died. Defoe stated that he paid £60 to Marsh and received a full £100 credit from a goldsmith to whom Marsh owed money. Hoyle's executor, Thomas Nisbet, discovered that the note was missing from Hoyle's papers, sued Defoe, and recovered damages of £41.10s. and costs of £15 10s. in January 1693. Although Defoe tried to have this verdict overturned, he was unsuccessful. It is hard to see this in any other light than Nisbet's view that Defoe and Marsh entered into a 'confederacy to deceive'. Defoe claimed that Hoyle owed Marsh the money and that he was merely taking what was due to him, but he gives

---

[1] Julian Hoppit, *Risk and Failure in Eighteenth-Century Business* (Cambridge: Cambridge University Press, 1987), 18–21.

every appearance of acting the part of a sharper, trying to cash the money of a dead man in the hope that the action would pass unnoticed.[2] Defoe spoke of the 'wicked' things that the bankrupt tradesman will do, and of 'what Shifts, what Turnings, and Windings in Trade to support his Dying Credit', but he usually avoided words like 'crime' and 'criminal acts'. True enough, he wrote of how the bankrupt feels like the criminal who is about to be executed, hoping for a reprieve and eventually giving way to despair when the 'dead warrant' comes down; but this is an analysis of the bankrupt's psychology rather than an ethical judgement on the acts that led to 'breaking'.[3] Defoe preferred to concentrate on those bankrupts who might be viewed as victims, as objects of pity, yet his incarcerations at this period were for a series of actions little different from theft. The experience was one of embarrassment and guilt, and it changed his character dramatically.

The long discussion of bankruptcy in *The Compleat English Tradesman* tends to portray the experience in terms of psychological theatre, with emphasis upon the anxiety suffered in the period leading up to the point at which the tradesman discovers that he must abandon his efforts at trying to save his failing enterprises:

Breaking is the death of a Tradesman; he is mortally stabb'd, or, as we may say, shot thro' the head in his trading capacity; his shop is shut up, as it is when a man is buried; his credit, the life blood of his trade, is stagnated; and his attendance, which was the pulse of his business, is stopt, and beats no more; in a word, his fame, and even name as to trade is buried, and the commissioners that act upon him, and all their proceedings, are but like the executors of the defunct, dividing the ruins of his fortune, and at last, his certificate is a kind of performing the obsequies for the dead, and praying him out of purgatory. (i. 70)

The imagery of sudden death is omnipresent, but Defoe's troubles continued for more than a year after the fatal first arrest on 29 October 1692.

I

Although he wrote only one full-length book during the thirteen-year reign of William III, *An Essay upon Projects*, this was the period when Defoe emerged as a powerful writer on politics and society in both prose and verse. If his greatest achievements lay ahead of him, in the reigns of Queen Anne and the first two Georges, most of his attitudes were formed

[2] PRO C8/548/96. The suit was dated 2 July 1692 and Defoe's reply 28 July 1692.
[3] *The Complete English Tradesman* (London, 1727), i. 73. References to this work will be included within parentheses in my text.

during this apprenticeship period when he first started to put his ideas on paper. He modified his ideas as he grew older, but in his attitudes toward society he remained a 'Williamite' to the end. What may be roughly called the 1690s was an extraordinary period in English life. The Glorious Revolution that drove James II from England brought in a new way of looking at the world, and the term 'Revolution Principles' (with which no one was more associated than Defoe), though usually applied to politics, carried with it the implications of that visionary time.

Although William was far more conscious of the privileges of rank and of monarchy than were the English who surrounded him at the court established after his and Queen Mary's coronation on 11 April 1689, he had to accept the fact that he and Mary were chosen as rulers by Parliament and that their claim to the throne was based on a secular, political act. As it was, the decision came only after an acrimonious debate in the Convention Parliament in which it was agreed to accept the fiction that James had abandoned his throne. The removal of the 'legitimate' monarch, James II, meant an end to certain metaphysical attitudes toward authority and toward society as a whole. Many sermons stressed the role of Providence in the Glorious Revolution, but the form of government established after the Glorious Revolution bore little resemblance to the system of divine monarchy. No one seems to have seriously thought that William was God's direct representative on earth. Yet Defoe was hardly alone in believing that God's hand was evident in the events leading to James's flight to France. For example, the Huguenot writer Pierre Jurieu urged such a vision upon his followers, but that was something less than the claims that Louis XIV made as King of France or that James II had made during his brief reign.

Belief in the older system persisted among the Jacobites, who longed for a return of James or his family to the throne. They fretted over the existence of an English king chosen by a Parliament, and placed their hopes in the power of France to return the 'king over the water' to his rightful place. They believed that if 6000 troops could land on English soil, the nation would rise up to support the family of James. Hindsight may suggest that the Jacobites never had a chance, but throughout most of the eighteenth century the Whigs lived in continual fear of a successful counter-revolution by the Jacobites. The last real opportunity that James had went up in smoke when the fleet that was to carry him and his forces to England was destroyed at La Hogue on 23 May 1692. After William retained his powers following the death of Mary at the end of 1694, Jacobite longings gradually came to assume the form of a romantic nostalgia.

Nevertheless, in 1708, 1715, 1723, and 1745, the Jacobites attempted to overthrow the government through armed force. Also, William had to dodge three attempts at assassination during his reign. For someone like Defoe, who grew up with the terror of the possible eradication of Protestantism by Louis XIV, confidence in the permanence of the Glorious Revolution was impossible. Only after 1723, when one more Jacobite plot was easily defeated, was he to relax his propaganda campaigns against the Jacobites.

The new social spirit that came over with William was immediately evident in the drama of the time. In the comedies written during the reigns of Charles II and his brother, the bourgeoisie was generally introduced only in the form of the foolish husband and the unfaithful wife who cuckolded him with some gallant wit of the town or court. Now, in plays such as Dilke's *The Lover's Luck*, characters from various classes mingled together with an awareness of a new spirit. The merchant was to emerge in the literature of the time as an important culture hero. If he could not claim gentility, if he was occasionally vulgar in his tastes and excessive in his desire for profit, he could at least argue for his usefulness to society, and if he was wealthy enough to free his children from the burden of labour, they, at least, could lay claim to the status of gentlemen and ladies.

Defoe's vision of a society open to the man of talent sprang from his interpretation of the significance of the Glorious Revolution and from the atmosphere that pervaded the 1690s. Throughout his *Tour thro' the Whole Island of Great Britain*, he went out of his way to list those members of the gentry and aristocracy whose family fortune had originated in trade. That he was doing this in a work published during 1724–7, when the lines of social distinction had grown more rigid, shows the extent to which he tended to view society through the vision he had formed in the 1690s. And in a work left unfinished at his death, *The Compleat English Gentleman*, he devoted the final chapter to a discussion of the ways in which aristocratic families had renewed their wealth through marriages into families which had grown wealthy through business. Defoe viewed such matches as advantageous for the aristocracy in every way. If the aristocracy was having difficulties, he argued, those problems were not being produced by some mythical diluting of their blood but rather by laziness, ignorance, and a contempt for learning.

Defoe usually started his discussions about gentility by denying that he was in any sense a 'Leveller'. Having established this point, he usually proceeded to attack false standards of gentility. In what he claimed to be his first published poem, *A New Discovery of an Old Intreague* (1692), he began by evoking the idea of gentility as virtue rather than birth, a concept which he found in Brathwait's *English Gentleman*, which he had read when he was a young man. Of course, such a concept had also long been a part of popular ideology:

> In Ancient Times when Men of Worth were known,
> Not by their Father's Actions, but their own,
> When Honours Sacred Pile could be come at,
> But by the Steps to Vertue dedicate;
> No purchas'd Fame our Panegyricks sung,
> Nor were our widdowed Harps on Willows hung.
> Renown by downright hazard was attain'd,
> And Deeds of Honour only Honour gain'd.[4]

In his *The Poor Man's Plea* of 1698, his speaker reminds his readers that wealth and gentility make no difference in the eyes of God, and in his most powerful statement about English prejudices, *The True-Born Englishman*, Defoe told his audience that the blood that flowed through the English nobility was the same as that which flowed through the tradesman—the same because so many families had their origins in or connections with what was becoming an increasingly more powerful business establishment:

> Innumerable City-Knights we know,
> From *Blewcoat-Hospitals* and *Bridewell* flow.
> Draymen and Porters fill the City Chair,
> And Foot-Boys Magisterial Purple wear.
> Fate has but very small Distinction set
> Betwixt the *Counter* and the Coronet.
> Tarpaulin Lords, Pages of high Renown,
> Rise up by Poor Mens Valour, not their own.
> Great Families of yesterday we show,
> And Lords, whose Parents were *the Lord knows who*.[5]

If some of Defoe's contemporaries thought they perceived what they considered a radical note in these comments, they were certainly right. Defoe was not a Leveller, in the sense of William Winstanley's programme to reduce the disparities of wealth within the social system, but he wanted a society that would reward energy, intelligence, courage, and imagination. A recurrent story in his 'Historical Collections' is one in which a poor but able man is instantly rewarded for some act which reveals or allows him to

---

[4] I am using the text in Mary Elizabeth Campbell, *Defoe's First Poem* (Bloomington, Ind.: Principia Press, 1938).

[5] *Poems on Affairs of State*, ed. Frank Ellis (New Haven, Conn.: Yale University Press, 1970) (*POAS*), vi. 279 (ll. 419–28).

reveal his abilities. Defoe had no real objection to a society that honoured admirals for a successful engagement that really depended upon the courage of the sailors fighting under his command, but he wanted the bravest of the sailors to receive some particular recognition as well. He frequently noted that one of his heroes, Gustavus Adolphus, would promote common soldiers to officers on the battlefield. He believed in a society that held out hope to its citizens—hope that cleverness, wit, ability, and industry would be rewarded by uncommon success.

The corollary to such attitudes would have been the notion that the idle, inept, and stupid did not deserve to hold any rank in a just society. This attitude was more radical, since it implied that those who had inherited wealth which they wasted or a title which they disgraced deserved to fall to the bottom of the social hierarchy. Defoe was certainly more cautious about expressing these attitudes than about his theories of upward social mobility, but he insisted in *The True-Born Englishman* that

> Fame of Families is all a Cheat
> *'Tis Personal Virtue only makes us Great.*[6]

Were such a doctrine to be taken seriously, the aristocracy of Defoe's ideal society would have to consist of those raised to such a position through their talents. Admittedly Defoe usually dealt with practical problems in a real world, and under these circumstances, he would accept the status quo of England at the time. But every now and then he would indulge in a bit of aristocracy-bashing in the context of political and economic discussions. At one point in the *Review*, he divided up society into those who made useful contributions and those who did not, a variant of Geofrey King's famous division of society according to the population's income. In King's work, the poor were classed among those whose wages were insufficient to provide their families with subsistence. Such people occasionally needed help from the parish and were therefore considered as subtracting from the wealth of the state.[7] In Defoe's calculations, only those who did not contribute to the state by their labour were to be considered as a problem. And among this group were the 'Drones' in the industrious hive of society—the wealthy and idle aristocracy.[8]

These ideas were deeply ingrained in Defoe's character. They could find their justification in the new theories of natural law that attracted him so

---

[6] *Poems on Affairs of State*, 309 (ll. 1215–16).

[7] *Natural and Political Observations and Conclusions upon the State and Condition of England* (1696), in George Chalmers, *An Estimate of the Comparative Strength of Great Britain* (London: Stockdale, 1804), 36–49.

[8] *Review*, vi. 135.

much, but while he might resort to theories of equality inherent in such systems as well as in his Christian beliefs to justify them, they were also an important part of his emotional makeup. During those years following his bankruptcy, when he was in prison or living with his wife's family, they must have loomed large in his daydreams. The arrogance and lack of humility of which his enemies complained had their sources in this cast of mind. Such attitudes were eventually to lead to the evolution of the English system of government toward representative democracy and in France, where they were suppressed, to violent revolution.

But if Defoe seems more enlightened than many of his contemporaries on this subject, he also was very much a seventeenth-century man in his belief that advancement in society was founded on a system of 'benefits'. The idea had its intellectual roots in Seneca's essay on this subject. Seneca saw society operating through a sense of gratitude for favours conferred. The recipient of favours was to show his gratitude by his loyalty and eagerness to make some return for the generosity shown by a patron or friend. Such notions were incorporated into the many theories of natural law familiar to Defoe and his contemporaries. If they tended to be undermined by prevailing theories of self-interest, they still constituted what many saw as a natural code of honour.

Defoe admired the man of talent who caught the eye of a monarch and received a just reward, but he also admired the generosity of the patron. In such acts true gentility might be perceived. 'Historical Collections' is as rich in these accounts of magnanimity as it is in stories about gratitude and ingratitude. Stung by an accusation of ingratitude by an old soldier who fought at Actium, Augustus takes the time from his duties to help the man in a legal case. Zopyrus, a follower of Darius, shows his loyalty to his master by disfiguring himself in order to convince the enemies of Darius, the Syrians, that he had been punished by his own people and longed for revenge. Having won their confidence, he then betrayed them to his master. Defoe even tells a number of stories about dogs who remain loyal to their masters, protecting their corpses and attempting to avenge their deaths. Defoe prided himself on his sense of gratitude, first to William III and later to Robert Harley. His loyalty to both reveals that ideal fidelity to a patron that had been part of his notion of ethical behaviour from his boyhood.

II

Just as Zopyrus lied to serve his master, so Defoe frequently lied when working in the cause of his masters. In his *Appeal to Honour and Justice*, which was supposed to be a sincere confession of his political involvements, he described how his *True-Born Englishman*—a defence of William III and the Dutch through an attack upon English xenophobia—had brought him to the attention of the King:

How this Poem was the Occasion of my being known to His Majesty; how I was afterwards receiv'd by him; how Employ'd; and how, above my Capacity of deserving, Rewarded, is . . . mention'd here as I take all Occasions to do for the expressing the Honour I ever preserv'd for the Immortal and Glorious Memory of that Greatest and Best of Princes, and whom it was my Honour and Advantage to call Master as well as Sovereign, whose Goodness to me I never forget; and whose Memory I never patiently heard abused, nor ever can do so; and who had he liv'd, would never have suffered me to be treated as I have been in the World.[9]

The difficulty with this scenario is that Defoe's work was published in January 1701. William died on 7 March 1702. Although it is possible that Defoe was able to set up his system of intelligence throughout England in so brief a period, and perhaps likely that his most extensive contact with the King occurred at this time, he had clearly been a propagandist for William's ideas during the 'Standing Army' controversy (1697–8), and perhaps before.

That there is no evidence currently available of the duties he undertook for the King has left historians sceptical about Defoe's claims to having an intimate relation with William. But when he transferred his services to Robert Harley, he wrote to him of the rewards he received from William and of his services to him. Since Harley would have had access to secret service records and would have been in a position to punish or reward Defoe, it is hardly conceivable that Defoe could have succeeded in deceiving Harley on this matter.[10] On the other hand, some of Defoe's recent biographers have suggested that he was the real force behind William's public utterances, writing speeches for him and orchestrating the propaganda for the monarchy. Frank Bastian's chapter 'The Closet of a King' presents the most extreme case for a chumminess between the obscure, bankrupt merchant and the monarch. The truth was probably somewhere in between. From his youth, Defoe had tended to admire the role of the secret counsellor and spy. He was particularly impressed by the

---

[9] *An Appeal to Honour and Justice*, in *The Shortest Way with the Dissenters and Other Pamphlets*, *Shakespeare Head Edition*, 195.
[10] See H 68.

adventurous comte de Rochefort, who operated in a clandestine manner on behalf of Cardinal Richelieu (his fictionalized *Mémoires de Mr. L. C. D. R.*, by Gatien Courtilz, had been translated as *Memoirs of the Count de Rochefort* (2nd edn., 1696)). Defoe probably tended to romanticize his relationship with the King, combining Rochefort's dashing spirit with his own powerful literary talent. Most probably he tended to exaggerate the intimacy of his relationship with William in his own mind, but at a time when a well-placed pamphlet could turn the opinions of the nation, William may well have taken a particular interest in the writings of an effective propagandist.

Since the works ascribed to Defoe during the period between 1689 and 1695 were unsigned, it is hard to tell if he gained any fame by them. On the other hand, the printing trade in London was like an extended family, and the presence of an effective political writer on the scene may have been known to many. And if Defoe gave copies to friends such as Stancliffe, they may have been read by various people in William's government. Most of these works have been claimed for Defoe because, by reading back from political treatises such as *Jure Divino*, they seem to come from the same intellectual set of mind, and because the style resembles his. The two works that are certainly his are poems: *A New Discovery of an Old Intreague* and 'To the Athenian Society'. The former, published in 1691, represents his first known effort at political poetry, and more particularly the kind of satirical poem that flourished during the Restoration, when they usually circulated in manuscript rather than print. They were always personal in their references and often libellous; and they represented the full political spectrum. William Trent remarked that if Defoe had not published *A New Discovery* in the second volume of his collected poetry and prose in 1705, no one would have bothered claiming it for him, but then Trent was not exactly an admirer of political poetry in general.[11]

Defoe's masters in this form of political controversy in verse were Andrew Marvell and John Dryden. In *A New Discovery*, Defoe writes as a defender of William and Mary against a combination of London's political figures and disaffected clergy who were inspired to express their dissatisfaction by petitioning the House of Commons on 2 December 1690 about their grievances. To Defoe this was all part of the 'old intreague' by the Jacobites to regain the throne, different only in kind from the active intriguing Jacobites such as Sir Richard Graham, Viscount Preston, and

---

[11] His extensively annotated MS bibliography in the collection of his papers at the Beinecke Library, Yale University, is filled with wry comments on Defoe's poetry. Trent's own poetry tended to be romantic.

John Ashton, who were captured on 31 December 1690 with correspondence that implicated them in an invasion plot. Ashton refused to give evidence and was eventually hanged. Defoe's poem in couplets imagines the petitioners as an army of enemies on the march to defeat William and, in the manner of Dryden's *Absalom and Achitophel*, he has the monarch drive them 'down to Hell' in exasperation after they have failed to understand that his generosity was not weakness.

His second poem, 'To the Athenian Society', appeared in 1692 in *The History of the Athenian Mercury*. That journal, published under a variety of names, first appeared on 17 March 1691 and continued with some interruptions until 14 June 1697. John Dunton, who initiated this work, had somehow guessed that there was an audience for a journal devoted to inviting queries on all kinds of subjects. Dunton tapped into a body of readers who were apparently eager to see themselves in print and to receive advice from what was supposed to be a society learned in the sciences, the arts, and religious casuistry. However, the ardour of the public cooled somewhat when it was discovered that the learned society consisted of men and women of talent rather than genius: John Dunton, Samuel Wesley (father of the founders of Methodism), and Richard Sault. It has sometimes been assumed that Defoe made some contribution to *The Athenian Mercury*. Certainly Dunton believed that Defoe was 'a very Ingenious Useful Writer', and he probably asked Defoe to contribute a poem to Charles Gildon's *The History of the Athenian Society*.[12] But whether Defoe ever actually worked with Dunton or was a close friend is questionable. Dunton married a daughter of Samuel Annesley, the minister of James Foe and his family, and they shared many of the same political opinions. But Dunton's emphasis on originality, his oddly introspective approach to many subjects, and his inability to sustain an idea for more than a few pages was to give him the reputation of someone close to insanity. J. Paul Hunter's suggestion that Swift's Hack of *Tale of a Tub*, who has just recovered from a bout of madness and who aimlessly writes page after page, may be modelled, at least partly, on John Dunton seems very likely.[13] At any rate, Defoe's references to Dunton always seem to contain a degree of amusement. If Dunton expected something original and witty from Defoe, he must have been disappointed, for Defoe wrote a traditional, complimentary verse tracing the history of learning in the world. Echoing the Earl of Rochester's great poem 'On Nothing', Defoe begins with a golden age during which man still retained something of the mental powers he

---

[12] John Dunton, *Dunton's Whipping Post: or, A Satyr upon Every Body* (London, 1706), 88.
[13] J. Paul Hunter, *Before Novels* (New York: Norton, 1990), 104–5.

possessed in the Garden of Eden. Equally important was longevity. Humankind lived long and remembered well. Books, the modern repository of learning, were unnecessary:

> *E're Science was, or Learning had a Name,*
> *Dilated Memory recorded Fame:*
> *'Twas long before* Forgetfulness *was born.*

Defoe's poem is about writing itself, and about books as a way of repairing the 'Forgetfulness' that descended upon the human race after the destruction of the Tower of Babel. Athens and Rome became the seats of the children of Knowledge, Wisdom, and Learning, and the works they produced became the enemy of 'Ignorance'. Defoe then goes on to praise the Athenian Society as continuing the revolution in learning begun in Greece and Rome. The poem shows another side of Defoe—the Defoe who thought of himself as a writer who might take his place among the great Restoration poets whom he admired so much. He seems to have thought that poems addressed to broad and lofty subjects such as that to the Athenian Society were more the work of a gentleman than his political poetry and pamphlets, but it was clearly in the messy reality of politics and social criticism that he was to excel as a writer.

III

Modern historians have dispelled any notion that after James left England there was much agreement about the lines along which a new constitution ought to have been written. What happened at the end of 1688 and the beginning of 1689 was a broad outpouring of opinion about the nature of politics in general and of the peculiar situation of England. Many of those who participated in the Glorious Revolution were soon to find themselves unwilling to abandon loyalty to a hereditary monarch—even a monarch as destructive to the English institutions as was James II. The Archbishop of Canterbury, William Sancroft, who had suffered for resisting what he considered to be James II's unjust and illegal actions against the Church of England, refused to sign an oath of allegiance to William and Mary and had to be replaced by a reluctant John Tillotson. The famous divine William Sherlock waited until past midnight to take the oaths and became the butt of numerous jests by wits of the time, including Defoe. Men like Sherlock and those who refused to take the oaths (the Non-jurors) faced a difficult problem. How was a fiction about a hereditary monarchy to be maintained when the 'true' ruler of England was living in France, exiled from the people who, according to the teachings of the Church of England, were to obey and love him no matter what he did? And how was William to be regarded? Was he another conquerer like a famous English monarch before him? He was certainly Dutch, and detestation of the Dutch was widespread after nearly a century of propaganda against England's chief commercial rival. Though many thought he had rescued England from a reign that would have been as unremittingly anti-Protestant as that of Bloody Mary, a large body of Englishmen regarded him as *Hogen Mogen*, a contemptuous term that the English used to express their feelings about what they considered to be an unwarranted claim by the Dutch to nobility and dignity. For such as these, William was a foreigner with no right to the throne. Paradoxes abounded.

Under these circumstances, as Defoe often noted, avoiding satire was difficult. His early pamphlets reveal the vein of irony that was to mark his writing throughout his life. Truth, embodied in common sense and that objectified form of rational behaviour known as the 'Laws of Nature', was clear enough. His expressed purpose as a writer, which is to say the rhetoric he employed, was to present a clear view of a given situation, ridicule those who failed to follow nature's first law of self-preservation and its corollary, self-interest, and indicate the rational solution to a given problem. In his first full-length pamphlet on politics, *Reflections upon the Late Great Revolution*, written in early 1689, Defoe emerged as a defender of government according to the laws of England and of the legality of replacing James. He accepted the notion of a balance of power between King, Lords, and Commons. England was a 'limited monarchy', and if the King violated the laws of the realm or threatened the wellbeing of the people, he was guilty of violating the 'Original Contract' between himself and the people who chose him. And since the safety of the people 'is the Supreme Law', James had forfeited his right to rule.

There is nothing very original in this work, and the subtitle, 'Written . . . For the Satisfaction of some Neighbours', suggests that he was explaining what was clear enough to those versed in political theory but not to those who had been reading court propaganda for the past six years. The salient features of Defoe's treatise involve his insistence that the relationship between the monarch and his subjects is essentially secular. The king is an executive who contracts to act as the 'Chief Magistrate', and so long as the ruler and his heirs obey this 'Original Contract', he and his family may stay in office. But his power comes from the consent of the governed. 'So that 'tis evident', Defoe wrote, 'that the Power of the People is not only antecedent to that of Kings, but also that the Kings did receive and derive their Authority at first from the People.'[14]

Although it has been common to derive Defoe's theories from Locke, at this stage, at least, they more than likely derived chiefly from the manuscript of Morton's political treatise, 'Eutaxia'. Morton attempted to synthesize the most up-to-date thinking on various subjects for his students, and this meant that in addition to a great deal of Aristotle, there would have been a sampling of the thinkers on natural law, Grotius and Pufendorf, and some theories drawn from those who examined man as a political animal operating purely from self-interest, Hobbes and the Libertines. As suggested previously, Morton must have met John Locke during his stay at Wadham College in Oxford, and he may have been familiar with the Constitution of Carolina with which Locke was involved. Some elements of Harrington and the 'Classical Republicans' must likely have found a place in the discussion. But if Samuel Wesley was to accuse 'Eutaxia' of advocating the overthrow of kings, Defoe was probably right in claiming that it accepted some form of limited monarchy as its ideal. When Defoe discussed the English government as embodying an Aristotelian mean, he was following Morton's tendency. 'For as Vertue does commonly lie in the mean,' wrote Defoe, 'so our Legislators have wisely pickt out all the good that was in all sorts of Government, but shunned the Extreams.' Defoe warns against the evils of 'a Democratical Confusion and Fury', but his broad concept of the 'people' as the entire population rather than a select part of it suggests the potentiality of a move toward a more radical position.[15]

In this and other pamphlets published at this time, Defoe played 'the card of sincerity', as Gracián called it. He writes from the country as a sincere well-wisher for his nation. His tone is usually conciliatory and questioning, except where he addresses the various Jacobite plots and the assassination attempts made against William. By 1694, when he came to write *The Englishman's Choice, and True Interest*, Defoe was ready to strike out more boldly. He presented William as the modern Gustavus Adolphus, a true Protestant hero in the fight against the aggression of Louis XIV and the Catholic Church. He suggested that the Dissenters ought to be allowed to serve in the army, and accused those who did not appear enthusiastic in the cause of William against Louis of being traitors. 'They who would be *Trimmers* in this Cause', he wrote, 'make it evident, they are for having the ship of State sink all at once; King *William's* and our Countries side, can

[14] *Reflections upon the Late Great Revolution* (London, 1689), 36–40.
[15] Ibid. 36.

never have too much weight against *France* and *Rome*.'[16] Defoe ended his tract with a rousing call to arms in the name of English freedom:

And should the issue of opposing *France* be as dismal as the most timerous, or most designing, pretend to foretell; it were better, that the last day of our being a free People, should overtake us doing our duty, and struggling against our Chains, than helping to put them on. And in truth, hardly any thing in this life can be a real affliction, till men begin to sink under the sense of having brought it upon themselves.[17]

Defoe liked this so well that he repeated it in a pamphlet of the same year in which he referred to William as the 'English David' fighting for the cause of freedom.[18] Such staunch support of William seems to have eventually attracted the attention of the government.

In any event, Defoe was in the employ of the government in a minor capacity from the autumn of 1695 onwards. In his *Appeal to Honour and Justice*, he recounted the progress of his career in a manner that moves rapidly over this period, leaving huge gaps but still suggesting some of his options:

Misfortunes in Business having unhing'd me from Matters of Trade, it was about the Year 1694, when I was invited by some Merchants, with whom I had corresponded abroad, and some also at home, to settle at *Cadiz* in *Spain*, and that with offers of very good Commissions; but Providence, which had other Work for me to do, placed a secret Aversion in my Mind to quitting *England* upon any account, and made me refuse the best Offers of that kind, to be concern'd with some eminent Persons at home, in proposing *Ways* and *Means* to the Government for raising Money to supply the Occasions of the War then newly begun. Some time after this, I was, without the least Application of mine, and being then seventy Miles from *London*, sent for to be Accomptant to the Commissioners of the Glass Duty, in which Service I continued to the Determination of their Commission.[19]

The tax on glassware and bottles (7 Wm III c. 18) was to take effect on 29 September 1695. Three surveyors were to be paid £200 each to administer the tax, and one of those was the person to whom Defoe was to dedicate *An Essay upon Projects* a few years later, Dalby Thomas. It was probably mainly through Thomas's influence that Defoe was appointed as 'Accomptant' at a salary of £100 to keep the books and supervise the work of two clerks. On 1 November of that year, Defoe's name appeared among

[16] *The Englishman's Choice* (London, 1694), 23.
[17] Ibid. 31.
[18] *Some Seasonable Queries on the Third Head* (n.d., n.p.), 4.
[19] *An Appeal to Honour and Justice*, 194–5.

thirteen 'Managers trustees' of 'The Profitable and Golden Adventure for the Fortunate', a lottery with which Dalby Thomas and an associate, Thomas Neale, were involved.[20] Since both Thomas and Neale were involved with a government venture, the Million Lottery, Defoe may have had some involvement with that as well, but his role may have been unofficial. Neither lottery was successful. He was later to disparage lotteries as a way of raising money, but in the 1690s he was very much a projector, and his schemes for raising money for the war may have included a variety of taxes and lotteries.

Although both Neale and Thomas had a certain respectability in being associated with the court, it may be said that this was a time when the government itself had turned projector in order to raise money to continue the war. Ingenious kinds of taxation were the order of the day. There was even a tax on bachelors at one point. State lotteries had been part of the English scene from 1567, when Queen Elizabeth sponsored one. They have ever been a way of getting money out of people through a form of gambling, and this was especially true during the reign of William and Mary. Neale had the title of 'Groom Porter' within the court, a post concerned with regulating gambling, and he was a natural person to sponsor the new lotteries. He lived long enough to see a law passed outlawing lotteries, and one contemporary wit, writing an elegy on both Neale and the lotteries, commented on his proclivity to spend his money freely, and on the lotteries that led England down the path of consumerism and waste:

> His Lady Gold, of the Consumption spent,
> Was gone long since! And when Fates call'd *HE* went;
> Having done the Work for which he here was sent:
> That is, to teach the Great Ones and the Small,
> How to get Money, and to spend it all.[21]

Thomas had the outward appearance of being more respectable than Neale. He sat on numerous government committees, some which seemed to be involved with charitable causes. But he was essentially a speculator and a projector. His name is attached to a variety of petitions to the government asking for new patents and aid in promoting the fishing industry or trade to Africa. Doubtless during the relatively idle days forced upon him by his business failure, Defoe, the economic speculator, who had dreamed of diving-engines and of a booming perfume industry, had come up with a number of ingenious schemes for raising money, communicated them to

---

[20] The notice first appeared in *The Post-Boy* for 3 Oct. 1695, and ran intermittently until March.
[21] *An Elegiack Essay Upon the Decease of the Groom-Porter and the Lotteries* (London, 1700), 3.

Neale and Thomas, and gained enough favour to be given a post—a post in which he joined the ranks of those involved in 'gauging' or assessing the indebtedness of the citizens to the state, a segment of that army of excise men who were so efficient in collecting taxes.[22]

In the description of his work as an accountant as well as in the newspaper advertisement for the lottery, the name 'De Foe' appears for the first time. This hesitant assertion of a claim to gentility through a change of name would have been in keeping with his ideas on the subject. He had an education at a Dissenting Academy, which in his mind was superior to any course of study he might have received at Oxford or Cambridge. He was a volunteer in the Royal Regiment. And his strong support of William III may have been instrumental in his being rewarded by a government position. Education, military rank, and royal favour were all ways of establishing gentility even if none of Defoe's particular credentials were quite legitimate. In addition, despite his bankruptcy, Defoe must have felt that sense of superior abilities that, in his mind, qualified a man to claim some status. Thirty years later, when he hinted at some relationship to a family named De Beau Faux, he may have been trying to find some noble bloodline to which he could attach his family, but despite this moment of vanity, he would have had no difficulty defending an ideal of an aristocracy based on character, achievement, and worth.

IV

What may be seen in the Defoe who emerged from his bankruptcy was a person divided in a number of ways. He was fiercely independent but still believed in a patronage system. But the patron—the father-figure to whom gratitude was always to be shown— was sometimes to be lied to and treated with contempt. He believed in the 'original contract' by which the people could overthrow their ruler when he was in violation of the agreement made between ruler and ruled, but he was also impressed by William as the powerful military leader. He believed in a world in which rank would be based upon merit and talents, but he was always eager to assert his own status as a gentleman.

There is no better example of the contradictions in Defoe's character than his first book, *An Essay upon Projects*, advertised on 25 January 1697 and published some time during that year. During the seventeenth century,

[22] See John Brewer, *The Sinews of Power: War, Money and the English State, 1688–1783* (Cambridge, Mass.: Harvard University Press, 1990), 102.

the word 'projector' had various connotations involving both dishonesty and the misuse of power. Defoe attempts to place the word in the context of the new *'Projecting Age'*.[23] The projector is now seen as a person with great powers of inventiveness and ingenuity. His motives—poverty and desperation—and abilities—cleverness and inventiveness—are not easily distinguished from those of the cheat, but he is able to apply his talents to benefit society through schemes that bring about social change and improvement. His character has some of the qualities of Marx's early capitalist in his adventurousness. Defoe, who moves in and out of the character of the projector, argues that society has a right to be suspicious of his motives while benefiting from his abilities. Some of Defoe's proposals belong to the category of the projector's special pleading, the work of that 'Contemptible thing' Defoe designates 'A Meer Projector'.[24] The most obvious of these is his proposal for allowing bankrupts to compound with their creditors and avoid the horrors of prison. As mentioned previously, just a few years earlier Moses Pitt had published his volume *The Cry of the Oppressed*, with illustrations showing bankrupts reduced to trapping mice for dinner and suffering outrageous torture from their gaolers, and the absurdity of incarcerating men and women and thus removing any chance of their earning money to pay off their debts was clear enough to many. Defoe avoids any detailed enumeration of the horrors described by Pitt; but his picture of the plight of the bankrupt represents a moving personal plea:

Nothing is more frequent, than for men who are reduc'd by Miscarriage in Trade, to Compound and Set up again, and get good Estates; but a *Statute*, as we call it, for ever shuts up all doors to the Debtor's Recovery; as if Breaking were a Crime so Capital that he ought to be cast out of Human Society, and expos'd to Extremities worse than Death. And, which will further expose the severity of this Law, 'tis easy to make it appear, That all this Cruelty to the Debtor is so far (generally speaking) from advantaging the Creditors, that it destroys the Estate, consumes in extravagant Charges, and unless the Debtor be consenting, seldom makes any considerable Dividends.[25]

Defoe speaks very much from personal experience here, and however much he writes about safeguarding the creditors, his heart is very much on his own problems.

The best-known proposals of the *Essay* are those for an academy of letters and an academy for women. The latter expresses clearly Defoe's

[23] *An Essay upon Projects*, ed. Joyce Kennedy, Michael Seidel, and Maximillian E. Novak (New York: AMS Press, 1999), 7.   [24] Ibid. 17.
[25] Ibid. 77.

belief in the equality of mind existing between the sexes and his feeling that an educated woman is '*a Creature without comparison*; her Society is the Emblem of sublimer Enjoyments; her Person is Angelick, and her Conversation heavenly . . . and the man that has such a one to Portion has nothing to do but to rejoice in her, and be thankful.'[26] Although he thought that the best education for women should involve a knowledge of the world, he reluctantly allows for the power of custom in this matter. 'I wou'd deny no sort of Learning,' he adds lest he be thought to be among those thinking women inferior. Much goes into Defoe's discussion—his reading in Locke's theory of education and Mary Astell's plea for educating women—but there is something in his praise of the woman of education and learning that sounds a personal note. Surely Defoe's wife, Mary, was not far from his thoughts as he wrote about the ideal woman.

Other sections of the *Essay* display his personal interests and, occasionally, surely a mild velleity that, as the proposer of his schemes, he might be employed in or be part of these projects. In proposing an academy for the language, Defoe must have thought that he would be considered one of those men of 'meer Merit' who would be among the thirty-six members of the academy to serve as 'a Sort of Judicature over the Learning of the Age' to judge the 'Stile and Language' of the time. He is careful to eliminate most of those 'meer Learned Men . . . whose *English* has been far from Polite, full of Stiffness and Affectation, hard Words, and long unusual Coupling of *Syllables* and Sentences, which sound harsh and untuneable to the Ear, and shock the Reader both in Expression and Understanding'.[27] Far better than these surely would be someone like Daniel Defoe, who had served the government with his pen and with his heart. In the same way, he may have seen himself as an agent for the great project of building roads throughout England, as an accountant on the board to distribute money on a regular basis to the nation's seamen or as a collector of the tax on authors that would be used to establish an asylum for the insane. Though Defoe may have had his tongue in his cheek when he composed this section on authors, he doubtless felt serious enough about the others and may have expected some benefit were any of his schemes put into action.

One way he might have benefited was through his involvement in building, particularly in the supplying of bricks to the various structures that would have been necessary for the new military academy, the new asylum, the new offices needed for administering the proposals concerning seamen. Defoe's involvement with building materials connects his interest in lumber, his apparent presence at Kensington when Queen Mary gave

[26] *An Essay upon Projects*, 112.   [27] Ibid. 91.

orders for laying out the gardens, and his role in supplying bricks for two other government projects, the building of the hospital at Greenwich under the guidance of Christoper Wren and his interest in the building at Christ's Hospital. He showed an extensive concern with architecture in the *Tour*, and he writes of Wren as if he had a direct acquaintance with both the man and his works.[28] And who can doubt that under the cover of supplying bricks Defoe went out of his way to become acquainted with Wren?[29]

All of this was made possible through the fact that one of Defoe's properties, a brick manufactury at Tilbury, near the mouth of the Thames, had been mortgaged at the time that he went bankrupt. He was able to get it back and embark on a new career manufacturing pantiles, the S-shaped tile that was popular in England during the reign of William and Mary, and bricks. One might think that government contracts would be a way of paying Defoe for his services, and at the very start of the ordering of bricks for Greenwich hospital Defoe was given a small order, probably through the services of Dalby Thomas, who was on the board. But it was probably not that easy to break into government supply. After the single order at the beginning, the committee reverted to the traditional suppliers of bricks for the government, even though on several occasions the products were found wanting. But if Defoe's proposals had been followed, there would have been ample need for bricks. This is not to say that his motives were entirely venal, that all of his ingenious proposals may be reduced to a desire to sell bricks to the government. What it does suggest is that Defoe the visionary and Defoe the schemer were inexorably joined.

[28] *Tour*, i. 335–7.

[29] The information concerning the building of Greenwich Hospital is at the PRO at Kew, Admiralty/ 67/2. Defoe is mentioned for 5 June 1696: 'A contract made with Mr Daniel Foe for Bricks order'd to be enter'd.' Compared to this one large order, brickmakers such as Goodwin and Huesthe were continually being called upon to supply bricks. Paula Backscheider estimates that Defoe only earned £85 12s. from the transaction, but for all the delay in payment, the possibilities of future advantage must have loomed large. See Paula Backscheider, *Defoe* (Baltimore: Johns Hopkins University Press, 1989), 64.

6

Propagandist for William III

From a political standpoint, Defoe was already what was called a 'Court Whig' by the middle of the 1690s, and he retained that identification proudly into the reign of Queen Anne. In *The Present State of the Parties*, written somewhat earlier than its publication date of 1712, he argued that whereas the junta of Whig lords who served William were mainly interested in their own advancement, the Court Whigs, who were so often attacked, were as 'true to the *Revolution Principles* as themselves'.[1] As Reed Browning has suggested, the Court Whigs argued in favour of a standing army when it was to be used in the service of a monarch who was trying to protect English liberties.[2] Although the Court Whigs posed as moderates, standing between the Jacobites on the Right and the Classical Republicans on the left, they actually avoided the elitism of the latter and shared with the Jacobites some elements of belief in direct appeals to the people. What Defoe wanted was a monarch who would act as a leader both in military engagements abroad and at home, putting into effect a programme of toleration and progress: toleration of the Dissenters that would extend to allowing them to serve without prejudice in all aspects of government, progress in following an expansive economic policy that would employ the labouring poor and find new markets abroad while encouraging trade within England. In the name of such potential good, Defoe was willing to sacrifice much in the way of checks and balances on executive power. It is in this sense that he may be seen as radical. He may be said to have defined his position through the sudden explosion of his pamphlets on the subject during 1697 and 1698. In countering the arguments of the Classical Republicans, the Country Party, the Tories, and the Jacobites, Defoe offered a new view of society and of political and social change. And it was

---

[1] Defoe, *The Present State of the Parties in Great Britain* (London, 1712), 51.
[2] *Political and Constitutional Ideas of the Court Whigs* (Baton Rouge: Louisiana State University Press, 1982), 190.

through this debate that he also began to define himself as a writer, thinker, and skilful tactician in the pamphlet wars of the time.

I

The strength and originality of Defoe's arguments in defence of a standing army are well summarized by J. G. A. Pocock, who views Defoe's response as the most powerful opposition to the Neo-Harringtonians and their able spokesman, Andrew Fletcher of Saltoun:

Defoe asserted that . . . true freedom was modern and could only be found in commercial society, where the individual might profit by wealth and enlightenment and did not risk his liberty in paying others to defend and govern him, so long as he retained parliamentary control of the purse strings. . . . The confrontation of Fletcher with Defoe supplies an antithesis between virtue and commerce, republicanism and liberalism, classicism and progressivism. The Old Whigs identified freedom with virtue and located it in a past; the Modern Whigs identified it with wealth, enlightenment, and progress toward a future. Around this antithesis, it is not too much to say, nearly all eighteenth-century philosophy of history can be organized, though it is obvious that in cultures other than the British, something other than Whig parliamentarianism must be located as the precipitating cause.[3]

Pocock is wary of generalizations. He sees the Old Whigs merging with the Tories in their attacks upon the monied interests, while the main body of the Whigs, who were to be content with the Hanoverians and Sir Robert Walpole, favoured the moderns against the ancients, and accepted the idea of a new society that was commercial and urban. 'The field of debate was not simple,' he remarks, 'and we should not hasten to resolve it.'[4] But he has no doubt that Defoe's vision, carried further in the direction of 'politeness' by Joseph Addison, was to set the tone for an original view of English culture.

An important element in Defoe's arguments was a concept of progress and change, and to reach this, he had to develop a method of viewing social and economic change in an entirely secular manner. As Paul Alkon has demonstrated, in any religious context Defoe's view of time was the traditional Christian one. There was to be an apocalypse that would bring an end to time with the second coming of Christ, and such an event was always to be expected.[5] Defoe could voice such a view as an aside when

---

[3] *Virtue, Commerce, and History* (Cambridge: Cambridge University Press, 1985), 231.
[4] Ibid.
[5] *Defoe and Fictional Time* (Athens: Georgia University Press, 1979), 40, 91. In this traditional

treating a topic in a religious context, but in his writings on politics, economics, and social problems it is replaced, for the most part, by a progressive and secular vision. In the *Review*, for example, he was to remark on changing economies and express the belief that at some distant time in the future English agriculture would change over to producing garden vegetables as the most profitable use of scarce land. In speculations of this kind there is no hint of an impending apocalypse that might cut short such endeavours.[6] Defoe loved to draw upon the past for historical parallels, but he was also an incorrigible futurist, projecting social schemes, inventions, and economic changes into a tomorrow that would be transformed by the introduction of such innovations.

When Defoe told his readers that he had been at work on the *Essay upon Projects* 'near Five Years', he may have been trying to cover himself both as to borrowings from his contemporaries and from the standpoint of the political issues he was raising. While some of his projects may have been the product of the enforced idleness produced by his bankruptcy in 1692, there is some possibility that his reasons for bringing these essays together in 1697 may have had much to do with the standing army controversy of that year. Defoe's proposal for a military academy is sandwiched modestly between his projects for two other academies, and the attempt at unobtrusiveness may have been deliberate. Although he states that he placed them together in one chapter because they all required academies of different kinds, he may have managed this juxtaposition to make his proposal more palatable by positioning it between some of his liveliest material. Defoe connected his military academy to his plans for an academy dedicated to improving the language by suggesting that such an institution could publish a journal with articles on the technical aspects of weapons and their use. He extolled the virtues of military exercises as a diverting spectacle for those interested in shows, and argued that the English could improve their health and general culture by regulating sports and organizing exercise around military activities. Placed just before the discussion of the necessity of improving the education of women, Defoe's essay on the ideal military academy has the appearance of establishing parallel categories, with a knowledge of war as a masculine activity, and educating women in languages and history as a way of providing them with the kind of knowledge that will enable them to reach their fullest capabilities as human beings.

Christian view, time did not exist for God and after the Second Coming would cease to dominate human life.

[6] *Review*.

The male students of his military academy learn history as well as the women, but most of their subjects involve what today would be called military science along with various forms of mathematics. Whatever political purpose Defoe may have had in making this proposal, there is no reason to doubt that he believed strongly in such an academy. His proposal to raise a regiment for the war in Flanders as an alternative to punishment in 1703, when he was being hunted by the government, reveals an interest in military activity that went beyonde quixotic posturing. Establishing a military academy would mean having a permanent officer corps and a standing army, and while Defoe does not put the matter in these terms, his very accurate picture of the inadequacy of the English in supplying William with well-trained military leaders highlights the need for a permanent institution to train soldiers.

In the context of the times, Defoe's proposal for this military academy was more radical than the other two. During 1696 the inevitability of a cessation of the hostilities became obvious. William did not have sufficient funds to conduct the war, and the defection of the Duke of Savoy, who made a separate peace with Louis XIV, meant an end to the war in Italy. Even before Louis showed himself willing to recognize William as England's king and to give up some of his conquests, a truce seemed likely. But William thought that another round of fighting might be expected in the future, and he wanted to have enough of an army on hand to make Louis think twice. The paper war over this issue was fought with considerable violence over the next few years, and there seems little question that Defoe was the main propagandist for the position of the court.

Defoe was probably engaged in answering a pamphlet by John Trenchard and Walter Moyle at the same time that he was completing his *Essay upon Projects*. Although both Trenchard and Moyle were Whigs, they adopted the position of the Classical Republicans and the Country Party in suggesting that a standing army would always be used by the monarch to strengthen his power at the expense of the power of Parliament. They argued, as Machiavelli had before them, that a militia was more suitable for the preservation of national institutions. Defoe's arguments in his *Some Reflections on a Pamphlet Lately Publish'd* was tuned to a very different wavelength. He wanted England to take its place among the powerful nations of Europe. A standing army was necessary for such a role at a time when the armies opposed to France had grown to 400,000 men during the war of the Grand Alliance. 'War', he wrote, 'is become a Science, and Arms an Employment.' He rightly argued that modern warfare involved too much techical knowledge for a militia to master, that

Parliament would still have the power to keep such a force on hand, and
that Louis would inevitably assert the rights of his family to the Spanish
throne. But the arguments of his opponents, which Defoe constantly
referred to as a '*Deceptio visus*' or illusion, had a strong appeal to a nation
tired of war. In 1697 few were willing to listen to the realities of what has
now been called 'the military revolution'.[7] Heavy taxes, the deaths of
thousands of soldiers, and a variety of economic disasters helped make the
attacks upon a standing army appear to be an assertion of English liberty.
But Defoe believed that the Glorious Revolution had established liberty
firmly enough; what was needed now, he thought, was the strength to
protect it. He may have been right, but he lost the propaganda war. No
academy was established; the army was disbanded; and England was back
at war with France within five years.

Defoe signed this response to Trenchard and Moyle with his initials,
D.F., but he did not include it in the collection of his works that he
published in 1703. Instead he reprinted *An Argument Shewing, That a
Standing Army, with Consent of Parliament, Is Not Inconsistent with a Free
Government* (1698), which was less tendentious and more theoretical in its
arguments. Here Defoe put forward an economic history of England that
saw a progress from feudalism to the present state of the country. In the
past, 'One Nobleman would Invade another, in which the weakest suffered
most, *and the poor Man's Blood was the Price of all*; the People obtain'd
Priviledges of their own, and oblig'd the King and the Barons to accept of
an *Equilibrium*; this we call a Parliament: And from this the Due Ballance is
deduced.'[8] Defoe praised the change from the time when 'the Misery and
Slavery of the Common People' was a fact of life, and stressed the significance of the growing wealth and independence of the House of Commons
with its power of the purse, a power stronger than that of the sword.[9] With
such economic power, the House can always prevent the King from
making war. More fearful than a standing army is a Parliament that goes
against the will of the people and a militia that has been misused in the past.

That Defoe printed only one of his standing army tracts in the first
volume of his *Collection* suggests that there may have been many more.
John Robert Moore continued to add titles to his *Checklist* that bore on this
subject which seemed to show Defoe's distinctive style and ideas, and I
have added *The Case of a Standing Army Freely and Impartially Stated*
(1698). The title of this work, along with Moore's ascription, *The Case of*

---

[7] See Geoffrey Parker, *The Military Revolution* (Cambridge: Cambridge University Press, 1988), 1.

[8] *An Argument Shewing that a Standing Army, with Consent of Parliament, Is Not Inconsistent with a Free
Government* (London, 1698), 15.

[9] Ibid.

Disbanding the Army at Present (1698), may suggest that both tracts were distributed to Members of Parliament during the debates. The theme of all of these pamphlets was pretty much the same: an attack on the 'Grumble-tonians' who opposed an army and an argument based on historical change: 'for 'tis not what our Ancestors did formerly, but what we ought to do now.'[10] This appears to be the first time that Defoe used the method of flooding the press with pamphlets to create the sense that there was a large body of opinion that was not being heard in Parliament. In some sense, it is this technique of manoeuvring the print media to sow confusion that may have been the most significant element in Defoe's involvement in the standing army controversy. He discovered that if he could write enough on any subject, he might be able to influence public opinion. Although there is some variation in the viewpoints offered by these pamphlets, they mostly repeat what has been said before. But Defoe may have learned from his failure to win this battle the advantage of exploiting a variety of viewpoints by using 'masks', or what would appear to be different attitudes expressed by a variety of writers.

II

Although much of Defoe's time during these years before the end of the century was taken up by the standing army controversy, he was still very much involved with the issues involving the Dissenters and religious controversy. As a future spokesman for unity among the Dissenting groups, he must have watched with some dismay as the alliance between the Presbyterians and Congregationalists unravelled in 1692. The occasion was the publication of the sermons of Dr Crisp by his son, Samuel Crisp. Lining up against Crisp were Richard Baxter and Daniel Williams; defending Crisp were Isaac Chauncey and a long list of divines. Baxter and Williams contended that Crisp's arguments for salvation by faith and grace alone led to the sense that there was no need for good works or for leading a moral life—that the sense of being among the elect who would receive the divine reward of Heaven after death might lead to so much confidence in a predestined salvation that the individual might feel that he could sin with impunity. The case of Jack of Leyden from 1538, whose community of believers felt that they were free of sin no matter what act they might commit and fell into debauchery, was always trotted out as an example of the terrible results of what was called antinomianism. Isaac Chauncey, who

---

[10] Daniel Defoe, *The Case of a Standing Army Freely and Impartially Stated* (London, 1698), sig. Aᵛ, 28.

noted that the Athenian Club had applauded Williams's *Gospel Truth Stated and Vindicated* (1692), accused Williams of reviving 'Justification by works' rather than by repentance and faith.[11] In actuality, Williams merely argued that God's terms for pardon of past sins were based on obedience to His will revealed by an upright life.

In writing a life of Daniel Williams in 1717, Defoe argued that Williams was simply wrong and his enemies right. The importance of this judgement may seem fairly obscure, but Defoe's opinion needs to be kept in mind. Max Weber and R. H. Tawney used Baxter's writing to argue for the Protestant basis of capitalism. In order to show themselves among the elect, Protestants worked hard in the world to give visible evidence of success. Gradually, so the thesis goes, success itself became evidence of God's favour, and the more successful the businessman, the more evidence he could show for his salvation. The Weber–Tawney thesis is subtle and convincing in many aspects, but it may be pointed out that Baxter, who is quoted at length by Weber, represented a part of English Protestantism that put a strong emphasis upon work and the evidence of success. Defoe seems to have come out against Williams and Baxter, and this should be remembered in view of attempts to impose the Weber–Tawney thesis on Defoe's fictional heroes and heroines.

A second event that occurred at this time was the death of Samuel Annesley, the minister of the Foe family, in 1697. Defoe published an elegy on the occasion, complimenting Annesley for having 'no Priestcraft in him, nor no Pride'. Defoe was fond of quoting the line from Dryden's *Absalom and Achitophel* to the effect that 'priests of all religions are the same'. Just as Dryden's anti-clericalism seems in no way to have diminished his religious faith, so Defoe, pious as he was, seems to have had little fondness for the clergy. It may have been part of what he brought out of his bankruptcy in the way of cynicism about human motivation. He was to adopt a typical seventeenth-century attitude that saw almost all human actions as having their source in self-interest. He later said that he was unable to attend church because he feared he might be arrested for debt, and this may have started as early as his first bankruptcy in 1692. But if he does not specifically exempt Annesley from his anti-clericalism and cynicism, he does attempt to present the 'character' of this 'Best of Ministers and Best of Men' in the most favourable light, following the 'worthies' tradition which flourished in the seventeenth century.

The attempt, however, was not entirely successful. He chose pentameter

---

[11] Isaac Chauncey, *Neonomianism Unmask'd: or, the Ancient Gospel Pleaded against the Other, Call'd A New Law or Gospel* (London, 1692), 1–7.

couplets for his elegy, and that form, unlike the hymn-like meditations of his youth, was better suited for satire than for an expansive elegiac statement. In fact, the poem alternates between sublime visions of Annesley as an ideal figure deserving of a heavenly reward and movements toward satire. Just as he argues a Lockean position that those on earth can only know of Heaven by 'negatives', so he digresses into satiric comments on some of his favourite subjects: that being a gentleman is a matter of '*Merit*' rather than birth; that on earth the 'Just and Wise' are often shoved aside by 'Knaves and Fools'; that 'Int'rest' rules mankind and limits the power of religious love. And his image of Annesley the minister seems to distinguish him from what might be expected of a clergyman.

> His *negative Vertues* also have been try'd,
> *He had no Priestcraft in him, nor no Pride;*
> No Fraud nor Wheedling Arts to be esteem'd,
> *But just the very Person that he seem'd;*
> Nor was he touch'd or tainted with a Bribe,
> *That universal Blemish of the Tribe.*

Defoe insists upon Annesley's innocence and sincerity in all things, particularly in his preaching. His remarks may suggest what he admired in pulpit oratory:

> *His native Candor, and familiar Stile,*
> Which did so oft his hearers Hours beguile,
> *Charm'd us with Godliness,* and while he spake,
> We lov'd the *Doctrine* for the Teacher's sake.
> While he inform'd us what those Doctrines meant,
> *By dint of Practice more than Argument,*
> Strange were the Charms of his Sincerity,
> Which made his Actions and his Words agree.

Even in the final section on heavenly love, this poem is calm, analytical and controlled rather than emotional. Dryden was his model, and while the poem is not badly done, who could deny that Dryden could write infinitely better?

The somewhat distanced effect of the poem may have been deliberate. Annesley was, after all, interested in cases of conscience or casuistry, and the basis of this type of religious exercise involved subjecting difficult 'cases of conscience' to rational analysis. Protestant casuistry was not a body of thought but a method. Difficult ethical problems were analysed in terms of religious thought, positive law, natural law. The latter was an effort at finding a universal, rational judgement based on permanent principles of human nature. Although the *Morning Exercises* at Annesley's church of St Giles Cripplegate were mainly sermons on various religious topics, they represented a genuine effort at thinking through difficult problems in morality. John Tillotson, who became Archbishop of Canterbury under William III, was a contributor to this series, and the lucid style that he developed in his later sermons may have owed something to Annesley's own sermon style. Defoe, who considered himself a connoisseur of sermon style, may have taken some hints from Annesley, but what is more important is that the method of his novels, in which heroes and heroines balance the weight of natural law against positive law and the message conveyed by their consciences, owed a great deal to Annesley and his students.

III

Two other sides of religion involved Defoe at this time. The first involved a movement for reform under the broad heading of 'reformation of manners'. The libertine spirit of England during the Restoration, with its willingness to tolerate a good deal of licentiousness, was gradually fading, and a new spirit of reform was in the air. The court of Charles II had been a scene which encouraged gallantry, and the King himself had led the way by the public display of a series of mistresses. Objections to the King's favourite, Louise Kerouaille, Duchess of Portsmouth, went so far as a parliamentary reprimand. Court writers had tried to put forward an image of magnificence and sophistication that was supposed to be part of absolute monarchy itself, but even the wit of Dryden and Wycherley could not succeed in firmly establishing a courtly ethic in the nation. James II too had had a number of mistresses, and not until William and Mary were ruling did the Court turn to reforming 'manners' as an ideal.

Although the sophisticated libertinism of Charles II and James II had a limited influence, there was an element of coarseness rooted in the populace that appears in the many inexpensive chapbooks that constituted popular reading.[12] In a lengthy work of fiction, *The English Rogue*, a character defecates in the middle of a barber's shop by way of an 'extravagant' gesture that the author clearly regarded as witty. To visitors from the Continent, the English often appeared somewhat barbarous in their eating of vast amounts of meat, in their stage plays that allowed scenes of murder

---

[12] See Margaret Spufford, *Small Books and Pleasant Histories* (Athens: University of Georgia Press, 1981), 156–85.

and brutality on the stage, and in their general behaviour. In such an environment, the poetry of Rochester could only keep its shock value by revelling in obscene language, by treating various forms of what was then considered sexual perversion, and by describing the body with detailed realism. Defoe never ceased to admire Rochester as a great satirist, and although he never adopted Rochester's use of obscenities, he retained the idea that only by shocking the reader in some way could the satirist succeed.

The great contemporary ideal involved reforming the morals of the nation, but the notion that gradually took hold was that the first step toward such a reform ought to be a reform of manners or outward behaviour. Many writers, such as Jonathan Swift, thought that by forcing an outward display of good manners even the vilest person might be improved, if only through force of habit. When *The Spectator* (1711–12), that great arbiter of right thought and behaviour, was to put forth as its goal the tempering of wit with morality and the improvement of morality with wit, it set the tone for the entire eighteenth century—a tone of politeness, feeling, and good humour. But before this could occur, the movement for reformation pulled in a somewhat different direction from that to be advocated in *The Spectator*. The Societies for Reformation of Manners, first formed in the early 1690s, printed 'black lists': the names of offenders against the moral standards of the society. These included those seen entering houses of prostitution, those guilty of public drunkenness, and those heard swearing in public. The dramatists of the 1690s, Southerne, Congreve, and Vanbrugh, who felt they were writing plays that approached moral treatises, had been under attack for a number of years for their vivid depiction of contemporary immorality. Nevertheless, they were astonished in 1698 to be attacked by a Non-juring clergyman, Jeremy Collier, in a witty and scurrilous work, *A Short View of the Immorality and Profaneness of the English Stage*. Despite its title, Collier's book was not all that short, and his notion of what constituted an immoral and profane passage encompassed almost any word that was used in the King James Bible; but Collier's atacks suited the public mood. Actors were attacked by audiences, and the texts of plays were expurgated to removed any offending expressions, particularly any reference to religion.

Defoe was a strong supporter of this movement for the reform of manners and morals, but he was never as polite a writer as, say, Addison or Steele. He believed in the duty of the writer to reflect the reality around him, and he continued to think that readers needed to be shocked out of their complacency. The future author of *Moll Flanders* was not one to avoid what was called 'low' subject-matter, and the admirer of Rochester may have enjoyed a kind of humour that readers of *The Spectator* would have considered coarse. One of Defoe's enemies reported that when he was arrested in 1703, he had a copy of a poem on the knighting of one of Queen Anne's physicians, David Hamilton, after he pronounced that she was pregnant. This was a period when the treatment of gynaecological problems as well as delivering babies was still mainly in the hands of women, and the final lines reflect a coarse kind of male humour over the nature of the female body. Lacking a sword, Queen Anne, knights Hamilton with her leg:

> The Queen rose up, the Doctor kneel'd,
> And lifting up the Royal leg,
> With gout and dropsie swel'd full big,
> Over his head she rais'd it high,
> As sword is brandisht in the skie,
> . . .
> Rise up, Sir David, says the Queen,
> The first Cunt knight that e'er was seen.

The writer of the attack on Defoe implies that Defoe was the author of the poem, and Defoe's biographer John Robert Moore also assumed this. There are all kinds of problems with such an ascription, but the details supplied about his having the poem on him have a ring of authenticity. Whether true or not, it should put us on notice that Defoe's involvement with the Societies for Reformation of Manners did not make him into a Protestant saint.

Defoe's earliest writings reflect the new movement for reform. He began his preface to *A New Discovery of an Old Intreague* with the announcement:

THE End of Satyr *ought to be exposing falshood in order to Reformation. As all Warrings are unlawful whose Aim is not Peace, so Satyrs not thus meant are no more* Satyrs, *but* Libels. *One great Character, and the Lines of which I liked as well as any, is left out here, because the Person is Attoning, as I am told for the past Errors of his Practice, by a future Loyalty to the Government.*[13]

Although Defoe's comments concern 'Reformation' of the hearts and souls of those opposed to William and Mary, the language suggests the movement for reform of manners and morals. In speaking of the individuals who were part of the plot against William, he examines the group of Londoners who were only too willing to betray the rights of citizens to James II,

---

[13] Repr. in Mary Elizabeth Campbell, *Defoe's First Poem* (Bloomington, Ind.: Principia Press, 1938), 189.

criticizing their sexual foibles and unethical behaviour. And nothing is less ethical in this context than the treasonable behaviour they demonstrated when they attempted to subvert the government in their petition to the Queen.

Equally filled with the spirit of reform is the section of *An Essay upon Projects* that treats the English habit of swearing. Defoe puts aside the religious implications and concentrates on the problems of manners. He attacks the senselessness of swearing—its lack of real meaning and faulty grammar. Language should make sense and not be a mere outburst of raw emotion, what he calls 'that scum and excrement of the mouth'.[14] Defoe gives a sample of what such language sounds like and takes a step toward the kind of fictional dialogue that he was to master in his journalism and fiction:

Some part ot them indeed, though they are foolish enough, as effects of a mad, inconsiderate rage, are yet *English*; as when a man swears he will do this or that, and it may be adds *God damn him he will*; that is, *God damn him if he don't*: This tho' it be horrid in another sense, yet may be read in writing, and is English. But what language is this? Jack, *God damn me* Jack, *How do'st do, thou little dear Son of a Whore? How hast thou done this long time, by God?*—*And then they kiss; and t'other, as lewd as himself, goes on;*

Dear Tom, *I am glad to see thee with all my heart, let me dye. Come, let us go take a Bottle, we must not part so; prithee let's go and be drunk by God.* (93–4)

Defoe eventually drops the question of the ungrammatical nature of this 'frenzy of the tongue' and 'vomit of the brain' to address the antisocial nature of the act:

Besides, as 'tis an inexcusable Impertinence, so 'tis a Breach upon Good Manners and Conversation, for a man to impose the Clamour of his Oaths upon the Company he converses with; if there be any one person in the Company that does not approve the way, 'tis an imposing upon him with a freedom beyond Civility; as if a man shou'd *Fart* before a Justice, or *talk Bawdy* before the Queen, or the like. (96)

Defoe never gave up preaching the necessity of good manners for the purpose of creating what he called 'conversation', that social encounter and discourse which he considered the essence of contemporary social life.

Although he never abandoned his distaste for swearing, Defoe did go on to treat more complex problems of legislating the morality of the society. For example, he wanted his academy to act as a screening body for all plays

---

[14] Daniel Defoe, *An Essay upon Projects*, ed. Joyce Kennedy, Michael Seidel, and Maximillian Novak (New York: AMS Press, 1999), 93. Subsequent references to this work will refer to this edition and be included within parentheses in my text.

that were to be performed. The context of Defoe's discussion appears to have been the withdrawal of Betterton and some of the leading actors and actresses from the united stage company to set up a rival company at Lincoln's Inn Fields in 1695. The consequent war between the two theatres was fought against a backdrop of increasing moral criticism directed against contemporary plays. Defoe joined with such critics in seeing a necessity for some moral scrutiny of plays, but by giving the task to an academy devoted to language and literature, he appeared to desire avoiding a rigid moral censor such as Collier. The imagery of the short poem he appended to his discussion is couched in terms of a witty analogy between church politics and theatrical politics, but he left little doubt that he would like to see some regulation of the stage:

> Wit and Religion suffer equal fate;
> Neglect of both attends the warm Debate.
> For while the Parties strive and counter-mine,
> Wit will as well as Piety decline. (97)

An *Essay upon Projects* had a strong reforming impulse, but the work most clearly connected with the new reform movement at this time was unquestionably *The Poor Man's Plea in Relation to . . . Reformation of Manners*, published at the end of March 1698. The preface, to which the initials, D.F. were added in the second edition, speaks of 'the present Torrent of Vice' that has inundated the nation and of necessity for members of the upper and middle orders to set an example for moral behaviour. Defoe appeals to 'Conscience' in acknowledging the rightness of what his Poor Man has to say. What follows is a Christian argument for equality of human beings in society. The Poor Man pleads that the laws against vice are used only against the poor, and calls upon the magistrates to enforce laws against drunkenness and immorality against the rich as well as the poor. If the law is not applied equally, England's system of justice is simply a method of crowd control. Poverty, Defoe argues, 'which is no Crime at all', is being treated as the key crime in society.[15] Defoe's Poor Man contends that the laws against 'Vicious Practices' are being enforced selectively:

These are all Cobweb Laws, in which the small Flies are catch'd, and great ones break through. My Lord-Mayor has whipt about the poor Beggars and a few scandalous Whores have been sent to the House of Correction; some Ale-house-keepers and Vintners have been Fin'd for drawing Drink on the Sabbath-day; but all this falls upon us of the Mob, the poor *Plebeii*, as if all the Vice lay among us;

---

[15] Daniel Defoe, *The Poor Man's Plea* (1698), in *Shakespeare Head Edition*, sig. a6 and p. 7.

for we do not find the Rich Drunkard carri'd before my Lord Mayor, nor a Swearing lewd Merchant Fin'd, or Set in the Stocks. *The Man with a Gold Ring, and Gay Cloths*, may Swear before the Justice, or at the Justice; may reel home through the open Streets, and no man take any notice of it; but if a poor man gets drunk or swear an oath, he must to the Stocks without Remedy.[16]

This statement is more suggestive of a desire for a complete reformation; the manners will follow. The Poor Man argues that the upper classes set the tone for society. It is upper-class vice that has permeated the lower orders, and it is the upper class that needs to reform: 'The Rich Man's Wickedness affects all the Neighbourhood, gives offence to the Sober, encourages and hardens the Lewd, and quite overthrows the weak Resolutions of such as are but indifferently fix'd in their Virtue and Morality.' Indeed, it is precisely the ability of the rich to 'be Lewd at a rate above the Common Size, to let the World see' that makes them more guilty than the poor.[17]

Toward the end of the century there was a general disaffection in the country. There had been riots over food shortages, and investigations into graft and corruption had disclosed both. The necessity of a recoinage had put a strain on the economy. Some people had grown rich and others had lost everything. Richard Newman, in a pamphlet called *The Complaint of English Subjects* (1699), commenced with the dire warning, 'Your Majesty is much abused, the Country most grievously injured, and opprest, their Trade is meerly lost, and in their Estates and Minds they are much decayed.' Newman went on to speak of how much the poor had suffered, arguing that many who knew how to get rich through the recoinage succeeded in breaking 'the Poor to pieces' and that 'many Hundred, if not Thousand, throughout *England*, gradually were then mearly Starved to Death'.[18] Another pamphleteer instanced a case of a 'Sweeper' who turned an office of £20 a year into an estate of £6000.[19]

Defoe's Poor Man does not blame the government at all, but rather deflects the hostility of the poor toward the 'Gentry' and away from King and Parliament. Still he does voice his discontent particularly on the breed of informers who, by turning in people for immorality, have created an atmosphere of terror. The very name of 'an Evidence or Informer', Defoe writes, 'is enough to denominate a Man unfit for Society; a Rogue and an Informer are synonimous in the Vulgar Acceptation.'[20] Defoe's acknow-

---

[16] *The Poor Man's Plea*, 6–7.

[17] Ibid. 11.

[18] Richard Newman, *The Complaint of English Subjects* (London, 1699), sig. A3, p. 21.

[19] For some typical complaints about the ways in which wealth had corrupted England, see L. Meriton, *Pecuniae Obediunt Omnia: Money Does Master All Things* (York, 1696), 40–57; and Edward Ward, *The Miracles Perform'd by Money* (London, 1692), 9–13.   [20] *The Poor Man's Plea*, 15.

ledgement of his authorship of this work by adding the preface with his
initials to the second edition, and later by including it in his two-volume
collection of poems and essays, suggests that he wanted to be known as a
radical supporter of 'revolution principles' in their fullest application. It
also announced his ability to assume the voice of the dispossessed in that
society.

For Defoe, reformation of manners had evolved into a larger social and
political programme. Just as he tried to counter the arguments of what he
considered to be a parliamentary elite in the fight over disbanding the
army, so he now voiced his dismay at Parliament in general. In 'An
Encomium upon a Parliament', distributed in manuscript some time in May
1699, Defoe set out their faults from the very beginning:

> Ye worthy Patriots go on
>   To heal the Nation's Sores,
> Find all Mens Faults out but your own,
> Begin good Laws, but finish none,
>   And then shut up your Doors.[21]

In this effective, swingeing doggerel, Defoe attacked Parliament for all the
follies of the past few years, from the disbanding of the army to the passing
of the unpopular tax upon leather. William had begun the session with an
appeal for laws for 'discouraging of Vice and Profaneness', but a bill to that
effect, authored by Sir John Philipps, was allowed to die in committee.
Thus the same Parliament which, in the face of an obvious threat from
French power, was responsible for reducing the army to 7000 men and
removing from its ranks all but native-born Englishmen seemed to be
doing everything else wrong for the nation. In their triumphant struggle
against the Whigs, the New Country Party, led by Robert Harley, had lost
sight of the national good. Things had come to such a pass that William
had been ready to abdicate at the end of December 1698. Defoe's poem
seems to have been timed for the end of the session of Parliament on 4 May
1699. Speaking with the assumed authoritative voice of the English people,
Defoe bade Parliament farewell:

> For shame leave this wicked Employment,
> Reform both your Manners and Lives;
>   You were never sent out
>   To make such a Rout,
> Go home and look after your Wives.[22]

---

[21] *Poems on Affairs of State*, ed. Frank Ellis et al. (7 vols., New Haven, Conn.: Yale University Press, 1963–75), vi. 49.　　　[22] Ibid. 57.

The strongest defence of King William, a pamphlet with the name *Cursory Remarks upon Some Late Disloyal Proceedings in Several Cabals* (1699), accused William's enemies of acting purely from self-interest and a lust for power. This pamphlet 'quoted' from 'An Encomium', but many of the verses in the style of Defoe's 'Encomium' are not in the original poem and are not as effective. Whether Defoe had anything to do with this work is difficult to say, but he would have appreciated the message: that William III truly represented the will of the people; that he wanted to help the country recover from the effects of the War of the Grand Alliance; and that he wanted to find ways of employing the poor. Parliament, on the other hand, in its obstruction of William's programmes, seemed to represent nothing but itself. A few years later, in his *Six Distinguishing Characters of a Parliament-Man*, Defoe was to advise his readers that what was truly needed in candidates for Parliament was that they be 'Men of Morals' who would usher in a true reformation of manners.

IV

If Defoe began finding his public voice as a writer on politics and moral reform, he also began to assume a role as a spokesman for the concerns of the Dissenters. But if his political positions are fairly clear, the same cannot be said for his relationship with the Dissenting community and its beliefs. He quarrelled with many Dissenters in his first published work opposing support for Count Teckely (Toekoeli) and the Hungarian rebels. He seemed inclined to shock members of his own group by taking uncomfortable positions. Yet he hoped for unity among a broad coalition of Dissenting groups, including Baptists and Quakers, on political issues affecting the entire community, and was particularly eager for a repeal of the Test Act, which excluded all but Anglicans from holding office and serving in the army. He regarded the Dissenters as the bulwark against the hegemony of the Catholic Church, and was always alert to signs of persecution and a renewal of the religious wars of the seventeenth century. But he could be irritatingly inconsistent, and occasionally he seemed deliberately to play the gadfly to the Dissenting groups he usually supported.

At the beginning of 1698, he published *An Enquiry into the Occasional Conformity of Dissenters, In Cases of Preferment*. The full title spelled out the occasion for the pamphlet 'With a Preface to the Lord Mayor, Occasioned by his carrying the Sword to a Conventicle', followed by a quotation from 1 Kings 18: 21: 'If the Lord be God, follow him: But if Baal then follow him.' The quotation comes from the scene in which the prophet Elijah challenged the priests of Baal to see whether Baal was as powerful as Jehovah in bringing down fire from the heavens. The priests of Baal failed, but Elijah's prayers were answered as fire consumed his sacrifice. The people of Israel acknowledged the power of God and, at the command of Elijah, slew the priests of Baal.

As he did in his pamphlets on the standing army controversy, Defoe began with a historical account—this time of the history of Dissent in England. Those who were called 'Puritans' during the reign of Elizabeth were those who sought the 'greatest Purity of Worship', and while the modern Dissenter is very different from these original saintly men and women, they still dissent on the same grounds. Defoe then proceeded to accuse those who conformed occasionally in the Church of England of being like Israelites who occasionally worshipped Baal, of being 'Christians of an Amphibious Nature', and he laid down the principle: 'He who Dissents from an Establish'd Church on any account, but from a real Principle of Conscience, is a Politick, not a Religious Dissenter.' He then pointed to the failure of logic in occasionally conforming in the Church of England: 'Nothing can be lawful and unlawful at the same time.' No one should use the desire to serve one's country as an excuse for acting against conscience. It was, as he said in what was to his contemporaries a memorable phrase, '*playing-Bopeep* with God Almighty'. It would be preferable to conform entirely, but to go from church to meeting-house had to be seen as sinful.[23]

Behind this pamphlet was a political motive. Defoe did not want to see Dissent weakened by a gradual movement toward the Church. He noted that there was greater unity among Dissenters in time of persecution, but that during the reign of William, when there was no significant penalty against the Nonconformists, those who were not truly committed to their beliefs would try to accommodate themselves to living in two worlds. Defoe felt that such an attitude weakened the position of the Dissenters in English society, and that it were better that the occasional conformist be cast out by the Dissenters. Defoe's logic might be seen as impeccable, but in some sense he was ruling on the consciences of others, and that made many of his fellow Dissenters very angry indeed. The quotation itself created a problem. Who were the followers of Baal? Was Defoe casting himself as a prophet? As a new Elijah?

It was also a pamphlet that gave comfort to the enemy. After its publica-

---

[23] Daniel Defoe, *An Enquiry into the Occasional Conformity of Dissenters, In Cases of Preferment*, in *A True Collection of the Writings of the True-Born Englishman* (2 vols., London, 1703–5), i. 315.

tion, the opposition of God and Baal came up frequently among Anglican controversialists as a way of arguing for the crushing of Dissent in England. The Dissenters wondered by what right Defoe took it upon himself to define their choices. In 1701 the Presbyterian Dissenting minister John Howe took him to task for this, and attacked his use of the God and Baal analogy:

Did you take this for a piece of Wit? 'twas uncharitable. Uncharitable? that's a Trifle in comparison; 'twas profane and most impious Wit; yet you are mighty fond of the Conceit, and we have it over and over in the Book, that the *Conformists*, and *Dissenters* serve two Gods (as the one of them is mis-call'd) and have two Religions! . . . But throughout the Book, such as are of this Christian Latitude, and benignity of Mind towards one another, and not so stingily bigotted to a Party, as he are treated with *this sort of Charity, to be styl'd Painted Hypocrites*, such as *Play Bo-peep with God Almighty*; that, if *such an occasion* offer it self to any of them, to serve God and their Countrey, in a publick Station, do what the law requires, and which they think they may Sinlessly do in order to it, do trespass upon their Consciences, and Damn their own Souls to serve their Countrey.[24]

Dissenters such as Richard Baxter, who had disagreed with the Anglican Church on only a few points, saw no problem with attending Anglican services, and Howe takes exactly this postion. What right had Defoe to tell the Dissenters how to behave? Defoe was to respond to Howe in his *A Letter to Mr. How* and again in a sarcastic preface added to his original essay in his *True Collection*. He identified himself as a Presbyterian. His attitude was essentially ironic and one he was later to express on several occasions: If I am the only person in the world who believes this, can I help it if I am right? Although Defoe was eventually to become a spokesman for dissent and for the Dissenters on many issues, he certainly did not go out of his way to make friends among his fellow Nonconformists.

If Defoe's religious views appear narrow next to what Howe praised as 'true Christian Latitude',[25] he appears even narrower in his attitude toward Catholicism. In *Lex Talionis: or, An Enquiry into the Most Proper Ways to Prevent the Persecution of the Protestants in France*, published at the end of summer 1698, Defoe turned to a subject dear to his heart, the persecution of the Huguenots under Louis XIV. Although he maintained that states were now governed mainly by self-interest rather than by religious motives, he suggested a course of action which he thought might well result in bringing the Huguenots back to their native land—the expulsion of Catholics as a

[24] John Howe, *Some Consideration of a Preface to an Enquiry, Concerning the Occasional Conformity of the Dissenters* (London, 1701), 28.
[25] Ibid. 19.

retaliation for the mistreatment of Protestants and the confiscation of their property in Catholic countries. Defoe stated that he knew of a letter among Milton's 'Letters of State' suggesting an alliance with Holland to force the Duke of Savoy to treat the Protestant Vaudois in a better manner and threatening the expulsion of all Catholics from England. This is the Law of Retaliation in Defoe's title. He speculated on what England might have been like under these circumstances—no Popish Plot, no wars with France. He foresaw an exchange of population that would enrich England by bringing in industrious and skilled workers and afford peace to Europe. He was a firm supporter of immigration, and later formed various schemes for absorbing the Protestant refugees from the Palatinate, but here I want to stress his strong anti-Catholic bias at this time. For Defoe, Louis XIV and France were the supporters of James II, the Turks, and Catholicism, and he often found it hard to separate these three. He was occasionally to bring up the Swedish practice of castrating Catholic priests discovered in that country as a possible solution to what he saw as an expanding Catholic presence in England. As will be seen, the mature Defoe could strike a more ecumenical pose, but despite his disclaimer, the young Defoe was still fighting the religious wars of the seventeenth century. From his standpoint, the presence of Catholicism in England was also equivalent to the sub-version of morals and might well stand as a project for groups such as the Societies for Reformation of Manners.

V

Defoe must have been extraordinarily busy during the last three years of the seventeenth century. His wife, Mary, had to be equally busy in her own way. Between the death of her first child, Mary, in 1688 and the baptism of Sophia on 24 December 1701, she gave birth to at least seven children: five daughters: Maria before 1690 and then Hannah, Henrietta, Sarah, and Sophia; and two sons: Daniel and Benjamin. If the family was living with Joan Tuffley, Mary's mother, it must have been a frantic household, even with servants to help out. Under these conditions, Defoe may have occasionally stayed with his sister Elizabeth. According to the London Marriage Assessments for the year 1695 to 1696, a Daniel Foe was living in London on the left side of Moore Fields in the parish of St Botolph's Bishopgate with two children, Daniel and Sarah and one servant, Hanah How.[26] Was Defoe occasionally living with his brother-in-law Robert

---

[26] Guild Hall Marriage Assessments, no. 103, St. Botolph's Bishopgate, 1 May 1695–1 May 1696.

Davis at this time? Certainly both Elizabeth and Robert Davis were involved in one of Defoe's schemes to use his resources as a maker of bricks and as a builder.

In May 1696 Defoe proposed to the London orphanage Christ's Hospital to build twelve brick buildings in the area where that organization owned several houses which it leased to various tenants. Defoe purchased two of the leases and some other property. He proposed creating a passage from the Thames to Westminster market, attempting an ingenious entry into the building industry in a rapidly expanding London. The governors of Christ's Hospital thought that there was not enough room for twelve houses (the lot was a mere 33 feet by 130), and the matter became complicated by the amount of money Defoe and his partner, a bricklayer named Gillingham, would put down as a 'fine' to guarantee that the work would be carried to completion. Defoe renewed his proposal in 1698, and Gillingham was still negotiating over the amount of the fine on one of the leases in 1704. Defoe retained control of the Sherman House lease, and probably kept apartments there for some time. He eventually fell behind in payments and by 1705 he had lost the lease.[27]

Despite noting that 'the diligent hand' creates riches, Defoe was anything but diligent in his business dealings. He was in every sense a projector, who imagined ingenious schemes and lost interest when confronted by the tedious business of carrying matters through to their conclusion. If, toward the end of his life, he revived many of the ideas put forward in the *Essay upon Projects*, it may be said that during that final decade he seems to have repeated the pattern of his business dealings: grandiose plans involving the manufacture of bricks and extensive building followed by a loss of interest and an abandonment of the project along with the loss of all the money paid to start it. That he should have returned to the manufacture of bricks suggests that he did enjoy the creative, manufacturing end of business. Just as Robinson Crusoe was to enjoy the creative energy of making his pots, so Defoe must have taken considerable pleasure in seeing the transformation of unformed clay into solid bricks and elegant pantiles. He probably spent a good deal of time at Tilbury observing the operations: the digging of the clay, the tempering of the material in a pit, and the firing of the bricks. He employed 100 workmen, and a clerk named Castleton, who died and was replaced by a man named Whitehurst. And while some of his enemies claimed that he was worse than the Egyptian pharaoh insofar

[27] See Spiro Peterson, 'Defoe and Westminster 1696–1706', *Eighteenth-Century Studies* 12 (1978–9), 306–36. Peterson reproduced the proposal of 1696 with Defoe's signature as Daniel D'Foe, an early version of the name by which he became famous.

as that monarch only commanded the Israelites to make bricks without straw while Defoe asked his workmen to manufacture bricks without wages, Defoe seems to have paid them well enough and provided drink for them.[28] He wrote in the *Review*:

Nor should the Author of this paper boast in vain, if he tells the World, that he himself, before Violence, Injury, and Barbarous Treatment Demolish'd him and his undertaking, Employ'd 100 Poor People in making *Pan-Tiles in England*, a manufacture always bought in *Holland*; and thus he pursued this Principle with his utmost Zeal for the good of *England*.[29]

In giving a short account of his life to Harley, his pride in that accomplishment is evident; the factory was to be the basis of his new life:

All my prospects were built on a Manufacture I had Erected in Essex; all The late kings Bounty to me was Expended There. I Employ'd a hundred Poor Familys at work and it began to pay me Very well. I Generally made Six hundred pound profit per Annum.

I began to live, Took a Good House, bought me Coach and horses a Second Time. I paid Large Debts Gradually, small Ones wholly, and Many a Creditor after composition whom I found poor and Decay'd I Sent for and Paid the Remaindr to tho' Actually Discharged. (H 17)

During these years he was still being pursued by his creditors. In 1694, a group of them complained that they were not getting anything out of the money that Defoe was making from rents and manufacturing at Chadwell and Tilbury, and Henry Lickbarrow, one of the tenants on the Chadwell land, sued for damages owing to an unrepaired sea wall. Defoe may have settled out of court with Lickbarrow, but he finally faced his other creditors, Maresco, Stamper, and Ghiselyn, in May 1699. The court gave Defoe until 29 September 1703 to pay far less than he owed. The sum was £466 13s. 4d. to Maresco, £408 6s. 8d. to Stamper, and £175 to Ghiselyn. He was allowed to keep his land and his brick factory. Perhaps his creditors, seeing the success of the latter enterprise, thought that he might be in a position to return some of their money to them at the end of the four-year interval.[30] At any rate, his statement to Harley, 'I began to live', seems to have been more the result of his resolve to do so based on what he thought might be his future prospects rather than a new way of life based on a dramatic change for the better in his present financial situation. He

---

[28] *The True-Born-Hugonot: Or, Daniel Defoe: a Satyr* (London, 1703), 1–2.

[29] *Review*, i. 34.

[30] See James Sutherland, 'Some Early Troubles of Daniel Defoe', *Review of English Studies* 9 (1935), 286–9.

moved into a house in Hackney, the fashionable London suburb, and began again.

Perhaps the 'Bounty' from King William that he spoke of to Harley may have been substantial. As I suggest previously, it is difficult to judge how close his work as a pamphleteer had brought him to William III and when he started his work setting up his spy network or system of intelligence. In his *Appeal to Honour and Justice*, he spoke of how John Tutchin's poem *The Foreigners* put him in a rage and inspired his reply, *The True-Born Englishman*, and how the poem brought him to the attention of William. He regarded himself as William's loyal follower, and he was proud to call him 'Master'. He would ever defend his memory, and he knew that William would always have protected him had he lived.[31] Defoe's sentiments seem genuine enough, but contact with William III, who in Defoe's mind was the exalted defender of the Protestant cause against Louis XIV, might have led him to imagine a more intimate relationship than actually existed.

As I have argued, Defoe was already a writer for the Court during the standing army controversy, and his usefulness should have been obvious from 1698 onward. He was in London on 16 November when William made his triumphant entry into London after the Treaty of Ryswick. He wrote of the celebration and of what he thought to be the ill omen that seemed to suggest that another war would not be long in coming:

just the very Evening, when we were making Bonefires, Illuminations and Rejoycings for the Peace of *Ryswick*—The Moon appear'd in a total Eclipse—As if it had told us, *and it really made me take the Boldness to say in Print, that heaven gave us Notice*, that the Peace we then rejoyc'd in should be soon eclips'd.[32]

We should not be surprised at an image of Defoe joining in the public rejoicing on this occasion. Of all the important writers of the time, he was the most completely rooted in what might be considered the ordinary pleasures of ordinary Englishmen. But the impulse that brought him to write about the impending war with France had for him a powerful urgency. The standing army controversy may have appeared to end with the victory of the New Country Party, but Defoe never let it die. He and William knew that a new war was coming. William tried to head it off by his barrier treaties, which guaranteed on paper that France and Spain would not be joined as a single nation. Defoe tried to do much the same by alerting his country to the dangers before it.

[31] Defoe, *An Appeal to the Honour and Justice Though It Be of His Worst Enemies*, in *Shakespeare Head Edition*, 195.
[32] *Review*, vi. 24.

7

The True-Born Englishman and
Other Satires

From this Amphibious Ill-born Mob began
The vain ill-natur'd thing, an Englishman[1]

Of the year 1699, William Peterfield Trent remarked that 1699 was a year in which Defoe seems to have gone 'without a single attempt to enlighten mankind'.[2] But Frank Ellis's ascription to him of *An Encomium on a Parliament* in May of that year removes the possibility that he ever put down his pen for very long.[3] Admittedly, one lampoon was not very much for one of the most prolific writers in the English language, and this brief hiatus was accompanied by changes in Defoe's life and in his attitudes. His position as accountant for the glass duty was coming to an end. The tax had been halved in 1698 and had been under attack in the Commons. They called for an examination of the accounts and it was presented on 17 April 1699 under the signature of Daniel de Foe, Accomptant.[4] The record revealed that £5124 had been raised at an expense of £727. William agreed to abolish the duty entirely as of 1 August 1699, and with that action, Defoe's life as a respectable civil servant came to an end. His patrons, Thomas Neale and Dalby Thomas, were in trouble with Parliament. Both were arrested and accused of embezzling funds from the Million Lottery. Neale was expelled from the Commons and died in December. Thomas, who had been released, was arrested again and charged with bribery in

---

[1] Defoe, *The True-Born Englishman*, in Frank Ellis (ed.), *Poems on Affairs of State: Augustan Satirical Verse, 1660–1714* (New Haven, Conn.: Yale University Press) (*POAS* vi), 270.
[2] Manuscript biography, Trent Collection.
[3] *POAS*, vi. 43–57.
[4] *JHC* 1803, xii. 647.

relation to a distilling Bill being considered by the House. Lotteries themselves were abolished in that year. The era of projects and projectors
seemed to be coming to an end, and the Whig managers were stepping
down as well. Charles Montagu resigned the Chancellorship of the
Exchequer in June and his position as First Lord of the Treasury in
November. Lord Somers, who may have masterminded the propaganda
for maintaining the standing army, stepped down from the position of
Lord Chancellor in April 1700. Defoe's interests remained the same, but
having lost his battles for William's army, he seemed to think that what was
needed was more radical action and yet more daring pamphlets.

I

We know little of what Defoe was doing between May 1699 and February
1700. Was he engaged in travelling about and setting up his spy network
for William? Or was he busy with his brick works and his growing family?
At any rate, on 15 February he celebrated the coming of the new century
by publishing a poem, *The Pacificator*, on the state of wit and poetry in
England. The poem is actually about the politics of poetry, since the
literary quarrels that had divided the nation were often allied to political
and social disputes. The former laureate, John Dryden, was a bitter
opponent of William III, and he insinuated into his translation of Virgil's
Aeneid and into the popular narrative modernizations and translations that
made up the *Fables* a steady attack upon the King and what he called the
'stupid military state' that he thought William had brought into England.[5]
As the master-poet of the age, Dryden was able to give a literary basis for
Country Party ideals and comfort to the Jacobites. The Wits tended to
form under Dryden's banner, with the satirist Tom Brown as a leading
spokesman.

One of the main targets of the Wits was Sir Richard Blackmore, a
mediocre poet whose two epic poems, *Prince Arthur* (1695) and *King Arthur*
(1697), were intended as compliments to King William. Blackmore, a
physician, stated that he wrote his poetry in a coach between house calls,
and he was an easy target for Brown and others. Blackmore replied in
November 1699 with his *Satyr against Wit*, an attack upon the excessive
striving after wit as destructive to the nation:

---

[5] John Dryden, 'To Sir Godfrey Kneller', in *Poems*, ed James Kinsley (4 vols., Oxford: Clarendon
Press, 1958), ii. 859.

> Wit does enfeeble and debauch the Mind,
> Before to Business or to Arts inclin'd.
> How useless is a sauntrying empty Wit,
> Only to please with Jests at Dinner fit?[6]

Blackmore saw the rage after wit destroying education and the moral fibre of the nation, and he urged a curb on satire and satirists. Before being allowed to publish, the satirists should be forced to establish their own moral rectitude. Blackmore aimed many of his attacks at Samuel Garth, whose *Dispensary*, published in the spring of 1699, had ridiculed another of the wars within England that had replaced the slaughter on the battle-fields of Flanders—that between the doctors and the apothecaries over pre-scribing medicines.

Defoe borrowed from Blackmore the opposition of the 'rich Sense' that dominates genuine satire from the 'empty Malice' that lies behind the products of the Wits. He also adopted the device of the French satirist Antoine Furetière, whose poem depicting a war between Rhetoric and Sense was popular enough to invite a number of translations around the same time. The intent of Defoe's poem was to urge peace between the antagonists, and his solution is similar to the proposal for an academy in his *Essay upon Projects;* he argues the need for a '*Grand Inquisitor* of Wit' who will bring order to the chaotic state of writing in England:

> Allow no Satyrs which receive their Date
> From *Juno*'s Academy, *Billingsgate*;
> No Banters, no Invective lines admit,
> Where want of manners, makes up want of Wit.[7]

Like Blackmore, he sees the struggle in terms of reformation of manners, and therefore his men of 'Sense' includes Jeremy Collier as 'A modest Soldier, resolute and Stout', even though he was a Non-juror, whose self-display at the execution of some Jacobites for treason must have left Defoe less than happy.

Defoe sides mainly with the forces of 'Sense', and gives the victory to Nokor (Blackmore), but the poem ends inconclusively with Dryden rally-ing the forces of wit and a new battle impending. In fact, Defoe's division between wit and sense has little in common with Blackmore's but rather resembles the common Restoration opposition between imagination and judgment. In Dryden's version of this image, the imagination was com-pared to a spaniel who ranges far but should always be under the control of the hunter. Defoe's list of those who combined the two qualities is

---

[6] *POAS*, vi. 140.   [7] Ibid. 179.

suggested by the army that Nokor attempts to recruit after his initial defeat:

> The General sent for help both far and near,
> To *Cowley, Milton, Ratcliff, Rochester,*
> *Waller, Roscommon, Howard,* and to *B[eh]n,*
> The Doubtful Fight the better to maintain;
> *Giants* these were of Wit and Sense together,
> But they were dead and gone *the Lord knows whether.*[8]

It was mainly these poets, along with Dryden and Marvell, that Defoe looked to for his models, and whom he continued to admire as the great poets produced by the age.

That Rochester could win a place among these poets of 'Wit and Sense together' suggests that Defoe placed a higher value on imagination as embodied in wit than he did on his category of sense. Thus his comparison of the two qualities gives the burden of compliment to Wit. Defoe's readers may not have known how to understand the opposition:

> *Wit* is a Standing Army government,
> And *Sense* a sullen stubborn *Parliament,*[9]

but Defoe, who was still fighting for an army after Parliament had doomed it, believed that his side in this conflict had possessed imagination and vision enough to see into a future in which a war with France would be inevitable. Defoe sticks with his intent at the end and calls for a combination of the two qualities:

> *Wit* is the *Fruitful Womb* where Thoughts Conceive
> *Sense* is the *Vital Heat* which Life and Form must give:
> *Wit* is the *Teeming Mother* brings them forth,
> *Sense* is the *Active Father* gives them worth.
> *United: Wit* and *Sense,* makes Science thrive,
> *Divided:* neither *Wit* nor *Sense* can live.[10]

When Defoe finally assigned everyone to their own genius, he included himself next to Congreve, the master of the 'Comick' as the ruler of the province of 'Lampoon', or that branch of satire dedicated to direct personal attack. Many contemporaries would have had little difficulty identifying Congreve with comedy, but one wonders how many readers in 1700 would have associated Defoe's name with any literary form. It may be that he had written a sufficient number of lampoons to have gained a local reputation. At least he seems to have thought that there were an adequate number of readers in 1700 who could have filled in the F— correctly. That action on

---

[8] *POAS*, vi. 165–6.   [9] Ibid. 177.   [10] Ibid.

the part of readers gave contemporary satires of this kind the pleasure of a crossword puzzle.[11]

Defoe's excursion into literary controversy reveals that he had a general knowledge of the commonplaces of criticism and a fair knowledge of the literary figures of his time. He always considered himself a man of culture combining the activity of a man of business with an understanding of music, painting, and literature, and the next controversy into which he plunged gave him some opportunity to demonstrate the superior degree of information he possessed compared to most Englishmen. In *The Two Great Questions Consider'd* and *The Two Great Questions Further Considered*, published respectively in November and December 1700, Defoe showed his command of the intricacies of European politics and geography. In the latter work, he boasted: 'truly I have Read all the Histories of *Europe*, that are extant in our Language, and some in other Languages', and he confronted the author of a reply to his first pamphlet with his personal knowledge of the Continent. 'I suppose this Gentleman never went up the *Rhine* into *Germany*', he noted by way of establishing his own wide experience.[12]

The two questions alluded to in the titles involve what Louis would do about the will of the King of Spain which left the Kingdom to the Duke of Anjou, the grandson of Louis XIV, and how the English should respond. Defoe enunciates the principle that the significant factor is the balance of power in Europe and English trade to Spain, which France will destroy:

If the French get the Spanish Crown, we are beaten out of the Field as to Trade, and are besieged in our own Island, and never let us flatter our selves with our Safety consisting so much in our Fleet; for this *I* presume to lay down as a fundamental Axiom, at least as the Wars go of late, 'tis not the longest Sword, but the longest Purse that conquers. If the *French* get *Spain*, they get the greatest Trade in the World in their Hands; they that have the most Trade, will have the most Money, will have the most Ships, the best Fleet, and the best Armies; and if once the *French* master us at Sea, where are we then?[13]

Defoe's great fear was that France would control Spain and with it the Spanish market for English cloth. And if this happened, the trade in woollen cloth or 'Bays', employing 40,000 people, would end, and all of those servicing the needs of these workers would also be put out of work, creating a cycle of unemployment that would impoverish the country.

[11] In Narcissus Luttrell's copy at the William Andrews Clark Memorial Library, someone, almost certainly Luttrell, gradually began filling in the names of the various authors. He succeeded in guessing correctly on Congreve and left the F-- blank. But he also missed so important a figure as Prior on the same page (14).

[12] *The Two Great Questions Further Considered*, in *True Collection*, i. 368, 377.

[13] *The Two Great Questions Consider'd*, in *True Collection*, i. 362.

What we see in these pamphlets is Defoe's growing confidence in his understanding of politics and the economic ramifications of political actions. He notes that the King of Spain had no right to will the nation to the Duke of Anjou. That is not the way rulers of nations are created. The people of Spain had already chosen to have the succession devolve on the House of Austria, and that decision could not be abrogated. 'Also,' he writes, 'if all Titles be deriv'd thus from the People, and any one that they will Accept, is Lawful King: Why should I be blamed for saying, 'twas a weak thing for the King of Spain to give away his Kingdom by his Will, which he had no Power to do?'[14] In the second of the pamphlets he returns to his defence of standing armies, arguing that so long as Parliament approves of the army there can be no threat to the liberty of the subject. Toland and the 'Club' of Classical Republicans had placed England in a weak posture. Defoe was right. France, a nation noted for governing its foreign affairs entirely on the basis of its interests, quickly took advantage of the situation. In *Six Distinguishing Characters of a Parliament-Man*, published in January 1701, Defoe urged the election of 'Men of Sense', who would not be fooled on matters of the army and who would help bring on the great reformation of manners that the nation needed so desperately.[15]

Defoe's gradual move toward a government more directly responsive to the needs of the people may be seen in his advice against voting for men of great estates. Honesty, he argued, was the more important quality. And what must be avoided at all costs was the election of 'Fools'.[16] This is one of the earliest appearances of his attack upon folly which will find its fullest development twenty-five years later in *Mere Nature Delineated*. He never ceased to be dismayed at the capacity for folly that seemed to defy the rational element that he felt ought to be dominant in human nature. After the sympathy with insanity he displayed in his *Essay upon Projects*, Defoe had come to see various forms of imbecility prevalent in every segment of society:

I desire to be understood here what I mean by a Fool, not a Natural, and Idiot, a *Ben* in the *Minories*, a Born Fool, no, nor a silly, stupid, downright Blockheaded Fool: But men are Fools or Wise-Men, comparatively considered with respect to their several Capacities, and their several Employments; as he may be a Fool of a Parson who is a very Ingenious Artificer; a Fool of a Clock-maker, and yet be a

[14] *The Two Great Questions Further Considered*, in *True Collection*, i. 374.
[15] *The Six Distinguishing Characters of a Parliament-Man*, in *True Collection*, i. 279.
[16] Ibid.

very good Sailor; so a Gentleman may be a good Horse-racer, a good Sports-man, a good Swords-man, and yet be a Fool of a Parliament-man.[17]

Defoe was clearly losing patience. In *The Danger of the Protestant Religion*, published just a few days after his advice about electing men with brains, he remarked that, however much one may believe in God's government of the world, 'he has ordered that we should Govern ourselves by Reason'. Defoe addressed this pamphlet to King William, and permitted himself this philosophical digression. Although God allowed himself the power of working miracles, what Defoe called 'the great Chain of Causes and Effects' is not customarily 'interrupted by God himself'. Reliance upon God is inadequate if it means passivity. Englishmen and the Protestants of Europe must act, must put aside their interests to defend their religion. He believed that reasonable men like King William and himself could lead the nation toward the war against France, Louis XIV, and 'Popery'—the war to save European Protestantism.[18]

II

Everything that Defoe wrote during 1701 was directed toward getting England involved in what was to be called the War of the Spanish Succession. In response to the difficulties he encountered in attempting to move Parliament to respond to what he considered a crisis, he was to formulate his ideological position on the role of the citizen toward government. He tried to get Englishmen to see beyond their island to what was happening on the Continent, and more especially to the growth of French hegemony. He pointed to Cromwell's concern for the Protestant Vaudois in Savoy and to Milton's many letters on the subject as a sample of England's traditional involvement with this cause. The standing army controversy had been narrowly nationalistic and isolationist in its insistence that all England needed was a wooden wall of naval vessels to protect the nation. Parliament had reacted against England's role as a player in the bloody War of the Grand Alliance. Now they had to see how wrong they had been and how necessary it was to understand the threat posed by France, not only to English religion and commerce but to the very lives of England's inhabitants.

In January 1701 Defoe published *The True-Born Englishman*, his first popular success and the most frequently reprinted poem of the reign of

---

[17] *The Six Distinguishing Characters of a Parliament-Man*, in *True Collection*, i. 280.
[18] *The Danger of the Protestant Religion*, in *True Collection*, i. 254.

Queen Anne. Besides the many official editions, if Defoe is to be believed, 80,000 pirated copies were sold. Writing in 1705 about the constant inability of authors to prevent piracy and collect their rightful profits, he estimated that he could have made £1000 had he been able to control the sale. His own ten editions of *The True-Born Englishman*, selling for a shilling, were undersold by copies priced at one or two pence. Such copies were probably passed around and read out of existence. A Dublin printer listed a twenty-fifth edition in 1749, though there is little likelihood that such a count was accurate. It was reprinted in Philadelphia at the beginning of the American Revolution and in London in 1788. The England of 1701 had no monopoly on a dislike of foreign immigrants, and whenever a similar prejudice would boil to the surface, someone was likely to rediscover Defoe's brilliant satire—at least this was true into the nineteenth century.

Although the immediate impulse behind the writing of *The True-Born Englishman* was clearly the publication of John Tutchin's poem *The Foreigners*, the background to Defoe's attack on English insularity, xenophobia, and absurd pride in purity of descent was part of the larger scheme to get his fellow Englishmen to see not only that their national affairs were tied to those of Europe but that they were connected to the Continent by a historic pattern of immigration. In his *Appeal to Honour and Justice*, written almost fifteen years after the event, he described his motivation entirely as a reaction to *The Foreigners*:

During this time, there came out a vile abhor'd Pamphlet, in very ill Verse, written by one *Mr. Tutchin*. and call'd THE FOREIGNERS: in which the Author, *who he was I then knew not*, fell personally upon the King himself, and then upon the *Dutch* Nation; and after having reproach'd his Majesty with Crimes, that his worst Enemy could not think of without Horror, he sums up all in the odious Name of FOREIGNER.

This fill'd me with a kind of Rage against the Book; and gave birth to a Trifle which I could hope should have met with so general an Acceptation as it did, I mean, *The True-Born-Englishman*.[19]

As we have seen, Defoe went on to state that it was this work which brought him to the attention of William III. Whatever doubts there may be about Defoe's becoming first known to the King at so late a date, there is little question about the services he performed for William and his reward.

Defoe did not mention Tutchin's poem at all in the 'Explanatory Preface' added to the ninth edition and frequently reprinted with Defoe's

[19] *Appeal to the Honour and Justice, Though It Be of His Worst Enemies, Shakespeare Head Edition*, 195.

poem, but instead he stressed the general ideological basis of his work. Far from mocking the English for their mixed descent, he intended rather to praise England for its intermingled races and merely attack the vanity of those who absurdly emphasized their nobility.

These sort of People, who call themselves True-Born, *and tell long Stories of their Families, and like a Nobleman of* Venice, Think a Foreigner ought not to walk on the same side of the Street with them, *are own'd to be meant in this* Satyr. *What they would infer from their long Original, I know not, nor is it easie to make out whether they are the better or the worse for their Ancestors: Our* English *Nation may Value themselves for their* Wit, Wealth *and* Courage, *and I believe few nations will dispute it with them but for long Originals, and Ancient* True-Born *Families of* English, *I wou'd advise them to wave the Discourse. A* True English *Man is one that deserves a Character, and I have no where lessened him that I know of; but as for a* True Born English *Man, I confess I do not understand him.*[20]

The concept of nobility of birth is absurd enough, Defoe argues, without having English men or women making a claim to it. The great puzzle is why English men and women should do it in a commercial nation:

> Wealth, howsoever got, in *England* makes
> Lords of Mechanicks, Gentlemen of Rakes.
> Antiquity and Birth are needless here;
> 'Tis Impudence and Money makes a Peer.[21]

The message of the work is radically egalitarian. Echoing the ideology of Brathwait, the author of one of his childhood books, and drawing upon the Roman satirist Juvenal, Defoe proclaims at the end:

> For Fame of Families is all a Cheat,
> *'Tis Personal Virtue only makes us great.* (vi. 309)

Tutchin and his poem made an easy target for Defoe's satire, and he was hardly the only poet to find Tutchin's attack upon the Dutch presence in England both narrow-minded and lacking in gratitude. Tutchin cast his poem in the 'parallel' pattern of Dryden's *Absalom and Achitophel* with its narrative of ancient Israel. This time the writer urges the Jews to cast out the foreign Gibeonites, and Tutchin displays all the classic attitudes of national prejudice even to the extent of complaining of the way the Dutch spoke the English language:

---

[20] Daniel Defoe, 'The Explanatory Preface' from *The True-Born Englishman*, in *True Collection*, i, sigs. B1v–B2.

[21] *The True-Born Englishman*, in *POAS*, vi. 279. Subsequent references to this work will refer to this edition and be included within parentheses in my text.

Our *Hebrew*'s murder'd in their hoarser Throats;
How ill their Tongues agree with *Jewish* Notes!
Their untun'd Prattle do's our Sense confound,
Which in our Princely Palaces do's sound:
The self-same Language the old Serpent spoke,
When misbelieving *Eve* the Apple took.[22]

Tutchin ignores all the help that the Dutch gave the English during the time of the Glorious Revolution, and reiterates the usual charge that William's friends, Bentinck and Keppel, were actually William's homosexual lovers. Although Bentinck (Tutchin's Bentir) fought with William at the Boyne and in Flanders, Tutchin sees no reason for English troops to be led by a foreigner. Admittedly there is no direct attack on William in Tutchin's poem, but Defoe and others took Tutchin's Dutch-bashing as aimed directly at William's right to reign.

Tutchin had excellent Whig credentials, but both Defoe and John Dennis regarded his politics as giving comfort and ammunition to the enemy. Compare, for example, Tutchin's lines:

When no Successor to the Crown's in sight,
The Crown is certainly the Peoples Right
If Kings are made the People to enthral,
We had much better have no King at all:
But Kings, appointed for the Common Good,
Always as Guardians to their People stood.
And heaven allows the People sure a Power
[To chuse such Kings as shall not them devour:][23]

with Defoe's discussion of government:

But if the *Mutual Contract* was dissolv'd,
The Doubt's explain'd, the Difficulty solv'd:
That Kings, when they descend to Tyranny,
Dissolve the Bond, and leave the Subject free.
The Government's ungirt when Justice dies,
And Constitutions are Non-Entities.
The Nation's all a Mob, there's no such thing
As Lords or Commons, Parliament or King.
A great promiscuous Crowd the Hydra lies,
Till Laws revive, and mutual Contract ties:
A Chaos free to chuse for their own share,
What Case of Government they please to wear. (vi. 292)

---

[22] John Tutchin, *The Foreigners*, in *POAS*, vi. 240.   [23] Ibid. 242.

In his response to Tutchin's poem (*The Reverse*), John Dennis, Whig though he was, denied Tutchin's notion that the people select their rulers. Defoe put forward a different theory. When the laws are violated, the contract between a ruler and the people dissolves and the state returns to its original state. That state is not Locke's social condition established by an initial social contract but a 'Chaos' more like Hobbes's state of nature. The state dissolves into the 'promiscuous Crowd' which comprises all members of society. The revolution that occurs uses the mob as its agent, though in England, the people who possess property will become the heirs of the revolution. What Defoe describes in this work and in several others written at the time is a classic bourgeois revolution. Even after he came to experience mobs at first hand and witnessed the seemingly misguided mobs of 1710, at the time of the famous Sacheverell Trial, he never renounced this idea.

The True-Born Englishman was a powerful political poem. It was intended to please and influence a wide audience by its wit and irony. In 1727 Defoe was to claim that, as the result of his attack, the kind of nationalism that inspired Tutchin's poem could no longer hide behind the common phrase 'a true-born Englishman'; that whereas it was once an extraordinarily common phrase and an unexamined platitude, it was hardly to be heard after 1701.

NATIONAL Mistakes, vulgar Errors, and even a general Practice, have been reform'd by a just Satyr. None of our Countrymen have been known to boast of being *True-Born English-Men*, or so much as to use the Word as a Title or Appellation ever since a late *Satyr* upon that National Folly was publish'd, tho' almost Forty Years ago. Nothing was more frequent in our Mouths *before* that, nothing so universally Blush'd for and laugh'd at *since*. The Time, I believe, is yet to come, that any Author printed it, or that any man of Sense spoke it in earnest; whereas, before you had it in the best Writers, and in the most florid Speeches, before the most august Assemblies, upon the most solemn Occasions.[24]

Defoe was always aware of the way language and gesture operate to convey meaning. The evidence for the mixture of nationalities in England is revealed in the language itself:

> From this Amphibious Ill-born Mob began
> *That vain ill-natur'd thing, an* Englishman.
> The Customs, Sirnames, Languages, and Manners,
> Of all these Nations are their own Explainers:

---

[24] Defoe, *Conjugal Lewdness* (1727), introd. Maximillian E. Novak (Gainesville, Fla.: Scholars' Facsimiles and Reprints, 1966), 400–1.

Whose Relicks are so lasting and so strong,
They ha' left a *Shibboleth* upon our Tongue;
By which with easy search you may distinguish
Your *Roman-Saxon-Danish-Norman* English. (vi. 270)

With a vocabulary, grammar, and syntax revealing signs of the mixed ancestry of the nation, those, like Tutchin, attempting to speak of racial purity reveal the absurdity of their arguments in every line.

Defoe was a great admirer of Dryden, who, indulging in a little self-praise, commended his portrait of the Duke of Buckingham in *Absalom and Achitophel* as creating so much laughter that the victim did not even know that his head was being cut off. Defoe was so witty on pride of lineage that all but those whose particular ox was gored should have been laughed out of the anti-Dutch bias that had afflicted England from the early seventeenth century. Doubtless members of the nobility did not enjoy being told that Arabian horses had longer blood-lines than they. And John Tutchin, whom Defoe bludgeons under the name 'Shamwhig' for some thirty lines, could not have appreciated being held up as an example of ingratitude. But the popularity of the poem suggests how thoroughly pleased the English reading audience was.

William Pittis, who was to cross swords with Defoe on numerous occasions in the future, criticized the poem for including the long section titled 'Sir Charles Duncomb's Fine Speech' toward the end (vi. 261 ff.). Versions of this piece were apparently being circulated in manuscript as a separate poem, but it is hardly out of place within *The True-Born Englishman*. Defoe began his poem with an amusing picture of the Devil subverting various nations through giving each a national character. Ingratitude, exemplified in Tutchin's poem, is made the central English vice, and Charles Duncomb is given a climactic position in Defoe's development of English ingratitude. He is provided with what amounts to an ironic autobiographical monologue in which he reveals that every step in his successful career has been achieved by being ungrateful to those who helped him. Now, just after barely being found innocent on a charge of forging exchequer bills, he has been knighted and made Sheriff of London. Without any intention of reforming his own wicked life, Duncomb notes that, though William had proclaimed that magistrates should follow through on reformation of manners, he need not be feared by any malefactor. Thus ingratitude makes a 'great man' of Duncomb, and the lasting effect is the corruption of the nation.

Unified structure was hardly the hallmark of contemporary satire. Defoe adopted a version of the loose 'instructions to a painter' form of satire in which the poet imagines himself in a gallery filled with portraits. The poet moves from one painting to another commenting on the foibles of the persons in the picture. As a variant, Defoe used 'Satyr' as a muse to guide him from one idea or character to another, but in its effect the device was nearly the same. Although *The True-Born Englishman* was not a highly unified poem, then, the tone of witty abuse directed against the English for their ingratitude toward William and the Dutch is kept constant throughout. Defoe had been reading Juvenal, and appropriated some of his attitude of moral indignation from the Roman satirist.

More will be said about Defoe's poetry later on, but it should be pointed out that this poem belongs to the category of political poetry, a genre that has not met with much appreciation among most critics. Some have argued that the meeting of poetry and politics is something of an accident, and that the important point is whether it meets the test of high art. Poems that are both effective political statements and great works of art are rare indeed. In English, Marvell's 'Horatian Ode', Dryden's *Absalom and Achitophel*, and perhaps a few poems of Yeats and Auden achieve this miraculous junction. Yet few English poets have succeeded in wedding the two forms in a manner that could appeal to readers high and low. Among those writing in languages other than English, Bertholt Brecht and Pablo Neruda appear to have been most successful. Defoe wrote a popular and effective poem, but it was not as finished a work as it might have been. Not that it was without its artistic effects: Defoe uses clever alliteration, assonance, and even complex rhymes, as in the passage on the return of Charles II to England:

> The Civil Wars, the common Purgative,
> Which always use to make the Nation thrive,
> Made way for all that strolling Congregation,
> Which throng'd in Pious *Charles*'s Restoration.
> The *Royal Refugee* our Breed restores.
> With *Foreign Courtiers*, and with *Foreign Whores*:
> And carefully repeopled us again,
> Throughout his Lazy, Long, Lascivious Reign,
> With such a blest and True-born *English* Fry,
> As much Illustrates our Nobility.
> When they look back on all that Crimson Flood,
> Which stream'd in *Lindsey*'s and *Caernarvon*'s Blood:
> Bold *Strafford*, *Cambridge*, *Capel*, *Lucas*, *Lisle*,
> Who crown'd in Death his Father's Fun'ral Pile.
> The loss of whom in order to supply
> With True-Born *English* Nobility,
> Six Bastard Dukes survive his Luscious Reign,

The Labours of *Italian Castlemain*,
French Portsmouth, *Tabby Scot*, and *Cambrian*.
Beside the Num'rous Bright and Virgin Throng,
Whose Female Glories shade them from my Song. (vi. 273–4)

This is a passage that is at once daring in its implications, delicious in its ironies, and extraordinarily well crafted. At a time when the Civil War, the execution of Charles I, and the restoration of the monarchy were regarded as tragic and sacred events, Defoe dismisses them as a common ritual that acts as a laxative to rid the nation of various ills, and mocks the religious import of these events with the image of Charles's court, as a 'strolling Congregation'. The import is that it was more like a company of strolling players than a group of religious believers. The double rhyme of 'Congregation' and 'Restoration' underscores the contrast.

Dryden had viewed Charles II as 'scattering his image throughout the land' at the beginning of *Absalom and Achitophel*, suggesting the munificence of kingship. Defoe sees it as an act of corruption lowering the vocabulary, with his description of Charles's 'Foreign Whores'. Having named some of them at the end of the passage, he will suddenly slip into a pastoral mode by referring to them as 'the Num'rous Bright and Virgin Throng', but by that point the irony is clear enough. Dryden had suggested something godlike in Charles's fertility. Defoe makes him into a ruler who knows the mercantile notion that numbers of people create wealth. Charles performs his duty through 'his Lazy, Long, Lascivious Reign'. The line has an extra syllable, and the liquid 'L' sounds attempt to suggest luxury and indulgence. Defoe follows it with lines in which the vocabulary is mocking. 'Illustrates' is used ambiguously to suggest either that the offspring of these assignations serve as typical examples of the English aristocracy or that they are the guiding lights of the aristocracy. Defoe then shifts into an ironic view of history to name the great men who gave their lives for the monarchy in the civil war only to be replaced by the children of women whose 'Glories' are so great as to be beyond the poet's talents to describe. The passage shows the magnitude of Charles II's ingratitude to the nation that welcomed him back.

Defoe could write this way if and when he wished. But he was more likely to sacrifice poetic artistry in the cause of making a forceful statement. Writing to answer the enquiries of the Duchess of Marlborough, Lord Halifax explained the problem away by saying that 'Defoe has a great deal of Wit' and that he would write 'very well' if his 'necessity's did not make him in too much haste to correct'.[25] Although Defoe was seldom without

---

[25] See the correspondence between the Duchess of Marlborough and the Earl of Halifax in Henry

some financial difficulties, money was not the main difficulty. Unlike a
Samuel Richardson, he was not the kind of artist who enjoyed revision.
When he revised prose works, he usually expanded the original material,
more interested in presenting new ideas than in changing what he had
already written. There is little doubt that he worked over the lines quoted
above, but he was writing on matters that could have been regarded as
libellous and doubtless wanted to get his words exactly right. And too
many sections of this kind would have changed the nature of the poem,
made it less available to a wide audience and less enjoyable to read. A case
has been made for the effectiveness of Defoe's prose as being particularly
open and forceful in a manner that compensated for loose structures.[26] The
same may be said for his poetry. Some passages clearly sacrifice poetic
complexity for forceful statement, but the meeting of poetry and politics
cannot be accidental. There has to be a kind of political poetry that gains
enough in the power of its vision and the force of its ideas to compensate
for the loss of some artistry. Defoe's vision of English history as a succession of one vagabond group after another is both comic and forceful. *The
True-Born Englishman* is not an example of Pope's 'Prose run mad'. It is
effective political poetry at its best.

Defoe's pride in the success of his poem was apparent in his decision to
identify himself as the 'Author of the True-Born Englishman' in most of
his writings—at least those he wished to acknowledge—over the next few
years. But not everyone was pleased by Defoe's combative tone. His
politics, and his dismissal of the importance of heredity and inherited titles,
produced around a dozen replies. The author of *The Female Critick*
assumed Defoe to be Dutch, and pointed out the weaknesses of some of the
rhymes. Nevertheless, she asked a question that was often asked about
works by Defoe: 'the Riddle is, Whom was this Poem calculated to
please?'[27] She saw it as insulting to William III, to religion, and to good
manners and suggested that the writer was inspired by the Devil. She also
suspected him of 'Commonwealth Principles'. This was a fairly typical
reaction. There was something in Defoe's way of writing that caused those

Snyder, 'Daniel Defoe, the Duchess of Marlborough, and the *Advice to the Electors of Great Britain*',
Huntington Library Quarterly 29 (1965), 56–8.

[26] P. N. Furbank and W. R. Owens, *The Canonisation of Daniel Defoe* (New Haven, Conn.: Yale
University Press, 1988), 125–33.

[27] *The Female Critick* (London, 1701), 123. Many critics thought it was inspired by the Dutch and
Huguenots. One writer suggested that it was written by an Irishman. See e.g. the broadside *Englishmen No
Bastards* (London, 1701) and *The English Gentleman Justified* (London, 1701). Bastian thought that this
latter work might have been by Defoe, but I doubt if Defoe would have written, 'I really Believe that this
man in Disguise has made his Verses run Lame, on purpose to Dwell Incognito' (8) in criticism of his own
talent as a poet.

who disagreed with him to rage against him; it is nothing very obvious to a
modern reader, but to some of his contemporaries it was equivalent to
hearing a fingernail scrape across a blackboard.[28] One author quoted the
section on Charles II and called Defoe 'the most murd'ring Viper of the
Earth'.[29] William Pittis, one of a number of pamphleteers in London who
were to make careers out of attacking Defoe's writings, wrote the most
thorough answer in which he questioned the anonymous author's status as
a poet and thinker. But as yet no one identified the work as Daniel Defoe's.

III

Defoe maintained his anonymity through the controversy surrounding his
most successful poem, but there is evidence in his behaviour during the
crisis over the Kentish Petition that he was about to make himself more
widely known. The political situation in England was deteriorating as the
Tory Cabinet, led by Laurence Hyde, Earl of Rochester, seemed to have
no control over the House, which had taken to criticizing William III in a
violent and insulting manner. Although the members of the House of
Commons were elected and a number of the contests for seats were open
enough, it was anything but a democratically elected body. Jealous of their
privileges, which they thought threatened by the House of Lords and the
King, the members felt that they mainly represented themselves. One of
their acts of defiance against the Lords was an attempt to impeach William
Bentinck, first Earl of Portland; Edward Russell, Earl of Orford; John,
Lord Somers; and Charles Montagu, Lord Halifax. The Commons also
refused to pay attention to the threat posed by France to the balance of
power in Europe. In an effort to take control of the Spanish monarchy,
Louis XIV violated the terms of the Second Partition Treaty which he had
signed with England, Holland, and the Empire just nine months before. He
moved forces to the Dutch frontier and occupied the barrier fortresses. On
8 May 1701, five gentlemen from Kent presented a petition to the
Commons requesting protection in the event of a French invasion and for
specific bills providing the King with the means to defend the nation. The
reaction of the Commons to this seemingly legitimate attempt to petition
was to place the five men under arrest and imprison them in the Gate House
for the remainder of the session.

[28] In *A Supplement to the Faults on Both Sides* (London, 1710), Defoe stated that he 'had been continually Persecuted, and at last effectually ruin'd by that very Party' he had affronted in writing his *True-
Born Englishman*. He probably meant the Jacobites and High Churchmen.
[29] *A Satyr upon Thirty Seven Articles* (London, 1701), verso.

What followed six days later, on 14 May, was the presentation of Defoe's *Legion's Memorial* to the Speaker, Robert Harley. It was sometimes rumoured that Defoe gave it to him while wearing a disguise—that of a woman. Defoe corrects this 'mistake', stating that ' 'twas deliver'd by the very Person who wrote it, guarded with about 16 Gentlemen of Quality, who if any notice had been taken of him, were ready to have carried him off by Force'.[30] There is little doubt that this person was Defoe. He then described in his *History of the Kentish Petition* how the *Memorial* 'struck such a Terror' in the members of the House that not only did they abandon their plans to punish the Kentish petitioners further but they began fleeing from London. The House did manage to pass the 'Money-Bills', and was prorogued on 23 June. By the prorogation, the five Kentish petitioners were discharged, and they were honoured at a banquet paid for by the citizens of London. In addition, there was a special place of honour for a person referred to as 'the Champion of the Party' by one unsympathetic commentator. That champion was almost certainly Daniel Defoe. The journey back to Kent was a triumph for the five, and Defoe remarked upon the enthusiasm displayed for them by the people, describing in detail the celebrations at Maidstone. Defoe remarked at the conclusion of the main section of his work that there was no ill feeling toward the institution of Parliament but only toward '*the Conspirators* and *Jacobite party* that are at present the Nation's burthen, and from whom she groans to be redeem'd'.[31] In a concluding section of both prose and poetry, Defoe quoted the act of the thirteenth year of the reign of Charles II making petitioning legal, and stressed the broad popular basis for the opinions expressed in the petition of the men of Kent. The poem, which he later incorporated into his *Jure Divino*, argued some of his basic political tenets, taken mainly from the writings of Hobbes and Rochester's *Satyr against Mankind*:

> Nature has left this Tincture in the Blood,
> That all men wou'd be Tyrants if they cou'd.
> Not Kings alone, not Ecclesiastick pride,
> But *Parliaments*, and all Mankind beside[32]

Defoe was expending some of his wit against the five hundred 'Tyrants' who had sought to replace James II in that role, but there is reason to believe that he had come to the conclusion that human beings—all human beings—were self-interested and acted mainly out of a desire for power. Defoe's radical politics were based upon a need to control this 'Tincture in

[30] *The History of the Kentish Petition*, in *Shakespeare Head Edition*, 91.
[31] Ibid. 95.
[32] Ibid. 100.

the Blood'. He was not content with having written *Legion's Memorial* and *The History of the Kentish Petition*. During the standing army controversy, Defoe had learned the value of writing a number of pamphlets and poems in support of a cause. Some time in June he produced *A New Satyr on the Parliament* in the ironic manner of his previous *Encomium*. He did not hesitate to remind the Commons that they were responsible for leaving the country defenceless, and he echoed the sentiments of *Legion's Memorial* in putting forward a theory of the subservience of the House of Commons to the national will.

> But you, although your Powers depend
>   On every Plowman's Vote,
> Beyond the Law that Power extend,
> To ruine those you should defend,
>   And sell the Power you bought.
> . . .
> You are the Nations darling Sons
>   The abstract of our Mobb;
> For City Knights and Wealthy Clowns,
> Stock Jobbers, Statesmen and Buffoons
>   You may defye the Globe.[33]

There was nothing very elegant in Defoe's rhymes, but as in his earlier lampoon, he showed considerable wit in attacking a House of Commons that was so sensitive about its status.

As one contemporary writer complained, Defoe had fired a barrage of poems and pamphlets at his enemies, and if my scenario is correct, in the role of 'Secretary of State' for the Kentish petitioners, he had actively participated in the events and then written their history. It was a cycle that he was to come close to repeating in his successful work for the Union between England and Scotland, but in many ways this was perhaps his least ambiguous triumph as a writer and activist. He had achieved it by taking a stance in *Legion's Memorial* that was truly revolutionary. His signature, 'Our Name is Legion and we are many', was an allusion to the reply of the devils to Christ (Mark 5: 9), when he cast them out of the body of the man who was possessed. Defoe was appealing to a satanic spirit of revolt, and if the overt message of *Legion's Memorial* did not carry this meaning clearly enough, the language code embodied in individual phrases would leave no doubt. He appealed to the 'Right' to correct the government by 'Englishmen' who were no more to be 'Slaves to *Parliaments* than to a King'.[34] In

---

[33] *POAS*, vi. 324–5.
[34] *Legion's Memorial*, in *Shakespeare Head Edition*, 112.

fact Defoe's part in staging this affair may have loomed large. He was certainly very close to the most active of the petitioners, Sir William Colepepper, during the following years, and the open admiration that Colepepper was to express about Defoe's abilities is suggestive of how important his role was.

Defoe's participation in this affair led him to formulate some theoretical positions concerning the nature of government, and he apparently felt it was time to make a more systematic statement than hitherto. At the end of December, he published a pamphlet with the title *The Original Power of the Collective Body of the People of England, Examined and Asserted*. This was partly a reply to Sir Humphrey Mackworth's *Vindication of the Commons of England* (1701), an attempt to set forth the view of the Commons as a body in no way dependent upon any kind of electorate. In response, Defoe argued that the members of the Commons were merely representatives of the property-holders of the nation. They served only so long as they were obedient to the laws—laws which were essentially based upon reason. The people, he argued, had a right to revolt against any of the three branches of the government on the first occasion of a breach in obedience to the law, since such a violation would dissolve the contract that established the government in the first place. The key to Defoe's system is property. If a king owned all of the land on which his citizens lived, he might rule as an absolute monarch. Similarly, if one person owned all of the land, he could dispossess the king. Defoe's argument that the rights and powers of the people derived from property has its main basis in Harrington's *Oceana* rather than in the writings of John Locke, with whom Defoe is often associated. On the other hand, the notion that the freeholders constituted a collective body that might reshape the government at the first sign of disobedience to the laws is somewhat more radical than what Harrington proposed.

Not surprisingly, such ideas led some observers to think that Defoe wanted to overthrow the government. A contemporary critic thought that 'One might read the Downfall of Parliaments in his very Countenance'.[35] And Edward Ward saw him as the representative of all the Dissenters in their politics:

> Their Notions Machiavellian, Hobbish,
> Draw *Multitudes*, because they're *Mobbish*.[36]

---

[35] *An Account of Some Late Designs to Create a Misundersanding betwixt the King and his People* (London, 1702), 18.
[36] Edward Ward, *The Dissenting Hypocrite or Occasional Conformist* (London, 1704), 12.

Indeed, though the property-holders were the ultimate governors of England in his scheme, Defoe gave a role to the mob in overthrowing a bad government. A decade later, an author attacked both Defoe and John Tutchin for precisely this concept:

> Who ascribe to the poor, undistinguishing Drudges,
> Both the Power of Kings, and the Wisdom of Judges;
> Till at length they believe, they've a Right of Chastizing
> Those that shew'd 'em the Method of thus Tyrannizing?[37]

Defoe was concerned as much with the more passive concepts of rights as with power, and the subject of the work may be better reflected in the sub-title to the main section in which 'Original Right' is the key phrase. He was later to refer to the work as 'Original Right' in the Review.[38] Defoe lays down the principle that 'all Government and consequently our whole Constitution, was originally design'd and is maintain'd, for the Support of the People's Property, who are the Govern'd'. This comes under the heading 'Salus Populi suprema Lex'. Everything follows from this assumption. Sometimes the voice of the people is indeed the voice of God, and some-times the 'Power' vested in a representative body may be reassumed by the whole. When the government stops following the law,

> *The Nation's all a Mob; there's no such thing*
> *As Lords and Commons, Parliament or King.*
> *A great promiscuous Croud the* Hydra *lies,*
> *Till Laws revive, and mutual Contract ties.*

Although he reserves control of the government to the citizens of property, he leaves no doubt that all the inhabitants form the 'Universal Mob' that carries out the violence often necessary for change.

IV

In addition to Defoe's triumphs as 'Secretary of State' of the Kentish peti-tioners, he had to regard 1701 as a year of brilliant successes. Looking backwards to this time in his *Appeal to Honour and Justice*, Defoe praised the new monarch of Britain, George I, and appealed to the wisdom of the decision made at that time to settle the succession on the House of Hanover and to give the power to make such a choice to Parliament. He pointed to William III as the force behind such decisions:

---

[37] *The Galloper* (London, 1710), 6.   [38] See *Review*, iii. 654; iv. 417.

call to mind who it was that first Guided them to the Family of *Hanover*, and to pass by all the Popish Branches of *Orleans* and *Savoy*, recognizing the just authority of parliament, in the undoubted Right of Limiting the Succession, and Establishing that Glorious maxim of our Settlement, (viz.) That *it is inconsistent with the Constitution of this Protestant kingdom to be Govern'd by a Popish Prince.* I say let them call to mind who it was that guided their Thoughts first to the Protestant Race of our own Kings in the House of *Hanover*, and that it is to king *William*, next to Heaven it self, to whom we owe the Enjoying of a Protestant King at this time.[39]

Although Defoe believed that it was necessary to have the union between England and Scotland to ensure the permanence of the Act of Settlement, the firm beginning was made on 12 June 1701, when William gave his agreement to the Act as passed by the Commons. The very personal importance of this event is demonstrated by Defoe's decision to baptize his daughter Sophia at Hackney parish church on 24 December 1701. She was certainly named after Sophia, the Electress Dowager of Hanover, whose family was named in the Act of Succession as the heirs to the English throne if neither Princess Anne nor William had any more children. So overjoyed must Defoe have been to think that his country, which had escaped the efforts of James II to move in the direction of Catholicism, was to remain a Protestant nation that he celebrated the future arrival of the House of Hanover in this manner. And not only did he celebrate by naming his daughter, he also felt enough confidence in the Protestant destiny of the nation to permit a ceremony that he refused to allow his other children to undergo. Did William III encourage Defoe in this regard? As he wrote of his relationship with William in his *Appeal*, it seems as if the subject of the successful passage of the Act of Succession was something both men delighted in at a time when so few good things were happening in the House of Commons.

Before the happy outcome of this issue, Defoe wrote several pamphlets on the succession. He dedicated *The Danger of the Protestant Religion*, published on 9 January 1701, to King William. He stressed the hatred of Louis XIV toward the Protestant religion and argued for the need to defend it at all costs. He pointed to the nightmarish extirpation of the Huguenots in France and raised the spectre of the religious wars against Protestantism in Europe over the past two centuries as likely to repeat themselves unless Englishmen prepared to fight for their beliefs. How much Defoe was writing to William and to the propaganda of the moment and how much he really believed his alarmist message is difficult to say.

[39] *An Appeal to the Honour and Justice*, 196.

A more complicated work on the subject of the succession by Defoe appeared shortly afterwards, *The Succession to the Crown of England Consider'd* to be followed by one written in an ironic tone, *An Argument, Shewing that the Prince of Wales, tho' a Protestant has no Just Pretensions to the Crown of England*. In the first of these, he apologized for trying to see what the future prospects of the country might be with the statement 'I am no Dreamer of Dreams, nor the Son of a Prophet', an allusion both to the warnings against false prophets in Deuteronomy and to the true prophet, Daniel.[40] In fact, Defoe's frequent attempts to judge the future on the events of the present led to a good deal of mockery concerning his resemblance to his biblical namesake. In this pamphlet, he argued that the succession depended not so much on heredity as on the choice of 'the People Collectively'.[41] He then put forward his own candidate, the son of the Duke of Monmouth, the man he had followed into battle. Raising the old notion that Charles had actually been married to Monmouth's mother, Defoe proposed a return to the cause for which Monmouth had fought and died. But Defoe's next candidate was the heir of Hanover, and he proposed that George ought to be brought over to England to learn about the institutions of the nation he was to rule.

His next pamphlet addressed rumours that there was a plot to kidnap the son of James II, turn him into a Protestant, and prepare him to assume the throne. Since Defoe supported the right of Parliament to select the monarch, as set forth in the Act of Succession, he thought the notion of England as a nation desperate for a legitimate heir absurd: 'But that which adds to the Banter too is that we shou'd steal him away, *Bless us all!* that we shou'd turn *kidnappers* for a king and spirit folks Children away.'[42] And he concluded in the mood which saw everyone motivated by self-interest. 'Mankind', he wrote 'is said not to be able to do that which their known Interest forbids them to do.' Why then, he asked, would anyone in England dream of doing such a thing so much to the disadvantage of all citizens? Then, in a style echoing Congreve's Lady Wishfort, he wondered whether it might not be better to make Louis XIV himself the next King of England. That, indeed, would bring reality home: 'And as to the Barr of Religion, pray what's that to a good Army; what's the Gospel to a Kettle-Drum? or Justice and Laws to a Regiment of Curiasseeres? If the French King comes once to have a fair Claim to the Crown of *England* for his

---

[40] *The Succession to the Crown of England Consider'd* (London, 1701), 3.
[41] Ibid. 6.
[42] *An Argument, Shewing that the Prince of Wales, Tho' a Protestant, Has No Just Pretensions to the Crown of England* (London, 1701), 18–19.

Grandson, and you have nothing to plead in Barr but his Religion, he'll talk with you about that in other Terms.'[43]

In this way even the question of the succession was ultimately tied to bringing the country to an awareness of the necessity of a war with France. In October he issued one of his first ironic titles, *Reasons against a War with France*. In some sense the title is not entirely ironic, since Defoe argues the advantages of thinking more in terms of a war with Spain. 'There never was yet a War between the *English* and the *Spaniard*,' he wrote, 'but that we made Extraordinary Advantages of their *West-India* Wealth.' [44] By putting the emphasis upon the profitability of a war with Spain as opposed to the grim series of battles that had been the War of the Grand Alliance, Defoe was trying to make the war more attractive, especially to the business community. But of course the war *was* to be with France, and in maintaining that there was no reason to go to war just because Louis had upset the balance of power in Europe and broken the Treaty of Ryswick, Defoe began his pamphlet with a series of those ironies at which he was soon to become expert. The coming war also aroused him to explain why he and other members of the livery companies refused to vote for a Jacobite, and he found time to write an appeal to Jacobites to abandon their stance and enter the mainstream of English politics. He probably wrote this after the death of James II in September 1701 and before Louis, somewhat foolishly, transferred his allegiance to James's son, despite his promise to recognize William as England's king.

Defoe's emphasis upon the advantage of a war with Spain and upon the possibility of taking away some of Spain's colonies in the New World may have had some connection with a scheme that Defoe and William Paterson presented to King William. A manuscript of this proposal, dated 12 December 1701, was in Defoe's possession and was later among some documents deposited by Defoe's descendants in the Bodleian Library. Patterson and Defoe proposed colonizing the areas of South America now equivalent to the southern parts of Chile and Argentina. Defoe was to propose such an adventure again to Robert Harley in 1711, and was eventually to write a fictionalized version of an explorative march through this area in *A New Voyage Round the World* (1724). But fiction was the furthest thing from Defoe's mind in 1701 as he saw himself part of a scheme that would open up the goldmines of South America for his exploitation. He was to tell Harley that the 'Wealth of the Place in Gold' was 'Incredible', and it should

---

[43] *An Argument, Shewing that the Prince of Wales . . .*, 24.
[44] *Reasons Against a War with France* (London, 1701), 15.

remind us that the Defoe who invested in a diving-engine to bring up sunken treasure had not disappeared, despite his plunge into politics.[45]

The only work Defoe wrote during this eventful year that was not entirely associated with these political struggles was an economic tract, *The Villainy of Stock-Jobbers Detected*, though even here there is some link. At the beginning of the pamphlet he refers to a work published a month before, on 23 January, *The Free-Holders Plea against Stock-Jobbing Elections of Parliament Men*. In that work, Defoe used the image of the newly flourishing stock market to protest against the evils of the system of voting in England. Because of rotten boroughs, places with small or no populations continued to send men to Parliament. Instead of an expanding role for freeholders in choosing representatives, it seemed as if more and more seats were being sold to the highest bidder. Not only did Defoe believe that a potentially representative form of government was being thwarted, but he argued that, with the buying and selling of seats, a situation was being created by which the French might be able to buy into English politics. The threat of a sinister French plot to subvert English politics connects this work to his interests during this year, but *The Villainy of Stock-Jobbers Detected*, despite its allusion to the pamphlet on elections was for the most part a conservative expression of Defoe's dislike of selling stocks. He regarded stock-jobbers as middlemen who made money by manipulating stocks far beyond any intrinsic value they might have. This had happened with East India stocks at a time when an older East India Company and a New Company were competing with each other. Defoe placed the blame on the Old Company, for their attempt to drain London of 'ready Money' and create a run on the Bank and the Exchequer, but he urged regulation of all stock negotiations.

Defoe was a great believer in the power of credit. He had gone far beyond the mercantilist tendency to worship precious metals, but he still thought that money and credit 'as the Sun and Moon alternately *Enlighten* and *Envigorate* the World'.[46] When a recoinage was necessary, the shortage of money resulted in a drying up of trade and inevitably of credit. He disliked the volatility of the stock market, the excessive reliance upon speculation, and the nature of making money in a way so far removed from labour, craft, and the management, buying, and selling of goods. And this extended to a dislike of the way successful stock-jobbers were entering Parliament and becoming a force in the land. Defoe's populism had an economic side as well, then, in a hearty dislike for financial manipulation. If

[45] See H 345–9.
[46] *The Villainy of Stock-Jobbers Detected*, in *True Collection*, i. 255.

the politics of this tract were only peripherally attached to his work against France and for the Protestant Succession, it nevertheless has much the same emotional origins and appeal.

Defoe was becoming increasingly visible at this time, and few of his pamphlets failed to provoke replies. As we have seen, his very countenance, as it was observed at the Mercers' Chapel following the release of the Kentish petitioners, was seen to contain the 'Downfall of Parliaments'.[47] A response to Defoe's lampoon, *The Ballad*, picked up his image as a satanic leader of the mob, accusing him of being 'a meer Devil in endeavouring to sow the Seeds of Discourd among thy Fellow Subjects'.[48] In addition to the works which he actually published, Defoe's name became associated with the *Black List*, a publication that appeared some time after William dissolved Parliament on 4 November. There was nothing ingenious in the writing of this list of 167 names of Tories whose voting records were regarded as especially awful. What was new was the use of the press to circulate such a list. It was very much in the manner of the lists of moral offenders published by the Societies for Reformation of Manners, and given Defoe's involvement with these groups and his understanding of how the press might be used for propaganda, it is hardly surprising that his name was associated with this enterprise. John Tutchin said in his *Observator* that he had heard 'Hundreds of his Party (I mean the Modern Whigs) affirm' that Defoe was the 'Author' of this work along with *Legion's Memorial* and other works associated with the Kentish petitition. Certainly Defoe was to deny any part in this work, but we have to balance his reasons for such a denial against Tutchin's extensive contemporary sources.[49]

Whatever role Defoe may have had in the listing of 167 members of the Parliament dissolved by William on 4 November 1701, he was not averse to naming individual members of the House of Commons whom he thought deserved notice for their behaviour. He did not name himself as master of the lampoon in his *Pacificator* without a reason. *England's Late Jury*, published in November 1701, selects twelve members of the House of Commons who were particularly active in opposing William III and in attempting to punish the King's friends, the four Whig lords. Frank Ellis suggests that Defoe's poem might have been one of the reasons why four of the members of Defoe's 'Jury' were defeated in the next election in December 1701: Charles Davenant, Anthony Hammond, John Howe, and

---

[47] *An Account of Some Late Designs*, 18.

[48] *The Ballad . . . Answered along with Memorial Paragraph by Paragraph* (London, 1701), 33.

[49] John Tutchin, *The Observator*, 6–9 Jan. 1703; and *The Second Part of the Mouse Grown a Rat* (London, 1703), 19.

Matthew Prior.[50] If Defoe worried about France buying off Parliament, he at least had some cause. Charles Davenant, one of Defoe's twelve-man jury, was discovered dining with the French chargé d'affaires in September, along with Anthony Hammond and a number of other Tory members of the House. Jack Howe, another member of the 'Jury', was also in the French interest. The defeat of some of these men and the election of a Parliament that would support William in his struggle against France ended the year on a note of triumph. Defoe was close to being famous, his brick and tile factory was prospering, and he had a new daughter, Sophia, who was to be his favourite. It must have seemed too good to last, and last it did not.

[50] POAS, vi. 344.

8

An Age of Plot and Deceit, of Contradiction and Paradox

In March 1702 William III died. He had been out riding in Richmond Park when a new horse, Sorrel, stumbled and fell as he started to gallop. William had suffered a similar accident in November 1700 without much injury, but this time he broke his collarbone and hurt his shoulder in the fall. The fracture had to be set again after a jolting ride from Hampton Court to Kensington. He was unable to write or put on a coat for eight days but otherwise conducted business in the usual manner, except that he found that he could not go to Parliament to recommend one of his greatest designs, a union between England and Scotland—the Union that his agent, Defoe, was to work on tirelessly in 1706. Though a broken collarbone was not serious in itself, William suffered through a series of fevers and agonizing pain, dying finally on the morning of 8 March. Toasting Sorrel or the mole who had made the obstruction that was thought to have caused the accident became common in Jacobite circles, in honour of horse or the rodent who had done what all the plots and all the missiles fired by the armies of Louis XIV had failed to accomplish.

William was extraordinarily generous toward those he liked, and Defoe knew that he had lost a patron of a character he would never see again. In his autobiographical *Appeal to Honour and Justice* of 1715, Defoe expressed his sense of abandonment in what may seem to us an accent of self-pity, as he remarked on:

the Immortal and Glorious Memory of that Greatest and Best of Princes, and who it was my Honour and Advantage to call Master as well as Sovereign, whose Goodness to me I never forgot [, neither can] forget; and whose Memory I Never patiently heard abused, nor ever can do so; and who had he liv'd, would never have suffered me to be treated as I have been in the World.[1]

---

[1] *An Appeal to Honour and Justice Though It Be of His Worst Enemies*, in *Shakespeare Head Edition*, 195.

Defoe was probably right. He had lost his protector, his guarantee that whatever he wrote or did, however outrageous, he would be forgiven. After William's death he should have been cautious, but he seems to have enjoyed the success of his satires, with their Juvenalian indignation, too much to have given them up easily. He should have remembered that Juvenal wrote about Nero's Rome after it was safe to do so.

Queen Anne's speech to Parliament following the King's demise must have provided some comfort to Defoe but also some apprehension. She spoke of 'maintaining the Succession to the Crown in the Protestant Line', of her 'true Concern . . . for the Laws and Liberties of *England*', and of a possible 'Union' with Scotland. But in speaking of 'our Religion' did she mean the Church of England exclusively? And what interpretation might be placed upon her moving statement, 'I know my Heart to be entirely *English*'?[2] Was it to be taken as a slap at William's memory? Certainly Defoe might have seen in her words an end to an emphasis upon England's role on the Continent.

For the moment, at least, Defoe did not grasp how complete a change had occurred. William was one of the heroic figures whom he imagined to be working out God's plan on earth. Thus in *The True-Born Englishman*, he had called upon Britannia to speak of William's greatness:

> *My Hero, with the Sails of Honour furl'd,*
> *Rises like the Great Genuis of the World,*
> *By Fate and Fame wisely prepared to be*
> The Soul of War, and Life of Victory. (vi. 296)

For Defoe, William was the living embodiment of the Glorious Revolution in every way: toleration for Dissenters, rights and liberties for every Englishman clearly stated and firmly established, a Protestant succession for England forever. Defoe's vision of history was progressive. He looked forward to the repeal of the Test Act forbidding Dissenters to serve in government, to the growth in trade that William had encouraged with plans to expand English colonies to South America, to reform of Parliament and elimination of its rotten boroughs, and to reform of manners that would give England the appearance of a polite and moral nation. He probably did not grasp emotionally that a relatively peaceful revolution such as that of 1688 might be followed by a period of reaction and that Anne would allow, if not encourage, turning back the clock on many reforms of the Glorious Revolution.

---

[2] William Cobbett, *The Parliamentary History of England* (London: Bagshaw, 1810–20), vi. 5.

I

The Duchess of Marlborough, whose husband had once been dismissed by William, complained that she did not get as much pleasure out of William's death as she had expected. Nevertheless, the English did not exactly surpass themselves in their funeral arrangements for a King who had rescued them from the tyranny of James II. Defoe added up the accomplishments of William's fourteen-year reign:

> The legislative Power he set Free,
> And led them step by step to Liberty,
> 'Twas not his Fault if they could not Agree.
> Impartial Justice He protected so,
> The laws did in their Native Channels flow
> From whence our sure Establishment began,
> And *William* laid the first Foundation Stone:
> On which the stately Fabrick soon appear'd,
> How could they sink when such a Pilot steer'd?
> He taught them due defences to prepare,
> And make their future Peace their present care:
> By him directed, Wisely they Decreed,
> What Lines shou'd be expell'd, and what succeed.[3]

The author of *The Mourners*, a poem Defoe may have had in mind when he wrote his elegy, saw matters differently. He blamed William for everything wrong from 'Taxes strung like Neclaces together' to the 'dismal Weather' England had been experiencing.[4] And as has been mentioned, there were poems in praise of William's horse, Sorrel, along with attacks on his favourites. He was buried at midnight in a private ceremony. Gilbert Burnet dismissed the excuses given for such an action, noting that the funeral 'was scarce decent, so far was it from being magnificent'.[5]

Defoe responded to this scarcely muffled joy at William's death with his poem *The Mock Mourners*, which he placed in a position of honour, just after the *The True-Born Englishman*, in his collection of poetry and prose. In some sense it was a continuation of the former, since that very ingratitude he had named as the quintessential English vice appears again in his personified rendering of the English nation which now is shown as newly aware of how important he was. The influence of Dryden, both *Absalom*

---

[3] *The Mock Mourners*, in *True Collection*, i. 44–5.
[4] In Frank Ellis (ed.), *Poems on Affairs of State: Augustan Satirical Verse, 1660–1714* (New Haven, Conn.: Yale University Press, 1970) (*POAS* vi), 362–3.
[5] *Bishop Burnet's History of His Own Time*, 2nd edn., ed. Earl of Dartmouth et al. (6 vols., Oxford: Clarendon Press, 1833), iv. 570.

and *Achitophel* and *Mac-Flecknoe*, is apparent in verse after verse as it was in his *True-Born Englishman*, and as with that poem he calls up the ideal concept of the nation, Britannia, to deliver a eulogy over William. Defoe dedicated the poem to Queen Anne and addressed her as someone who must continue carrying on William's work. The preface is a kind of wish list: Anne must feel resentment toward those who undervalued William, since William fought against all those who would oppose Anne's reign; she must continue the fight for Protestantism in Europe; and (as a final wish) may all those who opposed William find disfavour with her.

A few months later, Defoe published *Reformation of Manners*, a poem bound to make him enemies. If he had lampooned various members of the society before, he excelled himself in this rogues' gallery made up of members of the Societies for Reformation of Manners who had failed to practise what they preached. Defoe had made this point before in his *Poor Man's Plea*, where he argued that the purpose of the Societies was not or ought not to be punishing the poor for their misdeeds. If they functioned in this way, they were simply instruments of power wielded by the upper and middle orders to control the masses of poor men and women. Defoe now decided to name those members of the Societies whose private lives were shameful. 'Nor does the *Satyr* assault private Infirmity, or pursue Personal Vices,' he claimed, 'but is bent at those who pretending to suppress Vice, or being vested with Authority for that purpose, yet make themselves the Shame of their Country, encouraging Wickedness by that very Authority they have to suppress it'[6] Defoe was probably to resign, some years later, from the Edinburgh Society for Reformation of Manners, which he helped to found, on precisely these grounds—the refusal of members of the group to reform their own lives. But however principled may have been Defoe's stance, he seemed incapable of resisting the pleasure of revealing how paradoxical were the lives of these reformers.

Defoe's list of offenders included judges such as Sir Robert Jeffries and Sir Salathiel Lovell. He accused the first of enjoying the whipping of barebreasted prostitutes and the second of accepting bribes, but he really warms to his task with his portrait of Sir Henry Furnese:

> This is the man that helps to Rule the State,
> The City's New-reforming Magistrate.
> To execute the Justice of the LAW
> And keep less Villains than himself in Awe:
> Take Money of the Rich, and hang the Poor,

---

[6] *Reformation of Manners*, in *True Collection*, i. 65.

> And lash the Strumpet he debauch'd before.
> So for small Crimes poor Thieves Destruction find,
> *And leave the Rogues of Quality behind.*[7]

Defoe's satire carries him to a variety of topics, including a fierce attack upon slavery and the colonialism practised by the early Spanish conquistadors. Since he was a defender of English colonialism, this must appear odd. But *Reformation of Manners* is an ethical not an economic treatise. Defoe attacks the slave trade without ceremony, where greedy Europeans 'barter Baubles for the *Souls of Men*', and turn the slaves into beings who 'fear no Hell, *but where such Christians go*'. If the early Spanish explorers succeeded in killing 'thirteen Millions of Souls', the English colonists are seen as equally brutal.[8] Even in his economic treatises Defoe advocated decent treatment of slaves. However, his appeal for such treatment was to the greater profit to be made by such actions. He did not see a conflict between morality and trade, as has sometimes been suggested; rather he viewed trade as immoral in its very nature.

No one would claim much organization in this poem. Defoe ends the first part with an attack on atheism, and begins the second part by leaving the city for the vices of the nobility who live in the country. The exploits of the Cowper family occupy the first part. The father and his two sons succeed in committing a variety of sins from debauchery to polygamy, from hypocrisy to murder. Then Defoe takes up the growing drunkenness all over England. Admittedly it was a subject worthy of a Hogarth, and Parliament was eventually to pass a variety of acts during the eighteenth century to control the consumption of alcohol. Defoe sees it as dehumanizing the citizenry and destroying the nation's health. Yet here again, Defoe was an importer and dealer in wines and brandies. Even allowing for his separation of economics and ethics, it has to be said that as a businessman he was part of the problem rather than the cure. From drunkenness Defoe turns to religion and musters his gallery of fools and knaves, from the fierce High Churchman Edward Pelling, who once imagined that he had become pregnant, to a number of fanatical Anglican preachers. The final section gives the characters of a group of noble rakes, the 'Men of Wit' at Will's coffee-house and the poets. Again, this attack is about morality, aimed at poets who feel compelled to add a certain degree of lewdness to their poetry if they expect to attract readers and escape starvation. Defoe complains that a purely moral work would be turned down by the booksellers with the words, ''Twou'd not hit the Times, 'Twou'd never Sell.'[9] All of

---

[7] *Reformation of Manners*, in *True Collection*, i. 72.   [8] Ibid. 77.   [9] Ibid. 105.

this might make us think that Defoe was not averse to avoiding his own critique when he came to write *Moll Flanders* and *Roxana,* but at least these two women have excuses for their sins as a product of their poverty. The chief targets for Defoe are the rich and powerful, and he was certainly creating a long list of enemies, some of whom would play a role in his fall.

Neither of these poems had the power or skill of his *True-Born English-man.* The rhymes are sometimes awkward and the energy behind his satire occasionally flags. They were effective enough as political statements, but the powerful paradox that sustained his earlier attack on a narrow xeno-phobia was absent. Inspiration returned, this time not in poetry but in prose, with *The Shortest Way with the Dissenters*, which was continually enlivened by parody of what he considered to be the fanaticism of the High Church advocates. Always a good mimic, Defoe succeeded wonderfully in capturing the feverish rhetoric of the High Church sermons. In defending this work, he claimed he could show that his words were no more out-rageous than those he imitated and blamed himself for failing to supply examples of the passages he was imitating:

For that he did not quote either in the Margin, or otherwise the Sermon of *Sacheverell*, aforesaid, or such other Authors from whom his Notions were drawn, which would have justify'd him in what he had suggested; but these men do not see the Design of the Book at all, or the Effect it had. . . , The Case the Book pointed at, was to speak in the first person of the Party, and then, thereby, not only speak their Language, but make them acknowledge it to be theirs, which they did so openly, that confounded all their Attempt afterwards to deny it, and to call it a *Scandal* thrown upon them by another.[10]

If this were truly Defoe's only purpose, *The Shortest Way with the Dissenters* would have to be regarded as parody in the neutral sense of pure ventriloquism, but clearly much more was intended. Henry Sacheverell never wrote anything so outrageous as Defoe's piece. If Sacheverell had gone beyond innuendo and suggestive language imagery such as the 'bloody Banner', to which he alluded, he would have got into trouble with the authorities almost as quickly as Defoe. Defoe's High Churchman, on the other hand, calls for outright violence and persecution of the Dissenters. Parallel passages are instructive:

[Defoe] Alas! *The Church of England!* What with Popery on one hand, and Schismaticks on the other; how has she been Crucified between two Thieves. Now, *let us crucifie the thieves.* Let her foundations be Established upon the Destruction of her Enemies: the Doors of Mercy being always open to the

[10] *The Present State of the Parties in Great Britain* (London, 1712), 24.

returning Part of the deluded People: Let the obstinate be rul'd with the Rod of iron. Let all true Sons of so Holy and Oppressed a Mother, exasperated by her Afflcitions, harden their Hearts against those who have oppress'd Her. *And may God Almighty put into the hearts of all the Friends of Truth, to lift up a Standard against Pride and Antichrist, that the Posterity of the Sons of Error may be rooted out from the Face of this Land for ever.*[11]

[Sacheverell] In a word, Let Us be *True* to Our Selves, and Our Profession, Especially as it Concerns Us more Particularly of *This Place*, who are Entrusted with the Education of the *Future Patriots* of it, and Let Us Scorn to Trim, Waver, and Double with the Opinions and Interests of *These Halters betwixt God and Baal*, but let us Steadily Adhere to the Good Old Stanch Principlers of Our Church, and Fear not, *Tho She be Troubl'd on every Side, She shall never be Distress'd; thos he is Perplex'd, yet She shall not be in Despair; tho' She be Persecuted, She shall not be Forsaken; tho' Cast down, She shall not be Destroy'd; neither Shall the Gates of Hell be ever Able to prevail Against Her.*[12]

Sacheverell concludes with an appeal to the High Churchmen to stand fast by their principles, Defoe with a paean of hatred and destruction which drives home his main point: that the High Church has abandoned the very charity which is the essence of the Christian way of life.[13]

Defoe borrows the important passage on the crucifixion of the Church from Sacheverell. Noting the continual attack upon the Church of England by the 'Sectarists', the clergyman remarked that 'To Accomplish This Villainous Conspiracy, *Herod* and *Pontius Pilate* tho' never so much at Variance before, could immediately become Friends, Forget each Other's Interests and Resentments, and be Reconcil'd in the same Common Design of Crucifying *Their Lord and Saviour*, betwixt Thieves and Robbers.'[14] By his cry, '*Now let us Crucifie the Thieves*' Defoe's High Churchman identifies his cause with that of the enemies of Christ. Admittedly, Defoe must have gotten considerable private amusement at his depiction of the sufferings of the Church of England, since he thought the Dissenters had really been the ones to suffer, but there are elements which should have been available to any good reader that would have allowed him or her to understand that what was being read was a *reductio ad absurdum* of the High Church position. Indeed, one copy in the British Library has manuscript notes in a

[11] *The Shortest Way with the Dissenters*, in *True Collection*, i. 434.

[12] Henry Sacheverell, *The Political Union, a Discourse Shewing the Dependence of Government on Religion in General* (London, 1702), 24.

[13] For a discussion of the rhetorical strategies in *The Shortest Way with the Dissenters*, see M. E. Novak, 'Defoe's *Shortest Way with the Dissenters*: Hoax, Parody, Paradox, Fiction, Irony, and Satire', *Modern Language Quarterly* 27 (1966), 402–17.

[14] Sacheverell, *Political Union*, 62.

contemporary hand which list all the statutory violations that Defoe's speaker commits in his eagerness to rid the nation of these 'harmful Toads'. Sacheverell would never have been permitted to say:

If one severe Law were made, and punctually executed, that who ever was found at a Conventicle, shou'd be Banish'd, the Nation, and the Preacher be Hang'd, we shou'd soon see an end of the Tale, they would all come to Church; and one Age wou'd make us all One again.[15] (i. 430)

Defoe's speaker convinces not so much by what he says as by the force of his voice. He is a true fanatical visionary, egotistic and blind to the larger implications of what his slaughter would mean. We have none of the details about the speaker's private life that are present in Jonathan Swift's *Modest Proposal* to which Defoe's work has so often been compared. Instead we have the character type already sketched by Andrew Marvell in his *Rehearsal Transpros'd* thirty years before. It has sometimes been argued that Defoe failed because he wrote fiction rather than satire, but in an odd way Swift's speaker is closer to a complex fictional character than Defoe's one-dimensional fanatic. Yet if we recognize in Swift's creation the voice and language of the well-intentioned projector whose schemes, though presented in a rational and innocent manner, will destroy the fabric of society, we hear in the words of Defoe's clergyman something equally familiar, the message of the dangerous demagogue who dehumanizes his enemies to make their destruction appear both necessary and ethical.

Defoe may have thought that he could handle *The Shortest Way* in much the same manner as he managed the standing army contoversy and the affair of the Kentish petition. A controversial work would appear which would spark a national debate over toleration. There would be a massive outpouring of pamphlets on the subject of religious toleration, and the High Church would be exposed as a group advocating extreme measures. He may even have engaged his fellow Whig John Tutchin to support his efforts. Tutchin was brought to trial for arguing in his *Observators* that Defoe's picture of the dangers created by the High Church were essentially right, and managed to escape only because of a legal technicality. Tutchin's character listed some of the outrageous arguments of Defoe's High Churchman:

Here's a fine Rogue, A'nt Please your Worship! He's making out *Smithfield* for the way of Reformation, and is very sorry that the Spirit of Martyrdom is over, Hanging, Drawing, and Quartering! A pious Christian I'll warrant him: He commends the Discipline of Lewis the 14th towards the Hugonots, throughout his

---

[15] *The Shortest Way*, i. 430.

whole Book; and recommends the Gallies as things very necessary to row the
Dissenters into the Church of *England*. . . . This is certainly the most Impudent
Fellow in the World, to Prescribe Rules of Destruction, of any of Her Subjects to
Her Majesty.[16]

Indeed, Tutchin saw just how insolent the author was to all sides, and
though he denied knowing who wrote it, he probably knew or suspected
that it was a hoax and that Defoe was the author.

Defoe may have written *Reflections upon a Late Scandalous and Malicious
Pamphlet*, a work that appears to have been intended as the first reasoned
response to *The Shortest Way*. At any rate, Charles Leslie, a Non-juror and
future antagonist of Defoe, thought it was his.[17] The author of this work
displayed the kind of irony concerning the High Church that was typical of
Defoe; he begins by throwing some doubt on whether the author was a
Catholic, a Non-juror, or a Dissenter but says he will take the work at its
face value 'let him be serious or otherwise'.[18] The writer then proceeds to
identify the arguments with those of Sacheverell and Charles Leslie, and
suggest that the pamphlet undermines the 'Revolution Principles' upon
which Queen Anne's government is founded:

It were endless to animadvert upon all the extravagant Passages of this invenom'd
Libel, which is writ on purpose to set the nation in a Flame, and to engage us in an
intestine War, that the *French* King may have an opportunity to force the pretender upon us. His advising to send all our Dissenters to the Gallies and Gallows,
his sounding a Charge to a general Massacre of 'em, and his proposing the *French*
Kings Method with his Protestant Subjects, who he reproachfully call *Hugonots*, as
a fit Model and a proper Instance for our Incouragement to attempt it; his falling
foul upon the Act of Succession and the Family of *Hanover*, his outragious
Reflections upon the late K. *William* and his Government, and his Advice
to subdue the *Scots* instead of uniting 'em, are so unpolitick, inhuman and un-
christian, that I could not at first perswade my self that any man who calls himself
a Protestant, could be so much inspir'd by hell as to write such a Libel.[19]

It would not be unusual for Defoe, who signed himself 'Legion', to see
himself as a satanic provocateur. He took advantage of acting 'in Disguise'
to mount a defence of Occasional Conformity as acceptable if seen as a
public declaration that the parties were not Catholics and as an act to be left
to the conscience of the individual party. The author closed with the wish
that *The Shortest Way* would act as a warning for the moderates in the

[16] *Observator*, 71 (23–6 Dec. 1702).
[17] Charles Leslie, *The New Association* (London, 1703), ii. 7.
[18] *Reflections upon a Late Scandalous and Malicious Pamphlet Entitul'd the Shortest Way with the
Dissenters* (London, 1703), p. iii.
[19] Ibid. 22.

society to close ranks and realize that the real enemy was the threat of persecution and 'Arbitrary Power'.[20]

In 1705 the author of *The Diverting Post* remarked on Defoe's tendency to put himself in painful situations:

> As Quacks for Pence, and Praises from the Mob,
> Their Legs and Arms with seeming Pleasure Stab;
> So how, (and yet I own thy Wit) D.F.—
> Such a ridiculous Animal art thou.
> Else why so fond, like Bessus in the Play,
> To study thy own Kicking ev'ry Day?[21]

Defoe must have considered the possible disasters that could arise from his work. Somewhere in the back of his mind, he must have known that the government would be outraged and the Queen, who had expressed her devotion to the Church of England, furious. But Defoe was a gambler and could not resist the perverse pleasure of approaching the edge of an abyss.

In Defoe's defence, it should be pointed out that the *Poems on Affairs of State*, which appeared after the end of the Licensing Act in 1695, were filled with works using a mask or persona to establish a paradoxical position. 'This, Sir,' wrote Defoe, 'is an Age of Plot and Deceit, of *Contradiction* and Paradox.'[22] He grew up during the seventeenth century, when the 'sceptical' method of argument through paradox was considered to be more convincing because less dogmatic. In treating controversial subjects—luxury, political freedom, prostitution, drunkenness—Defoe preferred to raise questions, pretend to have no solution, and then insert his own opinion obliquely. That he should extend the innuendoes of the High Church into a stated attack upon the establishments of Church and State would have seemed to him similar to the satiric techniques used by his favourite poet, Rochester. Defoe issued an 'Explanatory Preface' in a second edition of his work which noted the imitation of passages from Sacheverell and claimed that he had employed 'an *Irony not unusual*'.[23] He referred to his piece as an 'Ironical Satyr' as late at 1710.[24] By satire he merely meant a didactic work containing a strong argument or attack; by irony, simply the idea that what he was saying was the opposite of what he believed. To this general genre concept he added the notion of 'dissimulation' or writing through a persona or mask. His critics did not think his method quite so traditional.

---

[20] *Reflections upon a Late Scandalous and Malicious Pamphlet*, 27.

[21] *The Diverting Post* 18 (24 Feb. 1705).

[22] *Review*, vi. E523.

[23] *A Brief Explanation of a Late Pamphlet, Entituled, The Shortest Way with the Dissenters*, in *True Collection*, i. 436.

[24] *A Supplement to the Faults on Both Sides* (London, 1710), 37.

One of them wrote that it was a very odd sort of irony, a 'dextrous Hocus Pocus', that resembled 'the most bitter Satyr or *Sarcasm*'.[25] Others objected to the obscurity of the technique, suggesting that the reader could not know when the irony stopped. Was the fanatical High Churchman's praise of Queen Anne intended ironically? If Anne was being praised by a person one author described as 'the worst of Men', could not such praise be taken ironically as an attack upon the Queen?[26] But perhaps the most telling complaint had to do with the effectiveness of Defoe's fictional creation. His audience was ill-equipped to read Defoe's text. One bemused commentator complained that Defoe 'Teaches us how to make other People's Thoughts speak in our words'.[27] Another accused him of 'invading the Conscience' by using a fictional speaker.[28] Defoe was not yet writing the prose fiction that is the basis of his modern reputation, but even in so highly rhetorical a work as *The Shortest Way*, he was able to give his readers the feeling that they could hear the voice of Defoe's High Churchman as if he stood in an imaginary pulpit in the mind of each reader.

II

The government was not amused. This time Defoe had slipped over the edge of the abyss. Some time after the publication of his work, he went into hiding. A High Church partisan who answered his work accused him of making Queen Anne into a monarch who would go back on her word. 'If this be not Sedition,' he wrote, 'What is an Incendiary; what is the Man that makes it his Practices to stire up Divisions, and sow the Seeds of Dissention?' This writer suggested that Defoe was wise to remain in hiding, since, if discovered, he would suffer 'a brutal punishment'.[29] Defoe's authorship was announced by Countryman in the *Observator* for 30 December–2 January 1702, giving Tutchin an opportunity to denounce Defoe as a false 'Modern' Whig, one of those who supported the need for maintaining an army during the standing army controversy. A week later, the *London Gazette* announced a reward of £50 for information leading to the apprehension of 'Daniel de Fooe', the author of a 'Scandalous and Seditious' pamphlet.

By the next issue they had a description of Defoe for their readers, and

[25] *The Fox with His Fire-Brand Unkennell'd and Insnar'd* (London, 1703), 4, 5.
[26] *Reflections upon a Late Scandalous and Malicious Pamphlet*, p. iii.
[27] *The Fox with His Fire-Brand*, 13.
[28] *The Sourse of Our Present Fears Discover'd*, 3rd edn. (London , 1706), sig. A4.
[29] *The Shortest Way with the Dissenters . . . Consider'd* (London, 1703), 9, 26.

while a bulletin of this kind is hardly the best way of picturing him, it is our first view of him:

He is a middle Sized Spare Man about 40 years old, of a brown Complexion, and dark brown coloured Hair wears a Wig, a hooked Nose, a sharp Chin, grey Eyes, and a large Mould near his Mouth, was born in *London,* and for many years was a Hose Factor in Freeman's-yard, in Corn hill, and now is Owner of the Brick and Pantile Works near *Tilbury-Fort in Essex.*[30]

Defoe was probably not more than five feet five inches, but by contemporary standards he may have fitted into the category of 'middle Sized'. Unfortunately, we have nothing in between the grotesque portrait of Defoe that emphasizes the sharpness of his chin, the hook of his nose, and the mole and the idealized engravings by Jeremiah Taverner and Michael Van der Gucht.[31] That he was easy to caricature suggests that he was also easy enough to recognize. Defoe may well have left London for a short time, and perhaps even went to Holland where a search was made for him. For the most part, however, he probably remained in London, aided by a radical Whig underground among tradesmen and craftsmen. One contemporary writer suggested that there were a number of times when Defoe barely escaped by leaping through a window.[32]

Whether or not Defoe actually jumped from a window just ahead of his pursuers, he was clearly dismayed by the revenge sought by the government. It was his old antagonist, Robert Harley, who set matters in motion. Defoe had expressed his contempt for the House of Commons during the Kentish petition debates, and without knowing the author of the work, Harley nevertheless considered that its comments reflected on the actions of the House. On 14 December he got the Lord Treasurer, Sidney Godolphin, to begin the investigation.[33] Godolphin assigned the job of ferreting out the author to Daniel Finch, Earl of Nottingham, Secretary of State for the southern region, and on 29 December Nottingham issued a warrant for Edward Bellamy, an agent of Whig propaganda. Taken into custody on 2 January, Bellamy admitted to carrying the manuscript to the printer, George Croome. On 3 January Nottingham ordered that Defoe be

[30] *London Gazette,* 11 Jan. 1702–14 Jan. 1703.

[31] The idealized portrait appeared before Defoe's *Jure Divino* (1706). The engraving was supposed to have been based on a painting by Jeremiah Taverner which formed the basis for the cruder engraving by Van der Gucht that appeared as the frontispiece to the first volume of *True Collection* (1703). The most detailed caricature was by George Bickham in *The Whig Medley* (1710).

[32] See *The Shortest Way with the Dissenters . . . His Name Exposed* (London, 1703), 22. This tract, which I have not seen, is quoted by William P. Trent in his manuscript biography, Trent Collection, 76.

[33] See H 5, n. 3. References to this collection of Defoe's letters have been included within parentheses in my text.

taken into custody and his papers seized, and that he should be brought before him for examination.

The arrest of Bellamy and the printer clearly alarmed Defoe. His *Brief Explanation of a Late Pamphlet* was almost entirely conciliatory in tone. He maintained that he had been misunderstood, and apologized for any misapprehension of what he intended. 'The Author', he wrote, 'humbly hopes he shall find no harder Treatement for plain *English*, *without Design* than those Gentlemen for their Plain Design, in Duller and Darker *English*.' He 'humbly hopes the Lords of her Majesties Council, or the House of Parliament, will be no longer offended, and that the Poor People in trouble on this account shall be Pardoned or Excused'. Again, on the confusion over his intention to expose the intolerance of radical elements among the High Church and Nonjurors, he lamented, ''Tis hard, after all, that this should not be perceived by all the Town, that no one man can see it, either Churchman or Dissenter.'[34] Defoe was attempting a pose of sincere apology, but he was not entirely convincing, partly because he continued to believe he had performed a public service. For all the language of humility in these passages, he was still boasting of his ability to write in a manner that attracted attention, still telling the House of Commons how to behave, and still suggesting that the real fault lay with the dullness of his readers, who could not understand what he was trying to do. Humility was not one of Defoe's most genuine emotions. He could show it when he was in prison or when he thought he was in danger of being hanged, but as soon as he escaped present danger, he would emerge as irritatingly cheeky as ever.

Defoe remained at large, and, his body being absent, Nottingham decided to punish the text. On 25 February 1703 he brought a formal complaint before the House of Commons, who resolved that 'this book being full of false and scandalous Refleections on this Parliament, and tending to promote Sedition, be burnt by the hands of the common Hangman, to-morrow in New Palace Yard'. They read particularly from pages 11, 18, and 26.[35] If Defoe was lurking about the apartments he had in Westminster near New Palace Yard, he might have smelled the smoke coming from his burning pages. He had remarked in his *Essay upon Projects* some six years earlier that nothing sold so well as a book treated in this manner. If there were any illiterate persons in England who had not read *The Shortest Way* before this bit of book-burning, they would certainly have known about it now.

[34] *Brief Explanation of a Late Pamphlet*, in *True Collection*, i. 436–8.
[35] *JHC* (1803), xiv. 207.

On 9 January 1703 Defoe wrote to Nottingham expressing his distress at those who had been imprisoned because of his pamphlet and attempting to make terms. He mentioned certain 'Menaces' made by the officers, and concerns about revenge 'as Respected former Things' thought to have been done by him. He expressed the fear of imprisonment as his chief reason for not surrendering, adding as he often did, the image of his long-suffering family:

My Lord a Body Unfitt to bear the hardships of a Prison, and a Mind Impatient of Confinement, have been the Onely Reasons of withdrawing My Self: And My Lord the Cries of a Numerous Ruin'd Family, the Prospect of Long Banishment from my Native Country, and the hopes of her Majties Mercy, Moves me to Thro' my self at her Majties Feet, and To Intreat your Lordships Intercession. (H 1–2)

He offered to come into custody if he could secure certain guarantees, noting that he knew that the Queen did not usually 'Capitulate with an Offending Subject'. He mentioned that he had sent his wife to see Nottingham, who had demanded that he surrender to the authorities and answer questions. Defoe then suggested that Nottingham make a list of questions for him to answer, suggesting that he hoped he would receive a sentence 'a Little more Tollerable to me as a Gentleman, Than Prisons, Pillorys, and Such like, which are Worse to me Than Death' (H 2). He then made an extraordinary proposal. Noting that prisoners were often spared a death sentence in exchange for volunteering to serve in the armed forces, he suggested:

If her Majtie Will be pleased to order me, to Serve her a year, or More at my Own Charges, I Will Surrendr my Self a Voluntier at the head of her Armyes, in the Netherlands, To any Collonell of horse, her Majtie Shall Direct, and without Doubt my Lord I shall Dye There Much More To her Service than in a Prison; and If by my Behaviour I Can Expiate This Offence, and Obtain her Majties Pardon, I shall Think it much More honourable to me Than if I had it by Petition. (H 3)

He then offerred to 'Raise her Majtie a Troop of horse, at my Own Charges, and at the head of Them Ile Serve her as Long as I Live'. He ended by suggesting his willingness to serve Queen Anne 'with my hand, my Pen, or my head' (H 3).

This is a remarkable letter, and the contents were by no means kept secret. One journalist was to mock 'Colonel' Foe's offer as an absurd gesture.[36] The modern novelist, Stefan Heym, has seen it as essentially

---

[36] John Tutchin, *Observator*, Wed. 7 July 1703.

rebellious.[37] It tells us a great deal about him. He was a man who thought highly of himself and his abilities. His notion of himself as a 'Gentleman' was not to be shaken. He was to write to William Paterson, just before he was to be imprisoned, that he lacked 'passive courage' (H 6). This letter shows that he had a great deal of active courage. He apologizes for seeming to make terms with the Queen, but for all the terms of humility, he believed fervently in the rights of the ordinary Englishman, even before his sovereign. He sent his wife to treat for him, a sign that he knew she would not break down before the likes of 'Dismal', as the dour Nottingham was called, and a sign of his trust in her. His offer to head a regiment in Flanders may have betrayed a romantic streak in him, but he was always fascinated by warfare. He may have seen this as a new life that he could begin—a life about which he may have dreamed for years. Robinson Crusoe's brother ran away from his home and his solidly middle-class father to become a soldier. Finally there is the offer of his mind and talents as an activist and a writer. Even if the government had merely heard rumours of his role in the controversies of King William's reign, Defoe's offer must have struck men like Harley and Godolphin as something to think about.

Defoe was attempting to bargain for some kind of position from which he could get some leniency. One biographer has suggested that he was acting like the hosier of Freeman's Yard, trying to buy low so that he could sell high, but Heym's intuition may be right. He was negotiating like a man who believed in the revolutionary principles that transformed England in 1689 and produced the Bill of Rights. He did not consider himself a criminal. He had written a work intended to alert the nation to what he thought really lay behind the threats of Sacheverell, and not for one moment did he genuinely believe he had committed a crime. For what reason, then, should he be punished? The biographer Wilson saw Defoe calmly surrendering himself to the authorities, but everything suggests that he was not for a moment ready to throw himself on the mercy of his enemies without a struggle. The person who discovered him would receive £50, enough money to live for a year, and Defoe would have been aware of the temptation. His account of how he was recognized by someone while he was walking in the fields near his home in Hackney has the ring of truth. Drawing his sword, he forced the man to his knees and made him swear that if he saw Defoe again he would shut his eyes until the fugitive from the law was able to move half a mile off. There is considerable violence in this account. Somehow in the back of his mind, Defoe seems to have carried an imaginative identification with such swashbuckling figures as the comte

[37] Stefan Heym, *The Queen Against Defoe* (New York: Lawrence Hill, 1974), 33–4.

de Rochfort, whose frequent duels and life as a fugitive had become the subject of fiction.[38]

In April 1703 Defoe wrote to William Paterson, whom he had once joined in formulating a scheme for an expedition to the base of South America. He rehearsed his offers to Nottingham about serving as a colonel of horse, and spoke convincingly of the psychological effect that being a fugitive had upon him. The thought of 'Jayls, Pillorys and Such like' had unnerved him, and after remarking on his inability to endure such thoughts, he added, 'I Shall Never for the Future Think my Self Injur'd if I am Call'd a Coward' (H 6). He noted that he had no difficulty earning a living, though he does not say how. But the main point of the letter was to get Paterson to reach Robert Harley. Defoe mentions Harley's standing with Queen Anne. Defoe may have been honest enough in expressing admiration for Harley's 'Character Among Wise Men' (H 5), despite having battled against Harley during the affair of the Kentish petition. Having realized how impossible dealing with Nottingham would be, he may have recognized in Harley someone with whom he could work. For some reason, Paterson did not send the letter to Harley until 28 May, eight days after Defoe was captured in the home of a French weaver named Sammen in Spitalfields.

Was Defoe relying upon the Huguenot community to recognize in the defender of the Dissenters someone who was undergoing the same experience they had suffered in France? Was he ready to leave for Scotland?[39] He was clearly unprepared. He had 'many Libells and papers' on his person when he was taken, and it cost £1 10s., charged against the Treasury, for Nottingham to go through all of them in several meetings.[40] According to the author of *The Republican Bullies*, they included the scandalous poem on Queen Anne's physician, Dr David Hamilton, which the author believed to be written by Defoe, and documents written in different types of disguised handwriting, all of which were produced by Defoe.[41] Nottingham wrote to Godolphin on 25 May that the person who had turned in Defoe wanted to remain anonymous but would be paid.

[38] Defoe knew Courtilz's *Memoirs of the Count de Rochefort* and drew upon it later for *Colonel Jack*.

[39] J. R. Moore used Defoe's account of a dream from Defoe's *History and Reality of Apparitions* about a man who had a vision that he would be captured by the agents of the Secretary of State if he went to London. He goes anyway and is captured. Defoe changes the time to 1701. If this is to be taken as factual, he was in hiding around Barnet. This was an area not far from Stoke Newington, where he was to live for the last years of his life, and there is a ring of truth to the account; but he was in no need of telling a true story, and it is hard to determine how much fiction entered this account.

[40] PRO T54 (18), fo. 365.

[41] *The Republican Bullies* (London, 1705), 3. The author of this pamphlet accused Defoe of ingratitude for not thanking Robin Stephens, who aided in his arrest, for removing the verses about Hamilton from the offending documents.

Defoe was sent to Newgate prison, and the stage was set for his enemies to even past scores. He was examined by Nottingham, but gave him no information that he wanted. Nottingham must have believed that Defoe was privy to many of the transactions by the Whig Junto during the reign of King William, and probably shared with Charles Leslie and others the notion that some sinister, secret group of plotters had put Defoe up to writing *The Shortest Way*.[42] Nottingham focused some of his questioning upon the Parliament of 1701. He probably knew something of Defoe's role in the events of that year, and Defoe seems to have given some account of his actions; but he implicated no one else. Leslie apparently believed that many Whigs and Dissenters knew about the 'Secret', of who wrote *The Shortest Way* and what its purpose really was. As late as 1712, Charles Hornby spoke of it as the work of the 'Party'.[43] Those who thought Defoe inspired by 'Devils' saw no difference between such supernatural inspiration and that of the 'Revolutionists' and 'Anarchists' with whom they associated the author. Defoe apparently told Nottingham that he acted entirely alone and pleaded ignorance of any secret knowledge. In a letter to William Penn, who apparently suggested that he could get out of Newgate if he told what he knew, Defoe assumes the moral position of those who, during the hearings led directly or inspired by Senator McCarthy during the 1950s, would admit their own involvement but refused to name others:

Sir The Proposall you are pleas'd to hint By your Son from My Ld Nottingham, of discovering Partyes is the same which his Lordship has often Put upon me before.

   Sir in Some Letters which I have Sent his Lorship I have Answer'd him with the Same Assurance . . . : That if my Life were Concern'd in it I would Not Save it at the Price of Impeaching Innocent men, No More would I Accuse my Friends for the Freedome of Private Conversation. . . . I have no Accomplices, No Sett of Men, (as my Lord Call'd Them) with whom I used to Concert Matters, of this Nature, To whom I us'd to show, or Reciev hints from them in Ordr to These Matters, and Therefore to Put it upon Condition of Such a Nature is to Offer me Nothing Attall. (H 8)

Good for Defoe! He may indeed have lacked some forms of courage, but he was not going to betray his friends.

   As Defoe's letter to William Penn reveals, Nottingham was not convinced that Defoe was telling the truth, but it was apparent that, short of torture, Defoe was not going to 'confess'. On 5 June Defoe was released on

[42] Defoe gave a brief account of his interview in *The Consolidator* (1705), where he made the unfulfilled promise to provide a full account some time in the future. See Defoe, *The Earlier Life and Chief Earlier Works*, ed. Henry Morley (London: Routledge, 1889), 366.
[43] Charles Hornby, *Caveat against the Whigs*, 2nd edn. (London, 1712), iv. 39.

bail for the very large sum of £1500. He put up the largest amount, £500; Robert Davis, his brother-in-law and intimate companion during these years, added £250; and the same sum was added by Joseph Whitaker, a 'Broker', Thomas Powell of Saroch Street, St Andrew, Holborn, and Nicholas Morris of Turnmill Street, Clerkenwell, identified as a baker.[44] Robert Davis was listed as a shipwright and his address as Tilbury, where Defoe had his brick and pantile works. Defoe had lived part of the year at his factory, keeping close supervision over production, and was even accused of having kept a mistress there. Davis was probably attempting to keep the business going in Defoe's absence, but it was a lost cause. Davis may have been ingenious enough, but he probably knew nothing of the way the clay, once mixed and refined, had to weather through the spring and how it had to be fired. This chief source of Defoe's wealth, bringing in an estimated £700 a year, was rapidly deteriorating, and he was faced with bankruptcy once more.

His freedom lasted just a month. On 5 July he appeared in court to be charged with libel. The indictment stressed his action in writing and publishing *The Shortest Way* as a direct affront to Queen Anne.[45] He had to confront a group of judges who were not at all friendly: Sir Edward Ward, Sir John Fleet, Sir Edwin Clarke, and Sir Thomas Abney.[46] Abney was the practitioner of occasional conformity who had been attacked by Defoe in the second printing of *An Enquiry into the Occasional Conformity of Dissenters*, Ward and Fleet were connected with the East India Company, which Defoe criticized on numerous occasions, Lovell was singled out as a hanging judge in Defoe's *Reformation of Manners* and was a good example of the kind of resentment Defoe might have had to encounter:

> He has his Publick Book of Rates to show,
> Where every Rogue the Price of Life may know:
> And this one Maxim always goes before,
> He never hangs the Rich, nor saves the Poor.
> God-like he nods upon the Bench of State;
> His Smiles are Life, and if he Frown 'tis Fate:
>
> . . .
>
> Fraternities of Villains he maintains,
> Protects their Robberies, and shares the Gains,
>
> . . .

[44] Corporation of London PRO, SF475, 5 June 1703.
[45] Ibid. SF472.
[46] For a full discussion of these men and their animus toward Defoe, see John Robert Moore, *Defoe in the Pillory and Other Studies* (Bloomington: Indiana University Press, 1939), 1–32.

With haughty Tone insults the Wretch that dies,
And sports with his approaching Miseries.[47]

It might be thought that anyone willing to write such a personal attack upon a villainous but eminent figure of the law would have the wisdom to make certain that he would never be in a position to face him. But it should be clear by now that Defoe seldom paid much attention to his safety. On 7 July a list of prisoners in Newgate included 'Daniel De Foe find for publishing a Seditious Pamphlett call'd the Shortest Way with the Dissenters'.[48] The trial had not been long. Defoe's attorney, Sir William Colepepper, one of the five Kentish petitioners and a close friend, persuaded Defoe to plead guilty and appeal for mercy. Sir Simon Harcourt, the Queen's Attorney-General, who had appeared in Defoe's *Reformation of Manners* as a magistrate who ought to be driven from a position of power, delivered a speech on the danger to the state of pamphlets such as Defoe's, and Defoe was sentenced to a fine of 200 marks (about £133), to stand three separate times in the pillory, to be on 'good behaviour' for seven years, and to remain in Newgate until he could give some evidence of that good behaviour.

Defoe was formally sentenced among a group of thirty criminals. If the future author of *Moll Flanders* could have taken his mind off his troubles long enough to observe them, he would have found them an intriguing group. There were two men accused of murder, and among the more notable figures was a famous prize-fighter. Seven were sentenced to death, nine were branded on the left cheek, two were ordered to be whipped. The ordeal of the pillory could end in death, but at the time Defoe might well have looked about him and thought that despite the humiliation involved, he was not the most unfortunate person in the world. The places assigned for his sentence were in Cornhill near the Royal Exchange, in Cheapside near the Conduit, and in Fleet Street by Temple Bar. He was to stand for one hour between 11 and 3 with a paper on his hat listing his offences. The original dates set aside for his first exposure were 19, 23, 26, and 29 July.[49]

Biographers have contrasted the severity of this sentence to that received by a variety of journalists, and John Robert Moore has suggested that Defoe's judges were taking their revenge upon him for the lampoons he had written. Certainly John Tutchin writing in his *Observator* for 10 July

[47] *Reformation of Manners, a Satyr* ([London,] 1702), i. 70–1.
[48] 'A True and Perfect Kallender of the Names of all the Prisoners in Newgate for Fellony & Trespisses the 7th Day of July 1703', Corporation of London PRO, SF475.
[49] *The Proceedings on the Queen's Commission of the Peace: Oyer and Terminer and Gaol Delivery of Newgate . . . On Wednesday, Thursday and Friday, being the 7th, 8th, and 9th Days of July, 1703* (London, 1703).

suggested that it seemed entirely unfair, but this was the view of a fellow Whig journalist who, despite his differences with Defoe, shared a great deal of common political ground as well as some feeling for a fellow author. The author of *The Scribbler's Doom; or, the Pillory in Fashion,* however, considered the sentence normal enough. He wrote about Defoe in the form of a dream vision in which Defoe is visited by William Fuller in Newgate. Fuller fabricated information in an attempt to convince the government of a plot. His first sentence was roughly equivalent to Defoe's. Fined 200 marks, he was ordered to stand in the pillory. The second time around, in 1702, he was fined 1000 marks, forced to stand in the pillory three times for two hours at a time, whipped, and sent to Newgate. In the pamphlet Defoe is seen as rejecting any resemlance to Fuller with scorn, but the writer insists that his vision is 'matter of Fact in several degrees'.[50] Charles Leslie thought that *The Shortest Way* was intended to get the Dissenters to start butchering members of the High Church before they became victims themselves, and others saw it as intended to frighten the Dissenters into another Rebellion.[51] In short, we are right to see Defoe as a defender of freedom of speech, but in attacking Defoe's pamphlet as a 'seditious libel', as a work intended to create significant disturbances in the state, Defoe's judges, in arriving at their punishment, were probably acting within parameters that appeared reasonable to them.

Defoe's account of his motives for pleading guilty appeared in a scarcely disguised allegory in *The Consolidator* two years later, and indicates that he felt that he and his attorney, Colepepper, had made a big mistake. As the allegory describes it, the prosecution had a major problem: it was obvious that Defoe did not endorse the words he put into the mouth of his High Churchman in *The Shortest Way*; and also that he was confident he could prove from High Church writings that his speaker indeed represented High Church views:

so they fell to wheedling him with good words to throw himself into their hands and submit, giving him that gewgaw the public faith for a civil and gentleman-like treatment. The man, believing like a coxcomb that they spoke as they meant, quitted his own defence, and threw himself on the mercy of the queen, as he thought; but they, abusing their queen with false representations, perjured all their promises with him, and treated him in a most barbarous manner, on pretence that there were no such promises made, though he proved it upon them by the oath of the persons to whom they were made. Thus they laid him under a heavy

---

[50] *The Scribbler's Doom; or, the Pillory in Fashion* (London, 1703), 8.
[51] See e.g. Leslie, *The Wolf Stript of His Shepard's Cloathing*, 3rd edn. (London, 1704), 60.

sentence, fined him more than they thought him able to pay, and ordered him to be exposed to the mob in the streets.[52]

Defoe then remarked upon Nottingham's attempt to extract information from him as a 'comical dialogue', but that Defoe himself found it at all 'diverting' at the time is questionable.

Could Defoe have pleaded innocent? One scholar has argued that it would have been impossible from a legal standpoint. Since the laws of libel simply asked the jury to decide only on two questions of fact, whether the accused writer was indeed the author and whether it had the meaning attached to it, there was hardly any room to decide that Defoe was innocent.[53] William Trent, who had considerable legal training, maintained that although an admission of authorship was practically equivalent to a guilty plea, 'by pleading guilty he cut himself off from the chance of bringing extenuating circumstances before the court'.[54] This may have been the key mistake. Whatever the instructions to juries in libel cases, the parallel with juries in criminal cases often produced similar results. Juries in libel cases frequently decided cases on 'matters of fact'. John Hawes, in a tract written in 1680, had argued that juries had this right.[55] The fact that Defoe appealed in a letter of 12 July 1703 to William Penn, who had been acquitted in a case by a jury that refused to follow the instructions of the prosecution, suggests that Defoe had some awareness of the legal history of such cases. It is surely possible that had Defoe been able to manoeuvre popular opinion in his favour, as he was to do at the pillory, he might have been acquitted or had his sentence reduced. It is even possible that, like John Tutchin, whose trial for libel was connected with Defoe's, he might have had the case dismissed on some kind of technicality. Defoe surely had some such possibilities in mind when he maintained that he had made a terrible mistake.

[52] Daniel Defoe, *The Consolidator*, in *Earlier Life and Chief Earlier Works*, 366.
[53] See Paula Backscheider, 'No Defense: Defoe in 1703', *PMLA* 103 (1988), 274–84.
[54] William Petersfield Trent, 'A Biographical and Bibliographical Study', MS biography of Defoe, Trent Collection, 81.
[55] John Hawes, *The Grand-Jury-Man's Oath and Office Explained: and the Rights of English-Men Asserted* (London, 1680), 13–14, 18–20. See also Henry Care, *English Liberties: Or, the Free-Born Subject's Inheritance* (London, 1680), 205–28.

9

From Pilloried Libeller to Government Propagandist

In his letter of 12 July 1703 to William Penn, Defoe pointed out that he was urged by some friends to take advantage of his bail to flee. 'I agreed', he wrote, 'to give the Court No Trouble but to plead Guilty to the Indictment, Even to all the Adverbs, the Seditiously's, the Maliciously's, and a Long Rapsody of the Lawyers et Ceteras; and all this upon promises of being us'd Tenderly' (H 8). He apparently thought that he might yet avoid the pillory, and urged Penn to continue his services. He had also sent his attorney, William Colepepper, to see Nottingham the day before, but Colepepper, while waiting to see Nottingham, asked an indiscreet question about whether the admiral, Sir George Rooke, was with the fleet or in Bath. Rook was a Tory, and the remark was taken as a political attack by a Whig. The injection of partisan politics at this point was unfortunate for Defoe. The Tory Secretary of State, Nottingham, would accept nothing more from Colepepper, who was to become the victim of physical assaults by the friends of the admiral.

Penn pleaded that Defoe's sentence be deferred, and Defoe may have offered to give some more information in the hope that something might come up. On 18 July, Nottingham wrote to postpone the sentence. Two days later, Defoe was taken from Newgate to be interviewed at Windsor.[1] Interestingly enough, the keeper of Newgate warned Nottingham that to remove Defoe might create technical legal problems, since it could be considered a discharge of his fine. Defoe was examined once more before Godolphin and Nottingham. The Queen too was present, and throughout the proceedings she seemed to be a major force in seeing that Defoe would be punished.[2] She was apparently a close reader of *The Shortest Way*, and

[1] Daniel Finch, Letter Book, PRO, SP44/104, fo. 316.
[2] BL Add. MS 29,589, item 46. This is signed by Godolphin.

had prepared the grounds for Defoe's persecution by her speech in the House of Lords on 27 February, arguing that the spread of 'Scandalous Pamphlets and Libels' had been harmful to the state and calling upon Parliament to pass laws to 'Prevent and Punish such Pernicious Practices.'[3] At any rate she was not impressed with Defoe's 'Confession', remarking to Godolphin that it amounted to 'nothing'.[4] She left the timing of Defoe's appearance in the pillory up to Godolphin and the 'Lords of the Committee', but she wanted it done within a few days. Nottingham thought he might yet discover something, and with the Lord Privy Seal, Buckingham, interviewed Defoe in Newgate on 23 July. What piece of information he hoped to obtain is impossible to say, but either Defoe did not know anything as Trent suggested or, as he claimed, he refused to betray any secrets. On the 27th Nottingham wrote to the Sheriff of London that he might proceed 'without expecting any further order'.[5] Defoe suffered the ignominy of standing in the pillory on the last three days of July. It was intended to be a memorable humiliation. The government had spent much more on Defoe's capture and prosecution than was usual in cases of this kind, and no doubt they wanted their money's worth. They were successful enough in some ways. From the lowliest Tory pamphleteer to acknowledged literary masters such as Swift and Pope, his enemies never let him forget this event. But what was most galling to them (whatever its real pyschological effect may have been upon Defoe) was that he turned it into a public triumph.

I

What could have happened may be seen from William Fuller's experience at the hands of the mob just a few months before. He had so much filth thrown at him that he could not stand; rocks shattered his legs and head, and he almost choked to death when his body was left hanging by his head after he fell from the stool on which he was standing.[6] Defoe's experience was very different. To the outrage of those who sought to destroy him, Defoe turned the event into an opportunity to sell his books and propagate his ideas. Charles Leslie complained about the 'Party' surrounding him while he was standing in the pillory, protecting him and offering various works for sale:

[3] *JHL* 1703, xviii. 322.
[4] BL Add. MS 29,589, item 46.
[5] Finch, Letter Book, fo. 318.
[6] George Campbell, *Impostor at the Bar* (London: Hodder & Stoughton, 1961), 214.

And the Party causing his Books to be Hauk'd and Publickly Sold about the Pillory, while he stood upon it (in Triumph!) for Writing them. And Writes on still. And the Advertisements in our News Papers are fill'd with New Editions of his Works, among which this Shortest way, for which he was Pillory'd still bears the Bell. For he has since Publish'd another Shortest way (as he calls it) to Peace and union, which is before Quoted, and puts upon it, by the Author of The Shortest way with the Dissenters, he Glories in the Title. And in his Verses since Publish'd, often bring in Rime, and the Burden of his Song—The Shortest way—so far is he or the Party from thinking the Pillory a Shame in such a Cause![7]

Defoe's first appearance in the pillory was near his warehouse and former residence in Freeman's Yard. This may have been done to increase his feeling of shame. But instead of exhibiting an emotion of this kind, Defoe, if Charles Leslie is to believed, took the occasion to sell copies of *The Shortest Way* among other works. As Leslie wrote elsewhere, Defoe 'Glory'd in it, and Quoted it 100 times in his after Writings'.[8] His enemies expected that, at the very least, the experience would make him 'uneasie'. Disappointed in this hope, they often suggested that since a sentence to seven years of silence had not been efficacious, hanging might be the only way to silence his pen. In some ways, his ability to keep on writing, indeed to write after this event as he had never done before, established his reputation as the Satanic 'Incendiary', and as the leading author of what many considered to be seditious publications. And what was worse, though vilified by his enemies as an agent of Satan, a leader of the mob, and a turncoat, Defoe had the irritating quality of pretending to complete sincerity and unruffled moderation. This was why Alexander Pope pictured him in his *Dunciad* as 'unabashed Defoe'.

Pope also showed him still in the pillory after twenty-five years, and Defoe helped to contribute to this image in some ways. If selling his *Shortest Way* at the pillory appeared impudent to his enemies, equally impudent, and in some ways even more effective, was his poem *A Hymn to the Pillory*, for, as J. T. Boulton has argued, it was a direct appeal to the ominous mob.[9] Defoe appears in the poem neither as a gentleman nor as a tradesman, but as a workman—an 'Author'—and the pillory is a symbol or 'Hi'roglyphic' of the machinery by which the state punishes 'Fancy' or creative criticism. Defoe speaks in his own voice as the satiric author of the poems on reformation and as the truth-teller of *The True-Born Englishman*.

---

[7] *The Wolf Stript of His Shepard's Cloathing*, 59.
[8] 'A View of the Times', *The Rehearsal*, 1 (94) (1706).
[9] J. T. Boulton (ed.), *Daniel Defoe* (New York: Schocken, 1965), p. 100.

As Robert Burns would do at the end of the century, Defoe appealed to a vision of himself as an honest and virtuous man whose inner knowledge of his own rectitude preserved him from the shame that the Pillory was intended to convey to the witnesses. By suggesting that the mob did not distinguish between the virtuous man being punished by vicious men and those who might genuinely deserve to be pilloried, Defoe confronted the mob with a challenge. Were they capable of understanding what was happening? Did they understand that the kind of action that might have won applause in a former reign was now being punished? Did they understand how just men had been punished by corrupt governments? Addressing the pillory as if it were a sentient being, Defoe turned the poem to the subject of the villains in the society who really deserved to be punished:

> Thou art no shame to Truth and Honesty,
> Nor is the character of such defac'd by thee,
>   Who suffer by Oppressive Injury.
>   Shame, like the Exhalations of the Sun,
> Falls back where first the motion was begun:
> And he who for no Crime shall on thy Brows appear,
> Bears less Reproach than they who plac'd 'em there.[10]

For most of the remainder of the poem, Defoe turned to the theme that he was to exploit later in his studies of crime, the theme stated by John Gay's Macheath in *The Beggar's Opera*: that if the wealthy and powerful were to be subject to such punishments for crimes that were far worse, the numbers would be too great for the machinery of the state to accommodate them. Suitably enough, Defoe began his list of rogues with Sacheverell, the fiery High Church clergyman whose work he had imitated. From there he moved through the various professions—the cowardly generals and admirals who had betrayed the national interest, the stockbrokers, judges, immoral priests, corrupt lawyers, and wicked women. At the end of the poem, he imagines the message pinned to his hat conveying the true reasons for his punishment:

> Tell them 'twas because he was too bold,
> And told those Truths, which shou'd not ha' been told.
> Extoll the Justice of the land
> Who Punish what they will not understand.
> Tell them he stands Exalted there
> For speaking what we wou'd not hear;

---

[10] Daniel Defoe, *A Hymn to the Pillory*, in *Shakespeare Head Edition*, 138–9.

And yet he might ha' been secure,
Had he said less, or wou'd he ha said more.[11]

Defoe then pointed out his refusal to betray his friends, and argued that his fate was intended as a warning to the people that those in power would not allow such independence from the citizens, and intended to 'make Men of their Honesty afraid'.

The message was clear enough, and Defoe probably shaped it in a way that would make his entire career understandable. He was the spokesman for the outsiders in the society, those seemingly unrepresented by a House of Commons that should have represented them, and certainly represented neither by the administrative apparatus with its lawyers and judges nor by the Anglican Church with its corrupt priests. Defoe's weapon was the printed word, and the efforts of the state to silence him were ultimately aimed at everyone outside the circles of power. His ability to use rhetoric in an extraordinarily effective manner aside, *A Hymn to the Pillory* was a deeply personal and extraordinarily effective political poem. If it did not create a revolution, it helped preserve his life from the 'Fury of the Street'. Defoe's courage in such difficult circumstances may have helped convince Robert Harley, the man who started the wheels turning that put him in prison, that Defoe would be the ideal man to help shape public opinion through manipulating the press.

For all the vengeance of the government, Defoe had succeeded. The Occasional Bill failed to pass, and in retrospect the Tory Charles Hornby in *A Caveat against the Whigs* blamed the changed attitude toward the Church of England on Defoe. He noted that *The Shortest Way* was

universally condemned by all Churchmen in general, yet it served the Purpose well enough to brand that whole Body with Blood-Thirstiness and a persecuting Spirit, till by the Diligence of the Government it appear'd that no Churchman had been so little a Christian, but that it was done by one of the chief Scribes of the other Party, with a worse Design to halloo the Mob to make the World believe that the Dissenters Throats were to be cut the Shortest Way, and to provoke those to begin first for their own Preservation, for which Attempt the Author had his Just Reward; but the Party were so little ashamed of it, that whenever it was objected against them it was only grinn'd off as a Piece of Wit and Management.[12]

The government had succeeded in punishing the body of Defoe, but his images of a type of persecution that most people in England were no longer willing to accept had blunted the attack upon the Dissenters. During the next decade Defoe was to use 'the shortest way' as an effective phrase to

---

[11] *A Hymn to the Pillory*, 151.
[12] Hornby, *Caveat*, pt. 4, 2nd edn. (London, 1712), 39.

conjure up images of persecution under a wide variety of circumstances. His readers had no trouble thinking at once of violent churchmen, of equally violent political leaders, and of the pillory, their instrument for enforcing their notions.

II

After appearing two more days in the pillory, at Cheapside and then finally, on 31 July, symbolically enough, at Fleet Street, now used metonymically as a synonym for the world of publishing in Britain, Defoe was returned to Newgate.[13] If he expected immediate release, he was to be disappointed. In his letter to William Penn early in July, he had signed himself somewhat melodramatically as 'An Unknown Captive' (H 9). But after spending over three more months in Newgate, he may indeed have thought that he had been forgotten by his friends. Unfortunately, his friends were not in as good a position to help him as his enemies, and ironically, two of those involved in prosecuting him, Robert Harley and Sidney Godolphin, sought to persuade Queen Anne that he would be useful to the government. James Stancliffe, who paid Defoe's fines with the prospect of receiving £150 from Godolphin, acted as the agent for his release on 4 November.[14] Defoe put up £200 bond and his brother-in-law Robert Davis £100. Charles Read, John Chase, and Thomas Fry also put up £100 each, in accordance with the formula set for releasing a prisoner who had committed a felony against the Crown.

Defoe was to tell the story of his release in moving terms in his *Appeal to Honour and Justice*. He was attempting to explain his sense of gratitude toward Robert Harley and Queen Anne as a justification for his loyalty to both of them from this point forward:

I will make no Reflections upon the Treatment I met with from the People I suffer'd for, or how I was abandon'd even in my Sufferings, at the same time that they acknowledg'd the Service it had been to their Cause; but I must mention it to let you know, that while I lay friendless and distress'd in the Prison of *Newgate*, my Family ruin'd, and my self without Hope of Deliverance, a Message was

---

[13] Although a painting by Eyre Crow shows Defoe being toasted and surrounded by flowers on a bright day, he may have been rained upon throughout his ordeal. John Evelyn noted: 'There hapend the last weeke of this moneth so great & long continual Raine, as had not ben know⟨n⟩ of late years, & the last day of it & the Sunday following I.Aug: Thunder lightning & raine, which hindered me from Morning Service &c at Church.' Evelyn was an old man at this time, but the rain might have reduced the crowds. Evelyn, *Diary*, ed. E. S. de Beer (London: Oxford University Press, 1959), p. 1099.

[14] Stancliffe did receive payment on 5 Nov. See PRO T 38/737, fo. 97.

brought me from a Person of Honour, who, till that time, I had never had the least Acquaintance with, or knowledge of, other than by Fame, or by Sight, as we know Men of Quality by seeing them on publick Occasions. I gave no present Answer to the Person who brought it, having not duly weighed the Import of the Message; the Message was by Word of Mouth thus *Pray ask that Gentleman, what I can do for him?* But in return to this kind and generous Message, I immediately took my Pen and Ink, and writ the Story of the blind Man in the Gospel, who follow'd our Saviour, and to whom our Blessed Lord put the Question, *What wilt thou that I should do unto thee?* Who, as if he has made it strange that such a Question should be ask'd, or as if he had said, *Lord doest thou see that I am blind, and yet ask me what thou shalt do for me?* My Answer is plain in my Misery, *Lord, that I may receive my Sight.*[15]

Defoe also tells of his gratitude to the Queen. He learned of her generosity to him through Harley and Godolphin. According to Defoe, Anne said that she did not think 'a certain Person' (Nottingham?) would have behaved so badly to him. She inquired after his family and through the Lord Treasurer, Godolphin, sent 'a considerable Supply' to his wife and family and saw that he was released from Newgate. 'Gratitude and Fidelity are inseparable from an honest Man', wrote Defoe by way of explaining his behaviour.[16] After he was taken into her service, his sense of gratitude was boundless, and he served her faithfully.

This is not exactly the way Defoe became a secret agent for the Queen and a propagandist for Harley. It is possible that Defoe believed this story, possible that, in addition to making a special plea for understanding from 'his Worst Enemies' in 1715, a dangerous time for him, Defoe may have been accustomed to rehearsing this narrative to himself as a rationale for his own behaviour. Certainly, we know that Harley deliberately allowed Defoe to remain in prison for so many months as a way of breaking down whatever resistance he might have to working for someone who, as Speaker of the House at the time of the Kentish petition and as one of those who worked to disband the army, was one Defoe would have regarded as an enemy to King William and to many of his ideas on government and society. If Defoe's brick and tile factory had dissolved and he was once more deeply in debt without the means to pay his creditors, the reason may be laid mainly at the door of the Secretary of State.

Harley was certainly acting in character. His correspondence with relatives and friends reveals him to be warm and generous, but as a statesman he was secretive and difficult. He was a subtle politician, interested in

---

[15] Defoe, *An Appeal to Honour and Justice Though It Be of His Worst Enemies*, in *Shakespeare Head Edition*, 199–200.

[16] Ibid. 200–2.

rendering what might be considered the far right of the Tory party ineffective while leading the government in the direction of moderately conservative Country Party ideas. In *Minutes of the Negotiations of Monsieur Mesnager*, Defoe's narrator provided an insightful analysis of this seemingly divided personality. Mesnager praises his 'vast Memory', his 'engaging Way of Conversation', and his complete lack of formality, but notes that as a public figure, 'he differs from himself', being reserved in the extreme and often communicating nothing at all. Mesnager noted that he took such 'exotick Measures' to bring his designs to pass that no matter how well-intended he might be, he often caused observers to doubt his motives. He was so untrusting that he would never tell people working for him the whole of any scheme. In this complaint, Defoe was surely registering a personal reaction.[17]

It has sometimes been said that Harley and Defoe got along well because they were very much alike. This seems an odd notion. True enough, they shared certain common ground. Defoe was only one year older than Harley; so they had gone through the same political battles even if they had often been on different sides. Both had been raised in the Dissenting tradition, and apparently Harley and his family attended a Dissenter conventicle until 1704.[18] Defoe knew that when he made a biblical reference, Harley would understand him. Interestingly enough, both were great admirers of the Restoration poet Rochester. They even shared some of the same attitudes. Harley's control over his emotions appears to have been truly stoical; Defoe fancied that he was a 'Stoic'. Both viewed the bills against occasional conformity as attempts to destroy the political influence of the Dissenters, both were eager to bring about a Union between England and Scotland, and both enjoyed secrecy. But for Defoe, secrecy was part of play and game. He threw himself with exuberance into establishing a spy network in England and into his secret work for the Union. Harley, on the other hand, sent spies to spy on his spies.

Mesnager commented on Harley's distrust of his fellow man. Defoe's enthusiasm and ingenuity bubbled over in a constant interest in new schemes; Harley was always cautious. Harley clearly thought he could use Defoe and keep him under control. Defoe had learned that if he was to continue to speak out on various issues in his usual outrageous manner, he would need some powerful patron or patrons to protect him. He had tried to function alone after the death of King William, and the results had been disastrous. I suspect that they liked each other in their own ways, but

[17] *Minutes of the Negotiations of Monsieur Mesnager* (London, 1717), 49–50.
[18] Brian W. Hill, *Robert Harley* (New Haven, Conn.: Yale University Press, 1988), 70.

Harley's secrecy in his public dealings and Defoe's rashness must have made an odd combination. We only have a few communications from Harley to Defoe, and one is a letter which warns Defoe to keep things secret.[19] Defoe's letters to Harley are informative, lively, and sometimes deceptive. He probably felt grateful for Harley's decision to free him from prison, but he could not have been entirely happy with his subservient position and with having to beg Harley for his secret service money. Their relationship always had a certain edge to it, and that may have made it interesting for both of them.

The question on the mind of Godolphin was whether the pillory had not made Defoe intractable. He soon came to see Defoe's resilience. Responding to what must have been a letter from Harley on using Defoe in Scotland, Godolphin replied on 13 August, 'Defoe would be the properest person in the world for that transaction.' We can surmise that in the frequent meetings between Harley and Godolphin, Defoe's name came up whenever the question of negotiations with Scotland was on the agenda. Godolphin even offered to send Charles Hedges, Secretary of State for Northern Affairs, to see Defoe on this matter. Harley apparently wanted to attach Defoe to himself through the usual tie of benefits and gratitude that both Harley and Defoe would have recognized as part of the seventeenth-century system of patronage. He had a particular interest in gaining some control over the press. Like Defoe, he had perceived the way newspaper reports and pamphlets could be manipulated to achieve control of information. This had been Nottingham's area of expertise, and once Harley had eased him out of office in April 1704, he assumed this power over the press.

On 23 August 1703 Defoe's former business partner and childhood friend James Stancliffe wrote in a letter to Harley, 'I saw mr. F yesterday, & he seems to be much dejected by the deferring of Hope which the Wise man says makes the heart Sick; but at the same tyme he & all men must know (that know any thing) tht Your Hurrys of late have been such as are not ordinarily met with.' But Harley had his own time table for Defoe's release. He notified Godolphin on 20 September that 'Foe is much oppressed in his mind', and the machinery was set in motion that brought him out of Newgate. Defoe's letter to Harley on 9 November is a kind of public document, stating his gratitude and offering his services by way of repaying the services rendered to him:

It Remains for me to Conclude my Present application with This Humble Petition

[19] See Paula Backscheider, 'Robert Harley to Daniel Defoe: A New Letter', *Modern Language Review* 83 (1988): 817–19. Healey also assumes that a letter written in Oct. 1706 is a communication from Harley to Defoe. See H 132.

that if Possible I may By Some Meanes or Other know what I am capable of
Doeing, that my Benefactors whoever they are May Not be Asham'd of their
Bounty as Missapplyed. Not Sir That I Expect to be able to Meritt So Much good-
ness, But as A Gratefull Temper is Allwayes Uneasy to be Loaded with Benefitts,
So the *Vertue* which I Call Gratitude, has Allwayes So Much Pride in it, as makes
it Push at a Retribution, Tho' tis Unable to Effect it. (H 11)

Although Defoe's feelings of relief at his release from Newgate and return
to his family were no doubt genuine, he surely knew what was expected of
him. His statement about being 'oppress'd in his mind' sounds like a
formula for 'Tell Mr. Harley that I am ready to be useful to their side'.
Whatever his Whig connections may have been, he was only going to get
out of that 'house of Bondage and affliction' (H 6) with the help of those
who put him there. Stancliffe probably conveyed a great deal more to
Defoe about Harley than what we have in writing, and Defoe must have
known that he could, indeed must, work with Harley. The next letter that
we have from Defoe to Harley, dated six months later, speaks of their 'So
Near and So Advantageous a Conversation' (H 12), and of his concern that
the times and places of their secret meetings have somehow become
known. He ends with a statement of his gratitude for what was to be a regular payment of secret service money and his desire for further instructions.

III

Defoe would have been more than human if his incarceration in Newgate
had not depressed his spirits, but he was a believer in action. He liked to tell
the fable of the wagoner whose cart becomes stuck in a ditch. The wagoner
prays to Hercules to help him and receives not help but advice. Hercules
chastises him for his failure to use all of his abilities to help himself. On his
island prison, Crusoe suffers a moment of fear and depression after he
saves himself from the threatening ocean, but as soon as he wakes from
his first sleep he throws himself into a frenzy of activity, swimming out to
the wrecked ship to salvage everything he can take on his raft. Defoe's
impulses were similar. In between moments of despair, he was probably his
usual self, arranging his affairs, scheming, plotting, and of course, writing.

   That his affairs were as thoroughly wrecked as Crusoe's ship there can
be no doubt. His family was forced to move back with the Tuffleys. Mary
was probably pregnant with Martha, who would be born some time in the
spring of 1704.[20] One may wonder how Defoe's mother-in-law greeted

---

[20] In the preface to *More Reformation* published on 16 July and written not long before, Defoe spoke of

these events. Defoe gave Harley an account of his situation at the time, estimating that he required £1000 to get free of his debts. £500 or £600 would hold off his creditors temporarily. He estimated his loss through imprisonment after the publication of *The Shortest Way* at £2500:

I forbear to Say all the Moveing Things to you I Could on This head. All my prospects were built on a Manufacture I had Erected in Essex; all The late kings Bounty to me was Expended There. I Employ'd a hundred Poor Familys at work and it began to Pay me Very well. I Generally made Six hundred pound profit per Annum.

I began to live, Took a Good House, bought me Coach and horses a Second Time. I paid Large Debts Gradually, small Ones wholly, and Many a Creditor after composition whom I found poor and Decay'd I Sent for and Paid the Remaindr to tho' Actually Discharged. (H 17)

He still owed a large debt, £1050, to Maresco, Stamper, and Ghisleyn, and he had other problems as well. He was sued by Paul Whitehurst about payment for supplying drink to the workers at Tilbury, and he was ordered to pay Francis Annesley £236 pounds and an additional £5 damages after Defoe had tried to palm off payment on a debt to a Matthew Clarkson. Clarkson said he did not owe Defoe that much money, and Defoe was forced to pay. Although Defoe presented an image of himself as a straightforward and honest trader, he seems to have taken a certain pleasure in balancing one debt against another.

His debts had not prevented his return to his attempt to 'live' as he thought a gentleman ought. All of this was ruined, as he says with some degree of self-mockery, 'The shortest way.' Defoe particularly blames himself for bringing troubles on 'a Vertuous and Excellent Mother', whose dowry of £3700 he wasted. But he tells Harley, 'I never Despaired' (H 17). Defoe gives as his reason for this his belief in Providence, but such resilience was certainly also an element in his character. Even as he was being hunted, he attempted to clear his reputation in a pamphlet that created the character of a 'Dissenter' who, in a dialogue with the author Tutchin, gave an 'objective' evaluation of his character touching on his courage and his honest behaviour toward his creditors. This pamphlet was included in *A Collection of the Writings of the Author of the True Born Englishman* published by John How on 17 April 1703. At one point in his career, John Robert Moore thought that Defoe may have had something to do with putting together this collection, but despite his continued conviction that all of the pieces included were by Defoe, he did not press the

his '*six innocent Children*'. In the spring of the next year, he mentioned 'Seaven Beautifull and hopefull Children' (*True Collection*, ii. 28; H 17).

point in his biography. Since Defoe retained the basic organization of this volume when he published *A True Collection* three months later on 22 July, and since the *Collection* appears to have been used as a copy text to set some sections of the *True Collection*, there may be some possibility that How somehow got hold of a copy Defoe was preparing to publish. In the preface to the *True Collection*, Defoe complained not only of How's inclusion of works not by him but of the inclusion of *The Shortest Way* at a time when he was subject to the resentment of the government.

Yet Defoe included *The Shortest Way* in his *True Collection* as well! Since Defoe believed that his work was the best antidote to attempts at passing some kind of bill against occasional conformity, he apparently could not resist the temptation to reprint it under the pretence of correcting errors in the text. Defoe took advantage of this preface to deny that he was an 'Incendiary', and to argue that his writings reflected more the 'Spirit of Healing than of Sedition'. His explanations for writing *The Shortest Way* were now addressed to those who might think him insane:

And as to the excepted Piece, since the general Vogue has Condemn'd it, I submit to the Censure, but must enter a Protestation that my Intention was not Seditious. I avoid Vindicating the Measures I took in the Method of the Argument, and rather acknowledge my self in the wrong than dispute it; but, however, I might by my Ill Conduct draw a Picture which shew'd a Face I did not design to Paint; yet, I never designed such a Face as should scare Mankind, and make the World think me Mad.[21]

Defoe hedged his apology so much that it would be hard to determine the exact nature of the crime for which he was excusing himself. In some sense it may be read as a compliment to his own powers as a writer. The High Church speaker of *The Shortest Way* was so real, so frightening in his persecuting frenzy that he frightened his readers more than Defoe intended. Defoe wrote about the possibility that the government might release him 'to Morrow', but this self-exoneration, published shortly after his conviction, could not have increased the slim chances of such an event. More pertinent was his attack on John How for violating the rights of authors, which he compared to highway robbery. Defoe was to champion the rights of authors to the rewards of their labours throughout his life, and devoted several numbers of his journal, the *Review*, to supporting the copyright law of 1710.

Defoe had originally warned against How's *Collection* in his poem *More Reformation*, published on 16 July 1703. This was the first of his works

---

[21] Daniel Defoe, 'Preface' to *True Collection*, i, sigs. A4–A4ᵛ.

written wholly, or in part, while he was in prison. The subtitle was 'A Satyr upon Himself', and it is the first of his works to exploit his personal situation in relation to the government. Defoe was no John Dunton, who made his private relationship with his wives the subject of his writings. Instead, Defoe transformed himself into an icon: the author as transgressor who, through that transgression, would be better equipped to hold up a mirror to society and reveal its sins. In his preface he returned to his image of the painter, instancing some unnamed Dutch artist who had to paint underneath his figures 'This is the Man' and 'This is the Bear' so that his audience would understand what he had done.[22] Although the anecdote was usually used by Defoe to criticize bad painters, he turned it around here to criticize the stupidity of his readers among the Dissenters. Unfortunately for himself, he adds, everyone else now does seem to understand it.

Defoe then went on to say that he would always attack hypocrisy where he found it, would always attack drunken clergymen and venal magistrates. Though uncomfortable with the public exposure created by *The Shortest Way*, he defended his character to a point, agreeing to '*act the Pharissee a little*': 'God I thank thee, *I am not a Drunkard, or a Swearer, or a Whore-master, or a busie-body, or idle, or revengeful*'.[23] But he finds these negatives not equal to a good character. Like everyone else, he is a sinner. Defoe assumes the fundamental Christian line here, and beginning with a pun on the very nature of human beings as making them incapable of avoiding sin, he puts the emphasis on honest recognition of human frailty and repentance:

> But since Mankind are all alike so frail,
> That Crimes with Life come like Estates in tail;
> All have an equal Title to reproach,
> Except some few, who sin a Knot too much:
> He that has all his own Mistakes confesst,
> Stands next to him who never has transgresst
> And will be censur'd for a Fool by none,
> But they who see no Errors of their own.[24]

The satirist, Defoe argues, should not 'banter the Misfortunes of Mankind', but should attack those hypocrites who want to punish sins in others that they practise on the sly.

There is much miscellaneous satire in *More Reformation*, including a restatement of his arguments against occasional conformity, but the thrust of the work went toward apologizing for having published *The Shortest*

---

[22] Defoe, *More Reformation*, in *True Collection*, ii. 28. [23] Ibid. 31. [24] Ibid. 36.

Way. Defoe faults satirists, such as Marvell, who attacked Charles II directly, suggesting that he intended no direct attack upon Queen Anne. And he finds fault with himself. He thought that his ironic method would be clear enough to all, but if it was not, it was his fault for overestimating the abilities of his readers to discriminate. He regrets having used the devices of lampoon in naming particular individuals deserving of criticism, since general satire should be able to make its point well enough. He is now repentant for his action, and prays that God will incline Queen Anne to consider clemency toward him.

Though the last few lines are humble enough, humility was hardly the poem's dominant emotion. Behind Defoe's attempt to eat humble pie was a sense of outrage and anger, and his efforts at restraining his feelings were not entirely successful. Defoe placed a high value on his abilities and on his accomplishments. Those who had feasted him along with the Kentish petitioners now seemed to find a certain pleasure in seeing his punishment:

> *Before thee* stands the Power of Punishment,
> In an exasperated Govenment.
> *Behind* the Vacant Carpet fairly spread,
> From whence thy *too well serv'd Allies* are fled.
> At a remoter distance, there they stand,
> And mock thy *Folly*; but thy *Fault* commend;
> Freely thy former Services disown,
> And slily Laugh to see thee *first undone*.[25]

Defoe accuses even his supporters of a certain *Schadenfreude*, and suggests that the inability of many to understand what *The Shortest Way* was all about was simply pretence. The trouble with *More Reformation* is that his need to conciliate his enemies resulted in a good deal of pretence on Defoe's part. He seems on the one hand to dislike naming names, but then he proceeds to do just that. His attack on Gildon for publishing Rochester's poems seems contradicted by his statements of admiration for Rochester's repentance, and the criticism of Marvell for writing attacks upon Charles II rings equally false. We know that Defoe admired and imitated the work of both poets, and that he believed that the people (and poets) could rebel against any monarch who threatened to violate the laws of the nation. Defoe clearly thought that flattering the Queen might get him some kind of clemency, but the anger apparent in his *Hymn to the Pillory* suggests that Godolphin's judgement, made a few weeks after Defoe's punishment, to the effect that Defoe would continue to feel resentment toward the govern-

---

[25] *More Reformation*, in *True Collection*, ii. 62.

ment, was accurate enough at the time. Harley's Machiavellian scheme to keep him in prison until he was ready to serve Harley's ends also reflects the assessments of a man experienced in the ways of human nature.

IV

Part of Defoe's sentence involved an insistence that he leave off writing for seven years. Defoe simply ignored this provision, continuing the flow of writings from Newgate. He followed *More Reformation* with *The Shortest Way to Peace and Union* on 22 July. It appeared during the days when Defoe was still trying to avoid the pillory by offering to give information, and its allusion to the infamous title of Defoe's unfortunate pamphlet could not have improved the temper of his enemies. Whether Defoe would have wanted the work identified as '*By the Author of the Shortest Way with the Dissenters*' is questionable, but he probably approved of the title itself. Defoe's preface suggests that he had written the work 'some Years' before, but if this was partly true, the additions turned it into a contemporary document, replete with quotes from Charles Leslie's *New Association* and attacks upon the 'Incendiaries' of the High Church such as Sacheverell.[26] His pleas for toleration and for an end to occasional conformity among the Dissenters were less interesting than his assertion that he would continue to defend his principles in print, principles that advised reconciliation between the Dissenters and the Church of England. 'Nor shall the Apprehension of the Severity of Her Majesty's Resentment', he wrote, 'cause me to cease the endeavour, of bringing, as far as writing can do it, a fair Reconciliation of Parties in View.'[27] If Defoe thought that no one could object to his writing on a subject that everyone could approve, he was mistaken. Many felt he should not be allowed to write at all.

But Defoe believed that as long as he was writing in opposition to Occasional Conformity there would be no way that he would be punished. He issued several more pamphlets on this subject from prison during September, and in one of them, *The Case of Dissenters as Affected by the Late Bill*, he seems to have regained some of his nerve. He argued that the Dissenters were loyal members of the state. Although they were not permitted to serve in state offices, they had served the nation well in municipal offices and had done nothing to deserve an act of Parliament that would have deprived them of such positions. Defoe may have found religion a

---

[26] Defoe, *The Shortest Way to Peace and Union*, in *True Collection*, i. 448.
[27] Ibid. 441.

somewhat safer subject than politics, however, and he turned his talents to two works which suggested that the soul might wing itself directly to Heaven in one way or another. His *Hymn to the Funeral Sermon* was an attack on Paul Lorrain, the chaplain (ordinary) of Newgate, for a sermon on a prize-fighter named Cook who had murdered a constable. For all his generosity toward sinners in *More Reformation*, Defoe was still too much of a Presbyterian to accept a vision of the boxer's direct transportation to Heaven. Defoe apparently classified Cook among those who 'sin a Knot too much', and insisted that there has to be some evidence of a virtuous life. Ironic about Newgate becoming famous for shipping 'so many Loads of *Saints* to *Heaven*', Defoe protested that such an attitude would overturn morality:

> Where's then the meer necessity to Pray?
> Or where's the great Reward of Honesty?
> Ne're think on't more, as well ye may,
> E'en lay aside *Morality*,
> And go to Heaven *The Shortest Way*.[28]

Defoe thought that Cook's wife, who paid £10 for the sermon, had been short-changed by Lorrain. It is significant that in Defoe's writings the ordinary of Newgate receives notably poor marks as late as 1722, when Moll Flanders finds him less than helpful.

Lorrain's sermon may have reminded Defoe of a commentary he had written a few years earlier on John Asgil's treatise concerning a direct transportation to Heaven. Asgil's expulsion from the Irish House of Commons may have afforded Defoe the occasion for publishing his commentary on what he considered to be a heretical work. The Christianity of Defoe's time was tinged with a variety of influences, from the science of Newton to the epistemology of Locke. Thinkers such as Defoe had no trouble accommodating their beliefs to such modern developments, but he tried all of his life to counter the arguments of deists, anti-Trinitarians, and atheists. Deists such as Toland and Gildon were given sections in his *Reformation of Manners* and *More Reformation*, and he was later to devote a number of volumes to refuting the ideas of such writers. His answer to Asgil is the first of these works, and gives us some insight into his religious views. However slight the likelihood of his fulfilling his parents' dream of his becoming a clergyman may have been, Defoe clearly enjoyed this kind of theological controversy. As different as his views were from those of his contemporary Thomas Burnet, one of the last of the Cambridge

[28] *A Hymn to the Funeral Sermon* (London, 1703), 2.

Platonists and a writer whose speculations spilled over into heresy, Defoe had clearly read his works carefully and with a certain appreciation. Thus he shows considerable admiration for Asgil's powers of reasoning and learning while regretting that Asgil's work had been published. Unfortunately, he speculated, reasoning and learning are not very helpful in matters of religion since they often awaken the fancy and eventually lead to believing false doctrines. Defoe argued that death was a natural process because the body was made of corruptible earth. Through Christian faith the soul, not the body, might live again. Defoe dismissed the idea of an instantaneous translation to heaven as absurd. Interestingly enough, *An Enquiry into the Case of Mr. Asgil's General Translation* was published on 4 November, the day that Defoe was finally able to translate his body out of Newgate.

V

Five days after he was back in the bosom of his family, Defoe wrote to Robert Harley to express his gratitude and to offer repayment in any way possible. The letter seems shaped to the expectations of a reader who, like the writer, knew of Seneca's essay on 'Benefits', an essay which had been widely popularized through the translation of Roger L'Estrange. Seneca considered the situation a delicate one both for the giver and the receiver, but the latter must show his entire appreciation, while the giver must not overplay his role. Defoe emoted with a proper sense of obligation:

Whoever Sir Are the Principalls in this Favour, I Can Not but Profess my Self a Debtor wholly to your Self, who Till I May be Otherwise Instructed Appeares the Originall *as to Me*. And in the kindness the Manner is So Oblidgeing, and all the Articles of it So Generous, that as a Man Astonish't at the Perticulars, I am Perfectly Unable to Express My Sence of it, Onely in the humblest manner I Can, Most Earnestly Pray That I May have Some Opportunity Put into my hands by Providence to Make More Explicit Acknowledgements; And that as I have Recd Such an Obligation as few Ever Reciev'd, I Might be Able to Make Some Such Sort of Return as No Man Ever Made. . . . I Take The Freedome to Repeat the Assurance of A Man Ready to Dedicate my Life and all Possible Powers to The Intrest of So Generous and So Bountifull Benefactors, Being Equally Overcome with the Nature as well as the Value of the Favour I have Reciev'd. (H 11)

Without doubting Defoe's sincerity in this outpouring of gratitude, the reader should be aware that all Defoe's letters to Harley contain an element of formality and distance, even when he was attempting to draw upon the familiarity that Harley apparently treasured in personal discourse. With the exception of the few letters to his family, Defoe's letters show traces of the lessons learned in Morton's academy about judging the nature of the reader. The particular self or personality that Defoe presented to Harley was within the range of what we know to be the real Defoe, but it was certainly shaped to suit Harley's own character. Both of them probably felt a sense of relief when, a few months later, he could write to Harley in plainer English, 'I am the Gratefullest wretch Alive' (H 13).

His meetings with Harley probably furnished him with hints about the kind of writing Harley wanted from him, but as familiar as Harley may have been in their secret meetings over the next few months, Defoe probably had difficulty getting Harley to provide exact orders about the kind of propaganda he wanted. The message Defoe began to preach, echoing a recent speech of Queen Anne, was the middle way between extremes—peace and union at home.[29] In *A Challenge of Peace Address'd to the Whole Nation*, which he published on 23 November, he had no difficulty assuming his own, recognizable voice with reference to *The Shortest Way* and quotations from *The True-Born Englishman*. There was a fair amount of humble pie eaten in the preface, but he continued to attack the High Church in something like his former style, along with a praise of the Low Church as representing the true ideals of the nation. Small wonder that a High Church supporter would eventually write:

> High Church for Allegiance to the Scripture does goe,
> But Low Church to the Devil and *Daniel de Foe*.[30]

Defoe preached a similar message to the Dissenters. Anne and her government were committed to protecting the toleration of the Dissenters, and they should join in the spirit of peace and union to make England great. Until Defoe started his *Review* with its broader agenda on 19 February 1704, he continued hammering at those who were still trying to push through a bill against Occasional Conformity and acts against the toleration of the Dissenters. In two pamphlets he returned to his attack upon the position of Sir Humphrey Mackworth, his old opponent on the matter of Parliament's power during the Kentish petition controversy. Mackworth had come out for having Parliament pass a bill that would eliminate toler-

---

[29] In her speech to the two Houses of Parliament on 9 Nov. 1703, Queen Anne stressed the need for an end to the quarrels between factions: 'I want Words to express to you My earnest Desires of seeing all My Subjects in prfect Peace and Union among themselves: I have nothig so much at Heart, as their gneral Welfare and happiness. Let Me therefore desire you all, that you would carfully avoid any Heats and Divisions, that may disappoint me of that Satisfaction, and give Encouragement to the common Enemies of our Church and State.' *JHL*, xvii. 332.

[30] *The New Loyal Members of Parliament's Delight* (London, 1710), broadside.

ation. In attacking Mackworth's position, Defoe also included critiques of the ideas of Charles Davenant, whom he associated with those championing the power of the House of Commons. In a work that was appropriately retitled in its second edition *Original Right: Or, the Reasonableness of Appeals to the People*, Defoe returned to his arguments on the power of the people, making only the faintest apology to those who might think he was advancing a 'Mob Doctrine'. People who own property and even those who pay rent in the cities 'are the Center of the other three Estates, from whom the constitution is deriv'd, and for whom 'tis formed'.[31] He followed this work with a frontal assault on Mackworth's notions as smacking of the behaviour of Louis XIV toward the Huguenots. Defoe was clearly leaving the jail rot of Newgate behind him. Instead of merely defending toleration of the Dissenters, he launched into an assault upon the Test Act that prevented the Dissenters from holding office.

'No Man is above the Dignity of Reasoning', wrote Defoe in his preface to *Peace without Union*. This appeal to rationality was hardly new with Defoe, but as he moved into 1704, the appeal to reason became a central element in his writing. Englishmen should aim at a society governed by enlightened ideals, and the rough edges of Englishmen, dominated by prejudice and passionate commitment, should give way to ideals of toleration and moderation. He had been reading writers on natural law over the past decade, and he tried to preach their notion of aiming at a concept of government and society based upon a rational assessment of human nature. Mackworth had argued for the need for a national church; Defoe countered with the ideal of toleration, as practised in the Netherlands, as a superior stance to a narrow nationalism. On 5 January he published what amounted to a historical review of what he considered to be the main reasons for the separation of the Dissenters, in response to Charles Leslie's *The Wolf Stript of His Shepherd's Cloathing*, which had attacked him as the leading antagonist of the High Church. Defoe depicted the willingness of the Dissenters to give in to the demands of the Anglicans at the Restoration, and listed five changes that would allow him to conform:

1. A change in the liturgy.
2. Freedom allowed to ministers for extemporaneous prayer.
3. Ordination permitted by presbyters and allowing all present ministers into the Anglican Church without reordination.
4. 'Kneeling at the Sacrament, Bowing at the Name of Jesus, the Cross in Baptism, the Use of the Surplice, and all those Things own'd by the Greatest

---

[31] Defoe, *Some Remarks on the First Chapter in Dr. Davenant's Essays* (London, 1704 [1703]), esp. 13 and 23.

Masters of the Dispute, to be Indifferent, may either be wholly left out, or so left at the Discretion of the People, as they may not be impos'd upon them without their Consent.'

5. Reduction of the power of the Episcopal hierarchy.[32]

He admitted that these changes were not all of his objections to the Church and certainly not sufficient for the Quakers, but they would be sufficient for him. He instanced the sufferings of Thomas Delaune, who died in prison, as a sample of the kind of persecution visited upon the Dissenters for their beliefs, but stated that the Dissenters were loyal subjects of Queen Anne who would never engage in rebellion. Then, after all this sweetness and light, he turned upon the High Church and accused them of fomenting a Jacobite plot in Scotland and of being the real enemies of a peaceful and united society. Small wonder that over the next few years the very use of the word 'moderation' would cause supporters of the High Church to fume with indignation.

Defoe continued his plea for toleration with two important pamphlets in the first few months of 1704. *An Essay on the Regulation of the Press*, published on 7 January expressed his belief that what the nation needed was not a return to a Licenser but clear laws about what could and could not be printed. Licensing by the government would merely result in works that would be passed about in manuscript. He argued that at a time when parties divided the nation, a free exchange of opinions was a necessary part of political life. Defoe does not mention his own name among those unfairly persecuted for their ideas, but there was more than a little pleading his own case in this work. He argued for author, publisher, and printer to have their names on the title-pages, and for a method of punishing the piracy of works by unscrupulous publishers. To say that this is a step down from Milton's high-minded *Areopagitica*, which he must have been reading around this time,[33] would be an understatement. Defoe thought that overtly profane and obscene literature should be prohibited, and a little less than a decade later he was encouraging the government to punish Sir Richard Steele for some of his writings. But this was at the height of the party squabbles during the reign of Queen Anne, when Defoe was hardly the only author to lose his bearings. From a biographical standpoint, Defoe's *Essay* should be read as the work of a professional writer attempting to protect his turf. He begins by opposing a tax that had been suggested

---

[32] *The Dissenters Answer to the High Church Challenge*, in *True Collection*, ii. 196–7.

[33] Defoe quotes from Milton's writings on numerous occasions in his pamphlets, but he gives a very specific reference to the edition of Milton's works in *The Parallel* (*True Collection*, ii. 385–7), referring to them as 'in every Library of any Value to be seen'. He published *The Parallel* at just about the same time as the *Essay*.

on printed news, wants a limitation on what the government would consider libellous along with clear laws that would prevent innocent writers from falling into traps, and ends with an argument for protecting the author's ownership of his work. Those moments in which he appeals to the ideals of 'the high Perfection of Human Knowledge', which would suffer were a licensing act to be passed, should not blind us to Defoe's practicality.[34] He was no longer the manufacturer who was also an occasional writer on politics. He had settled on his career, and was ready to throw into it all of his energies and talents.

At the same time that he was defending the press as an arena for the toleration of free political ideas, he stepped up his arguments for religious toleration, for an end to the campaign against occasional conformity, and for the repeal of the Test Act which disqualified Dissenters from holding government employment. In *A Serious Inquiry into This Grand Question; Whether a Law to Prevent the occasional Conformity of Dissenters Would not be Inconsistent with the Act of Toleration*, published early in 1704, he argued that the Act of Toleration, passed during the reign of William III, really guaranteed every Englishman freedom of worship, superseded the Test Act, and made present efforts at forbidding Occasional Conformity irrational and illegal. Because the Act of Toleration was 'built on Foundations of *Reason and Right*', he wrote, 'any Subsequent Law made in Prejudice of the Liberty, Granted by the Toleration is highly Unjust and Unreasonable'.[35] In *The Parallel*, Defoe took up the situation of the Dissenters in Ireland, who had fought against Catholic domination with courage and loyalty only to be deprived of the right to serve the government. In an address to Queen Anne, Defoe argued that while the Irish Dissenters were fully supportive of the attempts to limit the growth of 'Popery', they wished to be able to serve in the government.

John Robert Moore suggested that the way in which this tract was published, on fine paper and large print, suggests that it was almost certainly subsidized. That Defoe was commissioned to present the views of the Irish Dissenters suggests what was certainly true over the next few years—that he was considered the writer who would speak for the Dissenters and present their position to the nation. Defoe not only speaks of the service the Dissenters have done Ireland in contributing to the victory at the Boyne but threatens that if they are not treated well, they may soon abandon Ireland, leaving the nation so much the poorer. Defoe

[34] Defoe, *Essay on the Regulation of the Press*, ed. John Robert Moore (Oxford: Blackwell, 1948), 3.
[35] *A Serious Inquiry into This Grand Question; Whether a Law to Prevent the Occasional Conformity of the Dissenters Would not be Inconsistent with the Act of Toleration*, in *True Collection*, ii. 327.

accused the Church of a 'Persecution' that would destroy the kind of unity that Queen Anne was trying to establish in the state. Throughout all of these pamphlets, the figure of Sacheverell and his sermon threatening to hang out the 'bloody Flag' of massacre were invoked as an example of the potential for violence in the attitudes of the High Church.[36] The subtitle of *The Parallel* was *The Shortest Way to Prevent the Growth of Popery in Ireland*, an indication that as long as the High Church pressed its war against the Dissenters, Defoe would continue to fight the battle that brought him to the pillory.

VI

Some writers on Defoe have argued that, after his three days in the pillory and his total of five months in Newgate, at least a part of his soul remained forever in bondage. They see a major change in Defoe's ways of thinking about the world and society after these events. Some view it as the turning-point for a move from a radical stance toward society to a more conservative attitude. Certainly, the experience forced him to reassess his relationships to those in power and toward the group with which he most strongly identified—the Dissenters.[37] But it did not change his very strong identification with the ways of ordinary Englishmen. In the preface to *More Reformation*, when trying to appeal to the unfairness of his treatment, he drew for his analogy upon the sport of boxing as practised by his countrymen:

England *is particularly famous for the most generous way of Fighting in the World, I mean as to the common Peoples private Quarrels, while the* Dutch *mangle one another with Knives, the* Scotch *Highlanders knock one anothers Brains out with Pole-Axes, the* Irish *stab with their Skeins, and* Spaniards *with the Daggers; the* English *Men fairly Box it out, and in this way of Fighting the Rabble stand by to see fair Play, as they call it, which is, that when a Man is down 'tis counted foul Play, and the Trick of a Coward, to strike him, but let him rise, and then have at him.*[38]

Though the term 'Rabble' may seem to imply contempt, Defoe was clearly

---

[36] *The Parallel*, in *True Collection*, ii. 375.

[37] One traveller to England during this period remarked that people who were pilloried seemed to go on with their lives as if no earthshaking event had occurred. As a visitor from contemporary Switzerland, he thought this very odd. See Béat Louis de Muralt, *Letters Describing the Character and Customs of the English and French Nations* (London, 1726), 68. Muralt was in England for about two years, arriving in 1693 and leaving in Dec. 1694.

[38] Defoe, *More Reformation*, in *True Collection*, ii. [28–9]. Defoe used the same image in *The Shortest Way to Peace and Union*, in *True Collection*, ii. 441.

not contemptuous of the attitudes of the people, not ready to adopt the usual Augustan fear and hatred of the mob. The man who could look back on the time when every Englishman was master of the longbow for his diversion and for use in time of war may have had a tendency to romanticize the life of the ordinary English countryman, but he was unlikely ever to adopt Bernard Mandeville's notion that it was in the interest of the ruling orders to keep the poor ignorant, subservient, and drunk. And he never abandoned the theory of the legitimate sovereignty of the people in creating a revolution.

None of these attitudes prevented him from considering himself a gentleman. Such a notion lay behind his offer to lead a company of horse for Queen Anne. He was not treated as a gentleman by the authorities, who might have thought his various trade activities excluded him from such a category, but Defoe did not see any contradiction between being a gentleman and his various occupations as a wine merchant, hosier, and author. He often claimed that he did not write for 'Bread'. That may have been true from a variety of viewpoints, but his objections to the piracy involved in the publication of the *Collection* as a form of robbery suggests that he did not object to getting paid for his labours as an author. His portrait, painted by Jeremiah Taverner and engraved by Van der Gucht, appeared as a frontispiece to the first volume of his *True Collection* accompanied with a coat of arms—three griffins on a shield with the head of a griffin above.[39] Whether he obtained this distinction through the Heralds' Office or simply through the Painters' Company is impossible to determine, but he used the three griffins as a seal in his business transactions.[40] All of this suggests that in his own mind he was no one's servant or slave.

Nevertheless, he was a paid employee of the government, receiving about £200 a year in secret service funds, an income that would have made all but a few writers during this period more than a little envious. For this money, he did double duty as a spy and as an author. Though various writers tried to get rewards for doing similar work, his willingness to write more or less what his employers wanted may not appear suitable to the high standards of independence claimed by many modern authors. Judged by the realities of Defoe's time as well as by most modern standards, however, his position was perfectly understandable. He was not unlike a writer doing a column for a present-day periodical with a particular political slant. Harley, Godolphin, and Sunderland allowed him to say what he wanted on

[39] See *Bryan's Dictionary of Painters and Engravers*, ed. George C. Williamson (New York: Macmillan, 1905), v. 155.
[40] See his seal in the purchase of land around Colchester: Colchester Records Office.

most issues, but now and then they wanted a particular viewpoint expressed. Rather than give up so lucrative a position, he obliged. Not until 1710 was he actually writing things he did not believe, and not until 1713 and 1714 was he in the position of confronting a situation in which the ideas he was asked to support were truly detestable to him. But it should have been clear from the writings coming out of Newgate in 1703 that he was not going to stop writing about subjects that interested him and writing from his own angle of vision. It merely meant that, on occasions, where he disagreed violently, he would have to write surreptitiously. Defoe was so prone to taking risks that without the help of the government he might have been back in prison on numerous occasions. What those secret conversations with Robert Harley between September 1703 and May 1704 were actually about will never be known, but everything suggests that Defoe did not think that Harley was asking him to sell his soul as well as his pen.

10

'Writing History Sheet by Sheet': Defoe, *The Review*, and *The Storm*

On 19 February 1704, Defoe brought out his first issue of a newspaper. He used a number of titles throughout its ten-year run, but it began as *A Weekly Review of the Affairs of France: Purg'd from the Errors and Partiality of News-Writers, and Petty Statesmen of All Sides*. When it was published in the form of a volume at the end of the year, Defoe expanded his title considerably. Not only was he writing of France but of '*All Europe, As Influenc'd by that Nation: Being Historical observations, on the Publick Transactions of the World*', and he added an advertisement for one of the most popular features of his journal: '*With an Entertaining Part in every Sheet, Being Advice from the Scandal Club, to the Curious Enquirers; in Answer to Letters sent them for that Purpose*'. And it was no longer a weekly published on Saturday but a bi-weekly and then a tri-weekly. The *Review* was not a newspaper in the sense that it printed the daily news. That function was already the province of the *Daily Courant*. Rather it was very like the work of I. F. Stone, who published a kind of extended editorial every week during the 1950s and 1960s. In addition to the four-page essay on the power of France, economics, or any subject that interested him, Defoe included in the second number a page or two of entertainment. He borrowed the name of a French journal, the *Mercure Scandale*, which he translated as 'Advice from the Scandalous Club'.

I

Though most of Defoe's productions had been very serious indeed, his contemporaries appreciated the wit of his lampoons, and he thought he would attract readers by creating a mythical society to deal with errors of other newspapers and with various subjects, some light and some fairly serious. Although John Dunton thought that the idea for this feature had been stolen from his *Athenian Mercury*, Defoe had a number of models in mind, among which was the very popular *Advices from Parnassus* of Trajano Boccalini, which featured a court of Apollo to which various supplicants came with their problems to get a judgement from the patron god of the arts. This borrowing was more obvious at the beginning, when Defoe devoted most sections to the mistakes of various newspapers, mistakes of geography and history as well as errors in grammar and style. Like Apollo, the members of the Scandal Club would sentence the offending party to various acts of penance. Although Defoe had made comments on his fellow authors before, the Scandal Club gave him the opportunity to revel in his own ability as a writer of extraordinarily effective prose. That this kind of criticism did not please his fellow news writers needs hardly to be mentioned, but it had an effect that he probably intended. It set up an interaction between contemporary journals that occasionally produced some of the best political discussions of the period. Until Steele began his *Tatler* in 1710 and introduced a type of entertainment that better suited the polite social humour of the times, Defoe had no real rival among contemporary journalists.

If Boccalini furnished a model for the Scandal Club at the beginning, Defoe soon expanded the function of this section of the *Review* to handle discussions of various social and ethical issues of the period. Such commentary provoked letters from readers, and soon Defoe found that he had made contact with those kinds of readers who had previously sent their problems to Dunton's Athenian Society for solutions. The letters to Dunton's journal were often questions intended to puzzle, and Defoe gave official status to this aspect of reader interest by setting 'Enigmas' or riddles of the kind that were still providing domestic pleasure into the nineteenth century, when they were used to afford entertainment for the picnickers at Box Hill in Jane Austen's *Emma*. How many of the letters printed in the *Review* were composed or drastically revised by Defoe, we will never know. The form of Defoe's later essays in *Mist's Journal* and *Applebee's Weekly* were almost entirely epistolary contributions, and there is little doubt that he honed his abilities while writing his *Review*. But that the vast majority were genuine there can be little doubt. Defoe avoided the pedantry that filled the *Athenian Mercury*, and focused on what we would think of as pieces of 'human interest'. As Mr Review, he took on the character of a highly sympathetic and humane figure, so much so that one of his tasks involved distributing charitable donations. His readers trusted that he would select a worthy recipient. They knew him as the notorious Daniel Defoe and viewed him both as someone with wide experience in the world and as a person who, having suffered imprisonment and the pillory, could sympathize with suffering. If Defoe created a kind of fictional character as 'the Author of the Review' or 'Mr. Review', it was more in these sections than in his writing on politics. Even his worst enemies could agree that what he had to say on the sufferings undergone by bankrupts or his attacks upon those who controlled the coal trade or the trade in grain demonstrated his humane approach to England as a community in which no one should be forced to suffer because of the greed of a few or the unreasonableness of the laws. In many ways, it is a shame that he lost interest in this form of entertainment long before his readers did. Some of the exchanges give us glimpses into the domestic life of the period that are extraordinarily valuable.

But entertainment was surely not Defoe's main reason for starting the *Review*. He stated in the preface to the first volume that he conceived of the project while he was still in Newgate ('*in* Tenebris'), but the original idea was surely much less abstract than Defoe's description would have it. He probably intended to direct a subtle attack upon the bills against occasional conformity by way of a historical discussion of France's treatment of its Huguenots. Something similar had been done by Henry Care during the time of the Popish Plot. Instead of addressing the plot directly, Care, in his *Weekly Pacquet of Advice from Rome*, gave a running history of the plots fomented by the Catholic Church in the form of a weekly periodical.[1] Thus, in his first number, Defoe promised:

We shall particularly have a Regard to the Rise and Fall of the Protestant Religion in the Dominions of *France*; and the Reader, if the Author live, and is permitted to pursue the Design shall find this Paper a useful Index to turn him to the best historians of the Church in all Ages.

Here he shall find the mighty Struggle the Protestant Churches met with in that Kingdom for near 200 Years; the Strong Convulsions of their Expiring Circumstances; the True History of the vast Expence and mighty Endeavours of this nation to support them; and at last, the sudden and violent Destruction of them in *France*, by the Solemn Revocation of the Edict of *Nantes*.[2]

---

[1] In addition to the historical account that constituted 6 pages of the journal, Care devoted 2 pages, headed 'The Courant', to current topics. These were often in the form of a dialogue between Tory and Trueman, but he occasionally had poetry, commentary, and dialogues between other characters. Defoe followed a similar format with his 'Advice from the Scandal Club' and 'Miscellanea'. The journal ran from 3 Sept. 1679 to 13 July 1683, but the *DNB* says that the last volume was mainly the work of Thomas Salmon.

[2] *Review*, i. 2. Subsequent references to this work will appear in parentheses within my text.

And he promised to treat the experiences of the Huguenots' church 'in her Solitude and Sufferings' (i. 2), her behaviour under persecution, and the scattering of her worshippers around the world. He also promised to write about the present-day war with France in a manner that would be 'stript from the false Glosses of Parties' (i. 3) and all in the name of 'Truth' as written by an 'Impartial and Exact Historical Pen' (i. 4) When he came to assess what he had done over the first year, he had to admit that he had digressed. Like the future narrator of *Tristram Shandy*, who defended digressing on the grounds that there was always a wealth of possibilities to explore, Defoe had found too much to say about trade and other subjects to keep to his original purpose. Although one biographer has questioned whether Defoe was really following Harley's instructions in beginning his journal, certainly the *Review* that developed into a medium for commenting on England's foreign and domestic affairs took its cues from the soon-to-be Secretary of State. Harley had never been out of England, and Defoe's letters and enclosures to him on foreign affairs were often in the form of instructive memos. England was engaged in a major land war in Flanders, and Harley probably saw some necessity for keeping the English public informed about the reasons for this war as well as for English policy in the Great Northern War between Charles XII of Sweden and Peter the Great. Many Englishmen thought that England ought to worry only about a navy that would keep a 'wooden wall' around England. Defoe was interested in England's greatness as a world power. He knew that France was not only the major military power in Europe but also the dominant cultural force of the West—the seat of the academy which he admired so much and the possessor of a language which was spoken in almost all the courts of Europe.

The need to keep French power in check had been the burden of all he had written during both the standing army controversy and the affair of the Kentish petition. France was Catholic, the persecutor of the Huguenots, and the leading exponent of absolutism. By getting his readers to understand the reasons for the greatness of France, Defoe would enable them to make the kinds of distinction about foreign policy that, in turn, would enable the government to conduct the war in a proper fashion. They had to be made to grasp the concept of the balance of power that made keeping the Spanish colonies out of the control of France important, and they had to be made to understand the dynamics of trade that made France into a dangerous rival of England. They had to be made to comprehend how important the wool trade was to English prosperity and the ways in which France threatened to take over English markets.

Defoe's enemies liked to criticize his weak Latin and ungrammatical French, but he could answer such attacks by pointing to his knowledge of modern languages, his understanding of the workings of trade, and his grasp of large historical patterns. They may have attacked him for his 'self-conceit', but when they had to argue with him, his opponents had to try to match his level of expertise. Charles Leslie, author of *The Rehearsal* and an opponent of Defoe for many years, respected his thinking about politics enough to engage him in a lengthy debate over England's political establishment, and almost everyone acknowledged his expertise concerning trade. The *Review* was to become a formidable weapon in the propaganda wars for a succession of administrations. Whatever Harley's intentions, with the *Review* Defoe did not set himself up as a medium of information for Harley so much as establish himself as an indispensable figure in the machinery of government propaganda. As the Secretary of State for the Northern Department, Harley must also have seen it as an organ for informing the country and supporting the Union between England and Scotland. More than a year was to pass before Defoe was to write his essays on the progress of the Union from Scotland, but we know that while he was still in prison he was Harley's candidate for the ideal agent to be involved in getting the Union passed in Edinburgh. If he had supported the Kentish petitioners with pamphlets, open demonstration, and a brief history, now perhaps he could do something like that on a far grander scale.

By Tuesday 18 March 1704, with some apology to the 'Injury done the Eye-sight' of his readers, he settled into the format he would keep for the next ten years, a half-sheet of paper printed as four pages with double columns. Although the *Review* was not intimate in its personal details about Defoe's life, he did not hesitate to draw upon personal experience, and his choice of subjects reflected concerns so particular as to reveal his personality in a manner that someone like Swift would have found objectionable. He set himself strongly against duelling, and argued, contrary to gentlemanly standards of the time, that the husband who would put his life at risk because his wife was unfaithful to him was a fool. The Scandal Club ruled that a man might marry against his father's wishes if the father could not give good reasons against it, and almost invariably sympathized with the plight of women in their relationships with men. And Defoe frequently assumed the attitude that he had taken in *The Poor Man's Plea*, arguing that 'Punishing Vices in the Poor, which are daily practis'd by the Rich, seems to me to be, setting our Constitution with the wrong end upward, and making men Criminals because they want Money' (i. 353). He did not please all, but to one person who suggested that he was touching on dangerous issues, he wrote, '. . . may those Writers be for ever D----d to Silence, who seeing the laws broke, Good Manners Invaded, Justice Abus'd, the Innocent punish'd, and the Guilty sit in the Chair of Authority, are afraid to let the World know who is the Villain' (i. 354). If Defoe had undergone a dramatic change of character after being pilloried, it was not evident from the first year of the *Review*.

As a commentator on current events, Defoe liked to follow a story in depth. That was one of his thoughts in starting the *Review*, and he was to follow his idea even when some readers complained that they had had more than enough. He ended up giving more space to the Great Northern War than to the war in Flanders, where Marlborough's victory at Blenheim might have made that the preoccupation of the journal. Defoe was still trying to explain the reasons why the English should not support the Hungarian 'Protestants', as he had in the first piece he ever wrote. Perhaps the fact that Harley himself had found this difficult to understand convinced Defoe that there was a need to clarify the issues. The Turks were always to be regarded as the enemies of the Christian nations of western Europe, and when the Hungarians allied themselves with the Turks, they were not to be sympathized with however badly the Austrians treated them. England was allied with the Empire against France, and whatever detracted from that war, no matter how noble in itself, was bad for the nation. The Hungarian revolt under Rakoczy was a distraction for the imperialists and therefore bad for war against France. 'No Man can wish the *Hungarians* Success, without wishing the Duke of *Marlborough* to be beaten; his Army Destroy'd their Brethren and Countrymen under his Command, Trampled down by the *French* and *Bavarian*', he wrote (i. 222). He also had to explain why the English ought not to support the genuinely Protestant King of Sweden, Charles XII. That monarch, according to Defoe, was simply interested in pursuing his own glory without any interest in the Protestant forces allied against Louis XIV. He had also failed his people. The wellbeing of the people was, for Defoe, the highest law, and Charles XII, by allowing his nation to be invaded by Russia, had betrayed his trust.

If the main principle of foreign policy was the wellbeing of the state placed above any abstract concept of right, Defoe usually excluded ethical considerations in treating the sphere of economics. He praised the policies of Holland in this respect. The Dutch believed that nothing should cause a break in trade, not even war between two countries. They had agreed to a cessation of trade with France for one year at the beginning of the war, but were reluctant to continue such a policy. The Dutch system subordinated the interest of the state to that of individual merchants, and returning to trade with the enemy seemed as natural to them as it seemed unnatural to the English. Defoe argued that where trade was advantageous to a nation not even a war should interrupt it, instancing a time when the Dutch were at war with the Algerians yet traded ammunition to them. Defoe admitted that such a practice might seem odd, but insisted, 'they were in the Right of it' (i. 366), and that England too should consider trading with France. Though he was later to dramatize the conflict between trade and morality, Defoe never really believed that ethics could be applied to a world of activity dominated more entirely by self-interest than foreign affairs was dominated by national self-interest. This compartmentalizing of these modes of action was typical of Defoe's method of thinking, as a journal such as the *Review*, with its wide range of topics, was to make obvious.

II

Reading the *Review* is a good way of following Defoe's interests over the next decade of his life, but its focus on large, historical subjects often made it a less reliable reflection of his response to the events of his time than his individual pamphlets. Defoe liked to keep the drafts of certain projects in his desk to be worked on when inspiration or specific events of the time made them relevant. If he had conceived of his journal while in Newgate, he also kept busy on one other project there as well. He had started an epic satiric poem, which he was to call *Jure Divino*, and he may, as he states, have completed most of the poem before leaving prison. At any rate, he had written a sufficient number of verses to advertise in the *Review* of 26 September 1704 that a subscription for those interested in purchasing a copy was available for ten shillings. And in November 1703, the month he was released from prison, he apparently made plans for writing an account of a week-long storm that struck England on Wednesday 24 November.

This was no ordinary storm. In her proclamation of a fast day published in *The London Gazette* for 16 December, Queen Anne announced, 'A Calamity of this Sort so Dreadful and Astonishing that the like hath not been Seen or Felt, in the Memory of any Person Living in this Our Kingdom, and which Loudly Calls for the Deepest and most Solemn Humiliation of Our People.' There was no doubt that God had visited this storm upon the nation, but humility and repentance might let God know that the English people acknowledged his power.

The announcement proceeds to speak of the 'Crying Sins of this Nation', and offers the hope that such a fast might avert further evidence of God's wrath. The archbishops and bishops were requested to write special prayers for the occasion. If, then, to the modern reader, Defoe's work seems too strongly informed by a sense that God's presence might be detected in the winds, he was hardly out of step with the feelings of religious men and women throughout the nation.

Like most of his contemporaries, he believed that God manifested himself in great natural events such as plagues, earthquakes, volcanic eruptions, and storms. He collected accounts of the Great Plague of 1665 over the years, but he was a genuine witness to the storm, and he wanted the events captured in the fullest way possible. He contracted with one of his chief publishers, John Nutt, and advertised in the London Gazette on 6 December for all clergymen and others who had 'made Observations of this Calamity, that they would transmit as distinct an Account as possible, of what they have observed' to the 'Undertakers'. He added that he wanted only observations that the writers knew to be true and wanted the names of the writers of the reports.

By the standards of the day, Defoe was attempting to provide something like a scientific account of the cause and effects of the storm, and he was also following through on his efforts in the *Review* to write an authentic version of present-day history. His training under Charles Morton brought him into contact with the basic aims of the Royal Society in the way of verified accounts of places, things, and events. He tried to learn as much as possible about the causes of winds, just as he was later to try to learn as much as possible about theories concerning the causes of plagues when he was writing his *Journal of the Plague Year*. He was to collect the accounts he received with scrupulous care in weighing their authenticity, and he gave credit to those who sent him materials.

In signing himself at the end of his preface 'The Age's Humble Servant', Defoe was referring to his role as a historian of modern events that would be passed on to the future.[3] The preface is an interesting discussion of print culture and history. Defoe argued that the printed book had replaced the oral culture whose most common literary output was the sermon delivered throughout the land each Sunday. 'Preaching of Sermons', he wrote, 'is speaking to a few of Mankind; printing of book is talking to the whole world' (250). The modern historian passed his observations down to posterity in a medium available to every reader. He had an obligation to tell the truth and ran the 'risk' of ruining his reputation and of sinning against

---

[3] *The Storm* (1704), in *Works* (London: Bohn, 1855), v. 258. Subsequent page references to this work will refer to this edition and appear within parentheses in my text.

mankind when he made a mistake. Turning to the ancient myths, legends, and histories, Defoe argued that all the pagan gods as well as some of the figures appearing in the Bible were actually great men, whose real lives were distorted into mythological stories by the lack of true history. This argument, known as euhemerism, was to be an important element in *Jure Divino*, but here it was employed to throw doubt upon historical texts of the past and to warn against reading the fables of the ancient world, as well as those of the Middle Ages, as anything but fictions. His list of some of the popular English romances, including *Guy of Warwick* and *Bevis of Southampton*, suggests his familiarity with a contemporary type of fiction with which his enemies were sometimes to identify him, but here he named them as examples of the very opposite of what he was trying to achieve—a true account of a terrifying natural phenomenon.

Defoe was no cool and distanced observer of the storm. On the evening of 24 November he 'narrowly escaped' (273) being killed or badly injured by the collapse of part of a house near him, and the falling of tiles from the roofs of buildings must have made going outside extremely dangerous. He succeeded in reaching home, and being indoors seemed safe enough until the evening of Friday the 26th, when the velocity of the wind began to increase. Defoe made observations from his own barometer and found 'the Mercury sunk lower than ever I had observed it on any occasion whatsoever, which made me suppose the tube had been handled and disturbed by the children' (273). This is an intimate glimpse into the Defoe household, where apparently children were as mischievous as their modern counterparts and parents equally exasperated by the breaking of prized possessions. In this instance, however, the children were not at fault. After midnight the storm increased in force to the extent that sleep was almost impossible:

The author of this relation was in a well built brick house in the skirts of the city, and a stack of chimneys falling in upon the next houses, gave the house such a shock that they thought it was just coming down upon their heads. But opening the door to attempt an escape into a garden, the danger was so apparent, that they all thought fit to surrender to the disposal of Almighty Providence, and expect their graves in the ruines of the house, rather than to meet most certain destruction in the open garden for, unless they could have gone above two hundred yards from any building, there had been no security; for the force of the wind blew the tiles point blank; though their weight inclines them downward. (276)

Defoe observed some of the tiles flying thirty to forty yards and embedding themselves in the earth up to eight inches. As much as he may have tried to be a dispassionate observer, the scene in the Defoe household could not have been very different from that in the home of the minister John Gibbs, who wrote Defoe that the 'shrieks and cries of my dear babes perfectly stun'd me', and who added 'I think I hear them still in my ears, I shall not easily, I am confident, if ever, forget them' (392).

Despite the lasting shock that some experienced, on 3 December, the day after the wind stopped, Defoe went to the Thames to observe the 700 or so ships that had been tossed together in heaps by the wind. Defoe estimated the number of those killed on land to be 123, a relatively low figure considering the devastation, but the 8000 killed at sea had to appear appalling. Some of his most vivid accounts depict the horror of those wrecked mariners who managed to achieve a temporary safety on the Goodwin Sands, where the sea would eventually overwhelm them if they were not rescued. Though Defoe credits a Thomas Powell of the town of Deal with rescuing 200 of these men, he notes that the rest of the citizens of Deal ignored the agonized cries of these hapless men to search for booty among the wrecked ships. Powell is depicted as breaking the law in confiscating some boats from the customs officials to achieve his rescues, reminding us that Defoe continued to admire anarchistic acts of this kind. About a month after the storm, Defoe made a 'circuit' of Kent and tried to keep count of the trees that had been uprooted. He says that he stopped at 17,000 (344). One statistic that he gave in some detail must have left him longing to return to his former profession. The price of tiles went up almost six times and pantiles more than three times, from 50s. per 1000 to £10. And Defoe predicted that there would not be a sufficient supply for a year. The master of well-timed pamphlets must have wondered a little about his timing as a former manufacturer of roof tiles and trader in lumber.

Before publishing his full account of the storm, Defoe brought out *The Lay-Man's Sermon upon the Late Storm; Held forth at an Honest Coffee-House-Conventicle. Not so much a Jest as 'tis Thought to be* on 24 February 1704. The odd subtitle gives away the political nature of the work, since from their very inception during the Restoration, coffee-houses were considered sites of dangerous political exchange. Defoe begins in something like a sermon mode. Arguing that the 'Voice of his Judgements is heard in the Voice of Nature', he proceeds to argue that 'As God in all the Works of his Providence, makes use of the subserviency of means, so the whole Creation is Subordinate to the Execution of his Divine will . . . the most Powerful Elements are so subjected to his almighty power that the Clouds are but as Dust under his Feet'.[4] It was in the interpretation of the events

---

[4] *The Lay-Man's Sermon upon the Late Storm; Held forth at an Honest Coffee-House-Conventicle. Not so much a Jest as 'tis Thought to be* (London, 1704), 3.

that Defoe made his political points. He admitted that he was among those who believed that the storm might be a punishment for England's ingratitude toward King William, but he treated such a reaction as a 'feeling' rather than a reality. In fact Defoe did not believe that an event of this kind could be interpreted easily and certainly not on the basis of success or failure. He was to write in the *Review*, 'I most readily allow that the Justice of a Cause is not always to be found in the Success; and the most Wicked Designs in the World have often been the most Prosperous' (i. 266), and given the deaths of so many innocent sailors, the storm could hardly be read as a punishment of those in the coal trade who so often raised prices beyond the limits of the poor to pay.[5] Despite such attitudes and warnings, Defoe was willing to take some political advantage by turning the event into a chastisement of those men who refused to pursue a path of 'Moderation', particularly the High Church party and the Jacobites. He also managed to add a few satirical remarks directed at bad admirals such as Rooke and some of his particular enemies. The last part of the subtitle provided a clue to what Defoe was doing—wanting to have his cake and eat it too, as usual. He wanted his audience to be somewhat amused at the futility of trying to find explanations for events beyond the knowledge of human beings, but he also wanted his ideal reader to accept everything he was saying as correct.

III

One of the significant metaphors used by Defoe during 1704 was that of the author sentenced to a silence that was equivalent to a kind of death, yet, as W. P. Trent remarked, this year 'was one of the busiest and most important of Defoe's crowded life', and during this time Defoe emerged 'as the briskest and most scurrying genius in the annals of English Literature'.[6] But the year began slowly enough for a writer who could compose a pamphlet a day. He may have been reading and studying, preparing for writing the *Review* by organizing his knowledge of French history. What he refers to as his 'circuit' of Kent may have taken part of January. Whether this trip was connected with observations for his book on the great storm or whether he was engaged in some work for Harley is difficult to say. Certainly *The Storm* involved some reading in scientific literature

---

[5] *The Lay-Man's Sermon upon the Late Storm*, 9. He ascribes such judgements to others, but manages to inject it as a piece of social criticism.

[6] Trent Collection, fo. 98.

about winds and storms, but this would hardly have occupied all the time of Trent's 'most scurrying genius'.

During these early months of 1704 all sorts of exciting events occurred. There was another Jacobite plot to bring the Pretender to Scotland for an attempt at the crown; the two Houses of Parliament were feuding over who should try cases involving elections to the House of Commons; Marlborough was preparing to lead the allied forces to victory over the forces of France; and eastern Europe was in turmoil with a revolution in Hungary and an attempt to take over the Polish monarchy. Defoe was eventually to comment to some extent on all these events, but for a time he seemed content to limit himself to topics that picked up on remarks made by Queen Anne in her speeches to Parliament encouraging harmony among her subjects and upon the House of Lord's address to the Queen praising her 'Royal Moderation'.[7]

The trouble was that Defoe's notion of encouraging harmony and moderation was to attack what he considered to be the enemies of progressive thinking—the enemies of the Act of Succession, toleration for the Dissenters, and reverence for the accomplishments of King William III. Defoe's method, for the most part, involved an exercise in what we now think of as the Whig theory of history and what many of his contemporaries would have considered to be the Calves Head Club theory of history. In this view, the Stuarts were both immoral and tyrannical. He praised a sermon of White Kennet calling for a 'Compassionate Enquiry into the Causes of the Civil War', and noted that an antagonist who had called White Kennet another Milton had delivered the highest compliment possible to the clergyman. Defoe's own view, as stated in *The Christianity of the High Church Consider'd*, was that Charles I had 'aspir'd too greedily after Arbitrary Monarchy'. Englishmen would not bear an abridgement of their 'Civil Right' and rebelled. Cromwell was not the monster the Stuarts claimed. 'Everything was quiet and peaceable throught these Dominions,' Defoe wrote of Cromwell's rule, 'and the People in them (at least seemingly) Happy, and the Nation Wealthy, and all its Affairs Successful and Prosperous.'[8] If the Anglican Church had its way, it might have treated James II the same way Cromwell treated Charles I. The Glorious Revolution of 1688 brought an end to tyranny. Providence brought William to the throne and after him, Anne, the 'Queen of the Revolution'.[9] And Defoe suggested that this was the history accepted by all those in

[7] See *JHL*, xvii. 541.
[8] *The Christianity of the High-Church Consider'd* (London, 1704), 6–8.
[9] Ibid. 14.

favour of 'Moderation'.[10] Small wonder that Defoe's enemies choked on so innocuous a word.

All of this suggests that Defoe was gradually regaining his nerve. He began attacking his favourite target, the House of Commons, once more and assumed his old satanic guise of Legion. In *Legion's Humble Address to the Lords*, published in the spring of 1704, Defoe took the side of the Lords in the matter of Ashby v. White. The Commons did not have the right to deprive the people of the town of Maidstone of their right to elect their own members:

That whenever a house of Commons shall Part with, Expose, Neglect, or Suffer to be Infringed, the Liberties, Rights, and Peace of the People they Represent, they Betray their Trust, violate the Genral Reason and nature of their being Chosen, their Representing Power and Being ceases of course, and they become from that time forward a Mighty Conventicle, an Unlawful Assembly and may and ought to be Deposed and Dismist by the same Laws of Nature and Right that Oppressed Subjects may, and all Agree have, Deposed Bloody and Tyrannick Princes.[11]

Defoe accused the Commons of attempting to mislead the Queen by suggesting that she sat on the throne by right of hereditary succession rather than through the decisions of Parliament, and criticized them for their insistence upon reassuming the grants made by William III, taking them away from people without any thought of the merit of the rewards while the gifts of Charles II 'to Whores, Bastards, Papists, and Publick Enemies to the Nation' were allowed to stand without challenge.[12]

Defoe ended this pamphlet by playing on the theme of the Kentish petition. 'Our Name is *Million*, and We are more.'[13] As was his custom in these attacks upon the House of Commons, he composed one of his lampoons for the occasion. *The Address* has the same combination of wit, rough but successful versification, and effective attack that distinguished his earlier works in this mode. The Whig lords at this time seemed to Defoe to be the real guardians of liberty. It was the Commons that had attempted to abridge freedom of the press, who had urged the Queen to use her prerogative against the House of Lords, and who kept on trying to pass bills against Occasional Conformity and against the Dissenters in general. To say the least, it was an unusual House of Commons:

---

[10] He made this point more strongly in *Moderation Maintain'd* (London, 1704), 23. This work is advertised as the end of *The Christianity of the High-Church*.

[11] I am quoting from a text that incorporates Defoe's text and responds: *Legion's Humble Address to the Lords, Answer'd Paragraph by Paragraph* (n.p., n.d. [probably London, 1704]), 2.

[12] Ibid. 5. Defoe used the same argument and almost exactly the same language in *The Address*. See Frank Ellis (ed.), *Poems on Affairs of State: Augustan Satirical Verse, 1660–1714* (New Haven, Conn.: Yale University Press, 1970) (*POAS* vi), 639.   [13] Ibid. 8.

> In former Times, when Tyrants Reign'd,
> > Your Treatments were too rough,
> But if you'd have your Sense Explain'd
> You give the Queen to understand,
> > She's not Severe Enough.
>
> • • •
>
> This Nation has had Kings enough,
> That rul'd with Power Despotick,
> Who of Tyrannick Arts made proof,
> And us'd the nation much too rough,
> > By Means and Ways Exotic.[14]

As Frank Ellis suggested, Defoe had by now dropped any mention of his objections to Occasional Conformity.[15] It was one thing to quarrel with his fellow Dissenters on a narrow issue of conscience, when the Act of Toleration seemed to be the law of the land; it was quite another matter when the entire system of toleration installed by William III was under fierce attack. Now the issue was what Defoe called 'Civil Right'. The Lords had raised objections to the first bill, and it died for want of consensus between the two Houses. But the Commons were in the mood to try again, and William Bromley introduced another bill on the morning of 27 November 1703. One of the stanzas of *The Address* noted that the incredible storm that struck England a few hours later was surely a sign of God's displeasure.

None of these works indicates that Harley had decided to rein in Defoe in any dramatic way. An effort was made to have Defoe arrested for authoring these last two works, but it was ignored.[16] Harley was opposed to the attempts to pass the bills against Occasional Conformity, and as a 'Court Tory' he may have hoped for a House that would be more tractable; but he could not have been entirely happy with everything Defoe was writing. On the other hand, on matters such as King William's partition treaties and his grants, he probably knew that he was unlikely to change Defoe's mind. Harley was clever enough to know that Defoe would be more useful to him as a person offering independent ideas in private and maintaining those ideas in print than as someone acting entirely as his agent; and while Defoe was willing to write what Harley ordered, he also seems to have understood for the most part what Harley wanted. He gambled on the

[14] Ibid. 644. With a certain irony, the House of Lords remarked that they were 'still at a Loss to know what [the House of Commons] truly mean, by Your Majesty's re-assuming Your just Prerogative', *JHL*, xvii. 541. See also *JHC*, xiv. 362.

[15] *POAS*, vi. 632.

[16] Portland Papers, HMC (10 vols., London: Eyre & Spottiswoode, 1899), iv. 93. The message was sent by a J.W. on 14 June 1704.

belief that he would be thought useful enough to the government to allow him to take the kinds of risk that seemed to give a certain gusto to his life.

At any rate, Harley had no reason to feel displeased with his situation. The Earl of Nottingham, Defoe's hated enemy, resigned from his position as Secretary of State on 20 April 1704, and on Thursday 4 May Narcissus Luttrell noted in his diary the expectation that Harley would replace him as Secretary of State for the Northern Department. Harley's new status must have made Defoe even more useful than before. The move was not finalized for six more days, and some of the problems involved may have caused an interruption in what must have been a series of meetings between Harley and Defoe. On 12 May 1704 Defoe wrote to Harley expressing his disappointment in not seeing Harley the previous evening, revealing that he had been told that their meetings had been observed. He spoke of the shock this gave him and of his plan to make their meetings more secret in the future. Defoe suggested that Harley's reply should be sent to the maid-servant at the office of the Auditor of the Imprest, where Edward Harley, Robert's brother, was employed, or at Jones's Coffee House in Finch Lane.

As mentioned before, Defoe's entire correspondence with Harley was supposed to be secret, and the one letter we have from Harley to Defoe was mainly an injunction to destroy all his letters. From this point forward up until 1706, Defoe signed his letters with a symbol or with the initials of one of his pseudonyms, Alexander Goldsmith. Four days later he was once more having difficulty making connections with Harley, and ended with the comment: 'I Impatiently Wait to Reciev your Ordrs, and to Inform you of the Disappointment, Wishing if Possible the Time May Come, that you May find this Neglected fellow Servicable, or at least Make him So' (H 14). To conclude that Harley had made no use of Defoe's talents up to this point would be a mistake. Rather, it should be taken as part of the many expressions of gratitude toward Harley and his readiness to serve him further.

Harley's next proposal was to send Defoe to the Continent. The country is designated by Defoe as H-------, which Healey thought likely to be Hanover, although Holland is another obvious possibility. Defoe thought enough of what he had been doing to importune Harley for a position in the Auditor's office where Harley's brother worked. 'Accounts are my perticular Element,' wrote Defoe, 'what I have Allways been Master of' (H 15). He saw himself in possession of an office which he might pass down to his sons, and argued that he could put someone else in charge while he was away and keep his connection with it concealed. Barring this possibility, Defoe requested a reliable payment for his services, or, as he put it, 'a Convenient Private Allowance for subsistence' on which he could 'depend'

(H 15). What is clear from the refusal of a regular government position and Defoe's continual requests for funds is that Harley probably preferred him to be in a position of dependence.

Through Harley's intervention, the Queen provided immediate funds for Defoe and his family, and sometime toward the beginning of May Defoe wrote to thank Harley and the Queen. He was expecting some large assignment but still had not been given proper instructions. He referred to himself as 'a Man in the Dark' (H 16), wanting to know to what project he should direct himself. At this point he began one of his more confessional letters to Harley. Using a Crusoe-like metaphor, he compared himself to a man lost at sea who found the distance to the shore too great for him to manage. This great 'Gulph' is the £1000 he owes his creditors. He allowed that £500–£600 would free him sufficiently to put off paying the rest, but casting out a fairly obvious hint, he remarked, 'the Summe is Too Large for me to Expect' (H 16). He then informed Harley of his pantile business in Essex, the 100 families he employed there, and his £600 profit a year. After mentioning his seven 'Beautifull and hopefull Children', Defoe then explained that one of the reasons he stood out against Nottingham was that Nottingham tried to seduce Mary when she went to see him. Though doubt has been cast upon Defoe's account, it seems impossible that Defoe or Mary would have concocted such a story, and one can feel his anger rise in the telling of it.[17] Defoe ended this letter by saying that he never despaired and never lost his faith, and by apologizing for so detailed an account. 'The Miserable are allways full of Their Own Cases and Think Nothing Impertinent' (H 18). If Defoe was here following the advice of Baltasar Gracián and playing the 'card of sincerity', he was nevertheless doing it very well.[18] Trying to show himself as an open and honest personality who would play fairly with Harley, he attempted to interest Harley in his situation. This is not to say that Defoe did not have his genuine moments of sincerity and openness, but everything suggests that he never wrote a line to Harley which was not carefully considered in regard to the effect it would produce.

Thus, even in these early days of their relationship, Defoe was hardly entirely free and generous in dealing with Harley. In his next letter,

---

[17] See G. M. Trevelyan, *England under Queen Anne*, 3 vols., i. (*Blenheim*), 336. Trevelyan simply points to Nottingham's reputation for probity, and states that without further evidence such an accusation should be treated with some scepticism. On the other hand, Mary Defoe was the wife of a man engaged in trade. Surely an aristocrat such as Nottingham might have regarded her as fair game.

[18] The famous *Manual*, translated as *The Art of Prudence* (London, 1702), appears in his library. See *The Libraries of Daniel Defoe and Phillips Farewell*, ed. Helmut Heidenreich (Berlin: printed by W. Hildebrand for the author, 1970), 74, item 1187.

probably written in June 1704, he began by complimenting Harley on the 'Candor and Goodness' with which the Secretary of State had received him the night before, and quickly proceeded to the subject of Sir George Rooke, Admiral of the Grand Fleet. Defoe expressed his complete objectivity about the Admiral. He had 'No Manner of Personall Design', he wrote in his next letter, and added 'I Neithr kno' him, Nor am Concern'd with him, or with any that Does kno' him, Directly Or Indirectly. I have Not the least Dissrespect for him, or any Personall Prejudice, on Any Account whatsoever—I hope you will please to give Full Credit to me in This' (H 18–19). The letter contained an enclosure which outlined the reasons for removing Rooke from control over the fleet in the Mediterranean. Defoe claimed to be representing what he perceived as popular opinion, whether right or wrong, and then spelled out some reasons to consider Rooke's handling of an encounter with the French fleet under Admiral Toulouse in May as either incompetent or possibly deliberately traitorous. In fact, Defoe would have been antagonistic toward Rooke if only because he was a Tory who put Tory officers into important positions in the fleet. Defoe had satirized him on numerous occasions, holding him responsible for the loss of the Turkey fleet in 1693 and for a variety of other failures. Defoe's friend and lawyer, Sir William Colepepper, had been assaulted by friends of Admiral Rooke for what was taken to be a slighting query about Rooke's whereabouts during the ongoing war at sea, and Defoe may have written part of a work concerning the trial just a few months later. Defoe was also said to stay in Colepepper's rooms in the Temple. What Defoe stated about having no personal animus towards Rooke was entirely false. Strangely enough, he had written about the trial in the *Review* for 20 May, expressing his contempt for the behaviour of the friends of Rooke. Under these circumstances, Defoe's claim that his opinion of Rooke was unbiased by personal considerations must be regarded as a complete fabrication.

IV

While Defoe was writing on such subjects, he had not abandoned his attacks against the enemies of the Dissenters. He had been on the offensive for some time, proposing repeal of the Test Act which deprived Dissenters from serving in official state posts. But the continuing assaults upon Occasional Conformity by the House of Commons brought with them some additional proposals for eliminating religious Dissent among the nation's Protestants. One of these involved an attack upon the Dissenting schools. Samuel Wesley, a former Dissenter and a student at Morton's academy, attacked the education at the Dissenting academies as being politically dangerous (anti-monarchical) and immoral. Although Wesley absolved Charles Morton from these faults, he criticized the kinds of books read at the academies, particularly Milton. The students themselves, he argued, were debauched; some sold love powders, others passed around copies of the extraordinarily obscene play *Sodom*, ascribed then, as occasionally now, to John Wilmot, Earl of Rochester.[19] Wesley's main antagonist was Samuel Palmer, but Defoe also answered Wesley directly in *More Short Ways with the Dissenters* published on 28 April 1704 and more obliquely in *The Dissenter[s] Misrepresented and Represented* some time in May. Both these works attempt to push the theme of 'Moderation', and Defoe went out of his way to praise members of the Low Church such as Gilbert Burnet, who embodied reasonable attitudes. By way of counter-attack, he suggested that the children of Dissenters should be allowed into Oxford and Cambridge without having to take any oaths, something that did not occur until late in the nineteenth century. In the latter of these two pamphlets, Defoe returned to his familiar theme. Having already shown the true aims of the high Church in his *Shortest Way*, Defoe saw the new effort at destroying the education of children of Dissenting families as simply another attempt to imitate Louis XIV in his treatment of the Huguenots. The real aim, Defoe argued, was total extirpation of religious dissent.

Moderation, and the example of the persecution he had experienced, was all his theme in these works. He tried to demonstrate in *A New Test of the Church of England's Honesty* that he had been sacrificed to the fury of the High Church, which was preaching a message of intolerance entirely against the spirit of the Act of Toleration. If the pillory and his stay in Newgate had not convinced him that he had made a mistake in pleading guilty, he was now sure of it. Had he 'produc'd *Sacheverel*'s Book . . . Entituled *Political Union*, Licens'd by the Vice-Chancellor of *Oxford* before a jury of his peers, he argues, 'no *English* Jury wou'd ha' brought him in Guilty'.[20] The only difference between Sacheverell's '*Bloody Flag*' and his own '*Gallows* and *Galleys*' was a matter of class and privilege. One

---

[19] See Wesley, *A Letter from a Country Divine to his Friend in London, concerning the Education of the Dissenters in their Private Academies* (London, 1704); and *A Defence of a Letter concerning the Education of the Dissenters* (London, 1704). Wesley used a quotation from Defoe on the title-page of his *A Reply to Mr. Palmer's Vindication of the Learning, Loyalty, Morals and Most Christian Behaviour of the Dissenters* (London, 1707).

[20] Defoe, *A New Test of the Church of England's Honesty*, in *True Collection*, ii. 295.

was an 'Oxford Modern Dialect, and the other put into downright plain English: One is a church Phrase, and the other a City Comment'. The conflict over occasional conformity was not a religious issue at all, but 'a meer Farce' pursued for the purpose of hunting down the Dissenters 'with a full Cry, for being Dissenters'.[21] As for the Commons and men like Sir Humphrey Mackworth, they would have saved the nation a revolution had they passed the Exclusion Bill in 1682. This would have preserved the lives of many a Whig martyr and made the revolution unnecessary.

V

These pamphlets reveal an increasing cynicism about the roots of human action and perhaps a degree of self-pity concerning Defoe's efforts on behalf of the Whigs and the Dissenters. He quoted Machiavelli at the beginning of his True Test of the Church of England's Honesty on the wisdom of allowing an opponent a way out of having to admit total defeat, and there may have been some genuine feeling behind his rhetorical question, 'Alas, Poor De Foe! what has thou been doing, and for what hast thou suffer'd!'[22] Defoe had not changed his beliefs, but he certainly realized that those heady days when he sat in triumph with the Kentish petitioners were unlikely to repeat themselves.

His Elegy on the Author of the True-born Englishman, published on 15 August 1704, revealed him in a number of new roles. It showed him as a poet and pamphleteer who felt he was capable of earning an independent living and who could laugh to some extent at his own irrepressibility. Defoe began by remarking upon the silence imposed on him as a satirist and of the attacks made upon him for works he had written as well as for those, he claimed, he had not. Some copies were titled The Live Man's Elegy, and like Mark Twain a century and a half later, he well might have said that the reports of his (literary) death were a trifle exaggerated. In the poetic prologue he compared himself to a criminal who, because he was about to be hanged, was allowed a certain freedom in his speech. The purport of the analogy was that, though the wit and satire with which he had been associated were on the point of death, they refuse to depart without some final remarks. Defoe's own description of his 'Muse' as both 'vigorous' and possessed of 'strength of Thought' would have been challenged by few.[23] But now, he pretended, he had been silenced, while

---

[21] Defoe, A New Test of the Church of England's Honesty, in True Collection, ii. 309.
[22] Ibid. 313.
[23] Elegy on the Author of the True-born Englishman, in True Collection, ii. 67.

works he did not and would not have written were being ascribed to him:

> Hymn, Song, Lampoon, Ballad, and Pasquinade,
> My recent Memory invade;
> My Muse must be the Whore of Poetry,
> And all *Apollo*'s Bastards laid to me.[24]

Then Defoe imagined what he might have written about were he permitted, trotting out some of his usual subjects—vice, the power of the state in relation to the individual, the incompetence of England's admirals. Having stated that he was no longer allowed to attack those guilty of vicious acts, he then proceeded to lampoon a number of citizens who had gone beyond the pale. Taking up the rumour that he had been bailed out of gaol by the Whigs, Defoe compared himself to a woman friend of the poet Rochester, who never surrendered her virtue but still lost her reputation:

> Thus like old *Strephon*'s vertuous Miss,
> Who, foolishly too coy,
> Dy'd with the Scandal of a Whore,
> And never knew the Joy
> So I, by Whigs abandon'd, bear
> The *Satyr*'s unjust Lash,
> Die with the Scandal of their Help,
> But never saw their Cash.[25]

After this witty comment, Defoe then spoke of himself as an author who will not stop writing just because those in power have tried to suppress him and his works, and will not be starved by his enemies:

> I'm satisfy'd it never shall be said,
> *But he that gave me Brains will give me Bread.*[26]

He ended the poem with a continuation of this defiant posture, transforming himself into a symbol of the artist whom the state attempted to suppress by using what might seem legal means. By the actions of his enemies, he has been reduced to a mere 'Shadow of a Poet'.[27]

Although Defoe attempted to reveal that the elaborate machinery of justice was merely an intricate 'engine' to conceal the brutal use of 'Power', he distributed the blame freely among those who failed to rescue him and upon himself for his naivety. It is apparent that despite the remarkable prose of *The Shortest Way*, Defoe considered his poetic satires as the basis

---

[24] *Elegy on the Author of the True-born Englishman*, 71.
[25] Ibid. 85–6.   [26] Ibid. 86.   [27] Ibid. 89.

for his reputation. And to some extent his farewell to poetic satire was not entirely a staged fiction; he was indeed turning away from that form. Though he was yet to write *Jure Divino*, his longest satire, he was not growing creatively as a writer of poetry, and on some level must have been aware of this. The *Elegy* was as witty, in some ways, as *The True-Born Englishman*, but the complexity of the idea betrayed some of his weaknesses as a satirist—his carelessness and his willingness to sacrifice artifice for a clever comment. He stated that he wrote the poem 'several Months' before it appeared on 15 August, but one remark seemed in keeping with his mood during the summer months. Depicting himself as one who threw himself on the mercy of the government with a sense of his own innocence, Defoe demonstrated the folly of such a trusting attitude. Using the words of Edward Coleman, whose papers seemed to show that there was indeed a Popish Plot, and who seemed to believe that the Duke of York, later James II, would save him before his execution, Defoe echoed, 'I'll put no Faith in Man'.[28] And indeed, having failed to get help from those whom he had served, Defoe seems to have decided from this point on to avoid relying entirely on any single political figure or party. Yet as with *Legion's Address to the Lords*, he must have had good reason to think that Harley would intercede to prevent any attempt to prosecute him.

Harley appears not always to have understood what Defoe was attempting to do in his writings. Readers of the *Review* objected to what they considered too favourable a view of France, and Defoe had to explain to Harley, as to his readers, that they had to have a broader view of Europe now that England was beginning to play a role on the Continent. And that meant acknowledging the power of French armies, the attraction of French institutions and culture, and the potential strength of French trade. For Englishmen accustomed to laughing at frenchified characters in stage comedies and satires this was not always easy. Defoe was apparently questioned by Harley about what might have been perceived as a pro-French line, and was worried enough to need reassurance that Harley truly grasped his intentions.

Harley vacillated about the best way of using Defoe's talents. Some time in mid-summer the plan to send him abroad was scrapped in favour of one that would dispatch him on a tour of the eastern counties to sample public opinion about the government; but time passed while Defoe waited for orders, his horse saddled. Defoe had apparently convinced Harley of the importance of what he called 'a Scheme of General Intelligence' (H 28), a

---

[28] Ibid. 88. At least one of Defoe's detractors suggested that, like Coleman, he expected to be rescued from the pillory by those in power.

system of spies and agents who would send a constant supply of information to the Secretary of State. An agency would be set up to handle the
information, but it would appear to be just another harmless government
office. The machinery might be handled in so clever a way that even the
office clerks would not know what was actually happening. By these
means, Defoe argued, 'Openly and without the help of Mr *St Johns Back
staires* a Correspondence may be Effectually Settled with every Part of
England, and all the World beside' (H 28). The reference to the back
entrance in the dwelling of Henry St John, then Secretary of War, may
suggest that after the initial discovery of the meetings between Harley and
Defoe, they had resorted to this means for their secret conferences.

Defoe expanded upon his advice in a document named 'Maxims and
Instructions for Ministers of State', written some time around the end of
July 1704. Here Defoe does not simply outline a system of intelligence but
proposes a Machiavellian scheme for Harley to assume control of the
government from his position of Secretary of State. The tone suited
Defoe's hard-earned scepticism about human nature and his belief that self-
interest governed almost all actions. The 'Maxims' were about methods of
achieving and retaining power. Defoe argued that a 'prime' minister would
be accepted by the people if they felt that their leader was not interested in
personal wealth, and that the Secretary's office was the perfect place from
which an ambitious statesman might assume such a role. Once having
taken over this position, he could retain it by a spirit of generosity and by a
system of intelligence that would keep him in touch with any threats to his
popularity. 'A Man Can Never be Great That is Not Popular' (H 33),
Defoe advised. He then proceeded to suggest ruling through an inner
cabinet of six, but the real key to ruling would be in the organization and
processing of the information coming in from all parts of England and from
abroad so that he would have a clear idea of conflicts and change within the
various parties at home and in foreign governments. Instancing the
fictional *Letters of a Turkish Spy*, Defoe suggested the value of having
agents in Paris, Toulon, Brest, and Dunkirk to report all happenings. 'The
books I Take as They Are a Meer Romance,' commented Defoe, 'but the
Morrall is Good, A Settl'd Person of Sence and Penetration, of Dexterity
and Courage, to Reside Constantly in Paris, Tho' As tis a Dangerous Post
he had a Larger Allowance Than Ordinary, might by One happy Turn
Earn all the money and the Charge be well bestow'd' (H 38). Defoe overestimated the amount of money available to the Secretary of State for
intelligence operations of this kind, but he argued that proper use of spies
could have prevented Charles XII's conquest of Poland and the troubles

created by the Hungarian revolt against Austria by Francis Rakoczy. Both occurrences seemed to weaken the efforts against the French army along the Danube.

The spirit informing this document appears to have come from Defoe's favourable assessment of Cardinal Richelieu's method of governing France. Richelieu was mentioned frequently, and Richelieu's appeal to *raison d'état* in supporting the Protestants during the Thirty Years War seemed to lie behind Defoe's attack upon Charles XII, a Protestant king. Defoe reminded Harley that the war against France was not a religious war, and that the principle of the balance of power had to be put before any devotional considerations, whether in regard to Sweden or the rebels in Hungary. If a mixture of diplomacy and force appeared to work best in foreign affairs, 'Dissimulation' was the best method to achieve popularity at home:

Tho' this Part of conduct is Call'd Dissimulation, I am Content it shall be Call'd what They will, But as a Lye Does Not Consist in the Indirect Positioning of words, but in the Design by False Speaking, to Deciev and Injure my Neighbour, So dissembling does Not Consist in putting a Different Face Upon Our Actions, but in the further Applying That Concealment to the Prejudice of the Person; for Example, I Come into a persons Chamber, who on a Surprize is Apt to Fall into Dangerous Convulsions. I Come in Smileing, and Pleasant, and ask the person to Rise and Go abroad, or any Other Such question, and Press him to it Till I Prevail, whereas the Truth is I have Discovered the house to be On Fire, and I Act thus for fear of frighting him. Will any man Tax me with Hypocrisye and Dissimulation. (H 42)

The aim of such deception, argued Defoe, was 'the Reall happyness of us all', and he quoted St Paul on 'becoming all Things to all Men, that he might Gain Some'.[29] He concludes, 'This Hypocrise is a Vertue, and by this Conduct you Shall make your Self Popular, you shall be Faithfull and Usefull to the Soveraign and belov'd by The People' (H 43).

This advice may be read in a number of ways, but it is clear that Defoe believed that the ends justified the means. The person apt to have 'Convulsions' is clearly an allegorical representative for England and its politics. Defoe's political ends were by no means always the same as Harley's, but at this point they may not have been as divergent as they were to become. They both agreed on the importance of the Act of Settlement, which guaranteed a Protestant monarch, the idea of the Union with Scotland, which Defoe singled out in this letter, the necessity of war with France, and the Act of Toleration. These were among the basic views that,

---

[29] 1 Cor. 9: 22.

if properly championed, would make England into what, by contemporary standards, was a successfully functioning modern commercial state. In such a state the Dissenters could practice their religion without fear, trade would thrive, and English liberties would be protected. If achieving such a state meant engaging in deception and lies, Defoe had no objection. This ethical position informed both his actions and his writings, and had a particular role in his gradual turn toward writing a vividly realistic fiction.

11

From Public Journalist to
Lunar Philosopher

The dissimulation and lying that Defoe described to Harley included denying that he had written pieces for which he was clearly responsible. In the *Review* of 3 June 1704, the Scandal Club reported that it had received a letter from someone threatening to show that the author of the journal and of *Legion's Address to the Lords* were one and the same. One of two letters in the Portland Papers making the same claim reported that Sammen, the weaver in whose house Defoe was finally caught in 1703, had been picked up distributing '*The Address*'. The letter stated that Sammen was a 'Creature' of Defoe and established the connection.[1] In the *Review*, Defoe said that no one could 'prove' he wrote *Legion's Address*, and that it was not true that he had fled to avoid arrest.[2] Almost everything he published provoked attacks upon him and his ideas. Defoe was now a public figure, and if he had some right to complain about slanders concerning him and his life, he also had to expect them. One slanderous attack had him keeping Mrs Sammen as a mistress. If reporters did not literally go through his rubbish, as some modern reporters have done in search of a story, he and his family had to face a great deal of figurative garbage over the next two decades.

Defoe also had his defenders. William Colepepper, his lawyer in the trial over *The Shortest Way*, had been threatened with bodily harm by friends of Sir George Rooke, and he eventually took legal action against them. Naturally enough, Defoe came to his friend's defence. He may even have acted as a shorthand reporter during the trial, and he almost certainly wrote most of a pamphlet published on 22 August 1704 with the title *A True State of the Difference between Sir George Rooke, Knt., and William Colepepper, Esq.* Colepepper testified how he was assaulted for what he thought an

---

[1] HMC, *Portland Papers* (London: Eyre & Spottiswoode, 1899), iv. 93, 138.
[2] *Review*, Sat. 4 Nov. 1704, i. 300.

innocent remark while he was on the way to bring Defoe's petition to Queen Anne concerning *The Shortest Way*, and praised Defoe effusively:

If *W.C.* should here particularly add any thing of him, as an extraordianry Genius, tis presum'd Mr *De Foe's* greatest Enemies wou'd concur: and *W.C.* is not afraid of having his Judgment call'd into question by affirming, That the World has not in any Age produc'd a man beyond Mr. *De Foe*, for his miraculous Fancy and lively Invention in all his Writings, both Verse and Prose. And *W.C.* says farther, to justifie his Value for Mr. *De Foe*, That in an Age when the Heavenly Muses have become Syrens, and turn'd low Panders to the Senses, Mr. *De Foe* has giv'n Vice a stab, and writ up to the Test of moral Vertue.[3]

If readers may doubt whether Defoe would record praise of himself, it may be said in response that he may merely have taken down exactly what Colepepper said about him. On the other hand, no one ever claimed that modesty was Defoe's strongest suit. It was an age in which flattery was accepted with greater equanimity than in our period, and doubtless Defoe was as willing to put up with it as the next person. The pamphlet itself was on one of his favourite topics—the folly of duelling. Rooke's defenders claimed that there were twenty men who would defend the Admiral with their swords. Defoe noted that Colepepper had read Cervantes' *Don Quixote* and was no more ready to go out to fight twenty men than he would twenty windmills.

I

Defoe now began to diversify his writings. He continued his general commentary on politics and manners in the *Review*, treating everything from the benefits of imitating the French ban on duelling to the war in Italy, but he clearly craved a medium that would allow him to be more polemical. For a brief time, from 8 August until 25 September he ran another journal, *Master Mercury*. Not every number has survived, but Defoe publicized *Master Mercury* by mentioning it in the *Review* during a week in which four new periodicals had commenced publication. He noted that 'he [the author] appears in the World with a very great Stock of Asurance, under a Thundring Title, and abundance of great Things which he promises to do, bidding bold Defyance to all the World'. Referring to the writer of this periodical as 'this Dogmatick Gentleman', the Scandal Club objected to his inconsistent use of 'I' and 'We', suggesting that he 'Unmask himself' in his

[3] Daniel Defoe, *A True State of the Difference between Sir George Rooke, Knt., and William Colepepper, Esq.* (London, 1704), 5–6.

next number. As for his claim that he would write his articles 'without Respect to Persons or Powers', the Scandal Club suggested that he was likely to incur the displeasure of the government with remarkable speed if he was indeed committed to telling the truth and that he would likely find himself in Newgate soon enough.[4] This nearly happened when Defoe attacked one of his favourite targets, Admiral Rooke. His subsequent extravagant praise of Rooke's action around Gibraltar in that journal was probably a forced penance for once more overstepping the boundaries of what the government would accept from contemporary newspapers.[5]

Defoe began *Master Mercury* by commenting on the dilemma posed by a publishing industry that is forced to print news even when there is nothing worthy of printing. As he did with the beginning of the *Review*, he began by attacking the quality of other newspapers, including the *Review*. His description of the 'mythological Manner' of that journal represents an interesting commentary on Defoe's recognition of what everyone gradually came to recognize as his real talent—his ability at narrative.[6] *Master Mercury* may have been an experiment at amplifying this aspect of his journalism. The story of a recent encounter between Admiral Whetstone and a Swedish ship was intended to illustrate Charles XII's attempt to affront England, and used as a lead in to the story about how the English tried to provoke the Dutch fleet into an act of war by employing one yacht to fire on their fleet. The Dutch chose to ignore the incident and by so doing thwarted the plans of Charles II. Defoe then added a lively detail:

It was reported, how true we will not determine, that the Dutch Admiral caused ten Men on board every Ship, as the yacht passed by, to stand upon the fore-castle of their Ships, and letting down their Breeches, shew'd the *English-man* their Backsides as he passed by and then hallow'd him along, and let him go.[7]

Defoe followed his accounts of these naval engagements with numbers on the battle of Blenheim and the taking of Gibraltar. As short a run as *Master Mercury* had, it showed Defoe's interest in the kind of military history that was to form the basis for *Memoirs of a Cavalier* and parts of *Colonel Jack*.

The great events of 1704—events that brought an immediate response from so many writers of the period—were Marlborough's victories at Schellenberg on 2 July, followed by his even greater triumph at Blenheim

[4] *Review*, i. 200.
[5] See Frank Ellis and Henry Snyder, 'Introduction', *Master Mercury*, Augustan Reprint Society, No. 184 (Los Angeles: William Andrews Clark Memorial Library, 1977).
[6] *Master Mercury*, 8 Aug. 1704.
[7] Ibid.

on 13 August. Defoe thought the first battle had saved the Protestant cause, and gave a magnificent description of the battle at Blenheim in *Master Mercury*. But Blenheim was the occasion for poetry, and Defoe obliged with his *Hymn to Victory* on 29 August, ten days after the battle was mentioned in the *Review*. Defoe dedicated the work to Queen Anne, and devoted most of the poem to a historical survey of the military failures of the past when victory no longer seemed to favour the virtuous side. Though Defoe described modern warfare, with its sieges and avoidance of combat, accurately enough in his *Essay upon Projects*, it was clear that he longed for the kind of combat that he associated with the English Civil War. There is little doubt, then, of his enthusiasm for Marlborough's love of engagement:

> Fateaguing marches, Harass, and Surprize,
> Long Campings, Dodging, and Delays;
> These baulk an *English-man*, and make him mad,
> Make Valour droop, and hang the Head.
> There so impatient and uneasie there,
> The very Nation's *sick of War*.[8]

But with the opportunity to fight in an open field, the English finally had an opportunity to show their bravery. Defoe called upon Tallard, the French marshal taken by Marlborough, to testify to English courage, as the French troops chose to drown in the Danube rather than face the fury of the advancing troops. And Defoe ended with declaring Marlborough among the great heroes of the Protestant cause. Needless to say, Defoe argued that God was on Marlborough's side, but he paid him the compliment of winning with 'Old English Courage' and with '*higher Hearts*' than the opponents. Defoe was to complain that Addison refused to write a line of his poem on Blenheim, *The Campaign*, before he had received £50. Defoe may have hoped for reward for his poem, but there is little doubt that he wrote it out of the patriotism of the moment. And Defoe never abandoned his 'Hero'.[9] Years later, when his paymasters had turned against the war and used his pen to defend their cause, Defoe still found time to defend Marlborough and the army that defeated Louis XIV with his schemes of universal monarchy. On 31 August he sent one of his correspondents fifty copies of his poem with the comment that Samuel Elisha of Shrewsbury would see from reading his poem 'what wonderfull Things God is Doeing in the World' (H 56).

Although Marlborough's victory may have satisfied any worry that

---

[8] Defoe, *Hymn to Victory*, in *True Collection*, ii. 138.   [9] Ibid. 147.

Defoe may have had that the war on the Continent might be lost, he was still uncertain about the conflict between factions at home. Some time around the end of August and the beginning of September he wrote another of his long position papers to Harley. He began by arguing for a balance of factions, since no single party could dominate the country for long. The Queen's first speech, in which she expressed her love and support for the Church of England, let loose the hatred and ambitions of the High Church, with the consequent attacks on Occasional Conformity and plans to punish the Dissenters further. Yet only 'Moderate Measures' and 'Moderate Men' could effactually rule the nation. What followed this argument was a section which Defoe titled 'Methods of management of the Dissenters' (H 53–5). He argued that the Dissenters were weaker when there was no persecution and that the freedom they had enjoyed since James's Declaration of Indulgence to the present had weakened them. Were the Queen to guarantee that they would continue to have all the religious freedom they now had, there would be no agitation among them to increase their rights. Defoe referred to the Dissenters as 'Them' and spoke of managing them with a few secret agents as if he had nothing to do with them. The main thrust of his argument, however, was that such a declaration from Queen Anne would silence the High Church and ease anxiety among the Dissenters. Defoe's attempt to distance himself from the problems of the Dissenters in this document seems somewhat transparent. At one point he noted that if the Dissenters could unite and set up a system of intelligence in their own group, they would be powerful. This was precisely what he would have liked, and his avowal of the weakness of the Dissenters was hardly disinterested.

His commitment to fighting the enemies of the Dissenters may be seen in his ongoing exchanges with Charles Leslie, one of the most effective representatives of Jacobite views in England. He was effective because he offered his opinions under the disguise of a supporter of the government and the High Church. On 12 September Defoe advertised *The Protestant Jesuit Unmask'd* in the *Review*, and to underscore who might be meant, he added to the title, 'With my Service to Mr. Lesly'. Describing Leslie as the most dangerous of the pamphleteers on the radical right, Defoe, after stating his own attitude toward freedom and the rights of the people, remarked, 'I wonder he does not undertake to tell us, that we were born in *Fetters*, and that Slavery is entail'd on us like *Original Sin*'.[10] Defoe admitted that monarchy was a natural enough form of government, and not so bad if kings were capable of staying within the laws of any given

[10] *The Protestant Jesuit Unmask't* (London, 1704), 10.

society. But such restraint was impossible, and more important than any obligation to a monarch was 'the Duty to our *selves*', which was not discussed because it was 'written so deep in the Laws of Nature; for every Man's Inclination is to be happy'.[11]

Defoe had been reading the philosophers of natural law, particularly Grotius and Pufendorf as well as Hobbes. These writers formed the basis for his arguments in his ongoing poem *Jure Divino*, and he could confidently proclaim, 'The Great Fundamental Law of nature is *Self-preservation*. 'Tis a Principle so deeply radicated in Nature, that 'tis engraven upon every man's Heart.'[12] The contract between a king and his people was only conditional, and it was the right of Parliament to make war against any prince who proved himself to be tyrannical. And behind Parliament was the people, for whom the entire structure of government existed. If they felt threatened, they had the right to rebel, since the 'Safety of the People is the *Supremest Law*'.[13] Defoe then turned on Leslie to accuse him of Jacobitism, and to argue that this 'Jesuitical Author', rather than the author of *The Shortest Way*, deserved to be pilloried. Leslie had already spelled out his objections to Defoe's line of thought as well as the thinking of Locke in the second part of *The New Association* and its supplement dated 25 March 1703. Leslie had assured his readers that Defoe and his like were all members of the radically Whiggish Calves Head Club; Defoe replied that no such club existed outside of the nightmares of the High Churchmen and Jacobites. During the next few years they were to battle each other, sometimes in a clearly announced dialogue, sometimes simply as announced representatives of opposite points of view. They reached many readers who had never heard of Locke, much less read him, and they helped to clarify the debate over Revolution Principles that had yet to reach a mass audience.

II

Some time during the summer of 1704, Harley decided that Defoe would be more useful as a collector of information within England than as an agent on the Continent. In a letter written to Harley in June (H 19), Defoe had requested a Christopher Hurt, a fellow Dissenter and employee of the Customs Department, as a travelling companion and on 28 September asked for additional leave time for him (H 61). He set out on a tour of the eastern counties, acting out the role of Mahomet the Turkish spy, while

---

[11] *The Protestant Jesuit Unmask't*, 27.   [12] Ibid.   [13] Ibid. 8.

at the same time establishing a network for the distribution of his works by booksellers and other agents throughout the country. He sent his first report to Harley some time in September from Hertfordshire, north of London, under the heading, 'State of Partys in England'. He was apparently in Royston, and used the club of that town, dedicated to High Church politics and to drinking,[14] for his analysis of the party divisions within the county. He had moved on to Cambridge, from which place he had written a similar report on 16 September, when he was forced to return to London for two days to respond to the charge of libelling Admiral Rooke.[15] Like his friend Colepepper, Defoe may have had a run-in with one of Rooke's supporters, though whether the 'smart Rencounter with Mr. Toke' amounted to a duel, as Dottin suggested, is questionable.[16] Although he thought that he had managed to get Robert Stephens, the man charged with arrests of this kind, to acknowledge that there was no warrant out for his apprehension, he was forced eventually to announce his freedom from prosecution in the *Review*, first in a brief notice and finally in a full statement:

The said Daniel de Foe, hereby gives *Notice, That as soon as he came to Town, and before his Application to the Secretary of State, . . . he went, and in the presence of sufficient Witnesses, spoke with the said* Robert Stephens, *the Messenger, as he call himself, of the Press; and offering himself into his Custody, Demanded of him, if he had receiv'd any Order, to Stop, Take, or Detain him; and he denyed that he had any such Order, notwithstanding he had most openly, and in Villainous Terms, reported before, that he would Detain him if he could find him.*[17]

If Defoe thought that he had squelched the rumour by the time he wrote Harley from Bury St Edmunds in Suffolk on 28 September, he was mistaken. On that very day, Charles Hedges wrote to Harley to ask if he wanted Defoe picked up.[18] Luttrell had recorded the rumour two days earlier, and two months later Defoe specifically named Dyer's Newsletter, among others, as perpetuating the rumour that he had fled from justice.[19]

---

[14] He had criticized the club for specializing in epic forms of drunken revelry in *Reformation of Manners*, True Collection, i. 88. The enclosure Defoe sent Harley has been lost. For a picture of the club, see *Gentleman's Magazine* 50 (1780): 474; and 53 (1783): 813–15.

[15] Defoe may also have had some concern about *Legion's Address*. According to a newsletter, on 24 Oct. the printer, Rawlins, was charged with responsibility for this work. Defoe's confidence that no one could connect him with this pamphlet suggests that he may have had the piece delivered anonymously, but he may still have been concerned that his connection with it could emerge. See *Portland Papers*, iv. 144.

[16] Paul Dottin, *Daniel De Foe et ses romans* (3 vols, Paris: Presses Universitaires de France, 1924), i. 141.

[17] *Review*, 4 Nov. 1704 (i. 296). The first notice appeared on 7 Oct.

[18] *Portland Papers*, iv. 138.

[19] John Fransham sent Defoe a copy of the notice in *Dyers Newsletter* on the assumption that Defoe may not have see it. Defoe, on the other hand, was interested in a similar report in a newsletter circulated by Joseph Fox, since he suspected that Fox worked for the offices of the Secretaries of State. Defoe may have

Defoe expressed his hope to Harley that he would be more useful in the field than as a supplicant in London. He reported that while he was discovering the political mood in Bury, he had 'Perfectly Dissected' the situation to the north-east at Norwich through the agency of his companion, Christopher Hurt. Concerned about the possibility of arrest, Defoe told Harley that he was awaiting his instructions, avoiding populous areas such as Norwich, and visiting the towns along the coast, probably Lowestoft and Great Yarmouth.[20] He feared that were he arrested, papers might be 'Taken from me, and at Least Seen, which would be as bad' (H 59), and appealed to what he considered his moderation in treating the Admiral. 'I have Not Taken the freedome my Inclination guided me to, and which I Really Thot the Case of Sir G R Requir'd' (H 60), wrote Defoe, pointing to an unnamed person of whom Harley disapproved for having been critical of the government's handling of the war. Rooke's victory, he suggested, had been the occasion for the right-wing Tories to exalt him above Marlborough, and Defoe's 'Regard to your Orders, and that Onely, Restrains me On that head for the Case Requires to be Spoken to' (H 61). The letter ended with a request for permitting his assistant, Christopher Hurt, to extend his leave of absence, a plea for more money, and instructions to send a reply to Alexander Goldsmith via John Morley, Defoe's agent at Bury.

It was an astonishing performance. If, at the beginning, Defoe apologized for any offence he may have given Harley, he ended by proclaiming his own independence. He had restrained himself from expressing how strongly he actually felt about Rooke and his party, and he hoped Harley would appreciate his ability to moderate his true feelings and convictions. In short, were he not now working together with Harley for the good of the country, he would certainly have made Rooke the object of his satire. If the reminder to Harley of his alias, 'Alexander Goldsmith', served any purpose other than their mutual desire to keep matters secret, it was to draw Harley into the heart of the conspiracy that Defoe was waging against the High Church and its political allies. Small wonder that Harley too was drawn into Defoe's game, assuming the name 'Robert Bryan' to some of his correspondents.[21]

been hinting to Harley that better control ought to be exerted over the activities of government agents or obliquely asking for an explanation. See H 60, 65.

[20] In *Tour*, i. 66, Defoe mentions being in Yarmouth during the time of the 'fishing fair', which lasted through October.

[21] See Elizabeth Hamilton, *The Backstairs Dragon: A Life of Robert Harley* (London: Hamish Hamilton, 1969), 70. She describes Defoe's role as 'unofficial adviser and government spokesman' in addition to being an agent. Her remark that Defoe's 'loyalty to the man who had liberated him from Newgate never

Defoe's letters to Harley revealed a growing confidence in Harley's appreciation of his reports, and the letter of 2 November, despite the usual disclaimer, 'who am I that I Should Pretend to Advise you' (H 22), had some of the quality of Gulliver proposing to reveal the secret of gunpowder to the King of Brobdingnag—a revelation of secret knowledge that will advance the status of the writer. Appealing once more to the principles of Richelieu, Defoe attempted to advise Harley on the ways of using power. The new Parliament had convened on 24 October, and Defoe reported a move to oust Harley from power and end the rule of the 'Triumvirate' of Harley, Godolphin, and Marlborough. Whigs were to join with supporters of the High Church to support a new bill against Occasional Conformity, leaving the government without any constituency. Defoe's recommendation was that Harley should reward a few members of his enemies among the Whigs and thereby split his opposition. 'Sir,' he wrote, 'The Whigs are weak; they may be Mannag'd, and Allways have been So. What Ever you do, if Possible Divide Them, and they are Easy To be Divided. Caress The Fools of Them Most, There are Enough Among them. Buy Them with here and There a Place; it may be well bestow'd' (H 68). Defoe prefaced his advice by saying that it was the same he had given to King William and which William had acted upon. The man Defoe named as an ideal person to be 'bought' was John Somers, Baron Somers, former Lord Chancellor and member of the Whig Junto. Defoe wrote as if he were conveying advice from 'all I Can Talk with That are Friends' (H 69), but he may have had some personal reasons for suggesting someone disliked by the Queen and by Harley. He may have worked closely with Somers in the standing army controversy, and having such a person in a position of influence might have proved useful to him. As matters turned out, the Tories, acting without Whig support, tried to get a third Occasional Conformity bill through by tacking it to the crucial Land Tax Bill, gaining them the name of 'Tackers'. But Harley, who had become a fast friend of Queen Anne, was not threatened with a loss of power.

In some sense, the letter of 2 November reflected the first use of Defoe's system of intelligence for Harley. Defoe may indeed have been reporting conversations held and overheard in his favourite taverns and coffeehouses, but he insinuated that he was drawing on a larger sampling of public opinion. That some of this came from his system of correspondents throughout England there can be little doubt. A few letters from this period, to Samuel Elisha in Shrewsbury and to John Fransham in Norwich,

wavered' is generally true, though he never stopped expressing himself in print on issues where they disagreed.

gave hints of how extensive this correspondence might have been. Having
heard from Fransham on 10 November about the popularity of the *Review*,
along with an anecdote about a man who did not know the difference
between an address from the town of Marlborough and a letter from the
Duke of Marlborough, Defoe proceeded to elaborate on the latter in his
'Advice from the Scandal Club' in the *Review* of 2 December. He informed
Fransham of the defeat of the 'Tack' within the House of Commons four
days before, and of its reintroduction that very day. Defoe's hope that the
Commons would defeat this bill as well did not prove correct, but like the
others it was defeated in the House of Lords. He sent a copy of his *Queries
upon the Bill against Occasional Conformity*, offering to cover the costs of
distributing it without charge and mentioned a new pamphlet. 'I have now
in hand', he wrote, 'a small piece against Sir Humphrey Mackworth's Bill
for employing the poor, which unless you contradict I'll send you some of,
because it concerns you all as Manufacturers and employers and it is fit
when you are to be ruin'd you should know it' (H 72). The letter seemed to
have been fairly typical, giving up-to-date news on his activities and
supplying information on his latest publication to be distributed through
booksellers and private contact.

III

The 'small piece' Defoe referred to in his letter to Fransham was titled
Giving Alms No Charity. It represented Defoe's return to a systematic treatment of economic problems in a manner that he had not attempted since *An
Essay upon Projects*. He had vented his spleen against stock-jobbing in a
thorough enough fashion in *The Villainy of Stock-Jobbers Detected*, but his
plan to treat trade in the *Review* had been lost in the grand detour involving
discussions of the relationship between the revolt in Hungary and
England's war against Louis XIV. How much Mackworth's High Church
allegiance and attacks upon the Dissenters may have provoked Defoe is
difficult to say, but he was only too happy to point out how Mackworth's
plan to employ the poor in workhouses would have a disastrous effect on
the economy. It was a work that revealed Defoe's most conservative,
mercantilist side as an economist. As a follower of John Cary's theory of
creating wealth by means of the circulation of goods throughout the
nation, Defoe could not help but believe that the creation of workhouses
producing goods already manufactured elsewhere would have a disastrous
effect upon the established system of exchange. He exhibited the fear of

overproduction typical of mercantilists as well as a fear of change. If a manufacture of Bays was set up in London, unless a market for it was found, there would be less need for the same product to be made at Colchester. And the transportation of goods would circulate the wealth through the nation. 'By this Exchange of manufactures,' he wrote, 'abundance of Trading Families are maintain'd by the Carriage and Re-carriage of goods, vast number of Men and Cattle are employed, and numbers of Inholders, Victuallers, and their Dependencies subsisted.'[22] Inventions and new manufactures were good where they increased the consumption of products, enriched the worker, and increased the population of the nation upon which national wealth is based. Defoe instanced the invention of the knitting-frame as something of a disaster, since it moved the manufacture of cloth from the country to Spitalfields in London.

J. R. McCulloch thought he was complimenting Defoe in saying that he was free from 'all affectation of sentiment or philanthropy', but McCulloch was missing the point.[23] In employing 100 families at Tilbury in the manufacture of pantiles and bricks, Defoe was indeed acting as a kind of philanthropist. He was manufacturing a product needed by a London still rebuilding from the Great Fire, and allowing his families to live better than they had before. Among his concerns about Mackworth's plan was that it would drive down the price of labour and thereby impoverish the English workman, whose independence he admired. If Defoe had harsh words against beggars and told the story of a beggar who refused an offer of work because he said he could make more by mendicancy, it was because he placed such a high value on his idealized image of the ordinary worker who found pleasure in employment, cared for his family, and avoided the drunkenness that, in his eyes, plagued too many English workers. Nevertheless, he reminded his readers that 'Trade, like all Nature most obsequiously obeyes the great Law of Cause and Consequence; and this is the occasion why even all the greatest Articles of Trade follow, and as it were pay Homage to this seemingly Minute and Inconsiderable Thing, *The poor Man's labour*'.[24] The wealth of a nation was dependent upon a cycle of production and consumption, with the labourer creating value by his toil.

Defoe addressed *Giving Alms No Charity* to Parliament, writing anonymously as a freeholder and beginning with the assertion, 'He that has Truth and Justice, and the Interest of *England* in his Design, can have nothing to fear from an *English* Parliament. . . . Truth, *Gentlemen*, however

---

[22] *Giving Alms No Charity*, in *True Collection*, ii. 437.
[23] J. R. McCulloch (ed.), *A Selection of Scarce and Valuable Economic Tracts* (London, 1859), p. ix.
[24] *Giving Alms No Charity*, 428.

meanly dress'd, and in whatsoever bad Company she happens to come, was always entertain'd at your Bar'.[25] The opening appeared to adopt a somewhat less confrontational attitude toward Parliament, and reflected his increasing involvement with the *London Post* and its featured dialogue between Truth and Honesty. The confrontational style of *Master Mercury* was clearly unsuited to his new pose of moderation, and that journal was allowed to fade from the scene. Even if he could have turned that journal in a different direction, it would have been useless. In treating current issues Defoe wanted a degree of anonymity, and *Dyer's Newsletter* had revealed his authorship. It is significant that, when he reached some accommodation with Dyer some six years later, he insisted that the naming of names be stopped: 'That if what Either party are doeing, or Sayeing, that May Clash with the party we are for, and Urge us to speak, it shall be done without Nameing Eithers Name and without personall Reflections' (H 269). That they held different political opinions was not important; what *was* important was personal secrecy.

That secrecy permitted Defoe all kinds of latitude, as did the dialogue form of *The London Post*.[26] He could criticize the Dissenters freely and speak of the decline of the quality of preachers among them, attack the High Church, lampoon some of the vicious office-holders of London, and even turn on the voters who failed to elect Colepepper. Meanwhile everything he had to say about Defoe and the *Review* was, in one way or another, complimentary. One interesting passage had to do with the growing smugness of the Dissenting community, its glorying in its wealth. 'For it is now almost become a Maxim with them, that Poverty proceeds from want of Grace, Inverting the Scriptures That only . . . [rich] Men, can enter the Kingdom of Heaven, at least into their Congregation.'[27] As an example of their 'specious Promises and Ingratitude', Defoe named Daniel Defoe and Thomas Delaune as among those abandoned by the Dissenters while they suffered in Prison. When attacked, he insisted that he was just what he seemed to be: Truth and Honesty. But readers were becoming suspicious. In the issue for 9 April 1705, he denied that Defoe was the author, noting that Defoe was afflicted by an ongoing problem. If a work were anonymous and controversial, 'it must be *the Devil or De Foe*'. Despite his disclaimers, by June *The London Post*, as *Master Mercury* before it, had ceased to be a medium through which he could maintain an effective disguise and it too

---

[25] *Giving Alms No Charity*, 419.
[26] Although Defoe had Truth mention Bunyan in discussing the uses of allegory, the real source for Defoe's column were the dialogues in Henry Care's *Advices from Rome*.
[27] *London Post*, 12–15 Jan. 1705.

went silent. Through his characters, he had proclaimed: 'we are, and will be, what we profess, *naked Truth and Honesty*, that will neither disguise ourselves, nor suffer others to be Disguised, to act the *Wolf in Sheeps Clothing*.'[28] But 'to be Disguised' was precisely the role that Defoe assigned to himself.

On the other hand, Defoe continued an effort to advance his status as a public spokesman for certain political and economic positions. In the *Review*, he acknowledged himself the author of *Giving Alms No Charity*, having on 9 December announced, 'I Have at last, done with the Affairs of *Hungary*.' He could now talk about economic problems, and started on the need for a productive labour force. Attacking able-bodied beggars as people who were refusing to work, he argued that charity ought to go to destitute families who have been deprived of the labour and earnings of the working father or mother. Like the modern economist who focuses upon those thought to abuse the welfare system, Defoe revived the oft-told story of the beggar who is discovered to have thousands of pounds at his death. The important point was to see to it that the working poor were not deprived of their subsistence in an effort to establish workhouses. Defoe admitted the advantages of employing the poor, and in a proposal that he put before the Select Committee of the House of Lords concerned with investigating the navy, he revived some of the proposals that he had made in his *Essay upon Projects* for maintaining a constant supply of seamen for the navy. Although Defoe argued that the reason for the difficulty of recruiting men for the navy had something to do with the high wages paid on merchant ships, he was not so much interested in taking away these wages as in regulating the irregular lives of sailors. And his main suggestions had to do with establishing regular employment and a pension scheme for the families of seamen. He was essentially enlisting all sailors with the government and giving them steady if lower wages, arguing that they would appreciate the pensions for their families. When he revived this scheme once more in 1728, he noted of his earlier proposal that 'it was at last declined only upon some Scruples about Liberty and Compulsion' and put aside (H 73). Insofar as Defoe believed in a regulated, protected, and productive labour force, he was expressing the mercantilist notion of a state that used its resources to benefit its citizens and to increase its power and wealth. In suggesting that an 'English Gentleman' faced with dire need might better become a highwayman before stooping to begging, he was comparing what he considered to be two extra-legal responses to necessity. Both, it should be pointed out, reflected extreme aspects of individualism.

---

[28] *London Post*, 31 Jan.–2 Feb. 1705.

The correspondence suggests that the Select Committee received Defoe and his plan with respect. Whatever the dire financial and psychological results of the pillory may have been, it had given him the visibility he did not have when he wrote his *Essay upon Projects*.

IV

Defoe also had visibility as the chief spokesperson for Whig ideas and ideals. It was in acknowledgment of this role that John Fransham wrote to him on 29 March 1705 to report how a Mr Thomas Dunch, a wine merchant of Norwich, had been duly elected to the position of alderman but had been refused the right to assume his position by the Mayor and Sherriff on the grounds that he was a 'Contentious, Seditious and Pernicious' person (H 80). The case was an echo of the events following an election at Aylesbury which had embroiled the Commons and Lords in the major dispute of the day. Fransham's description of himself as 'a great admirer of your Writings' (H 79) might have been duplicated throughout the nation. Lord Halifax, one of the leading members of the Whig Junto, contacted him about supporting an act concerning bills of exchange, and Defoe was able to respond in a way that depicted himself as a martyr in the Whig cause, as one 'who scorn'd to Come Out of Newgate at the Price of betraying a Dead Master [i.e King William]' (H 82). He sent his brother-in-law, Robert Davis, on this secret contact and agreed to remain 'Incognito' in their relationship. Halifax was a figure of considerable reputation, and his desire to obtain Defoe's services suggests that the Whigs were beginning to turn to Defoe when they wanted propaganda in the cause of 'Truth and Liberty'.[29]

Defoe began the year by celebrating the return to England of the Duke of Marlborough with a poem, *The Double Welcome*. Although he did not put his name on the title-page, he announced himself with autobiographical references obvious to anyone familiar with his writings and his situation. The author of 'Truth and Honesty' followed a similar path in the opening couplets where he announced himself as one who scorn'd to flatter, '*tho' she sung to Kings*':

---

[29] James Sutherland thought that this letter revealed a certain familiarity between Defoe and Halifax that may have gone back to the reign of William, and Frank Bastian has expanded upon this possibility. Though a certain formality might be expected in a letter to a lord, still the tone reveals a polite distance of a kind which Defoe himself usually tried to abandon as quickly as possible in his correspondence. See Sutherland, *Defoe*, 2nd edn. (London: Methuen, 1950), 49.

> *Satyr has been her Talent*, Truth her Song,
> Truth *who can bear it!* sung too loud, too long.
> *Bright Truth!* that Stranger to the Jingling Train
> Makes all their praises Satyrs, all their Satyrs vain,
> While Truth can neither this nor that explain.
> *Th'Unspotted Standard* has been all her Aim,
> For this *she has felt her Fate*, and sunk her Fame:
> For this *they've* damn'd the Poet and his Rhimes,
> And slain th'unhappy Muse *for want of Crimes*.[30]

Without commenting on this verse picture of Defoe's sufferings, it should be pointed out that he had created an audience whom he expected to recognize him, at this stage of his career, both as Defoe and as a symbol of the writer of genius punished by a government whose shameful acts he has revealed. The impulse would have been viewed by a Swift as too autobiographical, but unlike John Dunton, he had not lost himself in a miasma of personal experience. The image of the suffering poet was to be used as a weapon against those identified as betrayers of the authority placed in them by the people. He was clearly battling with Addison for pre-eminence as the Whigs' major political poet. Allowing Addison to be 'our modern *Virgil*', Defoe put forward his own claims as a poet who had suffered in the cause, and as a writer willing to fight the enemy directly and on his own terms. To prove his point, he once more turned against the enemies of the Whigs, Charles Leslie and particularly that 'Noisy, Sawcy, Swearing, Drunken Priest', Sacheverell.[31]

He included *The Double Welcome* in the second volume of his collected writings and added a preface in which he launched an attack upon printers who plagiarize the works of authors and destroy their legitimate profits. He instanced the 80,000 copies of his *True-Born Englishman* that might have made him wealthy but which brought him no gain whatsoever. He was to argue his position strenuously and may have had some influence on the copyright act passed five years later. The focus of the preface reveals his conscious transformation into a professional writer. He would occasionally make the claim that he did not write for 'Bread', but he had clearly come to the point in his career when he could envision earning his living through writing. What he said of the popularity of *The True-Born Englishman* suggested an understanding of how works of this kind might reach a wide new popular audience, and Defoe was not one to neglect an economic opportunity.

---

[30] 'The Double Welcome', in *True Collection*, ii. 169.   [31] Ibid. 182.

In establishing his credentials as the leading proponent of Whiggish ideas, Defoe also began repairing some of his reputation among the Dissenters. His attack on Sacheverell and Leslie at the end of *The Double Welcome* certainly did not harm his position, and he published an essay on 19 February, *Persecution Anatomiz'd*, in which he again took up the battle against Sacheverell. He argued that persecution on grounds of religion was essentially an attack upon life and property; it was assuming the role of the Inquisition against the Dissenters and should be resisted like any other threat to self-preservation:

The Law of nature gives us a right to Act in Common with our Fellow *Country-men;* and whatever law is contrary to the Law of nature, is an Infringement of that Right, and so consequently, may properly be call'd a Persecution. All Law is founded on Justice and Equity; and whatsoever is not so founded is illegal, unjust and Unanswerable . . . 'Tis not this, or that Opinion in Religion, that ought to deprive a man of his Liberties, as an *Englishman*. Religion has nothing to do with a man in such Actions, as outwardly Respect, Morality only.'[32]

Neither the state nor a state church, Defoe argued, had any authority to force the consciences of its citizens. As for Occasional Conformity, to 'restrain a man from Conforming, when his Conscience allows him in it, is Persecution'.[33]

Defoe thought he had a perfect example of High Church persecution in the figure of Abraham Gill, a dissenting minister in the Isle of Ely. Comparing the treatment of Gill to that of a martyr's, Defoe argued that Gill had been arrested on several occasions and forced into the army by some soldiers. 'So much is Malice frequently forsaken of its Sence', wrote Defoe, 'that the just regard Providence always shews to Injur'd Innocence, is the Safety of all honest men, causing the Subtilty of wicked false Accusers to abandon them, and their Folly as well as Wickedness to go hand in hand, that Sin and Shame might come together, and their false Accusations carry its Detection in it self.' This sentimental doctrine represented a velleity rather than something he really believed. Defoe clearly identified himself with Gill, and wanted him to be an innocent victim not very different from himself.[34] Unfortunately, this impressive pamphlet was wasted for having been written in a bad cause. Gill was just the moral reprobate his enemies said he was. Even in this exculpation Defoe was willing to allow that Gill might have done some immoral things while he was

---

[32] *Persecution Anatomiz'd* (London, 1705), 3–5.

[33] Ibid. 2.

[34] The subtitle of *The Experiment* is *The Shortest Way with the Dissenters Exemplified*. The title continues with a description of Gill's persecution by the High Church, with an ironic comment on *Moderation of High Church Principles*.

an Anglican preacher and before he had become a Dissenter. As a condemnation of the behaviour of the Anglican establishment and of religious persecution, *The Experiment* was a powerful pamphlet. By getting his facts wrong, Defoe may have done more harm than good for his cause.

Defoe's interpretation of recent history as involving the counter-revolution by the High Church found its way into *The Consolidator*, a lengthy allegorical account of a voyage to the moon published on 26 March 1705. Given the sensitivity of the government, Defoe had good reason to wonder if he had not overstepped the bounds of toleration extended to the press. In sending a copy to Halifax, he noted that his work was 'likely to make Some Noise in the World, and perhaps to Come before your Lordship in Parliament' (H 82). What Defoe meant by the latter remark was that someone would bring a charge against it for libel, and he wanted Halifax to be aware of its nature.[35] He need not have worried. *The Consolidator* did not make the 'Noise' in the world that Defoe expected, either as a literary work or as a controversial view of English politics. The good news, then, was that Defoe was not once more thrown into gaol or threatened with such a fate. The bad news was that it received so little attention. John Fransham appears to have been one of the few who liked it. He wrote to Defoe around 5 April:

Your Consolidator (which I could have wish'd much longer) I have just now got through, which contains (according to the opinion of a high *Solunarian* Gentleman I had some discourse with about it) too much Wit for Mr De Foe to be the author of it; he will have it wrote by a Genius superior to any *Crolians*, which shews that let a man be never so great a Bigot to his party let him but have a Tast of starling sence and ingenuity such a one must be forc'd to confess that it abounds with masterly strokes of both. (H 83)

Fransham went on to report another reader who enjoyed it so much that he would have desired it to be as long as John Foxe's huge volume, *Acts and Monuments*.

Now Fransham and his fellow reader were not completely without a taste for what they called 'Wit', but Defoe's book was misconceived. He had read Swift's very successful *Tale of a Tub* and was much taken both by its wit and by its combination of chaos and order. But Defoe apparently believed that the key to Swift's achievement rested in the chaotic parts. His attempt at imitating the whirl of words that was part of Swift's method was unsuccessful. He ignored Swift's uncongenial suggestion that madness lay behind his narrator's effort at producing a work written according to the

---

[35] John Tutchin, writer of the rival Whig *Observator*, had been found guilty on 4 Nov. 1704. H 70; Luttrell, v. 484.

'modern' style. Defoe certainly recognized Swift's work as an attack upon modern philosophical treatises from John Locke to John Norris of Bemerton, but in joining the attack he failed to offer any serious critiques. He was too much of a modern himself truly to enjoy the wickedness of Swift's satire on contemporary philosophical systems, and too much a religious enthusiast to appreciate Swift's negative attitude toward enthusiasm in religion.

On the other hand, certain parts of *The Consolidator* were very clever. These included the satire on Chinese science and China itself as a source of all wisdom; the voyage to the moon and the description of the inventions to be found there; and the visionary alternate history in which the Crolians (Dissenters) of the moon (earth) band together and form their own bank and business, boycotting those of their enemies. In addition to the inventions they were usually credited with, Defoe's Chinese are imagined to have had a machine that allowed for simultaneous forms of copying—a machine that appears to us to combine a remarkable combination of tape-recorder and telepathy. Their library included a cabinet of curiosities with a working model of the brain revealing all its operations. These inventions were, of course, owing to the communication between China and the moon. On Defoe's moon itself there was a form of telepathy, a telescope that allowed the viewer to see the truth, 'Elevators' that permitted converse with departed souls, and a 'Chair of Reflection' that functioned as a form of lie detecting machine. That the machine for getting to the moon was an allegory for the House of Commons suggested that since some of their recent proposals were so much the product of hot air, getting to the moon with them would be no problem. Some of these concoctions were ingenious, and the entire work was informed by Defoe's reading in Harris's *Lexicon Technicum* (1704), with its discussion of the new steam-driven machines used to remove water from mines. The possibilities inherent in such a mechanism awakened Defoe's imagination and produced his genuinely interesting speculation on future machines.[36]

If there is universal agreement that the third book of *Gulliver's Travels* is inferior to the other three, it is because Swift decided to pick up on a variety of themes rather than dwell on a single concept with a single narrative. Although unified somewhat by the voyage to the moon, Defoe's work went in all directions at once. But his major mistake lay in making his moon a mirror image of the earth. This device allowed him to abandon the

[36] Defoe echoes the title of Harris's book. See *The Consolidator*, in *The Earlier Life and the Chief Earlier Works of Daniel Defoe*, ed. Henry Morley (London: George Routledge & Sons, 1889), 267. Page references to this work will be included in parentheses within my text.

imaginative and fanciful part of his work for satire. The lunar Philosopher who acted as his guide was an exact double for Defoe, to the extent of having been pilloried and received by the people with pity and 'loud shouts and acclamations when he was taken down' (297). The complicated telescope shown to him by the Philosopher allowed him to see the events on earth with complete clarity as to their significance, and the 'Cogitator or the Chair of Reflection' (311) did much the same. The Whig version of English history presented by Defoe covering the past forty-five years was pedestrian enough to make the use of his lunar names more of an annoyance than anything else, and his fancy dissolved into the mode of secret history.

The section which I have described as alternate history was strongly autobiographical. Since his three days in the pillory, Defoe had been telling parts of his history in almost every work he published. Now he portrayed the situation leading up to the event—the attacks upon the Crolians (Dissenters)—describing himself as 'a very mean, obscure, and despicable fellow, of no great share of wit, but that had a very unlucky way of telling his story' who wrote a work 'personating this High Solunarian [High Church] zeal' (364). Defoe's vision of his situation in prison had undergone revision over the years. Now he described how 'they fell to wheedling him with good words to throw himself into their hands and submit, giving him that gewgaw the public faith for a civil and gentleman-like treatment' (366). It was not Colepepper who advised him to plead guilty but the Earl of Nottingham and his cohorts who gave false information to the Queen, denied that they had made any promises, and ordered him to be fined excessively and 'exposed to the mob in the streets' (366). Defoe said they used this as a threat while offering him great rewards if he would tell all he knew. He refused and, abandoned by his fellow Crolians, he suffered through the terrible punishment of the pillory.

It is clear from this account that Defoe was anxious for a way of controlling his feelings by rendering them in a narrative. He now clearly made Sacheverell into a person who wrote political tracts in which 'he invited the people to murder and destory all the Crolians' (370) and called all those who would not agree cowards and traitors. Leslie was turned into a Jacobite. All this was concealed under Defoe's prevailing moon allegory. And by the same device he blamed the Dissenters for their failure to unite. In a moon fantasy he showed them finally opening their eyes to their self-interest. They sold, traded, and bought only within their group, created their own bank, and thereby brought the Solunarians to their knees.

Defoe ended his odd mixture of moon voyage, satire, and alternate history with a device borrowed from the French satirist Furetière and used in a variety of poems during the Restoration—the inventory of books in a library, or a catalogue of books to be auctioned, or, as Swift used it in *Tale of a Tub*, a list of books soon to be published by the author of a work. This device allowed for a series of wide-ranging satirical thrusts as unrelated as, say, a book auction catalogue organized, as was often the case, merely according to the size of the volumes. Defoe's moon voyager found a large number of works translated from earth languages, often with 'very hiero-glyphical' titles (423), including three volumes of 'European mysteries' and a series of tracts whose titles extend from a version of his own work ('"Alms no Charity", or the skeleton of Sir Humphrey Mackworth's bill for relief of the poor. Being an excellent new contrivance to find employ-ment for all the poor in the nation, viz., by setting them at work to make all the rest of the people as poor as themselves') to another reflection on the poor behaviour of the English navy (432–3).

One of these comments in the form of volume titles throws some light on Defoe's ideas and his associative thought processes: '"Killing no Murder", being an account of the severe justice designed to be inflected on the barbarous murderers of the honest constable at Bow, but unhappily pre-vented by my Lord Nottingham being turned out of his office.' This obscure reference even made Joseph Browne, author of *The Moon Calf*, a lengthy attack upon Defoe and *The Consolidator*, wonder why Defoe would allude to such old news. What happened was that a violent con-frontation between a press gang trying to recruit some innocent citizen for the armed forces had recently occurred on Bow Street in London, and this recalled an earlier case at Bow, a district of London. As reported through a letter in the Scandal Club section of the *Review* for 17 March 1705, a press gang had tried to take a cook at the Cock and Rummer and when a constable was called, the gang beat him severely. In both cases, Defoe argued that a citizen had the right to defend his life against the violence being offered to him by a press gang and that any violence committed by such an act of self-defence could not be considered criminal: Better to have killed them than not defend '*English* Liberties'. Employing a concept of power drawn from Hobbes, Defoe concluded that if the navy were capable of abridging the rights of a citizen in this way, sovereignty might be said to belong to 'Tom the *Tarr*' rather than to Queen Anne.

V

Defoe published *The Consolidator* at a time when attacks upon him and his views were mounting. His notoriety and his success in spreading his ideas on the nature of government and a wide variety of controversial topics provoked anger in the Tory camp, and he managed to hurl insults at practically everyone in *The Consolidator*. Satire and irony were dangerous weapons at the time. Swift, in his *Tale of a Tub*, succeeded in alienating every side in the religious disputes of the time. Defoe also hurled insults gratuitously at Addison, Steele, Prior, Swift, and Locke among others, but it was a miscellaneous writer named Joseph Browne, mentioned above, who seemed to take greatest offence at Defoe's remarks and pursued him in a series of printed attacks over the next four or five years. The first of these, *The Moon Calf*, picked up on Defoe's allegory in the form of a letter from the Man in the Moon denying Defoe's account of lunar history. Browne depicted Defoe as someone who dropped naked into the lunar world. Finding that he seemed not to understand the language of the moon, they called him a 'Moon Calf' or fool. Browne's account of Defoe is not very enlightening, being composed chiefly of attacks on his supposed ignorance and his belief in spirit as separate from the body, a possibility Browne denies. Like Charles Gildon, who was to attack *Robinson Crusoe* fourteen years later, Browne associated Defoe with popular literature and a reading audience of 'Chamber-maids, Cook-maids, Foot-men . . . and the like' and with works such as 'Gargantua, or Bevis of *Southampton*'.[37] But what is more interesting is his treatment of Defoe as someone possessed—as a person whose imagination has run entirely out of control and as a dreamer. He focused upon Defoe's fantasized world of a unified Dissenter community which could exert force within the state and remarked, 'What a Story of *Tom Thumb* is here! introduc'd without any Foundation for it in Truth or Reason, but the mere Imagination of his own Brain.'[38] Browne was to expand on this notion of Defoe in a second pamphlet devoted to Defoe:

He is always raising Apparitions in the Air, Encountering Fantastick Daemons in his Imagination, or Fighting with his own Shadow. . . . I fancy he keeps a Correspondence still with the Moon, or at least delights in strange and

---

[37] Joseph Browne, *The Moon Calf* (1705), ed. Maximillian Novak, Augustan Reprints No. 269 (Los Angeles: William Andrews Clark Memorial Library, 1996), 8.
[38] Ibid. 30.

monsterous Stories, Things that are not familiarly known or believed, but out of the common way of vulgar Thinking.[39]

If the image of the demonic Defoe was being reified in the public imagination by continued references to his satanic character and actions, it was being accompanied by an awareness that some of the power of his writing came from his ability to create imaginative fictions.

Browne was the first of Defoe's opponents to examine his work with care. He still attacked him as the 'Hosier' of Freeman's Yard, but compared to other enemies, he at least seems to have read through the poems and essays included in Defoe's *True Collection*. In attacks by less attentive critics, Defoe was more often than not coupled with John Tutchin, the author of the Whig *Observator*. In one of these attacks, *The Republican Bullies*, published in 1705, Tutchin and Defoe were presented as engaged in a dialogue in which Tutchin leveled various accusations against him, including the notion that he received £100 for the first volume of the *Review*, that irony was part of his character rather than a rhetorical figure to be used by a skilled writer, and that he had written a famous bawdy poem on Dr Hamilton, *Queen Anne's Midwife*. Defoe was allowed some degree of skill by this fictional version of Tutchin, and the two were shown as conspiring to coordinate their attacks. In *The Republican Bullies* Defoe is seen as accepting the role of '*Unserene Daniel Foe, Clergy-Flogger in Ordinary to his Highness the Prince of Darkness*'.[40] The leading 'Wit' among the writers of the 1690s, Tom Brown, took notice of Defoe in a number of works. In *Visits from the Shades* Defoe was introduced to Virgil, who proceeded to criticize his dead metaphors and 'Lifeless Expression'. On the other hand, Virgil did not object to Defoe's satiric poems and actually seemed to praise the *Review*;[41] it was the heroic poems to Marlborough that set the Roman poet's teeth on edge in Brown's attack. The author of *The Tacker's Vindicated* suggested that Defoe and Tutchin did the dirty work of the Whig Kit-Kat Club, and opined that *The Consolidator* might qualify Defoe for another trip to Newgate. These, of course, were mainly Tory attacks on Defoe and Tutchin as the leading spokesmen for Whig principles. This was made clear enough in *The Monster: or, The World Turn'd Topsy Turvy*, in which the two were seen as ruining the nation:

---

[39] Joseph Browne, *A Dialogue between Church and No-Church; or a Rehearsal of the Review* (1706) in *State Tracts* (London, 1715), i. 6, 35.   [40] (London, 1705), 8.

[41] Thomas Brown, *Visits from the Shades* (London, 1704 [1705]), 88. In another place Brown suggests that Defoe study the writing of Swift by way of improving the *Review*, but this is a relatively mild criticism. See Tom Brown, *The Last Will and Testament of Mr. Tho. Brown, to the Living Heraclitus* (London, 1704), 38.

This mov'd by Villany, and that by Pride,
Draw thousands of the giddy Mob aside
So fell these Monsters are, so direful fierce,
This kills in Prose, while that destroys in Verse.[42]

The moderation that both Defoe and Tutchin proposed as an ideal had now become anything but a virtue, and having lost the lexical high ground, the Tories decided they would destroy the word itself, associating it with the hypocrisy practised by the two Whig journalists.

Somewhat more complimentary and less politically antagonistic, John Dunton, in his *Life and Errors*, spoke of Defoe as one of the important writers of the age:

Mr. *Daniel de Foe* is a Man of good Parts, and very clear sense. His Conversation is ingenious and brisk enough. The World is well satisfy'd that he's enterprizing and BOLD; but alas! had his prudence only weigh'd a few Grains more, he'd certainly have writ his *shortest* way a little more at *length*. Had he writ no more than his *True Born English Man*, and spar'd some particular Characters that are too vicious for the very Originals, he had certainly deserv'd Applause; but 'tis hard to leave off when not only the ITCH and Inclination, but the Necessity of writing, lyes so heavy upon a Man.[43]

This was not entirely favourable, but a year later, in *Dunton's Whipping Post: or, A Satyr upon Every Body*, he confessed to holding a grudge against Defoe for employing a format (using letters and replies) that he had developed in the *Athenian Mercury*. In this new assessment, Dunton referred to Defoe as 'a First Rate Author' and '*a very Ingenious Useful Writer*', adding, 'He's Master of the English Tongue, can say what he please upon any Subject.'[44]

Defoe hardly needed such compliments. His handling of the *Review* gradually changed into an easy dialogue between himself and his audience. The letters grew more varied and his answers gradually created the character of Mr Review, a person of broad sympathies and interests. One moment he would be sympathizing with a female servant named Betty, who, much like his later fictional creation Moll Flanders, found herself seduced by a man who promised to marry her after the death of his wife; and the next he would be discussing the ability of the deaf to master reading and writing to an extraordinary degree. He would expand upon the importance of high wages for workmen and then argue that modern warfare was won by the wealthiest and not necessarily the bravest. In short, the *Review*

---

[42] *The Monster: or, The World Turn'd Topsy Turvy* (London, 1705), 3.
[43] *The Life and Errors of John Dunton* (London, 1705), 239.
[44] *Dunton's Whipping Post* (London, 1706), 89–90.

gave him the opportunity to reveal the depth of his thinking about his experiences: his understanding of ethics, science, warfare, economics, and history. He, who could wax eloquent on so many subjects, often expressed his longing for the ability to move and persuade his audience. Speaking of his desire for an end to the ceaseless political wars in England, he wrote:

were the Power of perswasion given me from high, were I blest with the Gift of Unresistible Eloquence, could I speak with Words that should be felt as well as heard, that should touch the very Soul, and make the Blood of the Readers turn within them; those Powers should be all Employ'd to Perswade, to Entreat, and, if possible, to prevail upon the English Nation at this time, above all times, TO STUDY PEACE. . . . For this I am Content to be Banter'd, Lampoon'd and Expos'd, to have my Name cry'd about Street to every Ballad, and every Villainous perjur'd Scribler ruffle me with Buffoonry and impertinence.[45]

He was still longing for such divine powers twenty years later when he wrote the *Compleat English Tradesman*, and insofar as a human being could have such a talent, Defoe was surely gifted with it.

If Dunton was only a somewhat half-hearted admirer of Defoe, we can be sure that Defoe had an enthusiastic circle of supporters such as Colepepper and Fransham. A year later, when he had gone up to Scotland, one of his enemies gave a picture of Defoe surrounded by his Whig supporters at Sue's coffee-house. 'One thing, Daniel, I want to know,' wrote this antagonist, 'that is, whether you keep up your Beau habit, your long Wig, with Tossels the End of it, your Iron-bound Hat, and your blew Cloak? As also whether you have left your old Wont, of holding out your little Finger to show your Diamond Ring?' This writer referred sarcastically to the 'man with the High Nose and long Chin', and dredged up the notion that Defoe had not merely used Sammen the weaver in a manner that had ruined his life but had engaged in an affair with the weaver's wife. Defoe, of course, always maintained that he had never engaged in any extramarital affairs, and there is no evidence that the author really knew much about Defoe's private life.[46] But the description of the gesture with

[45] *Review*, ii. 74–5.
[46] *The Review Review'd* [London, ?1706], 3. See M. E. Novak, 'A Whiff of Scandal in the Life of Daniel Defoe', *Huntington Library Quarterly* 34 (1970–1)/35–42. The author of *The Review Review'd. In a Letter to the Prophet Daniel in Scotland* did seem to know something about Sammen, since he stated that the weaver had been forced to work as a journeyman after his association with Defoe had ruined his economic prospects. We can accept Defoe's denials as better evidence than a scandalous report by an anonymous author, but Defoe was certainly very human, and very involved with questions of sex and sexuality in the Scandal Club letters. His Christian belief held that all humans were sinners and that repentance and faith were all that could be expected from a fallible humanity. He was also away from home for long periods of time. The rumours concerning an illegitimate child were persistent, and they should not be swept under the carpet in the manner practised by all previous biographers without some consideration of the nature of his sexuality.

the little finger with its diamond ring and the blue cloak suggested someone who had seen him in the midst of his circle of admirers. The engraving by Taverner shows him wearing a cloak, and both this and the Van der Gucht engraving before *Jure Divino* show him wearing a wig, but the other details had to come from personal observation.[47]

Defoe once told a story out of his experience in the brick factory. Two workmen got into a quarrel and one named Peter had another workman down on the ground and was beating him. Thinking he was shouting for help, Defoe rushed to separate the two, but the man on the bottom was not shouting for help but rather crying out that he would soon pay his opponent back. Defoe decided not to intervene, and indeed the man on the bottom soon took revenge on Peter, whose arms had apparently tired. Defoe too had taken a tremendous thrashing from his enemies. They were not entirely weary of trying to destroy him, but despite all their blows he was now recovered sufficiently to warn them that he might soon pay them back. It was a situation that his enemies found unendurable.

---

[47] Sue's coffee house or tavern was unquestionably the establishment mentioned in Dudley Ryder's *Diary* (ed. William Matthews, London: Methuen, 1939, 67). It was probably the same as Sew's coffee house in Bow Lane, Cheapside, described in Bryant Lillywhite's *London Coffee Houses* (London: Allen & Unwin, 1963), 564. Ryder speaks of a 'club' at Sue's, and it appears to have been patronized mainly by Dissenters.

12

Defoe as Spy and Whig Propagandist

Some time in 1705, Defoe had finally managed to move his wife and seven children out of Joan Tuffley's house to a residence at Kingsland in the parish of Hackney, where he had lived during the 1690s. He wrote to Harley on 30 July asking him to send money for his travels through the south of England to 'My wife who is my faithful Steward' (H 96). He assured Harley that she would see that the money got to him and that she 'will not Diminish One Penny'. Defoe's implication was that Mary was a special woman. If other wives might withdraw monies needed to maintain the household, Mary was made of better stuff. Besides, Defoe's financial fortunes during this period were growing rosier. In addition to the income collected from Harley, he also received a gift through Lord Halifax which must have been considerable. He wrote a humble letter of thanks describing himself as 'a Plain and Unpolish'd Man, and Perfectly Unquallify'd to Make formall Acknowledgements' (H 86). All he has written, he explains, has been for the cause of averting the destruction that the High Church and the Tories wished to visit on the country. Halifax had not identified the donor who had given this 'Exceeding Bounty', and Defoe requested the name of the person responsible for such 'Munificence'. He asked Halifax to convey his gratitude and his assurance that he would strive to retain 'the Homely, Despicable Title of *an Honest Man*' (H 86–7). Why Defoe thought that this kind of polite misrepresentation was required in addressing Halifax is difficult to say. That he was grateful there can be no doubt, but how did he expect to get away with the feigned modesty of describing himself as a 'Plain and Unpolish'd Man'? Defoe most probably thought that he was merely receiving his due—that having been engaged in some effective writing for the Whig cause, the party leaders were pleased enough to reward him. In fact, we know that the reward came from the Duchess of Marlborough, who was pleased by Defoe's defence of her husband's actions. The Duchess was to complain that she never heard anything more about the reward delivered to Defoe through Halifax, but Defoe remained an ardent defender of the Duke even during the days when, acting mainly as a direct spokesman for Harley's ideas, he was arguing for making peace with France.

Defoe was to continue his plea for harmony between those forces for unity and moderation in the nation and his attack on the Tories and the High Church in two works that had been drafted earlier but not entirely finished until 1705. These included *Advice to All Parties*, which Defoe said he had among his papers when Nottingham went through them on his arrest, and *The Dyet of Poland*, about which he had written to Harley in June 1704. He updated his slender and not very original *Advice to All Parties* at least to the extent that he questioned what the future would say about the ability or inability of the nation to put aside factional struggles in 1705. He clearly took more care with, and hoped for more of a sensation from, *The Dyet of Poland*, since he had told Harley, 'I Expect strange Effects from it as to the house' (H 19). Although the exact date of publication is not known, this remark suggests that he timed his poem to appear just before the May parliamentary election. The title-page introduces the fairly transparent comparison between events in Poland and in England with the use of a foreign-looking logo and the announcement '*PRINTED* At *Dantzick*', and the preface makes an ironic disavowal of any relationship between the events described in the poem and occurrences in England. Admitting some analogies, Defoe laments somewhat mockingly:

A poor Author must never Write at all, if he is not at Liberty to choose his *Metaphors*, and all the rest of the necessary Figures of Speech to help out his Expression. . . . 'Tis very hard, that a Man cannot Write of the Follies of other Nations, but People will be always comparing them with their own. One would ha' Thought the Author had Travell'd far enough to find out Histories and odd Passages to divert us; but if neither *China*, *Poland*, nor the Inhabitants of the Moon will protect Folks from being hang'd as the *Frenchman* said, *for Tinking*, go on Gentlemen, and if the *Cap* fits any Body let 'em wear it.[1]

In some sense, this is the beginning of a bantering relationship between Defoe and his audience—a relationship that involved an expectation that though a work was unsigned, Defoe's hand would still be recognized. It was a risky game as far as posterity was concerned and not entirely simple for contemporaries, but Defoe apparently found it irresistible.

Defoe also staked a claim against those who would charge him with libel in a work that pretended to be completely without any meaning beyond

---

[1] *Dyet of Poland* (Dantzick, 1705 [London, 1705]), sig. A2.

that on the surface. He argued that no one could 'Swear to a Man's Meaning, and know his Inside without the help of his Outside: For if the People your Profoundity pretends to describe are Affronted, the Action of Slander lyes against You, and not the Author. In the Writing 'tis a Poem, you, in the Reading turn it into a Libel, and you merit the Punishment for the Metamorphosis.'[2] The question of 'parallels' was a vexed one throughout the Restoration and into the eighteenth century. Performances of plays such as John Dryden's *The Duke of Guise* and John Banks's play about Mary Queen of Scots were held up because the historical situation depicted allowed the audience to apply a contemporary meaning and establish parallels between the past and the present.[3] Defoe's argument here is somewhat specious, since the characters he depicts under thinly disguised names were hardly to be found in the real Dyet of Poland. The notion that the author was not responsible for the reader's 'metamorphosis' of the work within him would hardly have protected him from libel laws had *The Dyet of Poland* created as much of a stir as Defoe expected.[4] As it was, Defoe brought in the members of Parliament and a number of characters such as Sacheverell (Sacharesky) and lampooned them in his inimitable style. He praised Halifax and Somers and pilloried his enemies and the enemies of the Dissenters—Nottingham, Sir Humphrey Mackworth, Rooke, and Toke—and ended the poem with encomiums upon Godolphin (Casimir) and Harley as heroic guardians of Queen Anne's government and upon Queen Anne (Augustus) as the ruler who rid her nation of fools and knaves.

I

In the *Review* of 10 May 1705, Defoe wrote an essay on the tumultuous scenes in Coventry at the election for Parliament. There had been rioting to the point of chaos: 'Parties draw up in little Armies in the Streets, and Fight with all the Fury and Animosity imaginable, 500, and some say, a 1000 of a side.' Though Defoe defended the mob as the chaotic centre of

---

[2] *Dyet of Poland*, Sig. A2.

[3] See Alan Roper's discussion of this problem and his remarks upon John Wallace's interpretation of contemporary attitudes toward concepts of application and parallels in Richard Ashcroft and Alan Roper, *Politics as Reflected in Literature*, introd. M. E. Novak (Los Angeles: William Andrews Clark Memorial Library, 1989).

[4] The author of *The Dyet of Poland Consider'd Paragraph by Paragraph* (London, 1705), sigs. A3–A4. suggested that there was no difference between Defoe's 'liberty to chuse what Metaphors he thinks fit' in this work and in *The Shortest Way*. Noting that everyone was aware that Defoe wrote *The Consolidator*, the author predicted that Defoe would eventually be hanged.

political change, it was the job of government to see that elections did not reach a point of outright physical warfare. The mob was, for Defoe, an aspect of the political sublime—powerful without limit and frightening in its terrible energy, instanced in the tearing apart of the De Witt brothers in Holland in 1672. The presence of troops at an election, he argued, might be a bad idea but whatever intimidation the troops might bring, it was better than that caused by rioting. At Coventry, the Church came armed with little clubs, and the mayor lost a tooth in the fray.[5] Some degree of order was necessary. A week later he returned to his theme. 'I cannot help saying', he wrote, 'in the View I have taken of the Elections, now carrying on in England, and in which the Nation is now so Exceeding Busie; I see nothing but Bribery, Corruption, Malice, Fury, Slander, Envy, and all sorts of Ill Practices.'[6]

The Coventry election was one reason for Defoe heading out on a tour of southern England to sample popular attitudes. The other was the publication of what he referred to as *The High Church Legion*, but which was actually titled *The Memorial of the Church of England*. It is usually ascribed to James Drake, but Defoe thought that whoever the ostensible author might be, one might detect the hand of the leader of the High Church faction, Bishop Atterbury, behind it all. The name he gave it associated the pamphlet with his own effort at a kind of mob rebellion. The difference was that his was a rebellion in the name of proper Whig principles; the author of the *Memorial* was attempting to lead a counter-revolution against the progress made since 1688. There were curious parallels between the *Memorial* and Defoe's arguments on government. The author of the *Memorial* also spoke of the 'Collective Right' of the people, and his attitude toward the power of the House of Lords bears an eerie resemblance to Defoe's attacks upon the House of Commons. But the *Memorial* contained a plea for 'Persecution' as the binding force of government, held up the image of the St Bartholomew's Day Massacre of the French Protestants as an understandable reaction to the growing power of a Protestant faction, and maintained that the political principles of the Dissenters were still the same as those who rebelled against and finally executed Charles I. The author suggested that the sin of rebellion had been passed on to the children and grandchildren of the defenders of Parliament and Cromwell as a taint in the blood, and threatened his readers with the spectacle of Scotland where the Episcopalians had been ousted by the Presbyterians.

[5] Elizabeth Hamilton, *The Backstairs Dragon: A Life of Robert Harley* (London: Hamish Hamilton, 1969), 76.
[6] *Review*, ii. 127.

As if these opinions were not inflammatory enough, the author of the *Memorial* accused the ministers, and particularly Godolphin, of leading Queen Anne astray. Even the Queen is accused of turning her back upon the Church and permitting the dismissal of some of the Church's most ardent friends while allowing the likes of Halifax, Somers, and Wharton back into power. The author argued that attempts of writers such as Defoe to divide the Church into a High and Low faction were insidious. There was only one Church, and those who believed in accommodations with the Dissenters or even in 'Moderation' were merely agents of the Dissenters who had managed to insinuate themselves into the ranks of true lovers of the Church. The pamphlet breathes an atmosphere of plot and conspiracy, suggesting that the author could name various individuals who were part of this attempt to overthrow the Church of England and turn the Presbyterians and Congregationalists into the established church of the land. Even some of the bishops sitting in the House of Lords appeared to be part of this plot. The only hope that the Church had was in the House of Commons and its bills against Occasional Conformity. The author defended tacking the occasional bill onto the Land Tax Bill as a perfectly legitimate manoeuvre, and accused the House of Lords of attempting to take away the liberties of Englishmen by bringing suit against the corporation of Aylesbury through five members who claimed they had been deprived of their right to vote. If the House of Commons did not have the right to determine the validity of elections, it could no longer be seen as a sovereign part of the English government.

It might be said that if *The Memorial of the Church of England* had not been published, Defoe would have been forced to invent it. Or, as Defoe argued, he had already invented almost everything contained in that work in his own *Shortest Way with the Dissenters*, including the fanatical character of the author. 'And as every Step this Party has lately taken, has been a Step backward as to their own Interest', so, he wrote in *The High-Church Legion*, an examination of the work would almost seem to reveal that it was written as '*an Irony* to Expose 'em, like *Defoe's Shortest Way with the Dissenters*'.[7] Defoe argued that, from the standpoint of his ability to predict future events, it revealed him as a true descendant of the prophet Daniel. The author of the *Memorial* had been particularly vehement about 'Moderation', distinguishing between true moderation, such as that shown by the Church of England toward the Dissenters, and false moderation, which was simply a screen for the activities of the Church's enemies. In response, ending every paragraph of one *Review* essay with the word

[7] Defoe, *The High-Church Legion* (London, 1705), 20.

'MODERATION', Defoe argued that the tactics of the Church of England were so blatant that they had antagonized the entire country:

What has turn'd the Nation, in general, so against the *Tackers*, [is] that in spight of Bribes, fighting, Drunkenness, Collusion, and all manner of ill Practices, in Spight of clubb'd Interest, small Burroughs, *Heaving* and *Thrusting*, with one another, Chopping and Changing of Places; yet above 40 of them are thrown out of the next Parliament, and 40 more of them asham'd to own their knowledge of the thing, testifie their Ingenuity by resolving to be wiser for the future; is not all this from the further spreading of this most dangerous Contagion among the People, and the Nations too generally embracing this Novel Invention of MODERATION.[8]

Defoe was certainly correct about the election, though the winners were not quite the centrists that Harley might have wished. In fact there was a notable swing toward mainline Whigs, and that did not bode well for Harley's future.

Harley thought Defoe would make a useful observer of the nation's mood, and sent him out to gather information as he had done for the eastern counties before. Defoe set out on 16 July on an extensive journey. Before leaving, he wrote asking Harley for a 'Certificate' (H 87) that would enable him to escape any situation arising from suspicions about the questions he might be asking. It would allow him to present himself as a person operating on state business and avoid any possible arrests—and 'which may be worse'—searching and seizure of papers. He requested leave time for his companion on his previous journey, Christopher Hurt, and wanted to be sure that proper arrangements had been made for passing on information. The departure was delayed. Harley wanted to see Defoe, and we have Defoe's letter following that meeting, a letter which is essentially a plea for regular payment for his services. He complained that to put a stop to his writing his enemies had attempted to worry him with old debts. He puzzled over whether Harley was paying him from his own pocket or whether the money was 'Publick' (H 88), and then made an appeal for a regular and permanent income from state funds:

Tho' the bounty to me is Equally yours, yet This Difference it will have; That tho' I hate to be craving, yet as I hinted Once, I was Fitter for a Pension than an Office, by which I Meant Respecting the Service I may do Among the Party. So Sir Might the Service I may do Merit a Private Allowance, by which The Necessary Craveings of a large Family of 7 Children might be answer'd, What Elce I Can Raise in the World would Soon Set me at Ease as to Creditors, whereas the

[8] *Review*, ii. 247.

Eager prosecution of Enemyes will at Last Disable me Either to Support the first or Discharge the Last. (H 88–90)

Defoe fills his letter with expressions of flattery toward Harley as well as something close to a threat. The opposition might be willing to bribe him to be silent, and, after all, 'No man Servs her Majtie for Nothing'. Reminding Harley of his usefulness, he informs his patron that he has written a pamphlet, *The High Church Legion*, in opposition to the *Memorial* and dedicated it to Godolphin. He assures Harley that he will be pleased by the performance, and ends with a postscript advising punishment for Dyer, his enemy. Everything was written to please the eye of Harley, including a quotation from the poet they both admired, Rochester. Defoe probably knew Harley well enough to know that he could understand the various innuendoes and appreciate the mixture of polite flattery and intimate confidences.

Defoe was unwilling to leave without the pass, and that did not come until 16 July. He had met with Harley at 4 in the afternoon on 10 July, writing a note in which he implicated a number of writers and publishers in the issuing of the *Memorial*, and reporting that Henry Pooley, a Tory Member of Parliament, had spoken in its praise. This was the kind of letter Harley received constantly and from all sorts of people.[9] It shows that Defoe took his role as a spy seriously, though he seems to have wanted to take some private revenge upon Dyer and Robert Stephens. On the 16th, as he was preparing to leave, he noted that Stephens had abetted the distribution of the *Memorial* by not exerting himself to prevent the distribution of a work which purported to reply to that work paragraph by paragraph. Defoe saw this as a device for distributing the original work, since such answers reprinted each paragraph of the original before commenting. He sent Harley six copies of his *High Church Legion* with that letter, and did the same in a letter to Halifax on that very day. He went south-west through Reading, Newbury, and Salisbury, reaching the south coast at Weymouth. Then he proceeded along the south coast into Cornwall until Bodmin, headed north through villages such as Launceston and Bideford and revisited Taunton and Bridgwater, the scene of his brief fling at soldiering with the Duke of Monmouth. From there he headed north-east through Bristol, Cirencester, and due north to Gloucester, Shrewsbury, Liverpool, Manchester, and Leeds. His return journey took him through Sheffield, Derby, and Coventry until he headed east, stopping at Northampton,

[9] Among the frequent writers of this kind of epistle to the offices of the Secretaries of State were William Patterson, John Dennis, and John Toland. At this time, William Greg was sending a regular series of reports from Edinbugh. See *Portland Papers*, iv. 195–7, 201–3, 205–11, etc.

Cambridge, and Bury St Edmunds. He had stopped at the latter two on his journey the year before, and he once more retraced his steps in returning to London through Colchester and Chelmsford. It was a hot, dry summer, and while Defoe did not have to face the problem of roads that resembled lakes, he found the heat exhausting.

The first letter we have from this circuit is on 30 July from Crediton, a town north-west of Exeter. Some rain had finally come to this part of England, and Defoe found the break in the 'Violent heat . . . Refreshing' (H 94). The story he had to tell was of Whig bishops trying to control the lower clergy, who tended to support the Tories. He noted the defeat of Gilbert Burnet's candidate at Salisbury. Violent mob behaviour in that town had been balanced in Exeter by the victory of the Bishop of Exeter (now a supporter of the Whigs and the ministry) over his clergy. His report on the way in which politics had gradually become a kind of religion for the populace was amusing:

all Our Party here are Politicians, Especially the Parsons (God bless us), who Once a week Settle the Consciences, Twice a week the state; and It Could not but afford me some speculation, to See, at This place, where the Dissenting parson is my Friend, the Post Comeing in on Sunday morning, The people Devoutly Resort to the News house as they Call it first, and then to the Church. (H 96)

Defoe was staying with, or in contact with, men who were later to appear on the list of agents recruited by him for the purpose of supplying intelligence. At Crediton it was Josiah Eveleigh, a Dissenting minister. Defoe's mail was to be sent to Francis Bere, a merchant at Tiverton, after he had been to Plymouth, where he would consult with Peter Baron. All of this was to destroy what Defoe referred to, in an allusion to his *Dyet of Poland*, as 'Seymskyes Western Empire' (H 100), the powerful hold that the violent Tory Sir Edward Seymour had over Devon and Cornwall.

In his next letter to Harley, Defoe had an adventure to tell. Although he may have set out with Christopher Hurt, Defoe was eventually to travel with a series of companions until meeting with his brother-in-law, Robert Davis, at Bath. The mail for Weymouth, addressed to 'Captain Turner', was picked up by the captain of the *Diligence*, a privateer, who delivered the letters to Defoe (Alexander Goldsmith) and his companion and then, piqued at being charged for a drink the cost of which he appears to have thought Defoe was defraying, reported the nature of the letters—with coded numerical replacements for names of persons and places—to the Mayor. The Mayor in turn passed on this information to the judges of the assize at Dorchester. This led to a warrant for Defoe's arrest and the questioning of the Dissenting ministers in the area. When Defoe came to Bideford, he received notice of the warrant for his arrest, but with the help of a friend, John Darracott, to whom he showed his pass, he was able to defeat the efforts to arrest him.

Defoe explained these efforts as a Tory plot. In the *Review* of 25 August, he wrote with indignation of how there had been an attempt to press him into the army when he was near Exeter. Paraphrasing the warrant that was issued against him, Defoe warned anyone thinking of travelling to that area:

Let him have a special Care of all those good Honest *Devonshire* Men, who when the Judge, according to his Duty, in his Charge to the Jury, tells them of Seditious Person, who *spread Libels* about the Country, to the Disquieting Her majesty's Subjects, and Directs them to put the laws in Execution, will have it to be no Body but the *Peace-making Traveller*, that being in the Country on his Lawful occasions, that brought neither Paper nor Pamphlet with him, has spread no Sedition but that which her majesty from the throne dictated to us all, viz. *The Absolute necessity of Peace and Union.*[10]

The *Review* account suggests that Defoe was far angrier than would appear from his version of the events in the letter to Harley. To Harley, he wanted to seem entirely in control of events. For the readers of the *Review*, he wanted to make the point that people such as Hugh Stafford are dangerous in that they attempt to curtail the freedoms of Englishmen. At the time, he was travelling with a teacher of sacred theology at a Dissenting academy in Exeter. It might well be wondered what *he* thought of these events. In response to Harley's speculation about the possibility that Defoe's travelling companions might betray his relationship with the Secretary of State, Defoe wrote to Harley that he deliberately kept such travelling companions in the dark about any connection with the government. Of course they may not have guessed, but a number of those in Defoe's intelligence net-

---

[10] *Review* ii. 302. The warrant was as follows: 'To all Constables and Tythingmen and other her majesties officers within the County of Devon and allso to Charles Sugg.

'Whereas I have received Information against Daniel de Foe for spreading and publishing divers seditious and scandalous Libels and false news to the great disturbance of the peace of this Kingdom and that he is a Person of ill Fame and Behaviour, and is now lurking within some or one of your Parishes, Tythings, or Precincts—These are in her Majties name to will and require you and every of you on Sight hereof to make diligent privy Search within your said parishes, Tythings, and Precincts, in all suspitious Houses and Places within the same, and to be assistant to the sd Charles Sugg in searching for and apprehending the sd. Daniel de Foe, and when found and apprehended forthwith to bring him before me to be examin'd concerning the Premises, and to be dealt with as the Law directs. Hereof you and every of you may not fail at your utmost Perils. Given under my hand and Seal the 9th day of august in the 4th year of the Reign of our soverain lady Ann over England &c. Anno Dom. 1705.' The warrant was signed by Hugh Stafford, and Defoe had written a reminder to Harley not to lose so important a document.

work, men like Benjamin Coole or James Pierce, were extraordinarily able men with exploratory and unconventional attitudes. All of them seemed deeply involved in contemporary politics, and some seem to have been able to guess at Defoe's connections with the government. Indeed, in his next letter to Harley Defoe puzzled over James Forbes's surmise about their association (H 104) after Forbes asked Defoe to give his regards to the Secretary of State.

It was partly the nature of Defoe's connections that made Hugh Stafford suspicious. Defoe wrote a letter to Stafford denying that he was distributing seditious materials and stating that he had a certificate from the Secretary of State for his activities, that he was not 'Lurking in the Country', and that he was on his way to Wells to confront the person who had accused him. Stafford, who thought that Charles Hedges was meant by Defoe's reference to Harley, sent Hedges a copy of Defoe's letter, describing Defoe's conversation about the young Members of Parliament—his complaints that they left everything to be managed by the leading figures and voted in imitation of their leaders. In addition, Hugh Stafford continued, 'Such Scandelous reflections as these are, which makes me very much doubt he comes into our country with noe good designe, for he keeps Company with none but presbyterian and Independent preachers, for he has made it his business to visitt them almost in every town and parish throughout our County' (H 102). Defoe had asked Stafford for the names of those who informed against him, and Stafford may have felt pressured by Defoe's obvious assurance and his evocation of a position synonymous with power.

Defoe was clearly a sharp observer of the contemporary political scene. He had mocked William Bromley's book on Italy as lacking in insight and precise detail, and made certain that Harley would not find these qualities lacking even in his relatively brief letters. He even provided a new vocabulary to describe how money has been used to buy elections:

Divizes and the wholl Country of Wilts are Corrupted and abused by the *Iron-Chest*, a Modern proverb now known in the Country as Universally as the Alphabet. The meaning is the Reciever Genll of the County is Sir Fra: Childs Bro: whose Influence so Rules by Lending Money that who ever is Needy is sure to be bought off. (H 104)

And he would occasionally be expansive about the boundless wealth to be found in England, as in his description of 'that Great Vale of Trade' between Warminster in Wiltshire and Cirencester in Gloucestershire. He was back in London on 6 November, writing his report for Harley after what he described in the *Review* as a circuit of hundreds of miles. Though he spoke in the *Review* of 'near 1100 Miles Riding'[11] he may have been including his earlier travels in this estimation. At any rate, he was often in the saddle for some seven hours before reaching his destination, settling himself down in a tavern to hear conversation, and making contact with his agents. Who can doubt that he loved it?

II

At the same time that he was collecting information for Harley, Defoe was continuing to write the *Review* three times a week every week and establishing himself as a commentator on almost all aspects of English life and thought. If he maintained his running commentary on politics in the main part of the journal, he continued his broader coverage of ethics, religion, and social commentary in what began as 'Advice from the Scandal Club' but which soon became a supplement to the *Review* or *Little Review*. Always an ingenious retailer of opinion, Defoe carried on his running analysis of practically everything in the same manner that he might have held forth to his circle at the local coffee-house. He had his opinions and was never reluctant to share them with his readers. He was still the man to regret that if he was the only person in the country to think correctly about Occasional Conformity, he could hardly help it.

One of the topics he was always willing to talk about was the failure of human perception to apprehend the crowd of spirits who inhabited the world but remained invisible to the senses. To a query concerning ghosts from one correspondent from Stamford, Defoe responded with the mixture of belief and scepticism that was to inform his later writings on the subject. His opinion was probably the same as that of Samuel Johnson at the end of the century: the Bible provides certain evidence for their existence:

It would be thought very Arrogant for the Society to Determine against Apparitions, when the Scripture positively tells us, That the *Witch of* Endor rais'd an Appearance of an *Old Man in a Mantle*, which the Text calls *Samuel*; and 'tis said of the disciples, when they saw our lord walking on the Sea, they thought *it had been a Spirit*, which they would not have suggested, if there had been no such thing. From this observation, the Society must agree to the General part of the Question, That *there may be such a thing as we call a Spirit*, an *Apparition*, a *Phantome*, a *Spectre*, a *Ghost*, or what you please to call it.[12]

---

[11] *Review*, ii. 378.   [12] Ibid. 43.

Defoe followed this affirmation with an attack on the 'teeming Imagination of Timerous People' whose fears create ghosts where none exist, whose minds seem to delight in the 'frighting its self for the meer sake of its own Delusion'. And as he was to do at the beginning of *A Journal of the Plague Year*, he mocked those whose minds create 'Devils in the Clouds', which dissolve under the gaze of reason.

Defoe saw the issue of ghosts in the larger controversy over the existence of the soul and the possibility of life after death. As we shall see, his three large volumes on the subject of magic and apparitions were to focus upon this subject at a time when the questions of deists and agnostics such as Collins, Toland, and Tindal had become more pressing. But Toland had already expounded his views at this time, and earlier writers such as Hobbes, Spinoza, and Blount had challenged traditional viewpoints. In a supplement to 'Advice from the Scandal Club' published in November 1705, Defoe asserted that 'Our Converse with the World of Spirits is a thing in our Opinion very certain'[13] and pointed out its connection to the immortality of the soul. He acknowledged the doubts expressed by 'Philosophy', but argued that such thinking leads to doubts about the existence of God. Defoe asked such potential materialists to consider the necessity for a 'first Cause', and challenged them to search for '*a Mighty Something*, a Great *First*, which was Pre-existent, Self-existent, Necessarily-existent'. At times Defoe simply resorts to Pascal's wager to encourage belief: if there is a God, salvation may be purchased, if none, little is lost. But this is a Defoe trying to argue with doubting philosophers. He was clearly a believing Christian, and that belief included an acceptance of ghosts and spirits.

Under these circumstances, his production of *A True Relation of the Apparition of One Mrs. Veal, the next Day after her Death: to One Mrs. Bargrave at Canterbury the Eighth of September 1705* at the end of the year is hardly surprising. Mrs Veal speaks of a world of spirits in exactly the way Defoe did. 'If the Eyes of our Faith were as open as the Eyes of our Body,' she remarks, 'we should see numbers of Angels about us for our Guard.' And Mrs Veal's comment is all the more weighty because she speaks as an apparition. She appears to Mrs Bargrave at noon, the exact moment of her death. The clues to her condition are suggested by her refusal to kiss Mrs Bargrave, her unwillingness to accept food or drink, her remarks on spirits, and cryptic comments about going on a long journey. The credibility of Mrs Bargrave's story turns on her knowledge concerning the dress that Mrs Veal was wearing—knowledge which, according to a Mrs Watson, she could only have had from the lips of Mrs Veal, whom, according to the

---

[13] Ibid. 6–7, suppl. 3.

account, Mrs Bargrave had not seen for two and a half years. Thus all the remarks Mrs Veal makes about the limitations upon our knowledge of Heaven and the books she admires, Drelincourt's *The Christian's Defence against the Fears of Death*, Anthony Horneck's *The Happy Ascetick*, and John Norris's *Friendship in Perfection*, carried particular weight, as if they were being recommended from beyond the grave. Defoe's work was attached to unsold sheets of the fourth edition of Drelincourt's book and apparently increased the popularity of that work, as it went into numerous editions throughout the century.

There is much that is problematic about the *True Relation of Mrs. Veal*, from the facts of its publication to Defoe's role in retelling a story which caused a considerable stir in Canterbury and, by way of journals such as *The Loyal Post*, throughout the country.[14] The traditional story of Defoe's involvement has him listening to a complaint about the slow sale of Drelincourt's work, inquiring if there was enough of the supernatural in it, and offering to write such an attractive piece. The anecdote was told by Chalmers, one of Defoe's earliest biographers—early enough to pick up information from publishers at a time when knowledge about Defoe was still fresh enough to have the ring of authenticity. Thus Samuel Johnson, who moved in this circle, could offer to give Mrs Elizabeth Montagu a list of works he knew Defoe had written, a list presumably far more extensive than any that existed up to that time.[15] Nevertheless, as William Lee suggested, 'All this is circumstantial', pointing to the errors in the account.[16] But what is perhaps most unfortunate is the way in which so anthologizable a piece has been allowed to become the quintessential work by Defoe. Leslie Stephen, believing the account to be a work of fiction, argued that 'it contains in a few lines all the essential peculiarities of his art'. Stephens did not mean this as a compliment. For him, Defoe's 'art' consisted of a few tricks of verisimilitude.[17]

The opening of the preface, 'This Relation is Matter of Fact; and attended with such Circumstances as may induce any reasonable man to believe it', reveals something of Defoe's attestations about evidence, and the account contains a blend of the real and the supernatural that became a

[14] See Manuel Schonhorn (ed.), *Accounts of the Apparition of Mrs. Veal*, Augustan Reprint Society No. 115 (Los Angeles: William Andrews Clark Memorial Library, 1965), 1–3.

[15] James Boswell, *Life of Johnson*, ed. George Birkbeck Hill (6 vols., Oxford: Clarendon Press, 1888), iii. 267–8

[16] Lee, i. 127–8. Although Lee threw doubt upon the narrative of Defoe's writing the work for a publisher of Drelincourt, he did not doubt Defoe's role in the work, though few works by Defoe have so little evidence for their inclusion in the canon.

[17] Leslie Stephen, 'Defoe's Novels', in *Hours in a Library* (3 vols., New York: Putnam, 1899), i. 4–12, 20.

hallmark of Defoe's style; but it is more an example of some of his more lively journalism than of his best work as a writer of fiction. What is intriguing is his handling of the doubts voiced by some, the attempt of Mr Veal to suppress the story, and his report of the questions he put to her along with her responses. His conclusion, that we should accept what appears to be 'Matter of Fact' even though it goes beyond the ability of science to explain things, is in keeping with his ideas on the existence of spirits and ghosts.

What Defoe had to say about ghosts in the *Review* was in many ways less important than his comments on problems involving love and marriage, human nature, society, and religion. In connection with matters of love, Defoe held steady to the line that a marriage without love was a form of legalized prostitution. He advised parents to be generous about dowries and to realize that they had obligations to their children. To those who complained about being in love with women without money, Defoe advised that love was the only important consideration in a marriage, and that neither rank nor wealth compared to it. He attacked men who were trying to escape their promises to marry as lacking in either religion or morality. If he tended to idealize family life, he warned of the difficulties of raising children: 'In short, a Wife ought to be capable of every part of her Office, or the Defects will spoil the Attainments; Children require Instruction as well as Provision; Examples of Piety and Prudence in Parents, are as useful adjuncts to a Mother, as their Nursing and Necessaries.'[18] He pretty much told a young woman thinking of marrying a widower with six children that it might be unwise. Like Mandeville, he tried to see into the realities of human life, and warned against any belief in an innate modesty in children who 'in the Bloom of Innocence, know nothing of it, have no Native Propensity to it, but see and do those things without Blushing, which they will afterwards Blush to think of'.[19]

He argued against the importance of rank and mocked the concept of noble blood. To a Celinda who was concerned about marrying a trades-man, he noted how adaptable concepts of gentility actually were: 'A Soldier is a Gentleman by his Profession, and his Sword pares off all the Dirt of a Mechanick Original'[20] And to a family objecting to the mean birth of a woman he advised,

Education, especially in *England*, has so much the Ascendant over Birth, that we see the Lady's Daughter a Paisant, the Tradesman's Daughter a Lady.

The Wealth of the Trading part of this Nation, is so Superiour to that of the

[18] *Little Review* No. 6, in *Review*, ii. 22. [19] Ibid. i. 20, suppl. 3. [20] Ibid. 9, suppl. 5.

Gentry, Especially of meer Ancient Families; that it has given the Tradesmen opportunity to give a more liberal Education to their Children, than the other; and Education has such strange Effects on children, that it makes these Mechanicks Gentlemen, and Join'd to Large Fortunes; has Erected such Great Families many of the Nobility, owe their Wealth and Birth to Trade.[21]

And as for the notion that the money was earned by immoral means, Defoe, who was to argue that all business was to a certain extent a form of criminal activity, urged the parties not to worry too much about that. At the same time, he could voice that opinion that 'the Partition Walls between Gentry and Rabble, Quality and Mechanicks, are all demolished'[22] and that, as he had maintained in the *True-Born Englishman*, only virtuous behaviour makes a difference between the orders of society and reveals true gentility.

On matters of religion and morality, however, Defoe could be strict. He objected to the use of cosmetics, to masturbation, and to maypoles. He did not object to 'Innocent Diversions, and the ordinary Sports and Pastimes of the People',[23] but he did not want the Church encouraging them. If the thrust of latitudinarian thought favoured the salvation of a good person of any religion, whether Jew or Turk, Defoe would have none of it. God might do it, of course, argued Defoe, but not without 'dissolving the Covenant of Grace'.[24] And he raged against a theatre benefit held to support the building of a church. How well this high religious tone accorded with his principles in politics and his pleas for moderation is hard to say. He doubtless touched a chord of sentiment among his audience with his attitudes toward love, and they may have accepted his religious principles as merely old-fashioned righteousness.

III

If his audience seemed unable to get enough of his forum for personal advice, Defoe himself was still mainly involved with his new political line on peace and union while trying to get *Jure Divino* into print before those who subscribed might demand their money back. He who had once attacked James Owen's *Moderation a Virtue* now gave the highest marks to moderation and toleration. The great evil was persecution, which was the product of passion rather than reason and was invariably self-defeating

---

[21] *Little Review*, in *Review*, ii. 46–7.   [22] Ibid. i. 22, suppl. 3.
[23] Ibid. ii. 338.   [24] Ibid. i. 11, suppl. 3.

because it produced sympathy for those oppressed.[25] It was in the name of this cause, that he wrote two pamphlets in defence of the Dissenters in Carolina, who were in the process of being deprived of their rights as citizens by the Governor. Defoe drew upon the reading in political theory that he had been doing for *Jure Divino* in responding to what he regarded as an attack upon the rights of citizenship guaranteed by the Constitution of Carolina, a Constitution that provided for religious freedom. Crediting Locke rather than Shaftesbury with the drawing up of this Constitution, Defoe argued that the attempt at passing a bill that would deprive Dissenters of the right of sitting in the Assembly of the colony would violate the spirit of the written laws as well as the 'Laws of Nature and Reason'.[26]

A few months later, on 18 March 1706, he published *The Case of the Protestant Dissenters in Carolina*, a pamphlet which was less particular about the events occurring in America and broader in its statement of political principles. Defoe now began speaking more fully about the liberties of the subject in society as the basis of all other principles:

Liberty being the only sure and lasting Foundation of our Quiet and Satisfaction in this World, a Community can never be reduc'd to any State, in which it will not have a right to use all Methods, absolutely necessary to secure that Liberty when it is in danger to regain it when it is lost: Nor can there be any Condition of any single Person in that Community imagin'd or devis'd, in which it will not be his truer Interest to give his Assistance to secure or recover the Liberty of that Community, than to endanger or destroy it, tho he were by that means to get all the Power of the Community into his own Hands.[27]

Defoe was not suggesting any degree of anarchy. He defined liberty as 'the Freedom of acting according to a known and stated Rule', but among those rules liberty of conscience had to be permitted. Since the 'state Rule' in this case was the constitution drawn up by Locke, it included a 'Universal and Absolute Toleration' of all religious beliefs, and any attempt to violate toleration by excluding Dissenters in Carolina was an example of tyranny. Defoe was plainly arguing as the agent for this Dissenting group in the colonies; they must have contacted him as the best spokesman for their cause in the same way that Cotton Mather planned to write to Defoe about

[25] See Daniel Defoe, *The Ballance: or, a New Test of the High-Flyers of All Sides* (London, 1705), esp. 44–5. Defoe wrote this tract in the guise of a moderate Anglican. Defoe draws upon Algernon Sydney for his defence of the mob and against the argument that the injustices of a tyrant are better than rule by the people. Defoe attempted to gain credibility by some mild attacks on himself.
[26] *Party-tyranny, or an Occasional Bill in Miniature* (London, 1705), 257.
[27] *The Case of the Protestant Dissenters in Carolina* (London, 1706), 3.

some pressing political issue.[28] He had assumed a role in English society as the spokesman for liberty and for those oppressed by the 'State Machine'.

All of this was a prelude to the appearance of Defoe's fullest statement about politics, *Jure Divino*, a work which he had begun in prison and from which he had been quoting for three years. After difficulties in setting the poem in type, Defoe wrote to his friend Fransham on 24 May that it was finally ready for distribution to subscribers in the country, though he may have been optimistic. In issuing his pirated version on 19 July, Benjamin Bragg spoke of the work being available in the country for about a month. Defoe had announced in the *Review* of 18 July that subscribers could obtain their copies at one of eight locations on the 20th; so in a sense Bragg, one of Defoe's own printers, had gained a step on Defoe, publishing the work in a cheaper format one day earlier. Defoe was furious. He considered Bragg's action as a form of theft little different from that performed by a robber on the highways; the work was his property, and Bragg had stolen from him whatever profit he hoped to make. Defoe based his view of government on various concepts of property, and he might justly view Bragg's action as a violation of his rightful control of his labours. Action by publishers such as Bragg eventually led to the passage of England's first Copyright Act, and, needless to say, Defoe was to be one of the Act's most enthusiastic supporters. Meanwhile, he appealed to his subscribers to do 'Justice to the Author' and avoid purchasing the cheaper version.

Defoe was particularly proud of the frontispiece, a portrait engraved by Van der Gucht, with his arms and the motto from Juvenal 'Laudatur et alget'. Bragg had published a picture that Defoe considered unrecognizable. 'The Picture put in the Book, which is but the copy of a Copy,' he wrote, 'is about as much like the Author, as Sir *Roger l'Estrange*, was like the Dog *Towzer*.'[29] He had written to Fransham about it, stating that it had been 'prepar'd at the request of some of my Friends who are pleas'd to value it more than it deserves' (H 124). Bragg's edition, he cautioned readers, was filled with errors, the print terrible, the paper worse. In the preface, he expressed his expectation that the work would be plagiarized. 'I have been forc'd into an open War with the Booksellers about this Book,' he wrote, 'having universally refused them subscribing . . . and in return I am assur'd they will reprint it, and sell it for half the Money.' But while he

---

[28] Cotton Mather, *The Diary of Cotton Mather, 1681–1724* (2 vols., Boston: Massachusetts Historical Society, 1911–12), ii. 74. Mather's daughter said that her father received letters from Defoe and read them to the entire family. See Paula Backscheider, *Daniel Defoe: His Life* (Baltimore: Johns Hopkins University Press, 1989), 573, n. 26.   [29] *Review*, iii. 360.

said that he was 'content' to 'let them turn Pyrates, and take away my Right', anticipation did not stifle resentment.[30]

Defoe probably expected considerable fame from *Jure Divino*. He apparently felt that the materials in it were dangerous enough to delay its publication, and he conceived his political ideology sufficiently radical to awaken outcries from the High Church and Tories. 'All those few and wiser Heads that had any respect for the Author', he wrote, 'earnestly press'd me not to attempt it while the last Parliament was sitting, Measures having been taken, and the Party then powerful enough to blast it in its Birth, seize it in the Press, and suppress both it and me together, by the heavy Weight of parliamentary Censure' (xxvii). He who had such success with his political poetry up to this point would surely create even more of a sensation with such a long poem. As the motto under the portrait and the motto on the title-page reveals, he had been studying Juvenal's satires, probably with the intent of achieving greater dignity, not realizing that, among all the postures he attempted to strike, that of the dignified man of letters was the least convincing. Thus the twenty-eight pages of prefatory material, the address to the Goddess of Reason, and the encomiastic poem addressed to him by A.O. give the impression of a parodic creation in the manner of Swift's *Tale of a Tub*. A.O. may have meant his praise of Defoe's 'Powerful Muse' sincerely, but the gifts he allows Defoe—those of wit and the ability to expose the evils of 'Despotick Power'—are hardly the highest compliments to a poet. In fact, *Jure Divino* is a didactic poem intended to present a compelling rational argument against the concept of the divine right of kings. That doctrine, with its attractive notion of authority was to be revealed as erroneous and replaced by one of individual freedom and toleration.

Up to this point, we have seen that the chief influences on Defoe's poetry were Dryden, Rochester, and Marvell. Defoe evokes Juvenal and praises Milton, but *Jure Divino* is only superficially anything other than a very long political poem in the manner of *The True-Born Englishman*. Defoe's aim was to show that the idea of absolute monarchy was irrational. As we have seen, France under Louis XIV had an immense appeal as a model government, and Defoe's praise of the efficiency of such a state often led antagonists to maintain that he was actually supporting England's enemy. Defoe attempts to demonstrate that the concept of absolutism was opposed to the laws of nature and reason and to prove his points through an analysis of human nature and human history as played out in the world and in

[30] Defoe, *Jure Divino* (London, 1706), p. xxvi. References to this work will be included within parentheses in the text.

England. Using a technique similar to that found in the 'Instructions to a Painter', he calls upon the muse of Satire to illustrate his arguments by calling up various examples of human actions both wise and foolish.[31] The poem ends with a survey of the major Whig politicians of the time—men capable of leading the nation to true greatness—and a final poem to Anne as the Queen who will eventually be responsible for the Union of England and Scotland.

The poem had a heuristic effect for Defoe, for he had to think through his ideas on politics in a manner he had never attempted before. The key to human political action is seen in the opening couplets of the introduction, a couplet he repeats throughout the poem to drive home his point:

> NATURE has left *this Tincture in the Blood*,
> That all Men *would be Tyrants* if they could.
> If they forbear their Neighbours to devour,
> 'Tis not for want of *Will*, but want *of Power*;
> The General Plague Infects the very Race,
> *Pride* in his Heart, and *Tyrant* in his Face;
> The Characters are legible and plain,
> And perfectly describe *the Monster, Man*. (Introd. 1)

As mentioned before, the echo of Rochester's *Satire upon Mankind* is deliberate. Defoe accepts Rochester's libertine political stance with its Hobbesian overtones. All men long for absolute power, and society is created out of fear that such power will attempt to enslave all others. True government is created out of a compromise by which everyone agrees to restrain the lust for power in themselves and every other member of society.

> The only Safety of Society,
> Is, that my Neighbour's *just as proud as I*. (Introd. 1)

Everyone is ruled by the passions, and that enslavement to the passions has allowed tyrants to enslave whole nations. The opening theme of the first few books is not very different from that of Rousseau's *Social Contract* half a century later: man is born free but everywhere he has been and is in chains. He should be able to negotiate a contract in the state of nature that gave him protection from the possibility of any individual becoming a tyrant. Laws were established to protect liberties and property, but because of the 'taint' in the human psyche, there will always be tyrants who will want to overthrow the laws, and cowardly citizens who will not resist.

---

[31] In the Introduction he calls upon Satyr to 'paint the Man that *thinks himself a God*'.

Since the drive to power is insatiable, the tyrant will eventually threaten the strongest drive of all—self-preservation. And when this happens, resistance becomes inevitable. The laws of nature, reason, and God dictate that tyrants will always be overthrown. Insofar as there is a divine right to rule, it lies in the people, not in monarchs. For his evidence, Defoe provides numerous footnotes with instances drawn from history, but as suggested by his dedication of the work to the Goddess of Reason, his greatest appeal is to the faculty of that very goddess. The metaphysical nature of authority during this period had not been dispelled by the Glorious Revolution. Defoe always instanced the behaviour of those who preached obedience to James II in 1688 as a perfect example of the way the necessity of self-defence overcame all principle, and he had little admiration either for those who followed their principles and allowed the tyrannical James to exploit them or for those who followed the law of self-preservation:

> They that resolve their Liberty to lose,
> Heaven is too just that Freedom to refuse,
> *But lets them have* the Slav'ry which they choose.
> Till Reason opens *their deluded Eyes*,
> Blinded with Notions and Absurdities;
> Instructs them *in the Rules* of Providence,
> And Guides *by Natures Laws* to Self-defence. (iii. 27–8)

Since all men are ultimately guided by laws of self-love and self-interest, the defender of passive obedience to tyrants is deluded or insane.

> Men may *sometimes* by Subtilty and Slight
> *Oppose themselves*, and Sacrifice their Right;
> *But all's a Blast*, the empty Fraud's in vain,
> Int'rest Instructs, and all's restor'd again;
> *Self-Love's* the Ground of all the things we do,
> Which they *that talk on't least* do most pursue (iv. 8)

Defoe's remark that he knew what Sidney, Locke, and others had said about government but that he was following his own system was true enough, though he drew extensively from those writers, from the writers on natural law Grotius and Pufendorf, and from Huguenot writers such as Pierre Jurieu. Defoe grounds all concept of rights and freedom in his reading of human psychology, drawn to a great extent from Rochester. He sees government as a natural result of human sociability and, like Locke, views laws and their enforcement as necessities arising from the inevitability of crime and aggression within society. He seems to have drawn his emphasis on the importance of property from Harrington,[32] though he goes beyond Harrington in allowing complete power to any monarch who actually owns all of a nation's lands. For Defoe, even God's power stems from His being the proprietor of the universe.

Defoe lamented that even before *Jure Divino* was published it was being criticized as a bad poem. He had some basis for this complaint. Those readers who had enjoyed the wit and energy of *The True-Born Englishman* would not have found much falling off in the first five books of *Jure Divino*. Admittedly, they would have been reading a more serious work, but there is no lack of clever analysis and wit. The sixth book aims at a different kind of seriousness. Defoe mentions Milton's *Paradise Lost* several times in the poem, and when he comes to the discussion of divine and secular history, he attempts a type of sublimity that does not reveal his best talents.[33] His discussion of Satan and the origins of crime bear direct comparison with Milton, and Defoe's standing as a poet does not emerge unscathed from such a contest in this book or in the following one. The final books, with their exposition of ancient and modern history, are heavy on ideas and light on inspiration. Book XI involves a specific discussion of the English government and its arguments about the divisions of power between King and Parliament, and Defoe has an opportunity to assert his belief in the 'Original Power' inherent in the people and once more to sing the virtues of his 'Hero', William III:

> *Till William came*, what Terrors press'd our Minds!
> What Dangers both from Enemies, *and more from Friends!*
> *How groan'd* the Land! with *Right Divine* opprest,
> And *Passive Pageantry*, the Parties Jest!
> With threatning Crouds of *willing Slaves* o'er run,
> Who courted Fate and *strove to be undone*;
> That *couchant Necks laid down* to rampant Pride,
> And their own Blessings purposely defy'd. (xi. 21)

This is what has been called 'Whig panegyric verse', and Defoe ended his poem in this mode. For those who agreed with his political positions, it probably seemed acceptable political poetry. If the passage above is not in the same class as Oliver Goldsmith's pessimistic 'Ill fares the land' section of *The Deserted Village*, his Tory message of decline, it is because the optimism with which Defoe regarded the future of England and its people may seem somewhat shallow in overlooking the realities of poverty and suffering in the nation. The last book, with its gallery of Whig leaders and

---

[32] Defoe refers to Harrington ('*Oceana*') in bk. ii. 10 of *Jure Divino*.
[33] He even tries his hand at a few epic similes. See ibid. vi. 15.

its address to Queen Anne, suffers most in this regard, and is certainly the weakest. *Jure Divino*, then, is hardly a failure as a statement of Whig political theories in verse, and is seldom entirely dull. The trouble was that Defoe's strong suits were his power in creating a fiction, his imagination, and his wit. *Jure Divino* hardly allowed him much of a platform for the kind of narrative he could write so well, and there was not much room for either imagination or wit in the second half. The modern reader of poetry is seldom taken by didacticism, but Defoe's contemporaries were. When John Clerk of Penicuik wrote to his father from London about his need to purchase the works of Defoe as a prelude to understanding English politics, *Jure Divino* was among them.[34]

IV

If Defoe was satisfying his patrons with his reports and writings, he was not able to prevent frequent attacks upon him in the print media. Accused of ignorance of Latin by John Tutchin in the *Observator*, he responded that he had read more books than Tutchin. He noted that his father had given him a good education and that it was his fault that, though he could read Latin, he could not speak it. He challenged Tutchin to a contest involving translation from Latin, French, and Italian into English and then back again into a combination of different languages, offering a wager of £20.[35] He replied to Joseph Browne's *Mooncalf* by suggesting that if he were less learned than his opponents, he had better manners.[36] His enemies stirred up his creditors, and he listed the names of those making claims on him in an advertisement in *The Review* along with the statement that he had not been arrested and taken to Newgate. By way of illustrating his plight in sustaining these attacks, he told an off-colour story of the behaviour of a black dog who barked loudly at one of his fellow brown canines. The brown dog, the recipient of this aggression, saw his enemy as the coward he was and 'finding him of a Currish cowardly Breed, and not worth his Notice, very Soberly and Unconcern'd, he holds up one leg, Pisses upon him, and so goes on about his Busines'.[37] This somewhat Rabelaisian story might be a sign of Defoe's frustration, but it was probably the kind of anecdote he was accustomed to tell among some of his friends.

In the *Review*, Defoe gave a picture of himself as one threatened continually with assassination and of his response to it:

---

[34] Scottish Records Office, GD 18/3135, item 6.   [35] *Review*, ii. 150.
[36] Ibid. 149.   [37] Ibid. 150.

I move about the World Unguarded and Unarm'd, a little Stick not strong enough
to Correct a Dog, . . . a Sword sometimes perhaps for Decency, but it is all harmless to a meer Nothing; can do no hurt any where but just at the Tip of it, call'd the
Point—And what's that in the Hand of a Feeble Author. . . . But now he has had a
Storm of a more Scandalous Assassination, Studying to Ruine, and Embroil him,
Crowds of Sham-Actions, Arrests, Sleeping Debates in Trade of 17 years standing Reviv'd; Debts put in Suit after Contracts and Agreements under Hand and
Seal; and which is worse, Writs taken out for Debts, without the Knowledge of
the Creditor, and some after the Creditor has been Paid. . . .[38]

Defoe's defiance of his enemies is apparent. He let them know that he
carried a sword and that he was ready to use it as well as his stick. If he was
being a little melodramatic, it made good copy. There he was again, the
Defoe of the *Hymn to the Pillory*, virtuous as always, surrounded by
enemies who know that they are wrong and that they represent the
betrayers of the nation.

Perhaps the most important element in these attacks and his replies
involved the question of what might be called his 'cover'. Defoe wanted to
be taken for an independent political writer of some dignity. He did not like
being hounded by rumours such as those spread by Dyer, and he especially
did not like anyone speaking of him as an employee of the government. By
way of revenge, he gathered together statements made by Dyer that he
considered libellous and printed them in the autumn of 1705 under the title
*A Collection from Dyer's Letters concerning the Election of the Present Parlia-
ment*. When he finally made peace with Dyer after years of feuding, he
reminded him of the events of 1705 and 1706 but said he would forget them
in an effort at a truce between writers on different sides:

But to State the Matter fairly between you and I, as writeing for Differeng Intrests,
and So possibly Comeing Under an Unavoidable Necessity of Jarring in Severall
Cases; I am Ready to make a fair Truce of Honour with you, (Viz) That if what
Either party are doeing, or Sayeing, that may Clash with the party we are for, and
Urge us to speak, it shall be done without Nameing Eithers Name and without
personall Reflections; and Thus we may Differ Still, and yet preserv both the
Christian and the Gentleman. . . . I See no Reason why I should affront a Mans
person because I do Not Joyn with him in principle. I please my Self with being
the first proposer of so fair a Treaty with you, because I beliv as you can Not
Denye its being Very Honble, So it is not the less So, in Comeing first from me,
who I believ Could Convince you of My haveing been the first, and the Most ill
Treated. (H 269–70)

Defoe was to write this in 1710, but his response to personal attacks may have been even more acute five years earlier, before he was able to arrange private treaties of this sort.

This attitude explains his response to a pamphlet written by Lord John Haversham concerning Defoe's attack upon him in the *Review*. Haversham heaped insults upon Defoe as a 'mercenary', a snarler', and 'scandalous', but it was his insistence that Defoe had been writing with the 'Charm and Protection' of a 'Minister' that probably upset Defoe most. Identifying himself as 'the Author of the Review', Defoe focuses on Haversham's description of him as a 'MEAN AND MERCENARY PROSTITUTE', and denies that he has had any 'Encouragement' from those in power or that anyone else has written any of his journal. He shifts the ground of his defence with a lengthy autobiographical description of his sufferings for the good of the nation:

how I stand alone in the World, abandon'd by those very People that own I have *done them Service*; how I am Sold and Betray'd *by Friends*, Abus'd and Cheated by Barbarous and *Unnatural Relations*, su'd for *other Mens* Debts, and strip'd Naked by Publick Injustice, of what should have Enabl'd me to *pay my own*; How, with a Numerous Family, and no helps but my own Industry, I have forc'd my way with undiscourag'd Diligence, thro' a Sea of Debt and Misfortune, and reduc'd them Exclusive of Composition from 17000 l. to less than 5; how in Goals, in Retreats, in all manner of Extremities, I have supported my self without the Assistance of Friends, or Relations, either to me or mine; how I still Live without this Vindicator's suggested methods, and am so far from making my Fortune by this Way *of Scribbling*, that no man more desires a Limitation and Regulation of *the Press*, than my self; especially that *Speeches in* Parliament might not be printed *without Order* of Parliament, and poor Authors Betray'd to Engage with Men too powerful for them, in more forcible Arguments than those of Reason; if I should still acquaint him, that whatever he suggests, I shall never starve, tho' this way of Encouragement were remov'd; and that were the Trade with *Spain* open, I shall Convince the World of it, by settling my self Abroad, where I shall receive a better Treatment from both Friend and Enemy than I have here.[39]

Defoe suggests that he might more likely have ended in the peerage than in the pillory had William III continued to live, and here makes one of the most defiant defences of his character and principles: 'I was ever True to one Principle, I never Betray'd my Master or my Friend; I always Espous'd the cause of Truth and Liberty, was ever on one side *and that Side was ever right*; I have Liv'd to be Ruin'd for it, and I have Liv'd to see it Triumph over Tyranny.'[40] He ends with a defence of the ministry, particularly Marlborough, and an apology for having offended Haversham.

[39] *A Reply to a Pamphlet Entituled The L[or]d H[avesham]'s Speech* (London, 1706), 7.
[40] Ibid. 9.

This is an impressive piece of rhetoric on Defoe's part. He succeeds in protecting himself and the ministry, and the ring of truth in his words is so great that one would hardly be able to detect that he was lying in the purely selfish cause of self-preservation. If he thought this vindication of his life and opinions would silence his critics, however, he was mistaken. Writers such as Joseph Browne found him too inviting a target. In *A Dialogue between Church and No-Church*, Browne introduced Defoe as a character in his pamphlet to confess to a variety of sins:

I D----l D'Foe, alias Foe of the Parish of St. *Nicholas*, alias *No-Church*, not having the fear of Law or Gospel before my Eyes, but presuming on the Assistance of my Familiar Associate, the Devil, did wittingly, willfully, and according to old Use and Custom forge, counterfeit . . . a Letter from the Town of *Blank*. . . . He has more cunning than a Fox, for when he has done Mischief, he will not come near the place again till 'tis forgot; and he has more Doublings and Windings than a Hare, to extricate himself out of a Snare, or to draw others into one. In short, . . . he's an Original Jugler, a meer *Proteus*, a Saint in his Expectations and a Devil in his Designs.[41]

Browne accused him of sedition, of possessing a '*Machiavellian* Head', and of loving 'mischief in his Heart'.[42] If this view of Defoe reveals an entirely opposite angle of vision from his self-image, it must be admitted that he not only manipulated the truth in presenting his autobiographical sketch in the response to Lord Haversham but had also come to accept his own version of events and his image of himself as an innocent martyr to the cause of liberty and progress.

Meanwhile, Defoe had been supporting a new bill to regulate the laws of bankruptcy. He devoted a month and a half of the *Review* to this subject, between 14 Feburary and 30 March 1706, and eventually published a pamphlet on the subject, *Remarks on the Bill to Prevent Frauds Committed by Bankrupts*, on 18 April 1706. In the *Review*, he had noted that the bill should have been titled in such a way that indicated its attempt to address 'the Frauds, frequently Committed, both by Bankrupts and their Creditors' (iii. 141).[43] The *Review* articles were mainly devoted to arguing the irrationality of a system that imprisoned the debtor in a way that made paying back the creditors impossible. Using some of the arguments employed by Christopher Pitt in the 1690s, Defoe drew attention to the horror of prison conditions and the families ruined. In addition he maintained that the nation itself loses by driving the bankrupt, with his potential skills, abroad,

---

[41] *A Dialogue between Church and No-Church* (1706), in *State Tracts* (London, 1715), i. 29–31.
[42] Ibid. 32.
[43] *Review*, iii. 141.

thereby forfeiting the wealth that might accrue to the nation by his and his family's consumption of goods. Defoe argued for a bill to force all the creditors to agree to the decision of the committees of bankruptcy. Otherwise, the bankrupt becomes a victim of a 'sort of *Trade-Murther*'. He is driven to despair, flees, commits suicide, or joins the army and dies that way. Defoe's comments on the psychological state of the bankrupt shows much about his own state of mind under those circumstances:

To support himself, and prevent Impending Destruction, and Flattering himself with Hopes that this or that Effort may save him, or at least may uphold him, till something else may happen to deliver him; he invades his integrity, breaks in upon his Conscience, and puts forth his Hand to the Accursed thing. Is he Entrusted with the Orphans Estate, or the Widows small Remnant, without which they must Starve and be Undone; he hopes to make it good again, and they may never know their Danger, and ventures to take it at all Hazards, to help in the Extremity of his Circumstances; he ventures to Buy, where he knows he cannot Pay; to promise where he knows he can't perform; to stop one Man's Mouth, with another Man's Money; pay one man's Debt with another Man's Goods; and innumerable Injuries he does that in the very doing them are like a Sword thrust into his Liver and Wound him to the Soul.[44]

Defoe was recalling his first bankruptcy, but the condition was still with him; he still had his creditors.

As a replacement for the present system, Defoe urged 'Humanity and Mercy'.[45] He instanced the numerous families ruined, the children starving, the horror of the debtors' prisons, all directed at men guilty of no worse crime than being unfortunate. But by 16 March, after it had been amended, he wondered if the law would do any good at all. In his pamphlet on this subject, *Remarks on the Bill to Prevent Frauds Committed by Bankrupts*, published on 18 April, he regretted that the bill did not reform the worst part of the system. The bankrupt might still be sent to jail, to perpetual imprisonment; this meant that he would struggle to avoid punishment and be forced to desperate measures. Defoe concluded 'That to make men desperate was the way to make them Knaves; and as there never was any law but some way or other might be evaded or avoided, this would put Men's Inventions upon the rack for new Methods to defraud their Creditors'.[46] At least the new bill allowed the bankrupt 5 per cent of his holdings to try to start anew. Defoe allowed himself some irony over the resulting loss of jobs among gaolers and those involved in arresting

---

[44] Ibid. 86.
[45] Ibid. 90.
[46] *Remarks on the Bill to Prevent Frauds Committed by Bankrupts* (London, 1706), 5.

debtors, and 'As to the Attorneys, Sollicitors, etc. they may turn their Hands to the more Laudable practice of picking pockets, *according to the letter of it*, and then in time may meet with the reward of their *former Merit*, by a way they have often deserv'd it'.[47] In short, he hoped they would be hanged.

Despite the passage of the bill, Defoe was uncertain of whether it would work for him. He had written to Harley after returning from his circuit, providing a list of his trusted agents throughout England. He apparently expected to put his system into operation immediately, but had heard nothing from Harley. Meanwhile his creditors were annoying him to the extent that he believed he needed 'Some Miracle' (H 119) to escape their grasp and remain useful. 'But Sir,' he wrote, 'The prospect of that Freedome looks Every Day More Dull upon me, and I foresee I shall Never master it, Unless I can Take off some of the most Furious people who Resolutely Oppose me' (H 119). He stated that he had been advised against taking advantage of the new Act, since he would have to surrender himself into the hands of his creditors. He begged help of Harley or the Queen; £200 or £300 would be needed to relieve him. He reminded Harley that the cause of all his problems was his prosecution by the Queen. He has been 'Unjustly Ruin'd and that in her Majties Name' (H 120) and now, because he is working for Queen Anne, his enemies have stirred up his creditors. Despite his doubts, Defoe decided to take advantage of the new law. Between 18 and 22 July a notice in the *London Gazette* stated that Defoe's bankruptcy was being examined by a committee, and a similar notice ordered him to attend a meeting.[48] All action was postponed, however. Defoe was needed in Scotland to speed the work on the Union.

---

[47] *Remarks on the Bill to Prevent Frauds Committed by Bankrupts*, 28.

[48] A stranger wrote to Robert Davis, Defoe's brother-in-law, offering proof that Defoe had an estate that brought him £400 a year and which had been sheltered from legal proceedings. Defoe denied the existence of such a fund. See *Review*, iii. 576.

13

A 'True Spy' in Scotland

In This Little scheme of their Affaires I have Acted a *True spy* to you.

(Defoe to Harley, 4 January 1707)

Defoe did not leave for Scotland until 13 September 1706, when he ended his letter of that date with the postscript, 'Just taking Horse'. If his letters to Harley are any indication of his state of mind, he had spent much of the summer trying to pacify his creditors and to get the new bankruptcy Act to work for him. He had suggested to Harley in his letter of 6 May that he might be given an apartment in Whitehall both as a way of having better access to Harley and as a means of avoiding his creditors. Reminding Harley of the 'Reserv' of monies that he believed had been put aside for him, he suggested that if he had to flee from those trying to extract money from him, he would be useless to the government. He hinted at the advantages of his being sent abroad to avoid his creditors, and while John Ogilvie (alias Jean Gassion, alias John Lebrun) was filling the position of Harley's agent on the Continent, Defoe (alias Alexander Goldsmith) would be the ideal person to send to Scotland.

I

Defoe's finances were very much uppermost in his mind when, in his letter to Fransham of 24 May 1706, he tried to justify himself against charges of dishonesty. He lamented that he had not followed his own advice about declaring insolvency (breaking) early, but maintained that when his fortunes improved, he had attempted to pay everyone he could. He blamed

the severity of his creditors ('perhaps the severest ever you heard' (H 124))
on attempts at political revenge by his enemies. Not until the end of 1706
did he succeed in staving off these 'severest' of creditors. He wrote to
Harley on 21 August that he had found relief under the new Act and
gained 'at last a Compleat Victory Over the most Furious Subtill and
Malitious Oposition That has been Seen in all The Instances of the Bankrupts act' (H 124).

The examination before the Commission of Bankruptcy must have been
painful. He spoke in this letter of being 'Exceedingly Fateagu'd with this
afternoons Struggle', but along with his exhaustion came some obvious
emotional relief. Although Defoe's statement in the *Review* of 20 August
that his financial embarrassments had caused him to live '14 Years in
Retreat ... most of the Time in Banishment from his Family' may be somewhat exaggerated, there can be little doubt that his situation sapped his
energy and took him away from that source of healthy feelings and
emotions from which he drew his strength—his family. If his continual
appeals to Harley to take care of Mary and his seven children may not seem
to have the same ring of sincerity to be found in his involvement in projects
that took him away from them, we should not conclude that his family
situation did not cause him considerable pain. In that same letter, he
reported propaganda being circulated against the Union and attempts to
win the Dissenters to an anti-Union position, and in balancing the needs of
the nation against his family concerns, he was clearly readying himself for
his new role.

If the struggle over his finances involved him emotionally during the
summer, there were many other events to occupy him as well. He wrote to
Harley on 21 May to congratulate him on Marlborough's victory over the
French at Ramillies. Tory propagandists had been increasing the number
and severity of their attacks upon Marlborough, and Defoe took time to
answer a particularly effective ironic tract, *A Letter to the Author of the
Memorial of the State of England*, with his own *Remarks on the Letter* in
which he described Marlborough as the first English general to win a
significant victory over the French. Defoe's opponent had suggested that
Marlborough might have taken money from France; Defoe refuted this
notion with indignation. 'But among all the men of Action now in the
World,' he wrote, 'the Duke of Marlborough appears to be the only man,
of whom it is to be said, He is allow'd no Rest; the Calms and Intervals of
Action are deny'd to him.'[1] In the *Review* of 21 May 1706, Defoe decided to
celebrate Marlborough's victory with a poem in blank verse, free from the

---

[1] *Remarks on the Letter to the Author of the State Memorial* (London, 1705), 28.

'Jingle' of rhyme.[2] If Defoe failed to attain a successful, sublime style in *Jure Divino*, he achieved little more than inflated rhetoric in his celebration of Marlborough's victory as the triumph of liberty over the tyranny of Louis XIV.

Defoe also engaged in a number of controversies during these months, particularly with the High Church. He wrote a preface to a work titled *De Laune's Plea for the Non-Conformists*, in which he underscored the degree of suffering endured by the Dissenters during 'the Days of that Merciful Prince King *Charles* the Second'.[3] Defoe maintains that 8000 Dissenters died in prison during those years. Among the great losses were Thomas Delaune himself, his wife and two children. Defoe also attacked the use of benefit performances at Drury Lane Theatre and at Oxford to help with the building and repairing of church structures as examples of pandering to immorality. It should be pointed out that Defoe's criticism of the stage had an undeniable political content. These projects belonged to the activities of the High Church, and he went out of his way to praise John Dennis's Whig tragedy, *Liberty Asserted*, as too 'sober' to satisfy the taste of the town.[4] Finally, he engaged in a running discussion of political theory with Charles Leslie, answering the Tory challenge to the ideas expressed in *Jure Divino*. Attacking Defoe and his ideas was hardly unusual for Charles Leslie, whose journal, *The Rehearsal*, frequently expressed horror at Defoe's various remarks on monarchy or the Anglican Church, particularly his sarcastic comparison between the 'dry Martyrdom' of James in which the Church of England played a major role and the 'wet Martyrdom' of Charles I, which was always blamed upon the Dissenters.[5] In number 94 of *The Rehearsal* he accused Defoe of stirring up the common people against the Church, and in number 104 he argued that Defoe's line 'To be as Wicked as an English Priest' summed up his contempt for the Church of England. For Leslie, the Dissenters were still in the state of revolt against the Church and government that they had declared in 1642, and deserved to be treated as rebels.

[2] It was published separately under the title *Daniel Defoe's Hymn for the Thanksgiving*.

[3] Preface to *De Laune's Plea for the Non-Conformists* (London, 1706), p. ii.

[4] The attacks upon the stage which had followed Jeremy Collier's *Short View* of 1698 had resulted in revision of texts to eliminate what Collier called 'immorality and profaneness'. But Queen Anne had encouraged continued reform, issuing a proclamation on 17 Jan. 1704 and appointing William Congreve and John Vanbrugh as overseers of the morality of stage plays. Arthur Bedford, a clergyman from Bristol, had continued Collier's researches into the texts of contemporary plays for the purpose of unearthing further violations of proper standards. Some time in Nov. 1706 Defoe received a letter from William Melmoth, congratulating him on his attacks on the stage and recommending Bedford's *The Evil and Danger of Stage Plays* to him.

[5] See Charles Leslie, 'A View of the Times', *The Rehearsal* 1 (94) (1706). Defoe's remark appeared in the *Review* of 18 Dec. 1705.

Leslie's attack was fairly typical of what might be thought of as the conservative view of political theory, much of which had been developed in response to Hobbes's ideas on the state of nature. Leslie questioned the very concept of a state of nature, which Defoe had adapted from Hobbes and the natural law philosophers, suggesting that it was merely a convenient fiction, and arguing that the only real right to government was directly from God, that it would not have come into existence without God's direct intervention. He suggested that Defoe had contradicted himself on the idea that there might have been a time when there was no government, and restated Filmer's theory of the concept of government proceeding entirely from the rule of Adam and the fathers of families. Without such a line of authority, Leslie maintained, power would have to be placed in the people. This, in turn, 'lays a Foundation for Perpetual Changes and Revolutions, without any Possible Rest or Settlement'.[6]

Defoe's running response to Leslie in the *Review* was a battle for the hearts and minds of contemporary readers of periodicals. Thousands of readers who could not afford *Jure Divino* could read the debates between Leslie and Defoe in their local coffee-house. Defoe took the opportunity to attack the notion of any direct line of succession for any contemporary king or queen and to dismiss once more the notion of rule by divine right. Rights come out of property which was given to humankind by God. Liberty too is a 'civil Right of Divine Original, the only Claim of mankind which is *Jure Divino* universally; he that won't fight for it, is a Fool, he that denies it *to any*, must be a Knave.'[7] He returned to Leslie's arguments again on 10 September, just before leaving for Scotland. Although appeals to Scripture are important, his 'Reasoning' must be convinced.

I know, what mr. *Lock*, *Sidney* and others have said on this Head, and I must confess, I never thought their Systems fully answer'd—But I am arguing by my own Light, not other Mens; and therefore my Notions may be new, yet I beg the Favour to be heard, and if confuted, no man shall be sooner silenc'd than I; if I cannot inform others by my Argument, I shall be inform'd my self by the Answers; so that some Good shall come of it, let it go which way it will.[8]

Defoe argues that what human beings take, say, from the sea by their labour is their property, and no one can take it away from them. As for dominion over others, God never gave Adam dominion over anyone. Human beings were actually never without government:

Government is an Appendix of Nature, one of the first rational Dictates to man from his Understanding; 'tis form'd in the Soul, and therefore of Divine Original;

⁶ Leslie, 'A View of the Times', 143.   ⁷ *Review*, iii. 350.   ⁸ Ibid. 429.

he would cease to be rational, when he ceased to live regularly; and if twenty Men born in the dark, and that had never known Men or things, were set on Shore in an Island, where they had no body to imitate, and nothing to do but to live; the first thing they would apply to by the Light of Nature after Food would be to settle Government among them.[9]

Thus government is simply natural to human reason. If it originally lay in the fathers of the first families, that system was broken long ago through war, conquest, and tyranny. These thoughts must have led Defoe to consider how far removed from the state of nature governments in modern Europe had become. Though he had finished his debate with Leslie over the nature of government, the image of what life must have been like before manufacturing, farming, and the use of animals for labour and food had transformed contemporary civilization led him to contemplate what society would be like if a human being were forced to 'tear his Food to pieces with his Teeth, or Claws', to hunt for food in the manner of the American Indians.[10] By a somewhat indirect method, Leslie may have led him in the direction to Robinson Crusoe's island.

II

Defoe began writing about the treaty of Union four months before he set forth for Edinburgh. The opening two parts of his *Essay at Removing National Prejudices against a Union with Scotland* were published in London and aimed at removing English objections to the treaty. The Parliament in Scotland, as it came into existence after the Glorious Revolution, was far less governed by rules of politeness than England's Parliament. Debates were often violent, and sentiments of feudal loyalty often dominated the behaviour of the members. Just a few years before, resentment against English hegemony had produced the famous Worcester Affair which saw the hanging of an English merchant ship's captain and crew on a trumped-up charge of piracy.[11] Considerable animosity had also been caused by the passage of the Act of Security in 1703 as a response to England's Act of Settlement in 1701. Dominated by English influence, the Scots thought they might be able to take a strong position before any discussion of a Union. They reserved the right to choose their own successor to Queen Anne and set up a different system of customs that would permit them to

[9] Ibid. 431.
[10] Ibid. 455–6.
[11] For a discussion of this matter with some possible connections to Defoe, see John Robert Moore, *Defoe in the Pillory and Other Studies* (Bloomington: Indiana University Press, 1939), 147–54.

trade with England's enemy, France. In response, England passed the Alien Act in March 1705 which threatened Scottish citizens with the status of aliens if they did not adopt the Hanoverian succession by Christmas Day 1705, and put a prohibition on the import of various Scottish goods such as linen and cattle. These disagreeents set the stage for the Union which appears to have been desired by a majority in both nations. The first meeting of the Commission appointed to consider the terms of the Union had taken place in London on 16 April 1706. Over three months later, on 22 July, the Commission agreed on a draft to be presented for ratification by each Parliament.

Defoe's first essay, published on 4 May, stressed the advantages of peaceful trade and of avoiding war. By way of emphasizing the advantages of peace, Defoe conjured up one of his most effective pictures of the horrors of war:

the *Groans* of the murther'd Innocents, the Cries of the Widows and Mothers for their Husbands and Children, the *Despair* of flourishing Families, ruin'd and undone; with their Fields *over run*, their Barns and houses *plunder'd* and burnt, their Cattle *driven away*, and their whole Substance *destroy'd*.[12]

And he presented a vivid image of the relief that would be experienced by all concerned once the Union was established—an image that suggests how much he carried with him certain emotions experienced by Robinson Crusoe:

As a man that is safely landed on a firm and high Rock, out of the Reach of the insulting Waves, by which he was in Danger of Shipwreck, surveys the distant Dangers with Inexpressible Satisfaction, from both the Sence of his own Security, and the more clear Discovery of the Reality of the hazards he had run, which perhaps he did not perfectly see before.[13]

This latter scene was a favourite of Dutch painters during the seventeenth century, and both images suggest that Defoe was attempting an artful creation of a visual scene to evoke a sense of both terror and of relief. Defoe was trying to persuade in these essays, and he was not above exaggerating the advantages he was advertising. His next essay in this series appeared on 28 May, and attempted to establish a sense of difference between the needs of the two nations and how that would affect the systems of taxation. He wanted to avoid taxes that would fall too heavily on the poor, such as a malt tax, and argued that as the nations became fully united, the circulation of trade would reach from Scotland to London, enriching all involved. Just as

[12] *An Essay at Removing National Prejudices against a Union with Scotland* (London, 1706), 19.
[13] Ibid. 25.

he held out the possibility of a rich fishing industry for Scotland in the first essay, so in the second he suggested that increased industry could exploit Scotland's mineral wealth. But for his English readers, he provided the comfortable assurance that under no circumstances would cheap Scottish labour undercut the prosperity of the English worker. Defoe's first two pamphlets were reprinted in Edinburgh and used by the opponents of the Union as pointing to all the advantages that the English would reap from the treaty.

Defoe wrote to Harley on 13 September requesting more instructions and materials. Meanwhile, he set down four aspects of his work as an agent, including secret operations, influencing people by conversation, convincing others by writing or what he called 'Discourse', and assuring everyone that England had no intention of harming the power of the dominant Presbyterian Kirk. Defoe assured Harley that he would husband his money, especially since it was coming directly out of Harley's funds, but noted that since he had had to surrender everything at the bankruptcy hearings, he was forced to purchase all his equipment—'horse, Sadele, bridle, pistols and Every thing new' (H 127). He raised the problems of his family (of 'a Widdo' and Seaven Children' (H 127)) once more along with the possibility of receiving some bounty from Queen Anne. He also arranged the addresses for 'Alexander Goldsmith' along the way, and he asked if Harley had any objection to his writing on the Union in the *Review*. It was probably at this point that Harley wrote him a series of instructions which included a secret place for sending his weekly reports. Harley told him that he must conceal any connection with England and pretend to be travelling on business.[14]

Defoe wrote to Harley from Leicester nine days later. The rains had slowed down his journey north, keeping him in one place for a period of forty-eight hours. If Defoe had complained about the roads in his *Essay upon Projects*, he would have had little to smile about a decade later. 'The Country here being Very Deep and wett', he hoped matters would improve once he passed the Trent. He had found no instructions at Coventry and was hoping that Harley's agent at Newcastle upon Tyne, John Bell, would have them. In addition, he provided some information about a new attack by the High Church, *The History of the Church, in Respect Both to its Ancient and Present Condition*, noting that in the area around Leicester, dominated by what Defoe would have considered

[14] *Portland Papers*, iv. 334. HMC Report 15, App. 4. This may have been what he meant when, in his letter to Harley on 30 Sept., he referrred to a 'Letter without your Name'. Healey thought these (H 132) were the instructions Defoe expected to receive, but those came later. See Paula Backscheider, 'Robert Harley to Daniel Defoe: A New Letter', *Modern Language Review* 83 (1988), 817–19.

reactionary forces, it was taken as 'a Defiance to the Court'.[15] From New-castle on 30 September, he complained that he had still not received Harley's 'Letter, Instructions, etc.', and attempted to put matters in an amusing light:

Methinks I look Very Simply when to my Self I Reflect how I am your Messengr without an Errand, your Ambassador without Instructions, your Servant without Ordrs. I beseech your Honr to let me Not be to seek for any thing which may furnish me to Answer your Expectations to do her Majsty & the Nation the Service which you Design, and for Justifyeing your choice in the honour you do me in Singling me Out for this work. (H 131)

Bell seemed to be suspicious of Defoe. He arranged for payment to him of twenty-five guineas in Edinburgh. Despite the use of his alias, Alexander Goldsmith, in Newcastle upon Tyne, Defoe told Bell his identity, adding that he would not try to hide that identity in Scotland, since he was so well known. Bell was even suspicious about Defoe's own name and hoped that what sharing a bottle had not revealed a dinner together would. But Defoe, who was apparently a remarkably lively conversationalist, soon won him over. Bell wrote on 4 October, 'I have had the favour of mr. A. G---'s conversation for two or three days and find him to be a very ingenious man and fit for that buisiness I guess he is going about. I wish him good success.' His suspicions removed, Bell advanced £40 17s. 6d. to buy a horse, in addition to the money to be used in Edinburgh. The term 'ingenious' is used so often by contemporaries to describe Defoe that a more guarded biographer might almost suspect that he introduced it into the conversation himself.

Defoe probably reached Edinburgh around 6 October, though the first letter to Harley that survives is dated 24 October. Defoe had not yet received his specific orders, and followed the general instruction about writing his observations about the progress of the Union. In so doing he chose to divide his comments between an account of the activities of those involved in a meeting of the General Assembly of the Church of Scotland and the actions of the mob. For all his interest in the politics of religion, Defoe found himself 'Much Out of Love with Ecclesiastic Parliaments'. Finding their debates futile and speaking to them on an individual basis exasperating, he concluded that 'in Generall They are the Wisest weak men, the Falsest honest men, and the steadyest Unsettled people Ever I met with. They Mean well but are blinded in their politicks and Obstinate in

---

[15] Interestingly enough, he implicated William Taylor, who would later become the publisher of *Robinson Crusoe* and some of his other works of fiction, in issuing this work.

Opinion.' He compared them to a mob and then moved on to speak of the real mob 'in the street', adding that of all rabbles, 'a scots Rabble is the worst of its kind' (H 133).

Defoe set the scene by noting that he had been kept inside for five days by a 'Violent Cold'. When he finally went out on 23 October, he was identified by one of the mob as 'One of the English Dogs', and was obviously concerned for his safety. He delayed going out until dark, when he found the streets filled with people shouting their support for the Duke of Hamilton, an opponent of the Union. Then, in a remarkable piece of narrative, he described the assault of the mob upon the house of Sir Patrick Johnstone, one of the Commissioners in charge of negotiating the Union treaty and the representative of Edinburgh in the Scottish Parliament. When Johnstone's wife called for help, a Captain Richardson marched to the rescue and arrested those at the head of the mob who were trying to batter down the door. Defoe finally decided to return to his own house between 8 and 9 o'clock only to be caught in the midst of the mob's fury:

I had not been Long There but I heard a Great Noise and looking Out Saw a Terrible Multitude Come up the High street with a Drum at the head of Them shouting and swearing and Cryeing Out all scotland would stand together, No Union, No Union, English Dogs, and the like.

I Can Not Say to you I had No Apprehensions, Nor was Monsr *De Witt* quite Out of my Thoughts, and perticularly when a part of This mob fell upon a Gentleman who had Discretion little Enough to say something that Displeased them just Undr my Window.

He Defended himself bravely and Call'd Out lustily also for help to the Guard, who being within Hearing and Ready Drawn up in Close Ordr in the street, advanc't, Rescued the Gentleman, and took the person he was Grappld with prisoner.

The City was by this time in a Terrible fright. The Guards were Insulted and stoned as they stood, the Mob put out all the lights, no body could stir in the streets, and not a light be seen in a windo' for fear of stones. (H 135)

Defoe's involvement in this action, his fear of being torn apart in the manner of the De Witt brothers in Amsterdam, informed his later treatment of mobs, from the one in Glasgow that would take over the entire city, going up and down the streets demanding to know 'Are you for the Union?' and threatening anyone who might hint at pro-Union sentiment, to the London mobs in *Moll Flanders*, who might visit a similar punishment on some pickpocket unfortunate enough to be captured by them. Defoe's account with its mixture of fear and excitement was surely intended to entertain Harley with its vivid scenes as much as inform him about significant events.

In his next letter, written on 29 October, Defoe decided to write of a third 'Mob'—the Scottish Parliament, but by this time irrationality was the order of the day:

There is an Entire Harmony in This Country Consisting in Universall Discords. The Church men in perticular are goeing Mad. The parsons are out of their wits and those who at first were brought Over, and pardon me were Some of them my Converts, their Country brethren being now Come in are all Gone back and to be brought over by no perswasion. (H 137)

Defoe reported on his efforts to overcome this anti-Union sentiment, and asked Harley to attend to an action taken against him because it was thought that a reference in the *Review* to a person who had spoken in opposition to the Union was taken as a slur upon Lord Chief Justice Holt. Defoe spoke of his 'secret Enemies being Very Vigilant and Furious' and asked Harley to have the charge dismissed. Defoe denied that Holt was intended in his *Review* of 21 November 1706, and apparently nothing further was done. Meanwhile the *Review* had been turned over to a celebration of the Union, including a poem, 'Peace and Union', which, while intended in a general sense for the need to mend factions within the nation, was allowed to play over the Union with Scotland as well:

> *UNION* is Nature's strong Cement;
> The Life of *Power*, and *Soul of Government*:
>   Without it, all the World's a Mob;
> Confusion's Universal Monarch of the Globe;
> Armies are *Crowds of Lunaticks* got loose,
> Whose Power for Want of Reason's our of Use;
>   Meer Hoords of *Tartars*, Wild and Rude,
>   Dissolv'd in Mother Multitude.[16]

These lines should remind us that Defoe's thoughts about the mobs in Scotland and the way in which he perceived them played in with his general theory of government. In its moment of merging with England, Scotland was almost in the process of turning into that chaotic mob which was the source of political power. This was one of his key arguments in the third part of his series, *An Essay at Removing National Prejudices*, where he tried to get his Scottish readers to understand that they were not giving up their freedoms. 'They may Dissolve themselves,' he argued, 'but Original natural Right must remain: if they dissolve the Form *whether shall* it

---

[16] *Review*, iii. 463.

return?—To its primitive State it cannot, because that is dissolv'd; to Confusion it must not, because Right must be preserved.'[17] A new choice, a new formulation must be made.

Defoe referred to what was happening as 'this stage of Confusion' in his letter to Harley of 2 November 1706. He described how he spent his time dealing with the politicians in the morning and the clergy in the evening. He blamed the clergy for inflaming the people; an association was being formed in the north and west in an effort to prevent the Union. Meanwhile, in order to convince the Scots that he was actually interested in settling in Scotland, he was at work upon *Caledonia, A Poem in Honour of Scotland and the Scots Nation* and using the *Review* to support the Union against its enemies. In the *Review* of 16 November he spoke of his moving his family abroad in response to the slanderous attacks upon him. Meanwhile he devoted various issues of his journal to demonstrating to his English readers that the forty-five seats in the House of Commons and sixteen in the House of Lords would not give the Scots overwhelming influence in the British government and not change the established Church, all along suggesting that the popular objections to the Union in Scotland were the work of the High Church, Jacobites, and their sympathizers. Defoe was involved in just the kind of situation he relished, extinguishing objections raised by pamphlets and sermons on one side, advancing his own ideas on the other.

To James Hodges, who had argued that Scottish and English institutions ought to remain separate, he replied in his *Fourth Essay at Removing National Prejudices* by rising above Hodges's particular comparison of the institutions of the two nations to a more generalized position drawn from natural law by which the rights of the freeholders constituted the basic claim to their freedom to choose who would govern them.[18] When Lord Belhaven made a rhetorically effective speech lamenting the passing of Scotland as an independent nation, Defoe wrote a serious pamphlet attacking him for misusing language and for depriving Scotland of the happiness and prosperity to be found only in a modern, tolerant, trading country such as Holland.[19] He then followed with a parodic lampoon, *The Vision*, in which Belhaven is compared to an 'Excorcist' rising 'Like a Ghost in a

---

[17] *An Essay at Removing National Prejudices against a Union with England, Part III* (Edinburgh, 1706), 13.

[18] Hodges argued for a 'Federal Union', a treaty between states remaining independent. Many of his arguments about the loss of trade that the Union would cause and the decline of Edinburgh as an important seat of government were accurate enough. See *The Rights and Interests of the Two British Monarchies* (Edinburgh, 1703), 80–5.

[19] Daniel Defoe, *An Answer to my Lord Belhaven's Speech* ([Edinburgh] 1706), esp. 4, 6, 8.

Circle' full of 'Extasies' to make his pronouncements.[20] Scotland, of course, was famous for those who claimed to have 'second sight', the ability to see into the future, but Belhaven's speech was supposed to be dignified oratory, not the kind of vision associated with the powers of a local fortune-teller.[21]

On Monday 4 November 1706, the 'Grand question', whether the Union should be approved, passed, and from this point forward the great task involved pacifying those who remained unreconciled and working out details involving economic compensation for disadvantages that Scotland might incur by the treaty. Money paid outright by England was called the 'equivalent', but adjusting trade involved a complicated system of draw-backs and adjustments on excise taxes. Defoe informed Harley that he had been called before the committee charged with this work to aid in calcu-lating the financial exchange. This was a committee composed of some of the leading men in Scotland, including Montrose, Argyll, and Sir Alexander Campbell of Cesnock. Defoe passed as one who intended to settle in Scotland, and they invited him to dine with them at their next meeting. On 9 November he informed Harley that he would be able to send him what was expected by way of compensation because he was now in their confidence and in a position to 'Influence them more than I Expected. . . . Their Ldships have Resolved to Committ the Drawing up the Explanations to me, and if Directed I might do more service to both Kingdomes than I Could have Expected' (H 144). In short, Harley had his

[20] *The Vision, A Poem* ([Edinburgh, 1706]). Belhaven's speech gained considerable fame, though its rhetoric caused laughter in Parliament. A sample of his visionary style is: 'I think, I see a *Free and Independent Kingdom* delivering up that which all the World hath been fighting for, since the days of *Nimrod*; yea, that for which most of all the Empires, Kingdoms, States, Principalities and Dukedoms of *Europe*, are at this very time engaged in the most Bloody and Cruel Wars that ever were, *to wit*, A Power to Manage their own Affairs by themselves, without the Assistance and Counsel of any other.' Among this series of paragraphs beginning 'I think I see' were visions of the Scottish army sent out to the West Indies or disbanded and the '*Honest Industrious Tradesman*' forced to drink 'Water in place of Ale, eating his saltless Pottage'. *The Lord Belhaven's Speech in the Scotch Parliament, Saturday the Second of November, on the Subject-matter of an Union betwixt the two Kingdoms of Scotland and England* ([Edinburgh] 1706), 4.

In his letter to Harley, Defoe seems to associate the activities of the mob directly with the effect of this speech. Despite his differences with Belhaven, Defoe came to a friendly understanding with him. See *Review*, 10 July 1708. For an account of the reaction to the speech, see Hume Brown, *The Treaty of the Union* (Oxford: Clarendon Press, 1914), 117; and David Daiches, *Scotland and the Union* (London: John Murray, 1977), 126–63.

[21] Defoe made his objections to the style of Belhaven's address even clearer in his response to Belhaven's answer to the *Vision, A Reply to the Scots Answer to the British Vision* ([Edinburgh, 1706]). He mocked Belhaven's poetry as even more absurd in its attempt at sublimity than his prose: 'Supream in Thought, to grammar unconfin'd/Thy lofty Genius soars above the Wind./So just the Numbers, so polite the Stile/So clear the Sense, and so exact the Pile;/The wondring World like Trees in *Orpheus* Wood/Admire those Strains they never understood.' Language used in this way, Defoe suggests, moves in a manner that appeals to pure emotion rather than reason.

spy involved in the very drafting of some of the most important economic aspects of the treaty.

While Defoe was managing the economic debates and hoping to hear any objections from Harley, he had to acknowledge the popular unrest over the Union through much of Scotland. Attempts were made to burn the printed articles of the treaty at Glasgow, and a successful burning had been achieved in the marketplace at Dumfries. In the *Review* of 30 November he printed the objections brought before Parliament by the Scottish Kirk through its Commission, with its special objection to being ruled by a House of Lords that contained twenty-six bishops of the Church of England. Without commenting on this matter, Defoe explained to his English audience that the settlement following the Glorious Revolution established the Presbyterians in Scotland as the Church of Scotland in the same way that the Anglicans were the established Church in England. From this standpoint, he maintained that the concerns of the Church of Scotland, however misplaced, were understandable.[22] He argued that the Union would establish a permanent friendship between the two Protestant churches, and indeed, he believed that one result would surely be an improvement of the status of the Dissenters in England.

He was still not certain if the Union would hold, and speculated about the possibility of moving up troops into Scotland from England. Since he considered the Union to be advantageous for both countries, he experienced a lesson in seeing the people violently opposed to what would surely be to their advantage. Although he thought the presence of a large number of Highlanders in Edinburgh suspicious and found hints of violence in their very appearance, he presented his fears to Harley in a humorous manner:

Indeed they are Formidable Fellows and I Onely Wish her Majtie had 25000 of Them in spain, a Nation Equally proud and Barbarous like Themselves. They are all Gentlemen, will Take affront from No Man, and Insolent to the last Degree. But Certainly the Absurdity is Ridiculous to see a man in his Mountain habit with a Broad sword, Targett, Pistol or perhaps Two at his Girdle, a Dagger and staff, walking Down the street as Upright and Haughty as if he were a lord—and with-all Driving a Cow. Bless us—are These the Gentlemen! Said I— (H 146–7)

Following this description, he provided his assessment of the 'Dark prospect' for a peaceful transition to the Union. He was to conclude that but for the incredible rains that fell at this time, the mobs from places such

---

[22] Although the Parliament did not follow the wishes expressed in this petition, it did pass an Act of Security for the Church of Scotland. See James Mackinnon, *The Union of England and Scotland* (London: Longmans, Green, 1896), 296–304.

as Glasgow would have descended upon Edinburgh. But he reported further progress in his work with the committee and the news that his former correspondent, Lord Halifax, had requested him to make a personal report on what was happening. Since the fifth article of the treaty involving customs was about to come up, on 22 November, he recounted how he had to coach members of the committee on how to answer questions that might arise. Among the members of the Scottish gentry and nobility, he must have passed for an economist of genius, and despite his disclaimers to Harley, it was probably an opinion he did little to discourage. 'I blush for them sometimes,' he wrote, 'and am asham'd to Instruct men, who I thought I had not been Able to Informe of any thing' (H 154). He was in the midst of things, debating the amount for the drawback on oatmeal exported to Norway and on salt, regulating the tax on ale, and debating prices with his old friend, Sir William Paterson.[23]

Surely, even in the days when he was reporting directly to William III, he could not have been in greater demand, and as he told Harley, no one suspected that he was actually a spy for the English government. His excitement in his achievement is evident in his letter to Harley on 26 November:

I Converse with Presbyterian, Episcopall-Dissenter, papist and Non Juror, and I hope with Equall Circumspection. I flatter my Self you will have no Complaints of my Conduct. I have faithfull Emissaries in Every Company And I Talk to Everybody in Their Own way. To the Merchants I am about to Settle here in Trade, Building ships etc. With the Lawyers I Want to purchase a House and Land to bring my family & live Upon it (God knows where the Money is to pay for it). To day I am Goeing into Partnership with a Membr of parliament in a Glass house, to morrow with Another in a Salt work. With the Glasgow Mutineers I am to be a fish Merchant, with the Aberdeen Men a woollen and with the Perth and western men a Linen Manufacturer, and stil at the End of all Discourse the Union is the Essentiall and I am all to Every one that I may Gain some. (H 158–9)

Harley would have caught the allusion to St Paul at the end, and might have thought to himself that however much his agent believed in the Union, he was surely no saint. Harley apparently wrote asking him to try to avoid any revisions of the treaty. Defoe thought the best that could be hoped for was to allow changes to be appended in an act of Parliament. He remained in Edinburgh working with the committee while warning Harley on 30 November that the 'war'—the rising of various groups against the Union—had commenced.

---

[23] Defoe may have seen Patterson as a rival. In his letter to Harley of 26 Nov., Defoe spoke slightingly of Patterson's useless statistics and his bad reputation.

III

No doubt the notion of rebellious mobs such as the one he witnessed in Edinburgh appealed to Defoe's imagination. Even events at Glasgow, in which a mob led by a man named Finlay attempted a small rebellion, never amounted to much, though in his *History of the Union* Defoe was to devote thirteen folio pages to this 'petty War', which ended anticlimactically with the arrest of Finlay. He never managed to gather more than forty-five men, and after frightening the Provost and collecting some arms, they melted away at the mere mention of the arrival of a squadron of dragoons.[24] But for Defoe, the notion of a rebellion seemed irresistible. He had written *A Letter from Mr. Reason to the High and Mighty Prince the Mob* shortly after he arrived in Edinburgh, trying to persuade his readers of the irrationality of mob action. Now with new riots, he used some of Harley's money to distribute copies of *A Short Letter to the Glasgow Men* with much the same message: 'You are a handfull of Poor Distempered Lunatick People, is *the kindest thing* can be thought of.' He reminded the mob that they were hardly the majority, and that if they were not property-owners they ought not to be expressing their opinions at all. Did they really believe that they were going to get their way by 'Tumult and Noise'?[25] Defoe followed this with *The Rabbler Convicted*, a work written, supposedly, by a reformed rioter. This agitator had come to the conclusion that his actions were wrong and that as a Presbyterian, he ought to realize the degree to which the riots were being instigated by papists. The true principles of Presbyterianism, he argues, 'tend to make a Man Good, and [a] peaceable Subject'. The former rioter praises the Duke of Queensbury, the head of the Commission in charge of the Union, as 'a truly Noble Man', and argues that riots were 'not to be tolerated in any Society where Law or Reason have any place'.[26] Meanwhile Defoe had sent one of his agents, J. Pierce, to calm the Cameronians, who were so angered by the Union that they were almost ready to ally themselves with their worst enemies, the Jacobites.

While trying to calm the storm among the rioters by these appeals to reason, Defoe was busy composing a series of pamphlets demonstrating that the changes involved in the treaty would not hurt Scottish trade. Mixing general principles of the circulation of trade with lamentations on the poor mathematics of his opponents, Defoe attempted to ease the fears of his readers about a large increase in the tax on ale and encourage them

---

[24] Mackinnon, *Union*, 311–13.
[25] *A Short Letter to the Glasgow Men* ([Edinburgh, 1706]), 7.
[26] *The Rabbler Convicted* ([Edinburgh, 1706]), 3–4.

with the prospect of increased trade with England's American colonies. Posing as a Scot in one of the pamphlets, he pointed out that the alternative would be allying with France and Catholicism. His readers, he argued, should not be swayed by the rhetoric of Lord Belhaven. He described how astonished he was 'to hear one in a Vision or Rapsody of Nonsense, Talking of *Hannibal, Caesar* and the Ancient Heroes of whom he knows little but the Names'.[27] He also assumed the pose of a Scot in one of his economic tracts, *The Advantages of Scotland by an Incorporate Union with England*, probably reasoning that he gave away much in identifying himself as an Englishman. Nevertheless, the attempt in this pamphlet and in such works as *An Enquiry into the Disposal of the Equivalent* and *A Fifth Essay at Removing National Prejudices* is the same—to demystify the economic situation through an explanation of the relationship between trade and money. Defoe adapted a somewhat simple mercantilist system for this purpose. The aim of trade, from the standpoint of the state, was to bring more bullion into the nation. This could only be achieved through a balance of trade that favoured the nation. 'Money', he wrote, 'is a real Intrinsick Species appointed by Custom, as the medium of Trade to bring Commerce in all its particular States to a Balance—So much as its real Value amount to, [s]o much real Wealth is in that nation, and their real Values is every where the same.'[28] The best trade is one that brings money into the country and does not send it out. Exporting raw materials for something like wine is equivalent to having 'piss'd against our Walls' the wealth of the nation.[29] 'But we Gain nothing but what is returned in unperishable Commodities'—bullion and permanent goods. 'That Trade', he wrote, 'only can be profitable, which employing their own People, carries out their own Growth or Product, and does not consume all the Returnes, but draws in the Surplus to it self in Bullion.'[30] Finally, it is more important that the state grow rich than the individual merchant. The complaints of any given trader must be weighed against the more important benefits to be reaped by the nation as a whole.

While he was engaged in arguing economic theory in his pamphlets, in his dealings with various committees Defoe was concerned with the

[27] *A Seasonable Warning or the Pope and the King of France Unmasked* ([?Edinburgh] 1706), 15.
[28] *An Enquiry into the Disposal of the Equivalent* (Edinburgh, 1706), 4. See also Defoe, *A Fifth Essay at Removing National Prejudices* ([Edinburgh] 1707 [1706]), 14: 'Money is an Intrinsick, plac'd as a medium in the Centre of Trade, to supply the differences in Value, between the Export and Import of one Nation to and from another.'
[29] *The Advantages of Scotland by an Incorporate Union with England* ([Edinburgh] 1706), 13.
[30] *Fifth Essay*, 28. Addressing the more sophisticated audience of the *Review*, Defoe could write of the various ways in which an economy could grow through new methods of production and inventions. For the most part, in these essays on Scottish trade he adheres to the most basic principles of mercantilism.

realities of the marketplace, as when he discussed the adjustment of draw-backs on salt for curing fish. He understood his task to be to discourage amendments as much as possible, and while he could not prevent certain changes, he did not think any of the revisions were of such a nature as to destroy the treaty. His agent, J. Pierce, had been out in the field calming the anxieties of the Cameronians and trying to convince their 'Bishop', John Hepburn, that the Union would not be a disaster. The Earl of Leven felt the situation was urgent enough to send Pierce back, and Defoe somehow found the funds to do this. There were still a suspicious number of Highlanders in Edinburgh, and armed men had been seen in the area. 'Tis Certain,' he wrote, 'there are some Secret Designs on foot; what they are Time and providence alone Can Discover' (H 182). That those opposed to the Union were becoming more desperate is likely enough.[31] Indeed, as the prospect of a general insurrection waned, the possibility of assassination increased. Defoe changed his lodgings after being told that he would be the first target, but his enthusiasm for the Union had not diminished. 'I dare not prophecy the Event but tis pity the two Nations would be divided any longer,' he wrote to John Fransham on 28 December. 'This people are a Sober, Religious and Gallant Nation, the country good, the Soil in most places capable of vast improvements and nothing wanting but English Stocks, English Art and English Trade to make us all one great people' (H 187).

The opponents of the treaty saved their last great effort for the debate over the twenty-second article, on representation in the British Parliament. Defoe now attempted to work his way into the opposition to discover what was afoot. He moved among the followers of the Duke of Hamilton, who, despite his opposition to the Union, would not abandon his adherence to the Hanoverian Succession, as well as among the adherents of the Dukes of Atholl and Gordon, who were close to being out-and-out Jacobites. 'In This Little scheme of their Affaires I have Acted a *True spy* to you,' he wrote Harley, 'for by an Unexpected success I have Obtaind a Converse with Some Gentlemen belonging to the D of Gordon who are Very Frank' (H 189). He managed to get a general plan of how they were going to launch their attack upon the treaty, but he was certain that the power of the opposition had been broken. He announced in this letter of 4 January that despite continuing 'Feares of Murther, Tumult, Rabble, etc' (H 190) he would persevere in obeying Harley's commands, but he wished to know

---

[31] Defoe printed a letter in his *History of the Union* that provided information about a plot to assassinate the Duke of Queensbury. Twenty-four men were supposed to be concerned in the attempt, which was to occur after the first day of the year. The letter was dated 20 Dec. 1706. See *History of the Union* (London, 1709), appendix, 63–4.

what Harley wanted done. He had hinted at the possibility of receiving some post in Scotland after the Union, but Harley's replies had apparently been so scant that Defoe was beginning to wonder if his letters were being received. Finally, on 9 January, he could write Harley, 'I hope I may Now give you Joy of the Union' (H 191). The Dukes of Atholl and Argyll had shouted at each other and almost came to blows, but the twenty-second article had passed.

IV

Defoe's trip to Edinburgh was a triumph in many ways. His opponents in England had attempted to insult his abilities as a writer, his knowledge, his understanding, and his morals. As a result, the caricatured image that his enemies had developed was that sketched in Joseph Browne's *A Dialogue between Church and No-Church*, that of 'a meer *Proteus*, a Saint in his Expectations and a Devil in his Designs'.[32] Browne viewed his ability to create a vivid fiction as a sign of the diseased imagination rather than as a genuine talent. Browne admitted grudgingly that the '*Consolidator*', as he called Defoe, had achieved a certain reputation; so that 'every trifling Coffee-House Statesman . . . crys up the *Consolidator* for one of the most penetrating *Politicians* of this *Nation*'.[33] But to Browne and other enemies, Defoe's fame had to be the result of some terrible mistake.

For the most part, Defoe's experience in Scotland had been without this kind of controversy. He had arrived as a person of considerable fame and without any apparent stigma from the pillory. He was now in a country where his religion did not make him a Dissenter from the beliefs of the majority, and where his work for the Union would bring him into contact with some of the most distinguished members of the Scottish nobility. His series of pamphlets *On Removing National Prejudices against a Union* showed him to have a persuasive understanding of political theory and economics, and he was soon to show his abilities as an economist in dealing with the drawbacks on salt. One of the earliest attacks upon him after his arrival in Scotland, grants much to him even in its mockery:

> Let Banter cease, and Poetaster's yield,
> Since fam'd *De Foe* is Master of the Field.
> What none can comprehend, he understands:
> And What's not understood, his Fame Commands.

[32] Browne, 'A Dialogue between Church and No-Church', in *State Tracts* (2 vols., London, 1715), i. 21.
[33] Ibid. 32.

This Mighty Bard, more mighty in Invention,
And most of all in humble Condescension.[34]

If the *Review* had begun to return a degree of respectability to Defoe in London, Scotland must have seemed like a return to the days when he was, or conceived himself to be, the chief propagandist for the causes of William III.[35]

In addition to his pamphlets and his work as a 'true Spy', Defoe broke into poetry over Scotland and the prospect of the Union. He had published *Jure Divino* through a subscription plan but apparently never published a subscription list, stating that the subscribers did not wish one published. Indeed, he had been accused of fabricating the existence of such a list.[36] On the other hand, *Caledonia. A Poem in Honour of Scotland, and the Scots Nation*, published in early December 1706, had a subscription list that included most of the Scottish nobility and, as Pat Rogers suggested, judged on the basis of the rank of the subscribers, was superior to any list of subscribers to be put together by Alexander Pope. Rogers was attempting to make a point about the nature of Defoe's readers.[37] Despite attempts to disparage his work, Defoe was always read by an audience that spanned the spectrum of the reading population. The list for *Caledonia* includes the Commissioner himself, the Dukes of Queensbury and Argyll, Earls of Buchan, Cromartie, and Stair, and Sir Alexander Campbell of Cesnock. And what is the more interesting is that Defoe seems to have had some acquaintance with these men.

He dedicated the poem to Queensbury, comparing himself to the painter who is perhaps better at conceiving the design than in executing the entire work. What was new about *Caledonia* was the attempt to praise Scotland for its present excellence and awaken it to future greatness—a greatness to be achieved by the proper directing of labour and capital. Defoe sees Scotland as ripe for exploitation:

> 'Tis Blasphemy to say the Climat's curst,
> Nature will ne're be fruitful till she's forc't;
> Nature's a Virgin very Chast and Coy,
> To court her's nonsense: If you will enjoy

---

[34] *An Equivalent for Daniel De Foe* ([Edinburgh, 1706]).

[35] Even the use of Defoe's *Original Right of the People* to attack him and his political ideas suggests that his enemies in Scotland regarded him with respect as a strong opponent. See *The Advantages of the Act of Security, of the Intended Union* ([Edinburgh] 1706).

[36] See *The Proceedings at the Examination, and Condemnation of a Certain Scribling, Rhyming, Versifying, Poeteering Hosier, and True-born Englishman, Commonly known by the name of Daniel the Prophet, alias Anglipoliski, alias Foeski . . .* ([London] 1705), 2–4.

[37] Pat Rogers, *Robinson Crusoe* (London: George Allen & Unwin, 1979), 102–3.

> She must be ravisht; when she's forc't she's free,
>   A perfect Prostitute to Industry.[38]

Defoe was attempting to be both deliberately outrageous and witty in this passage, which he repeated at the end. This is the Defoe who was typical of that early flourishing of the Enlightenment in England, a believer in the application of science to agriculture and industry in a way that would transform the social fabric economically and socially. He broke out into a hymn to science on contemplating the process:

> *What Infinites* doest thou pursue!
> The *Tangled Skeins of Nature* how undo!
>
> Pierce all her darkest Clouds, *her Knots untye*,
> And leave her naked to the wandring Eye.[39]

Both of these images suggest a deliberate form of violence toward nature which certainly does not accord well with modern concepts of living in harmony with the environment. Defoe sees the earth as given to man for exploitation, and the refusal to take advantage of nature as a sin.

He uses these images of ravishing nature, with their implicit concept of a cycle of freedom, labour, and prosperity, to attack the contemporary system of landownership in Scotland. By extorting exhorbitant rents from the tenants, the owners succeed in supressing desire:

> *Knowledge of Liberty*'s their only want,
> And loss of Expectation's their Content.
> Too much subjected to immoderate Power,
> Their *Petty Tyrants* all their Pains devour.[40]

Defoe argued that forcing the tenants into subsistence farming created a cycle of poverty that, by depriving the labourer of hope, made the worker slothful. Only by a combination of knowledge and liberty would this cycle be broken. Of course, Defoe devotes most of the poem to complimenting the Scots on their courage and achievements, but the real energy of the poem goes into a vision of a land in need of some of the same scientific developments that had started the agricultural revolution in England.

Defoe presented himself to various members of the Scottish gentry and nobility as a person knowledgeable in some of the new methods of agriculture. If the phrase 'improving the estate' was mainly applied to aesthetic changes in architecture and gardening during the eighteenth century, it

---

[38] *Caledonia* (Edinburgh, 1706), p. [viii]. Defoe may have borrowed this image from Southerne.
[39] Ibid. 8.
[40] Ibid. 22.

was also applied to new methods of farming. Probably the most important development in England had been the planting of turnips and their use as a food for cattle. With this new food source, farmers were able to keep their cattle alive during the winter rather than slaughtering them in the autumn. And new methods of ploughing in wider rows increased the yields of a variety of products. Agronomists such as Jethro Tull had been spreading the use of such methods throughout England, but they had yet to reach Scotland. John Clerk of Penicuik was one of those much taken by what Defoe had to say about the new agriculture. Defoe had told him in October 1706, after looking over his farmland, that he believed he could show him how he could double his yield on certain lands. Clerk stated that Defoe was 'very knowing' on this subject.[41] Apparently Defoe's involvement in building, lumber, and gardening extended to some understanding of contemporary experimental agriculture.

How many members of the gentry and nobility took advantage of Defoe's expertise on 'improvements' is difficult to determine, but to say that they were impressed by him would be an understatement. The elder John Clerk asked his son to send him various volumes by Defoe, including *Jure Divino*, the second volume of the *Review*, and the first volume of *A True Collection*. He already had the second volume and a number of pamphlets. Sir John wrote to his son that, though he admired poetry, he preferred to spend his time reading prose, mentioning *The Consolidator* as a work he would rather read than more poetry. Later, old Sir John comments on some remarkable things he discovers in Defoe's *Review*.[42] His son bought a copy of *Jure Divino* because, as one of the representatives from Scotland, he felt it 'absolutely necessary to let me Know a littel of the by past transactions of the house of commons'.[43] Although the younger Sir John came to realize that Defoe had been a 'spy among us', so far as one can tell he never ceased admiring Defoe, and considered everything in his *History of the Union* to be absolutely true.[44]

The response of the Penicuiks to Defoe may have been unusual, but it suggests the degree to which he was regarded as something of a genius in Scotland. Even his poetry must have met a better reception there than in the south. Scotland did not undergo the same revolution toward a highly allusive, compact, and complex verse that made the poetry of Dryden and

[41] Scottish PRO, Edinburgh, GD 18, 3131. John Clerk used variations on the word 'improve' 3 times in this short paragraph.

[42] Ibid, Penicuik, GD 18/3135.

[43] Ibid, letter of 17 Feb. 1707.

[44] Ibid, GD18/3202/7; GD18/2325. See also *Memoirs of the Life of Sir John Clerk*, ed. John M. Gray (Edinburgh: T. & A. Constable for the Scottish History Society 1832), xiii. 63–4.

Pope the norm. And the Scots continued to admire their earlier poetry and ballads. Defoe's Scottish readers may have admired his wit and the energy of his verse and been more forgiving of his faults. As a 'New-years Gift' for 1707 Defoe composed *A Scots Poem* much in the manner of *Caledonia*, urging the Scots to stop complaining about something that was as good for them as the Union, to throw off sloth, and to explore and colonize new lands. In his enthusiasm, he wrote some lines that must strike the modern reader with an anti-colonial bias as slightly absurd, but it is fascinating to see the future creator of fictions in which his protagonists were to sail around the world and trek across Africa indulging in an ecstatic vision over wandering the globe:

> I'd gladly breath my Air on Foreign Shores:
> Trade with rude *Indian*, and Sun-burnt *Mores*.
> I'd speak *Chinese*, I'd prattle *African*.
> And briskly cross, the first Meridan.
> I'd pass the line, and turn the *Caps* about.
> I'd rove, and sail the Earth's greatest *Circle* out.
> I'd fearless, venture to the Darien Coast;
> Strive to retri[e]ve, the former Bl[i]ss we lost,
> Yea, I wou'd view *Terra incognita*.
> And climb the Mountains of America.[45]

Of course, he assumed the identity of 'A NATIVE OF THE UNIVERSE' in writing the poem and was trying to awaken Scotland to the world outside its borders, but he seemed, in his enthusiasm, to have dreamt of making these mental travels along with the Scots.

V

Before the New Year and the votes that would assure the Union, Defoe had some terrible news from London. He wrote a short letter to Harley on 24 December about Pierce's activities among the Cameronians and in the Highlands and concluded with the confession that he found himself unable to keep his mind on what he was writing: 'But I Confess myself in Some Disordr to night, The Account of the Death of my Father Comeing just as I was writeing this' (H 180). The contrast between himself and his father could hardly have been stronger than at this moment. He was hundreds of miles from his wife and the seven children who were never far from his

---

[45] *A Scots Poem* (Edinburgh, 1707), 4.

mind. His father had led a steady life. His keeping of accounts for the Butcher's Company had been accomplished with the care of a tradesman accustomed to reckoning his losses and gains. He had been elected to various offices within the Company, and he probably represented for Defoe that notion of the middle way of life that Robinson Crusoe's father advised his son to follow. Defoe had not only failed to pursue a straight road but had gone bankrupt on two occasions. What could James Foe have thought of a son whose reputation among the merchants and tradesmen of the City was 'most foul'? Defoe's absence from London on this occasion was directly connected with the role he had assumed as Harley's spy. His father was around 76 when he died, and the fact that he made his will on 20 March 1706 suggests that he had been ailing during the past year. Nevertheless, Defoe must have experienced some strong pangs of guilt and a certain crisis of identity on receiving the news. His sense of doubt about how much good he was doing, doubt exacerbated by Harley's frequent failures to respond to his letters, is obvious in his next letter to Harley. In the *Review* of 9 January 1707, Defoe had a short notice denying reports that his journal was being written by someone else while he was in Scotland, and wondering how it could be possible that his particular style could fail to be recognized. The 'Judgment of the Gentleman that spread this Report, must be very good', he remarked sarcastically, 'that can neither guess at the Stile, nor guess by the Story or manner of it both, whether it be the Author's, and where the Author is'.[46] For someone accustomed to assume identities, he was being extraordinarily sensitive about a point of identity.

Defoe's father may have experienced some reverses in his health or finances before he died. He had moved from his house of seventeen windows in Throgmorton Street, where he and his second wife, Elizabeth, had lived for fourteen years or more, to rented rooms at the Bell on Broad Street in the autumn of 1705. Elizabeth died just a few months after the move in December and was buried in Bunhill Fields; and now her husband had died also, a year later. The pattern suggests that kind of withdrawal and narrowing of the scope of life experienced in old age which often seems to bring on death like a self-fulfilling prophecy. The couple were listed as having a child, but whether it lived or not is unknown.[47] James Foe's will shows a scrupulous regard for paying his debts, and some odd legacies. In regard to his grandchildren, he mentioned Benjamin first but only left him a gold watch in the possession of Mary, whereas he left his grandson Daniel

[46] *Review*, iii. 639.
[47] CLRO Ass. Box 19F (window tax), 32.6, 33.6. See also Frank Bastian, 'James Foe, Merchant, Father of Daniel Defoe', *N&Q* 209 (1964): 82–6.

£100 to be paid at the age of 21. His son, Daniel, was named as executor and given access to whatever money was available in case of necessity.[48] The £20 for the funeral suggests a desire to avoid any grand kind of event but to provide for a few rings or other customary gifts and refreshments for the 'drinking' that was traditional for the members of the Butchers' Company who might want to attend.[49] But Daniel Defoe, who doubtless grew up as the apple of his father's eye, would not be present.

[48] See PRO PROB 11/492/31/246. The will was written on 20 Mar. 1705/6 and superseded all other wills. It was proved on 25 Feb. 1706/7. James Foe left £20 to Elizabeth Roberts and the same to John Marsh. There is also a reference to paying his 'cousin', John Richards, money owed since the previous November.

[49] See Claire Gittings, *Death, Burial, and the Individual in Early Modern England* (London: Croom Helm, 1984), esp. 80–154.

14

In Limbo Between Causes and Masters

Defoe probably thought he could rely upon Mary to care for the necessary details after his father's death. Indeed, it might be said that, with so many children to care for, Mary was much like one of the many abandoned wives who would appear often enough in his fictions and conduct books. He had all the right theories about family life, but clearly relished being away from his own family amid the turbulent political scene. In fact, he might as well have returned to England, with the Union approved in Scotland and all of the excitement involving the treaty having moved south, but he was left in Edinburgh to engage in keeping the lines of communication open between England and Scotland and in defending the Union against those, such as the minister James Webster, who had suddenly turned against it.[1] He wrote to Harley on 27 January and again on 2 February that there might be anger if the treaty were returned to Scotland for further consideration: it might not be approved.[2] He also needed to sustain his position as the author of more than the half-hearted responses to Webster. He announced his intention of writing a *History of the Union* in the *Review* of 24 December,[3] reported some progress on it on 21 January 1707, and finally published an advertisement, on 29 March, in which he promised that the work would be finished in six months and asked prospective subscribers to contact his London printer, John Matthews. Defoe was overly optimistic. He might have been able to produce poetry with amazing rapidity, but he was trying

---

[1] He outlined all of his replies to Webster in his letter to Harley of 18 Mar. 1707, beginning with *Two Great Questions Considered*, published in Jan. 1707, in which he had argued that the Union did not have any impact on the National Covenant, to *A Short View of the Present State of the Protestant Religion*, which appeared in March of that year.

[2] 'But if This should be first Entered on and Amendments from England come after—Pardon my freedome Sir, It will Endanger breaking the wholl affair' (H 199). Defoe pointed out that the Scottish clergy were concerned about the oath to be taken of allegiance to the Queen. When the Regency Act was enacted in 1708, a clause that Presbyterians in Scotland thought applicable to the Church of England's dominance was omitted. See *Bishop Burnet's History of His Own Time*, ed. Earl of Dartmouth et al., 2nd edn. (6 vols., Oxford: Oxford University Press, 1833), v. 241, n. b.

[3] *Review*, iii. 611.

to be scrupulously exact in his *History of the Union*, and such a project would take time. It was not to appear until 1709, though different sections were printed over the intervening years by Andrew Anderson and his wife in Edinburgh. Information about the nature of the text leaked out during this interval, and Defoe had to engage in some fence-mending even before it appeared. Between composing this work and keeping the *Review* going, Defoe found little time to write quite the number of pamphlets that had issued from his pen during the past few years.

I

The Defoe who had passed through the excitement of the Edinburgh mobs was not unchanged by his experience. He who had depended so strongly on the popularity of his positions in his battles against Parliament, and who had escaped from the usual sufferings at the pillory through an appeal to the crowd, had experienced popular tumults directed against what he considered a good cause. The Scottish Parliament had simply ignored what were supposed to be popular petitions against the Union. These statesmen, not the mob in the streets of Glasgow and Edinburgh, passed the provisions of the Union, and this made Defoe more suspicious of the mob than he had been before. He had always believed that the mob was like a force of nature from which a new government might emerge, but now he saw more clearly the dangers involved in such a transition of power. What if the mob were not open to persuasion through the presentation of arguments appealing to reason and to self-interest? In Scotland, he had encountered Jacobite mobs that, from his standpoint, would have drawn Scotland and perhaps England into total disaster, into a reversal of the historical process by which the citizen progressed toward greater liberty and happiness.

In his poem celebrating the New Year of 1707, *A Scots Poem*, he attacked the intrusion of mobs into the real business of government:

> *A Mob*'s a Creature, never thinks, but raves,
> Hodge Podge of Women, Children, Fools, and Knaves.
> A malcontent, deluded Animal.
> *Without Grimace: within all* Spleen *and Gall.*[4]

Defoe explained in his answer to a critic who raised some of his earlier

---

[4] *A Scots Poem* (London, 1707), 11. Defoe described the mobs provoked into action by the Jacobites as a kind of mechanism: 'The Mob are a Machine; the Jacobites have wound them up to a Pitch and Nothing but Time, Mannagement, Temper and success Can Reduce them to the proper Medium. They must be let Run down Gradually or they precipitate at once into all Manner of Confusion' (H 202).

pronouncements against him, that the kind of situation he had been describing was one in which all authority was being called into question and the very preservation of the nation was in doubt. This did not mean, he argued, that the power of government was ordinarily in the mob. Normally power resided in the legislature and in the majority of representatives chosen by those having the power to vote.[5]

If Defoe may be seen as having taken a side-step to the right, it was by no means a large step.[6] The person who was singled out during the controversy over the Dissenting academies as the spokesman for radical theories of history and politics had moderated his views only slightly. He was never to adopt an 'Augustan' view of the mob or of the lower orders. However confused the members of the mob might be, they were always open to persuasion. False leaders might leave them bewildered, but Defoe did not believe that the bulk of the population would hold on to completely wrong ideologies—Jacobitism or support for the High Church—for very long. One attack upon him in 1707 rightly expressed what the Tories disliked about his beliefs. Judging Defoe a follower of Lucifer whose only reformation would lie in the terminal act of being hanged, the author attempted to describe his politics as based entirely upon the power of the people to choose their leaders:

> A hofeful Doctrine, drawn no doubt from Hell,
> To teach a stubborn People to Rebel:
> Which that there may be useful Rogues to prop,
> Such as *De Foe* the Devil conjures up.[7]

Without completely abandoning such doctrines, Defoe found himself forced to emphasize the power surrendered to representatives of the people in the legislature. He did this with some reluctance. 'As therefore, I would by no means lessen the Authority of the People, in the Reserves of Right left them, and *which are not Committed to the Representatives*,' he wrote, 'so I would by no means Reduce Parliaments to Mobs and Rabbles, and make them pay their Homage every day to the *Absolute Directions* of their Constituents; this were indeed, to sacrifice to Our Sovereign Lord, The People . . .'[8] On the other hand, he still believed in the literal, representative

---

[5] See esp. Defoe, *A Fifth Essay at Removing National Prejudices* ([Edinburgh] 1707), 2–7.

[6] Isaac Foote argued that Defoe had dropped a radical stance some time between 1704 and 1705. This is an overstatement. His business in Scotland was to see that the Union treaty was passed, and there is some possibility that he abandoned some positions simply to remain credible while he was in Scotland. See *The Pen and the Sword* (London: MacGibbon & Kee, 1966), 89.

[7] *Jure Divino Toss'd in a Blanket: or, Daniel De Foe's Memorial*, in *Poems on Affairs of State* (London, 1707), iv. 6.

[8] *Two Great Questions Considered . . . Being a Sixth Essay at Removing National Prejudices against the Union* ([Edinburgh] 1707), 15.

nature of members of the House of Commons and certainly had not abandoned the concept of rights still inhering in the people. Indeed, he was soon back defending what he might have called 'good' mobs—those that had chased Episcopal clergymen out of Scotland—describing them as being 'provoked . . . to the highest Degree'.[9] If Defoe was on the defensive about some of his previous statements concerning government, then, he was more aggressive about putting down attacks upon the Union and upon him personally. He complained in a letter to Harley on 2 February about being 'Entirely Taken up in Meer Cavil and Continuall Dispute with the Clamorous Clergy' (H 198). Among them was the Presbyterian minister James Webster, with whom he exchanged pamphlets in a manner suggestive of his wish to escape the dispute as soon as possible.[10] Defoe wrote an answer to Webster's *Lawful Prejudices*, which had raised doubts about the religion of the English Dissenters. Webster noted that English Dissenters such as Baxter, Howe, and Bates were willing at one time to accept a moderate episcopacy, and that they also were attracted by James II's offer of toleration. This questioning of whether the Dissenters in England were sufficiently pious for the Scottish Presbyterians brought forth Defoe's brief and moderate response in February 1707, *The Dissenters in England Vindicated*, and finally, a month later, as Webster persisted with his comments, *A Short View of the Present State of the Protestant Religion in Britain*, in which he attempted to give a short history of the Dissenters in England, illustrating the persecutions they suffered and defending their integrity and especially the intregrity of men such as Baxter and Howe. He also remarked on the sufferings of those who fled to America, and, as a parting shot he noted, 'But what will not People suffer for the Liberty of their Consciences?'[11]

Defoe was accustomed to such controversies, but he seemed particularly disturbed by the appearance of a number of personal attacks directed at destroying his reputation in Scotland. He took the opportunity of defending himself in his response to Webster:

They report me a Drunkard, a Swearer, a Sabbath-breaker, and what not—. Impotent Slanders! what Shift is Malice driven to? The issue is short and plain, and their Honesty shall be tryed by it, I challenge them to bring the man either here, or in *England*, that ever saw me drink to Excess, that ever heard me swear; or in short, can charge my Conversation with the least Vice or Immorality, with

[9] *Presbyterian Persecution Examined* (Edinburgh, 1707), 8.
[10] Webster's reply to Defoe commented on the weakness of Defoe's response, comparing it to a 'rickety Child, with a big Head and smal Body'. See *The Author of the Lawful Prejudices against an Incorporating Union with England, Defended* (Edinburgh, 1707), 3.
[11] *A Short View of the Present State of the Protestant Religion in Britain* (Edinburgh, 1707), 12.

Indecency, Immodesty, Passion, Prophaneness, or any thing else that deserves Reproach; when they can do this, I'll burn this Book at the Mercat Cross, and desire all the World to regard no more what I say, and till they can do it, all Honest Men will abhor the practice.[12]

Defoe challenged his critics to prove their charges and warned that if it came to trading charges of immoral conduct, he could join in a counter-attack 'with too much Advantage'. Though Defoe may indeed have been angry, we should be a little wary of accepting the rhetoric of sincerity as a spontaneous overflow of indignation. He was still meeting new people in positions of influence in Edinburgh, and he had a reputation to maintain.

In addition to his connections among the members of the Commission for the Union and his service to the committee charged with economic aspects of the treaty, Defoe had made a number of contacts with professional men and tradesmen of Edinburgh such as John Russell, a scrivener who continued to act as Defoe's agent in Edinburgh. Through his activities as a member of the Edinburgh branch of the Society for Reformation of Manners, he met merchants such as Baillie John Duncan, George Drummond, and Gilbert Elliot of Minto. He had been proposed for membership on 7 March and was apparently considered a valuable addition as a London contact. He was admitted in April, and the group occasionally met at Defoe's lodgings. Defoe led them in prayers and must have seemed a person of outstanding moral uprightness and fervent piety. He stopped attending meetings after a while but not until he had established sufficient trust to engage with several members of the city in a factory established for weaving linen. More particularly, he went into a partnership which allowed him to take advantage of the new emblems signifying the unity of the two countries.[13] In a letter to Harley of 27 January, he had written another version of his 'all things to all men' letter describing how he was still attempting to keep up a disguise of someone who was going to settle in Scotland. In addition to being there to write the *History of the Union*, he also had a scheme to do a new translation of the Psalms, noting 'by these things Sir I Effectually Amuse them and I am perfectly unsuspected'. He then added, 'Then I am Setting Weavers to work to make linen, and I talk of Manufactures and Employing the poor, and if that Thrives I am to Settle here and bring my Family Down and the like, by which Triffles I Serv the Great End Viz/ a Concealmt' (H 197).

---

[12] Ibid.

[13] Charles Burch suggested that Defoe gave up attending meetings because he knew that some of the members were guilty of the same sins for which they were faulting others. But given his function as a spy, who can doubt that he would have remained active had it proved advantageous? See Burch, 'Defoe and the Edinburgh Society of Reformation of Manners', *Review of English Studies* 16 (1940), 306–12.

The odd thing about this letter concerning his fictional identity was that he was certainly involved in two of these activities, and while he was hardly one to 'lock . . . [himself] up in the College 2 year for the performance' on the Psalms, he must surely have been contemplating that as well. The linen manufacture was to involve the weaving of linen damask tablecloths with a design of the united countries of Scotland and Ireland, but his mention of employing a hundred families 'at Work by my Procuring and Direction' in the *Review* of 29 March 1707 appears to be a grand projection paralleling the numbers he said he employed in his pantile and brick factory. In actuality, although he contracted with John Ochiltree, a master weaver, to set up such an establishment in New Greyfriars and although he had the encouragement of the Edinburgh town council, the operation did not actually commence until 30 November 1710, when those involved signed a contract. The number of the poor employed was listed as six men, twenty-nine women, and eighteen boys and girls.[14] Though the project clearly interested Defoe, like the others, their primary function was to conceal his work as a spy. Small wonder, then, if he was unnerved by those attacks from England that suggested he was not what he appeared to be.

The Review Review'd. In a Letter to the Prophet Daniel in Scotland mentioned some of Defoe's activities, especially buying salt, and spoke of his bankruptcies, his circle of admirers at 'Sue's', his blue cloak and habit of holding out his 'little Finger to show your Diamond Ring'. Perhaps worst of all it mentioned Defoe's agent, 'Jack' Pierce, as someone who went to Scotland with him. It raised the scandal of Defoe's relationship with Mrs Sammen along with some bad puns on salmon and herring and threatened a further response. However much these reflections may have disturbed him personally, the mention of his connection with Pierce, whose work with the Cameronians and with the Highlanders had been both dangerous and effective, seemed to link him to some kind of outside agency promoting the Union. John Clerk of Penicuik noted in his account of the period involving the Union that the mobs of Edinburgh would have 'pulled him to pieces' had they known he was an English agent.[15] Concealment was a matter of life and death. Defoe had not seen *The Review Review'd* when he was told about it by John Sanderland in the High Street of Edinburgh. Sanderland had apparently read a copy that had come from London to the elder John of

---

[14] See James Sutherland, *Defoe*, 2nd edn. (London: Methuen, 1950), 164–5; 289, n. 119; and Paula Backscheider, *Daniel Defoe: His Life* (Baltimore: Johns Hopkins University Press, 1989), 235, 572, n. 19. A fragment of a document at the Beinecke Library that appears to be another contract he signed in Edinburgh with James Wood and Walter Corkhouse on 1 June 1708 suggests even more business activity.

[15] *Memoirs of the Life of Sir John Clerk*, ed. John M. Gray (Edinburgh: T. & A. Constable for the Scottish History Society, 1892), xiii. 63–4.

Penicuik, and was worried that Defoe had been indiscreet. What is obvious from this report is that Defoe was extraordinarily concerned about the source of the publication and was contemplating ways of suppressing the danger it represented to him.[16] Whatever else he may have been doing in Scotland, whether dealing in horses, salt, linen, or wine and brandy, he was primarily a spy.

II

Defoe was restive during this period. Fighting against the enemies of the Union after the active work on its behalf was not particularly enjoyable. He worried about his future. He saw men like William Paterson leaving for London to collect his reward for work done to promote the Union, and wondered what was to be done for him. On 27 January 1707 he asked Harley to speak to the Queen about the family he had left behind and requested the Duke of Queensbury to do the same. He noted that he had surrendered all his money before leaving, and that Mary and the seven children were experiencing hardships. He wanted to go home, and suggested that he might make a short trip to London and then return to complete his labours in Scotland. Defoe discovered that Harley had been ill, not through Harley himself but through 'Accounts' that had reached Edinburgh. He wrote to Harley with some concern on 2 February 1707. After giving his patron some advice about preserving his health, he confessed that his own health had finally been affected by working too hard:

The body Sir is Not Made for wonders. And when I hint that Denying your Self Needfull and Regular houres of Rest will Disorder the best Constitution in the world, I speak Sir my Own Imediate Experience, who haveing Dispised sleep, houres, and Rules, have broke in Upon a perfectly Establish't health, which No Disstresses, Disasters, Jails or Mellancholly Could Ever hurt before—I Beseech you Sir, Pitty your Country in the spareing your Self For a work So Few but you are able to go thorow. (H 199–200)

Defoe was approaching 47 with his most productive years as a writer ahead of him. Whatever physical ill he was suffering could not have been improved by being far from home, in a cold, damp country, and doubtful about his future employment.

Harley's illness at the beginning of 1707 ushered in a year in which the Secretary of State found himself out of sympathy with Godolphin and

---

[16] Scottish PRO GD 18/4510. The letter was dated 6 May 1707.

Marlborough on many issues, and none more than their growing sense that the Whig Junto, whom Harley detested, should be given more power. His disaffection was to lead to his reluctant resignation of the seals of office in the following year. Defoe must have had some understanding of what might develop from the very beginning. His letter of 13 February 1707 is filled with a variety of false rumours, and in a cryptic passage he seems to assure Harley that although he has been asked to correspond with the new Secretary of State, the Whig Earl of Sunderland, he was still loyal and would not 'be pumpt or Sounded' (H 202). Defoe imagines a situation in which Sunderland or another Whig leader hints sympathetically that Defoe might not be receiving the kind of reward he deserves or might be dismissed:

We hope he is Not Dropt—Tis hard if the persons who *say they Employ him* do not stand by him. Pray let me kno' if you are in anything Uneasy, and the like:
   These *if Right* are kind things, and to one Circumstanced like me should be Improvd, but *if wrong* Sir I thank God Can have No Influence on me, who as before have neither hands to act, Mouth to speak, nor purse to Reciev favours but as you Direct. (H 202)

What Defoe is actually saying in this passage and in the lines preceding, which hint that he had some knowledge about Sunderland that might interest Harley, is perhaps something equivalent to the following: Sunderland, whom I know that you detest, has asked me to correspond with him about events in Scotland. The Whigs know my worth and are offering to employ me. I am still willing to continue in your employ provided that I receive a proper reward, but I had better hear soon about 'Supply' for me and my needy family.

   Although approval of the Act of Union seemed certain, the English Parliament continued to quarrel over minor provisions. And there was another period of anxiety between 6 March, the day of Queen Anne's signature to the agreement, and 1 May, when the treaty was to go into effect on a day set aside for national rejoicing. The chief problem during this stage of adjustment concerned the number of months in which goods could potentially be imported into Scotland at a low duty and then brought to England from Scotland duty-free. A bill attempting to deal with this matter was eventually passed by the Commons and rejected by the Lords, but the debate was so contentious that Queen Anne eventually decided to cool down the conflict, proroguing Parliament on 24 April for three days. Even that great enthusiast for the Union, Defoe, was uncertain how to respond to the problem of those taking advantage of the lower duties. He had already celebrated somewhat early by changing the name of his journal from the *Review of the State of the English Nation* to *A Review of the State of the British Nation*. In the issue of 29 March, he allowed the 'Strange Power of Imagination' to rise to a sublime expectation of the greatness a united Britain would achieve. It was in this context that he envisioned the growth of the coal and salt trades and pictured his '100 poor Families' at work in manufacturing linen.[17] But his first impulse concerning the importation of goods from Holland was to write Godolphin to see if the Treasurer wanted the names of the English merchants participating in this questionable way of making money.

Though he used the excuse of Harley's illness to write to Godolphin about the wines and brandies being imported into Scotland, Defoe made no mention of this problem to Harley in his letter of 4 March 1707. He may have been shrewd enough to guess that Harley had decided to break with Godolphin and lend his support to the 'fair traders' who were angered at the goods being brought into England at the lower duties.[18] By 10 March, however, he produced what may have been a subtext in his letter to Godolphin. He proposed buying a ton of claret for Harley. As he noted to Harley's agent, John Bell, he was an able judge of wine, 'This Trade being my Old bussiness' (H 207). A week later he wrote an entertaining letter to Harley about his activities as a spy, alluding to his acting 'the old part of Cardinal Richlieu', and boasting that he has been able to penetrate into every corner of Scottish life. 'I have spies in the Commision, in the parliament, and in the assembly,' he gloated, 'and Undr pretence of writeing my hystory I have Every Thing told me.' But at the end he asked for 'Directions about a Ton of Wine' (H 211). In a review, David Nokes rehearsed this series of letters and suggested that Defoe was not the most honest of businessmen and that a degree of sleaziness was part of his character. What is certainly true is that the projector in him could not resist a good deal.[19] If the government was going to allow an opening for some slight cheating through the provisions of the Act of Union, was it not almost his obligation to take advantage of it?

Defoe was dismayed when he heard of the debates in the House of Commons over preventing the importation of goods from Scotland without some duties, probably, in part, because the anti-Union forces in Scotland were using them as an example of the ways in which the English

---

[17] *Review*, iv. 81–2.

[18] Harley proposed that Scottish traders be made to prove that they were the owners of the goods being sent to England. In a grim incident the cargo of 40 ships were seized, but in the end the owners were not forced to pay duties.

[19] David Nokes, *London Review of Books*, 19 Apr. 1990, 18–19.

were breaking their word, and almost certainly because he was attempting to turn a profit for himself. Surely the ton of wine he offered Harley was not the only dabbling he did in his 'Old bussiness'. In his *Review* for 1 May, the day set aside for celebrating the Union, he pointed out that the profits being made from the loophole in the law were minuscule, and that there were actually few ships and a slight amount of trade involved. Harley, who had the traditional English dislike for the Dutch, was certain that they were the chief nation to profit from the period without duties, but Defoe seemed to think that the English merchants were those taking the most outrageous advantage of the situation.[20] When he reported complaints of merchants that they might be forced to travel to London to prove that they were indeed Scots, Defoe probably did not know that this distorted version of the law had its roots in a proposal made by Harley.[21] At any rate, throughout the month of May Defoe mocked English exaggeration of the trade involved and Scottish fears of English tyranny.

In the *Review* of 5 June, Defoe relieved himself of some of his frustration about trying to get those he met in Scotland to understand that the Union would not end in the English cheating and abusing them. 'I am, *without Vanity*, neither Ignorant of the Rules of Writing, nor barren of Invention,' he wrote in an effort to explain why he sometimes repeated matters; 'thousands see this, that never saw the other, and what is it to them that it has been said before.' His job, he argued, was to cure the people of their delusions and confusions:

The unhappy People are deluded, are impos'd upon, are fermented, and their Spirits disorder'd, *and how?* By raising false Reports, affirming forg'd and barbarous Allegations, raising scandalous Surmises, and pushing about absurd, ridiculous and incongruous Whymsies, among the well meaning but ignorant People in both Nations.[22]

He insisted in the *Review* that the Union was not broken by the attempts by the Commons to pass the 'Drawbacks Bill', nor should those in England be too outraged by the small amount of brandy and wine sent south. No one should be happy about what amounted to a fraudulent acquisition of government monies through the manipulation of drawbacks on tobacco, but, Defoe argued, the kind of hysteria that occurred was much ado about very little.

He attempted to bring his judgement on this matter, which had put him partly in opposition to Harley, more in line with what he must have come

---

[20] See Brian Hill, *Robert Harley* (New Haven, Conn.: Yale University Press, 1988), 107–9.
[21] *Bishop Burnet's History of His Own Time*, v. 299.
[22] *Review*, iv. 199.

to understand to be Harley's opinion. He made a circuit out of Edinburgh, travelling east to Glasgow on 15 May and then north to arrive in Stirling a week later. In his letter to Harley from Stirling, he warned against any stoppage of goods handled by Scottish traders, but the letter also made a direct appeal for some kind of government post that would allow him to draw a regular salary while still serving as an agent. He had learned that one position he coveted, that in the Custom House, had been given to someone else, and asked, 'Is there no Room for an Absent Servant to be admitted?' (H 223–4). He wondered about the possibility of a post similar to that of Charles Davenant, Inspector General of Imports and Exports, in England. At a time when goods were being brought into Scotland in a clandestine manner, such a position, he thought, would be particularly important. If he could be recommended for such an office by Godolphin or by Queensbury, he argued, he would no longer be a burden to Harley.

It was probably a few days later, on Sunday the 18th, that he attended a sermon by Robert MacAulay in Stirling and pronounced the preacher 'one of the best poets of the age'. When told that MacAulay had never written poetry, he replied, 'That is nothing . . . it may be he does not rhyme, but I see by his turns of speaking and lively images, that he has a poeticall flight and imagination, though he has not given himself to verse.'[23] Such a statement, which placed him among those who believed in a somewhat platonic concept of poetry, probably explains his statement concerning some of his companions who died in Monmouth's campaign as 'poets' cut off in their prime. He probably meant that they would have become inspirational preachers using an energetic prose rich in imagery. Defoe might have had some sympathy with Shelley's broad definition of poetry as equivalent to the spirit of inspiration whether in the form of verse or prose. The anecdote also suggests something about his feelings concerning the possibility of assuming a regular government position in the Custom House. He was an enthusiast in poetry, preaching, and life, and he believed in following his impulses. He was to idealize the settled domestic condition in his conduct books, but he found such a model difficult to sustain in his own life.

III

Defoe's travels took him to Wemyss Bay on the west coast of Scotland. He had not heard from Harley when he wrote on 10 June suggesting possible positions. He might do a survey of ports aside from Edinburgh, or rather

[23] Robert Wodrow, *Analecta* (4 vols., Edinburgh: Maitland Club, 1842), ii. 305.

the harbour of Leith. He might be an accountant or a controller of accounts. 'I thro' my Self wholly On your Concern for me, and perswade my Self while you are my Intercessor I Can not be Denyed' (H 227). This letter must have crossed Harley's extraordinary communication of 12 June 1707. Although he was to hold office for eight months longer, Harley was clearly feeling besieged, and the Whig Junto, he thought, were those ready to storm the gates.

I count upon all that impotent malice, inveterate spleen can do, by misrepresentations and notorious forgeries, to do me hurt. I am prepared for all. And the wrath is greater ag[ains]t me because their Weakness as well as villanous Arts happen to be detected; And if God Spares me Life; I think I Shall be able to pull off the Mask from the reall Atheists & pretended Patriots—but too much of this now. (H 227)

As his biographer Brian Hill has suggested, Harley regarded the members of the Junto as 'simply evil', maintaining that he was incapable of seeing anything good about this group of talented men.[24] Their influence in appointing Sunderland as Secretary of State for Southern Affairs in the previous December against Harley's wishes had apparently continued to irritate him.

Harley then suggested the route Defoe ought to take to obtain the position of surveyor of one of the Ports, including a formal letter to Godolphin as well as an appeal to the Duke of Queensbury, and then went on to his real view of the problem of goods pouring in from Scotland, just in case Defoe had not yet got it right. If Harley saw a plot by the Junto everywhere he looked, his view of the trade coming in from Scotland was equally conspiratorial. He was sure that most of the goods had been imported by 'Dutch, Jews, Swedes, Danes' (H 228) and one unnamed, sinister figure who was out to make an enormous profit.[25] It is unclear if his remark about wines and brandies of France being forbidden was intended to inform Defoe that he did not want his 'Ton of Claret', but his description of the actions of those taking advantage of the grace period before 1 May as masters of 'Cheat & Knavery' (H 229) certainly sounds as if he was attempting to let Defoe know what he thought of such a trade.

If Harley's vehemence goes beyond anything that Defoe put into the *Review*, he was generally on the right track in reminding his Scottish readers that some of the practices, particularly collecting drawbacks on tobacco on the pretence of exporting it, were simply illegal, equivalent to

---

[24] Hill, *Robert Harley*, 107.
[25] James Mackinnon seemed to think that most of the activity in importing goods from France came from Scottish merchants. See *The Union of England and Scotland* (London: Longmans Green, 1896), 356–7.

an attempt 'to meerly pick the QUEEN'S Pocket'.[26] But Defoe blamed English merchants for this particular fraud, and by turning the tables on the English opponents to the Union he deflected criticism directed at Scotland and Scottish traders. He also shifted the *Review* toward other matters, particularly the war against France, apologizing for not foreseeing the allied victory at Turin and advising about the necessity for more and more experienced troops in Spain. He predicted more victories in Flanders, and extolled the military tactics used by Gustavus Adolphus and his Swedish army during the Thirty Years War. A few French victories had given heart to the Jacobites, and there was once more the possibility of a rebellion in the Highlands. He wrote Harley about a riot by a group of men in women's clothes at Dingwall on 8 July 1707, suggesting that it was not a spontaneous action at all and asking if Harley wished him to travel to the area to investigate what looked like Jacobite activity preparatory to a general uprising. Supposedly the Jacobite heir, James VIII, was either already there or ready to come. Defoe offered to 'hazard' himself by going north to investigate.[27]

Defoe had heard nothing by 19 July when he wrote again about his doubts concerning his mission, wondering whether he should return to London. He once more raised the question of positions, pointing out that they were filling up and reminding Harley of his promise to find a place for him. In fact Godolphin had set aside a possible position for Defoe as Secretary at the Custom House several months before. Godolphin had already named a Mr. Henley as one officer and wanted Harley's recommendation to allow Defoe to have the position. This letter was dated 14 May 1707.[28] Defoe followed Harley's advice and wrote to Godolphin, who postponed acting until Harley's and Defoe's wishes became fully known.[29] Some three years later, on 19 June 1710, Defoe reminded Harley about this event and what followed:

Your Ldpp knows and I Presume Remembers That when your Ldpp Honord me with your Recommendation to the Late Ld Treasurer, My Lord Offred Me a Very Good Post in Scotland and afterward offred me to be Comissionr of The Customes There, and That I did Not Refuse Those offers, but it being your Opinion as well as his Ldpps That I Might be More Servicable in a Private Capascity, I Chose Rather to depend Upon her Majties Goodness That I Might be

---

[26] *Review*, iv. 214.

[27] He gave a full account of this incident in the *Review* for 14 Aug. (iv. 315–16). A meeting of the synod of Presbyterian clergymen was greeted with a shower of stones and oaths as they attempted to convene a lawful meeting. One Isabel Macka, 'a common notorious Whore and Vagabond', informed the ministers that she had 300 persons supporting her in preventing the ministers from preaching. The ministers decided to postpone their meeting and were stoned on the way out of town.

[28] HMC, *The Manuscripts of the Duke of Portland* (10 vols., London: HMSO, 1904), iv. 407.

[29] HMC, *Calendar of the Manuscripts of the Marquis of Bath* (3 vols., London: HMSO, 1904–8), i. 177.

Most Servicable Than to Secure My Family a Maintenance and be Rendred Uncapable to serve her Majties Intrest. (H 331–2)

Of course we do not know what passed in private conversation between Harley and Godolphin. If, in fact, Defoe was offered a position, from the standpoint of the security of his family he obviously made a huge mistake in not taking it, but it seems almost inevitable that he would not accept a post that might have meant attending to the duties of a public official in Scotland.

There were many government positions that required little or no attention. Defoe might have been able to live in London and farm out the real work to subordinates. But the keeping of accounts in the customs office required a great deal of attention, and books were open to the scrutiny of the committees of Parliament. As John Brewer has suggested, England was in the process of creating a remarkably efficient bureaucracy, and Defoe was just the kind of person who would have been ill-suited to be part of it.[30] Doubtless, Harley had his own agenda. He probably preferred to have Defoe dependent on an income that might prove to be as irregular as secret service payments usually were, rather than with a salary large enough to render him independent.[31] But in this case Defoe followed his heart. He was doing exactly what he liked most: responding to changing political events through his writings and acting as a secret agent. He might have done better for his family had he taken the position in the Custom House, but while he could write appealing letters about their sufferings, he does not seem to have attended very much to their needs.

Defoe wrote to Harley on 9 August mentioning 'the Choice I have Made of being Servicable Rather Than Proffiting of his Ldships Goodness' (H 236). He seems to have known that Godolphin would be 'pleased' by his decision, and from this point forward, Defoe drew his allowance from the government through William Lowndes, who apparently needed very specific orders before paying someone as notorious as Defoe. Some of the receipts for payment are still in the Public Record Office at Kew, and they are remarkable bits of evidence for anyone who puts credit in handwriting. Not only did Defoe seldom sign with the same name, varying between his alias, 'Claude Guilot', and assorted versions of his own signature, but all of these varied so much that one might suspect considerable uncertainty about his own identity. The £100 increments were for 'special service' or

---

[30] John Brewer, *The Sinews of Power: War, Money, and the English State, 1688–1783* (Cambridge, Mass.: Harvard University Press, 1990).

[31] On 10 June he was still asking about a possible position, naming Sir Alexander Rigby and James Isaacson among those appointed commissioners of the custom at a salary of £400 a year. See H 226.

'secret service', and however much he may have liked Harley, he must have experienced relief at not having to depend upon a person whose long silences sometimes made Defoe wonder if he had been forgotten.[32]

Not that the payments of the government were particularly regular. At the beginning the contrary was true. In his letter to Harley of 19 August, he wondered if Godolphin had received his decision and if he would be 'Delivred from the present Circumstance I am in here' (H 241). And a few weeks later, on 11 September, he wrote desperately to Harley for some help, suggesting that Harley would never let him suffer want. 'I have all-wayes Sir been bred like a Man,' he wrote, 'I Would Say a Gentleman if Circumstances Did Not of late Alter that Denomination, and tho' my Missfortunes and Enemies have Reduced me, yet I allwayes struggled with the World So as Never to want, till Now' (H 241). He reminded Harley that he had gone there at Harley's bequest, and 'without boasting I Ran as Much Risq of my life as a Grenadr in storming a Counterscarp' (H 242). The £40 he had received in April had vanished in the cause of settling the Union and now he was left 'without Subsistence, allmost Grown shabby in Cloths, Dejected' (H 242). He hinted at other embarrassments and, dropping into a military metaphor, compared himself to a town under siege and forced to surrender just before relief can arrive or 'like a Man hang'd Upon an Appeal with the Queens Pardon in his Pocket' (H 242). Edinburgh, he pointed out, was not like London: 'Pen and Ink and Printing will Do Nothing here. Men Do Not live here by Their Witts' (H 242). Small wonder that he decided Scotland was the wrong place for him.

Defoe did not receive any financial relief along with permission to return to London until late November 1707. The letters he sent Harley during this time bordered on hysteria. He reminded Harley of his needs and wondered how Godolphin could possibly be ignoring him. He finally received a letter from the Treasurer suggesting that he draw money from some unknown source, and asked Harley what Godolphin had in mind. Help, he had been assured, was on its way, but he found Godolphin's instructions exasperating. He was in debt in Scotland and had to borrow money in England. He suggested that the best way he could be useful would be to spend eight months in Scotland, one month in travelling and three months in London. He clearly wanted permission to leave, and compared himself to the sentry still at his post because orders to depart had not come through. He worried that the coming winter would make roads impassable if he did not soon leave, and when he received £100 on 28 November drawn upon Harley's agent, he wrote to Harley with gratitude, stating that he would be

[32] PRO, Lowndes Papers, T48/16, 17.

ready to leave in three or four days and promising that he would attempt to gather information about the state of Britain as he came toward London. The trip took some time. He was in Gainsborough on 20 December, writing to his old friend Fransham that he was back in the 'Land of the Living' despite 'Scotch Mobs, Swedish Monarchs or Bullying Jacobites' (H 248), and by 1 January he had arrived at his house and was awaiting orders.

IV

This had been a difficult period for Defoe, isolated in what he more and more came to feel was a 'Remote Country'. He wondered 'Why the Service as well as the Man is So forgotten' (H 244), and felt humiliated at being forced to beg for funds. When he referred to his situation as a form of 'Torture', he was mainly describing his mental state. Perhaps the most telling blow was the death of his daughter Martha. When he referred to debt that he had incurred 'On Family Account' in his letter of 31 October, he had probably just heard the news of her death or of her fatal sickness. His exasperation shows through in his comments on Godolphin's vague letter about drawing money. He told Harley that the instructions were impossible to follow and had the result of 'Trying My Modesty in a manner I Dare Not Venture On' (H 246). At that moment he must have been desperate. He printed a poem in the *Review* several years later which may well have been written during this difficult time. 'Of Resignation' is a poem about the comfort of religious faith:

> Happy the man confirm'd above,
>   And t' Heavens Dispose resign'd;
> Who by his Rule directs his Steps,
>   And on him stays his Mind.[33]

Such a man, he maintained, may remain calm even in 'the worst of Miseries.' Certainly Defoe needed all of his belief in himself and in God during those bleak months in Scotland.

It seemed as if nothing were going well. The agitation over the confiscation of Scottish exports sent to England was not relieved until special arrangements were made to allow the merchants to unload their cargo. The 'Equivalent', money sent to Scotland by way of balancing the economies of the two nations, arrived not entirely in the form of gold or silver but rather

[33] *Review*, vi. 510–12.

with three-quarters in the form of exchequer bills. Defoe reported how the mob threw stones at the drivers of the wagons and hurled curses at them. The criticisms of England as a 'Tricking, faith breaking Nation' (H 234) were quickly revived. Defoe had a long conversation with four merchants who came north with the bills, and perhaps as a result, £50,000 in gold was subsequently sent. Anyone asking for gold was paid in gold. In his concern about having sufficient funds to make his way south, Defoe pointed out that the exchequer bills were being sent into England discounted and that any kind of paper note would be difficult to cash. In August Defoe said he would be forced to give Harley a 'Very Mellancholly Account of Things', a phrase he repeated and punctuated with 'Really' (H 236). He reported how a preacher named John Anderson 'Railed at and Abused the English Nation, Denounc't Gods Judgment Against the people for Uniteing with a Perjur'd and a Godless people as he Call'd them—and it short flew in the Face of The Union and of the Governmet in such a Manner as Really is Unsufferable' (H 237). Robert Murray, a Jacobite agent straight from St Germains, was captured in the west of Scotland, and Defoe reported that rumour had it that if Louis XIV would land just '200 Officers, Arms and Ammunition, Artillery, etc. to furnish them & about 100000 Crowns in Money, he might soon Get Together 12 or 15000 stout fellows & Do a great Deal of Mischief' (H 244). If the situation in Scotland was deteriorating, Defoe also knew that the war on the Continent was going badly for Britain and her allies. Losing the battle of Almanza meant the likelihood that taking Spain would be difficult, even though he refused to admit that it would be impossible, and the siege of Toulon had failed miserably. In Flanders, the allies spent their time in quarrels, and the battle that Defoe thought might bring Marlborough to the gates of Paris was never fought.

As if matters were not bad enough during the autumn of 1707, the Tory newswriter Dyer printed a notice that the ambassador of Sweden had complained that Defoe's remarks on Charles XII were offensive to the King, his master. On 25 September, Luttrell reported that two days before 'an order was sent to Scotland to take into custody Daniel D'Foe for reflecting on the king of Sueden in his reviews'.[34] Defoe had dismissed rumours of this kind in the *Review* of 13 September, blaming Dyer for spreading false reports about himself and about the national disappointment in the failure at Toulon. In fact, Defoe had warned his readers about the difficulties of taking so well fortified a city and had to fend off those who suggested that he was a supporter of the French. Now he could attempt to turn the tables on Dyer. But Luttrell's notice suggests that the sniping continued even

[34] Luttrell, vi. 215.

after he had published two short pamphlets in Edinburgh attempting to rebut charges that he was about to be arrested again for libel.[35] He apologized for any offence to the King of Sweden in the *Review* throughout October, while at the same time insisting that English law protected the rights of the citizen. This was certainly in character. He had not given up his belief in liberty as the highest value in life. Writing on those who fled from French tyranny, he had argued:

Oppression may indeed last for a Season, and the Enemies of Peace may insult for a while, but Liberty always finds time and instruments some time or other to recommend her self to the World, and no Nation in the World, however Bigotted, however sold under the bondage of their own Customs, but first or last have taken Arms for Liberty, Dethron'd their most sacred Tyrants, and laid the Foot of Law upon the Neck of Power.[36]

Defoe may have needed the help of Harley and Godolphin to evade the malice of the Swedish ambassador, but his experience over the *Shortest Way* had taught him that reliance upon guaranteed English freedoms might be the best defence against the rights of a journalist to speak his mind. According to Luttrell, on the very day of the notice concerning the possible prosecution for his remarks on Charles XII, Defoe's sometime opponent, sometime friend, but fellow Whig, John Tutchin, died. He had apparently been set upon by some men who did not like his politics and beaten so badly that he did not recover. Defoe eulogized him as 'a very valuable Person', praising his 'zeal against Tyranny' in the *Review* of 20 November.[37] This was not a good time for Whig journalists or outspoken journalists of any kind.

For example, finding the right tone in dealing with recent military defeats had to be difficult. As mentioned previously, Defoe always had doubts about the siege of Toulon. At a time when Vauban had rewritten the book on fortifications, making them so effective that the taking of Namur by William III appeared almost miraculous, Prince Eugene's chances of success always appeared slim. This does not mean that Defoe was unaware of how such a defeat would depress the spirits of the nation. He gave the *Review* over to treating the defeat in a light manner and devoted the 'Miscellanea' section to amusing discussions of domestic issues. In the *Review* of 4 October he wrote of bad husbands, classifying the worst of them in five categories: the drunkard, the debauched, the wife-

[35] Defoe disliked the notion that Charles XII, a Protestant king, was not helping the Protestant cause. Gustavus Adolphus had been a true 'Hero' for the Protestants, but Defoe could not see how anyone could think pure military venturism was heroic. In his issue for 20 Sept. 1707, he returned again to criticize the actions of the King of Sweden (*Review*, iv. 373–6).   [36] Ibid. 321.
[37] Ibid. 483–4.

beater, the extravagant husband, and by far the worst of them all, the 'Fool'. Some good qualities might make the others endurable, but not the fool: 'the worst thing a sober Woman can be married to, is a FOOL; of whom whoever has the Lot, *Lord have Mercy*, and a † should be set on the Door, as of a House Infected with the Plague.'[38] Defoe was to put similar remarks on bad husbands into *Moll Flanders* and *Roxana*, and the reference to the plague recalls his *Journal of the Plague Year*. A few weeks later, he gave a *Review* over to the power of money ('O Money, Money!') to transform all appearances:

Thou art the Test of Beauty, the Judge of ornament, the Guide of the Fancy, the Index of Temper, and the Pole Star of the Affections; Thou makest Homely Things Fair, Old things Young, Crooked Things Straight; Thou has the great Remedy of Love, thou can'st give the Blind an Eye, the Lame a Leg, the Froward a Temper and the Scandalous a Character; Thou makest Knaves honest, Whores chast, and Bullies Justices of the Peace . . . Thou makest the Differences there between the Great and the Small, the High and the Low, and to thy Charge it is justly lay'd, why Sotts lead, Blockheads preach, Knaves govern, and Elected Fools make Aldermen and Mayors.[39]

Defoe continued this theme in his next issue, suggesting that the wealthy pirates of Madagascar should be pardoned (after paying the nation a suitable ransom) and accepted back into society as citizens. He was later to exploit this paradox in his tales of piracy. If critics have wondered at the speed with which he produced his novels fifteen years later, it should be remembered that he carried this kind of material around in his head, and that when he wanted to entertain the readers of the *Review* he could come up with amusing pieces of social satire such as these on short notice.

Aside from his work on the *Review*, Defoe's attempts at writing were not particularly successful at this time. He produced a defence of the Presbyterian Church in Scotland in relation to the Scottish Episcopal Church, attempting to show that, with the exception of some Episcopal clergymen who were particularly vicious in their lives, almost all the others were allowed to retain their positions. He maintained that he could produce a list of 165 such clergymen who had never sworn obedience to William and Mary but who were still allowed to hold their places. What was *really* needed, he complained, was a history of the sufferings of the Presbyterian Church in Scotland, and he attempted to fill this gap in historical writing some years later.[40] He published this pamphlet under the mocking title *An*

[38] Ibid. 404.
[39] Ibid. 423.
[40] Defoe published *Memoirs of the Church of Scotland* (London, 1717) to fill this need, and much of the research and writing was probably done during this period.

Historical Account of the Bitter Sufferings and Melancholy Circumstances of the Episcopal Church in Scotland, Under the Barbarous Usage and Bloody Persecution of the Presbyterian Government. This was a miscalculation. Apparently not enough readers responded to the joke, and the subtitle, *The Nature and Necessity of a Toleration to the North of Britain*, had all of the appearance of a tract by a real defender of the Episcopal Church. Defoe had to revise the title to the more neutral *Presbyterian Persecution Examined*, though he still kept the subtitle. Whether this change was the work of the booksellers or Defoe, it should have been a lesson to Defoe that if his irony had a hard time in England, it was hardly likely to succeed in Scotland.

Defoe announced his return to England in the *Review* with some general comments on how the nation appeared to someone who has just returned and by a series of reflections on England's North American colonies as being best treated with kindness. He argued that benevolent treatment would keep the natural ties between the colonies and England strong, and that prosperity would guarantee their continuing their relationship. But the tone of Defoe's journal reflects a kind of holding pattern as the crisis involving Harley worked its way out. Defoe had long been mocking the English tendency to believe in plots, and by way of warning against too much credulity, told the story of a practical joke played on a naive gentleman about a French conspiracy to steal the monument to the Fire of London. Nevertheless plotting against Harley had become the order of the day. Harley had begun to have conflicts with Godolphin in the House of Commons. Harley even failed to counter the Tory opposition in its criticism of the army's conduct at Almanza, and voted with the Tories and court supporters to prevent an investigation of the Admiralty. The revelation that William Gregg, one of the clerks in Harley's office, had been acting as a spy for the French further weakened Harley in the eyes of Godolphin and the Whig Junto. Gregg was sentenced to death on 18 January, refusing to implicate Harley in any way, but Harley was in trouble. Defoe wrote to him on 5 January offering his services, but no letter survives from between that date and 10 February, the day before Harley resigned. That letter arranged a meeting for the evening following, but Defoe made his position clear. He would stick with Harley. He saw the Whigs as a 'Tottering Party', and suggested that Harley would eventually return to power:

My Bussiness Sir was Onely in Duty and Gratitude to Offer my Self to you Against all your Enemies. My sphere is Low, but I Distinguish No body when I am speaking of The ill Treatmt of One I am Engag'd to as to you in The Bonds of an Invviolable Duty. I Entreat you Sir to use me in Any Thing in which I may

Serve you, and that More Freely Than when I might be Supposed following your Riseing Fortunes. Tis also my Opinion you are still Riseing. (H 250)

In offering his services to Harley as the 'Servant of your Worst Dayes', Defoe was embarking on a difficult road. He was suggesting that he would place his personal loyalty to Harley above his allegiance to the Whigs. As a Court Whig, Defoe might not have found this situation quite so odd, since he had supported William's views during the standing army controversy against prevailing Whig ideology. He probably had some notion of how shallow the support for such an ideology was throughout the country, and can be seen as opportunistic in his adherence to a still 'Riseing' politician. Nevertheless his decision to follow Harley in the future, even if it was to mean supporting Tory principles, was to lead him down a dangerous path. For the time being, however, Defoe was able to have matters both ways. He continued to work for the government under Godolphin, while Harley could be assured of his future support when and if he returned to power.[41]

Defoe conducted the *Review* with great discretion during the first months of 1708, entertaining his readers with puzzles ('Aenigmas') and quarrelling with the new writer of the *Observator* over what he considered to be a slight to William III and the ground war he pursued in Flanders rather than a naval war. During January, he pointed out that the Tories had been responsible for all that was evil in politics, and by March he was fully supporting the new Whig government with a series on '*French* Spectacles'. He noted that '*putting on Spectacles always makes Men Whigs*; for all Sorts of Illuminations tend to Liberty, and Love of Liberty denominates a *Whig*'. He defended the Queen in her contention that there was no corruption in the amount of supplies sent to Spain in relation to the troops there, and tended to strike a posture that proposed to mediate between the rage of the various groups and the two parties. But between the beginning of the year and his departure for Scotland again in the spring of 1708, Defoe chose some of his fairly safe, favourite topics: the abuse of debtors forced to remain in prison by their creditors, the bad treatment of Abraham Gill by the Church, the danger of a French invasion.

In his *Appeal to Honour and Justice*, Defoe covered this part of his life in

[41] Defoe was to write a letter to Harley on 20 Feb. 1708 with an enclosure that was critical of the handling of the shipment of Exchequer notes to Edinburgh rather than bullion as part of the Equivalent. Harley may have felt this was still part of the information gathered by Defoe when he had been in Scotland on business for him, and therefore justifiable though he was not longer in power. Or, more likely, the letter was written during the transition period when Defoe's employment by Godolphin was in doubt. Defoe expressed his willingness to serve Harley, and wished him 'Deliverance from all your Enemyes' (H 251).

extremely general terms. According to this version, Harley recommended that Defoe apply to Godolphin for continued employment and Godolphin had welcomed his offer, presenting him to the Queen 'for the second time'. Defoe noted that 'after an unhappy Breach had separated Harley from the government, Defoe thought of himself as 'lost, it being a general Rule in such Cases when a great officer falls, that all who came in by his Interest fall with him. And resolving never to abandon the Fortunes of the man to whom I ow'd so much of my own, I quitted the usual Applications which I had made to my Lord Treasurer.' Harley assured Defoe that Godolphin 'will employ you in nothing but what is for the publick Service, and agreeable to your own Sentiments of Things', and reminded Defoe that 'it is the Queen you are serving, who has been very good to you'. It would appear that although Harley was flattered by Defoe's loyalty, he thought of him as a government agent with his loyalty to the Queen. Defoe states that Godolphin 'receiv'd me with great Freedom, and told me smiling, *He had not seen me a long while*'.[42] Since Harley left office on 11 February and Defoe was already on his way to Scotland as a government agent by the end of March, the break could not have been very long.[43] It would seem that Defoe's contact with Godolphin, whether through letters or through personal meetings, had been fairly frequent. Defoe says that, in his meeting with Godolphin, he expressed his continued 'Obligations' to Harley, but that Godolphin did not think Defoe would be the less loyal to him on that account. 'I always think a Man honest', said Godolphin, 'till I find to the contrary'—a remark that was surely intended to imply that he expected Defoe to be more honest toward him than Harley had been.[44]

That Godolphin presented him to the Queen 'for the second time' suggests that although Defoe felt that his employment was a 'Continuance' of his former labours, the Queen and Godolphin wanted to be sure that he understood that he was under different management. 'Upon this second Introduction Her majesty was pleased to tell me,' wrote Defoe, 'with a Goodness peculiar to her self, That she had appointed me for another Affair, which was something Nice, and that my Lord Treasurer whould tell me the rest.' This was not exactly the kind of confidential relationship he had, or thought he had, with King William, but it was close enough. He was to be sent to Scotland with only three days to get ready. In the *Appeal*

---

[42] *An Appeal to the Honour and Justice Though It Be of His Worst Enemies*, in *Shakespeare Head Edition*, 202.

[43] Godolphin's letter introducing Defoe to the Earl of Leven was dated 22 Mar. 1708. Defoe says that his orders were ready for him the day after seeing the Queen, and that he departed three days after receiving his orders. See ibid. 203.

[44] Ibid.

to Honour and Justice, Defoe compared his former service in Scotland to the military service he had once offered the Queen as a way out of gaol and the pillory. It had been a time 'in which I had run as much risque of my Life, as a Grenadier upon the Counterscarp'.[45] Now, with the danger of a French invasion threatening, he was to return once more to renew his 'Services' or, to avoid Defoe's euphemisms, to continue his life as a spy.

Some things are more than a little odd about this account. Although Defoe had actually worked for Harley, he was certainly under Godolphin's control as well, and Godolphin was clearly extremely angry with Harley at the time for what he regarded as Harley's betrayal.[46] The brief remark Godolphin made about honesty was probably reported accurately enough, but we should not be deceived by Defoe's mastery of narrative, including the rapid time shift to the visit to Queen Anne. Much more must have been said, and Defoe's statement concerning his break with Harley over the next three years was probably part of the negotiated settlement that included Defoe's assurance of his complete allegiance to the government. Defoe refused to discuss his activities in Scotland in the *Appeal to Honour and Justice*, stating that it was never 'part of my Character that I reveal what should be concealed'. But he implied that it was of great importance, that it was 'far from being unfit for a Sovereign to direct, or an honest Man to perform,' reminding the Earl of Sunderland ('the greatest Man now in the Nation under the King and the Prince') of his service for the government.[47]

Defoe arrived in Edinburgh on 17 or 18 April, after what he described to Godolphin as 'the Severest Journey that Ever man had'. Defoe wanted to assure Godolphin that he was usually not so slow in responding but that he had lost a horse along the way and struggled through eight days of rain that left the roads almost impassable.[48] Scotland had just suffered an attempted invasion by a French Fleet of five ships carrying 5000 men. The fleet sighted Scotland on 23 March and not until two days later was it clear that they had been beaten off by the English fleet. Defoe arrived around the same time that the French admiral De Forbin straggled into Dunkirk with nine ships, including one carrying the Pretender. Events in Scotland were in turmoil, and in England the Whigs had gained new strength after news of the defeat of the French fleet reached London.[49] In his first letter of 20

---

[45] Ibid.

[46] See HMC, *Manuscripts of the Marquis of Bath*, i. 190. Godolphin ended by saying that he had lost the good opinion he had formerly had of Harley, and concluded, 'I am very far from having deserved it from you. God forgive you!' [47] *Appeal*, 204.

[48] Years later Defoe was accused of having stolen a horse in Coventry on his way to Scotland. See *A Hue and Cry after Daniel Defoe and his Coventry Beast* (1711). He denied the charge in the *Review* of 10 May 1711.

[49] Mackinnon, *Union*, 393–5.

April Defoe praised Carstares, who had been chosen Moderator of the Church Assembly, and was prepared to visit Lord Belhaven, who had been imprisoned after being accused of involvement in the invasion and planned Jacobite uprising. As it turned out, Belhaven, whom Defoe had satirized as an intransigent, visionary opponent of the Union several years earlier, convinced Defoe of his honesty in denying any involvement in a rebellion.[50] Upon Belhaven's death, Defoe, in the *Review* of 15 July 1708, praised his honesty and instanced their subsequent friendship as an example of how men may disagree about politics and still respect each other.

Defoe arrived with a letter of introduction from Godolphin to the Earl of Leven, recommending him as 'a person employed for the queens service in Scotland relating to the revenue'.[51] Leven was in charge of the castle in Edinburgh and commander-in-chief of the British forces in Scotland, and in what was probably the last *Review* written before leaving London, Defoe imagined the Earl marching his troops down to Leith to confront the French invasion force.[52] By the time he arrived in Scotland, although the threat of invasion was over, there was great ferment. As Gilbert Burnet pointed out, if so small a fleet and so few men were reckoned powerful enough to overthrow the government of Scotland and then England, Jacobitism, far from being dead, seemed to be a raging force throughout Britain. In England, the events had strengthened the Whigs, who gained the victory in the June elections. John, Lord Somers was made head of the council, and Queen Anne showed her support for the Whigs in referring favourably to those who supported the Revolution and in speaking disparagingly about the 'Popish *Pretender*'.[53] Defoe wrote to the Secretary of State, Charles Spencer, Earl of Sunderland, about the condition of Scotland after the attempted invasion. It had occurred when people were either apathetic about the Union or opposed to it. The invasion brought the people solidly behind Queen Anne and the Union, but ironically enough, those people who were most fully supportive of the Union were likely to be those who scrupled to take the oaths to Queen Anne. Defoe noted that the Jacobites had no such scruples.

Defoe's letters to Sunderland, sent through a Mr Shute, and to

---

[50] See his letter to David, Earl of Leven, expressing his disgust at being 'reputed amongst the herd of these disaffected Jacobitts'. See Sir William Fraser (ed.), *The Melvilles, Earls of Melville and the Leslies, Earls of Leven* (Edinburgh, 1890), ii. 215.

[51] See ibid. 217.

[52] See the *Review* dated 25 Mar. 1708. That De Forbin, the admiral of the French fleet, had decided to return to Dunkirk was not known for some time, and Defoe speculated on a landing at some other point. *Review*, iv. 698.

[53] See John Oldmixon, *The History of England during the Reigns of King William and Queen Mary, Queen Anne, George I* (London, 1735), 408. See also *Bishop Burnet's History of His Own Time*, v. 362–70.

Godolphin were much more formal than those he wrote to Harley. He began warning Sunderland against the Squadrone, the Scottish Members of Parliament who had allied themselves against Godolphin, pointing out that they had little support in Scotland. To Godolphin he also noted the criticism against Marlborough after the battle of Oudenarde on 11 July. The problem, Defoe argued, was that bits of news were picked up from the *Paris Gazette*, translated, and published by the *Daily Courant*. Defoe thought such misinformation coming from Paris ought to be stopped. Never a purist in the matter of freedom of the press and a firm believer in ends justifying means, he did not hesitate to suggest that the government's interests might be well served by a little censorship. We should remember this in judging his own role as a kind of censor some years later.

In the process of writing this letter to Godolphin on 3 August 1708, Defoe remarked that at one time he had been asked to translate the *Paris Gazette* for an 'Annual Summe' (H 263) but had refused. His own written French was not very grammatical, but we should remember that apparently he could speak it well enough to pass for a Claude Guilot when it suited. This is the last letter we have from Scotland. Defoe's activities during this period were probably much more secretive than they were during the time of the Union, and certainly more of a secret to us, since the next Defoe letter to turn up is from 8 March 1710, from England, and involved very different matters.

15

Journalism and History in 'An Age of Mysteries and Paradoxes'[1]

Defoe did not publish many pamphlets during the years 1708 and 1709. Much of his writing probably consisted of long reports to Godolphin and Sunderland, almost all of which have been lost. But if the letters that have been preserved are any indication of what the rest were like, the loss to posterity has not been great. He was a little more relaxed with Godolphin, but his letters to Sunderland are filled with too many formal 'your Lordship' this and 'your Lordship' that to provide much interest. Indeed, there is so much polite bowing and scraping that Defoe sometimes seems even to have difficulty getting around to appealing about his needs and the poverty of his family, a subject upon which he never before seemed short of words. But it was during these years that he emerged as an entertaining journalist and as a brilliant writer of prose narrative and description. Perhaps he was inspired by the competition. In 1708 Swift, Congreve, and a number of other wits started the brilliant hoax about the death of the astrologer Partridge. Creating the character of Bickerstaff, Swift announced through him the death of Partridge himself, and despite all that Partridge could do to proclaim that he was indeed alive, he had no adequate retort to the claim that he was dead and did not know it. 'O *Bickerstaff, Bickerstaff*, wonderful *Bickerstaff*', exclaimed Defoe in asking for an oracle who could explain the errors of the *Daily Courant*.[2] The brilliant journalism of the age of Queen Anne that would see the emergence of Addison and Steele's *Tatler* and *Spectator* was only a few years away, and Defoe was to make some of his finest contributions in these years as well.

---

[1] This attempt to describe the age appeared in the *Review* for 8 Dec. 1709.
[2] *Review*, v. 39.

I

Defoe was to complain in his preface to volume V of the *Review* of the inability of his readers to appreciate his concentration upon so important a subject as the Union. '*Novelty*, the Age's *Whore*', he wrote, prevents readers from liking what we might call 'in depth' reporting.[3] His complaint was justified. Never had he been more entertaining. In his issue for 8 April, he presented a vision of hell where the schemes of the Jacobites were being concocted. And he followed this with an issue containing a remarkable imaginary dialogue on the possibility of a Jacobite invasion between the Jacobite Charles Leslie (*Rehearsal*) and a Scottish boy, speaking in accent. Most of the pages of the *Review* were dedicated to assuring the English that the majority of the Scots were loyal subjects with no interest in returning the Pretender to the throne of the united country and in encouraging voters to select Whigs rather than Tories.

Although he attacked the Tories for their attempts to end the war, for the most part Defoe took the occasion to criticize an election system that was not truly representative of the people and corrupt in a variety of ways. He decided to tell the story of one district in which a '*Shock-Dog*' was put up as a candidate, apologizing for such an absurdity by saying that he believed the election took place on the moon. Pretending to be dismayed at the very idea, he used the device to point out that only men far gone in drink would do such a thing, thereby attacking the drunkenness at elections which allowed the candidate who expended the most money and supplied the most ale the best chance of winning. In the issue of 8 June he presented a series of vivid scenes, including one in which a candidate, to win her husband's vote, passes along two guineas to the wife while kissing her. Defoe followed these with some other examples of outright bribery. And he introduced a verbal depiction of what Hogarth was later to depict so effectively in his engravings—the embarrassments and humiliations that a candidate for office must endure:

and could I but give you a Picture now of the Baronet among the *Boors*, on one hand of him sits a Butcher greasie as the Master of of the Company, fat as a Bullock of 12 *l.* Price, drunk as a Drum, drivelling like a Boar, foaming at Mouth with a Pipe in his Jaws, and being in the open Yard, holds it so that the Wind carries the Smoak directly in Sir *William*'s Face; on the other hand sits a Tanner, not so fat, but twice as drunk as t'other, every now and then he lets a great Fart, and first drinks his Worship's Health, then spues upon his Stockings; a third gets up from the lower End of the Table to make a Leg, and drink to his

---

[3] Ibid. A2.

Worship; then comes so near him to give him the Flagon, that making his reeling Bow, he spills some of the Beer upon him, gives a great Belch in his face, and so scratching his Head, waits till his Worship must drink after him, and give him the Pot again; and making his Leg again a little too low, runs forward, being as the Sailors call too much by the Head, and over sets Sir *William*'s Chair and all, and falls upon him.[4]

The similarity to Hogarth's Election Prints is striking, including the up-setting of the chair, but while Hogarth provides a feeling of simultaneity, Defoe creates a speeded-up sense of time, something like an early Chaplin short feature.

Although Defoe was attacking the entire system, he implied that the Tories needed such methods to gain seats because they had no rational dis-course with which to persuade the voters. A Parliament of this kind, he noted after a reference to Milton's *Paradise Lost*, would be a 'House of Devils', imposing a tyranny that ought always to be resisted. He vowed 'without Fear' that he would not obey a government that failed to rule by the laws of the nation. 'I profess to believe, it is my Duty', wrote Defoe 'and the Duty of every Loyal Subject to resist and oppose all Sorts of Tyranny . . . and as long as I have a Head or a Hand, I shall oppose all Sorts of Tyranny.'[5] When the occasion rose, he could still express the same indignation about oppressive government that had inspired his earlier writings, and so long as he was working for the Whigs he probably had no reason to feel that he had in any way compromised his principles.

On 22 June, in an issue that expressed some satisfaction at the election of a Parliament that would be controlled by the Whigs, he introduced a 'Mad Man', a former inhabitant of the madhouse called Bedlam, whom he engages in a series of conversations that would appear off and on for five months in the *Review*. Though Swift's *Tale of a Tub* is the best-known example of this satiric device, it was common enough during this period. Defoe's Mad Man looks upon the author of the *Review* as a fellow sufferer, and offers to share his place among the lunatics with him. 'Review', on the other hand, warns his readers that he will continue his 'Discourses' with this person who is not as mad as he might seem. Mad Man begins with an attack both upon that kind of actual warfare that failed to give quarter to prisoners and to spare the civilian population and upon the figurative war-fare between parties. Defoe used this opening to defend the seeming lack of action in Flanders for which Marlborough was being blamed, by having Mad Man justify the British general's refusal to fight under conditions that were not advantageous. Although Defoe occasionally used Mad Man

---

[4] *Review*, v. 123–4.   [5] Ibid. 99.

simply as a prop, in the issue for 24 July he had him voice his amusing theory that all great generals are mad and that the madder general usually wins, Marlborough being the best example. And after Marlborough's victory at Oudenarde on 11 July, it is to Mad Man's question about the possibility of another poem from Defoe similar to his *Hymn to Victory* that Defoe announces his abandonment of poetry. He confesses that his 'Harps are long since hung on the Willows' and that his sufferings have destroyed his poetic 'Genius'.[6] The statement was not entirely true, but it might be argued that the real reason for the slackening of Defoe's poetic productions was the emergence of his true genius as a writer of prose.

Mad Man is sceptical about what he hears in the news and has come to doubt the existence of a victory at Oudenarde or any other victory. He is also doubtful about the claims of Charles XII to victory over the Russians, predicting that Charles will turn the Russians into a nation with a powerful army that would become a threat to Europe. He argues that instead of trying to attack Peter, Charles should help the allies against France. But in this opinion as in many others, Mad Man is not really so mad. Review tells him at one point that he has come to believe 'you talk by Irony, and expect to be understood so'. Defoe was back in England toward the end of September, and turned his dialogues toward the siege of Lille, a subject which brought to Defoe's mind the lack of any academy for training military engineers. Mad Man argues that all the English engineers at Lille behaved well in every respect, and the reason for this is that there were no English engineers there or anywhere else. The same paradox appeared in Defoe's criticism of the English nobility and their absence at the siege of Lille. With these exasperated comments Mad Man disappeared from the *Review*, and with him one of Defoe's most entertaining satiric devices. As he was to comment about his journal in the *Review* of 21 June 1709, 'it is grown old and grave, and has left off making you laugh a great while . . . because he thinks 'tis more for your Service to make you wise, than merry.'[7]

What probably occasioned this remark was the publication of the first number of Richard Steele's *Tatler* on 12 April 1709, with its stated end of entertaining the reader and with a lighter tone than the *Review* ever achieved. But *The Tatler* merely made Defoe aware of what had been true for some time. The materials that filled his pages were, for the most part, serious matters of human interest, the conduct of the war in Europe, the situation of those forced into bankruptcy, Scotland, the Palatine refugees, and anything having to do with trade. He commented at some length on

[6] Ibid. 212.   [7] Ibid. vi. 133.

the Pitikin lawsuit, a famous bankruptcy case of the time, and mused on the relationship between bankruptcy and the laws of self-preservation:

Let the Laws here say what they will, laws may be unlawful in their Nature, tho' they have the Sanction of the Legistlature of the Country—And he that will imprison a Man, when he knows he can neither pay him his Debt, nor feed himself there, is as much a Murtherer in the Sence of GOD's Law, as he that should go and pistol his Debtor in the Dark would be in the Eye of our Law. . . . For Human Nature cannot starve; and if the Creditor will not give him his hands to work, he must be content he eats up what is in his Possession.[8]

It was later in the *Review* that he argued that the natural response to the pressures of bankruptcy was to take to the road as a highwayman, and he expressed his entire sympathy with such a choice.

Whatever humour Defoe was able to generate over matters of war and peace disappeared with Mad Man. Peace efforts started at The Hague, but although Defoe argued that the French needed peace desperately, he eventually came to the conclusion that Louis XIV was merely stalling for time. Charles XII had finally fulfilled Defoe's prediction about eventual disaster as the Russians defeated him at Poltawa, and Defoe used the *Review* to moralize on the follies of wars of conquest. On 10 September 1709 Marlborough won a costly victory at Malplaquet. The allies lost 22,939 and the French only 11,000. If the Tory press had been able to suggest some doubt about the nature of Marlborough's victory at Oudenarde, they might, with every right, question whether Malplaquet could be described as a victory at all. Peace seemed as far away as ever.

Toward the end of 1709, Defoe devoted a number of issues to concepts of freedom of the press and to a new bill concerning the rights of authors which was going through Parliament.[9] Defoe believed wholeheartedly in the right of an author to his property, and advanced these arguments once again, attacking what he described as a form of robbery. Yet, as has already been suggested, Defoe had always been ambiguous about total freedom of the press. He opposed the idea of a Licencer such as existed up to 1695, but argued that certain forms of writing might be regulated without abandoning what might be considered Whiggish principles of liberty. On the other hand, attempts had been made to eliminate the *Review* and *Observator* as public nuisances, and a new journal, *The Rehearsal Reviv'd*, was demanding an end to controversial periodicals. Defoe was unkind enough to suggest

---

[8] *Review*, v. 582.
[9] Defoe associated 'Liberty of the Press' with the rights of authors to their property in the 'Miscellanea' section of the *Review* of 3 Dec. 1709.

that by numbering its issues 'Vol. I' that journal seemed to believe it would escape the 'general Conflagration'.[10]

If the *Review* lacked the charm of *The Tatler*, it had become a varied and well-written journal. In treating trade, Defoe often used amusing allegories. To illustrate the point that labour created wealth whereas stocks had 'no Intrinsick Value', Defoe presented an allegory of how 'Trade of *England*' was seduced by *Alderman AVARICE* and gave birth to the twins 'PROJECTING and ENSURING' (v. 427–8). Alderman Avarice committed adultery and incest with both daughters, and Projecting gave birth to an elder daughter, Monopoly, and a younger daughter, Patent. Ensuring produced Lottery, Bottomtree, and Wager. The terrible careers of these awful children is told in a clever manner, a manner unique to Defoe.[11]

II

Defoe's *History of the Union* was published some time near the end of 1709, though parts had been in print for several years. Perhaps Defoe wanted to be in Scotland when it was issued by Mrs Anderson, who ran the printing and publishing business after her husband Andrew's death. Defoe once more set out for Scotland some time in the middle of September 1709. He had started a series in the *Review* on 10 September analysing the Episcopal Church in Scotland, in an effort to show that those who refused to swear loyalty to Queen Anne were properly to be regarded as Jacobites and not worthy of charitable thoughts or deeds, especially if charity were to be withdrawn from the Palatine immigrants who had fled the scene of war and sought shelter in England. In the issue for 17 September Defoe advertised the loss of a bundle of the *Review* along the road, thereby making his journey public and using it as the basis for discussing the conditions of agriculture that he observed as he went north. In the number for 13 October he provided an account of his trip in the form of a report on the dearth in the 'corn' or wheat crop. Prices were up, yet there appeared to be no shortage as he went north; on the contrary, there appeared to be a 'great and very happy Harvest', yet the poor were miserable because the price of bread had risen.[12] The problem was that 'Engrossers, Fore-stallers, and With-

[10] The attack upon periodicals came, more often than not, from the High Church, and it was usually on these occasions that Defoe defended the freedom of the press. In the *Review* of 3 Dec. 1709, he argued that the Non-jurors were behind most of the anti-Union works written during 1709. Here (*Review* vi. 378) he speaks of attempts to silence the press 'for speaking too much Truth'. A similar assault was launched in 1718, and under these circumstances Defoe once more came to the defence of the press.

[11] Ibid. v. 427–8.

[12] Ibid. vi. 325–40.

holders' purchased the crop early and manipulated the price of grain.[13] Such middlemen, Defoe argued, had manipulated hops and coal as well. Defoe suggested that if the magistrates did not use force against such a practice, there might be wholly justifiable food riots. The entire subject put Defoe into an apocalyptic mood, and in issues of the *Review* toward the end of October he was predicting 'Plague, Famine, and Blood' throughout Europe.[14] He was especially eager to discuss the possibility of plague, having apparently collected materials on that subject throughout his life.

His chief job while in Scotland was defending the Union, particularly against charges in England that the Church of Scotland was persecuting the Episcopalian ministers in Scotland. He regarded these charges as inspired by the Jacobites and launched an attack upon James Greensheils, whom Defoe thought had not been properly ordained and had been thus rightfully prevented from preaching by the Church of Scotland. At the same time, he tried to calm the fears of the English Dissenters that actions of this kind would eventually cause trouble in England. But his best effort at achieving what he most aimed at—tolerance and understanding between the Church of England and the Church of Scotland and continued toleration for the Dissenters in England—was *The History of the Union*. Defoe attempted to strike a tone of impartiality and exculpation. The need for the Union and its ultimate benefits for everyone is the theme of the work, and there are few villains. Anti-Unionists such as the Dukes of Hamilton and Atholl are not treated kindly, but since the Union is made to appear as a supremely rational act, committed Jacobites aside, those opposed to the Union are presented as confused and uninformed rather than as villainous.

Despite Defoe's overall tone of sympathy, there is at least one modern critic who has argued that such a work might have been produced by Joseph Goebbels' propaganda machine.[15] Another, while admitting that Defoe was the most effective writer on the Union, insists: 'In 1706 he was a government agent, employed specifically to support the union in any way he could. He carried out the task zealously, but merely as another job, in the hope of immediate reward and a lucrative future in the Scottish customs.'[16] As we have seen, though Sir John Clerk of Penicuik lamented Defoe's status as an English spy, he still believed that everything Defoe

[13] *Review*, vi. 338. On 24 Nov. 1709, Narcissus Luttrell reported that attempts were being made in Parliament to prevent the export of grain to the Continent, where a famine had caused the prices to rise. The bill was approved by the Commons, and Luttrell reported that the Lords passed it on 8 Dec. 1709. Luttrell, vi. 515, 520.

[14] Ibid. 343.

[15] Sir Walter Scott, *Old Mortality*, ed. Angus Calder (Harmondsworth, Penguin, 1975), 17.

[16] P. W. J. Riley, *The Union of England and Scotland: A Study in Anglo-Scottish Politics of the Eighteenth Century* (Manchester: Manchester University Press, 1978), 240.

wrote was 'true', and indeed, one of the difficulties with *The History of the Union*, regarded as an artful work of history, is its concern with exact documentation. The lengthy appendices provide all sorts of documents that buttress Defoe's claim to objectivity, and he sets off his own comments on various events in a series of 'Observations'. He describes it as 'an Impartial and Unbyast History of Fact',[17] and notes that when he quotes an authority such as Buchanan, 'I put it down as Fact, giving my Author's Authority for it, and leave the Reader to believe as much as he thinks fit the Fact'.[18] Defoe lived during a period when great scepticism existed about the ability of any history to do more than record the prejudices of the historian's time, country, and beliefs. He once spoke of the need for a history of 'unprejudic'd Faithfulness' on a certain subject,[19] but despite all his documentation and his advantage of having been present during most of the events he detailed, no one would ever describe Defoe as lacking in opinions, and considered from a twenty-first-century viewpoint, he had not examined all of those opinions with sufficient care.

He believed in the progress of institutions toward the freedom of the individual, and from his standpoint Scotland was a country with what he would have considered 'backward' attitudes. He thought that the Scottish Constitution involved too much 'personal Tyranny of the Gentry over the Commonality', that the state of the common people was equivalent to 'Bondage', and that the Scots had lacked a '*Taste* of Liberty'. These opinions are expressed throughout the *History of the Union* but most clearly in the Dedication to Queen Anne. The Scottish mobs, as Defoe saw it, were in a state of ignorance, often being misled by their religious leaders, both Episcopalian and Presbyterian, and by their civil leaders. Such discordant voices did not understand what they were doing. The Union was actually a thing of beauty, constructed on the basis of 'Self-Denial' by a group of men acting for the good of the whole. Unaccustomed to the kind of liberty enjoyed by the English, the Scots could only see something monstrous, prefiguring the death of their country. Defoe laments their inability to see through the confusion:

Had they ever done this, they would have seen that Monster, as they call'd the Union, a most Beautiful Creature, Admirable in its Contexture, Agreable in its Figure, Squar'd like a most Exquisite Piece of Architect, both for Ornament, Strength, and Usefulness; They would have seen it a Compleat Circle, all the

---

[17] 'Of the Last Treaty Properly Called the Union', in *History of the Union* (Edinburgh, 1709), 6.
[18] 'A General History of Unions in Great Britain', in *History of the Union*, 12.
[19] See Lee, iii. 39. He was writing about the need for an account of the life of Marlborough that would be free of prejudice.

Lines of which were drawn from, and depended upon one General Centre, the Publick Good, a Mighty Arch, every Stone of which mutually contributed, not to its Private Support only, but to the Strength of the whole.[20]

Whig historian that he was, Defoe did not question that in bringing to the Scottish people the benefits of liberty inherent in the English Constitution the English were bestowing an enormous benefit upon Scotland. He depicts those who went about saying 'they were *Scots* Men, and they would be *Scots* Men still' as troglodytes.[21] For Defoe, the Scots were politically naive and needed to be guided by the gentle and forgiving hand of Queen Anne's Commissioner, the Duke of Queensbury, to act for their own benefit.

If Defoe's attitude made for less impartial history, it certainly created wonderful narrative, a narrative involving brilliant dramatic elements. He transformed his often frightening experiences of 1706 into some of his best writing. On the one side were the forces of reason, on the other the forces of darkness, and in the middle were the mobs, confused and led astray, acting against their own interests but also powerful, menacing, and dangerous. Defoe tells how they had been observing him and threw rocks at his residence; and how the wife of Sir Patrick Johnson, the former Provost, had to cry for help after they broke down the doors of her house. The mobs controlled the streets:

It is impossible to express the Consternation of the People: those that wished well to the Publick Peace, and who saw, that a Commotion at this Time, must immediatly involve the Nation in War, and Blood, not with *England* only, but with one another; these Trembled for Fear of the Desolation of their Country, the Blood and Ruine that always attends a Civil War, and the Danger of the Lives of themselves and their Relations.[22]

Armed rebellion, led by the agitator Finlay, broke out in Glasgow, and the Provost escaped a murderous mob by hiding in a bed folded into the wall. The mob went up and down the streets of that city asking, '*Are you for the Union?* And no Man durst owne it, but at their extremest Hazard.'[23] These are pictures of a nation struggling to discover itself. Throughout the work, Defoe praises Queensbury for his generous treatment of those arrested. These were 'poor depending, uninformed and abused People', more to be pitied than punished.[24]

[20] 'Of the Last Treaty', 9.
[21] 'Of the Carrying on the Treaty in Scotland', in *History of the Union*, 17.
[22] Ibid. 33.
[23] Ibid. 64.
[24] Ibid. 104.

In these scenes, *The History of the Union* is a brilliant work. As a whole, it is disorganized. The Preface discusses the attempted invasion of 1708 and what its consequences might have been. This is followed by a straight historical narrative of former attempts at uniting the two countries; the provisions of the Union Treaty as it was negotiated day by day in London with Defoe's 'Observation' on the important provisions; the reception of the Treaty by the Scottish Parliament and the people, with additional observations by Defoe. These were followed by the appendices, which included some of the individual letters and petitions sent to Queensbury, statistical tables on the English national debt, and the proclamation calling in the Scottish coin. Although some of these documents are tedious, many of them are in the spirit of 'scientific' history. Some documents, such as one outlining a threat against the Commissioner's life by a group of men who signed their names in blood, possess the same kind of interest as social history that the blackmail letters written at the end of the century by 'Captain Swing' and analysed by E. P. Thompson have to modern readers.[25]

Defoe's work was certainly a far cry from the kind of organized and selective 'philosophic history' that became the ideal during the eighteenth century, but as I have suggested, it contains some of his best writing. The discussion of the impediments to the Union, in the form of the massacre of the Scots by King William's forces at Glencoe and the Worcester affair, which involved the hanging of three innocent Englishmen, are treated with great tact and insight. Defoe saw the hanging of Captain Green and his two officers as an example of the judiciary yielding to mob hysteria. By balancing the two actions, which had no parallel from the standpoint of the numbers of lives lost, Defoe suggests that, as the proverb goes, 'to err is human' and that all should be forgiven.[26] Similarly, he treats the Scottish insistence on the right to choose an heir to Queen Anne mainly as Scotland's way of calling attention to the need for dialogue. That action, Defoe argues, was completely undeserving of the response by England's 'Tacker Parliament', which declared the Scots an alien nation. In the 'Observation' sections, Defoe is almost always shrewd and knowledge-

---

[25] E. P. Thompson, 'The Crime of Anonymity', in *Albion's Fatal Tree*, ed. Douglas Hay et al. (New York: Pantheon, 1975), 255–308.

[26] Some time during this decade, Defoe worked on an essay with the title 'Humanum est errare'. The MS at the Clark Library appears to have been written in at least two stages, and may have been updated later when Harley wanted something that eventually became *Faults on Both Sides*, usually ascribed to Harley himself. At the time I discussed this work, I thought that the continuation was in the hand of a scribe, but its similarity to some of Defoe's attempts at disguising his hand makes me believe now that the writing of the second part is also by Defoe. See Maximillian E. Novak, 'Humanum est Errare', *William Andrews Clark Memorial Library Newsletter* 4 (1983), 1–3.

able. It was the kind of history he believed in—that written by an eye-witness and concentrated on a single event. On the other hand, its focus on the crowds and popular disturbances, attractive as it is to us, was not the kind of history that would win praise from a polite audience. In short, modern readers should like it much more than did many of Defoe's contemporaries.

Defoe's account contains some important biographical details aside from his vivid description of being pursued by the anti-Union mob. He recounts how he was called in by the committee to lend his expertise on settling the tax on beer in Scotland, and he tells us that he discussed the massacre at Glencoe (1692) with King William and could therefore comment on the King's regret. It is such comments as these that would lead any biographer to suspect that Defoe's contacts with the King had to pre-date 1701. But more important than such specific details is the enthusiasm with which Defoe promoted the Union. Though historians like Riley see him as a secret agent with no real involvement in Scotland's future, he invested both financially and emotionally in the events of the Union.[27] And though he complained about the weather—that he could see his breath issuing from his mouth all the time in this cold, damp country—he sent his son Benjamin to Edinburgh University, kept up a steady correspondence with John Russell, his agent in Edinburgh, and continued the many friendships he made there. On the whole, he deceived his Scottish readers about the benefits of trade after the Union in the name of what he considered to be their political and institutional improvement. At the end of the *History of the Union*, he confessed that he did not know what the future would hold for Scottish trade but said he was hopeful. Later he confessed to knowing that, at least in the short run, there would be a decrease in trade.[28] But, as John Clerk pointed out, the trade to the colonies gradually grew to the extent that, by mid-century, the Union seemed advantageous from an economic standpoint as well.[29]

For all his attempt at an accommodating tone, Defoe ran into difficulties over the *History of the Union*. He had written that a clergyman named Clark

---

[27] See Riley, *The Union of England and Scotland*, 240. Although Riley's strategic reasons for downplaying Defoe's abilities are clear enough, Defoe's expertise in all forms of alcoholic beverages would have given him a special knowledge on the subject of ale, or 'beer', as he calls it. And he was an economic observer with no peer in his time. He knew, for example, that the Land Tax in England was never really collected as it was supposed to be, whereas taxes in Scotland were. A modern historian with the benefit of hindsight might think that Defoe knew less than he pretended to know, but everything suggests that the Scots who came into contact with him regarded him as little short of a genius.

[28] He knew that Edinburgh would decline as it lost its place as the seat of government, and he argued that though the trade in linen might increase rapidly, the English producers would inevitably crush the Scottish woollen trade.

[29] See Scottish PRO, GD18–3202/7.

had preached a sermon which, though it was undoubtedly not intended to incite rebellion at Glasgow, had just that effect. In 1708 Clark, who had somehow gained access to the unbound printed sheets, denied that he had any part in inciting the mob, and quoted some of the most vituperative attacks on Defoe as a 'Mercenary Prostitute' and 'a foul Mouthed Mongrel' as good reason for preventing the publication of the work. Defoe in the guise of a third party appears to have replied in *An Answer to a Paper concerning Mr. De Foe, Against his History of the Union*, defending his generosity in referring to Clark as 'a Weak Good Man' and insisting on the accuracy of his work. This battle continued through 1710, when another defence appeared, *A Reproof to Mr. Clark, and a brief Vindication of Mr. De Foe*. Although Moore assigns this work to Defoe, it reads more like something that one of his friends would write. This person argued that Defoe tried to get Clark's name removed but that his wishes were not obeyed. His admiration for Defoe went beyond anything that Defoe himself might say, depicting him as 'such a Phoenix of this Age, such a Rare, and Precious Gentleman, *the Envy and Glory of his Sex*'. For this writer, Defoe's works revealed even more. In them might be found 'Eminency of Gifts, Humility of Spirit, Elegancy of Style, Solidity of Matter, Height of Fancy, Depth of Judgment, Clearness of Apprehension, strength of Reason, and ardent zeal for Truth'.[30] No one could say Defoe did not have his admirers. Defoe's announced response, his *Advertisement from Defoe to Mr. Clark*, was more modest.[31] He insisted that he had received the testimony of five people who were present at the sermon who confirmed his report. He had given orders to Mrs Anderson, the printer and publisher, to remove Clark's name, but he would not change the facts as they were reported because they were true.

In some ways the narrative method of *The History of the Union*, with its glances backward, its dramatic plot, its focus on details and vivid scenes, and its repetitions, bore considerable resemblance to the kind of fiction Defoe would eventually write. But much closer to that future fiction was his *Memoirs of the Church of Scotland*, written about the same time but not published until 1717. Whereas *The History of the Union* attempted a high formal tone, in his *Memoirs of the Church of Scotland*, Defoe allowed himself much more room for exploiting his subject, including dialogues in accent, and vivid descriptions. Sir Walter Scott borrowed much of the atmosphere of Defoe's work for his novel *Old Mortality*, a work involving Scotland at

[30] ?Daniel Defoe, *A Reproof to Mr. Clark, and a brief Vindication of Mr. De Foe* (Edinburgh, 1710), 7–8.
[31] Defoe objected to the praise heaped upon him by the author of *A Reproof to Mr. Clark*. Aside from that, he approved of the pamphlet.

the time of the 'Rising of Bothwell', culminating in the battle at Bothwell Bridge and the severe persecution that followed. Defoe blamed the persecutions on the Scots themselves, particularly men like General Dalziel and John Graham, Laird of Claverhouse, and that might have been one reason not to publish it at a time when he was trying to promote the Union. But all of his sympathy goes out to the suffering of the Covenanters, who were subjected to inhuman torture. Defoe uses the biblical image of a people driven into the wilderness to describe the way the ministers and their flock were hunted down, and his account of the ambush of a troop of horse with prisoners at the side of Entrekein Hill is a wonderful blend of narrative, dialogue, and description. If indeed Defoe wrote these scenes in 1708, he already possessed most of the skills from which he constructed his fictions. What he lacked was the imaginative design. Without that, *Memoirs of the Church of Scotland* remains a superior literary version of the many 'Clouds of Witnesses' pamphlets published at the time, with their detailed accounts of torture and suffering.

III

On 13 December 1709 the House of Commons resolved that two sermons by Dr Henry Sacheverell, *Communication of Sin*, preached at the Derby assizes, and *The Peril of False Bretheren*, preached before the Lord Mayor on 5 November, were 'malicious, scandalous and seditious libells'.[32] Two days later he was examined at the bar of the House of Commons, with the decision to impeach him in the House of Lords. John Dolben was sent to the Lords, and a committee was established there to proceed against him. Lord Wharton, a member of the Whig Junto, (and a person hated by the High Church for an incident in which he was reported to have defecated on a church altar), was appointed to search for precedents. At the same time, Queen Anne was being urged to promote to a higher rank, perhaps to a bishopric, Benjamin Hoadly, a Low Churchman and a champion of the Whig cause. To the defenders of the High Church, it must have appeared as if the forces of Satan were about to dominate England.[33]

The trial of Sacheverell, which opened on 27 February 1710, became a grand event requiring special seating in Westminster Hall to accommodate

---

[32] 5 Nov. was the day of King William's landing and of the gunpowder treason plot against Parliament. Luttrell noted in his diary for that day (vi. 514) that instead of giving a sermon on the events associated with that day, Sacheverell had preached against the Presbyterians.

[33] Luttrell's abstract of the charges against Sacheverell on 12 Jan. 1710 included the notion that Church and State were being led astray by false brethren. Ibid. vi. 534.

the Lords, 450 members of the House of Commons, the Queen along with her ladies, and a variety of guests. On that day, Sacheverell was followed to his lodging in the Temple by an enthusiastic mob of supporters. On 2 March a mob attacked the meeting-house of a prominent Dissenting minister, Daniel Burgess, and several other meeting-houses. Reports had it that the mob was well organized and followed the suggestions of particular leaders, who were never identified. One group of rioters was on the way to the Bank of England in the City, when the Queen's own guards arrived under the direction of Captain Horsey and gradually restored order. The mobs following Sacheverell had grown as the trial progressed, and the violence that occurred should have been foreseen. The managers of the trial were subjected to the abuse of the mob, and Dolben, who led the attack on Sacheverell in the House of Commons, escaped on one occasion only by denying his identity. Trained bands were finally ordered in to prevent more such rioting. After the verdict, Sacheverell, sentenced to a ridiculously lenient ban on sermonizing for three years and having two of his sermons burned by the public hangman, made a progress about the country. In town after town he was greeted like a visiting monarch. He was wined and dined, rewarded with large gifts of money, sought after as England's most eligible bachelor, and eventually awarded St Andrews, Holborn, the London church offering the greatest financial reward in all of England. All of these events arose out of the Whigs' decision to 'roast a Parson'. At a time when the Whigs seemed fully in political control, it reversed public sentiment, eventually caused the downfall of the government, and created a widespread dislike for the political opinions of the Whig establishment and more particularly for the ideas expressed in the writings of Daniel Defoe.

The reasons why *The Perils of False Brethren*, preached by Sacheverell on an occasion usually used to celebrate the Glorious Revolution and subsequently published by him with a dedication to the Tory Lord Mayor of London, could have such a powerful effect is not difficult to understand for anyone who has lived through a period such as the McCarthy era in the United States. Sacheverell's text breathes the very same atmosphere of a nation being undermined by enemies from without and from within. Just as McCarthy saw Communists in the highest seats of power, so Sacheverell found these 'false brethren' in the highest offices of Church and State, spreading moral disease, corrupting the body of the nation. Only by exposing and driving out these 'false brethren' could the nation recover. Sacheverell's rhetoric was calculated to inflame first its listeners in London's vast St Paul's cathedral and then the readers of a work which may have found an even larger audience than the 100,000 copies circulated throughout Britain.[34] He complained of the corrupt works spewed out by the press, but he certainly knew how to manoeuvre the rhetoric of print, with his frequently capitalized and italicized words (a visual rhetoric added to a verbal pattern of violent metaphors), suggestive allusions and quotations, and sinister accusations. He also specialized in frenetic leaps of logic, by which the anniversary of the Glorious Revolution might be associated with the beheading of Charles I, the Dissenters with the Catholics, and the government of Godolphin and Marlborough with the obvious hypocrisy of the Occasional Conformists.

What he has to say of the Dissenters is a good sample of his style. After quoting Launcelot Andrews on the impossibility that they would ever merit Heaven, Sacheverell notes:

These FALSE BRETHREN in Our *Government*, do not *Singly*, and in *Private* spread their *Poyson*, but (what is lamentable to be spoken) are suffer'd to combine into *Bodies*, and *Seminaries*, wherein *Atheism*, *Deism*, *Tritheism*, *Socinianism*, with all the *Hellish Principles* of *Fanaticism*, *Regicide*, and *Anarchy*, are openly *Profess'd*, and *Taught*, to *Corrupt* and *Debauch* the *Youth* of the *Nation*, in all *Parts* of it, down to *Posterity*, to the *Present Reproach*, and *Future Extirpation* of Our *Laws* and *Religion*.[35]

The vision that Sacheverell had of the 'Constitution' of England was vague, utopian, and nostalgic, but he was able to convince a large part of his audience that the notion of a government based on concepts of liberty, property, and toleration and maintained by a right of self-defence was 'New-fangl'd' and smacked of the same kind of rebellion that produced the Civil War in 1642. In his eyes, no concept of 'Resistance' to the power of the monarchy could be drawn from the events of 1688, and to suggest that 'passive obedience' had died with the departure of James II was an insult to the memory of William III.[36]

Defoe did not comment on Sacheverell's sermons until 8 December 1709, when he devoted a number of the *Review* to considering how he thought the government ought to proceed. His first response was to suggest that Sacheverell be treated like an uncontrollable horse— permitted to run his course with all his fury until he was exhausted. If he and members of the High Church behaved like frightening, furious dogs, they were truly harmless because chained. The foundations of the British Commonwealth were set in stone and evident to everyone:

[34] For these figures, see Geoffrey Holmes, *The Trial of Doctor Sacheverell* (London: Eyre Methuen, 1973), 74–5.

[35] Henry Sacheverell, *The Perils of False Brethren Both in Church and State* (London, 1709), 14–15.

[36] Ibid. 12–13.

They expose their Designs, *Viz.* To embroil this Nation in the old Broils about Conscience, Liberty, Tyranny, and Oppression of Property, Things all happily settled by the Revolution, effectually confirm'd by the Succession, and for ever secur'd by the Union—And as it is apparent, these are their Grievances, let them grin, and snarl, and rail, the Mountain stands sure, the Glorious Pillar is rais'd, Revolution is the Basis, Protestant Succession is the Column, and Union is the Capital; Liberty, Religion, Peace and Truth are the beautiful Carv'd Work round it; and the QUEEN supported by Justice on one hand, and Strength on the other, is its Guard and Defence.[37]

Defoe's optimism about the triumph of reason in matters of politics and the demise of such nonsensical concepts as passive obedience was genuine enough, but his encounters with the irrationality of the mobs in Scotland could not have added much security to his assertion that nothing could shake the present political establishment. In the next issue, he repeated his opinion in different words drawing upon carnivalesque folk wisdom. 'But not to enter too far into the Doctor's Lay stall,' he quipped, 'Lest by stirring we raise an *English Proverb* . . .'[38] That proverb was, 'The more you stir a turd the more it stinks.'[39]

Unfortunately, like every other committed Whig, he could not take his own best advice. In the following issue of the *Review*, he accused Sacheverell of 'TREASON' for insisting on the Queen's hereditary right. To base the monarchy on so doubtful a principle rather than the Parliament's decision would be to open up the possibility of a return of the direct heirs of James II. This is precisely what Stanhope was to say during the trial:

to assert in general Terms, the absolute Illegality of Resistance, on any Pretence whatsoever, (as this Doctor and all the profesed Enemies of the government avowedly do) must be understood by all impartial and thinking People to overthrow Her majesty's Title and Government. . . . the true Object of these Doctrines is a Prince on the other side the Water.[40]

Defoe had put it more bluntly in an early number of the *Review*: 'In short, if *Jure Divino* comes upon the Stage, the Queen has no more title to the Crown than my Lord Mayor's Horse; all the People are bound by the Laws of God to Depose her as an Usurper.'[41] This passage was read at the trial as

[37] *Review*, vi. 422.
[38] Ibid. 426.
[39] See Morris Palmer Tilley, *A Dictionary of the Proverbs in England in the Sixteenth and Seventeenth Century* (Ann Arbor: University of Michigan Press, 1950), item T603. See also items S862 and T602.
[40] *The Tryal of Doctor Henry Sacheverell, before the House of Peers, for High Crimes and Misdemeanors* (Dublin, 1710), 63.
[41] *Review*, ii. 319. Quoted in *Tryal of Doctor Henry Sacheverell*, 216.

a particular example of Whig blasphemy, and Abigail Harley, who was upset by the mobs milling in the streets and hardly happy with Sacheverell, was nevertheless shocked enough to write to her nephew, Edward, at Oxford:

Yesterday was taken up by the Doctor's counsel in reading passages out of several books full of the horridest blasphemy that ever was vented among those called Christians, others full of base reflections upon the queen and her family, one passage that she had not more title to the Crown than my Lord Mayor's horse, Defoe's wet and dry Martyrdom was not forgot; none of common understanding but must think the Church and State too in danger from such christiened heathens if suffered to go one without notice taken of them. The Queen heard all of this yesterday.[42]

This was written on 7 March 1710. It was not until many months later that Defoe and the Whigs in Parliament would discover just how vulnerable they were to such outraged public opinion.

On the other hand, how could Defoe maintain the restraint of his initial reaction? Was not Sacheverell the author of *Political Union*, the work which he had parodied in *The Shortest Way with the Dissenters*, and had not its publication resulted in his sufferings at the pillory? Did not Sacheverell stand for everything he hated? Had he not demonstrated the folly of passive obedience and absolute monarchy in pamphlets, poems, and his journals? If Godolphin and the Junto could not restrain themselves, how could Defoe? The battle was drawn between the new rationalistic Whig ideology, the basis of which few contemporary writers had more thoroughly formulated than Defoe, and what must have appeared like a ghost from the past, the seemingly repressed metaphysical concept of Church and State returned to haunt the present. If the spirit was to be exorcised, who more likely than Defoe to perform the ritual? In the *Review* for 27 December 1709 he compared his punishment to the toleration with which Sacheverell had been treated, remarking on the way Sir Simon Harcourt, who was to be Sacheverell's strongest spokesman before the House of Lords, had berated him in 1703 for committing the 'mighty Crime' of suggesting what now was perfectly evident: that Sacheverell and the High Church believed 'that every Dissenter from the Church *is a Traytor to the State*.'[43] Defoe kept up such attacks in the *Review* through the opening day of the trial and for months afterwards. He returned to London in late January 1710, doubtless eager to be on the scene for what he probably thought would be a kind of self-justification in the form of Sacheverell's punishment.

[42] *Portland Papers*, iv. 434.   [43] *Review*, vi. 454.

Once in London, Defoe could see that matters were going badly. In the *Review* of 18 February he rehearsed some of the arguments of Sacheverell's supporters. While they were wrong in thinking that the entire trial would be dropped, some of their judgements would prove prophetic: that the Whigs had made a mistake in attacking a member of the High Church; and that the entire matter would turn into a religious debate rather than a civil procedure. Defoe could still trumpet the folly of Sacheverell's supporters and argue that it would be a showcase trial for the Revolution itself, but the dangers must have been becoming more obvious to him. He was still hopeful that the trial would explode theories of non-resistance, but by 2 March he was commenting on the crowds gathering in the streets, the insistence of other High Churchmen, such as Higgins and Milbourne, on preaching inflammatory sermons, and of Sacheverell's popularity among women. Although Defoe tried to treat some of these matters with a light touch, he was not jesting on 4 March after the burning of the meeting-houses. While he could rejoice that the 'Mask has been thrown off', and that the Dissenters could now see the dangers they faced, he could hardly have viewed the mobs with anything but dismay.

He wrote to Stanhope on 8 March because he had heard that Stanhope had sent for some copies of the *Review* to learn about Sacheverell's character. Just a week earlier, a great mob had rampaged through London, burning down the meeting-house of Daniel Burgess, and in offering some insight into the Doctor's character, Defoe noted that he had been 'severely and openly threatened' by Sacheverell's 'rabble'. Defoe reported on Sacheverell's well-known drunkenness, his Jacobitism, and an overheard comment on King William that expressed his hope that he would see William torn apart by the mob. By this date, passages of the *Review* had been read before the House of Lords, and Defoe, more than ever, was made to seem like the chief fomentor of sedition within the state. When Sacheverell was asked how he could relate the rhetoric of the 30 January sermons with a sermon celebrating the Glorious Revolution, he and Sir Simon Harcourt could point to Defoe's connection between the 'wet martyrdom' of Charles I and the 'dry martyrdom' of James II. Indeed, some of Defoe's more witty comments on the Anglican clergy were trotted out. On 9 March Defoe said that he believed in English fair play, on never hitting an opponent when down, and that he resented being singled out as a seditious writer. Although he argued that nothing could be found in these quotations that he would not defend and for which he was ashamed, he indulged in a palliative praise of the wisdom and generosity of Queen Anne in her treatment of the Dissenters that amounted to an apology for his language if not for his ideas. By the *Review* of 14 March, he could lament that the Sacheverell affair 'gives the nation more Trouble than there is Occasion for'. For Defoe, what had begun as a long-delayed bit of *Schadenfreude* had turned into a trial of his ideas and the ideas of the Whig interpretation of the Glorious Revolution.

Defoe had regarded the mobs in Scotland as confused, but he found the notion of a London mob going about shouting 'No Resistance' somewhat baffling. He devoted an '*Advertisement to the Street-Gentry*' in the *Review* of 14 March to disabuse them of the idea that the Queen was a whole-hearted supporter of Sacheverell, and borrowing something of the mood of the crowd itself, he argued that it must have consisted entirely of Jacobites and Catholics. Geoffrey Holmes tended to dismiss the notion that the riots were related to the bad harvests and unemployment, arguing that none of the rioters pleaded poverty and hunger.[44] What cannot be dismissed so easily, however, is the feeling that the price of bread and the cost of coal were being manipulated by a few powerful and greedy men. Holmes gives evidence for the willingness of the mob to take money, and for the fact that a segment of the rioters wanted to march on the bank. Sacheverell himself had inveighed in his sermon against the venality of those in power. He aroused a vague suspicion that power had deserted authentic sources of legitimacy and authority such as the Queen and the Church for those conspiratorial forces who manipulated the wealth and resources of the nation. A vague sense of insecurity and powerlessness probably lay behind the rioting more than any specific adherence to Queen Anne and the High Church.

The important point about Defoe's adopting a conspiratorial theory about the mobs supporting Sacheverell is that from the very beginning he assumed the attitude that they were not what they seemed to be. Indeed, his first pamphlet on the Sacheverell affair expressed these doubts about Sacheverell's motives. 'This, Sir, is an Age of Plot and Deceit, of *Contradiction* and *Paradox*,' he wrote, adding 'It is very hard, under all these Masks, to see the true Countenance of any Man.'[45] The same sense that a deception had been practised appears in another pamphlet involving the address of the traditional head of the English mob, Captain Tom, to his cohorts in *A Letter from Captain Tom to the Mob*. Tom states that they resemble no English mob he has ever encountered, that a true English mob is not interested in fighting for money, that indeed he would have hanged anyone who stole. The mobs he, Tom, has led in the past were fighting for liberty in the same way the armies in Flanders were fighting under

---

[44] Holmes, *Sacheverell*, 177.   [45] *A Letter to Mr. Bisset* (London, 1709), 10.

Marlborough. After careful consideration, then, he has decided that the Sacheverell mob is actually part of a French plot. Certainly the image of such dissension at home weakens the English at a point when the French seem about to be ready for peace.[46]

As Sacheverell made his 'progress' about the nation to be greeted by hysterical crowds of supporters, the larger implications behind the victory of the Tories and the High Church and its influence on the future of the Whigs was becoming apparent. Defoe fought the tide of irrational adoration as well as he could. In *A Speech without Doors*, published around the middle of April, he appealed to the 'Laws of Nature and Reason' to attack the concept of non-resistance with which the enthusiastic crowds supporting Sacheverell seemed so taken. Quoting the great Dutch jurist Grotius, he argued that such a principle was a political impossibility. In a nation such as England, power was divided between the monarchy and the Parliament, and if any one segment of the government—whether the monarchy, the House of Commons, or the House of Lords—attempted to assume more power than the laws allowed, resistance was mandated by the Constitution. Otherwise, all of Britain would become like France, a nation of 'Black Bread, Garlick, and Wooden Shoes', in short, a nation in which poverty was a natural consequence of absolute monarchy.[47] Defoe attempted to show how the English might start upon that ruinous path in a pamphlet purporting to be a set of instructions from the Pope to his agents in England informing them how they might best conspire to bring England into the fold. Interestingly enough, his description of what ought to be the behaviour of these agents sounds much like his description to Harley of his activities in Scotland:

In the mean time let your Emissaries alter their Shapes; be one thing to Day, another to Morrow, now a Courtier, by and by a formal Cit, or a Soldier; sometimes a Taylor, other-times a Shoemaker, or Valet-de-Chambre; a Beau among the Ladies; and Atheists among Wits; or any other Variation or Transposition, agreeable to our Interest.[48]

After the trial, Queen Anne received a series of 'addresses' from around the country stating their loyalty to her. The collection of these statements of

---

[46] This pamphlet is typical of Defoe's attitude toward the mob at this point. He still believed that the English mob was a force for revolutionary liberty. Hence his conclusion that this cannot be a true English mob but rather a group bribed by the French and Jacobites.

[47] Defoe, *A Speech Without Doors* (London, 1710), 6, 13.

[48] *Instructions from Rome, in Favour of the Pretender, Inscrib'd to the Most Elevated Don Sacheverellio, and His Brother Don Higginisco. And Which All Perkinites, Non Jurors, High-flyers, Popish Desirers, Wooden Shoe Admirers, and absolute Non Resistance Drivers are obliged to pursue and Maintain* . . . (London [1710]), 12. In the *Review* Defoe had compared Sacheverell to Don Quixote, and he carries the comparison further in this mock title.

loyalty, as they were published by John Morphew, suggests an enormous variation in the political views of various parts of the country. Although the early versions of these addresses, with their promise to select members of Parliament who will be more respectful and loyal than those who voted to impeach Sacheverell, appear to be highly formulaic and part of an organized campaign by the Tories to support new elections, they eventually varied greatly. Some begged Anne to assume more power and others vowed loyalty while blaming Sacheverell for a lack of it.[49] Defoe had some reason to feel ambivalent about these particular petitions, since all of them show the kind of humility and respect noticeably lacking in Defoe's treatment of Queen Anne's hereditary right to her throne.[50] But Defoe knew that loyal addresses of this kind were appearing in the *London Gazette* up to the time that James II was fleeing from his very unloyal subjects, and reprinted several for the edification of his readers.[51]

Though Sacheverell was hailed as a kind of saint by the crowds, Defoe knew enough of his personal life to make the adoration he was receiving that much more absurd. In *A New Map of the Laborious and Painful Travels of Our Blessed High Church Apostle*, Defoe created an allegorical fiction concerning Sacheverell's progress to various cities, depicting him as the agent of Louis XIV (Grandoso) and the Pretender, mocking his almost royal reception in Oxford and at Banbury, and suggesting that his somewhat cool reception at Worcester was more in keeping with the true attitude of the English people. At Banbury, the procession is supposed to include a person carrying the motto 'Unlimited Passive Obedience', various symbols of the power of the Pope and Catholicism, followed by 'a vast Mob, Hollowing, Hooping, and playing the Devil'. Everywhere the image of Benjamin Hoadly, the Low Churchman who was a spokesman for Whig concepts of government based on liberty, property, and toleration, was ritually defaced as a symbolic gesture of the nation's rejection of such ideas. Defoe thought that it was all nonsense, a conspiracy of the Jacobites

[49] For objections to and a defence of one of the more moderate addresses, see *The Worcestershire Address: with an Account of some Remarks upon it in Dyer's News letter of April 27, 1710* (London, 1710), 3–6.

[50] Queen Anne appears to have disliked references to anything resembling divine right and seemed to have had no objection to considering her title to the throne based on the revolutionary settlement made by Parliament. See Geoffrey Holmes, *Politics in the Age of Queen Anne* (London: Macmillan, 1967), 187.

[51] He announced his publication of this rival to *A Collection to the Addresses that have been presented to the Queen since the Impeachment of Dr. Henry Sacheverell* in the *Review* of 4 July 1710. The title of Defoe's proposed collection announced the support of the people for all of James's 'Arbitrary' policies, and promised to choose a Parliament that would help him in implementing them. He argued that the real expectation of how the nation would be acting at the election of a new Parliament might be discovered in such tangible indicators as the stock market, the behaviour of the nation's allies, and the reaction of its enemies. In fact, Louis XIV seemed to think that the Tories were likely to win and to be more eager to end the war than the Whigs.

and Louis XIV to destroy Britain's resolve to fight against arbitrary principles in politics at home and in the battlefields of Flanders and Spain. He felt certain that reason would prevail and that the mobs were simply confused and abused, yet he had to admit that they had created doubts about the government in power. '*As for me*,' he wrote in the *Review* of 3 June 1710, 'I can say nothing, nor see nothing but *Confusion, Confusion, Confusion.*' He liked to quote the line, 'whom the Gods wish to punish, they first drive mad', but he hoped that the madness was temporary.[52] Of course, we know now that Defoe was right. Concepts of liberty, property, and union were to triumph. The Church, rather than the State, was in crisis, and the Sacheverell affair was to prove its last moment of genuine popular power. But for a frightening few years, the last four years of Queen Anne's reign, Defoe, for all his optimism, was to have moments of doubt.

[52] The time will come, he argued, when the same rabble that shouted for Sacheverell would turn upon him and his supporters: 'Then shall the same Rabbles Tear them to Pieces, and break all the Jacobite-Schemes of Tyranny and Oppression, which they are now laying to Ensnare and Betray their Native Country; and resolving to reassume their Liberty, shall drive them before them like Smoak before the Wind, as they did once before' (*Review*, vii. 134).

16

How to Sell Out While Keeping
One's Integrity (Somewhat) Intact
in That 'Lunatick Age'[1]

Defoe expressed his despair over what he saw to be the coming downfall of the Whigs and the triumph of the Tories and High Church in a series of essays in the *Review* beginning 17 June 1710. Queen Anne had just dismissed Sunderland as Secretary of State, and Defoe could read the writing on the wall as well as his biblical prophetic namesake. Defoe stated that he would not 'give up a Cause which God himself has not yet given up', but he blamed the Whigs for selfishness, pride, and a false sense of security. 'The Game was all in their own Hands,' he lamented. 'It was in their Power to have Crush'd the Party, and to have kept them where they were, *viz*. Undermost for ever; had they thought fit to have used that Power for the just purposes for which it was Entrusted with them: But their Day is over.'[2] Godolphin did not resign until 8 August 1710, but Defoe had no illusions about the inevitable downfall of the Whigs. He proceeded to praise Sunderland for his honesty and service, retelling the story of how Sunderland had turned down Queen Anne's offer of a pension with the words, '*He was glad her Majesty was Satisfy'd he had done his Duty; but if he could not have the honour to SERVE his Country, he would not PLUNDER IT*, and so refused the Pension.'[3] Defoe must have thought in the back of his mind that Sunderland, a powerful, wealthy nobleman, could afford such a gesture. On the other hand, such generosity of spirit was hardly a possibility for Defoe, who needed both financial and political protection. Might not the mobs that had inquired after him during the Sacheverell riots in

---

[1] 'Lunatick Age' is one of Defoe's many attempts to give a name to his era. See *Review*, 24 Aug. 1710, vii. 253.
[2] Ibid. 137.
[3] Ibid. 143.

London be incited against him with greater effect once the Tories were in power? At the very least, he seems to have thought that he might suffer a very literal loss of liberty by being arrested once more.

Defoe's principles were Whiggish to the tips of his fingers. He was still the defender of the liberties of the people, of moderation, and of toleration. He still admired Marlborough and detested Louis XIV, the Jacobites, and the High Church. But he clearly thought that he needed to be shielded from his enemies. The Whigs had misplayed their hand and once out of power, they were in no position to defend him. On the same Saturday that he wrote so despairingly in the *Review* about his future, he took the opportunity to mend fences with his enemy, John Dyer, the author of a Tory newsletter, arranging for a mutual cessation of name-calling and apparently offering an exchange of news sheets and publications. At this point in his career, the business of journalism must have provided a relief from the dangers of its political conflicts.

I

During May and June Defoe tended to keep a low profile, low, that is, for him. He turned to problems of trade and economics, areas in which he had established a reputation as a supporter of sensible and humane ideals. He defended the African Company as a good monopoly, operating in hostile territory and so requiring an outlay of money to maintain forts. And he came out on the side of the keel men at Newcastle who were protesting the low wages paid by those running the coal trade. Here was a clear case of Defoe's mercantile view of how industry should function. The price of coal, he argued, should be regulated by the state, allowing even the poor to buy it. If wages were so low that working men could not feed their families, the system was unjust, and Defoe asked his readers to sympathize with them and to support them in their strike against the 'Combination' of lightermen. That they should refuse to work was less wonderful than their patience in the face of starvation. 'Hunger', he wrote 'knows no Laws; and as Oppression makes a wise Man mad, so want of Bread makes honest Men Thieves.' The real violators of the law were those in control of the coal trade and not these honest strikers.

Indeed, what could any Body expect from above 4000 Poor Men, Most of whom have Families, who by the unhappy Project of 20 or 30 Men, for their meer private Gain, are at once depriv'd of their Employment, and by consequence of their Bread. I must tell you, Gentlemen, had such a Stop of Trade, and in such a manner, happen'd to your *Weavers* in *Spittlefields*, the Authors must have fled the Town before now.[4]

Defending so righteous and reasonable a cause must have been a welcome respite to Defoe, who was still recovering from the Sacheverell affair. Of course, he was incapable of staying away from politics entirely. On 29 June, in the *Review*, he dared the defenders of '*Hereditary Right*' to define what they meant: 'Not an *Engraver* can Cut the Figure of it. Not a *Limner* Paint it. Not a *Poet* Illustrate it, neither by Simily or Allegory. Not an *Arithmetician* give the Square Root of it. Not a *Geographer* the Scituation of it.'[5] The concept made no sense, but almost every address to the Queen expressed faith in it; and if the High Church were to gain influence, journalists who thought that Queen Anne had no more right to her crown than the Lord Mayor's horse, and seemed incapable of silencing themselves on this subject, might find themselves in deep trouble.

Defoe made his crucial move on 17 July 1710, when he decided that he would try to work with the new Tory administration. He wrote a letter to Harley suggesting that the future Chancellor of the Exchequer and Lord Treasurer would be the ideal person to steer between the extremes of party. He said that he knew that Harley was 'blest with Principles of Peace and Concern for your Country and a True Tast of its Liberty, and Intrest'. Harley, he continued, would be the perfect leader to steer the nation between the 'preposterous Conduct On Every Side' (H 271), and Defoe, who was still grateful to his former employer, wondered if he might operate for 'the Service of my Country' under Harley's direction. At this point, Harley was attempting to form a government that would reflect a balance between the parties.[6] Somerset, who had left the Whigs, the Duke of Shrewsbury, who had been installed as Lord Chamberlain, and Argyll joined with Harley to form a middle force. For a time, after Godolphin's resignation on 8 August, Walpole was left as Secretary of War. It may have seemed to Defoe, then, that Harley wanted no rapid transition to the Tories. But whatever his real reasonings, he presented two versions of his motivations for supporting the new goverment. During 1710, he stated that he had no strong sense of loyalty to the Whig *party* as such, and was remaining steady and true to his principles while events changed about him. A second position, which he held to five years later in *An Appeal to*

---

[4] *Review*, vii. 171.
[5] Ibid. 158.
[6] In his letter dated 2 Sept. 1710, Defoe reminded Harley that he had written to him before the departure of Godolphin as Lord Treasurer, but someone as perspicacious as Defoe would have had little difficulty seeing that Harley was returning to power. Nevertheless, it gave him an advantage in arguing for his continuing loyalty to Harley.

Honour & Justice (1715), was that his true allegiance was to Queen Anne. Quoting Godolphin whom he supposedly visited on 8 August 1710, he reported that the departing Lord Treasurer had told him 'That I was the Queen's Servant. . . . My Business was to wait till I saw things settled, and then apply my self to the Ministers of State, to receive Her Majesty's Commands from them.' Only after Godolphin's wise advice did he realize that it was his 'Duty . . . to go along with every Ministry, so far as they did not break in upon the Constitution, and the laws and Liberties of my Country; my Part being only the Duty of a Subject, (*viz*) to submit to all lawful Commands'.[7] Of course, we know that he had contacted Harley a month and a half before this supposed meeting and that Godolphin, who died in 1712, could hardly refute such an account. Of course, Defoe also averred in this work that he had never written anything at the command of Harley or for anyone else. The trouble was that Defoe knew, and most of his contemporaries seemed to sense, that these accounts contained more fiction than truth.

It was little to the purpose to argue that Harley actually represented Whig ideals. As part of the earlier compromise government composed of Godolphin and Marlborough, Harley had been only barely endurable to the Whigs, who had not forgot his hatred of the Junto and his attempts to impeach Somers. Intent on ending the Whig war with France at almost any price, Harley apparently shared this goal with Queen Anne. Harley was suspicious of the Dutch and thought nothing of sacrificing them, even though they had been dissuaded from making peace with France in 1709 by British promises of what would have amounted to military control over the Spanish Netherlands, the equivalent of modern Belgium. The Dutch were to feel betrayed. They had suffered terrible losses at the battle of Malplaquet, and their nation was in financial ruin; but Harley was willing to go back on all promises to them. In his history of this period, John Oldmixon pictured Harley as the real force behind the Sacheverell riots and every other sinister event that propelled the Whigs out of office in 1710.[8] The Duchess of Marlborough described Harley as a demonic figure in league with his cousin, Mrs Masham, both working together with Machiavellian skill to displace the once beloved Sarah Jennings as the Queen's favourite. Finally, Harley's insistence upon an end to the war meant the eventual removal of the Duke of Marlborough, commander of the allied forces, England's greatest military leader, and a true hero in

[7] *An Appeal to the Honour and Justice Though It Be of His Worst Enemies*, in *Shakespeare Head Edition*, 207–8.

[8] *The History of England During the Reigns of King William and Queen Mary, Queen Anne, King George I* (London, 1735), 430, 436.

Defoe's eyes. In his *Appeal to Honour and Justice*, Defoe denied having ever stated that he 'approv'd of the Peace', which is to say, allowing for a broad equivocation, that he did not approve of the Treaty of Utrecht in its final form despite his having written in its favour at great length.[9] The tone of sincerity that rings throughout this autobiographical defence of his integrity has won over many a biographer, but there is not the slightest doubt that Defoe was now a hired pen for Harley and the Tory party.

There were more risks than to his integrity. The Tories, particularly St John, were not entirely happy with Harley's relatively moderate measures. He was continually having to placate the right wing of his party, and if he had not become a national martyr after being stabbed by the suspect Frenchman and friend of St John, Antoine de Guiscard, on 8 March 1711, Harley might have been displaced by his rival within a matter of months. Thus Defoe committed himself to abandoning Whig foreign policy and supporting Tory economic policies for what might have amounted to little more than a year's relief from persecution by the Tory right wing. For St John had proposed to Harley an alliance with the 'Church of England party' shortly after the two men had resigned their offices in 1708.[10] St John felt more comfortable with Jacobites and those willing to take another look at some alternative to the House of Hanover as the possible successor to Queen Anne than Harley ever might have been. A Secretary of State longing to be Prime Minister, he had a falling out with Harley in February 1711. Would Defoe have written a conciliatory letter to St John as he did to Harley had St John taken over the government? Defoe was to have considerable dealings with him in 1714, but how long he could have allowed himself to do St John's bidding is questionable. In short, Defoe gambled his entire career in July of 1710. He hazarded alienating his reading audience entirely, and worst of all, he risked putting himself in a position in which he would have been forced to write publicly for the Tories even while assuaging his conscience by occasionally writing privately against them. Now and then 'caught in the act', he experienced acute embarrassment, and that embarrassment increased in exact proportion to the degree that he found himself working for those whose opinions were almost directly opposed to his own. By the time Queen Anne died at 7:30 a.m. on 1 August 1714, he was regarded as a traitor by the Whigs and as a seditious writer by the Tories.

---

[9] *Appeal to Honour*, 229–32.
[10] HMC, *Calendar of the Manuscripts of the Marquis of Bath*, i. 191.

II

Even before he took the critical step on 17 July 1710 of offering his services to Harley, Defoe devoted the *Review* of 8 July to attacking those who might have thought that the new elections and changes in the ministry would roll back the clock to a time before the Act of Settlement, when Parliament did not have power over the succession to the throne. Equally wrong were those who thought the new ministry would ruin the nation's economy. Defoe argued that Parliaments do not surrender powers they have gained, and that the general direction of the government toward greater individual freedom could not be reversed. 'Liberty,' he wrote, '*like a rowling Stone*, will go over the Belly's of the Party, and Crush them all to an Equality with their Neighbours.'[11] And for all the anxiety about the nation's economy, it would be found that stocks and credit, the purchase price for annuities, would remain fairly stable. In assuring the public that the transition to the new ministry would not prove disastrous for the country in any way, and in raising the possibility of a series of discourses upon credit, Defoe may have been preparing himself for the interview with Harley that followed his opening letter.

If this seems like a somewhat cynical reading of Defoe's motives, it should be pointed out that, even as he was establishing his arrangement with Harley and the winning side, he was not betraying his own ideas in his treatment of credit. (At any rate, he knew that his pose of steering between extremes would have pleased Harley.) National credit appeared to be threatened by two forces: the powerful monied interests centred in the Bank, and the Jacobites trying to destabilize England through the Sacheverell riots and demonstrations. In June, four representatives of the financial community with connections to the Bank, Sir Gilbert Heathcote, Sir William Sawen, Mr Eyles, and Mr Nathaniel Gould, had informed Queen Anne that a change in the ministry might cause a decline in credit.[12] The Tory bias against the City, the Bank, and the manipulators of trade and finance was scarcely a secret. Richard Steele's exemplary merchant, Sir Andrew Freeport, feels the necessity of putting forth a defence of trade

[11] *Review*, vii. 175.

[12] For the position of the Bank in relation to the Whigs and Tories, see Geoffrey Holmes, *British Politics in the Age of Anne* (London: Macmillan, 1967), 170–6. For Anne's meeting with the representatives of the moneyed interests, see the comments of Robert Harley in his letter to Arthur Moore: 'This is a matter of a very extraordinary nature, that private gentlemen (for it cannot be conceived for their own sakes that the Bank deputed them), that private persons they should have the presumption to take upon them to direct the sovereign. If this be so let us swear allegiance to these four men and give them a right to our passive obedience.' Harley's final comment seems to contain a mild criticism of the extremists behind Sacheverell. *Portland Papers*, iv. 545.

against those who regard it as ungentlemanly and vulgar. Partly on account of this attitude, partly because of the times, and though it was slow in coming, a Tory economic policy based more strongly on land than trade was taking form, being shaped through the speeches of St John and by the writings of Swift.[13] Defoe, no admirer of the great monied interests of the City, and genuinely detesting the East India Company, was yet hardly dishonest in suggesting that Heathcote, Sawen, Eyles, and Gould had overstated their case. His greater fear was that the Jacobites were attempting to undermine the national credit through their extravagant support for Sacheverell. Compared to the prospect of a Jacobite resurgence, the prospect of Harley at the helm must have seemed by far the better bargain. If the Whigs had not succeeded in keeping the Jacobite devil in chains, perhaps Harley would be the one to restrain him.[14]

In his next letter to Harley of 28 July Defoe reported that he had been spreading word about the advantages of a Harley-led government, saying that a ministry with the Duke of Shrewsbury and Harley would retain a moderate stance and do nothing to endanger the three goals important to the Whigs—the Hanoverian succession, toleration, and the Union. Already Defoe was formulating his publishing plans for Harley. Some of these he outlined in this letter emphasizing particularly ways of sustaining credit. By 12 August, he was congratulating Harley on his elevation to the post of Chancellor of the Exchequer and expressing regret that he had been 'Oblig'd by Circumstances to Continue in the Service of your Enemyes' (H 273). Defoe was ready to show Harley the sheets of an essay he had written, dropped some hints about his financial needs, and complimented Harley on his previous generosity. Since Harley had formerly recommended him to Godolphin, surely he would be willing to follow his own recommendation:

But Sir in Recommending My Self to you, I would fain have an Eye to your Service, I would Not be an *Invalid*, and My hope is, That as you were pleased to Recommend Me to Another, As One That Could be Made Usefull, and who it was worth while to Encourage; The Same Argumt will Move you to Entertain The

---

[13] St John was one of the leaders in the attacks upon the Bank and the monied interests. See Holmes, *British Politics*, 174–6.

[14] John Robert Moore ascribed to Defoe a work with the title *Seldom Comes a Better*, published by Sarah Popping around the beginning of August. It is a retelling of the fall of the Whigs and the rise of the Tories during the summer of 1710 and very much in Defoe's manner—the events reduced to a domestic dispute within the household of an old lady whose property is threatened from without by a 'Great Man' and from within by a new group of favourites. Written before the elections and even Godolphin's resignation, the moral is that the Tories, if they are to get in, should try to earn the respect of the nation by behaving with moderation, honesty, and wisdom. If Defoe wrote this, as I believe he did, it was a private gesture warning the Tories to behave themselves.

Man your Self, Since your Merit, and the Voice of the Nation, place you in The Same Point, in which you were pleased to present me to Another. (H 273–4)

Although this is a somewhat different sequence of events from that which appears in Defoe's *Appeal to Honour and Justice*, the results were the same. As Defoe makes clear in his letter of 2 September, Harley was to present him to the Queen again, and his secret service payments were to be continued.

Gradually Defoe eased the *Review* into what seemed at first to be a neutral position in relationship to the new ministry, but this did not prevent his enemies from accusing him of changing sides, perhaps in return for some kind of government position.[15] Defoe denied all charges. If the government were to go over to the 'High Flyers', he would certainly oppose it. 'I hate turning sides,' he wrote, 'never did turn in my Life, nor can I ever heartily trust a man that does.'[16] All he was doing, he argued, was supporting the Queen. Besides, the government accepted the principles of the Glorious Revolution, the war, toleration, succession, and the Union. That, he maintained, was Whiggish enough for him. And taking the offensive, he engaged in a discussion of the nature of government and of being a Whig, concluding that anyone who resisted arbitrary power could be designated a Whig and that even a Tory ministry would have to govern by Whig principles. He refused to accept the motto, 'They must be *WHIGS or TRAYTORS*', and as long as he could maintain that posture with any credibility, he held to his position of being above factional squabbles.[17]

From the first letter to Harley to the end of the year, Defoe engaged in producing a whirlwind of pamphlets intended to boost Harley's position and to destroy the forces behind Sacheverell. He had been accustomed to taking advantage of the freedom that Harley and anonymity permitted him, and whatever Harley may have suspected about Defoe's other writing activities, he was apparently satisfied so long as Defoe wrote what he specifically wanted at any given time. Defoe's *Essay upon Publick Credit*, published on 23 August, was precisely the kind of pamphlet needed by the new ministry. He argued that the machinery of credit depended on Parliament's ability to provide funds for the government and the Queen's ability to select the right men to administer them. According to Defoe, credit owed its existence to a sense of trust in the stability of the nation, not to a single person such as Godolphin, the former Lord Treasurer.

---

[15] Defoe turned the question about his writing for a 'Place' in the government into a jest. 'Indeed I have not yet Enquir'd whether there is a Vacancy in the Press-Yard, but I know no *Place* any Body can think I should be writing for, unless it be *a Place in Newgate*' (*Review*, vii. 258). [16] Ibid. 261.

[17] Ibid. 262.

Godolphin had been capable, but hardly perfect, and there was no reason to believe that the new ministry would not do as well or better. Defoe then addressed the problem of the supporters of Sacheverell:

I must profess to think, if Dr. Sacheverell thinks he serves the Interest he pretends to appear for, by his mobbing and riotous Progress, he is as much mistaken *as they were*, who made him Popular by a hasty Prosecution, instead of committing his Sermon to the Hang-man and kicking him from the Bar for a Lunatic; which if they had done, the nation had been more in Debt to *their Prudence*, than I think they are now for *their Justice*.[18]

This passage seems to apply especially to Godolphin, for if the Lord Treasurer had handled the Sacheverell affair properly, the country would not be experiencing the kind of rioting that this 'hasty Prosecution' had produced. He wrote to Harley triumphantly that many readers had thought the work to be by Harley himself, and that he had planned both an *Essay upon Loans* and 'an Essay upon Banks'.[19] As Defoe described the *Essay upon Loans* to Harley, it was going to demonstrate to the monied men that they could not withhold money from the government, since 'Gain is the end of Commerce', and where a profit is to be had, those who have the money will lend it. To think that some action of the type we would call a boycott could be maintained would be absurd. 'To pretend . . . that Parties shall Govern Mankind against their Gain, is to Philosophize wisely upon what *may be*, and what would be Politick to bring to pass; but what no Man can say was ever put into practise to any Perfection.' In business dealings it would be utopian to believe that principle would govern human behaviour, since 'the stream of Desire after Gain runs too strong in mankind'.[20] Near the beginning of his study of credit, Defoe suggested that had people looked at the expense of the war they would have ended it long ago, and toward the end he hinted that the real basis of wealth was to be found in land rather than trade. Defoe's two essays on the crisis in credit were supplemented with a light series in the *Review* on 'that *Coy Nice* Gentlewoman called CREDIT'.[21] The 'Essay upon Banks' seems never to have been written.

---

[18] *Essay on Public Credit*, 3rd edn. (London, 1710), 26.
[19] Another sign of Defoe's renewed relationship with Harley may be found in the sudden turn against the Dutch in the *Review*. He suggested that, though allied in the war, the Dutch were simply more aware of the necessary pursuit of self-interest in trade, and that, through such awareness, they had succeeded in enriching themselves through the African trade. It is they who understand the principle: 'Trade knows no Friends, in Commerce there is Correspondence of nations but no Confederacy . . . he that would get *from me* is my Mortal Enemy in Trade, tho' he were my Father, Brother, Friend, or Confederate.' See the *Review* for 29 July 1710 (vii. 210).
[20] *An Essay upon Loans*, in *The Works of Daniel Defoe*, ed. William Hazlitt (London: John Clements, 1843), iii. 5.
[21] *Review*, vii. 225. Defoe's 'Lady Credit' articles continued through much of Aug. 1710.

Perhaps Harley thought that two essays were sufficient to frighten the financial community into proper behaviour.

In addition to such relatively straightforward publications, Defoe could hardly resist creating the kind of hoax that that was one of his journalistic specialties. On 5 September an anonymous pamphlet appeared with the title *A Letter from a Gentleman at the Court of St. Germains, to One of his Friends in England; Containing a memorial about methods for Setting the Pretender on the Throne of Great Britain, Found at Doway, after the Taking of that Town.* The work was purportedly published at Cologne, and the introductory account on the discovery of the manuscript among the papers of an Irishman is typical of Defoe's methods. The 'Doway' letter, as Defoe often called it, is a conspiratorial document outlining the best procedures for getting the English to accept the Pretender. The 'Gentleman' advises Jacobite agents to assure everyone that the Pretender will turn Protestant, spread the rumour that the Church is in Danger, and attack the Nonconformists as engaged with Low Churchmen in an attempt to establish a republic. The best political argument, however, is to insist that the succession is hereditary, and the surest tactical method is to get the clergy to win over the mob. The letter is dated 12 January 1710 to make all of the popular unrest surrounding the prosecution of Sacheverell appear to be part of a Jacobite conspiracy. Defoe quickly exploited the evidence contained in the *Letter.* In the *Observator,* for which he wrote briefly following the death of the publisher, Benjamin Bragg, he devoted several numbers to discussing the plans of the Catholic Church for assuming a political as well as a religious role in England.[22] He was a little more coy in the *Review* about the genuineness of this publication. The important point was that the 'very Spirit and Temper of the *Jacobite* Party, is there fully explain'd, in the Instructions given to his Friend'. Defoe also noted that the document advises attacking the memory of William III, and could not resist remarking upon the sufferings he had undergone as an admirer of the late king:

This poor Unfortunate Author of the *Review,* who had the Honour once to serve, and, *if I may say it with the Humblest Acknowledgment,* be BELOV'D by that glorious Prince, has run a strange variety of Fate for his Zeal to the Honour and memory of his Person and Actions; by Governments Ruin'd, by pretence of Justice Punished, by Enemies Reproach'd, and even by Protestant Writers

---

[22] He devoted Nos. 68–70, 6–16 Sept., to the information contained in the *Letter from St. Germains,* and in *Queries to the New Hereditary Right-Men* (London, 1710), 13, he asked if 'the St. *Germains* Letter was not Prophetical, in case it was not indeed a real Account of the jacobite Scheme, agreed on by the Young Prince abroad; seeing it was publish'd there in French many Months ago, and has been followed since here, by our new Politicians'.

pretending the Defence of our Constitution, Scurrillously Insulted for adhering to his Service, and Vindicating his Character—And now it appears, that the Blackening the Memory of this prince, is the first Maxim of the Politicks of St. *Germains*, towards preparing a Way for the Pretender.[23]

Defoe was to write this at the end of October, and he was clearly showing some irritation over the attacks being made upon him by the Whigs. He was able to show his former friends that he had been right about Jacobite subversion and to remind them of all he had suffered for the cause.

Such irritation with the Whigs probably explains his attack upon Richard Steele in September. Though Defoe had congratulated Steele on his attempts at reform in founding *The Tatler*, he certainly could not have felt much empathy with Steele's particular style, whether in his life or in his writings. As a writer on politics, Steele adhered to the Whigs as a party, taking an anti-Harley line. He did this despite the fact that Harley, at the beginning of his government, when he was attempting to achieve a hold on domestic and foreign affairs, for the most part continued Whig policies. Indeed, the growing power of the radical right, represented by the October Club, had only increased with the elections. Queen Anne's speech to the House of Commons reflected a desire for moderation and a continuance of the war, 'particularly in Spain',[24] and some thought that Harley's quarrels with Rochester, the head of the Council, might lead to his joining with the Whigs once more.[25] Under these circumstances Steele's posture may well have irritated Defoe as being mere party politics without any principle— or, to view Defoe's motivation in a less favourable light, having decided to support Harley's new government, Defoe was annoyed by Steele's party-oriented stand. But most of all Defoe, in his *Condoling Letter to the Tatler*, was responding to a direct attack upon him by Steele.[26] Defoe now criticized Steele for the very attacks upon Partridge that had before amused him, and mocked him for ending in debtor's prison through luxurious living and drunkenness.

As an example to be drawn from the wrong kind of life Steele had lived, Defoe now advanced a psychological and ethical guide in the form of striving toward a mean between excesses. Using some of Steele's suggestions about an emotional barometer, Defoe offered his own in which 'FAMILY' occupied the moral centre:

---

[23] *Review*, vii. 372.
[24] G. M. Trevelyan, *England under Queen Anne* (3 vols., London: Longmans, Green, 1930–4), iii. 107.
[25] Brian Hill, *Robert Harley* (New Haven, Conn.: Yale University Press, 1988), 147.
[26] See Donald Bond (ed.), *The Tatler* (3 vols., Oxford: Clarendon Press, 1987), iii. 124–5; and M. E. Novak, 'The Defoe Canon', *Huntington Library Quarterly* 59 (1997), 189–207.

Madness
Poverty
Extravagance,
Excess or Profusion,
Waste, Generous Liberality,
Plenty,
FAMILY,
Frugality,
Parsimony,
Niggardliness,
Covetousness,
Sordidly Covetous
Wretchedness or Rich Poverty,
Madness.

Defoe offered this as a personal psychology, since, as he explained, the concept of family and individual was the same, since 'every Man is a Family to himself'. In arguing that Steele had failed to regulate his life in a manner that kept at least within the degrees of 'Generous Liberality and Parsimony', Defoe was establishing a concept of behaviour by which family relations were to be internalized in a manner that would have made every action referrable to behaviour toward the members of a group of loved ones. It is impossible to avoid the notion that Defoe was contrasting the naturalness and sympathy inherent in family relationships to the polite social relations promulgated by Steele and his collaborator, Joseph Addison.

The elections took place in October, and Defoe was busily engaged in advising the nation about the best way of casting its votes. Harley, it might have been thought, was eager for a Tory landslide, a national expression of dissatisfaction about the perceived mistreatment of Sacheverell, but in fact he was anxious about having too strong a Tory majority, since it would surely make the House of Commons unmanageable. This left Defoe free to preach against voting in the supporters of Sacheverell, whom he depicted as being guilty of deceiving the people:

In Government they Embrace absolute Tyranny, for Legal Monarchy, Hereditary Right instead of Parliamentary Limitation, and Arbitrary Will, for Law, by which they are led Blindfold to practice Absolute Submission with Pleasure, giving up Liberty, with Delight, like the True Tribe of *Isacher*, Couching, even before the Load is laid on. Court their own Chains, and Address their Soveraign for Slavery.[27]

---

[27] *A Word about a New Election* (London, 1710), 4.

The tract put out by the Harley camp that represented 'a full-scale exposition of Harleian ideology' was titled *Faults on Both Sides: Or, An Essay upon the Original Cause, Progress, and Mischievious Consequences of the Factions in this Nation.*[28] The work was anti-Marlborough, effusively pro-Harley, and against the Bank and monied interests in a way that neither Defoe's *Essay upon Credit* nor his *Essay upon Loans* were. At one point the writer suggested that everyone would be better off if they kept their money at home 'as their grandfather's did'. Defoe's notion of steering between parties was very different, and that his manuscript version of such a pamphlet, 'Humanum est Errare', was never published is hardly surprising. What he put forward was the possibility of Whig ideology being administered by nominal Tories such as Harley. This is the thrust of his substantial pamphlet *A Supplement to Faults on Both Sides*, staged as a dialogue between Steddy and Turn-Round. Since Steddy has always been a Whig, related to Algernon Sidney Steddy,[29] and Turn-Round a Tory for just a short period ready to turn Whig again, they have no major disagreements. Both are concerned about having 'a *Whigg* Constitution administered upon *Tory* Principles', but they take consolation in what they consider the likelihood that Harley will soon turn Whig. Unlike the original pamphlet which it is supposed to 'supplement', Defoe insists that the monied sector of the economy is necessary to sustain credit. Although Defoe has Steddy pose the very good argument that the allies demanded too much from France in 1709, Steddy answers that objection himself with reference to the insincerity of France and the necessity for a peace which would truly safeguard the interests of those opposed to France. He actually ends the pamphlet on a note of warning about the folly of making a bad peace. Harley had other plans, but while Defoe was eventually to write anti-war propaganda for Harley, he was certainly not convinced of its wisdom.

III

In Defoe's letter to Harley dated 2 September 1710, he spoke of his financial difficulties as being made worse by a certain 'Step' he took some five months earlier that prevented his working as effectively for Harley as he might:

[28] See J. A. Downie, *Robert Harley and the Press* (Cambridge: Cambridge University Press, 1979), 119–22. The work is ascribed to Simon Clement and praises Harley as a person able to govern the nation while being above party strife. Downie points out that the pamphlet occasionally seems to reflect Harley speaking in his own voice.

[29] That Defoe should choose Algernon Sidney as the crucial Whig saint and ideologist suggests that, in his mind at least, Locke had not yet reached that position.

1. Defoe by Van der Gucht after the painting by Jeremiah Taverner

2. Popish Plot playing card:
the Fire of London

3. Popish Plot playing card: Titus
Oates before Charles II

4. Title-page and illustration of debtors in prison from Moses Pitt,
The Cry of the Oppressed, 1691

5. King William engraved by Smith after the painting by Sir Godfrey Kneller

6. Robert Harley, Earl of Oxford

7. Sacheverell Trial playing card showing Queen Anne and Sacheverell

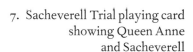

A

REVIEW

OF THE

Affairs of FRANCE:

AND OF ALL

EUROPE,

As Influenc'd by that NATION:

BEING,

Historical Obſervations, on the Publick Tranſactions of the
WORLD; Purg'd from the Errors and Partiality of
News-Writers, and *Petty-Stateſmen* of all Sides.

WITH AN

Entertaining Part in every Sheet,

BEING,

ADVICE from the Scandal. CLUB,

To the Curious Enquirers; in Anſwer to Letters ſent them
for that Purpoſe.

_____

LONDON:
Printed in the Year MDCCV.

8. Title-page of Defoe's *Review*

9. Frontispiece of the 1719 edition of
Robinson Crusoe

10. Moll Flanders from a chapbook illustration

11. Frontispiece of the 1724 edition of *Roxana*

The Famous ROXANA.

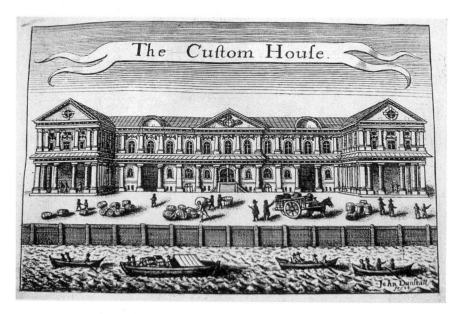

12. The Custom House, from Robert Morden and Philip Lea,
A Prospect of London. London, *c.*1700

13. Engraving of Defoe's house at Stoke Newington

14. Peter the Wild Boy, a
woodcut after the portrait
by William Kent, 1726

15. Frontispiece to *A System
of Magick*, 1727

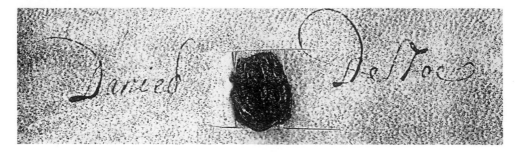

16. Defoe's signature and seal on a deed to the Colchester property

17. Henry Baker engraved by Nutter after the
portrait by Thompson

And Really These Things too Much Dissable the Very Capascity of Serving Usefully, and is a great Reason why I Move in This Matter with More Assureance, haveing No Reason Sir to Expect from you any Thing but as it May Render me Servicable to you. Tis with too Much Experience Sir That I Express to you That the Anxieties and Impatience of Perplext Circumstances lessen the Very Capascity of Service, Sink the spirits, and leave Neither the hands Free, or The head Clear, for any Valluable Performance. (H 275)

Such a reference to what he had communicated in conversation to Harley is perplexing. He cannot be referring to his accommodation with his creditors, since that occurred two years earlier, yet in dragging in the condition of his 'wife, and Six Children allmost Grown up, and Perfectly Unprovided for' (H 274), he is clearly referring to his needs for additional money. What comes to mind is that Defoe may have undertaken some kind of time-consuming position in relation to the distribution of news and newsletters, perhaps involving the same work he mentioned in his letter to John Dyer at the beginning of June, and that he was offering to abandon this work for a proper reward. His suggestion that he would be happier working with Harley than with Godolphin and Sunderland because he could now serve 'both with Principle, and Inclination' (H 275) should be taken with a grain of salt.[30]

Harley successfully applied to the Queen on Defoe's behalf, and Defoe offered on 21 September 1710 to go to Scotland to 'Argue with, perswade, and bring to Their Temper and Eye-Sight a Certain people who are but too Apt to Reciev Impressions from Some here who want both' (H 287). He had prepared the way for this request by writing about Scotland in several letters. One contained a warning against the creation of a naval base in Leith, suggesting Queens Ferry as a better spot in the Firth and outlining the necessity for docking facilities in the north. Defoe presented this with a general outline of his theory of trade. The dry docks and other facilities would stimulate employment, which in turn would stimulate various trades and businesses in a circular pattern of prosperity. On 12 September he had warned that a Presbyterian minister from the London area had plans to

[30] Healey's note is typical of Defoe's biographers: 'Harley, though nominally a Tory, was a professed Moderate who shared Defoe's distaste for faction and extreme measures. It was Harley's moderation, not his Toryism, that Defoe was so willing to support with "Principle, and Inclination" ' (H 275, n. 3). Defoe was shrewd enough to have read in the popular support for Sacheverell how dangerous the years ahead would be and how difficult a time Harley was likely to have in restraining adherents of the October Club. He knew that Harley would have to make concessions to the right-wingers among the Tories, and that Harley would probably find such concessions more palatable than he. Defoe was clearly offering his remark as a compliment, and it should not be turned into a genuine expression of opinion. What is probably true is that Defoe found Harley easier to work with on a personal level, since his informality and ability to make people feel at ease were famous.

travel to Scotland and might spread discontent. Defoe argued that were he to go north at the same time, he would be able to counteract any anxiety that might be spread concerning the new ministry's adherence to principles of popery and persecution.

Defoe received £100 on 27 September and promised to be worthy of the trust placed in him by the Queen, but first he discussed the appearance of letters concerning an invasion by the Pretender. Defoe thought that this was part of a plot intended to produce a situation in which the letters might be found in the houses of those supporting the government. He saw the purpose of such letters to be the arousal of fear and suspicion. Defoe clearly recognized this because, in some sense, they represented a type of subversion not very different from what he attempted in a few of his own publications. He ended this letter with a contrast between those 'Men of Peace and Patience' as opposed to those who have been devoured by the 'Zeal of Parties', in short, between Harley and his enemies. This is called telling the boss what he likes to hear. Harley obviously wanted to be told that rumours about an invasion by the Pretender were not to be taken seriously, and Defoe did just that.

Defoe's brief trip to Scotland may have been as much for his own interests as for service to the Queen and Harley. He had established a number of businesses there, including a trade in horses. The Earl of Hundsford, commander-in-chief of the Scottish forces, had made an arrangement for paying Defoe a commission to buy horses for himself and his officers. Defoe also supplied horses to Major Coult, the governor of Edinburgh Castle, for £85, and dealt in Canary wine, ale, and pickles.[31] Though most of these activities were carried on through Defoe's agent, John Russell, Defoe probably wanted to oversee matters at first hand. In the *Tour thro' the Whole Island of Great Britain*, he was particularly attentive to the horse fairs throughout the country, and showed a first-hand knowledge of the methods of horse-trading. He also completed the arrangements with John Ochiltree for a linen manufacture, appointing Hanna Goodale as his factor to run the business, and Russell's letters inform us that he was dabbling in the production of brass to manufacture farthing coins.

More important than these business ventures, however, were his interests in the education of his son, Benjamin Norton, and his involvement with his various publications in Edinburgh. In sending his son to Edinburgh University, Defoe was following the scheme of Daniel Williams and

---

[31] See Paula Backscheider, 'John Russell to Daniel Defoe: Fifteen Unpublished Letters from Scotland', *Philological Quarterly* 61 (1982), 161–77.

others, who thought that the Scottish universities would serve as excellent places to educate the children of Dissenters. Defoe seems to have been an enthusiastic supporter of Edinburgh University, while Daniel Williams had been an advocate for Glasgow and may even have written a proposal sent to Carstares, the principal of that university, to encourage increased enrolment by the children of English Dissenters.[32] But as matters turned out, Benjamin Norton was not an ideal student. He neglected his studies and was running up debts, despite some lectures about his behaviour from John Russell. At the beginning of September 1711, following his father's orders, Benjamin Norton departed for London.[33] Russell offered Defoe the consolation that his son would eventually abandon the follies of his youth, but Benjamin Norton was not one of those children to be made wiser by time and experience. Russell hoped that Defoe would exercise careful supervision over his son, but Defoe was closer to the real Rousseau than to the idealized mentor of *Émile*, better at theorizing over the benefits of the education offered in Edinburgh than in seeing that his son was well suited to engaging in such a course of study. Defoe's involvement in Edinburgh publishing shows a similar pattern—an interest in the possibilities of an activity followed by a failure to involve himself in the day-to-day operations of the business. He arranged to have a special edition of the *Review* published in Edinburgh by Agnes Campbell Anderson, beginning 31 March 1709. And he attempted to gain control of the *Edinburgh Courant* and the *Scots Postman*. Charles Eaton Burch once offered the suggestion that Defoe may have planned to gain overall control of the press in Edinburgh with the idea of putting Benjamin Norton in charge of these enterprises.[34] This seems far more likely than the notion that Defoe entertained for very long the idea of settling himself and his family there, and indeed Benjamin Norton was present at one of the negotiations between Mrs Anderson and Defoe's agent, Russell, over publication, litigation, and debts she believed were owed her by Defoe.[35]

[32] The proposal, titled 'Considerations and Proposals Encouraging Parents in Sending their Youth to the University of Edinburgh 1709/10', was mainly concerned with improving the supervision of students through a controlled environment consisting of a dormitory ('public boarding house') and selected lodgings. Students would be brought together in a study hall to supervise their reading and study and checked twice a week to see if they remembered what they had learned. Charles Eaton Burch reprinted the document with the strong suggestion that Defoe wrote either all or most of it. Paula Backscheider argued for Defoe's sole authorship of the document but did not include it in her bibliography. Without further evidence, Burch's more modest claim should be allowed to stand. See Burch, 'Benjamin Defoe at Edinburgh University 1710–1711', *Philological Quarterly* 19 (1940), 343–8; and Backscheider, *Daniel Defoe: His Life* (Baltimore: Johns Hopkins University Press, 1989), 309–10.

[33] See Backscheider, 'John Russell to Daniel Defoe'.

[34] Burch, 'Benjamin Defoe at Edinburgh University', 348.

[35] See Russell's letter of 30 Oct. 1712; Backscheider, 'Russell to Defoe', 171.

Defoe settled into his official work of obtaining information about what was happening in Scotland with the ease of someone who had done much the same job before. He wrote to Harley that he was intimately acquainted with two of those elected to office in the Edinburgh city elections. John Brown, chosen Lord Mayor, and John Duncan, elected to the Edinburgh Dean of Guild Court, devoted to mediating disputes among merchants, were both members of the Edinbugh Society for Reformation of Manners. Duncan had actually put forward Defoe as a member. Through such sources of information, Defoe believed he could calm the fears of those who had become unhappy with the Union over the past few years. And he hoped he could aid in the election of moderates. He believed that the view of English affairs presented by a disaffected English Presbyterian, Joshua Olfield, had created fears of the extinction of Scottish rights almost equal to the hysteria present at the time of the Union treaty, and he vowed to work against such forces of disorder.

Defoe's description of the election in Scotland in his letter to Harley of 18 November 1710 is somewhat perplexed. As Defoe argues, Toryism in Scotland was a very different animal from what it was in England. Thus, though the government, through the management of the Earls of Mar, Islay, and Argyll, carried all sixteen of the peers for Harley, the group included a number of out-and-out Jacobites such as Marischal, Ilsyth, Blantire, and Hume. The rumour had been spread that Queen Anne truly wanted the Pretender to be King and was ready to resign the throne in his favour. Indeed, a test had been imposed in choosing the new members of the House of Lords—the willingness to support an impeachment of both Marlborough and Godolphin. The forces of history were moving strongly in favour of the Tories and immoderate measures, and Defoe was clearly having a difficult time staying atuned to what he considered a retrograde movement. Surely, he stated to Harley, the claim that there was actually a list of candidates approved by the Queen had to be an exaggeration. To quiet the apprehensions of his Scottish friends he had been telling them that it was impossible that such a list existed. But he was not absolutely certain that the Duke of Argyll's list of those favoured by the Queen was a complete fabrication. In fact such a secret list did exist.[36] Harley still favoured the Hanoverian succession, but he was not averse to giving some power to known Jacobites. Defoe's letter to Harley of 25 November shows him grasping at straws. Did not the Queen know that almost every

[36] See *Portland Papers*, iv. 626. The Earl of Islay notes how they were able to present a clear choice of candidates by this means, and writes of those 'who received the Queen's commands upon promise of secrecy'.

Episcopalian in Scotland was a Jacobite? Did not the Queen know that to put the military in Scotland under the Tories was equivalent to putting the Pretender in possession of Scotland? And he was worried about being exposed as an agent of the goverment. John Bell, the person through whom Harley distributed his money, had given him only £20 and, according to Defoe, had let everyone in Edinburgh know about that payment.

The Claude Guilot letters from Edinburgh are written in a disguised hand. Defoe was worried enough about Bell to ask for a different conduit for funds, and some of his letters are simply requests for assurance that his previous letters have been received. On 18 December he informed Harley that only the terrible weather was keeping him from returning, and took up the notion of a law that would extend toleration to the Episcopalians in Scotland. Since Defoe believed that almost all of them were Jacobites, he could not but handle Harley's opinion on this issue with caution. He urged that it was not the proper time for such an action. The Scottish Episcopalians, he argued, were not eager for it at this point, and it would inflame the mass of the population. Defoe had been writing on this issue for several years, excoriating an Episcopalian minister named James Green-shields who had opened a meeting-house for Episcopalians in the centre of Edinburgh and had made an ostentatious display of using the English Book of Common Prayer, which had seldom been used in Scotland before. Defoe argued that from the standpoint of the Church of Scotland, Green-shields had not been properly ordained and that the entire controversy had been created with the aim of drawing England's attention to what was supposed to be persecution of their Church; in other words that, like Sacheverell's sermon, an attempt was being made to create a problem where none actually existed.[37] Since he believed in toleration between Protestant Churches, Defoe had no difficulty accepting Harley's notion that it ought to be the same in Scotland as it was in England, but he was much more sensitive to the hysteria that might be caused by what would be surely regarded as an attack on their church by Scottish Presbyterians.[38]

Defoe was not prepared for the coming confrontation with the Scottish Members of Parliament over the next few years—a confrontation that was

[37] See the entire argument of Defoe's *Greenshields Out of Prison and Toleration Settled in Scotland* (London, 1710). The House of Lords ruled in favour of Greenshields, and eventually established toleration of the Episcopalian Church in Scotland.

[38] In his letter to Harley dated 1 Jan. 1711, Defoe made this case: 'I am No biggot, and farther yet from a friend to Coertions of any kind. But Sir, The Liberty Obtained here by Connivance is So great, the people that will Accept of a Tolleration Except without Oaths to the Governmt So few, the Design of Seeking it So Manifestly a plot upon the public peace, and the Consequences apparently so Distracting to the people here, who are Now So happily Easy Under all her Majties Measures, that I Can not but in Duty to her Majtie . . . Offer it to your Consideration whether at Least this may be a Time for it' (H 308).

to result in a Parliamentary vote to annul the Union that failed by only four votes. While Defoe was insisting, 'I Conciev my proper Work here is to Calm and quiet the minds of the people here, Reconcile them to her Majties measures, and keep them Easy' (H 303), he did not see the willingness for resistance soon to be displayed in Parliament. Harley had received such documents as a list of pensions that had been promised to people in Scotland, and was soon to state during a debate that it was absurd for the Scots to consider cancelling the Union when the English had really paid the Scots for their country and provided pensions to the nobility that enabled them to live well for the first time.[39] If that was in a future that Defoe was not prepared to contemplate at this point, he had enough sense of his differences with Harley to practise some deception.

Defoe decided to publish his version of the events leading to the choice of the Members of Parliament in Scotland in the form of a secret history, *Atalantis Major*, purportedly printed in 'Olreeky, the Chief City of the North Part of Atalantis Major'. In his title, Defoe was taking advantage of the popularity of the scandalous *roman à clef* fictions of Mary Delariviere, usually known as Mrs Manley. The scarcely veiled pun-name for Edinburgh (Olreeky) reflects on the inhabitants' custom of emptying human waste into the streets.[40] Although Defoe's overall method is closer to the kind of history he wrote in *The Consolidator* than to Mrs Manley's outrageous tales of sexual liaisons, he was not above learning some of her techniques.[41] He noted that the situation arose because of the removal of two excellent leaders, not for any error in the conduct but rather because the government 'was so much in debt to their Services, that they could not be capable of rewarding it, therefore like the corrupted nature of the whole Race of Man, they hate the Men, as a late Author say, because they hate to be in debt beyond the Power of Payment'.[42] Defoe presents the entire episode of the list which allowed Jacobites into the government as a disaster for the nation. The only optimistic note is the retention of Marlborough as leader of the forces in Flanders, This turns out to be a shock to those who had plotted against him, as well as to those who had thought that the Pretender was about to arrive at any moment.

[39] See *Portland Papers*, iv. 638; and James Mackinnon, *The Union of England and Scotland* (London: Longmans, Green, 1896), 408–35.

[40] In his *Tour* (ii. 300), Defoe commented on the 'stench and nastiness' of Edinburgh, but noted that the causes included a rocky and mountainous situation, incredible crowding, and a shortage of water.

[41] The series of remarkable historical 'characters' owes something to the character sketches used by Manley in her secret histories.

[42] *Atalantis Major* (n.p., 1711 [1710]), 13. Defoe's discourse upon feeling hatred toward those to whom we owe so much that we are incapable of repaying the debt appeared most notably in *The True-Born Englishman*, where he selected it as the particular vice of the English.

Atalantis Major is a cleverly written tract with some excellent assessments of some of the leading players in the politics of contemporary Scotland, but what is even more interesting is the way in which Defoe reported it to Harley. He informed him of the publication of 'Two Vile Ill Natur'd Pamphlets', both of which had fallen into his hands and which he was attempting to stifle before they were printed. The first, he noted, was called 'the Scots atalantis'. He knew the printer of this work and warned him against printing it. He suspected that it was written in England, and detailed some of the objects of satire in the work. Then he came to his own work:

The Other Pamphlet is called *Atalantis Major*; and is a Bitter Invective against the D of Argyle, the E of Mar, and the Election of the Peers. It is Certainly written by Some English man, and I have Some guess at the Man, but dare not be positive. I have hiterto kept this also from the Press, and believ it will be Impossible for them to get it printed here after the measures I have Taken. The Party I Got it of pretends the Coppy Came from England, but I am of Another Opinion. . . . I will Transmit the Coppy by Next post, for I have the Originall in My hand. They Expect I shall Encourage and assist them in the Mannageing it, and Till I can Take a Coppy I shall not Undeciev them. (H 307)

Defoe not only wanted to have the pleasure of having written an attack upon the Jacobite interests in Scotland; he also wanted to take credit for having intercepted the work and for having deceived those on the side of the Whigs or the 'old court' who thought he would help to get it published. In a letter written on New Year's Day he continued this little drama, telling of his endeavours to prevent publication of the work and promising to send it to Harley as soon as possible. Defoe's behaviour may be read wholly in terms of self-interest—of seeming to do a useful task for his employer— but to do so would be to miss the obvious pleasure he took in deceiving Harley. He enjoyed the game he was playing perhaps the more because Harley had the reputation of being remarkably astute in his handling of men and policies, a true disciple of Machiavelli.[43] And most of all he had the pleasure of presenting his own viewpoint on what he considered to be corrupting the election process to eliminate the Whigs. Defoe had apparently resolved that if he was going to be loyal to Harley, it would be in his own way, and that way included publishing whatever he believed whether Harley liked it or not.

At the end of the year he turned out a work called *British Visions*. In Europe, at least, it had been a year of natural disasters. The entry in

---

[43] See the broadside *A New Ballad to the Tune of Fair Rosamond*, where he is identified as Machiavel. In this Whig fantasy, his relative Mrs Masham, is turned out by the Queen and Harley is hanged.

Narcissus Luttrell's *Brief Relation of State Affairs* for 9 December 1710 reports the plague raging in Hungary, Poland, and parts of Germany, an earthquake at Mecca that destroyed the city, and storms at sea. It was a perfect time for the publication of prophecies of doom of the kind that the astrologer Partridge used to issue. Indeed, Defoe assumes the mask of Isaac Bickerstaff for the purpose of his prophecies, putting them in the same humorous category as the prophecies perpetrated by Swift and his fellow wits. Defoe deliberately reminds his reader in the preface of his former role in predicting the death of Partridge. But whereas Partridge's prophecies were as deliberately vague as Swift's prediction of Partridge's demise was intentionally specific, Defoe has his Bickerstaff utilize both of these methods in his predictions, along with the manner of the mad Valentine in Congreve's *Love for Love*— commonplace commentary on what the reader will recognize as events certain or very likely to happen. Bickerstaff claims to possess the prophetic power of 'Second sight' that ensures what he says will come to pass.[44] His prediction of the death of King Philip of Spain is amusing, since it was the death of his rival, King Charles, who was supported by the Allies that undermined the arguments for the Whig's motto, 'No Peace Without Spain'. And the veiled prediction that Marlborough may be killed and that, by his death, the envy of his greatness would finally be stilled is mingled with terrifying warnings of continued wars and plagues:

As the hot Weather comes on, men's Blood grows warm, this subjects and exposes them to fatal mischiefs, the plague of War, and the War of Plague, *Italy* and *Germany* have by this time felt the fury of the Contagion, and dreadful Ravages have been made in all the populous Nations on that side. Shall *Britain* be free! flatter not your selves with Expectations of it, many Plagues visit this Nation and whole Parties of Men suffer the Infection; all sorts of Men shall die, some politickly, some really; the Grave makes no Distinction of *Whigg* or *Tory*, High or Low *Church*. Three bishops go off the Stage first, Dukes, Earls, Barons and Privy-Counsellors follow; a great Rot falls among the Court-Sheep, and the Murrain upon the Stallions of this *Sodomitish* City. The Infection spares none: But alas, for the Sheepherds of our Flocks! they fly and leave their Flocks to be Scattered.[45]

---

[44] Defoe, *British Visions* (London, 1710), 5. Defoe would eventually treat second sight in a number of places, treating prophecy in much the same way. See e.g. his *The Second-Sighted Highlander* (London, 1713). For Defoe, such works involved a fraction of seriousness, since he believed that prophecy of the Bible revealed it as possible; but he also enjoyed revealing the cheats of conjurors. The dominant mode in such works is comic. For a different view, see Rodney Baine, *Defoe and the Supernatural* (Athens: Georgia University Press, 1968).

[45] Ibid. 10.

Only the labouring poor seem to escape this partly real plague. They are blessed with plentiful harvests, and since the plague has reduced the population, the survivors live in abundance. Defoe would eventually develop these ideas a little over a decade later in his *Journal of the Plague Year*, ranging from the image of the ministers leaving their congregations to the Malthusian view of war, plague, and population. But the seed of that brilliant work is visible in this partly playful, partly serious pamphlet. As for the war-weariness demonstrated throughout, Defoe shared this with almost everyone in Great Britain after the failure of negotiations in 1709 and 1710. It was not peace but the nature of the peace treaty that was already the main point of contention.

IV

Defoe was prevented from leaving Scotland by an incredible period of bad weather that lasted almost ten weeks. He had complained of a shortage of funds and had been issued £50 on 27 December 1710, a sum sufficient to pay his debts and to make his stay more pleasant. Defoe wrote to Harley that while he was waiting, he had succeeded in defusing some explosive suggestions about the question of toleration at the meeting of the Presbyterian ministers, the Commission of the General Assembly. Healey suggests that Defoe may even have been sent to London by the group to act as a London correspondent. At any rate, he was finally back in London seeing Harley in person, and on 13 Feburary 1711 he listed the current subjects on which he had some ideas—subjects involving both Scotland and England. Among the latter were problems of trade with France, the African Company, and the Post Office. As was common with letters in which he held out the possiblity of new ideas, Defoe added a plea for additional funds, arguing that he had expended all that had been given on his activities for Harley and on his journey. He noted that he did this 'in spight of Blushes', though one would have thought that whatever embarrassment he might have felt about such requests had vanished long since.[46]

Harley apparently liked to have Defoe's ideas on subjects even when he did not take his advice. He asked Defoe to present a list of those who might serve as Queen Anne's Commissioner to the General Assembly of Ministers. Defoe offered to make his judgement based on a consideration of

[46] This request for funds was successful, and Harley apparently paid Defoe out of his own pocket rather than from the secret service funds. See H, 315. In this letter he stated that Harley's generosity had actually succeeded in 'Preventing My Blushes'.

what might be wanted by the present goverment in England and what would be acceptable to the ministers in Scotland. Harley gave Defoe a number of names, including the person who was eventually appointed, William Johnstone, first Marquis of Annandale. Defoe thought that he would command no confidence and rejected him, as he did William Kerr, second Marquess of Lothian, because he was a libertine. Among those Defoe recommended were James Carmichael, second Earl of Hyndford, for whom he had purchased horses under commission, and David Erskine, first Earl of Buchan, who learned of Defoe's recommendation and was pleased by it. A correspondence commenced, and when Erskine came to know Defoe's son-in-law, he asked him to give his regards to Defoe as a person he knew and respected. When Defoe was vilified as a hireling scribbler over the next few years, he could always know that he continued to be appreciated in some quarters.

At the beginning of 1711, then, Defoe was offering to be as serviceable as he could be to Harley on problems in Scotland and England while attempting to balance his writing along the lines of 'one for them and one for me'. He had yet to arrive at the position of writing a work for Harley which was entirely against his principles. *Rogues on Both Sides* was certainly written against the Whigs and in favour of what he described as the 'Modern Tory' position, but for the most part Defoe attempted to strike a stance between parties, falling back upon Halifax's concept of the 'Trimmer', who attempts to achieve a middle position or 'Balance' between parties. As has been seen, in the *Review*, Defoe was able to argue that the Tories were forced to act according to Whig principles. In treating the subject of credit in the *Review*, he could claim that credit was not a party question but a matter of national concern, and that by attacking the Whigs for undermining credit he was rising above party concerns. 'If this be to serve *Tories*,' he wrote, 'I must serve *Tories*; I'll rather Sacrifize my private Peace to a *Tory Party*, than Sacrifize a Nation's Bread to Misery, and a Nation's Poor to Famine and Distress.'[47]

Under the cover of an anonymous pamphlet, he was able to go further along these lines, and whereas the theme of his *Supplement to Faults on Both Sides* was essentially conciliatory, this new pamphlet accused both sides, but particularly the Whigs, of misbehaving. 'I confess,' he wrote, 'for my own Part, I was always so unfortunate as not to be able to continue long of any Part, that was uppermost; because both *Whig* and *Tory* have still been Guilty of Things complain'd of in each other.'[48] He urged his readers to distinguish between 'Men and Things', between present reality and the

[47] *Review*, vii. 471. See also 457–9.   [48] *Rogues on Both Sides* (London, 1711), 6.

notions surrounding a word like 'Whig', for if the old connotation had involved concepts of liberty, the 'Modern Whig' was chiefly defined in the actions of members of the Bank to threaten the ruin of the national credit if the Whigs were not kept in power. As for the 'Old Tory', he was chiefly distinguished by his subservience to James II and his willingness to enslave the nation.

Defoe then proceeded to define the qualities of a good political leader as possessing 'CAPACITY, INTEGRITY, COURAGE, AND APPLICA-TION', and while he does not state that Harley is the perfect embodiment of such qualities, what he describes under the heading of 'CAPACITY'— '*Justness* and *Firmness of Wit* or *Genius; Solidity* of *Judgment*; a moderate Degree of *Learning*; a general Knowledge of History . . . *Constancy*, *Deliberation*, and *Modesty*: It absolutely excludes *Pride*'[49]—was clearly intended to describe the image of himself that Harley wanted projected. Defoe was reflecting the new rancour between the parties, for while a moderate Whig such as Shrewsbury continued in the government, Robert Walpole, who had refused to cooperate with Harley, was dismissed from his post as Treasurer of the Navy in January and promptly accused of having appropriated funds. Although he defended himself ably at the time, a year later he lost his seat in Parliament and was imprisoned in the Tower for six months.[50]

Rogues on Both Sides included a somewhat negative view of the Whigs' support for the army, but Defoe attempted to make up for this in his *A Short Narrative of the Life and Actions of His Grace John D. of Marlborough*. If the former pamphlet was purportedly the work of an anonymous Trimmer, the latter was supposed to have been written 'By an Old Officer in the Army'. Published on 20 February 1711, the work appeared when Marl-borough and the army were under attack for Stanhope's defeat in Spain at Brihuega on 9 December 1710. Although Marlborough had been persuaded by Harley to fight one last campaign, St John was in the process of mount-ing a continual attack against a man he had formerly admired to the extent of urging Oxford's Christ Church College to set up a statue of the general.[51] Defoe never lost that admiration. For him, Marlborough was a true hero, of the stamp of Gustavus Adolphus and William III. They were unique and irreplaceable: 'A Finish'd hero does not grow up every Day, they are Scarce Plants and do not thrive in every Soil; He may be easily

[49] Ibid. 30.
[50] Holmes, *Politics in the Age of Anne*, 115, 140.
[51] Even Swift, whose contempt for Marlborough knew no bounds, wrote to Stella, 'I think our friends press a little too hard on the duke of Marlborough.' *Journal to Stella*, ed. Harold Williams (2 vols., Oxford: Clarendon Press, 1948) i. 159. See also Trevelyan, *England under Queen Anne*, iii. 115.

lost, but then that Loss cannot easily be repair'd; therefore there is great Reason to Value and Esteem him.'[52] In addition to picturing Marlborough and the Duchess in this favourable light, Defoe also attempted to counter the negative image that Tory ideology projected of the common soldier by a vivid presentation of the aura of death and danger that soldiers had to face. In his picture of the 'intolerable Marches, men and Horses dying and dead together' and the 'Stinks of Mortality', he tried to show what the experience of war was like.[53] Defoe was clearly remembering those days of marching in the rain with Monmouth in this moving passage. He was not ready to give up on his great ideals just yet.

Defoe's attempt at balancing his party commitments reached a crisis on 1 March 1711, when the House of Lords repealed the decision against Greenshields and paved the way for the repeal of the Toleration Act that, in Defoe's mind had been part of the Treaty of Union. He had written only a few months before that such an action would be impossible, since

There are Things which are stipulated expressly by the Treaty, not to be left, no, not to the Parliament of *Britain to alter*; such as the Church of *Scotland* in particular, and the Church of *England*; in both which, it is expressly agreed, That the Worship, Discipline, and Government of either Churches, shall *be and remain*, to the respective Subjects, *without any Alteration*; mark that Word ANY, whether by *Parliament* or otherwise, *to all succeeding Generations*.[54]

He wrote to Harley in genuine distress the next day. What he had stated in the *Review* had been true enough. 'I . . . Never Thought the affair Could ha' been Carried This Length—Especially considering what Assurances were given by her Majties Express Direction at the Time of the Union' (H 318). The Treaty would probably never have been approved, he argued, if he and others had not worked on its behalf and promised that the agreements contained in it were inviolable. The best thing to do, Defoe advised, was to maintain that the actions of the House of Lords did not have the approval of the Queen, who would do everything to see that the rights of the Church of Scotland would be upheld.[55]

[52] *A Short Narrative of the Life and Actions of His Grace John, D. of Marlborough* (London, 1711), 45.
[53] Ibid. 41.
[54] *Review*, vii. 458.
[55] Defoe produced at least one pamphlet in an attempt to raise the spirits of the Scottish Presbyterians, *A Seasonable Caution to the General Assembly in a Letter from a Member of Parliament of North-Britain to a Minister in Scotland* (Edinburgh, 1711). Moore suggests that it was probably published in Edinburgh, and it was certainly intended to fulfil what he told Harley (H 318–19) would be necessary in the way of calming the fears of the ministers. Defoe had argued during the Union controversy that the Treaty was an established part of the constitution, impossible to change. Now, as he notes, one Scottish peer had said that Parliament could do what it wished. In response, Defoe noted that Queen Anne was the 'Protector, and Royal Preserver' (18) of the Church of Scotland and would see to its continued welfare, and that as long as the Church continued to be as it had been, 'Famous for the most undivided Church in the World' (27), the

He had agreed to act as the representative of the Scottish Presbyterian ministers in London; therefore, he reasoned to Harley, it would be better if he remained in the capital, rather than return to Scotland and open up the possibility of replacing him. Meanwhile he would write to his correspondents about the Queen's displeasure so that 'If possible The Antidote may Spread as far as The Poison, and as fast' (H 320). Defoe thought that the news would result in tumults throughout Scotland, though he knew nothing could be done about the situtation: 'But it is Not a Time to look back. The business is how to prevent the Mischief That will Other Wise Follow' (H 318). This was the way Defoe was to proceed during the coming years. However much he may have been motivated by self-interest, he had also made his decision to remain within the government structure because he conceived that he could do more good for what he believed in by working within than by attacking from the outside. From some standpoints this was true. The Tories had all the power to themselves, and until they could be dislodged, working with Harley might be the most effective method of exerting some control. A writer such as Steele continued writing for the Whigs and against the government, but unlike Defoe, he had various protectors. Defoe needed all the influence he could find. Nevertheless it was the wrong decision. The tide was running against Harley and against moderation, and Defoe had to participate in supporting a peace he detested, defending a treaty in which he did not believe, attacking a general he admired to the point of hero-worship, and in seeing almost everything promised to Scotland—everything he had promised the Scots—withdrawn, and punitive measures taken against that nation. In some ways, particularly from the standpoint of his sense of his own integrity, the next few years would prove more trying than imprisonment and the pillory.

activities of its enemies would pass the way the enthusiasm for Sacheverell had passed in England. The prediction, however, that the ruling on Greenshields would not change the status of the Episcopalian ministers and their meeting-houses was one that Defoe knew to be false when he wrote it. The pamphlet was mainly an exercise in pouring oil upon troubled waters.

17

These Dangerous Times:
Or Wild Doings in This World[1]

Having chosen to retain his identity as a Whig while accepting the policies of what was looking more like a Tory government with each passing day, Defoe was much like the referee who tries to separate two brawlers: he managed to be hit by both of them. And this was not merely with words. He reported being accosted by men disguised as officers who pretended to have orders (but no warrant) to arrest him, 'and whether *to Murther*, or deliver me up to them *that should*, is like, for want of Justice, to remain a Secret'.[2] A Tory who threw a bottle at Defoe was arrested, but immediately released when the Justice discovered who the target was. A Whig refused to unload his goods on discovering who their owner was. His brother-in-law fought a duel over an insult offered about him. These were hardly the only incidents of this kind; Defoe's problems echoed the divisions in society. A murderous duel between Hamilton and Mohun was related to party differences. And Harley was fortunate to survive his wounds from a knife thrust at his body by Antoine de Guiscard, a French spy, on 8 March 1711. If, as some believe, violence is infectious as well as capable of releasing uncontrolled emotions, at this time it had the appearance of becoming epidemic. But the threat of physical harm was probably less real than the outpouring of verbal violence from the press. The satiric rhetoric of Jonathan Swift was honed to razor sharpness during these years, and his attacks wounded Defoe more deeply than most. But the effect of such attacks had to be blunted by their very number. Somehow Defoe, though embittered and unhappy, gradually managed to slip into the role of Tory propagandist, arguing as well as he could for what he did not believe while occasionally throwing himself into anonymous pamphlets that actually expressed his ideas.

[1] The title of this chapter is drawn from two quotations appearing in *Review*, vii. 489, 497.
[2] Ibid. 490.

I

On 8 February 1711, Swift threw out the line 'party carries everything' in his letter to Stella. He had complained to her of being ignored by his former Whig friends, Steele, Somers, and even Addison. If it was a difficult time for Swift and Defoe, the same was true for Harley. He had tried to steer between violent extremes, but found that his friend and Secretary of State, St John, had joined the violent wing of the Tories, the October Club; after the beginning of that month, Harley never again entered St John's house. Harley had not yet come to the point of playing the game of party politics required by the times. The end of that game was winning at all costs, including any sacrifice of principle that might be necessary. Defoe too had to learn how to survive in this maelstrom of politics. He had mastered the use of the press, overwhelming his opponents through the variety of his arguments, but now he had to learn the lesson of the paid journalist. If he were to survive and exert a certain amount of power, he was going to have to do his best for his employers in their time and do the best for himself in his own.

The crucial moment came with the attempted assassination of Harley by Guiscard. In pursuit of his duty, the Chancellor of the Exchequer was wounded by a French spy, and all of the concern about Louis XIV's attempts to assassinate William III, about French perfidy, and about the safety of Queen Anne created an outpouring of sympathy for Harley that restored his power, brought him the post of Lord Treasurer, which had remained vacant after Godolphin's resignation, and raised him to the peerage as Earl of Oxford and Mortimer. St John, whose behaviour during the assassination attempt was equivocal, received a setback in his pursuit of power that was to prove fatal to his career. The possibility that Guiscard had intended to poison the Queen gave a new strength to her friend Harley and to his group of court Tories and court Whigs. He was greeted with a congratulatory speech from the Speaker of the House of Commons when he returned on 28 April 1711, and the bickering that had prevailed during his absence made him seem indispensable.[3] And Defoe, who at this point would hardly have been able to accommodate himself to St John and the October Club, found that a reinvigorated Harley still had need of his services despite the rise of Swift as the chief Tory propagandist.

---

[3] In his broadside *Captain Tom's Remembrance to His Old Friends the Mobb of London*, written during the weeks following Guiscard's attempt on Harley's life, Defoe has Captain Tom, the leader of the London mob, congratulate Harley on his recovery and signal a change in the mob from concern for Sacheverell and the High Church to true English worries about Jacobitism and the danger to the Protestant Succession.

Renewed contact came after a period during which it appears that some of his suggestions were rejected. He proposed a series of pamphlets to the Scots in the manner of his early series on the Union, and he suggested that Whig attacks upon Harley's proposed lottery might prove harmful enough to require an answer. But Harley seems to have had little interest in Scottish sensibilities on the issue of Greenshields and toleration, and the lottery turned out to be enormously successful and in no need of help from Defoe.

On 25 April Defoe wrote a letter to Harley congratulating him on his recovery. The opening line, 'Tho I am comforted with the Sight of your Personall Safety, which No Man has More Reason to be Thankfull for Than my Self' (H 326), suggests that Defoe had visited Harley in the interval between the stabbing and the letter. Nevertheless, Defoe took the occasion to see Harley's preservation as a sign that God had had a hand in it and that the reason for his recovery would lie in the future good he would do for his country:

May The Same hand Still Guard you, The Same Goodness protect you. May you be filled with Wisdome and Counsell For the Great Things Heaven has Reserv'd you for, and as I Doubt Not your Eyes are up to him who has bid us if We want wisdome to ask it of him; So I am Perswaded he has Not placed The Weight of This Great Nations affaires on your Shoulders, and Thus Miraculously Preserv'd your life, But he will (for his Works like himself are all Perfect) He Will Compleat what he has Purposed to Do For us, by your hand; to his Own Glory and The Great Honour of The Instrumt also—and Great is your happyness That They are Joyn'd to gether. (H 327)

Though a cynical reading of Defoe's feelings of relief at Harley's recovery might centre on the Lord Chancellor as his continuing source of funds, Defoe rightly understood that, with the Whigs willing to do almost anything to get back into power and the Tories likely to be swallowed up by the machinations of the October Club, Harley was the surest means through which the Protestant Succession would be assured. That would remain the bottom line for Defoe. He was ready to write in defence of anything Harley wanted, provided that the heir of the House of Hanover would be sitting on the throne after the death of Queen Anne. Harley certainly had a serious, deeply religious side that could appreciate Defoe's pieties, while he was also able to spend an evening in light conversation and drinking with Swift. Both were writing for Harley at this time, but the difference between Harley's relationship with the two is not entirely encompassed in the image of Swift entering by the front door and Defoe by the back,[4] or by the fact that Swift was insulted by a gift of £50 that Harley sent him whereas Defoe was happy to receive the reward for his labours. Swift represented a lighter, more social type of existence, and his writing displayed a masterful use of rhetoric in the Tory cause. Defoe too had conversation as his social ideal, and lacked neither wit nor a kind of serious play in his writings, but it would be difficult to imagine him trivializing the deaths of children as Swift did in his *Journal to Stella*. Behind Defoe's most humorous work was always a profound sense of the seriousness of existence, whether in personal relationships or in a political cause. Swift was genuinely distressed by the stabbing of Harley, but, at least in his correspondence with Stella, the event does not lead him to contemplate the meaning of life or whether the event might lead Harley to some significant reconsideration of how he should conduct himself and the politics of the nation. Defoe and Swift had different ways of looking at the world, and Harley had room for both in his psychological makeup.

Defoe's *A Spectator's Address to the Whigs, on the Occasion of the Stabbing of Mr. Harley*, published on 17 March 1711, takes advantage of the concept of the seemingly unbiased viewer of mankind promulgated by the journal of that name. The *Spectator* of Addison and Steele had started publication on the first day of that same month. But Defoe used the term to reflect upon the actions of the Whigs toward Harley's ministry. That the French seemed to have singled him out for assassination suggests that just because he might favour a good peace with France did not mean he was opposed to the best interests of Britain. Harley, he argued, was the only person to restrain the 'Madness and Extravagencies of the State Lunatics of the Nation'. Defoe then proceeded to attack the former Whig 'Management' for running the nation into debt, for losing Spain, and for not knowing how to make peace. Through his prudence, management, and conduct, Harley had preserved all sections of the nation from the Churchmen to the Dissenters, and through his 'Vertue' he had defeated the forces of France and Popery. Even the Whigs should have been able to realize the sacrifice he had made and should have desisted in their attacks upon his measures.[5]

The view of Defoe's 'Spectator' was anything but distanced and

---

[4] James Sutherland, *Defoe*, 2nd edn. (London: Methuen, 1950), 185, suggested this image partly as an explanation of why the two probably never met. It is suggestive of the office of a modern psychiatrist, where the incoming and outgoing patients do not usually see each other. London was a very small place, and both shared Morphew as a publisher. The likelihood is that, even if Harley kept them separate, they knew each other at least by sight. Defoe considered Swift a member of the High Church and an enemy of the Dissenters. Defoe was also one of Swift's early targets, and took mortal offence at Swift's attacks on his learning and intelligence. He accused Swift of lacking manners as well as real learning in matters of economics, and boasted of his own knowledge of five langauges, mathematics, logic, geography, and astronomy. See *Review* vii. 449–51.   [5] Defoe, *A Spectator's Address* ([London] 1711).

objective, but he used a somewhat similar technique in his *Eleven Opinions about Mr. H[arle]y*. To avoid the effect of a single adulatory angle of vision, Defoe broke up his work into what turned out to be only seven viewpoints, but all the 'opinions' added up to a Harley whose moderation protected the nation from the extremes of politics.[6] Putting forward an ecumenical view of Christianity, Defoe attacked contentions over religion and all the petty squabbling over politics. The Queen, the Dissenters, the allies, all admired Harley, while only the Whigs, members of the former ministry, the October Club, and the Jacobites were against him. Defoe accomplished almost the same effect in the two parts of his *Secret History of the October Club*. In these pamphlets he gave a somewhat jaundiced history of the Whigs, distinguishing among the Old Whigs, Modern Whigs, and Court Whigs and the complexities of the Whig Party in Scotland, represented for the most part by the Squadrone. He accused some of those in power of pursuing their interests to the extent of allowing Jacobites into positions of influence in order to sustain their own position. The ideal, Defoe states, was 'to have continued the management of Affairs in the hands of the Disinterested Honest Men of both sides, without respect to *Whig* or *Tory*', but the Whigs did not understand this. He then enunciated the Harleian principle 'That the Government should be of no Party'. If Harley seemed to be leaning toward one side or another, that was merely temporary.[7] Harley was made Lord Oxford and Earl Mortimer on 23 May and Lord High Treasurer six days later. When Defoe had predicted, on Harley's leaving office in 1708, that he would yet triumph over his enemies and rise to new eminence, he was right. The man whom he had advised on the role of prime minister was that in all but name.

Defoe argued, as he had before, that in governing the country the Tories had to behave as Whigs, though the list of the policies that supposedly had to be followed is interesting from the standpoint of what was eventually to be reversed. At this point, however, Defoe could confidently enumerate the continuance of policies:

[6] John Chamberlain wrote to Harley on 29 May 1711 to praise this 'ingenious pamphlet'. He thought that Swift was the likely author. See *Portland Papers*, iv. 697.

[7] Daniel Defoe, *The Secret History of the October Club* (London, 1711), i. 26 and 29. See also the preface to vol. vii of the *Review*, where he enunciated the same principle: 'the Ministry, the Government is a party by itself, and ought in matters of Parties, to be Independant; when they cease to be so, they set the Shoe upon the head, they set the nation with the bottom upward, and must expect to be Mob-ridden, till they cease to be a Party at all, but become Slaves to the Party they espouse, and fall under the Party they oppose: and this is what has Ruin'd all the Ministries that have been these last 20 Years' (*Review*, vii. sig. A4). Curiously enough, however, he ended his preface by criticizing the 'Party that have so long regretted that Old Branch of *English* Liberty, Freedom of Speech'. This criticism of a proposed tax on newspapers is directed at the Tories. It might be said that Defoe believed in governing above parties provided the governor behaved like a Whig.

For Example, They no sooner came to Administer the Publick Affairs, but they kept on foot the same Alliances, engag'd in the same War, resolved upon the same foot of Peace without abatements, made the same Capitulations, paid the same Subsidies, declared their Resolution to stand to the same Succession of the Crown, allow'd to the Dissenters the same Tolleration, Raised Money by the same Methods, and Lay'd Taxes and Funds of the same kind as the old Ministry had done before them.[8]

Defoe then proceeded to show, in this rewriting of history, that almost everyone saw that no real change was intended and that it was simply a matter of those who were formerly on the outside coming into power. He then dramatized the disappointment of the Jacobite members of the October Club in one of his extraordinarily effective dialogues (here between Sir Thomas and Sir John), expressing their frustration. This section functions as a dramatic scene, and Defoe was to get better and better at this kind of prose dialogue. Nevertheless it is significant that he mastered it as political dialogue before he turned to his moral conduct books, where it was given a religious turn. Defoe continued the same techniques in the second volume, which came out two months later in June, but here his main purpose was to throw the blame for the attacks upon the Tories and Jacobites. It is they who were against all credit, against all taxes; it is for them that Swift conducted his *Examiner* with its 'unintelligible Jingle, fine-spun Emptiness, and long winded Repetition, without truth, without evidence, and without meaning'.[9] In Defoe's fictive depiction of the October Club, its members are shown as voting pensions for both Swift and the author of the *Post Boy*, along with promises of preferment whenever the Pretender set up his court in Great Britain. Defoe ended this second part with what appears to be one of his first lampoons in almost a decade, but very much in the manner of his attacks upon Parliament. He bid the October Club dissolve itself and go home:

> Leave your Mobs and your Riot
> Go home and be quiet
> For your Party's grow quite out of Fashion;
> First we us'd you like Tools,
> Now Cashire you like Fools,
> And your P[iss]t upon by all the Nation.[10]

Whether Defoe actually believed what he wrote is hard to say. St John was already deeply involved with the October Club and its policies, and the Swift–Manley *Examiner* advanced a view of government that was

---

[8] *Secret ... Club,* i. 52.   [9] Ibid. ii. 27.   [10] Ibid. ii. 93.

distinctly Tory. Harley doubtless appreciated Defoe's political angle of vision, for he found himself fighting a desperate battle against a militant Tory right wing. As he gradually yielded to these intransigent Tories on a variety of issues, having Defoe around to argue that his policies were ever those of a true moderate must have been invaluable.

How many of Defoe's readers would have been convinced by his explanation of historical change as more of a conjuror's trick managed by leaders of the various parties out of power than a real change in policy would be difficult to determine. Over the next few years, he would have to defend the government's insistence upon signing a peace treaty with France (a treaty that showed little gain for a decade of war) whether her allies liked it or not; the establishment of a kind of rival to the Whiggish Bank in the form of the South Sea Company; the passage of a Toleration Act for Scotland which gave new status to the Episcopalians and which seemed, in Defoe's eyes, a violation of the Union Treaty; and a Commercial Treaty with France that would have permitted French wines to enter England with little or no duty. He would even have to try to make palatable to the Dissenters the passage of an Act against Occasional Conformity as well as an Act preventing Dissenters from educating their children according to their deeply held beliefs. The ultimate difficulty of taking such positions in the face of the government's dramatic changes in policy was reflected in the evident loss of popularity sustained by the *Review* over the next few years. But Defoe continued his basic pattern of argument in his pamphlets until the middle of May 1712, when he published his lengthy *Present State of the Parties in Great Britain*. Before that work appeared, he had published works with titles indicative of the rising party strife in Britain: *Reasons Why a Party among Us, and also among the Confederates Are Obstinately Bent against a Treaty of Peace with the French at this Time*, *An Essay on the History of Parties*, and *The Conduct of Parties in England*. These works, along with a rash of other pamphlets, give us some opportunity to see where Defoe actually stood on a variety of issues as events caused him to compromise and sometimes forced him into opposition.

The areas of concern were: the peace with France, the new attacks upon the Dissenters in the form of a bill forbidding Occasional Conformity, apparent violations of the Union Treaty by Parliament, and the South Sea Company. What a relief it must have been for him to find some uncomplicated issues to write about during 1711 and 1712. Whenever Jacobitism came into sight, he could summon his indignation effectively enough. Thus, during the summer months of 1711, when the Faculty of Advocates at Edinburgh were presented with a medal by the Duchess of Gordon containing a half-hidden allusion to the return of the Pretender and initially accepted it, Defoe was quick to point out their mistake.[11] And when a Mr James Dundas made a speech in favour of the son of James II, he wrote a direct attack upon those involved and upon Dundas, who had proposed that another medal be struck of William III with a devil at his ear.[12] Then he followed this with a piece in Scottish accent, *A Speech for Mr. D[unda]se the Younger of Arnistown*, in which Dundas confesses that he got his ideas from the addresses to the Queen after the Sacheverell affair. These told him that the rights of the Queen were purely hereditary:

I might safely with the Whigs have believ'd the Lawfulness of Resistance in Cases of outter Necessity; that the Subversion of our Constitution by King *James* was sik a Case, and it was therfore lawful to resist him; that it will be alike lawful to resist ony of our footer Princes gif ever the sam Breeches of the Constitution sou'd be repeeted; that in sik Cases it wad be lawful for the Estates to make a new Settlement of the Crown, and aw the People wad be bund to conform to the Terms of this new Settlement. Aw this I might have affirm'd to be the Case of the Revolution, without contenancing the least Resistance against the Q. wha they say has sa gloriously restor'd and preserv'd our maist excellent Constitution.[13]

He also found the keel men of Newcastle upon Tyne in trouble once more from the greed of those controlling the coal industry, this time over a hospital they had funded themselves and which the owners were trying to control. He wrote on this in pamphlets and in the *Review* and lobbied Harley and the House of Commons in their cause.[14] This was one battle from which he emerged with a clear victory, the Commons acting in favour of the workers. And he took time to defend the Royal African Company as a necessary monopoly for trading to countries where forts were necessary to protect the traders from barbaric tribes. However uncomplicated such writing was, it should be noted that even in this work, Defoe complained

[11] See H 350–2. For a description of the medal, see the *Review* for 31 July 1711. Sir David Dalrymple was soon dismissed for his failure to handle both the medal and Dundas in a proper fashion.

[12] *The Scotch Medal Decipher'd, and the New Hereditary-Right Men Display'd* (London, 1711), 4. Defoe took up the notion of a comparison between Cromwell's usurpation and that planned by the Pretender, remarking that whereas the Pretender operated by fraud, Cromwell used open force, 'which is the more honourable of the two because we have a Chance to defend our Purse from a Highway-Man, which we cannot so easily do from a Pick-pocket or Night-strouler, that does his Work in the dark' (12).

[13] *A Speech for Mr. D[unda]se the Younger of Arnistown* (London, 1711), 12–13. Defoe was intrigued by matters of language, and was to comment on accents in his *Tour*. He probably had to restrain himself from imitating the Scots accent more often than he actually did. He was likely torn between his deep respect for the Scots and his love of imitation and comedy.

[14] See two folio half-sheets, *The Case of the Poor Skippers and Keel-Men of Newcastle* ([London, 1712]) and *A Farther Case Relating to the Poor Keel-Men of Newcastle* ([London, 1712]); *Review* for 12, 14, and 17 Feb. 1712. See also his letter to Harley for 19 June 1711 and the note (H 332).

about the difficulties of writing and living in an age in which everything
was judged by 'Parties . . . or Interests'.[15] But when it came to parties,
nothing caused Defoe more agony than Harley's attempt to make peace
with France.

II

The preliminary agreement to what was to be the Treaty of Utrecht was
not to be signed until 27 September 1711, and the final treaty on 31 March
1713, but Harley started the peace process moving before the end of 1710
after the battle of Brihuega on 9 December seemed to doom the chance of
winning Spain. The years between the preliminary agreements arranged
by Mesnager and Torcy, the final treaty, and the aftermath involving an
attempt to arrange a Commercial Treaty with France saw some of the most
violent factional disagreements ever experienced in England. Images of
women in the *Spectator* wearing what were called 'patches' on their faces to
indicate their party preference tried to laugh people out of their partisanship, but the nation had indeed become a 'Divided Society'; and entertained as a growing body of readers were by Addison and Steele's journal,
they were unwilling to abandon their partisanship. Defoe described it this
way:

Unhappy Nation! What End can these Things lead us to? Not a Publick Society,
not a Coffee-house, not a Meeting of Friends, not a Visit; but like *Jehu* to *Jezabel,
who is on my Side?* Who? Who is for Peace? Who is for carrying on the War?
Society is converted into Cabal, all Publick Meetings appear sorted into Committees, or bandyed into Sides as their Notions of Peace or War encline them.[16]

Almost everyone in England expected a peace in 1709, and only article 27
of what was called the Treaty of Gertruydenburgh, with its insistence that
Louis XIV wage war against his own grandson, prevented its achievement
early in 1710. It is unlikely that Defoe would have been opposed to an
advantageous peace. On the other hand, he admired Marlborough and
longed for the military defeat of the king who had invaded nations without
warning, aided the Turks, persecuted the Huguenots, and ravaged
southern Germany. His brief experience of warfare with Monmouth had
left him something of an armchair strategist, and his faith in Marlborough

---

[15] *An Essay upon the Trade to Africa* (London, 1711), 4. Defoe was not entirely without 'Interests' in this
matter himself, since he occasionally held stock in the Royal African Company.
[16] *An Essay at a Plain Exposition of that Difficult Phrase of a Good Peace* (London, 1711), 7.

and William III was much like that of his fictional contemporary, Laurence Sterne's Uncle Toby. Defoe would have preferred a clear victory over Louis XIV, but he was willing to accept less. On the other hand, had he known during the summer of 1711 that he would be asked to defend a peace that involved the firing of Marlborough, the abandonment of Britain's allies, and the refusal of the army to fight, he might have decided to abandon Harley and the government and gone into opposition. But he was led gradually to defend all of the government's actions. At the beginning, he thought that his job was to provide what would seem a good Whig argument for peace. By the end, though he never ran out of arguments, he seems to have lost every principle except defending what must have seemed to him the indefensible actions of his government.

He began his *Review* of 27 February 1711 with the ringing statement: 'I am for opening a Trade with France.'[17] What Defoe meant by this, as his discussions proceeded over the next months, was not a free exchange of goods, but a trade that would keep the duties on French wines so high that there would be no possibility of their being imported at a price that would allow any but the very wealthy to buy them. What he wanted, then, as his opening argument to the possibility of a peace, was an arrangement whereby France would be open to English manufactures, but Britain would be able to exclude anything that would interfere with her own manufactures, and to place so high a tariff on French luxury products such as wine that they would be effectively excluded as well:

Whoever thinks, that by opening the *French* Trade, I should mean bringing us back to Trade with *France* upon the same Terms that we Traded with them in 76, and to 86, from the sham Prohibition mention'd before, to the real one; that we should come to Trade with them 850000 *l. per Ann.* to our Loss, must think me as Mad as I think him for suggesting it.[18]

He would prove, he maintained, that his notion of trade to France would produce £600,000 profit a year. Defoe must have known that a peace was in process, but at this point his argument was to follow the pattern of Holland, which did not stop trading with its enemy, France, during hostilities. That Defoe should suddenly be a strong advocate for commercial relations with France is more than suspicious. This was a Tory project which was to find its fulfilment in the attempt at passing a Commercial Treaty as part of the peace package and one of St John's favourite schemes.

Defoe's earliest pamphlets strongly supporting peace did not come out

[17] Defoe was supporting a bill in the House of Commons on this matter. See *Review*, 15 Mar. 1711. The notion of trade to France was probably more a product of St John's mind than of Harley's.
[18] Ibid. vii. 574.

until after the preliminary agreement had been signed, though the death of Emperor Joseph of Austria on 17 April 1711 caused him to wonder about the wisdom of giving Spain to the new Emperor.[19] In a pamphlet published on 2 May 1711, *The Succession of Spain Consider'd*, he had taken note of the death of the Emperor and the problems this event would entail as far as 'THE BALANCE OF EUROPE' or European power was concerned. Charles III of Spain, now Charles VI of Austria, might grow so powerful as the head of both the Empire and Spain, Defoe argued, that he might be able to conquer all of Italy with no difficulty at all. Defoe's solution at this time was the juggling of the map of Europe to create a powerful Lombardy under the Duke of Savoy,[20] with the Spanish Netherlands going to Prince Eugene. But as of 1 September 1711, he was unwilling to entertain the possibility of Spain being left in the hands of Philip and the Bourbons. And when, after Tory policy became clearer, he was challenged on this issue, he equivocated. We have to say first 'what we understand by the Word *Spain*,'[21] he wrote to one of his detractors, and he soon fell back on emphasizing the impossibility of permitting the Emperor of Austria and the Holy Roman Empire to control so much land and power. By the *Review* of 22 November, the Austrians were to be seen as much more dangerous than the French. And by the next number, seeming to forget Louis XIV's treatment of the Huguenots, he stressed the cruelty of the Emperor to Protestants and the weakness of France after so many years of war. When challenged on his contradictions in attacks by the Tory *Post Boy* and the Whig *Observator*, he resorted to bluff and bluster. And then, with some help from Boileau's ninth 'Satire', he engaged in a dialogue with himself, wondering why he worried so much about his critics. He did this by a running prose commentary—a mixture of loose translation and extrapolation—mocking his own involvement in journalism and acknowledging that much of his work, though not bad, was also not always as polished as the *Spectator*, the brilliant new journal of Addison and Steele. A healthy exercise in self-

---

[19] Defoe's reaction was not very different from that of the Duke of Marlborough, who wrote to Godolphin, on hearing the news, that it would cause some adjustment in any treaty of peace. See *The Marlborough–Godolphin Correspondence* (3 vols., Oxford: Clarendon Press, 1975), iii. 1665–6.

[20] Trevelyan writes that at a crucial point in the treaty negotiations, St John made a proposal to redraw the map of Europe: 'With lightning rapidity he made a new and ingenious proposal. As an alternative to the renunciation of the reversion of the French Crown by Philip, let him, wrote Bolingbroke, retain his rights thereto, on condition that he at once hands over Spain and the Indies to the Duke of Savoy. In compensation, he is himself to become ruler of the Duke's territories of Savoy-Piedmont, together with Montferrat, Mantua and Sicily. If and when Philip becomes King of France, these North Italian territories are to be added to the French dominions, but Sicily is to pass to Austria.' G. M. Trevelyan, *England under Queen Anne* (3 vols., London: Longmans, Green, 1930–4), iii. 214. He did this without any consultation with Britain's allies, and one wonders if he had some dim memory of Defoe's somewhat similar proposal.

[21] *Review*, viii. 351.

mockery, it probably kept him from writing a dangerous and savage reply to his enemies.[22] Abel Roper, the author of the *Post Boy*, was to get into trouble with the authorities during November, and the best that can be said for Defoe is that, for a few months at least, he avoided that fate.

If all of this suggests more than a certain reluctance on Defoe's part, he nevertheless hurled himself into the defence of the necessity for peace and of what would become the Treaty of Utrecht under the cover of anonymity with his usual barrage of pamphlets, intended to give the impression of a national opinion on the side of Harley's decision to end the war at all costs. The first of these appeared on 6 October 1711, *Reasons Why this Nation Ought to Put a Speedy End to this Expensive War*, taking its title from the kind of argument he had derided several years before. Picturing the financial situation of Great Britain as desperate, he argued that continuation of the war would involve either a tax on food and clothing, 'a Thing which our Parliament, in all Ages, have avoided, and will avoid, till they are brought to the last Extremity', or stopping payment on interest. The former, particularly, would put 'Heavy, Insupportable and oppressive Burthens on the People, and especially on the Poor', and go far to ruin the state. Defoe accused the Dutch of demanding too much in the early attempts at a treaty, raised the possibility that the plague that had been raging in Europe might come to England, and argued that Philip would permit a trade with Spain's colonies that would enrich England. Defoe probably knew that the accusation against the Dutch was unjust, since they had been persuaded against seeking peace by the bribes offered to them by England, but a little Dutch-bashing made for effective rhetoric. Defoe's pamphlet ran to three editions. If no single work was as effective as Swift's *Conduct of the Allies*, published almost two months after Defoe entered the field in defence of the Treaty, Defoe prepared the way for Swift by familiarizing the reading public with a variety of issues. Also going into three editions was Defoe's *Reasons Why a Party among Us . . . Are Obstinately Bent against a Treaty of Peace with the French*. Published shortly after Defoe's opening salvo, as an attack upon the Whig effort at sabotaging the Treaty, it accused the Whigs of using every underhand means of stopping the peace, including an attempt to stir up the mob. Arguing that everyone was happy to see an end to the loss of life, Defoe contended that the Whigs were simply waging a party war against the peace negotiations, just as they had opposed the sensible establishment of the South Sea Company.

---

[22] It also served as a reply to comments in the *Observator* on 7 Nov. 1711, suggesting that Defoe's use of the *Atlas Historique* had been faulty because he could not read French.

The arguments in the pamphlets that followed attempted to see the peace from a variety of angles. Writing from a Whig standpoint, Defoe argued that the Whigs desired a peace as much as the Tories, that peace would bring a rise in stock prices and benefit the monied sector more than anyone. Still insisting upon the importance of Spain, he nevertheless rehearsed the arguments about the power Austria might wield.[23] Having raised the image of Austrian persecution in earlier works, he returned to it in detail with accounts of the horrors committed against the Protestants during the Thirty Years War along with earlier persecutions. Having Philip as King of Spain was better for preserving the balance of power in Europe. Besides, the Spaniards seemed to want him, and he would gradually grow less French and more Spanish.[24] Defoe was probably the author of *Worcester-Queries about Peace*, in which a Tom Flockmaker, a clothier, come to London from Worcester, complains that those Whigs who oppose the peace efforts are 'quite another sort of Folk than Honest *Whigs* used to be', since in wanting the war continued, 'they never Enquired into the ruine of the Clothiers, *the Poor* unemploy'd, *the Wool* unconsum'd, *the Price* sunk to half Value, and 5 Years Stock *in quantity* upon Hand all over the Nation'.[25]

Defoe finished the year, 1711, with two tracts that he signed 'By the Author of the Review', and in *An Essay at a Plain Exposition of that Difficult Phrase a Good Peace*, he complained about the 'Bastards'—all those unsigned works that he was accused of writing—and asked to be judged on his signed works. Comparing himself to the lady in the poetry of Rochester who refused the sexual advances of the libertine but enjoyed his company and wit too much to stop associating with him, he commented wryly, 'I have the Scandal without the Joy, the Reproach without the Profit of the Charge'. Since Defoe was soon to get into trouble for three anonymous pamphlets, what this meant, in fact, was that he believed that the publication of unsigned works or writings employing a mask or pseudonym amounted to a request for anonymity, a request that he believed ought to be honoured. Samuel Johnson quoted Castiglione approvingly on this matter; so there was nothing unique about Defoe's opinion.[26] At any rate, the *Essay* was a well-written pamphlet setting forth Defoe's concept of the

---

[23] *Armageddon: or, The Necessity of Carrying on the War* (London, 1711). The title is somewhat deceptive, since the thrust of the argument is to support the idea that Whigs as well as Tories long for peace and that Britain will do nothing against the will of its allies. The longing for one decisive battle in Flanders (39) suggests some of Defoe's mixed feelings about ceding Spain to Philip, as well as about the necessity for more leverage in getting concessions from France.

[24] Defoe, *The Ballance of Europe* (London, 1711).

[25] *Worcester-Queries about Peace* (London, 1711), 9 and 15.

[26] Quoted by Samuel Johnson in *The Rambler*, No. 208.

balance of power in Europe, arguing that the demands made at Gertruydenberg had been a mistake and that Philip V ought to get something out of a partition of all the Spanish territories. He also repeated his contention that 'a few Years would make King *Philip* as much a *Spaniard* and *as much* an Enemy to *France* as any King of *Spain*'. If this meant abandoning Parliament's vow 'No Peace without Spain', it should be considered that 'Alteration of Circumstances must for ever be allowed to be a Reason for Alteration of Opinion'.[27] Under no circumstances must Charles VI be allowed to control Spain.

Defoe was shifting his argument here. He too had maintained that Spain should not fall into the hands of Louis XIV, but now new circumstances ought to be met with a certain flexibility. He still tried to convince his readers that his principles had not really changed; they had merely shifted a little because events had changed. Reason dictated that everyone should make similar adjustments. *The Felonious Treaty*, the second of the signed pamphlets, began with an historical review of William III's reasons for his Partition Treaties, '*that the Crown of* Spain *should never be or revolve to the same Person that should have any Title, or at least any Possession, either of the Kingdom of* France, *or the* Empire *so as that the same Person should Govern both at the same Time*'. But 'the Malignant Influence of the Terrestrian Stars' had made such a decision along with the ensuing war absurd: 'Upon this nicety we push'd on the War for three Years, and, as I may say, spent Twenty Millions Sterling for our share, and the whole Alliance above 120,000 Mens Lives, purely to give *Naples* and *Sicily* to King *Charles* III; a strife which some compar'd to Ten Years War against *Troy* for the Rescue of a Whore.'[28] Somewhat in the manner of Chaplin's *The Great Dictator*, which has the equivalents of Hitler and Mussolini tossing a globe of the world around like a beach ball, Defoe compared these attempts to regulate European politics to a football game: 'the Foot-ball is thrown down amongst the Gamesters, France gave it a hand-kick, as we call it, and Philip catch'd it; Charles the III. pushes at him and bids him give up the Ball.' By trivializing the wars against France, Defoe was attempting to get his readers to accept the absurdities of history and give up expecting too much. He tried to clarify what he meant by the possibility of 'Partition' in his earliest numbers of the *Review*. From the very start of the war, Spain's American colonies had been fair game for the Allies, and to grab Spanish

---

[27] *An Essay at a Plain Exposition of that Difficult Phrase of a Good Peace*, 4, 20, 48.
[28] Defoe was now beginning the campaign of laying on Austria and Holland the blame for the failure of the war to bring any substantial reward. See e.g. the *Review* for 18 Dec. 1711 where he noted, '*The Emperor will part with nothing*, and we must fight on till we get him all.' The Emperor was delaying attempts to meet for a peace treaty, and was to send Prince Eugene to London in an effort to change the government's mind.

land for the purpose of colonization was one element of partition that had always been a worthy goal. Britain, he insinuated, must avoid being tied down too much by 'the Ceremony of Words'. That this phrase might be taken to lessen the value of the nation's solemn obligations to its allies was an implication Defoe's readers could hardly avoid.

Defoe's pamphlet appeared on 6 December 1711, the day before Queen Anne, who had been proroguing Parliament, finally addressed the two Houses with a request for peace, while assuring her listeners that the Hanoverian succession would be protected and Holland not mistreated. Though the Commons voted in favour of a peace without any consideration of a Spanish settlement, the Lords refused, affirming the popular slogan 'no peace without Spain'. What followed was the creation of twelve new peers on the first day of 1712 who would give the Tories and the peace forces the majority. The Whigs were in disarray. By 22 December accusations had been made against both Marlborough and Walpole for illegally taking money from the army accounts, and before the month was out Marlborough had been dismissed. Walpole was soon to be imprisoned in the Tower. Britain's allies, including Hanover, were furious, as a formal peace conference was set to meet at Utrecht.

Some historians have argued that peace was absolutely necessary, that the Tories were right and the Whigs wrong.[29] This would put Defoe on the right side in this quarrel, and doubtless he could tell himself that he believed some of his arguments. He also had the comfort of knowing he was supporting the Queen's viewpoint. But the historical hindsight that he used in his pamphlets and in the *Review* would not have consoled him for the humiliation of Marlborough, whom he considered a brave soldier, and the betrayal of Holland, a nation he greatly admired. If Defoe was to engage in what was for him an unusual appeal to a malignant fate, he may well have included himself along with the Allies as victims.

III

Defoe still retained some hope that in the final treaty, in whatever partition might be made of Spanish territories, some part of South America would yet go to Britain. During this period he had been an enthusiastic proponent of Harley's South Sea Company Scheme. There were actually two schemes in one package presented to Parliament in May 1711. The first was a holding company for consolidating government debts under a single roof with

[29] See e.g. Trevelyan, *England under Queen Anne*, iii. 176–230.

the payment of 6 per cent interest. The second involved the creation of a new company to trade to the South Seas. The financial part of the scheme had been designed in 1710 by a London financier named John Blunt, and Defoe probably had little to do with this. But he probably influenced Harley considerably on the notion of a colony in South America, since it was a scheme that he favoured during the days of William III.[30] Defoe argued that although the war had hitherto cost the nation vast sums of money, this proposal would 'open a new Vein of Wealth', stimulating all aspects of the economy, providing work for the poor, a new market for the colonies already established in North America, increasing the seamen employed in shipping, and ultimately advancing the value of land in England. Defoe harked back to the days of Sir Walter Raleigh, quoting a speech by Sir Benjamin Rudyerd with much the same proposal. Such a company, he argued, could play a major role in the slave trade, and allowing his imagination full play, he imagined a commerce with the wealthy pirates of Madagascar, arguing that it was no worse than when the Italians first traded with the Romans, who were then no better than a 'Company of Publick Robbers'.[31] Ideal places for settlement might be present-day Chile, or perhaps California, which Drake had explored. He boasted in his *Essay on the South Sea Trade*, published on 13 September 1711, that William was so delighted with the idea that, had he not died, he would have put it into effect. Although Defoe acknowledged that such a colony would probably have to be established by force, he argued that, once established, it would succeed in every way. And after a time Spain would find it necessary to trade with it.

Defoe did not publish these pamphlets until September, and he may have had some questions about the financial aspects of the scheme.[32] Initial doubts by Whig financiers depressed the stock at first, but one may wonder

[30] Brian Hill notes Blunt's role in the financial aspect of the Company, but thinks Harley merely took suggestions from Defoe. Elizabeth Hamilton maintains that Harley and Defoe worked it out in close cooperation. Compare Hill, *Robert Harley* (New Haven, Conn.: Yale University Press, 1988), 144, and Hamilton, *The Backstage Dragon: A Life of Robert Harley* (London: Hamish Hamilton, 1969), 186–9. The Bodleian Library has a manuscript, owned by Defoe, containing a proposal made by William Paterson for colonies in the land claimed by Spain.

[31] *A True Account of the Design and Advantages of the South-Sea Trade* (London, 1711), 21.

[32] See John Robert Moore, 'Defoe and the South Sea Company', *Boston Public Library Quarterly* 5 (1953), 176–88. Moore's argument that Defoe had little to do with Harley for almost six months is based on doubtful evidence. We do not know how often they spoke or how complete the letters are. And to sustain his position, Moore has to remove from the canon of Defoe's writings *A Letter to a Member of Parliament*, published by one of Defoe's publishers, Abigail Baldwin, with many marks of his style. But that Defoe seems to have stressed the concept of colonization rather than the financial aspects of the South Sea Company is unquestionably true. His attack upon 'STOCK-JOBBING the Funds' at the end of July and the beginning of August (*Review*, vii. 221–7) has a broader target than the South Sea Company, but it certainly follows his essays in the *Review* in support of the new trading institution.

about Defoe's comment that if the wealth of America is opened to traders, 'it will be Stockjobb'd up as fast as we are now Stockjobb'd down'. He disliked stocks that had no real financial basis in something with intrinsic value, and may have wondered whether the issuing of stock should not have waited until colonies were established and trade begun. What is certain, however, is that he had no doubts at all about the advisability of establishing colonies. The thought seemed to awaken that part of his imagination that dwelt on distant lands and the possibilities of finding treasure. He enumerated the wealth of the Madagascan pirates at £20,240,000, and just as he had previously advised accepting them back into English society for an appropriate ransom, so he thought trading with them legitimate enough.

Defoe's letters to Harley on the subject begin on 17 July 1711 with Harley's command to put his ideas in writing. Presumably he had spoken to Harley over some time and at some length about one of his favourite projects, and was now in the process of communicating his private thoughts. He had already written a number of essays in the *Review* on the subject, but the letters were not entirely for public consumption. He argued that, although the public announcement of an open trade to the Spanish colonies would bring immediate opposition from Spain, some quiet smuggling of goods would accompany the Asiento—the right to trade in slaves which, according to the ongoing peace negotiations, would be under the control of the South Sea Company. But the really important aspect of the trade would be a colony that would act as a place from which goods would be distributed without the tariffs imposed by the Spanish government on any goods traded first to Spain itself and then sent out to the colonies.

In his letter of 20 July 1711 Defoe suggested that, at first, the emphasis should be on a colony 'on the Continent of America, and in the Midst of The Gold, Silver and Other productions with which the Spaniards have So Enrich't Themselves, and which The English are Much more capable to improve Than They' (H 343). It would be the ability of the English to organize industry in such a way that a colony which would 'Perish and Starv' under the administration of the Spaniards could prosper in much the same manner as the colony of Barbados, where the numbers of people relative to the ability of the land to support them were such that 'if it were in The Governmt of the spaniards [they] would Eat up one Another'. That Defoe's mind dwells on cannibalism when thinking of these colonies may have some ramifications for his fiction a decade later. Certainly *A New Voyage Round the World*, with its proposal for a colony in the area of Chile and Argentina, has a direct relation to the thought he gave to the South Sea project. In providing Harley with a specific plan, he pointed out that the original had been burned so as not to fall into the hands of Nottingham at the time he was being hunted for *The Shortest Way with the Dissenters*. One may wonder what it was about his notion of a colony in Chile and trading with Peru that he thought dangerous and inflammatory, but it gives us some sense of how vivid his writing could be even when his geography was somewhat off.[33] 'Here', he wrote, 'The Climate is good, The Country Fruitfull, the The Natives Courteous and Tractable, and the Wealth of the Place in Gold Incredible' (H 347). Defoe's language was to be repeated in his novelistic version of exploring this area in his *New Voyage*,[34] and we should always be aware that a form of fictional narrative was never far from anything he wrote, and that his description in the letter to Harley implies the story of human settlement and development:

The Soil here will Encourage The Industry of Our People, who will Settle and plant, produceing rice, Cocoa, Wine, Exceeding Rich and Pleasant, and on the North Side Sugar and spices in abundance, but Especially Gold and Salt peter.

The Air here is pleasant, Agreeable, and Healthy. The Mountains of Andes being Exceeding high, The winds from Their Tops keep The air Cool; and on the Other side The breezes from the Sea keep it Moist and Moderate; and being in the Latitude of 39 to 40 Degrees, it Answers to Our Collony of Carolina, which is Esteemed the Most Healthy of all Our Colonys in the North Parts of America. (H 348)

He also proposed a colony somewhere near the middle of Argentina, describing it much in the manner of someone writing an advertisement to attract settlers, again pointing to the excellent climate. Some six years later, writing under the mask of the French envoy who arranged the preliminary peace with France, Defoe praised Harley for courage, but in speaking of the South Sea Company as a scheme for 'ascertaining a precarious Debt, and appointing an unpracticable Commerce', he seems ambiguous about Harley's accomplishment. He admitted that it was eventually 'thought by some . . . the best Scheme of its Kind that ever was laid in that Nation', and that the Whigs eventually invested more in the company than the Tories. But his interest lay in exploring and exploiting strange lands, and he must have been disappointed that this part of the South Sea Scheme never came to fruition.[35]

---

[33] Healey notes that his image of a river from Valdivia to Santiago is in error. See H 347, n. 3.
[34] Healey annotated this passage with reference to Defoe's fictional voyage.
[35] Defoe, *Minutes of the Negotiations of Mr. Mesnager* (London, 1717), 50–1.

IV

Compared to what was happening in matters of religious toleration, the
difficulties with the peace and with the South Sea Company must have
seemed relatively simple. On 20 December 1711 Defoe wrote to Harley, 'I
confess my Self So much Surprized with the Perticulars which your Ldpp
did me the honor to Communicate to me On Tuesday of the Conduct of a
Set of Men with Respect to the Dissenters, That I could not Express my
Self on Severall Things' (H 363–4). What amazed Defoe was that the
Whigs had offered Harley the opportunity of passing a bill against
Occasional Conformity in exchange for a rejection of the terms of the
treaty of peace and some reorganization of the government. Harley
refused, but the Whigs had managed to entice Defoe's old nemesis, the
Earl of Nottingham, and his followers into their camp with the same bait.
For his support of the 'No peace without Spain' resolution in the House
of Lords on 7 December, the Whigs agreed to vote in favour of
Nottingham's favourite project, which passed its second and third readings
on the very day on which Defoe wrote his letter. By the time Harley had
spoken with Defoe, he knew that his government would not fall and that
the Queen would appoint twelve new peers.

If Harley had triumphed over his enemies, the Dissenters would have
been thrown to the wolves by the very party in which they had placed their
faith. Harley had not spoken out against the Occasional Conformity Bill
which would either disenfranchise many mayors and office-holders or
cause them to abandon attendance at Dissenting conventicles. Not even the
Dutch and French Churches were spared the indignities of this act, which
included registering ministers and fines of £40 for those violators found
attending conventicles. In a bitter letter to the eminent Presbyterian divine
Dr Daniel Williams, Harley blamed the Dissenters for putting their faith
in the Whigs, whom he described as 'deists' and 'libertines', but pledged
that, despite their folly in following the Whigs, he would not turn against
them.[36] The bill passed through the Commons on 20 December, and an
issue that had aroused burning passions for more than a decade hardly
caused comment in a period transformed by Sacheverell's trial and
triumph.

Defoe's confession to momentary speechlessness at the manoeuvrings of
the Whigs on this issue seems to have been genuine. He thought that the

---

[36] Hill, *Robert Harley*, 172. For the provisions of the bill itself, see *The History of the Proceedings of the
House of Lords, from the Restoration in 1660 to the Present Time* (London, 1742), 352–7. Defoe also reproduced it in its entirety in his *The Present State of the Parties in Great Britain* (London, 1712), 105–10.

cause of the Dissenters would be 'Ruind' by this action, and he urged Harley to take the opportunity of emerging as a hero to them by getting the Queen to reject it. He thought it an infringement on 'her Royall Promise to the Dissenters, to Preserv The Tolleration Inviolable' (H 364–5), and in the *Review* of 22 December, he lamented the absurdity of it all: 'What *Cameleon* Disposition is Mankind made of! How are there some in the World *given to Change!*' He put his hope in a petition to the Queen reminding her of her promise to preserve toleration and in his introduction to the petition, asking Anne to picture what it will mean:

Let us suppose them [the Dissenters] at her Majesty's Feet, with their Petition, Presented by Ten Thousand starving Infants, the Children of the poor Dispossess'd Parents, turn'd out of their Employments, and left without Bread, meerly because, in Conscience, they cannot and dare not, take the Sacrament in the Church of England; and suppose their Petition in these moving Expressions . . .[37]

In his next *Review*, Defoe picked as his main theme the betrayal by the Whigs, a betrayal similar to Brutus's of Caesar. He quoted from an essay he passed around in manuscript, a visionary speech by the stone chimney-piece in the House of Lords objecting to what has been done. Though composed of stone, the chimney-piece argues that its heart is not as hard as those members of the House of Lords who passed the bill, and begs for someone to speak up in defence of those who always trusted them.[38] But the chimney-piece's call to the Lords to repent went unheeded, as did Defoe's petition to Queen Anne. At the end of his *Essay on the History of Parties*, which was written in stages, Defoe's optimism showed some signs of returning. Persecution, he argued, could sometimes make a group stronger. The Dissenters needed to turn inward, and he quoted that source of scepticism concerning human behaviour, Ecclesiastes, for the sentiment 'Put not your Trust in Princes'.

But Defoe's real feelings appear at the beginning of that work, a strenuous argument against the Test Act that kept the Dissenters from assuming positions in the government and army. That Act, he argued, had been intended for the Catholics and was wrongly applied to the Dissenters. 'The Wholesomest Laws have been perverted to the most wicked Purposes,' he wrote, 'as Establishments of Civil Rights to Oppression, Corporation-Privileges to Monopoly.' What had seemed like a steady

[37] *Review*, vii. 474–6.
[38] Defoe reproduced most or all of this exercise in Gothic allegory in his *Present State of the Parties*, 102–5. Defoe gives the title as 'The Speech spoken by the *Stone Chimney-Piece* in the House of Lords', which is somewhat different from Moore's made-up title as item 233 in his bibliography.

progression toward civil liberties had been subjected to what seemed to him a dramatic retrogression. Defoe had been arguing his own vision of history for more than twenty years. The fault with England did not rest, as the Houses of Convocation of the Church of England believed, with the Civil War and religious and political dissent, but rather with the *Book of Sports* and the suppression of religion during the reigns of James I and Charles I. Defoe had noted in his *True-Born Englishman* that the Civil War had actually benefited England, but now the Church of England's version of history seemed to have triumphed.[39] If Defoe lamented the passage of this Act for its effect upon England, he had to feel even more embarrassed by the series of measures that appeared in his eyes to be violations of the Union Treaty. The decision in favour of Greenshields by the House of Lords opened the way for granting the Episcopalians in Scotland the same rights held by the Dissenters in England. A Toleration Act for Scotland was prepared in the 1711 session and passed on 26 February 1712, doing just what the Church of Scotland feared. Along with compulsory prayers for Queen Anne and Princess Sophia, it also contained the oath of abjuration that Defoe was afraid would alienate many among the Presbyterian clergy. Carstares, whom Defoe knew well, pleaded for a change in the oath but was unsuccessful.

If religious rights, seemingly guaranteed by the Treaty of Union, were being flaunted, on 20 December, a few days after passing the act against Occasional Conformity, the House of Lords ruled against recognizing the English title of the Duke of Hamilton (Duke of Brandon), and did so with considerable reflection on Scotland's status. Even before this, during discussion of a tax on exporting linen cloth, Harley had somewhat unguardedly asked, 'Have not we bought the Scots, and may we not claim the right to tax them?' These were the beginnings of a series of attacks upon the Union Treaty, a treaty that Defoe had argued was permanent and unchangeable. As mentioned before, several years later this attitude toward Scotland was to result in a motion to dissolve the Union that failed in the House of Lords by just four votes.

[39] During the summer of 1711, Defoe published *The Representation Examined* in response to the conclusions of the Lower House of Convocation of Canterbury, *A Representation, of the Present State of Religion* and *A Representation Drawn Up by the Upper House*. Although the Upper House rejected the contentious report of the Lower House, both agreed that the causes of impiety and profanity in England might be found in the enthusiastic sects so prevalent during the Civil War. The Lower House was more insistent in blaming the freedom of the press to publish heresy, and Defoe's pamphlet is an attack upon their reading of history and a defence of freedom of speech and therefore of the press as the right of every Englishman.

V

Defoe made the familiar Latin proverb *Tempor Mutantur, nos et Mutamur* ('the times are changing and we are changing with them') the motto for his *Review* of 22 December 1711. He had found himself caught up in a bewildering round of change, and was trying his best to control it and himself within the whirlwind of events. He wrote to Harley on 30 November, complaining about his treatment by the *Observator* and asking for protection from his enemies in his effort to turn his readers toward the peace. What the *Observator* did in its issues of October to December was to attack what it called the 'Summer Campaign' of the government to convince the nation of the necessity for peace. Although the main target was Abel Roper's *Post Boy*, the author of the *Observator* began to attack Defoe's position on the peace as early as 24 October, when he singled out *Reasons Why This Nation Ought to Put a Speedy End to this Expensive War* for special denunciation. A few days later the *Observator* was wondering how a person who pretended to support the Hanoverian succession could defend the peace, and finally, on 24 November, it accused the *Review* of errors. In the next issue he spoke of those who 'employ' Defoe, and in the issue for 5 December, after naming several works issued anonymously as being by Defoe, he stated, 'profess'd Jacobites are now become his Admirers, and extoll him in Coffee-Houses *etc.* and glory as much in their Convert, as the Whigs despise their loss of him.'[40] On 26 December the *Observator* described Defoe as 'a Tool whom no Man that knows believes, or will trust to the Value of a shilling . . . for considering who act him behind the Curtain, 'tis an Argument of Merit to incur his Displeasure, and a Blemish for any Man to have his Good Word'. In short, Defoe the government agent was being exposed to the light of public knowledge in a manner that he hated. After having stated that he would indicate his authorship of all the essays he published, Defoe was being revealed as the author of a variety of anonymous pamphlets in addition to those that he admitted to having written.

He was running the risk of alienating many of his former supporters and felt in need of protection. The letter to Harley on 30 November 1711 seemed to prepare for what he thought would be the inevitable attack:

I have my Lord Openly Declared against and Opposed Them, my Own Principle Concurring with my Duty to your Ldpp Therein; and as my Entire Dependence is

---

[40] The works named were *The Ballance of Europe* and *An Essay upon Credit*. The world of London printing and publishing was small indeed, and usually it was not difficult to discover who wrote what. This is why contemporary ascriptions such as these are so valuable.

That I Shall not be left Unsupported in The prosecution of That Duty; This gives me Confidence with all humility to Represent my Condition to your Ldpp, and How if Ever This Party Prevail I am to Expect No Quarter Or Favour, and in the Mean time am Onely Supported by This Bounty of her Majtie, which is all Owing to your Ldpps Goodness, and The Arrear whereof has So Much Reduced me. (H 363)

Defoe's request for what was essentially a quarterly salary aside, the feeling of being placed in danger from new enemies must have seemed very real. The *Observator's* claim that Defoe was now a favourite of the Jacobites was an exaggeration. But the reality was that he now had enemies of all sorts. He had continued to be hated by the Tories, and now he was detested by many Whigs.

Attacks upon him were now again reaching the level they had attained around 1705. *The Whig's Medly trompe-l'œil* print of 1711 by George Bickham did him the honour of showing him in the pose where some Whig prints put Sacheverell and where some Tory prints put Benjamin Hoadly—between the Pope and the Devil—as 'The Three False Brethren'.[41] He is surrounded by a variety of cards and printed sheets, including two playing cards, both knaves (jacks of hearts and clubs), a print of Cromwell, a small poem 'On the Calves Head Feast', a picture of a Whig and Tory wrestling, and a grotesque portrait of Defoe in the pillory with a poem identifying him as quintessential Whig. In the main picture he is holding an open book with a seditious inscription, and below is a poem:

> Here's Daniel, the Pope, and the Devil well match'd
> By whose Crafty Inventions all mischief is hatch'd:
> In deceiving poor Creatures their chief Talent lies,
> Altho' to us Mortals they'd seem otherwise.
> From crafty deceivers, Good Lord, set us free,
> And keep us secure from the snares of these *Three*.

The image of Defoe as the master deceiver, which had been present in some of the earlier attacks on him, now emerged more fully.

One work, *Hell Broke-Loose; Upon Doctor S-ch-ve--ls Sermons*, written earlier but not published until 1713, has Defoe in hell with all of the other Whig worthies, plotting to silence Sacheverell, but he is given prime place

---

[41] The picture hardly looks very much like Defoe, and one might suspect that the Daniel intended in the main section was Daniel Burgess, a flamboyant minister. But the figure holds a book with the inscription 'Resistance Lawful', a sentiment easily connected to Defoe, and Defoe was frequently associated with the Devil. In addition, as Hallett remarks, the portrait appears to draw upon the Taverner portrait of Defoe. Burgess was usually identified iconographically by his 'puritan' outfit. Bickham may have been trying to conflate the two Daniels. See Mark Hallett, 'The Medley Print in Early Eighteenth-Century London', *Art History* 20 (2) (1977), 214–37.

as 'the Ringleader of the Whiggish Party and Dictator General in *UTOPIA*'. It is he who mocked the Queen's hereditary right and aimed at 'Anarchy'.[42] Defoe had a major place in the anthology *Whig and Tory: or, Wit on Both Sides*, where he was depicted as one of the 'grand Incendiaries of the Age' and made the subject of an 'Epigram':

> To speak the Truth, is criminal now,
> Whilst vilify'd by such as thou;
> Who hast the Policy *of Devil*,
> *An Head* to work the Nation's Evil;
> Detacht from *Hell*, thou did'st commence
> Thy daring Pride and Impudence,
>
> . . .
>
> Whereby thou do'st the Croud delude,
> The poor unthinking Multitude.[43]

In *The Gates of Hell Open'd: In a Dialogue Between the Observator and the Review* (1711), Defoe is again the arch-deceiver. 'I write all *Moderation*,' he states, 'yet I am bold.'[44]

If his image with the Tories was mainly satanic, the Whigs were more concerned with his relationship with Harley and his inconsistencies. The author of *A Caveat to the Treaters* wondered how a true Whig could support a peace treaty and where he could have learned such principles. And, although written several years earlier, a witty poem entitled 'To My Generous Friend, and Worthy Patriot, Harlequin Le Grand. The humble memorial of Your Little Scribler, Spy, Champion, Closet-Counsellor, and Poet, D----l D'F-e', seemed to capture a good deal of the Defoe–Harley relationship as perceived from outside. Defoe is made to boast to Harley:

> For who can doubt my Cunning, or my Wit,
> Since I am Courtier, Poet, Prophet, and a Cit.
> You know my Parts, for you have try'd em oft,
> I've been the Tool that rais'd you up aloft;
>
> . . .
>
> For my keen Wit, without your ill Nature join'd,
> Blacken'd the Wise, and did the Foolish blind:
> Or, by the sacred Stile of my R[evie]w,
> There never had been Room for such as you.

But in his poem Defoe is shown to be concerned for his safety and wants some assurance of Harley's continued protection:

[42] *Whig and Tory: or, Wit on Both Sides* (London, 1713), 13.
[43] Ibid., 'An Epigram on Dan. de F[oe]', 2: 31.
[44] *The Gates of Hell Open'd: In a Dialogue Between the Observator and the Review* (London, 1711), 10.

> For tho' I'm thought to be a Saint by some,
> I'm really unprepar'd for Martyrdom.[45]

The poet then imagines Defoe warning Harley that he will uncover all of his secrets if he is threatened with being hanged at Tyburn.

One of the virtues upon which Defoe prided himself was his refusal to give information to Nottingham that might have implicated William III and the Whigs in some kind of scandal. But these critics of Defoe's writings and character were satirizing someone who had become a public figure. To most of them, particularly those writing after 1711, he appeared an enigma. His early image as the 'incendiary from Hell' remained, but now, to the Whigs, he seemed to have unaccountably swung to the side of the Tories. Given the seemingly inexplicable nature of *The Shortest Way*, he appeared to some as a malicious anarchist with no principles other than a delight in argument for its own sake. What we can see from his letters is very different. He did indeed feel he needed the protection of the government if he was to struggle for the Hanoverian succession. At a time when the Tories had triumphed, he remained at his post as a court Whig willing to support Harley so long as the succession was not in danger. His sense of insecurity was based on the realities of his situation. He was being reviled by the very Whigs from whom he had been accustomed to receive applause, and he doubtless felt bitter, isolated, and misunderstood.

[45] In *State and Miscellany Poems* (London, 1715), i. 143–5. It was originally published in 1708 as a prefatory poem to the prose work *A Dialogue between Louis le Petite, and Harlequin le Grand*. The authorship of these two volumes is disputed, though Joseph Browne and William Oldisworth are candidates. For a date of 1708 for this poem and the possible authorship of a Robert Mann, see J. A. Downie, 'Defoe and *A Dialogue between Louis le Petite, and Harlequin le Grand*', *American Notes and Queries* 12 (1973–4), 54–6.

18

'A Miserable Divided Nation'[1]

As if stung by attacks upon his defence of the preliminary articles of peace, Defoe seems to have set out at the beginning of 1712 by boldly, perhaps foolishly, trying to pursue an independent line. Swift's *Conduct of the Allies* had appeared at the end of November 1711 and was a tremendous success. Swift captured a xenophobic sense of indignation against Britain's allies, particularly against the Dutch, creating the image of a noble and virtuous nation generously sacrificing its men and wealth for a selfish, worthless, mercenary country. Of the Barrier Treaty of 1709, created to discourage the Dutch from making a separate peace, little was said. Instead, Holland was portrayed as the nation that insisted on trading with France during the war and refused to provide an equal number of troops. Similarly, Britain was seen as conquering various parts of Europe for Austria while the Emperor enriched himself. Swift even insinuated that the treaty with the Dutch had 'put it out of the Power of our own Legislature to change our Succession'.[2] He clarified this statement by adding some lines about the possibility of tyranny in the future, but for Defoe, the suggestion must have smelled of Jacobitism and duplicity. Defoe answered, first with *A Defence of the Allies and the Late Ministry* in which he remarked on Swift's 'Frenchified Principles', and pointed out that Britain was not fighting for the Dutch but that they were equally involved in opposing France. With what must have been more hope than certainty, he enlisted the Queen among those 'who yet abhor the Thoughts of abandoning our Allies'.[3] And he followed this with another pamphlet having the descriptive title *A Justification of the Dutch*, in which he spoke of the attitude of writers such as Swift as revealing 'Unparallel'd Ingratitude' toward a nation that had entered the war to help Britain and not the other way around. He praised

---

[1] *Review*, viii. 489.

[2] See Jonathan Swift, *Prose Works*, ed. Herbert Davis et al. (14 vols., Oxford: Blackwell, 1951), vi. 27, 65.

[3] *A Defence of the Allies and the Late Ministry* (London, 1712), 46.

the Dutch for their reputation for 'a due Observation of their Oaths and Treaties', and worried that England might gain a reputation for bad faith[4] and that somehow French plotting lay behind the attacks on Holland.[5]

I

These two pamphlets represented Defoe's only indication of the discomfort he must have felt with his assigned role during this year. Beginning with *No Queen: or, No General*, published on 10 January 1712, Defoe was writing straight government propaganda. On that same day he wrote to Harley of the rage shown to him by the Dissenters, 'God Grant your Ldpp Victory over This New Possession, for however I May Fare while your Ldpp holds the Reins; I am Sure to Sink if any Thing happen to The prejudice of your Intrest' (H 365–6). This is a new note for Defoe, and his subsequent remarks on the dismissal of Marlborough ('The Idol Man, who Coveted to Set himself up as the head of a Party' (H 366)) were clearly directed at what he knew Harley would want to hear. His attack upon his favourite living hero came almost as a way of validating his willingness to be less independent in his course of writing. Yet even here Defoe uses a form of irony which cuts both ways:

I shall be far from reproaching him with long Sieges in *Flanders*, instead of entring the Heart of *France*, that I shall own his Prudence and Conduct in attacking *Aire*, rather than piercing to the Gates of *Paris*: Nay, to go as far as any Man can do in his just Praise I'le call the taking of *Bouchain* a Prize suitable to the Expence of a Year, and the passing the *French* Lines a glorious Campaign; I'le forbear to lessen his Glorious Character by reckoning the Number of the Slain, or counting up the Cost of the Towns we have recovered.[6]

Defoe was obviously being sarcastic, but at the same time as criticizing Marlborough he was also summing up his achievements. The essential thrust of the essay was to suggest that Marlborough was a challenge to the power of the Queen, that he had ambitions to take over the government and defy the power of the monarch, and that Anne simply could not permit it. Marlborough was worshipped in a way that made him a rival, and, like

[4] *A Defence of the Allies and the Late Ministry*, 14, 22.
[5] There was considerable debate over the original notion in the Barrier Treaty of 1709 involving Holland's protection of the succession. The Treaty of Utrecht watered down Holland's obligation to guarantee the succession by force if necessary, but during the last years of Queen Anne, when the Duke of Cambridge and his followers were insisting that he be allowed to come over to Britain to guarantee the succession, there was some speculation about an invasion of Dutch and Prussian troops to ensure the peaceful transition to the reign of George I.
[6] *No Queen: or, No General* (London, 1712), 2.

Mary Tudor with Lady Jane Grey, Anne had to rid herself of him. If that comparison contained a hidden threat that Marlborough might bring punishment upon himself, Defoe did not press the matter. Doubtless Defoe was happy when, after being questioned in the House of Lords for possible peculation, the Duke and Duchess went into a form of exile in Holland.

The course of Defoe's writing on England's withdrawal from the war followed the events that eventually led to the formal Peace of Utrecht in the spring of 1712. At first Holland refused to sign, and orders were given to the Duke of Ormond to avoid any encounter with the enemy. In fighting on her own, during 1712, Holland lost Bouchain and Douai, which had been taken at great cost, and had to accept fewer of the barrier fortresses that were to protect her from French power. Austria made peace a year later. But both nations bitterly resisted the fate that Britain had thrust upon them. Austria even sent the great Prince Eugene to England in 1712 in an attempt at changing minds. Defoe's pamphlets on the war were mechanical exercises in journalism, picking up the arguments of the Tories against Dutch venality and Austrian ingratitude, as if England were not showing just these same qualities. He had not lost his talent for titles: *Imperial Gratitude*, *Peace or Poverty*, *The Validity of the Renunciation of Former Powers*, and *The Justice and Necessity of a War with Holland*. The latter, published toward the end of July, revealed attitudes almost exactly opposed to the position with which he had begun the year. Now, instead of Holland being a friend and ally, its inhabitants were seen as a belligerent and treacherous people who threw impediments in the way of Queen Anne's desire to make peace. Defoe even threatened that England might join with France in a war against them. From arguing that Britain would never desert an ally, he came to justify Ormond's shameful failure to engage the enemy, stating that to Dutch requests for participation, Ormond might have answered that he was not ready 'to butcher their Men for the meer Name of a Victory, as was done at Malplacquet'.[7] When quarrelling with an opponent five years later who taunted him for accepting money to write against the war and for the Treaty of Commerce, Defoe responded to the taunt by admitting its accuracy and saying that he did as good a job 'in a bad Cause' as he could. To argue for peace at this time might have been a very good cause indeed, but he had to acknowledge that he did not think so at the time.

Defoe's discussion of the peace was closely bound up with his treatment of party warfare—of the Whigs' struggle to gain control of the government by a variety of means. And this, in turn, led him to the relationship of

[7] *Reasons against Fighting* (London, 1712), 18.

the Dissenters to the two parties. He had treated this subject in 1711, in *An Essay on the History of Parties*, but at that time he was still hopeful that Anne might refuse to sign the Whig-supported Occasional Bill. Much of what he was to write on this subject is repetitious, but in addition to flooding the press to win his point, he also seems to have been attempting to sort out what it all meant. For the Whigs to have abandoned the Dissenters in this way seemed to be a relinquishing of reason for self-interest. That they should abandon all principle for the sake of a tactical manoeuvre intended to consolidate the power of the party amounted to a cynicism that seems to have left him angry and frustrated.

There is no question that having thrown in his lot with Harley, Defoe's own feelings about the Whigs had been bruised, and in *The Conduct of Parties in England* he commenced his attack upon the behaviour of the Whigs that was to lead to some vindictiveness on his part further down the road. He pointed out that the Whigs had begun the attacks upon Marlborough and Godolphin because they had not been bred within the party, a party that Defoe associates not with a certain ideology so much as with thirst for power. Their only desire was for 'getting into Places and taking hold of the Publick Administration to raise their Families and Fortunes out of the Spoil of the Nation'.[8] Under these conditions, he argued, the Dissenters should not be surprised by their support of a bill to prevent Occasional Conformity. Joining with Nottingham served their interest, and that, in the end, was the only thing that mattered.

What, then, were the Dissenters to do? Defoe gave his answer in a full treatise with the title *The Present State of the Parties in Great Britain*, published on 17 May 1712. Defoe states at the beginning that '*These Sheets have been written above Eight Years*', but while some parts may have been composed in earlier moments of frustration and anger against the Dissenters, the central intent of the work was to argue for an abandonment of political ties and to urge an effort at consolidation and revitalization. His historical survey of persecution against the Dissenters and his own efforts at restoring an atmosphere of toleration and moderation through writing *The Shortest Way with the Dissenters* is not very different from his autobiographical account in the *Consolidator*, but his focus is more clearly on how his behaviour helped the Dissenters:

Some People have blam'd the Author of the aforesaid Pamphlet, called *The Shortest Way*, etc. for that he did not quote either in the Margin, or otherwise the Sermon of *Sacheverel*, aforesaid, or such other Authors from whom his Notions

---

[8] *The Conduct of Parties in England* (London, 1712), 33.

were drawn, which would have justify'd him in what he had suggested; but these men do not see the Design of the Book at all, or the Effect it had on the People it pointed at . . . The Case the Book pointed at was to speak in the first person of the *Party*, and then, thereby, not only speak this language, but make them acknowledge it to be theirs, which they did so openly, that confounded all their Attempts afterwards to deny it, and to call it a *Scandal* thrown upon them by another.

Defoe continued his history from his own suffering at the pillory forward to the present time, defending Harley and his government as supporters of moderation and attacking the Junto Whigs as greedy for *'Advancement'* and, for all their posturing, no more committed to 'the *Revolution Principle*' than the 'Court Whigs' with whom Defoe apparently continued to identify himself.[9] Eventually, their adherence to party rather than principle turned people against them, and the Sacheverell affair showed just how disaffected the people were with them.

Having blamed the parties for a variety of ills, Defoe then turned to the treatment of Scotland by the British Parliament, rehearsing the case of Greenshields and the general effort to undermine what the Union Treaty had promised—the preservation of the Church of Scotland. As he rehearsed the various violations of the Union, with yet another privilege of the Presbyterian clergy about to be destroyed (in the restoration of patronage in appointing ministers), Defoe showed both his irritation and his faith that these attacks could not endure. He noted that Parliament had been playing with the *'Unalterable'* nature of the Treaty in an effort to change it, but argued that 'without it *the whole Union* is a Cheat, a Snare laid to Entrap a whole Nation, a Politick Fraud, back'd with Court Assurances, Royal Authorities, and Parliamentary Ratifications, on purpose to draw in an Innocent People'.[10] Whatever changes might be made temporarily, he suggested, would eventually be removed by a Parliament true to its principles. In Defoe's eyes, party politics had caused Parliament to lose its integrity in relation to the Union Treaty, and when, a little over a year later, Swift was to describe Scotland as a beggarly country with whom the Union Treaty was made only to avoid the annoyance of having to conquer it, and whose nobility were so poor that their income hardly came to that of a Welsh parson, Defoe rushed to defend the Union as a major accomplishment.

If Defoe felt that the Scots had been unfairly victimized, he was somewhat harder on the English Dissenters, whose declining prestige as mirrored in the passage of the Occasional Conformity Act might be laid as

[9] *The Present State of the Parties in Great Britain* (London, 1712), 24, 48–51.
[10] Ibid. 237.

much at their own door as at that of an indifferent Parliament. Those who Dissented after the failure of the Savoy Conference were men and women of great integrity, and their ministers were preachers who inspired their congregations.[11] What had gone wrong might be ascribed to a poor system for selecting and educating ministers. In this combined criticism of sermon style and treatise on education, Defoe revealed some of that ability to probe a subject that was to be an important feature of both his fictional and didactic writings during the 1720s with its combination of satire, humour, and insight. The wrong men were often chosen for the most important task:

If the Boy be a Clod, a meer Stupid, a Block without a head, or if he be a Flutter, a meer Feather, the one too hard, the other too soft; one too thick, and the other too thin for a Stock of Learning; one so contracted in the Head there is no room to hold it, the other so thick ther's no Power to retain it, to what Purpose should Schoolmasters go to invert Nature, and force the Current? . . . Give a Fool Learning, you make him a *Rake*, a *Fop* and at last quite a *Lunatick*. Letters, like fine Cloaths, let them be never so well made, so gay, or so rich, they will never make the Man Genteel, if he has no Shapes.[12]

Defoe saw nothing wrong with the Dissenting academies, but he wanted them strengthened and structured in such a way as to produce dedicated, learned, and enthusiastic ministers. He attacked pedantry and foppishness as no replacement for one 'Eaten up with the Zeal of God's House', and in the process gave one of the best descriptions of the kind of style he disliked:

How is the Energy of the Spirit of God, which accompany'd the last Age, succeeded by Formality, Gaiety, empty Un-meaning Sound and Jingle of Words, without the Power and Force, either of Religion or of true Eloquence, and how are the People pleas'd with it? Metaphors without Meaning; Stile without Cadence; letters wihout Learning; and which worst of all, Divinity without Gospel.[13]

He wanted the Dissenters' schools to provide the kind of 'Conversation' imparted by England's two great universities. It would allow their ministers to preach as they are accustomed to speak, with an 'Easie, Free, Plain' manner. If the Dissenters could just rededicate themselves to the religious life, he argued, how bad could the Occasional Conformity Act be?

He offered the same message in *Wise as Serpents*, a work focused less on the political situation of the Dissenters and more on their condition as

---

[11] He named Drs Goodwin, Manton, Owen, and Bates, along with Charnock, Pool, Clarkson, Baxter, Flavell, How, Collins, Allen, Gilpin, and Mead, and one woman, Mrs Richard. See ibid. 290 and 352.

[12] Ibid. 300–1.

[13] Ibid. 313.

practising Christians.[14] He confesses once more that he has been deprived of 'the Advantage of Publick Worship' ever since it became possible for him to be arrested by his creditors on Sunday. The wealthy Dissenter might join with some of his friends to hire a minister, but what of the effect of the Occasional Conformity on the poor office-holder who may risk starving his family?

This is a Martyrdom equal in Degree to a Faggot and a Stake. A Tender Father can no more see his Children starve, than he can leave the World. A Tender Affectionate Husband can no more see his Wife perish for Want, than he can burn: This breaks the Soul, invades the Bowels, and pulls at the very Vitals of a Man's Principles; and he must have a Strong Faith, a Flaming Affection, a Burning Zeal, for his Profession, that can stand this Shock.[15]

Defoe's sympathy for the poor had not diminished, nor had his solidarity with the Dissenters. He saw this as a time to go underground in the manner of the Huguenots in France. The office-holder in genuine need, who might lose his position were he to openly attend a Dissenting congregation, should practise deception. In going to a meeting-house, he should be sure he was not followed, but if caught, he should not abandon his faith. He should do business only with Dissenters and boycott all trading outside the group. Defoe had advised the same kind of economic pressure in his *Consolidator*, but now it would have to be done as part of a more or less secret conspiracy against the establishment. He had lived through this before. It was a time for the Dissenters to act inconspicuous and wait for better days.

II

With everything else going wrong, Defoe threw most of his energies into the war against Jacobitism. Harley had been reluctant to give those with Jacobite sentiments any positions of power, and while he had spoken to Gualtier about the possibility that the Pretender might succeed to the throne, the conditions he set forth for a second restoration of the Stuarts were impossible to fulfil. Defoe too had gone among Jacobites to discover their plans, and Harley seems to have been doing little more than that. In his final struggles with St John (now Viscount Bolingbroke) in 1714, he was to move toward the Whigs for help rather than to the right. Whatever the

[14] Though it was published on 13 May, a few days before *The Present State of the Parties*, it is unlike that work in showing no indication of some parts having been written earlier. The title is taken from Matt. 16: 10: 'Behold I send you forth as sheep in the midst of wolves: be ye therefore wise as serpents, and harmless as doves.' [15] *Wise as Serpents* (London, 1712), 38.

man he now addressed more formally than before, as 'your Lordship', might be doing as far as the peace was concerned, Defoe clearly thought he needed no special instructions to write against Jacobitism. Indeed, what he mainly did to earn his payments from the secret service was to guess at the kind of work Harley wanted from him. From this standpoint, his boast in his letter of 19 August 1712, 'What Ever your Lldpp has done for me, you Never So much as Intimated, (tho' Ever So Remotely) that you Expected from me The Least Byass in what I should write, or That her Majties Bounty to me was Intended to Guide my Opinion; Your Ldpp has too Much honour in your Principles to look That way, or to Think me worth your Notice, if I Could have been So Moved' (H 379), is wistful in many respects. Harley may have preferred that Defoe's imagination be allowed to range free, but he surely expected that Defoe would understand what was wanted of him. And that letter contains Defoe's own reminder, 'as I am Driven by the Torrent Upon a More entire Dependance On your Ldpp, So have I No Humane Appeal But to your Self' (H 380). As we have seen, Defoe's association with Harley was well known, and if Defoe did not admit that the *Review* was specifically a publication in direct support of the ministry, almost everyone understood it as such. The *Mercator*, with which his name was quickly associated, was to be taken as ministerial propaganda. And Defoe himself was to argue, after the *Review* was defunct, that a statement in that journal to the effect that the ministry would support the succession was to be taken as equivalent to a government announcement.[16]

When he travelled north to Derbyshire and Scotland in the autumn of 1712, mainly to take the baths in Derbyshire at Matlock and Buxton, he reported that everywhere he went—Lynn, Newcastle, Edinburgh—he found certain notions universally accepted: that the Queen favoured the Pretender as her heir, that the ministry was in the pay of France, and that there was to be a war with Holland. His brief excursion north to Scotland, where some of the ministers were in revolt against taking the Oath of Abjuration, was very different from his earlier journeys. This time he spoke of his relief in being 'Return'd From a land of Distraction and Confusion' (H 389). The trip convinced him that something had to be done both to attack Jacobitism and to assure the people that the government was not in support of the Jacobite cause.

In *Hannibal at the Gates*, published at the end of December, Defoe lamented the fact that a cause which seemed so dead should suddenly seem to have new energy. He tried to assure his readers that the rumours would all disappear again and that the nation would remain steady in its attach-

[16] See *Hannibal at the Gates*, 2nd edn. (London, 1714), 39 [51].

ment to the Protestant Succession. Even the most violent of Tories was actually a Whig to the extent that he supported the settlement established by the Glorious Revolution. He was to admit, in a second edition of this work published in 1714, that things had got worse, and there was a kind of nostalgia about James that seems incredible considering the realities of history. But at the end of 1712 he was still trying to argue the absurdity of anyone thinking that the heir of James could return. On the other hand, he was having to convince his readers in the *Review* that, despite his support of the peace, he was not himself a Jacobite. At the beginning of 1712 he had written:

I have look'd as narrowly into my own Thoughts, as the worst Enemy I have can do; and I thank God I find in myself no Propensity, no Inclination that Way; if my Friends fear it, or my Enemies hope it, they will be equally deceived; I know no Man can answer for himself; but this Justice I'll do the Devil, That he never tempted me to it yet.[17]

That Defoe had to defend himself in this way may seem extraordinary, but he was still fighting this battle in what was supposed to be the last number of the *Review* in 1713, as he ended the number on 29 July with a ringing defence of peace and a wish that Holland would soon agree to join Britain in accepting France's terms. After a prayer for peace, he wrote, 'Other than this I *never did say*, and *never shall say*; let the man that will not say *Amen* to such a Prayer stand forth and shew himself; *and my Life for yours, he is a Mad Man or a Jacobite.*'[18]

Of course the connection between the peace and Jacobitism was not as absurd as Defoe tried to make it seem. Queen Anne had originally selected as her ambassador to the meeting at Utrecht the Duke of Hamilton. She was apparently thinking in terms of his important rank rather than his political standing as the leader of the Scottish Jacobites, but the association between Jacobitism and the peace was by no means accidental. Before he could leave for Utrecht, on 15 November 1712, he engaged in a duel with Lord Mohun with whom he was engaged in a lawsuit. He killed Lord Mohun and subsequently died of the wounds inflicted by his opponent or, as the Tories had it, by Mohun's second, a major-general under Marlborough named MacCartney, who was reported by one witness to have pushed his sword at the Duke of Hamilton while he lay on the ground. The Jacobites felt that the death of Hamilton was a Whig plot which successfully destroyed the possibility of a return of the Pretender.[19] That such a

[17] *Review*, viii. 497.
[18] Ibid. 848.
[19] See George Lockhart, *Lockhart Papers* (London: William Anderson, 1817), i. 377, 402, 482.

duel could be politicized shows just how much a 'miserable divided nation' Britain had become.[20] Though Shrewsbury, a moderate Whig, was chosen as the Duke of Hamilton's successor, the Treaty of Utrecht seemed to many to be tainted with Jacobitism.

Defoe's pamphlet on the subject of the duel, *A Strict Enquiry into the Circumstances of a Late Duel*, appeared at the beginning of 1713. Insofar as the treatment of evidence, the details of criminal trials, were to have a major influence on the novel, and in particular on Defoe's novels, this work has to be seen as one step on the path toward Defoe's later fictions. Swift, in writing to Stella of the duel and in his version of the same in his *History of the Last Four Years of the Queen*, viewed Mohun as a 'Rake' and MacCartney a murderer. Swift was always partisan, always convinced that a man such as the Duke of Hamilton, because he was his friend, must have been in the right. Defoe, on the contrary, attempts a tone of complete impartiality. The duel had nothing to do with politics and everything to do with two men of passionate temperament being so transported by their sense of 'Honour' that they felt they had to come to this violent confrontation. Defoe's actual position favoured the Whig view. He argued that the Duke had been affronted by remarks made by Lord Mohun over a Chancery suit, and had issued the challenge. Neither of the two could claim much in the way of a 'Character' that would avoid the duel, but an examination of the evidence suggested that MacCartney did not run his sword at the Duke after he had been wounded by Mohun. Neither the testimony of the witnesses nor his behaviour afterwards suggested MacCartney's guilt. The pamphlet has some resemblance to a detective story. Defoe examines the varying accounts and weighs the evidence before coming to his decision, supplying a letter from MacCartney corroborating Defoe's conclusions and stating that he had left the country for fear he could not receive a proper trial at a time, when, as Swift described it, there was 'a Devilish Spirit among People'.[21]

Like Sir Richard Steele, Defoe attacked duelling as a remnant of an obsolete concept of gentility and chivalry. In his early numbers of the *Review*, Defoe had praised the French for their strict laws against duelling and printed them in an appendix. Interestingly enough, he did not return to

---

[20] *Review*, viii. 489.

[21] Jonathan Swift, *A Journal to Stella*, ed. Harold Williams (2 vols., Oxford: Clarendon Press, 1948), ii. 570–4. Colonel Hamilton, the Duke's second, testified that MacCartney had thrust a sword through the Duke's left breast while the Colonel was helping the wounded Duke up. This account had him winning his duel with MacCartney and disarming him; MacCartney's letter suggests that he won the duel between the seconds and left Hyde Park without further violence. When MacCartney returned to England after the Whigs were in power, Colonel Hamilton's account was discredited, but in 1712 the Tories considered the duel to be a Whig Plot. See *Portland Papers*, v. 246–7.

the subject until Swift's attacks upon him, when he was apparently angry enough to recall how he felt when he had engaged in something resembling a duel against a '*Rascal*' and expressed his personal 'Penitence' for it.[22] As for the duel between Hamilton and Mohun, Defoe argued that both of them were guilty:

Nothing of Purity reaches there; Provocation, Point of Honour. Heat of Blood, and all the Pretences which Fools form, to cover themselves with, will Argue nothing then; he that needlessly or unjustly puts his own Life in hazard, is a Murtherer as much as he that takes his Life away; he that foolishly and wickedly exposes his Life, is a Self-Murtherer, as much as he that hangs himself, or cuts his own Throat; and in this Sense, every Dueller is a Murtherer, nay every Duel is a Murther, whether any one is kill'd there or no.[23]

Drawing upon his 'own unhappy Experience', he dismissed reports that the Duke of Hamilton had spent the night in religious devotions as both uncharacteristic of the man and absurd from a Christian standpoint. 'I am of the Opinion', he wrote, 'such times are taken up, in the rolling of the Passions, the boyling of the Blood, the furious agitation of the Animal Spirits.' A high sense of honour is merely a pretence. Under these circumstances, the duellist is stricken with a sense of shame that seems worse than death, but, Defoe argues, it all amounts to the fear of being branded a coward by the outside world. And from this fear, the duellist acts against reason and against the law.

Defoe's pamphlet on the Hamilton–Mohun duel was structured so as to give a feeling of complete authenticity as well as objectivity, and the exercise in restraint may have whetted his appetite for the kinds of playing with point of view he delighted in. That Defoe should have kept away from irony for as long as he did was, for him, remarkable, but the line from Juvenal, to the effect that it was impossible not to write satire given the condition of the world, was always in Defoe's mind, and in the end he could not resist. *Reasons against the Succession of the House of Hanover*, published on 21 February 1713, mocked the absurdity of the arguments

22 See the *Review* for 14 and 16 Dec. 1710. Frank Bastian has formed Defoe's references to duelling here and in both *Memoirs of Major Ramkins* and *Colonel Jack* into an autobiographical confession. In both the *Review* and in his fictions, the occasion for the duel is not political but an affair with the injured party's wife. The story in the *Review* involves the argument that the husband ought not to risk his own life because his wife has been unfaithful but rather demand as his revenge the right to have intercourse with the wife of the man who has injured him. The man who makes this demand is described as 'A Gentleman of a Courage that had been try'd upon many Occasions'. What it suggests, I think, is that a Defoe who had been absent from his wife for many months at a time, whether because he was in hiding, in gaol, or working as a government agent, fantasized about the possibility that his wife might prove unfaithful and how he would act under those circumstances. Of course turning such fantasies into fictional narratives was his speciality.

23 *Review*, ix. 67.

being put forth by the Jacobites by adding a few that were even more absurd. He began with a picture of the nation divided downstairs as well as upstairs:

You Gentlefolks, if you please to listen to your Cook-maids and Footmen in your Kitchens, you shall hear them scolding, and swearing, and scratching, and fighting, among themselves; and when you think the Noise is about Beef and Pudding, the Dish-water, or the Kitchen-stuff, alas you are mistaken, the Feud is about the more mighty Affairs of the Government, and who is for the Protestant Succession, and who is for the Pretender.[24]

He proceeded from this vision of political warfare among all classes to the question of whether, by the time the future George I was ready to assume the throne, the nation would be in a condition to receive him. And would he want to come into so quarrelsome a nation? Would the nation be capable of defending him? As desperate diseases required desperate remedies, so surely bringing in the Pretender was desperate enough to cure anything. Since good and evil lie in the 'Intention', perhaps it would be possible to intend to bring over the King of Hanover but really bring in the Pretender. Toward the end he raises the question of hereditary right and passive obedience, but points out that none of this makes any difference because James fled the country and abandoned any claim that his family might have. The Latin motto for the pamphlet was '*Si populus vult decipi, Decipiatur*' (If the people wish to be deceived, they will be deceived), and that was really the purpose of Defoe's satire—to suggest that all the words and arguments in a cause that would mean the loss of liberty are absurd.

Defoe's third pamphlet of visions from the 'Second-Sighted Highlander' focused mainly on the striving for peace and its uneven success, but he also saw no possibility that the Pretender would manage to take over the throne. Some, he foresaw, would try, 'but the Fruit is not ripe, and some who pretend to pull it before it is come to Perfection, make much of it Fall to the Ground in the shaking'.[25] Having taken the high ground from anyone having mystical visions involving the arrival of the Pretender, Defoe returned to his ironic stance with *And What If the Pretender Should Come? or, Some Considerations of the Advantages and Real Consequences of the Pretender's Possessing the Crown of Great Britain*. This time he limited his absurd arguments to one—the benefits of having someone on the throne who was a true friend of the French. If this occurred, he opined, 'then we shall on the contrary say to the World, the stronger the King of *France* is,

[24] *Reasons against the Succession of the House of Hanover* (London, 1713), 3.
[25] *The Second-Sighted Highlander: or, Predictions and Foretold Events: Especially about the Peace* (London, 1713), 10.

the better for the King of *England*; and what is best for the King, must be so for his People; for it is a most unnatural Way of Arguing to suppose the Interest of a King and of his People, to be different from one another'.[26] There is much in this argument that the Tories would have accepted, and the argument for the benefit of trade with France was what Defoe was advancing in *Mercator* at the time. Indeed, he was trying to draw his readers into his discourse gradually, pointing to the problems with 'this Trifle we call Liberty'. The Pretender would wipe out the burden of the national debt, and England would be more like so great a nation as France:

And when will they learn to know, that the Absolute Government of a Vertuous Prince, who makes the Good of his People his Ultimate End, and esteems their Prosperity his Glory, is the Best, and most godlike, Government in the World. . . . Tyranny is no more Tyranny, when improv'd for the Subjects Advantage; perhaps when we have tried it we may find it as much for our Good many ways, nay, and more too, than our present Exorbitant Liberties . . . a little *French Slavery* . . . as yet may do us a great deal of Good in the Main, as it may teach us not to *Over* (Under) *Value* our Liberties, when we have them, so much as sometimes we have done; and this is not one of the least Advantages which we shall gain by the Coming of the Pretender, and consequently one of the good Reasons why we should be very willing to receive him.[27]

The parenthesis that Defoe adds to create the neologism 'Over (Under) Value' shows that he was uncertain whether his audience would understand his irony. The argument becomes gradually more ridiculous as he speaks of the money saved by people not having to travel to Parliament, the fine fortified cities built by the presence of a large standing army, the end of stock-jobbing, and the useful destruction of all freedom of the press. Some of Defoe's arguments might have seemed fairly good to some of his readers, especially those who did not pick up passages such as 'your new Monarch will suffer none to Insult or Plunder the City *but himself*'.[28] But most readers would have got the message that many of the faults of British government and society were part of the price paid by a free people for their liberties. One section, however, was straight enough: his comments on a Scotland that would eagerly end a Union which, by 1713, 'not one Man in Fifteen, throughout Scotland' would vote for. [29] This was a brilliant pamphlet, but not without its ambiguities. Defoe's irony on the wonderful advantages of the trade to France for England could not have made St John

---

[26] *And What If the Pretender Should Come?* (London, 1713), 12.

[27] Ibid. 20–1.

[28] Ibid. 36.

[29] Ibid. 27. Apparently Defoe did not find himself greeted by the Scots as one of the heroic builders of the Union Treaty during his last trip to Scotland.

very happy, and his comment on the happiness of Spain in receiving a king from France, read within the pamphlet's ironic context, does not seem to be the work of a writer willing to accept Philip III as the ruler of Spain. In short, it was hardly calculated to avoid trouble.

The third of these pamphlets, *What If the Queen Should Die?*, published in April 1713, had the most provocative title but was actually the least ambiguous of the three that were soon to be cited for sedition. In a sober response to Jacobitism, Defoe argued that the ministry could not support the Pretender 'without such Inconsistencies, Contradictions, and Improbable things happening in, which render it highly *Irrational*, so much to suppose it of them'.[30] Nevertheless, he argued that there were Jacobites in the government and that the situation was fraught with danger. The Queen was not to die until 1 August 1714, more than a year later, but had she not appointed Shrewsbury as Lord Treasurer and as head of the committee charged with handling the transition to King George I, the change would not have been half so smooth. As it was, there were to be riots in parts of England and a rebellion in Scotland.

III

Naturally enough, with titles such as Defoe gave his three pamphlets, they sold remarkably well, but they also gave an opening to his enemies, who began organizing against him. On 23 March 1713 he was arrested on an escape warrant and committed once more to prison. The matter this time was an old debt that he thought he had satisfied. It went back to his first bankruptcy of 1691 and had been the cause of some difficulty for him in 1705 and 1706 when, during his visit to the eastern counties, the creditor had spread malicious rumours about Defoe's character.[31] Now he was accused of owing £1,500 to a Yarmouth citizen. Defoe wrote to Harley from prison, begging for help and complaining of the actions of 'a private Set of Men' (H 401) who had acted behind the scenes in stirring up this creditor. While rumours floated that Harley had advanced the full sum, Defoe stated that the creditor had settled for 10 per cent of what he had requested.[32] Defoe remained in prison for eleven days, and seven of them

---

[30] *What If the Queen Should Die?* (London, 1713), 7–8.

[31] In his letter to Harley, Defoe mentions difficulties that he had when he 'Travelled a journey into the West', and credits Harley with having protected him at this time. But the letters that we have from and to Fransham (H 115, 123) reveal that he was still having trouble with debts contracted in Yarmouth.

[32] A comparison of the letters that Defoe wrote to Harley at this time is useful. In 1706, when Defoe first informed Harley of the attempt to collect this debt, Defoe was engaged in his trip to the eastern

passed before he wrote to Harley. Since he stated that the arrest occurred in the evening when he was on his way to visit the Lord Treasurer, his remark about writing only because Harley would wonder what had become of him seems genuine enough. He was apparently unwilling to involve Harley if he could help it, and the embarrassment expressed in the letter seems equally real. If his attempt to describe his arrest as arising out of the activities of a 'Faction rather than a Creditor' (H 402) involved a degree of self-pleading, it was probably accurate enough. Those who had complained of Defoe's 'self-conceit' sought to undermine his confidence by shaming and embarrassing him publicly. If the attacks in the public press and numerous pamphlets would not succeed, perhaps an arrest in the full sight of his neighbours would. Little more than a week after his release, Defoe was back in prison, this time on a charge of libel. Three Whig journalists, William Benson, Thomas Burnet, and George Ridpath, joined in filing a complaint against Defoe before Lord Chief Justice Parker. As Defoe pointed out in his letter to Harley of 12 April 1713, all these journalists were at that time under prosecution by the government for seditious and libellous publications. Revenge may have been their motivation, a private grudge against someone whom they regarded as benefiting from the kind of protection against prosecution that they lacked,[33] but the likelihood is that their action was known and encouraged by other members of the Whig party. At any rate, Parker issued the warrant for the printer, Richard Janeaway, who implicated Defoe's publisher, John Baker, and Defoe himself. The printers swore that they recognized Defoe's writing in the manuscripts of the pamphlets, and were to form part of the mob audience when Defoe was taken into custody. The arrest was intended to resemble a kind of street theatre with a group of spectators brought along to hiss the villain, a miniature re-enactment of Defoe's public shaming when he had appeared in the pillory a decade earlier.[34]

Defoe was arrested on the morning of Saturday 11 April 1713 and led into London with a cavalcade of arresting officers and some of the printers from the Janeaway shop. These were the same printers who said that they had seen these pamphlets in Defoe's handwriting, or rather handwritings, since they claimed that they could recognize the variety of disguised scripts

counties to discover the temper of the nation, still enjoying his role as a spy. In 1713, his letters to Harley sound a note of desperation. See H 123, 401–2.

[33] 'they were heard to Say that they had all been prosecuted and the Review had a full liberty, but They would bring him in whether the Ministry would or no' (H 406).

[34] In the *Review* for 14 Apr., Defoe stated that one of those who filed the warrant against him were heard to vent their anger at being prosecuted and add, *'. . . damn him, why should not he have some Trouble? They shall see that we can bring him upon the Stage, whether they will or no.'*

that he used. The printers joined with the substantial group sent to arrest him, and his enemies spread word that his house was fortified[35] and might have to be forced open:

> But the Design was plain, (*viz.*) To execute the Warrant, and carry on the whole afterward, with as much Insult, Rage and Noise, and as little Humanity as they could, the Tip-Staff himself being asham'd of them.
>
> To Illustrate this piece of Malice, let the Reason of the Case be considered, if I had had *the least knowledge* of the thing, Why was I not gone from Home, which had been better than ten Fortifyings of my House? And if I had *no knowledge of it,* how could I strenthen the House against them?—Whereas the truth is, all that know my House, know there is not a Lock, Bolt, or Bar in it, more than when I came first to it.[36]

If Defoe is to be believed, the plan to carry him to Newgate in an embarrassing manner failed, as the arresting officer allowed him to ride his horse into town in a manner that created a considerable distance between him and those who wanted to make the arrest into 'a Mobbing Business'. Defoe suggested that the incident would be difficult for the ministry as well as for himself, since by arranging his release the government could be accused of being against the Protestant succession, a prediction that proved to be true enough. By bringing him to Newgate on Saturday, his enemies made sure that he would spend a few miserable nights in the prison he hated and feared most of all, but on Monday he was free again. Harley smoothed over the process of arranging bail, and £1600 was paid, £400 each by the publisher Thomas Warner and the printer, John Grantham, and £800 by Defoe himself. But as Defoe foresaw, the Whigs credited the government with putting up the money as well as influencing Lord Chief Justice Parker.[37]

These painful and significant events might be ascribed directly to Defoe's increasing efforts at defending the position of the ministry in the *Review*. He not only found the Peace of Utrecht acceptable but began arguing that were the Dutch and the Austrians successful in their attempts to bring France to its knees, England would have to go to war on the side of France to retain the balance of power in Europe. Why he persisted in this paradoxical position is difficult to say. He suggested it to Harley in a

[35] There were accounts of secret trap-doors and other devices in the house. William P. Trent, who spent a considerable amount of time investigating descriptions of the house, concluded that although the windows were inset, presenting the appearance of a house that might resist an assault, Defoe's dwelling at Stoke Newington had none of the heavy locks and bars that some of his enemies implied were there. See MS biography, Trent Collection.

[36] *Review*, i[ix]. 169–70.

[37] The Solicitor to the Treasury, William Borret, approved Defoe's bail. Healey points out that Borret figured in Defoe's arrest in 1703 and in an investigation of the *Review* in 1708.

letter of 27 May 1712 after the Dutch had published a series of effective 'memorials' defending their actions as proper and attacked the behaviour of the British as perfidious. As the Dutch and Prince Eugene absorbed a series of defeats throughout the summer of 1712, Defoe had less occasion to raise the dreadful notion of fighting an ally. He tried to explain how much he disliked the notion of a war against the Dutch, Britain's partner in maintaining Protestant power in Europe, but in advancing and dwelling upon this idea, he seems to have allowed his ideas too much play. It was hardly the first or last time that he allowed his love of paradox to triumph over his common sense. A contemporary pamphlet with the title *A Letter from a Tory Freeholder to his Representative in Parliament* shows how perplexing his arguments must have appeared. The Tory speaker points to Defoe's arguments as those being offered by someone with good Whig credentials, but his opponents dismissed that notion as absurd:

Here I thought I had a Loop-hole to escape, and told 'em I know of no body who writ more for a War against the *Dutch* than *Daniel Foe*, of their own Party. This they entertain'd with a Scoff, and answer'd, it was evident that since the Change of the Ministry, that Scribler had chang'd his Conduct, and was visibly retain'd on Our side; adding, that he was always a mercenary Tool, that they could prove he had taken mony on both sides, and that the Whigs do now universally disown him as much as they did . . . other infamous Tools, who were always the Disgrace of the Whig-Party, tho now some of the brightest Ornaments of ours.[38]

As Defoe went from defending the Peace to arguing for the benefits of St John's Commercial Treaty with France, whatever credibility he retained as spokesman for the Whigs waned rapidly. More than ever before, he reminded the readers of the *Review* of his allegiance to Whig principles. The fault was not in him but with the party strife that had brought the Whigs over to the side of men such as the Earl of Nottingham. 'O DISMAL', he lamented, using the satirical name usually applied to Nottingham, but now applied by Defoe, in a symbolic fashion, to the behaviour of the entire party.[39]

At a time when he was attempting to align his arguments with those of the government, Defoe allowed himself a certain degree of indulgence in complaining about the treatment of Scotland. After what were distinctly anti-Scottish rulings on the abjuration oath and on toleration, Parliament turned to the problem of levying a malt tax upon Scotland. Defoe had been

[38] *A Letter from a Tory Freeholder to his Representative in Parliament* (London, 1712), 15. The Whigs refer to Defoe as a 'Convert' to Tory ideas, and dismiss his arguments on maintaining the balance of power as having 'been answer'd a hundred times without a possibility of Reply'.

[39] See *Review* for 9 June 1713 for one of his last expressions about party warfare.

instrumental in getting the compromise on this matter through one of the many committees involved in crafting the Union Treaty. Taxation had been deferred until the end of the war, and Defoe could point out that there was no real violation of that Treaty in imposing a tax after the Treaty of Utrecht. The trouble was, as Defoe argued in the last numbers of the *Review*, that Scotland was a poor country and the malt used in the making of beer was different from that used in England, being of an 'inferiour Quality'.[40] By taxing Scotland at the same rate as England, Parliament was subjecting the Scots to an intolerably heavy burden—a tax that would probably put many breweries out of business. Nevertheless, Defoe argued, the actions of Parliament did not break the Treaty of Union. Since that had been agreed upon by a Scottish Parliament that no longer existed and an English Parliament without any representatives from Scotland, there was no way in which the two nations could separate themselves. Defoe still clung to his accomplishments in bringing about the Union, even during a period when he was abandoning almost all principles except loyalty to the government that employed him.

The other belief in which he still prided himself was his constant adherence to the House of Hanover. The three ironic pamphlets on the succession were anything but government-approved propaganda. They represented his own attempt to show how essential to the wellbeing of the nation adherence to the Protestant succession actually was. When he wrote to Harley about the attempt to accuse him of treason, he felt some need to explain to his employer the 'Reason for The Manner of writeing in all these books, the Necessity There has been to give a Turn in all I Wrot, which should gratifye Some of the Weaknesses of those poor people to Detect the Rest' (H 407). It seems that Defoe was writing to attract not only Jacobites, who would find that, despite the titles, they had purchased works supporting the Hanoverian succession, but also those Whigs who, in a time of party strife, would buy Jacobite pamphlets to feed their anger and anxiety. In the *Review* he insisted upon his loyalty to the Hanoverian succession, and affirmed, 'I never could think of the Pretender's coming in, or being set up here to Rule over us, but with Horror and Aversion.'[41] That he should be arrested for attempting to spread Jacobite propaganda for these works must have appeared to him a complete outrage, the kind of absurd lie of the type that often renders its victims speechless.[42]

His arrest made Defoe realize that the *Review* could no longer be an

---

[40] *Review* i [ix]. 203.
[41] Ibid. 167.
[42] For an analysis of this kind of experience, see Jean-François Lyotard, *The Differend: Phrases in Dispute*, trans. Georges Van Den Abbeele (Minneapolis: University of Minnesota Press, 1988), esp. 3–31.

effective voice for him. When he appeared before the Court of the Queen's Bench on 22 April to answer the charge of treason in connection with the three pamphlets, Parker, the Lord Chief Justice, asked if he was the author of the *Review*. Parker, it turned out, had taken offence at some of Defoe's remarks about the proceedings against him in that Journal for 16 and 18 April 1713. He claimed that Defoe had libelled both him personally and the laws of England in general. Defoe had drawn a picture of his being persecuted and prosecuted for defending the House of Hanover and writing against the Pretender. 'If the Prosecutors will not see their own Knavery,' wrote Defoe, 'they shall never say other People do not see it.' He added, 'This is not an Age to complain of Injustice, but to expect it', a remark which might have seemed innocuous enough as a speculative reflection on the unfairness of life but which might be taken as a direct accusation of malfeasance when applied to a particular case.[43] Parker left it to the other justices to consider the charge, and they promptly threw Defoe into the Queen's Bench prison. Defoe was in jail once more, the third time in the month of April.

On this occasion, the charge against him was for libel rather than for treason, but that could hardly have been much consolation. Defoe's argument in one of the offending issues of the *Review*, was that he had written in a recognizably ironic mode:

If I have really written a Word in my Life, in prejudice of the Interest of *Hanover*, I am content to have an Act of Parliament pass (even now) *ex post facto*, to make it *High Treason*, and I'll submit to the Punishment. But if what I have written be the strongest Irony, and consequently the greatest push that I could make against the Pretender's Interest, then this Prosecution must be Malicious and Abominable. Nor is this Irony concealed, *as has been suggested formerly*; but it is express'd plainly, and explicitly, in words at length.[44]

But when he made a similar defence at his trial, one of the justices replied that 'he might come to be hang'd, drawn, and quarter'd' for such irony.[45] That of course was the punishment for treason, and indeed Defoe's three pamphlets were ruled to be 'Scandalous, Wicked, and Treasonable Libels'.

If Defoe sought to set the stage for his trial by the wholly justified cries of righteous indignation in the *Review*, his enemies were depicting him as a person of such deviousness that all his protestations about his love for the House of Hanover and his hatred for the Pretender might be viewed as part

---

[43] *Review*, i [ix]. 168–69.

[44] Ibid. 168.

[45] Trent speculated that it was Sir Thomas Powys who made this remark, though Parker was certainly the judge who ruled that the themes of Defoe's three pamphlets were 'not Subjects to be play'd with'. MS biography, 332; PRO, SP 34/21/241, repr. in H 410–11.

of the elaborate system of pretence that seemed to govern his life. The author of *Judas Discuver'd, and Catch'd at last: Or, Daniel De Foe in Lobs Pound*, however inept a writer, was able to bring together all the charges against Defoe that had been made over the past decade:

Of all the Writers that have Prostituted their Pens, either to encourage *Faction*, oblige a party, or for their own *Mercenary Ends*; the *Person* here mentioned is the Vilest. An *Animal* who shifts his Shape oftner then *Proteus*, and goes backwards and forwards like a Hunted hare; a thorough-pac'd, true-bred *Hypocrite*, an *High-Church Man* one Day, and a *Rank Whig* the next: Like the *Satyr* in the *Fable*, he blows Hot and Cold with the same Breath, and is in reality a downright *Fanatick*. This same too and fro *Antimonarchial-Loyal-Person*, imagining no doubt that he began to decline in the Eye of the World, he Ushers into the World a Scandalous and Seditious Libel, call'd *Reasons against the Succession of the House of Hanover*, etc. with a melicious and treacherous intent to Poyson the Minds of Her majesty's *Subjects*, foment Divisions, raise Jealousies, and cause a Commotion among the *People*.[46]

Asking for a rational analysis of these works seemed futile to this author; they might seem ironic, but who knew what else they might be? Such attacks created a dangerous environment for Defoe. Imprisonment for libel was one thing, suffering the terrible punishment for treason was quite another. To the outrage of the Whigs, Defoe received a direct pardon for his offences from Queen Anne on 16 October 1713 and escaped in a far more successful manner than he had at the time of his arrest and punishment related to the *Shortest Way*. To Whigs and enemies of Defoe, such as John Oldmixon, the Queen's action seemed to be a violation of the laws of England, but what they really regretted was that, after seemingly having cornered him, they found that if he did not actually have a trapdoor in his house, he had equally deft ways of escaping from the grasp of his enemies.[47]

As for the charge of libelling the Lord Chief Justice, Defoe was released after apologizing before the court. He repeated his apology in print as the substance of identical issues of the *Review* for 28 April and 5 May. No one can say that he did not know how to grovel when it became necessary: he confessed his error 'in the humblest Manner possible, and with the lowest Submission', promising that he would 'never take the Liberty to mention any thing in Publick which relates to Your Lordships Proceedings, in any rspect whatsoever'.[48] It must have seemed both to himself and to his audience that 'Mr. Review' had lost the ability to avoid offending or of having his offences ignored.

[46] *Judas Discuver'd, and Catch'd at last* (London, 1713), 3.
[47] *Read's Weekly Journal* for 24 Aug. 1717 accused Defoe of having a '*Trap-Door*' by which to escape from his enemies. [48] *Review*, i [ix]. 177–8, 181–2.

This was the swan-song of the *Review*. Defoe announced its demise in the issue for 6 June 1713 along with the image of his retreating from the world 'as to writing', but like many a performer, he tended to extend his farewell somewhat. 'I shall be a quiet Spectator of those wretched abominable Divisions, that I can do no good in attempting to Cure,' he lamented, 'and I shall be a silent Mourner over the Miseries of my Country, which I expect this Rage, that now governs our Parties, will bring us to.'[49] Even on his death bed Mr Review could not avoid preaching. He lingered for another month after the apology, attacking some safe targets such as his enemy George Ridpath, the editor of the *Flying Post*, or 'Lying Post', as Defoe liked to call it. Ridpath avoided the wrath of the government by leaving the country. The event reminded him of his own opportunity to escape the pillory by forfeiting his bail and how he would not take so dishonourable a way out. In his final issue, he attacked the sins of the nation under the term 'Whoring', admitting in his final paragraph before going to his 'Retreat', perhaps hundreds of miles from London, that 'Writing upon Trade was the Whore I really doated upon', and lamenting that his true 'Whore' had been 'ravish'd out of . . . [his] hands by the *Mercator*', a new journal devoted entirely to that subject. It was characteristic of Defoe to end his journal on a satiric note and not so sad after all, since the supposedly silenced Defoe was certainly the author of that new journal.

IV

Mercator: or Commerce Retriev'd appeared for the first time on 26 May, at approximately the same time as he published two numbers of the *Review* offering the challenging idea that the high quality of English woollen manufactures would overcome lower-priced goods from other countries and help to destroy any effort of the French to compete. These essays were plainly supportive of Bolingbroke's Commercial Treaty, but it became clear that a different type of journal was needed for performing the task of defending the Treaty, a journal on trade. A year later, Defoe reminded Harley that he had been hired to write *Mercator* by Arthur Moore, Bolingbroke's financial adviser. He claimed that he had not been paid for some time, meaning, presumably, that he had not been given money, beyond what he usually received from the Secret Service payments, to defend the Commercial Treaty:

[49] *Review*, i [ix]. 209.

So that I perform it wholly without any Appointm[en]t for it, or benefit by it; which I do Singly as I hope it is of Service, and That it may be agreeable to your Ldpp to have it Continued; Tho' my Circumstances render it hard to me to do So because it is Expensive to me. But I lay it all and my Self at your Ldpps Feet. (H 441)

That Defoe's work on *Mercator* was purely a labour of love is much to be doubted, but that it constituted work for Bolingbroke rather than Harley seems obvious.[50] The real question is, how comfortable was Defoe with an assignment from a man who was hand in glove with the High Church party and even suspected by some of leaning toward Jacobitism?[51] Did Defoe simply regard himself now as a government official taking orders unquestioningly from his superiors? Was this what he had in mind when he wrote of his retreat into another kind of world in the last numbers of the *Review*? One thing is certain: he was determined to keep a lower profile than previously and to take advantage of the power that anonymity, of writing in a mask, could give him. His statement about his authorship of *Mercator* was for Harley's eyes only. To everyone else, a W. Brown, alias Mr. Backstroke, was the author.

Now although Defoe did indeed delight in writing about trade, the situation in 1713 made such discussions highly political. Bolingbroke's negotiation of the Commercial Treaty with France would have oriented British trade in a wholly new direction, away from the highly profitable trade to Portugal negotiated in the Methuen Treaty and toward the former national enemy. At a time when trade was regarded as a form of warfare by other means, the aim of any nation was to gain the balance of trade and perhaps destroy certain aspects of a trading partner's economy. The great fear of the English was that French wines would replace those of Portugal in the English diet, and that French silks would cause a decline in the use of woollens at home. High tariffs could be used to balance matters by making the price of foreign products prohibitive, but what was most important to any nation operating under these principles of mercantilism was to emerge victorious from the trade war. When Defoe had advised trading with France while the war was continued, he did so because he thought that Britain could maintain its high tariffs on wines and other products while taking advantage of France's need for British goods, particularly woollen

[50] He mentioned *Mercator* in a letter to Harley on 1 Aug. 1713. Defoe never commented upon the well-publicized quarrels between Harley and Bolingbroke in his letters to Harley, and not until the day before Harley was dismissed on 27 July 1714 did he inform him that he had heard rumours about such an event.

[51] There were rumours that during his stay in Paris, while negotiating terms for peace, Bolingbroke had actually met with the Pretender. They were certainly both present at the performance of an opera. See Sheila Biddle, *Bolingbroke and Harley* (New York: Knopf, 1974), 243.

cloth. The Commercial Treaty posed a more difficult scenario; he would have to stress the advantages of the commerce while somehow trying to ignore the possible danger of having French wines dominate the home market and cause the nation to lose the balance of trade.

Defoe must have enjoyed the challenge. He came up with some ingenious ideas which flirted with concepts close to the ideals of free trade to be proposed by the Physiocrats in France and Adam Smith in Britain later in the century. But while Defoe was always extraordinarily inventive under difficult circumstances of this kind, his ingenious suggestions did not always ring true. From the very first number, he argued that trade with France had always been to England's advantage. He obtained access to the custom house records on the trade to France and tried to turn them to his benefit by claiming that only in those years in which the French raised the tariff did British trade suffer. Unfortunately, his journalistic opponent Henry Martyn, in the *British Merchant* managed to show that he had played with the figures to buttress his position. In fact, Martyn had most of the accepted economic arguments on his side and won his battle with Defoe easily enough.[52] As has been mentioned, several years later, when Defoe answered one of his opponents who had attacked him for carrying on arguments for a treaty that might have destroyed English trade, he commented tartly that having a 'bad Cause to handle, I did the best for my Clients; as he having a bad Cause now in his Hands does the best for his'.[53] Defoe was inventive and often skilful, but from his standpoint, any trade with France that would not provide proper protection was dangerous. Though the treaty was defeated in the House of Commons on 23 June 1713, to Bolingbroke's irritation and embarrassment, the debate over trade continued at fever pitch for another year, not only because Bolingbroke considered reviving the bill in some form during the next session of Parliament, but because the question of trade had become a part of the war between the various factions.

The real problem with the Commercial Treaty lay with the eighth and ninth articles, which involved giving France equal trade status with nations such as Portugal. In a separate pamphlet in favour of the Treaty, Defoe could offer the hope that in negotiating these issues, 'I think it easie to make out, that the Commissioners who are to meet to Regulate Duties, Remove

---

[52] The strongest 'maxim' that Defoe had on his side was that 'manufacturing Nations ought never to prohibit the exportation of their own Manufactures to any place whatsoever. Importations may be Prohibited as Emergency may offer, and sometimes are made necessary by the Circumstances of Trade, but exportations never' (*Mercator* 23 (14–16 July 1713)). But compared with the maxims offered by a 'Generosity Thrifty' in a letter to No. 170 of *The Guardian*, Defoe had few enough traditional arguments. See *The Guardian*, ed. John Calhoun Stephens (Lexington: Kentucky University Press, 1982), 552–6.

[53] *The Manufacturer* 10 (2 Dec. 1719).

Difficulties, and State the Proportions and Differences of Things, may so order it, that the General Interest of Trade in *Britain* shall be bettered very much by the Treaty'.[54] But in *Considerations upon the Eighth and Ninth Articles of the Treaty of Commerce*, he was less sanguine. Since the trade to France would undoubtedly undermine the trade to Portugal, which supplies Britain with gold in exchange for English products, the treaty must provide an 'Equivalent' or else be worthless. Since fashion and taste are fickle, and a taste for the primitive ('*Indian* Pictures') in art may 'become more valuable than the Finest Paintings of *Italy*', and 'since Our Fancies are thus debauch'd; if possible then, whatever Treaties of Commerce are made', care must be taken to protect British trade. On the whole, he thought the treaty would disrupt employment intolerably:

It is humbly recommended then to those in whose Hands Power is or shall be lodg'd to do these Things, that they would consider the many Thousand Families of our Poor, as well *Weavers* as others, who depend upon the *Silk Manufactures* in this Nation, as also the Great and truly Beneficial Trade to *Turkey* and the *Levant*, from whence our *Silk* is chiefly Imported, and to purchase which, our *Broad Cloth* is sent in such great Quantities, as to make a very considerable Figure also in the Employment of our People in the Country; all which must sink in a very great Degree, if some immediate Care is not taken, and Means used to keep up the Value of our own *Broad Silks*, and keep down and discourage, as much as may be, the Importation of *French Silks*, upon this New Opening.[55]

In short, where he was able to take advantage of anonymity, Defoe argued that the Commercial Treaty posed considerable risk.

Defoe's official propaganda, from *Memoirs of Count Tariff* to the *Mercator*, attempted to be more optimistic and innovative. He proposed that the superior workmanship of the English would give them an advantage over their French competitors and that even if the balance in an exchange of French wines for English wool favoured the French, it would nevertheless benefit the labouring poor at home. Only the wealthy would be able to afford French wines, and if they wanted to ruin themselves in expenditures of this kind, so be it. He wanted all prohibitions against exporting manufactured goods removed, and advocated severe punishment for anyone caught exporting raw wool. But what he maintained above all was this: 'It is an undoubted rule of trade, that the employment of our own poor, and Consumption of our own Growth, is the first Principle of Commerce.'[56] This was indeed a general maxim of mercantilist

---

[54] *An Essay on the Treaty of Commerce with France* (London, 1713), 37.
[55] *Considerations upon the Eighth and Ninth Articles of the Treaty of Commerce* (London, 1713), 34, 36.
[56] *Mercator* 8 (9–11 June 1713).

economics, but his emphasis on the wellbeing of the poor and upon consumption was somewhat unusual. At a time when driving down the wages of the poor as much as possible was a very real ideal for many economists, he envisioned a nation of healthy and prosperous workers whose very prosperity would enable them to work harder and more skilfully than their foreign competitors.

19

A Change of Monarchs and the Whig's Revenge

When Defoe published one of the three pamphlets that brought him so much grief, *An Answer to a Question that No Body Thinks of, Viz. But What if the Queen Should Die?*, Queen Anne's health was clearly failing. She had been ill on and off throughout 1712, and the meeting of Parliament had been delayed until December for that reason. She grew worse during the following year, and fell so ill at Windsor around Christmas time that her ministers were summoned to her bedside. In his usual fashion Defoe had put in print what was regarded as a taboo subject, and Lord Chief Justice Parker thought he should be punished for it. In fact, succession was in everyone's mind. The Whigs were struggling violently to succeed the Tories, and within the government, Bolingbroke was struggling mightily to take over power from Harley. Harley felt that he had lost real control by 25 July 1713, but not until the end of that year was it clear to all that Bolingbroke's measures were winning favour and Harley's were losing. Though Harley was prepared to resign by 19 March, he actually staged a belated rally in July only to be dismissed by Queen Anne on 27 July 1714. The Queen died a few days later, on 1 August, but not before approving the choice of the Duke of Shrewsbury as Lord Treasurer and assuring the Protestant succession and the transition from the House of Stuart to the House of Hanover. But before that event, party quarrels, the battle over the nature of English trade, the continuing controversy over the Peace of Utrecht and its provisions, and renewed legislation against the Dissenters created divisions in society seldom matched in English history. Defoe's response to these events seemed to be similar to that of some of his later fictional characters in his adventure tales. He was adrift in stormy seas with a damaged compass, few provisions, and a desperate need to know which way the wind would be blowing.

I

Faced with such uncertain times, Defoe attempted to conceal his activities as best he could, but by now he was anything but a part-time writer. The arrest in April and the accompanying testimony by his publishers revealed a great deal about his work as a journalist. He sent his work, usually in his own hand, to the printer, and the proofs were returned to him by the printer's messenger either to his chambers in the New Temple or to his house. He often used his sons to carry the corrected proof back to the printers and for other errands; on 1 April 1713, when he was in prison, one of them carried his letter to Harley. At least one pamphleteer accused Defoe of having neglected the education of his sons so that he could use them in this way, though the evidence would suggest that Benjamin Norton himself neglected the opportunity offered by study at Edinburgh. Whatever the truth of this charge, his sons could hardly have been pleased by being employed in this way, and Defoe may have planted the seeds of future family discontent in this attempt to make them serviceable. He received four guineas for tracts of forty-eight octavo pages and twenty-five copies for every 1000 printed. John Baker, Defoe's major publisher at this time, testified to paying two guineas per 500 copies. The printer, Janeaway, worried that Defoe might sell his copies in London at a reduced price, but with his system of intelligence around the country, Defoe seems to have been able to distribute them easily enough. Since he seems to have been able, when he wished, to compose at least one pamphlet of this kind within a day, and since he appears to have been involved in a number of journalistic ventures at any given time, his income from writing was probably more than equal to his pay from the government. Defoe was not really going to retreat from the world as he had promised when putting an end to the *Review*, but he did try to be more circumspect about his activities as a writer. In the case of *Mercator*, for example, after being singled out for attack by Henry Martyn in the *British Merchant*, he created the elaborate fiction of having the 'real' author, Mr Backstroke, visit the wrongly attacked Defoe:

When I saw this paper, I made it my business with a Friend or two, for Witness of Fact to find out and speak with the person it related to, whom I never had occasion to know before, and shewed him the Paper.

I was surprized to find him receive it without the least Concern; he told me, he would place it all to the Account of the General Injury he suffers for other Mens Writings; and began to talk very calmly of the Necessity every one was under in this World of going thro' Evil Report and Good Report; and smiling upon me with the greatest Calmness imaginable, told me he had a secret Witness within himself, which testified, that these Men did him Wrong; and that brings him to a full Satisfaction, he begg'd of me that not a word might be said to it, for it was *to use his own Words, Une Bagatelle,* a meer Trifle, what Opinion Men had of him, and that he had learnt to *pray for them that despightfully used him.*[1]

Here is Defoe as he wanted to be seen, above the fray and having forgiven his enemies with proper Christian charity. The visit sounds suspiciously like the encounter between Job and his three friends who are dismayed by the sufferings that their formerly prosperous friend has undergone. It was passages of this kind that led W. P. Trent to record in one of his commentaries, 'the sign of the snake'. Formerly playful in concealing himself behind fictional masks, Defoe had now become elaborately devious in his self-presentation.

One pamphlet suggested that Defoe met frequently with Bolingbroke's agent, Arthur Moore, and it is possible that Defoe had more contact with the agent of the Secretary of State than with Harley at this time. Though he wrote occasionally to Harley of ways to get a trade to France going with or without some kind of commercial treaty and of various strong-arm methods to get Portugal to accept an increase in the tariff on wines, neither man was very well at this time. Engagements to meet seem to have been broken off. Harley had rheumatism, gout, gravel, and inflammation of the eyes. Defoe had a cold caught when he was taken off to prison and a variety of other ills. Actually, the subject of trade, with which Defoe was pre-occupied during much of 1713 and 1714, was really more Bolingbroke's department, and the tone of *Mercator* little resembled the attempt at a middle way that Harley preferred. Instead Defoe depicted the exchange between nations as the product of aggressive self-interest and the merchant as *homo economicus*:

We know no Parties in Commerce, no Alliances, no Enemies; they are our Friends we can Trade with to Advantage, tho' otherwise hating us and hated by us; no Differences of State-Matters are concerned here; we know no *Whig or TORY* in Trade: There is no *Popery* in Commerce; it matters not to use what God they worship, what Religion they own, with whom we Trade; our Commerce worships but one Idol, *viz.* GAIN; we trade with Mahometans in Turkey, Pagans in India, Savages in Africa, Papists in Spain, Italy and France, and nearer home with Jews, Christians, and Hollanders.[2]

The anti-Dutch sting at the end drives home the point. The Dutch were notorious for their pursuit of gain, to the point of trampling on the crucifix

---

[1] *Mercator* 101 (12–14 Jan.).   [2] Ibid. 155 (18–20 May 1714).

in Japan to show that they were not Christians. But if Harley harboured unfriendly feelings toward the Dutch, he was hardly eager to imitate their rapacity. In a letter to Harley on 22 October 1713, he remarked that he thought the ministry should have pretended that the Commercial Treaty was of little real importance. By stressing its significance, the government had turned it into 'an Arrow Shot at the present administration, a handle taken hold of, and an Opportunity which They think is given Them, to Raise a Tumult against the Ministry, and Enflame The People' (H 419). After Moore had stopped paying Defoe what must have been a special supplement for writing the *Mercator*, Defoe wrote to Harley about changing that journal into something 'More usefull'. What is clear, then, is that Defoe adapted his style and content to suit Bolingbroke's more aggressive attitudes in economic matters. Whether he would have been as willing to adapt Bolingbroke's political ideas is difficult to say, but there is little doubt that Defoe was now willing to stray far from his customary positions to support in print the government that was supporting him financially.

While waiting for the pardon from Queen Anne that would free him from the prosecution over the three infamous pamphlets, Defoe turned his mind toward a more general discussion of trade in a monthly publication called *A General History of Trade*. Though the first number was ostensibly written for June 1713, it apparently did not appear until July, after the Commercial Treaty had been defeated. If Defoe's purpose was ever political—to bring the reader gradually to a consideration of a freer trade with France—he seemed so charmed by the abstract concepts of trade that he may have found turning his work to the gritty task of arguing the government's position too much to endure while, at the same time, he was fighting that battle in the *Mercator*. At any rate, the *General History* never strayed far from the theoretical problems of how trade transformed the primitive environment of self-sufficient labour into the modern world of beneficial exchange.

In exploring this subject, Defoe almost certainly found the germ of ideas that were to go into *Robinson Crusoe*. Operating in a world created in such a manner that an exchange of goods was necessary, Defoe continually dwelled upon the primitive state of man. He pictured ancient England as barbarous:

The People were Wild and Barbarous, the Lands Untill'd, Uncultivated, and almost Useless. . . . Instead of flourishing Towns and Cities, the People unacquainted with the World, lived like Wild Beasts in Woods, Bays, Dens, and Caves; and instead of the Riches of Clothes, Jewels and Furniture, which we now flow in, they went in Glorious Nakedness; their Skins cut and mangled; the

Figures of Lyons and Dragons Drawn upon them, to make them look Terrible and Majestic: The Ladies, instead of Patches and Painted Faces, appeared with their Skins Painted over, in such manner as might be most agreeable to the Men, and Draw or Invite them to View their Naked Beauties, which now they hide with the utmost Modesty and Art.[3]

If trade rescued the British from this situation, it is God the Creator who must be thanked, since he might have made the world in such a way 'as that every Man should have been his own Labourer, or his own Manufacturer'.[4] If the July issue had a political tone to the extent of arguing that God put Dunkirk where it was and man should not destroy it—this at a time when Sir Richard Steele was complaining about the stipulations in the Treaty of Utrecht that promised France's destruction of the harbour and the fortifications of Dunkirk—the basic argument continued to be the Providential arrangement of trade. Defoe dedicated the third issue to a consideration of labour and the ways in which it transformed nature, ending with a subtle plea for allowing freedom of export throughout the world. The last issue was unquestionably the most political in its arguments against the restrictions of the Methuen Treaty between Britain and Portugal, but the tone was so much more reasonable than that of *Mercator* that it seems a shame that this journal had so short a life. Defoe was always interesting when he spoke of the relationships between nature, labour, and the production of wealth.

If concepts of primitive economic existence emerged in the *General History of Trade*, so the debate over dropping some of the regulations against trade to France and favouring trade to Portugal led Defoe to create the first of the many 'memoirs' that he produced over the next decade. Published on 20 August 1713, *Memoirs of Count Tariff* was certainly closer to the kinds of allegorical accounts of trade that appeared in the *Review*, allegories of 'Lady Credit' and 'Necessity', than to the kind of memoirs, both real and fictional, turned out in great numbers by contemporary French writers. As in his earlier economic allegories, Defoe traced the family origins of the Tariffs back to the beginning of commerce itself, but his story, replete with characters—the villainous Dutchman, Coopmanschap, the Englishman, Sir Pol., and the friendly Traffick—is far closer to realistic fiction than these earlier works. Of course Defoe had already written allegorical history in *The Consolidator*, but the presentation of character in *Memoirs of Count Tariff* is not very far from his more realistic *Memoirs of the Duke of Melfort*, published some six months later.

---

[3] *A General History of Trade* (June 1713), 14.   [4] Ibid. 33.

There can be little doubt that Defoe took a certain creative pleasure in writing these works defending the ideals of the Commercial Treaty and offering speculations about trade that were at a considerable remove from the accepted maxims about trade. A tract with the title *A Letter to the Honourable A[rthu]r M[oo]re*, dated 26 May 1714, pictured Defoe as a mere 'Secretary' to Moore, the Commissioner of the Treasury and Boling-broke's agent, visiting him every night in Bloomsbury Square to receive dictation on the next issue of *Mercator* and other tracts on trade. Moore may have been a powerful enough figure to have insisted on having direct control over the nature of the debate, but if he gave Defoe directions, he most surely left the writing up to him. In that anti-ministerial tract, Moore is allowed to speak in the first person of his income, his various activities, and his intentions, and in one of these statements he confesses that the reasons he was keeping alive the debate over trade was that he was secretly in the employ of the Whigs and was actually trying to bring down the government. In fact, Moore was soon to be involved in a growing scandal over a private cargo on the first ship to be sent under the Assiento Treaty that permitted the South Sea Company to trade with the Spanish posses-sions in America. The other investors were Queen Anne, Lady Masham, and Bolingbroke. That scandal was one of the reasons that Harley remained in office so long, for Bolingbroke knew his position was being weakened. Queen Anne quickly renounced at least a part of her share in the South Sea Company venture, but too late to restore confidence in the government's trade policy. Small wonder that Defoe thought that he should turn to other matters.[5]

II

The somewhat immoderate tone of the *Mercator* was a reflection of those changed times to which he said everyone must adjust, and Defoe had certainly changed with them. The series of arrests between March and April of 1713, at a time when he was not well, seems to have changed his political attitudes considerably, if not his political beliefs. The Whigs now seemed to be his enemy. They revenged themselves upon him, and he was apparently seething inside. The image that he tried to give of a man above the fray who prayed for his enemies was apparently just the reverse of his

---

[5] Harley actually played a part in organizing the investigation started by the House of Commons con-cerning these events. See Brian Hill, *Robert Harley* (New Haven, Conn.: Yale University Press, 1988), 216–19.

true feelings. He was suspicious of the Tories' attitude toward the Hanoverian Succession, and in his darker moods he may even have doubted Harley's full commitment to this cause. Working for Arthur Moore and Bolingbroke, whatever its financial compensations, could not have made him entirely happy. Some time around the point at which his payment from Arthur Moore stopped, Defoe announced the commitment of *Mercator* to the 'Protestant succession', and soon after insisted that he was not allied to any party.[6] As a result of this situation, his letters throughout the remainder of 1713 up until Harley's fall from power are extraordinarily vindictive both toward individuals and toward groups. He was continually pointing to various persons whom he felt deserving of punishment by the government. He once told a story in the *Review* about such turnabout emotions. A boy who was punished by his father for frequent pranks 'had this unhappy piece of Malice rooted in his very Nature'; he would severely beat the first boy he encountered who was smaller than he, blaming his behaviour, with some degree of self-satisfaction, on the treatment he had received. The story was intended to point to the absurdity of such behaviour, and this bully eventually got what he deserved when he was severely thrashed after selecting the wrong victim.[7] But if Defoe understood the absurdity of such an emotional response, he was nevertheless ready to indulge his own anger.

He complained on 18 July 1713 about insults offered to Queen Anne, and of some people's glee at news of her ill health, blaming the Whigs for creating an evil political environment and volunteering to write an attack upon them. Two weeks later he singled out the Dissenters for special blame, expressing his 'Just Indignation' and separating himself from the group with which he had identified all his life:

I That have all my Life been brought up among and Conversant with Those People profess my Self Amazed at Them. I allwayes Thot *However Mistaken* They Meant well, acted from Principle, and lookt up, as well as about Them, in The Measures They Took; But I am Astonished to See Them Implacable, Outrageous, and Flying to all Those abhorr'd Methods of Compassing Their Own Designs, which they allways Censur'd and Condemn'd in Others. (H 414)

Doubtless Defoe was stressing his loyalty to the government more fervently than ever before in order to get Harley to put through Queen Anne's pardon, and he continued the flurry of letters to the end of the month. The toll upon his health may have been too much, for on 28 October, he had to put off a meeting with Harley after experiencing 'an

---

[6] See *Mercator* 129 (18–20 Mar. 1714); 131 (23–5 Mar. 1714).
[7] *Review*, i [ix]. 170.

Indisposition So Violent as has obliged me to be Carryed home and lay all bussiness aside' (H 422). Two days later he wrote to Harley about his *Letter to the Dissenters*, about which Defoe said he had 'a hint' from the Lord Treasurer. On 18 November 1713, Defoe expressed his relief and gratitude for the pardon and for Harley's willingness to help with the costs of this episode. He was free from the malicious prosecutions concocted by his enemies, but this freedom did not improve his state of mind.

A Letter to the Dissenters, published on 3 December 1713, was hardly written in a tone of conciliation and is not without an air of threat and intimidation. He began by maintaining that the Dissenters got just what they deserved in the act prohibiting Occasional Conformity. The practice was morally offensive to the Church of England and 'Scandalous to Religion' in general. But the act would never have passed were it not for the Whigs who voted for it. Why then, Defoe asked, should the Dissenters continue to support the Whigs? He then went on to argue that there were really only two parties: those who supported the present ministry and those who supported the old ministry. The latter did not constitute a party with a political agenda but merely a faction within the state, and as such, they and their supporters might be crushed by a government that had won the autumn elections and was the legal government. Activities against the present ministry might be construed as 'the mere Essence and Spirit of Sedition'. Warning that too avid a longing for a change in the monarchy and the succession of the House of Hanover might drive the government in an unspecified wrong direction, Defoe urged the Dissenters to support the present ministers with loyalty or risk being punished.

Two replies to Defoe's pamphlet viewed it as posing the possibility of a threat to civil liberties. The author of *Remarks on the Letter to the Dissenters* argued that Defoe, whom he recognized as the author of the anonymous tract, intended 'to wheedle and frighten the whole Body of the *Dissenters* out of that *Spirit* of *Liberty* and *Zeal* for the *Publick Good*' that had distinguished them as a body. The author's fundamental image throughout the work involved a Defoe who was an agent of Satan, who was motivated in the same way as his master, having 'the same Pleasure as the *Devil* has in drawing Men on to their Destruction'. Referring to the pardon Defoe had lately received, the author compared him to a conjurer protected by his magic circle from which he could 'set *Devils*' to work, and he concluded:

If he was but an *Honest* Man, no matter whether or no he was a *Scholar*; and if he wanted not *Veracity*, there is no body wou'd accuse him for his want of *Wit*. The Craft he so much values himself upon might pass for it, were it not that wicked

Craft which deciev'd our Mother *Eve*; and without *Redemption* wou'd have damn'd her whole Posterity.[8]

The author of *A Letter to the People of England, occasion'd by the Letter to the Dissenters* was more analytical, commenting on Defoe's division of the two factions and concluding that Defoe was arguing for Harley's government as 'the *New Court Party*'. For the most part this author gave over most of his time to showing that the present government was more corrupt than the former, but he too saw the scarcely veiled threat to the liberty of the subject, calling to his readers, 'YOUR LIBERTIES ARE IN DANGER! AWAKE, AWAKE.'[9]

Defoe wrote Harley of the success of his pamphlet, of the tendency of some people to ascribe it to the Lord Treasurer, and of distributing it throughout the nation.[10] Defoe put on a brave front for Harley, blustering about the need for the Dissenters to heed the advice. 'Either My Lord These men Must alter Their Conduct to the Governmt or the Governmt Must alter its Conduct to Them,' he wrote to Harley, explaining that 'Justice Must Exert it Self or Suffer a Contempt Dangerous even to Governmt it Self' (H 428). The need of the government to exert itself against its enemies was the theme of most of the letters of the spring. At the same time, Defoe wrote a preface to the second edition of the pamphlet, singling out the charge made in the *Flying Post* that he had threatened the Dissenters. While denying that anything was intended but the kind of gentle warning a father might give his son, Defoe noted:

That they have generally, I do not say universally, join'd with the Hot Whigs, they will not deny: That some among them have been Leaders and General Officers in the late Party-Expeditions against their QUEEN and Country, I need not dispute, for they will not deny it: That they have begun to bring Faction and Party-Politicks into their Pulpits, shewing the Lawfulness of Resisting their Sovereign, under the Shadow of taking Arms against a Tyrant: This they will not deny.[11]

As for the Whigs, he threatened them further with the '*Iron Hands of . . . Justice*', while denying that any threats were implied. He boasted of the

---

[8] *Remarks on the Letter to the Dissenters* (London, 1714), 2, 8 (note 28).

[9] *A Letter to the People of England, Occasioned by the Letter to the Dissenters* (London, 1714), 8.

[10] Edmund Calamy felt that Defoe's pamphlet 'insulted . . . [the Dissenters] in a cruel manner'. Agreeing with Defoe that the work was generally ascribed to Harley, Calamy notes that it was ignored for the most part, 'For, as great as he was they genrally took him to be now their enemy, whatever he might have been formerly; and to be more governed by a regard to his own interest than to that of his country'. Calamy's summary of the pamphlet shows that the subtext of threat and bullying was well perceived by contemporary readers among the Dissenters. *An Historical Account of My Own Life* (London: Henry Colburn and Richard Bentley, 1829), ii. 274–7.

[11] *A Letter to the Dissenters*, 2nd edn. (London, 1714), p. vii.

strength of the pamphlet, and momentarily at least must have felt some exhilaration at his literary power.

After this seeming success in suggesting some kind of retribution upon the Whigs, Defoe indulged himself in taking revenge upon some of his fellow journalists. He started with Sir Richard Steele, for whom he had always felt a mixture of admiration, respect, and envy. Although the pillory and gaol were common enough experiences for contemporary journalists, Steele, Addison, and Swift seemed to have received special protection. In his present mood, Defoe would have loved to have seen them all suffer some of the indignities that he had had to endure. Steele had accused the government of failing to force the French to follow through on their promise to destroy Dunkirk, and he had used his journal, *The Guardian*, and a pamphlet, *The Crisis*, to argue his positions. Defoe had answered a letter, purporting to be written by an anti-French 'English Tory', in the *Guardian* of 7 August 1713, with a series of essays refuting the arguments purely on economic grounds and with only an occasional irony. But in a letter to Harley of 19 February 1714, following one more plea that the government exert itself against its detractors, Defoe urged that Steele's writing was 'Seditious' and that he ought to be expelled from Parliament. He maintained that such an action 'would break all Their projects at Once'[12] (H 430). Defoe was hardly the first to argue that Steele should be treated in this way, but as another voice added to the chorus, he could take pleasure in seeing Steele expelled from the House of Commons for the nature of his writings even as his election was being disputed on grounds of bribery. Defoe celebrated that event in the edition of *Mercator* for 18–20 March. He stated that he was sure that his readers would appreciate the irony of witnessing the embarrassment of a writer who had built his career upon raising the morals of the nation and who had now 'justly fallen under the censure of many thousands of the most judicious, sober and sensible people of this nation'. After all, had not Defoe castigated the immorality of the nation in his *Reformation of Manners* and its sequel, and had he not been severely punished? He was not so foolish as to publish such a question, but that it was going through his mind there can be no doubt.

Defoe's *Schadenfreude* over Steele's troubles shows something of his state of mind at the time. If he had his true desires fulfilled, he would probably have selected Swift as the author upon whom he would have heaped indignities. But Swift, as he well knew, was a friend of Harley.

---

[12] The occasion for Defoe's criticism of Steele's behaviour was the publication of a speech he made in the House of Commons supporting the election of Sir Thomas Hanmer for Speaker. Though the speech was brief, it was published in a quarto format as if it were of great importance.

Thus when Swift's anonymous pamphlet *The Publick Spirit of the Whigs* was attacked in the House of Lords on 2 March 1714 and a reward of £300 offered for the discovery of the author two weeks later, Defoe did not mention Swift at first beyond a vague reference to 'Unsteaddy Friends of the Administration' (H 431). Instead he took the occasion to advise Harley to treat the war between the parties as a genuine military battle in which the only possible course of action would be 'To Conquer' (H 432).[13] If the Whigs had really become a faction, as he had argued in his *Letter to the Dissenters*, then there was no ideological problem in opposing them with all possible weapons:

Your Ldpp has but One way left with These Men. They Must be Conquer'd; Or the nation is Undone, The Queen Undone, and all her Majties Faithfull Friends and Servants Sacrifiz'd to a Rageing and Mercyless Party.

I Presume your Ldpp is Not destitute Either of Means or Council. You have The Fountain of Honour, The strength and The Right on your Side. All Legall steps are justifyable in Such a Case. If a slack Rein is held Now, They will Run down all before Them. Clemency and Kindness will prevail No More with Men that Can be Ingratefull, or justice and Reason with Men who Resolv to play the Bully.

They Openly Declare That they have Thrown away the Scabbard, and as They Expect, So They will Give, no Quarter. (H 432)

Defoe followed this letter with one dated 10 March in which he listed the 'Collection of Scandal' to be found in a variety of Steele's publications. He did not merely list the passages which he regarded as potentially libellous but provided explanations, some of which, in their distortions, resemble the charges against Defoe's three pamphlets. For example, he quotes Steele as saying, 'That the Duke of Marlbro' was not permitted to Enjoy the Fruits of his Glorious Labour', and argues that this is libellous because 'Here he acknowleges Takeing Away his Employment as an Injury to The Duke; and That prolonging The War was the Fruit of his Glorious Labour; which he Expected but was not Permitted to Enjoy' (H 436). Under these circumstances, what appears to be an innocent enough statement is construed into a libel against the Duke of Marlborough, the government, or both at the same time.

At the end of this letter, Defoe decided to throw his old acquaintance John Dunton into the stew of enemies to the government that he was stirring. He described Dunton's *Neck or Nothing* as 'One Continued Breath

---

[13] Defoe quotes Davila's account of the advice of the King of Navarre to Henry III when faced by something resembling an insurrection. Davila is also quoted in the 27 Apr. issue of *The Monitor*, a journal in which Defoe may have been engaged at the time.

of slander and Scurrillity on The administration, Calling The Ministry Vile Names and Charging The Queens faithfull Servants with Treason, Robbery, Drunkness and all Manner of Crimes' (H 438). He was willing to admit that the ministry need not be concerned with a work by Dunton, but urged that such an attack was symptomatic. The next day he pointed his finger at William Hurt, printer of the *Flying Post*, who had already been sentenced to prison for a libel published in June 1713. 'I am far From Prompting justice', he wrote, 'but No faithful Subject can be Satisfyed to See justice Thus affronted, and I Move your Ldpp The Rather because I See This as a forerunner of Greater Insults under the Same protection' (H 439). Defoe's advice about crushing the opposition and the opposition press appear to show him as a ministry loyalist. What is also abundantly evident is that by the spring of 1714, in those works written for Harley and Bolingbroke, he was willing to abandon any pretence at being a Whig of any kind, 'Court Whig' or 'Old Whig', and was producing unadulterated Tory propaganda.[14]

Defoe may have been emotionally enmeshed in the war between the parties, but so thorough a conversion in his way of thinking about history and politics has to raise suspicions. He had never been wholly honest in his dealings with Harley, even during the days when, as Secretary of State, Harley was at the height of his popularity and ruling the nation with a government that drew strength from both Whig and Tory. Now, when Harley's power was waning, Queen Anne ailing, the Succession in doubt, Defoe continued to 'play the card of sincerity', as La Rochefoucauld called it, in his letters to Harley while keeping his own counsel. In writing further of Swift in relation to that author's *Publick Spirit of the Whigs*, he expressed regret that Swift had left himself open to prosecution by some of his comments, but privately, on 23 February 1714, Defoe published *The Scots Nation and Union Vindicated from the Reflections Cast on them in an Infamous Libel*, a vicious attack on Swift and his attitude toward the Union. Defoe began by stating that dealing with Swift was like pursuing an enemy

[14] John Robert Moore ascribes *The Monitor* to Defoe in his *Checklist* (Hamden, Conn.: Archon, 1971), 233, item 530. If Defoe was involved with this journal, which first appeared on 22 Apr. 1714 as a critic of the opposition press from 'Lunatick' Dunton to Richard Steele, it represents a willingness to be associated with a publication which was strongly oriented toward the Court and Toryism. Its chief target was Steele, and after the letter to Harley of 10 Mar. listing seditious passages in Steele's *Guardian* and his pamphlet *The Crisis*, Defoe may have seemed the ideal person to start such a journal. On 20 May, the writer of that issue states that there were a number of contributors. Defoe may have been one of them, but I doubt if he could have indulged in the encomium on James II or in the vicious attacks upon Marlborough made in the issue of 29 June. On the whole, the tone of the journal is essentially that of the Tory *Examiner*, and it might be wiser to look among the writers of that journal for the author of the *Monitor*. However, having made this sensible assessment, I should point out that both John Dunton in his *Queen Robin* (31) and the *Flying Post* of 4–7 Dec. 1714 attributed *The Monitor* to him.

'that has neithr acted the Gentleman or the Christian' or like hunting a wild, ravenous beast which is to be 'knock'd down any how, as we can find them'. Swift had acted like a 'slanderous Lybeller' in comparing the Union to the marriage of a man to a woman who, though much inferior to himself in wealth, boasted that she was his equal because she had as many servants and relations as he. Most of the pamphlet is devoted to a defence of the Scottish people, particularly for their military service, and Defoe noted that he possessed evidence in the form of a frequently mentioned manuscript about the wars of the seventeenth century, probably a draft of what he would eventually publish as *Memoirs of a Cavalier*.[15] He argued that the real impulse behind the work was Swift's opposition to the Protestant succession.

That Defoe would imply that Swift was a crypto-Jacobite is hardly surprising. The succession and the Schism Act were the two most crucial objects of Defoe's interest during 1714. The latter was introduced by Bolingbroke's friend Sir William Wyndham on 21 May. It was part of Bolingbroke's attempt to curry favour with the High Church party by proposing a law that would forbid the existence of any Dissenting schools and academies. The measure resembled those pursued by Louis XIV in his attempt to destroy the Huguenots, and Defoe must have been horrified at the prospect that it might pass.[16] He concealed his feelings from Harley. Perhaps he knew that Harley was in such a weak position that he would have to pretend to have no objections. Harley may even have said as much. Defoe began his letter of 21 May with a reference to their 'Usefull' conversation, and wanted to put what he had to say about the Dissenters in writing. He expressed 'fear' that the bill would pass but maintained that the Dissenters deserved what they were getting. 'I Pity Them,' he wrote, distancing himself from his own religious community, and refused to enlist Harley's sympathy for them. Perhaps, he mused, there would be no loss:

As to Their Accademies, if there had never been any, I kno' not but Theyr Intrest had been as Good, and Fewer beggars and Drones had been bred up for Ministers Among Them: But for The Schooles for Common Introduction of Children, I think Their Loss will be Irreparable. It is True That They will have schooles still; They will be No More Illegal Than before; but it Seems hard upon the Nation in Generll to make Laws which it will be Necessary to Break, Like That of the late Abjuration Oath act in scotland. (H 440)

---

[15] 'The Manuscript I have had in my hands many years, neither is it to be Contradicted, the histories of those Times making frequent mention of all their Names': *The Scots Nation and Union Vindicated* (London, 1714), 24. See also 3, 13, 19.

[16] Richard Steele made this comparison. See *A Letter to a Member of Parliament*, in *Tracts and Pamphlets*, ed. Rae Blanchard (Baltimore: Johns Hopkins University Press, 1944), 246.

Although Defoe had criticized the decline in the quality of the ministers being produced by the Dissenting Academies in his *Present State of the Parties in Great Britain* (1712), he was eager that their education be improved. When he wrote that tract, abolishing Dissenting Academies was the furthest thought from his mind. Although amendments gave the Dissenters the right to give their children a basic education, the Schism Bill seemed to doom them to being a perpetual underclass. As matters turned out, the bill passed but was not to go into effect until 1 August, the day Queen Anne died.[17] As a consequence the bill was never enforced, though attempts to repeal it did not succeed until 1719. Some of the most distinguished thinkers of the eighteenth century were to owe their education to the Dissenting academies; so the death of the Queen at this juncture may have saved the Dissenters as well as the Protestant succession.

Despite Defoe's seeming coolness toward the Dissenters in the presence of Harley—a coolness that extended even to warning about an apocalyptic spirit of revolt among some of them—his real response was anything but calm. In his *Letter to Mr. Steele*, he posed as a fair-minded Tory and supporter of the Church of England who could nevertheless applaud Steele's *Letter to a Member of Parliament* for its just attack against the Schism Bill.[18] The speaker argued that the toleration granted by William III after the Glorious Revolution implied a right to educate their children as they saw fit. 'Mankind', wrote this right-minded Tory, 'is Born with a natural liberty both of Body and Mind; and it is infinitely a less Crime to Imprison the Body without Cause, than to burthen and confine the Conscience.'[19] He added that the bill was an abridgement of the 'Natural Right' that parents had to raise their children as they wished, and that it might cause a mass exodus of Dissenters to other nations and with that a decline in Britain's wealth and power. In *The Remedy Worse than the Disease*, published on 9 June, he once more enunciated his theory of a parental 'Natural Right to Educate' children, and, with a glance in the direction of John Milton, he launched into a defence of the 'Heavenly

---

[17] Edmund Calamy put a Providential interpretation on the confluence of these two events on this day. His editor, John Towill Rutt, noted that as late as 1758 a sermon was given at Salters' Hall in which the speaker, Dr Benson, stated that 'God once more appeared for us, in the most remarkable and distinguishing manner; took away the life of that Princess, who had so far been seduced, as, causeless, to seek our destruction . . . O that glorious first of August! that most signal day, which ought never to *be* forgot.' See *An Historical Account of My Own Life*, ii. 293.

[18] Steele's arguments were similar to Defoe's in a number of ways. He has an especially effective passage imagining the arrest of a schoolteacher barely beginning to teach her charges how to write letters. See *A Letter to a Member of Parliament*, 251.

[19] *A Letter to Mr. Steele, Occasion'd by his Letter to a Member of Parliament, Concerning the Bill for Preventing the Growth of Schism* (London, 1714), 19.

Principle' of Toleration.[20] With the single exception of a religion allowing human sacrifice, Defoe argued for toleration of all private worship, and while he protested against allowing the Catholic Church to function in Britain, since it constituted a faction sworn to the destruction of all other religions, he expressed no objection to Jews in Britain practising their religion in a private manner, noting that the Bill did not exempt them, and that it would have the effect of driving them and their trade out of the country. What is notable about these two works is the obvious ease and effectiveness which Defoe revealed when writing in a Whig cause and manipulating Whig rhetoric. They suggest how uneasy he must have felt with some of his more recent Tory propaganda.

As has been mentioned, at the time of the passage of the Act against Occasional Conformity two years earlier, Defoe had published a pamphlet with the title *Wise as Serpents*. Aside from his usual search after historical causation, this work was a survival guide for living under a law that had the effect of threatening the survival of the Dissenters. He even seemed to foresee the coming Schism Bill, for he lamented the failure of the Dissenters to get specific protection for the Dissenting schools and academies. The title, drawn from Matthew 10: 16, advises caution and a degree of cunning. He wanted the Dissenters to withdraw themselves from their neighbours in a political as well as a spiritual manner, to grow strong again, and to exert their power once more. He urged the Dissenters to assume the same attitude now. *The Weakest Go to the Wall* urged the Dissenters to strive for political power that would enable them to 'bear some weight in the Commonwealth, and make it worth while to the Parties' to try to win their support.[21] In its suggestion that the Dissenters might find succour from the court rather than from the two parties, this piece was probably mild enough to have been shown to Harley, who at this time may have been somewhat more receptive.[22] On the other hand, *A Brief Survey of the Legal Liberties of the Dissenters* was much more defiant. Defoe argued that the Toleration Act passed at the time of William gave the Dissenters the right to worship as they wished as well as the right to educate their children. The Schism Bill was attempting to assert a right over the conscience, a thing which

[20] *The Remedy Worse than the Disease: Or, Reasons against Passing the Bill for Preventing the Growth of Schism* (London, 1714), 12, 20, 29.

[21] *The Weakest Go to the Wall* (London, 1714), 40. This pamphlet was essentially a discussion of the failure of the Dissenters to achieve a position of power during the past four reigns. Since the Whigs had failed the Dissenters and the principles of the Tories seemed unacceptable, a direct appeal to Queen Anne was suggested as an alternative.

[22] Harley was under so much pressure from Bolingbroke that, in an attempt to save his position, he had begun to consult with the Whigs.

could not be permitted, 'Human Power Having no Judicial Right over it'.[23] Given the inevitable revival of persecution, Defoe held out one positive result. It would 'Revive the Antient Family Discipline and Instruction';[24] in short, the family would become the unit of religion and education for the Dissenters. This idea would eventually lead to Defoe's creation of the first volume of *The Family Instructor* in the following year, a work dealing with conflicts within families, usually over matters of religion. It was rendered in a dialogue form that was to stand somewhere between the old moral dialogues of the seventeenth century and the novel, that new, realist form devoted to stories of domestic life. Even though the Schism Act was never enforced, it nevertheless had an unintended effect on the history of fiction.

III

More central to Defoe's concerns than even the Schism Bill was the question of the succession. He had managed to get into trouble on this matter in the affair of the three pamphlets, but nothing could prevent him from treating a question so crucial to the future of Britain. The official ministry line was that there was no possibility that the Pretender would play a role in the succession, but few were convinced. The House of Commons actually debated a motion affirming that the succession was not in danger on 17 April 1714, and while the court won, the margin of forty-eight made this a Pyrrhic victory.[25] The Whigs wanted the son of the future George I, at this point the Duke of Cambridge, brought over to Britain as a guarantee of good faith, but Queen Anne hated the idea. An official invitation was extended, but the offer, merely a face-saving device, was rejected after Harley indicated how much the Queen objected. In his *Mercator* Defoe maintained the party line, but his anonymous pamphlets allowed him the freedom to keep the issue constantly before the British public. In these he attacked those who swore oaths of obedience to Queen Anne while being practising Jacobites. Such men, he felt, having allowed their consciences to fall asleep, might eventually confront such '*HORRIBLE ideas* of *GUILT* and *PUNISHMENT, as none could bear.*'[26]

---

[23] *A Brief Survey of the Legal Liberties of the Dissenters* (London, 1714), 8.

[24] Ibid. 14.

[25] See the comments of Sir John Perceval quoted in *The Divided Society*, ed. G. S. Holmes and W. A. Speck (New York: St. Martin's Press, 1968), 112.

[26] *Whigs Turn'd Tories and Hanoverian-Tories, From Their Avow'd Principles Prov'd Whigs* (London, 1713), 13.

In *Memoirs of John, Duke of Melfort*, Defoe created the first of his feigned memoirs and a tract which, if accepted as genuine, would lead a reader to believe that the Pretender and his servants were constantly plotting to take over the government from Queen Anne. The Duke of Melfort, a Jacobite residing in the court of James II and the Pretender, was famous for an absurd indiscretion in sending an easily intercepted letter about a Jacobite-French invasion of England in February 1701.[27] He had died at the beginning of 1714, and his connection with a previous invasion plot made these memoirs, 'Published from the original Papers found in the Closet of the said Duke since his Death', an excellent vehicle for raising the nation's consciousness about the Jacobite threat. In this work, interestingly enough (along with the accounts of how the Pretender would feign turning Protestant and how much the Jacobites felt the loss of the Duke of Hamilton), Defoe was already attempting to defend Harley from any future retribution. Melfort is made to testify that Harley was a 'Riddle' and that despite efforts to uncover his intentions, no Jacobite in England could give the slightest 'Encouragement of his being in the Chevalier's Interest'.[28] This suggests that whatever optimism about the future Harley and Defoe may have felt, Defoe may have suspected that his employer might need some helpful testimony about his loyalty in the not too distant future.[29]

At a time when Queen Anne was so ill that she had to be hoisted up between floors of her palace, the Whigs had seized upon their best gambit in the war between the parties, and Defoe hovered nervously between upholding the ministry's commitment to the Protestant succession and his own sense of how vital such a commitment must be. With Bolingbroke supporting the appointment of known Jacobites to government positions, Defoe had to be concerned. He produced *A Letter to the Whigs, Expostulating with them upon their Present Conduct* at the beginning of the year, reproving the Whigs for creating a dangerous hysteria over the

---

[27] See George Hilton Jones, *The Main Stream of Jacobitism* (Cambridge, Mass.: Harvard University Press, 1954), 59. The article on him in the *DNB* questions whether the discovery was accidental. It depicts him as a possible double agent, mentioning rumours that the abortive invasion of 1708 may have been revealed by someone in his household at the court of St Germain. Given his knowledge of Scottish politics, Defoe must have known of these rumours, but portrayed him as Machiavellian but devoted to the Jacobite cause.

[28] Defoe, *Memoirs of John, Duke of Melfort; Being an Account of the Secret Intrigues of the Chevalier de S. George, Particularly relating to the Present Times* (London, 1714), 33. The blurb about the manuscript source is taken from the title-page.

[29] Harley was depressed during these months, and there is no assurance that he did not encourage Defoe to establish a clear trail of information and misinformation that would seem to establish his refusal to have any dealings with Jacobites in case Anne should die suddenly. For his general mood, see Hill, *Robert Harley*, 193–222; and for his brief flirtation with Jacobitism, see ibid. 174–5.

Hanoverian Succession. He did not 'see one thing of Moment' that would lead anyone to think that the ministry was not firmly committed to the Hanoverian Succession. He noted the way in which the stock market had fluctuated dangerously in response to rumours about the succession and urged a unified national approach to the eventual change of monarchs:

The true Interest of the Protestant Succession, would certainly be to compose our Disorders, heal our Breaches, quiet our Minds, reconcile our Animosities, bring all the Nation to rejoice in his Accession to the Throne, and spread a Universal Smile upon the Countenances OF his People; with a Face of Beneficence TO his People; and National Affection IN them, to his Person, forming a general Unanimity in Prince and People to the Publick Safety.[30]

In April Defoe reissued two earlier pamphlets, *Hannibal at the Gates: or, the Progress of Jacobitism* and *A View of the Real Dangers of the Succession*, revising them slightly to meet new developments. What he had discovered in his trip to Derbyshire was what he perceived as a kind of amnesia about the reasons for the Glorious Revolution, and some success by Jacobite propagandists in suggesting the possibility of accepting the Pretender rather than the House of Hanover. If he was not ready to give the Whigs an inch of ground on the government's support for the Hanoverian succession, he was nevertheless not eager to see the anxiety of the populace assuaged. For the former pamphlet, he wrote a new section urging that those who tried to minimize the threat posed by Jacobitism were to be regarded with suspicion. In the latter, to which he added the word 'Protestant' (lest there be any doubt of his subject), he pointed out that the Treaty of Utrecht guaranteed the Protestant succession, but also confessed that the issue was of such importance that it 'very much justifies the Anxieties of our Minds about it'.[31]

Whether Defoe would have trusted anyone on so crucial an issue is questionable. He probably had few doubts about Harley's commitment to the Hanoverian succession, but how long could Harley maintain control of the government? And how much trust did Defoe have in Bolingbroke? Was he prepared to assume the role of a loyal civil servant even under a ministry that might have been ready to change the succession? Everything we know of Defoe's principles would have made this almost impossible, but he was certainly disillusioned about politics and still the only support of a large and needy family. Would he have taken the course he advocated when he extended his advice to the Dissenters to be 'Wise as Serpents' in

---

[30] *A Letter to the Whigs, Expostulating with them upon their Present Conduct* (London, 1714), 33, 39.
[31] *A View of the Real Dangers of the Succession* (London, 1713), 3.

the face of oppression, to appear to do the work of the new ministry while secretly subverting it? He probably could not have answered these questions himself. He was spared the necessity of such decisions by the speed of events. Harley was finally relieved of his position as Lord Treasurer on 27 July. This was followed by the sudden illness of the Queen, by her appointment of the Duke of Shrewsbury to succeed Harley, and by her death a few days later on the morning of 1 August 1714.

As has been suggested, Harley had attempted to rally his forces during July, and while Defoe could not have been ignorant of the rumours concerning Harley, he may have been indulging in some wishful thinking. At any rate, he wrote to Harley on 26 July to report the rumours that Harley's enemies were about to take power. He began the letter by thanking Harley for his stipend of £100 (the usual sum) and returning the receipt. He then turned to what he had heard from some of those in the government who spoke of removing the Lord Treasurer even though they owed everything to his bounty:

But My Lord, when They speak of their haveing Power with the Queen to dispossess and Succeed your Ldpp, I must Confess it Amazes me, as Well to Think whether Such a thing Can be, as what Ruine The Nation will be Exposed to if it should.

I hope still your Ldpp, who has been Victorious Over worse Enemyes than These, will Easily Baffle their projects; if Not I Think it my Duty to Repeat my assurances of my following your Worst Fortunes, and of being, fall it foul or fair, your Constant, faithfull and Steddy as Well as Humble and Obedt Servt. (H 443)

The letter is not very different in some ways from the letter Defoe wrote to Harley on 10 February 1708, when Harley was dropped by Godolphin and Marlborough, and he may have recalled that letter when he added the 'still' to his hopes for Harley's ultimate victory. Both Harley and Defoe were six years younger when Defoe wrote the letter that resulted in his transferring his allegiance to Godolphin and Sunderland at Harley's recommendation. Now they were less resilient both mentally and physically. Harley's decline in health was almost mirrored by Defoe's. During the past year Defoe had complained of lameness and various pains that prevented him from leaving his home, and while he shows no sign of Harley's psychological depressions, he must have felt some degree of despair over the retreat of civil liberties and toleration under the Tories. At any rate, Harley seems to have been willing to take Defoe at his word this time, and Defoe may have been grateful to have been spared the humiliation of a transfer of his services to those he regarded as his enemies. As the letter of 3 August makes clear,

Harley had assured Defoe of continued financial support, and Defoe apparently told him of his plans to publish a defense of Harley's actions as Lord Treasurer. He had already written one of his typically paradoxical pieces offering reasons why Harley deserved (or rather did not deserve) to be impeached, but the new work was to be a more straightforward defence. He apparently had part of that work in the press when the Queen died. With that event, the question of Harley's future status probably caused him to change the tone of the work. He wanted to consult Harley to consider how to proceed. Harley too must have thought that waiting was the best idea, and the first part of *The Secret History of the White Staff* did not appear until October.

The letter that Defoe sent on 3 August was written after King George I had been proclaimed the next ruler of England. Defoe opened the letter by mentioning 'the Surprising Turn given by The Immediate hand of Providence to the State of things'. He was careful to mute his joy in writing Harley. The Protestant succession was safe, and England was once more to have the kind of soldier-king that remained the dominant model of monarchy for the rest of the century. Defoe undoubtedly knew that George I would prove to be no William III, but he must have looked very good to a Defoe who feared what the Pretender would do to the nation. As for himself, he probably thought that he would be able to survive whatever revenge his enemies might take for his support of the ministry, but Harley's future must have seemed more problematic. Defoe wrote to Harley of the 'Change in The judgement Men Make of things' (H 444) in response to new situations, and both appeared to think it best to test the waters before plunging into a defence that now had become more crucial. Three weeks later, Defoe wrote to Harley of the 'Furious Tempers' of most of the Whigs and of their desire for revenge. Since they were not in a mood to listen to 'Moderation' (H 444–5), Defoe urged that the work that was to become the three parts of *The Secret History of the White Staff* should begin by establishing general principles of what had occurred and then gradually move to justification of Harley's political actions. Both men may have underestimated just how angry their opponents were.

George I came to Britain with a distrust of Whig political ideology and a desire to govern through a balance of parties, but he had a particular animus toward Harley and Bolingbroke for their roles in making the separate peace with France. From George's viewpoint, by withdrawing its forces from the conflict, Britain had frozen out Hanover's role in negotiating a peace, and George had expressed his displeasure at the time.[32]

[32] See Ragnhild Hatton, *George IV* (Cambridge, Mass.: Harvard University Press, 1978), 105–7.

George's first action as King—restoring Marlborough to his post as commander of the armies after dismissing the Duke of Ormond—was less a reflection of his allegiance to the Whigs than a restatement of his position on the handling of the peace. George blamed Harley more than Bolingbroke for the events of 1712, and could not have been displeased by the attempts to impeach the former Lord Treasurer and by his imprisonment in the Tower. In his efforts to aid Harley, Defoe had allied himself with a lost cause. To think that he was unaware of this would be to drastically underestimate his political acumen; but he thought that he owed Harley a debt of gratitude—a debt that he was going to repay in his own way whether Harley approved of what he was to do or not.

Defoe was soon to realize just how little power the former Lord Treasurer had. On 31 August he asked Harley to help him out of one of his typical scrapes. Defoe began by suggesting that the reason for this attack upon him was directly connected to his known association with Harley. The narrative that follows, however, is somewhat puzzling:

It has been long That I have been Endeavouring to Take off the Virulence and Rage of the Flying Post. Mr Moore has been wittness to the Design and to Some of the Measures I took for it, which were Unsuccessfull.

After Some Time an Occasion Offred me which I Thought might be Improv'd Effectually to Overthrow it; The Old Author Redpath Quarrell'd with his Printer Hurt and Takes the Paper From him; Hurt Sets up for himself and applyes himself to a Certain Author to write it for him but being Not Able to get any One to Publish it, he lost ground.

It Occurr'd to me That To Support Hurt would be the Onely Way to bring the Paper it Self Out of Redpaths hand, and to this Intent I frequently at his Request Sent him paragraphs of forreign News but Declin'd Medling with home Matters.

The publisher Recd a letter Very Unhappily for me and finding it full of Reflections desir'd it to be Softn'd as he calld it, and Sends it to me. I left out indeed a great Deal of Scandalous Stuff that was in it but added Nothing and Sent it back. This they have printed from my hand, and I am Charg'd as the Author of the Letter, am Sent for by a warrant and held to Bail. (H 446)

What is surprising about this letter is its clear admission that Defoe was engaged in the business of attempting to control anti-government propaganda while he was working for the Tories. When he states that he has been attempting to exert some control over the *Flying Post* for a 'long' time, he must mean at least as long as April 1713, when its editor, George Ridpath, fled from government prosecution. It is also likely that, as a collector and distributor of information contained in newsletters coming from abroad, Defoe acted in this capacity as well. Since he appears to have been working under Bolingbroke's agent, Arthur Moore, in a cause which he had to distrust, it undercuts his claims to high principle during the ensuing years, when he was to do the same job for the incoming Whig government. Defoe had acted as a spy for close to two decades, and it should be clear enough by now that he was no boy scout.

There is another part of this account that merits some scepticism—the account of his attempt to soften the edge of the letter that appeared in the *Flying Post* on 19 August 1714:

Sir, You cannot be ignorant of the late Journey of a N[oble] Pe[e]r to Ireland . . . part of the Design of which we are assur'd was, to new model the Forces there and particularly to break no less than 70 of the Honest Offices of the Army, and to fill up their Places with the Tools and Creatues of Con[stantine] Phi[pp]s, and such a Rabble of Cut-throats as were fit for the Work that they had for them to do.

The men referred to were Arthur Annesley, fifth Earl of Anglesey, whose position as a seemingly diehard Hanoverian Tory had earned him the honour of being one of the eighteen regents (one of four Tories) who, along with seven members of the government, would oversee the transition to the rule of George I, and Sir Constantine Phipps, Lord Chancellor of Ireland, who was certainly a Jacobite. The possibility that Defoe was the author of the letter should not be discounted. Brought up on tales of the massacre of Irish Protestants by the Catholic population during the seventeenth century, Defoe would have been extremely sensitive to what Phipps was doing. He knew of Anglesey as a fierce enemy of the Dissenters, and may well have suspected the worst. But even if the letter was not his, and Hurt truly wanted it 'Soften'd', surely Defoe had spent enough time in gaol to know what might be regarded as offensive, and printed enough letters, composed by himself as well as his correspondents, to know how to transform such a letter into a more general reflection on the danger threatening in Ireland. By this time the printer Hurt was issuing the journal with Defoe's publisher, John Baker, and Defoe must have gained more influence over it. He clearly wanted the letter published, and was taking advantage of his position as a kind of editor to spread anti-Jacobite propaganda. In short, there is no way that he could have been ignorant of the risk involved.

Anglesey complained to the other Regents, and the machinery for a prosecution was put in motion by William Bromley, the Secretary of State.[33] A warrant was issued for Hurt's arrest on 21 August, and two days

---

[33] Examinations of Baker and Hurt are dated 23 Aug. 1714. BL Loan 29/8, newsletter for 24 Aug. 1714, says 'yesterday': the examinations were enclosed in Bromley's letter to Attorney-General Northey and recorded as dated 23 Aug. PRO SP 44/115 for 27 Aug. 1714. Warrant for the seizure of papers, PRO SP 44/79A for 24 Aug. See also PRO SP 35/1 pt 1, fol. 29. For a thorough summary, see Paula Backscheider, *Daniel Defoe: His Life* (Baltimore: Johns Hopkins University Press, 1989), 595.

later John Baker, the publisher of the majority of Defoe's works over the past three years, was arraigned. Bromley informed Northey that the regents wanted to prosecute Hurt, Baker, and Defoe, and that they wanted 'an Account of the last Prosecution against Defoe'. Defoe was in custody by 28 August, and the manuscript of the letter in his hand seemed to complete the case against him.[34] In ending his missive to Harley, Defoe urged his patron to intercede with Anglesey and to tell him that what he did 'was to prevent their Printing Severall Scandalous Reflections on his Ldpp which I therefore struck quite out and Wrot the Rest Over again' (H 447). In this sense, if Defoe is to be believed, he was being punished for rendering Anglesey a service.

To have persuaded Anglesey of this would probably have taken more rhetorical power than even Harley could command. Defoe was out on bail on 7 September, but the machinery of justice had been set in motion. He wrote to Harley three weeks later with a reminder of the action he had taken in regard to Anglesey 'with a Sincere Design to Serv him' (H 448), asking Harley once more to try to use his influence. But in the same letter (along with a letter he had intercepted intended for *Dyer's Newsletter* that he thought might be useful to his patron) Defoe mused on the dangers of the present political situation:

I presume The Artifice of the present Politicians is Now to have it believed That all who acted under The late administration were Enemies to the Succession of the Present King, and in Such a Stream as Now Runs Such Absurdityes may go down; how Evedent So Ever the Contrary May be; Honest men then must Reserv themselves for better Fortunes, and For times when Truth May be more quietly heard. (H 447)

Those times were not to come soon. On 12 July 1715, almost ten months later, Robert Harley, Earl of Oxford, heard the articles of impeachment against him read in the House of Lords and was ordered to be taken to the Tower four days later. On the same day, Defoe was tried in King's Bench Court. The charge might have come out of a piece of existential fiction about the hopelessness of finding justice in an absurd world, for, although the letter on the dangerous revamping of the army in Ireland was mentioned, for the most part he was accused of being a 'seditious and malicious man' and of creating 'perturbation' in the state. The references to 'intending evil . . . to the Queen' seemed to go directly back to the charges

---

[34] A newsletter in the Portland Papers at the British Library (v. 28) dated 28 Aug. records the arrest. The Attorney-General expressed some doubt about the reliability of Hurt's testimony concerning the paragraph being in Defoe's handwriting, and wondered whether there was sufficient evidence against him. See PRO SP 35/1/item 29.

in the three 'seditious' pamphlets.[35] To add to the multiple ironies in this situation, the case was heard by Chief Justice Parker, who had presided over the former case. Defoe was found guilty but the sentence was postponed for three months, crucial months during which he managed to find a way of escaping from punishment one more time.

IV

Though the paragraph in the *Flying Post*, with its renewal of trouble for Defoe, appeared just eighteen days after the death of Queen Anne, the successful transition to the House of Hanover provided a kind of stability to the Protestant succession and to the toleration of the Dissenters that Defoe had long desired. It was probably Defoe who wrote in the *Flying Post* of 'The happy Time being come that honest men may speak the Truth without any Fear of Informations in the Queens Bench', and in a pamphlet, he sketched his vision of George's reign:

The Succession is secured, and in that our whole Demands are secured: In a Protestant King, Rightful, Lawful, Parliamentary *Hanover* King all we can wish for is contained; the Protestant Religion is secured; the Church of *England*, and the *Kirk* of *Scotland* Reciprocally established; the toleration of Dissenters is contained in a temper of Moderation; the Laws are protected; Liberty and Property engag'd for; Parliamentary Authority recogniz'd; every thing that was in Danger is made safe, that was in doubt ascertain'd, that was disputed, settled, and nothing remains for us but for every Man to *Study to be quiet and to do their own Business*.[36]

Defoe proclaimed that the Jacobite threat was over and asked for a return to moderation and peace. He also suggested, in what has to be seen as a bit of self-pleading, that no revenge ought to be taken against the supporters of the previous ministry.

Defoe had lost his government stipend of £400, but during the past four years he had learned how to make a living from his writing and from distribution of the news. As he reminded his enemies, whatever happened to him, so long as he could move his pen, he and his family would never starve.[37] One indication of this new sense of optimism may have been his decision to move from the house that had the appearance of a miniature

---

[35] Northey, the Attorney-General, was ordered to bring the three infamous pamphlets to the court, and it is clear that, for the most part, Defoe was being retried for them. For the court documents involved, see Backscheider, *Defoe: His Life*, 595, n. 77.

[36] See *The Flying Post: and Medly*, No. 10 (17 Aug. 1714); and *Advice to the People of Great Britain* (London, 1714), 14–15.

[37] See esp. *An Elegy on the Author of the True Born Englishman*, in *True Collection*, ii. 86.

fortress to a larger house in Stoke Newington with four acres of land attached to it. Here Defoe had room for his large collection of books upon which he might draw for the information needed in his writing, and here, like Alexander Pope, he had room to practise what an age that saw nature as the product of God's creative power regarded as a fine art—the art of gardening. John Robert Moore imagined him leading a life detached from the struggles in which he had been recently engaged—cultivating his garden like Voltaire's Candide—but so long as he was to write on controversial subjects, such an existence would be impossible.[38]

The two main tasks Defoe set for himself at this time were Harley's defence and, eventually, his own. The three parts of *The Secret History of the White Staff* appeared at the end of September 1714, 27 October, and 29 January 1715, following the plan laid out to introduce the arguments gradually, to impose a given view of history upon events, and then to show that Harley was a well intentioned political leader, attempting to do his best for the nation at a time of violent factionalism. The title, with its reference to the symbol of the Lord Treasurer's office, caught some of the quality of the memoirs of the period as well as those half-fictional accounts in which historical figures were presented under barely disguised names, but Defoe aimed at a mixture of biography and history told by what was supposed to pass as an impartial narrator. He insisted in the third part that 'this History enters not into any Defence', and to the extent that the narrator admits Harley's mistakes and faults of character, it is anything but an encomium. He judges Harley as a person given to delay and 'Caution', and who was so reluctant to spend the government's money that he reduced the monies for the secret service from £97,000 to £22,000. He notes how Harley kept people waiting for monies owed to them and even expresses some sympathy for Guiscard, who tried to stab Harley, since he was among those 'kept languishing with Expectations'. Harley's behaviour showed 'more Exactness than Wisdom', wrote Defoe, and in a world in which self-interest was the dominant force, Harley found himself outspent by his enemies:

Moreover, it is the most impolitick thing in the World in any Administration, wherein there are opposite Parties, to commit a Confidence in things of Moment to any Person, and then neglect to support that Person in his just Pretensions; such Conduct will lose a Minister of State, the best and most faithful Servants in the World. . . . the Sum of the Business amounted to this, *viz.* That no body did

[38] For Defoe's house, see Arthur Secord, 'Defoe in Stoke Newington', *PMLA* (1951): 211–16 ; Adam John Shirren, *Daniel Defoe in Stoke Newington* (London: Stoke Newington Public Libraries Committee, 1960), 18–23.

any thing for nothing; and the STAFF, endeavouring to serve himself of every body, without rewarding, brought them to this pass, that no body would stir a Foot farther in the publick Business than they were paid for it.[39]

The important points established by all three parts of Defoe's *Secret History of the White Staff* were that Harley was free from any involvement in bringing in the Pretender, that he had little power during his last six months in office, that in making peace with France he was obeying the wishes of the Queen, and that he was opposed to that group among the Tories who favoured 'making the Ministry absolute'.[40] Mistakes were freely admitted. Harley had appointed known Jacobites to positions in the government with the intention of exerting control over them, but had found they were not easy to restrain. Establishing the South Sea Company had been an error. But if Harley had committed errors, so had the Whigs, from failing to conclude a peace at Gertruydenburgh to attempting to persecute Sacheverell. The moral seemed to be that no leader, no party, was ever without faults and that Harley had behaved as a loyal public servant.[41]

The Secret History of the White Staff is usually treated as one of Defoe's failures insofar as he is supposed to have miscalculated the reaction of the audience. Alan Downie compared it to Defoe's similar miscalculation over *The Shortest Way with the Dissenters*, pointing out Harley's advertisement in the *Gazette* for 5–9 July 1715 denying that he had any role in its composition and the writing of another piece by Defoe, *An Account of the Conduct of Robert Earl of Oxford*. Harley stated that 'he has reason to believe from several passages therein contained, that it was the intention of the author or authors to do him a prejudice'.[42] Defoe's pamphleteering certainly did not prevent Harley's impeachment; indeed, Harley's notice appeared a few days before he was sent to the Tower. But both Harley and Defoe knew that the Whigs would attempt to have their revenge. The very concept of the gradual publication of the three parts was to stall for time and sow seeds of doubt. Harley was rumoured to be the author, but in a letter of 23 November 1714, after the publication of the first two parts, Harley wrote to a correspondent about the outrageous behaviour ('madmen's contrivances') of both parties during the elections, adding 'The Whigs brag in print they caused the two books of the White Staff to be written; and the

---

[39] *The Secret History of the White Staff, Part III* (London, 1715), 74, 79–80. See also 53, 70.

[40] Ibid. 60. Although Defoe clears Bolingbroke of any serious flirtation with the Pretender, this accusation was clearly aimed at him and with some justice. Bolingbroke thought that once Harley was removed he would be able to wield greater power over the opposition and even over the succession.

[41] He listed 9 basic errors of the Whigs, including their error in removing Harley from power. See *Secret History of the White Staff, Part III*, 16.

[42] See J. A. Downie, *Robert Harley and the Press* (Cambridge: Cambridge University Press, 1979), 186–8.

policy is plain. He ought to be treated as a fool who had the staff, if he ever encouraged a vindication.'[43] In 1715 no vindication could have been successful. The ultimate justification of the strategy was Harley's eventual acquittal when he was tried in the House of Lords two years later.

Perhaps only Defoe and Harley could have concocted such a strategy, but there is another scenario. Harley may have followed Defoe's method only as far as the first two parts and may have been offended by the criticism levelled by Defoe in the third part. He may also have misunderstood Defoe's method of flooding the press with pamphlets which vindicated his actions in only the most oblique manner, and he may have thought that the severe criticism of Bolingbroke and of the behaviour of the Tories as depicted in the work mentioned in the *Gazette*—*An Account of the Conduct of Robert Earl of Oxford*—would alienate him from some of his friends. All of this is possible, but the latter pamphlet did not pretend to the view of the 'impartial historian' to be found in *The Secret History of the White Staff*; it was a well-reasoned, ardent defence, and John Robert Moore is probably right in thinking that Defoe had something to do with reissuing it in July 1717 before Harley's trial.[44] No letters between Harley and Defoe after 1714 have survived to inform us whether they continued to coordinate a strategy. Defoe persevered in defending Harley into 1717, perhaps, as some biographers believe, out of high principles of gratitude in spite of Harley's disapproval, or perhaps with Harley's approval and financial support.

What must be said, finally, about *The Secret History of the White Staff* is that the three parts represent Defoe's best writing as a pamphleteer. Downie notes that it was 'remarkable for its lucid and accurate picture of the power struggle between Oxford and Bolingbroke', but it was also startling in its depiction of a man of high principle and moderation skilfully attempting to mediate between violent forces. Harley's vices—a refusal to act with dispatch on important issues, a reluctance to take advantage of political power, and a kind of penuriousness in regard to spending public money—emerge as virtues in a world of party rage and the universal desire to accumulate as much wealth as possible. Defoe chose to write almost all of his fictions through first-person narrative, but he showed in this account how well he could handle third-person narrative. In another sense the 'Staff', as Defoe calls Harley throughout, may also be said to be Defoe's

---

[43] HMC, *Papers of the Duke of Portland*, v. 501. See also v. 513, where an observer reported on the atmosphere in the House of Lords after the vote to send Harley to the Tower. The Earl of Anglesey, when he commented that 'such cruel proceedings would shake the sceptre in the K[ing's] hand', was forced to make up the excuse that he was speaking of the riots occurring at the time.

[44] *Checklist*, 127, item 323.

first well-developed character. And since Defoe knew that every word and every innuendo would be carefully scrutinized, he wrote with a purity of style that was almost unique for a writer accustomed to rushing out copy to reflect upon each passing event.

Replies to *The Secret History of the White Staff* appeared rapidly. Most of the attacks complained that Harley blamed the Queen or Bolingbroke for everything. Bolingbroke assumed, 'from the Correctness of Stile, and notorious Sincerity', that Harley was the author, and gave a completely different picture of the former Lord Treasurer, complaining that 'when you had a Mind not to be understood, your L------p could be effectually unintelligible, without putting your self to much Trouble'. Bolingbroke read behind the 'broken sentences' for which Harley was famous the qualities of an 'Adroit Kn[a]ve'. He denied that Harley strongly favoured the Hanoverian succession, and suggested that had he been more loyal to the principles of those who belonged to the Tory October Club, their party might still have been in power.[45] Though Harley was often credited with the authorship of *The Secret History of the White Staff*, Defoe was soon accused of being the author and transmitter of Harley's ideas.[46] Defoe had at least managed to do one thing right; he had succeeded in dictating to Harley's opponents the terms of the argument.

---

[45] *Considerations upon the Secret History of the White Staff*, 2nd edn. (London [1714]), 5, 7, 15, 27, 34.
[46] See e.g. *The White-Staff Speech to the Lords* (London, 1714), 29.

20

Times When Honest Men Must Reserve Themselves for Better Fortunes

When a Man has chang'd his Principles which are his very nature, 'tis not a Work of much Labour for him to do the same Thing by his Name; and if such a one puts on the Resemblance of a Person of Honour or a Countess, he does but Act the Second Part of the same Farce.

William Pittis?[1]

Defoe had not changed all of his principles, but with the *Mercator* and some of his pamphlets of 1713 and 1714 he had involved himself in writing through a persona supporting ideas and positions that he would have found problematic, if not outright false. Although such writing had some benefits in stretching his imagination, it also left him with a restricted core of beliefs. He was still the ardent defender of the Hanoverian succession, of the Union with Scotland, and of the English Dissenters. He was still ready to attack wealthy merchants who encroached upon the rights of the labouring poor, still indignant over certain aspects of privilege in society, and he still held the belief that Britain ought to be a society that allowed individual talent to develop to its fullest extent. Whether he was still the thoroughgoing Whig idealogue who composed *Jure Divino* is doubtful, but he believed more firmly than ever in that right of self-defence that formed the basis of his argument in that work. Indeed, during the years

---

[1] *Queen Anne Vindicated from the Base Aspersions of Some Late Pamphlets Publish'd to Screen the Mismanagers of the Four Last Years from Publick Justice* (London, 1715), 10

following the death of Queen Anne, he may well have come to understand better than ever that undeniable right of self-preservation. And of course, he was still the ardent believer in Christian revelation and a world of invisible spirits whose influences might lie behind all sorts of human impulses.

The threat of the Anglesey accusation hung over him during the end of 1714 and lasted until the end of autumn of 1715, but Defoe was never more busy. Such Whigs as John Dunton looked into the future and thought they could envision there the execution of Harley for treason and the punishment of all who served him.[2] In defending Harley, Defoe was also protecting himself, for if all the members of the government were to be found guilty of various crimes against the state, who could tell where the revenge of the Whigs would stop? Defoe's own defence, *An Appeal to Honour and Justice, Though It Be of His Worst Enemies*, has to be seen as part of the same project, and a desperate one at that. Joining in the debate on the ground rules established by those who, like John Dunton, had prejudged the issue would be futile. The best way to protect himself would be to sow confusion, to show that there were many ways of seeing the actions of the ministry and that truth was never all that simple.

I

The 'Person of Honour' and the 'Countess' mentioned in the quotation at the start of this chapter were both versions of Defoe, as was the author of *A Secret History of One Year, Impeachment or No Impeachment, The Secret History of the Scepter*, and *The Secret History of State Intrigues*. With such titles as *The Secret History of the Secret History of the White Staff, Purse and Mitre*, Defoe was undermining the possibility of ever determining truth in judging the previous ministry as well as mocking the press's attempts to satisfy the curiosity of readers. This work projected an image of an audience like the scandalmongers of Sheridan's *School for Scandal*, the 'truth' of whose narratives depended not on their accurate description of real events but on the degree of detail that gave an air of verisimilitude to the most improbable story. He returned to the reign of William III to show how that monarch pardoned all those who opposed him, and even in

---

[2] Dunton has a poem on Harley in which he writes of bringing the former Lord Treasurer 'to the Ax', and he expressed the hope that 'every honest Briton' would soon hear the streets ring with Harley's '*last dying Speech and confession*'. See *Queen Robin: or the Second Part of Neck or Nothing* (London, [1714]), vi. 11.

pamphlets urging support for George I and concern over the Jacobite threat, he attempted to spread the theme of moderation and an avoidance of internal strife ('Civil Peace') as the best way for George I to begin his reign.[3] In what would seem a violent Whig attack upon the former ministry, he called for punishing all or none with the implication that since condemning everyone would be impossible, it would be better that none were punished. In *The Secret History of State Intrigues in the Management of the Scepter*, he suggested that 'the Check, every Party is to each other' might be 'needful to the whole, in Order to restrain them from Tyranny and Oppression', and defended Harley as a party politician within an established system of party politics.[4] Continuing in this vein, Defoe's Countess of ----, a lady close to Queen Anne, suggested that all of the talk of impeachment was absurd, since the ministry submitted everything to Parliament. Besides, it was the Queen who wanted peace and who, on one occasion, had rebuked Harley for suggesting that the war be continued.

The 'Person of Honour' who was the supposed author of *The Secret History of the Secret History of the White Staff* raised an even more complicated smokescreen, while complaining that the purpose of these discussions of Harley was '*To raise a Dust that he* [Harley] *may be lost in the Cloud*'. Beginning with an attack on the authenticity of *The History of the White Staff*, the author suggests that both Whig and Tory have 'been bubbled to accept these Romances for a true Narration, and have taken the Fable for a History, without enquiring into the Things whether they were impos'd upon *Yea* or *No*'. Everything is made to appear as if the press has been engaged in making money off the credulity of its readers:

It shall appear that the same People employing other Hands, have been the Editors not only of the Books themselves, but also of several of the Answers to these Books, causeing the deceiv'd People to Dance in the Circles of their drawing, while these have enjoy'd the Sport of their own Witchcraft; and like the Hangers-on of the Camp, have taken the Spoil of the Field of Battle, as well of the Victors, as of the Vanquished.[5]

And by some odd sleight of hand, Defoe manages to hint that William Pittis, one of those who attacked him as the author of these works, may himself have been the author.

William Pittis understood well enough what Defoe was attempting to

[3] See e.g. Defoe, *Advice to the People of Great Britain* (London, 1714), 4 and *passim*.
[4] *The Secret History of State Intrigues in the Management of the Scepter* (London, 1715), 13.
[5] Defoe, *The Secret History of the Secret History of the White Staff* (London, 1715), 8. See also 5–6.

accomplish. In *Considerations on the History of the Mitre and Purse* he vilified Defoe as the Machiavellian presence behind all of these works:

He is capable of such Drudgery as any Wretch alive, and can with a quiet Conscience publish a *Satyr* and a *Panegyrick* on the same Person, as very often he writes and answers himself. In this he sometimes is oblig'd to be honest by Necessity, and to make himself appear as great a *Knave* and a *Dunce* in one Scription, as he pretended to be a *Politician* and an *Englishman* in another. This juggling would be of great service to the late *Managers*, if it could take off People from talking on their Crimes, and make 'em the more indifferent of their Punishment. If by using them to look upon 'em as Guilty all alike it could prevent *Distinction*, which by *dividing* the *Guilty* among them all, would lessen in proportion every man's share of it. . . . 'Tis in this Case as in *Hunting*, where the *Game* is lost by the plenty of it, and the true Scent sunk in many.[6]

Pittis believed that, behind all these masks and appearances, Defoe was single-minded in defending Harley and forestalling the punishment being prepared for him by the Whigs. Yet Pittis did not give Defoe any credit for loyalty; the image of the unscrupulous journalist was the one that lingered.

In attempting to defend Harley, Defoe also managed to defend himself. In his *Secret History of the Secret History*, he introduced a dialogue between a renegade Quaker and his neighbour in which the Quaker dismisses *The History of the White Staff* as 'no other than Fable, being compos'd by Evil Persons for Lucre and Gain', and speaks of his understanding that Harley reacted with indignation upon reading them. He then asked a friend to visit Defoe to see whether he had composed them at Harley's dictation:

It seems, he found the poor Man in a very Dangerous Condition, having had a Fit of an Apoplexy, and being very Weak, insomuch, that his Life was despair'd of; but, mentioning the said Books to him, and that the Town charg'd him with being the Author of them, and that he had Written them by Direction of the said Lord *Oxford*, the said Person answer'd, That they did him a great deal of Wrong; neither did he believe, that the Lord *Oxford* was in any Way concern'd, directly or indirectly in the said Books, and that he believ'd his Lordship had never heard of them till they were publish'd. It was true, he said, that he happen'd to see some of the Copy, while it was at the Press, and that being desir'd to look upon it, he did Revise Two or Three Sheets of it, and mark'd some Things in them, which he dislik'd; but for the rest he could safely Swear he never saw them, or knew what was in them, till after they were printed, nor did he know whether the Things which he had mark'd (as above said) were alter'd in the Print, *Yea* or *No*.[7]

---

[6] William Pittis, *Considerations on the History of the Mitre and Purse* (London, 1714), 2–3.

[7] *Secret History of the Secret History*, 16. It should be pointed out that this work was published on 4 Jan. 1715, after the publication of the first two parts of *The History of the White Staff* but before the publication of the third. The strategy worked out between Defoe and Harley seems to have involved allowing the

What follows this pathetic scene of Defoe seemingly on his deathbed is an account of the press—the 'Hackneys' who sell their services and the publishers who purchase their labour with the single intent 'that the said Books *may Sell*' exemplified in the characters of Pittis and the unscrupulous publisher Edmund Curll. Pittis had attempted to expose Defoe, and Defoe had no qualms about insulting his enemy. But the commentary at the end suggests much more than is stated. After the Anglesey incident, Defoe had apparently discovered the wisdom of destroying his original copy. What he could not control so well were the corrections he made on the proof sheets. Since these were probably used by the printers up to the last moment, some might elude his care. He now had a story that could explain why his handwriting might appear on the copy.

The story of Defoe's apoplexy has been doubted by both Defoe's contemporaries and modern biographers. Defoe's autobiographical account, *An Appeal to Honour and Justice*, breaks off dramatically with a 'CONCLUSION BY THE PUBLISHER' stating that before he could finish 'the Author was seiz'd with a violent Fit of an Apoplexy, whereby he was disabled finishing what he design'd in his farther Defence, and continuing now for above Six Weeks in a Weak and Languishing Condition, neither able to go on, or likely to recover, at least in any short time'.[8] His friends, who have urged the publication of the fragment, blame his languishing condition on the treatment he has received from the world. James Sutherland thought that this brief announcement sounded very much like Defoe himself.[9] To question the reality or seriousness of Defoe's sickness might seem excessively cautious, especially when we know that Defoe was ill at various times during the previous two years. The difficulty hinges at least as much on his productivity during this period as upon the serpent-like cunning he thought necessary for survival during these months. The *Appeal* was published on 24 February 1715.[10] John Robert

controversy over the first two parts to subside before publishing the last and crucial part of the argument. That both of them should deny any part in writing the work seems to have been part of the plan. Defoe may have altered the third part to be more critical of Harley in order to bolster Harley's contention that he was not involved, and it is hard to conceive that he would have been ignorant of Defoe's purpose, however much he may have disliked the manner in which he was portrayed.

[8] *An Appeal to the Honour and Justice Though It Be of His Worst Enemies*, in *Shakespeare Head Edition*, 238.

[9] For scepticism about Defoe's illness both contemporary and modern, cf. *Queen Anne Vindicated*, 14, and James Sutherland, *Defoe*, 2nd edn. (London: Methuen, 1950), 210.

[10] Trent followed William Lee in believing that the writing was complete by 1 Oct. 1714, but Lee based his judgement on Defoe's statement, 'I have meddl'd neither one way or other nor written one Book since the 1st of October'. Such a statement has to be taken as part of Defoe's created image of himself as one withdrawn from the field of conflict. Since the discussion of his sons' education in response to an attack upon his failure to have his sons properly educated came in the *Flying Post* for 4–7 Dec. 1714, the statement cannot be true. See Trent, MS biography, 368, 380; and Lee, i. 236.

Moore's *Checklist* offers eighteen items from the beginning of the year. Even if some of these are doubtful, the number suggests that, if he was indeed ill, he was neither 'languishing' nor 'disabled'.[11] By turning his autobiography into a fragment with all the sublimity and pathos that the age associated with unfinished forms, Defoe was apparently hoping to win some sympathy at a time when he seemed to have been abandoned by all sides. In fact, any careful reading would suggest that he had actually said all that he had wanted to say. Just as Pope had ended his poetic defence in the *Epistle to Arbuthnot* with a sudden appeal to the virtues of his father and mother, so Defoe, after comparing himself to Jeremiah, wronged by his enemies, pointed to an attack in the *Flying Post* upon his family and his failure to pay for the education of his children.

The *Appeal* contains a great deal of information as well as some disinformation. Just as Harley had decided to plead his case on the basis of actions taken through loyalty to the Queen, so Defoe made the same plea. Pointing to the time of his life when he joined the forces of Monmouth against James II, he claimed to have remained steady to his principles— 'Revolution Principles'—while others were swayed by loyalty to party and rage against the opposition. 'I never once changed my Opinion, my Principles, or my Party; and let what will be said of changing Sides, this I maintain, That I never once deviated from the "Revolution Principles," nor from the Doctrine of Liberty and Property, on which it was founded.'[12] Some of these statements have a ring of truth; in his mind he was still the Whig radical who defied Parliament during the time of the Kentish petition. But the *Appeal* was mainly a political document, and we can be confident that his denials of ever having written certain works—*Mercator*, for example—fly in the face of what we know of his activities from his own statements in his letters.

If, at this stage of his life, Defoe was not the master liar that Minto called him, surely few humans have ever mastered the art of equivocation so thoroughly.[13] He was almost 55 years old and had survived political persecution, warfare, and the rage of mobs. He was a bankrupt, a gaolbird, a Dissenter, and a writer living by his wits. He may have bowed and scraped when confronted with the powers of the state, but in his heart he hated the various forms of authority that were attempting to crush him

---

[11] See J. P. W. Rogers, 'Defoe and *The Immorality of the Priesthood* (1715): An Attribution Reviewed', *Papers of the Bibliographical Society of America* 67 (1973): 245–53. Rogers ascribes this pamphlet convincingly to John Oldmixon. [12] *Appeal to Honour and Justice*, 232.

[13] William Trent, *Defoe and How to Know Him* (London: Macmillan, 1879), 169. Trent was extremely critical of Minto's hyperbolic description of Defoe's abilities along these lines, but at one point in his biography he reconciled contradictions in Defoe's accounts by suggesting that it reflected a satanic tendency to deception.

physically and spiritually. Behind the *Appeal* and all that he wrote in his and Harley's defence during the first half of 1715 was a kind of defiance—a defiance based partly on a conviction that neither of them had done anything criminal and partly on a sense of his own power as a writer to manipulate a readership that belonged to that unique body of eighteenth-century Britain that Jürgen Habermas has called 'the public sphere'.[14]

One of the crucial arguments in the *Appeal* is connected with what Defoe calls the 'Ballance of Parties'. Bolingbroke had apparently hoped to make the Tories so dominant that the Whigs and other opposition groups would be powerless, and now the Whigs were attempting a similar move to power. Defoe had previously attacked the concept of parties as unfortunate. Harley was always trying to govern in such a way that no single party would dominate, and Defoe seems to have appreciated the advantages of such an arrangement. Now Defoe was defending parties as institutionalized parts of the British government, partly because that view seemed to preserve their followers from any charge of treason, but also because he now actually saw the state in this way. He may even have seen some financial benefit in such a situation, since the continued existence of the two parties would mean prolonging the kind of party journalism that abounded during the last four years of Queen Anne's reign, and it was clear that Defoe's talents as a writer could flourish in such a situation.

Although Defoe printed a copy of the pardon he had received from Queen Anne for publishing the three pamphlets against Jacobitism and for the House of Hanover in *An Appeal to Honour and Justice*, he might well have suspected that the charges laid against him in 1713 would figure in the verdict against him in July of 1715. In some sense, he had done better for Harley than for himself. The items of impeachment read in the House of Commons on 10 June and 30 July had already been answered in *The History of the White Staff* and some of Defoe's other writings. The charges used phrases like 'the Iniquity of his Heart', and argued that Harley had sought 'the final Destruction of his Country' and was 'an Enemy to the common liberty of Europe'. But proof that Harley violated any laws in being a party to the peace with France or the creation of the twelve new peers must have seemed questionable. The additional charges brought in at the end of July were more specific. They blamed him for the disastrous expedition to Quebec, of embezzling £13,000, of supporting the Pretender, and of betraying the Catalans. By this time Harley was already in custody,

---

[14] See Jurgen Habermas, *The Transformation of the Public Sphere*, trans. Thomas Burger (Cambridge, Mass.: MIT Press, 1989). Defoe discussed the coffee house as a unique institution where custom had accepted the notion that treasonable ideas would be exchanged.

but he may well have believed that none of these charges would succeed in convicting him in the House of Lords and that, in the end, his determination to fight the charges was wiser than Bolingbroke's decision to flee to France and, eventually, to the Jacobite court. Harley wrote a lengthy and moving answer to the charges against him, claiming that 'with all the assurances of an innocent man, . . . he ever acted , according to the best of his skill and judgment, with sincere desires and intentions to serve the public, and without any view to his own private advantage'.[15] Interestingly enough, Swift and Defoe were oddly joined in the response of the Whigs. Walpole argued that Harley's version of the Peace of Utrecht might be found in writings which everyone knew to be by Swift, and Aislabie noted that Harley's defence of his actions 'was a contexture of the shifts, evasions, and false representations', contained in the three parts of *The Secret History of the White Staff*, which despite all their denials was thought to be the work of Defoe and Harley.[16] The impeachment went forward to the House of Lords. Harley's political career was over, but following two years in the Tower, he was to be freed after the House of Commons failed to reply successfully to a demand by the House of Lords that the charges against him be accompanied by evidence that he was guilty of them. Since the Treaty of Utrecht had become the basis for the Whigs' efforts at establishing a new treaty with France which was to make that nation part of the Quadruple Alliance, any effort at establishing Harley's guilt might have proved both difficult and embarrassing. Harley was eventually freed to take up a new life among his beloved books.

Though Defoe's situation seemed desperate, he was even more fortunate. His letters to Harley on the Anglesey affair were futile, since Harley had little influence at this time. Defoe had entered a plea of not guilty, but having alienated his friends among the Whigs, he was unlikely to be found innocent or pardoned. On 12 July 1715 he was tried for libel in the King's Bench along with John Wine and the printers, Gibbs and Watson. All four were found guilty, fined heavily, sentenced to be whipped from Newgate to Charing Cross, and to be imprisoned for two years. Defoe was singled out as a person of vicious character and a danger to the state, but he did not come up for sentencing on 19 November. The *Flying Post* of 15 November reported that he had forfeited his bail by not appearing before the court and that actions were being taken. But Defoe's name had never been called. He had once more struck a deal with the government, an event that he was eventually to view as close to miraculous.

---

[15] William Cobbett, *Parliamentary History*, vii (London: Longman et al., 1811), 210.
[16] Ibid. cols. 211–12.

He had felt a strong 'Impulse darting into his mind' to write Lord Chief Justice Parker. The words seemed to come from some supernatural source:

It was immediately impressed on his mind, and the words flowed upon his pen in a manner, that even charmed himself, and filled him with expectations of success.

The letter was so strenuous in argument, so pathetic in its eloquence, and so moving and persuasive, that as soon as the Judge read it he sent him word he should be easy, for he would endeavor to make that matter light to him, and in a word never left till he obtained to stop prosecution and restore him to his liberty and to his family.[17]

The passage is from *Serious Reflections of Robinson Crusoe* and is told about someone Crusoe knew, but there is no question that Defoe was talking about himself. As told in his work of fiction, it would seem as if Defoe had achieved the high point of his literary talents through taking dictation from some angelic force. Fortunately, in 1718, he gave an account of this event in more direct language to a government official, Charles de la Faye:

It was in the Ministry of My Lord Townshend, When My Ld Chief Justice Parker to whom I stand Obliged for the favour, Was pleased So farr to state my Case, That Notwithstanding the Missrepresentations Under which I had Suffred, and Nothwithstanding Some Mistakes which I was the first to Acknowlege, I Was So happy as to be believ'd in the Professions I made of a Sincere attachmt to The Intrest of the Present Governmt; and speaking with all Possible Humillity, I hope I Have not Dishonourd My Ld Parkers Recommendation. (H 451)

Defoe says that it was the then Secretary of State, Lord Townshend, who came up with the idea 'That I should still appear as if I were as before under the Displeasure of the Governmt; and Seperated From the Whiggs; and That I might be more Servicable in a kind of Disguise, Than If I appeard openly' (H 451). He then recounted his work for the ministry in publishing or assisting with Tory newspapers, newsletters and journals, *Mercurius Politicus*, *Dormer's Newsletter*, and *Mist's Weekly Journal, or Saturday's Post* with the intention that 'mistakes accepted' they would 'Pass as Tory Papers, and yet be Dissabled and Ennervated, So as to do no Mischief or give any Offence to the Governmt' (H 453). Defoe then noted that such a situation meant that he was 'Posted among Papists, Jacobites, and Enraged High Torys, a Generation who I Profess My Very Soul abhorrs'.

John Robert Moore lamented the loss of the letter to Parker on the

---

[17] *Serious Reflections of Robinson Crusoe*, in *Novels and Romances of Daniel Defoe*, ed. George A. Aitken (London: Dent, 1895), 281. Defoe says that this event occurred when the man was in hiding. Allowing for the elaboration of fiction, it may still indicate that Defoe had finally decided that, if the letter to Parker did not work out as he hoped, he would forfeit his bond rather than go to prison.

grounds that it would have been a literary masterpiece. What one would like to know is whether in fact Defoe included in the letter the scheme of subverting the Tory press. Was this not exactly what he had been doing during 1714 with the *Flying Post* for Bolingbroke and the Tories? Since it was in this journal that he had libelled Anglesey by calling him a Jacobite, would it not have seemed the proper service to offer? How much difficulty would Defoe have had in convincing Townshend that he was loyal to the house of Hanover? And in his position as a translator and distributor of foreign news was he not perfectly positioned for such work? The usual explanation for Parker's willingness to serve Defoe is that by this time Anglesey had been exposed as a Jacobite and that the charge of libel was moot; but what is more likely is that other events had made Defoe's services valuable.[18] Rumours of a Jacobite invasion had been given official status from 20 July 1715, when George I announced that the various riots throughout the country were part of a plan to foment insurrection in preparation for an invasion by the Pretender. The Duke of Ormond made two unsuccessful attempts at an invasion of England, but on 6 September, the Earl of Mar raised the standard of rebellion in Scotland and by October his forces held most of Scotland. Though the Pretender did not land at Peterhead in Aberdeenshire until 22 December 1715, it would have been apparent to Parker how useful Defoe might be to the government at so critical a juncture.

The morality of Defoe's activities as a spy on the opposition press has taxed the ingenuity of Defoe's biographers. Lee did not see that it posed any moral dilemma, while Minto was outraged. Moore argued that Defoe was a good soldier, obeying orders and manning the dangerous post to which he had been assigned. In fact, for all his protesting that he would keep his beliefs pure while being forced to associate with vile Jacobites and High Tories, who can doubt that Defoe enjoyed every moment, who can doubt that the 'Disguise' which he says Townshend suggested he assume in

[18] Although Anglesey was angered enough by the attempts to impeach the former leaders of the Tory party to state in the House of Lords that 'it was to be feared these violent measures would make the scepter shake in the King's hands', subsequently being forced to apologize for his words when other members threatened to send him to the Tower, there is no evidence that he ever entertained Jacobite sentiments. On 5 Apr. 1714 he had broken with the Tories and voted with the Whigs on the question of whether the nation was in danger. On the other hand, Constantine Phipps, the Lord Chancellor of Ireland, was overtly Jacobite in his opinions. He would have liked to have turned the army over to Jacobite officers, but his battles with the Whigs in Dublin and in the Irish Parliament had resulted in a stalemate. At the same time, something similar to what the news article had reported had been happening in Scotland, where the Tory government had been accused by the Duke of Argyll of encouraging Jacobitism in the army by eliminating Whig officers. See John Robert Moore, *Daniel Defoe* (Chicago: University of Chicago Press, 1958), 206–7; Cobbett, *Parliamentary History*, vii. cols. 1333–7; T. C. Nicholson and A. S. Turberville, *Charles Talbot Duke of Shrewsbury* (Cambridge: Cambridge University Press, 1930), 206; 'Constantine Phipps', *DNB*, xv. 1114–15.

running the Tory press had become so much a part of his character that he would have been unhappy without it? He was to start a number of Whig journals in the years after 1715 alongside the Tory journals he was controlling in various ways, but whatever we may think of his attempts to express his true opinions in journals of this kind and in separate pamphlets, can there be any question that he had come to find a certain excitement and imaginative stimulation in treating forbidden ideas?

That this arrangement continued for about seven years is a tribute to Defoe's talents. He was accused of being 'Corrector General' of the Press as early as 24 August 1717, and his role in various publications was to be revealed off and on during this time. But despite an embarrassing exposure in 1718, no one seemed to mind too much.[19] This was as much a tribute to him as a writer as it was a commentary on the relative stability of the political system that the Whigs were to establish along with the cooling off of some of the heated contentions of the reign of Queen Anne. It was already apparent that Defoe could be as entertaining a journalist as might be found, and for Nathaniel Mist, at least, the desire to sell newspapers was one reason for keeping Defoe in charge even after his connections with the government had become obvious.

II

Although the transition to the reign of George I had gone relatively smoothly, there had been some disturbances, most notably in Bristol, and the government was determined not to let riots get out of control.[20] There had also been a series of provocative acts throughout England during the summer of 1715, and with the rebellion begun in Scotland in September, the real battle seemed ready to take place. Staunch as he was for the Hanoverian succession, Defoe was not going to remain silent even when threatened by prosecution. Often the pamphlets he wrote during this period were intended to do more than merely vindicate George and the

---

[19] Sir David Dalrymple wrote to the Earl of Stair on 3 Oct. 1718 of his shock at discovering that Defoe was writing for both Whig and Tory journals. But by this time Defoe had become legendary for his subversive journalistic methods. See Paul Dottin, *Daniel Defoe et ses romans* (Paris: Presses Universitaires de France, 1924), 236.

[20] John Robert Moore ascribed two pamphlets on the Bristol riots to Defoe on a tentative basis (*Checklist*, items 286 and 288). The attack upon Sacheverell in *The Bristol Riot* is similar to the kind of comment Defoe would make, but Defoe was hardly the only contemporary pamphleteer who blamed Sacheverell and the High Church for popular discontents. John Oldmixon, to whom Pat Rogers has ascribed another work Moore thought to be by Defoe, might be a more likely candidate. See Rogers, 'Defoe and *The Immorality of the Priesthood* (1715): An Attribution Reviewed', *Papers of the Bibliographical Society of America* 6 (1973), 245–53.

Protestant succession; he usually took the opportunity to defend his own actions by describing a situation in which those loyal to George might work with a Tory minister. Harley too needed to be defended, first against the impeachment proceedings and then against the trial itself. Of course, once he had re-established his relationship with the Whig Secretaries of State, he was more than willing to use his pamphlets for supporting the government.

On 7 October 1714 Defoe published a pamphlet that would be the prototype for the many that followed over the next few years. He hailed the coming of George as a new era in British politics. With the succession firmly established and the jacobite threat over, the confusions that swayed Britain since the Exclusion Crisis in 1680 will be replaced by a new political paradigm dominated by a 'general Union of Affections':

The Danger of the pretender will be lost, the very Remembrance of it will dye, a brave and a magnanimous Prince at the head of an united Nation can leave us no room for Apprehensions, nor the Friends of the Pretender any room for Hope: Popery, and jacobitism must no more shew their Faces, or have the least Pretences for their Cause; let them make what Efforts they can, they will be Laught at by the World[21]

Of course, as part of this halcyon period, an amnesty ought to be proclaimed in which the members of the former government and its supporters would be forgiven. Even 'a quiet passive Jack' would be allowed to live his life in peace, though 'not an intreaguing, ploting busy turbulent Jacobite'. Defoe's inoffensive Jacobite would hold his belief as part of what one historian has called 'the politics of nostalgia', but he viewed an active Jacobitism as something that 'will be Laught at by the World'.[22] Defoe was right in the long run, but even he must have found his confidence shaken by the rebellious spirit that prevailed at the time, and which saw the Pretender go through his coronation at Perth on 23 January 1716. The French troops the Pretender thought necessary for his success never arrived, and he sailed back to France just a few weeks after that event on 4 February in order to, as he stated, preserve the Stuart cause for the future. With his withdrawal, the Jacobite army faded into the remote areas of the Highlands. True to Defoe's prediction of a new age of moderation, the government acted with caution. There were few executions, and eighteen months later a general amnesty was issued.

---

[21] *Advice to the People of Great Britain* (London, 1714), 32–3.

[22] Ibid. 24, 32. See also Isaac Kramnick, *Bolingbroke and His Circle: The Politics of Nostalgia in the Age of Walpole* (Cambridge, Mass.: Harvard University Press, 1968). See also Manuel Schonhorn, 'The Limits of Jacobite Rhetoric', *English Literary History* 64 (1997), 871–86.

Being an accurate prophet of what would happen in the long term did not save Defoe from all kinds of doubts about the safety of the nation, the safety of Harley, and, for that matter, his own safety until November 1715. At the beginning of 1715 he had begun publishing with Samuel Keimer, a former member of the Sect known as the French Prophets, and this was eventually to give a special character to some of his publications.[23] But the message, sometimes hidden, sometimes overt, was very much the same: the Jacobites and the clergy of the High Church need to be controlled, and an 'Act of Oblivion' should be passed in favour of the supporters of the previous Tory government so that recriminations between the parties would cease.[24] He paused in this effort to urge the election of Whigs to office when he felt the need to respond to a pamphlet by Atterbury, *English Advice to the Freeholders of England*, attacking George I and raising the old cry that the 'Church was in Danger'. These efforts gave birth to one of Defoe's best pamphlets. Published on 27 January, *The Candidate*, unlike his specific attacks upon the attempts by the High Church to blacken George I, was addressed to the general problem of corruption in the process itself. With a vividness foreshadowing Hogarth's series on electioneering, Defoe expressed doubts about the eagerness of English gentlemen to win posts in Parliament that paid nothing and were an open road to accepting bribes. He pictured scenes of candidates delivering a guinea to the wives of the voters by placing the bribe on their tongues and passing it to them with their kisses. Defoe also showed voters, sick from excessive drink, vomiting over candidates, and deplored the betrayal of the ideal of carefully choosing the 'Conservators of . . . Liberty' by those 'made Slaves to . . . Liquor'.[25] Indeed, since winning elections amounted to bribing voters with drink or money, it would be inevitable that one form of bribery would lead to another. Defoe printed part of a play 'never made Publick' in this pamphlet to illustrate the buying and selling of seats in Parliament through brokers in Exchange Alley. Though the writer of the pamphlet does not claim to be the author of the play, it is interesting to think that at a time when Defoe had lost his payments from the government, he may have toyed with the idea of writing for the stage. But whether it is by Defoe or

---

[23] See Hillel Schwartz, *The French Prophets* (Berkeley: University of California Press, 1980), 114, 128, 193. In his autobiographical memoir, *A Brand Pluck'd from the Burning*, Keimer described how his association with this group brought him to the wildest forms of enthusiasm and ultimately to complete poverty. It is significant that this work was published in 1718 by Defoe's own publisher, William Boreham.

[24] See Defoe's *Strike While the Iron is Hot* (London, 1715); and *The Secret History of State Intrigues in the Management of the Scepter, in the Late Reign* (London, 1715).

[25] *The Candidate* (London, 1715), 12. Defoe's other pamphlets on the election were *Treason Detected* (London, 1715) and *A Reply to a Traiterous Libel, Entituled, English Advice to the Freeholders of Great Britain* (London, 1715).

not, it certainly represents his vision of a system that ought to be the basis of free political expression corrupted by a stock market willing to buy and sell anything.[26]

However much Defoe may have become emotionally involved in defending Tory ideas on the peace and on trade, he certainly had to consider himself subjected to a form of intellectual slavery, expecially while labouring under Bolingbroke's yoke and while trying to please a Harley who was becoming less and less clear about his own ideals. In a work such as *The Protestant Jubilee* published on 8 February, a day set aside for celebrating George I's 'Happy Accession' to the throne, he could allow himself to speak freely on precisely those issues about which he had needed previously to restrain himself. The Schism Act was a 'Murthering of Souls' in taking away from children the 'Key of Knowledge'; the peace was a disaster and a betrayal of the Dutch; Sacheverell was 'the French King's Trumpeter'. George I would bring a new wealth to the nation with 'the Manufacturers diligent and full of Employ, enriching themselves, and supplying and feeding the Poor, *viz*. Employing the Labouring, and Cloathing the Hungry Poor'.[27] Even allowing for the specific nature of Defoe's celebration in this tract, his real feelings on these issues are clear enough. If he was to bow in the House of Rimmon once more by the end of the year, he must nevertheless have enjoyed his period of freedom even with Justice Parker's sentence hanging over him.

Oddly enough, Defoe took the opportunity of publishing with Samuel Keimer to indulge in what is probably the first of his tracts assuming the voice of a Quaker. Keimer must have been aware of the deliberate stylistic exaggeration in Defoe's rendering of Quaker speech, but Keimer, though a member of the French Prophets, a sect that was the target of even more opprobrium than the Quakers for their enthusiasm, must have enjoyed the joke.[28] The Quaker disguise enabled Defoe to resume the mode of reproof

[26] Paula Backscheider speculates on some relationship between Susan Centlivre's unperformed play, *The Gotham Election*, and the section printed by Defoe. Keimer published the first act of Centlivre's play. See Paula Backscheider, *Daniel Defoe: His Life* (Baltimore: Johns Hopkins University Press, 1989), 594, n. 68.   [27] Defoe, *The Protestant Jubilee* (London, 1714), 15–16, 25.

[28] During this period, Keimer was in a state approaching madness, and after one of the leaders of that group, John Potter, had him arrested for debt, Keimer turned against them. After examining many systems of Christianity, he eventually came to believe that 'the true Quakers' were the least offensive of the lot, but he opposed oaths even more strongly than the Quakers. And though he wore a yard of green cloth and wrote on apples under the influence of the French Prophets, he apparently found the Quakers odd enough to perform a skit in which he parodied Quaker mannerisms. 'I used to divert the Company', he wrote of his prison experience, 'either with Stories I'd read formerly, singing, or Preaching (as it was impiously call'd) a Quakers Sermon, which I several Times acted with great Applause from the Company, mixing my Discourse with somewhat filthy.' See Keimer, *A Brand Plucked from the Burning* (London, 1718), 96, 99; and *The Platonick Lady* (London, 1718), 4 and 7. For a discussion of the French Prophets, see Schwartz, *The French Prophets*, esp. 47–8, 117, 193.

he had used in *The Poor Man's Plea*.[29] In this instance, he was exhorting
Thomas Bradbury, a clergyman who had urged revenge against Harley
and the other members of the ministry, to spend his efforts at more serious
moral violations in the society, particularly the corruptions to be found in
the theatre. The pamphlet went into numerous editions, and must have
been profitable for Defoe. The fact that it irritated the Quakers so much
may have helped its sale, since a postscript was added dealing with 'Threats
and Menaces' made by the Quakers over its publication. The Quakers
published a repudiation of the work in the *London Gazette* for 5 March and
in the *Daily Courant* two days later.[30] Though Defoe was eventually to
apologize to the Quakers for one of his Quaker tracts, he was not ready to
give ground yet. In another pamphlet, titled *A Sharp Rebuke from One of the
People Called Quakers to Henry Sacheverell, The High-Priest of Andrew's
Holbourn*, published around 26 March 1715, he commented upon a sermon
delivered by Sacheverell on 31 January, the day set aside for commem-
morating the beheading of Charles I and the occasion for High Church
attacks upon Dissenters, Whigs, and Low Churchmen. The style is a comic
parody of Quaker dialect:

Verily, *Henry*, thou hast troubled Israel for some Years of thy Life past; and If I
should look upon thee for the Days of thy Youth, thou has not only spent them in
much Vanity, but even in the Abomination of unclean Things; howbeit I shall not,
at this time rebuke thee as thou art a Sinner against the Lord, there is one that
rebuketh thee, even thy Conscience, who is the Minister of the Spirit within thee,
who, if thou wouldest listen to its Voice, would with Faithfulness witness against
thee, for thy vile Conversation, thy Drunkenness, thy Swearing, thy Abusing of
Women, and many of thy said Practices, as well during thy Residence at *Oxford*,
where thou oughtest to have been an Instructor of Youth, and a Teacher of
Vertue, as in *Staffordshire*, Worcestershire, and other Places where thy Name is
become a Stink in the Nostrils of the People.[31]

---

[29] In some ways Defoe was turning his attack upon the new world of the eighteenth century. In *The
Fears of the Pretender Turned into the Fears of Debauchery* (London, 1714), Defoe attacked Addison and
Steele for creating a culture that approved of plays and gave them a certain moral status. While praising
the *Spectator* for reforming the manners of society, Defoe questioned whether it had not harmed the
morals of the nation. Addison is reproved for seeming to approve of suicide in his *Cato* and Steele for
being a continuing advocate for the stage.

[30] See Lee, i. 244–5; and Moore, *Checklist*, item 305.

[31] Defoe, *A Sharp Rebuke from One of the People Called Quakers to Henry Sacheverell, The High-Priest of
Andrew's Holbourn* (London, 1715), 4. Defoe may have written all or part of another criticism of this
sermon, Moore's item 306, *Reflections upon A Sermon Preach'd January 31 1714/15 by Henry Sacheverel,
DD* (London, 1715). Moore may have thought this to be by Defoe because it refers to *The Justice and
Necessity of Restraining the Clergy*, but that pamphlet is almost certainly by John Oldmixon. On the other
hand, the 'Remarks', with its comments on Charles I and Clarendon's *History*, is consistent with Defoe's
ideas and is written in a style very much like that of Defoe.

As the danger that the Tories might have brought in the Pretender became more obvious to Defoe, he seems to have experienced a kind of revulsion from the entire situation in which he had been placed. This attack on Sacheverell is also directed against the Tories, and after accusing Sacheverell of being a Jacobite, Defoe's Quaker pronounces the real danger to the Church of England to lie with the defeated party, 'the Heathen People called Tories', and with clergymen like Sacheverell. If Atterbury's *English Advice* could depict the Tories as saintly preservers of liberty and the Whigs as vicious demagogues, and if Sacheverell could continue to attack all those who opposed Charles I as the blackest of villains, it might well seem that some kind of restraint on the clergy would work a remarkable improvement in Britain's political climate.[32]

Defoe assumed his Quaker mask once more in *A Seasonable Expostulation with, and Friendly Reproof unto James Butler, Who, by the Men of this World, is Stil'd Duke of O[rmon]d*, published on 31 May. Ormond had taken over the army in Flanders after Marlborough had been removed, and while he was an object of hatred for the Whigs, he had considerable popularity throughout Britain. He was to flee to France after 31 July 1715, when the news of a planned invasion by the Pretender brought sharp reprisals against the Jacobites at home, and his flight, at a time when he was thought to be the ideal person to lead a rebellion in Britain, was considered one of the major reasons for the failure of the hopes of the Pretender and of Bolingbroke, the Pretender's new Secretary of State at this time.[33] Defoe's Quaker addresses Ormond as the leader of the Jacobite mob and warns him of the fate of those who put themselves at the head of popular causes against a ruling monarch. The Whigs continued to hold Ormond responsible for withdrawing British troops from the allied effort against the French, but the Quaker refuses to attack him for this action, 'because as thou knowest *Friends* approve of none of those Things; neither do we go out to Fight, or make War upon any Occasion whatsoever'.[34] The central irony of the work is that Ormond's refusal to fight is linked to a principled pacifism, understandable enough in a Quaker but completely incongruous in a general. The Quaker position on war never ceased to amuse Defoe, who believed it contrary to the law of nature that dictated self-

---

[32] See e.g. *An Attempt Towards a Coalition of English Protestants* (London, 1715); *His Majesty's Obligations to the Whigs Plainly Proved* (London, 1715); and *Bold Advice: or, Proposals for the Entire Rooting out of Jacobitism in Great Britain* (London, 1715).

[33] See Wolfgang Michael, *England under George I* (London: Macmillan, 1936), 148–9. The other reason for the failure of Jacobite schemes in 1715 was the death of Louis XIV on 1 Sept. after a long illness.

[34] Defoe, *A Seasonable Expostulation with, and Friendly Reproof unto James Butler, Who, by the men of this World, is Stil'd Duke of O[rmon]d* (London, 1715), 21.

preservation. William, the fictional Quaker pirate of *Captain Singleton*, may have taken shape in his imagination at about this time.

The possibility of a repeat of the Sacheverell mobs of 1710 which had brought the Tories to power caused him to write a series of pamphlets attacking Ormond and the mobs supporting him. Defoe objected to Ormond's actions as despicable, and he has no difficulty placing the blame upon Bolingbroke whom he accuses of having had 'the greatest Hand in all the Villainous Management'.[35] As for the mobs, Defoe appealed to them to come to their senses. In the preface to his poem, *A Hymn to the Mob*, Defoe identified the tumultuous behaviour of the people throughout the country as inspired by the Jacobites, and put forward a somewhat more conservative view of mobs than he had espoused at the time of the Kentish petition, though the basis for his view was still essentially drawn from Hobbes. 'Mobs of any Party', he wrote, 'are in their Nature destructive of Government itself, ruinous to all Purposes of Civil Society, Enemies to Safety, Order, Justice, and Policy among Men.'[36] Government, he argued, was created by the mob to overcome or prevent tyranny, but a well-functioning government must always prevent mob rule: 'It is True, we have a Notion, That in England the People govern; I do not grant the Fact, tho' I am for Preserving the People's Priviledges of every Kind in their full Extent; but suppose it to be true, This is properly the People represented, not the People gather'd together.'[37] He has moved slightly from his view of Parliament as a symbolic representation of the mob, but not so much that he has abandoned his belief in the mob as a formative part of government. 'Justice and Law derive from thee,' he wrote, and Parliament remained the 'Creature' of the mob.[38] He also argued that however much the mob had been misled by Jacobites and the High Church, it would eventually understand its true interest and loyalties:

> Nor is thy Judgment often wrong,
> Thou seldom are mistaken, never long;
> However wrong, in Means thou May'st appear,
> Thou gener'ly art in thy Designs sincere.[39]

[35] *A Brief History of the Pacifick Campaign in Flanders* (London, 1715), 38.
[36] *Hymn to the Mob* (London, 1715), p. i.
[37] Ibid. p. ii.
[38] Ibid. 13.
[39] Ibid. 11. In *A Humble Address to our Sovereign Lord the People* (London, 1715), published in early summer, Defoe wrote from a more conservative standpoint. The speaker urges the mob not to attack the meeting-houses of the Dissenters, insisting that such actions were never sanctioned by the High Church, despite the fact that the mobs supporting Sacheverell marched and burned meeting-houses under the pretence that they were acting in support of that cause.

Though dangerous when raised in the cause of religion or political party, the mob was still useful for controlling tyranny.

In these works, Defoe speculated on the relationship between the mob and the army, which he regarded as a mob under the discipline and control of a leader who might merely claim credit for the exploits of his men or who might be a genuine hero such as Gustavus Adolphus, William III, or Marlborough. Defoe's interest in military affairs was hardly new. He considered himself an expert on all kinds of building and was particularly involved with methods of fortification, which at this time had their master in Vauban. From this standpoint, he had to like the new monarch. George I may not have lived up to the military ideals with which his mother, Sophia, had imbued him from childhood, but he showed himself to be a courageous leader. George's involvement in the Great Northern War, which was to continue as long as Charles XII was alive, kept Britain interested in military affairs, despite the state of peace which the Tories had imposed upon the nation. As early as April 1715 Defoe was writing under the mask of an officer in praise of the army and in expectation of a new war. He gave a rationale for warfare (a love of honour and a desire to do good) that might have pleased that idealist on military affairs, Laurence Sterne's Uncle Toby, and stressed the sufferings undergone by the soldiers in Spain, who fought often without encouragement or pay. Despite the brevity of the campaign with Monmouth and the refusal of the government to accept his offer to lead a troop of horse in Flanders, Defoe's imagination was still with the soldiers who had fought so gloriously under William and Marlborough. Though the quest for loot after battle was regarded as a legitimate part of the reward of soldiering throughout the eighteenth century and into the next, such actions were often considered ignoble. Defoe attempts to defend the soldier as less mercenary than many of the more respectable professions. The soldier was 'constrained almost by an absolute Necessity to *Rob* or *Starve*', yet no profession turned its practitioners into gentlemen the way soldiering did.[40] Over the next decade, Defoe was to treat feats of arms and accounts of battle with great skill, transforming his own fantasies into fictional accounts of courageous enterprises.

Even before the Earl of Mar's proclamation of rebellion in September 1715, when he was to follow the campaign and its political ramifications with great care, Defoe was putting together the first of his book-length military memoirs, *The History of the Wars, of his Present Majesty Charles XII*, published on 6 July 1715. Little need be said about this work, which he

---

[40] *An Apology for the Army* (London, 1715), 16. Defoe also assumed the mask of an officer in *A Brief History of the Pacifick Campaign in Flanders* (London, 1715).

was to expand in 1720 as *The History of Wars of his Late Majesty* . . ., nor about his *An Impartial History of the Life and Actions of Peter Alexowitz, The Present Czar of Muscovy*. Both are compilations of information about the battles fought by the two leading actors in the Great Northern War, and while they have narrators in the form of two Scottish officers serving on opposite sides, Defoe was merely taking advantage of the available sources from contemporary newsletters and doing little more than some occasional editing and rearranging of the texts. As might be expected, the Scottish officer serving with the Swedes attacks the barbarity of the Russians, and the Scottish officer serving with the Russians finds the Swedes barbaric. But Defoe thought Charles XII a monarch who had failed to fight for the Protestant cause in Europe and Peter the Great a barbarian who had sold the Christian prisoners he took in battle to the Turks as slaves. Given his dislike of both monarchs, it is hardly surprising that neither work was very inspired; they are hardly more than an account of one battle after another, with little attempt to explain the reasons for fighting.

Defoe's authorship of these works has been challenged, but it is clear that he had a particular interest in Scottish officers serving in European wars.[41] Trent points out that it was given a puff by a journal with which Defoe had some association, and there is no doubt that Defoe gave particular attention to events involving Sweden over the next few years.[42] *The History of the Wars* was written at a time when Defoe was no longer on the government's payroll, and was attempting to earn a living by projects such as these. Although the touches from Defoe's hand are clear enough to establish his editorship, they are only occasional. The *History of the Wars* was also the first work to be issued by a combination of publishers or conger, which was to become Defoe's usual method of publication. Those involved included John Baker, one of Defoe's regulars, A. Bell and J. Osborn, who were to publish a number of Defoe's works, and William Taylor, who was eventually to publish *Robinson Crusoe*.

[41] See *The Scots Nation and Union Vindicated* (1713), where Defoe provided a list 3 pages long containing the names of those serving under Gustavus Adolphus. See also P. N. Furbank and W. R. Owens, *The Canonisation of Daniel Defoe* (New Haven, Conn.: Yale University Press, 1989), 17–28. The argument against Defoe's authorship is based mainly on the inferiority of the work, but Furbank and Owens do not take into account the possibility of other hands being involved. Without showing any reason to doubt the judgement of Defoe's numerous editors or offering a possible alternative author, they try to undermine the rationale for ascribing these works to Defoe by impugning the intelligence and motives of the many scholars who have worked on Defoe in the past. Although they do not consider the presence of a quotation from one of Defoe's works to be significant, it was a quotation that Defoe used frequently, and which, to my knowledge, is employed by no one else. In her biography, Paula Backscheider ignored the objections entirely.

[42] See Trent, MS biography, 397–8. According to Trent, the *Weekly Pacquet* for 16 July 1715 noted that it had been ordered translated into 'the German and Sclavonian tongues'. Trent also added that 'the traces of Defoe's hand are so numerous that it's practically impossible to assign the volume to anyone else'.

III

On 31 March 1715 Defoe published the first of his three volumes of *The Family Instructor*, the others appearing in 1718 and 1727. Although the last volume appeared as *The New Family Instructor* and claimed to be by the author of the former volumes, it is a relatively rare volume. The first two volumes on the other hand went into dozens of editions during the eighteenth and nineteenth centuries. As J. Paul Hunter has suggested, there were many such didactic guides to virtuous, religious behaviour during the century, some more popular than Defoe's, but to lump Defoe's productions in this genre together with the work of less talented writers would be an error.[43] Although Defoe started writing these works in response to the punitive, repressive legislation that was to accompany life under the Schism Act, they were not merely guides for Dissenters who decided to educate their sons and daughters at home. This was certainly an important element in their construction, but they were also fictions with plots and well-developed characters. In length they were about the same as the novels he was to produce in a few years, and form a part of Defoe's turn toward longer works. Yet their intent was different from his experiments in historical and fictional memoirs. Humour is never permitted to intrude. These were serious works intended to inculcate serious lessons.

The passage of the Schism Act, with its resemblance to the revocation of the Edict of Nantes, seemed destined to destroy the Dissenters. Under these circumstances, Defoe saw the Dissenters as embattled, and he hoped that from the difficulties and sufferings they experienced would come a new dedication to religious faith. The French Prophets who came to England from the Cevennes, had experienced most fully Louis XIVth's effort at extirpating Protestantism in France. They spoke of their 'desert' experience, and their sufferings had led to the rise of very young men and women, sometimes even children, acting as the centre of prophecy among the group.[44] Similarly, the Covenanters in Scotland, about whom Defoe was to publish his *Memoirs of the Church of Scotland* in 1717, were depicted as 'wandering about in Sheep-skins and Goat skins, in Dens, and Holes, and Caves of the Earth', after the defeat of their army at Bothwell Bridge in 1679.[45] In describing them, Defoe alluded to Hebrews 12: 37–8, which included 'Deserts and Mountains' as the scene of sufferings, and to the

---

[43] Defoe remarked that the 'method is new', and while his enemies mocked its use of dialogue as a 'play', he was willing to call it a 'dramatic poem'. *The Family Instructor*, in *The Novels and Miscellaneous Works* (Oxford: Thomas Tegg, 1841), vol. xv, pp. ix, 4.

[44] See Schwarz, *The French Prophets*, 17–36.

[45] *Memoirs of the Church of Scotland* (London, 1717), 231.

story of the Maccabees, who would not yield to and who eventually triumphed over their enemies.

That Defoe viewed the Schism Act as an exact equivalent of such violent repressions is doubtful, but he was certainly willing to evoke the rhetoric of violent persecution, with the High Church cast as the villain. In fact, he expressed scepticism about the behaviour of the French Prophets and pity for their delusions.[46] And toward the Covenanters he felt a mixture of superority and envy—envy because he reported that, as a result of their sufferings, they grew strong. He knew that the Schism Act would not thrust the Dissenters into a literal wilderness, but transforming London into a figurative desert had not been all that difficult for the French Prophets.[47] Until the end of his life, Defoe thought that contemporary Britain with its heretics, deists, and atheists formed a kind of wilderness through which the true Christian was forced to wander, and the religious controversies of the coming years were to reinforce that belief in him. The three volumes of *The Family Instructor* were calculated to war against such dangers, and to do that, Defoe was to create a domestic scenery of convincing reality.

The first volume begins and ends with the story of a single family. Although the main body of the work is told in dialogue, Defoe acted as the stage manager or editor to set and comment on the dramatic scenes he presented. As with the French Prophets, the key to the conversion of the group is to be found with a child; but whereas the children among the Protestants of the Cevennes uttered inspired statements about the millennium to come, the setting for Defoe's opening dialogue, between a child and his father, foreshadow the beginning of Pope's *Essay upon Man*, a work still two decades in the future. It takes place in a field outside the father's garden and involves a precocious child interrogating his father about the creator of the universe. The questions of the child gradually open the father's eyes to the ways in which he has neglected the religious and moral training of his family, and lead him to bring his wife and all of his children back to a religious and moral life.

Though this first dialogue is embarrassingly sentimental to modern taste, Defoe defended its role in his 'main design' as establishing the basic motifs 'running through the whole course of the work'.[48] Indeed, the little

---

[46] *Review*, v. 125–32. Defoe thought that Christianity confered a 'Sedateness' upon the true believer, and that the 'Extasies, the Agitations, Distoritions, Convulsions, and other Extravagancies' displayed by the French Prophets seemed more likely to come from the Devil.

[47] See Schwarz, *The French Prophets*, 222.

[48] *The Family Instructor*, xv. 37. This is one of Defoe's only attempts to defend his method of constructing a work of fiction. Here the psychological reactions to the questionings of the child produces a gradual awakening of conscience. The innocently formed views of the child are supposed to reverberate throughout the work.

boy's observations on the ways in which the family has transformed true religious fervour into something merely social, along with the boy's own fervid expressions of faith, are the foundations upon which the reform of the family are constructed. The conflict in the family arises from the intransigence of the eldest son and stubbornness of the eldest sister. Their refusal to go along with their parents' wishes drives the plot forward. When the parents move to destroy their plays and novels, the two prodigals are as outraged as any modern teenager would be at such high-handedness. The son eventually defies his father, enlists in the army, and returns with his arm amputated, an event he had foreseen in a dream. Although his sister eventually accedes to parental demands, the eldest son refuses to accept the terms of reconciliation—religious reformation and complete submission to his father.

There are no happy endings here. The sister, who had shared his rebellion and his love of plays and novels, tries to help her beloved brother, but the downward course of the eldest son is summarized for a reader prepared for the worst:

She takes him home in her coach, where she used him with all the kindness and tenderness in the world, but could never bring him to any sense of his duty to God or his father; after some time, having still his allowance from his father, he grew melancholy and disturbed, and offered two or three times to destroy himself; but being recovered from that, he removed from his sister's, and God having not pleased to grant him either the grace of repentance for his former sins, or to prevent future, he fell into an extravagant life, ill company, and drinking, and died in a miserable condition, atheistical and impenitent; having never seen his father, nor so much as desiring it, till on his death-bed, being delirious, he cried out for his father! his father! That he had abused his father, and begged to see his father, that he might ask him forgiveness; but he died before his father, who happened to be in the country, could be sent for.[49]

This kind of summary is very different from the detailed dialogue in which tempers flare and misunderstandings seem more the result of emotion than any principled stance. But two notable concepts in this passage are basic to Defoe's beliefs. Avoiding any differences in Christian doctrine that might be based on specific denominational divisions, Defoe relies almost entirely on a broad concept of 'Repentance' as the key to all belief. For a Christian to repent meant a full recognition of past sins, or the nature of original sin, and a thorough belief that such an awareness brought with it a sense of salvation. Since he cannot repent, the eldest son slips easily into a form of despair. The second notion that fills this passage and the entire work is the

---

[49] *Family Instructor*, xv. 392–3.

equating of the father of the family with God. Lawrence Stone has shown
how much authority surrounded parents at this time, and there was nothing
unusual in Defoe's presentation of the role of the father.[50] Nevertheless it is
impossible to avoid thinking that Defoe may have been having trouble
with his two sons at this time. Daniel's rejection of his family obligations
seems clear enough from some of the late letters, and Benjamin Norton was
soon to pursue his independent and undistinguished career as a journalist.

What is most lively for the modern reader, however, is the revolt of the
sister and brother rendered vividly and convincingly. When one of the
younger brothers urges reform on his sister, she is as sassy as anyone might
wish:

Sist. No, no, I'll learn anything too, but I won't be taught to be a hermit; if they
have a mind to breed me up for an abbess, let them send me to a monastery; I'd as
lieve be in a real cloister, as be cloistered up at home; use none of your new cant
with me; I tell you, brother, my mother may ruffle me as much as she will, I'll have
my way still.[51]

It was in such scenes of domestic conflict that Defoe succeeded in painting
the lives of contemporary Britains convincingly, but perhaps more important is his dialogic method. He intended his readers to see the eldest son and
sister as sinners who were rejecting the sudden, stern reformation of the
family. Many modern readers will find identifying with these two easier
than with the book-burning, 'narrow-minded' parents, and while Defoe
leaves no doubt about where his sympathies lie, he made his wayward
family members so real that it might be wondered whether some of his
readers might have indulged in a subversive reading of his text.

Defoe prided himself upon his knowledge and skill at theology, but he
probably knew that the success of the first volume would come through his
fictional method. When he was to publish his second volume of *The Family
Instructor*, the impulse behind the first had disappeared. George was on the
throne, and although the need to appease strong supporters of the Church
of England during the first year of his reign meant that any effort at
revoking the Schism Act had to be postponed, its inevitable repeal came in
1718. Defoe, then, has some justification in arguing that the second volume
should not be read as an insipid continuation but rather as a work in which
'the whole scene now presented is so entirely differing from all that went
before, and so eminently directed to another species of readers; that it
seems to be as perfectly new as if no other part had been published before

[50] Lawrence Stone, *The Family, Sex, and Marriage in England, 1500–1800* (New York: Harper & Row, 1977).
[51] *Family Instructor*, i. 82.

it'. Alluding to *The Turkish Spy*, with its predominantly secular emphasis, Defoe argues that this volume is given over to depicting 'the different scenes of human life' and the various 'duties' that exist in relationships within families. He writes of the new volume as devoted to the education of youth, particularly when children ought to be punished and how it should be done.

Religion is still central to the family life he depicts, but the first dialogue involves a family quarrel in which both the husband and wife are devout Christians but argue so violently over their religious beliefs and actions that the family is torn apart. The passions that dominate this couple are so overwhelming that one may suspect that the wife, at least, uses her disagreements over religion as an excuse for a general expression of unhappiness. She is victimized by the relative powerlessness of women in her society, and her decline into depression and madness seems inevitable under these conditions. She recovers somewhat but appears to suppress all memory of what occurs. In many of these dialogues, arguments erupt from the most trivial situations. In the first, a witty conversation between husband and wife over the eclipse of 22 April 1715 leads to bitter recriminations, and in the story of a friend of the husband, a violent quarrel starts over the proper direction for an evening stroll. Of course, behind this last disagreement lies a sexual conflict. The wife wanted her husband to come to bed with her, but he insisted that he had to say his evening prayers. Although Defoe seems to come out on the side of the husband, we are allowed to see the wife's side as well.

From a fictional standpoint, Defoe manages to weave together his dialogues and stories in an intricate pattern. The characters in the dialogues not only dramatize themselves but tell tales of other men and women whose passions have led them astray. For example, Dialogue II, on the subject of fathers who are either too cruel or too lenient toward their children, concludes with the recovery of one father after he had come close to madness. The agent of this recovery is a good, religious housekeeper who reconciles him first to his daughter and then to his other children in scenes of domestic distress in which the participants are sometimes too overwhelmed with emotion to speak and in which tears flow freely. The main participants in this dialogue, identified as the Father and Neighbour, agree to meet again the next day to discourse on the effect of such religious servants upon various households. The story that follows introduces a new cast of characters in what is a novella of about 100 pages about domestic conflict within a family. The volume ends with one of the main participants in these dialogues, the Father, coming to understand the necessity of controlling passions within a family after being told a new story of a man (whom a modern psychiatrist might say had symptoms of paranoia) whose suspicions bring him close to murdering an innocent workman. Many of these characters are fascinating psychological types, and the way story is woven into story, character contrasted with character, is anything but haphazard. Defoe had little to learn about the way fictions beget fictions after writing this second volume of *The Family Instructor*.

In 1728, at a time when Defoe was writing a number of treatises on education, he returned to this form with *The New Family Instructor*. Little need be said of this work here except to note that, written years after Defoe's triumphant career as a writer of fiction, there is nothing like the outpouring of stories that appeared in the first two volumes. In choosing to concentrate on one family he was to gain some sense of unity, but was also to lose some of the inventiveness that makes the earlier volumes more lively. The great educational subject in this volume was the evil of the Catholic Church and the dangers inherent in going to Catholic countries without an adequate grounding in Protestant principles and a knowledge of the wicked wiles of the Catholic Church. Yet it is not so much about the family or education as a defence of what Defoe considered to be orthodox Christian principles against the various modern 'heretics'— Anti-trinitarians, Socinians, and deists. This theme was to be among his main concerns after 1725, and he may have tried to call attention to his ideas and enlarge his reading audience by using the *Family Instructor* format. For those interested in Defoe as a writer of fiction, probably the most interesting section is a debate between a father and his children over the uses of fiction in which the thrust of the debate attempts to make serious fiction a valuable moral product for society. While romances were dismissed as trivial, those writers of fiction with a serious moral message are extolled as valuable contributors to the wellbeing of society.

Much of the subject-matter of these volumes involved inculcating basic Christian thought in the young. Because the message was supposed to be practical and the medium dialogic, Defoe avoided anything that would smack too much of enthusiasm or statements of a private nature. But if anything so elusive as an origin for Defoe's longer works of fiction is to be sought, these works cannot be ignored. Defoe depicted the middle class with understanding and clarity at a time when increasing prosperity and secularism was accompanied by a resulting anxiety. Wives quarrel with husbands, husbands worry that their sons are attempting to steal their businesses from them, and some of the sons and daughters reject their parents' claims of authority. All of this has not been lost upon cultural historians such as Lawrence Stone, who drew upon them extensively in his *The Family, Sex and Marriage* (1977), but literary historians have been more reluctant to find any virtues in them. When William Lee published his biography of Defoe in 1869, the first two volumes were 'still popular', and he could say with pride that they had found their way 'into the libraries of kings, and into the cottages of peasants'. James Sutherland expressed a preference for the second volume but dismisses the religious content of both as lacking in true feeling and sincerity.[52] That is probably a little hard on Defoe. These volumes contain some excellent dialogue and some stories rendered with a skill that he would put to better use in his later fiction.

[52] See Lee, i. 248, and Sutherland, *Defoe*, 211. I have tried to explain Defoe's religiously inspired children with some reference to the French Prophets, but to the modern ear, and particularly for someone living in the United States, children such as Jacky of the second volume have some of the quality of the child preachers to be found among fundamentalist Christian sects in the American South.

21

Corrector General of the Press: A Digression on Defoe as a Journalist

Anybody who was once caught up in journalism, or is caught up in it still, is under the cruel necessity of greeting men he despises, smiling at his worst enemy, condoning actions of the most unspeakable vileness, soiling his hands to pay his aggressors out in their own coin. You grow used to seeing evil done, to letting it go; you begin by not minding, you end by doing it yourself. In the end, your soul, spotted daily by shameful transactions always going on, shrinks, the spring of noble thoughts rusts, the hinges of small talk wear loose and swing unaided. . . . A man degenerates, the belief in works of beauty evaporates. A man who wanted to take pride in his pages spends himself in wretched articles which sooner or later in his conscience will tell him were base actions. You came on the scene . . . intending to be a great writer, you find you have become an impotent hack.

Honoré de Balzac, *A Harlot High and Low*
(*Splendeurs et misères des courtisanes*)[1]

---

[1] Trans. Rayner Heppenstall (Harmondsworth: Penguin, 1970), 24. The original reads: 'Quiconque a trempé dans le journalisme, ou y trempe qu'il méprise, de sourire à son meilleur ennemi, de practiser avec les plus fétides bassesses, de se salir les doigts en voulant payer ses agresseurs avec leur monnaie. On s'habitue à voir faire le mal, à le laisser passer; on commence par l'approuver, on finit par le commettre. A la longue, l'âme, sans cesse maculée par de honteuses et continuelles transactions, s'amoindrit, le ressort des pensées nobles se rouille, les gonds de la banalité s'usent et tournent d'eux-mêmes. . . . Les . . . caractères se détrempent, les talents s'abâtardissent, la foi dans les belles œuvres s'envole. Tel qui voulait s'enorgueillir de ses pages de dépense en de tristes articles que sa conscience lui signale tôt ou tard comme autant de mauvaises actions. On était venu . . . pour etre un grand écrivain, on se trouve un impuissant folliculaire.' Pléiade ed., *La Comédie humaine* (11 vols., Paris: Gallimard, 1977), vi. 437.

It was not until 24 August 1717 that *Read's Weekly Journal* noted Defoe's apparent control over a large number of journals and particularly over what was the most forceful anti-government newspaper, the *Weekly Journal*, sometimes called *Mist's Weekly Journal* after the nominal editor, Nathaniel Mist:

> *Daniel Foe*, the Author of the Weekly-Journal on Saturday's list, we find is turn'd *Corrector-General* of all the News-Papers, excepting his own; which wants as much correcting as the illiterate Author, who, by the Virtue of a *Trap-Door*, can shew how to abscond from Justice, as well as any of the Faction. . . . He alarms the World with other News Papers being erroneous, but never takes any notice of the palpable Untruths he imposes on it.

This report was quickly followed by another in the *St James Weekly Journal* complaining that Defoe 'industriously follows his old Trade of Writing against himself, and frequently scolds in Controversy, wherein no one else is concerned'. In other words, his fellow journalists were certain that he often generated journalistic quarrels by writing on both sides of an issue. Not until the following year did this paradox gain wide publicity through the pages of *Read's Weekly Journal*, but if Defoe's new role as a double agent and subverter of the opposition press demanded considerably more secrecy than he maintained during his years as the author of the *Review*, he was anything but invisible. What he desired was the kind of bond between journalists that he tried to strike with Dyer—an agreement to avoid using the names of journalists when attacking their principles or methods.

On just this basis, Defoe appears to have struck up a brief relationship with Edmund Curll, the renowned publisher of pornographic works such as *Onanism Display'd*. Defoe attacked what he called 'Curlicism' in two numbers of *Mist's Weekly Journal*, published on 5 and 12 April 1718, arguing that the pornographic literature published by Curll was bad for the morals of the nation, a corrupting force within society. Curll responded in a witty pamphlet with the title *Curlicism Display'd*, in which he spoke of Mist's 'superannuated letter writer' while pretending to confess that he did not know whether the writer of the letters was indeed an old man.[2] In short, he never mentioned Defoe's name but showed that he knew who was responsible for the attack upon him and his methods. This occurred not very long after Defoe published his *Memoirs of the Life and Eminent Conduct of the Learned and Reverend Divine, Daniel Williams* with Curll. The *Memoirs* were a fairly straightforward biographical account of the

---

[2] Daniel Defoe, *Curlicism Display'd* (London, 1718), ii. 26, 28.

events in Williams's life. Defoe might have flattered himself with the notion that he was publishing the kind of work that someone like Curll ought to publish by way of reforming, but he also gave Curll an item that had some value for both the publisher and the writer. And then, by stirring up a controversy with Curll, both benefited from the sales of newspapers and the pamphlet. It is difficult to avoid the conclusion that there was some collusion between Curll and Defoe in this exchange of thought. Defoe may have wanted to be treated in the manner that Curll used, but Curll's professional behaviour toward a fellow worker in the writing and publishing industry was so close to the standard Defoe desired that it was, as the saying goes, too good to be true.

If Curll had shown by his deference to Defoe that he could restrain himself, what Defoe usually received from his fellow writers was more of the same kind of personal abuse that he had received during the reign of Queen Anne, and the allusion to the trapdoor through which he was supposed to have escaped his pursuers in 1713 indicates that he had far to go before he would be able to rid himself of the reputation of being gifted with great talent for eluding arrest and punishment at the hands of justice. It is small wonder that he was inspired to write some of his best fiction about those who were incapable of escaping from their situation as well as a criminal biography of Jack Shepherd, one of the greatest escape artists.

I

Between Defoe's letter to Harley on 28 September 1714, asking for assistance with the Anglesey case, and the fascinating explanation to Charles de la Faye on 26 April 1718, the only extant letter from Defoe is one to Samuel Keimer, the printer of Defoe's 'Quaker' tracts. Under these circumstances, attacks upon him by his enemies are some of the best sources of information about him and his writing. After nothing in the way of punishment seemed likely to develop from his sentence for libelling Anglesey, there was a brief period of silence for which no one could have been more grateful than Defoe.[3] It came at a time when he was undertaking one of the more questionable tasks of his career in attempting to control the opposition

---

[3] Two of Defoe's most determined foes, John Oldmixon and Abel Boyer, were engaged in writing historical accounts of the reign of Queen Anne. In these works they took the opportunity to vilify Defoe at some length. See e.g. Oldmixon, *The Life and Posthumous Works of Arthur Maynwaring* (London, 1715), 168; Oldmixon, *The History of England during the Reigns of King William and Queen Mary, Queen Anne, King George I* (London, 1735), 37, 301, 456, 509–10, 518; and Boyer, *The History of Queen Anne* (London, 1715), 633.

press while defending the government in some more acknowledged publications. As we have seen, some of Defoe's biographers tried to see high motives of patriotism in Defoe's action, but William Trent was more sceptical. He argued that Defoe had become a very different kind of writer as well as a different person from the part-time commentator on public affairs who had begun the *Review*. He was now a professional journalist with a large acquaintance among printers and publishers. Trent argued that 'he had become so accustomed to intrigue that he probably liked it for its own sake'. Trent also suggested that writing could become like a 'disease'. If so, Defoe had certainly come down with a fatal case.[4]

If 1716 was a quiet year for Defoe as he settled into performing his tasks for the government, he was soon to be back in the thick of the journalistic controversies of the time. Abel Boyer renewed his battle with Defoe in the summer of 1717. On 17 June a work was published that purported to be by Nicolas le Baillif Mesnager, one of the French diplomats sent over to Britain to negotiate the agreement that became the basis for the Treaty of Utrecht. Mesnager's death in 1714 at the age of 56 opened the possibility of a fictional memoir, and Defoe, who was beginning to specialize in this form, quickly obliged.[5] *Minutes of the Negotiations of Monsr. Mesnager at the Court of England* was a hoax which apparently was to have had a title-page that announced its place of publication as Antwerp and its publisher a Jean van Borscelen. Such a device was hardly unusual for the author of *The Dyet of Poland*, but it eventually appeared with the announcement that it had been translated from the French and with the name of the real publisher, S. Baker.[6] Boyer, who may have been irritated by Defoe's decision to start a rival Tory monthly journal, *Mercurius Politicus*, in May 1716 to compete with his *Political State*, pounced upon Mesnager's account as an obvious counterfeit. As a Huguenot refugee, he had no difficulty spotting the errors in French history as well as the mistakes in the remnants of French that were scattered throughout the text. Calling the attempt at counterfeit history 'shameless', Boyer went on to identify Defoe as the author, describing him as a writer who had 'prostituted his Pen to the *vilest Purposes*'. For Boyer, Defoe's greatest sin was writing *Mercator* in defence of the Commercial Treaty.[7] For Boyer, Defoe was a man 'famous for writing upon, for, and against all manner of Persons, Subjects, and Parties'. Worst

---

[4] See Trent's MS biography, Trent Collection, 406.

[5] See Geoffrey Sill, *Defoe and the Idea of Fiction, 1713–1719* (Newark: University of Delaware Press, 1983), esp. 24–5.

[6] *Checklist*, 148–9, item 377.

[7] In his *History of Queen Anne* (London, 1715), 633, Abel Boyer referred to *Mercator* as 'the product of an ambidexterous mercenary scribbler, employed . . . by the Earl of Oxford'.

of all, unlike many of the authors who managed a meagre living from their work on what was known metaphorically as 'Grub Street', Defoe had succeeded in doing extremely well for himself.

The Beneficence of his Masters, and in particular of the E[arl] of O[xford], enabled him to repair and beautify his Habitation at *Newington*, where he had set up his Forge of *Politicks* and *Scandal*, for which, for these Six Years past, he supplies *Monthly*, often *Weekly*, the *Publishers* in and about *Pater noster-Row*.[8]

Boyer chose his words carefully, almost certainly punning on the word 'Forge' in much the same way Joyce would at the end of *Portrait of the Artist*. Boyer's use of the word suggested a writing factory producing its goods with the heat and fury of a blacksmith's shop along with the implication of a place producing fraudulent documents. This might suggest the locale of the print shop with its own furious combination of typesetters, proofreaders, correctors, and machine operators. But instead, Defoe seemed to be doing it all from his estate at Stoke Newington, a property with a large garden that he had 'improved' in the manner of many an English gentleman of the period, shading the elegant walks with various trees. The outrage against Defoe had shifted focus somewhat. His fellow writers were less annoyed with his opinions than by the apparent prosperity he had been able to achieve.

Boyer then listed thirteen pieces that he claimed Defoe had written anonymously during the preceding three years, concluding with *Minutes of the Negotiations*. 'That this last *doughty* Piece comes from the same *Forge* with the rest, will immediately appear to any who shall take the Pains to consider the *loose Stile*, and *long-winded, spinning way of Writing*, which is the same in all the Productions of this celebrated Author.'[9] That Defoe had a unique style for the period—a style *entirely* distinguishable from that of his contemporaries—is open to debate.[10] On the other hand, as we have seen, he once expressed surprise that one of his enemies could not recognize his mannerisms. Certainly the '*loose*' and '*long-winded*' feel to his writing of which Boyer complained owed more to seventeenth-century style than to the more elegant writing of Defoe's younger contemporaries Addison and Steele, upon whose style most younger writers had modelled their own. Defoe had some individual quirks, particularly in the ways in

---

[8] Abel Boyer, *The Political State of Great Britain*, xiii (London, 1717), 632.

[9] Ibid. 633.

[10] William Lee argued that Defoe had no double in the age: 'I have utterly failed to discover any contemporaneous imitator of Defoe or to sift out any book or pamphlet that will bear all the requisite tests of critical comparison except those written by himself.' *N&Q*, 4th ser. (19 Feb. 1870), v. 205. This contention has been challenged over the past decade by P. N. Furbank and W. R. Owens.

which he began his paragraphs and his method of arguing his points, and Boyer may have observed some peculiar habits in the way he used bits of French; but Boyer had no need to engage in stylistic analysis. He had worked as a journalist for many years and undoubtedly had a wide acquaintance among publishers and printers in what was a relatively small circle engaged in that profession. Discovering who wrote what, especially in the case of controversial pamphlets, could not have been that difficult.

Some of Boyer's ascriptions were obvious enough. In ascribing the three parts of *History of the White Staff* to Defoe, he was merely reporting common knowledge. And in naming Defoe as the author of *An Argument against Employing and Ennobling Foreigners*, he was reporting on a quarrel between Defoe and Toland that involved an open exchange between two old enemies. Written at a time when a schism developed in the Whig government between Sir Robert Walpole and his brother-in-law, Lord Townshend, Defoe shows the degree of freedom his new position gave him. After all, the more he could demonstrate that he was independent of the influence of the government the more credible was his position as an editor of and contributor to the opposition press. Thus when Toland wrote his *Anatomy of the State of Great Britain* in defence of Stanhope's attempt to pass an act that would create British titles for foreign noblemen, fix the numbers of the nobility, and employ them in the administration, Defoe accused the government of acting out of wrong principles. The granting of noble titles ought to be done on the basis of merit alone:

for that very Reason that his Majesty being also the encourager of Virtue, may animate the Emulation of his Subjects, and teach them to aspire in the just Ambition of doing well; that Nobility may be the Reward of Virtue, not the Reward of Money only.[11]

Defoe's position was essentially that of Sir Robert Walpole, whose speech in the House of Commons turned the vote against the government, and it should be pointed out that Defoe's sympathies seemed to lie strongly with Walpole and the Whig opposition. Walpole argued that by making membership in the House of Lords more difficult, the members of the House of Commons would be closing off opportunities for their children.

Defoe apparently did not consider either of George I's advisers, Bothmar and Bernsdorff, worthy of joining the British nobility, and the notion of titles as a reward for merit goes back to his reading in Brathwait when he was very young. He was to take up the subject of nobility and the

---

[11] *An Argument Proving that the Design of Employing and Enobling Foreigners, Is a Treasonable Conspiracy against the Constitution* (London, 1717), 36.

ideals of gentility in his fiction and in several of his later tracts. The real
trouble was that in debating Toland he thought nothing of making derogatory comments on various European nations, and he seemed to think that
Toland's arguments in favour of a standing army were a good target for
attack. Neither the fact that he had achieved early fame for defending the
utility of a standing army with the support of Parliament as an excellent
notion nor his attack upon the narrow hatred of anything foreign that was
common in Britain provided much strength to his arguments. Boyer had
revealed his knowledge of Defoe's authorship of the tract in the *Political
State* and reproached him for failing to be 'consistent . . . with himself'.[12]
Defoe took the only way out. He denied having written the attack upon
Toland; he denied everything. In *A Farther Argument against Ennobling
Foreigners*, published on 8 May 1717 under the smokescreen of anonymity,
Defoe posed as an unbiased observer, who stated that he wrote in defence
of an ailing, bedridden Defoe, obviously not the author, and claimed that
both Toland and Boyer had chosen to attack the wrong man. Certainly
Boyer, 'in his Monthly Fables, called falsely *the Political State*', should
never have mentioned Defoe's name. Defoe wanted to be sure that what he
considered the ethics of political writing should be understood, while still
denying that he (the sickly Defoe) had any part in this controversy.

    Boyer had apparently not been convinced either on the matter of who
wrote the *Argument* or on the question of ethics, and the publication of the
counterfeit account by Mesnager gave him the opportunity to renew
the attack. This time Defoe did not resort to a third party to deny his
authorship. He responded directly in the *St James Post*, and somewhat less
directly in the July 1717 issue of *Mercurius Politicus*, a journal in which
Defoe only barely retained his 'Lover of Old England' mask, in attacking
Boyer and defending himself. That Defoe truly believed that Boyer had
based his attributions on his ability to detect Defoe's style is questionable,
but to show how little Boyer could accomplish along those lines, he went
back to an issue of the *Political State* for April 1716, when Boyer had
judged *The Triennial Act Impartially Stated* to be by Defoe on the basis of
its 'loose Stile' and weak arguments, while *Arguments about the Alteration of
the Triennial Election of Parliaments* was assigned by Boyer to 'the
ingenious and judicious Joseph Addison'.[13] Pointedly referring to Boyer as
a 'Frenchman', Defoe noted that he was so poor a judge of English style
that he could not tell that 'the Book which he praised so impertinently I was
the Author of, and that Book which he let fly his Dirt upon, I had no

---

[12] *Political State*, xiii. 147.   [13] Ibid. xi (Apr. 1717), 484–5.

concern in'.[14] William Trent, convinced that there was no end to Defoe's deviousness, thought Defoe had probably written both of them; John Robert Moore, following William Lee, apparently thought that the best course was to eliminate both from his *Checklist*.[15] Lee argued that Defoe must have forgotten what Boyer had written, but if this was true, it was certainly unusual. On all other occasions Defoe seemed to have a clear enough grasp of what his enemies were saying about him. For him to deny having written a certain work was common enough, but for him to lay claim to a work that was not his would be extraordinary.

The problem may arise from Boyer's characterization of *The Triennial Act Impartially Stated* as a work written against the proposal to extend the time of election from three to seven years. In fact, what that tract argued was that the Triennial Act had been one of the basic liberties brought by the Glorious Revolution, and that it should be abridged only under an absolute necessity. Very likely Defoe thought that such a statement should be made even though he felt that the rebellion of 1715 and Jacobite activity that followed constituted a clear danger to the state. None of the pamphlets assigned to him by John Robert Moore expresses unmitigated joy at so long a period between parliamentary elections. Rather, they point to the advantages of such a law, at that particular historical moment, as a means of destroying Jacobitism.[16]

In stating that he had not written *Minutes of the Negotiations*, Defoe maintained that he had not written the works assigned to him by Boyer or rather that 'of all that Number, there is but one that I was sole Author of, not above three that I ever had any Hand in, and five or six that I never saw in my Life'.[17] This denial, however, shows that in addition to the newspapers he was controlling, Defoe was also very much the writer and distributor of much of the pamphlet literature of the time. What seems like a disclaimer was actually a confession of remarkable activity. He was not ready to admit to the authorship of all of the pieces assigned to him by Boyer, but even in denying the authorship of works that were obviously his, he suggested that his 'Hand' had been in some of them. A few years later, when he was to engage in some amusing comparisons between the writer and the manufacturer and to write of authorship as a branch of

[14] *Mercurius Politicus* (July 1717), 473.

[15] See Trent, MS biography, 414.

[16] See e.g. *Some Considerations on a Law for Triennial Parlaments* (London, 1716), 16, where Defoe asks 'whether there may not be some necessity to break in upon some of our own Privileges for a Season, to prevent the Enemy's breaking in upon the whole Constitution, for want of the prudential Stop I am speaking of'.

[17] Repr. in *Mercurius Politicus*, July 1717, 473, from the *St James Post*.

commerce, he was advancing an amusing paradox. Authors were supposed to be inspired by the muse, not hired to write by the number of lines or pages completed, but Defoe thought the parallel clear enough:

And really it is inconceivable, what a Number of Poor, we that are Masters and Undertakers *in the Pen and Ink Manufacture*, do daily employ: For Example, *poor* Authors, *poor* Publishers, *poor* Printers, *poor* Paper-makers, and above all *poor Readers*; without whom, indeed, the Manufacture would be in great Danger of being ruin'd, and the Nation of being depriv'd of so eminent a branch of her Commerce. For it is by these last that we *Writing Manufacturers* are chiefly supported, to the manifest Encouragement of the whole Trade, and the immediate creating of News-houses, Coffee-houses, *etc.* by whom the King's Revenues of Excise are considerably increas'd, and the Poor kept, in the Country. . . . Nor are we so remote in our Employment from the Weaving Trade, that any of the Woollen Manufacturers should take it ill that we claim Kindred of them; for do we not weave both with *Woof* and *Warp*, when we write Dialoguewise, or when we dispute, cavil, and work it up with Cross-Questions, brocade it with Allegories, Allusions, Quirks, Punns, Connundrums, *Quidlibets,* and *Quodlibets,* which we have our *Draw-boys* to Embellish and our *Doublers* and *Twisters* to wind up for us, by which we make innumerable Flourishes, Figures, Tropes, Squares, Circles, *etc.* to make the coursest Stuff *we weave* look gay and pleasant to the Eye, when they are really good for nothing.[18]

Defoe was eventually to argue for journalism as a profession that differed little from the more accepted professions of lawyer, surgeon, and merchant. Since the members of these professions were not embarrassed to accept pay for their services, why should the writer?[19] Aware of the materials of the writer's craft as no other writer of his time, he was eventually to comment on printing, pens, paper, and ink, on which every writer depended.[20]

Mesnager's account of the peace negotiations was much more, however, than an occasion for the revelation of Defoe's involvement with the contemporary press. It was a defence of Robert Harley, not through some panegyric on his character but through the kinds of passing comment that might actually be made by a diplomat who found Harley difficult to deal with and completely evasive about anything regarding the Pretender. Thus at one point Mesnager admits that he never had a 'secret' conference with

---

[18] *The Manufacturer* 44 (18 May 1720).
[19] Lee, iii. 391.
[20] See Defoe's *An Essay on the Original of Literature* (London, 1726), 99–127. At the end of this work, he speculated on the numbers of copyists who would have been employed had the printing press not been invented. He argued that cheapness encouraged consumption, and that printing was responsible for the spread of books, but he could not help contemplating the effect that an equal degree of consumption would have had on employment if the labour-saving and efficient printing press had not existed.

Harley and that he found getting Harley to concentrate on a serious issue a difficult matter. Mesnager came to understand that despite Harley's interest in making peace with France, 'he would be for making his Court to the House of *Hanover*, at the Expence of his Mistress and of all his Friends'.[21] Seen in one way, Defoe had created an entire fictional memoir for the purpose of a few seemingly offhand remarks; seen in another way, he was beginning to get himself into a frame of mind for the writing of fiction. Despite a number of factual errors, Defoe kept the character and angle of vision of Mesnager very well. He is ever the Catholic, ever the servant of Louis XIV, and ever the Frenchman critical of British barbarism.[22]

The *Minutes* served a specific function. In May of 1717 Harley petitioned the House of Lords to try his case. The proceedings became bogged down in wrangling over parliamentary privilege, and Harley was simply released. Defoe's account was published on 17 June 1717, and he reissued an earlier defence of Harley under the title *Memoirs of Some Transactions During the Late Ministry of Robert E. of Oxford* five days later.[23] Whether Harley knew of Defoe's actions on his behalf or not is unknown. In the absence of evidence to the contrary, it may be judged possible that Defoe was following his own code of honour in creating one more piece of information that might lead to Harley's freedom. At any rate, Harley was out of politics, and this was the end of an association between the two men that even at this terminal point produced some remarkable writing from Defoe.

[21] *Minutes of the Negotiations of Monsr. Mesnager*, 185. Drawing on his own experience with Harley, Defoe had Mesnager state, 'I have heard of some who have waited upon him, by his own appointment, on Business of the Greatest Consequence, and have been entertained by him, from one Hour to another on some Trifle, 'till at last the main Affair has been confin'd to a Minute or two, or perhaps deferred to another Occasion.' *Minutes*, 183.

[22] Mesnager is particularly critical of the verbal violence of British political life, arguing that in any other European country the insults thrown about would cause duels that would easily equal the losses at the battle of Malplaquet: 'But here, a foul Tongue has a full Liberty to abuse every Man absent or present; the Language of Rogue, Villain, Rascall, *etc.* is reciprocal, and is both given and received without Resentments; the highest Quality is not free from the Raillery and Insults of the Coffee-houses, and the Streets; and when I came to understand a little of the *English* Tongue, I was amazed to hear the great Lords of the Court, the Ministers of State, and especially Mr. H[*arley*], then High Treasurer, called Rogues, Villains, Thieves'. Ibid. 88.

[23] It had been published as *An Account of the Conduct of Robert Earl of Oxford* in July 1715 just before the original impeachment proceedings. Reissued by Defoe's friend and publisher Thomas Warner, the pamphlet would have reminded everyone of Harley's personal integrity in office and of his refusal to have anything to do with Jacobite plans for changing the succession. It would have supported what the 'unfriendly' Mesnager reported about Harley. The change in the title to suggest that the work was a form of memoir suggests the popularity of that form at the time.

II

As noted above, the one letter that exists for this period is from Defoe to the printer and publisher Samuel Keimer. Keimer had been forced into bankruptcy and then into the Fleet prison by his creditors. He was also a printer for *Mist's Weekly Journal*, which had started publication at the end of 1716, and while still in the Fleet he fell under the displeasure of the government for the appearance of some questionable statements in that newspaper. Keimer was removed from the Fleet to the Gatehouse prison only to be returned to the Fleet after seventeen weeks. Written apparently in 1717, Defoe's letter attempts to console Keimer in his hours of trouble, and gives us little information except to see Defoe as someone sympathetic to a friend in distress. The ending, though, suggests that Keimer must have known enough of Defoe's connection with the government to have thought that Defoe could aid him. 'I should be glad to render you any Service within my Power,' wrote Defoe, then warning Keimer that such influence as he had was probably less than Keimer thought.

Those with whom Defoe would have had some influence during this period were the Secretaries of State for Northern Affairs, Charles, Viscount Townshend, under whom he worked until December 1716, James Stanhope, who served in that office until 15 April 1717, and Charles Spencer, third Earl of Sunderland, who succeeded Stanhope. Defoe's letter to Charles de la Faye seems to suggest that although he was able to start up the pseudo-Tory journal *Mercurius Politicus* in May 1716 and to gain effective control of *Dormer's Newsletter* in the following month, some time elapsed before he achieved effective control of *Mist's Weekly Journal*, which issued its first number on 15 December 1716.

with his Ldpps [Shrewsbury's] Approbation, I Introduced my Self in the Disguise of a Translator of the Forreign News to be So farr Concernd in This Weekly Paper of *Mists*, as to be able to keep it within the Circle of a Secret Mannagement, also, prevent the Mischievous Part of it, and yet Neither Mist or any of those Concernd with him have the least Guess or Suspicion By whose Direction I do it. (H 453)

Defoe's relationship with *Mist's Journal* presents the great difficulty here. His impact on *Dormer's Journal* is difficult to assess, since the only copy of that publication known to have survived is the one for 21 July 1715—the issue that brought Dormer into trouble with the authorities and that dated from a period prior to Defoe's control. From the six copies in the Public Records Office we know that *Dormer's Newsletter* was written in the form of a piece of private correspondence and that it was sometimes attached to a printed newspaper. In that particular issue, Dormer had remarked that the burning of meeting-houses was no problem, since they would undoubtedly be rebuilt at public expense, and that news of an invasion by the Pretender was probably nothing more than a Whig hoax. Dormer apologized to the government for this number and promised that such remarks would never be made again.[24] Apparently Defoe saw to it that the promise was kept.

The relatively balanced, uncontroversial manner of *Mercurius Politicus* may give some idea of the tone that Defoe gave to *Dormer's Newsletter*. He reported on various controversial publications, but the bland judgments of the 'Lover of Old England' could only be considered 'Tory' in that they were not positively adulatory toward the government or toward George I. Occasionally, as with his attack upon Toland in the issue for August 1716, he could accuse the Whigs of being unwilling to disown a writer whose militant deism led him to attack the very foundations of Christianity, but in defending orthodox Christian thought, Defoe must have felt that he could take a few risks. In fact such a concern with religious controversy was hardly unusual. Defoe tended to turn his journal away from political conflict to matters of ethics and morality. Admittedly, he was writing during the years of two major religious conflicts—the Bangorian controversy and the Salter's Hall controversy—but even in treating the riots of the weavers over the importation of calicoes, he turned the discussion toward the growth of luxury throughout Britain. To add spice to his journal, he might include such pieces as a translation of a letter from the admiral of the Turkish Fleet on the necessity of abandoning the siege of Corfu, with its criticism of Catholic ritual. The editor of the journal offered it as something no other journal had discovered, and while there is always the possibility that it is genuine, it has the distinct sound of some of the epistles in Defoe's *Continuation of the Letters of a Turkish Spy*.[25] If the news was dull, Defoe was always willing to improve it through a little fiction.

More problematic was Defoe's relationship to *Mist's Weekly Journal*. From the time that Samuel Keimer acted as printer for the first issue of 15 December 1716 until it was replaced as the main opposition paper by *The Craftsman* in 1726, the publisher and its printers were in constant difficulties with the government.[26] Aside from political idealism (and there is no question that Nathaniel Mist was a Jacobite sympathizer), daring news items in such journals sold well and earned money for the publisher. Samuel Keimer attempted to pay his creditors by just this kind of printing

---

[24] PRO SP 35/1/3/78, items 5 and 6.
[25] See *Mercurius Politicus*, Oct. 1716, 371.
[26] George A. Aitken, 'Defoe and Mist's "Weekly Journal"', *Athenaeum*, 26 Aug. 1893, 287–8.

after he had fallen into debt. An issue of one of Keimer's papers, which claimed (wrongly) that the Pretender had won a major victory, earned him £15, and needy as he was, he found the profit impossible to resist.[27] In trying to undestand Defoe's relationship with the *Weekly Journal* and with its owner, Nathaniel Mist, biographers have spent too much time speculating on the clash of character and ideology between Defoe and Mist and not enough on the money. The early issues of the *Weekly Journal* were dull and almost unreadable, and Mist must have greeted Defoe's early contributions with a sigh of relief. Whatever his real political affiliations, Defoe could interest his readers, and Nathaniel Mist must have been willing to ignore almost everything else.

Defoe's account in his letter to De la Faye manages to protect himself entirely while leaving a number of questions unanswered. After describing his early work on the journals that were to 'Pass as Tory Papers and yet be Dissabled and Ennervated', Defoe distinguished between publications such as *Mercurius Politicus* and those such as the *Weekly Journal*:

But here it becomes Necessary to Accquaint My Lord (as I hinted to you Sir) That This paper called the journall is not My Self in Property, as the Other [*Dormer's Newsletter*]; Onely in Mannagemt; with this Express Difference, that if any thing happens to be put in without my knowledge, which may Give Offence; Or if any thing slips my Observation which may be ill Taken; His Ldpp shall be Sure allways to kno', whether he has a Servant to Reprove or a stranger to Correct. (H 453)

The problem with this account is that so much that we would like to know and that De La Faye undoubtedly would have wanted to have known was omitted. Defoe had been a translator and distributor of foreign news for some time, but how he could control a journal without raising the suspicions of the owner and some other mysterious advisers connected with the newspaper is difficult if not impossible to understand. Perhaps Defoe had already made the case with Mist that he understood what would and would not pass with the government, so that he was allowed to delete whatever he considered offensive. Had he simply acted as a convert to Tory principles, he might have been able to avoid hard questions. The problem is, how long did Defoe think that his writing for journals on both sides of the political spectrum would pass unnoticed?

In January 1718 he began a Whig version of *Mercurius Politicus* with the title *Mercurius Britanicus*, and on 18 September 1718 he started up the long-running Whig journal, the *White-Hall Evening Post*. In a series of issues following the arrest of Nathaniel Mist by Defoe's correspondent De la

---

[27] Samuel Keimer, *A Brand Pluck'd From the Burning* (London, 1718), 75, 84.

Faye, *Read's Weekly Journal* (which had noted Defoe's activities with some suspicion for more than a year) revealed his extensive and ambiguous journalistic involvement. The letters from Defoe to De la Faye, written in the spring of 1718, show how much difficulty Defoe experienced in trying to keep Nathaniel Mist and the *Weekly Journal* out of trouble. De la Faye was in the position of explaining the nature of the job Defoe was doing for the government to James Stanhope, who had succeeded Sunderland as Secretary of State for Northern Affairs on 2 March 1718, and Defoe was careful to provide a narrative history of the work he had been doing for the government. From the letter of 4 June 1718, announcing, 'I have Entred into a New Treaty with Mr. Mist', it would appear that Mist must have understood that Defoe was speaking for the government in warning him about the extent of his offences and in getting them pardoned. Defoe stated that he did not reveal the 'Secret of who I spoke from', but Mist must have been incredibly dense not to understand what Defoe was saying. Defoe even managed to get information from Mist about some seditious publications. To some extent, then, Defoe was enlisting Mist for the government as well. But the optimism of Defoe, expressed in his letter of 13 June, that he believed 'the Time is Come when the Journall instead of affronting and Offending the Government may many ways be made Serviceable to the Government' proved to be wrong.

Read's Weekly Journal for 1 November 1718 printed an allegorical cartoon showing the arrest of Mist, and as part of this campaign against the opposition press, that journal also revealed Defoe's connection to the *White-Hall Evening Post*. A correspondent in a letter dated 28 October 1718 stated that there was no necessity to say that Defoe was behind it all, since everyone already knew that he was the sinister agent behind the press:

for all who have heard of him, knew that no other person would be guilty of such vile Prevarication. The Impudence which he treats the Governemnt withal in the former *Paper* makes one think that the White-Hall Post is like to be well furnished, after the fine Ideas that must be necessary for equipping out the *Saturdays Libel*. 'Tis very true, as you say, that if he has Security from *Mist* not to discover him, he may write with the greater Insolence, but it is to be hop'd the Persons Concern'd in the *White Hall Post*, will not offer to Skreen him under such an Indulgence, but let him stand, and fall by his own Works, unless they wou'd be thought Men of such Principles as wou'd Encourage *Mists Journal*. But Sir, there needs no other Proof of his binomical Performance, than the Agreeablenes of the stile and manner; the little Art he is truly Master of, of forging a Story and imposing it on the World for the Truth.[28]

---

[28] [*Read's*] *Weekly Journal. Or, British Gazetteer*, Sat. 1 Nov. 1718.

This revelation was followed by a series of notices which established Defoe as the archetypal unprincipled journalist. One poet pretends to have heard of his death and ironically celebrates the example he set as a journalist:

> He wrote for all cause[s] that did yield him most,
> *Mist's Weekly Journal, White-Hall Evening Post*,
> Two *Mercurys* each Month one for the Whiggs,
> The t'other fraim'd to please the Tory Priggs.

In a poem describing Defoe's death and descent into hell, his encounter with Charon, and Pluto's judgement against him, another contributor attacked him as '*Satan's* eldest Son', the evil force behind contemporary journalism, and a letter attempted to refute Defoe's claim that he merely translated foreign news in *Mist's Weekly Journal*, accusing him of being 'an Enemy to the Government'.[29] That Defoe received a government stipend during these years was not discovered until 1864, to the consternation of his hagiographer, William Lee.[30] Needless to say, his contemporaries would have had little trouble with seeing Defoe in such a role.

James Sutherland had a chapter in his biography of Defoe with the title 'Mist's Man', in contrast with an earlier chapter, 'Harley's Man', but while Defoe had clearly tied his fortunes to Harley's career, he was so far from being tied to the service of Nathaniel Mist that he functioned as the Whig ministry's watchdog over Mist and those opponents of the government who wanted to use *Mist's Weekly Journal* as their vehicle for anti-government propaganda. According to the testimony of Thomas Warner, one of Defoe's publishers, Mist paid Defoe 20s. a week when he began his editorial duties and raised his salary to 40s. in the autumn of 1718.[31] Defoe always thought that he should be compensated for his services, and did not object to being paid by both Mist and the government for his labour. But

---

[29] [*Read's*] *Weekly Journal*, 22 Nov. 1718, 1187, 1191, 1195, 1204, 1206–8. The author of 'A Dream by a Gentleman as he slept in Westminster Hall, in Imitation of *Don Quevedo's*, Vision of H[el]l', covered a number of Defoe's writings and the events of his life, including a reference to '*Keimer's* Visions and his Dreamers' and his civet cat venture.

[30] Lee, vol. iii, pp. ix–xix. Defoe was apparently drawing only £50 a year from the government compared to up to £400 when working for Harley. Defoe remarked in his letter to Charles de la Faye of 23 May 1718 that 'the half year Expired The 17th' without his having received any compensation from the government. He gave Sunderland a receipt for £25 received from Samuel Buckley on 17 Nov. 1717. See HMC, *Eighth Report*, 27.

[31] Warner reported that at the outset Mist was supposed to be paying the money to a Samuel Moorland Esq., and that this caused some problems. Defoe may have been attempting to use a new alias or a go-between by this name. At any rate, he finally decided to take the money in his own name. Warner also testified that Defoe promised to help Mist if he concealed his part in the article. It is hard to grasp what kind of influence Defoe had, unless they suspected that it involved the government. See Aitken, 'Defoe and Mist's "Weekly Journal" '. Aitken was quoting from documents in the PRO, SP Domestic, George I, bundle 15, Nos. 30, 33, 115. The latter document suggested that Defoe had delivered the offending letter through a Jonathan Marshall, supposedly Defoe's gardener.

while Mist probably regarded him as his servant and labourer, Defoe undoubtedly saw matters in a different light.

It could not have been an easy relationship. Defoe withdrew from the paper after Mist was arrested in October 1718 and rejoined in January 1719. When Mist managed to get into trouble with the government again in June 1720, Defoe apparently offered to help him. But when Mist insisted that Defoe was the author of some paragraphs that had annoyed the Bishop of Gloucester and on another occasion of a letter signed 'Sir Andrew Politick', Defoe pointed out that there was no evidence tying him to these works. He had grown wise over the years and routinely destroyed all his copy. He edited and published a collection of letters to *Mist's Weekly Journal*, two volumes in 1722 and two in 1727, to help Mist after he was pilloried and imprisoned by the government. In his biography of Defoe, William Lee concocted a violent quarrel between Defoe and Mist some time after 24 October 1724, supposedly after Mist discovered Defoe's connection with the government.[32] Although Defoe's reference to a man who drew his sword upon a benefactor who had rescued him from prison three times may refer to Mist's behaviour to Defoe, it would be a mistake to underestimate Defoe's ability to create fiction or, as he put it in his defence of fiction in *Serious Reflections of Robinson Crusoe*, 'to represent anything that really exists by that which exists not'.[33]

The possibility of such a quarrel will be taken up later in this work, but at this point, it should be noted that Defoe found himself in an unusual position for a person whose opinions were often eccentric. That he would wholly oppose the war with Spain or attack the Palatines, as the offending passages in *Mist's Weekly Journal* did, is very doubtful. He believed that any war with Spain could be potentially advantageous to Britain, and he was a firm supporter of resettling the Palatine immigrants in England or abroad.[34] On the other hand, there were occasions when he disagreed with the policies of the ministry, and being in the position of writing 'Tory' papers enabled him to express his disagreements and doubts. For example, Sir Andrew Politick expressed concern over the immediate effects of a war: the seizure of British businesses in Spain and the taking of British ships in the West Indies. It was followed by a commentary from 'Mist' which insisted that 'Jack Spaniard may be made to pay for the Supper, whoever

---

[32] Lee, i. 393–5.

[33] *Serious Reflections of Robinson Crusoe*, in *Romances and Narratives*, ed. George A. Aitken (London: Dent, 1895), p. xii.

[34] Warner stated that Defoe had spoken to him about the war with Spain in the same tones that appeared in the letter of Sir Andrew Politick, but Defoe may merely have been staging a debate, since the letters answering Sir Andrew are far more convincing. See Aitken, 'Defoe and Mist's', 287.

pays for the Breakfast'. The government did not think that the refutation was adequate in view of Sir Andrew Politick's ten strong points. Not long before the letter appeared in *Mist's Weekly Journal*, Warner stated in his deposition, Defoe had engaged him in a conversation about the war that resembled the views of Sir Andrew, and the letter certainly reads as if it were written by Defoe. Being a spokesman for the Tory viewpoint may have forced him to see two sides to every argument, and he may have discovered more of himself in the Tory and Whig opposition position than he might have supposed possible. Certainly the need to present multiple views helped to shape him into a masterful writer of fiction.

Like Townshend and Walpole, who had gone into opposition, Defoe was not very enthusiastic about pursuing the goals of George I and Hanover in the Great Northern War. When George I had the Swedish ambassador, Gyllenborg, hunted down and arrested, he could complain in *Mercurius Politicus* that such an action was a violation of the law of nations and the law of nature. War with Spain was one thing; war with a Protestant nation such as Sweden was quite another. He thought it might be harmful for English merchants, and printed a letter from a British merchant in Sweden that cast doubts upon the seriousness of Sweden's preparation for war.[35] In short, his position gave him an opportunity to write against the prevailing attitudes of the government when he wished and encouraged that side of his personality that enjoyed defying authority. His printer, Morphew, was put in prison for a number of *Mercurius Politicus* that picked up a story about a man hanged for the theft of three halfpence. He remarked that it was 'a very small Sum to be hang'd for'. Defoe tried to interest De la Faye on Morphew's behalf. He had apparently managed to obtain Townshend's pardon for his own role in the offensive comment, but it was just the kind of tyranny by what was supposed to be a system of justice that Defoe could hardly resist criticizing. If, then, he had deliberately turned his interests toward social and ethical problems in these opposition newspapers, he still had his outlet for that spirit of defiance and contradiction that had ruled him for so much of his life.[36]

---

[35] *Mercurius Politicus*, Feb. 1717, 68, 98–100. Although Defoe should have known that nothing was beyond Charles XII, the concoction of an alliance with the Jacobites along with the possibility of invading Britain was among the more bizarre episodes of his career. See R. Nisbet Bain, *Charles XII* (New York: Knickerbocker Press, 1895), 280–2; and Defoe, *An Account of the Swedish and Jacobite Plot* (London, 1717); *What if the Swedes Should Come?* (London, 1717); *A Short View of the Conduct of the King of Sweden* (London, 1717). These pamphlets are essentially Whiggish in tone. The third exploits the curiosity that many Britons must have felt about Charles XII. It extols his military genius and appears to appreciate the grandeur of his actions. *What if the Swedes Should Come?* warns the British against behaving like the citizens of Constantinople, who lost their city by being too concerned with their individual possessions. Defoe never seems to have taken the likelihood of a Swedish invasion very seriously.

[36] H 456, including nn. 1–3.

III

In one of the many poems written during the early eighteenth century concerning the contest for the laureateship among contemporary poets, Defoe is rejected for his poetry but sent away with the relatively gentle recommendation that he continue to write newspapers.[37] The periodical essay, as it was developed by Addison and Steele in the *Tatler* and *Spectator*, was applauded by all sides and won even the grudging praise of Defoe. Addison gained the reputation of being the best author of the time, and as Donald Bond, the most recent editor of *The Spectator*, has indicated, the popularity of the journal in eighteenth-century Britain came to rival that of the Bible.[38] Samuel Johnson, who gave the form a weight and complexity very different from the relatively light tone of Addison and Steele, still gave an honoured place to it in his *Lives of the Poets*. But the collections of the best of the essayists which appeared in the nineteenth century suggested that the form was moribund. The title of a recent book, *Addison and Steele Are Dead*, announces an inevitable truth.[39] Not only is the mediating temperament of these two writers nearly unavailable to modern readers, but almost everything about them—their gentle humour, their stilted allegories, their light moralism—is slightly irritating to the modern sensibility. Johnson alone has some remaining admirers because his morality was never light and because his genuine seriousness of purpose reaches across the centuries. But most of this lay in the future. In Defoe's day, Addison rose in the government to become Secretary of State, and Steele, whose life was far more stormy, still sat in the House of Commons. Yet, despite such success, journalists had quickly earned a shabby reputation.

What Balzac said of the journalists of his day, that they eventually found their souls irretrievably damaged, has been the more common experience. Oddly enough, however, in Defoe's case, his experience as a journalist ultimately served to broaden his view of the world. Of course, there were essays in his *Review* which appeared to have been written without very much thought, and his defence of the Treaty of Commerce led him far in the direction of writing things in which he did not believe in order to pick up his government salary. Now, by an odd twist of government policy, he was engaged in writing Tory propaganda, and while his efforts earned for *Mist's Weekly Journal* the greatest circulation for the time, he could hardly

---

[37] *The Battle of the Authors Lately Fought in Covent Garden* (London, 1720), 39. Defoe eventually wins second place, with Steele first and Cibber third.

[38] Donald F. Bond (ed.), *The Spectator* (3 vols., Oxford: Clarendon Press, 1965), vol. i, p. lxxxvi.

[39] Brian McCrea, *Addison and Steele Are Dead* (Newark: University of Delaware Press, 1990).

have been pleased by some of the strange stances he was forced to take. If Richard Burridge, the editor of *Read's Weekly Journal*, could express ironic wonder at Defoe's sudden enthusiasm for the Church of England, he had every reason to doubt Defoe's sincerity. If any contemporary reader knew that the first number of *Mercurius Politicus* was written by the foremost propagandist for the Dissenters, he or she might indeed believe that Defoe was an agent of Satan. Commenting upon his fellow journalists' treatment of the Church of England, the 'Lover of Old England' (Defoe) accused them of a '*scandalous Crime*' in their combination of neglect and insolence:

It must fill the Minds of Honest Men with Horror to read some Papers written by Known Presbyterians, and see them pretending to Vindicate the Church; others who call themselves Churchmen, falling upon the Clergy with Reproaches, and scandalous Language: Again to see Atheists, Deists, hereticks, Prophane and Irreligious Persons, and real Schismaticks, all falling upon the Church by invading her Doctrine, by defaming her Clergy, and the best members of the Church, in their false and partial relating of Fact, as well as in their Ignorant and Scandalous Reflections; these Things, I say, must fill the Minds of Honest Men with Horror. . . . It is therefore more than time that some Body began to do Justice to Truth and the Church of England, in a Time when she has so many Enemies in her own Bowels.[40]

Defoe as the loyal defender of the Church of England? Few notions could be more absurd. So long as the fiction could be maintained that the 'Lover of Old England', who was supposed to be the author, was not Defoe, the passage above may be seen as an example of the extent to which anonymity conferred power upon the writer. Like Gyges in the ancient Greek parable or like H. G. Wells's invisible man, the writer could do almost anything when protected by his device of invisibility. Yet his fellow journalists saw Defoe's hand behind *Mercurius Politicus* soon enough, and tried to warn the periodical-reading audience of his presence behind a pro-Tory, pro-Church journal. It would be fascinating, had we the ability, to find some readers of *Mercurius Politicus* who knew that Defoe was the author but who continued to read the journal. Would they have said that they knew that Defoe's opinions were suspect but that they liked the way it was written? Had they come to the point of suspecting that Defoe was the author but that it did not make any difference to them because Defoe had become part of the surveillance system that was accepted as an inevitable part of contemporary life? Whatever the reaction of his readers, this much is clear: Defoe did write against his known and stated opinions and managed to make a very good living by doing so. Like Balzac's quintessential

---

[40] *Mercurius Politicus*, May 1716, A3.

journalist, on any given day he found himself lying, cheating, and playing the hypocrite.

The standard form Defoe used for *Mist's Weekly Journal* was the letter to the editor from a given personality, expressing some kind of opinion or raising a problem, whether ethical, political, or moral. If indeed he was Sir Andrew Politick, he managed once more to create too convincing a personality for the authorities, but it was typical enough. The cast of characters might have filled more than one long Russian novel. There were Quakers, Sir Foppling Tittle-Tattle, Miranda Meanwell, Frank Faithful, Boatswain Trinkolo, Quinquampoix, White Witch, Woman Witch'd, Lionel Lye-alone, and Timothy Trifle. The man who signed himself 'Woman Witch'd' tells of a man's relationship with a woman everyone took to be his wife. Only they know that a marriage has never taken place. Though delighted with her in every way, he has doubts about marrying her. 'Mr Mist' then gives advice in a somewhat more eccentric manner than a modern adviser on love and marriage might do. '*Go you Fool!*,' he replies, Marry her and be happy; and hug yourself in being a fortunate Sinner . . . and marry her, before you once close your Eyes;—for if you ruin her, you ruin yourself too.' And so it went, each week bringing up a new difficulty to be solved by 'Mr. Mist'. Small wonder that one female correspondent signing herself 'Arina Donna Quixota', but with some stylistic devices oddly like those of Defoe, could begin her letter, 'Mr. Mist, as I find by many late Instances, you are now the grand Oracle for resolving all Doubts and Scruples, the Receptacle of all just Complaints and particularly the patron of all that are unmarried'.

Some letters of praise were probably less solicited, such as one in which the writer expressed his appreciation of an account of floods in Europe during a particularly severe winter. For Defoe did not limit himself to advice to the lovelorn. Though the letter of Arina Donna Quixota, with its comments on the marriage market, was to resonate through *Moll Flanders* and *Roxana*, there were other ways in which his journalism played an important role in the brilliant fiction to come. On 8 March 1718, for example, Defoe provided three narrative accounts that were to sink deeply into his imagination. The first involved reports of a floating island, the second an account of wild beasts in the Pyrenees, and the third a description of a feast in Paris displaying a remarkable example of conspicuous consumption, which was eventually to lead Defoe to raise questions about the function of luxury in society. The first two incidents were to play a role in *Robinson Crusoe*. For if Crusoe's island was anchored solidly enough, the 'Roaring of wild and ravenous Beasts, such as Lions, Panthers, Tygers' who made 'a most horrible and frightful Roaring and Howling' on the floating island off Gibraltar was to play a role in the early episodes, when Crusoe escapes with Xury from his slavery in North Africa. Similarly the 'Armies' of wild beasts driven mad by hunger add one final adventure to Crusoe's life as he returns to England. The third narrative, which Defoe promised his readers would be more 'diverting', was an entertainment given by the Duchess of Berry, daughter of the Duke of Orléans, the regent of France during the minority of Louis XIV. Defoe notes that the Duchess of Berry 'was so covered with Diamonds, that she was, as the French call it, (we want a Word suitable) *Tout Brilliant*'. Though the meal is larger than that provided by Roxana's Prince, Roxana was also covered with diamonds when she dined, and the masquerade and dance with which this description ends would resonate in Roxana's famous 'Party' and dance. In short, Defoe's reporting was to function as an aid to his imagination. He was storing up impressions for his coming works of fiction.

On 25 June 1720 he began his work for Applebee's *Weekly Journal*, and unlike his work on journals such as *The Manufacturer*, *The Commentator*, *The Director*, and the *Citizen*, which served specific goals, this represented a shift in emphasis. Applebee's *Weekly Journal* was intended more for the entertainment of its readers than for their edification, and specialized in accounts of criminals and in light material. If Defoe supplied a degree of humour and pure entertainment in his work for Mist, he now had to draw more fully on his talent to entertain, through his sense of the comic and satiric. As one correspondent put it, 'I conjure you, therfore, good Mr. *Original*, let us have some simple Stuff to be Merry with, that we may *Laugh and be Fat*'.[41] Was this Defoe describing the audience for which he had just begun to write? On 16 July 1720, the *Original Weekly Journal* printed a letter from 'an *Elder*, and well known Sister, of the *File*', which Lee labelled 'Precursor of Moll Flanders', and with considerable justification.[42] The writer is a transported thief who has returned to Britain. Her attitude toward her life shows a genuine pride in her previous accomplishments, though she is finding life hard both because of blackmail by those who recognize her and because picking pockets is not as good a 'Business' as it once was.

Defoe found more room for the comic aspects of love in the *Original Weekly Journal* than in *Mist's Weekly Journal*. He had a man who signed himself 'Hubble-Bubble' describe how, after being rejected by a lady

[41] Sat. 30 July 1720. This was written as a response to the complaints of an A.B., who called for the section entitled 'Letters Introductory' to be devoted to more serious materials.
[42] Lee, ii. 256–8.

because he was poor, he comes to her again as the possessor of £200,000. Thinking that his wealth gives him sufficient right to claim a woman who had rejected him for his poverty, Hubble-Bubble visits the lady and attempts to make physical advances at once, only to find himself turned over to her footmen and doused in a horse pond. It was with such social comedy that Defoe entertained his readers. He gave them accounts of the plague in France and satirical narratives involving the fate of speculators in the South Sea Scheme; discussions of freedom of the press and of highwaymen; debates upon assassinating rulers and comments upon the revealing nature of slips of the tongue; descriptions of Jack Sheppard's escape from Newgate and of the condition of imprisoned debtors. In some of these essays Defoe managed the kind of good-natured 'humour' that was to be exploited by later essayists from Fielding to Goldsmith,[43] but compared to what appeared in the journal before he came upon the scene, he also introduced a serious note into the 'Letters Introductory'. There are essays on suicide and painful deaths, on the sufferings of the poor, and on ingratitude. W. P. Trent thought Defoe's work for Applebee's *Original Journal* his best achievement as a journalist after the *Review*.

In the first number of Defoe's journal *The Commentator*, which appeared at the beginning of 1720, the author reports that when he mentioned his plan to begin a journal to one of his friends, the friend suggested that he might consider becoming a highwayman instead.[44] Though Defoe did not expand on the similarity between what the friend clearly considered one of two desperate choices, the comparison is obvious. Both depended on short adventures which might or might not succeed. Both were attended with a lack of real respect, and in Defoe's time, both activities might result in severe punishments. Unconvinced by these warnings, the author feels he must persevere in the cause of 'Truth' to enlighten the 'Common People'. Defoe certainly felt some of that impulse, and a journal such as *The Commentator*, with its direct essay structure, provided him with a good opportunity to state his ideas. In the journals printed by Mist and Applebee Defoe was always in disguise, always speaking through a fictional character. Could his statements on avarice be collected from his journals or from the *Original Weekly Journal* alone, they would stand as a powerful indictment of what to Defoe was a new world dominated by the desire to make money for its own sake. But as it was, his comments on human nature

---

[43] See Stuart Tave, *The Good Natured Humorist* (Chicago: University of Chicago Press, 1960).

[44] The first number of this journal appeared on 1 Jan. 1720. Though it was aimed at a Britain in the midst of the South Sea Company crisis, Defoe kept his subject matter fairly broad compared to a paper such as *The Manufacturer*, devoted specifically to the riots by the weavers over imported calicoes, or *The Director*, devoted exclusively to the South Sea Bubble.

were scattered over many years, issues, and numbers of these journals. Small wonder, then, that he eventually abandoned journalism to focus his energies on writing entire books on his favourite subjects. He was a brilliant journalist, but he was not able to overcome the insubstantiality of the form. His work on these journals was to be important for his fiction and for his book-length studies of contemporary Britain. It gave him a sense of the complexity of character and point of view as well as a world of experience on which to draw.

22

The Year Before *Robinson Crusoe*: Intellectual Controversies and Experiments in Fiction

During 1717 and 1718 Defoe responded to a number of important events in a manner that reveals a deepening of moral and ethical views. His position as a government agent overseeing both Whig and Tory journals forced him to view events from all angles, and this produced a kind of relativism. He never doubted the evils of Jacobitism or the benefits of the Whig succession, but as the government grew stronger after the suppression of the Jacobite revolt in Scotland, he was not averse to making judgements about the government's positions or even opposing them on occasions. In battling against John Toland on the issue of ennobling foreigners, as Toland suggested with some glee, Defoe seemed to be betraying the position he had taken years before in his *True-Born Englishman*. Although both Toland and Abel Boyer seemed to find his position contradictory, Defoe felt there was little relationship between the situation that had produced *The True-Born Englishman* and that involving George I's attempt to reward foreigners. In Defoe's eyes, George I and the recipients of his favours bore no resemblance to William III and his heroic Dutch forces who had rescued England from James II. Yet in another controversy where he took a stance against the government, his opposition to the attempts to close off admission to the aristocracy and the House of Lords to deserving commoners, he took a stand that was essentially more Whiggish than the Whig government. For the most part, however, his belief that in matters of economics and politics human beings were ruled entirely by self-interest had been reinforced by his experiences. Such a cynical position came hard to him, going against his natural enthusiasm and ebullience, but he was more than ever convinced that it was true.

Self-interest, he felt certain, was the force that lay behind Richard
Steele's sudden conversion to treating the Jacobite rebels with leniency.
Appealing to that 'Dear Self' that the Earl of Rochester knew to be at the
core of most men, Defoe dramatized Steele's decision to speak against the
policies of the government as a way of reminding those in power of a
certain neglect with which he had been treated. Defoe argued that what
Steele wanted was a form of 'Hush-Money' of the sort that Charles II paid
Members of Parliament.[1] He was convinced that Steele would be successful
in wringing favours from the government, as would all those who paid
sufficient attention to their interest. Though he admired Robert Walpole,
he saw the split in the Whig ministry as an inter-party struggle for power.
'Their aim has been all along their own Interest,' he wrote, 'the satisfying
their own voracious Appetites, and the most unbounded Avarice; that
Pride, and the worst sort of Ambitions, has been the Helm that steers all
their Actions.'[2] And again on Walpole, he commented upon the prevailing
'Self-interested Spirit among great Men' which makes them willing to
ignore the people in an effort to 'serve themselves'.[3]

I

The most thorough discussion of this matter comes in the pamphlet *The
Old Whig and Modern Whig Revived*, published on 1 August 1717. The only
difference between the two groups among the now divided Whigs could be
summed up as 'Whigs out of Place, and Whigs in Place'. After 1688 the
'Modern Whigs' were those acting upon Revolution Principles, but they
soon found themselves without any power. Walpole and his followers who
were out of power in 1717 claimed to be acting from principle too, but self-
interest lay at the bottom of all their actions:

So much are the greatest men apt to stretch the Pretences that they make to a disinterested Principle, and so easily do they shew us that SELF lies at the Bottom of
the most popular Actions they go about; that the Outside indeed may seem to
shew something of the *Patriot*, but at the Bottom their own Grandeur, Gain, and
the unsatiable Desire of Power and Profit, is the *Pole Star* by which they steer; the
Center of their Designs, and the Point in which all the Lines of their Practice
meet.[4]

---

[1] *An Essay upon Buying and Selling of Speeches* (London, 1716), 29, 36.
[2] *The Danger of Court Differences: or the Unhappy Effects of a Motley Ministry* (London, 1717), 41.
[3] *The Conduct of Robert Walpole* (London, 1717), 52.
[4] Defoe, *The Old Whig and Modern Whig Revived . . . or, the Difference betwixt Acting upon PRINCIPLE
AND INTEREST* (London, 1717), 27.

From the very beginning of his career, Defoe had been a believer in self-interest as the chief motivation of human kind. He was an admirer of the political writings of Thomas Hobbes and of Lord Rochester, whose poetry is echoed in the quotation above, and liked to quote their ideas on power and human egotism. But at this stage of his life, he seems to have appre-hended emotionally what he had previously grasped only intellectually. Thus, in *Mist's Weekly Journal* of 26 April 1718 he pictured the eagerness of those out of power 'to expose the Self-Interest-Transactions of those in Place, when, in Truth, the only Motive to this Zeal was, their being deprived of Power to act in the same manner themselves'. Speaking through the mask of one of the letter-writers to the journal, he longed for some way to communicate this truth to the people, to 'open their Eyes'. It would result in an end to parties and the creation of a citizenry who voted entirely for the 'Interest of the Nation'. That this letter ends on a utopian note shows that Defoe had difficulty sustaining so negative a view for long. A few years later he was to object to La Rochefoucauld's dour view of mankind as being excessively pessimistic about human nature, however accurate it might have been.[5] By that time he had come out of this period of pessimism, but during 1717 and 1718 it pervaded his thinking.

Of course, the opposition often attempted to take the moral high ground in depicting George I and his government as lacking in probity, integrity, and feelings of love for the British people. In addition to seeing that such accusations were relatively muted, Defoe's job was to defend George I and the motives of the government, particularly on the question of mercy to those identified as traitors. A number of events, from the execution of Jacobite sympathizers captured in the rebellion of 1715 to the trials and punishments of a variety of plotters and would-be assassins, occupied him over the next three years. The Tory press, often in the form of journals for which Defoe was writing, called upon George I and his government to show mercy to these men, while the government defended its right to punish those who would attempt to destroy it. Most notable among the cases were those of the seven lords captured at Preston, a Non-juring priest named William Paul, John Hall of Otterburn, and a young man named James Shepheard. The crucial point in the arguments of those who wanted mercy for these rebels and assassins was that they acted according to their consciences. Pleading a tender conscience had for decades been the special

[5] *The Commentator*, 5 Feb. 1720. Defoe wrote of La Rochefoucauld, 'I never observed in any Writer, so deep Penetration with so little Distinguishing, nor so much Good Sense, with so little Good Nature'. He modified this judgement by admitting the dominance of '*Self-Love*' in most human beings. At the same time, he allowed for some acts of charity that could be traced more to 'Good-will to our Fellow Creatures, than to Vanity and Ostentation'.

province of the Dissenters. They fully believed that they were justified in separating from the established Church, and writers like Jurieu among the Huguenots and Defoe among the English Dissenters defended their right of self-defence in cases where their lives were threatened by a repressive state. How then did such a position differ from that of a Jacobite who was convinced in his heart of the rightness of the Stuart cause?

In *An Address to the People of England*, published in the autumn of 1715, Defoe had raised the question of rebellion for the sake of conscience only to dismiss it with a rhetorical flourish as 'a most heinous Sin against God; and those who resist this King's Authority, do as certainly run into the danger of being damn'd in the next World, as of being hang'd in this'.[6] Those who had taken the oaths of loyalty to George I were doubly guilty. Even Defoe's mock Quaker, who stated his general opposition to oaths, could inform the rebels of this additional sin while assuring his readers that they were fighting on the side of Satan and would be defeated by those fighting for a righteous cause.[7]

After the rebellion in Scotland had been crushed, George I tended toward mercy by the standards of the time. About forty common soldiers had been executed after the rebels' defeat at Preston, but much leniency was shown afterwards.[8] Cadogan, in charge of British forces, more or less winked at the escape of prisoners from jail. Seven hundred ordinary soldiers were brought to trial and sentenced to be indentured servants in Britain's American possessions. Some would turn up in Defoe's novel *Colonel Jack* seven years later to threaten the prosperity of Defoe's hero. A death sentence was passed against the seven lords captured at Preston, but only two, Kenmuir and Derwentwater, were actually executed. Nithsdale and Wintoun escaped, and the rest were released under the Act of Grace passed in 1717. Walpole and the House of Commons would have hanged them all, but the House of Lords appealed to the King to show mercy.

An aura of romance and nostalgia was already surrounding the rebels. Derwentwater excused his actions on the basis of his youth and his belief that mercy would be shown to him if he surrendered. Lord Nithsdale's escape was engineered by his wife, who exchanged clothing with her husband on the night before his scheduled execution. She was left behind in

---

[6] *An Address to the People of England: Shewing the Unworthiness of their Behaviour to King George* (London, 1715), 9.

[7] *A Trumpet Blown in the North and Sounded in the Ears of John Erskine ... Duke of Mar* (London, 1715), esp. 28. This was one of the pamphlets published by Keimer.

[8] See Abel Boyer, *The Political State of Great Britain*, 11 (May 1716), 542–65; (July 1716), 31–72. Boyer gave a lengthy treatment of the execution of Richard Gascoigne, upon whose fate Defoe did not comment, but otherwise concentrated on the same executions as Defoe. Boyer notes that 22 of those sentenced to death had their sentences reprieved.

prison, but the general admiration for her courage made any prosecution impossible, and she was soon released. If some consideration was given to the appearance of equality under the law after the execution of forty common soldiers, the aura of romance did not extend to those implicated in a riot in London in July of 1716. Five Jacobites ('Jacks') were arrested, sentenced to death, and hanged.[9] Defoe insisted that Derwentwater and Kenmuir, the two lords who were actually executed, neither confessed their guilt nor showed repentance. 'He that implores Mercy', wrote Defoe, 'must first put himself into the Condition that denominates him a proper Object of Mercy, or he has but little Reason to expect it.'[10] Such a position was consistent with Defoe's religious views. Not even God pardoned sinners who had failed to confess all and sincerely repented, and from Defoe's viewpoint Derwentwater and some of the other lords had certainly not shown themselves sufficiently contrite.

But Defoe was to acknowledge that the word 'Mercy' had become a key word in contemporary political discussion. Brooding over the way 'certain *Words* put in the Mouths of a deluded Populace' will sometimes take on an uncontrollable force and implication, Defoe attempted to narrow the meaning of the word. In addition to repentance, he added the concepts of circumstances and reparation. Given the weakness of human nature, it might be possible to take into consideration the strength of temptation. But in the case of the rebels, Defoe argued, there were no mitigating circumstances, living as they did under a good government. Since they showed no desire to make reparations for their crime, they deserved no mercy. A government, he argued, has to protect itself. And he complained of writers such as Bishop Atterbury, who acted as if the rebellion were nothing more than 'a fit of the Spleen'. What Defoe learned from the response to the execution of the two lords, the failure to distinguish between mercy and 'foolish Compassion', was that almost three decades had passed since the Glorious Revolution and that a new generation needed to be educated about the evils of Jacobitism and the obligation of individuals and the state to follow the principles of self-preservation.[11]

The executions of William Paul and John Hall of Otterburn on 13 July 1716 brought this lesson home. Paul, who had acted as a preacher among

[9] See Ragnhild Hatton, *George I* (Cambridge, Mass.: Harvard University Press, 1978), 179–80; and Wolfgang Michael, *England under George I* (London: Macmillan, 1936), 207–13.

[10] *The Conduct of Some People about Pleading Guilty with some Reasons Why It Was Not Thought Proper to Shew Mercy to Some Who Desire'd It* (London, 1716), 36.

[11] See Defoe, *The Mercy of the Government Vindicated* (London, 1716), 5, 28; and *A Dialogue between a Whig and a Jacobite, upon the Subject of the Late Rebellion* (London, 1716), 8–22. For a discussion of the way in which key words may be used to indicate political attitudes, see Richard Ashcraft and Alan Roper, *Politics as Reflected in Literature* (Los Angeles: William Andrews Clark Memorial Library, 1989).

the rebels, tried every dodge before succumbing. Originally pleading innocent, he changed his plea and threw himself upon the mercy of George I. He conducted a writing campaign that included among its addressees both Lord Townshend and the Archbishop of Canterbury, but when all failed, he went to the gallows at Tyburn in the full regalia of a member of the Church of England. Enough of the emotion that fuelled the Sacheverell riots seven years before remained to create the spectacle of a number of women weeping at the sight of a minister apparently being oppressed by an unfeeling government. Paul's speech, delivered for publication at the gallows, expressed loyalty to James III and suggested that the government of George I was lacking not only in mercy but also in legitimacy. The speech of John Hall was even more defiant:

I offer my self as a Victim for the Liberties and Happiness of my dear Country and my beloved fellow Subjects; that I fall a Sacrifice to Tyranny, Oppression, and Usurpation; in short consider that I suffer in defence of the Commands of God and the Laws and Hereditary Constitution of the Land, and then know, and be assured, that I am not a Traytor but a Martyr.

Referring to George I as the Elector of Brunswick and impugning the legitimacy of the judges who sentenced him, Hall described his execution as an act of murder. He also claimed that the rebels would have gained the upper hand at Preston had they not been deceived into surrendering, and he expressed the hope that James III would soon defeat his enemies.[12]

Defoe viewed these executions as an unfortunate form of street theatre through which Jacobite propaganda could be disseminated to the crowds who gathered at Tyburn and along the routes leading to it.[13] He doubted that either Paul or Hall of Otterburn had written the speeches published in their name, but felt that the arguments about the legitimacy of the Glorious Revolution and the ruling House of Hanover were absurd. He returned to the arguments that had shocked so many when they were read at the Sacheverell trial. A people had a right to rebel against a bad monarch and to change their government. There was no hereditary right, only the will of the people expressed through Parliament.[14] In 1717, when the split in the

---

[12] Boyer, *Political State* (1716), xiii. 32–72. See also Arthur Ashley Syckes, *The Thanks of an Honest Clergyman for Mr Paul's Speech at Tybourn July the 13th, 1716* (London, 1716), 7–20.

[13] Defoe resorted to the comparison of William Paul and Hester Davenport, the actress whose 'marriage' to a nobleman was not accepted as legitimate because the clergyman who performed the ceremony was actually a servant in disguise. Defoe was commenting both on the priest's garb worn to his execution and on his claim to being a Non-juror. Similarly, a famous attack upon George I, *The Character of Sultan Gaga*, noted that he enjoyed executions both on the stage and in reality. See Defoe, *Remarks on the Speeches of William Paul Clerk* . . . (London, 1716), 8; and Bodleian Library, MS Rawl, D 383, fo. 80.

[14] *Remarks on the Speeches of William Paul Clerk*; and *The Layman's Vindication of the Church of England* (London, 1716), 26–50. Defoe uses the term 'Revolution Principle' (26) in the latter pamphlet, a phrase notably absent from his writing after the Tories regained power in 1710.

ministry weakened the government and the Jacobites threatened to invade Britain with the help of the King of Sweden, it might have been thought that George would move to execute more of the Jacobite prisoners, but he wisely decided to issue a general pardon which, though it had been in the air since May, took final form on 15 July 1717. Defoe argued that it would give the opportunity to those who had repented of their crimes to make reparations, and that 'Mercy in a Prince is so heavenly a Disposition' that such action gave even those who 'have the greatest Aversion to the Crimes which are forgiven, . . . a secret involuntary Pleasure, in seeing other People forgiven'.[15] But despite his praise of George I, he noted that some of those pardoned were not repentant, that instead of being grateful they continued to harbour a rebellious spirit. 'What indeed can be a greater Testimony of their abusing the Mercy shewn them', he wrote, 'than the open Endeavours to undervalue it?' Defoe may have admired monarchs for displaying such a 'God-like Principle', but he wanted there to be no question about the type of punishment that the Jacobite rebels truly deserved.[16]

That no mercy was shown to James Shepheard, a young man executed in March 1718 for planning to poison George I, seemed fitting to Defoe. Since he never repented of the action that he planned, he should receive no pardon. Shepheard was reported to have said that he would be 'justified at the righteous Bar of his Redeemer', but Defoe thought he saw in Shepheard's brief life a sign that God had consented to his destruction. The government attempted to forbid the publication of Shepheard's speech from the gallows, and while Defoe thought that wise, he also believed that those in power should have known that the attempt to suppress such a document would only lead to a secret and wider dissemination. On the other hand, he did not see why the government should open itself to such attacks. Shepheard was only 18 when he was hanged, and the spectacle of a young man possessed of such an intense conviction that assassinating George I was a religious and moral obligation was not one that the government would have wanted publicized.[17]

As Michel Foucault has shown, the law was supposed to reveal itself as a demonstration of the revenge of the state against the criminal, but a major part of the ritual, an essential element in the pattern of criminal justice with

---

[15] *A General Pardon Consider'd* (London, 1717), 6.

[16] *The History of the Clemency of Our English Monarchs* (London, 1717), 8, 27.

[17] See Defoe's *Some Reasons Why It Could Not Be Expected the Government Wou'd Permit the Speech or Paper of James Shepheard which He Delivered at the Place of Execution to be Printed* (London, 1718), 13, 27. At the beginning of *A Vindication of the Press* (London, 1718), Defoe mentions the ban on the publication of Shepheard's speech as one of the points of contention about freedom of the press; but the movement for some regulation was coming mainly from the High Church and the Tories.

its accompanying literary forms—the report of the crime, the capture of
the outlaw, the trial, execution, and life of the criminal, with his final words
at the gallows—was the confession.[18] At the moment before death, human
beings were supposed to be in a unique position to tell the truth, having
nothing to gain by lying and facing the possibility of divine retribution
after death for having lied. In all the cases of the Jacobites executed during
these years, defiance of the House of Hanover and complete faith in the
ultimate triumph of James III was the established pattern. Such a failure to
confess had been a force in turning the public against the Popish Plot
during the reign of Charles II, and it had to be a concern of the ministry led
by Sunderland and Stanhope. Defoe was eventually to confront this issue
in an introduction to a series of 'dying speeches' of state criminals. That the
Jacobites were firmly convinced of the righteousness of their cause meant
very little. Such men were under 'strong Delusions', dedicated to their
cause beyond the reach of any appeal to reason or the hopelessness of their
cause. Defoe justified his argument with a reference to the opinions of the
Bishop of Bangor, 'who tells us to be perswaded in the Mind of this or that
Way being the Right, is, in Matters of Religion, a sufficient authority'.[19]
The King might choose to exercise mercy toward the Jacobite prisoners,
but whether he chose to do so or not had nothing to do with the sincerity of
their convictions.

In an undated broadside attack upon the government with the title *A
Dialogue between P. Lorena, and James Sheperd*, the writer launched an
attack upon what he called 'the Bangorian Doctrine' of sincerity. 'I shall
not impose upon the Ignorant by insinuating that this unfortunate Young
Man, was induced to meditate so horrible a crime by reading Bangorian
Authors,' he wrote, 'But where Sincerity is the only Plea, we can wonder to
hear of a Ravilace, a King killer.' Within the dialogue itself, Shepheard
pleads 'Sincerity of Conscience' as his justification for his act. And in one
of the pieces printed as Shepheard's last writings, the condemned man

---

[18] Michel Foucault, *Discipline and Punish*, trans. Alan Sheridan (New York: Vintage Books, 1979),
65–8. Defoe reported Shepheard's refusal to admit any guilt to Paul Lorrain. See *Mercurius Politicus* (Apr.
1718), 163.

[19] *Collection of Dying Speeches of All Those People Call'd Traytors, Executed in This Reign* (London,
1718), 14. He also noted in the same work, 'We are come to an Age in which the Dying Words of Men are
little more to be credited than their Living Words; and tho' one would in Charity suppose that at the
Gallows and on a Death-bed, Men were past Disguises, and that it was not worth their while to speak
doubtfully, or deal deceitfully, and therfore we ought to lay an uncommon Weight upon Words spoken at
those Times, let the Persons who speak them be of what denomination soever: Yet there are some
Circumstances attending the Quarrel of the Age, and upon which most of our State Criminals are brought
to Execution, which render it less possible to judge of the Men, or of their Cause, by their Last Words,
than has been the Case perhaps in any other Age of the World' (3–4). See also Maximillian E. Novak,
'Defoe's Authorship of *A Collection of Dying Speeches*' (1718), *Philological Quarterly* 61 (1982), 92–7.

accused George I of 'Bangorian Sincerity' in his treatment of the Church of England. The references here are to a tract of 1716 by Benjamin Hoadly, Bishop of Bangor, with the title *A Preservation against the Principles and Practices of the Non-Jurors*, in which Hoadly had argued that the 'sincerity' of each man in his beliefs, as he expresses them, cannot be disputed by others. Hoadly was responding to an attack upon the sincerity of the Anglican clergy by the Non-juror George Hickes. This work, along with a sermon preached in the following year, on the text 'The Kingdom of God is not of this world', which urged the Church to assume a diminished political role and preached again the impossibility of judging sincerity of belief, brought about a successful effort by the lower house of Convocation to condemn Hoadly's ideas. This, in turn, produced a counter-attack from the government which resulted in an end to meetings of Convocation for more than 100 years.

II

The ensuing pamphlet war, which centred on the concept of sincerity, continued for several years. Opponents such as William Law argued that according to Hoadly's doctrine, 'sincere Jews, Turks, and Deists, are upon as good a Bottom, and as secure of the Favour of God, as the sincerest Christian', while defenders such as John Balguy extrapolated from Hoadly's ideas to make sincerity into a social and moral good, a stance of honesty and fairness. The debate took a personal turn when one of Hoadly's antagonists, Andrew Snape, accused the Bishop of having a former Jesuit in his employ and of having originally written his sermon in a far more offensive form. Snape gave as the source of his information about the early draft of the sermon the Bishop of Carlisle, who in turn named White Kennett, Dean of Peterborough, as his informant. When White Kennett denied any knowledge of the contents of an earlier version of the sermon, it raised the question of sincerity once more, and to make matters worse, the clergymen resorted to the public press to make their charges. Who was lying and who was sincere? And did they know themselves? But so far from discrediting the term, these arguments about the nature of sincerity gave that word a crucial meaning for the entire eighteenth century.[20] Elsewhere I have referred to this episode as a 'sincerity crisis', and Daniel Defoe played no small role in it.[21]

---

[20] On 25 July 1718, in the middle of the controversy, the *Freethinker* defined the ideal man as one 'who will upon no account violate the Sincerity of his Soul'.

[21] See Maximillian E. Novak, 'Sincerity, Delusion, and Character in the Fiction of Defoe and the

Sincerity, after all, had been a term associated with the Dissenters, whose refusal to conform to the discipline of the Church of England was usually defended on grounds of sincerely held religious convictions and a tender conscience. Now it was appropriated by the Bishop of Bangor to defend the essential individuality and privacy of belief. Not only could Defoe appreciate the irony of the situation, but as a Dissenter he could write from a position of strength. The King and his ministry strongly favoured repealing not only the recent Schism Act and Occasional Conformity Act but also the Test Act, dating from the Restoration, that prevented Dissenters from serving in the army and in positions of government.[22] Defoe agreed with Hoadly on most issues, and as mentioned above, Defoe found his arguments useful. But Hoadly had been an opponent of the Dissenters, and Defoe could hardly deny himself some fun at the Bishop's expense.[23] In *A Declaration of Truth to Benjamin Hoadly,* Defoe resumed his Quaker voice to applaud Hoadly for coming over to the Quaker position on sincerity which the Quaker interprets as being the same as that sect's concept of 'inner Light'. To be consistent, however, Hoadly needed to become a Quaker.[24] But this Friend is far less gentle with Hoadly's opponent, Andrew Snape whom he finds contentious and overly passionate in dispute. '*O Andrew! Andrew,*' writes Defoe's Quaker, 'hadst thou been guided by the Light of Truth shining in thy inward Parts, thou wouldest have known that the Light leadeth to Peace.'[25]

There were times when Defoe could hardly conceal his delight in seeing the leaders of the Church of England—the Church that had persecuted the Puritans before the Interregnum and the Dissenters for close to five decades after the Restoration—in so much discomfort. In *The Conduct of Christians Made the Sport of Infidels*, published on 1 August 1717, Defoe assumed the guise of an Armenian convert to Islam, Kara Selym, writing

"Sincerity Crisis' of His Time', in *Augustan Studies*, ed. Douglas Lane Patey and Timothy Keegan (Newark: University of Delaware Press, 1984), 109–26.

[22] The government also favoured closer control over Oxford and Cambridge, which served as positions of power for the Anglican clergy. For some of Defoe's writings on the repeal of the legislation passed against the Dissenters, see *The Question Fairly Stated, Whether Now Is Not the Time to Do Justice to the Friends of the Government, as Well as Its Enemies?* (London, 1717); and *The Danger and Consequence of Disobliging the Clergy Consider'd* (London, 1717). Jeremy Black has argued that the split in the Whig ministry weakened the government sufficiently to delay the repeals of the Occasional Conformity Act and the Schism Act. See 'Parliament and the Political and Diplomatic Crisis of 1717–18', *Parliamentary History* 3 (1984), 92–4.

[23] Defoe certainly sympathized with Hoadly's arguments about the role of the clergy in politics. Quoting Dryden to the effect that 'Priests of all Religions are the same', he argued that the clergy should never again be allowed to inflame the nation as they did during the Sacheverell affair. See *Misere Cleri: or, the Factions of the Church* (London, 1 (1718)), esp. 23, 26, 34.

[24] Defoe, *A Declaration of Truth to Benjamin Hoadly* (London, 1717), esp. 19–26.

[25] *A Letter to Andrew Snape* (London, 1717), 18.

about the Bangorian controversy to his friend Muli Ibrahim Esad. Selym expresses his dismay at British behaviour in general, remarking: 'Christians deviate from the Rules, and dishonour even that Nature, whose Dictates they know as well as feel in their own Breasts with other Creatures.' In Britain parents are not honoured by their children, the universities enforce oaths upon students that they cannot observe, and politicians are motivated entirely by greed and self-interest. But nothing matches the spectacle of the Bangorian controversy—a spectacle which provided considerable amusement to the Dissenters who were

well pleased to see the Confusion which this Breach among the Priests of that Church had put them into, and insulted them most openly upon that Occasion; jesting in particular with them, for that they on one and the same Side preached up the Schismatick Doctrines, and yet possessed as they said, the Episcopal Authority, and the Profits of it, both which they preached down by their Words and Doctrines.[26]

Selym feels that it would be better if they all joined him and converted to Islam, a religion without strife or contention. In a similar vein, after pointing out how petty were the attempts to associate Hoadly with his secretary, De La Pillonniere, a former Jesuit, Defoe wrote a pamphlet from the standpoint of the Jesuits attempting to convince De La Pilloniere to return to the fold. The Jesuits urge De La Pillonniere to imitate Hoadly's opponent, Snape, a cleric who follows his passions rather than reason. Once De La Pilloniere has thrown off reason, he can once more become enslaved to the doctrines of their order.[27]

Defoe was still writing on aspects of the Bangorian controversy in 1719, but whatever satisfaction he experienced from seeing the Church of England in disarray must have been lessened by the outbreak of doctrinal conflict among the Dissenters, often known as the Salters' Hall controversy. At issue was belief in the Trinity, a religious concept that had been under attack from all sides during the past thirty years. Sir Isaac Newton's disciple William Whiston saw this mystery of three beings in one as a corruption of the original ideas of Christianity, and Newton himself held a similar belief, although, like many contemporaries, he kept his ideas on this subject to himself. James Pierce, a minister of Exeter who had been one of Defoe's correspondents, was ejected from his congregation for refusing to

[26] Defoe, *The Conduct of Christians Made the Sport of Infidels* (London, 1717), 30. Defoe allows himself a somewhat private joke in suggesting that the practice of strangling an evil political grand vizier in the Ottoman Empire (22) was superior to Britain's system of competing political parties and ambitious politicians.

[27] Defoe, *A Letter from the Jesuits to Father de la Pillonniere* (London, 1718), 7, 8, 21.

acknowledge his belief in the Trinity.[28] The debate involved the minister
of the Dissenting congregation at Stoke Newington, Martin Tompkins,
and it touched Defoe deeply. When a kind of test of orthodoxy was applied
at a gathering of ministers at Salters' Hall in April 1719, a majority refused
to sign the document affirming their faith in the Trinity. Although many of
those who did not sign stated that they refused because of the nature of
such a test, Defoe accused them of lacking sincerity in such protestations.
In a pamphlet titled *Some Remarks upon the Late Differences among the
Dissenting Ministers and Preachers*, Defoe argued the 'orthodox' position,
the position of the believers and the signers, and remarked that 'a wound is
given to the Interest of Religion in this Nation, too deep, I fear, for any of
you to heal'.[29] He accused Pierce of reviving the heresy of Arius. Some
seven years later, in his *Political History of the Devil*, he was to accuse
Milton of fostering the same heresy. But most of all, he was horrified that
the Dissenters would match those involved in the Bangorian controversy
in making a public display of their basic disagreements.[30]

Although Defoe's personal beliefs were unlikely to have been changed
by the chaos that ensued in the ranks of the Dissenters after the conference
at Salters' Hall, he may have lost much of his respect for the Dissenting
clergy. And this came at a time when there is evidence that he had again
begun attending church services after a long period of time during which
he had abandoned this practice for fear of being arrested.[31] During the last
decade of his life, he presented a number of dramatic situations in which
the natural religion of savages, particularly sun worship, was shown as a
rational form of belief in the absence of revelation. Defoe's intent, however, was to lead his readers to some basic form of Christianity. Defoe was
clearly allowing himself more play in his writings about religion than he
had before, while clinging more firmly than ever to a private belief that he
considered to be strictly orthodox. He even assumed the name 'Orthodox'
in a letter to *Applebee's Journal* of 18 March 1721 in which he argued:

[28] Defoe thought that the confrontation at Salters' Hall was bad in itself, and hoped that the matter
might be smoothed over without the kind of violent disagreement that eventually occurred. He aimed his
Memoirs of the Life . . . of . . . Daniel Williams, published on 25 Feb. 1718, at Pierce, using the example of
Williams as a person who always attempted to mediate disputes and avoid quarrels.

[29] *Some Remarks upon the Late Differences among the Dissenting Ministers and Preachers* (London, 1719),
17. For Defoe's authorship of this pamphlet and a discussion of his attitudes, see Maximillian E. Novak,
'Defoe, the Occult, and the Deist Offensive during the Reign of George I', in *Deism, Masonry, and the
Enlightenment*, ed. Leo Lemay (Newark: Delaware University Press, 1987), 93–108.

[30] See *A Letter to the Dissenters* (London, 1719), esp. 15.

[31] Trent quoted *Heraclitus Ridens* for 24 July 1718, in which the author wondered why Defoe should
appear to be defending the Church of England in some of his writings while attending a Dissenting congregation. Trent also mentions an additional contemporary comment about Defoe's churchgoing. See MS
biography, 446.

'Freethinkers are profane, and *Free Actors* also; for,—erasing the Awe of God in their hearts, they plead immediately, and of Course, for a Freedom in all Manner of Vice,—using the Pretence of Liberty for a Justification of Crime, as if the Liberty God gave to Man of being a free Agent disengaged him entirely from the restraint of Laws, whether Human or Divine.'[32] The real enemies of religion had become atheism, a complete disbelief in the existence of spirit, and a militant deism with its mockery of the supernatural in general, its direct attack upon the credibility of the Bible, and its tendency to subvert Christianity by exalting other religious systems. During the last years of his life, Defoe was to set himself against the heresies of Toland and Collins as fiercely as he could through a wide variety of rhetorical approaches.

III

All these subjects managed to work their way into the fictional writing of 1718: his second volume of *The Family Instructor*, *A Continuation of Letters of a Turkish Spy*, and *The Memoirs of Majr. Alexander Ramkins*. In his preface to *The Family Instructor*, Defoe made what would be one of his most forceful arguments for fiction. Maintaining that the method of the second volume was entirely different, he defended his practice as following necessary principles of order. If he exhibits two bad wives, that is necessary to show how the husband must behave. As for novelty, though the insistance upon the new may be 'the modern Vice of the reading Palate', he has provided it:

the whole Scene now presented, is so perfectly new, so entirely differing from all that went before, and so eminently directed to another Species of Readers, that it seems to be more new than it would have been, if no other Part had been publish'd before it; nay, to any considering People that reflect upon the differing Scenes of human Life, and the several Stations we are plac'd in, and Parts we act, while we are passing over this Stage; it cannot but be known that there are Follies to be exposed, Dangers to be caution'd against, and Advices to be given, particularly adapted to the several Stages of Life.[33]

Comparing his work to Marana's popular *Letters of a Turkish Spy*, which ran to eight volumes, Defoe suggested the possibility of a similar series of moral dialogues.

I have discussed the general purport of these volumes before, but it

---

[32] Repr. in Lee, ii. 353. [33] *The Family Instructor* (London, 1718), ii. 3.

should be pointed out that the second volume, while less unified than the first, is more effective as an account of domestic life. The quarrels between husband and wife, the kind of bitter wit that exasperates each partner as the domestic warfare increases in warmth and intensity, is rendered brilliantly. At one point the images drawn from an eclipse of the sun that occurred on 22 April 1715 takes over the dialogue and has a life of its own. The Husband makes the mistake of comparing a 'cross Wife' to the moon that prevents the sun from shining. She, 'being of a sharp Wit', rejoins that some men think that their wives receive their light only from them and refuse to acknowledge that wives can eclipse their husbands. He retorts that the result of such action is to spread darkness, and with that the battle begins:

[*Upon this she came close to him.*] *Wife.* I suppose you think you have been Eclips'd lately, we don't see the House is the darker for it. *Husband.* That's because of your own Darkness; I think the House has been much the darker. *Wife.* None of the Family are made sensible of it, we don't miss your Light. *Husb.* It's strange if they don't, for I see no Light you give in the room of it. *Wife.* We are but as dark as we were before; for we were none of us the better for all your Hypocritical shining. *Husb.* Well, I have done shining, you see; the Darkness be at your Door.
    [*It is evident that both meant here, his having left off Family-Worship; and it is apparent, both were come to a dreadful Extremity in their Quarrel.*] *Wife.* At my Door! am I the Master of the Family! don't lay your Sins to my Charge. *Husb.* No, no; but your own I may; It is the Retrograde Motion of the Moon that causes an Eclipse. *Wife.* Where all was dark before, there can be no Eclipse. *Husb.* Your Sin is, that my Light is your Darkness.[34]

And with this the imagery stops as she eventually accuses him of 'A fine Delusion of the Devil! or rather an Artifice to throw your Burden on me', and he says all she wants is that he obey her in all things.

This dialogue, filled with sarcasm, is not intended as an example of brilliant wit but rather a rendering of the way people who are not great wits may use language games to wound. Defoe had read his Congreve, but this disputing couple resemble Fainall and Marwood of *The Way of the World* only in their ability to quarrel. Defoe's realist dialogue was intended to show quarrels as they are heard in everyday life. They would be impossible on the stage. As Dryden suggested, stage dialogue requires exaggeration, and what might appear to be the wittiest dialogue in real life would not seem amusing were it literally transcribed and made part of a play. But Defoe's stage imagery in the preface to the first volume of *The Family Instructor* was deliberate. He wanted to create a form of fiction that would

---

[34] *The Family Instructor*, 5–6.

possess the power and vividness of stage presentation, but he appears to have understood that prose fiction could capture the dullest and most stupid quarrel without ever becoming dull itself. Although he begins with a stage direction to bring the quarrelling couple physically close, his next direction is novelistic, a comment on the awareness of the couple to the effect that they understand what lies behind their imagery. He thought the situations so various and fascinating that (like a soap opera on radio or television) they could continue almost endlessly. He never doubted the power of a lively rendering of domestic life to fascinate the reader, and while he wrote only one more work in the series, he used similar techniques in a variety of volumes produced during the coming decade.[35]

The 1718 volume of *The Family Instructor* also presents a dialogue between a man who is seen beating his son without mercy and a friend who offers advice about the evils of such actions through a series of stories that illustrate how actions of this kind, performed through emotional rather than rational responses, can destroy the peace of a family. The form is that of 'midrash', in which one narrative comments on another, and also resembles that contemporary rococo form sometimes likened to a 'chinese box' in which one fits inside the other. This child-beater is a man who cannot control his passions, and his friend attempts to tell him stories of similar men by way of warning. The final story is about a father who cannot control his passions or behave mercifully, and the ending is sombre. Of course mercy here is almost equivalent to the kind of love that should exist in all family relationships. The father does not believe that his sons are behaving honestly, and acting out of a deep sense of distrust that we would call paranoid behaviour, he dismisses his sons from the business and takes it over himself. Finally, he almost kills a worker in a fit of passion and spends the rest of his life repenting his folly. The Neighbour's message is not lost on his listener, who feels that he can now reform his own life after examining the behaviour of this 'other' father and recognizing that his behaviour might deserve to be treated as a form of madness.

The second volume of *The Family Instructor* also contains one of Defoe's few attacks upon slavery and is a good illustration of the way he compartmentalized his views of the world. This was intended as a moral work, and within this category slavery might be criticized as an inhuman institution. The very religious Boy whose conversion to an active Christianity is something of an embarrassment to the family is given a 14-year-old 'negro'

[35] His *New Family Instructor* (London, 1727) added little to the kind of material that appeared in the earlier volume except, perhaps, for a strong defence of fiction, including romances, where such works provide a useful moral. The techniques perfected in the first two volumes were used in such volumes as *Religious Courtship* (1722) and *Conjugal Lewdness* (1727).

named Toby as his servant. Toby uses a variety of curses common to those working in Barbados, and the Boy is so shocked that he lets him go. On being informed that Toby has never been taught anything about Christianity, the Boy engages him in a conversation about life in the West Indies. Toby explains that the slaves do 'much great work, weary work, all day, all night', and that they are not allowed to go to church because baptism would turn the slave into a free man. The Father, who is given an account of the conversation, agrees. 'That is too true,' he remarks; 'they are rather afraid they should be Christians and get their liberty than that they should be infidels and go to the devil.' Upon hearing this story, the Boy weeps; he resolves to teach Christianity to Toby and does so with his father's permission. Toby is baptized and learns how to read through the good graces of a woman who volunteers to teach him. While theoretically a free man, he refuses to leave his master until he becomes a full adult and dismisses him.

The moral lesson is clear. Slavery, especially slavery purchased through keeping slaves ignorant and depriving them of any religious training, was an evil system. That Toby proves to be a loyal servant is a sign of the natural system of benefits that compels gratitude from the recipient of both knowledge and eternal life in a world to come. There is no contradiction between this treatment of slavery and Defoe's advocacy of the slave trade as a way to increase British wealth. The world, Defoe knew, was governed by economic self-interest, and no moral consideration could stand in the way of the gain to the nation. He attempted to prove that economic considerations dictated generous treatment of slaves, but questions of the morality of slavery itself could not be allowed to enter into economic discussions. I believe it is clear enough, however, that at a time when little distinction was made between the servant and the hired worker, Defoe hoped to see the slave system transformed into one of hired labour, with a structure of benefits tying master and worker together in something resembling a kind of 'family'. But all this is kept at a distance here. Though the world of *The Family Instructor* is convincingly real in the delineation of character and emotion, economic considerations are not allowed to intrude upon its purely moral realm.

IV

A second important experiment for Defoe in 1718 was his *Continuation of Letters of a Turkish Spy*, a ninth volume of a work that had first appeared in eight volumes in French in 1684. According to the second edition, published in Amsterdam, the 'translator' of these letters from the Arabic was a Jean-Paul Marana, and he is given credit for the authorship of the first few volumes. Who wrote some of the later volumes is hard to say, though John Dunton maintained that his brother-in-law, Richard Sault, wrote them in a matter of days.[36] Certainly there was not much of a trick to it. The mannerisms of the letter writer, supposedly a Turkish spy living in Paris, were easy enough to copy, and the observations on various events occurring in Europe during the seventeenth century merely required a knowledge of history and a sense of how a Turk, contemptuous of Western manners and religion, would react to a century filled with political intrigue and a good deal of religious hypocrisy. Although the letters seem contrived enough to a modern reader, they obviously appeared genuine enough to some readers at the end of the century. One episode, concerning the Wandering Jew appearing in Vienna, raised only a slight hint of incredulity from the diarist Robert Wodrow, who wrote from Glasgow to a friend at Paris on 6 December 1698 asking his opinion of both the Spy himself and his account. He learned shortly thereafter of Sault's possible involvement, but the first inquiry shows that audiences unaccustomed to reading a form of fiction so imbued with history were ready enough to take the account as real.[37]

Defoe's praise of the work of Marana and his successors is hardly surprising. Not only did the work convey its vision of history in an entertaining manner, but Defoe, more than a little of the spy himself, could hardly resist some identification with this secret agent and outsider. Mahmut, the letter writer, was small, anything but handsome, and given to philosophy and contemplation. Defoe would have appreciated his feeling that women were the equals of men and deserved to be better educated, his interest in Descartes, and his scepticism about the rituals of the Catholic Church; but Marana was clearly a francophile, and Defoe's main purpose was to turn the work into another anti-Jacobite tract, to demonstrate the hypocrisy of Louis XIV and the French in the promises they seemed to hold out to James II and, by implication, his descendants. The letters cover the period from 1687 to 1693, when French power once more seemed to threaten 'Universal Monarchy' and only William III and his allies prepared

[36] For some discussions of authorship, see Joseph Tucker, 'On the Authorship of *The Turkish Spy*: an *Etat Présent*', *Papers of the Bibliographical Society of America* 52 (1958), 34–47; William McBurney, 'The Authorship of *The Turkish Spy*', *PMLA* 72 (1957), 915–35; and Arthur Weitzman (ed.), *Letters Writ by a Turkish Spy* (London: Routledge & Kegan Paul, 1970), pp. viii–x.

[37] Wodrow, *Early Letters, 1698–1709*, ed. L. W. Sharp (Edinburgh: T. and A. Constable, for the Scottish Historical Society, 1937), 3, 30, 92.

to thwart the ambitions of the French King. For those Jacobites who might believe that Louis XIV would restore Catholicism and James III to England, Defoe presented a France that supported the Turks against the Christians and was attempting to 'embroil in War all the Courts and Princes of *Europe*' while concealing all their actions behind a 'Mask of Devotion'.

Defoe also used Mahmut for a number of other purposes, particularly for attacks upon the religious controversies that were undermining all religious belief. Although the world described is purportedly that of the end of the seventeenth century, Defoe was clearly aiming his barbs at the situation in Britain in 1718. But what is more important is his development of Mahmut as an exile suffering the pangs of loneliness and alienation in a foreign land. His description of his psychological state, without a friend with whom he can converse, his 'Lunatick' gestures during fits of despair, and his fear that he will explode emotionally are all preparations for those moments in *Robinson Crusoe* when Crusoe finds himself gnashing his teeth in frustration at his loneliness and longing for a companion. Thinking that there is a chance that he may be relieved of his post, Mahmut writes, 'My Heart has been ready to burst for these thirteen Moons past, with the violent Agitations of joy and Despair, revolving in their Turns, equally strong and equally unsupportable.'[38] Mahmut compares his experience to the ways in which wine may sometimes explode, bursting the iron bonds of its cask, or a volcano will suddenly erupt. Mahmut may not have known much about this subject, but Defoe, the former wine merchant, with an amateur interest in explosions of all kinds, and the former secret agent who felt abandoned in his post in Scotland a few years earlier, had no difficulty reaching for these comparisons or describing Mahmut's sense of isolation.

Defoe published his *Continuation of the Letters of a Turkish Spy* on 20 August 1718 with William Taylor, the future publisher of *Robinson Crusoe*, but his major publisher was now William Boreham, who, along with Thomas Warner, had taken over much of the business of the recently deceased John Baker. On 9 December 1718 Boreham published Defoe's *Memoirs of Maj[o]r Alexander Ramkins*, Defoe's first, if somewhat halting, effort at producing the type of realist fiction that was to occupy him for the next six years. Mahmut had been a ready-made character and the letter-essay form was easy enough to imitate. Ramkins, on the other hand, was a new character in need of shaping. Defoe's strong commitment to various messages about society and Jacobitism had to be filtered through the mind of a young man strongly committed to the Jacobite cause. His convictions

[38] Defoe, *Continuation of Letters of a Turkish Spy* (London, 1718), 267.

had to be shown as waning under increasing evidence of the indifference of France toward restoring James III to the British throne. This was not to be another *Memoirs of Monsieur Mesnager* with its emphasis on external afffairs. Ramkins was supposed to come alive as a convincing character. The lengthy title that followed the seeming promise of a military memoir may merely reflect Boreham's desire to sell his product, but it may also reflect some of Defoe's indecision:

A Highland-Officer, Now in Prison at Avignon. Being An Account of several remarkable Adventures during about Twenty Eight Years Service in Scotland, Germany, Italy, Flanders and Ireland; exhibiting a very agreeable and instructive Lesson of Human Life, both in a Publick and a Private Capacity, in serveral pleasant Instances of his Amours, Gallantry, Oeconomy, etc.

As Moore pointed out, the twenty-eight years may have suggested Robinson Crusoe's equivalent stay on his island, and a reissue in 1719 changed the title to reflect the excitement caused by Defoe's masterpiece. But what is most interesting here is Defoe's entrance into the world of fiction-writing. Jacobite memoirs were common enough, but the title promises to include a 'Private Capacity' as well as the usual public nature of memoirs, and adds the expectation of a discussion of 'Amours, Gallantry, Oeconomy', suggesting to the prospective reader that he or she might discover between the covers the kind of scandalous fiction that Delarivière Manley had claimed as the province of women writers when she published her *New Atalantis* less than a decade earlier.

In fact, Eliza Haywood would soon emerge as the real master of literature involving love, and from the standpoint of popularity, her *Love in Excess* was a strong rival of both *Robinson Crusoe* and *Gulliver's Travels*. But Defoe was not ready to write this type of novel, however much he or his publishers may have attempted to capture its audience through misleading titles. *Maj[o]r Ramkins* actually is mainly a more direct attempt than the *Continuation* to discredit France as a possible ally for the Jacobites. Ramkins along with his brothers enlists with King James's forces without any second thoughts. Only 17, he fights for James at the battle of Killiecrankie (27 July 1689), a short-lived victory for the Highlanders loyal to James, followed by a devastating defeat at Dunkeld less than a month later. From the very beginning, Ramkins is warned by a Highland officer that Louis XIV is merely using James II for his own purposes, and Ramkins discovers the truth of this and provides the reader with the same moral throughout the work. He goes to France, where he receives further training, and buys a commission in time to fight in Ireland for James at the battle of the Boyne.[39] He blames the failures of the Irish campaign on Louis XIV's refusal to send troops, and points to the advantages gained by France in being able to recruit 150,000 Irish soldiers. And like Mahmut, he is astonished by the hypocrisy of Louis's pretending to be a loyal Catholic while supporting the Turks in their battles against the Christians in eastern Europe. He learns later that Louis has no intention of supporting any invasion of England by the deposed King, and that James is hardly more than a prisoner of the Sun King. He also discovers the dangers of open speech in France when he suffers two days' imprisonment for making derogatory remarks about the French King. In the end, he recommends a work with the title *A Roman Catholic System of Allegiance*, which demonstrates how Catholics in England may give their loyalty to George I without betraying their principles.[40]

Defoe had considerable difficulty maintaining a connection between his message and his narrative. He had not yet discovered how the two might be merged, and Major Ramkins drops his narrative entirely at the end to preach his sermon on the wickedness of the French and the futility of the Jacobite cause. But Defoe was resolved to continue his narrative to the extent of manufacturing some kind of an ending. For example, there is a love and marriage plot of a type not very different from that which he was to exploit a few years later in *Colonel Jack*. First Ramkins finds himself involved in a case of mistaken identity. His brother had flirted with a lady in Paris and so enraged a relative of the lady, a French officer, that he challenged Captain Ramkins to a duel. The duel proves fatal for the Frenchman, and Captain Ramkins departs at once for Ireland to fight for James II. On arriving at Paris from Strassburg, the younger Ramkins

---

[39] Ramkins's training among the French cadets at the military college of Strassburg is reminiscent of Defoe's proposal for a military academy in his *Essay upon Projects*: 'This I look'd upon as an excellent method of educating young Officers; for it qualify'd them to be serviceable to their Country under a double Capacity; that is, as well to argue as to Fight for it, and defend it equally with their Tongue and Sword.' *Memoirs of Maj[o]r Ramkins* (London, 1718), 21.

[40] The author of this work, published by Lintot in 1716, is identified by the initials P.R. Since Defoe so commonly referred to his own writings, some suspicion might arise as to his authorship of this work, but the style is completely unlike that of Defoe. On the other hand, a work published by Boreham in 1718 with a title obviously influenced by this work, *A General Claim to Allegiance*, may indeed be by Defoe. The writer of this work falls asleep in Westminster Hall and dreams of a quasi-judicial hearing to determine which social, religious, and political groups in contemporary Britain might be acceptable in their claims to allegiance to George I. Although the Quakers, Jews, and even the Turks are found acceptable, atheists and Tories are excluded. The tract concludes with the author's meditations on the Shepheard case and the role of the Non-juring clergyman Orme in encouraging Shepheard's intransigent stance toward George I that led to his execution. In the same manner as the author of another Boreham tract that I have identified as Defoe's (*A Collection of Dying Speeches*), the author points out that there was no moral or religious significance in the possibility that Shepheard was following his conscience in attempting to assassinate George I.

finds himself arrested for murder and has to obtain proof of his innocence by demonstrating that he was elsewhere when the duel took place.

Back in Paris once more after his campaign in Ireland, Major Ramkins begins to court a Spanish lady of Irish descent and finds himself carried away by his passions, particularly jealousy, as he comes to believe that he might have a rival for the lady's affections. Just as the French officer involved himself in a duel with his brother because he could not control his passions, so Major Ramkins almost fights a duel with a man he suspects of displaying a snuffbox similar to one which he gave the lady. Fortunately, he has enough control to realize that there might be similar snuffboxes available in Paris, and upon discovering a jewellery shop displaying similar boxes, he manages to realize how close to danger he had come. When the lady leaves for Spain he has few regrets, and the emotional and financial expenses of his courtship teach him a lesson. When he decides to marry, he chooses the widow of an extravagant colonel who had brought his wife and himself to poverty. She seems to be a sensible woman, and he believes that he has learned his lesson from the 'perplex'd State' he was in during his courtship of the Spanish lady: 'to consult my Reason rather than my Passions' (159). Yet, as with Colonel Jack later on, Ramkins discovers that what might seem like a prudent marriage may not turn out well. Ramkins finds that his wife has spent his £1000 within a year. Because they 'did really affectionately love each other', they are able to retrench their expenses and live within their means. Although Ramkins made mistakes about her, they end up as 'two inseparable Companions' (164).

Along with this series of love encounters, *Major Ramkins* maintains a running account of Ramkins's adventures in maintaining the funds in his Amsterdam account before his wife succeeds in wasting it. Despite his initial idealism and enthusiasm for the Jacobite cause, he is able to say proudly, 'though I have frequently hazarded my Life, I never risqu'd my Substance'. While he is at Strassburg, he finds that his fellow officers are only too eager to get him to pay for various entertainments and suspects that they covet his account at Amsterdam. He has to invent reasons to escape from this situation, only to find himself having to spend money to rescue himself from the difficulties created by his brother's duel. Later on, he discovers that an attempt has been made to obtain his money through a false will. It turns out that the company clerk had thought Ramkins had been killed at the battle of Landen and that the money was merely waiting to be claimed. As if this were not enough, Defoe adds an interpolated story of a runaway footman who, after robbing his master, has posed as a nobleman and lived a life of 'meer Romance' (133) until he hangs himself. This pattern of desperation and indigence finds its fullest expression in Ramkins's experiences during his visit to England. On a sight-seeing trip to areas around London with an Irish gentleman, he is robbed by two highwaymen. The landlord of the inn at which they arrive informs them that the men who had robbed them were now part of a 'Gentleman-like Employment', adding that

younger Brothers of very good Families are not asham'd to spend their time that way; besides the Practise is very much refin'd as to the manner, there's no Fighting or Hectoring during the Performance, but these Gentlemen approach you decently and submissive, with their Hat in their Hand to know your Pleasure, and what you can well afford to support them in the Dignity they live in: 'Tis true, says he, they often for Form sake have a Pistol in their Hand, which is part of their riding Furniture; but that is only in the Nature of a Petition, to let you know they are Orphans of Providence just fallen under your Protection. In a Word, demanding Money upon the Road, is now so agreeably perform'd, that 'tis much the same with asking an Alms. The poor Beggar wou'd rob you if he durst, and the Gentleman Begger will not rob you if you will but give him a decent Alms suitable to his Quality. (151–2)

Ramkins is delighted with the landlord's theory about the improvement in the 'Employment' of highway robbery, and it does seem to fit in with the larger image of a rapacious society in which theft is hardly distinguished from other professions. Certainly Ramkins can understand the landlord's argument well enough, since getting loot on the battlefield was an important part of the soldier's profession.[41] Defoe had made similar remarks a decade earlier in a variety of numbers of the *Review*, but these comments have a new significance, for they have to be read in terms of the coming business crisis—the South Sea Bubble— that was to envelope the entire society of Britain and its social institutions. The theme of Ramkins's struggle to hold onto his wealth and his ultimate failure, like the love– marriage theme, is never fully integrated into the main thrust of the work—the discrediting of Jacobitism and demolishing the image of France as a trustworthy nation. But *Major Ramkins* held the promise of better things to come.

[41] See John Keegan, *The Face of Battle* (New York: Viking, 1976), 180–1.

23

Robinson Crusoe and the Variability of Life

How strange a Chequer Work of Providence is the Life of Man! and by what secret differing Springs are the Affections hurry'd about as differing Circumstance present! To Day we love what to Morrow we hate; to Day we seek what to Morrow we shun; to Day we desire what to Morrow we fear; nay even tremble at the Apprehensions of; this was exemplify'd in me at this Time in the most lively Manner imaginable; for I whose only Affliction was, that I seem'd banished from human Society, that I was alone, circumscrib'd by the boundless Ocean, cut off from Mankind, and condemn'd to what I call'd silent Life; that I was as one who Heaven thought not worthy to be number'd among the Living, or to appear among the rest of his Creatures; that to have seen one of my own Species, would have seem'd to me a Raising me from Death to Life, and the greatest Blessing that Heaven it self, next to the supreme Blessing of Salvation, could bestow; *I say*, that I should now tremble at the very Apprehensions of seeing a Man, and was ready to sink into the Ground at but the Shadow or silent Appearance of a Man's having set his Foot on the Island.[1]

For all the writing that Defoe had done before the composition of *Robinson Crusoe*, indeed for all the prose fiction that he had written, *Robinson Crusoe* must have come to him as almost as wonderful a surprise as it was to his readers. In the process of writing, he must have recognized how original, how ingenious it was. For all the descriptions of alienation and loneliness in his *Continuation of the Letters of a Turkish Spy*, that work was essentially a

[1] *Robinson Crusoe*, ed. J. Donald Crowley (Oxford: Oxford University Press, 1990), 156.

work of wit rather than imagination. The form was pre-established, and all Defoe had to do was add his own observations on European culture through the eyes of a Turk. *Robinson Crusoe* was very different. For the first time Defoe created a work that drew upon all of his talents, knowledge, and experience. As early as his first bankruptcy, he might have composed a letter from some fictional character on the contingencies that make life so uncertain, but by 1719, like Lear, Defoe was able to understand such matters 'feelingly'. And he was able to transfer such a concept to the despairing Crusoe and turn it into an observation that seems to come from the bottom of his soul. The immediate popularity of *Robinson Crusoe* did not arise from some easily duplicatable 'trick' in Defoe's realistic narrative method or, as his detractors suggested, because of some trick of style that would deceive the reader into believing that he was being presented with a true narrative. Rather it succeeded because it drew conclusions from experience that seemed to possess a sense of self-discovery for the adult Crusoe, while being simple enough for a child to grasp.

To modern critics it has appeared as an economic parable, a spiritual autobiography, an adventure story, and a fable illustrating human development and education. And to a certain extent, the hint of such interpretations was present from the very start. Although the original frontispiece, with Crusoe in his island costume holding his two guns over his shoulder, suggested adventure, the first French edition, illustrated by Picart, showed Crusoe with his saw and hatchet, hinting at Crusoe as a builder and creator. Jean-Jacques Rousseau was the first commentator to discuss the work seriously and thoroughly as a fable of education. He argued that his ideally educated man, Émile, should be raised free from the prejudices of traditional European pedagogy, and the first book he should be given ought to be *Robinson Crusoe* because it would give the boy a sense of the thingness of nature. Just as Crusoe had to learn how to construct his cave and cooking utensils, Émile might learn something about his place in nature from Defoe's work. More modern versions of the Crusoe story have been critical of its colonialist attitudes, but such works have also shown how Defoe's text continues to raise basic questions about human relationships and encounters. Like a painting by Dali that may appear to be a head of Voltaire at one moment and then a group of ladies dancing, it tends to have enough in it to support what might seem to be entirely separate readings.

I

The problem of interpretation arose almost immediately with Charles Gildon's forceful critical assault on the work, *The Life and Strange Surprising Adventures of D[aniel] De F[oe]*, a work which sought both to attack Defoe and to gain some notoriety from the popularity of Defoe's novel. *Robinson Crusoe* had gone into four authorized editions between 25 April 1719, when it was published, and 7 August 1719. An unauthorized abridgement was published by T. Cox on the day before the fourth edition, and it was serialized in a London newspaper from 7 October 1719 onward, a practice unique at the time. Its popularity and its originality were immense. Gildon's attack has to be understood, at least partly, in the context of the low opinion in which prose fiction was held. It had no standing among what were considered, at the time, the serious literary genres. When Gildon tried to find parallel works, he could only come up with *Pilgrim's Progress*, a popular work of morality, *The Practice of Piety*, and Reynolds's *God's Revenge Against Murther*, a series of narratives illustrating the bad end to which those guilty of violent crimes came. For Gildon, none of these had any literary standing; they were merely the product of what he would have considered religious fanaticism. If Gildon attempted to condemn *Robinson Crusoe* as the product of religious Dissent, he also compared Crusoe to the heroes of the popular chapbooks that then made up much of the reading of British children. 'Your Hero!', wrote Gildon, '*Your Mob Hero*! on a foot with Guy of Warwick, Bevis of Southampton, and the London Prentice.'[2] Though Gildon maintained that he had nothing against 'Fables' which had a 'useful Moral, either express'd or understood', he argued that Defoe's work was 'design'd against a publick good' in a variety of ways. Gildon's charge that Defoe was once more playing his subversive games would certainly have won easy recognition from an audience which, only a year earlier, had learned that Defoe was seemingly writing for both Whig and Tory papers.

In a section depicting Defoe in an encounter with his fictional characters, Friday and Crusoe, Gildon shows Defoe at first frightened by them and then insistent they are simply his creations, 'airy Fantoms' with whom he may do as he pleases. But when threatened by them, he argues, 'Then know, my dear Child, that you are a greater Favorite to me than you imagine; you are the true Allegorick Image of thy tender Father D[anie]l; I drew thee from the consideration of my own Mind; I have been all my Life

[2] Charles Gildon, *The Life and Strange Surprising Adventures of D[aniel] De F[oe]*, in *Robinson Crusoe Examin'd and Criticis'd*, ed. Paul Dottin (London: Dent, 1923), 72. See also 71 and 82.

that Rambling, Inconsistent Creature, which I have made thee.'[3] Aside from being a forerunner of Pirandello's *Six Characters in Search of an Author* or of some postmodern work of fiction, Gildon's dialogue displayed a recognition of how much of a novelist's own character goes into his fictional creations. It also gave Defoe a way into defending his work when he came to write *Serious Reflections of Robinson Crusoe*, the third and last of the Crusoe volumes. In that work, still writing as Robinson Crusoe, Defoe announced, in the formulaic style of a will, that all of his critics were mistaken:

I, Robinson Crusoe, being at this time in perfect and sound mind and memory, thanks be to God therefor, do hereby declare their objection is an invention scandalous in design, and false in fact; and do affirm that the story, though allegorical, is also historical; and that it is the beautiful representation of a life of unexampled misfortunes, and of a variety not to be met with in the world, sincerely adapted to and intended for the common good of mankind, and designed at first, as it is now farther applied, to the most serious uses possible.

Farther, that there is a man alive, and well known too, the actions of whose life are the just subject of these volumes, and to whom all or most part of the story most directly alludes; this may be depended upon for truth, and to this I set my name.[4]

This statement, like most of those in the preface, was an attempt at obfuscation. The work is 'real', 'true', and 'sincere' in its intent, yet it is also true that the reality was one created by the fabulist and that the truth was that of serious realist fiction.

In Europe, where *Robinson Crusoe* was reviewed extensively after being translated into German and French, it was treated as a 'sort de Roman Moral'.[5] And it was this new kind of fiction that Defoe was defending along with his own integrity as the creator. 'All these reflections are just history of a state of forced confinement', wrote Crusoe-Defoe, 'which in my real history is represented by a confined retreat in an island; and it is as reasonable to represent one kind of imprisonment by another, as it is to represent anything that really exists by that which exists not.' Only Albert Camus, who placed it as a motto before his novel *La Peste*, seems to have found this statement significant, but for Defoe it was an argument for a serious type of fiction sustained by a vivid method of representation. Though he used the word 'allegory' to describe his rendering of Crusoe's story, Defoe meant what we would call a novel rich in symbolic meaning. In its

---

[3] Ibid. 72.

[4] *Serious Reflections of Robinson Crusoe*, ed. George A. Aitken, in *Romances and Narratives by Daniel Defoe* (16 vols., J. M. Dent, 1895), vol. iii, pp. ix, x.

[5] See e.g. Jean Le Clerc (ed.), *Bibliotheque ancienne et moderne* (29 vols., Amsterdam, 1721), xv. 441.

own way, the preface was as much of a manifesto for the kind of fiction he was to write over the next four years as anything that Henry Fielding or Samuel Richardson were to produce some thirty years later. Like these later novelists, who claimed to have invented a 'new species' of writing, Defoe had created a new form. As Robert Shiels argued in 1753, 'It was indeed written upon a model entirely new'.[6]

The shaping of *Robinson Crusoe* was, of course, anything but pure inspiration. The most obvious source for the island episode is to be found in well-publicized accounts of a sailor named Alexander Selkirk, who voluntarily went ashore on the island of Juan Fernandez located in the Pacific Ocean off the coast of Chile and remained there for four years and four months. He succeeded in surviving on the island by singing hymns, reading his Bible, dancing with the goats he had tamed, and running swiftly through the forest after the wild ones. Since contemporary thought had it that man could not live in isolation, Selkirk's story seemed miraculous. He was rescued on 31 January 1709 by Captain Woodes Rogers, whose account of his voyage and of this event, *A Cruising Voyage Round the World* (1712), had been published in a second edition in 1718, just a year before the appearance of Defoe's *Surprizing Adventures*. The story drew immediate attention, for it fed into certain notions about man in a state of nature that held a particular fascination for the age. For example, Selkirk survived without salt for his food and became accustomed to live without this luxury. He expressed a dislike for alcoholic drinks when they were offered him, and he seemed to have lost some of his ability to use language, a fact that supported those who believed that language was neither a natural nor a necessary human acquirement.

As Arthur Secord suggested, it would be impossible to think that Defoe was unfamiliar with and uninfluenced by Selkirk's story, but it would be an equal mistake to believe that the character of Crusoe was merely modelled on Selkirk and Crusoe's adventures a somewhat expanded version of those experienced by him.[7] On the contrary, Selkirk, a Scot from Largo, where he lived most of his life, had a character that was, unlike Crusoe's, notoriously irascible, and his adventures, aside from his success in taming some goats and making a costume of goatskins and his ability to survive his isolation, bore little resemblance to Crusoe's. The notion was widespread at the end of the eighteenth and the beginning of the nineteenth centuries that Defoe had stolen Selkirk's manuscript and claimed credit for a work

---

[6] See his life of Defoe in *Lives of the Poets*, ed. Theophilus Cibber (London, 1753).

[7] Arthur Secord, *Studies in the Narrative Method of Defoe* (New York: Russell & Russell, 1963 (repr. of 1924 edn.)), 24, 32.

that was not his. This misconception, popularized by such diverse agents as
the poet William Cowper and the *Encyclopaedia Britannica*, had an adverse
effect on Defoe's reputation at this time, when the probability of the story
was increased by a general unfamiliarity with the extent of Defoe's other
writings.[8] Defoe was supposed to have encountered Selkirk in Bristol and
either absconded with the manuscript or pretended to take it away to make
improvements, a story which may have had its origin in Richard Steele's
account of Selkirk in his journal *The Englishman*.[9]

   In fact, Defoe drew upon the same techniques that he had perfected in a
work such as *Memoirs of the Negotiations of Monsieur Mesnager*, the creation
of a fiction through drawing information from a wide variety of sources.
But in addition to the many sources Defoe consulted, even more works had
stuck in his imagination. Noting the large number of passages from travel
literature that went into a relatively short narrative poem such as
Coleridge's *Rime of the Ancient Mariner*, Arthur Secord suggested that as
with Coleridge, Defoe may have recalled a myriad of travel accounts
which he had read in his earliest years. Secord's book appeared three years
before John Livingston Lowes published his *Road to Xanadu*, a work
which explored Coleridge's imaginative use of such source material, and
Secord's concept of a source remained something that could be thought of
as a work that Defoe could have had open on his desk as he worked.[10]
Secord would have rejected the notion of an imaginative Defoe whose
unconscious might combine four or five different works into a single
image. Everyone knew of Coleridge's fecund imagination, but the image
of Defoe that Secord would have inherited—that of the practical man of
business who half-stumbled into literary creation— would have excluded
Defoe from such a concept. As admirable as Secord's scholarly tools were
and as useful his work, it is only fair to say that our Defoe is less narrow and
more interesting.

   For example, Secord was not interested in biblical parallels—Adam in
the Garden of Eden, the story of Jonah, the prodigal son. It seemed
inevitable that, once he embarked on his story, Defoe would have drawn
upon material part of which he literally knew by heart. Biblical echoes
carry throughout the work, particularly in Crusoe's meditations upon his

---

   [8] In Sir Herbert Croft's novel *Love and Madness*, published in 1776, an extended and adulatory discussion of *Robinson Crusoe* is followed by a condemnation of Defoe's treatment of Alexander Selkirk.
   [9] The number for 1–3 Dec. 1713. Steele, who tended to mythologize the story into an account of the
benefits of the simple life, stated that he met Selkirk in 1711, 'soon after his arrival in England', which was
14 Oct. of that year. Steele was sometimes credited with authorship of *Robinson Crusoe*, particularly by
Continental critics.
   [10] This remained Secord's method in his posthumously published *Robert Drury's Journal and other
Studies* (Urbana: University of Illinois Press, 1961).

experiences, and J. Paul Hunter has reminded us of the ways in which such parallels set up specific expectations.[11] Yet the island is not the biblical Paradise, and Crusoe is neither Jonah nor the prodigal son. Certainly Crusoe sees himself somewhat in the mould of Jonah, the prophet who boards a ship to avoid doing the work of God only to be the victim of a terrible storm and cast into the ocean. Expansions upon such narratives in contemporary sermons were common practice, and Crusoe alludes to Jonah on several occasions. But it is hard to see anything but the loosest parallel with Crusoe's story. Defoe seems to use his references to such biblical narratives more as a form of allusion than as an attempt at creating a serious typological structure.[12]

This is even more true of the story of the prodigal son, for if Crusoe returns from his island to his native England as a wealthy man after twenty-eight years of punishment for his sinful defiance of his father's desire that he find a calling in the 'Middle Way of Life', he has no living father to welcome him back. If Ian Watt saw in Crusoe's life a fable of indivi-dualism, it is precisely because he earns his own rewards. What greets him when he returns is a great deal of money—the accumulated wealth of his plantations in Brazil. The news of his newfound wealth leaves him over-joyed, and it might be said that the story of the prodigal son's loving recep-tion by his father is replaced by an accumulation of money, that family relationships are replaced by the power relationship of capitalist accumu-lation. Friday's emotional encounter with his father, after Crusoe and he rescue the father from the cannibals, may be seen as a truly natural, emotional scene of love between parent and child. For Crusoe, the venture capitalist, money replaces human relationships. Defoe turns the story of the prodigal son on its head. In the world of Crusoe, a pot of gold is a far more concrete reward than the embraces of a doting father.

II

Writing of adaptations of British fictions during the time of the American Revolution and its aftermath, Jay Fliegelman has pointed out that *Robinson Crusoe* was one of the texts revised better to suit readers in a nation that was

[11] *The Reluctant Pilgrim* (Baltimore: Johns Hopkins University Press, 1966).

[12] In one corner of the Pine illustration there is the depiction of a ship in stormy seas. Although such a scene, which formed a major element in Dutch sea painting, bore an allegorical meaning related to the Christian's experience of life—its dangers and transitoriness—particularly in the works of the early seventeenth century, by the end of that century such a message had become less important than the visual display of the violent sea and the struggling vessel. Thus Pine's illustration can be given a specific alle-gorical reading or a purely representational one.

in the process of throwing off all ties to the parent state.[13] *Robinson Crusoe* is a work peculiarly suited to images of successful revolt against parental authority. This is true despite all the warnings that he would not prosper so long as he was disobedient, true despite Crusoe's own recriminations, in his sufferings, about his failure to obey his father's wishes. Although slavery at Sallee might make him believe that he was an object of God's wrath, it failed to change his ways. His shipwreck after leaving his Brazilian plantations, where he seemed to be attaining just that balanced point of achievement which his father had extolled, brought with it a similar sense of guilt but failed to change his basic character. The fact is that after his escape from drowning, and after his fears about being devoured by wild beats have passed, Crusoe finds great delight in his island life. His display of energy in looting the wrecked ship that brought him to his island has a distinct feeling of pleasure attached to it. And the same may be said for his attempt to transform the island into a self-sufficient utopia. The restlessness that drove him so relentlessly before his stay on the island is consumed in enjoyable, hard, physical labour. Like a new Adam, Crusoe has an opportunity to shape his island according to his wishes. Admittedly, he might have become as wealthy had he directed his ambitions to putting in the long hours in a shop or office as his father wished, but who can doubt that he feels pleasure in his outdoor life and in exploring his new environment? If he experiences terrible loneliness before the arrival of Friday, he also takes pleasure in the creation of his new world with its Castle, Country House, and grotto. And none of this could have been experienced had he been obedient and followed the calling chosen for him by his father.

We have to conclude that Crusoe's rebellion, his overthrowing the authority of the father, has its rewards within the work, and that its creation had some psychological rewards. We have no written evidence to suggest what James Foe thought of his son's life, but the chances are that the careful keeper of books for the Butchers' Company was horrified at his son's early bankruptcy and even more horrified to see him pilloried for writing seditious literature. In the *Family Instructor* of 1715, the son who revolts against his father is wounded in body and spirit and dies miserably. But in the second volume (1718), published in the year before the appearance of *Robinson Crusoe*, the villain is the father who cannot control his passions. After agreeing to surrender his business to his children, he becomes darkly suspicious of what appear to be perfectly well-intended actions, accusing them of plotting against him. He reassumes control of his affairs, only to

---

[13] *Prodigals and Pilgrims* (Cambridge: Cambridge University Press, 1982), 67–83.

relinquish his power once more when his irrepressible passions provoke him to a near-murderous outburst against one of his workmen. Although Crusoe's father is far from violent, his attempt to control the lives of his children seems to have alienated all of them. And although Crusoe's sense of guilt over his disobedience and his repentance is real enough, *Robinson Crusoe* was not a book intended to inculcate lessons of obedience in the young. Rather it was an imaginative and exciting exploration of a series of adventures which occur because Crusoe was disobedient. And the entirely satisfactory plot has him embarking upon those adventures against his father's wishes. That all should end well suggests that to the degree that Defoe identified with Robinson Crusoe, Defoe was creating a narrative in which defiance of the parents, however much guilt might be entailed in the process, could produce a relatively happy conclusion—that the father might be seen as little more than a representative of dull, conservative ideas of the past which the enterprising son must sweep aside to achieve his success. It was a fantasy which clearly had considerable emotional significance for Defoe.

That Defoe shows more than a degree of ambivalence about the conflict between father and son suggests that his fiction functioned in a different manner from his moral conduct books. One of his last pieces, *Chickens feed Capons* (1730), a revision of his *Protestant Monastery* (1726), returned to this theme with such vehemence in its denunciation of the poor treatment children give their elders that one might suspect that he had been reading *King Lear*. But aside from his personal involvement, he had to be intensely aware of how much the theme belonged to the times. On the level of royalty, conflict between sons and fathers seemed to be reaching new heights. In Britain, the Prince of Wales and King George I began to find each other's company unbearable, and the prince moved his family away from his father's court. Defoe considered this event too dangerous to write about directly, stating that he was leaving any analysis of these events to future historians, 'when our Posterity shall speak with an unrestrained liberty'.[14] It was easier to write about the conflict between Peter the Great and his son Alexei, allowing the readers to draw parallels if they wished. Defoe followed this story in his journals, and in those that pretended to a Tory or an opposition point of view, all the sympathy was for the son. Peter accused his son of leaving the country without his permission, and in so doing,

he acknowledged himself incapable and unworthy of our Succession, desiring us to discharge him of the same . . . But forgetting the Fear and Commandment of

---

[14] *Mercurius Politicus*, Jan. 1718, 5.

God, who enjoyns Obedience even to Private Parents, and much more to those who are at the same time Sovereigns, Our Cares had no other return than an unheard of ingratitude from him.[15]

Peter, accepting Alexis's supposed request that he be relieved of his rightful claim to the throne, stated that he had put his son under his 'Protection'.

Defoe remarked of these events that he believed 'no History can equal it and perhaps never may'. He reported that those who protested Peter's treatment were severely punished, including one woman who received what Defoe called the '*Potoque*', which involved being stripped naked and suffering 400 lashes.[16] Although what Western Europe considered Russian barbarism may have seemed distant enough from contemporary Britain,[17] Defoe could not resist drawing certain parallels:

Who could honestly stand up for such a Father, or pity such a Son, where irreconcileableness and Stubborness meet? Where the Father embraces all the Opportunity he can find to distress the Son, who in return not only repels his Efforts, but labours to ruin his interest by disturbing his Measures? Can anyone imagine that he can love any Person that hates his own Son? Or that such a Son can esteem, obey, honour, reverence, or be grateful to anything Human or Divine that can dash Nature out of his Constitution?[18]

Accused of plotting against his father, Alexis was rumoured to have died 'for fear of Death'—out of terror that his father would kill him. Defoe had little respect for those who succumbed to despair, and his sympathy for Alexis faded rapidly. There was some truth to the story, but Defoe apparently did not know that Alexis had been subjected to forty brutal blows by a whip called the knout which stripped ribbons of flesh from his back.[19] Whatever may have been a weakness of character in Alexis, the vividness of the struggle between father and son made a deep impression on Defoe.

At almost the same time that such family conflicts were occurring on the level of royal families, Defoe insisted upon following a story of private domestic conflict in his journals. The sons of a Quaker potter named

---

[15] *Mercurius Politicus*, Mar. 1718, 199.

[16] Ibid. Apr. 1718, 258.

[17] Saint-Simon remarked of Peter, when he visited France during May and June of 1717, that he 'was not exempt from a strong flavour of his country's past lack of culture', and that his manners were 'rough, even violent'. He was apparently entirely without interest in anything beautiful, and his eating habits were 'unseemly' by French standards. See *Historical Memoirs*, ed. and trans. Lucy Norton (New York: McGraw-Hill, 1972), ii. 121–30.

[18] *Weekly Journal*, 2 Aug. 1718, 509.

[19] See Robert Massie, *Peter the Great and His World* (New York: Knopf, 1980), 698–705. See also Defoe, *Weekly Journal*, 22 Mar. 1718, 129. Alexis was not guilty of actively leading a revolt against his father, but he did speak to his mistress Afrosina of his wishes to become czar.

William Oades apparently schemed to have their father arrested in an attempt to assume control of the family business. According to reports in the *Weekly Journal*, the sons fired a gun from a window in their home in an effort to kill their mother; they missed and hit a stranger instead. The father, rather than taking revenge in the manner of Peter the Great, actually attempted to free his sons after they had been arrested. And despite rumours that the sons might be transported to the colonies, Oades succeeded in obtaining their freedom.[20] The story of the conflict between George I and the Prince of Wales ended better than that of the Czar, though George I might have envied the brutality and barbarism of Peter's Russia. The Prince of Wales remained irritatingly alive until his father's death in 1727. As for Crusoe, he continued to believe that his disobedience was his 'original Sin' for which he was punished by being forced to remain on the island for twenty-eight years, but he succeeded in changing his prison into a paradise.

Of course, it is a paradise from which Crusoe would, at any time, flee, and at one point, when he is giving thanks to God for all the benefits He has bestowed upon him on the island, he hesitates because he knows that if the opportunity permitted, he would leave the island at once. The Crusoe of Michel Tournier's *Friday* refuses to abandon the island and remains behind as Friday goes off. But this is a very different Crusoe from Defoe's creation. Defoe's Crusoe is restless—a wanderer for whom the island is a form of prison. Crusoe longs for a companion, and obtains Friday after a dream that combines wish-fulfilment with problem-solving. But while he finds himself gnashing his teeth in longing for a human being with whom he might communicate, Crusoe is not a particularly companionate character. He tends to treat people as objects. His sale of Xury to the captain who rescues him after his flight from Sallee suggests that he does not really take much pleasure in human contact. His effort at isolating himself on a self-sufficient farm in England, after his return to his native country, implies a longing to be apart. What the island experience should demonstrate to him is that his restlessness might be put to use in the form of productive labour. What is notable, however, is his refusal to accept such labour as valuable outside a European context of monetary exchange, and his reluctance to admit that the pleasure he receives in manufacturing pots has genuine value for him in the form of creative gratification. Crusoe passes his pleasure in such work on to his readers, but in the end it hardly cures his restlessness. Friday is accepted as a servant who may give him the knowledge that work is being done even if he is resting. While he regards

[20] *Weekly Journal*, 1 Mar. 1718; and *Mercurius Britannicus*, Mar. 1918, 401.

his 'Man Friday' with some affection, Crusoe establishes a relationship with him that is essentially that between a capitalist and a worker or, more precisely, that of colonist and colonial subject. No money is exchanged, but Friday owes a debt of gratitude to Crusoe that he will be paying off throughout his life. Defoe does not create this relationship blindly. The descriptions of the two companions show Crusoe in a grotesque 'Sketch', in his shaggy goat skins and with a long Turkish mustache. Friday, on the other hand, is given a description that shows him as an almost classical figure. Although modern readers may find the insistence upon his European features and good complexion patronizing, Defoe clearly intended to contrast the grotesque, restless colonial entrepreneur with the innocent native. When Crusoe states that Friday was a 'better Christian' than he, we should not take it lightly. Defoe could hardly imagine a higher compliment.

Certainly one impulse behind *Robinson Crusoe* was a colonial enterprise. In the *Weekly Journal* of 7 February 1719, Defoe announced a new scheme for a colony at the mouth of the Orinoco River where Crusoe was to be shipwrecked. It was far from Selkirk's Juan Fernandez but better suited to Defoe's continuing interest in creating a British enclave among the Spanish and Portuguese colonies:

We expect, in two or three Days, a most flaming Proposal from the South Sea Company, or from a Body of Merchants who claim kindred of them, for erecting a British Colony on the Foundation of the South Sea Company's Charter, upon the Terra Firma, or the Northermost Side of the Mouth of the great River oroonoko. They propose, as we hear, the establishing of a Factory and Settlement there, which shall cost the Company 500000 £. Sterling, and they demand the Government to furnish six Men of War, and 4000 regular Troups, with some Engineers and 100 pieces of Cannon, and military Stores in Proportion for the maintaining and supporting the Design; for which they suggest, that the Revenue it shall bring to the Kingdom will be a full amends. it is said they will send over Workmen to build 12 Sloops with 12 Guns each, and able to carry 300 Men, which are to maintain a Commerce up the Great River to the Province or Empire of Guiana, in which they resolve to establish a new Colony also, above 400 Leagues from the first Settlement, to be always supplied with forces as well as Merchandizes from the first Settlement, and they doubt not to carry on a Trade there equal to that of the Portuguese in the Brazils, and to bring home an equal quantity of Gold, as well as to cause a prodigious Consumption of our British Manufactures. This, it seems, is the same Country and River discovered by Sir Walter Rawleigh, in former Days, and that which he miscarried in by several Mistakes, which may now easily be prevented.[21]

[21] *Weekly Journal*, 7 Feb. 1719, 56.

If, as I have argued elsewhere, *Robinson Crusoe* took its inspiration as much from Defoe's interest in expanding British colonization as it did from Selkirk's tale of isolation, this outburst of enthusiasm for the possibilities inherent in the South Sea Company might be the point of departure for any discussion.[22] *The Farther Adventures of Robinson Crusoe*, the second volume of Defoe's Crusoe trilogy, was often retitled in later editions to reflect this particular aspect of the work.

Although the notion of colonialism strikes a discordant note in the modern reader, the recent celebration of Columbus's discovery of America sounded the even more discordant note of the 'conquest' of America—a conquest carried on with a brutality matched only by the Holocaust created by Nazi Germany during the Second World War. In composing *Robinson Crusoe*, Defoe had such a distinction very much in mind. As an avid reader of all kinds of voyages, he was certainly familiar with the situations that arose during the early conquest, particularly the dehumanization of the natives, extending to a refusal to accept their languages as true human speech. After discovering the footprint of the cannibal in the sand of the island, Crusoe experiences a mixture of fear and horror. Like the Spaniards who encountered human sacrifices, Crusoe thinks that the natives deserved nothing but the most savage destruction at his hand:

I was so astonish'd with the Sight of these Things, that I entertain'd no Notions of any Danger to my self from it for a long while; All my Apprehensions were bury'd in the Thoughts of such a Pitch of Inhuman, hellish Brutality, and the Horror of the Degeneracy of Humane Nature; which though I had heard of often, yet I never had so near a View of before; in short, I turn'd away my Face from the horrid Spectacle; my Stomach grew sick, and I was just at the Point of Fainting, when Nature discharg'd the Disorder from my Stomach; and having vomited with an uncommon Violence, I was a little reliev'd; but could not bear to stay in the Place a Moment. (165)

He prepares ambushes for the cannibals and has fantasies of slaughtering twenty or thirty of them in one attack. But then he conquers his 'Thoughts of Revenge' (169) by an examination of his own motives, concluding that the massacre which he planned 'would justify the Conduct of the *Spaniards* in all their Barbarities practis'd in *America*, and where they destroy'd Millions of these People, who however they were Idolaters and Barbarians ... were yet, as to the *Spaniards* very innocent People'. Crusoe recalls that

[22] I argued this in my *Economics and the Fiction of Daniel Defoe* (Berkeley: University of California Press, 1962), 36. Although Defoe probably had nothing to do with titles describing how Crusoe 'colonised' his island, such a view was hardly the invention of twentieth-century commentators.

all the nations of Europe condemned the Spaniards for their actions as a people lacking 'Pity to the Miserable, which is reckon'd to be a Mark of generous Temper in the Mind' (172).

Writing at a time when self-interest was considered the chief motivating force in human beings, Defoe cannot allow Crusoe quite this much generosity. He contemplates the dangers involved in the kind of assault that he planned and concludes that leaving matters alone would be the wisest course. Yet self-interest is not his only motivation. The barbarity of the conquest is to be avoided at all costs. But it is clear that Crusoe sees nothing wrong with colonialism or even slavery. He dreams of rescuing some natives and making them his slaves. He feels that Friday owes him his life, and that in bestowing upon him Christianity (and thereby the possibility of eternal life) he has given Friday things for which he ought to be forever grateful. He insists that Friday learn English and that he perform many of the tasks he used to do for himself. That Defoe is aware of some of the problems inherent in colonialism is plain enough, from Friday's questioning Crusoe on the problem of evil in the system of Christianity that Crusoe has taught him to the genuine emotion displayed by Friday when he discovers that one of the prisoners rescued from the cannibals is his father. Friday seems capable of probing more deeply into the problems of religion than Crusoe, and he shows just the kind of emotion that the suspicious and alienated Crusoe cannot express. Crusoe is an exploiter of others and jealously guards his power. Friday is a being of warm and natural emotions whose gratitude toward Crusoe for rescuing him is much more engaging than Crusoe's willingness to take advantage of it.

III

In addition to so specific an event as the possibility of new British colonies in South America, a number of other events contributed to *Robinson Crusoe*, some that consciously provoked Defoe's mental powers and others that aroused his imagination. For example, the scene in which Crusoe expatiates upon the uselessness of gold on his island was as interesting to the contemporary *Journal des Scavans* as it was to Coleridge a century later.[23] Encountering the money in a drawer on the wrecked ship along with 'two or three Razors, and one Pair of large Sizzers, with some ten or a Dozen of good Knives and Forks', he is amused:

[23] See the *Journal des Scavans* (Paris, 1720), 505; and Samuel Taylor Coleridge, *Miscellaneous Criticism*, ed. Thomas Raysor (Cambridge, Mass.: Harvard University Press, 1934), 293.

I smil'd to my self at the Sight of this Money, O Drug! Said I aloud, what art thou good for, Thou art not worth to me, no not the taking off of the Ground, one of those Knives is worth all this Heap, I have no manner of use for thee, e'en remain where thou art, and go to the Bottom as a Creature whose Life is not worth saving. However, upon Second Thoughts, I took it away. (57)

As if to leave no doubt about the centrality of the situation, he repeats the scene when he finds a tobacco pipe and two pieces of eight in the pocket of a drowned boy whose body has washed ashore. Speaking of the pipe, he remarks that 'the last was to me of ten times more value than the first' (189). And when he discovers 1100 pieces of eight and some gold coins and bars on the wrecked ship on which the boy served, he spends most of his time detailing the few other useful items he discovers:

Upon the whole, I got very little by this Voyage, that was of any use to me; for as to the Money, I had no manner of occasion for it: 'Twas to me as the Dirt under my Feet; and I would have given it all for three or four pair of *English* Shoes and Stocking, which were Things I greatly wanted, but had not had on my Feet now for many Years: I had indeed gotten two pair of Shoes now, which I took off of the Feet of the two drown'd men, who I saw in the Wreck; and I found two pair more in one of the Chests, which were very welcome to me; but they were not like our *English* Shoes, either for Ease, or Service; being rather what we call Pumps than Shoes. (193)

As in the previous instance, Crusoe carries this money along with some additional money discovered back to his cave. This time he thinks specifically of the use that such money would be if he ever escaped to Europe, but he is also more oriented toward and more discriminating about use-value than he was before.[24]

Although most critics have focused upon the insight into human nature in Crusoe's inability to resist the attraction of money, some contemporaries would have recognized in the scene a reflection of a current debate over whether gold and silver money was merely a form of exchange that might be replaced by paper money or whether it had a kind of intrinsic value in itself. In Paris, John Law, who believed in paper money, had been appointed head of a new national bank,[25] and during 1718 discussions about

---

[24] John Locke had given his prestigious reputation to the notion that money, whether silver or gold, had mainly an 'imaginary value'. John Law objected to this idea, as did those who generally agreed with him. See Law, *Money and Trade Consider'd*, 2nd edn. (London, 1720), 8; and anon., *An Essay on Money and Bullion* (London, 1718), 20. Law's essay was originally published in 1705.

[25] Defoe came out strongly against Law's theory in *The Chimera: or the French Way of Paying National Debts* (London, 1720), predicting (76) the terrible collapse that would follow his policies. Though he admired some of Law's efforts to create a fund of credit, he argued that eventually there would be a run on the bank.

regulating British coinage resembled the debates of the 1690s, the last time coins had been called in and new coins issued.[26] In *Robinson Crusoe* Defoe seems to come out on the side of those who, like John Locke, recognized that, although money was mainly a neutral form of exchange, it was useful insofar as it had a value in itself—a value, however, that did not extend to a world such as Crusoe's island.[27] On the other hand, in the real world wealth, with all the power it could command, was anything but imaginary. Confronted by the wealth that he has accumulated from his plantations in Brazil, Crusoe experiences a rush of emotion that almost kills him. 'In a Word,' writes Crusoe, 'I turned pale, and grew sick; and had not the old Man run and fetch'd me a Cordial, I believe the sudden Surprize of Joy had overset Nature, and I had dy'd upon the Spot' (285). Just as Crusoe can be an absolute monarch only when he is alone on his island and ruling over his parrot, dog, cat, and goats, so he can express contempt for monetary wealth only when value upon his island depends entirely on the use and the pleasure that he receives from the objects he gathers around him and creates through his labour.

The crucial word here is 'pleasure'. In the gospel according to Milton, Adam and Eve are capable of finding pleasure in all of their activities, from sex to tending the crops that grow naturally in the Garden of Eden. Their expulsion and the curse placed upon mankind for their transgression condemns them and their descendants to tedious work on the land. Although he labours hard during his time on the island, beginning with his looting from the wreck everything useful for his survival and comfort, Crusoe's island is truly Edenic. What Marx said of his religious exercises, that they constituted a form of recreation, may in part be said of Crusoe's labours.[28] Marx has Crusoe using his diary as a form of ledger to record the quantity of time he puts in on his various projects, but since the ocean alone would be able to supply all of his wants, even without the guns and ammunition he has from the wreck, his labour too is mainly a form of recreation. The time he logs in perfecting himself as a potter, inventing a proper clasp for his

[26] Defoe mentioned an early phase of the debate when it was thought that too many silver coins were being exchanged for the guinea. On 22 Dec. 1717 King George ordered his 'Loving Subjects . . . upon Pain of highest Displeasure' to lower the amount of shillings paid for the guinea by six pence. See Defoe, *A History of the Last Session of the Present Parliament* (London, 1718), 57–9.

[27] In his *Tour*, Defoe described the cycle of labour and reward as 'sweet', in contrast with the cycle of poverty that produced indolence. In this, he is very much part of the new consumption society that was to dominate the eighteenth and later centuries. 'People tell us', he wrote, 'that slothfulness begets poverty, and it is true; but I must add too, that poverty makes slothfulness.' On Crusoe's island, useful labour produces an almost instantaneous gratification. See *Tour*, ii. 734–5.

[28] Karl Marx, *Capital*, trans. Samuel Moore and Edward Aveling (London: Glaisher, 1949), 47–50. For my critique of Marx's analysis of Crusoe's use of time in connection with the labour theory of value, see my *Economics and the Fiction of Daniel Defoe*, 58.

umbrella, and attempting to manufacture a form of beer is actually equivalent to a modern man or woman taking a class in some craft. In having his
protagonist recapitulate the development of crafts in society, Defoe makes
him into a character involved in recapturing, for each individual, tasks
which had long ago been assigned to the artisans and tradesmen who
peopled the streets of London.[29]

How much genuine use-value these products have is difficult to say.
Crusoe discovers all kinds of fruit, and the seeds of grain from the ship
eventually provide him with his bread. The convenient flock of goats
afford an ample supply of meat. Before the coming of the cannibals, he is
able to enjoy his 'country house' in the beautiful vale, his grotto, and his
'castle'. In his imagination, he lives the life of a country gentleman,
involved with his crops and cattle but also capable of relaxing and enjoying
the pleasures of nature. The discovery of the cannibals reveals the degree
to which the island is not an Eden; but before that moment, and afterwards
with Friday as his companion, Crusoe actively enjoys his life. As Gonzalo's
contemplation of an island utopia in Shakespeare's *The Tempest* suggests,
islands had long been considered scenes for speculation on ideal existence.
But Crusoe's island is no allegory for Eden, and a utopia only in a very
practical sense. This is *our* island—the perfect Caribbean spot for a
vacation. As Pierre Bachelard remarked in quoting Van Gogh, all of us
should 'retain something of the original character of a Robinson Crusoe.
Make and remake everything oneself, make a "supplementary gesture"
toward each object, give another facet to the polished reflections, all of
which are so many boons the imagination confers upon us.'[30] Crusoe's
island is the vacation world in which we rediscover ourselves by getting to
see the world around us—its things, its objects—in a new way. Just as it
provided Crusoe with an enforced escape from his commercial ventures, so
it is for us. Of course not many of us take twenty-eight-year vacations.
Crusoe's island provides fiction with a wonderfully viable daydream. 'A
dreamer of refuges dreams of a hut, or a nest, or of nooks and corners in
which he would like to hide away like an animal in his hole,' wrote
Bachelard. Doubtless this daydream existed long before *Robinson Crusoe*,

[29] Ian Watt (*The Rise of the Novel* (Berkeley: University of California Press, 1957), 44–9) was the first
to suggest the connection between Crusoe's task on the island and a London in which people shopped for
bread rather than bake it themselves. Watt, however, does not treat the question of audience interest in
Robinson Crusoe at this point in his work. Since many of the tasks undertaken by Crusoe—cooking,
making clothes, arranging his supplies—were jobs usually performed by women, it may be that this part
of Defoe's fiction had as much appeal for women as the adventurous part had for men. For a modern
example of a fiction in which a woman forms her life around the Crusoe experience, see Jane Gardam,
Crusoe's Daughter (New York; Athenaeum, 1986).

[30] Pierre Bachelard, *The Poetics of Space*, trans. Maria Jolas (Boston: Beacon Press, 1970), 69–70.

but Defoe imagined it for us, and through his art was able to move it from daydream to realist fiction of a kind never seen before.[31]

A central element of the real involved economic concerns. The financial speculation that began in 1718 and 1719 and culminated in the South Sea Bubble gave Defoe a unique view into a world dominated entirely by avarice. On one front he attacked those who were speculating in stocks and on the other he defended the 'poor' weavers of Spitalfields who were being deprived of their livelihood by the importation of cotton goods. The great villain in this drama was the East India Company, guilty in Defoe's eyes of exporting bullion to the East without benefiting Great Britain. Although his battle against what he saw as corporate avarice followed the publication of the first volume of *Robinson Crusoe*, the ideas were clearly already in his mind in the spring of 1719, and the subsequent volumes of the trilogy repeat this theme even more emphatically. *The Anatomy of Exchange Alley*, ostensibly written 'by a Jobber' and published on 1 July 1719, has much in common with a tract he published eighteen years earlier, *The Villainy of Stock-Jobbers Detected*. But in the intervening years Defoe's arsenal of weapons had expanded greatly, particularly his skill at dialogue.

The 'Jobber' begins by predicting that the government will eventually be forced to abolish the entire system of buying and selling stocks, but then notes that the government itself is so much involved that if they set out to 'hang the Stock-Jobbers, . . . they will be apt to hang themselves'.[32] Defoe knew well enough that the King himself had become an honorary officer in the South Sea Company, and that the Company's willingness to accept the debts of the nation meant that this predatory body had become part of the national economic system. He depicts the gulling of a 'landed gentleman' by these men who willingly admit that their business is 'founded in Fraud, born of Deceit, and nourished by Trick, Cheat, Wheedle, Forgeries, Falshoods, and all sorts of Delusions'. The landed gentleman loses enough to enrich this gang of swindlers. Afterwards he engages in a comparison between the honest thief and such men:

Have I not heard *T.W.B.O.* and *J.S.* a thousand times say they know their Employment was a Branch of Highway robbing, and only differ'd in two things, *First in Degree, (viz.)* that it was ten Thousand times worse, more remorseless, more void of Humanity, done without Necessity, and committed upon Fathers,

[31] Bachelard, *The Poetics of Space*, 32. Although tourism in Defoe's day was more or less limited to the Grand Tour through Europe, Defoe saw the possibilities of tourism as a source of pleasure. His suggestion about touring through the Highlands with the use of a military tent comes many years before Boswell and Johnson made such travel popular. See Defoe, *A Tour thro' the Whole Island of Great Britain* (London: Dent, Everyman edn.), 417–18.

[32] Defoe, *The Villainy of Stock-Jobbers Detected* (London, 1719), 2.

Brothers, Widows, Orphans, and intimate Friends, in all which Cases Highwaymen, generally touch'd with Remorse, and affected with Principles of Humanity
and Generosity, stop short and choose to prey upon Strangers only. *Secondly in
Danger, (viz.)* that these rob securely; the other, with the utmost Risque that the
Highwaymen run, whereas these rob only at the Hazard of their Lives, being sure
to be hang'd first or last, whereas these rob only at the Hazard of their Reputation
which is generally lost before they begin, and of their Souls, which Trifle is not
worth the mentioning.[33]

Defoe had written much the same thing often enough in the *Review*, but
outrage at what Michel Foucault called the 'illegality of rights'—the notion
that the 'white-collar criminal' had to be treated more leniently than those
whose crimes might arise from poverty—had increased during these
years.[34] Though he concealed Sir Josiah Child, one of England's leading
merchants during the Restoration, in the initials Sir J----- C----, no one
could have mistaken the target of his attack on the man he called the
'Original of Stock-Jobbing'. In describing how Child would deliberately
float false rumours to deflate or raise the price of stocks, Defoe made continual comparisons to whores and thieves. He concluded with the notion
that 'the encroaching Nature of Immortal Avarice' might lead men of this
kind to sell their own country for a percentage of the profit. Defoe argued
that, although such men were capable of bringing a disaster upon the
nation, they would destroy themselves in the process and that, like the
visitation of a plague or any other 'common Calamity', such an event,
terrible as it would be, might ultimately restore the nation to its moral and
spiritual unity.[35]

The connection between financial disaster and plague would stick in
Defoe's mind when he was to write about the terrible plague in southern
France that threatened to spread to England. But during 1719, perhaps
because of certain thoughts left over from the first volume of *Robinson
Crusoe*, he was more concerned with the ways in which individuals and a
society tended to behave during and immediately after periods of stress. A
major element of stress during 1719 and 1720 were the riots by the weavers
against those wearing cotton clothing imported by the East India
Company. Considering the animus that Defoe vented against someone
who was so important a figure in the East India Company as Sir Josiah
Child in *The Anatomy of Exchange Alley*, it is hardly surprising that
his sympathies lay with the weavers. He was placed in the position of

[33] Defoe, *The Villainy of Stock-Jobbers Detected*, 8.
[34] Michel Foucault, *Discipline and Punish*, trans. Alan Sheridan (New York: Vintage Books, 1979), 87.
[35] Ibid. 54, 55, 60.

defending mob violence, since the rioters sometimes tore the clothes off women wearing the offending material. In pamphlets such as *The Just Complaint of the Poor Weavers Represented*, published on 11 August 1719 and in his new journal, *The Manufacturer*, which first appeared on 30 October of that year, Defoe argued that the poor could not be starved for the good of wealthy and powerful business interests. While stating his dislike of mobs, he nonetheless argued that the nation ought to regard those arrested as 'Objects of our Pity'.[36] Elsewhere, in *A Brief State of the Question between the Printed and Painted Callicoes and the Woolen and Silk Manufacture*, he contended that the wellbeing of the worker was the chief interest of the state, and that he had no objection to a new product if the 'Employment can be lost and the Workman not suffer'.[37] It is significant that at the end of this pamphlet he was once more reminded of the national stress caused by the plague.

Of all the works Defoe composed in close temporal juxtaposition to the three volumes of *Robinson Crusoe*, however, *The Manufacturer* comes closest to revealing his mindset. The title, of course has none of the resonance that it has in American English, where it describes a factory owner; indeed, at this time it may have had the clear implication of someone who works with his hands. As such, the journal seemed to announce itself, in much the same manner as Defoe's 'Poor Man's Plea' of 1698, as being the voice of the lower orders—a voice that had scarcely been heard in England since the time of the Levellers. Unfortunately, whatever shock value the title had was dissipated in Defoe's relatively conservative economic stance. Although he insisted that any economic force that caused permanent unemployment was bad and had to be removed, he held to a standard mercantilist position on the power of foreign trade to enrich a nation compared to the power of circulation merely to distribute that wealth. The important point, however, was that importing calicoes was ruining the woollen manufacture upon which the nation depended, and that it was being done for no other purpose than to enrich the East India Company. He took on the women who felt they had the right to follow fashion even at the cost of driving workmen into poverty, and he mounted a defence of a weaver who was sentenced to transportation for, as Defoe

[36] *The Just Complaint of the Poor Weavers Represented* (London, 1719), 5. Defoe was arguing against writers such as the author of *A Further Examination of the Weaver's Pretences* (London, 1719), who described the weavers as 'an insatiable sort of people' whose poverty should concern no one.

[37] (London, 1719). In *The Trade to India Critically and Calmly Consider'd*, published in Feb. the following year, Defoe expanded the target of his attack by claiming that all of Europe was being ruined by 'Gaiety and Trifles' imported from the East, amd that the rise of unemployment throughout England and the Continent had been caused by the East India Company. Like the former tract and *The Manufacturer*, this was printed by Boreham.

remarked, 'pulling a *Callicoe* Madam by the Elbow'. Fortunately for Defoe, who was quickly exposed as the author, this time he was on the winning side.[38]

Although Parliament recessed without deciding on a prohibition, it was obvious that matters were moving in that direction. Defoe took the waiting period to amuse his readers by writing an intriguing series of numbers on the variety of manufactures in society, including a few on the writer as a manufacturer and writing as a branch of British industry. I have quoted this before as an example of what was Defoe's possible use of a workshop of writers to block out material, but what I want to stress here is his sense of writing as an employment in which 'Allegories, Allusions, Quirks, Punns, Connundrums' are to be considered materials to be used by the writer in his work.[39] Defoe was jesting to a certain extent, yet when he speaks of his intention for the future to comment more broadly on subjects—'whether I talk of Peace or War, Trade, Law, Politicks, or Religion, 'tis all Weaving still'—he is using the word in the sense that we speak of a 'weaver of tales'. For all his jesting, Defoe is announcing with some degree of ironic reticence that writing is his trade.

IV

The *Farther Adventures of Robinson Crusoe* was published on 20 August 1719, approximately four months after the appearance of the first volume. Defoe had ended his work with an outline of the various events that Crusoe experienced after his return to England, including his marriage, the death of his wife, his return to the island with his nephew, a ship's captain, an account of how the inhabitants of the island fared since his departure, and the statement, 'All these things, with some very surprizing Incidents in some New Adventures of my own, for ten Years more, I may perhaps give a farther Account hereafter'. Defoe sometimes ended his works of fiction with the possibility of a sequel, but this is the only time that he was to give so thorough a projection of how he might proceed.[40] It suggests that he was already at work on the sequel before the original was printed. He was shrewd enough to realize just how remarkable his achievement had been, and while he probably had not grasped that he had written a work that

[38] For the quotation in the previous sentence, see *The Manufacturer* 84 (23 Feb. 1720), in the facsimile edn. with an introduction by Robert Gosselink (Delmar, NY: Scholars' Facsimiles and Reprints, 1978).

[39] *The Manufacturer* 44 (18 May 1720).

[40] For example, the preface to *Moll Flanders* ends with the possibility of an account from the point of view of her husband but gives few details.

would rapidly spread beyond the shores of Britain to most of the nations of Europe, he must have realized that if the world did not really need another volume of *Letters of a Turkish Spy*, it might be willing to pay for additional adventures of his unique hero.

If the first volume was influenced by the religious quarrels among the Dissenters, the war with Spain, and the prospect of new colonies, so the discontent in Britain seems to lend a kind of impetus to *The Farther Adventures*. Whereas at the end of the first volume the explanation for why he decides to continue his roving life is laid upon the persuasions of his nephew, the restlessness that he once described as his 'Original Sin', and curiosity about what happened to the inhabitants of his island, a new rationale is added at the beginning of *The Farther Adventures* in the form of a criticism of British society. True enough, Crusoe's longing to return to his island becomes a kind of obsession. It seizes his imagination to the extent that he has waking visions of being on the island and talking to the Spaniard and Friday's father, visions so real that they have at least the sub-stantiality of apparitions. Crusoe's visions appear to be driven by a longing for a particular kind of delight rather than anxiety. It is for this reason, probably, that he is able to control his imagination after his wife offers to embark with him on his voyage. 'I struggled with the Power of my Imagination,' he writes, 'and reason'd myself out of it.' By way of subli-mating his 'wandring Fancy', Crusoe attempts to duplicate the life he experienced on his island through the purchase of a farm in Bedford:

I farm'd upon my own Land; I had no Rent to pay, was limited by no Articles; I could pull up or cut down as I pleased; what I planted was for myself, and what I improved was for my Family; and having thus left off the thoughts of Wandring, I had not the least Discomfort in any Part of Life, as to this World. Now I thought indeed, that I enjoy'd the middle State of Life, that my Father so earnestly recom-mended to me, and liv'd a kind of heavenly Life, something like what is described by the Poet upon the Subject of a Country Life.

> Free from Vices, free from Care,
> Age has no Pain, and Youth no Snare.[41]

His attempt to become 'a meer Country Gentleman' (ii. 16) re-enacts the fanciful version of his life on the island, and indeed Crusoe's farm exists as a kind of economic island. That Defoe was to purchase the land in Col-chester in 1722 partly for its possibilities for manufacturing bricks but also

---

[41] *The Farther Adventures of Robinson Crusoe*, in *Robinson Crusoe* (3 vols.), included in *Shakespeare Head Edition*, ii. 115–16. All subsequent citations of this work will refer to this edition, with page numbers included in parentheses within my text.

for farming suggests that this dream of an existence independent of the hurry of commerce in a world suddenly dominated by the South Sea Company's expansion was as much a part of Defoe's daydreams as it was of Crusoe's. The paradisical idea of the country in the song of the Restoration composer Thomas Hart echoes in Crusoe's utopian depiction of his farm.[42]

But everything changes with the death of his wife, and Crusoe's elegy to her has to echo Defoe's feeling for his wife, Mary. In a metaphoric sense, Mary too had been willing to embark with him on his many voyages. Though he says he will not indulge in the 'Flattery of a funeral sermon', what he says is moving enough:

She was, in a few Words, the Stay of all my Affairs, the Center of all my Enterprizes, the Engine that, by her Prudence, reduc'd me to that happy Compass I was in, from the most extravagant and ruinous Project that fluttered in my Head, as above; and did more to guide my rambling Genius than a Mother's Tears, a Father's Instructions, a Friend's Counsel, or all my own reasoning Powers could do. I was happy in listening to her Tears, and in being mov'd by her Entreaties, and to the last Degree desolate and dislocated in the World by the loss of her. (ii. 117)

This vision of what Crusoe feels after the death of his wife is a projection of what Defoe conceives that his life would be without Mary, and echoes what he wrote a decade earlier about the importance of family for sustaining a degree of sanity.[43]

Without his wife, Crusoe experiences an intense sense of isolation, and the feeling of anomie which strikes him is exacerbated by a powerful alienation from the economic and social experience of British society:

When she was gone, the World look'd aukwardly round me; I was as much a Stranger in it as I was in the *Brasils*, when I went first on Shore there; and as much alone, except as to the Assistance of Servants, as I was on my Island. I knew neither what to do, or what not to do. I saw the World busy round me, one Part labouring for Bread, and the other Part squandring in vile Excesses or empty Pleasures, equally miserable, because the End they propos'd still fled from them; for the Man of Pleasure every Day surfeited of his Vice, and heaped up Work for Sorrow and Repentance; and the Men of labour spent their Strength in daily Strugglings for Bread to maintain the vital Strength they labour'd with, so living in a daily Circulation of Sorrow, living but to work, and working but to live, as if daily Bread were the only End of wearisome Life, and a wearisome Life the only Occasion of daily Bread.

---

[42] For a discussion of the source of this quotation, see my 'Crusoe and the Country Life', *N&Q* 237 (1992), 48–52.

[43] See Defoe's *A Condoling Letter to the Tatler* (London, 1710), 14.

This put me in Mind of the Life I liv'd in my Kingdom, the Island; where I suffer'd no more Corn to grow, because I did not want it; and bred no more Goats, because I had no more Use for them: Where the Money lay in the Drawer 'till it grew mouldy, and had scarce the Favour to be look'd upon in 20 Years. (ii. 117–18)

Crusoe draws his moral against a background of an England that was increasingly indulging in excess, luxury, and display. He had already rejected the idea of spending his time in attempting to increase his wealth beyond what he considered reasonable, eschewing 'Servants, Equipage, Gayety, and *the like*' as 'Things . . . [he] had no Notion of, or Inclination to' (ii. 112). But what is even more striking than the vision of excessive expense is the implication that such excess has been purchased through exploiting the poor and forcing them to live in a cycle of subsistence labour. There is a clear implication that the newly elegant and luxurious Britain had been built on the backs of the labouring poor. Defoe had always allowed considerable dignity to men and women willing to work hard. The contemporary England he depicts is one in which the drones in the hive have managed to achieve too much power. In Crusoe's mind, the island has become a utopia in which money was useless and overproduction folly.

Somewhere in Defoe's mind was the sense that a commodity culture was beginning to obscure genuine feelings and needs. He was far from conceiving of a society such as ours, concerning which writers such as Jean Baudrillard, have argued that reality has been replaced by hyperreality and that use-value (as Marx conceived of it) has disappeared, but it would be a mistake to underestimate the degree to which Defoe experienced the shock of change during his sixty years. The dynamics of the rise and fall of the South Sea Company and comparable institutions in Europe produced hysterical outbursts of greed, elation, and despair and had a dramatic impact upon the life of the time. In part, *The Farther Adventures* attempts to represent what human needs really were. That Crusoe once more sets sail at the beginning of January 1695 may even have some autobiographical significance, for this was approximately the time that Defoe ventured into some kind of role in the government apparatus of William III. But what Crusoe encounters in his first adventure is a scene of desperate thirst and starvation, of existence at the limit of human endurance. First Crusoe's ship encounters the crew of a ship that had caught fire. The ship had been successfully abandoned and the passengers and crew were in boats, but all knew that their chances of arriving at Newfoundland were slight. As a result, their joy at this rescue has the effect of temporary madness. Crusoe describes how they were thrown into Extasies and a kind of Frenzy, and it was but a very few that were compos'd and serious in their Joy. . . . A Man that we saw this Minute dumb, and as it were stupid and confounded, should the next Minute be dancing and hallowing like an Antick; and the next Moment be tearing his Hair, or pulling his Clothes to Pieces, and stamping them under his Feet, like a mad Man; a few Moments after that, we should have him all in Tears, then sick, then swooning, and had no immediate Help been had, would, in a few Moments more have been dead. (ii. 128–9)

Thus he finds that the simple recovery of life after hope had been abandoned produced emotional outpourings of a kind that exceeded even Friday's joy at the discovery of his father. Crusoe, whose author may have been thinking of the French Prophets, explains that the crew was French and that it was a nation that tended to be more expressive than the British. The focus, however, is upon what Defoe considers a *normal* psychological response to the turn from dread to joy, and while the modern reader probably finds Defoe's preoccupation with the external appearance of those rescued somewhat strange, his message is apparent enough. This is real emotion operating in a real situation.

Soon after they send these people safely back to Canada, Crusoe and his nephew encounter a ship adrift after an encounter with a hurricane. The crew and particularly the three passengers are close to starvation and have to be forcibly restrained from grasping the food before it is properly cooked, though Crusoe and his nephew attempt to prevent the sickness that would occur from such unrestrained eating. The passengers, a mother, her son, and a maid, are close to death. When their lives were threatened, the crew followed the sure road of self-preservation and saved the food for themselves. The mother dies that night, and saving the son and the maid is not easy. The vivid description of the maid's agonized posture, 'like one that had fallen down with an Apoplexy and struggled for Life' (ii. 140), vividly enforces the idea that Defoe wants to impress upon the reader— that real suffering from forces such as hunger and fire is part of human experience. The son regards the members of the crew as murderers of his mother, and Crusoe agrees to the extent that they might have saved her life by sparing her some food. 'But Hunger', writes Crusoe, 'knows no Friend, no Relation, no Justice, no Right, and therefore is remorseless, and capable of no Compassion' (ii. 142). Throughout these early scenes Crusoe's own compassion, earned by his sufferings on the island, is contrasted with his nephew's willingness to take financial advantage of the crew of the burning ship. The nephew is not evil in any respect, but as an ordinary self-interested merchant he stands in contrast to this somewhat new and wiser

Crusoe, who will act as an observer of and commentator on human weakness.

Defoe continues to exploit this established pattern throughout *The Farther Adventures*. When he arrives at the island, Crusoe listens more or less passively to the account of the quarrels between the marooned English mutineers and the Spaniards. If the account functions as an allegory for the ways in which a people come together as a nation under the threat of external invasion,[44] it also serves to suggest that Britain itself, divided among Anglicans and Dissenters, defenders of Bishop Hoadly and his detractors, the signers of the pledge of belief in the Trinity and the non-subscribers, Whig and Tory, Whigs in power and Whigs out of power, followers of George I and followers of the Prince of Wales, wealthy stock speculators and impoverished workers, women who insisted on wearing printed calicoes and weavers who saw them as a threat to their livelihood, might unite if faced by a terrible enemy from the outside. Certainly Will Atkins and the two other Englishmen are, at first, as thoroughly unreconcilable to living in peace with the Spaniards as any of the groups who refused to heal the divisions in Britain. Indeed, they are willing to murder or enslave all the others on the island, and only the mercy of the Spanish Captain saves their lives. The enemy need not be something as literal as a boatload of cannibals. Even something as insubstantial as a plague would serve just as well.

But on Crusoe's island, nothing works quite so well as the prospect of being devoured by the cannibals. If Crusoe's preoccupation with such a fate seems to evoke psychological nightmare rather than reality, Defoe expands upon the theme as wave after wave of savages invade the island. After one victory, the Spanish captain describes the horror that such a fate evokes:

This Deliverance tam'd our *English* Men for a great while; the Sight had fill'd them with Horror, and the Consequences appear'd terrible to the last Degree, even to them, if ever they should fall into the Hands of those Creatures, who would not only kill them as Enemies, but kill them for Food, as we kill our Cattle. And they profess'd to me, that the Thoughts of being eaten up like Beef or Mutton, tho' it was suppos'd it was not to be till they were dead, had something in it so horrible, that it nauseated their very Stomachs, made them sick when they thought of it, and fill'd their Minds with such unusual Terror, that they were not themselves for some Weeks after. (ii. 171)

[44] This theme becomes even more explicit in the *Farther Adventures*. When Will Atkins and his two brutal companions set up places to live separated from that of the Castle and the two other Englishmen, Crusoe speaks of them as three separate 'Towns'.

The fear of being devoured encourages the inhabitants of the island to fight courageously, and none more so than the most untameable among the English mutineers, Will Atkins. Thus society may find the true warrior a nuisance in peacetime but invaluable during a period of war. And it is as a colonial war that the battle against the cannibals must be seen. After killing 180 of the 250 invaders, the victors regard the scene of battle with the sadness of any soldiers after a battle in Europe. On viewing those wounded beyond help, the Spanish captain remarks that it was 'a Sight disagreeable enough to generous Minds; for a truly great man, tho' obliged by the Law of Battle to destroy his Enemy, takes no Delight in his Misery' (ii. 211). The vocabulary chosen tends to elevate this skirmish to what might have been a scene after the battle of Blenheim. This extensive section on the war against the cannibals served as a preparation for Defoe's treatment of warfare in *Memoirs of a Cavalier* and *Colonel Jack*.

Significantly enough, for a work tending to a spirit of reconciliation, thirty-seven of the savages who survive the major battle are eventually welcomed into the colony after agreeing to live in peace with the other inhabitants. They are given a section of the island and remain as more or less permanent inhabitants. If Crusoe could jest about the toleration of pagan, Protestant, and Catholic on his island when Friday's father was the lone pagan, toleration now functions truly as the Christians become the minority. Perhaps the most surprising moment of reconciliation comes when Crusoe agrees to allow the young priest on the island to minister to the needs of the inhabitants. For the most part, Defoe's anti-Catholic attitudes remained a consistent element in his thinking throughout his life, but during the brief interval during which the Crusoe volumes were written, Defoe seemed to favour even the hated Catholic Church as an antidote to atheism and paganism. Admittedly the creed of the young priest exhibits the kind of generalized Christianity that later informed Jean-Jacques Rousseau's Savoyard vicar, but to have Crusoe accepting so broad a faith suggests what may have represented a shift in Defoe's thinking during the last decade of his life. Sinister as the Catholic Church remained in his mind, he came to believe that the real enemies of Christianity were those who denied all belief in spirit and spirituality, or believed in some grotesque and demonic god whose powers seem inspired by the forces of Satan.

The Crusoe we observe in *The Farther Adventures*, then, is not a different personality but rather a person who has been transformed by his experiences into someone more tolerant and accepting than the young slave trader who had been cast on the seemingly deserted island. The same may be said for Crusoe's creator. Though he could still strike a rigid and self-righteous position when the occasion arose, he had moved far from the prim and puritanical young man who had recorded his favourite stories for his future wife in *Historical Collections*. As he voyages to the East, Crusoe objects strenuously to the cruelty shown by the ship's crew toward the natives. The crew members shoot them and pour boiling oil on them for their amusement. Refusing to remain silent in the face of such barbarism, he earns, as his reward, the hatred of the mutinous crew and is put on shore. Of course, neither Crusoe nor his creator idealized what they considered to be barbaric about the pagan world. As he travels to China, Crusoe expresses contempt for a civilization that many of his contemporaries had idealized, and he insists on blowing up a pagan idol worshipped by the Tartars because he considers it a representation of evil. Still, the Crusoe of the *Farther Adventures*, while still capable of impulsiveness and excess, which is part of his character, is for the most part a wise and moderate figure.

V

Serious Reflections of Robinson Crusoe appeared on 6 August 1720, and except for the opening discussion in which Crusoe laid his claim for his work as a realist allegory, it has never been either widely read or discussed. The first two parts were often printed together; this third volume was ignored from the start. The first two volumes were successful because they rendered all events through exciting narratives and captured the fascination for narrative that was to make prose fiction a respectable mode during the century. The last volume was a series of essays followed by a 'Vision of the Angelick World', but while even contemporaries considered this work to be a direct statement by the author, Defoe never drops his Crusoe mask. Without denying that there is much of Defoe in the work, these essays have to be regarded as part of the Crusoe fiction. They are imbued with the character of toleration and moderation that Crusoe has earned through his personal sufferings. From this standpoint, Crusoe's comments on honesty may have greater force coming from someone who has lived long in contact with nature. This experience entitles him to argue the position of the natural law philosophers on the artificial nature of laws against poverty-induced theft far better than if such observations came from so infamous a writer as Daniel Defoe.

There is some preparation for the vision Crusoe experiences at the end, partly in his concern with dreams and impulses and partly in the remarks of one of the Spaniards to his captain when he learns that his leader had been moved by some unnamed anxiety just before the discovery of the Cannibals:

Well, says the *Spaniard*, there is something in it, I am persuaded from my own Experience; I am satisfied our Spirits embodied have a Converse with, and receive Intelligence from the Spirits unembodied and inhabiting the invisible World, and this friendly Notice is given for our Advantage, if we know how to make Use of it. (ii. 166)

But a more likely inspiration might have been the reading that Defoe had done in *Letters of a Turkish Spy* when he was preparing his *Continuation* of that work. In a letter dated 6 November 1682, Mahmut says that he is no longer interested in exciting his imagination by observing the ghosts in the pyramids but needs some more expansive experience. He imagines himself on a 'ramble through an infinite Space' in which he would encounter the 'Essence of all Beings', and he conceives of himself flying through the skies to investigate the comets. This letter ends with a vision of God as the supreme creator:

Oh God! thy Praises are without Beginning or End: Thou art an Eternal Circle of Wonders and Miracles. Thou surpassest all our Sublimest Thoughts; no Words can Decypher the Skirts of thy Garment. On thee Infinite worlds have rested from Eternal Ages. Thou art no Niggard of thy Gifts.[45]

Defoe, who was occasionally willing to reveal himself an admirer of religious enthusiasm, began at about this time to show special concern about asserting the existence of spiritual force and spirits in the face of attacks by deists and heretics such as Toland and Collins.

The tone of Crusoe's 'vision' begins with solemn attestation to the existence of a world of invisible spirits all about us. It is to them that we owe those impulses of good or evil in the world, and we would do well to trust them. Yet despite this solemnity Defoe has Crusoe indulge occasionally in the kind of half-serious, half-bantering treatment of the supernatural that he was to adopt in *The Political History of the Devil* six years later. When it comes to picturing heaven, Crusoe insists that we are only capable of conceiving of this state in terms that we know. Hence the image of palaces of gold and gems are to be taken merely as an example of the limitations placed upon human knowledge. 'We can form no idea of anything that we know not and have not seen but in the form of something

---

[45] Giovanni Paolo Marana et al., *Letters Written by a Turkish Spy* (8 vols., London, 1723), viii. 30–2.

that we have seen.' The context for such a judgement was essentially Locke's discussion of our ideas of God and of spirits as being limited by the nature of the mind.[46] Although writers could see elements of religious 'Paradoxe' in Crusoe's 'Vision', Defoe's protagonist differed little from most of his contemporaries.[47] For most traditional Christian believers, God's presence in the world was hidden but knowable—knowable to all who were capable of reading the signs of His providence in the nature which He had created.[48] To such believers the signs of his presence were everywhere. Not everyone would have been comfortable with Crusoe's visionary mental flight, but for Defoe, his hero was a traditional Christian in a world that suddenly seemed replete with atheists and deists.

[46] John Locke, *An Essay concerning Human Understanding*, ed. Alexander Fraser (2 vols., Oxford: Clarendon Press, 1894: repr. New York: Dover, 1959), i. 415–23 (bk. ii, ch. 23).

[47] See Le Clerc, *Bibliotheque ancienne et moderne*, xv. 440.

[48] See Douglas Patey, *Probability and Literary Form* (Cambridge: Cambridge University Press, 1984).

24

After *Crusoe*: Pirate Adventures, Military Memoirs and the South Sea Scandal

The success of *Robinson Crusoe* did not appear to change Defoe's reputation very much with his fellow authors. Alexander Pope's private comment to Joseph Spence to the effect that it was 'good' and that 'there was something good in all he has writ' did not transform his public stance.[1] In *The Dunciad*, Defoe was to appear in the pillory once more as a shameless journalist, and in an anonymous tract, published in 1720, depicting a contest for the Laureateship before the Goddess of Ignorance, he is made to lay claim to the position on the grounds that he has advanced the Goddess's cause more than anyone:

I take it great Goddess, that Ignorance here is the chief Claim, and in that I think I have as great a Right as any Author this Nation ever beheld: Let me add, that my Ignorance has found the greatest Success, Hundreds of Volumes have I printed, both in Prose and Rhime, which have been greedily swallow'd, not only in *England, Scotland* and *Ireland*; but even as far as the *East* and *West-Indies*: The Gentleman who spoke last [Sir Richard Steele] indeed has had good Luck in some Penny Papers, but when did he venture upon such volumes as *Jure Divino*, and *Robinson Crusoe*? Which my very Enemies own to be extraordinary Triumphs of Ignorance, there is still this difference between the Knight and my self that he seems to deserve a Suspicion of some Knowledge . . . whereas, I without either *Free-School* or *House Learning*, started from my *Stocking-Shop*, and in a Trice became a Voluminous, and taking Author.[2]

---

[1] Spence, *Observations, Anecdotes and Characters of Books and Men*, ed. James Osborn (2 vols., Oxford: Clarendon Press, 1966), i. 213 (item 498).

[2] *The Battle of the Authors Lately Fought in Covent-Garden, between Sir John Edgar, Generalisimo on One Side, and Horatius Truewit on the Other* (London, 1720), 14–15.

Charles Gildon had written sarcastically about Defoe's description of Crusoe's education, and he is a likely candidate for this tract, which sentences Defoe to limit his writing to newspapers. Prose fiction was not yet a respectable genre, and Gildon had already expressed his contempt for *Robinson Crusoe*.

Yet this tract tells us something about the envy with which Defoe's success among the reading public was greeted.[3] He is described as entering 'with a Pertness, Self-conceit, and over-weaning sufficiency in his Countenance' suggestive of his sense of his own talents, and as being accompanied by the booksellers and printers responsible for producing his works. In short, Defoe is presented as the leading figure in the rise of a publishing industry that was interested in making money off books and eager to appeal to as wide an audience as possible. Although the commercial aspects of publishing are hardly shocking to us, Pope was to hold the printers and publishers up for ridicule in *The Dunciad* for issuing trash and failing to disseminate works of the highest levels of art and learning. That Pope was to manoeuvre the press in a manner at least as expert as Defoe's was something known to his contemporaries but mostly forgotten or ignored by the admirers of Pope's poetic pyrotechnics in *The Dunciad*. Defoe, who was the master hand behind seven or eight newspapers, at the time of *The Battle of the Authors Lately Fought in Covent-Garden*, probably resented this attack bitterly, as he always did, but he could certainly afford to be amused by it.

One change that occurred in publishing at this time was the development of congers, or groups of publishers who would join together on various publishing ventures. Taylor published *Robinson Crusoe* by himself, but some six years after his death his name appeared as 'the Executors of William Taylor deceas'd', the last of twelve publishers of *Atlas Maritimus & Commercialis*, a work that contained an extensive contribution by Defoe. John Robert Moore speculated that this was the same as the atlas advertised by Taylor at the end of *The Farther Adventures* and argued that it was essentially Taylor's project.[4] The significance of such an undertaking was that a conger might sponsor a major enterprise of this kind and pay an advance to the author. For example, six publishers sponsored Defoe's *Tour Thro' the Whole Island of Great Britain*. In addition to the possibilities inherent in

---

[3] Discussions about the money Taylor and Defoe made from *Robinson Crusoe* was not limited to London. Joseph Spence records a comment from one of his friends at Oxford to the effect that Defoe's work 'cleared £1,000', and that although *The Farther Adventures* also made money, it reduced the profit on the first volume. James Osborn notes that the speaker, William Walter, was in error, in that Taylor made a great deal from both volumes, but what is evident from this 'hearsay' is that discussions of Defoe's financial success were widespread. See Spence, *Observations*, i. 391–2 (item 1011).

[4] *Checklist*, 217.

large projects of this type, there was clearly an audience for books of all kinds that had not existed at the beginning of the century. *Robinson Crusoe* was a huge success but so, as we have seen, was Haywood's *Love in Excess*, also published in 1719. Defoe had written about the special quality of books as opposed to other forms of publication in his preface to *The Storm*, but the age of Queen Anne seemed to call for pamphlets and newspapers. Now novels costing four to six shillings attracted purchasers, along with books on a variety of subjects.[5] Everything suggests an expanded reading audience interested in books providing entertainment and instruction.[6] Defoe was still very much an active journalist up to 1724, but he was to produce fewer pamphlets and an ever larger number of books. His eventual shift toward fiction and toward works focused on voyages to distant lands, on economic geography, and on the occult certainly reflected his interests, but he was surely responding to what he thought to be the tastes of the reading public.[7] No contracts between Defoe and his publishers have survived, but it is difficult to believe that the author of *Robinson Crusoe* had a difficult time getting good terms from the eager printers and booksellers whom the author of *The Battle of the Authors* imagines supporting his nomination to the Laureateship. If his support from the government may not have equalled the £400 he once received from Harley, he could probably add to his income a much larger share of earnings from his writings.

Under these circumstances, it is hardly surprising that, between 1719 and 1724, Defoe came more and more to speak of himself as a 'professional writer'. I put this in quotation marks because the common image of the writer was still that of the man of genius whose abilities were recognized by wealthy and distinguished patrons. But a number of publications written during the eighteenth century, such as Richard Savage's *An Author to Be Lett* (1729) and James Ralph's *The Case of Authors by Profession* (1758), attempted to argue the need for writers to take a more professional approach to their work. As has been mentioned, in *The Manufacturer*, a journal that he ran between the end of 1719 and the beginning of 1720,

[5] Even current events seemed to demand publication in book form. At the end of 1717 and 1718, Defoe produced a compilation under the title *The Annals of King George*. This was a joint venture in which William Taylor joined with A. Bell, T. Vernon, J. Baker, and J. Osbourn.

[6] During these years, Defoe frequently expressed his disapproval of having to entertain his readers in works that were intended to be fairly serious. In the preface to the *The Family Instructor* of 1718, he described 'Novelty', 'the modern Vice of the reading Palate', as his reason for a new method of presenting his dialogues, but since his real talent lay in making any topic entertaining, it is difficult to take seriously his objections to the taste of this new reading public.

[7] Paula Backscheider points to the number of voyage accounts published in the years before *Robinson Crusoe* by way of suggesting Defoe's response to the taste of the reading public. See *Daniel Defoe: Ambition and Innovation* (Lexington: University Press of Kentucky, 1996), 219.

Defoe paused in his defence of the weavers of Spitalfields to compare the work of a writer to that of the manufacturers of woollen cloth. Although the tone was facetious, other statements in his journals echoed similar thoughts. By the end of the century, writers were being listed among the professional occupations in the city of London. And by the nineteenth century, the ability of novelists such as Sir Walter Scott and Charles Dickens to make a great deal of money by their efforts often created the same kind of admiration for the author that was lavished upon those considered captains of industry. Defoe's image of the writer as manufacturer, then, while distinctly playful and perhaps even ironic at his own expense, predicted the future accurately enough.

I

This Money-getting Age[8]

Although writing *Robinson Crusoe*, its sequels, and other works of fiction must have kept Defoe busy enough between 1719 and 1720, he was particularly involved with the great event of these years—the swelling wealth of the South Sea Company and its demise. Although it was called a 'Bubble', an insubstantial effervescence that enlarges until it must burst, its inevitable end was not at all evident to those who watched and participated in its fatal growth. In France, the Scottish financial projector, John Law had worked what seemed like a financial revolution. He had assumed control of the Mississippi Company, which was to exploit the wealth of France's expansive territories in America, replaced the French currency with a system of paper money, and created a boom which raised the stock of the Mississippi Company to fantastic heights. The author of a pamphlet *Considerations on the Consequences of the French Settling Colonies on the Mississippi*, reprinted in Abel Boyer's *Political State* for April 1720 (accompanied by an elaborate map of what became known as the Louisiana Territory), described the way in which Law had enriched France and urged the British to look to their own interests at home and in America in the face of the new French threat. He argued that what Law had created

is justly looked upon as one of the most prodigious Events any Age has produced; and is scarce to be parallel'd in History. That it has been the general Topick of Coversation in most Countries in Europe; and as every man finds himself in a manner forced to say something or other about it, all your heavy Fellows, who would pass for wise, but who

[8] *The Commentator*, 26 (28 Mar. 1720).

have neither Parts nor Application sufficient to examine so great a Scheme, have thought it the shortest Way, to tell us gravely it will certainly come to nothing, and to treat it as a meer Chimera. . . . yet if we would give our selves the Trouble to reflect seriously on all the happy Circumstances which concurred to favour Mr. Law's Projects, our Wonder will in some measure be abated.[9]

To the possibilities inherent in the exploitation of new colonies that excited so many investors had to be added a certain optimism about progress that seized people's imaginations at this time. Scientific discoveries seemed to promise the development of new technologies. Behind Law's belief in paper money was the notion that by circulating more money the state might stimulate enterprise and invention. Aside from such idealistic purposes, Law's schemes seemed to have awakened forces of greed and avarice in a way that must have surprised even that great projector.

The South Sea Company had been approved by Queen Anne on 12 June 1711 and was part of Harley's plan to diminish the power of the Bank of England and the Whigs who supported it. Although Defoe was sometimes credited with being the mastermind behind Harley's move, John Robert Moore has forcefully demonstrated how little contact Defoe had with Harley at the inception of the South Sea Company and how little enthusiasm he had for the project in general.[10] Defoe was sceptical about the Asiento treaty that would allow England to supply South America with slaves and various goods, feeling that Spain would never permit it, and although he supported the idea of establishing a British colony in South America, his *True Account of the Design and Advantages of the South-Sea Trade* (1711) shows more enthusiasm about trading with the pirates who had established what looked like an incipient state in Madagascar. By 1715, when he came to write *The History of the White Staff*, he took the freedom to express his opinion about Harley's scheme more openly. The company should never have been created. It was not capable of giving investors a real return on their money because the likelihood of earning money through trade to South America was slender.[11]

Indeed, when the Company actually did manage to send a ship to the Spanish colonies, the results were disastrous. However much Law may have overestimated France's ability and desire to exploit the wealth of her American territories, the potential of those resources was real enough. Law was a visionary economist who overreached and failed. On the other hand,

[9] *Considerations on the Consequences of the French Settling Colonies on the Mississippi* (19 Apr. 1720), 360.

[10] John Robert Moore, 'Defoe and the South Sea Company', *Boston Public Library Quarterly* 5 (1953): 175–88.

[11] Defoe, *The Secret History of the White Staff*, Part III (London, 1715).

many of the South Sea Company directors were speculators who hoped to grow rich through what is now called 'an endless chain'—a process now recognized to be criminal.[12] The House of Commons's Secret Committee, chaired by Thomas Brodrick, which was to begin its business on 14 January 1721, was dealing with a new phenomenon, but in handing out punishment to the directors of the South Sea Company they had no difficulty recognizing fraud when they saw it. Hundreds had been ruined, but while Robert Walpole, the new head of the government, acted to protect the King, Sunderland, and a few highly placed parties, most of those responsible were forced to return large sums of money to the government. The effects of the South Sea Bubble reverberated through the entire decade during which Defoe wrote his novels and some of his best prose works, but the country got off relatively lightly. There was a time when people expected a Jacobite insurrection, or, at the very least, some divine punishment upon the nation in the form of a devastating plague. Nevertheless, the epidemic of greed that seized so many in England and Scotland in 1720 was not easily or quickly removed from the national consciousness.

Defoe could not help a sense of *déjà vu*, for if the 1690s had not produced anything of the magnitude of the South Sea Bubble, it had been a time of projects and financial schemes. Economic tracts that had been published originally in the 1690s or a few years after suddenly found a new audience. These included the works of John Asgil and John Cary along with John Law's *Money and Trade Consider'd* written originally in 1705.[13] As we have seen, Defoe had invested in a number of projects, including a diving-machine to recover sunken treasure. The Bank proved to be a viable financial institution, but there had been schemes for other banks of various kinds. There had also been state-sponsored lotteries, and while the recoinage that had occurred at that time was not reduplicated, there had been discussions about the coinage in 1718, concluding in an official adjustment of the relationship between gold and silver coins.[14] Although Defoe believed strongly that paper letters of credit extended the powers of commerce, he himself had been involved in problems concerning a paper

---

[12] John Carswell, *The South Sea Bubble*, rev. edn. (Stroud: Alan Sutton, 1993), 65–74, 129, 144–8.

[13] Law's *Money and Trade Consider'd*, originally published in 1705, was reprinted in 1720 with an introduction by the Earl of Islay. Law apparently developed his ideas on paper money while he was in Holland during 1696. See H. Montgomery Hyde, *John Law* (London: W. H. Allen, 1969), 38–40. John Asgil's *Several Assertions Proved*, first published in 1696, was a proposal for paper money issued by a bank drawing its value from land. John Cary's *Essay on the State of England in Relation to Its Trade* provided a forceful argument for the importance of the circulation of money, reappearing in 1719 as *An Essay towards Regulating Trade*.

[14] See Defoe, *A History of the Last Session of the Present Parliament* (London, 1718), 56–9; anon., *An Essay on Money and Bullion* (London, 1718), 1–38.

letter of credit in 1691. But however fast and loose he played with such documents, however much he extolled credit as a wonderful creation of the imagination, he never believed that a system of paper money, or bills of credit based exclusively on paper money, could be viable.[15] John Locke had argued that gold and silver had mainly imaginary value, but Crusoe knew better. He made speeches on the uselessness of gold on his island, but then made sure to put it away in a safe place.

II

The Anatomy of Exchange Alley, Defoe's first substantial attack upon the South Sea Company, was published on 1 July 1719, appeared while he was still writing *The Farther Adventures of Robinson Crusoe*. I mentioned this work in the previous chapter as background material for my discussion of *Robinson Crusoe*, but I want to treat it here on its own merits. His comparison between white-collar crime and actual theft in *The Anatomy of Exchange Alley* had been a paradoxical theme for Defoe throughout his life. That he was to revive it in his discussion of 'Honesty' in *Serious Reflections of Robinson Crusoe* was no more surprising than that he took to writing about pirates, thieves, and prostitutes for the next five years. He looked upon Jacob Sawbridge, Sir George Caswell, and Elias Turner, the manipulators behind the Sword Blade Company, the financial arm of the South Sea Company, as 'a true Triumvirate of modern thieving', and they were no different in kind from the highly respected Sir Josiah Child, whom Defoe regarded as the villainous founder of stock-jobbing.[16] If, when he came to write his *Complete English Tradesman* in 1726, he concluded that all trade was a species of 'Crime', he was reflecting an attitude that had grown stronger toward the end of his life.[17] It did not mean that commerce was bad in itself, but it certainly suggested that in the many instances where the self-interest of the merchant might endanger the health of the state, it was the duty of the King and Parliament to regulate and inflict punishment upon those whose greed seemed to know no bounds. Quoting his earlier tract, *The Freeholder's Plea*, he compared the activities of stock-jobbers to those who commit treason against the state. And indeed, the image of the merchant who would bring plague into a nation rather than forgo his profit was much in the air. Although no plague was to strike Europe for a year,

[15] See Carswell, *South Sea Bubble*, 15.

[16] *The Anatomy of Exchange Alley* (London, 1719), 13–14, 37, 40. See also William Scott, *Joint Stock Companies* (3 vols., Cambridge: Cambridge University Press, 1911), iii. 440–1.

[17] *The Complete English Tradesman* (London, 1726), i. 108–18.

when on 31 July bubonic plague appeared suddenly at Marseilles, Defoe had already waxed prophetic about the possibility of such an event:

The Truth is . . . that these men by a mass of money, which they command of other Peoples as well as their own, will in Time, ruin the Jobbing-Trade. But 'twill be only like a general Visitation, where all Distempers are swallow'd up in the Plague, like a common Calamity, that makes enemies turn Friends and drowns lesser grievances in the general Deluge.[18]

The elegiac note of this warning reflects the dilemma of many who feared that too violent a reaction to the situation might endanger the entire political establishment—the Whig ministry, George I, and the Protestant succession.[19] In his newspapers, Defoe maintained a relatively moderate position. In Tory papers, such as *Mist's Weekly Journal*, he blamed the directors but urged stoicism for those who had suffered financial loss and even argued that too much grief over the loss of wealth and worldly goods was shameful. 'There's one Merchant sits raving at the Gaming-House in Exchange-Alley, and swears he was worth forty thousand Pound but yesterday, and to Day is not worth a Shilling,' wrote Defoe, asking how much sympathy men of this kind deserved: '[W]ho could pity them? What have Merchants to do to turn Gamesters? What have Linnen and Woollen men to do with Box and Dice? Every man to his Business! Let them mind their Calling, and leave the Bites and the Cullies to the Place of Bites and Cullies.'[20] In *Applebee's Journal*, which tended to avoid politics in the name of entertainment, Defoe, under the pseudonym of 'Anti-Jobber', attacked avarice and rejoiced at the end of trading in South Sea Stock. And on 1 April 1721, when he came to consider the final decisions of the Secret Committee, while appearing to demand justice, he tended to obscure the question of guilt and innocence by distinguishing between legal innocence and moral innocence.[21] On the other hand, in one short-lived journal, *The Director*, he attempted to defend the actions of the directors, even appealing to his readers to pity honest men led into imprudence.[22] In his writings for

[18] *Anatomy of Exchange-Alley*, 40–1.

[19] This was the situation of Thomas Brodrick, who chaired the secret committee in charge of investigating the actions of the directors of the South Sea Company and those in the government, such as Stanhope and Sunderland, who took bribes. See Carswell, *South Sea Bubble*, 184.

[20] In Lee, ii. 203.

[21] Ibid. 290.

[22] Defoe struck a similar note in *The Commentator*. On 7 July 1720 he argued that the South Sea Company would be able to meet its obligations, but he may have been urged by the government to write a journal that would defend the South Sea Company and the government more forcefully. *The Director* began on 5 October 1720, just a few weeks after the last number of *The Commentator*. Although he eventually abandoned any direct defence of the Directors of the Company, Defoe did assume an attitude of Christian charity: 'for my Part, I will always be among the Number of those that would assist them while they Stand, and will pity them if they Fall, let their offence be what it will' (18 Nov. 1720).

newspapers, then, Defoe attempted to work toward establishing stability. This was also the goal of the new leader of the Whigs, Sir Robert Walpole. Walpole earned the contemptuous name 'Skreen Master General' for his successful efforts to deflect the revenge of the Secret Committee of the Commons toward those actually responsible and away from members of the court and government who had profited from the situation.[23]

Defoe remained a loyal supporter of the government for the rest of his life, but he could hardly have appreciated Walpole's methods. A natural enthusiast and idealist, he wrote as a moralist who accepted a degree of corruption as an inevitable part of existence, a stance well suited to the decade following the South Sea Scandal. But he had never believed that the inflated stocks of the South Sea Company could hold the value set at their height, and he took some pleasure during 1720 and 1721 in attacking the theories of John Law. '*No Credit, no Bank*', he wrote, 'is as much a Maxim in Trade, as any Principle or Fundamental can be allowed to be in other Things.' A bank, he maintained, must back up all bills with specie, and when Law's *Banque* failed to understand this principle, it proved 'ill Stewards' to the French people.[24] In *The Chimera, or the French Way of Paying National Debts*, published on 5 January 1720, when Law's success had astonished Europe, Defoe gave a history of Law's actions which included some praise of his 'Genius and Capacity' but which refused to accept Law's theories of credit and paper money. 'When I begun this Work,' he wrote, 'it was not possible to imagine but I might have given some account of the Ebb, as I have of the Flood of this *Phantosme*, for I call it yet not more; its fate without question must come ere long, since there is no Foundation equal to the Structure that now stands upon it.'[25] Almost two years later, in *The Case of Mr. Law*, published in November 1721, Defoe supplied the epitaph to Law's career that he had already imagined. In responding to a work that defended Law's theories and morals, Defoe reminded his readers that Law had attempted to destroy English credit and that there was no way the French economy could continue to function after all the money had been collected from the victims. Law had been a successful gambler before becoming a financier, and Defoe viewed his activities in terms of his former profession: 'like a Board of Play, when the Box has got all the money of the Gamesters, if it does not think fit to lend it out to them

---

Eventually he fell back to a defence of the government and of the government's solution to the crisis—a reconstituted Company that would function as a distributor of annuities.

[23] These included George I, his mistress the Duchess of Kendal and her two daughters, and the two leading Whig ministers.

[24] *Commentator*, 12 Aug. 1720.

[25] *The Chimera, or the French Way of Paying National Debts* (London, 1720), 76.

again, the game is at an end.' And he judged Law as 'bold, enterprizing, rash, and adventurous beyond the Reach of the Plan on which he proposed to act'.[26]

Defoe's undoubted fascination with John Law was partly like that of Conrad's captain for his criminal double in 'The Secret Sharer', and perhaps observing Law's dangerous gamble with the French economy gave him the strength to resist getting involved himself. He could identify deeply with the kind of excitement engendered by Law, and praised his attempt to relieve the poor of their burdensome taxes. If he criticized Law's risk-taking, Defoe too knew the mixture of excitement and despair in wagering all on a final roll of the dice—on one more scheme that might rescue him from bankruptcy. Although his writings display a seeming self-assurance in taking a conservative economic stance in relation to both the Mississippi scheme and the South Sea Bubble, everything we know of him suggests that the restraint he showed in this period caused him considerable anxiety. For these reasons, his display of indignation over those Directors of the South Sea Company whom the government was willing to sacrifice was sufficiently unrestrained. When John Aislabie printed a speech in which he complained of the punishments inflicted upon him by the House of Commons on 21 April 1721, Defoe defended the rights of the House of Commons to act as a quasi-judicial body on behalf of the public good at a time when 'the Nation has been cheated, the Powers granted by Parliament abus'd, innocent People most scandalously Ensnar'd, and the publick Credit . . . irreparably injur'd'.[27] Indeed, Defoe's last pamphlet on the South Sea 'Scheme', *A Brief Debate upon the Dissolving the late Parliament*, probably published in March 1722, accused the House of Commons of excessive leniency toward James Craggs, John Aislabie, and the other directors. To a great extent the pamphlet represents a return to the scathing irony of his early work. The punishments inflicted by the Secret Committee are compared to the biblical injunction of repaying fourfold. Like so many of his countrymen, Defoe would have liked to have seen blatant white-collar crime, which often led to the suffering of thousands, punished more severely than the action of a poverty-stricken robber, but in neither Defoe's time nor in ours has such justice been possible. As frequently happens with works employing the machinery of irony, there is difficulty keeping the ironic effect from spilling over into those parts which are intended to be read without any implication of sarcasm. The effect is

[26] *The Case of Mr. Law* (London, 1721), 16, 25. For Law as a successful gambler, see H. Montgomery Hyde, *John Law* (London: W. H. Allen, 1969), 49.

[27] *A Vindication of the Honour and Justice of Parliament against a Most Scandalous libel Entitul'd, The Speech of John A------, Esq* (London, 1721), 15.

one of indeterminacy, for, while he praises the stability of the monarchy and maintains that Walpole surely could not use secret service money to secure elections, such statements seem to pose a threat to both the monarch and the prime minister. For what Defoe suggests—that money might overwhelm the free choice of the electors—is presented as a subversion of the liberty of the subjects:

... if People, who we call Electors, will sell their Votes, will be brib'd, be bought, be corrupted, and chuse those who bid most without respect to their own Safety, and without regard to what may be the Consequences; I say, if they will do so ... why who can doubt but he that has the money will have the Election, let him be what or who he will. . . . The Injustice of it to our selves, the loss of Privileges to the People, and the like; I say, what is this to the purpose? What are all those Things to the Money.[28]

What was plain to Defoe was that what he feared had come true. Money, whether in the hands of stock-jobbers or in the hands of the government, could destroy what, in Defoe's mind, was the promise of the 1690s—a body politic moving toward representative government.

The pamphlet tergiversates, then, between urging the government to avoid bribery and hoping that the electors would select men who were not tainted by the South Sea Company's bribery. He suspects the worst, particularly in the case of Robert Knight, the cashier of the Company. Defoe argued that the government's efforts to have Knight extradited appeared to be half-hearted at best. We now know that Walpole, in collusion with the King, persuaded the agents of Austria to see to it that Knight would never be brought back to embarrass members of the court and the former Whig ministers.[29] While he suggested that any sentence against the former directors less than death should be considered lenient, Defoe was not ready to sacrifice everything in what was shaping up as Walpole's version of the Whig establishment. On the other hand, Walpole's cynicism would have shocked him, despite his sense that self-interest governed most human actions. The effects of the South Sea Bubble remained with Defoe throughout the rest of his life; it permeates all the major fiction in which individual criminal actions of one kind or another have to be set against corporate crime and government collusion. In this, Defoe was hardly unusual. A highly publicized criminal trial of 1722 involved an attempt by Arundel Coke of Bury to engage a man named Carter in helping with a murder with the argument that the deeds of the South Sea directors and their mild punishment had freed ordinary men and women from moral

[28] *A Brief Debate upon the Dissolving the Late Parliament* (London, 1722), 3–4.
[29] Carswell, *South Sea Bubble*, 195–218; Defoe, *A Brief Debate*, 18.

laws and obligation.[30] As a writer deeply involved in matters of economics and social reform, Defoe appears to have viewed the South Sea Bubble as an event that changed Britain's social fabric. He seems to have purchased an annuity for his daughter Hannah from the now safe South Sea Company,[31] but he is also likely to have been the person who wrote of the pirate Captain England, who had accumulated a considerable treasure after committing the crimes usually associated with pirates:

I can't say, but if they had known what was doing in *England*, at the same Time, by the *South-Sea* Directors, and their Directors, they would certainly have had this Reflection for their Consolation, *viz.* that whatever Robberies they had committed, they might be pretty sure they were not the greatest Villains then living in the World.[32]

England and his crew surrendered to the Governor of Porto Bello and managed to keep a good part of the money they earned, and in such an economic environment Defoe was hardly ready to criticize them for their enterprising spirit. Defoe's nineteenth-century biographer, William Lee, noted a chronological connection between Defoe's first appearance, on 25 June 1720, in *Applebee's Journal*, a journal carrying accounts of criminals and other entertaining materials, the same day on which the Act for the suppression of Bubbles became law. Lee thought it his duty to apologize for Defoe's descent into writing literature of this kind on the grounds of his financial needs. Since he viewed Defoe as one of the founders of early capitalism, Lee would hardly want to look too closely at Defoe's analogy between crime and business. Yet, as we shall see, in Defoe's mind there was a profound connection between the lives of criminals and the financial schemes that nearly brought the nation to ruin.

III

Contributing to that association between criminal activity and business was what Defoe regarded as a particularly flagrant example of the type of com-

---

[30] *The Tryal and Condemnation of Arundel Coke* (London, 1722), 15. For a typical exploitation of Coke's arguments for murdering Edward Crispe, see John Dennis, *Vice and Luxury: Publick Mischiefs: or, Remarks on a Book Intituled, The Fable of the Bees* (London, 1724), 72–3.

[31] Lee (i. 362) quotes a document from Hannah ordering the payment of her dividend. Lee's assumption that Defoe purchased this stock for Hannah after it had been stabilized with the backing of the Bank and the East India Company seems to be based entirely on Defoe's assertions about the purity of his intentions when writing about the South Sea Company. But given his hatred for stock-jobbing, it is doubtful that he would have been caught up in the frenzy that ruined so many investors.

[32] Defoe, *A General History of the Pyrates*, ed. Manuel Schonhorn (London: Dent, 1972), 133.

mercial activity that appeared to be harmful to the economic health of the
nation—or rather to the wellbeing of the labouring poor: the importation
of cotton cloth from the East through the East India Company. The
weavers of Spitalfields and throughout Britain regarded these importations
as a threat to their livelihood. In 1707 Defoe had actually praised the manufacture of cotton cloth, provided that the raw product came from English
plantations in America, but a few years later he classified calicoes among
the 'Baubles and Knick Knacks' that were taking the place of trading in the
'True-born English Broad-Cloth and Kerseys'.[33] The situation appealed to
his deeply held belief that, however important economic innovation might
be, no new industry ought to be introduced into Britain without some
special provision for those workers who might lose their present employment. This time the villains were the East India Company and others who
were taking advantage of making money by importing calicoes from the
East. The Company might claim that it was merely satisfying the craving
for a new fashion in women's dress and that women had the right to wear
what they wished, but for Defoe what this meant was the destruction of a
native clothing industry that employed large numbers of the labouring
poor. England had grown rich over the past few centuries on the quality of
its wool, and while the wool industry may have been declining, Defoe still
viewed it as the basis for English wealth. In his *Tour Thro' the Whole Island
of Great Britain*, the first part of which was published in 1724, he was to
exalt the view of the weavers working in their cottages as an example
of what might be called the economic sublime, for after crossing a mountainous area that was 'horrible' in its bareness, he encounters a scene of
human industry in the midst of the mountains of Yorkshire:

After we had mounted the third Hill, we found the Country, in short, one continued Village, tho' mountainous every way, as before; hardly a House standing
out of a speaking distance from another, and (which soon told us their Business)
the Day clearing up, and the Sun shining, we could see that almost at every House
there was a *Tenter*, and almost on every Tenter a Piece of *Cloth* . . . from which the
Sun glancing, and, as I might say, shining (the White reflecting its Rays) to us, I
thought it was the most agreeable Sight that I ever saw, for the Hills, as I say,
rising and falling so thick, and the Vallies opening sometimes one way, sometimes
another, so that sometimes we could see two or three Miles this Way, sometimes
as far another; sometimes like the Streets near St. *Giles*'s, called the *Seven Dials*;
we could see through the Glades almost every Way round us, yet look which

---

[33] Though Defoe loved to see paradoxes between economic theory and human activities, he
was consistent enough on this matter, having, in the *Review* of 12 Feb. 1713, praised a recent act of Parliament that prohibited the 'wearing of *East India* Silks, and *foreign Printed Callicoes*'. *Review*, iv. 51; [ix]. 83b,
114b.

Way we would, high to the Tops, and low to the Bottoms, it was all the same, innumerable Houses and Tenters, and a white Piece upon every Tenter.[34]

Defoe sees a providential plan in the interaction between the natural environment and the way entire families—men, women, and even young children—are employed. He indulges in the myth of the nobility of labour, seeing the workers in the houses of the master manufacturers as 'lusty fellows'. There is ample evidence to show that long before 1724 Defoe would have regarded anyone who interrupted such a scene as an enemy to God, humanity, and nature. He was the perfect person to defend the weavers, and, as I have emphasized, he threw himself into the task not only with a journal, *The Manufacturer*, but with a series of pamphlets that vilified those who would cause unemployment for their own selfish aims.

If Defoe looked upon the dissolution of Dissenter unity over the Trinitarian dispute as the triumph of Satan and the rise and decline of the South Sea Company as a revelation of the victory of human greed, he might take comfort in a temporary triumph in the battle over imported calicoes, for in this case Parliament eventually sided with the weavers and passed more prohibitions. But it was one of the last examples of Defoe's propaganda campaigns. Beginning with *The Just Complaint of the Poor Weavers Truly Represented* on 11 August 1719, which appeared just nine days before *The Farther Adventures of Robinson Crusoe*, and ending with *The Trade to India Critically and Calmly Consider'd* on 13 February 1720, he kept up a steady barrage against the East India Company. William Boreham seems to have published most, if not all, of Defoe's writings on this matter, including the eighty-six numbers of Defoe's bi-weekly journal, *The Manufacturer*, but Defoe reprinted some of his pamphlets in his monthly review, *Mercurius Politicus*, published by John Morphew. And it was in this journal, in the issue for June 1719, that he first defended the rioters:

And this brings me to the main Point, which I believe no body will deny, that tho' the Weavers have been wrong in the Manner of their Complaint, and wrong in the Time of it, yet that without Question the matter of their Complaint was just; that is to say, for I must be very cautious how I speak, for I would give no offence to our Superiors, nor would I give Encouragement to Tumults and Riots: But this is certainly a Truth that cannot be contradicted, that the Humour of our People running so much upon the wearing of painted *Callicoes* and Linnen, is a great interruption to our Woollen and Silk Manufacturers, lessens their Consumptions, and by Consequence takes from the Poor so much of their Employment as bears a Proportion to the Decrease of Consumption.[35]

---

[34] *Tour*, ii. 601.   [35] *Mercurius Politicus*, June 1719, 381.

The poverty of the weavers was of little interest to the opposition, who took up the cudgels for free trade, but Defoe presented a double argument—that the starving workers should be 'Objects of our Pity', and that the real wealth of the nation came through employing the poor.[36]

From a literary standpoint, the best pamphlet to come out of this debate was Defoe's *The Female Manufacturers Complaint: Being the Humble Petition of Dorothy Distaff, Abigail Spinning-Wheel, Eleanor Reel, Etc. Spinsters, to the Lady Rebecca Woolpack*, published in January 1720. The work is purportedly written by women workers representing 'Thousands of the Female manufacturers of Wooll and Worsted Yarn in the said County, and in the Counties of Norfolk, Essex, Huntington, Cambridge, Herford, etc.'. It is very much in the mode of Defoe's Kentish petition pamphlets—a protest from the roots of English life and this time coming from women workers, some of whom say they are the support of their families who are in danger of falling into destitution, some of whom complain that they have lost their sweethearts. They request Dorothy Distaff to consider that she was descended from the 'Woolpack' family and that her ancestors would be horrified to see her 'dress'd up in your painted Trangums, and *East-India* Rags, while all the poor Spinners hung about you crying for Bread and for Work'.[37] Defoe concluded this exercise in using a female voice with a letter to Sir Richard Steele from Tisserando de Brocade, who comments severely on the importation of women's clothes from Italy, Venice, and Paris. Brocade notes how ironic it is that the French often import their cloth from the weavers in Spitalfields and then sell them back to the ladies of Britain with the false glitter of being imported.

Both sections of the pamphlet reveal how much Defoe was learning from his stint as a writer for *Applebee's Journal*. He had developed a lighter touch, an ability to entertain his audience without apologizing, and an ability to convey a serious message in an amusing manner. Even his response to the author of *The British Merchant*, who taunted him with being the former author of *Mercator* and who called him Robinson Crusoe, shows a new maturity. After pointing out how irrelevant such charges were, he turned to the dispute at hand. He pointed out that, so far from being willing to argue any economic position for money, he had actually turned down the opportunity to write against the weavers, and that while he had not

[36] *The Just Complaint of the Poor Weavers* (London, 1719), 5, 10; for the arguments of the opposition, see e.g. *A Further Examination of the Weaver's Pretences* (London, 1719), 13, 24; *The British Merchant* (London, 1719). A sample of the latter is reprinted with Defoe's *The Manufacturer*, ed. Robert Gosselink (Delmar, NY: Scholars' Facsimiles and Reprints, 1978), Nos. 1–12.

[37] Defoe, *The Female Manufacturers Complaint* (London, 1720), 12.

refused the job, his opponent 'had never been employ'd in it'.[38] Although Defoe still maintained that he was not paid in any direct way for his work on *The Mercator*, he shows a willingness to accept his role as a journalist and a writer on economic subjects. This is certainly what he was during this period and for the rest of his life, and he seems to have found a new dignity in such a role. The implication is that, having such power, he could choose the side on which his principles lay. Though polite enough, his dismissal of his opponent is devastating.

Defoe was not to be put off by references to him as 'Robinson Crusoe'. The accusation that he was a popular writer never seemed to annoy him. He had revelled in the extended audience for his *True-Born Englishman*, and long before the end of 1720 must have known that *Robinson Crusoe* had achieved an extraordinary popularity throughout England and a readership on the Continent unmatched by any previous work by an English writer.[39] But such success would have confirmed what he already knew as a writer deeply involved in what we would call the writer's market, a concept which Defoe practically invented. His first attempt at a work of fiction after the first two volumes of *Robinson Crusoe* came on 10 December 1720, under the auspices of members of the conger who would publish most of his future work: A. Bettersworth, C. King, J. Brotherton, W. Meadows, W. Chetwood, and William Boreham. The full title was: *The King of Pirates: Being an Account of the Famous Enterprises of Captain Avery, The Mock King of Madagascar. With His Rambles and Piracies; wherein All the Sham Accounts Formerly Publish'd of Him Are Detected*. In some ways, this work may be dismissed as a prelude to *The Life, Adventures, and Pyracies, of the Famous Captain Singleton*, published six months later, yet it has a peculiar interest for that very reason: it is like a proleptic sketch, as if Defoe were anticipating future fictions in the very process of writing.

Next to Captain Kidd, Captain Avery was probably the best-known pirate to Defoe's contemporaries. Defoe had suggested the possibility of offering him a pardon in exchange for a portion of his wealth in the *Review* of 18 October 1707, where he emphasized a number of themes that would

---

[38]   *The Manufacturer*, 10 (2 Dec. 1719).

[39]   The popularity of Milton and Shakespeare in Europe emerged during the second half of the eighteenth century, but the contempt for popular literature was almost axiomatic during this period. For this reason, the argument against Defoe's role in *A Vindication of the Press* (1718), which praises *The True-born Englishman* and compares Defoe to Shakespeare, seems paradoxical. Such notions were limited to Defoe and his circle of admirers. See M. E. Novak, '*A Vindication of the Press* and the Defoe Canon', *SEL* 27 (1987): 399–411; P. N. Furbank and W. R. Owens, *The Canonisation of Daniel Defoe* (New Haven, Conn.: Yale University Press, 1988), 160–1; and '*A Vindication of the Press* (1718): Not by Defoe?', *Bibliographical Society of America* 78 (1984): 355–60. Laura Curtis, 'The Attribution of A Vindication of the Press to Daniel Defoe', in *Studies in Eighteenth-Century Culture*, xviii (Baltimore: Johns Hopkins University Press, 1988), 433–44.

appear again in *The King of Pirates* and elsewhere: pirates were no worse than respectable financiers to be found at the stock exchange; most nations at their beginnings were little more than groups of pirates and brigands; the amount of money that the pirates were supposed to have amassed would always exert influence in the world and England might as well take advantage of it. There was a component of piracy and mutiny in the first and second parts of *Robinson Crusoe*, and Cox's abridgement, which retained this material, may have made Defoe realize that he could expand upon it in future writings.

Avery provided a ready-made character with mythic dimensions, and Defoe reached back to much of this early material in creating his more imaginative fiction of piracy. Even the form of the work, with its two letters divided into the adventurous gathering of treasure and the story of his escape with his loot, has some resemblance to the structure of *Memoirs of a Cavalier*, and the escape through Persia and Turkey seems to be an experiment in varying Crusoe's caravan journey across Siberia. Significantly enough, Avery is Defoe's first attempt at examining a character who takes a turn toward a life of roguery and never looks back. Crusoe acts out his role as Governor of his island, but like Mahmut and Ramkins he is sincere in his beliefs and feelings. Once Avery turns from the life of a privateer to being an outright pirate, he becomes adept at deception and misinformation. And although he distinguishes himself from the dedicated cruelty of Captain Redhand, with whom he serves, he is not chosen captain of this group of cutthroats for his adherence to morality and virtue.

Manuel Schonhorn has suggested that Defoe tended to soften the genuine violence and cruelty of piracy, and the same is true of his tales of criminality, prostitution, and warfare.[40] He manages to do this mainly by the use of what Pierre Machery has called 'silences'.[41] Sometimes we are told by the narrator that he or she will not speak about certain events; at other times, the narrator is extremely brief about matters about which the reader might want more information. During the period of the New Criticism, it was argued that the critic could not speak of what was not directly in the text. Macherey maintained that once the novelist created a fictional world, the reader became involved with both what was actually depicted and what might be inferred. Thus the great event in Avery's career—the capture of a ship belonging to the Great Mogul, carrying his daughter and a large number of her female servants—is long on

[40] Manuel Schonhorn, 'Defoe's *Captain Singleton*: A Reassessment with Observations', *Papers on Language and Literature* 7 (1971): 38–51.

[41] *A Theory of Literary Production* (London: Routledge & Kegan Paul, 1978).

descriptions of the treasure but relatively brief on a scene which one historian described as a prolonged gang rape. Captain Avery avers that he never had sexual relations with the Mogul's daughter, only consensual sex with one of her attendants, and that all of the rest of the women on the ship proved perfectly willing to have sexual intercourse with his crew.

Such a view of piracy tends to make it more attractive for the reader, and Defoe tends toward building his own mythology of piracy at the same time that he mocks the absurd stories about Avery's adventures. In his role as narrator, Avery denies any basis to an earlier biography about him, but then adds, 'and tho' it may be true, that my extravagant Story may be the proper Foundation of a Romance, yet as no Man has a Title to publish it better than I have to expose and contradict it'.[42] Defoe created a fictional biography for the young Avery that attached him to the buccaneers who filled the pages of Alexander Esquemiling's account of the pirates of the seventeenth century. Avery says that he served under Captain Sharp and 'was among that Party who fought their Way Sword in Hand thro' all the Detachments of the *Spaniards*, in the Journey over land, cross the Isthmus of *Darien*, to the North Seas'.[43] He amasses a considerable treasure, which he buries at Campeachy and which he later recovers and adds to the wealth he accumulates in Madagascar. On that savage island, his position gave rise to the myth of Avery as the founder of a new nation, often depicted as a kingdom based on just laws.[44] But in Defoe's version this is merely a piece of propaganda deliberately passed on to some prisoners to be disseminated to a gullible world. The misinformation included an exaggerated view of the strength and wealth of the community, the notion that they were in the process of forming themselves into a nation, and their willingness to welcome pirates into their community who had become rich through their adventures. Speaking under the disguise of one of Avery's lieutenants, Avery tells them that 'the *Romans* themselves were at first, no better than such a Gang of Rovers as we were; and who knew but our General, Captain *Avery*, might lay the Foundation of as great an Empire as they'.[45]

So much of *The King of Pirates* represents an early draft of *Captain*

---

[42] Defoe, *The King of Pirates* (London, 1720 [1719]), 1.

[43] Ibid. 3, 4.

[44] For one example of the way in which the story of Avery invited utopian thinking, see Charles Johnson, *The Successful Pirate*, ed. Joel Baer, Augustan Reprint Society, Nos. 203 and 204 (Los Angeles: William Andrews Clark Memorial Library, 1980). Although John Robert Moore was wrong in saying that Johnson's play was not about piracy at all and merely drew on Avery's fame, it is basically a mingling of heroic drama, farce, and satire, entirely different in tone from Defoe's treatments of piracy.

[45] *King of Pirates*, 79.

Singleton that it might appear that Defoe had a habit of beginning with a relatively short narrative and only gradually came to realize the full possibilities in his material. This is true of the relationship between *Major Ramkins* and *Colonel Jack* as well as between some of the military memoirs and *Memoirs of a Cavalier*. Certainly one of the most intriguing characters in *Captain Singleton*, the Quaker William Walters, was expanded from a brief account of a Quaker captain whose behaviour seemed to belie the pacifism of his religion. The Quaker in *The King of Pirates* commands a ship too lightly armed to battle Avery and his crew, and is eventually captured after three days, but Avery feels certain that 'had he been equal to us in Force, it appear'd by his Countenance he would not have been afraid of his Flesh, or have baulk'd using the Carnal Weapon of Offence, *viz.* the Cannon-Ball'. This captain refuses to join the pirates, but does so in a way that makes it appear that were he forced to sail with them (as were his mate, carpenter, and surgeon) he might have acted the part of a freebooter as well as any of them. From this character Defoe fashions William Walters, who is cautious enough to arrange with Singleton to have the appearance of being coerced and who refuses to engage directly in any fighting, but who willingly participates in every other way and becomes Singleton's chief adviser. William regards piracy merely as a slightly unusual form of trade, one likely to show higher profits than its slightly more legitimate relation. His role is that of Singleton's grey eminence, somewhat similar to Defoe's own role when he was advising Harley on affairs of state.

Captain Singleton is not Defoe's best work of fiction, but in terms of an imaginative projection of his own divided ego, he never came so close as the combination of Singleton and Williams. Neither of them is entirely respectable by ordinary standards, both committing capital offences, but by 1720 Defoe must have known that, from any outside view, he too did not seem very respectable. Captain Singleton, as one of his companions remarks, is a born pirate—enterprising, bold, and careless of the consequences of his actions. Although he goes through the motions of accumulating money, he is really interested only in action and adventure. As he remarks in his self-characterization:

I was perfectly loose and dissolute in my Behaviour, bold and wicked while I was under Government, and now perfectly unfit to be trusted with Liberty; for I was as ripe for any Villainy, as a young Fellow that had no solid Thought ever placed in his Mind could be supposed to be. Education, as you have heard, I had none; and all the little Scenes of Life I had pass'd thro', had been full of Dangers and desperate Circumstances; but I was either so young, or so stupid, that I escaped the Grief and Anxiety of them, for want of having a Sense of their Tendency and Consequences.[46]

It was not in his education that Defoe found something of himself in Singleton but in his tendency to action, adventure, and even violence. Defoe must have wondered what he would have been like if he had been spirited away from his parents as a child and raised without any care at all. Singleton eventually ends up as the servant to a number of seamen and finally to a Portuguese pilot who mistreats him. He is saved from the likelihood of having to murder his master by joining a mutiny among the men after the ship has been blown to Madagascar by a storm. And though the Gunner among the twenty-seven men left at Madagascar after the mutiny predicts of Singleton, 'thou has commenced Pyrate very young, but have a Care of the Gallows, young Man; have a Care, I say, for thou wilt be an eminent Thief', the Singleton who emerges from this first section of the novel is an adventurer and an explorer, with almost no sense of property and without any real interest in accumulating wealth.

The trek across Africa that Singleton and his followers make after leaving Madagascar for the mainland has been criticized sometimes for its lack of realism, sometimes for its lack of imagination. Defoe occasionally mocked map-makers who drew designs or monstrous figures where they had no information about the terrain, but in *Captain Singleton* he too had to create an imaginary Africa. What emerges forms part of the myth of the 'Dark Continent'—a land filled with strange beasts and even stranger men.[47] They are accompanied by a 'Black Prince', and enter the 'Heart of the whole *Continent*' (105). Shades of Haggard and Conrad! They discover some gold, but there are other lessons to be learned. They are able to barter for food only after the Cutler begins manufacturing what silver and iron they have into jewellery. The metal by itself is as worthless in Africa as it was on Crusoe's island, and indeed, after first learning of the discovery of some gold, Singleton refers to it as 'the *Makebait* of the World' (94), meaning the thing that causes division among mankind. But beyond Africa is the outside world, and Singleton discovers among the savages a white man, entirely naked, who sees Africa as a land that needs to be exploited for its

[46] *The Life, Adventures, and Pyracies, of the Famous Captain Singleton*, ed. Shiv K. Kumar (London: Oxford University Press, 1969), 11.

[47] As with the wolves and bears who attack Crusoe after his return from the island, Defoe tends to see animals engaging in a kind of organized warfare. This is true not only of the animals who attack Singleton and his men but among the animals themselves, for the elephants are described as forming a line and charging their enemies in such a way that nothing can withstand them. The natives who have not encountered too many Europeans, tend to be friendly, but their willingness to trade anything for the Cutler's ornaments is presented as a constant from tribe to tribe.

riches. This ancestor of Conrad's Kurtz was a real figure named Freeman, an employee of the Royal African Company, in which Defoe always took some interest. Though he appears in 'the most wretched Condition that ever Man was reduced to' (122), he is cultivated enough to speak several languages. After having been tempted to leave one of the settlements of the Royal African Company, he has spent years of wandering from tribe to tribe. Yet he is less interested in returning to his native land than in mining the gold that fills the rivers and lies in vast deposits in the mountains. After Singleton and his Portuguese followers work for a few weeks, they are anxious to continue their voyage home, and they reject the arguments of Freeman, who wants them to remain for several more years to exploit the wealth of the country. Singleton's thoughts on the subject are typical of those of the other seamen. He is eager to leave:

for I had no Notion of a great deal of Money, or what to do with my self, or what to do with it if I had it. I thought I had enough already, and all the Thought I had about disposing of it, if I came to *Europe*, was only how to spend it as fast as I could, buy me some Clothes, and go to Sea again to be a Drudge for more. (132)

Only Freeman's persuasion gets them to stay for six more months, during which time Freeman makes a separate expedition to gather gold dust and ivory, bringing in fifteen tons of the latter with the help of 200 negroes whom he persuades to help 'partly by good usage, partly by bad' (133). 'Our friend the *Englishman*' (135), as Singleton calls him, teaches these pirates how to use their time. He gets Singleton's crew to stay another month and then two more, not long enough to satisfy the avaricious Freeman but certainly long enough to make each man wealthy. It is difficult to know how to deal with this dream of golden treasure gained through exploitation of the natives; insofar as it was an imaginative projection of accumulating immense wealth, it belongs very much to the time of the South Sea Company's inflation of paper stocks. Defoe may well have been contrasting the real wealth that could be gained by exploiting the mineral wealth of the earth with the imaginary value of inflated stocks. But whatever criticism of the search for wealth in paper investments might be contained in his fiction, it also shows that Defoe too had his daydreams set on mountains of riches.

The story of how Singleton quickly loses his money through trusting of 'the keeper of a Publick House in *Rotherhith*' has its basis in the stories surrounding Captain Avery, but for the most part Singleton finds himself to blame for the 'Folly and Wickedness' and the 'Luxury' that brings him to poverty once more. The word 'Luxury' has distinct sexual connotations, and we may presume that, like the sailors described by Ben in Congreve's *Love for Love*, Singleton wasted much of his wealth on women, and was ready to go to sea again. Once more the image of a fortune thrown away only to be regained has to be seen as one of Defoe's fantasies. He who had received so wonderful a dowry on marrying Mary would now, in his imagination, recover all. For Singleton this is achieved through his Quaker adviser, William Walters. For William, who acts as a ship's surgeon, everything must be subordinated to making money. True to his beliefs, he tells Captain Wilmot with whom Singleton has joined that he will not fight, but when Wilmot suggests that he will be only too happy to share in the booty, William replies, 'Those things are useful to furnish a Surgeon's Chest . . . but I shall be moderate' (144). Although William always seems to speak in jest, he is serious enough about transforming this group of men who enjoy adventure and trouble into businessmen of a somewhat unusual cast. He helps the sailors when they engage a Portuguese warship out to destroy them, but he believes that the Quaker way dictates a prudent avoidance of such encounters. When Captain Wilmot wants to engage in fighting rather than in looting, William reminds Singleton of their true purpose:

Why, says *William* gravely, I only ask what is thy Business, and the Business of all the People thou has with thee? is it not to get Money? Yes, *William*, it is so, in our honest Way: And wouldst thou, says he, rather have Money without Fighting, or Fighting without Money? I mean, which wouldst thou have by Choice, suppose it to be left to thee? O *William, says I,* the first of the two to be sure. Why then, *says he*, what great Gain has thou made of the Prize thou has taken now, tho' it has cost the Lives of thirteen of thy Men, besides some hurt? It is true, thou has got the Ship and some Prisoners, but thou wouldst have had twice the Booty in a Merchant Ship, with not one Quarter of the Fighting. (153–4)

William proves equally sensible when they come upon a ship filled with slaves who have revolted against their white masters. Combining a sense of natural law with an ever-active eye to profit, William first calms the murderous racist rage of the pirates by arguing that the 'Negroes had really the highest Injustice done them, to be sold for Slaves without their Consent; and that the Law of nature dictated it [their revolt against the white crew] to them' (157). Then he convinces the pirates that no amount of torture will get these victims of the slave trade to confess what happened until they could communicate through language. He cures one of the slaves whose leg has been broken in the struggle and eventually teaches him a sufficient amount of English to piece together a story. One member of the crew of the slave ship raped ('abused' (161)) the 16-year-old daughter of one of the slaves and then his wife. Angered by this, the husband took his revenge, and the slaves eventually took over the ship, resisting a counter-attack that killed large numbers of them. There were no arms aboard because they had thrown them into the ocean. Concocting a story about being short on provisions, William eventually finds a way of trading the slaves to various Brazilian planters for money and provisions and exchanging the large ship for a more convenient sloop.

If Melville's tale of revolt aboard a slave-ship, *Benito Cereno*, has its ambiguities, they are contained within certain imaginative possibilities; Defoe's narrative is unsatisfactory from a variety of standpoints. If William's arguments about the evils of slavery and the slave trade are correct, why not free the slaves on some island or uninhabited part of the coast? And why spend so much time on matters such as language and communication when everything is resolved into teaching the Africans sufficient English to allow them to describe what happened? Why give over several pages to William's remarkable abilities as a surgeon, when the man whose leg he saves is simply to be sold into slavery? The answer to some of these questions is plain enough. Slaves represented profit, and although William believes that they should be treated mercifully and with attention to their moral and sexual integrity, they were nevertheless valuable economic commodities. If everything that William does smacks of hypocrisy, it is important to note that, after he tells a series of lies to the planters about the origin and destination of the slaves, Singleton notes that William 'past for what he was; I mean, for a very honest Fellow' (165). 'Honesty' is defined by Singleton within the linguistic parameters of a pirate milieu. He sells the slaves and returns to the pirate ship to split the returns with the crew.

Such 'honesty' was rare enough among pirates; it was also rare enough among the men of Exchange Alley. Because Europeans possessed superior technology, they were more powerful than the natives of Africa, and power was not to be ignored in a world that took seriously the lessons of Thomas Hobbes on this subject. Indeed some of these lessons had been revived by Bernard Mandeville, whose *Fable of the Bees* (1704, 1714) preached a somewhat similar vision. The Africans are adrift in the middle of the ocean without any knowledge of how to work the sails of their captured ship or the understanding of navigation that might bring them back to their land. They would undoubtedly have fallen prey to death by thirst or starvation had not Singleton rescued them. The Black Prince who helps Singleton and his crew cross Africa is sent back to his country, richer and more knowledgeable about European weapons and crafts than when he set out. All that Singleton holds out is the possibility that native peoples may be capable of absorbing enough of European inventions to compete with them in a hostile world. Singleton does not present William as a great humanitarian; he was merely 'honest' enough by the economic standards of the day, for while pirates could not claim to be engaged in legally sanctioned commerce, they were still trading in commodities.

The fascination for communication through language was a quality Defoe shared with Singleton. The early voyagers to America often thought they understood the completely alien languages and gestures of the natives, particularly when they wanted them to be pointing to some area that was rich with gold. Some even had the awareness to make jokes about it.[48] In Singleton's voyage across Africa, he and his crew come upon a tribe at the very beginning of their journey whose gestures are almost understandable but still in need of translation. 'When we ask'd for some to guide us, they shrunk up their Shoulders as *Frenchmen* do when they are afraid to undertake a thing.' Some gestures were universal enough. Crusoe has no difficulty understanding what is meant by one group which 'moons' at them, turning up their rears in contempt. But as Singleton remarks, communication is never easy:

We conversed with some of the Natives of the Country who were friendly enough. What Tongue they spoke, I do not yet pretend to know. We talked as far as we could make them understand us, not only about our provisions, but also about our Undertaking; and ask'd them what Country lay that Way, pointing West with our Hands. They told us but little to our Purpose, only we thought by all their Discourse, that there were People to be found of one Sort or other everywhere. (48)

The Black Prince's signs for peace have no meaning to some of the ferocious tribes they enounter. Gestures and signs are not universal. Even gold proves to be of less interest to the natives than ornaments made of silver. Only the firing of the guns, with their noise and killing power, speak a universal language of terror and amazement. Defoe's scepticism about language was to find a richer field for exploration among the English-speakers of his future fictions, but it was a constant element in his fiction from the beginning.

Although it is always lively enough, *Captain Singleton* tends to lose momentum toward the end. Singleton and his crew meet Captain Avery on Madagascar, but unlike this mythic pirate they have no desire to create a

---

[48] See *Portuguese Voyages*, ed. Charles Ley (London: Dent, 1965), 45.

state on Madagascar. On the other hand, Avery's riches inspire Singleton to further adventures, and with the taking of a junk belonging to the Mogul's court, he certainly approaches the goal of possessing enormous wealth. To lend some variety to this tale of successful piracy, Defoe dropped in the story of Robert Knox, who was forced to live among the natives on Ceylon. But the only suspense toward the end of the narrative involves the problem of finding some way for Singleton and Walters to return to Europe with the spoils. Defoe gives Captain Bob a brief period of conversion and repentance through the guidance of William Walters, but no one would confuse this work with a spiritual autobiography. Singleton is intent on telling his adventures as a pirate to his readers, and he emerges as a successful pirate indeed. Captain Singleton marries William's sister at the end, and the two friends settle down in England to share a prosperous retirement. *Captain Singleton* is Defoe's most light-hearted book. In a world in which the pirate and the businessman were barely distinguishable, Defoe allowed his fantasy free reign.

IV

Memoirs of a Cavalier was published shortly before *Captain Singleton*, but while it is set back in the first half of the seventeenth century, there are some clear connections between this historical novel and the other works of fiction Defoe was writing. In *Captain Singleton* the Portuguese sailors, in their fight with the African natives, fire their guns in the manner used by the army of Gustavus Adolphus, in three rows so that there is a constant volley as those who have fired reload, and in *The Farther Adventures of Robinson Crusoe* the attack upon the native village with its indiscriminate massacre of the entire population is compared directly to the sacking of Magdenburgh during the Thirty Years War, when the imperial army under Tilley's command killed the inhabitants indiscriminately. And in the method of the narrative—one in which the narrator gradually comes to understand the political and human meaning of the wars in which he has engaged—there is much that resembles *Major Ramkins*. Nevertheless, *Memoirs of a Cavalier* was written with a different purpose in mind. Anti-Jacobitism would have been difficult to squeeze into a work set in the 1630s and 1640s, and by 1720 some of the religious disputes of the previous year had begun to fade. An issue that seemed more important at the time was the condition of the Protestant states in Europe in relation to what appeared to be the expansion of Catholic power.

George I was particularly concerned about events occurring only too close to Hamburg, and remarks in his addresses to Parliament about strengthening the Protestant interest were understood to apply both to Britain and to the Continent. Westphalia had fallen into the Catholic camp, Protestants in Hungary were subjected to a steady harassment, and the newspapers had been reporting a variety of incidents in Germany, from beatings of Protestants by Catholic students in Heidelberg to insults to the ambassadors from Holland and England. It hardly seemed likely that such events would produce anything like the horrendous religious wars of the seventeenth century, but they were important enough to Protestant states such as Hanover; and England now shared the same monarch with that state. The first part of *Memoirs of a Cavalier*, after the narrator sets out on his adventures, deals briefly with the condition of Protestants in France, where they were already suffering the persecution that would lead to the revocation of the Edict of Nantes in 1685. A Protestant gentleman in the work reads the Cavalier a lesson: the English and Dutch actually aided France in its war against its Protestant citizens and were at least partly to blame for the coming extermination of Protestantism in France. And if this lesson of what happened when Protestants failed to help their own was not clear enough, the horrors of Magdenburgh and the victories of the unified Protestant camp under the command of Gustavus Adolphus should have left no doubt in the readers' minds. Protestants needed to stand united against the Catholic threat.

Defoe stated on a number of occasions that he possessed manuscripts about the wars in Germany, and particularly the involvement of Scottish soldiers enlisted under Gustavus Adolphus, but whether these remarks applied to works he had composed during that idle period following his first bankruptcy or to genuine documents, such raw materials could not have had the particular political and historical thrust of *Memoirs of a Cavalier*. If they were works that he had written earlier, they would certainly have lacked the narrative skill that Defoe developed only with the writing of *Robinson Crusoe*.[49] Writers of memoirs were supposed to tell of the events they experienced; they were not supposed to write auto-biography or make themselves the heroes of their own romance, an effect often criticized by contemporary critics. Certainly Defoe's focus is upon the battles and the nature of the leaders. He had to have worked with the histories of the time: *The Swedish Intelligencer* by Thomas Roe or William

---

[49] The British Library has a copy (call no. 154. d. 1) of *The Swedish Intelligencer* with notes in pen on a variety of subjects, and different types of list of those serving with Gustavus Adolphus. Defoe may have meant little more than this in referring to his manuscripts.

Watts, Ludlow's *Memoirs*, Clarendon's *History of the Rebellion*, open at his desk in the extensive library at his house in Stoke Newington. We can see the seams of these texts as he moved from one to another, but many contemporaries could not. *Memoirs of a Cavalier* was associated with a Colonel Newport, and many good readers, including Dr Johnson, thought it genuine. The very limitation of the Cavalier's experiences to what his eyes saw and his ears heard gives the work a sense of authenticity. The Cavalier misses what was perhaps the most important battle of the Thirty Years War for the frivolous reason that he was pursuing some lady, and he tells us little about those parts of the battles that he did not experience personally. He does not engage in long passages of novelistic self-examination, but he is a rich character for all that.

Without unnecessary elaboration, he shows the reader a scene in southern France in which a mob protests against the policies of the government. It is a violent situation and the Cavalier finds himself reacting emotionally against popular disturbances and regarding the Queen with great admiration. Such a response suggests why he eventually fights on the King's side during the Civil War in England. On the other hand, his strong admiration for the 'Swedish Discipline' that he observes in the army of Gustavus Adolphus was to be a significant element in English Puritanism. His willingness to promote his servant to the status of a 'Gentleman' after he shows his ability to collect booty following the battle of Leipzig reveals an egalitarian streak in him that mirrors the policies of his leader. Gustavus Adolphus was famous for promoting men on the field of battle, and the risks which he took in fighting alongside his men led to his early death. The Cavalier's distaste for the charming Italian courtesan who attempts to seduce him also suggests a puritanical streak in his nature. And he blames the clergy for bringing on the storm clouds of war that will envelop England. He charges furiously with Prince Rupert but comes to realize how foolish such heroism is when the cavalry wins its part of the battle while the infantry is routed and the field is lost.

He is Defoe's version of the ideal cavalier—brave, idealistic, fair—the model created by Clarendon in the character of Falkland in his *History of the Rebellion*. Puzzling over Defoe's creation, Macaulay complained that there was 'nothing' in it, and indeed, had Sir Walter Scott created the Cavalier, he would have given him speeches about fairness and aristocratic ideals, as he did with Henry Morton in *Old Mortality*. But that is precisely an aspect of Scott that strikes the modern reader as absurdly anachronistic. Until the end, we judge the Cavalier through his actions rather than through his stated opinions; so that when he does tell us what he thinks of the war, he has earned our respect. He does not find the fighting distasteful until he is forced to engage in a massacre at a private house. He never recovers from this experience, and when he finally surrenders with the promise that he will not fight against the forces of Parliament again, he appears to be genuinely relieved. The Cavalier finally tells us that his ideal was not the King but General Fairfax, the leader of the Parliament. For the real ideals of the gentleman—courtesy, honour, and courage—were as much to be found among the opposition to Charles I as among Charles's Cavaliers.

Although *Memoirs of a Cavalier* looked back to the military memoirs that Defoe partly wrote and partly edited during the past five years, it also led him toward new ventures. The march that the Cavalier makes through England after losing a battle may suggest something of his future work on the *Tour Thro' the Whole Island of Great Britain*, but the interest in the Cavalier as an ideal gentleman points forward to *Colonel Jack* with his quest for gentility, and, ultimately, to *The Compleat English Gentleman* and *Of Royal Education*. The possibility of cashing in on the coat of arms that Defoe displayed in the frontispiece to *Jure Divino* may have once more seemed a possibility. His claim to the status of a gentleman had been ignored during the quarrel over *The Shortest Way*, and to his enemies, during the attacks upon him in 1718 and 1719, he was still the hosier who dared to write as if he were a gentleman. But the success of *Robinson Crusoe* and the commissions that seemed to follow it may have turned his thoughts toward gentility once more. Though the Cavalier is born to his status, the rest of Defoe's protagonists snatch at gentility through any means at hand. In his study at Stoke Newington, Defoe may have thought of working toward the ideal of his Cavalier by commanding his empire of words.

25

Creating Fictional Worlds

There was an intimate relationship between Defoe's fiction and his way of thinking about the world, even though he probably did not, in the manner of Balzac, call for his fictional surgeon, William Walters, when he was ill. Crusoe's self-sufficient English farm was part of a fantasy world that Defoe might have wanted to come true for himself, and his gentlemanly Cavalier was deeply rooted in his dreams. His claim to gentility during the crisis over *The Shortest Way with the Dissenters* had been rudely brushed aside by the government. His willingness to raise a regiment to fight under Marlborough received not a flicker of response, and while he printed his coat of arms under the portrait that accompanied his *Collected Works* of 1703 and *Jure Divino* some five years later, it must have seemed like a distant vision to the embattled journalist of the early years of the reign of George I. But for the successful writer of *Robinson Crusoe* anything might be possible. He had begun dealing in various food products in the 1720s—cheeses, honey, anchovies, oysters—and even had a warehouse for some of these goods on Brewer's Key, a street off Tower Dock, one of three streets between the Tower of London and the Custom House.[1] He continued such activities until 1730, when we learn through the *Proceedings of the Sessions* of London's Old Bailey for 1730 that '*Paul Croney, of Al[l]hallows Barkin[g]*, was indicted for feloniously stealing a Barrel of Anchovies, the Goods of *Daniel de Foe*, the 6th of February last'.

Although the first evidence of this type of trading appears in 1724, the chances are that Defoe embarked on such commercial enterprises as soon as his finances permitted. But such activities were also accompanied by efforts at establishing a family estate. On 6 August 1722 he signed an agreement to lease for ninety-nine years a large area of land in the parish of

[1] See James Sutherland, 'A Note on the Last Years of Defoe', *Modern Language Review* 29 (1934), 141; George Starr, 'Sauces to Whet our Gorg'd Appetites', *Philological Quarterly* 54 (1975), 531–3; Paula Backscheider, *Daniel Defoe: His Life* (Baltimore: Johns Hopkins University Press, 1989), 470, 606 n. 7.

St Michael Mile End from the Commonality of Colchester.[2] He was given the right to exploit the lumber on the property except for twenty trees. Defoe appears to have convinced the city leaders that he would be able to put the land to use as a source of lumber, as a farm, and as a site for manufacturing bricks.[3] It was an ambitious scheme for a 62-year-old, but unlike Robinson Crusoe on his farm, Defoe did not intend to run the operation himself. He hired a John Ward to oversee the operation. As with so many of Defoe's projects, this one proved disastrous and ended in a lawsuit. But when he signed the lease, which identified him as Daniel Defoe Esq., he sealed it using his coat of arms. If Crusoe could have his island, so Defoe could have his piece of land to use as he thought fit.

The possibility of becoming a gentleman merchant-farmer-writer must have loomed large for him. Many have been amused by his specious derivation of the Foe family from the 'antient *Norman* Family of the Name of *De Beau-foe*', but it was probably not a comic moment for him.[4] Or, if it was a joke, it was a very private one. What was a little rewriting of history for someone who was a specialist in the field? Merely getting a coat of arms demanded the creation of a fictional inheritance, and Defoe was not in the mood to separate himself from his fantasies. Yet even as he was planning the improvement of his estate, he must have known how fragile his plans were.

I

His sons must have found life with such a father difficult, and their roles as messengers for their father's various publishers irksome. They must have been eager to start their independent lives. The conflicts between father and son that appear in *Robinson Crusoe* and four years earlier in the first volume of *The Family Instructor* suggest that such conflicts were as normal in the eighteenth century as today. Both sons married at about this time, Benjamin to a Hannah Coates of Norwich on 22 September 1718 and Daniel to a Mary Webb of St Mary, Aldermanbury, London.[5] If his elder son, Daniel, was off to a modest start in business as a merchant in Cornhill, Benjamin's life had already taken a nightmarish turn. Through the eyes of

---

[2] Colchester Public Record Office, CPl 1176/18.

[3] Defoe paid £500 for the right to cut and set the timber on the property. A later law suit describes part of the land as a 'Forest'. See Colchester Public Records Office, Assembly Book, fo. 134; and Colchester Muniments, Miscellaneous Deeds, under the law suit against Daniel and Mary Webb, 4 Aug. 1756.

[4] *Tour*, ii. 484–5.

[5] See John Robert Moore, *Daniel Defoe: Citizen of the Modern World* (Chicago: University of Chicago Press, 1958), 331–2.

the diarist Dudley Ryder, we can see him a few years earlier as a young man with pretensions to gentility and strong political opinions. Ryder noted that he 'is a talkative sort of young man, tells a story tolerably but does not seem to have very good sense, seems to be mighty superficial and talks the notions he had from his father'.[6] Whether or not Defoe still had direct ties with the dissenting community in Hackney, his reputation among them would probably have been that of the radical Whig who wrote *The True-Born Englishman*. Ryder's comment, then, suggests that Defoe's son had picked up his father's principles without his father's hard-won wisdom concerning the need for discretion.[7]

Benjamin was soon to leave the Inner Temple and abandon whatever thoughts he may have had about a legal career in order to pursue his vocation in the dangerous world of journalism, and not surprisingly, he began working for the *London Journal*, whose chief editors, Thomas Gordon and John Trenchard, represented a radical Whig position untainted by the temporizing practised by court Whigs such as Daniel Defoe. As James Sutherland pointed out, for the press it was a time of heated language and opinions when journalists had to come close to libelling the government to hold their readership.[8] Defoe had barely escaped punishment while writing for *Mist's Journal*, and Mist was once more in difficulties. On 28 May 1721, Nicholas Lechmere raised objections to a letter that appeared in *Mist's Journal* on the previous day. The letter described the nation as being 'ruined by footmen, pimps, pathicks, parasites, bawds, whores, nay what is more vexatious, old ugly whores! such as could not find entertainment in the most hospitable hundreds of old Drury'.[9] The House of Commons ruled the piece to be a 'false, malicious, scandalous, infamous, and traitrous Libel, tending to allienate the affections of his majesty's subjects'. Mist was arrested and, as a result of rumours that he was planning to escape to

---

[6] *The Diary of Dudley Ryder*, ed. William Matthews (London: Methuen, 1939), 128–9. Matthews mentions a correspondence between Ryder and Benjamin Norton carried on in a pastoral, artificial style.

[7] Much has been read into Ryder's brief comments on Benjamin Norton Defoe. For example, John Robert Moore suggests that Ryder's comments reveal that Benjamin was a drunkard; but that Ryder was concerned that Benjamin would expect to be entertained with a bottle of wine says more about Ryder's worry about spending money than about Benjamin's drinking habits. Since Ryder envied those who spoke with ease and possessed an ability to tell stories as part of their conversational gifts, he may have found Benjamin's gifts annoying in the light of his own self-consciousness. For a fuller picture of Ryder's character, see William Matthew's full transcription of 'The Diary of Dudley Ryder', Special Collections, UCLA Research Library, Los Angeles. For Moore's analysis, see *Daniel Defoe*, 331.

[8] James Sutherland, 'The Circulation of Newspapers and Literary Periodicals, 1700–1730', *The Library*, 4th ser., 15 (1934–5), 110–24.

[9] William Cobbett, *The Parliamentary History of England* (36 vols., London: Longman et al., 1806–20), vii. 806. The reflection was mainly directed against the King's mistresses, Mlle Schulenburg and Mme Kielmannsegge, but particularly against Schulenburg, who had made a fortune through illegal dealings with the directors of the South Sea Company.

France, moved on 3 May from the King's Bench prison to Newgate. A committee was established to investigate similar libels spawned by indignation over the collapse of the South Sea Company. No one could say that journalists did not have fair warning of the perils ahead.

Few journalists had suffered so notoriously from the charge of libel and the vagueness of the laws against it as Daniel Defoe, and while not defending Mist directly, he wrote an essay in *Applebee's Original Journal* on 8 July 1721 complaining about laws against libel that gave no notion of the limits of free speech. Once the jury had determined whether a given work was a libel or not, the degree of punishment was left entirely to the whim of the judges hearing the case. In their vagueness, Defoe complained, the laws relating to libel were different from crimes such as murder or burglary, where the violations and punishments were clear:

But here alone, the Case is left to the Mercy of the Court, both to resolve the Crime and adapt the Punishment. When the Fact alone is not Criminal, the Indictment is loaded with the usual Adverbs, seditiously, maliciously, or traitorously and seditiously, and the like; when perhaps the mistaken unhappy Scribbler has had no Sedition, or Treason, or Malice in his Head,—and the Indictment ought only to have said greedily, covetously, and avariciously,—the Man having no Design at all, but merely to get a Penny, and perhaps to buy him Bread; in which Case a Court of Justice, were they fully satisfy'd of the Thing, would commiserate his Poverty, and mix the more Mercy with their Justice.[10]

During the following weeks, Defoe was to examine the question of freedom of the press from a variety of angles, and while he was particularly hard on John Aislabie, one of the directors of the South Sea Company and Secretary of State, he also criticized those journals which, in their zeal to ferret out political corruption, were undermining the wellbeing of the nation. On 14 August 1721, while his father was attempting to prevent a swing to the Tories through excessive indignation against the government, Benjamin was arrested for writing an article in the *London Journal* of 12 August that commented upon the examination of Aislabie before the Secret Committee of the House of Commons: 'Here we find the source of all our Misery and Woe; here we see who have been Traytors, harpies, Parricides; who their Aiders, Confederates, and Abettors; to whom we owe the National Calamities we labour under; and who has contributed to destroy us at Home, and make us contemptible Abroad.'[11]

There have been a number of scenarios about Defoe's response to

---

[10] In Lee, ii. 403.

[11] Quoted in Charles Bechdolt Realey, '*The London Journal* and Its Authors, 1720–1723', *Bulletin of the University of Kansas* 36 (1935), 15.

his son's situation, most of which suggest that Defoe was angry and disgusted—angry that he had been willing to work with Thomas Gordon and John Trenchard in the first place and disgusted at Benjamin's confessing that what he had written was at the direct promptings of Gordon. But the essay on libels quoted above suggests that Defoe may have seen that Benjamin would eventually get into trouble if the *London Journal* continued its war of words against the government. And although Benjamin took the stance that Thomas Gordon forced him to write the article, the fact is that he did write it and told Peele, the publisher, Wilkins, the printer, and various workers connected with printing and distributing the paper that he took complete responsibility for the contents of the essay. The notice that appeared in *Applebee's Journal* of 26 August 1721, to the effect that Benjamin was 'but a Stalking Horse and a Tool. to bear the Lash and the Pillory . . . to skreen the true Proprietors from Justice', simply repeats Benjamin's line of argument. He was merely earning his 'Wages' from the real masterminds.[12]

Benjamin Defoe was to live his life on the edge of complete destitution. His wife gave birth to seventeen children, fourteen of whom were dead along with their worn-out mother when he wrote to the various members of the government between 1730 and 1739.[13] His first child had been baptized in Norwich in June 1719, and his wife apparently gave birth continually from then on. If the 'Historical Collections' that Defoe gave Mary during their courtship suggested a capacity for self-restraint, it was that quality that his son appeared to lack completely. If he took to working for the *London Journal*, it was probably because he preferred the unrestrained attacks on the government to his father's concern that the South Sea affair might result in empowering the Tories once more and perhaps give new life to the Jacobites.[14] A chastened Benjamin Defoe was eventually employed by the government as one of its journalists, and while William Lee's suggestion that this was done out of regard for his father appears to overstate matters, it may be that Defoe had a hand in convincing the government that his son might be useful. A year later the *London Journal* appeared as a pro-government paper, and this is not necessarily an example of how Benjamin sold out to Walpole and abandoned all of his principles.[15]

---

[12] See Lee, i. 353.

[13] See the Benjamin Defoe letters among those concerning problems involving the government and the press in the Cholmondeley Houghton MSS at Cambridge, esp. No. 1700 for 25 Mar. 1730; and various letters in the British Library: Add. MSS 32691, fos. 390–1; 32692, fos. 480–1, 454–5.

[14] Arguing the government's position, Defoe attacked *The London Journal* as poisoning 'the Morals and Loyalty of People', and therefore opening itself to condign punishment. See *Appleby's Journal* for 3 Feb. 1722, in Lee, iii. 485.

[15] Charles Realey, for example, views *The London Journal* as directed against Walpole, but the main

The stance taken by Gordon and Trenchard in *The Independent Whig* had been anti-clerical in a manner that might not have been very different from the way Defoe was supposed to be when he was hired to write against the pro-church journal *The Shift Shifted*. And although the letters Gordon and Trenchard wrote under the name of 'Cato' were to be used by the anti-Walpole opposition and the Tories, Gordon later objected to this as a mis-use of attacks mounted at a time of corruption. The quarrels that Benjamin Defoe, Gordon and Trenchard, and even Daniel Defoe had with the government were spats within the Whig family.[16] Walpole came on the scene late, and there was little resemblance between this attack upon corrupt dealings between Stanhope and Sunderland and the South Sea Company and the unceasing attack upon Walpole conducted by *The Craftsman* beginning in 1726. Defoe may have resented his son's attempt at early independence, but he probably helped him as much as he could under the circumstances.

II

At the end of 1721 and the beginning of 1722, Defoe was embroiled in journalism. In France a plague was raging around Marseilles that threat-ened to cross the Channel. He was to report the developments with fascina-tion. In *Applebee's*, he carried on a running battle against the *London Journal* on the issue of 'Liberty'. Whereas Trenchard and Gordon had defended the republicans of Rome and justified Brutus' assassination of Caesar, Defoe wrote a series of letters defending the Whig establishment under Walpole and George I.

Rebellion then can never be call'd Liberty, or justify'd on pretence of Liberty, unless we call that Liberty which all wise Men abhor. And this is the True Reason why all the Murmurers against just Government set up a Claim of Liberty; not that Liberty, rightly understood, and properly so call'd, is their Design, or that

target of the attacks upon the government were Sunderland, Stanhope, and those close to the King who profited from the rise in the price of South Sea stocks. See '*The London Journal* and Its Authors', 33–4.

[16] See Marie McMahon, *The Radical Whigs, John Trenchard and Thomas Gordon* (Lanham, Md.: University Presses of America, 1990), esp. 111–33, 185–90. McMahon certainly overstates her case, and her remark that 'Walpole and Townshend probably paid Gordon but they did not have to buy him' has comic overtones. Nevertheless, she is right in arguing that both Trenchard and Gordon were ardent supporters of the House of Hanover and detested Jacobitism. When information about a Jacobite plot gradually emerged in 1722, Trenchard, writing in the *British Journal*, was to lament the necessity of curb-ing free speech at a time when the government was threatened by insurrection and possible invasion. Trenchard viewed such a threat as preventing the proper function of a free press; but he had no doubts about the reality of the Jacobite threat.

they really intend to heal the Breaches which may have been made upon the People's Rights; but that the Word is popular, and taking with the People, and the most likely to prevail upon their Minds to raise a popular Tumult.[17]

Defoe had certainly unfurled the banner of Liberty often enough in his younger days, but he feared that agitation of the kind practised in many of the 'Cato Letters' could ignite riots. He does not deny that the events of the South Sea scandal have created 'Breaches . . . upon the People's Rights'. He simply argues that keeping the Whig government running was better than the alternatives. Though he still retained some of his Revolution Principles, along with most of the Whigs who had been shaken by the revelations about Stanhope and Sunderland, Defoe was ready to plead for a stable government that continued to exemplify the principles of the Protestant succession and freedom within the limits of established laws. The agitation for repeal of the Test Act had failed, but even so Defoe thought that the Dissenters should count their blessings under a government that supported religious toleration. By the end of the year, a new Jacobite plot was to make such a position even more desirable.

At the same time that he was trying to defend the government from some of the dangerous attacks of the *London Journal*, Defoe was also preoccupied with crime and prisons. While Nathaniel Mist was in prison for libel, Defoe seems to have been involved in collecting some pieces out of the *Weekly Journal* and publishing them in two volumes. But the threat of imprisonment for libel appears to have been of less interest to him than the outbreak of violent crime in England and on the Continent. The notorious French criminal Cartouche, whose murders and thefts were the material of legend, had been captured at the end of October 1721. *Applebee's* continued to report the alarming increase in crimes throughout Britain, and comments on criminal behaviour, along with a related body of language and images, seemed to invade much of what Defoe was writing. In dealing with the subject of political assassinations, for example, he launched into an attack upon the Romans as no better than a 'Race of Thieves and Mighty Robbers', whose conquests were no more than a species of robbery. Yet none of this seems to be an adequate preparation for the appearance of his remarkable *Fortunes and Misfortunes of the Famous Moll Flanders* on 27 January 1722.

Critics have been accustomed to say that Defoe just put himself in Moll's place and asked himself, 'What would I do next?' Seen in this light *Moll Flanders* may be read entirely as an autobiographical document. We should

---

[17] *Applebee's Journal*, 20 Jan. 1722, in Lee, ii. 480.

be able to read Defoe's mind through Moll's. In 1968, Gerald Howson argued in an article that Moll Flanders was really an imaginative construction drawn from several female criminals of the time. The two who appeared closest to Moll Flanders were Moll King and Callicoe Sarah. Since 'flanders' was a kind of cloth, a combination of the two names might easily become conflated into Moll Flanders. Howson reasoned that since Defoe was probably visiting Nathaniel Mist in prison at the time, he might easily have made a slight detour to interview these two ladies who were in Newgate at the time. After all, Moll's story is partly about Newgate. She is born there and almost ends her life there, and Defoe, who knew a great deal about prisons, also knew the psychological horror of such a place. Moll King succeeded in surviving between five and eight sentences of transportation without being hanged, and the outlines of her life could easily have provided the mythic sense of endurance that surrounds the narrative of Moll Flanders. *The Family Instructor* volumes contain dozens of narratives about families with whom Defoe was acquainted either directly or through gossip; why not take the basic pattern of his story from the notorious Moll King? Of course, Defoe's method of writing fiction was to combine a variety of characters and events to give his story depth and resonance. Throughout the seventeenth and eighteenth century there had been a series of real and fictional female rogues from whom Defoe could draw, including the notorious Moll Cutpurse and a much more direct influence, the 'German Princess', who managed to gull a series of victims.

Although the basic pattern of *Moll Flanders* draws upon the tales of roguery usually identified with the literary genre known as the picaresque, Defoe changed the form by adding certain ingredients of spiritual autobiography and psychological depth, and in so doing he transformed the entire way we, as readers, experience her narrative. But, as one critic pointed out, Moll appears to be somewhat confused about the nature and purpose of her story; she *thinks* she is telling a spiritual biography while actually doing something very different.[18] Moll's story is told by a woman who has reached a certain period of calm in her life. She is married to the man she truly loves; she is wealthy; and she even has a son from her third marriage to dote upon now that she has the leisure for such an emotion. As a result she is distanced from her story sufficiently to maintain an ironic pose in certain sections.[19] But she is never so distanced that she does not feel

[18] Richard Bjornson, *The Picaresque Hero* (Madison: University of Wisconsin Press, 1977), 193–6.

[19] Lincoln Faller maintains that using the word 'irony' is not helpful in treating Moll's and Defoe's attitudes, but his analysis of Defoe's complex stance in *Moll Flanders* amounts to the same thing. Irony is the most common word for this kind of complexity, and we should not be afraid to use it. See *Crime and Defoe* (Cambridge: Cambridge University Press, 1993), esp. 88.

the sadness of her youth. I once compared this stance to that of a shaman described by Franz Boas, who told the story of his life and medical cures with a mixture of sympathy, disbelief, and awe. I raised this comparison because Moll, without insisting on a metaphysical basis for all the events of her life, nevertheless regards everything as shrouded in a certain mystery and wonder. She is no Crusoe to perceive God's design behind the 'chequer work' of her life, but the reader feels spiritual forces at work when she is in prison toward the end of her narrative and in the scene in which she seems to hear the voice of her beloved Jemmy after they have separated. The result is a truly magical type of realism that defamiliarizes her world, transforming it into something concrete and valuable to the reader.

In addition to the originality of the narrative itself—its mixture of irony and sympathy—*Moll Flanders* is structured around a questioning of the world that is constructed by language. Understandably enough, as a child, she does not understand what words such as 'gentlewoman' or 'Miss' can mean. She confuses the first with the idea of being able to support herself and discovers that the woman she selects as her notion of a 'Gentlewoman' turns out to be 'a Person of ill Fame' who has several 'Bastards'. The ironies of this part of the novel abound. The members of the Colchester family who come to see the little girl in the workhouse who wants to be a 'gentlewoman' consider such an attitude both ridiculous in a child of her age and in her situation and also charming and precious. They do not understand her desperate desire to avoid a life of drudgery; instead they see her as a toy to amuse themselves. Despite the fact that Defoe was to publish the first of his lengthy attacks upon the newly independent servant class just a few months later, he allows us to see the world through Moll's eyes, and for Moll, it is a world that would deprive her of the liberty she desires so much. We feel her tears as she cries again and again at the prospect of being sent out to service, and we are allowed to feel that the Colchester family's amusement at her antics is foolish. When they mock her with the term 'Miss', Moll finds it a 'strange' word, strange because she was too young to know it as a word for a prostitute and too ignorant to hear the ironic use of it as applied to a young gentlewoman. The older Moll understands the mockery; the child is merely bewildered.

III

With his sons out of the house in Stoke Newington, Defoe found himself in
a society dominated numerically by the women members of the family.
Maria had married, but still at home with Mary and himself were Hannah,
Henrietta, and Sophia. It is no accident that Defoe's two brilliant women
characters, Moll Flanders and Roxana, emerge from this period between
1722 and 1724 and that one of the central themes of *Colonel Jack*, as well as
of the novels named for the heroines, involves marriage; but in some ways
the most typical work of these years was one with the title *Religious
Courtship*, published in February 1722, a month after *Moll Flanders*. Surely
something of Defoe's own family life went into this depiction of a family
with three daughters of marriageable age. If later reports of Hannah and
Henrietta are to be believed, they might well fit the profiles of the Eldest
and Youngest Sisters, who insist they will never marry unless they find
men suitable to their religious beliefs and temperaments. Defoe had a
seemingly endless resource of stories concerning the tradesmen and their
families who inhabited London and its suburbs, but the central family of
Religious Courtship and its experiences seems to strike some personal
notes.[20]

Easy enough to overlook in the year that saw Defoe's genius as a writer
of fiction flourish, *Religious Courtship* is a fascinating transitional work—
more novel than conduct book. From a purely technical standpoint it
would seem to show little advance over the two volumes of *The Family
Instructor*, and its message—that women are better off marrying husbands
of similar religious temperament and religions—shows Defoe at what
might seem to be his narrowest frame of mind. Yet the marriage theme that
was to loom so crucially in *Moll Flanders* and *Roxana* was developed with
considerable subtlety in this story of three sisters and their experiences in
marriage. If Defoe was to insist on some kind of compatibility between the
religious temperament of those planning to marry, we should not forget
that, ninety years later, even Jane Austen's Anne Elliot in *Persuasion*
broods over her suitor's sinning by travelling on Sundays. There is something slightly sinister in the depiction of the religious painting in the house
of the sister who marries a man who turns out to be Catholic, but, in fact,
the sisters are delighted with the paintings. In none of his fictions was

---

[20] For the characters of Hannah and Henrietta, see Walter Wilson, *Memoirs of the Life and Times of
Daniel De Foe* (London: Hurst, Chance, 1830), iii. 644–5. Both became staunch members of the
Dissenting community in Wimborne after Henrietta married John Boston and settled there. Wilson's
description of their 'peculiar' character seems to have been connected with the strictness of their religious
observance.

Defoe to give a better representation of contemporary life among what we would call the upper middle class. Although the three sisters are only identified by their ages and never given names of any kind, each of them has different attitudes toward the religion of her suitors and defines herself for the reader in relation to this issue. The opening story, about the conversion of the lover of the youngest daughter to a more serious life through the help of William, a poor ploughman, moves the plot of religious conversion in the direction of transformation of character. And while the characters do not have names, perhaps Ian Watt's arguments on the importance of this matter for the growth of the novel was overstated.[21] It is hard to see how *Religious Courtship* is very much less of a novel than the tendentious *Millenium Hall* (1762) of Sarah Scott. For while Sarah Scott names her characters 'Mrs. Selvyn', 'Mrs. Trentham', and 'Lady Mary Jones', they are no less representative of typical marital experiences than Sisters 1, 2, and 3. Characters in both works are shaped to advance various viewpoints. And, as for Defoe's attempt to drive home his argument, as Paul Hunter reminds us over and over again, eighteenth-century fiction always had a strong didactic bias.[22]

If Defoe succeeded in blending didacticism and fiction in *Religious Courtship*, he nevertheless had a tendency toward separating those works with a clearly didactic message from those which put a premium on holding the attention of the reader through narrative. The clearest case of such a separation appears with his *Due Preparations for the Plague*, published on 8 February 1722, and *A Journal of the Plague Year*, published on 17 March of the same year. It may be argued that Defoe was attempting to appeal to two different audiences, those seeking religious meaning in the plague that was causing such havoc in the south of France during 1721 and those seeking a fantasy of escape from such a terrible visitation. The separation probably manifests itself in Defoe's selection of publishers. He published the first volume with Matthews and Battey, Matthews having published his *Family Instructor* volumes and acted as one of several publishers of *Religious Courtship*. *A Journal of the Plague Year* was published by a consortium of publishers including Nutt, Dodd, Roberts, and Graves. Defoe may have been contemplating these compositions for many years. References to the Great Plague of 1665 are scattered throughout his early writings, and in the *Review* he suggested that he collected the bills of mortality published during that time. It was an event that subjected human beings to incredible stress. He had shown a fascination for such moments when he compiled

[21] Ian Watt, *The Rise of the Novel* (Berkeley: University of California Press, 1957), 18–21.
[22] J. Paul Hunter, *Before Novels* (Chicago: University of Chicago Press).

The Storm in 1704, and he had already shown his ability to turn such material into exciting fiction in his recent work. Given the anxiety about a punishment from God for the excesses of the South Sea Bubble, Defoe's publishers must have fought to get their hands on a work by Defoe dealing with so terrifying a prospect as the plague coming to Britain.

Due Preparations for the Plague advertised itself as being about care for the 'Body' as well as the 'Soul', but the key 'preparation' of the title has to do with the preparation for dying as a Christian. Defoe begins his book with a discussion of the plague in France, but he is quick to strike a note of warning about the likelihood that Britain is ripe for God's punishment because of the immorality of the age, particularly 'the raging avarice of the times, by which the civil interest of the nation is ruined and destroyed'.[23] Although the work has sometimes been taken as vigorously supporting the government's policies on the plague, Defoe's strong endorsement of the good will of the government should not disguise his disagreement with its original decision to quarantine all of London. Defoe argues strenuously that, even by employing the most brutal measures, including shooting small children and soldiers who had done their duty, the French had not been able to contain the plague. Predicting what he would show in *A Journal of the Plague Year*, he argued that no lines could be so strong as to contain a force of thirty men trying to break through. In his journal accounts, Defoe gave vivid depictions of the cruelty of French troops.[24] He could not see this happening in his own country. What he advises instead are forms of dispersal throughout the countryside and voluntary separation of families to avoid contagion. His two families follow this scheme, one by locking themselves in a house within London, the other by boarding a ship in the Thames and waiting for the plague to subside.

But in this work Defoe was mainly intent on the preparation of the soul. He noted that the debates over the Trinity had weakened religion throughout Britain, and urges a revival of Christian faith in the face of an illness that seemed capable of wiping out the entire city. In a dialogue among a family of merchants, Defoe allows the women of the family, first the widowed mother and then her daughter, to carry the weight of argument. And the substance of the discussion allows no room for arguments about the commerce of the nation or what the Mother calls 'politics'. When her son argues that warning the people will injure trade, she remarks,

[23] *Due Preparations for the Plague*, in *Romances and Narratives by Daniel Defoe*, ed. George A. Aitken, 2nd edn. (London: Dent, 1901), xv. 6. Page references to this work will be included within parentheses in my text.

[24] For a fuller discussion of Defoe's position on the effect of quarantining London, see my 'Defoe and the Disordered City', *PMLA* 92 (1977), 241–52.

I have nothing to do with your politics, all your reasons of state are of no weight here; it were better all those mischiefs followed, and the people were prevailed upon to begin a general sincere repentance, than all those things should be avoided, and the poor stupid people be left to sleep in security till they sink into destruction. (109)

The Eldest Son, who pleads for keeping 'public peace', is also the one who does not experience sincere repentance. Hence his terror is revived with each publication of the lists of those who died during the week. Whereas the Mother and Daughter achieve a full religious preparedness for whatever may happen, the Eldest Son never does and is punished by his state of anxiety. Defoe had gone beyond the kind of physical punishment meted out to the son in the first volume of the *Family Instructor*. The world, he knew, did not operate that way.

Compared to *Due Preparations*, *A Journal of the Plague Year* has many of the trappings of an adventure novel. The running title was 'Memoirs of the Plague', and despite the effect of measuring the progress of the plague through the weekly bills of mortality and the occasional internalization of experience by H.F., the narrator, the work is essentially told in memoir style. There is little doubt that H.F. was modelled upon Defoe's uncle Henry Foe, who like H.F. was a saddler, living in London at the time of the plague. Frank Bastian speculated on a full biographical treatment, and made the very likely assumption that the brother who fled out of London to Lincolnshire was no other than Daniel's father, James Foe. Did Henry Foe tell his nephew stories about the plague of 1665 that awakened his imagination so many years later? Or did Defoe merely keep the character of his uncle in mind as a convenient way of creating his work of fiction? Both are likely to be true. Certainly events such as the scene in which a crowd of women enter the warehouse of H.F.'s brother to appropriate his supply of hats has an intimate and personal touch. But the greatness of *A Journal of the Plague Year* is not dependent on its many anecdotes, wonderful as they are. Rather it is the sense of the city under siege by a terrible and unseen enemy that awakens the imagination of the reader—the terrible and isolated cries and the sound of shutters flapping in the wind as a city once full of life is reduced to near-silence and immobility.

If that effect is reminiscent of Wordsworth's famous sonnet 'On Westminster Bridge', it is hardly surprising. Defoe was intent on showing a city in crisis—a city full of sounds and crowds reduced to emptiness and disuse. As was true of the city during the time of the South Sea Bubble, during the plague, grass grew in the unused streets. Defoe was a master of the ineffable and, for all his realism, of the sublime. The horror of the plague dominates every aspect of life in Defoe's London. We know through other accounts that it was not really like this. Pepys lived through this period and could sum up the year in which so many had died as one of the best and most joyful of his life. Defoe concentrates the mind of the reader on pain and suffering. Even more Wordsworthian than the vision of the city devoid of people is the amazing scene in which H.F. comes upon an impoverished waterman whose wife and daughter have caught the plague. He works hard during the day and then comes to bring them whatever he can. Defoe captured the simple intonation of the Waterman as H.F. questions him about the condition of people in that area of the city:

Here I saw a poor man walking on the Bank, or Sea-wall, as they call it, by himself. I walked a while also about seeing the Houses all shut up; at last I fell into some Talk, at a Distance, with this Poor Man; first I asked him how People did thereabouts? *Alas, Sir!* says he, *almost all desolate; all dead or sick: Here are very few Families in this Part, or in that Village,* pointing at *Poplar, where half of them are not dead already, and the rest sick.* then he pointed to one House, *There they are all dead,* said he, *and the House stands open; no Body dares go into it. A poor Thief,* says he, *ventured in to steal something, but he paid dear for his Theft; for he was carried to the Church yard too, last Night.* Then he pointed to several other Houses. *There,* says he, *they are all dead; the man and his Wife, and five Children. There,* says he, *they are shut up, you see a Watchman at the Door;* and so of other Houses. *Why,* says I, *What do you here all alone? Why,* says he, *I am a poor desolate man; it has pleased God I am not yet visited, tho' my Family is, and one of my Children dead. How do you mean then,* said I, *that you are not visited. Why,* says he, *that's my House,* pointing to a very little low boarded House, *and there my poor Wife and two Children live,* said he, *if they may be said to live; for my Wife and one of the Children are visited, but I do not come at them.* And with that Word I saw the Tears run very plentifully down his Face; and so they did down mine too, I assure you.[25]

Pity and sympathy are triangulated in this scene in which the emotions of Robert the Waterman convey themselves to H.F. in a way that expands his (and the reader's) capacity for empathizing with the plight of those who suffered most from the plague—the London poor.

Within the passage quoted above, and throughout the work, the word 'poor' moves from a neutral description of the lower order of society to an adjective charged with emotion. Robert's sympathies extend beyond his wife and two children to include the 'poor thief' who died after attempting to rob the houses of those who fled or died from the plague. H.F. addresses Robert as 'Poor Man' and even 'honest Friend.' After witnessing the con-

[25] *A Journal of the Plague Year*, ed. Louis Landa (London: Oxford University Press, 1969), 106. Page references from this edition will be included in parentheses in my text.

versation between Robert and his wife, Rachel, H.F. feels that he must help the man and gives him a little over four shillings. The result of this gift is an inability to find words to express feelings, on the part either of Robert or of the narrator. 'I have not Words to express the poor Man's thankfulness,' writes H.F, 'neither could he express it himself; but by Tears running down his Face.' In scenes of this kind, Defoe achieved that kind of power that Coleridge spoke of in relation to *Robinson Crusoe*. Defoe, he wrote, 'raises me into the Universal Man—Now this is Defoe's Excellence you become a man while you read.'[26] In *A Journal of the Plague Year* Defoe was able to expand the sympathies of his readers, to understand that all humanity shared a common fate and should reach out in charity and understanding to his or her neighbours. It may sound like a common enough Christian theme, but perhaps never before had it been presented with the representative power that only realist fiction could provide.

IV

Toward the end of this miraculously productive year, on 20 December, Defoe published *Colonel Jack*, or, *The History and Remarkable Life of the truly Honourable Col. Jacque*. Eight publishers had a share in this venture, a fact which probably meant that they all thought a volume by Defoe would be an excellent investment.[27] What is certain is that whether the hero be called Jacques or Jack, the name would have been understood to mean 'Jacobite', and the lengthy title suggested that Jack 'came over, and fled with the Chevalier, and is now abroad compleating a Life of Wonders, and resolves to dye a General'. None of this promise is fulfilled by the text. How much of this part of the title was occasioned by the enthusiasm of Defoe's publishers and how much by his initial description of the work is difficult to say. On the other hand, the rest is relatively accurate in describing him as 'born a Gentleman, put 'Prentice to a Pick-Pocket, was Twenty Years a Thief, and then kidnapp'd to Virginia. Came back a Merchant, married four Wives, and five of them prov'd Whores; went into the Wars, behav'd bravely, got Preferment, was made Colonel of a

---

[26] F. D. Klingender, 'Coleridge on *Robinson Crusoe*', *Times Literary Supplement*, 1 Feb. 1936, 96.

[27] They included Brotherton, Chetwood, Dodd, and Mears, who published numbers of works by Defoe in the last decade of his life, J. Stagg and Payne, who were apparently never again to publish a work by Defoe, and Chapman and Graves, who were associated with Defoe on several occasions. Although the large number of publishers probably suggests Defoe's popularity, it is also possible that the publishers did not wish to take too much of a risk. But even if the latter is true, Defoe's name probably made spreading the risk easier.

Regiment.'[28] Even if Defoe was not responsible for promising more than he could perform, it should have been clear that he was going to have a problem with merging so many themes. As critics have suggested, the novel succeeds in following up some of these subjects at the expense of making them work together effectively.[29]

The overarching theme of *Colonel Jack*, the subject that runs through almost all aspects of the work, is gratitude. This was hardly something new for Defoe. Hobbes had called it the fourth law of nature, and in his autobiographical *An Appeal to Honour and Justice* Defoe had cited gratitude toward Harley as the chief reason for all of his actions. Crusoe is a believer in written contracts, but Friday's loyalty to the man who saved his life arises from his sense of gratitude. And the Cavalier's sense of loyalty toward Lord Fairfax at the end of *Memoirs of a Cavalier* represents a similar sense of obligation. As that epitome of Senecan thought for the Restoration, Sir Roger L'Estrange's *Seneca's Morals*, would have it:

To pass . . . to the matter of Gratitude and Ingratitude; there never was any Man yet so wicked, as not to approve the One, and detest the other; as the two things in the whole World, the one to be the most Abominated, the other the most esteem'd. The very Story of an Ungrateful Action puts us out of all Patience, and gives us a loathing for the Author of it . . . which plainly shews the sense we naturally have, both of the one, and of the other, and that we are led to't by a common Impulse of Reason, and of Conscience.[30]

Rumours about a singular act of ingratitude in the form of a treasonable Jacobite plot against George I and his government, the so called Atterbury Plot, spread about London through most of 1722.[31] In his speech to Parliament on 11 October 1722, George I spoke of the conspiracy and of the arrest of several of those involved. He later addressed a 'Declaration' by the Pretender which had been circulating since early October, which Parliament condemned as 'a false, insolent, and traiterous libel'. The man who called himself James III suggested that George I should abdicate, in view of his lack of any support from the people of Britain.[32]

---

[28] *The History and Remarkable Life of the Truly Honourable Col. Jacque Commonly Call'd Col. Jack*, ed. Samuel Holt Monk (London: Oxford University Press, 1965), title-page. All subsequent references to this work will refer to this edition and be included within parentheses in my text.

[29] See e.g. Faller, *Crime and Defoe*, 170–211.

[30] *Seneca's Morals by way of Abstract*, trans. and ed. Sir Roger L'Estrange, 6th edn. (London: J. Tonson, 1696), 57.

[31] Although there was some knowledge of a plot in April, on 21 May 1722, with the arrest of George Kelly, the plot or plots began to unravel. Christopher Layer was eventually executed and Francis Atterbury banished. See George Hilton Jones, *The Mainstream of English Jacobitism* (Cambridge, Mass.: Harvard University Press, 1954) 150–7.

[32] See Cobbett, *Parliamentary History*, viii, cols. 25–7, 47–51.

In general, the plot was not viewed so much as a serious threat to the government as an example of the persistence of the delusional state of the Jacobites. At the time of the execution of one of the plotters, Defoe, who probably thought his own life might have been forfeit at the time of his various imprisonments, argued that the horror of waiting for a verdict under such conditions was inexpressible:

O! that a Painter could be found, who in lively Colours could describe, on his Cloth, the inside of the Man's Soul, in those two or three Hours; while the Jury are contending with one another, whether the Man shall be a Man, or a Corpse; an Embodyed Soul, or a dislodged Soul, and a macerated, quartered Carcase; whether he shall be delivered, or deliver'd up; in short, whether he shall Live or Die!

But it is not in the power of Art. It is not to be done. No Colours are lively enough, any more than they are to paint real Light, or the full brightness of the Sun. No, not only not Colours, but not Words. Language is deficient; nothing can Express it. No Ideas of it can be received by any one, but him who has been in the same Condition.[33]

But in *Colonel Jack*, Defoe was more intent on portraying a moral system based on the stoic notion of benefits than in tracing the psychology of a Jacobite. A few years later he was to identify strongly with a painting of the death of Seneca, and in Seneca's view of society, everyone owes debts of gratitude and obligation to those who treat them with generosity. Towards the end of *Colonel Jack*, the protagonist is pardoned by George I for participating in the battle of Preston. His response represents a full renunciation of whatever Jacobite symphies he had and a commitment of complete loyalty to George I 'from a Principle of Gratitude and a Sense of . . . Obligation to his Majesty' for sparing him punishment. Jack expands upon this:

I mention this to hint how far in such Cases Justice, and Duty to ourselves comands us; namely, that to those who graciously give us our Lives, when it is in their Power to take them away; those Lives are a Debt ever after, and ought to be set apart for their Service, and Interest, as long as any of the Powers of Life remain, for Gratitude is a Debt that never ceases while the Benefit receiv'd remains; and if my Prince has given me my Life, I can never pay the Debt fully. (276)

Jack appeals to the 'laws of Honour, printed by the Laws of Nature in the Breast of a Soldier, or a man of Honour' (277) as evidence of a universal code of gratitude.

Defoe did not see any conflict between a belief in gratitude as the key to

---

[33] Lee, iii. 124.

the social system and the Revolution Principles which he emphasized in his earlier writings, but that this represented a shift in ideology there can be no doubt. Jack's system of gratitude advances a stronger sense of hierarchy than appeared in Defoe's earlier writings, and it also suggests a swing from a willing acceptance of self-interest as the motivating force in life toward an ethical position that emphasized moral obligation. Almost all his later writings on moral and social subjects reflect this shift in his way of thinking, and if he was to portray the sphere of economics as inevitably ruled by self-interest, even here he often felt it necessary to remind his readers of the disparity between real morality and what was acceptable behaviour among tradesmen and merchants. Defoe did not disagree with Mandeville's insistence upon self-interest as the major motivating force in human nature, but in battling against Mandeville's ideas—his opposition to Charity Schools and his arguments in favour of prostitution—Defoe, in *Applebee's Journal*, held a running argument over the years in favour of gratitude and principles stemming from it, such as charity and friendship. He continued to present the view of Mandeville and his followers, but he gave the strongest arguments to the defenders of gratitude.[34]

Jack's speech about gratitude is the culminating moment of his education but, as the title-page promises, Defoe touches on a number of other themes, including poverty, theft, what might be called the 'American success story', and the search for a good wife. To a great extent *Colonel Jack* is very much a kind of *Bildungsroman* in which the protagonist's desire to become a 'gentleman' eventually culminates in outward proof of gentility along with some comprehension that true gentility lies in an understanding of the system of benefits, obligation, and gratitude. The title suggests that Jack is born a gentleman, but from a legal standpoint he is merely an abandoned, illegitimate child. His foster mother or 'Nurse' tells him that his real mother was a 'Gentlewoman' and his father 'a Man of Quality'. According to his Nurse, his father left a message to be delivered to him when he reached some stage of cognition to the effect that he was a 'Gentleman' with the expectation that 'the very hint would inspire me with Thoughts suitable to my Birth, and that I would certainly act like a Gentleman, if I believed myself to be one' (3). In his later writings on gentility, Defoe makes it clear that 'blood' is not a significant aspect of being a gentleman, but some aspects of character appear innate. The three Jacks, Captain, Major, and Colonel, are distinctly different; nevertheless, the environment in which they are raised guarantees that each will be a thief. In Jack's case, the very notion of belonging to some unknown higher state—the trad-

---

[34] See the selections from *Applebee's Journal* printed ibid. 154, 286–8 344–51.

itional family romance that Freud saw as the universal daydream of youth— is enough to inspire him. His Nurse allows him to name himself, stating that he could call himself 'Mr. Any-thing' (4) if he wished. True to ideals of self-fashioning, he accepts the name of Colonel Jack from his Nurse in view of his status as a 'Gentleman' (5), and he accepts the name with a full sense that his 'rank' gives him a status superior to those of his brothers, the Captain and the Major.

The name is absurd in view of his early life as an impoverished boy wandering the streets of London. Defoe drew mainly from picaresque novels for the adventures of the young boy. He learns the 'Trade' of picking pockets and of begging from his companions, and when he makes his first large sum from his efforts, having no sound pockets in which to deposit the money, he fears it will be stolen from him and attempts to hide it in a tree. When the loot appears to drop down a hole to be lost forever, he weeps in despair and frustration:

I cry'd, nay, roar'd out, I was in such a Passion, then I got down the Tree again, then up again, and thrust in my Hand again till I scratch'd my Arm and made it bleed, and cry'd all the while most violently: Then I began to think I had not so much as a half Penny of it left for a half Penny Roll, and I was hungry, and then I cry'd again: Then I came away in dispair, crying and roaring like a little Boy that had been whipp'd, then I went back again to the Tree, and up the Tree again, and thus I did several Times. (25)

It is instructive to compare this passage with its source in the picaresque novel *The French Rogue*. As in that novel, the protagonist discovers that the money has fallen through to the other side of the tree and is ecstatic at its recovery. But Defoe was fascinated by the psychological situation of a dramatic change from grief to joy, and he dwells on the way Jack's emotions operate. And Jack's story is ultimately not that of a rogue. His brother the Captain has 'the very look of a Rogue' (9), but not Jack. Nevertheless, Jack identifies himself with the crew of poor, hungry children who sleep in the ashes of the Glass House to keep themselves warm:

As for my Person, while I was a dirty Glass-Bottle House Boy, sleeping in the Ashes, and dealing always in the Street Dirt, it cannot be expected but that I looked like what I was, and so we did all; that is to say, like a *Black your shoes your Honour*, a Beggar Boy, a Black-Guard Boy, or what you please, despicable, and miserable to the last Degree; and yet I remember, the People would say of me, that Boy has a good Face, if he was wash'd and well dress'd, he would be a good pretty Boy, do but look what Eyes he has, what a pleasant smiling Countenance, 'tis Pitty! (7)

Like Moll, then, Jack is very much a part of the society of thieves, yet somehow apart. If he is different in appearance, he is also unusual in his interest in learning from the old soldiers and sailors about the wars and battles, becoming 'a kind of an Historian' (11) without any knowledge of how to read or write. He also has a gradual education in the use of money, from his first purchases of breeches with pockets to his investment of his money at interest with a businessman. No matter how much Defoe drew from the picaresque, then, his emphasis was different.

An additional difference lay in Defoe's treatment of Jack's sensibility. Although the beggar boys of Spanish painters like Ribera and Murillo were depicted as objects of sympathy, for the most part the rogues of the picaresque novel were chiefly distinguished by their resilience—their ability to endure punishment and turn it into jest. On the contrary, Jack weeps easily and is affected strongly by his experiences. When Captain Jack is lashed for participating in the 'Trade' of kidnapping, the scene of the punishment appears so awful to Colonel Jack that he is literally 'frighted almost to Death' (12) at the sight of the blood and cries of his foster-brother. When he recounts his manner of life to the businessman with whom he leaves his money, he frequently weeps over his ignorance about the nature of money, over his innocence of the theft of the bills for which he receives a £30 reward, and over fear that he will be robbed of his money. And even at the age of 20, when he returns the money that he had stolen from a poor nurse in a wide-ranging series of thefts, he is once again almost moved to tears. Samuel Monk argued that Defoe's novel was an early form of the novel of sensibility, and there is much to be said for such a view.[35] Sir Richard Steele had his sentimental comedy *The Conscious Lovers* produced just a year before, in 1721, and there is no question that Defoe was still very much a part of the age's attempt to reform manners in the direction of greater sensitivity to the sufferings of the poor. He also dwelled on traditional themes of sensibility dear to the heart of writers such as Steele—the attack upon duelling, the dignity of the merchant class, the importance of friendship and true love. Dickens's criticism of Defoe's lack of sentiment, particularly in his rendering of Crusoe's emotions on the occasion of Friday's death, is still used to question Defoe's proper rendering of true emotion, but that Dickens's rendering of emotion, particularly in relation to children, should be held up as normative seems rather odd.[36] Crusoe, a born colonialist, may not wear his heart on his

---

[35] 'Introduction', *Colonel Jack* (London: Oxford University Press, 1965), p. xiv.
[36] See e.g. Patrick J. Keane, *Coleridge's Submerged Politics: The Ancient Mariner and Robinson Crusoe* (Columbia: University of Missouri Press, 1994), 47–8, 102.

sleeve, but Colonel Jack surely does. To be properly grateful, one must *feel* grateful.

Seneca's system of benefits does not create a society based on democratic principles. The social principle is that which has been called the 'Noble Household', a vision of society as an extended family. When Jack is unlawfully transported to Virginia to labour as a slave, he brings his principles with him. Eventually, he is able to apply them to the treatment of slaves. By arousing the gratitude of the slave Mouchat and his fellows, by providing good and generous treatment, he gets the slaves to work harder and serve contentedly. And by demonstrating the economic viability of his method, Jack himself rises in status and eventually becomes the owner of his own plantation, helped by his grateful former master. Defoe probably thought he was at the cutting edge of reforming the treatment of slaves, but for the modern reader warning flags go up all over the place. Lincoln Faller properly quotes Althusser on methods of getting workers to accept subjection under the illusion that they are free subjects.[37] Jack may find punishing the slaves difficult. We are intended to see that his heart is in the right place. But after all, what is he but an exploiter of slaves, not very different from Crusoe?

Admitting that Jack's use of gratitude creates a system of exploitation and that any modern reader would have to find Jack's method repellent, it must also be said that Jack thinks of Mouchat and his fellow workers as 'Servants', just as he was a servant before being made an overseer. After treating Mouchat with mercy, Jack expects Mouchat to show gratitude, but unlike Crusoe, he is uncomfortable with Mouchat's weeping and his attempt to abase himself before him. 'I would have taken him up,' Jack writes, 'but he would not Rise, but I Cry'd as fast as he, for I could not bear to see a poor Wretch lye on the Ground to me, that was but a Servant the other Day like himself' (139). Jack conceives of servants as part of the extended family of a household. He wants them to work voluntarily and enthusiastically. And if they succeed in working hard, he wants to reward them. Defoe doubtless had in mind the utopian notion of the patriarchal and protective owner of a business who sees that his workers are taken care of, well fed and housed. I see in it one of the specious utopias of capitalism—the delusion of the ideal boss and the happily subservient worker. The only thing to be said in its favour is that recently it has tended to be replaced by something worse—an idealization of the boss who, in his dedication to the laws of the market, lacks any concern for his workers. Defoe would not have thought much of the social Darwinism that has

[37] *Crime and Defoe*, 190.

resurfaced in our time; for him, under no circumstances was the honest labourer in a decent society supposed to have that most ironic of freedoms, the freedom to starve.

After he achieves his breakthrough method of exploiting the plantation workers and acquires his own plantation, Jack decides to pursue his ideal of becoming a gentleman. He turns one of his indentured servants into a tutor after the man promises to lead Jack in the direction of the kind of education a gentleman ought to have. Like Jack, the tutor had been a thief, and his appearance gives Defoe an opportunity to return to the theme of poverty and what it does to people. The Tutor paraphrases Proverbs 30: 8–9, 'Give me not poverty lest I steal'. The Tutor refuses to say that he has reformed to the extent that he would rather starve to death than steal, and given Defoe's belief in self-preservation as a force from which there was no appeal, there is every reason to believe that Defoe was supporting the arguments of the Tutor. The Tutor's role is to have Jack read history and geography and to implant in him the desire to return to Europe, where all the important actions of history occurred. Eventually, Jack is to go to Europe, fight with the Irish regiments of Louis XIV, and rise to the rank of colonel in the French army. By becoming an officer, Jack cements his claim to being a true gentleman, since no one would deny that status to someone serving in so high a station in a profession that was held in such high esteem in eighteenth-century society.[38]

Unfortunately, Jack's achievement is undercut in a number of ways; it is not so much an education as a mis-education. True enough, he is not fighting directly against Defoe's hero, William III, but he is certainly on the wrong side. And his victories in the field are accompanied by a series of marital disasters which leave him in the position of the cuckold of comic tradition. When he arrives in England, he is completely unprepared for any kind of career either as a military officer or as a husband. He is trapped into marriage by a woman who pretends to be virtuous, but who quickly takes a lover. She also takes advantage of the laws that saw her as a mere appendage of her husband, and spends his money. When he tries to protest, he is treated with contempt by a representative of his wife and beaten soundly. By the time he confronts his second wife's lover, he is an experienced enough swordsman to wound him severely, but his inability to control his anger forces him to flee the country. The courage that Jack manages to learn on the battlefield is just what the experience of soldiering teaches him. He turns out to be something less than the coward thrashed by

[38] See André Corvisier, *Armées et sociétés en Europe de 1494 à 1789* (Paris: Presses Universitaires de France, 1976), esp. 13–30.

a bully, but there is not much to boast of in his defeat of the Marquis. His next two wives are good women, but the one becomes an alcoholic and is raped by a friend and the second, his 'Moggy', a plain country woman, had been seduced in her youth by a neighbouring member of the gentry. Jack finally discovers a wife who will be true to him, who loves him and whom he can truly love, when he does something that no one involved in the genteel life would do. He remarries his first wife. She comes to him as an indentured servant, as someone who has suffered deeply. The child she had with another man has died and she has sunk into poverty and crime. She has grown with adversity, and it is with complete trust that Jack allows her to manage his affairs during the period when he is trying to get his pardon for fighting with the Pretender at Preston. It is with such a wife that Jack is finally able to become a more complete human being. His education, his becoming a gentleman, is completed not so much by his military career as by the full realization of his social relations to others.

Colonel Jack is useful as a gauge of Defoe's attitudes, those that had changed and those that remained the same. As mentioned earlier, considered as a novel, it suffers from attempting too much. Defoe tried to tie together the themes and with some success; but at the end he sets Jack on a series of voyages around the Caribbean colonies of Spain in an effort to make a great deal of money by selling goods illegally. Although this section reveals Defoe's interest in the illegal trade to the colonies and in creating fictional voyages, it is a disaster for the structure of the novel. That Jack should suddenly become incredibly avaricious and turn toward making a fortune by such a risky series of adventures has little to do with the rest of the work. Defoe may have been trying to fill in pages to satisfy a promise to the booksellers about the length of the book, but from an artistic standpoint it was a catastrophic decision.

V

Defoe did not publish very much throughout 1723, but there is good reason to believe that he had advances on some long-term projects, such as the lengthy *Atlas Maritimus*, and was hard at work on them. Most of these projects involved geography and that 'Whore' upon whom he always 'doated'—'Trade', or economics. But it is clear from his journalism in *Applebee's* that he continued to be interested in moral and ethical problems. Nothing of earth-shaking importance occurred during these twelve months, and as so often happens today with the media, he frequently focused upon journalism itself, its status as a form of news and entertainment, and the problems raised by the presence of someone like Bishop Hoadly writing for the *London Journal*. Between arguments to the effect that it was beneath the Bishop to act as a journalist and attacks on what he had to say, many columns were filled up. Concern about the Atterbury plot and its ramifications took up space during the early part of the year, not so much fear of an invasion as questions about the need to suspend habeas corpus and to impose oaths of loyalty. And he carried on debates over the degree to which parties contributed to governing the country and, as we have seen, on the degree to which the state had an obligation to help poor children through charity schools. But throughout 1723 and 1724 he also devoted a number of weekly essays to the condition of women and the problems of marriage. These are usually in the form of letters from women outraged by their treatment by the men they have married. On 8 August 1724 he wrote a defence of the capabilities of women in a manner similar to what he had written in 1697, in his *Essay upon Projects*:

I might enlarge upon the usage of Women in many Nations in *Europe*, even the most civilized; and Argue the inhumanity of setting up to Tyrannize over the Sex. Also the Cruelty of denying them that early Erudition, which would make them Equal, if not Superior in all manner of Science, and even more capable of all possible Improvement than the Men.[39]

On 29 February 1724 Defoe published *Roxana*, a novel about an extraordinary woman and the last of his narratives treating the social problems of his times.

Like *Colonel Jack*, this novel had an extensive title: *The Fortunate Mistress: Or: A History of the Life and Vast Variety of Fortunes of Mademoiselle de Beleau, Afterwards Call'd the Countess de Wintselsheim, in Germany. Being the Person known by the name of the Lady Roxana in the Time of King Charles II*. And as with the title of *Colonel Jack*, contemporary readers would have found their curiosities aroused. Was it a scandalous history in the manner of Mrs Manley? The promise of German countesses would have raised images of George I's two German mistresses, Fräulein von Schulenberg, later Duchess of Kendal, and Mme Kielmannsegge, later Countess of Leinster and Countess of Darlington, and perhaps his Italian mistress, the Duchess of Shrewsbury. None of them was a British native and all of them were 'Fortunate Mistresses'. Defoe was also playing with the title of a work by Eliza Haywood, a novelist whose contemporary success rivaled that of Defoe's fiction and who specialized in a kind of soft

[39] Lee, iii. 290–1.

porn featuring fallen women. The name Roxana, coupled with the name of Charles II, would also have raised an image of Hester Davenport, one of the first women actresses, who was dubbed Roxana for one of the most famous of her roles and who lived many years as the mistress of a wealthy nobleman. The entire title is redolent of the mixture of sex, scandal, and thinly veiled biography that was part of the form known in England as the 'secret history'. Defoe was to promise his readers a salacious narrative and give them a number of moral lessons.

But what kind of moral lessons? Not everyone has been able to agree. There are two basic critical camps. One has seen *Roxana* as a novel of degradation in which the protagonist slips into sin and moves step by step toward damnation. In this camp, the more it is possible to prove Roxana to be evil, the more successful Defoe is seen as a novelist, since we are always asked to observe the disparity between her growing wealth and her moral decline. More recently, the second camp has judged Defoe to be morally insensitive, presenting an argument that has gone something like this. Defoe was a writer very much involved in commerce. True, he wrote on politics, morality, and social problems, but at heart he was a businessman who himself desired to accumulate wealth, and who wrote for an audience who enjoyed nothing more than reading about characters, fictional or otherwise, who recorded with book-keeping precision the profits they earned with each adventure. Samuel Macey, in *Money and the Novel*, maintained that Defoe's audience enjoyed adding up the ever-growing hoard because they were middle-class, because during their daily lives they spent much of their time compiling accounts, and because they could get considerable pleasure from these fantasy accounts of Robinson Crusoe, Moll Flanders, and Colonel Jack.[40]

This work was followed by Bram Dijkstra's extraordinary argument in his *Defoe and Economics* to the effect that Defoe was an ardent proponent of the new capitalism, that his novels simply present scene after scene of unrestrained acquisitiveness, and all with the wholehearted approval of Defoe and the expectation of his audience. Dijkstra focused particularly upon *Roxana*, a novel in which Defoe's heroine consults with Sir Robert Clayton, a scrivener who has made a fortune through unscrupulous dealings during the Restoration, arguing that Defoe approved completely of Clayton and of Roxana's financial dealings. This argument depended on deliberately omitting Defoe's judgement that Clayton was as 'greedy as the grave', as well as his attacks upon Clayton for selling land that had been used for the burial of victims of the plague of 1665. Nevertheless, Dijkstra's

[40] Samuel Macey, *Money and the Novel* (Victoria, BC: Sono Nis Press, 1983), esp. 17–83.

view of *Roxana* and his image of Defoe as an economist and immoralist has found some supporters, particularly among those unfamiliar with Defoe's economic ideas.[41]

Without disagreeing entirely with Samuel Macey's comments on the pleasures provided to readers by the prospects of wealth afforded the protagonists of eighteenth-century fiction, I would suggest that Defoe's audience would have been capable of finding a variety of pleasures in Defoe's texts, including that of absorbing a moral lesson. Supporting Macey's argument is the frontispiece to the 1740 edition of *Roxana* with its spurious continuation. Roxana is depicted in bed having just given birth to a child by her lover, the Prince. She asks that the child be made a nobleman, while the delighted prince holds up a purse. Nevertheless, it is obvious that neither Macey nor Dijkstra have a full grasp of the complexities surrounding concepts of luxury during this period. Debates over luxury had been heating up throughout the early part of the eighteenth century and broke into flame with the spectacle of Regency extravagance in France, the South Sea Bubble, and the publication of the 1723 edition of Mandeville's *Fable of the Bees*. Mandeville might well protest that the edition of 1714, with its prose explanation of the unannotated poem of 1704, had made his positions on luxury abundantly clear. But the events of the past few years had given an entirely different context for his work when it was reissued in 1723. Defoe's *Roxana*, published in 1724, was part of that debate. What I want to do here is to clarify a few points which appear to have been ignored.

A well-known article by Hans H. Andersen published in 1941 had argued that Defoe experienced a conflict between his moral judgement and his love of what he called 'Trade'.[42] In fact, Defoe did not see this as a true conflict. He did indeed view trade, as regulated by the state, to be essential to the functioning of society. He knew it to be sometimes criminal in its nature, but insofar as it was beneficial to the state he regarded it as entirely outside the realm of moral judgement. He saw the state as struggling for power with other states abroad and trying to protect the wellbeing of its citizens at home. But notions such as self-interest and self-preservation at any cost, which were axiomatic for the state, were far more problematic concepts for the individual.[43]

---

[41] Bram Dijkstra, *Defoe and Economics* (New York: St. Martin's Press, 1987).

[42] 'The Paradox of Trade and Morality in Defoe', *Modern Philology* 39 (1941), 23–46.

[43] Defoe used the term 'luxury' in three different ways: he sometimes applied it to the consumption of all products unnecessary for sustaining existence; secondly, he applied it particularly to importations that depleted the wealth of the nation, and sometimes, as in the case of imported material from the Far East, caused English workers to lose their jobs; and thirdly, he also employed the term to describe that manner of life that was wasteful of time, energy, and morals. In this latter sense, luxury was a sin against chastity. See my *Economics and the Fiction of Daniel Defoe* (Berkeley: University of California Press, 1961), 136.

Defoe's fiction is often a theatre of moral struggle in which the protagonist, yielding to the demands of necessity to lead an immoral life, attempts to find an accommodation between the imperative of self-preservation and his or her struggle toward leading a moral life. As G. A. Starr suggested years ago, they belong to the realm of casuistry, with its dramatized conflicts between conscience, religious law, conventional law, and natural law.[44] At the time in which they were published, Defoe's fictions reflected these general moral conflicts while also appealing to the particular ethical issues that bemused contemporaries. The stage on which the characters acted out their struggles had as an invisible, usually anachronistic, backdrop all the corruptions of the South Sea Bubble, including the involvement of the court and some of Britain's leading figures.

By 1723, when Mandeville's expanded edition of *The Fable of the Bees* was published, none of his detractors was ready to argue with him on the need for some degree of luxury. The new, consumer-oriented nature of English society had been furiously defended by Nicholas Barbon throughout the 1690s, and Defoe was one of the strongest advocates of projects that would enrich society through circulation and consumption. If he borrowed unashamedly from writers such as Nicholas Barbon, Charles Davenant, and John Cary, he was not behind them in enthusiasm. Almost all of his businesses were essentially luxury-based, from manufacturing perfume extracted from civet cats to importing wines and spirits from Spain. If he believed in the necessity for the government to limit aspects of consumption that were harmful to the economic wellbeing of the state, he was content enough with an England that imported goods that did not interfere with the productivity of the English worker. On the other hand, like Richard Fiddes, William Law, George Blewitt, and others, Defoe did not accept Mandeville's eagerness to use labourers, prostitutes, and poor children as so much disposable material for maintaining a well-run state. Though filled with economic and sociological information about contemporary Britain, Defoe's novels were essentially aesthetic and moral texts.[45] And accepting as he was of the sinful nature of humanity, he was not going to applaud in his fiction all the aspects of modern luxury—masquerades, practices that he considered sexual perversion, and over-indulgence in food and drink.

Of Defoe's characters, only Roxana finds herself involved in a world of luxury and corruption. If he drew on imagination for his early scenes of a

[44] *Defoe and Casuistry* (Princeton, NJ: Princeton University Press, 1971).

[45] For an excellent analysis of the difficulties of reading Defoe's fictions, see Faller, *Crime and Defoe*, esp. 229–44, where he argues that in *Roxana* Defoe was indulging in consciousness-raising in relation to his readers.

destitute mother and her starving children that he described earlier in his journal, the *Review*, he appears to have taken some aspects of Roxana's character from the notorious Duchesse de Berry, the daughter of Philippe II, Duc de Chartres et d'Orléans, and Regent of France. The Duchesse de Berry participated in the nightly debaucheries of her father, and was even rumoured to have had incestuous sexual relations with her father.[46] Her pride in her position and vanity were notorious, almost approaching madness. As we have seen, Defoe, who acted as a translator of the foreign news for Mist's *Weekly Journal*, appears to have been deeply involved with the issue of 8 March 1718, which contained an account of the actions of the Duchesse de Berry. That issue reported a reception and dinner given by her, a dinner whose menu was so lavish that it was published by the *Mercure galant* in ten pages of the February 1718 issue with apologies that there was not more space to describe the incredible variety of rare dishes. This 'magnifique' feast, prepared by M. de Pesié, along with other activities in honour of the Duchesse de Lorraine, was described as 'une des plus brillantes Festes que l'on on vûë à Paris'.[47] Although Defoe introduced his description of this occasion as 'diverting', he could hardly have been pleased by the extravagance of the feast and the masquerade that followed:

. . . there were at the Table . . . three Course 270 Dishes, all of Plate, Covers and all, five beaufaits, which were filled with three several Services of Gold Plate of different Fashion and Workmanship, the others with an infinite Variety and number of Glass Works for all Occasions necessary to the Day.

For their Repast there was first as above, 270 Dishes of meat, 200 several sorts of Soop, all differing from one another, 215 several Dishes of Pastry, 70 Stands of Rings upon every Stand eleven Rings, and every Ring holding Sweetmeats, Preserves, and Fruit of an infinite Variety, dry'd and green; with 70000 China Oranges, 5000 Lemons and Citrons, 1000 Gallons of perfumed Lemonade for the ladies, and a Profusion of the choices of Wines of Burgundy and Campaign for the Gentlemen. Before they sate down, the ladies made a Ball, and danced with such Persons of the first Rank as presented, and after they had supped, they had a Masquerade and Ball, when the King came incognito to see them, and the Company did not begin to separate till Day-light appear'd.

Defoe did not comment adversely on this scene of extravagance, but the reader has the sense that he experienced this account with some of the same feelings as the governors of Lilliput watching Gulliver devouring the needed produce of their country. It was a magnificent spectacle, but

---

[46] See duc de Saint-Simon, *Historical Memoirs*, ed. and trans. Lucy Norton (3 vols., New York: McGraw-Hill, 1968), i. 181; H. Montgomery Hyde, *John Law* (London: W. H. Allen, 1969), 94–5.

[47] *Le Mercure Galant*, Feb. 1718, 223–4.

how much could any nation afford? Luxury as a necessary display of monarchical power and magnificence had still some time to grow and expand before it began to be challenged by the revolutions that broke out at the end of the eighteenth century. In 1718, seen through Defoe's eye, this kind of extravagance must have appeared wasteful and evil. A year later the Duchesse de Berry, the Messalina of the Regency, was dead, apparently burned out at the age of 24.

At one of the celebrations, the Duchesse de Berry, along with other ladies of the court, appeared dazzlingly covered with their gems ('toutes brillantes de pierreries').[48] Defoe reported this with the remark that the phrase 'toute brillante' was not truly translatable into English. Similarly, Roxana, who has obtained the jewels of her first lover after he has been murdered and other jewels from subsequent lovers, appears before her future husband, the Dutch Merchant, in the Turkish dress she had worn when she danced before the King of England, along with a diamond necklace and diamonds in her hair that made her '*Tout Brillant*, all glittering with Jewels'.[49] Defoe's reading of the relationship between food and sex is obvious from the gradual progression of Roxana from her yielding to the advances of the jeweller out of sheer necessity, to her accepting the fine feast set for her by the Prince who becomes her lover, to her own role as the hostess of 'what they call'd, a Party', which, in addition to the gaming tables and the room in which she received guests resplendent in her jewels, provided three rooms with tables 'cover'd with Wine and Sweet-Meats'. It is in these rooms that she gives the lascivious, pseudo-Turkish dance that earns her the name 'Roxana'.[50] The dress appears to have allowed her to dance with her breasts only partly concealed, and introduced into the already luxurious court of Charles II a note of Near Eastern luxury.

Scholars have long been aware of the double historical time-scheme of *Roxana*, with its attempted analogy between the luxurious time of Charles II and the contemporary court of George I. Despite Dijkstra's attack on David Blewitt's forceful statement of the case, Blewitt's arguments are sound.[51] But in many ways the spectacle of contemporary France presented

[48] *Le Mercure Galant*, Feb. 1718, 223.

[49] *Roxana*, ed. Jane Jack (London: Oxford University Press, 1964), 247. All subsequent page references to this edition will be included within parentheses in the text.

[50] For a discussion of all the echoes in this part of *Roxana*, see my 'Crime and Punishment in *Roxana*', *Journal of English and Germanic Philology* 65 (1966), 445–65. It might be added that the court of the Regency was often associated with the Turkish seraglio, and that the court of George I, in celebrating his birthday on 28 May 1720, was dressed in clothes imported from France. Like the duchesse de Berry, the women were covered with jewels. See *The Original Weekly Journal*, 28 May 1720.

[51] The frame of reference for the ambience of Charles's court is much clearer than for the court of George I, and the figure of Sir Robert Clayton, who died in 1707, makes no sense in the context of the court of George I. His role as an active financial adviser and womanizer belongs entirely in the seven-

an even more vivid scene to exploit. Roxana, who is as much French as she is English, carries the burden of the geographical allusion. Defoe was certainly reflecting upon the excesses of the court of George I and his times, with its financial corruption, its masquerades, and its official mistresses.[52] If the Regency of the Duc d'Orléans in France provided a scene that was sometimes described as a 'seraglio', the English court, with its aping of French fashions and its grotesque speculations in the South Sea Company, afforded an almost equal example of corruption.[53] And that Roxana should proceed from being mistress of a king to mistress of an older nobleman whose special interest was anal intercourse seems predictable from the pervasive Turkish influence surrounding her sexuality.[54]

Defoe punishes Roxana in the end. I do not mean so much the somewhat enigmatic final paragraphs but the state of near madness that descends upon her when she is at the height of her prosperity. Having replaced any notion of family by values based on vanity and wealth, Roxana finds herself alienated from all around her. Much of this is predictable from the frontispiece, which reveals her emblematically as a traditional figure of vanity, examining herself in the mirror in all her elegant costume. But even this emblematic scene had taken on certain aspects of ambiguity over time, since a similar emblem from the seventeenth century was used to illustrate a kind of proper pride in self.[55] If Roxana does sin a little too successfully, she is nevertheless both the victim and the product of a society dedicated to luxury and consumerism. Defoe noted in his *General History of Trade*:

This new method of Living, saving the Errors of it, as it May be recon'd a Vice; is however the great support of Trade in the World; again, that Trade encreases

teenth century. For a general discussion of the double time scheme, see David Blewett, *Defoe's Art of Fiction* (Toronto: University of Toronto Press, 1979), 121–7.

[52] Defoe was not the only one to make the comparison between the times of Charles II and George I. See e.g. the specific attack on the practice of masquerades during both reigns in George Blewitt, *An Enquiry Whether a General Practice of Virtue Tends to the Wealth or Poverty, Benefit or Disadvantage of a People* (London, 1725), 148–57.

[53] See James Breck Perkins, *France under the Regency* (Boston: Houghton Mifflin, 1901), 580–2.

[54] See e.g. Joseph Pitts, *A True and Faithful Account of the Religion and the manners of the Mohammetans* (Exeter, 1704), 18. One of Defoe's main sources for discussions of Turkey was Jean Dumont's *New Voyage to the Levant*, 2nd edn. (London, 1696), with its ample account of dress and dancing among the Turks. See Defoe's *Conjugal Lewdness* for the suggestion of anal intercourse practices in Turkish marriages and the recourse to the law available to wives.

[55] See George Whither, *A Collection of Emblems* (London, 1635), 249. In his musing over the difficulties of reading Defoe, Lincoln Faller argued that where Defoe seemed to be emblematic, it was incumbent upon him to avoid ambiguity, but pictorial emblems often had texts whose interpretations varied greatly. And in Defoe's time, contemporary Dutch still life had moved from emblematic warnings about the brevity of existence to a glorification of luxury while often retaining, in muted form, some of the pictorial symbolism.

Wealth, raises Families, lifts the Poor up from the low and necessitous way of living to subsisting comfortably and plentifully on their Labour.[56]

Roxana's forceful arguments about the vicious treatment of women in contemporary society and the need for female independence may go too far in the direction of libertinism for Defoe when he was in a less paradoxical mood, but we are not to take the arguments as evil in themselves. As I once suggested, she functions as a satirist upon the manners of her society.[57] If, like so many satirical figures of the Restoration, she is deeply implicated in her critique, this does not mean that we must reject all of her comments as fallacious. She is somewhat like Manly of Wycherley's Restoration comedy *The Plain Dealer*, wrong-headed but still admirable in many ways. She refuses to be reduced to starvation despite being abandoned by her husband, and whatever her end may be, she is certainly not pathetic. Defoe, who disliked characters who succumb to despair, would have liked that aspect of Roxana's character. She achieves financial success as a participant in the new consumer society. It is part of the irony of her role in this milieu of luxury and self-interest that she raises the ghost that comes to haunt her, by trying to provide for the children she had been forced to abandon in her struggle to survive. If, as modern readers, we feel that she deserves a better fate, it is not at all certain that Defoe would have entirely disagreed.

[56] *A General History of Trade* (London, 1713), No. 2, 27.
[57] Maximillian E. Novak, *Defoe and the Nature of Man* (Oxford: Clarendon Press, 1963), 112.

26

Describing Britain in the 1720s

Roxana was by no means Defoe's last work of fiction, but it was his final effort at creating the kind of fiction we think of as a novel of manners. Defoe's ability to place a character within a complex milieu and to show how that character interacts with others, his ability to dramatize the moral implications of actions, and his continuing awareness of individual personality and the way it sees the world all found their fullest development in *Roxana*. In her combination of passivity and daring, her self-awareness and her resolve to plunge into an immoral world, her willingness to use sex to achieve status, and her burning avarice, Roxana is very much a creature of her age—very much a 'Whore'. It is also clear that Defoe was ready to go on to other things. He wanted to speak in a voice closer to his own, and for this purpose he was soon to invent the cantankerous old Andrew Moreton, who did not like what he saw in the world of the mid-1720s and was ready to complain about it. Defoe was not quite Andrew Moreton—at least, he had given only part of his personality to that kind of vision—but there are signs that he was tiring of the kind of entertainment required by his column in *Applebee's* and his novels.

A more practical consideration may have turned him away from novels. *Robinson Crusoe* had been an enormous success, and *Moll Flanders* and *Colonel Jack* had both rapidly gone to three editions. *Roxana*, on the other hand, appears not to have been half so successful, and neither was *A Journal of the Plague Year*. Defoe and Eliza Haywood had both come on the scene at approximately the same time, creating a mass market for prose fiction, but after five years public interest may have started to decline. By the early 1730s Haywood had abandoned fiction for an acting career. She only returned to fiction after 1740, when Richardson had given a new respectability to the novel. In *Roxana*, Defoe had attempted to write a moral version of the Haywood love novel, turning it on its head in the process. He probably thought it was time to move on to other, more profitable enterprises. It is perhaps vain to speculate on what might have followed *Roxana*. Would it have been a new breakthrough in the art of fiction? However interesting Defoe's ideas and however permanently valuable works such as his *Tour thro' the Whole Island of Great Britain* were to prove, it is impossible not to regret his decision to turn from an arena in which he was to gain lasting fame and in which he was to discover his true genius.

I

After publishing *Roxana*, Defoe turned to writing the first of a series of books and pamphlets on the social problems of England. In some sense these works were continuations of *An Essay upon Projects*, but while they were essentially secular in orientation in the manner of his first book, they lacked the optimism of the earlier work. Now the stress was often upon the ills of Britain and the best methods to repair them. Defoe was still capable of envisioning his improved future, but now his utopian stance existed in counterpoint to a darker view. *The Great Law of Subordination* was addressed to investigating that perennial difficulty, the servant problem. In his younger days Defoe had been accused of failing to pay the workers at his brick factory, but as we have seen, he had rushed to the defence of other workers, from the Newcastle dockmen to the weavers, protesting the conditions of their employment and objecting to the loss of the profits of their labour caused by the importation of calicoes. On the other hand, Defoe seems to have thought of house servants as, ideally, part of the extended family. Their refusal to perform their duties, then, had the potential to disturb the family peace. At a time when servants were cheap and when there were no machines to ease the burden of domestic chores, everyone who could pay £5 to £7 a year had a servant or two. As Defoe was to note in his best-known tract on this subject, it was *Every-body's Business*, at least everybody above the level of a labourer or servant, and it was likely, then, that Defoe and the booksellers would have thought that a book complaining about the 'Insolence and Insufferable Behaviour of Servants in England', as the extended title promised, would sell very well indeed. The preface, however, suggests that the contrary was true, that '*tho' they own'd the Fact,* [the booksellers] *did not think it important enough to appear; that it was below the Dignity of the Pen, and wou'd not influence the World, as it hop'd it wou'd, to attempt a Cure*'. As proof of his foresight, the writer of the preface points to a new law passed by the House of Commons on this very subject.

The six publishers who ventured on this project were doubtless disappointed in the result. The remaining unsold sheets, accompanied by a less polemic title, were issued by H. Wittridge some two years later. In telling a number of stories of domestic distress, Defoe used a format generally similar to that employed in the second volume of *The Family Instructor*, but this time he used the device of a series of ten letters, purportedly written by a Frenchman living in England to his brother in France. That may have been a mistake, since it is not certain that the British wanted to be lectured about anything by the French, especially on 'the great law of subordination', which might well conjure up images of tyranny, popery, and poverty. In addition, the attack was not as focused as Defoe's more successful *Every-body's Business*. In the end, *The Great Law of Subordination* was as much an attack upon the behaviour of the masters as upon that of the servants, as much about swearing and the increase in drunkenness as about anything else. As Defoe had argued in *Colonel Jack*, once completely inebriated a person might do anything. In the *Great Law of Subordination*, he was particularly intent on arguing that it led directly to the abuse and beating of wives.

The complaints about overthrowing the class system might well come from a Frenchman, or from that naturalized Hollander Bernard Mandeville, but it does not sound much like Defoe:

. . . the miserable Circumstance of this Country is now such, that, in short, *if it goes on, the Poor wil be Rulers over the Rich,* and the Servants be Governours of their Masters; the Plebeij have almost mobb'd the Patricij; and as the Commons, in another Case, may be said to be gotten above the Lords, so the Cannaille of this Nation impose Laws upon their Superiors, and begin not only to be troublesome, but in time, may be dangerous; in a word, Order is inverted, Subordination ceases, and the World seems to stand with the Bottom upward.[1]

But after this diatribe, the letter writer couples the 'common sort' (18) with the nobility, the one seeking a liberty to commit crimes, the other sunk in a vicious manner of living. Would he were back in France, he muses, where servants know how to be servants. There even seems to be a note of nostalgia in the narrator's lament that masters cannot kill servants in England.

Though the letter-writer has horror stories enough about the threat of combinations—early forms of unionization among workers—many of the tales are ambiguous. What did Defoe really think about the master who shoots and kills the footman whom he discovers in the act of eloping with

[1] *The Great Law of Subordination Consider'd* (London, 1724), 17. Subsequent quotations from this work will be included within parentheses in the text.

his daughter, or about the jury verdict to the effect that the footman was guilty of theft in attempting to 'steal' the daughter, who was to be regarded as a possession of the father? And what are we, as readers, to think of the master who kills his servant, Humphry, with his sword in a drunken rage? Defoe's letter-writer extends his attacks to gamekeepers, who actually take game from their masters to make huge profits; such clever and wealthy servants are contrasted to the poor thresher who violates the law by carry-ing off a little wheat from his master's field to feed his family. In the end, Defoe's main proposal involves institutionalizing letters of recommenda-tion in the form of 'Certificates' of good behaviour. His other proposals—punishment for drunkenness among servants and punishments for servants guilty of assault—were surely within the bounds of contemporary laws and, considering the freedom that Justices of the Peace had in retaliating against servants, were relatively lenient.

Whatever may be said concerning Defoe's general plan for reform, a plan that sounds little different from the kind of proposal that might have come from one of the Societies for Reformation of Manners with which Defoe was associated in his younger days, it should be said that his treat-ment of servants lacks the bite of Swift's brilliant *Directions to Servants*, a work which leaves the impression that the nation would be happier if all servants were sent to the gallows. Swift was writing satire; Defoe was still operating in a fictional mode. There are certain aspects of the work which are intended to be more in character with the letter-writer than with some of Defoe's opinions. For example, he was generally a defender of the theory that high wages result in the production of superior goods which, in turn, will find a market through their excellence. In *The Great Law of Subordination*, he takes up the complex of attitudes knows as the 'hard times' theory. Defoe's letter-writer argues that workers do not benefit by receiving higher wages, because they will use the extra money to get drunk and ruin their families in the process. 'I never knew a servant or a Work-man in England, one farthing the better for the encrease in his wages,' (78) writes the French letter-writer. But a few years later, Defoe's Andrew Moreton was to comment drily on this matter, 'As they have had Wit enough to get 'em, so will they, I doubt not, have the same Sense to keep them.'[2] The implication, as above, is that they probably will not be capable of benefiting from the additional money, but Moreton is willing to leave open the possibility of an industrious servant improving his or her lot in life.

As I mentioned above, Defoe was to make up for the lack of success of

[2] Defoe, *Augusta Triumphans*, 2nd edn. (London, 1729), 24.

The Great Law of Subordination about a year later with *Every-body's Business, Is No-body's Business*, which went into five editions within a month and a half. Whereas the former work cost 3s. 6d., his new work could be bought for only 6d. He avoided the broadly based attack upon the decline of morals and focused particularly on women servants. In the preface to the fifth edition he argued that his work was directed against bad servants, not servants in general, and within the body of the work he spoke of his willingness to pay £5 or £6 a year for a good servant. But what is best about *Every-body's Business* is his vivid picture of maidservants coming to London and transforming themselves: 'in short plain country Joan is now turned into a fine London madam, can drink tea, take snuff and carry herself as high as the best.' As suggested above, Defoe wanted these maidservants to save their money, and not spend it on clothes in an effort at mimicking the conspicuous consumption of their mistresses. Toward the end of the pamphlet Defoe wandered into regulating this and that—homeless children, who ought to be put to work in agriculture or in helping to clear the sand bars in the Thames, or the aged poor, who needed to be given employment. What is clear is that in these later years Defoe was revisited by his desire to reform society through social engineering. As we shall see, it was a terminal delusion which only came to an end with his own end, but there is little question that his opposition to the ideas of Bernard Mandeville lay behind much of what he proposed.

Although Mandeville believed in regulating society where it came to preserving the status quo, particularly where it came to keeping the poor in their place, his theories were based to a great extent upon an early concept of *laissez-faire*. Society was like a great punchbowl, a working mixture of many ingredients, including even a little virtue. Attempts to 'improve' or reform it, particularly in the direction of greater virtue (superior taste), were likely to be destructive to the balance that made the mixture work. Mandeville did not see a perfectly static mixture. What was on top sometimes sank to the bottom (the wealthy and powerful often had sons who spent the family fortune and fell into poverty), and the ingredients at the bottom sometimes rose to the top. But, dropping Mandeville's simile for the moment, it was certainly in the interest (and for Mandeville self-interest was always the guiding principle of behaviour) of those ruling society to keep it as stable as possible, and since they had the power, they ought to see to it that the poor were kept ignorant, hard-working, and even drunk— anything to keep them from disturbing the wellbeing of the rich and powerful. In Mandeville's view the greatest danger was a misplaced sense of Christian virtue, which argued for charity toward the poor, reform of a society based on fashion and luxury, and an ill-conceived urge toward selflessness.[3] Part of the extended title of *Every-Body's Business, Is No-Body's Business* is *Private Abuses, Publick Grievances*, a play on Mandeville's own subtitle to *The Fable of the Bees, Publick Vices, Private Benefits*. The subtext of Mandeville's pithy phrase is: accept human nature for what it is—entirely self-interested—and take pleasure in contemporary life; the subtext of Defoe's comment is that since individual abuses lead to evils which adversely influence everyone in society, the government should act to improve the social wellbeing of its citizens. I hardly need to comment on the modern resonance of these viewpoints.

Although Defoe's ideas on social and economic problems were more or less in place before his encounter with Mandeville's writings, there is no doubt that Mandeville's paradoxical ideas got Defoe's mind working. He may even have conceived his French letter-writer of *The Great Law of Subordination* in Mandevillian terms. Aside from Defoe's attraction to new intellectual approaches, Mandeville's ability to irritate people certainly had commercial possibilities, and Defoe was not unwilling to exploit that potential. In *Applebee's Journal*, he attacked both Mandeville's contempt for the charity schools that educated the poor and his advocacy of legalized prostitution, which Mandeville, in his *Modest Defense of the Publick Stews* (1724), had defended as a way of protecting the virtue of women in the middle and upper orders.[4] Defoe would have found much to agree with in Mandeville's *An Enquiry into the Causes of the Frequent Executions at Tyburn* (1725), but the thrust of Mandeville's arguments was in the direction of contempt for the poor, while Defoe was always ready to remark on the causes that brought people to steal. But Mandeville proposed the possibility of seeing all social action in terms of self-interest, and Defoe filled the columns of *Applebee's* with debates over this issue. Like Mandeville, he believed firmly in human evil and saw Shaftesbury's view of human nature, with its tendency to dismiss the idea of any type of natural wickedness,

---

[3] See Bernard Mandeville, *The Fable of the Bees*, ed. F. B. Kaye (2 vols., Oxford: Clarendon Press, 1924). For the image of the punchbowl, see 'Remark K', i. 105; for a general statement of his moral and social position, see 'A Search into the Nature of Society', i. 323–69.

[4] See Lee, iii. 154, 286. Defoe is usually ascribed *Some Considerations upon Street-Walkers* (London, 1726), though recently the ascription has been questioned. The anti-Mandevillian thrust of the argument is obvious enough. 'Sure no body will urge', writes the author, 'that the Consumption of Commodities and Manufactures which she helps towards is a sufficient Atonement for the Mischief she does; and the want of that Good she is capable of doing' (6). The insistence both upon the value of life and upon the evils of thinking that prostitutes justify their existence by consumption of goods are very much like Defoe, as is the general sympathy toward women at a time when marriage without a dowry was impossible. The reasons for ascribing it to Defoe is his obvious involvement with the subject in *Applebees*, the style, and the ideas. These are the reasons for ascribing most works to Defoe. But see P. N. Furbank and W. R. Owens, *Defoe De-attribution* (London: Hambledon Press, 1994).

as wrong headed. In his later attacks upon deism, Defoe was far more
vehement about the errors of Shaftesbury and his followers than he ever
was about Mandeville. There are few of Defoe's writings after 1724 that are
not in some way touched by Mandeville's ideas.

II

Two aspects of *The Great Law of Subordination* that stray somewhat from
the main theme of the work involve discussions of travel within England
and the increasing growth of criminal activities. The latter subject,
attached as it is to discussions of crime among servants, is not as surprising
as the discussion of the French letter-writer's wanderings through the
nation during the years 1684–8, close to the time when Defoe was in hiding
after the Monmouth episode. That Defoe did some wandering after
Monmouth's defeat seems very likely, but the leisurely 'Tours' of the
French letter-writer could have little resemblance to what must have been
Defoe's frantic efforts at escape. He stresses his effort at 'critically observing, and carefully informing . . . [himself] of every thing worth observing
in all the Towns and Counties through which . . . [he] pass'd'. He takes
along an 'ancient Gentleman' who acts as 'a walking Library, a moveable
map' (47), and examines all 'Curiosities of Nature or Art' to be seen. But he
particularly stresses his attempt to assess the nature of 'the common
People, what their general Employment is, and what the particular
Employment is in the several Counties respectively'. Through his companion he learns of the gradual changes in the nation from the halcyon
years of 1634–48 until the present, changes brought on by the Stuart
monarchs who introduced 'all manner of Luxury not . . . to mention the
more wicked Parts of it' (55). Interestingly enough, the first volume of *A
Tour thro' the Whole Island of Great Britain*, published a little over two
months after the appearance of *The Great Law of Subordination*, shows little
of this kind of gloom-and-doom vision of the nation. Though the author of
the *Tour* sees evidence of economic decline in some areas along with moral
decline in others, and duly notes the Rotten Boroughs that distort any
notion of a properly elected Parliament, on the whole the work is a
panegyric on English wealth, power, and potential for growth. Defoe
noted in his preface that there was room for criticism, but stated that he was
going to write as an admirer 'of the most flourishing and opulent country in
the world'.[5]

---

[5] *Tour*, i. 1. Subsequent references to this work will be included within parentheses within my text.

In some ways, then, Defoe divides his view of Great Britain in the same way as Milton constructed his twin poems, *L'Allegro* and *Il Penseroso*, as two views of the human soul. Just as *The Great Law of Subordination* presented everything in decline, in *The Tour*, the 'Author' criticizes those who

strive to write a History of her Nudities, and expose, much less recommend her wicked Part to Posterity; he has rather endeavour'd to do her Justice in those things which recommend her, and humbly to move a Reformation of those which he thinks do not; In this he thinks he shall best pay the Debt of a just and native Writer, who, in regard to the Reader, should conceal nothing which ought to be known, and in regard to his Country, expose nothing which ought to be conceal'd. (2)

This doubleness of vision was pure Defoe. There was much of Defoe in the French letter-writer and in Andrew Moreton, but in all important ways, the 'Author' of the *Tour* was closer to the real Defoe. Although he is never given a name, the distance between the Author and Defoe is practically nil, and this means that we get the full Defoe, including the writer of novels and imaginary voyages. Small wonder that Charles Lynn Batten, in his study of voyage literature in Britain during the eighteenth century, concluded that the *Tour* was actually a 'novel' in disguise, while Pat Rogers, noting the large amount of 'direct experience' that went into the *Tour*, also comments on the way the factual is balanced by 'personal commenatry . . . and travellers Tale . . . myth . . . and impression . . . and informal anecdote'.[6] In short, aside from its brilliant observation of the British social and economic landscape, the *Tour* was at least partly a kind of imaginative autobiography.

Defoe's statement that he actually started on the first of his thirteen circuits on 3 April 1722 may certainly be possible, since by 1 August 1722 he had signed a lease on the Mile End Estate just outside Colchester, and the likelihood is that he would have looked into the possibilities of exploiting the property during the early part of the year. *Moll Flanders*, published at the end of January 1722, sets all of Moll's early life in Colchester. It suggests that Defoe may have been doing a considerable amount of travelling about Britain between 1722 and 1725, but it is also true that he was drawing from his memory of earlier journeys.[7] Some of these may have

[6] Charles Lynn Batten, *Pleasurable Instruction: Form and Convention in Eighteenth-Century Travel Literature* (Berkeley: University of California Press, 1978); 'Introduction', *A Tour through the Whole Island of Great Britain*, ed. Pat Rogers (Harmondsworth: Penguin, 1971), 15, 29.

[7] For a balanced discussion of Defoe's real and imaginary wanderings and of when the real travelling was done, see Pat Rogers, 'The Making of the *Tour thro' Britain*', *Prose Studies* 3 (1980), 109–37. This article revises some of his suggestions in 'Defoe at Work: The Making of *A Tour thro' Great Britain*', *Bulletin of the New York Public Library* 78 (1975), 431–50.

been taken during the period in which he was in hiding from the Monmouth incident; some when he was setting up a spy network for William III; and several were taken on behalf of Harley and Godolphin, during the time that he was a spy. But there are also times when Defoe has to rely upon accounts of earlier writers.[8] Historians have warned against regarding the work as an entirely precise picture of Great Britain during the years 1724–6. His estimates of population are often extremely inaccurate, and he does not always get his family histories right in writing about the estates of the nobility and gentry; but for historians who consider the early part of the eighteenth century as 'the world of Defoe', such warnings are unnecessary. Even where his statistical estimates may have been wrong, his judgements were always valuable. Defoe was writing about the social and economic state of England in the *Tour*, and as a spy, tradesman, projector, and self-proclaimed expert on world geography, he was the ideal person to comment on the state of Britain during this period. If on occasions he got his facts wrong, his was nevertheless a personal vision of the nation told by the most compelling writer of prose narrative England had produced up to that time. Even when he was mistaken about the facts, his ideas were interesting. He had dealt in timber, and on 6 August 1722 paid £500 for the rights to exploit the timber on the Mile End property.[9] If he was quite wrong about England's timber reserves being sufficient to supply any future need of industry, we need to ask why he was in error rather than presume that he was entirely ignorant. In his introduction to the *Tour*, Cole suggests that, as a tradesman, Defoe knew of agricultural products as they came into the market rather than in the field, but Defoe says a good deal about the agricultural revolution of the time, particularly the growing of turnips to allow more to be done during the winter months.

But what makes the *Tour* so remarkable is Defoe's enthusiasm for an England at work and his sympathy for the people in it. He loves to indulge in moments of what might be called the economic sublime—an awe at the changing, pulsating nature of Britain. Change is everywhere. In the preface to the second volume, he stated his hope that his book would encourage others to follow his lead and in a visionary manner, projects into the future:

As we observ'd in the first Volume, and frequently in this, there will always be something new, for those that come after; and if an Account of Great Britain was to be written every Year there would be something to describe, which had its

---

[8] He often follows the 1695 edn. of Camden's *Britannia*, and was aware of contemporary guides such as John Macky's works on England and Scotland. See Rogers, 'The Making of the *Tour thro' Britain*', 119, 129.
[9] Coventry PRO: CPL 1176/18, p. 2.

Birth since the former Acounts: New Foundations are always laying, new Buildings always raising, Highways repairing, Churches and publick Buildings erecting, Fires and other Calamities happening, Forturnes of Families taking different Turns, new Trades are every Day erected, new Projects enterpriz'd, new Designs laid; so that as long as England is a trading, improving Nation, no perfect Description either of the Place, the People, or the Conditions and State of Things can be given. (i. 252)

On the most banal level, this seems like a remarkable prediction of the annually updated tourist guide book, and indeed, in his advice that the Highlands of Scotland could best be seen by the use of a tent for camping, Defoe does seem like the prophet of modern tourism. But what is truly remarkable is his willingness to embrace future change with genuine joy. This is not very long before Pope will write his apocalyptic vision of English poetry and society, *The Dunciad*. Even Defoe embraces a pessimistic view of Britain's ills in *The Great Law of Subordination*. But in the *Tour* almost all is visionary and England an 'improving Nation'.

In embracing change and growth, Defoe also embraces the chaos and disorder that it produces. His sublime vision contains its element of horror. Thus London, which is placed at the middle of the English section of the *Tour* as the geographical hub of all trade, is both wonderful and monstrous in its constant growth and formlessness:

It is the Disaster of *London*, as to the Beauty of its Figure, that it is thus stretched out in Buildings, just at the Pleasure of every Builder, or Undertaker of Buildings, and as the Convenience of the People directs, whether for Trade, or otherwise; and this has spread the Face of it in a most straggling, confus'd Manner, out of all Shape, uncompact, and unequal; neither long or broad, round or square; whereas the City of *Rome*, though a Monster for its Greatness, yet was, in a manner, round, with very few Irregularities in its Shape. (i. 316–17)[10]

Although he comes out in favour of city planning and regulated growth, Defoe is also fascinated by the exuberance of a city that seems to devour the hamlets that formerly surrounded it, and while he imagines the city shrinking with the wished-for disappearance of the stock-jobbers who 'bewitched the Nation almost to its Ruin' (338) at the time of the South Sea Bubble, he mentions this briefly in the midst of his account of expanding residential and business areas.

Another aspect of what I call the economic sublime emerges at times when Defoe imagines those supporting the great staple of English commerce, the woollen industry, busily at work in their cottages creating

[10] For a discussion of the growth of London in Defoe's time, see Jack Lindsay, *The Monster City: Defoe's London 1688–1730* (New York: St. Martin's Press, 1978).

wealth for the nation through their labour. On the occasion of passing from Lancashire to Yorkshire, crossing over some mountains where the travellers are terrified of falling into a ravine, he is startled by seeing so many cottages with entire families at work. The description of the scene is enlivened by Defoe's vision of nature improved by the presence of human beings and their industry. He has a similar experience when he comes upon a scene during the night in which the lights from the cottages seem like so many jewels in the landscape.

Defoe has his other moments of excitement as well. Attending the horse races in Nottinghamshire, he is carried away by a fit of historical nostalgia to the games of Greece and Rome, imagining himself in the Circus Maximus in Rome, 'where the Racers made a great Noise, and the Victors made great Boasts and Triumphs: But where they chiefly drove in Chariots, not much unlike our Chaises, and where nothing of the Speed, or of Skill in Horsemanship could be shown, as in our Races' (ii. 553). Once a seller of horses, Defoe fancies himself an expert on horse-racing as well, and takes the occasion to disparage antiquity in favour of contemporary Britain. This movement in time and space is present throughout the *Tour*. Not only are the races at Nottingham superior to those of ancient Rome, but they surpass the meetings at Newmarket during the Restoration:

I cannot but say, that in King *Charles* II.'s Time, when his Majesty used to be frequently at *Newmarket*, I have known the Assembly there have been with far less Company than this at *Nottingham*; and, if I might go back to one of these *Nottingham* Meetings, when the Mareschal Duke *de Tallard* was there, I should say, that no Occasions at *Newmarket*, in my Memory, ever came up to it, except the first time that King *William* was there after the Peace of *Ryswick*.

Nor is the Appearance of the ladies to be omitted, as fine and without Comparison more Bright and Gay, tho' they might a little fall short in Number of the many Thousands of Nobility and Gentry of the other Sex; in short, the Train of Coaches filled with the Beauties of the North was not to be described; except we were to speak of the Garden of the *Tulleries* at *Paris*, or the *Prado* at *Mexico*, where they tell us there are 4000 Coaches with six Horses each, every Evening taking the Air. (ii. 553)

Passages of this kind create in the reader much the same confidence in the narrator that Fielding was to establish as a narrator in *Tom Jones*. He can reach back to antiquity in his imagination and to the days of Charles II in his memory; he has travelled through France and Spain and can establish a large geographical frame through which Britain may be seen; and he has read widely enough to enable his readers to stretch their imaginations to America. He functions in a manner similar to that of Colonel Jack's

Tutor—he educates his readers about geography and history while informing them about their own country. If Fielding had the more difficult task of transforming his readers into believers in a fiction, Defoe had the equally daunting work of establishing himself as the teller of true accounts as opposed to the falsehoods and exaggerations associated with the tales of travellers.

In addition to winning the confidence of readers about his knowledge, he also scores points in his commentary on the moral state of the nation and in his sympathy for those somehow excluded from the general prosperity that he sees everywhere. Though never as stern as the Frenchman of *The Great Law of Subordination*, the narrator of the *Tour* finds some satisfaction in the destruction by some puritanical youths of an area around Box Hill devoted to pleasure, and is unhappy with the 'Assemblies' or gatherings for dancing and company that had spread throughout the nation. Where these appear to be innocent gatherings for the purpose of promoting social life, Defoe is hesitant to condemn them, but he suspects that they will lead to a decline in morality. And when he encounters a poor family in Derbyshire, he tells about it to point a moral—'to shew the discontented Part of the Rich World how to value their own Happiness, by looking below them, and seeing how others live' (ii. 568). The Derbyshire family dwells in a cave, though without squalour, and the five childen appear to be healthy enough. As for the husband, he manages to earn five pence a day in the lead mines, but Defoe describes his employment as almost subhuman, as he descends perilously into the earth great distances through narrow holes in the rock. Defoe depicts the man as 'lean as a Skeleton, pale as a dead Corps, his Hair and Beard a deep Black, his Flesh lank, and, as we thought, something of the Colour of the Lead itself' (ii. 571). The horror of being forced to labour at such an occupation is used to suggest how awful life can be. In typical fashion, having moralized about this experience at length, Defoe remarks that he will 'leave Moralizing to the Reader'. Defoe and his companions give the man two shillings, and, suspecting he will want to spend it at a local alehouse, they meet him there, tell him to keep the money for his family, and pay for his drinks.

Compared to such experiences, Defoe tells us, the usual task of seeing the sights are 'Trifles', and, as he promises in the introduction to the third volume of the original text, 'these Letters shall not be a Journal of Trifles' (ii. 540). Defoe regards poverty as the worst of evils, and does not consider religious faith a replacement for the happiness that comes from the rewards of industriousness. Faced by the combination of idleness, religious faith, and poverty in Scotland, Defoe remarks, 'they might at the same Time be industrious, and apply themselves to Trade, and to reap the Advantages that Nature offers them' (ii. 735).

Although Defoe does not include his comments on art and architecture among the more 'Manly' parts of the *Tour*, he does not relegate such matters to the level of 'Trifles'. He praises the interest in paintings and collecting works of art as an important advance in English culture, crediting William III with introducing this improvement into England. Defoe's own involvement with painting goes back to his earliest writings, when he expressed a longing to be able to make his prose function as clearly and concretely as a painting or drawing in getting close to a representation of what he called 'the Thing itself'. His usual term for a false argument was a '*deceptio visus*', or optical illusion, and it may be argued that his growth as a writer owes much to this impulse. It was only when he began to combine description with a sense of the inability of language to approximate reality that he achieved a method that, in his mind, came close to the concrete imaging of painting. Painting, nevertheless, remained important to him. In addition to his verse paraphrase of Du Fresnoy's *De arte graphica* as *The Compleat Art of Painting* in 1720, he devoted a section of *Religious Courtship* (1722) to the story of the woman married to the Catholic collector of religious paintings. He would speak contemptuously of a person who purchased paintings for their value as trading commodities and would himself pass judgement on the poor quality of some of the Dutch paintings that had recently been imported into Britain. In the *Tour* itself, he describes himself as having 'some Pretension to Judgment in Pictures' (i. 306), and comments on the quality of paintings at the great houses he visits. He singles out five paintings for special attention. At Wilton House, he admires the Tintoretto rendering of Christ washing the feet of the disciples and the Van Dyck painting of the family of the Duke of Pembroke. At Hampton Court he praises the Raphael cartoons of Paul preaching at Athens and passing a death sentence upon Ananias, and at Burleigh House the painting of the death of Seneca by Lucca Giordano. As we might expect, what is clear from his comments on these paintings is his appreciation of realist representation, but he also reveals an admiration for large-scale works of art (all are of heroic proportion) and for an ability to render character and the passions. Of the death of Seneca, he comments that 'the Passions are in so lively a Manner described in the Scholars, their eager Attention, their generous Regard to their Master, their vigilant Catching at his Words, and some of them taking Minutes, that it is indeed admirable and inexpressible' (ii. 506–7). Similarly, he praises Raphael for rendering the faces of those witnessing Ananias' death as well as the main figure, surprised by 'Terror and Death' (i. 177). Defoe may not have been as sophisticated an observer of art as, say, the third Earl of Shaftesbury, but I think it is undeniable that art's power to convey feeling so immediately influenced him throughout his life. His *Tour* was dedicated to depicting Britain as a trading and industrial nation, but he also tried to demonstrate that its many collections of paintings, its architecture, and its gardens were also causes for pride.[11]

III

Defoe decided to combine his intense involvement in economic geography and his mastery of story in *A New Voyage Round the World*, published on 7 November 1724. In the *Tour*, he had contrasted the traveller who is mainly concerned with taking exact measures of the days on which he visited places and their names with one who is concerned with analysing the meaning of what he experiences. 'The Difference between these two Gentlemen in their travelling, and in their Remarks upon their Journey', writes Defoe, 'is a good Emblem of the differing Genius in Readers, as well as Authors' (ii. 540). If he could fill in sections of the *Tour* with imaginative projections re-created from his sources, why not write an account of a tour around the world that would make better observations about savages encountered, goods traded, and gold discovered than any written before?

The title clearly invokes William Dampier's work of the same title published in 1697 and Woodes Rogers's *A Cruising Voyage Round the World*, which began publication in 1712. Defoe certainly knew both these accounts of circumnavigations of the globe. Rogers's account includes the most thorough narrative of Alexander Selkirk's life on the island of Juan Fernandez, and Defoe drew upon various details for *Robinson Crusoe*.[12] But Defoe's account of a voyage across the Pacific by a southerly route similar to those which Captain Cook would take during the 1770s, was a work of fiction pointed in a specific direction. Defoe was trying to spur English exploration and colonialism at a time when many people seemed to feel that what was needed as regards the lands in the New World was to consolidate what was already possessed. Defoe did not think that Britain had been

[11] For a fuller discussion of Defoe's attitude toward painting, see my 'Describing the Thing Itself, or Not: Defoe, Painting, Prose Fiction, and the Arts of Describing', *Eighteenth-Century Fiction* 9 (1996), 1–20.

[12] Aitken suggests that Defoe might have read George Shelvocke's *Voyage Round the World* before it was actually published in 1726 . Shelvocke's account shares with Defoe's *A New Voyage* a lengthy account of the island of Juan Fernandez, but if Defoe had seen Shelvocke's account, he does not appear to have borrowed anything very specific from it that he could not have found in other sources.

enterprising enough. There were new lands to be discovered and exploited, and he wanted to see Britain at the forefront of such discoveries. Like so many of his contemporaries, Defoe would have found it difficult to separate out his feelings about exploration. The Royal Society itself had urged travellers to record new species of fauna and flora, but behind its instructions to those travelling to new lands was the distinct notion that the explorer was laying the groundwork for future colonizing and exploitation. The spirit of adventure has always been contaminated by the desire for wealth and, along with that, the inevitable exploitation of native peoples. As we have seen in the discussion of *Robinson Crusoe* and *Captain Singleton*, despite his awareness of the brutality of Westerners in their contact with natives, Defoe could never bring himself to question the entire enterprise.

With the exception of those ventures which were clearly piratical, the voyage of Woodes Rogers and some of the voyages of Dampier were financed by the government in hopes of immediate or eventual profit. Defoe's *A New Voyage Round the World* is more directly connected with business enterprise. What is evoked at the beginning is the effort of a group of European investors hoping to make inroads upon the established national companies such as the East India Companies of Britain and the Netherlands. Defoe's shadowy organization was clearly intended to remind his readers of the very real Ostend Company, an enterprise organized by the southern Netherlanders in the area then under the control of Charles VI. Ships were actually sent out to the East Indies in 1715 and 1716 to demonstrate the commercial possibilities of such a trade. And in December 1722, persuaded of the value of the enterprise by John Ker of Kersland, Charles VI agreed to incorporate an Ostend East India Company.

The involvement of English and Scottish investors and English and Dutch captains in the early formation of what was to be the Ostend Company persuaded the Commons to threaten heavy penalties against those who might be involved. And the fact that some of the investors, like Ker of Kersland, had Jacobite political sympathies made the Ostend Company seem particularly sinister. Since *A New Voyage Round the World* was published in November 1724 and probably completed some time earlier, Defoe could not have known either of the conflict that followed the signing of the Treaty of Vienna between the Emperor and Spain in April 1725, which gave the Ostend Company the right to trade with the Spanish Colonies in the West Indies, or of the secret negotiations sponsored by Philip V and Elisabeth Farnese to restore the Stuarts to the throne of England. He writes in 1724 of plans for trade to the East Indies that were eventually abandoned despite the enormous possibilities that such trade offered. Since his fictional expedition is shrouded in mystery and clearly illicit, he seems to have known of the British and Dutch opposition to such a venture. How much he knew of the Jacobite connections of the investors is unclear.[13]

Some knowledge of what we now call Australia as a possible site for colonial exploitation already existed at the time Defoe wrote *A New Voyage Round the World*. William Dampier had recorded his landing at Shark's Bay on the west coast of Australia, and the maps of this time revealed the possibility of a huge continent attached to New Guinea.[14] In addition the explorations of Dampier and others had suggested that the South Pacific might be filled with islands possessed of unimaginable wealth and peopled by a mass of potential consumers of European products. Defoe was to refer to Dampier and Woodes Rogers as 'illiterate sailors' in his *Compleat English Gentleman*, arguing that an imaginative and creative student of geography could follow these two circumnavigators of the world while learning 'a thousand times' more than they put down in their texts. The reader, Defoe argued, had the ability to combine the accounts of various explorers into a 'whole' vision, while those who actually experienced what they told in their narratives were confined to 'the narrow compass of their owne actings'.[15] And just as the reader may create a more imaginative experience than may be discovered in any single text, so the writer of fiction might fashion a more exciting image of a voyage round the world than might be discovered in the genuine accounts. Dampier had a good eye for detail and Rogers had the fascinating account of Selkirk to enliven his narrative; but, unburdened by the necessity to relate history and truth, Defoe could always draw upon his imagination to write an exciting series of adventures.

In the manner of what the critic Mikhail Bakhtin considers typical of the adventure novel, Defoe does not concern himself with character at all. The narrator gradually merges with the unnamed captain, who is intent on making a profitable trading voyage. Defoe takes the opportunity to suggest that Britain should pursue a trade policy with the lands in the area of Australia rather than pursuing the trade with India—a trade that consumes British gold in exchange for luxury items such as tea and fans or goods that

---

[13] For an account of the Ostend Company and England's attempts to counter the threat of a rival commercial enterprise, see Ragnhild Hatton, *George I* (Cambridge, Mass.: Harvard University Press, 1978), 268–73; and I. S. Leadam, *The History of England from the Accession of Anne to the Death of George II*, in *The Political History of England*, ed. William Hunt and Reginald Poole (12 vols., London: Longmans Green, 1921), ix. 321–32.

[14] William Dampier, *A Voyage to New Holland*, ed. James Williamson (London: Argonaut Press, 1939); see esp. the map between pp. viii and ix.

[15] *The Compleat English Gentleman*, ed. Karl Bülbring (London: David Nutt, 1890), 225–6.

compete with the products of native British workmen. Although there are some well-written scenes involving encounters with natives who are essentially deists in their worship of nature itself rather than idols, the best section involves an exploration of the area now known as Chile (or 'Chili' for Defoe) and the brilliant rendering of the crossing of the Andes by a number of the sailors. An initial exploration of the possibility of such a crossing leads to a brilliant rendering of the sublime horror of the Andes—terrifying volcanoes, frightening precipices, raging streams. Heaps of gold lie about untouched, and Defoe makes a strong pitch for British colonization of the entire southern section of South America. *A New Voyage Round the World* has some exciting scenes of adventure, but he may have been tiring of the indirectness of fiction for conveying his arguments about the desirability of colonial expansion. He had a great deal to say about the social and economic realities of his country, and he may have concluded that a more direct approach was needed.

IV

A large part of Defoe's writing during this period was devoted to dealing with the criminal activity that appeared so prevalent during the 1720s. And to a certain extent the relationship between trade and crime was to be one of the themes of his *Complete English Tradesman*. He had already treated the subject of urban crime and crime on the high seas in *Captain Singleton*, *Moll Flanders*, and *Colonel Jack*, and were a publisher interested in hiring someone to write on criminals, the two notable authors to approach would have been Alexander Smith, author of *The Lives of the Highwaymen*, and Defoe. Although P. N. Furbank and W. R. Owen have attempted to argue against Defoe's link with the publisher Applebee, every other Defoe scholar since 1869, when Lee first argued the connection, has accepted it. Does this mean that every pamphlet on crime ascribed to Defoe in the *Checklist* compiled by John Robert Moore is by Defoe? George Aitken, Defoe's editor, was convinced that he could see obvious signs of Defoe's authorship in works such as the account of the criminal career of Louis Cartouche, *A Narrative of the Proceedings in France* published in 1724; and of *A Brief Historical Account of the Lives of the Six Notorious Street Robbers executed at Kingston*, published in 1726, he noted that 'the piece abounds in Defoe's favourite phrases'.[16] In fact, both do show signs of Defoe's authorship and should not be lightly dismissed from the canon.

---

[16] Aitken (ed.), *Romances and Narratives*, vol. x, p. xviii.

The most important of these works concerned two criminals, Jonathan Wild, the master criminal, and Jack Sheppard, whose famous escapes from Newgate excited great interest among the reading public. Both achieved a form of immortality as models for John Gay's wonderful presentation of the criminal world in *The Beggar's Opera*, with Wild sitting as the model for Gay's Peachum and Sheppard transformed into the dashing Captain Macheath. Defoe may have written the two works on Sheppard ascribed to him as well as the two works on Jonathan Wild, but he is certainly responsible for *A True and Genuine Account of the Life of Jonathan Wild*, which was issued by John Applebee on 8 June 1725.[17] What is most impressive about this work is the consistent moral tone of the narrator. Defoe treats the career of Wild as an example of individual evil. He recognizes the new social conditions, particularly the extensive development of urban crime, that made possible Wild's ascendancy, but he is mainly interested in Wild's mind and character. Defoe sees Wild in much the same way as Shakespeare saw Macbeth, as someone who possessed a kind of 'brutal courage', as 'rather bold than courageous',[18] and describes Wild's domination over the criminal world in terms of a monarch ruling over his minions.

We who can look back upon periods in which cities were dominated by criminal groups can recognize Defoe's error in predicting that there would never be another Jonathan Wild; yet he was right in some respects. Because there was no official police force in his day, Wild was to lay claim to being a 'thief taker', to fulfilling the function of the police. He captured thieves and turned them over to the courts for a reward.[19] That some of these criminals had been trained by him in their younger years made him that much more guilty in Defoe's eyes. Unlike the social bandit, with whom the lower classes might identify, Wild was the illusory hero of the propertied classes.[20] He seemed to be protecting them from the new breed of criminal who made house-breaking a speciality, and if they were robbed of some item of particular personal value, he would usually be able to find it

[17] P. N. Furbank and W. R. Owens argue (*Defoe De-attributions* (London: Hambledon Press, 1994), 139) against inclusion in the Defoe canon. Yet this is a work which bears such obvious signs of Defoe's unique style that their attempt to exclude it comes close to throwing complete doubt on their entire method. In their first book, *The Canonisation of Daniel Defoe* (New Haven, Conn.: Yale University Press, 1990), they argued against the use of 'stylometry' in determining what Defoe wrote. If this means that a mechanical application of principles of style cannot be used to determine authorship, anyone would agree. But in the case of a work such as *A True Relation*, anyone familiar with Defoe would recognize certain unique aspects of his style. Listing five bibliographers who considered it to be by Defoe is disingenuous. They would have to include all of Defoe's biographers and critics as well.

[18] *A True and Genuine Account of the Life of Jonathan Wild*, in *Romances and Narratives*, xvi. 238–9.

[19] For a discussion of Wild in the context of contemporary London crime, see Gerald Howson, *Thief-Taker General* (London: Hutchinson, 1970).

[20] I take the term 'social bandit' from Eric Hobsbawm, *Bandits* (New York: Delacorte Press, 1969), 13–23.

and return it to its rightful owner for an appropriate reward. Of course, the thief was usually working for Wild, but for sixteen years he was able to avoid the mistake that would prove such behaviour. But by the time he was captured, tried, and executed no one had any doubts about his guilt. Defoe described the execution as a riotous scene of 'cursings and execrations, abhorring the crimes and the name of the man, throwing stones and dirt at him all the way' (xvi. 278).

For the most part in *A True and Genuine Account*, Defoe avoided satire. The final line comments on Wild's attempts at making what he did pass 'for merit, even with the government itself' (xvi. 278). By turning Wild's career into a social tragedy, Defoe deflected the possibility of satirical attacks which transformed Wild into a criminal version of Sir Robert Walpole, Britain's prime minister. In Gay's *Beggar's Opera*, produced three years after Defoe's *True Relation*, Wild is easily transformed into Peachum, and Peachum into a satirical version of Sir Robert Walpole. Defoe was content with presenting him as what we would think of as an early version of Charles Dickens's Fagin, a corrupter of children, a blight on the moral fabric of society. It is tempting to think that Defoe was the author of *The Life of Jonathan Wild* by a purported H.D., published at the end of May, because this version sees in Wild's career an economic parable of the kind Defoe, who was surely already working on *The Complete English Trades-man*, would have appreciated.[21] The satirical tone is entirely compatible with that which Defoe assumed in attacking stock-jobbing, and several later pamphlets on Wild blended the two versions. When Henry Fielding came to publish his bitterly satirical version of Wild's life in 1743, he drew extensively from both works. Another kind of work with which Defoe appears to have had some association was *A History of the Robberies of the Most Notorious Pyrates*, published originally on 14 May 1724 and expanded through a number of editions until a second volume appeared on 25 July 1728. Much in these volumes is a collection of already published accounts of the outbreak of piracy after the end of the War of the Spanish Succession, when crews accustomed to attacking Spanish and French ships as privateers went over to outright piracy. John Robert Moore's attempts to show that Defoe wrote almost all of the lives was based in part on drawing parallel passages from ascriptions that were themselves doubtful, and his

---

[21] John Robert Moore included it in his *Checklist* as item 471. George Aitken notes (*Romances and Narratives*, vol. xvi, p. xvi) that it had been ascribed to Defoe by Crossley, but while he recognizes a number of characteristic elements of Defoe's style, he judges it 'doubtful'. P. N. Furbank and W. R. Owens argue that it does not have the 'feel' of Defoe (*Defoe De-attributions*, 139), but what is needed is a careful analysis of style and vocabulary. If it is not actually by Defoe, it might, in the manner of a painting, be considered to belong to the 'school of Defoe'.

arguments about parallel passages seldom win unanimous consent. On the other hand, no one doubts Defoe's authorship of *Captain Singleton* and *A New Voyage Round the World*, and both of them involve accounts of piracy. He had been working on *Atlas Maritimus* with its treatment of global geography from some time after his success with *Robinson Crusoe*, and he would have been the ideal writer to introduce some excitement into this somewhat tedious account of piracy.

The second volume of this collection begins with a parable about two pirates, Captain Misson and Captain Tew, and their approaches to social and economic life. Misson, with the help of his companion, Caraccioli, preaches a new political doctrine to the crew of the *Victoire*, a French warship, to turn them toward liberty and equality as social ideals:

he fell upon Government, and shew'd, that every man was born free, and had as much Right to what would support him, as to the Air he respired. A contrary Way of arguing would be accusing the Deity with Cruelty and Injustice, for he brought into the World no Man to pass a life of Penury, and to miserably want a necessary Support; that the vast Difference betwixt Man and Man, the one wallowing in Luxury, and the other in the most pinching Necessity, was owing only to Avarice and Ambition on the one hand, and a pusilanimous Subjection on the other; that at first no other than a Natural was known, a paternal Government, every Father was the head . . . but Ambition creeping in by Degrees, the stronger Family set upon and enslaved the Weaker; and this additional Strength over-run a third, by every Conquest gathering Force to make others, and this was the first Foundation of Monarchy. Pride encreasing with Power, Man usurped the Prerogative of God over his Creatures, that of depriving them of Life, which was a Privilege no one had over his own.[22]

Upon the deaths of the superior officers in a sea fight, Misson offers each member of the crew the chance of 'following his Fortune'. The choice was simple: pursue freedom as pirates and as citizens in the colony of Libertalia in Madagascar or go back to dancing to 'the Musick of their Chains' in the Europe of the *ancien régime*.

V

In a very real sense *The Complete English Tradesman*, which eventually appeared in two volumes in 1727, was actually two different books, reflecting what were to be Defoe's major interests at the time of publication. The first volume, which though dated 1726 appeared on 7 September

[22] Defoe, *A General History of the Pyrates*, ed. Manuel Schonhorn (London: Dent, 1972), 389–90.

1725, was 'Calculated for the Instruction of our Inland Tradesmen; and especially Young Beginners', as the title-page of the first edition indicated.²³ Defoe was becoming ever more interested in matters of learning and education, both from an abstract standpoint that was to be embodied in *Mere Nature Delineated* in 1726 and from a more practical standpoint, as in *The Compleat English Gentleman* and *Of Royal Education*, neither of which was published during his lifetime but upon which he worked during his last years. This section allowed him to act as a mentor to those who were just starting out, and it is filled with Defoe's thoughts about his own youthful mistakes. Defoe's second impulse, reflected in the second volume, was to write on inland trade in Britain, a subject that he was also to treat throughout the remainder of his life. In the preface to the second edition he outlined his interest in the 'circulation of trade' by which goods travelled to London 'as the blood in the body to the Heart', the way in which London functioned as the centre for consuming the products of the nation, and the operation of credit as the instrument that allowed for the exchange of goods within society (i. xiii). Defoe's general optimism about trade contrasts with his dire warnings about the errors that tradesmen commit, whether in marrying too early or in avoiding the inevitability of bankruptcy, and creates an artful counterpoint throughout the work.

Related to this counterpoint of optimism and pessimism is Defoe's undercutting of his encomiums on the tradesman's life with consistent reminders that, of necessity, that life is always hypocritical and occasionally criminal. After presenting a dialogue about a patient tradesman dealing with a woman whose attitudes toward buying would drive most people insane, Defoe comments:

The short inference from this long discourse is this, That here you see, and I could give many examples very like this, how, and in what manner, a shop-keeper is to behave himself in the way of his business; what impertinences, what taunts, flouts, and ridiculous things, he must bear in his Trade, and most not shew the least return, or the least signal of disgust: he must have no passions, no fire in his temper, he must be all soft and smooth; nay, if his real temper be naturally fiery and hot, he must shew none of it in his shop; he must be a perfect *complete hypocrite*, if he will be a *complete tradesman*. (i. 94)

In a perceptive passage Defoe comments on the tradesman who holds in his anger and releases it upon his wife and children, 'furious for two or three

---

²³ *The Complete English Tradesman* (London, 1726 [1725]), title-page. Citations will be included within my text in parentheses and, unless otherwise indicated, will refer to the modern reprint published by Augustus Kelley in New York in 1969. This includes the 2nd edn. of the first volume (1726) with a supplement, and the second volume of 1727.

minutes, as a man chain'd down in *Bedlam*' (i. 95). Defoe's ideal tradesman is patient, cheerful, and dedicated. He warns against all excess—too much pleasure, expensive living, even excessive practice of religion. Diligence is all.

In *The Complete English Tradesman*, as in his fiction, Defoe is an advocate of what has been called the 'companionate marriage'. He exonerates the wives of tradesmen from most of the blame for business failures, presenting them as caring and loving in response to husbands who often refuse to tell them the truth about their finances. It would be useful to know if Defoe was recalling the situation of his youth in the dialogue between husband and wife in which the wife instructs the depressed husband about how to cut expenses, or if the tale the wife tells of a G--- W--- whose wife knew nothing of her husband's difficulties before finding herself 'turn'd into the street with five small children to take care of' (i. 140) was based upon an extrapolation from his own bankruptcy. The stories are probably partly personal and partly about people he knew. What is important for us is that Defoe, the master of so many stories about the Londoners of his time, seems in this work to be reaching into his deeply felt knowledge, from his accounts of wine merchants tricked by sharp traders to his psychological analysis of the shame, anxieties, and grief of a tradesman slipping inexorably toward bankruptcy. The worst part of these experiences is the isolation and secret life of the failing tradesman, and Defoe may have learned much from his bankruptcy about keeping wives thoroughly informed. To the shock of some nineteenth-century commentators on this work, he strongly advocated teaching women the skills that would enable them to operate the business alongside the husband.

Probably because, as a mid-nineteenth-century Englishman, he tended to read it as a paean to the English business temperament and as a prophetic text heralding the nation's economic triumph, William Chadwick, one of Defoe's early biographers, thought *The Complete English Tradesman* not only Defoe's best book but 'the best book that ever was written in the English language'.[24] Yet the final chapters, which attempt to argue against any moral reform of the economic system, have a melancholy tone. 'It must be confess'd,' Defoe laments, 'Trade is almost universally founded upon Crime' (ii. 2. 108). He exonerates the tradesman who participates in the ever-growing demand for luxury products. The tradesman, he argues, is merely satisfying the cravings and follies of the consumer. Defoe accepts

---

[24] William Chadwick, *The Life and Times of Daniel Defoe* (London: 1859), 454. For a similar judgment, see Walter Wilson, *Memoirs of the Life and Times of Daniel De Foe* (London: Hurst & Chance, 1830), iii. 587.

parts of Mandeville's ironic view of the 'Grumbling Hive', but he has little of Mandeville's cheerful acceptance of a society based upon oppressing the poor and keeping them ignorant and drunk. He sees the terrible price that gin is exacting from Britain's poor, but he is unwilling to abandon the benefits of this industry along with all the other luxury trades. Such businesses, he argues, 'find Employment for millions of People in all parts almost of the World (ii. 2. 109), and for Defoe the system of production and the circulation of goods has been responsible for raising the living standards of the poor and, indeed, for creating modern civilization. So when he states, 'It is not my business here to write a Satyr upon Luxury' (ii. 2. 107), he means it to the extent that he knows that everyone in Britain is complicit in that wonderful and awful system of trade.

Although *A General History of the Discoveries and Improvements in Useful Arts* was not a work of education in the same sense as the first volume of *The Complete English Tradesman*, it attempted to educate its readers by providing a survey of inventions and a vision of human progress. Published in monthly numbers beginning with October 1725, the four parts that had appeared were gathered together as a single volume on 13 December 1726. When he published *An Essay upon Projects* in 1697, Defoe looked to the 'Art of War' as the sphere where innovations in methods and inventions had transformed an activity that was still honoured on the Continent as having a status only matched by religion. But when he began publishing *A General History of the Discoveries and Improvements In Useful Arts*, he could look back on almost thirty years of scientific accomplishments during a period sometimes called 'the age of Newton'. As the subtitle, which stresses 'Commmerce, Navigation, and Plantation', suggests, Defoe was actually more interested in trade and exploration than in new inventions. In discussing inventions, however, he did take the opportunity to diminish the importance associated with new military weapons as compared with the discovery of the compass and Newton's theory of gravity. Since he never actually completed the work as planned, it appears to us mainly historical, discussing the achievements of the Romans and carrying the account of inventions and improvements only up to the compass. He did, however, devote a chapter to one of his favourite projects—the founding of a British colony in the area of Argentina, the same project that is so strongly advocated in *A New Voyage Round the World*.

Much in *The History of the Principal Discoveries and Improvements* is propaganda for technological progress in Britain and should be seen in the light of what has been thought of as the 'Whig' view of society—a view which saw life in terms of a gradual improvement in human existence.

From this standpoint, Defoe has to be seen as the contemporary of the much younger James Thomson, who championed industry in *The Seasons* (1726–30) and later in *The Castle of Indolence* (1748). Yet it would be an error to accuse Defoe of a naive optimism about progress. In fact, one of the major events of his literary career during 1725 was the invention of a new persona in writing *Every-body's Business, Is No-body's Business*—Andrew Moreton. Now 65 or close to it, Defoe was able to exploit that part of himself that discovered much to criticize in contemporary life.

Everything in his writings of these last years suggests that the real Defoe was at some remove from the cantankerous Moreton, who takes advantage of his advanced age to attack the manners and morals of the present age. Moreton depicts himself as a bachelor who lives with his sister. His style is far removed from that of the Defoe who pretended to be a defender of moderation. The women servants are called 'Pert Sluts', 'Creatures', and 'Whores', and he coins the term 'Chamber-Jade'. Indeed, the author of *Every Man Mind His Own Business, or Private Piques no Publick Precedents*, who had no difficulty identifying the new work with 'D----l de F----s *Great Law of Subordination*', launched into an attack upon Defoe as a 'peevish old Fornicator', whose style lacked all economy. He did, however, add some interesting details in response to Defoe's vivid picture of Moreton's complaint about his inability to get the attention of a waitress when he was trying to order some 'Rice-Tea' at a coffee-house:[25]

No wonder you complain of Non-attendance at the Coffee-Houses, when the Boys hate and shun you like the Devil. You eat six or seven Rusks with a Three-penny Dish of Chocalate, which is your common Dinner when abroad: But for Rice-Teas I dare affirm you never drank a Dish at your own Charge in your Life.[26]

The notion of Defoe as someone deliberately avoided by waiters and waitresses sounds much like the rantings of enemies such as John Old-mixon, but the details of his eating habits may be true enough. This writer reluctantly attests to the popularity of Defoe's work, and by way of taking advantage of his renewed fame, Defoe, in his preface to the fifth edition of *Every-body's Business*, revealed that Andrew Moreton planned to put forward other proposals for the betterment of Britain in the future. At 65 Defoe revived his career as a reformer and a gadfly.

---

[25] *Every-Body's Business, Is No-Body's Business*, 3rd edn. (London, 1725), 21.
[26] *Every Man Mind His Own Business*, 32–3. See also 10, 15.

27

Enter Henry Baker

Following Defoe's train of thought during these years is easy enough, because he was writing so much and because, more and more, he was calling upon his memories of the past in assessing the present. Some time in 1724 Henry Baker, an aspiring poet with a unique ability to teach deaf children to speak and to give them a general education, began to travel from Enfield to Stoke Newington where, between Wednesday and Saturday, he remained with a local family. He was at leisure after the morning hours spent in instructing a young pupil, Master White, and describes how he spent his time either reading by himself or consorting with the 'People of Fashion', playing cards or drinking tea. Baker states that Defoe first sought him out and that after he accepted his first invitation, he 'was so pleased with his Conversation, that he seldom came to Newington without paying a Visit to Mr. D----.' If this is so, Baker met with Defoe for almost three years before he began his courtship of Defoe's younger daughter, Sophia, on 11 August 1727. The story that Baker wanted to tell involved the difficulties entailed in the courtship—difficulties caused by Defoe's unwillingness to provide what Baker considered a satisfactory dowry. As a result, we learn a great deal about the sufferings of the two lovers and very little about Daniel Defoe.

I

Baker was 26 and Defoe 64. To Baker, who clearly overestimated Defoe's wealth, he appeared to live as a prosperous old gentleman who had retired from the troubles of London to a house in the country:

Amongst the first who desired his acquaintance at Newington was Mr. D----, a Gentleman well known by his Writings, who had newly built there a very handsom House, as a Retirement from London, and amused his Time either in the

Cultivation of a large and pleasant Garden, or in the Pursuit of his Studies, which he found means of making very profitable. He was now at least sixty years of Age, afflicted with the Gout and Stone, but retained all his mental Faculties intire.[1]

Their conversations generally continued until tea, when they were joined by Mary and the three daughters who still lived at home, Hannah, Henrietta, and Sophia. The picture Henry Baker gives of the Defoe household suggests how much it must have exerted a strong emotional appeal to him. Unlike the Foster family, with whom he stayed at Enfield, here was no deaf child who needed instruction. When he complimented Sophia for her beauty, he also included the 'Bloom of Health that tinctur'd every Charm'. He did not perceive in Defoe's seeming Horatian retirement the violent political battles that had marked most of his life. And he seems not to have seen Defoe working away with unabated energy behind the closed doors of his study. It seems more than likely that on some days when Defoe sent word that he was too ill to join Henry in their weekly conversation, he was actually in his study, with its extensive library, writing and organizing his various projects. This is not to say that Defoe did not have his aches and pains. 'Gout' was a general term often used to include arthritic illnesses,[2] and Defoe's vivid description of the operation for removing stones from the bodily organs suggest that he may have contemplated some type of operation for relieving the excruciating pains from kidney or gallstones.[3] But there is also little doubt that Henry's view of Defoe was that of a young man who tended to exaggerate Defoe's debilities.

On the other hand, if Baker took pleasure in his dialogues with Defoe, it is not at all difficult to believe that Defoe enjoyed Baker's conversation and even learned a great deal from him. Baker's system of teaching deaf children appears to have involved bonding with each of them as a kind of surrogate father or older brother. After winning the confidence of these children, he succeeded in teaching them to vocalize. He recognized the intelligence of these deaf children and spoke of their ability to use sign language to express the most complicated ideas.[4] Having perfected his techniques in the home of his relative, John Foster, he spent much of his life on this humanitarian task.[5] He had a rigid system of fees, but no

---

[1] George Potter, 'Henry Baker, F.R.S. (1698–1774)', *Modern Philology* 29 (1932), 310.

[2] Robert James, 'Arthritis', in *A Medical Dictionary* (3 vols., London, 1743).

[3] 'Here's a Man cut for the Stone, and perishes in the Operation, torn and mangled by the merciless Surgeons, cut open alive and bound Hand and Foot to force him to bear it: the very apparatus is enough to chill the blood, and sink a Man's Soul within him.' See Lee, iii. 430.

[4] The volume titled 'Literary Correspondence' at the John Rylands Library in Manchester contains 'An Essay upon Speech', dated 1723, in which Baker discusses the ways in which sound actually comes from the mouth in order to form words.

[5] In a letter of 21 Aug. 1739, Baker expressed his feelings about the 'useful' purpose he had served by his

contemporary appears to have accused him of greed. Aside from what he earned as a teacher of the deaf, he had no other income that would enable him to achieve the level of life he admired in Defoe and his family. His scientific interests, particularly those that were to produce his popular treatise on the use of the microscope, eventually brought him the honour of being elected president of the Royal Society. He translated Molière and wrote competent poetry. In short, he was close to being the ideal man of mid-eighteenth-century Britain: a person of sensibility who dedicated himself to literature and to the progress of science and a benefactor to the handicapped.[6] Small wonder, then, that Defoe enjoyed talking with Baker, and that Baker found his conversation as ingenious as those who knew him during the reign of Queen Anne. Doubtless much that Defoe had to say about theories of language and education during the last years of his life was influenced by this knowledgeable young man.[7]

When Henry Baker came to visit the Defoe family in 1727, he described the scene in a manner that has somewhat comic overtones to the modern reader. After Defoe withdrew to his study, Baker found himself in the garden with Mrs Defoe and three of her daughters. Then, by some seemingly magical process, he discovered himself alone with Sophia, the youngest of the sisters. Having already sensed himself falling deeply in love with her, he had tried to resist making what might prove an imprudent match, but now he felt himself impelled to take her hand and ask her if she were engaged. Sophia replied, 'Yes, Sir, engaged,—to God and to my Father; but to none beside.'[8] Probably she had most of his attention from the beginning and perhaps it was obvious enough to have caused everyone to leave them alone. For anyone but an eager young man such as Henry Baker was, it might have seemed as if they were being deliberately thrown

methods. This included a system of sign language that he developed to relate ideas to words. See his Letter Book, Beinecke Library, Yale University.

   [6] See G. L'E. Turner, 'Henry Baker, FRS: Founder of the Bakerian Lecture', *Notes and Records of the Royal Society of London* 28 (1974), 53–4.

   [7] They both probably had the reservations that might have been expected in a friendship between the young and the old. Defoe must have thought Baker's effusive love poems silly enough. If he recognized Sophia as the Amanda of the volume, he would have experienced a mixture of pleasure and annoyance, pleasure at Baker's description of Amanda's character: 'Without Affection, gay, youthful and pretty;/Without Pride, or Meanness, familiar and witty;/Without Forms, obliging, good-natur'd and free;/Without Art, as lovely as lovely can be.' He would have been less pleased with a passage from 'The Beauties of Enfield': 'With Beauty blest, *Amanda* trips along,/And all around the *Loves* and *Graces* throng,/Bask in her Smiles, and wanton in her Eyes,/Whilst each Beholder sighs, adores, and dies.' See Baker, *Original Poems* (London, 1725), 29, 82. On the other hand, Baker probably found Defoe's conversation too anecdotal, since it is difficult to believe that his narrative gifts did not spill into his ordinary talk. In No. 53 of *The Universal Spectator* 11 (Oct. 1729), Baker argued that storytelling was a fault in conversation: 'Old Folks are most subject to this Error, which is one chief Reason their Company is so often shunned.'

   [8] Potter 'Henry Baker', 312.

together. What is important for our purposes is that the Defoe household that he perceived would have seemed essentially stable and prosperous in 1724.

Defoe had indeed begun to tend more to his home and family by this time, and we should not be surprised to see the man who advised the Scottish nobility on the improvement of their estates in 1706 improving his own garden in Stoke Newington. William Lee concludes that Defoe's last essay for *Applebee's Weekly Journal* appeared on 5 March 1726, and while Defoe certainly dabbled in journalism after this date, he no longer felt it necessary to be tied to daily deadlines. In one of his last essays, Defoe wrote on what Lee titled 'the Folly of Hazardous Pleasures', ruminating on those who derive a thrill from running unnecessary risks. He concluded with an image of the solider who knows when bravery is required and when it is not: 'No man runs needless hazards in War; it is enough to be bold and daring when he is drawn out to the Action.' This was a lesson that Defoe seldom heeded himself, but it had been years since he had to answer to the Secretary of State for the materials printed in *Mist's Weekly Journal*. From 1726 onwards Defoe is visible mainly in his didactic treatises, and it is chiefly in these works that I intend to trace the final five years of his life.

In addition to his ability to obtain advances from the conger of book-sellers for large projects such as *Atlas Maritimus*, a family event that may have enabled Defoe to distance himself from the life of a journalist was the death of Mary Defoe's brother, Samuel Tuffley, whose will, made in 1714, was proved on 3 August 1725.[9] He ordered the three overseers of the estate to pay Mary Defoe 'absolutely and Independently' of her husband, Daniel, all of the profits from his estate, probably because he was wary about Daniel's financial difficulties and wanted to be sure that his sister would have sufficient money to support herself, despite whatever difficulties Daniel might be in at the time. Were Daniel to die, the 'Trust' would be dissolved and everything be put under the power of Mary Defoe. Perhaps the oddest aspect of the will is the statement concerning his nephews and nieces to the effect that 'if any of the said Children shall behave undutifully disobediently or disrespectfully either to their said Father or Mother and continue obstinate to do so without humbling thmselves to their parents and obtaining their pardon that it is my declared Will . . . that . . . not one Shilling of my Estate shall be given' to them. Certainly by his behaviour in Scotland Benjamin Norton may have caused some concern about his future as early as 1714, but the inclusion of all the children may suggest a certain strain within the Defoe family. The departure of the two sons from the

---

[9] PRO Prob, 11/604/364ᵛ.

house may have solved most of the problems. Visible to Henry Baker was a harmonious family, and after the addition of the wealth of Samuel Tuffley, the Defoes seemed to have the prospect before them of a comfortable old age.

But if Defoe was approaching the end of his career as a journalist, he remained a projector at heart. In an agreement of 23 November 1724, Defoe gave a John Ward a share of the profits of the Colchester property that Defoe had obtained in 1722 and along with it, he leased his daughter's farm to Ward. A lawsuit filed by Defoe against John Ward dated 25 November 1728 suggests that Defoe turned over entire management of the property to him. In exchange, Defoe was to teach Ward how to exploit the soil of the Colchester property for making bricks, and Ward was to pay him a share of the profits. One ominous line suggests that Defoe was acting secretly, without informing his family. Ward stated Defoe had urged him to sign a paper that was intended for the ease of Defoe's family, since Hannah and his wife would be

uneasy if they knew that he had joined with this Defendant in taking and occupying the said farm and therefore under that Color and Pretence prevailed on this Defendant to Sign another paper Dated as this Defendant believes on the same day with the former purporting an agreement for this defendant to take the said farm singly but for what time or for what terms this defendant cannot say or whether the same was signed by the complainant or not this Defendant having no copy and taking very little notice thereof being assured by the Complainant that same was only to make his family easy and should be of no other use.[10]

It is clear enough that Defoe was not only refusing to consult his family entirely but probably taking advantage of John Ward, who seems to have been somewhat naive. In the agreement, Defoe said that some money was soon coming and promised that he would be able to advance his share of the stock. Defoe argued that Ward owed him £253 1s. 11d. In addition to these dealings, Defoe appears to have been speculating on commodities, selling cheese and oysters. William Trent, in his manuscript biography of Defoe, wondered what Defoe's family would have thought of these transactions if they had known of them.[11] The answer is clear enough: they would have been hysterical. Beneath the idyllic scene witnessed by Henry Baker, then, dark currents were flowing.

---

[10] PRO C11.2578.31, Ward v. Defoe.   [11] Trent Collection, 584.

II

Between 1726 and 1727 Defoe published a number of works dealing with magic and the occult, the best known of which are *The Political History of the Devil* (1726), *A System of Magick* (1726), and *An Essay on the History and Reality of Apparitions* (1727). At a time when Defoe was deeply immersed in writing on worldly problems, in expanding *The Complete English Tradesman* (1726) and finishing the third volume of his *Tour thro' the Whole Island of Great Britain* (1727), these books might seem oddly out of place. James Sutherland considered them as the product of an interest that Defoe had held for many years, but he also thought that Defoe was mainly turning out trash for what was, for the time, a large reading audience. 'He was making some money out of the Devil and the world of evil spirits,' Sutherland commented, 'and once more it was the readers of *Mist's* and of *Applebee's* that he had in mind.'[12] Sutherland judged *The History and Reality of Apparitions* as the most serious of these studies, but thought that Defoe knew well enough that his personal belief in a spirit world would fascinate readers who would match his accounts of premonitions that came true with their similar experiences. In response to Sutherland's somewhat irritable tone over the notion that Defoe was writing potboilers, Rodney Baine stressed instead the continuity that might be found between Defoe's most famous ghost story, *The Apparition of Mrs. Veal*, written in 1706, and these later works.

Much truth may be discovered in both viewpoints. Defoe knew that books of this kind would be popular enough to go into many editions. A 1965 paperback edition of *The Political History of the Devil* advertises the work as 'a spine-chilling exposé of Evil Incarnate'. On the cover is a lustful-looking devil holding a scantily draped woman in his arms. Although the flames of Hell roar beneath her body, her face reveals a distinct smile, reflecting her expectation of some form of pleasure. As Sutherland suggested, it is still possible to make money out of Defoe's Prince of the Air. Yet Baine was certainly correct in emphasizing Defoe's attraction to the occult. The problem with his approach is that Defoe was the kind of writer who responded to contemporary events. His earliest writings reveal how much he was intrigued by the plague of 1665, but he did not write *A Journal of the Plague Year* until 1722, when the plague in the south of France posed a threat to the citizens of Great Britain. Neither Sutherland's venal Defoe nor Baine's spiritual Defoe tells us about the intellectual climate to which Defoe was reacting.

[12] *Defoe*, 2nd edn. (London: Methuen, 1950), 264.

If juxtaposed against three other treatises that Defoe published during these years, these works reveal that Defoe was responding to a group of writers on religious subjects who, starting with John Toland's *Nazarenus* in 1718 and ending with Anthony Collins's *The Scheme of Literal Prophecy Considered* in 1727, raised questions about the origins of Christianity and the doctrines associated with the teachings of Christ. Although they are usually grouped together, they had vastly different motives and beliefs, but many of them fit the general pattern of the deist as outlined by Alfred O. Aldridge in *Shaftesbury and the Deist Manifesto*. Some, like William Whiston were Arians, but as a group they put forward a challenge to orthodox Christianity that a religious controversialist such as Defoe would have found difficult to ignore.

That Defoe should appoint himself as a defender of what he considered to be religious orthodoxy during the reign of George I is hardly surprising. In his early works he seldom missed an opportunity of attacking John Toland's unmysterious Christianity, and he devoted a number of pamphlets as well as a large section of his *Consolidator* (1705) to assaults upon both the deists and those whose principles seemed to smack of one heresy or another. After Collins published his *Discourse of Free-Thinking* in 1713, Defoe frequently expressed his distate for what he believed lay behind this plea for freedom of thought, and he was convinced that all of William Whiston's abilities lay in the area of astronomy and mathematics rather than theology. It is doubtful that Defoe ever seriously contemplated a career as a Dissenting clergyman, but his pronouncements on the decline of the clergy and of preaching in *The Present State of the Parties in Great Britain* (1712) show that he regarded himself as something of an expert on both the form and substance of religion.[13]

As we have seen, before the great deistic offensive of the 1720s, two important controversies (scandals might be the better word) attracted Defoe's attention, one within the Church of England and the other among the ranks of the Dissenters. In 1716 Benjamin Hoadly, Bishop of Bangor, began a series of disputes that lasted in one form or another until 1721 and resulted in a very real and permanent diminution of the political power of the Church of England, along with a temporary loss of its credibility as a religious institution. A few years after the beginning of the Bangorian

[13] In this work, Defoe is more interested in the method of preaching than in the substance, supporting spontaneity in the pulpit and scorning the pedantically prepared text. Frank Ellis has raised the question of whether Defoe did some preaching himself, but the report of one such occasion, which he quotes, suggests, on careful reading, that Defoe was listening to the Scottish preacher Robert M'cala and commenting on his poetic style rather than preaching himself. See Ellis, 'Defoe's "Resignacon" and the Limitation of "Mathematical Plainness"', *Review of English Studies*, n.s. 36 (1985), 338–54; and Robert Wodrow, *Analecta* (Glasgow: Maitland Club, 1842), ii. 305.

Controversy the Dissenters engaged in an equally disastrous controversy, a violent disagreement over the nature of the Trinity. Defoe played an active role in both of these disputes, and they must have influenced him in a variety of ways. Although Defoe's personal religious convictions were unlikely to have been changed by the chaos that ensued in the ranks of the Dissenters after the meeting at Salters' Hall, he may have lost much of his respect for the Dissenting clergy. The ecumenicalism of *The Farther Adventures of Robinson Crusoe* and his appreciation of the natives who worship the sun in *A New Voyage Round the World* suggests that during the last twelve years of his life Defoe was searching for a Christianity purified from the controversies among the clergy. Yet despite his willingness to play with utopian notions, he set himself firmly against the powerful attacks upon the literal reading of the Old and New Testaments by those who seemed heartened by the Bangorian controversy and by the events at Salters' Hall. The deist offensive that Defoe had to face in the 1720s was waged by writers who were confident that they were putting an end to an irrational and barbaric religious system.

Defoe's objection to these writers may have been as much concerned with the moral issues raised by the deists as with religious principle. He was one of those who held the not uncommon belief that morality could not be separated from religion. Writing under the name 'Orthodox' in *Applebee's Journal* of 18 March 1721, he argued:

Freethinkers are profane, and *Free-Actors* also; for,—erasing the Awe of God in their Hearts, they plead immediately, and of Course, for a Freedom in all Manner of Vice,—using the Pretence of Liberty for Justification of Crime, as if the Liberty God gave to Man of being a free Agent, disengaged him entirely from all the restraint of Laws, whether Human or Divine.[14]

As an active advocate for the Societies for Reformation of Manners from their inception, Defoe viewed the civilizing of English behaviour during the transition from the Restoration to the eighteenth century as the product of a moral code enforced by religious sanctions. Writers such as Toland and Collins regarded themselves as soldiers in the cause of Enlightenment, but to Defoe, they seemed enemies to the progress of both manners and morals.[15]

[14] Lee, ii. 353.

[15] Both Defoe and Swift shared the common contemporary notion that an outward show of manners, even when not accompanied by any sincere moral reform, was good for what they considered a somewhat barbarous society. This has led to the charge that Swift's *A Project for the Advancement of Religion and the Reformation of Manners* had to be either ironic or hypocritical, but as Irvin Ehrenpreis remarked, the central idea was to propose something 'immediately efficacious'. *Swift* (3 vols., Cambridge, Mass.: Harvard University Press, 1962–82), i. 289.

Defoe's first full-length attack upon the position of the deists appears to have been *An Essay upon Literature*, which, according to John Robert Moore, appeared in April or May 1726. Although it has a title that would naturally attract literary critics hoping to discover clues to Defoe's methods as a writer or to his literary taste, such readers would be disappointed. It is actually about what we would now call the semiotics of writing. Asserting that God communicated writing to mankind at Sinai with the Ten Commandments, Defoe urges the miraculous nature of such an invention:

Mankind had no Idea of such a thing among them, it was not in them to make a piece of Paper speak, and to stamp a Voice and Words, which were neither more or less than meer Sounds to stamp them on a Paper and empower other People to speak over again by the help of those dumb Figures, the same Word that the first Person had uttered at a hundred or a thousand Miles distance; no Man could imagin such a thing feasible.[16]

It was a miraculous gift that gave the possibility of communicating knowledge not merely over distance but over time as well. Through writing, it became possible to stand 'upon the Shoulders of our Fore-fathers Learning', and man quickly 'improv'd upon their invention; carry'd on progressive Knowledge upon the foot of their Discoveries, and brought experimental Knowledge both in Arts and in Nature to that Prodigy of perfection to which it is now arriv'd' (2).[17] Although he sometimes longed for the power of hieroglyphics to communicate directly through the combination of picture and word, here he speculated on the awkwardness of the Egyptian system for communicating complex ideas.[18] Ultimately they were 'lame, unintelligible, aenigmatic' (29). Defoe raised many questions in this work, more than he answered. He speculated on writing as a profession and upon what would have happened to the production of books if printing had not been invented. He wondered at the numbers who would have been employed in an age of so much book production, and asked his readers to marvel at the number of manuscripts that might have been saved had printing been invented in an earlier age. But he also established what he considered to be an orthodox chronology for the events recorded in the Old

[16] Daniel Defoe, *An Essay upon Literature* (London, 1726), 16. Subsequent references to this work will be included in parentheses within my text.

[17] Defoe used much the same image in his *General History of Discoveries and Improvements in Useful Arts*, which was still being issued in numbers at this time.

[18] Reversing the deists' attack on the Jews as a barbarous people who borrowed all their ideas from the Egyptians and the Chaldeans, Defoe tries to show that the admired hieroglyphs were less effective than words for communication. For Defoe's ideas on language, see my 'The Unmentionable and the Ineffable in Defoe's Fiction', *Studies in the Literary Imagination* 15 (1982), 85–102.

Testament at a time when the chronology of Sir Isaac Newton and Fréret's reply to it were creating doubts about the accuracy of previous calculations. Throwing uncertainty upon the historicity of the Bible was one of the main weapons of the deists. In response, Defoe affirms the coming of letters in 2415 BC and makes God the 'first *Writing Master* in the World' (62).

Although *An Essay upon Literature* contains many of Defoe's favourite ideas about writing as a form of industry and about the decline of education in contemporary England, it is unique in being a tribute to the variety of mediums involved in writing, from shorthand, at which Defoe had considerable skill, to cyphers of several kinds, a medium that he used when acting as a spy for Robert Harley. The most significant contribution of writing, however, has been to spread truth throughout the world:

How little a Way wou'd the Fame of the greatest Heroe have reach'd? The Noise of a Victory would have scarce been heard farther than the Noise of the Cannon: much less could Things have continued in Time longer than the Memory of the Persons concern'd wou'd preserve them, . . . of which already we see so many fatal Effects, and by which Things of the greatest Moment done as it were but Yesterday, that is to say, within the Compass of two or three Ages, turn into Fable and Romance; Scoundrels are made Heroes, and Heroes are made Gods. (114)

Defoe was sceptical enough concerning the ways in which history was transmitted even with books and printing.[19] Without them, almost nothing in the past could be reported accurately. But it was God himself who gave mankind the means by which his message could be preserved for all to know the truth.

In July of 1726, Defoe published *Mere Nature Delineated*, a fascinating study of a wild child who had been discovered in the woods of Germany in 1725. Peter, as he was called, was brought to England and created a considerable stir. For Defoe, it was an occasion for commenting on one of his favourite topics—the condition of human beings in the state of nature. He devoted a large section to various forms of human folly, to theories of education and language, and, guessing that Peter was actually deaf, he speculated on this subject as well. But the main thrust of Defoe's argument undercut the notions of Shaftesbury and the deists on the natural goodness of humankind, a doctrine which he considered to be against all notions of original sin. The title echoes William Wollaston's *The Religion of Nature Delineated* (1722) and its argument that virtue was achievable through squaring every action with an ideal standard of truth. In Wollaston's vision

[19] For Defoe's attitudes toward recording events through the writing of history, see my *Realism, Myth, and History in Defoe's Fiction* (Lincoln: University of Nebraska Press, 1983), 47–70.

of the world in which this high level of virtue might be achieved, concepts of a fallen world or a natural human tendency toward evil played no role at all. *Mere Nature Delineated* was Defoe's opportunity to ally himself with Mandeville's assessment of Shaftesbury's view of humanity's natural tendency toward virtue, by arguing that the problem with such concepts was that they were incompatible with any real vision of human behaviour. Defoe's wry, half-playful manner may have been dictated by the graceful style of Shaftesbury and, more particularly, Collins, whose extraordinarily effective irony was disguised behind a pose of openness and a seemingly innocent quest for knowledge. To make his reply more cogent as satire, Defoe pretends for a time to accept what he never actually believes: that Peter is a true natural man who, after some education, would be capable of taking his place in society.

But after jesting over the notion of Peter among the beaux, wits, and court ladies, Defoe gets down to his main subject—the problem of natural good and evil. The example of Peter shows that virtue does not come through contact with nature: 'Let those who deny original Depravity, answer this for me, if they think they can; for my Part, I acknowledge it to be out of my Reach, upon any other Foot.'[20] Defoe argues that even if Peter were mentally retarded (a 'natural'), he was nevertheless a good example of what a human growing up in the state of nature, without the benefits of society and education, would be like: 'Such a plain coarse Piece of Work is a man in the mere Condition he is born in, just coming out of Nature's Hand: and by Consequence, the Improvement of the Soul by Instruction which we call Educating, is of the highest Importance' (68).

Both the *Essay on Literature* and *Mere Nature Delineated* are concerned with the nature of language and of learning. Both assert the miraculous gift of writing at Sinai, but only in the latter does Defoe consider the ways in which language is transmitted. In examining the kind of control over learning that can be exerted in teaching the deaf to understand their world, he contemplates what would be necessary to turn Peter into a Christian:

As for that Trifle called Religion, I reckon no Time at all to that Part, in which I know I please many of my Sceptical, Deistical, Ante-Enthusiastick Readers. I call them Ante-Enthusiasts, because they place so little Weight upon Religion in general, that they never are at Pains to make Pretensions to Inspirations or Revelations of any kind whatsoever. (83)

Although he states that he intends to avoid the subject of religion, he adds

[20] *Mere Nature Delineated* (London, 1726), 44. Subsequent references to this work will be included in parentheses within my text.

that he assumes that Peter will receive some kind of religious instruction among the other subjects that he will be taught. For all his mockery of human folly, in the end Defoe found it difficult to maintain a comic tone on a subject he regarded as being of the highest importance. Indeed, in the following year he abandoned all kinds of irony and indirection. Published in September 1727, after the three works on the occult with their bantering tone, his *New Family Instructor* went directly to what he considered the heart of the matter—the attack upon traditional Christian values by the deists.

Although Defoe considered his own orthodoxy beyond suspicion, like so many of his contemporaries, he had amplified his religious ideas with concepts drawn from the philosophy of Locke and the science of Newton, particularly from Newton's notion of God as the ruler of infinite space. 'The utmost Perfection of Human Knowledge that can be attained to by us, and the best use that Knowledge can be put to in this World', he wrote, 'is to lead our Thoughts into Extasies of Admiration, Wonder, and Astonishment, at The Wisdom and Powr of the great Author of Nature, who has made all these glorious Bodies, and directs all their Motions.'[21] He gives over one of his dialogues to a character who has some of the qualities of Anthony Collins, but who is misled, despite his 'Knowledge and Wit . . . with the new Errors as to the Trinity; and withal a little of a Deist, or Sceptick, or Free-Thinker call them what you will' (253). This new type of thinker looks at the same world as the believer but fails to read correctly what, at the time, were called the 'probable signs'.[22] He refuses to see the pattern of divine retribution 'covering Things with Words, and amusing us with being quite wrong, as they call it, about hell, and a Future State of Perdition, which they make a jest of' (255). Defoe had moved far from the notions of a horned and cloven-footed devil, but he never abandoned the idea of punishment for sin.[23]

The Bible, which was under attack from Whiston for its inclusion of what he considered immoral sections such as the *Song of Songs* and from Toland, who considered it as the product of Jewish fanaticism and ignorance, was,

---

[21] *A New Family Instructor* (London, 1727), 251. Subsequent references to this work will appear within parentheses within my text.

[22] Douglas Patey's *Probability and Literary Form* (Cambridge: Cambridge University Press, 1984) has demonstrated how important this concept was for the Restoration and eighteenth century. Defoe's ideas on this subject were not unlike those of his fellow novelists two decades into the future, Richardson and Fielding.

[23] D. P. Walker has shown that while most religious thinkers of Defoe's time had come to consider the iconography of hell as childish, they were divided on the question of eternal punishment, some suggesting that the translation of the words describing the length of torment indicated something less than an eternity. See *The Decline of Hell* (Chicago: Chicago University Press, 1964).

for Defoe, divine in every part. Defoe argued that the deists were simply trying to manufacture a God after their notion of what a God ought to be:

The problem is that the Deists want a God who is limited in his power: a God without a Devil, according to Epicurus; a God Wise and Powerful, but not infinitely so, not Omnipotent, not Self-sufficient, and All-sufficient; a God that having created the World (and 'tis with some difficulty they go so far) has not power to guide it, but has abandoned it to the Government of it self; to that foolish *Nothing*, that unexisting piece of Nonsense, call'd Chance; or like the Followers of Zeno, the Deist Philospher, a God depending upon (they know not what, of a) blind Destiny; a God who not being able to break the Chain of second Causes, is carry'd away with them himself, being obliged to act by the Course of natural Consequences, even whether he will or no. (263)

The notion of a God who was incapable of intervening in the affairs of human kind was something Defoe could never accept. However much his God may have remained hidden behind the physical nature through which He worked, Defoe never appears to have doubted His continued presence.

III

The anti-deistic nature of the three works I have been discussing suggests that Defoe was conducting his private crusade against the heresies of the time. I want to turn now to Defoe's explorations of the occult, where the comments on deism are less direct but equally important. *The Political History of the Devil*, published on 7 May 1726, shares with the far less successful *Mere Nature Delineated* a mocking style intended to meet the ironic tone of Collins on equal ground. Although Defoe boasted of the popularity of this work in the preface to the second edition, he noted the disapproval expressed by one 'Reverend Gentleman' over the lack of gravity.[24] He raises this objection, however, only to dismiss it. Defoe's Devil has certain comic elements, but for the most part he is used as a fictional angle of vision to contemplate the follies of mankind, follies extended to include the theological wars of the time. Behind the often deliberate buffoonery there is a serious purpose, for just as the man who believes in a world of spirits is likely to believe in a God, the same might be said about the belief in the Devil. From this standpoint, Defoe's aim was not very different from that of the seventeenth-century divine Richard Baxter in his entirely humourless treatise on apparitions.

---

[24] [*Political*] *History of the Devil*, 2nd edn. (London, 1726), sig. A2ᵛ. References to this work will be included within parentheses in my text. The title was changed to *The History of the Devil* with the 2nd edn.

Defoe's Devil is a far cry from the dragon-winged fiend embodied in Bunyan's Apollyon or in folk tradition. He is a spirit who lives in continual envy of man, or rather of those elect humans who will find eternal life through grace. His only major role in human history was the temptation of Eve. After that event and the subsequent taint that dwells with humanity in the world, he functions mainly as a regulator of the evil that he introduced on earth and which will remain forever. Occasionally he would extend that taint of evil into such a major horror as warfare, and he might dwell constantly with someone like Richelieu; but mostly he was simply an observer. The evil in human beings was such that he would often find himself astonished by their invention of new sins. Defoe's Devil represents the spirit of negativity and destruction. His dwelling-place is not some local hell filled with fire and the varied places set aside for select torture. He dwells with humanity itself, and is present whenever human passion drives a soul to commit an evil action:

Pride swells the Passions; Avarice moves the Affections; and what is Pride, and what is Avarice, but the *Devil* in the Inside of the Man? ay, as personally, and really as ever he was in the Herd of Swine. . . . In like Manner Avarice leads him to rob, plunder and destroy for Money, and to commit some times the worst of Violences to obtain the wicked Reward. How many have had their Throats cut for their Money, have been murther'd on the High-Way, or in their Beds, for the Desire of what they had? It is the same Thing in other Articles, every vice is the Devil in a Man. (403)

Whatever the past may have been, Defoe noted, the present suggests a world in which human ingenuity in the invention of evil has surpassed anything the Devil might have imagined.

One of the oddities of this book is Defoe's attack upon Milton, whose poetry, as might be suggested from the extraordinary compliments he was soon to lavish on it in *A New Family Instructor* (368), was never more in Defoe's mind and heart. But in the context of the religious controversies of the 1720s, Milton might be seen as an intriguing target. If Milton's greatness had ever been in doubt, Addison's papers on *Paradise Lost* in *The Spectator* would have firmly established his eminence as an epic poet. Under Milton's influence, the turn of English poetry toward blank verse was given a major impetus in the very year of publication of Defoe's book with the publication of James Thomson's *Winter*. And even Defoe was to imitate what he surely thought to be Miltonic blank verse in 1727.

However much he admired Milton as both a poet and thinker, Defoe knew that he took poetic liberties with the Bible. Defoe's Devil may seem a very modern spirit compared with Milton's Satan, but he was also free from some of Milton's imaginative embellishments. Defoe had no real objections to Milton's poetic fictions, but at a time when the text of the Bible was being probed for errors and ambiguities, at a time when Collins was insisting that only by an allegorical reading could Old Testament types be made the foundation of New Testament antitypes, Defoe was reminding his readers that Milton's brilliant epic was not equivalent to a biblical text.

Having taken the high ground in freeing the Devil from the form that medieval iconography would have imposed upon him, and having admitted that most cases of witchcraft were nothing more than the persecutions of poor old women, Defoe could turn to the subject of Milton's adherence to 'the corrupt Doctrine of Arius' (75). Focusing on Milton's scene in which God summons the angels to pay homage to Christ, Defoe objects to what seems to be the creation of Christ as a kind of after-thought:

This is, indeed too gross; at his meeting he makes God declare the Son to be *that day begotten* as before; had he made him not begotten that day, but declared General that day, it would be reconcilable with Scripture and with sense; for either the beginning is meant of ordaining to an office, or else the eternal Generation falls to the ground. . . . And *Milton* can have no authority to tell us there was any Declaration of it in heaven before this, except it be that dull authority called *poetic Licence*, which will not pass in so solemn an affair as that. But the thing was necessary to Milton, who wanted to assign some cause or original of the *Devil's* Rebellion; and so, *as I said above*, the design is well laid, it only wants two trifles called *Truth* and *History*; so I leave it to struggle for it self. (74)

In revealing that he considered one of his favourite poets an Arian, Defoe must have experienced some ambiguity. He praised Milton's powers of invention and argued that the imagery was 'exceeding magnificent, the Thought rich and bright, and in some respects truly sublime' (73). Knowing that nothing served so well for a stick to belabour his real opponents as what he regarded as orthodox Christianity, he must have consoled himself with the belief that Milton's reputation as a poet was strong enough to survive his accusations of heresy.

The real Arians he set out to attack had only oblique relations with Milton. They were the new objectors to the concept of the Trinity, whether someone like Whiston, whose explorations of the documents of the early Church convinced him that that notion of the Trinity was not grounded on the firmest historical evidence, or those among the Dissenters, such as Martin Tompkins or Thomas Emlyn, whose opinions created such discord at the Salters' Hall conference. As I suggested previously, Defoe was writing at a time when the Dissenters, particularly the Presbyterians, were still in disarray from the refusal of so many to sign the agreement over a fundamental belief in the Trinity. From Defoe's standpoint, those who did not sign were, as Blake might have put it, of the Devil's party without knowing it.

Before the end of 1726, Defoe had produced another work in his fight against the heresies of the time. *A System of Magick*, published on 24 November and advertised on the title-page as 'An Historical Account of Mankind's most early Dealing with the Devil', has clear connections with *The Political History of the Devil* and with Andrew Moreton, whose name was added in later editions. Though less satirical here than in his earlier study of the Devil, Defoe continues to preserve a certain scepticism toward accounts of the supernatural, especially toward stories of apparitions and accounts of miracles. He depicted the prophets of the past as the equivalent of contemporary scientists—Newton, Halley, and Whiston— and suggested that those who possessed some knowledge of science often had to disguise it under a form of magic that would please the ignorant. From this account of true prophets forced to conceal their knowledge, Defoe moves on to his main point—the evils done by the deists and Arians of his time.

After remarking on the ways in which the princes of the East were accustomed to punish false prophets, Defoe contemplates the possibility of using such methods with 'the Broachers of Atheistical, Deistical, and Enthusiastic Whymsies in our Age'.[25] In a manner not very different from that of Swift, he concludes with regret that considering the numbers of these heretics, such severe penalties could not be practical, since they might have the effect of depopulating the world:

But I am loth to seem vindictive in my Notion, nor would I set up Fire and Faggot; no, not against the *Devil* and his Agents; they may have enough of that hereafter. . . . And besides, such a Persecution must necessarily at this time be so bloody, that I know not what City, or Town, Inns of Court, Palace, College or University, (our own excepted) which it would not almost lay waste, desolate, and make void of Inhabitants. Mercy on us! persecute and punish Men for being Atheists, and Deists; for dividing the Trinity and unsanctifying the Holy Ghost, who is the Sanctifier of the World, and such difficult Trifles as these? where would it end! and what would become of all the religious Part of the World! what a Schism, in the most literal Sense would this make among us? (124–5)

Although Defoe expresses mock 'fear of laying waste the Globe' (125) by

---

[25] *A System of Magick* (London, 1726), 124.

such measures, one feels that, as Swift remarked of his enemies, he 'would hang them if he could'.

As in his *Essay on Literature,* Defoe defends the authenticity of the Bible, calling it, with deliberate understatement, 'a tolerable good history' (185). Relying on the chronology in Raleigh's *History of the World,* he shows how Moses would have had access to the traditions of Noah and the Creation. And after all, Moses had direct inspiration from God, whereas those such as Whiston who were ready to question the propriety of sections of the Old Testament were merely relying upon their reason. As for writers such as Collins, who wanted every aspect of religion subjected to the ideals of 'criticism' or open discussion, they too suffered from an excessive dependence on reason. Defoe wrote that these men believe that 'humane Judgement is in its self infallible, and therefore in some manner equal to the divine Being; a Light issued from Heaven, and darted by Emanation into the Souls of Men; which, if rightly cultivated and improv'd, and especially if sincerely follow'd, adher'd to, and obey'd guides the Soul to understanding things in a superior way' (196). The new deists, Defoe argued, tend to treat reason as a magical faculty, but reason failed mankind in the Garden of Eden and would always fail when too much is expected of that faculty.

Later in this work, following an attack upon contemporary atheism, Defoe develops the notion of the ways in which reason has functioned as a replacement for faith in magic or in some supernatural force:

It may be ask'd of me, why I will Insist upon this matter in a Treatise of Magick; that this relates to the Atheists, not to *Magicians,* and that by the same Rule, all Enthusiasm, Heresies and mysterious things in Religion as well as in Science, may be rated in the same Class, and be called by the same Name, and so we shall make a Magick of Religion at last.

But let a short Answer suffice to this weak Objection; All Errors in Religion are not equally Diabolic, no, nor equally mischievous; and as I have said above, that this seems to be of an Original deeper than Hell, and out of the Reach of the *Devil;* so as far as it is a Crime which derives from the Man as Independent, and acting the *Devil* by himself, I think it must have the Height of human Imagination and Invention in it, and so may be call'd Magical, as Magick is a Science or Art of doing Superlative Evil. (239)

Defoe questioned the motives of these new heretics, but he never questioned their ingenuity.

The purpose of these studies of the occult is even more obvious in the last of this group, *An Essay on the History and Reality of Apparitions,* published on 27 March 1727.[26] In his introduction, Defoe tries to steer a

[26] As with *A System of Magick,* this work was also identified with Andrew Moreton. See the title page of

middle course between gullibility and complete scepticism. Having asserted that everyone feels impulses and apprehensions that seem to come from outside, he suggests that the spirits responsible for these warnings should be capable of assuming the form of an apparition. At the same time, he states, 'I affirm nothing that will not bear a Proof' (5). Once again Defoe expresses his disdain for pictures of the devil 'with a Cock's Bill, Ass's Ears, Goats's Horns, glaring Eyes; Bats's Wings, cloven Foot, and Dragon's Tail', but he maintains that the existence of spirit itself is so evident as to make debate on this issue unnecessary. Having made this assertion at the beginning of his book, Defoe allows himself to express doubts about various stories of ghosts that have been accepted by the gullible John Aubrey, and scorn for the accounts of apparitions in Homer. After telling the story of a student at Cambridge who heard a voice warning him that his atheism was folly, Defoe hints that the entire story might have been the effect of the student's imagination. He ends his work with the judgement that the British seem to delight in ghost stories: 'our Hypochondriack People see more *Devils* at noon-day than *Gallilaeus* did Stars, and more by many than ever really appear'd' (394). Yet he affirms his belief in the reality of apparitions in the midst of considerable scepticism about individual tales of supernatural experiences.

Defoe is more at home in discussing dreams and impulses as genuine monitions from an invisible world of spirits. He attacks a variety of modern heresies and their proponents, from those who, like Thomas Burnet, believed that the soul experienced a form of sleep after death, to the Boyle Lecturers, who emphasized the littleness of earth in the entire universe and the unlikelihood that there could be a special dispensation for 'this despicable Species called Man' (56) that would not be extended to beings on other planets. While allowing for the possibility of beings on other planets, Defoe indulges in considerable play over the creatures on Saturn without eyes and those on Jupiter who would be capable of living in freezing temperatures.

In suggesting that Defoe's main intent was to attack contemporary heresies rather than viewing him as having a sudden desire to write on the fantastic and the occult, I do not want to argue that he did not enjoy telling these ghost stories. But at times he appears to show some genuine irritation at having to please as well as educate a naive audience.

But hold! wither am I going? This looks like Religion, and we must not talk a

the 'second edition', published by Thomas Worral in 1735. Page numbers will be taken from the first edition and included within parentheses in the text.

Word of that, if we expect to be agreeable. Unhappy Times! where to be serious, is to be dull and grave, and consequently write without Spirit. We must talk politely, not religiously; we may show the Scholar, but must not show a Word of the Christian; so we may quote profane History, but not sacred; and a story out of *Lucan* or *Plutarch, Tully* or *Virgil* will go down, but not a Word out of *Moses* or *Joshua*.

Well, we must comply however; the Humour of the Day must prevail; and as there is no instructing you without pleasing you, and no pleasing you but in your own way, we must go on in that way; the Understanding must be refin'd by Allegory and Enigma; you must see the Sun through the Cloud, and relish Light by the help of Darkness; the Taste must be rectify'd by Salts, the Appetite whetted by Bitters; in a word, the Manners must be reform'd in Masquerade, Devotion quicken'd by the Stage not the Pulpit, and Wit be brighten'd by Satyrs upon Sense. (42)

Perhaps Defoe did tire of the satirico-comic method of these attacks against modern heresies. *The History of Apparitions* was his last effort of this kind. He may also have exhausted the market, since it did not sell as well as its predecessors. But what is more likely is that this statement of despair about having to titillate his audience represents a feeling of impotence about getting his message across. *The History of Apparitions* is in some ways the most personal of the works on the occult, with several stories drawn from what would appear to be his own experiences. And in this work, as in *The New Family Instructor*, he defended his fictions as being similar to the parables used by Christ: 'the most perfect Representations and Illustrations of the things which they were brought to set forth' (51).

'I am Orthodox in my Notions' (44) Defoe asserted, but he obviously had a different concept of the uses of fictions from that of most of his contemporaries. He accepted the notion that many sections of Scriptures were allegories and parables. He clearly did not appreciate the irony with which Collins approached biblical narrative in *A Discourse of the Grounds and Reasons of the Christian Religion*, or his assertion that Christianity was mainly a form of mystical Judaism, but he would probably have been less shocked by Collins's allegorical approach than were many of the distinguished Anglican clerics who attempted to answer their mocking opponent. Defoe's claim to be an 'Orthodox' Christian did not mean that he was unsophisticated in his approach to religion. His *Essay on Literature* reveals that he had read Theophilus Gale's *The Court of the Gentiles* and Edward Stillingfleet's *Origines Sacrae*. His first reaction to Addison's essays on *Paradise Lost* was to contemplate what Milton would have made of an apocryphal version of the Genesis story in which Eve separated from

Adam after the Fall.[27] What we would now consider 'comparative religion' captured his imagination because it offered alternative fables to what he had learned in his early religious studies. It is hardly surprising that, when he came to answer the writings of the heretics of his time, he should have approached his subject first through the analysis of the mechanics of language and then through the power of illustrative fictions.

The writer of fiction has a certain freedom inherent in his form that the author of the most illustrative didactic thesis lacks. The Defoe who appears in this chapter, the writer of 1726 and 1727, is explorative and lively, but he is also a writer who would seem an unlikely author of novels such as *Moll Flanders* and *Roxana*. And to explain how he could have written passages appearing to praise natural religion and a form of deism in *A New Voyage Round the World*, not to speak of that to be found in some later works, might be difficult. But it is important to try to understand Defoe's full response to religious heresies during the last years of his life. The freedom that anonymity and fiction provided him is apparent enough in *The Farther Adventures of Robinson Crusoe*, in which Crusoe permits a Catholic priest with ecumenical attitudes toward Christianity to assume the religious duties of his island. Curiously enough, Defoe was writing anti-Catholic propaganda at much the same time. He could create a sympathetic Jacobite hero in the narrator of *Colonel Jack* during a period when his hatred for the Jacobites was unabated. And, as we have seen, he could say of the sun-worshipping natives of a mythical Australia, compared with the idol worship of some other tribes, 'these people seem to act upon a more solid foundation, paying their reverence in a manner much more rational, and to something which it was more reasonable to worship'.[28]

What this suggests is that Defoe could see the attraction of deism, and that at times he considered it superior to what he thought to be the corruptions of the Catholic Church, which during the 1720s was continuing its attacks against Protestants, particularly in the city of Thorn (modern Torun). If he considered atheism and idol worship the worst religious developments, he also fought battles on small points of faith throughout his life. He could, on the one hand, accept the Quakers as a true branch of Christian Dissent at a time when many of his fellow Nonconformists thought otherwise, and, on the other, in his younger days, he could oppose the majority of his fellow Presbyterians in arguing the wickedness of Occasional Conformity with the Church of England. He thought he recog-

---

[27] *Review*, vii. 637–49.
[28] *A New Voyage Round the World, in Romances and Narratives by Daniel Defoe*, ed. George A. Aitken (16 vols., London: Dent, 1895), xiv. 148.

nized wrong religious thought when he saw it, and he permitted himself all kinds of freedom to explore interesting possibilities, especially when he was writing fiction. Such contradictions should tell us something about the complexity of Defoe, but it should also warn us against oversimplifying the thought of the age in which he lived, particularly in matters of politics and religion.[29]

IV

Although Defoe's attack upon deism gives a central organization to all the above works, they were remarkably diverse and inventive. The litany of fools in *Mere Nature Delineated* is one of his finest satires, and his attack on Milton's theology, though directed toward revealing Milton's heresies, is actually a remarkable piece of extended criticism of the poet. In *The History and Reality of Apparitions* (374), the account of the 'roguish London boys' at a boarding-school in Dorking who set out to fool the gullible inhabitants into believing that a ghost haunted an uninhabited 'Mansion House' in the neighbourhood is autobiographical to some extent and reveals a young Daniel Defoe who appreciated mischief if he did not personally participate in it.[30] Similarly, *A System of Magick* exhibits a Defoe who is familiar with the shows of Britain's fairs and the soothsayers who deceive the young girls who compose the bulk of their customers. Near the end of the work, he gives an account of a conjurer who gets a young woman to confess that she is pregnant by a young man named Thomas. Using his assistant, George, who plays the role of a ghost, the conjuror tricks Thomas into believing he is haunted. Confessing his affair with the girl and his refusal to marry her, Thomas is tricked into marrying his sweetheart, whom he admits 'is a good honest Girl, and loves me too mainly, and she'll be a good Wife' (377). Defoe's magician is more of a psychologist than a true manager of the 'real Black Art' (378), and by his clever ruses saves a poor woman from despair and disgrace.

[29] One explanation for the diversity in Defoe's thinking is his tendency to compartmentalize his approach to any subject along separate political and religious grounds. It might be argued that Defoe's Whiggish politics were considerably more 'radical' than those of the 'classical republicans' who generally held the extreme left among the Whigs. Yet when *The True-Born Englishman* was published in 1701, Robert Wodrow and one of his friends (*Analecta*, i. 7) ascribed it to John Toland, a deist whom Defoe detested. What this demonstrates is the complexity of contemporary political and religious thought. Although the appearance of similarities between Toland and Defoe may represent a confusion in the minds of these contemporaries, it is not something that we should ignore.

[30] For the suggestion that Defoe was the leader of this group, see Frank Bastian, *Defoe's Early Life* (London: Macmillan, 1981), 35–6.

This is a set piece reminiscent of the scenes in the paintings of Jan Steen, with its combination of realist detail, comedy, and morality, but it is also a reminder that, even in these works, Defoe had not abandoned his role as a commentator on society. While he was completing the second volume of *The Complete English Tradesman*, he produced a number of shorter pieces that were in a sense spin-offs from the larger study. These included *A Brief Case of the Distillers*, published at the beginning of 1726, which argued for a *laissez-faire* approach to the consumption of alcohol in Britain, and *A Brief Deduction of the Original, Progress, and Immense Greatness of the British Woollen Manufacture: With an Enquiry whether it be not at Present in a very Declining Condition*, which appeared a year later, on 15 March 1727. As is often true of works by Defoe, this work is not exactly what it might seem at first glance. On the surface it represents the kind of gloom-and-doom economics that the Tories often practised in these years. It argues that the manufacturing of wool cloth has reached a point of overproduction that will eventually destroy the industry as a 'Dropsy' eventually destroys the body. Defoe drew upon the same statistics and historical accounts of the wool industry that he was using in other works he was writing at the time, but instead of his usual optimism about the quality of British woollen manufactures overwhelming the poor cloth of France and Spain, he laments that even Germany and northern Europe were developing their own industry and closing off available markets. Yet he proposes two solutions at the end: regulating imports of foreign cloth and French fashions; and discovering new markets for English products. The first echoes his attack upon French fashions in *The Complete English Tradesman* and the second is part of his attempt to encourage new British exploration and colonization, which made its most recent appearance in his *General History of Discoveries and Improvements in Useful Arts*, the numbers of which had been bound as a single volume at the end of 1726. He was finding new ways of packaging old arguments.

He continued his arguments for expanding English trade in two related tracts: *The Evident Approach of a War; and Something of the Necessity of It, in order to Establish Peace and Preserve Trade*, which appeared at the beginning of the year on 10 January 1727, and *The Evident Advantages to Great Britain and Its Allies from the Approaching War*, published less than a month later, on 2 February. These tracts treat the sabre-rattling of Spain and the Empire at this time, accusing both of a form of 'Quixotisme'.[31] The two nations were threatening to stop the importation of British goods, encouraging the creation of the Ostend Company to compete with the

---

[31] *The Evident Approach of a War* (London, 1727), 6.

Dutch and the British in trading to the Far East, and demanding that
Gibraltar be given back to Spain. According to the agreement between the
two nations, Spain was opening up its colonies to trade by the imperialists,
and it was rumoured that, as a secret part of the negotiations, the House of
Stuart was to be encouraged in its attempt to regain the throne of England
and Scotland. Defoe argued that the combined forces of the British, the
Dutch, and the French would be too much for Spain and Austria even with
the help of Russia. He also alluded to a tract he had written in 1712 with
the title *Imperial Gratitude* by way of commenting on the failure of the
Austrians to realize how much was owed to Britain and her allies in the
War of the Spanish Succession, and used the occasion to discuss one of his
favorite themes: ethical obligation:

GRATITUDE is a Branch of *Honesty*; and it is very hard to say, or even to think a
man can be Honest that is not Grateful; for as *Gratitude* respects an obligation
past, or a Kindness receiv'd; so it is no more or less, than paying a Debt; and tho'
the Debt be not such perhaps as can be demanded by Process (if it were the
Creditor could oblige the Debtor to Payment) yet the Obligation is the stronger.[32]

Having established how just a war Britain would have on its hands, Defoe
was ready to spell out how advantageous it might be if Spain and Austria
were foolish enough to act upon a treaty that appeared to be mostly bluff.

In the first of these pamphlets, Defoe showed how thoroughly he knew
the wine trade in Spain in the area of Cadiz, where he probably worked for
some time during his younger days as an importer of wines. He maintained
a half-mocking tone of disbelief that Spain and Austria could actually be
moving toward a war they could not win. But the second pamphlet was
devoted to the advantages that Britain might find in such a war. These
included the punishment of the Spaniards for pride and cruelty, but the
most obvious gain would be financial—the possible taking of a Spanish
treasure ship as a consequence of a vigilant naval blockade and the harvest-
ing of riches were Britain to establish a trading centre on Cuba at the Bay of
Honda, about 50 miles west of Havana. Legitimized by war, the formerly
illegal trading with Spanish colonists in the Caribbean would now become
a way of enriching the nation. 'Trade knows no Religions, no Sects, no
Parties, no Divisions,' writes Defoe by way of chastising Spain's seemingly
foolish refusal to trade with the Moors.[33] While insisting upon the justness
of the coming war on the basis of the behaviour of Spain and the
imperialists, Defoe appears to suggest that the Spanish deserve to be

---

[32] *The Evident Approach of a War*, 39.
[33] *The Evident Advantages to Great Britain and Its Allies from the Approaching War: Especially in Matters
of Trade* (London, 1727), 16.

punished for refusing to allow Britain to engage in a free trade with Spain's colonies, and by way of illustrating a generous national spirit, he suggests that both France and Holland could join Britain in a newly opened trade. Defoe states as a maxim, '*England* may Gain by a War with France, but never Loses by a War with *Spain*'.[34] Just as he never gave up his role as a proposer for projects that would improve Britain at home, so he never abandoned his hope to see England renewing the visions of discovery and colonization that Raleigh and Drake had inspired in their countrymen. When Austria took a second look at the forces arrayed against her and decided to end her bellicose stand, Defoe, identifying with his nation, probably felt like the gambler with an excellent hand who sees his mark fold his cards and refuse to play further.

V

In his concern for mounting his offensive against the enemies of Britain both domestic and foreign, Defoe did not ignore his role as Andrew Moreton, scourge of bad servants. During 1726 and 1727 he chose two new targets for Moreton's wrath: the mistreatment of the elderly by the young and the power of parish officers over the purse of the citizens. If the latter concern might seem like personal pique related to what he considered outrageous levies against him, the former has some of the power of a prose King Lear. Defoe published *The Protestant Monastery: or a Complaint against the Brutality of the Present Age. Particularly the Pertness and Insolence of our Youth to Aged Persons* on 19 November 1726, despite the 1727 date on the title-page. The full title, which is extensive, warns the older citizens of Britain against depending upon 'the *Mercy of others*'.

Moreton presents himself as a public-spirited citizen and an old man who is offering his proposals not as a '*despised . . . Projector, the most contemptible Character in this Part of the World*' but as one who hopes he may yet do some good for '*the Service of my Country*'.[35] He states that he is in his sixty-seventh year and 'almost worn out with Age and Sickness' (vi), adding that he would not have published his work in pamphlet form but was 'baffled and disheartened by Journalists' (vii). Defoe was actually 66.[36] It is possible that he was uncertain about his age, but since Moreton was supposed to be a

---

[34] *The Evident Advantages to Great Britain and Its Allies from the Approaching War*, 13.

[35] Daniel Defoe, *The Protestant Monastery* (London, 1727 [1726]), p. v–vi. Subsequent references to this work will appear in parentheses within my text.

[36] Defoe may have been aware that the publisher had made the decision that the title-page date would be 1727, but it seems hardly likely that he would have been informed of so minor a detail.

very old man, Defoe may have put an additional year on his own for emphasis. How sick Defoe was at the time is hard to say. Sophia wrote Henry Baker on 4 December 1727 that she was 'alarmed by my father's complaining of a violent sudden pain, which spread itself all over him', but even this devoted daughter thought it was 'not dangerous'.[37] It would probably be safe to say that while his infirmities were real enough, they were probably not as bad as those portrayed in the character of Andrew Moreton. Certainly Henry Baker thought of him as a sick old man. Yet 1726 and 1727 were still amazingly productive years for Defoe. Doubtless he was occasionally in pain, but not to such an extent that he was incapable of overcoming it. As for his difficulty in obtaining the attention of the editors of London's journals, it is difficult to see how he could have managed to get a thirty-one-page pamphlet into a journal. Moreton was never to be associated with the world of periodic journalism. He was Andrew Moreton, Esq., 'Author of *Every-Body's Business is No-Body's Business*', for us another side of Daniel Defoe, but for those readers not in the know, an elderly gentleman disgruntled with the modern world.

The Protestant Monastery portrays the mistreatment of the old by their children. One of the stories illustrates the lesson of King Lear—the aged should never misjudge the character of their children and should never surrender their power over their wealth in the expectation that their own generosity will be rewarded. Moreton tells of a retired merchant who, after abandoning control over his wealth to his daughter, finds himself forced into a miserable garret, ill-fed and mistreated. Moreton uses this tale to launch into an attack upon the younger generation as addicted to external manners rather than to the high ideals of gratitude which Defoe preached throughout his life. 'With them,' writes Moreton, '. . . a good Shape is Merit, a scornful toss of the Head, and despising every Body, but their own dear selves is Wit, an everlasting Giddiness, and an eternal Grin is Affability and good nature, fancy in Dress is Understanding, a supine Neglect of every thing commendable Gentility' (20). Defoe's cure for this condition, aside from educating children to respect their elders, is indeed a project—a home for the aged supported by the contribution of the members to the tune of £400 for each person. The scheme resembles some of those in his *Essay upon Projects*, written thirty years before. What is different is the tone. Instead of the voice of the optimistic projector for whom all things are possible, we have the desperate urgency of a man writing 'under many bodily Infirmities' (28), sometimes forgetting what he wants to say, but still offering his ideas for benefit of society.

[37] Thomas Wright, *The Life of Daniel Defoe* (London: C. J. Farncombe, 1931), 376.

Similar in many ways to the former pamphlet was an attack upon parish government with a lengthy title, *Parochial Tyranny: or, the House-Keeper's Complaint against the Insupportable Exaction and Partial Assessments of Select Vestries. . . .* The rest of the title lists a variety of abuses practised by parishes, with a suggestion about how to cure this ill. It was published a year after *The Protestant Monastery*, and despite Moreton's name on the title-page, it is much more like Defoe than Moreton. There are no complaints about bad health or even personal, anecdotal accounts of how he was mistreated by the officers of his own parish. Instead, Moreton focuses on the lack of representative parish government and responsible distribution of taxes and fines against the members of the parish. 'Why', he demands, 'should these parish Tyrants tax us at random, and make it penal to be industrious?'[38] If they actually used the money collected to take care of the poor of the parish, Moreton says he would have but mild objections to the high-handed way in which taxes are collected, but instead of spending the money upon the poor, they feed 'their own Guts' (9). Men die of want, women die in childbirth because of inhuman treatment, and the streets are filled with beggars. 'In short,' writes Moreton, 'they are quick to Contract, slow to Pay, severe in Assessing, unrelenting in Redressing. What Tyrants would these men be, were more Power lodg'd in their Hands!' (11) If the subject-matter is not as compelling as his picture of filial ingratitude in *The Protestant Monastery*, it serves the purpose of addressing the problems of the poor and the middle class. If Gray was to consider such subjects off the scale of history in his *Elegy in a Country Churchyard*, Moreton (here very much Defoe) argues, after a graphic picture of a London filled with prostitutes and criminals, that such subjects of 'Low Life' must be addressed by the civil powers, since 'nothing which is necessary or conducive to publick Peace, is below the Cognizance of a Commonwealth' (21). If Defoe was reverting to many of the projects of his youth, here he was also returning to the radical politics of 1700 when he asserted the superior right of the people over the machinery of government. His solution was to make parish government more responsible to the people, with annual elections of a treasurer and monthly meetings to oversee the distribution of funds. The ills of England, as he saw them in his youth, remained unredressed, and now, as an angry old man named Andrew Moreton, Defoe was going to do his best to bring his reforms before the public.

---

[38] *Parochial Tyranny: or, the House-Keeper's Complaint against the Insupportable Exaction and Partial Assessments of Select Vestries . . .* (London [1727]), 5. Subsequent references to this work will be included within parentheses in my text.

28

Last Productive Years

Ruin and wild Destruction sport around him.
    Henry Baker on Defoe

We come weeping into the World and go groaning out of it.
    Defoe, *Conjugal Lewdness*

Free from the obligations of his journalism, Defoe might have been able to nurse his ailing body and wander in the garden of his house at Stoke Newington contemplating the 'Chequer-work' of events that had been his life, but such an ending was hardly compatible with his restless spirit. He did not decide to wander off to distant lands in the manner of Robinson Crusoe, but for Defoe also a peaceful retirement was hardly a possibility. Some of the problems that were to overwhelm him were apparently not his fault—an unpaid note from his first bankruptcy suddenly surfaced in the hands of a third party, a Mrs Brooke, and despite his insistence that the bill had been paid, he could not bring convincing evidence to prove it. Perhaps he had never paid it, and hoped it would disappear; perhaps it was paid, and he had lost the receipt that would have shown his innocence. But if this represented a belated punishment for over-extending himself financially, there is no reason to believe that he was ever to learn his lesson. His purchase of the Five-Mile property in Colchester was also running into difficulties and lawsuits. And worst of all, the engagement between Sophia and Henry Baker began to founder over questions involving the extent of Sophia's dowry.

I

Defoe's most recent biographer has tended to blame Henry Baker for a venal approach to the marriage and to life in general.[1] But this is certainly not in keeping with everything we know about him. What Defoe said about trade as a form of crime without morality seems to have applied to his dealings over Sophia's dowry. On 23 August 1728 he delivered an 'ultimatum' to Baker stating that Baker would have to take Sophia on Defoe's terms. This was a question of money, and the author of *The Complete English Tradesman* knew all about that. Defoe's motives were not all bad. After all, he had three other daughters to worry about. He saw Henry Baker as a young man earning good sums by treating deaf children. It seems as if Defoe thought he could take advantage of him, and it would appear as if this is what he tried to do, plunging Henry Baker and Sophia into complete misery. The marriage finally took place on 30 April 1729, but only after Sophia appears to have suffered a nervous collapse. Shortly before the ceremony, Defoe wrote to Baker about a technical problem with the agreement, remarking that he had caught the error even though he had to read it 'but Hastily and in Disorder that night on Account of our family being So Disscomposed' (H 470).

James Sutherland puzzled over negotiations that stalled over a difference of £5 a year, the 5 per cent interest on £500 that Baker wanted or the 4 per cent Defoe considered 'the ordinary Interest of Money' (H 463).[2] Baker was not making extraordinary demands, and that may have been apparent to more members of the family than Sophia. Defoe's picture of a disordered household in the letter to Baker quoted above may have involved more than a distraught Sophia. Other members of the family may also have expressed their anger at the way Defoe had been handling the matter. In a letter to Sophia written a little over a month after the marriage, Defoe expresses his unhappiness at something Sophia said to him, stating that the reason for his sadness was his love for his daughter 'beyond the Power of Expressing' (H 471). He then goes on to say that 'Had Deb, The *Hasty*, the *Rash*, and so far *Weak*, Said Ten Times as much to me it had Made no Impression at all' (H 471) compared to the unkind words that Sophia had delivered. If, as is likely, 'Deb' was a nickname for one of Defoe's other daughters, it would appear that Defoe's behaviour toward Sophia and

---

[1] See Paula Backscheider, *Daniel Defoe: His Life* (Baltimore: Johns Hopkins University Press, 1989), 502. For a favourable account of Baker, see B. L'E. Turner, 'Henry Baker, F.R.S: Founder of the Bakerian Lecture', *Notes and Records of the Royal Society of London* 28 (1974), 53–80.

[2] *Defoe*, 2nd edn. (London: Methuen, 1950), 260.

Henry was not without repercussions within the Defoe household as a whole.

It seems clear that once the marriage became a matter of business, of money and property, Defoe treated it without decent feeling. Henry Baker's letters to Sophia speaking of Defoe as 'dark and hideous' in his dealings might show his frustration more than keen character analysis, but it suggests that there was a hard side to Defoe's character that cannot be ignored.[3] However unpleasant, the negotiations involved dealing with leases, mortgages, interest, deaths, and wills. These matters are best handled by lawyers, and John Foster, the attorney of Enfield with whom Henry Baker was living, was perfectly right to suggest that certain matters should be absolutely unambiguous. Although Defoe resented having to renegotiate the lease on his house in Stoke Newington, Baker was right to insist that the title be clear. Defoe expressed resentment at Baker's insistence that Sophia's portion be kept by him in case his wife died before him and without issue. He suggested that the very image of Sophia's death was a terrible thing to contemplate and that Baker was putting him through unnecessary anguish in forcing him to contemplate such a possibility. Anyone who has ever made out a will can sympathize with Defoe's uneasiness about being forced to imagine the future death of a favourite child and, far more significantly, his own mortality. But Defoe was clearly using this display of emotion to make Baker feel guilty about raising such matters. It is impossible not to think that he was trying to manoeuvre Baker into taking less. That he would gamble at driving his daughter into a near-psychotic depression and eventually arousing the anger of his entire family is hardly surprising in someone who loved to take risks.

Baker's behaviour toward Sophia throughout this agonizing struggle appears to have been admirable. Contemporary love letters were bound by conventions, but Baker's feelings appear to have been genuine. His mother opposed the match, but Baker persevered, staging the relationship between Sophia and himself as a battle of young lovers against parents incapable of understanding their passion. He thought that Defoe felt 'contempt' for him. 'You', he wrote to Sophia, 'are my good genius, and your father is my evil one. He, like a curst infernal, continually torments, betrays, and overturns my quiet; you like a divinity, allay the storm he raises and hush my soul to peace. Ruin and wild destruction sport around him and exercise their fury on all he has to do with, but joy and happiness are your attendants and bless where'er you come.' This satanic image of Defoe may

[3] Thomas Wright, *The Life of Daniel Defoe* (London: C. J. Farncombe, 1931), 387.

be the product of an emotionally distraught lover—a lover who went so far as proposing a double suicide to Sophia—but it bears an eerie resemblance to the satanic representations of the incendiary Defoe created by his enemies throughout his life. Again, Baker saw him as 'One who is under the necessity of being crafty, ungenerous, dishonest'.[4] Sophia defended her father against her lover's accusations, but the anger that appears to have emerged a month after she became Baker's wife suggests that, as a result of this quarrel, she harboured considerable resentment toward the father she had worshipped only second to God.[5]

II

As if his relations with Sophia and Henry Baker were not sufficient cause for him to worry about the vicissitudes of marriage, Defoe had been writing about the role of women in marriage for a number of years. He had explored this subject extensively in his novels, but his essays in *Applebee's Journal* were filled with discussions such as that for 20 March 1725, in which a group debates the value of marriage. All agree on the difficulties for both men and women, and though the women eventually vote in favour of marriage as an institution, they do not come to this conclusion easily. And all agree that women are better off marrying after the age of 25. As if matters were not complicated enough, Bernard Mandeville published his *Modest Defense of the Publick Stews* in August 1724, arguing, as usual, that the public vice of prostitution had benefits for the state as a whole. Mandeville's paradoxes always set Defoe's mind working, and while he first reacted with outrage, it turned him once more in the direction of considering the problems involved with luxury and fashion and toward seeking ways of dealing with prostitution in modern London.[6] It also set him thinking about the problem of sex in marriage and of the sexual abuse of

---

[4] *The Life of Daniel Defoe*, 372–81, 384–9. See also George R. Potter, 'Henry Baker, FRS (1694–1774)', *Modern Philology* 29 (1932) 301–21. Collections of Baker's autobiographical notations may be found at the John Rylands Library, Manchester, in the Foster Collection at the Victoria and Albert Museum, London, and at the Beinecke Library, Yale University.

[5] From the information in Henry Baker's Letter Book at the Beinecke Library, the marriage of Sophia and Henry was extraordinarily successful. When she died in 1762, Henry seems to have experienced a long period of depression. The letters from Baker's correspondents Brooke, Mounsey, and Wolfe speak of her as 'the worthiest of Women' and urge him to consider the happiness she had brought him during the 33 years of marriage. See Letter Book, fos. 167–73.

[6] See *Applebee's Journal*, 1 Aug. 1725, Lee, iii. 286–8. Defoe was to reject Mandeville's arguments about prostitutes helping to support the economy by their purchase of clothes, but his attack upon fashion at the end of *The Complete English Tradesman* is related to some of the problems raised by Mandeville. Although the style of *Some Considerations upon Street-Walkers* (London, 1726) is not markedly like Defoe's, the paradoxical attitude toward Mandeville's arguments is very much in Defoe's manner.

wives. The result was a book with the title *Conjugal Lewdness; or, Matrimonial Whoredom*, published on 30 January 1727.

That the sheets of this work had to be reissued a few months later with the more polite title *A Treatise Concerning the Use and Abuse of the Marriage Bed* suggests that Defoe was falling out of step with his times. Assuredly *Conjugal Lewdness* is not a polite work. It returns to the sexual honesty of the Restoration and the equally honest 'Black Lists' issued by the Society for Reformation of Manners between 1695 and 1705. Defoe loved the direct sexual language of Rochester's poetry, and he liked to use the word 'whore' to shock his readers.[7] He may even have been hoping that his original title would capture readers who had been titillated by titles such as *Onanism Display'd*, the infamous treatise on masturbation issued by Edmund Curll. Defoe's formula was simple enough. Entice the readers with a suggestive title and then deliver an attack upon sexual immorality protected by the legal limits of marriage. Defoe had a good subject, and even preaching against sexual excess had a certain prurient interest which he did not ignore. One of the more interesting aspects of this text is Defoe's struggle with sexually suggestive language. How, he asks, was he to write of what he considered sexual perversions without doing what he loved to do—describe the 'Thing itself'? Since language often fails, since the wife is often incapable of putting the sexual abuse she suffers from her husband into words, Defoe longs for a device employed by Turkish women, who could go before a magistrate, hold up a slipper, and turn it about by way of indicating the crimes which their husbands inflict upon them.

Some aspects of this text must seem to the modern reader overly severe in advocating a stoic control of passion, even appealing to the practices of the Catholic Church in subduing sexual desire.[8] But what Defoe is defending is what Lawrence Stone, who cited this work extensively, called the 'companionate marriage'.[9] Men and women should marry only for love, which he conceives as sexual desire and affection under the control of reason.[10] Defoe may have been thinking of his marriage to Mary when he he wrote about love and marriage constructed

[7] 'I cannot guild their Crimes, a Whore's a Whore.' See Defoe, *Conjugal Lewdness* (London, 1727; repr. Gainesville, Fla.: Scholars' Facsimiles and Reprints, 1968), 48. Subsequent page references involving this work will be included within parentheses in the text.

[8] Defoe was particularly angered by the anti-Protestant events that occurred at Thorn in Poland, and his *New Family Instructor* (1728) was vehemently anti-Catholic.

[9] Lawrence Stone, *The Family, Sex and Marriage in England, 1500–1800* (New York: Harper & Row, 1977), 361–74.

[10] Defoe's psychology in this work is similar to the system employed by Shakespeare and other Renaissance writers. Reason is supposed to control the will, the passions, and the imagination. When the sex drive rules the imagination and controls the reason, the ordinary processes no longer function properly. See *Conjugal Lewdness*, 263–8.

upon the solid Foundation of real merit, personal Virtue, similitude of Tempers, mutual Delights; that see good Sense, good humour, Wit, and agreeable Temper in one another, and know it when they see it, and how to judge of it. . . . It would call for a Volume, not a Page, to describe the happiness of this Couple. Possession does not lessen, but heighten their Enjoyments; the Flame does not exhaust it self by burning, but encreases by its continuance; 'tis young in its remotest Age; Time makes no Abatement; they are never surfeited, never satiated. (113–14)

In contrast to the portrayal of this ideal state, are the many perverse forms of unions which Defoe labels 'Matrimonial Whoredom'. Marrying for money, position, or purely out of sexual desire are all likely to prove disastrous; they cannot possibly lead to happy marriages. For the woman particularly, marriage is a 'Leap in the Dark', and he follows this caution with tales of men who infect their wives with venereal diseases, use violence against their wives, and force their wives to perform various per-versions of the sex act. But for Defoe, any marriage which does not involve mutual love is a type of torture. He compares it to a particularly gruesome form of capital punishment involving the binding of the criminal to a corpse, the putrefaction of which gradually kills the malefactor. When Moll Flanders spoke of her feelings of nausea associated with sexual relations with the husband who turns out to be her brother, she was describing a similar horror, for the unloved spouse is perceived as literally little more than a disgusting, decaying body by the partner in the marriage who has become completely disaffected.

At the end of this study of marital problems, Defoe threatens a sequel in which he will name names and give exact facts, since no author 'in a Christian Government, as this is, need be afraid of laying hell open, or drawing the Picture of men when they are turn'd Devils' (405). Although he has some depictions of women who cannot control their sexual desires, this work is mainly an attack upon men and a defence of women. If he did indeed begin the composition of this book some thirty years earlier as he suggests, it originated at the time of *An Essay upon Projects*, when he was under the influence of the early feminist Mary Astell and enthusiastically advocating academies for women. Even the defence of his work as a 'Satyr' seems more in keeping with his earlier writing, but for the most part, as he states in his introduction, this is the work of a very old man: 'despising all unjust Reproaches from a vitious Age, he closes his Days with this Satyr' (v). Utilizing the prose style of the great seventeenth-century moralists, particularly Sir Thomas Browne and Jeremy Taylor, Defoe conveys a sense of doom and decline:

The lawful Things of this Age will make the next Age lawless; their Father conveyed Blood, and they convey Poyson; our Parents handed on Health, and we Diseases; our Children are born in Palaces, and are like to die in Hospitals. Debauchery is the Parent of Distemper; Fire in the Blood makes a Frost in the Brain; and be the Pleasures lawful or unlawful, the effect of Folly is to leave a Generation of Fools. (399)

Despite this particular focus—that of an aged man delivering a moral condemnation of contemporary times—Andrew Moreton's name was never attached to this work, and quite properly. This is a work not so much of projected reform as of moral reproof.

III

Much that Defoe wrote during the last years of his life shows a pattern of repetition. Especially toward the end he was recycling material, reissuing earlier tracts, and reviving old ideas. There was no loss of vigour in his style, but occasionally there was a note of urgency of the kind that enters into the Andrew Moreton tracts. Just as much of the writing of the past decade had been shaped by the writing of his treatise on world trade, *Atlas Maritimus*, so his late social writings are formed to some extent by the two treatises on education that he left unfinished at his death—*The Compleat English Gentleman* and *Of Royal Education*. He wanted to leave an impress on his society—a vision of a world in which each citizen would have the opportunity to achieve a degree of wealth and gentility through a process of hard work and a lifelong effort at self-education. He also wanted to leave his readers with a utopian vision of a more orderly, more cultured, more civil society than that in which he found himself in the late 1720s. Much of this material could have been extracted from his earlier didactic works and fiction by a careful reader, but because Defoe wanted to be sure that everyone understood what he meant, and because he believed that one could never repeat things too much, he launched into a series of pamphlets and books on the subject.

He started the year by reviving a scheme for enlisting all sailors in a national system that would care for them from the cradle to the grave, one that he had originally broached in his very first book, *An Essay upon Projects* (1697). As we have seen, he had presented his arguments to the Select Committee of the House of Lords at the end of January 1705, but it had been ignored then just as *Some Considerations on the Reasonableness and*

Necessity of Encreasing and Encouraging Seamen was now.[11] Defoe was never shy about a desire to create large bureaucratic mechanisms for running society, and it is equally clear that Parliament was reluctant to follow such suggestions. The English, as Defoe was to note a few months later, did not particularly like 'Schemists' and despite his insistence that he was not a projector, this was one of his classic projects.[12]

Despite Defoe's argument that his pamphlet differed from the many works which had complained about the difficulties suffered by sailors and their families in that it was proposing a practical cure for the problems, some of the most effective pages present the plight of the individual seaman and his family. And in the section in which he proposes a 'Hospital' for training homeless children 'to good Letters and good Manners' for the navy or merchant fleet, he evokes a vivid image of the children living in poverty on the streets of London who might benefit from his system:

for it snatches a Breed of Imps (as they may many of them be call'd) out of the Clutches of the Devil, out of the very jaws of eternal Destruction, whose Fate is summed up in a few Words, these, That they are born Beggars, bred Thieves, and dye Criminals.

Nor would the Number of them be inconsiderable; 'tis scarce what a black Throng they are; many of them indeed perish young, and dye miserable, before they may be said to look into Life; some are starv'd with Hunger, some with cold, many are found frozen in the Streets and Fields, some drowned before they are old enough to be hang'd.[13]

If some might view Defoe's scheme as excessively paternalistic, it would have to be seen in the light of a disorderly and cruel system of naval recruitment—of impressing seamen and ordinary citizens in a manner that, to his mind, violated the rights of everyone living in Britain.

A month later, on 16 March 1728, he published a work the contents of which echoed his earlier *Essay upon Projects*. This new work had the grand title *Augusta Triumphans: Or, The Way to Make London the Most Flourishing City in the Universe*; not the world, one might note, but the '*Universe*'.[14] There is surely a hint of Defoe the moon voyager of *The Consolidator* in the title. Indeed, in keeping with his goal of creating a London of present and future greatness, the work contains a mixture of utopian project and moral

---

[11] See H 73–7; and *Manuscripts of the House of Lords*, 1704–6.

[12] *Augusta Triumphans* (London, 1728), 2.

[13] *Some Considerations on the Reasonableness and Necessity of Encreasing and Encouraging the Seamen* (London, 1728), 44.

[14] Although the title-page does not connect this tract with Andrew Moreton, it was listed among tracts by Moreton in an advertisement at the end of Defoe's *Second Thoughts Are Best* (1729 [1728]). Like the Moreton tracts, it draws attention to the age of the writer with the statement in the preface, 'As I have but a short time to live, I would not waste my remaining Thread of Life in vain' (p. viii).

reform. If he could praise London as the heart of British commerce, the centre into which trade poured like blood circulating through the veins of a body, he was also fascinated by a combination of architectural adventures and institutional reform, and had blended them together in his *Essay upon Projects*. Now he tended to separate the two. In his *Atlas Maritimus* he was to laud Naples and Venice as the greatest cities of the world for their magnificent public buildings. In *Augusta Triumphans* he is less interested in the city as a site for great architecture than its human dimensions. For the creation of a new university to be launched in London, he maintained that any old building might be appropriated, and the same applied to his arguments for establishing academies of music and art.

The title speaks of a 'University where Gentlemen may have an Academical Education under the Eye of their Friends'. Defoe had long regarded Oxford and Cambridge as places where youth are more likely to be seduced into Toryism and Jacobitism than places of education. This time, he avoided any need for government action by calling for a subscription. 'In a Word,' he wrote, 'an Academical Education is so much wanted in London, that every Body of ability and Figures will readily come into it.' Students would continue to live at home while attending; Professors would not have tenure but serve 'during good Behaviour'. Defoe is not very specific about the curriculum, but he envisions London transformed into a 'Scene of Science'.

His additional educational scheme was a plan for an Academy for Music. He was later to add a notice to the retitled and slightly revised version of this tract about an academy of art, but whereas we can tell little about his knowledge of painting from so brief a statement, he reveals considerable command of information about music in *Augusta Triumphans*. The author tells us that he performed upon the viol and the lute in his youth, and there is no reason to believe Defoe is not speaking about himself.[15] What he wants is not an academy in the sense that Handel established the various versions of his academies but a school that would train musicians. The nation that had given birth to a Purcell, he argued, should be able to match the musicians of Italy and the Italian style: Corelli, Handel, Bononcini, and Geminiani. They would provide excellent entertainment in the form of concerts. If there is an economic component in this—a sense of art as a kind of industry and craft—he nevertheless praises music as a form of entertainment that was 'innocent' and capable of composing the mind. However much he may have deemed it necessary to stage a struggle over the legitim-

---

[15] See my discussion of a song mentioned by Crusoe and its implications, 'Crusoe and "The Country Life": Defoe and Music', *N&Q* 237 (1992), 185–205.

acy of prose fiction, here at least there is absolutely no evidence of a puritanical objection to art.

A considerable number of the tracts published after *Augusta Triumphans* serve as appendices—often quite extended ones—to Defoe's vision of London as a reformed city. *Second Thoughts Are Best*, published on 8 October 1729 (for 1728), another Andrew Moreton tract, makes frequent references to both *Augusta Triumphans* and *Parochial Tyranny*. It attempts to deal with street crime and its causes by promoting a physically strong watch, one armed with sword and guns, better street lighting, and stricter regulation of vagrants, prostitutes, and beggars. In his urgency over having his reforms accepted, he dedicated this work to George II and, as the extended title-page suggests, called upon Parliament to consider his scheme. His admiration for the house of Hanover is hardly news, but his address to George as his 'Hero' seems to hark back to his hero-worship during the time of William III. Defoe may have actually received favourable recognition from the court at this time for his proposals, and whatever his personal problems may have been, this emergence of Andrew Moreton as the voice of a dissatisfied middle class, weary of crime and disorder, must have given Defoe great satisfaction.[16]

But, of course, there were still elements of the more radical Defoe. He ended *Second Thoughts Are Best* by lashing out at the combinations of tradesmen—coal dealers, bakers, butchers, and sellers of candles—for forcing the poor into crime by raising their prices unfairly. By concluding on this note, Defoe seems less the defender of the propertied class from a naturally wicked *Lumpenproletariat* than a populist longing for some kind of order. And he continued to attack what he considered immorality within the middle class. A year later, in the fourth edition of *Chickens Feed Capons*, published on 17 December 1730, essentially a reissue of the Moreton tract *Parochial Tyranny* (1727), Defoe revelled in his power. The family he had exposed for mistreating an aged father had not only threatened him 'in his own House'[17] but, after futilely trying to buy up earlier editions, had hired a hack to attack him in a pamphlet titled *No Fool Like an Old Fool*. Defoe pointed out that the pamphlet against him was thoroughly ineffectual and that the entire affair was enriching his own bookseller to whom he had 'given the Copy and Bond of Indemnification'.[18]

---

[16] The author of *Villainy Exploded: or, the Mystery of Iniquity Laid Open* (London, 1728) grudgingly admitted that many of Defoe's ideas were excellent while mocking a 'grave Alderman' (53) whom he thought gave Defoe too much credit. Newspapers reported that the author of *Augusta Triumphans* and *Second Thoughts* had been honoured by the court.

[17] Defoe, *Chickens Feed Capons*, 4th edn. (London, 1731 [1730]), sig. A2.

[18] Ibid. sig. A2ᵛ. Defoe's amusement at *No Fool Like an Old Fool* (London, ?1730) is amply warranted.

Defoe's allusion to abuses of freedom of the press in *Second Thoughts Are Best* seems to be directed at the anti-Walpole journal, *The Craftsman*, which often strayed dangerously into what looked very much like Jacobitism. Defoe may have been the master of the digression, but here his tendency to wander from his subject suggests some decrease of intellectual rigour. Advocacy of a return to home industry—the baking of bread and making candles in the household—is redolent of the ideology behind Crusoe's exercises in craftsmanship, and the lament on the decline of manly sports (the reason why finding athletic watchmen was so difficult) seems to echo schemes in his very early *Essay upon Projects*. These repetitions suggest signs of a failing imagination.

How much Defoe had to do with *Street Robberies Consider'd*, published in early November, is difficult to say. The autobiography of a thief and the subsequent discussion has much in common with Defoe's style and vocabulary, and as with *Second Thoughts Are Best*, the author attacks John Gay's *Beggar's Opera* for glorifying thieves and making them into heroes. 'Criminals go to Execution as neat and trim', writes the author, 'as if they were going to a Wedding.' We then are given a dialogue between two men who curse and praise the courage of the hanged criminal in his last moments.[19] The condemnation of swearing has much in common with the Defoe of *An Essay upon Projects*, and it contains criticism of the weakness and advanced age of the watch. If this is not by Defoe, it is certainly by someone who was a close reader of Defoe's tracts on this subject.

If one might wonder at Defoe's tendency to repeat ideas, it is true that his last pamphlet, or the last pamphlet in the canon, *An Effectual Scheme for the Immediate Preventing of Street Robberies,* published in mid-December 1730, goes over many of the familiar themes once more. Here he concentrates mainly on the 'Night-Houses' which he had treated in *Second Thoughts*, the places where prostitutes and thieves created a combustible mixture that led inevitably to crimes. Now Defoe sees an entire community of thieves undermining society. His mind wanders to the plague of 1665 that existed for him from his youth as both symbol and reality. What London has now is a plague of thieves, and their movement through the warren of houses resembles the spread of the plague from one section of London to another. He compares eliminating the 'Night-Houses' and their occupants to the

Although the author claims that the daughter was innocent of mistreating her father and attacks Moreton as 'a peevish old Fellow' (4) who believes that the young ought to be enslaved by the old, he/she agrees that age ought to be honoured, drifts off into irrelevant narratives, and concludes that children should venerate their parents.

[19] ?Daniel Defoe, *Street Robberies Considered*, ed. Geoffrey Sill (Stockton, NJ: Carolingian Press, 1973), 48–52.

kind of crusade undertaken by Charles V in his attack upon Algiers, a subject that crops up in a number of places in Defoe's last writings.[20] He returns once more to the image of the young thieves who sleep in the ashes of the Glass House, which he had rendered so brilliantly in Colonel Jack, and even digresses on the appearances of the guilty and the way the pulse may be used to detect guilt, an idea he had floated in his *New System of Magick*. Sections of this pamphlet, especially the historical tracing of the increase in crime and violence in England from the Restoration when 'Lewdness poured in upon us like a Flood' and the arguments on why those receiving anonymous threats should not give in to extortion, are excellent, but it is clear that toward the very end Defoe was having some difficulty organizing his ideas and a genuine problem with keeping his mind from falling into ever-familiar patterns—perhaps the inevitable fate of one who had written so much.

IV

When Henry Baker mentioned Defoe working in his extensive library, he spoke of a 'Pursuit of his Studies' in his 'Retirement', which his future father-in-law nevertheless managed to make 'very profitable'. As has been demonstrated, despite his various ailments Defoe was anything but retired from the writing profession. Along with his social commentary, he continued to write on matters associated with economics, the condition of debtors, and upon education. On 23 March 1728 he published his extensive survey of the British economy, *A Plan of the English Commerce* (a work upon which he was to improve with the addition of an appendix in 1731). And a few months later, on 3 June 1728, he was to publish his contribution to *Atlas Maritimus*, an extensive survey of the commerce of the entire world in over 300 folio pages. When Baker noted that Defoe 'retained all his mental Faculties entire', he was writing as a very young man who probably expected a man in his 60s to be showing signs of senility. If, as I have suggested earlier, there are signs of repetition in his very last works, no such indications are evident in these two volumes. They display his optimism about the trade of Britain, his vision of an entire world united by the exchange of products, and a world growing ever more civilized through this exchange.

[20] See esp. *Atlas Maritimus* (1728), 240, 266. Furbank and Owens make what strikes me as an ineffective argument for de-attributing this pamphlet from the Defoe canon; as with so many of their other arguments, they fail to take into account a combination of arcane references which could only belong to Defoe.

There are utopian elements in both works. In *A Plan of the English Commerce*, Defoe returned to his idea of a self-sufficient community which produces wealth through the labour of each person involved. Starting off with fifty farmers who are to 'live in a Kind of Circle within themselves' with the land arranged in a circular pattern, he sees how they will gradually attract craftsmen and various shopkeepers until the centre of the circle becomes a town with 1400 people.[21] And these are happy people because their life is shaped by their work. Among trading nations, Defoe argues, the workers are 'merrier at their labour, than others are at their Play; their hearts are warm, as their Hands are quick; they are all Spirit and Life, and it may be seen in their Faces; or which is more, it is seen in their Labour; as they live better than the Poor of the same Class in other Countries, so they work harder.'[22] Although it would be too much to argue that Defoe develops a theory of work as the means to societal happiness and individual wellbeing, it is certainly presented more systematically here than in his earlier economic writings. 'Employment is life,' he writes, 'Sloth and Indolence is Death.'[23] There is no idealizing of an idle aristocracy here; it is the working population who will eventually inherit the estates of the old and decaying upper orders.

Defoe sees many problems in the shape of English commerce. Will luxury overwhelm the nation? Will the American colonies separate? Will the woollen industry decline? But he also proclaims that English commerce is at a high point. And the main reason is a perpetual circulation of goods, people, and labour, including the ever-growing trade to the American colonies. Unabashed in his admiration for colonies, Defoe argues, 'An Encrease of Colonies encreases People, People encrease the Consumption of Manufactures, Manufactures Trade, Trade Navigation, Navigation Seamen, and altogether encrease the Wealth, Strength, and Prosperity of *England*.'[24] The author's voice in this work shows little sign of the irritable tone of Andrew Moreton, who was always assuring his readers that he was not long for this world. *A Plan of the English Commerce* is written with the verve of someone prepared to voyage to new lands and start a new colony, or to begin a new industry that will bring employment and happiness to thousands. The appendix to this work, treating recent developments in British commerce, may have been the last piece he was to publish.

[21] *A Plan of the English Commerce Being a Compleat Prospect of the Trade of this Nation, as Well the Home Trade and Foreign*, in *Shakespeare Head Edition* (Oxford: Basil Blackwell, 1927), 16.

[22] Ibid. 26. Defoe begins with an egalitarian note, dismissing the division of society into classes.

[23] Ibid. 52. Defoe's attitude is predictive of many nineteenth-century thinkers. For a general discussion, see Hannah Arendt, *The Human Condition* (1958) (Chicago: University of Chicago Press, 1971), 79–174.

[24] Ibid. 276.

Defoe knew British trade well, but an attempt at surveying world trade must have been an adventure even for the master of surprising adventures. Defoe was like the geographer he was fond of depicting, who could imagine the world through books and make it seem real. In composing *Atlas Maritimus* he had to rely on the accounts of others, from Sir Walter Raleigh to Nicolas Sanson, but he succeeds in creating his own particular tone. For one thing, he is even more insistent on the geographical sublime than he was in the *Tour*. Confronting the famous Maelstrom that was to fascinate Edgar Allen Poe a century later, Defoe calls it 'the greatest Wonder of this Country [Norway] and perhaps of the World of its Kind', describing 'the thing itself' as being beyond description:

at the Tide of Flood there is a violent perpendicular Indraft, and at the Ebb as furious an Expulsion of the Water, into and out of some vast Cavity, which no Mortal is able so much as to make any probable Guess at, or by any Philosphy to account for. At the time of the Indraft, 'tis believed the largest Ship in the World might be swallow'd up in it, tho it was made tight Top and Bottom as a Cask, and perhaps at the Ebb be cast up again, broken and dash'd to Pieces by the violent Agitation of the Waters.[25]

He indulges in similar moments of astonishment in describing a variety of subjects: 'the Circulation of Trade' in Britain, the expansion of the drinking and cultivation of coffee, what the more sensational press of the twentieth century used to call 'the elephant's graveyard', and that 'Wonder of the World', the Grand Canal of China.[26]

Defoe also refuses to resist at least one moment of imaginative empathy with the long-dead citizens of Carthage. He imagines what the world might have been like if the trading empire of Carthage had been allowed to flourish instead of being devastated by those 'Destroyers of Industry and Trade', the Romans. Like the mid-eighteenth-century poets and the Romantics, Defoe cannot resist shedding his tear over the ruins of the city that had once encouraged trade:

And here we may crave leave to drop a Tear over the Ruines, not the City of *Carthage* only, but the whole Carthaginian Empire, whose Monument and Grave are together seen in the heaps of faded Glory huddled together, where that once flourishing City stood; the broken Columns of Marble, the Arches, the Vaults; in a word, the Bones of the City lie cover'd with their own Ashes, and bury'd by Time. . . .

In our way from *Algier* to *Tunis*, we see the ruinous Heaps where that famous City once stood, the haven of *Biserta*, of little use, and almost choak'd up with Sand; the numberless Villages, like the *Bastides* of *Marseilles*, which contained the

---

[25] *Atlas Maritimus & Commercialis* (London, 1728), 45.   [26] Ibid. 108, 199, 238, 255.

country Lodgings, or Summer Retreats for the Citizens are now lost . . . and not so much as a Remembrance that any such Habitation had been there; nay, to jest a little with the Idolatry of that Day, how many Gods lie buried among the Bones of their Worshippers, who can neither restore Life to their Votaries, or give themselves a Resurrection from the Rubbish of their Temples.[27]

By devices such as these, quarrels with previous writers and their absurd accounts of unexplored areas, narratives of various kinds, and discussion of current happenings that throw light on the history of remote areas, Defoe managed to retain the interest of his readers. Inevitably there are passages of straight description which fail to be very lively or imaginative, but *Atlas Maritimus* is a neglected work. The account of the first landing on the Bermuda Islands throws light on *Robinson Crusoe*, and the story of a white man lost in Africa indicates the material which formed the basis for much of *Captain Singleton* as well as prefiguring Conrad's *Heart of Darkness*. Such narratives attracted Defoe because they involve what Defoe liked to call 'the Nature of Man'—the psychological components of human beings that make them act the way they do both as individuals and as social beings.[28]

The section of *Atlas Maritimus* treating British trade was, more or less, an encomiastic reworking of what he had said in his *Plan of the English Commerce*, but Defoe felt he could never say enough on this subject. On 15 March 1729 he published *An Humble Proposal to the People of England*. The full title hinted at commentary on the struggle with Spain and its efffect upon trade, but it introduced Defoe's usual themes—the need for expanding trade in general, encouragement of the wool trade, and prohibitions on imported printed fabrics. His call for everyone to join in this great effort, however, was perhaps never more urgent. The 'Voice of Nature' calls out to Britons to open their eyes and awake to the potential prosperity of the nation: '*Dig* and *Find*, *Plow* and *Reap*, *Fish* and *Take*, *Spin* and *Live*; in a word, *Trade* and *Thrive*.'[29] A year later, he was at his task again with *A Brief State of the Inland* or *Home Trade*, published in the spring of 1730. Once more his great theme was the way the 'CIRCULATION' of trade and the division of labour enriches the nation. If Robinson Crusoe could wonder at all the tasks required to make a loaf of bread, Defoe now describes,

How the meanest Trifles accumulate a Value, as they pass from Hand to hand: How they become Important, Rich, Useful, and Beautiful, by the addition of Time, Labour, and the Improvement of Art; and how the meanest Labourer or

---

[27] *Atlas Maritimus & Commercialis*, 239.
[28] See my *Defoe and the Nature of Man* (Oxford: Clarendon Press, 1963).
[29] *An Humble Proposal to the People of England for the Encrease of Their Trade, and Encouragement of Their Manufactures* (London, 1729), 8–9.

Mechanick contributes by an unwearied Application, to finish in a mere Road of instructed workmanship those Beauties in nature, which even he himself does not at all understand.[30]

The serpents in the garden of such a beautiful scheme were the pedlars who, by moving about with their wares from house to house, interrupted the symmetry of this providential plan. Defoe echoed the discussions and legislation in the House of Commons which was attempting to control these interlopers. Despite such dangers, he leaves no doubt that British trade and industry will continue their amazing triumphs.

V

Defoe left two works unpublished at his death. *The Compleat English Gentleman* was almost ready for publication, the first section having already been set in type, but with Defoe's death the publisher appears to have abandoned the project. It was not published until 1890, when George Bülbring brought it out along with a shorter and perhaps less complete *Of Royal Education*. Defoe had been working on the manuscript for several years, but it gives us a unique opportunity to examine his most mature thought and to observe his methods of composition. It is clear from the manuscript that, contrary to the impression left by Ian Watt in his *The Rise of the Novel*, Defoe did revise his work extensively. Most of his revisions tended to be expansions on ideas that he felt needed further development. His was a mind brimming over with ideas and examples, and he was always ready to amplify his original text. He tended to use dashes within paragraphs, leaving general instructions about punctuation—commas, semicolons, and colons—to the printer. He did underscore words for emphasis; so while some of the italics in his texts may be part of the printing conventions of the time, others probably reflect his own choices. The handwriting of this work is a far cry from the ornate script he often used when writing to his political patrons, but the clearly formed letters are still typical of his manner. Whatever Defoe's final illness may have been, it did not influence his handwriting, which remained firm in this last manuscript and in his final letters to Sophia.

That the subject of education was on Defoe's mind at the time is apparent from his proposal for a London university and academy of music in *Augusta Triumphans*, as well as from his argument in *Atlas Maritimus*

---

[30] *A Brief State of the Inland or Home Trade of England* (London, 1730), 6.

that had Spain chosen to educate some of the native children of America
rather than slaughtering them, these natives would have grown into 'true
born *Spaniards*' and emerged 'as polite, and as capable of all manner of
Improvements, as the Children of the wisest and best polish'd Nations'.[31]
The echo of Defoe's 'true-born Englishman' here is no accident. If, in 1701,
Defoe was to mock the notion of a pure English stock that was supposedly
being polluted by William III and his Dutchmen, so at the end of his life he
set out to undermine all such theories of superior status inherent in the
blood of particular nations and of the ancient nobility. Gentility, Defoe
argues, owes everything to education, and little to 'blood'. Indeed,
perfectly aware that most of the wealthy members of society had used the
services of wet nurses, Defoe mounts an elaborate argument to the effect
that the milk of such poor women is more likely to influence the lives of
their charges than other hereditary factors. This is couched in an appeal
for a return to mothers nursing their own children, but while Defoe may
have been convinced of the value of such an action, he knew that, insofar
as his readership was likely to include members of the gentry and nobility,
he was addressing an audience which might not want to believe that most
or all of their noble blood had been washed out in the milk of their wet
nurses.

Having disposed of any literal pride in noble 'blood', Defoe undertakes a
twofold task: to demonstrate that the nobility and gentry are in desperate
need of a proper education, and to argue that the well-educated heir of a
successful tradesman is far more of a gentleman than an ignorant land-
owner, however ancient his family might be. This seeming return to the
levelling principles of his youth may have emerged the stronger for his
having made a false start. He had begun a work on the education of princes
which he had titled 'Of Royall Education' and had completed the historical
introduction up to the time of Henry VIII, when he launched into an attack
upon anyone who might read his work as a 'satyr' upon George II and education of the royal children. At a time when the legitimacy of the succession
and of the house of Hanover was under attack by journals such as *The
Craftsman* and by Tory and Jacobite satirists, Defoe hesitated to provide
such an easy target. He wanted to write a work that 'may be servicable at
least as much in ages to come as now'.[32] After all, had not his *True-Born
Englishman* and *Robinson Crusoe* demonstrated signs of permanence within
the literary canon? Why should not an extensive treatise on education do

---

[31] *Atlas Maritimus*, 160–1.
[32] *Of Royall Educacion*, ed. Karl Bülbring (London: David Nutt, 1895), 62. I doubt if Defoe would have
ever allowed the spelling of 'educacion' to appear in print as Bülbring renders it from the manuscript.

equally well? So he turned to *The Compleat English Gentleman*, his treatise on the neglect of education among the nobility and gentry, as a topic that was far less dangerous and ultimately much more interesting. Curiously enough, it was in this abortive work on the education of princes that he expressed his strongest protest against the widespread lack of literacy among the poor.

Free from the risk of being misunderstood, Defoe drove his messages home through example, invective, and dialogue: it is education alone that makes life fulfilling, and the gentleman who refuses to learn 'will be but the shadow of a gentleman'.[33] Although Defoe concedes that the usual definition of gentility involved ancient family and blood, he argues that the most prosperous contemporary families were actually raised through learning and education. Defoe not only points to those families among the gentry and aristocracy whose fortunes came originally through trade but also to those given new life through marriage between the daughter of a tradesman and a member of the nobility. Defoe mocks the English squire who values only the language of his dogs and horses while scorning those who study history and travel to gain knowledge. Such a person is 'one of the most deplorable objects in the world' (60).

Since the milk from wet nurses has as much influence on the child as the blood which he or she inherits from the parents, Defoe concludes that the notion of inherited gentility is absurd. We are what we learn. He recounts the story of the ignorant gentleman who buys a library from a bookseller without having the faintest idea of what the books are about. The gentleman feels embarrassed by his ignorance and rejects the idea of inherited tendencies. 'Nature', says the Lord, 'is the virgin bride, Learning is the bridegroom. Nature produces nothing till she is marryed to Learning and got with child of Science. In a word, Nature is ignorance and Learning is knowledge' (163). Defoe holds out hope to the ignorant nobility. It is never too late to learn. Latin and Greek are to be jettisoned in favour of the study of history and geography. Defoe mocks the notion that no one may be designated a scholar except those who are learned in the classical languages. He instances a man who speaks numerous languages, knows geography and astronomy, 'is a master of History' (200), yet is considered, as the refrain goes after the list of his accomplishments, 'NO SCHOLLAR'. Defoe asks the reader to join with him in rejecting such an absurdity. Many a scholar learned in Greek and Latin is incapable of writing a good English sentence, whereas Defoe's true scholar is a man

[33] Defoe, *The Compleat English Gentleman*, ed. Karl Bülbring (London: David Nutt, 1890), 5. Citations from this text will be included in parentheses within my text.

who has a knowledge of 'things, not words' (212), and this may be achieved through reading:

If he has not travelled in his youth, has not made the grand tour of Italy and France, he may make the tour of the world in books, he may make himself master of the geography of the Universe in the maps, atlasses and measurements of our mathematicians. He may travell by land with the historian, by sea with the navigators. He may go round the globe with Dampier and Rogers, and kno' a thousand times more in doing it than all those illiterate sailors. He may make all distant places near to him in his reviewing the voiages of those that saw them, and all the past and remote accounts present to him by the historians that have written of them. (225)

The imaginative possibilities of learning remove the 'Compleat English Gentleman' from the 'meer state of nature' (236) and transform him into an active citizen and a good husband and father, living in perfect family harmony.

It is a shame that Defoe never finished this work. It would have been interesting to see what impact his arguments would have had upon the age. But perhaps the fullness of life had finally overcome his unique ability to contain and describe it. The number of exemplary narratives seemed to have overwhelmed him as the work expanded into a second part. Defoe's letter to the printer John Watts, written on 10 September 1729, excuses the delay in getting back the revised sheet by his having been 'Exceeding ill' (H 473), but it is also clear that he was having trouble shortening *The Compleat English Gentleman* according to the specifications set by Watts. Was he in so much pain that he could not keep his mind from wandering in familiar paths?

He could still function well enough in writing on relatively limited projects until the end of 1730. His forty-page appendix to the second edition of *A Plan of the English Commerce* turned into a piece of government propaganda glorifying the advantages of British commerce in the Treaty of Seville. An indication of its value as an index of Defoe's best thinking is his praise of the Treaty of Utrecht and of treaties of commerce in general, a clear allusion to the 1712 Treaty of Commerce that Defoe had been forced to defend at Harley's behest. For the most part, however, all he had to do was repeat the upbeat arguments of the original work. More complicated, certainly, though fairly mechanical for the former editor of *Mercurius Politicus*, was his undertaking to edit Abel Boyer's *The Political State*. An old antagonist of Defoe, Boyer died on 16 November 1729, and Defoe appears to have gradually involved himself in editing the journal until December 1730. He did not have to change its Whig cast, but he did turn it in the direction of economic subjects. At the end of the March issue, he introduced a list of imports and exports, and one sign of his leaving the journal is the discontinuing of its emphasis on economic matters with the issue of December 1730.

Although Defoe was mainly excerpting the news in *The Political State*, he managed to puff his own writings, such as the remarks on *A Brief State of the Inland or Home-Trade*, which he describes as 'Extraordinary'. One highly problematic issue concerns his treatment of the Masons. A. J. Shirren stated that Defoe was connected to the Masonic lodge which convened at the 'Three Crowns' on the corner of Church and High Streets.[34] Lodges certainly differed in their emphasis on various matters, but it is hard to see what, aside from its anti-Catholic bent, would have attracted Defoe to Masonry. But one of his last pamphlets was an attack on Samuel Pritchard, whose *Free-Masonry Detected* published some of the secrets of the initiation ritual. In *The Perjur'd Free Mason Detected*, Defoe attacked Pritchard for failing to respect the oath of secrecy. Defoe held all oaths as sacred: 'for the Obligation is not fix'd upon the form, but it is fix'd in the Soul, and an honest man will do what is honest from an inherent Principle of Justice, tho' there were no Laws to bind him.'[35] But in the *Political State*, he argued that the ritual was nothing but a 'Piece of Frippery', despite the fact that 'many . . . noted for eminent Virtues' had joined the organization.[36] One can only conclude that Defoe's interest in the Masons was hardly very serious. As Paula Backscheider has insisted, Defoe loved tavern conversation. He may have been willing to endure what he considered a silly ritual for the sake of the friends he had among them.

Fortunately, Defoe had other subjects to deal with in *The Political State* that must have interested him more. He seemed particularly eager to place contemporary events in the perspective of history by comparing the present with what happened during the reign of William III. Thus in treating discussions about opening up the trade to India, he reminded his readers of the battle between the two companies during the 1680s and 1690s. He retold the story of the English ship captured by Algerian rovers just off Harwich and contrasted the excellent harvests in Europe with the famines during the time of William III. It had the advantage of keeping his

[34] E. Forbes Robinson, *Daniel Defoe in Stoke Newington* (London: Stoke Newington Public Libraries Committee, 1960), 26. There is always the possibility that he was confusing Defoe with his son Daniel.
[35] *The Perjur'd Free Mason Detected* (London, 1730), 24. The work was published by one of Defoe's most steady printers, Thomas Warner. Warner published Defoe's *Political History of the Devil* five years before, and the author of *The Perjur'd Free Mason Detected*, using similar material, digresses to the subject of the person who confessed to being a wizard toward the end of the Salem witch trials and found that the jury refused to believe him (25).
[36] *The Political State of Great-Britain* (Aug. 1730), 210, 216.

mind on the events of the day, but there is much repetition of old arguments on trade and almost no spark of the amusement and irony that for
many decades gave his writing so much energy.

29

Sinking Under the Weight of Affliction

Hence Caesar Tho' of a Spirit Invincible Gave up to Death, when he felt a stroke from his Adopted Brutus, and Said no More But (et tuo quoque mi fili! Tue Brute!) What! and Thou too Brutus! My Son! Nay, Hence the Wise man Says, a Brother offended is harder to be Won, than the Barrs of a Castel. Love is of So Nice a Nature, That like the heart, it faints with the least Touch. Where it is not So, it must be because Such kno' not how to Love.

Defoe, *Letters*, 471

Defoe wrote the above lines in a letter to his daughter Sophia in one of two entirely personal letters preserved by the Baker family. The family also preserved the letters wrangling over Sophia's dowry, but in the letters of 9 June 1729 and 12 August 1730 Defoe wrote as a father about his illnesses, his anger, his despair. Most of all, however, he wrote about his love for his family. Sometimes, with good reason, we tend to suspect Defoe when he talks about himself in his published writings and even in his letters to Harley. Present in such passages are a sense of his personality, his likes and dislikes, but usually it is to some purpose—an attempt to give his writings an aura of sincerity to convince his readers to support one thing or another. But in these two letters we see Defoe as he really was, at least in his old age.

The letter of 9 June is about love and the misunderstandings arising from family intimacy and disagreements. He had felt betrayed by a remark made by Sophia, probably having to do with the quarrel between her father and her husband, Henry. If she had once expressed her complete submission to her father, she was now a married woman, and her allegiance was to her husband whose bitterness toward Defoe was understandable. Defoe's anger had flared up, much like one of his characters in his volumes of *The Family Instructor*. Now he was writing to explain that his anger was the fiercer because he had loved her so intensely:

Had Deb, The *Hasty*, the *Rash*, and So far *Weak*, Said Ten Times as much to me, it had Made no Impression atall: But From Sophi, Thee Sophi! whose Image Sits close to my affections, and who I Love beyond the Power of Expressing: I acknowledge it Wounded my Very Soul; and my Weakness is So much the more, as that Affection is strong; So that I can as ill Express The Satisfaction I have from your Letter, as I could the grief of what I thot an Unkindness. (H 471)

No one has ever solved the problem of who Deb was, but, as I have suggested, it was most likely one of his unmarried daughters, Hannah and Henrietta, who still lived with Defoe and his wife at the house on Church Street in Stoke Newington. Whoever Deb was, it is clear that the Defoe household was typical enough—replete with love and disagreements.

Defoe begs Sophia to understand and forgive him. His love for her is so great that the mere hint of an affront was enough to set him off. Sophia apparently had no idea of the exact word she used that angered her father and he refused to, would not tell. Apparently Mr Foster, Henry Baker's client and friend, was involved in everything. He had tried to represent Henry Baker's interests in the negotiations over the marriage. Defoe had resented it, but now all is forgiven. He insists upon his 'Sincere heart' and urges a kiss of peace to be shared among the three of them. Defoe probably found the communication of such emotion easier on paper than it might have been when he sat together with his family. Perhaps Sophia never heard such heartfelt love directed at her from her father before, but it seems from the way he spoke of her to Henry Baker that his love for this youngest daughter was very real.

He concluded the letter with a postscript. After signing himself as her 'Most Affectionate Father', he added after the signature, 'But Very much Tormented with Pain Ever Since' (H 472). Whether the illnesses afflicting Defoe involved arthritis, gout, or some form of bladder, kidney, or gallstone, there seems no question that the pain was intense. In a letter of 10 September 1729 that was intended to be sent to the printer John Watts, along with the corrected sheet of *The Compleat English Gentleman*, Defoe said he had been 'Exceeding ill' (H 473) and unable to finish his work on the manuscript. He insisted, however, that he was still working on it, and apologized for revisions that would probably require resetting everything that had been done. He was clearly working and arriving at new approaches to his subject despite the pain. The last letter that we have from him, dated 12 August 1730, reveals him sick in both body and spirit. The end was approaching.

I

During the last six months of his life, Defoe was once more in hiding. He had been fighting a suit filed against him by a Mary Brooke since in 1727. She opened proceedings against him in the King's Bench. The case was a complicated one. The money had been owed to Defoe's childhood friends the Stancliffes. After his first bankruptcy, Defoe was obliged to satisfy his debtors, including Samuel Stancliffe. After Samuel's death, his brother James Stancliffe became the administrator of his brother's estate. He was also the person to whom Defoe surrendered all of his assets after the bankruptcy of 1704. James Stancliffe should have arranged the payments to all of Defoe's creditors from Defoe's assets, including any debt owing to himself and his brother. When Stancliffe died suddenly, without having rendered a full account of his trusteeship, Samuel Brooke, a weaver, became the administrator of his estate. Brooke noticed Defoe's indebtedness to the Stancliffes, but, according to Defoe's account, he accepted the explanation that the debt had been discharged. When Samuel Brooke died, his wife took over the administration of her husband's estate.[1] She refused to believe that the debt had ever been paid and in 1727 began proceedings against Defoe in the courts of King's Bench. Defoe tried to hold her off by filing bills in Chancery in 1728 and again in 1730.[2]

When Mary Brooke eventually won her suit, Defoe apparently decided on two courses of action.[3] He was not going to pay her a penny if he could help it, and he was not going to be sent to prison as a debtor.[4] He fled, first

---

[1] This is Defoe's version of matters in his Chancery suit, PRO, C11/1473/18. Defoe claimed that he had turned all his goods over to the Stancliffes and that they and all of his other creditors were satisfied. In response to Mary Brooke's request that he show documents proving that he did not owe the Stancliffes any money, Defoe could name only one document associated with his bankruptcies, and that was in possession of an Aaron Lamb, who would not cooperate with Defoe because he too believed that Defoe owed his family money. See PRO, C11/679/2.

[2] PRO, C22/1473/18; C33/351/154; E13/880 rot. 3; C11/679/2; Ind 4533; C33/353/191.

[3] For interpretations of the events, see James Sutherland, 'A Note on the Last Years of Defoe', *Modern Language Review* 29 (1934), 137–40.

[4] The court was having difficulty serving a judgment on Defoe, and Mary Brooke seems to have been in the dark about where he was and whether he was alive or dead. She placed his death in Jan. 1732 in a document claiming her rights to his property. See the PRO documents dated 4 Mar. 1729, C33/353/191; 26 June 1733, PROB 31/117/376; Probate 29/125, fo. 181, 7 Sept. 1733; and PROB 6/109, Sept. 1734. She managed to win her original suit against Defoe, but her efforts to track down Defoe's goods and members of his family were futile. She never mentions the younger Daniel Defoe among Defoe's children and could not locate Benjamin Norton, believing he must have left England. For her vain effort to collect a clock, see Sutherland, 'Last Years'.

to lodgings in London and then to an area south-east of London in Kent, a place isolated enough to be some distance from any coach transportation and hence from the agents of Mary Brooke. The letter that he wrote on 12 August 1730 indicates that he was 'About two Miles from Greenwich, Kent', but that seems dangerously close to London for a hiding-place. The letter, nominally addressed to Henry Baker but certainly intended for the eyes of Sophia, shows Defoe old, sick, and perhaps for the first time in his life in a state of despair.

He opens with a complaint that Henry Baker's letter, which had been sent on the first day of the month, had not reached him until the tenth. There is the implication of a conspiracy against him, though he states that he views Henry as 'Nathaniel like, without Guile' (H 473).[5] But he seems to see the rest of the world lined up against him. He sees himself 'sinking under the Weight of Affliction too heavy for my Strength, and looking on myself as Abandon'd of every Comfort, every Friend, and every Relative, except such only as are able to give me no Assistance' (H 474). He urges Sophia to avoid seeing her father in his present state. Defoe then explains that the cause of his depressed emotional state is traceable to 'the injustice, unkindness, and . . . inhuman dealings of . . . [his] Son.' It is this that has broken his heart and brought on a 'very heavy Illness, which I think will be a Fever' (H 474). Defoe lived on for eight months after writing this letter. The physical illness that he thought sure to follow as the result of his low spirits did not arrive immediately. Although Defoe was clearly feeling sorry for himself, his most moving images are reserved for his two daughters, Hannah and Henrietta, and his wife, all supposedly left penniless. He begs Henry to

Stand by them as a Brother; and if you have anything within you owing to my memory, who have bestow'd on you the Best gift I had to give, let them not be injured and trampled on by false pretences, and unnatural Reflections. I hope they will want no help but that of Comfort and Council; but that they will indeed want, being too easie to be manag'd by words and Promises. (H 475)

For all his seeming cruelty in the battle with Henry Baker over the dowry, Defoe appears to have believed that all animosity between them had ceased and that he was addressing the young man whom he had formerly accepted as both a friend and something of a disciple. He was, after all, the husband of his Sophia, the daughter of his heart and mind. In suggesting that his wife and two other daughters were ruled by their emotions and credulity,

---

[5] These, of course, are the words of Jesus to his new disciple (John 1: 45). One would not want to read too much into an eighteenth-century father seeing his relationship to his son-in-law in this light. What is now loosely called 'patriarchy' was probably the reigning spirit of the Defoe household.

Defoe was not saying he did not love them. But in Sophia he saw the caution and scepticism with which he conducted his own life.

He ends the letter with an expression of longing to see his seven-month old grandson, and the wistful hope that Sophia's child will be that impossible thing—an offspring who will bring her complete happiness. But before that he offers one more scheme:

It is not possible for me to come to Enfield, unless you could find a retired Lodging for me, where I might not be known, and might have the Comfort of seeing you both now and then; upon such a circumstance, I could gladly give the days to Solitude, to have the comfort of half an Hour now and then, with you both, for two or three Weeks. But just to come and look at you, and retire immediately, 'tis a Burden too heavy. The Parting will be a Price beyond the Enjoyment. (H 475)

If there is just a touch of *Robinson Crusoe* in this image of Defoe as the prospective hermit of Enfield, there is also the hint of a new kind of sentimental fiction in the narrative that Defoe appears to be weaving for Henry and Sophia. The innocent, aged father, pursued by an inexorable enemy whose success in finding him would ruin his entire family, disguises himself and moves to humble quarters just to be near his beloved daughter and grandson.

Even more than Mary Brooke, the real villain of this story in Defoe's eyes was his son Daniel. Little is known about this son except for his pursuit of a moderately successful career in business. Defoe had transferred all his assets to his son's name by way of protecting them from Mary Brooke, and it is clear from this letter that Daniel junior was not acceding to every wish of his father concerning what Defoe considered his property. He explains to Henry Baker that the cause of his unhappiness

has been the injustice, unkindness, and I must say, inhuman dealings of my own Son, which has both ruin'd my Family, and, in a Word, has broken my Heart; and as I am at this Time under a weight of very heavy Illness, which I think will be a Fever, I take this Occasion to vent my Grief in the Breasts who I know will make a prudent use of it, and tell you that nothing but this has conquered or could conquer me. *Et tu! Brute.* I depended upon him, I trusted him, I gave up my two dear unprovided Children into his hands; but he has not Compassion, but suffers them and their poor dying Mother to beg their Bread at his Door. (H 474–5)

That there is a degree of exaggeration in Defoe's image of his wife and daughters as abandoned and poverty stricken seems inevitable. Mary had been provided for and her money protected by the will of her brother, Samuel Tuffley. Her death in 1732, a year after her husband, had nothing to do with her poverty. Her will distributed her property to three of her daughters, Maria Langley and Hannah and Henrietta Defoe.[6] The latter two lived long lives at Wimborne in Dorset, where they went after Henrietta married a John Boston, who was appointed supervisor of the excise in that town. One of Defoe's early biographers, Walter Wilson, comments of Hannah, 'As she lived upon her own property, which after-wards passed to a nephew, it may be concluded that De Foe's daughters succeeded in recovering their estates out of the hands of their brother, and that they were converted into money for the purpose of being divided.'[7] Wilson, of course, believed Defoe's account of Daniel junior as the quintessential cruel son along the model of the offspring in Defoe's *Chickens Feed Capons*, but there is a more likely interpretation.

After Daniel junior had been invited to take over his father's business affairs, he probably found everything hopelessly enmeshed.[8] Defoe's purchase of the Colchester property had been carried on in considerable secrecy, and the revelation of so vast a use of the family's resources must have struck Daniel junior as irresponsible. He had lived through many of the surprising adventures of his father's life and would have had a vivid memory of some of the imprisonments his father had undergone, particu-larly that of 1715. In Defoe's eyes, Mrs. Brooke was 'a wicked, perjur'd, and contemptible Enemy', but he should have kept some evidence that he had paid this particular debt.[9] From his son's standpoint, this may have been another example of the way his father was threatening the wellbeing of his mother and sisters. For all Defoe's hyperbole, there is no indication in this letter that Defoe was himself in any need, even at the very end.

Defoe's letter to Henry Baker on 12 August 1730 does not contain the final words we have from his pen, but they are certainly the last that add very much to our knowledge of him. There is nothing in the appendix to *A Plan of the English Commerce*, published in 1731, that was not already

---

[6] See PRO PROB 11/655/fo. 126. Mary wanted to be sure to provide for her two unmarried daughters, Hannah and Henrietta. She gave her married daughter, Maria Langley, a third of the rents from the property at White Cross Alley in Moorfields, but provided that, in case Maria were to die, such money should be equally divided between Hannah and Henrietta. And she specified that Hannah and Henrietta should receive the farm at Dagenham in Essex and the rest of her effects. Sophia had already been pro-vided for in her marriage settlement. Mary also left money to purchase mourning rings for her two sons.

[7] Walter Wilson, *Memoirs of the Life and Times of Daniel De Foe* (London: Hurst, Chance, 1830), iii. 644.

[8] We have no idea what Defoe's debts may have been, but one amounting to £437 was still being recorded in 1737. See the Guildhall Court of Orphans Inventory for 11 Oct. 1737, Box 41, Com. Serv. Book 6, fo. 160.

[9] PRO/C11/1473/18; PRO/C.11/679/2. Defoe wrote on 13 Jan. 1728 that he was so happy to be released from debt that he did not ask for a receipt. He argued that all evidence of his indebtedness ought to have been destroyed by James Stancliffe. In Defoe's statement, dated 30 Apr. 1730, he claimed that all the records were kept by Stancliffe, who was the trustee overseeing Defoe's bankruptcy. He claimed that Stancliffe's widow agreed to discharge any debts, but apparently never obtained proper evidence.

present in his writings on the Treaty of Seville in 1728 and 1729, and as we have already mentioned, in *An Effectual Scheme for the Immediate Preventing of Street Robberies*, published on 15 December 1730, almost everything focuses on the past—Charles V's crusade in Tunis, Charles II's luxurious court, and the Great Plague. It has some good passages, but Defoe was no longer able to function effectively as a writer. His last, entirely characteristic writing appears in the very brief preface to the fourth edition of *Chickens Feed Capons* some time around the middle of December.

Defoe complained to Henry Baker about 'some Fits of a Fever that have left me low' (H 475), and if he was not quite 'dying', he was certainly unwell. He probably had a combination of ailments, including arthritis and rheumatism, that often left him in agony. One contemporary medical work describes how the pain often begins in the hands and feet and from there

ascends to the Elbow and Knee, and seizes on the Acetabula of ossa Femoris, where altering its course, and winding about, it makes a Transition to the Muscles of the Back and Thorax. The Disorder spreads at an incredible rate, takes Possession of the Vertebrae of the neck and spine, and fixes itself on the Extremity of the Os Sacrum; and though all these parts labour under one common Disease, each Part has its peculiar Pain.[10]

Perhaps the best evidence of the seriousness of his illness and the pain he was experiencing was his silence. Apparently he was unable to do any extensive writing after the autumn of 1730 and perhaps unable to write very much at all after December.[11] One of the most prolific and brilliant writers in Britain had put down his pen for the last time.

Some time between August and the day of his death on 24 or 25 April, Defoe moved back to London, to the general area of his boyhood ramblings and not far from some of the labyrinthine alleys where Colonel Jack would run from his pursuers. He took lodgings in Ropemaker Alley. In his revision of John Stow's survey of London, John Strype describes this street as 'pretty broad, with several Garden Houses; which are well built and inhabited'. There is no reason to think that Defoe had slipped into poverty, like the protagonist of a naturalistic novel, but despite a number of decent streets in this area and its proximity to Moorfields, it also contained narrow alleys, which Strype described as 'but indifferently built and inhabited'.[12] Were Defoe inclined to flee the agents of Mary Brooke at a

[10] See the discussion of arthritis in Robert James, *A Medical Dictionary* (London: T. Osborne, 1743), i. sig. 8C4.

[11] Of course Defoe's correspondence with his wife has not been preserved, but given the danger that any exchange of letters might have revealed his hiding-place, the likelihood is that he communicated secretly and through brief notes.

[12] John Strype (ed.), *A Survey of the Cities of London and Westminster* (London, 1720), i, B.3, p. 92.

moment's notice, he could wind his way through Butler's Alley into nearby Grub Street. Pierre Dottin suggested another reason why Defoe may have selected this area.[13] It was not too far away from White Cross Alley, where his wife, Mary, owned property. She and her daughters might reasonably enough go there to oversee the houses they had there while surreptitiously meeting with their beloved husband and father. He had mentioned to Henry Baker in his last letter, 'I have not seen Son or Daughter, Wife or child, many Weeks, and kno' not which Way to see them. They dare not come by Water, and by Land there is no Coach, and I kno' not what to do' (H 475). His plan to become the hermit of Enfield, had been a familiar flight of fancy, but surely in moving to Ropemaker's Alley he managed to contact Mary and his children again.

It was here that he died of a 'Lethargy', a diagnosis that has often caused comment from biographers on the irony of a person of such seemingly inexhaustible activity departing the world so quietly. But at the time this term may have merely meant that the physician believed that he had died in his sleep of what was perhaps a relatively mild stroke.[14] Defoe was over 70 years old. In his last letters, in addition to the various fevers and pains that he listed, he revealed a distinct sense of weariness. He had been imprisoned at least five times during a period when typhus and other diseases killed off more inmates than the gallows. He had survived the pillory, which hostile mobs often made into a fatal experience for the victim. He had travelled through the British countryside on horseback through storm and cold. He had endured the psychological trauma of two bankruptcies and a barrage of attacks upon his integrity, his beliefs, and his character. And during the last decade of his life he saw one son, Benjamin, imprisoned, his beloved daughter, Sophia, turn against him, and his other son, Daniel, refuse to obey him over financial matters. As was said of King Lear, 'the wonder is, he . . . endured so long'.

Defoe was buried in Bunhill Fields on 26 April 1731, where his grave may be found among the great Dissenting Englishmen of his century, not far from those of John Bunyan, Isaac Watts, and William Blake—an eye-opening companionship in death. What conversations their ghosts might have! His beloved Mary survived her husband only by a year and eight

[13] *Daniel Defoe et ses romans* (3 vols., Paris: Presses Universitaires de France, 1924), iii. 283.

[14] James, *A Medical Dictionary* , sig. 11Q1. This work includes both ancient and more modern opinions. In the article on 'Lethargy', James classifies it as related to apoplectic and paralytic disorders. Defoe's complaints about fevers would have been appropriate for such a diagnosis, but more than likely it was a convenient diagnosis for death among the elderly. It should be noted, however, that Defoe's Moll Flanders uses the term to describe the demise of her bank manager, who is clearly psychologically depressed.

months. He was such a presence in her life that the loss must have been difficult, if not impossible, for her to bear. Lee speculated that Mary was probably buried in the same grave as her husband. Although there is little evidence for this posthumous reunion, it was reported on the occasion of the reopening of Defoe's grave in 1871 that it contained two other coffins placed on top of his. His was apparently identified by a brass plaque with his name.[15] Surely the others were the coffins of Mary and the mysterious Mrs Deffoe buried on 19 January 1737 and mentioned in the burial records of Bunhill Fields.[16]

When the diggers finally reached the coffin containing Defoe's skeleton, they found the remains of a man who, for all his literary stature, stood only five feet four inches tall. Those involved also noted that Defoe had a 'peculiarly massive under-jaw', a characteristic that hardly appears in the flattering portrait of him done by Van Der Gucht or any of the uncomplimentary prints made by contemporaries.[17] The occasion for this disinterment on 16 September 1871 was the erecting of a monument to the author of *Robinson Crusoe*, with its seventeen-foot marble pillar resting on a four-foot base.[18] The financial support for this project came from girls and boys who had been delighted by Defoe's work. What should have been a solemn scene of dedication was marred by what came close to being a riot, when violent attempts were made to take off bones of the skeleton. The police had to be called to keep the remains intact. If the spirit of Defoe still hovered around the grave, it must have retained sufficient irony to be amused at seeing his bones treated as saintly relics, an aspect of religion for which he had considerable contempt and which he associated with the superstitions of the Catholic Church.[19]

There was no one to carry on Defoe's literary legacy. His library was sold, along with the books of Phillips Farewell, in an auction conducted by Olive Payne in 1731.[20] Before that event, however, the family divided up some of the precious manuscripts. Hannah, for whom Defoe had purchased an annuity based on safe South Sea Company stocks, and who had

---

[15] See Samuel Horner, *A Brief Account of the Interesting Ceremony of Unveiling the Monument Erected by the Boys and Girls of England to the Memory of Daniel Defoe* (Southampton: Hampshire Independent Office, 1871); and Wilson, *Memoirs*, iii. 610–11.

[16] Located at the London PRO in Islington.

[17] Horner, *Brief Account*, 5.

[18] This monument replaced a modest stone identifying him as the author of *Robinson Crusoe*. For an engraving of this stone, see Thomas Wright, *The Life of Daniel Defoe* (London: C. J. Farncombe, 1931), 385.

[19] See Horner, *Brief Account*. This pamphlet, which reprinted newspaper accounts of the event, also functioned as an advertisement for Horner as a seller of monuments.

[20] See *The Libraries of Daniel Defoe and Phillips Farewell*, ed. Helmut Heidenreich (Berlin: printed by W. Hildebrand for the author, 1970).

sufficient money to live with her sister Henrietta, kept Defoe's *Historical Collections* and the volume containing the *Meditations*.[21] Some of the books went to Henry and Sophia Baker and show up in the catalogue of Henry Baker's library, sold in March 1775. About Benjamin Norton Defoe there is little information. We do know that he was condemned to do hack work for the remainder of his life and lived in abject poverty.[22] Daniel may have emigrated to America with his family, but nothing certain is known about his descendants. The closest thing to a literary descendant was Sophia's son, David Erskine Baker (1730–67), who became fascinated by the stage and compiled a useful theatrical dictionary. But Defoe's fame, as Tristram Shandy would have it about his own literary efforts, had to swim down the stream of posterity on nothing more than the genius he had imprinted on his writings.

II

The Aftermath

A few Days ago dy'd Mr. Defoe, Sen. a Person well known for his numerous and various Writings. He had a great natural Genius; and understood well the Trade and Interest of this Kingdom. His Knowledge of Men, especially those in High Life, (with whom he was formerly very conversant) had weakened his attachement to any party; but in the main, he was in the Interest of Civil and Religious Liberty, in behalf of which he appeared on several remarkable Occasions. (*Read's Weekly Journal*, 1 May 1731)

Obituaries something like the above appeared in a number of newspapers. Its emphases upon his 'great natural genius', his special talent as a writer on trade, and his connections with those in 'High Life', along with the praise of his defence of 'Civil and Religious Liberty', suggest that it was a document produced by one or more members of the family. In other

[21] These volumes are now in the possession of the William Andrews Clark Memorial Library, Los Angeles, and the Henry E. Huntington Library, San Marino, Calif.

[22] Benjamin Norton Defoe's letters to the government in 1739 reveal a man pleading for financial help to keep him and his children from literally starving to death. He confesses to writing for the opposition in *The Craftsman* at a time when he and his children were 'reduced to the last bitt of Bread'. He offers his services to the government and pleads for an act of charity that would rescue him 'from a condition consumately miserable and wretched'. Although Defoe was always asking Harley for money to help his family, the picture that Benjamin Norton creates is a good example of the horrors of Grub Street: 'I live every day in the dreadfull apprehension that they will be turn'd Naked into the Streets; I beeing reduc'd to the greatest Extremity, and utterly unable to protect or supply them; and will your Grace, give me leave to add, that they have not had a Morsel to Eat this day, had not Mr. Hutchins moved to uncommon compassion by their calamatous condition lent me a little money . . .'. See BL MSS, Newcastle Papers, vol. vi, 32691; and BL Add. MS 32692, fos. 454–5, 480–1.

words, if Defoe did not write it himself, those close to him knew what he would have wanted said. William Lee counted fifteen notices in monthly, weekly, and daily papers, though his attempt to view this as a sign that Defoe's greatness was universally recognized is undercut by his inability to see the irony in the review that appeared in *The Grub Street Journal* of 29 April depicting Defoe as a 'Great Author'.[23] In fact, Defoe's name lived on in a variety of ways. He was frequently mentioned among economic writers who based their arguments on what we would call statistics and which was then labelled 'political arithmetick'. The reputation of *Robinson Crusoe* continued to grow throughout the century, and Robert Shiels' life in Theophilus Cibber's *Lives of the Poets* in 1753 praised Defoe as a man of great moral and political integrity, providing a short list of his writings at the end. Even Pope in the *Dunciad* severed the connection between Daniel Defoe and his son Benjamin Norton as denizens of Grub Street on the grounds that the father did have 'Parts' or talent. But if the passage of time seemed to help Defoe's reputation, in the years immediately following his death, somehow the attacks on Defoe had transformed him from a writer who would serve all sides for pay into a convinced Jacobite. In reprinting a work by Defoe in 1735, the editor of the *Corn-Cutter's Journal* praised the writing and arguments, despite Defoe's conversion to Jacobitism. And the Queen's pardon to Defoe for the three ironic tracts on the succession was frequently quoted as an example of an unlawful act of favouritism to a Jacobite sympathizer.[24] One of the strangest examples of this transformation I have encountered is an edition of *The True-Born Englishman*, published in London in 1780, with an illustration of the Young Pretender, the last of the Stuarts to make a serious claim to the throne of Great Britain. One of Defoe's most outrageously Whiggish poems was being utilized for Jacobite propaganda.

By the time Chalmers published the first edition of his biography in 1785, Defoe had begun to attract the attention of critics and an audience searching for writers of genius—in this case, the genius who produced *Robinson Crusoe*. Although toward the end of the eighteenth century Francis Noble had published editions of some of the other novels, often in a form far from that which Defoe had originally written, Defoe only emerged as a novelist comparable to Richardson, Fielding, and Smollett with the Ballantyne

---

[23] Lee, iii. 462.

[24] See e.g. the quote from *The Corn-Cutter's Journal* 74 (1735), where the writer comments on 'the late Daniel De Foe; I know not whether to say of *famous*, or *infamous*, memory, for I think, before his fall into jacobitism he as fairly merited the former epithet, as he justly deserved the latter'. Quoted in *An Alphabetical Catalogue of an Extensive Collection of the Writings of Daniel De Foe* (London: Whitmore & Fenn, 1830), 41. See also William Arnall, *The Case of Opposition Stated, between the Craftsman and the People* (London, 1731), 49–50.

edition of 1810 and its introduction by Sir Walter Scott. *Robinson Crusoe* became a romantic text for Coleridge, and Lamb contributed an essay on Defoe's realist fiction to Wilson's *Life of De Foe* in 1830.

Nineteenth-century biographers, such as William Chadwick, writing in 1859, saw in Defoe an early exponent of free trade, and Defoe often was conflated with Robinson Crusoe—the ideal Englishman, hard-working, a venture capitalist, a defender of empire. It was this image of Defoe that impelled the erection of the monument over Defoe's grave in 1870 paid for by the 'Boys and Girls of England'. William Lee's biography, accompanied by two volumes of his journalism, is adulatory throughout, but it uncovered Defoe's duplicity in dealing with the opposition journals. Although Lee merely viewed this as an example of his patriotism, William Minto, using the same material, judged him to be a master prevaricator. Such a judgement might be seen as completely damning, but in fact it conjured up the figure of Defoe the trickster—clever, scheming, always shifting his positions to survive—a far more fascinating figure for us than the Whiggish saint of some earlier studies.

And so it has gone. Virginia Woolf saw Roxana as an early feminist, and E. M. Forster, in his *Aspects of the Novel* (1927), used Moll Flanders as his example for discussing character in fiction. During the time of the New Criticism, when biographical interpretation was out of fashion, Defoe the novelist emerged with new force. The first-person technique seemed to create character without obvious interference from the narrator, and *Moll Flanders*, *A Journal of the Plague Year*, and *Roxana* have emerged as being among the finest works of fiction produced in Britain during the eighteenth century. *Robinson Crusoe* has retained its interest as a book for readers young and old. Recently it has become a classic text for postcolonial studies, though it is uncertain whether its protagonist and its author are to be regarded as heroes or villains. Defoe will never be without controversy. Would he have wanted it any other way?

WORKS CITED

ABERCROMBY, PATRICK. *Advantages of the Act of Security, Compar'd with These of the Intended Union.* Edinburgh, 1706.

Account of Some Late Designs to Create a Misunderstanding betwixt the King and His People, An. London, 1702.

AITKEN, GEORGE. 'Defoe and Mist's "Weekly Journal"'. *Athenaeum* (26 Aug. 1893): 287–8.

ALDRIDGE, ALFRED O. *Shaftesbury and the Deist Manifesto.* Philadelphia: American Philosophical Society, 1951.

ALKON, PAUL KENT. *Defoe and Fictional Time.* Athens: Georgia University Press, 1979.

ANDERSON, HANS H. 'The Paradox of Trade and Morality in Defoe'. *Modern Philology* 39 (1941): 23–46.

ARENDT, HANNAH. *The Human Condition.* 1958. Chicago: University of Chicago Press, 1971.

ARMYTRAGE, GEORGE, ed. *Allegations for Marriage Licences Issued by the Vicar-General of the Archbishop of Canterbury July 1679–1687.* London: Harleian Society 30 (1890).

ARNALL, WILLIAM. *The Case of Opposition Stated, between the Craftsman and the People.* London, 1731.

ASGILL, JOHN. *Several Assertions Proved In Order to Create Another Species of Money than Gold and Silver.* London, 1696.

ASHCRAFT, RICHARD and ROPER, ALAN. *Politics as Reflected in Literature.* Intro. by Maximillian E. Novak. Los Angeles: William Andrews Clark Memorial Library, 1989.

ATTERBURY, FRANCIS. *English Advice to the Freeholders of England.* [?London,] 1714.

Author of the Lawful Prejudices against an Incorporating Union with England, Defended, The. Edinburgh, 1707.

BACHELARD, PIERRE. *The Poetics of Space.* Trans. Maria Jolas. Boston: Beacon Press, 1972.

BACKSCHEIDER, PAULA R. *Daniel Defoe: Ambition and Innovation.* Lexington: University Press of Kentucky, 1986.

BACKSCHEIDER, PAULA R. (cont.). *Daniel Defoe: His Life*. Baltimore: Johns Hopkins University Press, 1989.

—— 'John Russell to Daniel Defoe: Fifteen Unpublished Letters from Scotland'. *Philological Quarterly* 61 (1982): 161–77.

—— 'No Defense: Defoe in 1703'. *PMLA* 103 (1988): 274–84.

—— 'Robert Harley to Daniel Defoe: A New Letter'. *Modern Language Review* 83 (1988): 817–19.

BAIN, R. NISBET. *Charles XII and the Collapse of the Swedish Empire*. New York: Knickerbocker Press, 1895.

BAINE, RODNEY. *Defoe and the Supernatural*. Athens: University of Georgia Press, 1968.

BAKER, HENRY. 'An Essay on Speech'. In *Literary Correspondence*, 1723. John Rylands Library, Manchester.

—— 'Letter Book'. Beinecke Library, Yale University.

—— *Original Poems, Serious and Humorous*. London, 1725.

—— ed. *The Universal Spectator*. London, 1729–31.

Ballad . . . Answered along with Memorial Paragraph by Paragraph, The. London, 1701.

BALZAC, HONORÉ DE. *A Harlot High and Low. Splendeurs et misères des courtisanes*. Trans. Rayner Heppenstall. Harmondsworth: Penguin, 1970.

—— *La Comédie humaine*. Paris: Gallimard, 1977.

BASTIAN, FRANK. *Defoe's Early Life*. London: Macmillan, 1981.

—— 'James Foe, Merchant, Father of Daniel Defoe'. *Notes & Queries* 209 (1964): 82–6.

BATH, MARQUIS OF. *Calendar of the Manuscripts*. London: His Majesty's Stationery Office, 1904.

BATTEN, CHARLES LYNN. *Pleasurable Instruction: Form and Convention in Eighteenth Century Travel Literature*. Chicago: University of California Press, 1978.

Battle of the Authors Lately Fought in Convent-Garden, between Sir John Edgar, Generalissimo on One Side, and Horatius Truewit on the Other, The. London, 1720.

BAYLY, LEWIS. *The Practice of Piety*. London, 1720.

BELHAVEN, JOHN HAMILTON. *The Lord Belhaven's Speech in the Scotch Parliament, Saturday the Second of November, on the Subject-Matter of an Union betwixt the Two Kingdoms of Scotland and England*. Edinburgh, 1706.

BICKHAM, GEORGE. *The Whig Medley*. London, 1710.

BIDDLE, SHEILA. *Bolingbroke and Harley*. New York: Knopf, 1974.

Biographia Britannica. Ed. Andrew Kippis, Joseph Towers et al. 2nd edn. 5 vols. London, 1778–93.

BJORNSON, RICHARD. *The Picaresque Hero in European Fiction*. Madison: University of Wisconsin Press, 1977.

BLACK, JEREMY. 'Parliament and the Political and Diplomatic Crisis of 1717–18'. *Parliamentary History* 3 (1984): 92–4.

BLACKMORE, RICHARD. *King Arthur, an Heroic Poem*. London, 1697.

—— *Prince Arthur, an Heroic Poem*. London, 1695.

BLEWETT, DAVID. *Defoe's Art of Fiction: Robinson Crusoe, Moll Flanders, Colonel Jack and Roxana*. Toronto: University of Toronto Press, 1979.

BLEWITT, GEORGE. *An Enquiry Whether a General Practice of Virtue Tends to the Wealth or Poverty, Benefit or Disadvantage of a People?* London, 1725.

BOND, DONALD F., ed. *The Spectator*. Oxford: Clarendon, 1965.

—— ed. *The Tatler*. Oxford: Clarendon Press, 1987.

BOSWELL, JAMES. *Life of Johnson*. Ed. George Birkbeck Hill. Oxford: Clarendon Press, 1888.

BOULTON, J. T. *Daniel Defoe*. New York: Schocken, 1965.

BOYER, ABEL. *The History of Queen Anne*. London, 1715.

—— *The Political State of Great Britain*. London, 1711–29.

BRATHWAIT, RICHARD. *The English Gentleman: Containing Sundry Excellent Rules or Exquisite Observations*. London, 1630.

BREWER, JOHN. *The Sinews of Power: War, Money, and the English State, 1688–1783*. Cambridge, Mass.: Harvard University Press, 1990.

BROOKS, THOMAS. *Apples of Gold for Young Men and Women, and a Crown of Glory for Old Men and Women*. London, 1662.

BROWN, HUME. *The Treaty of the Union*. Oxford: Clarendon Press, 1914.

BROWN, TOM. *A Letter from the Dead Thomas Brown, to the Living Heraclitus*. London, 1704.

—— *Visits from the Shades: Or, Dialogues Serious, Comical, and Political*. London, 1704.

BROWNE, JOSEPH. 'A Dialogue between Church and No-Church; or, A Rehearsal of the Review (1706)'. In *State Tracts*. 2 vols. London, 1715.

—— *The Moon Calf, or, Accurate Reflections on The Consolidator*. 1705. Ed. Maximillian Novak. New York: AMS Press, 1996.

—— *State and Miscellany Poems*. London, 1715.

BROWNING, REED. *Political and Constitutional Ideas of the Court Whigs*. Baton Rouge: Louisiana State University Press, 1982.

BRYAN, MICHAEL. *Bryan's Dictionary of Painters and Engravers*. New edn. Ed. George C. Williamson. New York: Macmillan, 1903–5.

BUNYAN, JOHN. *The Poems*. Ed. Graham Midgley. In *Miscellaneous Works of John Bunyan.*, vi. Oxford: Clarendon Press, 1980.

BURCH, CHARLES. 'Benjamin Defoe at Edinburgh University'. *Philological*

Quarterly 19 (1940): 343–8.

BURCH, CHARLES (cont.). 'Defoe and the Edinburgh Society of Reformation of Manners'. *Review of English Studies* 16 (1940): 306–12.

BURNET, GILBERT. *Bishop Burnet's History of His Own Time*. 2nd edn. Ed. Earl of Dartmouth et al. 6 vols. Oxford: Clarendon Press, 1833.

CALAMY, EDWARD. *An Account of the Ministers, Lecturers, Masters and Fellows of Colleges and School Master Who Were Ejected or Silenced after the Revolution in 1660*. [The second volume of Calamy's *Abridgement of Mr. (Richard) Baxter's History of His Life and Times*. 2 vols., 2nd edn. London, 1713.

—— *An Historical Account of My Own Life*. London: Henry Colburn and Richard Bentley, 1829.

CAMPBELL, GEORGE. *Impostor at the Bar: William Fuller, 1670–1733*. London, Hodder and Stoughton, 1961.

CAMPBELL, MARY ELIZABETH. *Defoe's First Poem*. Bloomington, Ind.: Principia Press, 1938.

CARE, HENRY. *English Liberties, or, The Free-Born Subject's Inheritance*. London, 1680.

CARSWELL, JOHN. *The South Sea Bubble*. Rev. edn. Stroud: Alan Sutton, 1993.

CARY, JOHN. *Essay on the State of England in Relation to Its Trade, Its Poor, and Its Taxes, for Carrying on the Present War against France*. Bristol, 1695.

—— *An Essay towards Regulating Trade and Employing the Poor of This Kingdom*. London, 1719.

CATO, BRUTUS. *A Letter to the People of England, Occasion'd by the Letter to the Dissenters*. London, 1714.

CHADWICK, WILLIAM. *The Life and Times of Daniel De Foe with Remarks Digressive and Discursive*. London, 1859.

CHALMERS, GEORGE. *The Life of Defoe*. London, 1790.

—— 'Life of De Foe'. In *The History of the Union*. London, 1785.

'Character of Daniell de Foe, Writer of the Pamphlet Called the Review, A'. (1704). MS 28,094, fo. 165. British Library, London.

Character of Sultan Gaga, The. n.p., n.p., ?1714.

CHAUNCEY, ISAAC. *Neonomianism Unmask'd, or, the Ancient Gospel Pleaded against the Other, Call'd a New Law or Gospel*. London, 1692.

CIBBER, THEOPHILUS. *Lives of the Poets of Great Britain and Ireland*. London, 1753.

CLEMENT, SIMON. *Faults on Both Sides: Or, an Essay upon the Original Cause, Progress, and Mischievious Consequences of the Factions in this Nation*. London, 1710.

CLERK, JOHN. *Memoirs of the Life of Sir John Clerk*. Ed. John M. Gray. Edinburgh: Scottish History Society, 1892.

COBBETT, WILLIAM. *The Parliamentary History of England, from the Earliest*

Period to the Year 1803. 36 vols. London: Longman, Hurst, Rees, Orme, & Browne, 1806–20.

COETZEE, J. M. *Foe.* London: Secker & Warburg, 1986.

Colchester Public Record Office, CPI 1176/18.

Coleman Ward Records. Boxes 21.3 and 37, MS 5. Guildhall Library and Record Room, London.

COLERIDGE, SAMUEL TAYLOR. *Miscellaneous Criticism.* Ed. Thomas Raysor. Cambridge, Mass.: Harvard University Press, 1936.

COLLIER, JEREMY. *A Short View of the Immorality and Profaneness of the English Stage.* London, 1698.

COLLINS, ANTHONY. *A Discourse of Free-Thinking.* London, 1713.

——*A Discourse of the Grounds and Reasons of the Christian Religion.* London, 1724.

COMB-BRUSH, CATHERINE (pseud.). *Every Man Mind His Own Business, or Private Piques No Publick Precedents.* London, 1725.

'Considerations on the Consequences of the French Settling Colonies on the Mississippi'. *Political State* 19 (Apr. 1720).

Considerations upon the Secret History of the White Staff. 2nd edn. London [1714].

Corn-Cutter's Journal, The 74 (1735), quoted in *An Alphabetical Catalogue of an Extensive Collection of the Writings of Daniel Defoe.* London, 1829.

Cornhill Ward, Jury Duty Wardmote. MS 4069/2, fos. 358 and 379. Guildhall Library and Record Room, London.

Cornhill Ward Records, 1st Precinct Poll Book. March 1692. Guildhall Library and Record Room, London.

——Box 37, MS 5. Guildhall Library and Record Room, London.

Cornhill Ward Taxation Rolls. Box 6, MS 10. Guildhall Library and Record Room, London.

Corporation of London Public Record Office. 'A True and Perfect Kallender of the Names of all the Prisoners in Newgate for Fellony & Trespisses the 7th Day of July 1703'. SF475.

Corporation of London Public Record Office. SF472 (1703).

——SF475.5. 5 June 1703.

CORVISIER, ANDRÉ. *Armées et sociétés en Europe de 1494 à 1789.* Paris: Presses Universitaires de France, 1976.

Court Minutes. MS 6443–1. Guildhall Library and Record Room, London.

CROFT, SIR HERBERT. *Love and Madness.* London, 1780.

Cursory Remarks upon Some Late Disloyal Proceedings, in Several Cabals. London, 1699.

CURTIS, LAURA. 'Defoe's "Captain Singleton": A Reassessment with Observations'. *Papers on Language and Literature* 7 (1971): 38–51.

DAICHES, DAVID. *Scotland and the Union*. London: John Murray, 1977.

DAMPIER, WILLIAM. *A Voyage to New Holland*. Ed. James Williamson. [London:] Argonaut Press, 1939.

DEFOE, BENJAMIN NORTON. Unpublished Letters. Chalmondeley Houghton MSS, Cambridge University; British Library Add. MSS 32691, fos. 390–1; 32692, fos. 480–1, 454–5.

DEFOE, DANIEL et al. *Accounts of the Apparition of Mrs. Veal*. Introd. Manuel Schonhorn. Augustan Reprints No. 115. Los Angeles: William Andrews Clark Memorial Library, 1965.

DEFOE, DANIEL. *An Account of the Conduct of Robert Earl of Oxford*. London, 1715.

—— *An Account of the Swedish and Jacobite Plot*. London, 1717.

—— *An Address to the People of England: Shewing the Unworthiness of Their Behaviour to King George*. London, 1715.

—— *The Advantages of Scotland by an Incorporate Union with England*. [Edinburgh,] 1706.

—— *Advertisement from Defoe to Mr. Clark*. Edinburgh, 1710.

—— *Advice to All Parties*. London, 1705.

—— *Advice to the People of Great Britain*. London, 1714.

—— *The Anatomy of Exchange-Alley*. London, 1719.

—— *And What If the Pretender Should Come? Or, Considerations of the Advantages and Real Consequences of the Pretender's Possessing the Crown of Great Britain*. London, 1713.

—— *The Annals of King George*. London, 1717–18.

—— *An Answer to a Paper Concerning Mr. De Foe, against His History of the Union*. [Edinburgh, 1708]

—— *An Answer to a Question That No Body Thinks of, viz. But What If the Queen Should Die?* London, 1713.

—— *An Answer to My Lord Beilhaven's Speech By an English Gentleman*. Edinburgh, 1706.

—— *An Apology for the Army*. London, 1715.

—— *An Appeal to the Honour and Justice Though It Be of His Worst Enemies*. In *The Shakespeare Head Edition of the Novels and Selected Writings of Daniel Defoe*. 14 vols. Oxford: Blackwell 1927–8.

—— *An Argument Proving that the Design of Employing and Enobling Foreigners, Is a Treasonable Conspiracy against the Constitution*. London, 1717.

—— *An Argument Shewing that a Standing Army with Consent of Parliament, Is Not Inconsistent with a Free Government*. London, 1698.

—— *An Argument, Shewing that the Prince of Wales, Tho' a Protestant, Has No Just Pretensions to the Crown of England*. London, 1701.

—— *Armageddon: Or, the Necessity of Carrying on the War*. London [1711].

—— *Atalantis Major*. n.p., 1711.

—— *Atlas Maritimus & Commercialis, or, A General View of the World so Far as it Relates to Trade and Navigation*. London, 1728.

—— *An Attempt Towards a Coalition of English Protestants*. London, 1715.

—— *Augusta Triumphans, or, the Way to Make London the Most Flourishing City in the Universe First by Establishing an University*. 2nd edn. London, 1729.

—— *The Ballad, or, Some Scurrilous Reflections in Verse, on the Proceedings of the Honourable House of Commons: Answered Stanza by Stanza [. . .] Repl'd to Paragraph by Paragraph*. London, 1701.

—— *The Ballance of Europe*. London, 1711.

—— *The Ballance: Or, a New Test of the High-Flyers of All Sides*. London, 1705.

—— *Bold Advice: Or, Proposals for the Entire Rooting Out Jacobitism in Great Britain*. London, 1715.

—— *A Brief Case of the Distillers and of the Distilling Trade in England*. London, 1726.

—— *A Brief Debate upon the Dissolving the late Parliament and Whether We Ought Not to Chuse the Same Gentlemen Again*. London, 1722.

—— *A Brief Deduction of the Original, Progress, and Immense Greatness of the British Woolen Manufacture: With an Enquiry whether it be not at Present in a Very Declining Condition*. London, 1727.

—— *Brief Explanation of a Late Pamphlet, Entituled, The Shortest Way with the Dissenters*. London, 1703.

—— *A Brief Historical Account of the Lives of the Six Notorious Street-Robbers Executed at Kingston*. London, 1726.

—— *A Brief History of the Pacifick Campaign in Flanders*. London, 1715.

—— *A Brief State of the Inland or Home-Trade of England and of the Oppression it Suffers*. London, 1730.

—— *A Brief State of the Question and the Woolen and Silk Manufacture between the Printed and Painted Callicoes*. London, 1719.

—— *A Brief Survey of the Legal Liberties of the Dissenters*. London, 1714.

—— *British Visions: Or, Isaac Bickerstaff's Twelve Prophecies*. [?London, ?1711].

—— *Caledonia, &c. A Poem in Honour of Scotland, and the Scots Nation*. Edinburgh, 1706.

—— *The Candidate*. London, 1715.

—— *Captain Tom's Remembrance to His Old Friends the Mobb of London*. [London, 1711]

—— *The Case of a Standing Army Army [sic] Fairly and Impartially Stated: In Answer to the Late History of Standing Armies in England*. London, 1698.

—— *The Case of Disbanding the Army at Present, Briefly and Impartially Considered*. London, 1698.

DEFOE, DANIEL (cont.). *The Case of Dissenters as Affected by the Late Bill Proposed by Parliament.* London: A. Baldwin, 1703.

—— *The Case of Mr. Law, Truly Stated, in Answer to a Pamphlet Entitul'd A Letter to Mr. Law.* London, 1721.

—— *The Case of the Poor Skippers and Keel-Men of New-castle.* [London, 1712]

—— *The Case of the Protestant Dissenters in Carolina.* London, 1706.

—— *A Challenge of Peace, Address'd to the Whole Nation.* London, 1703.

—— *Chickens Feed Capons, or, A Dissertation on the Pertness of Our Youth in General Especially Those Trained up at the Tea-Tables.* 4th edn. London, 1731.

—— *The Chimera: Or, the French Way of Paying National Debts.* London, 1720.

—— *The Christianity of the High Church Consider'd.* London, 1704.

—— *Collection of Dying Speeches of All Those People Call'd Traytors, Executed in This Reign.* London, 1718.

—— *A Collection of the Writings of the Author of the True-Born Englishman.* London, 1703.

—— *The Commentator.* London, 1720.

—— *The Compleat Art of Painting, a Poem.* London, 1720.

—— *The Compleat English Gentleman.* Ed. Karl Bülbring. London: David Nutt, 1890.

—— *The Complete English Tradesman.* 2nd edn. 2 vols. London, 1727. New York: A. M. Kelley, 1969.

—— *The Complete English Tradesman in Familiar Letters Directing Him in All the Several Parts and Progressions of Trade.* London, 1726.

—— *A Condoling Letter to the Tattler on Account of the Misfortunes of Isaac Bickerstaff, Esq., a Prisoner in the [Gatehouse] on Suspicion of Debt.* London [1710].

—— *The Conduct of Christians Made the Sport of Infidels.* London, 1717.

—— *The Conduct of Parties in England.* London, 1712.

—— *The Conduct of Robert Walpole, Esq.* London, 1717.

—— *The Conduct of Some People About Pleading Guilty : With Some Reasons Why It Was Not Thought Proper to Shew Mercy to Some Who Desire'd It.* London, 1716.

—— *Conjugal Lewdness; or, Matrimonial Whoredom.* Ed. Maximillian Novak. Gainesville, Fla.: Scholars' Facsimiles and Reprints, 1967.

—— *Considerations upon the Eighth and Ninth Articles of the Treaty of Commerce and Navigation.* London, 1713.

—— *The Consolidator.* In *The Earlier Life and the Chief Earlier Works of Daniel Defoe.* Ed. Henry Morley. London: Routledge, 1889.

—— *Continuation of Letters Written By a Turkish Spy.* London, 1718.

—— *The Danger and Consequence of Disobliging the Clergy Consider'd.* London, 1716–17.

—— *The Danger of Court Differences: Or, the Unhappy Effects of a Motley Ministry.* London, 1717.

—— *The Danger of the Protestant Religion Consider'd, from the Present Prospect of a Religious War in Europe.* London, 1701.

—— *Daniel Defoe's Hymn for the Thanksgiving.* London, 1706.

—— *A Declaration of Truth to Benjamin Hoadly.* London, 1717.

—— *A Defence of the Allies and the Late Ministry.* London, 1712.

—— *A Dialogue between a Whig and a Jacobite, upon the Subject of the Late Rebellion.* London, 1716.

—— *The Dissenters Answer to the High Church Challenge.* In *A True Collection of the Writings of the Author of the True-Born Englishman.* London, 1703–5.

—— *The Dissenters in England Vindicated From Some Reflections in a Late Pamphlet, Entituled, Lawful Prejudices, &c.* [Edinburgh, 1707]

—— *The Dissenters Misrepresented and Represented.* London, 1704.

—— *The Double Welcome. A Poem to the Duke of Marlbro'.* London, 1705.

—— *Due Preparations for the Plague, as Well as for Soul as Body.* In vol. 15 of *Romances and Narratives by Daniel Defoe*, ed. George A. Aitken. 16 vols. London: J. M. Dent, 1895.

—— *The Dyet of Poland a Satyr.* Dantzick [London], 1705.

—— *The Earlier Life and Chief Earlier Works*, ed. Henry Morley. London: Routledge, 1889.

—— *An Effectual Scheme for the Immediate Preventing of Street Robberies and Suppressing All Other Disorders of the Night.* London, 1731.

—— *An Elegy on the Author of the True-Born Englishman.* In *A True Collection of the Writings of the Author of the True-Born Englishman.* London, 1703.

—— *Eleven Opinions about Mr. H[arle]y.* London, 1711.

—— *England's Late Jury: A Satyr.* London, 1701.

—— *The Englishman's Choice, and True Interest in a Vigorous Prosecution of the War against France.* London, 1694.

—— *An Enquiry into the Case of Mr. Asgil's General Translation.* London, 1704.

—— *An Enquiry into the Disposal of the Equivalent.* [?Edinburgh, 1706]

—— *An Enquiry into the Occasional Conformity of Dissenters, in Cases of Preferment.* London, 1697.

—— *An Essay at a Plain Exposition of that Difficult Phrase of a Good Peace.* London, 1711.

—— *An Essay at Removing National Prejudices against a Union with Scotland.* Edinburgh, 1706.

—— *An Essay on the History of Parties.* London, 1711.

DEFOE, DANIEL (cont.). *An Essay upon Publick Credit*. 3rd edn. London, 1710.

—— *An Essay on the Regulation of the Press*. Ed. John Robert Moore. Oxford: Blackwell, 1948.

—— *An Essay on the South Sea Trade with an Enquiry into the Grounds and Reasons of the Present Dislike and Complaint against the Settlement of a South-Sea Company*. London, 1712.

—— *An Essay on the Treaty of Commerce with France*. London, 1713.

—— *An Essay upon Buying and Selling of Speeches*. London, 1716.

—— *An Essay upon Literature: Or, an Enquiry into the Antiquity and Original of Letters*. London. 1726.

—— *An Essay upon Loans*. In *The Works of Daniel De Foe*. Ed. William Hazlitt. 3 vols. London: John Clements, 1843.

—— *An Essay upon Projects*. Ed. Joyce Kennedy, Michael Seidel, and M. E. Novak. New York: AMS Press, 1999.

—— *An Essay upon the Trade to Africa*. [London,] 1711.

—— *Every-Body's Business, Is No-Body's Business: Or, Private Abuses, Publick Grievances Exemplified in the Pride, Insolence, and Exorbitant Wages of Our Women-Servants, Footmen, &c*. 3rd edn. London, 1725.

—— *The Evident Advantages to Great Britain and Its Allies from the Approaching War: Especially in Matters of Trade*. London, 1727.

—— *The Evident Approach of a War and Something of the Necessity of It*. London, 1727.

—— *The Experiment: Or, the Shortest Way with the Dissenters Exemplified*. London, 1705.

—— *The Family Instructor*. In *The Novels and Miscellaneous Works*. 20 vols. London: Tegg, 1840–1.

—— *The Farther Adventures of Robinson Crusoe*. In *The Shakespeare Head Edition of the Novels and Selected Writings of Daniel Defoe*. 14 vols. Oxford: Blackwell, 1927–8.

—— *A Farther Case Relating to the Poor Keel-Men of Newcastle*. [London, 1712]

—— *The Fears of the Pretender Turned Into the Fears of Debauchery*. London, 1714.

—— *The Female Manufacturers Complaint: Being the Humble Petition of Dorothy Distaff, Abigail Spinning-Wheel, Eleanor Reel, Etc., Spinsters, to the Lady Rebecca Woolpack*. London, 1720.

—— *A Fifth Essay at Removing National Prejudices*. [Edinburgh,] 1707.

—— *The Flying Post: and Medley*. London, 1714.

—— *The Fortunes and Misfortunes of the Famous Moll Flanders*. Ed. G. A. Starr. London: Oxford University Press, 1971.

—— *A Fourth Essay at Removing National Prejudices* [?Edinburgh,] 1706.

—— *The Free-Holders Plea against Stock-Jobbing Elections of Parliament Men.* London, 1701.

—— *A General History of the Discoveries and Improvements in Useful Arts.* London [1725–7].

—— *A General History of the Pyrates.* Ed. Manuel Schonhorn. London: Dent, 1972.

—— *A General History of the Robberies and Murders of the Most Notorious Pyrates and also Their Policies, Discipline and Government.* London, 1724.

—— *A General History of Trade, and Especially Consider'd as it Respects the British Commerce.* London, 1713.

—— *A General Pardon Consider'd, in its Circumstances and Consequences.* London, 1717.

—— *Giving Alms No Charity.* In *A True Collection of the Writings of the Author of the True-Born Englishman.* 2 vols. London, 1703–5.

—— *The Great Law of Subordination Consider'd: Or, the Insolence and Unsufferable Behaviour of Servants in England Duly Enquir'd Into.* London, 1724.

—— *Greenshields Out of Prison and Toleration Settled in Scotland.* London, 1710.

—— *Hannibal at the Gates: Or, the Progress of Jacobitism.* London, 1714.

—— *The High-Church Legion, or, The Memorial Examin'd.* London, 1705.

—— *His Majesty's Obligations to the Whigs Plainly Proved.* London, 1715.

—— *Historical Collections or Memoires of Passages and Stories Collected from Severall Authors.* MS H6735M3. William Andrews Clark Memorial Library, Los Angeles.

—— *The History and Remarkable Life of the Truly Honourable Col. Jacque, Commonly Call'd Col. Jack.* Ed. Samuel Holt Monk. London: Oxford University Press, 1965.

—— *The History of the Clemency of Our English Monarchs.* London, 1717.

—— *The History of the Kentish Petition.* Oxford: Blackwell, 1927. In *The Shakespeare Head Edition of the Novels and Selected Writings of Daniel Defoe.* 14 vols. Oxford: Blackwell, 1927–8.

—— *A History of the Last Session of the Present Parliament.* London, 1718.

—— [Scots Gentleman in the Swedish Service]. *The History of Wars of His Late Majesty.* London, 1720.

—— *A Humble Address to Our Sovereign Lord the People.* London, 1715.

—— *An Humble Proposal to the People of England for the Encrease of Their Trade, and Encouragement of Their Manufactures.* London, 1729.

—— *A Hymn to the Funeral Sermon.* London, 1703.

—— *A Hymn to the Mob.* London, 1715.

—— *A Hymn to the Pillory.* London, 1703.

DEFOE, DANIEL (cont.). *An Impartial History of the Life and Actions of Peter Alexowiz, the Present Czar of Muscovy.* London [1722].

—— *Impeachment or No Impeachment.* London, 1714.

—— *Imperial Gratitude: Drawn from a Modest view of the Conduct of the Emperor Ch ... es VI, and the King of Spain Ch ... III, with Observations on the Difference, &c.* London, 1712.

—— *Instructions from Rome, in Favour of the Pretender, Inscrib'd to the Most Elevated Don Sacheverello, and His Brother Don Higginisco. And Which All Perkinites, Non Jurors, High-Flyers, Popish Desirers, Wooden Shoe Admirers, and Absolute Non Resistance Drivers Are Obliged to Pursue and Maintain ...* London [1710].

—— *A Journal of the Plague Year.* Ed. Louis Landa. London: Oxford University Press, 1969.

—— *Jure Divino: A Satyr.* London, 1706.

—— *The Just Complaint of the Poor Weavers Truly Represented.* London, 1719.

—— *A Justification of the Dutch from Several Late Scandalous Reflections.* London, 1712.

—— *The King of Pirates.* In *Romances and Narratives.* Ed. George A. Aitken. 16 vols. London: Dent, 1895.

—— *The Lay-Man's Sermon upon the Late Storm: Held forth at an Honest Coffee-House-Conventicle. Not So much a Jest as 'tis Thought to be.* London, 1704.

—— *The Layman's Vindication of the Church of England.* London, 1716.

—— *Legion's Humble Address to the Lords, Answer'd Paragraph by Paragraph.* [?London, c.1704]

—— *Legion's Memorial.* Oxford: Blackwell, 1927. In *The Shakespeare Head Edition of the Novels and Selected Writings of Daniel Defoe.* 14 vols. Oxford: Blackwell, 1927–8.

—— *The Letters of Daniel Defoe.* Ed. George Healey. Oxford: Clarendon Press, 1955.

—— *Letter from a Gentleman at the Court of St. Germains.* London, 1710.

—— *A Letter from Captain Tom to the Mob.* London, 1710.

—— *A Letter from the Jesuits to Father De La Pillonniere.* London, 1718.

—— *A Letter from Mr. Reason, to the High and Mighty Prince the Mob.* [Edinburgh, 1706]

—— *A Letter to a Dissenter from His Friend at the Hague, Concerning the Penal Laws and the Test.* The Hague [London], 1688.

—— *A Letter to a Member of Parliament, Shewing the Necessity of Regulating the Press.* Oxford, 1699.

—— *A Letter to Andrew Snape.* London, 1717.

—— *A Letter to the Dissenters.* 2nd edn. London, 1714.

——— *A Letter to the Honourable A[rthu]r M[oo]re*. London, 1714.

——— *A Letter to Mr. Steele, Occasion'd by His Letter to a Member of Parliament, Concerning the Bill for Preventing the Growth of Schism*. London, 1714.

——— *A Letter to the Whigs, Expostulating with Them Upon Their Present Conduct*. London, 1714.

——— *Letter to Mr. Bisset*. London, 1709.

——— *Lex Talionis: Or, an Enquiry into the Most Proper Ways to Prevent the Persecution of the Protestants in France*. London, 1698.

——— *The Life, Adventures, and Pyracies, of the Famous Captain Singleton*. Ed. Shiv K. Kumar. London: Oxford University Press, 1969.

——— *The Life and Strange Surprizing Adventures of Robinson Crusoe*, ed. J. Donald Crowley. London: Oxford University Press, 1981.

——— *The London Post* (25 Sept. 1704–8 June 1705).

——— *The Manufacturer* (1719–1721). Introd. Robert Gosselink. Delmar, NY: Scholars' Facsimiles and Reprints, 1978.

——— *Master Mercury*, ed. Frank Ellis and Henry Snyder, Augustan Reprint Society No. 184. Los Angeles: William Andrews Clark Memorial Library, 1977.

——— *The Meditations of Daniel Defoe*. Ed. George Healy. Cummington, Mass.: Cummington Press, 1946.

——— *Memoirs of a Cavalier*. In *The Shakespeare Head Edition of the Novels and Selected Writings of Daniel Defoe*. Oxford: Blackwell, 1927–8.

——— *Memoirs of Count Tariff, &c.* London, 1713.

——— *Memoirs of John, Duke of Melfort: Being an Account of the Secret Intrigues of the Chevalier de S. George, Particularly Relating to the Present Times*. London, 1714.

——— *Memoirs of Majr. Alexander Ramkins, a Highland Officer*. London, 1719 [1718].

——— *Memoirs of Some Transactions During the Late Ministry of Robert E. of Oxford*. London, 1717.

——— *Memoirs of the Church of Scotland, in Four Periods*. London, 1717.

——— *Memoirs of the Life and Eminent Conduct of the Learned and Reverend Divine, Daniel Williams*. London, 1718.

——— *Mercator: Or, Commerce Retrieved*. London, 1713–14.

——— *Mercurius Politicus*. London, 1716–20.

——— *The Mercy of the Government Vindicated*. London, 1716.

——— *Mere Nature Delineated: Or, a Body without a Soul*. London, 1726.

——— *Minutes of the Negotiations of Monsr. Mesnager at the Court of England*. London, 1717.

——— *Miserere Cleri: Or, the Factions of the Church*. London, 1718.

DEFOE, DANIEL (cont.). *Mistakes on All Sides, an Enquiry into the Vulgar Errors of the State*. MS D324M1. H918. William Andrews Clark Memorial Library, Los Angeles.

—— *The Mock Mourners. A True Collection of the Writings of the Author of the True-Born Englishman*. London, 1703.

——*Moderation Maintain'd, in Defence of: A Compassionate Enquiry into the Causes of the Civil War, &c*. London, 1704.

—— *The Monitor*. London, 1714.

——*More Reformation: A Satyr Upon Himself*. In *A True Collection of the Writings of Daniel Defoe*. London, 1703.

——*More Short Ways with the Dissenters*. London, 1704.

——*A Narrative of the Proceedings in France, for Discovering and Detecting the Murderers of the English Gentlemen, September 21, 1723, Near Calais*. London, 1724.

——*A New Discovery of an Old Intreague*. London, 1692.

——*A New Family Instructor: In Familiar Discourses between a Father and His Children, on the Most Essential Points of the Christian Religion*. London, 1727.

——*A New Map of the Laborious and Painful Travels of Our Blessed High Church Apostle*. [London,] 1710.

——*A New Satyr on the Parliament*. In *Poems on Affairs of State: Augustan Satirical Verse, 1660–1714*. Ed. Frank Ellis. New Haven, Conn.: Yale University Press, 1970.

——*A New Test of the Church of England's Honesty*. London, 1704.

——*A New Voyage Round the World*. In vol. 14 of *Romances and Narratives by Daniel Defoe*, ed. George A. Aitken. London: Dent, 1895.

—— *No Queen: Or, No General*. London, 1712.

—— *The Novels and Miscellaneous Works of Daniel de Foe*. 6 vols. London: Henry Bohn, 1854–6.

—— *Of Royall Educacion a Fragmentary Treatise*. Ed. Karl Bülbring. London: David Nutt, 1895.

—— *The Old Whig and Modern Whig Revived . . . Or, the Difference betwixt Acting upon Principle and Interest*. London, 1717.

—— *The Original Power of the Collective Body of the People of England, Examind and Asserted*. London, 1702.

—— *Original Right: Or, The Reasonableness of Appeals to the People*. London, 1704.

—— *The Original Weekly Journal [Applebee's Original Weekly Journal]* London, 1720–6.

—— *The Pacificator, a Poem*. London, 1700.

—— *The Parallel*. In *A True Collection of the Writings of the Author of the True-Born Englishman*. 2 vols. London, 1703–5.

—— *Parochial Tyranny, or, The House-Keeper's Complaint against the Insupport-able Exactions and Partial Assessments of Select Vestries, &c.* London [1727].

—— *Party-Tyranny: Or, an Occasional Bill in Miniature As Now Practised in Carolina.* London, 1705.

—— *The Perjur'd Free Mason Detected.* London, 1730.

—— *Persecution Anatomiz'd.* London, 1705.

—— *A Plan of the English Commerce Being a Compleat prospect of the Trade of this Nation, as Well the Home Trade and Foreign.* In *The Shakespeare Head Edition of the Novels and Selected Writings of Daniel Defoe.* 14 vols. Oxford: Blackwell, 1927–8.

—— *The Political History of the Devil: As Well Ancient as Modern.* 2nd edn. London, 1726.

—— *The Political State of Great-Britain.* Dec. 1729–Oct. 1730.

—— *The Poor Man's Plea.* In *The Shakespeare Head Edition of the Novels and Selected Writings of Daniel Defoe.* 14 vols., Oxford: Blackwell, 1927–8.

—— 'Preface'. In *De Laune's Plea for the Non-Conformists.* London, 1706.

—— *Presbyterian Persecution Examined.* Edinburgh, 1707.

—— *The Present State of the Parties in Great Britain.* London, 1712.

—— *The Protestant Monastery, or, A Complaint against the Brutality of the Present Age.* London, 1727.

—— *The Protestant Jesuit Unmask'd.* London, 1704.

—— *The Protestant Jubilee.* London, 1715.

—— *Queries to the New Hereditary Right-Men.* London, 1710.

—— *Queries upon a Bill against Occasional Conformity.* [London, 1704]

—— *The Question Fairly Stated, Whether Now Is Not the Time To Do Justice to the Friends of the Government, As Well As Its Enemies?* London, 1717.

—— *The Rabbler Convicted: Or, A Friendly Advice to All Turbulent and Factious Persons.* Edinburgh, 1706.

—— *Reasons Against a War with France, or, An Argument Shewing That the French King's Owning the Prince of Wales as King of England, Scotland and Ireland is no Sufficient Ground of a War.* London, 1701.

—— *Reasons against Fighting.* London, 1712.

—— *Reasons against the Succession of the House of Hanover.* London, 1713.

—— *Reasons Why a Party among Us, and also among the Confederates are Obstinately bent against a Treaty of Peace with the French at this Time.* [London,] 1711.

—— *Reasons Why This Nation Ought to Put a Speedy End to This Expensive War.* [London,] 1711.

—— *Reflections upon the Late Great Revolution.* London, 1689.

—— *Reformation of Manners, a Satyr.* [London,] 1702.

Defoe, Daniel (cont.). *Religious Courtship*. London, 1722.

—— *Religious Courtship: Being Historical Discourses, on the Necessity of Marrying Religious Husbands and Wives Only*. London, 1722.

—— *Remarks on the Bill to Prevent Frauds Committed by Bankrupts*. London, 1706.

—— *Remarks on the Letter to the Author of the State Memorial*. London, 1705.

—— *Remarks on the Speeches of William Paul Clerk, and John Hall of Otterburn, Esq*. London, 1716.

—— *The Remedy Worse Than the Disease: Or, Reasons against Passing the Bill for Preventing the Growth of Schism*. London, 1714.

—— *A Reply to a Pamphlet Entituled the L[or]d H[avesham]'s Vindication of His Speech*. London, 1706.

—— *A Reply to a Traiterous Libel, Entituled, English Advice to the Freeholders of Great Britain*. London, 1715.

—— *Reply to the Scots Answer to the British Vision*. Edinburgh, 1706.

—— *The Representation Examined*. London, 1711.

?—— *A Reproof to Mr. Clark, and a Brief Vindication of Mr. De Foe*. [Edinburgh, 1710]

—— *A Review of the Affairs of France: and of All Europe, as Influenc'd by That Nation*, ed. Arthur Wellesley Secord. 22 vols. New York: Columbia University Press, 1938.

—— *Robinson Crusoe*: see *The Life and Surprizing Adventures* ...

—— *Rogues on Both Sides*. London, 1711.

—— *Roxana, the Fortunate Mistress*. Ed. Jane Jack. London: Oxford University Press, 1964.

—— *The Scotch Medal Decipher'd, and the New Hereditary-Right Men Display'd*. London, 1711.

—— *The Scots Nation and Union Vindicated*. London, 1714.

—— *A Scots Poem: Or, A New-Year's Gift*. London, 1707.

—— *A Seasonable Caution to the General Assembly in a Letter from and Member of Parliament of North-Britain to a Minister in Scotland*. Edinburgh, 1711.

—— *A Seasonable Expostulation With, and Friendly Reproof unto James Butler, Who, by the Men of this World, is Stil'd Duke of O[rmon]d*. London, 1715.

—— *A Seasonable Warning or the Pope and the King of France Unmasked*. [?Edinburgh,] 1706.

—— *The Second-Sighted Highlander: Or Predictions and Foretold Events: Especially about the Peace*. London, 1713

—— *Second Thoughts Are Best, or, A Further Improvement of a Late Scheme to Prevent Street Robberies*. London, 1729.

—— *A Secret History of One Year*. London, 1714.

——— *The Secret History of State Intrigues in the Management of the Scepter.* London, 1715.

——— *The Secret History of the October Club.* London, 1711.

——— *The Secret History of the Secret History of the White Staff, Purse and Mitre.* London, 1715.

——— *The Secret History of the White Staff.* 3 parts. London, 1715.

——— *The Secrets of the Invisible World Disclos'd: Or, An Universal History of Apparitions Sacred and Profane.* 2nd edn. London, 1735.

——— *Seldom Comes a Better: Or, A Tale of a Lady and Her Servants.* London, 1710.

——— *A Serious Inquiry into this Grand Question: Whether a Law to Prevent the Occasional Conformity of Dissenters Would not be Inconsistent with the Act of Toleration.* London, 1704.

——— *Serious Reflections of Robinson Crusoe.* In vol. 3 of *Romances and Narratives by Daniel Defoe*, ed. George A. Aitken. 16 vols. London: J. M. Dent. 1895.

——— (transcriber) Sermons by John Collins. MS, Huntington Library, San Marino, Calif.

——— *A Sharp Rebuke from One of the People Called Quakers to Henry Sacheverell, the High-Priest of Andrew Holbourn.* London, 1715.

——— *A Short Letter to the Glasgow Men.* Edinburgh, 1706.

——— [Old Officer in the Army]. *A Short Narrative of the Life of His Grace John D. of Marlborough from the Beginning of the Revolution to This Present Time with Some Remarks on his Conduct.* London, 1711.

——— *A Short View of the Conduct of the King of Sweden.* London [1717].

——— *Short View of the Present State of the Protestant Religion.* London, 1707.

——— *The Shortest Way with the Dissenters.* In *A True Collection of the Writings of the Author of the True-Born Englishman.* 2 vols. London, 1703–5.

——— *The Six Distinguishing Characters of a Parliament-Man.* London, 1700.

——— *Some Considerations on a Law for Triennial Parliaments, with an Inquiry.* London, 1716.

——— *Some Considerations on the Reasonableness and Necessity of Encreasing and Encouraging the Seamen.* London, 1728.

?——— *Some Considerations upon Street-Walkers.* London [1726].

——— *Some Reasons Why It Could Not Be Expected the Government Wou'd Permit the Speech or Paper of James Shepheard Which He Delivered at the Place of Execution to Be Printed.* London, 1718.

——— *Some Reflections on a Pamphlet Lately Publish'd, Entituled, An Argument Shewing that a Standing Army is Inconsistent with a Free Government.* London, 1697.

——— *Some Remarks on the First Chapter in Dr. Davenant's Essays.* London, 1704.

DEFOE, DANIEL (cont.). *Some Remarks upon the Late Differences among the Dissenting Ministers and Preachers*. London, 1719.

—— *Some Seasonable Queries on the Third Head*. [?London, c.1694]

—— *A Spectator's Address to the Whigs, on the Occasion of the Stabbing of Mr. Harley*. [London,] 1711.

—— *A Speech for Mr. D[unda]se the Younger of Arnistown*. London, 1711.

—— *A Speech without Doors*. London, 1710.

—— *The Storm*. London: Henry G. Bohn, 1855.

—— *A Strict Enquiry into the Circumstances of a Late Duel*. London, 1713.

—— *Strike While the Iron is Hot*. London, 1715

—— *The Succession of Spain Consider'd*. London, 1711.

—— *The Succession to the Crown of England Consider'd*. London, 1701.

—— *A Supplement to the Faults on Both Sides: Containing the Compleat History of the Proceedings of a Party Ever Since the Revolution*. London, 1710.

—— *A System of Magick, or, A History of the Black Art Being an Historical Account of Mankind's Most Early Dealing with the Devil*. London, 1726.

—— *Third Part of Advice to the Painter, Concerning the Great Turk*. London, 1684.

—— 'To the Athenian Society'. In *The History of the Athenian Mercury*. London, 1692.

—— *Tour thro' the Whole Island of Great Britain*. 2 vols. Introd. G. D. H. Cole. London: Peter Davies, 1927.

—— *The Trade to India Critically and Calmly Consider'd*. London, 1720.

—— *Treason Detected*. London, 1715.

—— *A True Account of the Design and Advantages of the South-Sea Trade*. London, 1711.

—— *A True and Genuine Account of the Life of Jonathan Wild not Made Up of Fiction and Fable*. London, 1725.

—— *The True-Born Englishman*. In *The Shakespeare Head Edition of the Novels and Selected Writings of Daniel Defoe*. 14 vols. Oxford: Blackwell, 1927–8.

—— *A True Collection of the Writings of the Author of the True-Born Englishman*. 2 vols. London, 1703–5.

—— *A True Relation of the Apparition of One Mrs. Veal* (1706), in *Account of the Apparition of Mrs. Veal*, ed. Manuel Schonhorn, Augustan Reprint Society, no. 115. Los Angeles: William Andrews Clark Memorial Library, 1965.

—— [?and William Colepepper] *A True State of the Difference between Sir George Rooke, Knt., and William Colepepper, Esq.* London, 1704.

—— *A Trumpet Blown in the North and Sounded in the Ears of John Eriskine . . . Duke of Mar*. London, 1715.

—— *The Two Great Questions Consider'd*. In *A True Collection of the Writings of the Author of the True-Born Englishman*. London, 1703.

—— *Two Great Questions Considered . . . Being a Sixth Essay at Removing National Prejudices against the Union*. [Edinburgh,] 1707.

—— *The Two Great Questions Further Consider'd*. London, 1700.

—— *A View of the Real Dangers of the Succession*. London, 1713.

—— *The Villainy of Stock-Jobbers Detected*. In *A True Collection of the Writings of the Author of the True-Born Englishman*. 2 vols. London, 1703–5.

—— *A Vindication of the Honour and Justice of Parliament against a Most Scandalous Libel Entitul'd, The Speech of John A——, Esq*. London, 1721.

—— *A Vindication of the Press: Or, an Essay on the Usefulness of Writing, on Criticism, and the Qualification of Authors*. London, 1718.

—— *The Vision, a Poem*. n.p., 1706.

—— *The Weakest Go to the Wall*. London, 1714.

—— *The Weekly Journal Being an Auxiliary Packet to the Saturday's Post* [*'Mist's Weekly Journal'*]. London, 1717–26

—— *What if the Swedes Should Come?* London, 1717.

—— *Whigs Turn'd Tories and Honverian-Tories, From Their Avow'd Principles Prov'd Whigs*. London, 1713.

—— *Wise as Serpents*. London, 1712.

—— [Flockmaker, Tom, (pseud.)]. *Worcestershire-Queries about Peace*. London, 1711.

—— *Word about a New Election*. London, 1710.

DENNIS, JOHN. *Vice and Luxury Publick Mischiefs: Or, Remarks on a Book Intituled, The Fable of the Bees*. London, 1724.

Dialogue between Louis le Petite, and Harlequin le Grand, A. London, 1708.

DICKSON, P. G. M. *The Financial Revolution in England: A Study in the Development of Public Credit, 1688–1756*. New York: St. Martin's Press, 1967.

DIJKSTRA, BRAM. *Defoe and Economics: The Fortunes of Roxana in the History of Interpretation*. New York: St. Martin's Press, 1987.

DILKE, D. *The Lover's Luck, a Comedy*. London, 1696.

DOTTIN, PAUL. *Daniel Defoe et ses romans*. 3 vols. Paris: Presses Universitaires de France, 1924.

DOWNIE, J. A. 'Defoe and "A Dialogue between Louis le Petite, and Harlequin le Grand"'. *American Notes and Queries* 12 (1973/4): 54–6.

—— *Robert Harley and the Press: Propaganda and Public Opinion in the Age of Swift and Defoe*. Cambridge: Cambridge University Press, 1979.

DRAKE, JAMES[?]. *The Memorial of the Church of England, Humbly Offer'd to the Consideration of All True Lovers of Our Church and Constitution*. London, 1705.

DRYDEN, JOHN. *The Poems of John Dryden*. 4 vols. Ed. James Kinsley. Oxford: Clarendon Press, 1958.

DUMONT, JEAN. *A New Voyage to the Levant: Containing an Account of the Most*

Remarkable Curiosities in Germany, France, Italy, Malta and Turkey. 2nd edn. London, 1696.

DUNTON, JOHN. *Dunton's Whipping Post, or, a Satyr Upon Every Body.* London, 1706.

—— *The Life and Errors of John Dunton.* London, 1705.

—— *Queen Robin: Or, the Second Part of Neck or Nothing.* London [1714].

DYER, JOHN. *A Collection from Dyer's Letters Concerning the Election of the Present Parliament.* London, 1705.

EARLE, PETER. *Monmouth's Rebels: The Road to Sedgemoor, 1685.* New York: St. Martin's Press, 1977.

—— *The World of Defoe.* New York: Atheneum, 1977.

EHRENPREIS, IRVIN. *Swift: The Man, His Works, His Age.* 3 vols. Cambridge, Mass.: Harvard University Press, 1962–83.

Elegiack Essay Upon the Decease of the Groom-Porter and the Lotteries, An. London, 1700.

ELLIS, FRANK. 'Defoe's "Resignacon" and the Limitation of "Mathematical Plainness"'. *Review of English Studies* 36 (1985): 338–54.

—— ed. *Poems on Affairs of State: Augustan Satirical Verse, 1660–1714.* New Haven, Conn.: Yale University Press, 1970.

Epigram on Defoe, An. In *Whig and Tory: Or, Wit on Both Sides.* London, 1712.

English Gentleman Justified, The. London, 1701.

English Men No Bastards, or, a Satyr Against the Author of the True-Born English-Man. London, 1701.

Equivalent for Daniel Defoe, An. [?Edinburgh, ?1706]

ETHICUS. *The Way of Good Men for Wise Men to Walk in.* London, 1681.

Evening Post, 21–3 Mar. 1723.

Every Man Mind His Own Business, or Private Piques no Public Precedents (London, 1725).

FALLER, LINCOLN. *Crime and Defoe: A New Kind of Writing.* Cambridge: Cambridge University Press, 1993.

Female Critick, or, Letters in Drollery from Ladies to Their Humble Servants, The. London, 1701.

FOOTE, ISAAC. *The Pen and the Sword.* London: MacGibbon & Kee, 1966.

FORSTER, E. M. *Aspects of the Novel.* New York: Harcourt, Brace, 1927.

FOUCAULT, MICHEL. *Discipline and Punish.* Trans. Alan Sheridan. New York: Vintage Books, 1979.

Fox with His Fire-Brand Unkennell'd and Insnar'd, The. London, 1703.

FRASER, WILLIAM, ed. *The Melvilles, Earls of Melville, and the Leslies, Earls of Leven.* Edinburgh, 1890.

FURBANK, P. N., and OWENS, W. R. *The Canonisation of Daniel Defoe*. New Haven,Conn.: Yale University Press, 1988.

————— *Defoe De-Attributions: A Critique of J. R. Moore's Checklist*. London: Hambledon Press, 1994.

————— ' "A Vindication of the Press" 1718: Not by Defoe?' *Bibliographical Society of America* 78 (1984): 355–60.

GARDAM, JANE. *Crusoe's Daughter*. New York: Atheneum, 1986.

GARTH, SAMUEL. *The Dispensary, a Poem*. London, 1699.

Gates of Hell Open'd: In a Dialogue Between the Observator and the Review, The. London, 1711.

GAY, JOHN. *The Beggar's Opera* (1728). Ed. Edgar Roberts. Lincoln: University of Nebraska Press, 1969.

General Claim to Allegiance, Atheists, and Tories Excluded, A. London, 1718.

GILDON, CHARLES. 'The Life and Strange Surprising Adventures of Mr. D——— De F———'. In *Robinson Crusoe Examin'd and Criticis'd*. Ed. Paul Dottin. London: Dent, 1923.

GIRDLER, LEW. 'Defoe's Education at Newington Green Academy'. *Studies in Philology* 50 (1953): 573–91.

GITTINGS, CLAIRE. *Death and Burial and the Individual in Early Modern England*. London: Croom Helm, 1984.

GOLDMANN, LUCIEN. *Pour une sociologie du roman*. Paris: Gallimard, 1964.

GOLDSMITH, OLIVER. *The Deserted Village*. In *The Poems of Gray, Collins and Goldsmith*. Ed. Roger Lonsdale. London: Longman, 1969.

GOODWIN, JOHN. *Anti-Cavalierisme, or, Truth Pleading as Well the Necessity . . .* London, 1642.

GRACIÁN Y MORALES, BALTASAR. *The Art of Prudence, or, A Companion for a Man of Sense*. London, 1702.

GRASSBY, RICHARD. 'Social Mobility and Business Enterprise in Seventeenth-Century England'. In *Puritans and Revolutionaries: Essays in Seventeenth-Century History Presented to Christopher Hill*. Ed. Donald Pennington and Keith Thomas. Oxford: Clarendon Press, 1978.

HABERMAS, JÜRGEN. *The Structural Transformation of the Public Sphere*. Trans. Thomas Burger. Cambridge, Mass.: MIT Press, 1989.

HALLETT, MARK. 'The Medley Print in Early Eighteenth-Century London'. *Art History*, 20 (June 1977): 214–37.

HAMILTON, ELIZABETH. *The Backstairs Dragon: A Life of Robert Harley*. London: Hamish Hamilton, 1969.

HARE, FRANCIS. *A Caveat to the Treaters*. London, 1711.

HARRIS, F. L. 'Charles Morton: Minister, Academy Master and Emigrant (1627–1697)'. *Journal of the Royal Institution of Cornwall* 4 (1963): 326–52.

HATTON, RAGNHILD. *George I: Elector and King*. Cambridge, Mass.: Harvard University Press, 1978.

HAWES, JOHN. *The Grand-Jury-Man's Oath and Office Explained: and the Rights of English-Men Asserted*. London, 1680.

HAYWOOD, ELIZA. *Love in Excess, or, the Fatal Enquiry, a Novel*. London, 1719–20.

HEAD, RICHARD. *The English Rogue: Containing the Life of Meriton Latroon, and Other Extravagants*. London, 1671.

HEIDENREICH, HELMUT, ed. *The Libraries of Daniel Defoe and Phillips Farewell: Olive Payne's Sales Catalogue (1731)*. Berlin: printed by W. Hildebrand for the author, 1970.

Hell Broke-Loose: Upon Doctor S-ch-ve--l's Sermons. London, 1713.

HEYM, STEFAN. *The Queen Against Defoe, and Other Stories*. New York: Lawrence Hill, 1974.

HILL, BRIAN. *Robert Harley: Speaker, Secretary of State and Premier Minister*. New Haven, Conn.: Yale University Press, 1988.

History of the Proceedings of the House of Lords, from the Restoration in 1660 to the Present Time. London, 1742.

HOADLY, BENJAMIN. *The Nature of the Kingdom, or Church of Christ*. London, 1717.

——*A Preservative against the Principles and Practices of the Nonjurors both in Church and State*. London, 1716.

HOBSBAWM, ERIC. *Bandits*. New York: Delacorte Press, 1969.

HODGES, JAMES. *The Rights and Interests of the Two British Monarchies*. Edinburgh, 1703.

HOLMES, GEOFFREY. *British Politics in the Age of Anne*. London: Macmillan, 1967.

——and SPECK, W. A., eds. *The Divided Society: Parties and Politics in England, 1694–1716*. New York: St. Martin's Press, 1968.

—— *The Trial of Doctor Sacheverell*. London: Eyre Methuen, 1973.

HOPPIT, JULIAN. *Risk and Failure in Eighteenth-Century Business, 1700–1800*. Cambridge: Cambridge University Press, 1987.

HORNBY, CHARLES. *A Caveat against the Whigs, in a Short Historical View of Their Transactions*. London, 1710.

HORNER, SAMUEL. *A Brief Account of the Interesting Ceremony of Unveiling the Monument Erected by the Boys and Girls of England to the Memory of Daniel Defoe*. Southampton: Hampshire Independent Office, 1871.

HORNSBY, CHARLES. *Caveat Against the Whigs*. 2nd edn. London, 1712.

HOWE, JOHN. *Some Consideration of a Preface to an Enquiry, Concerning the Occasional Conformity of the Dissenters*. London, 1701.

HOWSON, GERALD. *Thief-Taker General: Jonathan Wild and the Emergence of*

Crime and Corruption as a Way of Life in Eighteenth-Century England. London: Hutchinson, 1970.

—— 'Who Was Moll Flanders?', *Times Literary Supplement*, 18 Jan. 1968, pp. 63–4.

Hue and Cry after Daniel Defoe and his Coventry Breast, A. London, 1711.

HUNTER, J. PAUL. *Before Novels: the Cultural Contexts of Eighteenth-Century English Fiction*. New York: Norton, 1990.

HYDE, H. MONTGOMERY. *John Law: The History of an Honest Adventurer*. London: W. H. Allen, 1969.

JAMES I. *The King's Majesties Declaration to His Subjects Concerning Lawfull Sports to be Used*. London, 1618.

JAMES, ROBERT. 'Arthritis'. *A Medical Dictionary*. 3 vols. London, 1743.

JOCELYN, J. *An Essay on Money and Bullion*. London [1718].

JOHNSON, CHARLES. *The Successful Pirate*. 1713. Ed. Joel Baer. Augustan Reprint Society, Nos. 203–4. Los Angeles: William Andrews Clark Memorial Library, 1980.

JOHNSON, SAMUEL. *The Rambler*, No. 208. In *Works*. 11 vols. London, 1787.

JONES, GEORGE HILTON. *The Main Stream of English Jacobitism*. Cambridge, Mass.: Harvard University Press, 1954.

Journal des scavans. Paris, 1720.

Journals of the House of Commons. n.p., 1803–.

Journals of the House of Lords. n.p., 17xx–.

Judas Discuver'd, and Catch'd at Last: Or, Daniel De Foe in Lobs Pound. London, 1713.

Jure Divino Toss'd in a Blanket: Or, Daniel De Foe's Memorial. Poems on Affairs of State: Augustan Satirical Verse, 1660–1714. Ed. Frank Ellis. New Haven, Conn.: Yale University Press, 1970.

KAPLAN, LAWRENCE. *Politics and Religion During the English Revolution: The Scots and the Long Parliament, 1643–1645*. New York: New York University Press, 1976.

KEANE, PATRICK J. *Coleridge's Submerged Politics: The Ancient Mariner and Robinson Crusoe*. Columbia: University of Missouri Press, 1994.

KEEGAN, JOHN. *The Face of Battle*. New York: Viking, 1976.

KEIMER, SAMUEL. *A Brand Pluck'd From the Burning*. London, 1718.

—— *The Platonick Lady*. London, 1718.

KENYON, JOHN. *The Popish Plot*. London: Heinemann. 1972.

KING, GEOFFREY. *Natural and Political Observations and Conclusions upon the State and Condition of England*. 1696. In *An Estimate of the Comparative Strength of Great Britain and of the Losses of Her Trade*. Ed. George Chalmers. London: Printed for J. Stockdale, 1804.

Kippis, Andrew et al., eds. 'Defoe'. In *Biographica Britannica*. 5 vols. London, 1793.

Klingender, F. D. 'Coleridge on *Robinson Crusoe*'. *Times Literary Supplement*, 1 Feb. 1936, 96.

Knolles, Richard. *The Generall Historie of the Turkes*. 5th edn. London, 1638.

Kramnick, Isaac. *Bolingbroke and His Circle: The Politics of Nostalgia in the Age of Walpole*. Cambridge, Mass.: Harvard University Press, 1968.

Law, John. *Money and Trade Consider'd: With a Proposal for Supplying the Nation with Money*. London, 1705; 2nd edn. London, 1720.

Law, William. *Three Letters to the Bishop of Bangor*. 9th edn. London, 1753.

Le Clerc, Jean, ed. *Bibliotheque ancienne et moderne*. 29 vols. Amsterdam, 1721.

Leadam, I. S. *The History of England from the Accession of Anne to the Death of George II*. London: Longmans & Green, 1921. Vol. ix of *The Political History of England*. Ed. William Hunt and Reginald Poole. 12 vols. 1909–34.

Lee, William. *Daniel Defoe: His Life and Recently Discovered Writings Extending from 1716 to 1729*. London: J. C. Hotten, 1869.

Leslie, Charles. *The Diverting Post*. (24 Feb. 1705)

—— *The History of the Church, in Respect Both to Its Ancient and Present Condition*. London, 1706.

—— *The New Association with Farther Improvements*. London, 1703.

—— *Reflections upon a Late Scandalous and Malicious Pamphlet Entitul'd the Shortest Way with the Dissenters*. London, 1703.

—— 'A View of the Times'. *The Rehearsal*, 1 (94) (1706).

—— *The Wolf Stript of His Shepard's Cloathing*. 3rd edn. London, 1704.

Letter From a Tory Freeholder to His Representative in Parliament, A. London, 1712.

Ley, Charles David, ed. *Portuguese Voyages, 1498–1663*. London: Dent [1960].

Lillywhite, Bryant. *London Coffee Houses*. London: Allen & Unwin, 1963.

Lindsay, Jack. *The Monster City: Defoe's London, 1688–1730*. New York: St. Martin's Press, 1978.

Locke, John. *An Essay Concerning Human Understanding*. 2 vols. Ed. Alexander Fraser. Oxford: Clarendon Press, 1894. Repr. New York: Dover, 1959.

Lockhart, George. *Lockhart Papers*. London: William Anderson, 1817.

London Gazette, 11 Jan. 1702 and 14 Jan. 1703.

'Lord Mayor's Waiting Book'. Guildhall Library and Record Room, London.

Lowes, John Livingston. *Road to Xanadu: A Study in the Ways of the Imagination*. Boston: Houghton Mifflin, 1927.

Luttrell, Narcissus. *A Brief Historical Relation of State Affairs from September 1678 to April 1714*. Oxford: University Press, 1857.

Lyotard, Jean-François. *The Differend: Phrases in Dispute*. Trans. Georges Van Den Abbeele. Minneapolis: University of Minnesota Press, 1988.

MACEY, SAMUEL. *Money and the Novel: Mercenary Motivation in Defoe and His Immediate Successors*. Victoria, BC: Sono Nis Press, 1983.

MACHEREY, PIERRE. *A Theory of Literary Production*. Trans. Geoffrey Wall. London: Routledge & Kegan Paul, 1978.

MACKINNON, JAMES. *The Union of England and Scotland: A Study of International History*. London: Longmans, Green, 1896.

MACKWORTH, HUMPHREY. *Vindication of the Rights of the Commons of England*. London, 1701.

'Managers Trustees'. *The Post-Boy* (3 Oct. 1695).

MANDEVILLE, BERNARD. *An Enquiry into the Causes of the Frequent Executions at Tyburn and a Proposal for Some Regulations Concerning Felons in Prison, and the Good Effects to be Expected from Them*. London, 1725.

—— *The Fable of the Bees*. Ed. F. B. Kaye. 2 vols. Oxford: Clarendon Press, 1924.

—— *Modest Defense of the Publick Stews: Or, An Essay upon Whoring, as it is Now Practis'd in These Kingdoms*. London, 1724.

The Manuscripts of His Grace the Duke of Portland, Preserved at Welbeck Abbey. 6 vols. London: HMSO, Historical Manuscripts Commission, 1891–9.

MARANA, GIOVANNI PAOLO et al., *Letters Writ by a Turkish Spy*. Ed. Arthur Weitzman. London: Routledge, 1970.

—— et al., *Letters Written by a Turkish Spy*. 8 vols. London, 1753–4.

MARLBOROUGH, JOHN CHURCHILL. *The Marlborough–Godolphin Correspondence*. Ed. Henry Snyder. 3 vols. Oxford: Clarendon Press, 1975.

Marriage Assessments, no. 103 St Botolph's Bishopgate. 1 May 1695–1 May 1696.

MARVELL, ANDREW. *An Account of the Growth of Popery and Arbitrary Government in England*. Amsterdam [London], 1677.

—— *The Rehearsal Transpos'd*. London: A.B., 1672.

MARX, KARL. *Capital*. Trans. Samuel Moore and Edward Aveling. London: Glaisher, 1949.

MASSIE, ROBERT. *Peter the Great: His Life and World*. New York: Knopf, 1980.

MATHER, COTTON. *The Diary of Cotton Mather, 1681–1724*. Boston: Massachusetts Historical Society, 1911–12.

MATTHEWS, A. G. *Calamy Revised: Being a Revision of Edmund Calamy's Account of the Ministers and Others Ejected and Silenced, 1660–2*. Oxford: Clarendon Press, 1934.

MAYNWARING, ARTHUR. *The Life and Posthumous Works of Arthur Maynwaring, Esq*. London, 1715.

McBURNEY, WILLIAM. 'The Authorship of "The Turkish Spy"'. *Publications of the Modern Language Association* 72 (1957): 915–35.

McCREA, BRIAN. *Addison and Steele Are Dead: The English Department, Its Canon, and the Professionalization of Literary Criticism.* Newark: University of Delaware Press, 1990.

McCulloch, J. R., ed. *A Selection of Scarce and Valuable Economic Tracts.* London, 1859.

McMahan, Marie. *The Radical Whigs, John Trenchard and Thomas Gordon: Libertarian Loyalists to the New House of Hanover.* Lanham, Md.: University Presses of America, 1990.

Memento for English Protestants, A. London, 1680.

Merchant (pseud.). *A Further Examination of the Weaver's Pretences being a Particular Answer to a Late Pamphlet of Theirs, Entituled The Just Complaints, &c.* London, 1719.

Mercure Galant, Le. Paris, 1718.

Meriton, L. *Pecuniae Obediunt Omnia: Money Does Master All Things.* York, 1696.

Michael, Wolfgang. *England under George I: The Beginnings of the Hanoverian Dynasty.* London: Macmillan, 1936.

Minto, William. *Daniel Defoe.* London: Macmillan, 1879.

Monster: Or, The World Topsy-Turvy, The. London, 1705.

Moore, John Robert. *A Checklist of the Writings of Daniel Defoe.* 2nd edn. Hamden, Conn.: Archon Books, 1971.

—— *Daniel Defoe, Citizen of the Modern World.* Chicago: University of Chicago Press, 1958.

—— 'A Defoe Allusion in Gulliver's Travels'. *Notes & Queries* 3 (1940), 79–80.

—— 'Defoe and the South Sea Company'. *Boston Public Library Quarterly* 5 (1953): 175–88.

—— *Defoe in the Pillory and Other Studies.* Bloomington: Indiana University Press, 1939.

Morton, Charles. *An Essay Towards the Probable Solution of this Question, Whence Come the Stork and the Turtle, the Crane and the Swallow . . .* London, 1703.

—— 'The Improvement of Cornwall by Sea Sand, Communicated by an Intelligent Gentleman well Acquainted in those Parts to Dr. Dan Cox'. *Philosophical Transactions of the Royal Society for the Year 1675.* New York: Johnston Reprint Corp., 1963.

—— *The Little Peace-Maker.* London, 1674.

—— *The Spirit of Man.* Boston, 1693.

Mundy, P. D. 'The Ancestry of Daniel Defoe'. *Notes & Queries* 174 (1938): 112–14.

—— 'The Ancestry of Daniel Defoe'. *Notes & Queries* 175 (1938), 44.

Muralt, Béat Louis de. *Letters Describing the Character and Customs of the English and French Nations.* London, 1726.

New Ballad to the Tune of Fair Rosamond, A. [?London, c. 1710]

New Loyal Members of Parliament's Delight, The. London, 1710.

NEWMAN, RICHARD. *The Complaint of English Subjects, Delivered in Two Parts.* London, 1699.

NICHOLSON, T. C., and TURBERVILLE, A. S. *Charles Talbot Duke of Shrewsbury.* Cambridge: Cambridge University Press, 1930.

NICOLSON, MARJORIE. *Newton Demands the Muse: Newton's Opticks and the Eighteenth Century Poets.* Princeton, NJ: Princeton University Press, 1946.

No Fool Like an Old Fool: Or, A Pertinent Answer to an Impertinent Libel Call'd Chickens Feed Capons. London, ?1730.

NOKES, DAVID. Review of Paula Backscheider's *Defoe. London Review of Books,* 19 Apr. 1990, 18–19.

NOVAK, MAXIMILLIAN E. 'Crime and Punishment in "Roxana"'. *Journal of English and Germanic Philology* 65 (1966): 455–65.

—— 'Crusoe and "The Country Life"; Defoe and Music'. *Notes & Queries* 237 (1992): 48–52.

—— 'Defoe and the Disordered City'. *Publications of the Modern Language Association* 92 (1977): 241–52.

—— *Defoe and the Nature of Man.* Oxford: Clarendon Press, 1963.

—— 'The Defoe Canon: Attribution and De-Attribution'. *Huntington Library Quarterly* 59 (1997): 189–207.

—— 'Defoe, the Occult, and the Deist Offensive During the Reign of George I'. In *Deism, Masonry, and the Enlightenment.* Ed. Leo Lemay. Newark: Delaware University Press, 1987.

—— 'Defoe's Authorship of "A Collection of Dying Speeches"'. *Philological Quarterly* 61 (1982): 92–7.

—— 'Defoe's "Shortest Way with the Dissenters": Hoax, Parody, Paradox, Fiction, Irony, and Satire'. *Modern Language Quarterly* 27 (1966): 402–17.

—— 'Describing the Thing Itself or Not: Defoe, Painting, Prose Fiction, and the Arts of Describing'. *Eighteenth-Century Fiction* 9 (1996): 1–20.

—— *Economics and the Fiction of Daniel Defoe.* Berkeley: University of California Press, 1962.

—— 'Humanum est Errare'. *Clark Library Newsletter* 4 (1983): 1–4.

—— *Realism, Myth, and History in Defoe's Fiction.* Lincoln: University of Nebraska Press, 1983

—— 'Sincerity, Delusion, and Character in the Fiction of Defoe and the "Sincerity Crisis" of His Time'. In *Augustan Studies.* Ed. Douglas Lane Patey and Timothy Keegan. Newark: University of Delaware Press, 1984.

—— 'The Unmentionable and Ineffable in Defoe's Fiction'. *Studies in the Literary Imagination* 15 (1982): 85–102.

Novak, Maximillian E. (cont.). ' "A Vindication of the Press", and the Defoe Canon'. *Studies in English Literature* 27 (1987): 399–411.

—— 'A Whiff of Scandal in the Life of Daniel Defoe'. *Huntington Library Quarterly* 34 (1970–1): 35–42.

Ogg, David. *England in the Reign of Charles II.* 2 vols. Oxford: Clarendon Press, 1966.

—— *England in the Reign of James II and William III* (Oxford: Clarendon Press, 1966).

—— *Europe in the Seventeenth Century.* 4th edn. London: Black, 1946.

Oldmixon, John. *Considerations on the History of the Mitre and Purse.* London, 1714.

—— *The History of England During the Reigns of King William and Queen Mary, Queen Anne, King George I.* London, 1735.

—— *Remarks on the Letter to the Dissenters. By a Churchman.* London, 1714.

Owen, John. *A Brief and Impartial Account of the Nature of the Protestant Religion.* London, 1690.

P.R. *A Roman Catholick System of Allegiance.* London, 1716.

Parker, Geoffrey. *The Military Revolution: Military Innovation and the Rise of the West, 1500–1800.* Cambridge: Cambridge University Press, 1988.

Parker, Irene. *Dissenting Academies in England: Their Rise and Progress and Their Place Among the Educational Systems of the Country.* Cambridge: Cambridge University Press, 1914.

Patey, Douglas. *Probability and Literary Form: Philosophic Theory and Literary Practice in the Augustan Age.* Cambridge: Cambridge University Press, 1984.

Pepys, Samuel. *The Diary of Samuel Pepys.* Ed. Robert Latham and William Matthews. 11 vols. Berkeley: University of California Press, 1970–83.

Perkins, James Breck. *France under the Regency with a Review of the Administration of Louis XIV.* Boston: Houghton, Mifflin, 1901.

Peterson, Spiro. *Daniel Defoe, a Reference Guide, 1731–1924.* Boston, Mass.: G. K. Hall, 1987.

—— 'Defoe and Westminster, 1696–1706'. *Eighteenth-Century Studies* 12 (1978–9): 306–36.

Philips, Ambrose and Hugh Boulter. *The Freethinker.* London, 1718.

Pitt, Moses. *The Cry of the Oppress'd.* London, 1691.

Pittis, William. *Queen Anne Vindicated from the Base Aspersions of Some Late Pamphlets Publish'd to Screen the Mismanagers of the Four Last Years From Publick Justice.* London, 1715.

Pitts, Joseph. *A True and Faithful Account of the Religion and Manners of the Mohammetans.* Exeter, 1704.

Pocock, J. G. A. *Virtue, Commerce, and History: Essays on Political Thought and*

History, Chiefly in the Eighteenth Century. Cambridge: Cambridge University Press, 1985.

Poems on Affairs of State . . . From 1620 to this Present Year 1707. 4 vols. London, 1704–7.

POTTER, GEORGE. 'Henry Baker, F.R.S. (1698–1774)'. *Modern Philology* 29 (1932): 301–21.

Proceedings at the Tryal Examination, and Condemnation of a Certain Scribling, Rhyming, Versifying, Poeteering Hosier, and True-Born Englishman, Commonly Known by the Name Daniel the Prophet, Alias Anglipoliski, Alias Foeski, The. London, 1705.

Proceedings of the Sessions of London's Old Bailey. London, 1730.

Proceedings on the Queen's Commission of the Peace: Oyer and Terminer and Gaol Delivery of Newgate . . . on Wednesday, Thursday, and Friday, being the 7th, 8th, and 9th Days of July, The. London, 1703.

RALPH, JAMES. *The Case of Authors by Profession or Trade.* London, 1758.

REALEY, CHARLES BECHDOLT. '*The London Journal* and Its Authors, 1720–1723'. *Bulletin of the University of Kansas* 36 (1935): 1–38.

Reflections upon a Sermon Preach'd January 31 1714/15 by Henry Sacheverel, DD. London, 1715.

Register of St. Michael's Cornhill 1546–1754, The. London: Harleian Society, 1882.

Representation of the Present State of Religion, A. London, 1711.

Reproof to Mr. Clark, and a Brief Vindication of Mr. De Foe, A. [Edinburgh, 1710]

Republican Bullies, or, A Sham Battel between Two of a Side, The. London, 1705.

Review and Observator Review'd, The. London, 1706.

REYNOLDS, JOHN. *The Triumphs of Gods Revenge against the Crying and Execrable Sin of Murther . . . To which is added Gods Revenge against the Abominable Sin of Adultery.* 6th edn. London, 1679.

RILEY, P. W. J. *The Union of England and Scotland: A Study in Anglo-Scottish Politics of the Eighteenth Century.* Manchester: Manchester University Press, 1978.

ROCHESTER, JOHN WILMOT, EARL OF. 'Satyr against Mankind'. In *The Complete Poems of John Wilmot, Earl of Rochester.* Ed. David Vieth. New Haven, Conn.: Yale University Press, 1968.

ROGERS, J. P. W. 'Defoe and "The Immorality of the Priesthood" (1715): An Attribution Reviewed'. *Papers of the Bibliographical Society of America* 67 (1973): 245–53.

ROGERS, PAT. 'Defoe at Work: The Making of "A Tour Thro' Great Britain"'. *Bulletin of the New York Public Library* 78 (1975): 431–50.

—— 'Defoe in Fleet Street Prison.' *Notes & Queries* 216 (1971): 451–5.

ROGERS, PAT (cont.). 'Introduction'. In *Tour thro' the Whole Island of Great Britain*. By Daniel Defoe. Harmondsworth: Penguin, 1971.

—— 'The Making of the "Tour Thro Britain"'. *Prose Studies* 3 (1980): 109–37.

ROGERS, WOODES. *A Cruising Voyage Round the World First to the South-Seas, Thence to the East-Indies, and Homewards by the Cape of Good Hope*. London, 1712.

ROSCOMMON, WENTWORTH DILLON. *An Essay on Translated Verse by the Earl of Roscommon*. London, 1684.

Rough Master's and Warden's Accounts. MS 6441/1–5. Guildhall Library and Record Room, London.

Rough Master's and Warden's Accounts. MS 6443a. Guildhall Library and Record Room, London.

ROUSSEAU, JEAN-JACQUES. *Émile*. Amsterdam, 1762.

RYDER, DUDLEY. *The Diary of Dudley Ryder, 1715–1716*. Ed. William Matthews. London: Methuen [1939].

SACHEVERELL, HENRY. *The Communication of Sin: A Sermon Preach'd at the Assizes Held at Derby, August 15ᵗʰ, 1709*. London, 1709

—— *The Perils of False Brethren, Both in Church, and State*. London, 1709.

—— *The Political Union, a Discourse Shewing the Dependence of Government on Religion in General*. London, 1702.

Saint Giles Cripplegate Parish Register (June 1659): film 6419/5, 6, 7. MS 64196.

Saint Giles Cripplegate Parish Register (Nov. 1657): film 6419/5, 6, 7. MS 64196.

SAINT-SIMON, LOUIS DE ROUVROY. *Historical Memoirs*. Ed. Lucy Norton. New York: McGraw-Hill, 1972.

Satyr Upon Thirty-Seven Articles, A. London, 1701.

SAVAGE, RICHARD. *An Author to Be Lett*. London, 1729.

SCHONHORN, MANUEL, ed. *Accounts of the Apparition of Mrs. Veal* Augustan Reprint Society No.115. Los Angeles: William Andrews Clark Memorial Library, 1965.

—— 'The Limits of Jacobite Rhetoric'. *English Literary History* 64 (1997): 874–86.

SCHWARTZ, HILLEL. *The French Prophets*. Berkeley: University of California Press, 1980.

SCOTT, SARAH. *A Description of Millenium Hall, and the Country Adjacent*. London, 1762.

SCOTT, WALTER. *Old Mortality*. Ed. Angus Calder. Harmondsworth: Penguin, 1975.

SCOTT, WILLIAM. *Joint Stock Companies*. 3 vols. Cambridge: Cambridge University Press, 1911.

Scottish Public Records Office. GD 18/2325; 18/3131; 18/3135, item 6; 18/3135; 18/3202/7; 18/4510. Edinburgh.

Scribbler's Doom, or, The Pillory in Fashion Being a New Dialogue between Two Loop-hole Sufferers, William Fuller and De Fooe, The. London, 1703.

Seasonable Warning to Protestants from the Cruelty and Treachery of the Parisian Massacre, August the 24ᵗʰ 1572, A. London, 1680.

SECORD, ARTHUR. 'Defoe in Stoke Newington'. *Papers of the Modern Language Association* (1951): 211–16.

——*Robert Drury's Journal and Other Studies.* Urbana: University of Illinois Press, 1961.

——*Studies in the Narrative Method of Defoe.* New York: Russell & Russell, 1963.

SENECA. *Seneca's Morals By Way of Abstract.* Trans. and ed. Roger L'Estrange. 6th edn. London: J. Tonson, 1696.

SHIELS, ROBERT. 'Daniel De Foe'. In *The Lives of the Poets of Great Britain and Ireland.* Ed. Theophilus Cibber. 4 vols. London, 1753.

SHIRREN, ADAM JOHN. *Daniel Defoe in Stoke Newington.* London: Stoke Newington Public Libraries Committee, 1960.

SILL, GEOFFREY. *Defoe and the Idea of Fiction, 1713–1719.* Newark: University of Delaware Press, 1983.

SMITH, ALEXANDER. *The History and Lives of the Most Noted Highway-Men, Foot-Pads, House-Breakers, Shop-Lifts, and Cheats, of Both Sexes, in and about London, and other Places of Great Britain, for above Fifty Years Last Past.* 2nd edn. London, 1714.

SNYDER, HENRY. 'Daniel Defoe, the Duchess of Marlborough, and the *Advice to the Electors of Great Britain'. Huntington Library Quarterly* 29 (1965): 56–8.

Sourse of Our Present Fears Discover'd, or, Plain Proof of Some Late Designs against Our Present Constitution and Government, The. 3rd edn. London, 1706.

SPENCE, JOSEPH. *Observations, Anecdotes and Characters of Books and Men.* Ed. James Osborn. 2 vols. Oxford: Clarendon Press, 1966.

SPUFFORD, MARGARET. *Small Books and Pleasant Histories: Popular Fiction and its Readership in Seventeenth-Century England.* Athens: Georgia University Press, 1981.

STACE, MACHELL. *An Alphabetical Catalogue of an Extensive Collection of the Writings of Daniel De Foe.* London: Whitmore & Fenn, 1830.

STARR, G.A. *Defoe and Casuistry.* Princeton, NJ: Princeton University Press, 1971.

——'Sauces to Whet our Gorg'd Appetites'. *Philological Quarterly* 54 (1975): 531–3.

STEELE, RICHARD. *The Conscious Lovers, a Comedy.* In *Plays.* Ed. Shirley Kenny. Oxford: Clarendon Press, 1971.

STEELE, RICHARD. et al. (cont.). *The Guardian*. Ed. John Calhoun Stephens. Lexington: University Press of Kentucky, 1982.

——*A Letter to a Member of Parliament*. In *Tracts and Pamphlets*. Ed. Rae Blanchard. Baltimore, Md.: Johns Hopkins University Press, 1944.

STEPHEN, LESLIE. 'Defoe's Novels'. In *Hours in a Library*. 3 vols. New York: Putnam, 1899.

STERNE, LAURENCE. *The Life and Opinions of Tristam Shandy*. Ed. Melvyn and Joan New. 3 vols. Gainesville: University Presses of Florida, 1978–84.

STONE, LAWRENCE. *The Family, Sex, and Marriage in England, 1500–1800*. New York: Harper & Row, 1977.

STOW, JOHN. *A Survey of the Cities of London and Westminster Containing the Original, Antiquity, Increase, Modern Estate, and Government of Those Cities*. Ed. John Strype. London, 1720.

SUTHERLAND, JAMES. 'The Circulation of Newspapers and Literary Periodicals'. *The Library*, 4th ser., 15 (1934–5): 110–24.

——*Defoe*. 2nd edn. London: Methuen, 1950.

——'A Note on the Last Years of Defoe'. *Modern Language Review* 29 (1934): 137–40.

——'Some Early Troubles of Daniel Defoe'. *Review of English Studies* 9 (1935): 286–9.

SWIFT, JONATHAN. *The Conduct of the Allies, and of the Late Ministry*. In *Prose Works of Jonathan Swift*. Ed. Herbert Davis. 14 vols. Oxford: Blackwell, 1939–68.

——*A Discourse Concerning the Mechanical Operation of the Spirit*. In *A Tale of a Tub*. Ed. A. C. Guthkelch and D. Nichol Smith. 2nd ed. Oxford: Clarendon Press, 1958.

——*Gulliver's Travels*. In *The Prose Works of Jonathan Swift*. Ed. Herbert Davis. 14 vols. Oxford: Blackwell, 1939–68.

——*Journal to Stella*. Ed. Harold Williams. 2 vols. Oxford: Clarendon Press, 1948.

——*A Modest Proposal for Preventing the Children of Poor People from Being a Burthen to Their Parents or the Country*. In *The Prose Works of Jonathan Swift*. Ed. Herbert Davis. 14 vols. Oxford: Blackwell, 1939–68.

SYLVESTER, MATTHEW. *Elisha's Cry After Elijah's God, Consider'd and Apply'd with Reference to the Decease of the Late Reverend Richard Baxter*. London, 1696.

TAVE, STUART. *The Amiable Humorist: A Study in the Comic Theory and Criticism of the Eighteenth and Early Nineteenth Centuries*. Chicago: University of Chicago Press, 1960.

Thamasis's Advice to the Painter from Her Fridgid Zone, or, Wonder upon the Water. London, 1684.

Third Part of Advice to the Painter, Concerning the Great Turk. London, 1684.

THOMPSON, E. P. 'The Crime of Anonymity'. In *Albion's Fatal Tree*. Ed. Douglas Hay et al. New York: Pantheon, 1975.

TILLEY, MORRIS PALMER. *A Dictionary of the Proverbs in England in the Sixteenth and Seventeenth Century*. Ann Arbor: University of Michigan Press, 1950.

TOLAND, JOHN. *The State-Anatomy of Great Britain*. London [?1717].

TRENT, WILLIAM PETERFIELD. 'A Biographical and Bibliographical Study'. MS biography of Daniel Defoe. Trent Collection, Beinecke Library, New Haven. Conn., *c*.1900–27.

TREVELYAN, G. M. *England under Queen Anne*. 3 vols. London: Longmans, Green, 1930–4.

—— *English Social History: A Survey of Six Centuries, Chaucer to Queen Victoria*. London: Longmans, Green, 1942.

Triennial Act Impartially Stated Shewing, The. London, 1716.

True-Born Hugonot: Or, Daniel Defoe: a Satyr, The. London, 1703.

Tryal and Condemnation of Arundel Coke, The. London, 1722.

Tryal of Doctor Henry Sacheverell, before the House of Peers, for High Crimes and Misdemeanors, The. Dublin, 1710.

TRYON, THOMAS. *Modest Observations on the Present Extraordinary Frost*. London, 1684.

TUCKER, JOSEPH. 'On the Authorship of "The Turkish Spy": an État Présent'. *Papers of the Bibliographical Society of America* 52 (1958): 34–47.

TURNER, G. L. E. 'Henry Baker, F.R.S.: Founder of the Bakerian Lecture'. *Notes and Records of the Royal Society of London* 28 (1974): 53–4.

TUTCHIN, JOHN. *The Foreigners*. In *Poems on Affairs of State: Augustan Satirical Verse, 1660–1714*. Ed. Frank Ellis. 7 vols. New Haven, Conn.: Yale University Press, 1970.

—— *The Observator*, 23–6 Dec. 1702; 6–9 Jan. 1703, and 7 July 1703.

—— *The Second Part of the Mouse Grown a Rat: Or, The Story of the City and Country Mouse*. London, 1703.

Villainy Exploded: Or, the Mystery of Iniquity Laid Open. London, 1728.

WALKER, D. P. *The Decline of Hell: Seventeenth-Century Discussions of Eternal Torment*. Chicago: Chicago University Press, 1964.

WALZER, MICHAEL. *The Revolution of the Saints: A Study in the Origins of Radical Politics*. 2nd ed. New York: Atheneum, 1968.

WARD, EDWARD. *The Dissenting Hypocrite or Occasional Conformist*. London, 1704.

—— *The Galloper, or, Needs Must When the Devil Drives. A Poem*. London, 1710.

—— *The Miracles Perform'd by Money: A Poem*. London, 1692.

WATT, IAN. *The Rise of the Novel*. Berkeley: University of California Press, 1957.

WATTS, WILLIAM[?] *The Swedish Discipline*. London, 1632.

WESLEY, SAMUEL. *A Defence of a Letter Concerning the Education of the Dissenters in Their Private Academies*. London, 1704.

—— *A Letter from a Country Divine to His Friend in London, Concerning the Education of the Dissenters in Their Private Academies*. London, 1704.

—— *A Reply to Mr. Palmer's Vindication of the Learning, Loyalty, Morals and Most Christian Behaviour of the Dissenters towards the Church of England*. London, 1707.

Whitehall Evening Post, 25–7 Jan. 1728.

White-Staff Speech to the Lords, The. London, 1714.

WHITHER, GEORGE. *A Collection of Emblems, Ancient and Modern*. London, 1635.

WILLIAMS, DANIEL. *Gospel-truth Stated and Vindicated*. London, 1692.

WILSON, WALTER. *Memoirs of the Life and Times of Daniel De Foe Containing a Review of His Writings and His Opinions upon a Variety of Important Matters, Civil and Ecclesiastical*. 3 vols. London: Hurst, Chance, 1830.

WODROW, ROBERT. *Analecta, or Materials for a History of Remarkable Providences Mostly Relating to Scotch Ministers and Christians*. Ed. Matthew Leishman. 4 vols. Glasgow: Maitland Club, 1842–3.

Worchestershire Address: With an Account of Some Remarks upon it in Dyer's Newsletter of April 27, 1710, The. London, 1710.

WRIGHT, THOMAS. *The Life of Daniel Defoe*. London: C. J. Farncombe, 1931.

WYCHERLEY, WILLIAM. *The Complete Plays of William Wycherley*. Ed. Gerald Weales. 2nd edn. New York: Doubleday, 1962.

—— *The Gentleman Dancing-Master: A Comedy*. London, 1693.

ZWICKER, STEVEN. *Politics and Language in Dryden's Poetry: The Arts of Disguise*. Princeton, NJ: Princeton University Press, 1984.

INDEX